LEE'S LIEUTENANTS

A Study in Command

Douglas Southall Freeman

VOLUME I
Manassas to Malvern Hill

SCRIBNER CLASSICS

SCRIBNER
1230 Avenue of the Americas
New York, NY 10020

Copyright 1942 by Charles Scribner's Sons
Copyright renewed © 1970 by Inez Goddin Freeman

First Scribner Edition
SCRIBNER *and design are trademarks of Simon & Schuster Inc.*
Manufactured in the United States of America

3   5   7   9   10   8   6   4   2

The Library of Congress has cataloged the
Charles Scribner's Sons edition as follows:

Freeman, Douglas Southall, 1886–1953.
Lee's lieutenants, a study in command, by Douglas Southall Freeman.
New York, C. Scribner's sons, 1942–44.
"Short-title index": v.3, p. 781–784. "Select critical bibliography":
v.3, p. [797]–825.
Contents: v.1. Manassas to Malvern hill.—v.2. Cedar mountain to
Chancellorsville.—v.3. Gettysburg to Appomattox.
1. United States—History—Civil War, 1861–1865—Campaigns.
2. Confederate States of America—Biography. 3. United States—
History—Civil War, 1861–1865—Biography. 4. United States—
History—Civil War, 1861–1865—Regimental histories. 5. Confederate
States of America. Army of Northern Virginia. I. Title.
E470.2.F7   973.73   42-24582
MARC

ISBN 0-684-83783-8

TO

John Stewart Bryan

WHO HAS KEPT THE FAITH

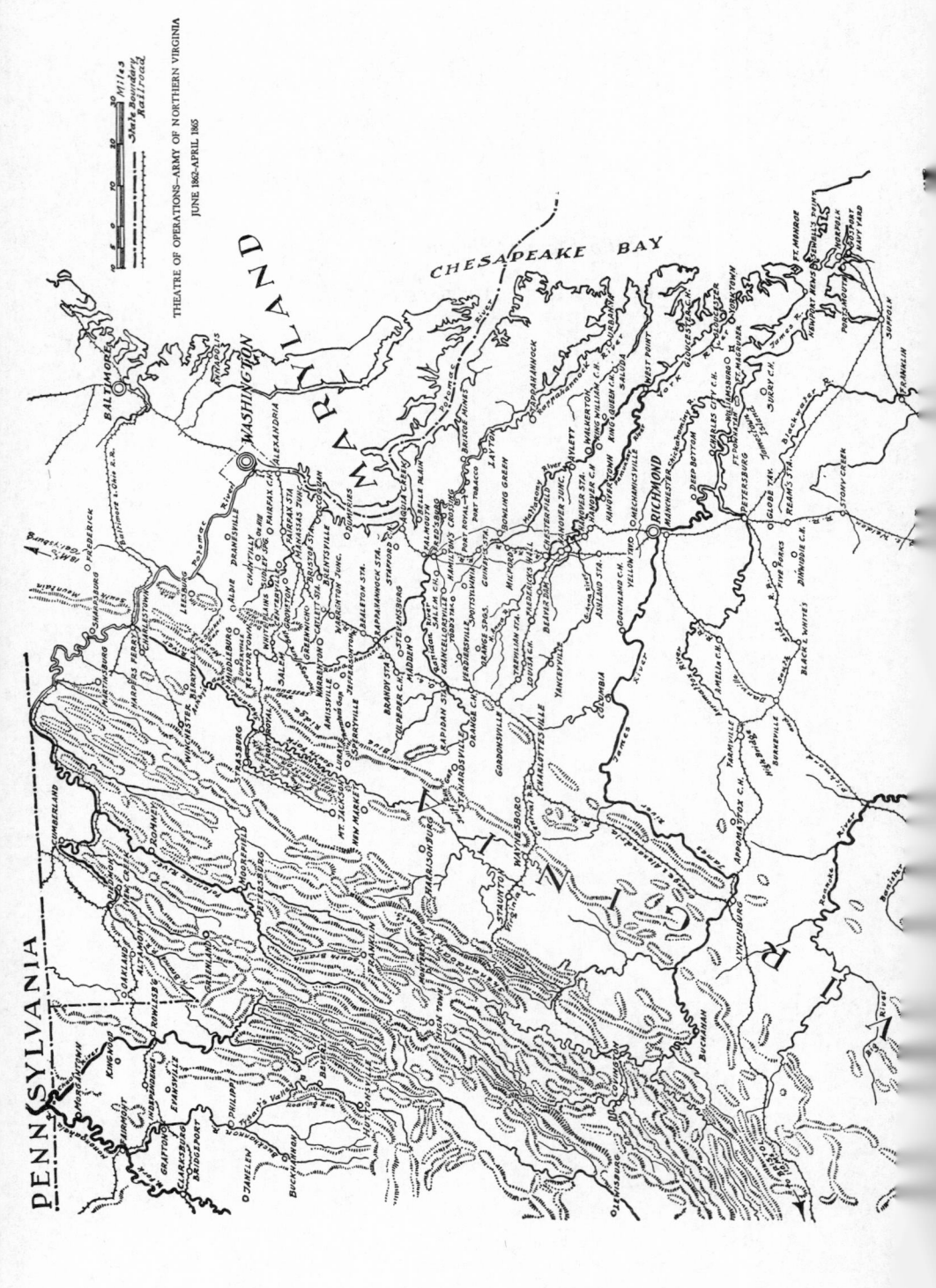

THEATRE OF OPERATIONS—ARMY OF NORTHERN VIRGINIA
JUNE 1862–APRIL 1865

CONTENTS

Foreword   xiii

"Dramatis Personae"   xxxi

   I. "Old Bory's Coming"   1

   II. Magruder and D. H. Hill Emerge   14

   III. First Loss of a Leader   23

   IV. Beauregard Essays Grand Strategy   38

   V. Beauregard Plans a Battle   45

   VI. Beauregard's Star at Zenith   62

   VII. Pursuit and a Confused Council   73

   VIII. Subordinates of Promise   81

   IX. The Star of Beauregard Is Beclouded   99

   X. Johnston Passes a Dark Winter   111

   XI. Johnston's Withdrawal from Manassas   137

   XII. Johnston Retreats Again   148

   XIII. The Army That Left Yorktown   156

   XIV. Williamsburg   174

   XV. Eltham Introduces John B. Hood   193

   XVI. Twenty-four Unhappy Days   201

   XVII. Seven Pines: A Battle of Strange Errors   225

   XVIII. Grim Fruits of Anniversary   244

XIX.	Old Snarls Are Untangled	264
XX.	Stuart Justifies His Plume	275
XXI.	General and Deacon Jackson at Odds	303
XXII.	The Building of a "New Model" Army	321
XXIII.	"Dick" Ewell Sticks by a "Crazy Man"	347
XXIV.	Jackson Launches His Offensive	362
XXV.	Cedarville to Winchester—a Dreadful Night	383
XXVI.	A Victory Ends at a Manse	395
XXVII.	"From the Snare of the Fowler"	411
XXVIII.	A Crowning Double Victory	435
XXIX.	"The Hero of the South"	470
XXX.	Jackson Marches to a Confusing Field	489
XXXI.	The New Organization Fails	503
XXXII.	First Battle of A. N. Va.	517
XXXIII.	Magruder Stays Up Too Long	538
XXXIV.	The Delay in the Reconcentration	557
XXXV.	Two Columns Are Halted	565
XXXVI.	Holmes Advances and Magruder Gallops in Vain	581
XXXVII.	Malvern Hill: A Tragedy of Staff	588
XXXVIII.	The End of Magruder and of Huger	605
XXXIX.	Discontent and Dyspepsia as Problems of Command	620
XL.	Stuart Makes a Second "Raid"	633

XLI. The Juniors Who Vied with Veterans   645

XLII. The Enigma of Jackson's State of Mind   655

XLIII. A New Organization for New Battles   670

APPENDIX

I. The Military Geography of Virginia   677

II. Southern Resources of Command   701

III. The Distribution of Beauregard's Combat Order
     of July 20, 1861   726

IV. Order of Battle of Confederate Infantry,
    July 21, 1861   728

V. Origin of the Name "Stonewall"   733

VI. Jackson's Plans and Marches of May 24, 1862   735

   Manuscript Sources   741

   Short Title Index   745

   Index   749

ILLUSTRATIONS

Pierre Gustave Toutant Beauregard	*Facing Page*	XXXII
John Bankhead Magruder	"	XXXIV
Daniel Harvey Hill	"	XXXVI
Joseph Eggleston Johnston	"	XXXVIII
Gustavus Woodson Smith	"	XL
Thomas Jonathan Jackson	"	XLII
James Longstreet	"	XLIV
Richard Stoddert Ewell	"	XLVI

MAPS

The district between Warrenton and Washington and the Shenandoah Valley from Front Royal to Harpers Ferry   11

The region of Gen. R. S. Garnett's operations in Western Virginia   26

Rich Mountain and Pegram's position at Camp Garnett   30

Confederate Forces on Bull Run, July 21, 1861, sunrise   47

Fort Magruder and redoubts, woods, and abatis, May 4–5, 1862   178

Advance of Early's Brigade in the Battle of Williamsburg, May 5, 1862   184

Advance eastward from Richmond to Seven Pines, May 31, 1862   227

Route of Stuart's "Ride around McClellan" (Chickahominy Raid)   287

The Parallelogram of the Massanuttons   331

The Central Shenandoah Valley in relation to the passes of the Blue Ridge and the railroads of Midland Virginia   334

Jackson's alternative lines of advance, end of April, 1862   343

The environs of Front Royal, action of May 23, 1862   375

Battle of Winchester, May 25, 1862   397

Jackson's choice of position on his retreat before Frémont and Shields   428

Port Republic and environs   436

Battle of Port Republic, June 9, 1862   453

General line of Jackson's advance, June, 1862   493

Route of Jackson, Ewell and Branch, June 26, 1862   507

Battlefield of Gaines' Mill, June 27, 1862   521

The environs of Savage Station   549

White Oak Swamp, New Road and Charles City Road   559

The vicinity of White Oak Swamp Bridge   573

Malvern Hill, July 1, 1862   593

The northeastern frontier district of Virginia   687

The Shenandoah defensive area   689

Rappahannock-North Anna area and the Mid-Tidewater district   693

The Peninsula, Norfolk zone, and Richmond-Petersburg area   696

The order of battle of the Confederate Infantry on the left, First Manassas, July 21, 1861   729

Theatre of operations—Army of Northern Virginia, June 1862–April 1865   *Following Page* 774

FOREWORD

FOREWORD

AFTER completing in 1934 a life of General R. E. Lee, the writer began to collect material for a biography of a great American of an earlier period but found that mentally it was not easy to leave the struggle about which one had been writing for twenty years and more. A question plagued and pursued: In holding the light exclusively on Lee, had one put in undeserved shadow the many excellent soldiers of his army? "Stonewall" Jackson undoubtedly has won a permanent place in the history of American wars; Longstreet and "Jeb" Stuart probably have; but at least a score of other able officers, who fought under the same leader and added to his fame, rapidly are being forgotten. Had so modest a man as General Lee ever foreseen this, he would have lamented any presentation of his own services that might depreciate, even by silence, those of his comrades in arms. For this reason, it did not seem permissible to pass to another period of military history until that company of gallant gentlemen had been placed in their proper relationship to their chief. It was beyond one's capacity to paint all of them fully, but it might not be impossible to prepare, so to say, a succession of sketches. In June, 1936, this was undertaken.

Temerity has had due punishment. It was assumed that this work could begin with a brief review of the status and personnel of the Confederate command on June 1, 1862, the date when General Lee opened the headquarters of the Army of Northern Virginia. Before inquiry had proceeded far, it became apparent that many of Lee's problems of personnel were set for him in advance. His hopes and plans were circumscribed by appointments and by organization, good and bad, that went back to the Spring of 1861. Command was not created but was inherited by Lee. Most of his assigned lieutenants had been Johnston's. The failures of the Seven Days could be explained in no other way than by tracing the career of the men through whom Lee undertook his first major offensive. Inquiry had to be extended to the secession of Virginia, to the lists of the Southerners graduated at West Point and at the Virginia Military Institute, and to the roster of those who got their schooling in the Mexican War. This background, once assembled, could be put into appendices that need not trouble the hurried reader; but the material of command had to be examined, and the employment of that material during the fourteen months that preceded the wounding of Joseph E. Johnston had to be explained.

As for battles prior to June, 1862, many of the officers Lee used in his first campaign in Eastern Virginia had acquired their combat experience in one or more of Johnston's three engagements or in Jackson's Valley campaign. Examination of the literature brought to light a curious historical neglect of the early actions under the direction of Joseph E. Johnston. Consequently, to understand why some men were entrusted confidently with field command in June, 1862, while others were regarded as excitable or timid, it became necessary to make a detailed study of the battles of First Manassas, of Williamsburg and of Seven Pines. It had been hoped, for the next engagements, that Henderson's glorious biography of Stonewall Jackson would supply a proper introduction to Ashby and Ewell and Trimble and Charles Winder. Instead, it was found that documents which had been disregarded by Henderson, or brought to light after the appearance of this book, made imperative a complete re-examination of the operations from Kernstown to Port Republic. For months of labor spent on those battles, any student cheerfully would admit himself compensated *in toto*. The actors are as interesting, on close view, as the drama is different in many details from the familiar presentation.

Subsequent to Port Republic, no battles until Cedar Mountain, and then none of importance until those of Early in 1864, had to be treated *in extenso* from the standpoint of the commanding General. While these Virginia battles not described in *R. E. Lee* were under review, it seemed proper to sift the evidence on several troublesome and obscure historical questions connected with those actions. These inquiries were not an essential part of the task at hand, but it was thought the summarized results would round out the story of the battles without burdening too heavily the completed work. This is the reason for the inclusion of several of the appendices, which may seem to deal with matters of small importance.

During the two years spent in studying events prior to Lee's assumption of command, June 1, 1862, the choice of a method of presenting these sketches was a continuing puzzle. Manifestly, to write a succession of separate articles would be to duplicate what had been done in the *Confederate Military History,* in the *Dictionary of American Biography,* or in both. Gamaliel Bradford, to be sure, followed the traditional method successfully in his *Confederate Portraits* but, with two or three exceptions, he chose men who had different roles. In the present work, it sometimes would be necessary to write of as many as a dozen soldiers who had a conspicuous part in the same battle. If in separate studies of these men, a reader were confronted with essentially the same details of, say, Sharpsburg, he would damn the battle, the soldiers, the method and the writer.

What alternative was there to this traditional method of treatment? That question prompted another: What had these Confederates in common; what bound together their lives in all the similarities and contrasts? Obviously the nexus was their service in the same Army and, for three years of the war, under the same commander. That answer suggested a history of the Army of Northern Virginia, but such a book would parallel *R. E. Lee* too closely. At length there came to mind the General's letter of May 21, 1863, to John B. Hood. That officer evidently had sent Lee on May 13 a plan of campaign, which Hood had realized some critic might assail as exacting too much of the troops. The Texan must have expressed belief that the Army was capable of greater feats than it had performed. Lee answered: "I agree with you . . . in believing that our Army would be invincible if it could be properly organized and officered. There never were such men in an Army before. They will go anywhere and do anything if properly led. But there is the difficulty—proper commanders-- where can they be obtained?" Enough was known of Lee's difficulties to make it clear that he constantly was seeking "proper commanders." Was not that a possible basis for a study of Lee's Lieutenants? Might not the book be a review of the command of the Army of Northern Virginia, rather than a history of the Army itself?

As this approach was examined, it was apparent that the high command of the Army of Northern Virginia was subject to a constant and heavy attrition—by death, by disabling wounds, by intemperance and by incompetence. The Army always was being built up and torn down. Aside from man power, no aspect of the whole tragedy meant more than "proper commanders—where can they be obtained?" The connecting thread of this book well might be that of the effort to create and to maintain competent senior officers. As they emerged in battle or in administration of the Army, the various leaders could be introduced. If they rose, the scene of their new successes would be the proper setting for their reappearance. In the event they fell, they could be appraised and committed to posterity. All the while, the Army would be marching and fighting under such leaders as it had at a given moment. Where familiar battles again were described, the viewpoint would not be that of Lee but that of the men executing his orders or making decisions for themselves.

A manifest first difficulty in using this method of sketching so many persons is that they appear and disappear, speak or hold their peace, according to their share in particular scenes. One of Lee's Lieutenants may not "have a line" in the drama, so to say, for hundreds of pages, and then, perhaps when forgotten, will be found to be the central figure. To meet the difficulty of keeping individuals in mind, it has been thought that cross references can be used to bind together the different parts of the various sketches. Often, to avoid interruption of narrative, the connecting events of a career are put in footnotes, but each sketch can be integrated and, where so desired, may be detached from the larger story. Though Longstreet, D. H. Hill, Ewell, Hampton and others are examples in the first volume, this method of tying together the sketches with cross references is not so frequently used as in the second and third volumes, because four of the most conspicuous figures of the opening period—Beauregard, Joseph E. Johnston, Gustavus Smith and Magruder—are in the narrative almost continuously until they disappear permanently. Another large section of the first volume is allotted Jackson. Subsequently, a score of men who pass silently through the opening acts, or have one or two brief scenes, begin to shine as leaders. Dorsey Pender is typical. He appears first, casually, in a Richmond hotel lobby, where he asks a question of Johnston. Then he is mentioned in one report on Eltham. He is seen again in the Seven Days and at Second Manassas, but it is not until Chancellorsville that he becomes a major character in the drama. On the road to Gettysburg, for the final scene in Pender's life, the reader spends a night or two in the camp of the North Carolinian and, over his shoulder, reads some of the last letters written the young wife at Salem.

Equal to the difficulty of finding a suitable method of presentation has been a second, that of making a score of men stand out as distinguishable individuals where hundreds of actors, literally, crowd the stage. Animation and reality inhere in "Stonewall" Jackson and "Dick" Ewell, because of their eccentricities, though there always is danger of historical distortion in overstressing peculiarities. Besides Jackson and Ewell, perhaps half a dozen of the men treated in these pages have personalities that can be caught, as it were, and held. In addition, the frequent eulogies in the *Richmond Examiner* and the details of the quarrel with Jackson may fix, in some measure, the elusive personality of A. P. Hill. One may not say even that much of that modest gentleman, the easy-going, generous "Dick" Anderson. Still again, certain of Lee's Lieutenants were unsensational in behavior or had emotional control so complete that they seemed colorless or even stolid. For the painting of other portraits, the pigments were scanty and dim. Nothing remains but the monochrome of formal, impersonal reports with which to paint a personality.

To vitalize all these men without cartooning them is impossible. It would be a simple matter to adopt the technique Carlyle employed in his *French Revolution* and to use a catchword description for each of them; but where all the skill of Carlyle did not suffice to relieve that method of painful artificiality, lesser writers should shun it. Besides, men usually are too complex to carry on their backs the labels of assured classification. In the case of John B. Gordon, one might be justified in calling him "Ram-rod" because of his thinness and posture. "Jube" Early's habit of turning his chewing tobacco in his mouth in moments of great excitement may be mentioned occasionally to identify him. About "Jeb" Stuart there always is jingle and loudness. That is as far as the device of Carlyle may be borrowed without making it ridiculous. As a permissible substitute for catchwords. an elaboration of a

Dramatis Personæ, in the form of brief characterizations of the men sketched in each volume of this work, follows the Foreword. It may be consulted if, from the *mise en scène,* some man of remembered name but forgotten qualities steps out.

In order to adhere to the realities of a war in which old idols fell fast and new demigods rose overnight, few of those sketched here have been characterized upon their first appearance. Such a man as Beauregard showed his essential ego at a glance. Nothing ever was disclosed that was not plain after one day's association with him, except such a peculiarity as his mastery of his tongue and his utter lack of control over his pen. Jackson, on the other hand, had a nature not shown in all its contrasting lights until one had been with him for months. Quick portraiture is easy for Beauregard. Presentation of Jackson must be by a process of color printing, where each impression brings out something different. He probably will not be understood by readers of this book prior to the winter at Moss Neck, and perhaps not until he is on his deathbed. In most of the complex men who cross these scenes, as in Jackson, new experiences of the war brought new qualities to light. Consequently, the actors in the drama are not presented as definite personalities until they attract some attention by their performance. "Jeb" Stuart, for example, is mentioned several times in the early pages, but he is treated as one of many promising but not pre-eminent officers of the army until, in June, 1862, he made his "ride around McClellan." This approach has the virtue of placing a man where he belongs chronologically in the campaign. A further advantage, it is hoped, will prove to be that of sparing the reader the embarrassment of being introduced, in a single breath, to a large company. One description after another of the dozen officers and more who were around Manassas in the summer of 1861 would have confused all of them hopelessly in the reader's mind. That treatment, incidentally, would have given the early chapters a length disproportionate to the importance of the events described.

After method had been determined and a gradual introduction of the actors had been arranged, the third question was, Who of Lee's many companions in arms should be presented? No arbitrary standard has been applied for inclusion in these pages. At the outset, it was thought that all corps and divisional commanders should be presented; but it was apparent early in the research that some of the chiefs of division in 1862 were not historically important, and that some who never attained to the coveted rank of Major General, or even to that of Brigadier General, had a place in the history of the army command or of the army morale. Joseph E. Johnston and P. G. T. Beauregard stood in another category. Was it proper to list them among Lee's Lieutenants when he had no command over Beauregard until June, 1864, and none over Johnston until January, 1865, when Lee became General in Chief? To assert for Lee an authority he never exercised over these men would be to misrepresent him. On the other hand, both Beauregard and Johnston bulked large—perhaps out of proportion to their true military stature—in the history of the army command in Virginia. General Johnston, in particular, did much to shape the military outlook and esprit de corps of many of the higher officers who served under Lee. Were Johnston and Beauregard omitted, moulding influences would be disregarded. The decision was to sketch them and to enter this disclaimer.

In the main, it may be said that each man treated here won his own place, as it were, and determined by his deeds the extent of the treatment he received. If, as a result, Jackson commands almost a fourth of the first and second volumes, that is not thought to be a misplacement of values. It is hoped that no man has been portrayed solely because he was picturesque and readily characterized, or omitted because he was colorless or difficult to describe; but in several instances space is given to humble men of gallant behavior whose feats diverted or thrilled the Army. In the one category belongs Private William Hood, of the Thirty-third North Carolina, who "shinnied" up a tree at Sharpsburg to count for Jackson the enemy's flags. Among those of heroic mould and inconspicuous station who inspired his fellow soldiers, Richard Kirkland stood out at Fredericksburg. Some hundreds of others have been mentioned without being characterized. Certain of the anecdotes that have been a part of the South's endowment of sentiment and of humor for two generations have been reprinted. This has been done primarily because so grim a narrative needs to be lightened with laughter.

When the relevant facts, somber and sunny, concerning Lee's

principal lieutenants had been examined, four surprises were encountered. First among them was the disregard in the Confederacy of officers' training. Prior to secession, much reliance was placed on the leadership of those Southerners who then had or previously had held commissions in the United States Army. Although militiamen were left out of account as unqualified, former officers of volunteers in the Mexican War and the graduates of Southern military schools were expected to supplement the regulars. Virginia listed more men in each of these categories than any other Confederate State could count, but the total was low. The extensive summary in Appendix II shows that if every Virginia officer in the Federal Army at the beginning of 1861, every retired West Point graduate, every native veteran officer of the Mexican War and every living graduate of the Virginia Military Institute had supported the Confederacy, they would have supplied trained officers for the equivalent of fourteen regiments only. Actually, that number of available professional soldiers was not approximated. Twenty Virginians were on the active list of the regular Army in 1861 at the grade of field or general officer. Nine, and no more than nine, sided with the South. Of active company officers, sixty-four were Virginians. Forty-seven of these threw in their fortunes with the Confederacy. Thirteen retired officers shared in the defense of their State. Because of age, scarcely more than one fourth of the officers of volunteers of 1846–48 could take the field. All these sources yielded a total of ninety-four officers of greater or less military experience.

Small as was this number, virtually nothing was done in any organized way to train the required hundreds of new officers. Sometimes the artillerists had a little instruction, but the infantry and cavalry officers usually went into camp with no previous training. They had to acquire the elements of tactics on the drill ground, with troops, and in the tent at night with a book but with no instructor. The preservation, after seventy-five years, of copies by the score of Hardee's *Tactics,* of the various *Manuals* and of the many editions of the *Regulations* shows that many officers earnestly and diligently sought to learn the theory ere they undertook the practice of war. Comparatively few drilled "by the book" as "Extra Billy" Smith is alleged to have done (page 66, note 14), but the reports of early battles contain grim admission that some officers had to direct troops in action before they themselves knew even the simple evolutions of the line.

The rapid improvement of the troops in drill and in discipline would be inexplicable were two facts overlooked. One was the immense service rendered by graduates of the Virginia Military Institute and of the South Carolina Military Academy as drill-masters and then as company and regimental officers. Second was the success of the few professional soldiers of the Confederacy in having their government accept and support the standards of discipline and of military usage that had prevailed in the "Old Army." Insistence on those standards provoked endless gibes at the "West P'inters," but it explained many things. Professional soldiers applied all they had learned at the Academy and on the frontier. They administered the Army as if there always had been and always would be a Confederacy. One never gets the impression, after the first few months of war, that one is reading of a revolutionary, haphazard organization. It was, in the minds of its leaders, a "Provisional Army," but it had a permanent, professional corps of officers. Fascinating and monitory as all this is to the student, it makes necessary the reminder that in the first volume of this work are described the choice and the *combat* training of the Army's leaders—*combat* training because there was no other.

The second surprise in studying the command of the Army of Northern Virginia was something for which the writer should have been prepared—the unhappy sharpness of the contrasts of character in the men portrayed. After the War between the States, the Southern code for the judgment and treatment of soldiers and public men was explicit. President Davis, Cabinet members, Congressmen and officers of the general staff, especially of the quartermaster's and commissary service, could be denounced freely; deserters were shunned; men who had profited by the war and those who had dodged conscription were avoided but were not entirely beyond the pale; notorious cowards were the subject of jest but, if they had not deserted, they were not barred socially though rarely approved politically. If any veteran went over to the Republican Party or consorted with Negroes, that never was forgiven him. It cancelled his military record, no matter how fine that had been. A boastful Major might be ridiculed privately; on rare occasions a politician might assert that a rival, though a Confederate veteran, "never had smelt gunpowder"; former Generals, if necessitous, had first call on all offices that paid well; one-armed or one-legged men were preferred for political sinecures and, when chosen, must be retained. Apart from these distinctions, there was democracy in defeat. All ex-soldiers were to be rated gallant and all officers able. Among men who had lost everything, comparisons were not in order. The sons and daughters of Southern soldiers were reared in the unquestioning belief that Confederate Generals were great warriors who never would have been defeated had not the odds been overwhelming. A certain sacredness that attached early to the name of General Lee came in time to embrace the high command generally. As bickering and rivalries were forgotten, the Army and the Southern cause took on a spiritual symbolism that must have been experienced to be understood. Criticism was disloyalty. To mock was to betray.

On cold reappraisal, after seventy-five years, some Generals have diminished in stature. The failure of two or three of them is found to have been due to definite and discoverable peculiarities of mind. There is, for example, no mystery about the unwillingness of the Confederate President to give Beauregard or D. H. Hill a post commensurate with their rank. Beauregard never could be rid of his Napoleonic complex or be induced to shape his strategical plans in terms of available force and practicable logistics. Hill, a fine combat officer, would not accept the responsibilities of departmental command. Other men, in unpleasant number, were boastful and were willing to warp the historical verities in order to glorify themselves or to extenuate error. Some of Lee's Lieutenants were jealous and some were stupid; some were self-seeking and many were vaingloriously ambitious. In two or three cases, the evidence is all too explicit that men of honored name were physical cowards. Several military blunders and no little of chronic inefficiency had their source in the bottle.

In contrast with this dissipation, this smallness, this indiscipline and this selfishness stand gloriously the character and the fortitude of Lee and of other morally unshakable leaders. In case after case, Lee patiently assuaged the victims of hurt pride, stimulated the discouraged, appealed to the better nature of wavering men, and by force of his own righteousness more than by the exercise of his authority, reconciled bitter differences or induced personal enemies to work together. The seeming absence from the Army of Northern Virginia of such rivalries and animosities as hampered nearly all the other large forces, Confederate and Union, was not in reality absence but control. In the hearts of Lee's subordinates were all the explosive qualities that existed elsewhere, but the General himself possessed the combination of tact, understanding, prestige, firmness and personal character necessary to prevent the explosion. It may be remarked, also, that discovery of new details of Jackson's ceaseless controversies with his subordinates, and review of his failure to maintain efficient divisional and brigade leadership, are an all-sufficient answer to the question asked for two generations, whether Jackson, separated from Lee, would have been a great army commander. Strategically he would have been; administratively, he could not have been.

In employing the history of the army command as the framework for a study of these Confederate officers, the next surprise was the discovery that skill in the administration of a command had an even closer relationship to morale than had been supposed. Army morale does not depend exclusively, or even primarily, on the C. in C. He can do little more than give the dynamic of his personality, the stamp of his character, to that which his subordinates have achieved. Insofar as it reflects the command, morale is the mirror of the faith, the administrative skill and the leadership in training and in combat displayed by the average officer. What is shown in battle is created in camp.

The final surprise came in the study of the third major reorganization of the Army of Northern Virginia. Those successive periods of large-scale promotion do not permit of swift and easy investigation, nor does the description of them make diverting reading; but, needless to say, an account of the replacement of general officers is an essential part of the history of the command. When the Army was organized in 1861, few responsible leaders foresaw difficulty in procuring qualified commanders. The South was thought by most public men to be opulent in leadership. Arms were as readily the avocation of the gentleman as the profession of the soldier. In terms of confident ambitions, the material for a corps of officers seemed abundant. Joseph E. Johnston

felt, in the winter of 1861–62, that he had numerous officers qualified for brigade command at the least. By the summer of 1862,
General Lee, who was more cautious in his judgment of leadership, was not so sure that Colonels in large number could be promoted to the grade of general officer. He was hampered then and
increasingly thereafter by the necessity of maintaining a rough
balance of commissions among the Generals from the different
States. Still more was he hindered in the upbuilding of command
by the rules of seniority which, at least in theory, prescribed that
the senior Colonel or, in any event, a Colonel within a given
Brigade, should be elevated to its command if the General were
slain.

Despite these rules, which are among the inherited abomina-
tions of military service, little difficulty was experienced in maintaining at a promising level the quality of general officers in the
first major reorganization, which followed the campaign of the
Seven Days, and in the second, which was necessitated by the
losses at Cedar Mountain, Second Manassas and in the Maryland
expedition. When this study reached the third reorganization, that
of May, 1863, undertaken after the death of "Stonewall" Jackson,
the evidence quickly proved that the Army of Northern Virginia
did not then have a sufficient number of qualified Colonels of the
line to fill vacancies. Stated explicitly, after the second year of
hostilities, in an army of nine infantry Divisions, roughly 150
regiments, two officers only, John B. Gordon and William Mahone,
added materially to the vigor of the high command. A few others
suggest the possibility of development; at least three who might
have become noteworthy commanders—Dorsey Pender, Dodson
Ramseur and Robert Rodes—were killed in action. The remaining new general officers scarcely attained to the standard of performance established prior to Gettysburg.

This raises a question of present and continuing importance.
The necessary qualities of high military command manifestly are
administrative skill and diligence, strategical and logistical sense,
military imagination, initiative, resourcefulness, boldness coupled
with a grasp of practicality, ability to elicit the best of men, and
the more personal qualities of character, endurance, courage and
nervous control. Are these essential qualities possessed, or may
they be developed, by more than a minute fraction of those who

can perform well the lesser military duties? Ere the Army of Northern Virginia passed the high noon at Chancellorsville, it was plain that a good General had been a good officer from the time of his first commission. No less was it plain that a man would not of necessity be a good General because he had been an excellent Captain or had a creditable record as a Colonel.

On the basis of that established truth of command in one great American army, it perhaps is a mistake to assume that when a small nation wages a long war it trains in the exacting but instructive school of battle an inexhaustible supply of competent general officers. Instead, where capable officers rise fast, their death or invalidism may mean that less competent men will succeed them. Whether the necessary standard of command can be sustained, in the face of heavy casualties in the corps of officers, may depend less on training and combat experience than on the size of the population. A martial tradition, public respect for the profession of arms, and the long-continued service of an ample and well-trained general staff may be ponderable factors; but unless there is vast man power from which to sift and develop soldiers, mere experience may not be enough to assure continuing good field command above the grade of Colonel.

May three matters be added that relate directly to the preparation of this book? First is the plenitude of source material concerning some officers and the paucity of the records of others. None of the corps commanders of the Army of Northern Virginia, except Jackson, left any large number of contemporary personal letters. This is a lamentable, an irreparable gap. What would not one give for the letters Longstreet presumably wrote his wife after Gettysburg, and those A. P. Hill penned during the heat of his quarrel with Jackson? Concerning other officers of high rank, Dr. J. G. de R. Hamilton of the University of North Carolina, the best-versed authority on the manuscript sources of Confederate history, has found that the abundance or the scarcity of letters and contemporary memoirs is in a measure geographical: the worst ravages of time and of neglect have been in the papers of Virginia and of South Carolina officers. In comparison, the letters of many North Carolina officers are quite numerous. With the assistance of the friends whose kindness is recorded more specifically at the end of Volume III, many "trails" have been followed with results the most varied. Of all the manuscripts graciously made available to the writer, much the richest are the papers and maps of Maj. Jed. Hotchkiss. On them primarily is based the new treatment of the Valley Campaign of 1862. Complete failure has attended efforts to procure material on certain soldiers and most notably on "Jeb" Stuart's famous scouts, William Farley, Redmond Burke and Franklin Stringfellow, whom the writer had hoped to sketch. For the pre-war career of those mentioned in these pages, no attempt has been made to use primary sources. It is as soldiers in one war, and not for their achievements before 1861 or after 1865, that Lee's Lieutenants are portrayed here through the military records, the judgment of their contemporaries and their own private papers.

Those war letters and diaries of the eighteen-sixties, so informative when available, so deplored when lost, exhibit, in the second place, as marked a difference from present-day thought on religion as perhaps ever has been wrought in seven decades. Many of the men who appear in these pages kept religion in the same sanctuary of the heart with patriotism and love of home. Acceptance of traditional Christianity was almost universal. Mild and reverent deism was viewed with horror. Doubt was damnation. Agnosticism was service to Antichrist. What was believed was professed. The example of Lee and of Jackson in attributing victory to God was duplicated in thousands of letters. Every escape from death in battle was acknowledged to be a special mercy of a personal God. Premonition of the "inevitable end" was regarded as a definite and not uncommon reality. The dying soldier must be warned unhesitatingly that his time was short and that he must "make his peace with God"; the believing soul was encouraged to voice faith and farewell. All the circumstances of a man's last hours became later the subject of eager review and, if they were edifying, often were the theme of letters and sermons. This is emphasized here because the spirit of the times would be violated were one to pass lightly over the reflections of soldiers on religion, to eliminate the deathbed scenes, or to omit the alleged "last words." If those incidents give a sentimentality to some of these pages, it is enough to say, in justification, that the book in this respect must mirror the era it describes.

Finally, it has to be remembered that the speech of the eighteen-sixties had a formality half eloquent, half artificial. The simplest observation might become a declamation. Any remark might evoke an oration. This ornate conversational style has been reflected in much of the dialogue quoted in these pages; but on occasion it has been necessary to apply a critique that may have been somewhat arbitrary. Particularly in writing down the words attributed to "Stonewall" Jackson, and above all, in recording what that soldier is alleged to have said during the last few days of his life, one has to be circumspect in employing direct discourse. Accustomed as Jackson was to the rhetorical speech of the clergymen whose company he much enjoyed, it scarcely seems possible that he could have shaped in the half delirium of his pneumonia some of the flights credited to him. One has to conclude that his eloquent clerical attendants rounded their sentences in reporting his. This probably is true of several other incidents, but it does not alter the main fact that even the casual conversation of the period was, by present-day usage, deliberate and stiff. Perhaps the best for which one may hope, in reporting the verbal exchanges, is that they will not distract or appear stilted.

To make the requisite investigation, to decide upon a method of treatment, to assemble the notes, to write and to revise has been a labor of eight years, but they have been pleasant years. A writer of biography can ask for nothing more interesting than to begin with a score of names in printed military dispatches and then to work over historical materials of many sorts until names become personalities, characteristics emerge, and reports take on the sound of a voice. At first, one had the feeling that these Confederates had ridden so far toward oblivion that one could not discern the figures or hope to overtake them before they had passed over the horizon of time. In the end, there was the sensation of reaching their camp, of watching the firelight on their faces, and of hearing their brave and genial conversation.

In times less out of joint, publication of this study would have been delayed until it could have appeared in its entirety. The disadvantages of issuing a three-volume work as if it were a serial story are manifest; but something, perhaps, may be gained by printing in the first year of this nation's greatest war, the story of the difficulties that had to be overcome in an earlier struggle before the command of the army became measurably qualified for the task assigned it. If the recountal of the change of officers in the first fifteen months of the war in Virginia seems discouraging, the events that followed the reorganization of July, 1862, are assurance that where the supreme command is capable, fair-minded and diligent, the search for competent executive officers is not in vain. The Lee and the "Stonewall" Jackson of this war will emerge. A Second Manassas will follow the blundering of backward-looking commanders and of inexperienced staff officers during any Seven Days' Battle the new army must fight.

DOUGLAS SOUTHALL FREEMAN

Westbourne,
Richmond, Virginia,
September 21, 1942.

Lee's Predecessors and Lieutenants

IN THE FIRST PART OF THE
TRILOGY OF THE HIGH COMMAND
ARMY OF NORTHERN VIRGINIA

Listed in substantially the order of their
appearance in the narrative. Ages are
those of the birthday nearest
the outbreak of hostilities,
April, 1861

PIERRE GUSTAVE TOUTANT BEAUREGARD

Professional soldier, "Hero of Sumter," who comes to Virginia with high reputation easily won during the initial hostilities at Charleston, S. C. He is 43, an admirable actor in a martial role, and he displays great self-confidence on the basis of limited experience with troops. From the outset, he shows a lack of the sense of logistics and he grossly overestimates the strategical combinations possible with green troops and inexperienced staff, but he has the good fortune to rout the enemy at Manassas, July 21, 1861. The aftermath of this victory brings to light some curious mental qualities and a singular infelicity in writing. All these combine to get him into trouble with the President and the War Department. Latin in look, he is of medium height and middle weight. His soldiers call him "Old Bory" and say he has the eye of a bloodhound. Lettered admirers insist he might have been the reincarnation of one of Napoleon's marshals.

JOHN BANKHEAD MAGRUDER

"Prince John" he is to all his acquaintances, 51, a professional soldier with some antebellum experience as an artillerist. He is handsome, perfectly uniformed, insistent, impatient and theatrical, and he always appears at a gallop. Despite a slight lisp, he loves to talk and he writes ceaselessly to his superiors. A certain aptitude for independent command he possesses, and with it ability to bluff an adversary. After winning much applause for the first Confederate victory in Virginia, he gradually becomes entangled in a large military organization, which irks him unreasonably. In the end, when his great opportunity comes, he shows a weakness not uncommon in war—an excited, overzealous desire to do all his work in person.

DANIEL HARVEY HILL

Former professional soldier, educator, text-book author and distinguished Presbyterian layman, age 40, who has an accidental spine injury and an exceedingly sharp tongue. In looks he is cadaverous and has haunting eyes. He is in combat as capable as in camp he is critical. Off duty he is unpretending. His judgment of men always runs to an extreme. Ere this part of the military drama in Virginia closes, there are vague indications that he lacks some quality of leadership, but wherein he may fail to realize promise is not yet clear.

JOSEPH EGGLESTON JOHNSTON

He considers himself the ranking officer of the United States Army who joins the Confederacy and he resolves that he shall be so accepted. About him, at 54 years of age, are some magnetic and winning qualities which make his friends and most of his subordinates devoted to him. He has, also, unmistakable strategical sense, though doubts concerning his administrative capacity and his attention to detail gradually accumulate. Early he acquires a grievance which embitters all his dealings with the Administration. Johnston is alarmed, also, to discover how readily secrets of military importance leak out, and probably for this reason he is excessively reserved in dealing with the President and the War Department. His peculiarities clash with those of the Commander in Chief until his acts are hampered and his response to orders or to suggestions is unpredictable. A difficult and touchy subordinate he is, though a generous and kindly superior—in sum, a military contradiction and a temperamental enigma. In appearance he is small, soldierly and graying, with a certain gamecock jauntiness.

GUSTAVUS WOODSON SMITH

Street commissioner of New York City, former army engineer and private engineering contractor, age 39, a somewhat late arrival on the battlefield. Bulky, occasionally frowning and always determined to impress, he is an assured administrator, who maintains suavely pleasant relations with his superiors and subordinates and enjoys high rank and reputation though he had little experience with troops. There is a suggestion of politics in his eminence. Somewhat pompously he proceeds to his first great hour of responsibility and then disappoints the army. To his intimates, he is "G. W."

The portrait is from a photograph furnished by Cook, Richmond

THOMAS JONATHAN JACKSON

Mediocre teacher at the Virginia Military Institute and a former professional soldier, age 37, profoundly and, some say, fanatically religious, with a precise regard for discipline and army regulations. A man he is of contrasts so complete that he appears one day a Presbyterian deacon who delights in theological discussion and, the next, a reincarnated Joshua. He lives by the New Testament and fights by the Old. Almost 6 feet in height and weighing about 175 pounds, he has blue eyes, a brown beard and a commonplace, somewhat rusty appearance. From the first scene he grows in importance until he becomes the hero of the drama, and then, abruptly, he fails in a climactic hour and raises a question whether he can work in harness. His students called him "Tom Fool Jackson." To his soldiers he is "Stonewall" or "Old Blue Light" and then "Old Jack."

The portrait is from a photograph furnished by Cook, Richmond

JAMES LONGSTREET

He first seeks staff appointment as paymaster, the position he had held in the United States Army, though he is a graduate of West Point. He receives line commission and soon displays administrative capacity, power to win the respect of his subordinates, and a calm imperturbability in battle. Until an epidemic kills three of his children, he is a somewhat gay comrade; thereafter he is absorbed in his duty. Blunt and roughly bantering, he is not ill-natured. If he is not brilliant, in strategy or in conversation, he is solid and systematic. Ambitious he is, also, but not disposed to pick quarrels. In height he is about 5 feet 10½ inches, age 40. He is slightly deaf, but a dignified, impressive man, known to his soldiers as "Old Pete." The secret of his power is his incredible nervous control. He never gets tired.

The portrait is from a photograph furnished by Cook, Richmond

RICHARD STODDERT EWELL

From graduation at the United States Military Academy a trooper, and for most of his career as a soldier, an Indian fighter. Forty-four years old, he is, at his quarters, an unsoldierly person, bald, pop-eyed and long-beaked, with a piping voice that seems to fit his appearance as a strange, unlovely bird; he probably has stomach-ulcers and chronically complains of headaches, sleepless nights and indigestion; but he quickly shows that he has a chivalrous, fighting spirit along with a sharp tongue and an odd sense of humor. He acquires friends unnumbered. They are not quite so irreverent as the soldiers who style him "Old Bald Head."

ROBERT SELDEN GARNETT

A solitary, professional soldier, age 41, of intellectual stock, wholly devoted to his profession, frozen by grief to seeming austerity, but regarded as a leader of great capacity and high promise. He passes from the stage in the first act of this tragedy.

WILLIAM HENRY CHASE WHITING

Son of a Lieutenant Colonel in the United States Army, he had a higher rating at West Point than any cadet ever had won prior to his time. Thereafter, until 1861, he had been a conspicuous younger officer in the Corps of Engineers. He is 47, thoroughly conscious of his position and somewhat disposed, perhaps, to lord it over men like Jackson, who had no distinction among his contemporaries at the Military Academy. Quite soon Whiting clashes with the President, on whose black books his name is entered. Somehow -none knows exactly how—he does not quite fulfil expectations. He is below middle height but handsome, martial and aristocratic in appearance. His troops call him "Little Billy."

JAMES EWELL BROWN STUART

By training and by preference a cavalryman, though not without an affection for artillery. At 28 years of age, with an excellent army record, he still is a good deal of a boy, with a loud, exhibitionist manner, a fondness for spectacular uniforms and theatrical appearance and a vast love of praise. Soon he shows, also, that he is disposed to somewhat reckless adventure, but he has remarkable powers of observation, great physical strength and immense endurance. He is just emerging, in this part of the trilogy, as a major figure in command. His peculiarities are not generally known, nor are they yet of interest to the Army. The troopers call him. "Jeb." His old classmates at West Point, mindful of his roughhewn features, which his heavy beard scarcely softens, satirically call him "Beaut." He is about 5 feet 9 inches, massive and nearly square.

AMBROSE POWELL HILL

Almost five years of Powell Hill's career as a professional soldier have been spent in the office of the Superintendent of the United States Coast Survey. That has given him a certain knowledge of the inner workings of the machinery of government but it has not improved his temper. At 35 years of age, and a Confederate Colonel of the line, he trains what proves to be an excellent regiment and in his first battle he shows good brigade leading. He then wins promotion to the grade of Major General and almost immediately shows certain explosive qualities. As this part of the trilogy closes he still is a man of uncertain future and of undetermined capacity for cooperation. In person he is thin, of average height and frail health, with heavy beard and hair of an auburn brown. He dresses picturesquely but not so conspicuously as "Jeb" Stuart.

JUBAL ANDERSON EARLY

Lawyer, prosecuting attorney and West Point graduate, age 44, notoriously a bachelor and at heart a lonely man He comes from an unrenowned region, has no powerful family connections, and by a somewhat bitter tongue and rasping wit has isolated himself. During this part of the Confederate drama, he has two scenes only. In one he distinguishes himself while still a Colonel; in the other, he raises a question of impetuosity: Is he too reckless to be entrusted with command he otherwise is qualified to discharge? He is about 6 feet in height, thin and stooped by arthritis. His eyes, his hair and his beard are black. Amused by his odd name, soldiers call him "Old Jube," or "Old Jubilee."

WILLIAM NELSON PENDLETON

Clergyman of the Protestant Episcopal Church. He is 52 years of age and is on a friendly footing with the President and with Generals Lee and Johnston because he was at West Point with them. Circumstance and a certain aptitude for organization give him advancement to the post of Chief of Artillery, but he does not appear prominently until the last scene of this drama. Then he makes the younger men of the artillery wonder if he has the basic qualities of command. Pendleton looks and dresses like the commanding General, for whom he sometimes is mistaken. He suffers from a curious form of that unhappy disease *cacoëthes scribendi,* which produces some remarkable distortions.

MINOR FIGURES OF THIS PART OF THE TRILOGY OF THE HIGH COMMAND, ARMY OF NORTHERN VIRGINIA

PHILIP ST. GEORGE COCKE

Great planter, philanthropist and writer on farm management, a graduate of West Point, age 52. He is a renowned man in civil life and most useful there, but under the spur of duty and the rowel of ambition, he tenders his service to the Confederacy and has a succession of humiliations and one opportunity.

1

NATHAN GEORGE EVANS

Of the devil-may-care type of soldier, he is, age 37, bold, reckless, schooled in Indian fighting. Savage in appearance until he smiles, he has one fine scene and then leaves the stage to return in the late summer of 1862. His nickname is "Shanks."

ROBERDEAU CHATHAM WHEAT

Clergyman's son, 35, lawyer and soldier of fortune in Mexico and in Italy under Garibaldi, he has the dubious distinction of commanding the toughest battalion in the Army and, ere his end, he shares in three of the most dramatic scenes of the drama.

WADE HAMPTON

Probably the richest planter in the entire South, 42 years of age, he has had no previous military education but he possesses high intelligence, superb physique and the training of a thorough sportsman. He is fighting from a sense of duty, not from love of combat, but by the time the smoke clears from Malvern Hill, he shows distinct promise as a cavalry commander.

RICHARD HERON ANDERSON

Like Hampton, he is a South Carolinian of high station. Aged 40 and a West Pointer, he is proving himself capable of handling troops in battle and of hitting hard; but he is of a kindly, generous and easy-going nature, and, though he receives early promotion to the grade of Major General, he has no inclination to advertise or to advance himself.

li

LAFAYETTE McLAWS

Stout, short and more intense than his round face would indicate, this Georgian, aged 40, had a good record as an officer of the "old army" and he has shown administrative capacity as a soldier of the Confederacy. By the summer of 1862 he is entrusted with divisional command but as yet he is not appraised finally because his opportunities in combat have been few.

JOHN BELL HOOD

By birth a Kentuckian and by choice a Texan, he appears as a somewhat ungainly Lieutenant of cavalry, age 30, but he develops amazingly as a commander and as an individual. On every battlefield where he can put his men into action, he shines. There is reason to believe his magnificent personality, blond, towering, blue-eyed and handsome, will advance him as surely as his fighting will. Altogether promising he is as a combat officer; as an administrator and a strategist, he is inexperienced.

ROBERT EMMETT RODES

Graduate of the Virginia Military Institute, a teacher there and a former civil engineer for an Alabama Railroad. He is 32 years old, more than 6 feet in height, blond, with a drooping sandy mustache and a fiery, imperious manner on the field of battle. As yet, he is a hard-hitting fearless young Brigadier General, but at his grade he is a marked man.

SAMUEL GARLAND

A lawyer of wide literary taste and cultural interests, a graduate of the Virginia Military Institute and, at 30, a man of recognized standing. With more of the look of a scholar than of a soldier, he does admirably in all the battles he is privileged to share and ahead of him appears to lie a career of great distinction. Perhaps he scarcely cares for fame, though he will do his full duty. At the time of his appearance, he has lost both wife and child and finds himself the last of his line.

MICAH JENKINS

After he was graduated from the South Carolina Military Academy, he was one of the organizers of the King's Mountain Military School and, at 25, he was Colonel of a fine regiment. He is bold and ambitious and, as the battles multiply, he throws himself more furiously into them. He is full of promise—clear-eyed, with dark waving hair and a firm, determined but not unfriendly mouth.

JOHN BROWN GORDON

Mining promoter and lawyer, age 29, who already has risen from Captain to Colonel and, during this phase of the drama, has opportunity of leading Rodes's Brigade. With a fine head and penetrating eyes, Gordon is so thin and so straight that he resembles a ramrod. Although he has had no military experience before the war, he quickly learns the art of procuring the full obedience of his men and he possesses an oratorical power which inspires his troops to undertake anything.

FITZ LEE

This rollicking nephew of General R. E. Lee is 25 and a West Pointer with some experience as a Lieutenant in the United States Cavalry. He begins his Confederate service as a Captain and he rises steadily until, in July, 1862, he wears the wreath and three stars of a Brigadier General. Florid, after the manner of the Lees, he is long-bearded, strong and already too fat; but he is active, cheerful and on terms of laughing intimacy with "Jeb" Stuart. Those in the Army who do not enviously attribute to "family influence" his rapid rise, say he is a typical cavalryman.

TURNER ASHBY

Farmer, noted horseman, age 30, with little formal education, though born of good stock, he shows himself so bold and resourceful a leader, so flawlessly courageous in the presence of the enemy, that he attracts to him every boy in the Shenandoah Valley who loves horses and craves adventure. Soon Ashby gets more soldiers than he can direct well, but he performs some amazing feats before a certain day in June, 1862. In appearance he is strange, almost mysterious—of the darkest olive complexion, "an Arab type" some insist, small but agile and of great strength. About him, while still living, myths gather.

RICHARD TAYLOR

Son of a President of the United States, he is a wealthy sugar-plantation owner, sometime student at Edinburgh and Harvard and graduate of Yale. At 35 he accepts election as Colonel of a Louisiana regiment and comes to Virginia, where he has little fighting to do until he gets a Brigade under Ewell and marches to join "Stonewall" Jackson in the Shenandoah Valley. There a multitude of adventures befall him. He is absolutely self-reliant and indisposed to accept any judgment as sound merely because it is authoritative. This does not cost him either his admiration or affection for other men, or deny him their friendship. Observant, he has a fine sense of the dramatic. His nickname is "Dick."

ISAAC RIDGEWAY TRIMBLE

Railroad executive, engineer and old-time West Pointer, who, at 59, leaves ease in Maryland to share the fortunes of the South. At first he shows awkwardness in handling troops but he learns fast. He is a dark, handsome man with a flaming eye and deep ambition—perhaps disposed to be contentious and certainly a dandy in dress, but of the most conspicuous courage and a furious, insatiable fighter.

MAXCY GREGG

Savant and lawyer is Gregg, a rich South Carolina bachelor of wide literary and scientific interests, who has counted politics among his avocations. He had a commission, though he saw no active service in the Mexican War and he appears here first as a Colonel and then as a Brigadier. In station, in influence, in bearing and in entourage he is a considerable person, whose ability to adapt himself to command is of some interest to his friends. He is dignified, unfailingly courteous, 47 years of age and slightly deaf.

ROBERT TOOMBS

This well-known Georgia politician, former United States Senator and first Confederate Secretary of State, age 51, is a furious, fascinating person who believes that the war will be brief but that participation in it will give him more prestige than can be had in civil life during the sectional quarrel. He is ambitious, insubordinate and quarrelsome, the impersonation of the "political general." A few of his friends hold loyally to him and share his belief that he is a great man. His hatred of President Davis develops through the whole of this part of the trilogy.

THOMAS LAFAYETTE ROSSER

West Point cadet of the class of 1861, who resigns before he is graduated. He procures a commission as First Lieutenant and, before the Seven Days, rises to be a Colonel of cavalry. Not yet 25, he is 6 feet, 2 inches tall, powerful, brown-eyed and handsome.

JOHN PELHAM

Like Rosser, a West Pointer of the Class of 1861 who resigned on the secession of Alabama and prior to his graduation. He is 20 and commands as Captain the Stuart Horse Artillery, which he organized. Of all the young artillerists, none is braver, more promising or physically more magnificent. He is a tall, clear blond, who blushes red when he is praised. In camp he is quiet, and is without a touch of exhibitionism—a glorious boy in the estimation of both sexes.

WILLIAM JOHNSON PEGRAM

Until secession, he was a student of the University of Virginia, and was regarded merely as an intelligent, retiring boy of high character. At 20, he appears in this drama as a tireless Captain of artillery whose tactics seemed to be summed up in three orders—get close to the enemy, stay there, fire fast and accurately. He is a small young man, so near-sighted that he always wears spectacles, but he is of the type that battle develops.

AND MANY OTHERS

—who will make their appearance later.

LEE'S LIEUTENANTS

CHAPTER I

"Old Bory's Coming"

He would go at once. The request from the President that he come to Richmond offered an opportunity as surely as it conveyed an order. Federal troops had crossed the Potomac. A battle that would assure the triumph of the new Confederacy would be fought ere long in Virginia. Command there was much to be preferred to the post at Pensacola, from which Mr. Davis had excused him. Virginia was more inviting, even, than New Orleans, whither his fellow Lousianians had asked the Chief Executive to send him. At the same time, departure from South Carolina would be regrettable. From the hour of his arrival there, March 6, 1861,[1] the patriots of Charleston had welcomed him. After he had forced the surrender of Fort Sumter on April 14, without the loss of a man, they had acclaimed and adopted him Some of them seemed to find a certain Huguenot kinship in his name—Pierre Gustave Toutant Beauregard—and all of them united to do him honor.[2] Before he left those friendly and gallant South Carolinians, to win the battle in Virginia, he would write a farewell address.

It was done with dispatch and was, in its final form, a message not to South Carolinians only but to the entire Confederacy also. Beauregard wrote: ". . . it seems my services are required elsewhere, and thither I shall go, not with joy but with firm determination to do more than my duty, if I can, and to leave as strong a mark as possible on the enemies of our beloved country, should they pollute its soil with their dastardly feet. But rest assured . . .

[1] *War of the Rebellion. Official Records of the Union and Confederate Armies*, 1, 266. This work is cited as *O. R.* All references are to Series I, except when Roman numerals, preceding *O. R.*, indicate Series II, III or IV. Where a volume is in one part only, the volume and page number, as in this initial reference, follow *O. R.* without "pt." or "p." Where a volume is in more than one part, the reference will be to part and page; e.g., *O. R.*, 12, pt. 2, p. 514.

[2] Alfred Roman, *The Military Operations of General Beauregard* (cited hereafter as *Roman*), 1, 52 ff, 64. Although Colonel Roman was responsible for the original draft of this book, General Beauregard reviewed the whole of it so carefully that it is, in effect, his military autobiography.

that whatever happens at first, we are certain to triumph at last, even if we had for arms only pitchforks and flint-lock muskets, for every bush and haystack will become an ambush and every barn a fortress. The history of nations proves that a gallant and free people, fighting for their independence and firesides, are invincible against even disciplined mercenaries, at a few dollars per month. What, then, must be the result when its enemies are little more than an armed rabble, gathered together hastily on a false pretence, and for an unholy purpose, with an octogenarian at its head? None but the demented can doubt the issue." [3]

Before it was possible to ascertain what impression was made by this address, the General and his staff left on May 29, 1861, for Richmond, the newly selected capital of the Confederate States.[4] The staff itself included many Carolinians of distinguished name and of the highest political station. At the moment, it was fortunately so. Along the railroad, advance word had been spread that General Beauregard was aboard the northbound train. Multitudes gathered at every station to have a look at the "Hero of Sumter." Their demand, voiced in every key, was, "Speech, speech, speech!" He bowed his acknowledgments, but he did not reply. Where the crowd was insistent, Beauregard would glance at one of his volunteer aides, Col. John L. Manning, who then would step forward and would deliver a brief oration. Often, also, on the journey, Judah P Benjamin, former Senator from Louisiana, and Attorney General of the Confederacy, who chanced to be aboard, would appear on the train platform and would stir the throng with his eloquence.[5]

The journey confirmed everything the General had been told of the incredible popularity he had won by his success in Charleston Harbor. How quickly fame had come to him! When he had resigned from the United States Army, Feb. 20, 1861, he had been fifth ranking Captain in the Corps of Engineers and had a brevet as Major for gallant conduct in the Mexican War. Late in 1860,

[3] Anon. [W. P. Snow], *Southern Generals*, edition of 1865 (cited hereafter as *Southern Generals*), 214.

[4] *O. R.*, 51, pt. 2, p. 120. Beauregard was not sure, 1 *Roman*, 64, whether the request from President Davis to come to Richmond was received by him on the 28th, but Roman said it was "on or about" that date. The order is not in *O. R.* or in Dunbar Rowland, *Jefferson Davis, Constitutionalist, His Letters, Papers and Speeches* (cited hereafter as *Rowland*).

[5] 1 *Roman*, 64.

he had been named Superintendent of the United States Military Academy, but because of known Southern sympathy had held the post five days only—Jan. 23–28, 1861. In his profession he was esteemed; outside of it he was little known till hostilities had been opened at Charleston.[6] Now, seven weeks after the fall of Sumter, and less than three months from the time he had arrived at Charleston, he had received the thanks of Congress[7] and the laudation of the Southern press as one of the greatest soldiers in the world.[8] Napoleonic myths had grown up about him. He was said to have warned President Lincoln to remove all noncombatants from Washington by a given date, as if he were determined forthwith to take the city.[9] Southern people even were told that a frightened North hoped and believed that he was dead and that his body had been shipped to France.[10] Not one doubt of his military genius was admitted.

At the fullest of this valuation, Richmond was prepared to welcome him. On May 31, ere his train puffed importantly into the station, hundreds of townfolk had gathered there. A carriage and four were waiting to carry the General to the Spotswood Hotel, where a suite had been reserved for him. All the honors that had been paid President Davis upon arrival two days previously were to be repeated for General Beauregard. He was most grateful when he stepped from the car and shook hands; but, if the committee would permit, he would take a simpler carriage and, in the company of one or two of his staff officers, would go quietly to the hotel. With even more of admiration for his modesty than of regret that he might not be seen by all who had come to welcome him, the committeemen acquiesced. Quickly he was wheeled up the hill to the Spotswood. The band and the crowd followed. Music and cheers and appeals for a speech were in

---

6 He was born near New Orleans, in the Parish of St. Bernard, May 28, 1818, and was graduated No. 2 in the Class of 1838 at West Point. For his army assignments, see G. W. Cullum, *Biographical Register of the Officers and Graduates of the U. S. Military Academy . . .*, 3rd edition (cited hereafter as *Cullum* and with the "Number" of the individual on the roster of West Point graduates, rather than by page and volume, which differ materially in the several editions), No. 942. Beauregard's rank in the Corps of Engineers is given in the Army Register, June 30, 1860.

7 May 4, 1861; *O. R.*, 53, 160.

8 *Richmond* (Va.) *Dispatch*, Apr. 24, p. 1, col. 4; May 23, p. 2, col. 1; *Richmond Examiner*, Apr. 11, p. 1, col. 4; May 31, 1861, p. 1, col. 4. *Cf.* J. B. Jones, *A Rebel War Clerk's Diary*, edition of 1935 (cited hereafter as *R. W. C. D.*), I, 15; Mary Boykin Chesnut, *A Diary from Dixie*, edition of 1929 (cited hereafter as *Mrs. Chesnut*), 31.

9 *Richmond Dispatch*, May 1, 1861, p. 2, col. 3.

10 *Richmond Dispatch*, May 11, 1861, p. 3, col. 1.

vain.[11] His mission was war. He must waste no time in needless words.

The next day, he conferred with the President and with General R. E. Lee who, in an ill-defined manner, was responsible for military operations in Virginia. Old friends these were, old and admiring. Davis as United States Secretary of War had known Beauregard well and, in March, 1861, had commended the General to Governor Pickens of South Carolina as "full of talent and of much military experience." [12] This favorable judgment had been strengthened by Beauregard's direction of affairs in South Carolina. In planning immediate steps to combat the fast-developing Federal threat against Virginia, Jefferson Davis felt that he could rely on Beauregard.

No less did the President have self-reliance. He had hurried to Richmond in answer to earnest representations that he and he only could direct aright the defense of the frontier. Montgomery newspapers had reported not long previously that Mr. Davis was having his old Mexican sword sharpened at a gunsmith's in Market Street and that numbers of visitors had called to see that famous weapon. A man who was having his blade made ready of course intended using it. Little doubt was expressed that the President would take the field in person.[13] Rumor had it he had written Governor Letcher of Virginia that he would do this and, with Lee and Beauregard to execute his orders, would himself plan operations.[14] Such a course, the *Richmond Examiner* asserted, would inspire confidence, order and energy. With others, the paper explained, the soldiers would fight and perhaps would win, but "with him, the victory would be certain, and chance become certainty." [15] He was acclaimed "a tower of strength, with the iron will, the nerve, the energy and decision of Andrew Jackson and more than Jackson's knowledge and general education." Davis, it was asserted, was a statesman in every way qualified

[11] 1 *Roman,* 66. *Richmond Examiner,* p. 3, col. 1; *Richmond Dispatch,* p. 2, col. 3, June 1, 1861; "A Richmond Lady" [Sally Brock], *Richmond during the War* (cited hereafter as *Miss Brock*), 46.
[12] 5 *Rowland,* 58.
[13] *Richmond Semi-weekly Examiner,* April 26, 1861, p. 2, col. 3.
[14] *Richmond Dispatch,* May 2, p. 3, col. 2; May 11, 1861, p. 3, col. 1—false reports, of course.
[15] *Richmond Semi-weekly Examiner,* May 7, 1861, p. 2, col. 2.

for his task; he had foresight, judgment, fertility of resources and wonderful composure of spirit.[16] As for comment in the Northern press, the South was flattered when the *Cleveland Plain Dealer* styled the President a "genuine son of Mars," and when the *Bangor Democrat* pronounced him "one of the very, very few gigantic minds which adorn the pages of history."[17]

If there were error of judgment in these estimates, the new President did not deprecate it. He was not flattered by praise, but neither was he frightened by responsibility. Without vainglory or belief that he had genius for swift strategical combinations, he felt, as he sat down with Beauregard and with Lee, that he had been trained as a soldier and that, as a commander, he had been tried. To his four years of administrative experience as Secretary of War—an experience that no other living man in the South except John B. Floyd could boast—he had added that of chairman of the Military Committee of the United States Senate. Who had so diversified an equipment, who a better reason for self-reliance? Difficult he knew his task was; capable of discharging it he believed himself to be. Systematic, swift and with a memory that was not quite so accurate as he assumed it to be, he was confident he could discharge in more than a perfunctory sense his prerogative as commander in chief of the military forces of the Confederacy.

The third man at the council on May 31 was in public estimation the least distinguished of the three. Robert Lee was the son of a renowned Revolutionary soldier and had enjoyed the high admiration of Winfield Scott. In the Mexican War, Lee's work as an engineer had been brilliant, and when he had resigned from the "old army" he had reached the rank of Colonel of Cavalry; but he had no such reputation as Beauregard had won at Sumter and no prestige, other than social, that compared with that of President Davis. Inasmuch as Lee had returned to Richmond from Manassas on the 30th,[18] he was asked by the President to explain what had been done to prepare that important railroad junction against the Federals, who, on the night of May 23–24,

---

16 *Richmond Dispatch*, May 23, 1861, p. 2, col. 1.
17 Quoted in the *Richmond Dispatch*, May 20, 1861, p. 2, col. 2.
18 *O. R.*, 2, 894; D. S. Freeman, *R. E. Lee* (cited hereafter as *R. E. Lee*), 1, 512–14

had crossed the Potomac and had seized Alexandria.[19] Beauregard listened and reflected. He soon perceived that the President intended to send him to Norfolk. Later, when Lee had explained the situation in Northern Virginia, the President decided that Beauregard should have the post of instant danger, that of the Alexandria line.[20]

Beauregard exhibited neither concern nor satisfaction. If that was the post the President wished him to have, he would proceed immediately to Manassas. He needed to outfit himself, but he could leave that assignment to some of his entourage. The next morning he would start for the Northern frontier of the Confederacy.[21]

Promise was performance. By way of Hanover Junction, Gordonsville, Orange and Rappahannock Station, names destined to be written red, he travelled on June 1 to Manassas and forthwith assumed command.[22] "Old Bory's come!" cried the South Carolina troops who had served under him at Charleston. The Virginia recruits, hearing the cheers, sought this first opportunity of observing him.[23] If they expected a theatrical personality, they were disappointed. What they saw was a small man, 43 years of age, and five feet seven inches in height. He weighed about 150 pounds and had much strength in his slight frame,[24] though often he fell sick. With graying hair, cropped mustache, a good brow, high cheekbones, a belligerent chin and sallow olive complexion, he was as surely French in appearance as in blood, though not disposed to flashing uniform or to caparisoned steed. Imaginative Southern writers already pictured him as the reincarnation of one of Napoleon's marshals, but they said that his eyes, which were his most pronounced physical characteristic, were those of a bloodhound, large, dark, melancholy, half-inflamed as if from long vigils and obscured sometimes by their heavy, drooping lids. In manner, he was quiet but cordial. Privately talkative, he was officially uncommunicative. His gravity was adjudged the mask of

---

[19] O. R., 2, 42. For the relation of that city and of subsequently mentioned positions to the defense and the military geography of Virginia, see Appendix I. The military situation as it developed between April 17 and May 23 is described in the closing paragraphs of Appendix II.
[20] 1 Roman, 66.
[21] Ibid.
[22] O. R., 2, 896, 901.
[23] J. E. Cooke, Wearing of the Gray (cited hereafter as Wearing of the Gray), 83 ff.
[24] Southern Generals, 212.

kindliness. If he was unsmiling, he cancelled that by lack of ostentation. His tongue manifestly was his ally; it was not equally apparent that his pen was his enemy.[25]

With little ado Beauregard proceeded to inspect his troops. In command was Milledge L. Bonham, who had fought the Seminoles and the Mexicans as a citizen-soldier and had resigned his seat in Congress to the defense of his native South Carolina.[26] Under Bonham were two fine regiments,[27] more than 1500[28] of the best young men of the Palmetto State. In addition, a regiment was being organized at Manassas by Col. J. F. Preston,[29] another was being recruited rapidly by Col. R. S. Ewell, and a third by Col. Samuel Garland, a graduate of the Virginia Military Institute.[30] From Alexandria had arrived in retreat a few companies under Col. G. H. Terrett. At Culpeper, collecting men as rapidly as possible, was Col. Philip St. George Cocke,[31] a rich planter who had been graduated from West Point in 1832 and had been for two years a Lieutenant in the United States Army.

The smallness of this force alarmed Beauregard. Two days after his arrival at Manassas, he sat down and wrote directly to the President, without reference to Lee.[32] His position, Beauregard explained, his troops, and his service of supply alike were inadequate. "I must therefore," he said, "either be reinforced at once, as I have not more than about 6000 effective men, or I must be prepared to retire, on the approach of the enemy, in the direction of Richmond, with the intention of arresting him whenever and wherever the opportunity shall present itself, or I must march to meet him at one of [the] fords [of Bull Run or Occoquan], to sell our lives as dearly as practicable."[33]

25 Cooke, *op. cit.*; T. R. R. Cobb in 28 *Southern Historical Society Papers* (cited hereafter as *S. H. S. P.*), 287; David Macrae, *The Americans at Home*, 2, 139. If Beauregard has another biographer, excellent personal descriptions of the General will be found in *Richmond Whig*, July 26, 1861, page 2, col. 3, and in "A Distinguished Southern Journalist" [E. A. Pollard], *The Early Life, Campaigns, and Public Services of Robert E. Lee, with a Record of the Campaigns and Heroic Deeds of His Companions in Arms* (cited hereafter as *Companions in Arms*), 268–69.

26 5 *Confederate Military History* (cited hereafter as *C. M. H.*), 377–78.
27 *O. R.*, 2, 879.   28 *O. R.*, 2, 831.
29 *O. R.*, 2, 879.
30 *O. R.*, 2, 841; *Report of the Adjutant General of Va. for 1861–62*, p. 7.
31 *O. R.*, 2, 846.
32 It is quite probable that this was by verbal direction of the President, who seems, at this period, to have directed the major operations in Virginia and to have left the minor to Lee.
33 *O. R.*, 2, 902.

It would not suffice, Beauregard concluded, merely to exhort the President. The populace must be aroused. To that end, he issued on June 5 a formal proclamation in which he told the "good people" of the counties covered by his command: "A restless and unprincipled tyrant has invaded your soil. Abraham Lincoln, regardless of all moral, legal, and constitutional restraints, has thrown his abolition hosts among you, who are murdering and imprisoning your citizens, confiscating and destroying your property, and committing other acts of violence and outrage too shocking and revolting to humanity to be enumerated. All rules of civilized warfare are abandoned, and they proclaim by their acts, if not on their banners, that their warcry is 'Beauty and booty.' All that is dear to man, your honor, and that of your wives and daughters, your fortunes, and your lives, are involved in this momentous contest." With this preamble, Beauregard urged the farmers to "rally to the standard of our State and country, and by every means in your power compatible with honorable warfare to drive back and expel the invaders from your land." He became more specific: "I conjure you to be true and loyal to your country and her legal and constitutional authorities, and especially to be vigilant of the movements and acts of the enemy, so as to enable you to give the earliest authentic information to these headquarters or to the officers under my command. I desire to assure you that the utmost protection in my power will be extended to you all." [34]

The phrase "in my power" had limitations the "good people" of Northern Virginia might not realize. In their complete reliance upon Davis and Beauregard and the valor of their own sons, they did not understand, in those first furious days of half-organized war, how difficult it was to muster and to equip enough men to meet the four offensives that were being forged against their State.

Virginia was singularly vulnerable. From the Northwest, the North and the East, she could be assailed so readily that her defenders would lose much of the advantages of inner lines and of railways that ran from Richmond like spokes from a hub. The Federals held Fortress Monroe on Hampton Roads and commanded the deep water everywhere Although earthworks had

[34] *O. R.*, 2, 907.

been constructed on the tidal rivers of Virginia and had been armed with heavy guns captured at the Norfolk Navy Yard, there was no assurance that Federal warships could not silence or pass those defenses. In particular, there was danger of joint land-and-water operations by the Unionists against the Peninsula between the James and the York Rivers.

That operation would be no particular threat to Beauregard. Nor was there immediate danger to his front from an expedition that was in process of organization around Grafton on the Baltimore and Ohio Railroad. This town in Taylor County is about 120 miles west of Harpers Ferry and is situated in the Tygart Valley. By ascending Tygart River and then turning eastward over the Alleghenies, an enemy might reach Staunton; but not until then would he be in rear of the forces fighting in the lower or northern end of the Shenandoah Valley. Beauregard could afford to disregard this threat, unless and until he was called upon to detach troops to combat it.

Much nearer Beauregard's line was the prospect of a Federal attack from Pennsylvania and Maryland in Harpers Ferry, where the Shenandoah flows into the Potomac. The terrain and railroad communications were such that if Beauregard's position at Manassas were taken, an adversary might turn westward along the Manassas Gap Railroad, cross the Blue Ridge and cut the line of retreat of the forces at Harpers Ferry. Conversely, loss of Harpers Ferry would endanger Beauregard's position at Manassas.[35]

The Virginia authorities had seized Harpers Ferry and its valuable arms machinery on the night of April 18.[36] Militia officers had been placed temporarily in charge, but on April 30 [37] they had been superseded by Col. Thomas J. Jackson, Virginia Volunteers. Beauregard probably remembered Jackson, who had been a young artillerist during the Mexican War and had been brevetted Major for gallantry at Chapultepec. Whether or not he recalled the Major of the gallant days of '47, Beauregard soon heard of the work Tackson was doing at Harpers Ferry. The

[35] See Appendix I. The specific references to the northeastern and Shenandoah areas are on p. 688.

[36] 1 R. E. Lee, 473.

[37] D. S. Freeman, ed., Jackson MS. Order Book at Harpers Ferry, cited in Calendar of Confederate Papers, 282. For Jackson's earlier career, see infra, p. 706.

Colonel had been Professor of Physics and Instructor in Artillery at the Virginia Military Institute, to which position he had been appointed on the recommendation, among others, of D. H. Hill.[38] Serious-minded persons at the seat of the Institute, Lexington, Virginia, respected Jackson's piety, his diligence as a Presbyterian deacon, and his zeal in the religious instruction of the Negroes; the irreverent cadets and the recent graduates of V. M. I. said he was a "curiosity," a dull teacher who hewed to the line of the text and showed much embarrassment when forced to depart from it. At Harpers Ferry, he had been a different, an infinitely more competent, man. Terse, clear in direction, positive in orders, he was declared to be every inch the soldier. With the assistance of some of the cadets from V. M. I., he diligently had been drilling his raw volunteers. Despite the lack of level ground for the parade of even a battalion, he fast was developing to competent performance some of the 8000 men who had been assembled.[39]

A large invading force might shut up the Confederate troops in the angle made at the Ferry by the rivers, but, for the time, Jackson seemed reasonably safe. The cavalry would give him warning. When Col. George Deas—an old inspector of the United States Army—had made an official visit to Harpers Ferry about ten days before General Beauregard reached Manassas, he had noted the alertness of a handsome, spirited young cavalryman, small but vigorous, who was commanding Jackson's mounted outposts. "I am quite confident," Colonel Deas had reported, "that, with the vigilance . . . exercised by Capt. Ashby, no enemy can pass the point which he is directed to observe."[40] Besides, to quote Deas, all five of the companies of cavalry, which included Ashby's two, were "in very good condition, and quite effective."[41] Their commander was the stocky, broad-shouldered Lt. Col. James E. B. Stuart, "Beauty" Stuart, the boys at West Point during Lee's superintendency had called him, in tactful tribute to his notorious lack of good looks. Stuart had arrived in Richmond from the West on May 7, had received commission as Major of Infantry

[38] William Couper, *100 Years at V. M. I.*, v. 1, p. 253.
[39] *O. R.*, 2, 867 ff. For details of this neglected period of Jackson's career, see *Richmond Examiner*, May 6, p. 2, col. 5; May 21, p. 1, col. 6; June 29, p. 2, col. 4; *Richmond Dispatch*, May 17, p. 1, col. 4; July 4, 1861, p. 3, col. 1; 19 *S. H. S. P.*, 83; *O. R.*, 2, 809, 814, 824–25, 849; *O. R.*, 51, pt. 2, p. 78.
[40] *O. R.*, 2, 868.
[41] *O. R.*, 2, 869.

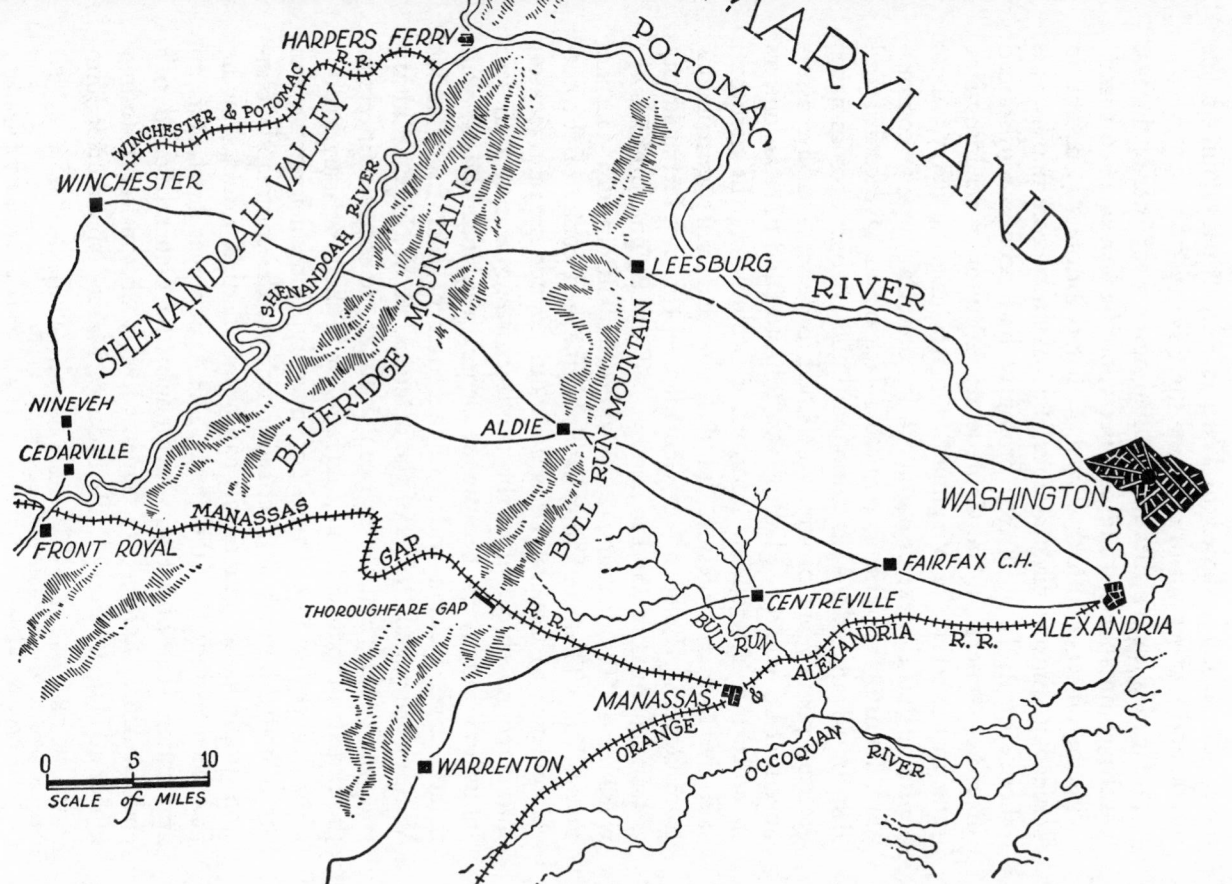

Sketch of the District between Warrenton and Washington and of the Shenandoah Valley from Front Royal to Harpers Ferry, to illustrate how the strategical areas were so related that the occupation of the one by the enemy threatened the security of the other.

and, after being assigned to Harpers Ferry, had mounted one grade and had set out to organize the Cavalry.[42]

So far as is known, Beauregard had never met either of the two cavalry commanders at Harpers Ferry, but he was well acquainted with the officer who had arrived at that point on May 24 and in somewhat unusual circumstances had assumed command. This officer, Joseph E. Johnston, promptly had been commissioned Brigadier General in the Confederate Army after declining like rank in the service of Virginia.[43] On reaching the Ferry, where he found Jackson exercising authority under a Virginia commission, Johnston in writing requested Jackson to have copied and distributed an order that announced the change of command. Jackson politely but promptly declined to do so. He gave assurance that he would be glad to assist Johnston and the staff officers in procuring "appropriate information" concerning the post, but, said the former professor, "until I receive further instructions from Governor Letcher [44] or General Lee, I do not feel at liberty to transfer my command to another." This he signed in his awkward hand, "T. J. Jackson, Col. Virginia Vols., Comdg. at Harpers Ferry, Va." Then he immediately dispatched copies of the correspondence to General Lee's adjutant. Either because Jackson interposed no objection to the transfer of engineering duties to Johnston's staff, or else because the General's engineer did not wait to ask leave, Jackson added to the letter he sent Lee: "Major Whiting has taken charge of the defences." [45] W. H. C. Whiting —it was a familiar name to Lee and to all the older engineers of the corps and soon to be no less familiar in the new army.

As Beauregard in due time got the story, General Johnston was not offended by Jackson's refusal to transfer the command. Johnston simply looked among his papers for one that would show he had been assigned to the post. The search was brief. On an application sent him from Richmond, the General found this endorsement: "Referred to General J. E. Johnston, commanding officer at Harpers Ferry.[46] By order of Major-General Lee: John

---

[42] J. W. Thomason, *"Jeb" Stuart* (cited hereafter as *Thomason*), 63, 82, 83. For the first detailed references to Stuart, see *infra,* p. 275 ff.

[43] See Appendix II, pp. 714, 722.   [44] John Letcher, Governor of Virginia.

[45] *O. R.,* 2, 871.

[46] This document carried an apostrophe in the name of the town, as did many contemporary papers, but as the present spelling is Harpers Ferry, that form is used in the text.

A. Washington." Shown to Jackson, this was accepted instantly by him as evidence of Johnston's authority. The Colonel circulated the desired order and transferred the command. Harpers Ferry formally became a Confederate post.[47] The correspondence was a trivial incident, but it might have been read even then as an indication of the precise military standard of Colonel Jackson: authority was bestowed to be exercised; responsibility was not lightly to be shifted; orders were to be obeyed. If this meant that Jackson for the moment had no command, he would await one.[48]

Soon Beauregard heard that Jackson's successor was having difficulties similar to those encountered at Manassas. Neither Johnston's position nor his troops pleased him. As an engineer he saw that Harpers Ferry could be turned, in his words, "easily and effectively from above and below." The volunteers, in his opinion, were so utterly lacking in "discipline and instruction" that it would be "difficult to use them in the field." When told by a young surgeon of a certain volunteer regiment, "If these men of the Second Virginia will not fight, you have no troops that will," Johnston replied, "I would not give one company of regulars for the whole regiment!"[49] He wrote for instructions within forty-eight hours after assuming command;[50] and within a week he asked whether it would not be better to withdraw altogether from Harpers Ferry and to "join one of our armies, which is too weak for its object."[51]

Of all this and of much that followed, Beauregard was informed. He listened; he pondered; he planned. French he was . . . French strategy he would employ, Napoleonic strategy.[52]

[47] O. R., 2, 877.
[48] The next detailed reference to Jackson is *infra*, p. 81.
[49] Hunter McGuire and Geo. L. Christian, *The Confederate Cause and Conduct . . .*, 2d ed., 207.
[50] O. R., 2, 881.
[51] O. R., 2, 896. Whiting meantime had concluded that an army of 12,000 to 15,000 would be required south of the line of the upper Potomac. If such a force were placed where he suggested, he was sure he had a plan that would "absolutely force the enemy to very great delay and vastly extended preparations." O. R., 2, 890.
[52] The sketch of Beauregard is continued on p. 38.

CHAPTER II

MAGRUDER AND D. H. HILL EMERGE

BEFORE the ranks of Beauregard began to swell or his strategy to take form, the actors between the James and York Rivers commanded the stage. The Federals were concentrating at Fort Monroe, which apparently they intended to use as a base for operations up the Peninsula.[1] If, simultaneously, the mouth either of the James or of the York could be opened, vessels of the United States Navy might pass the hastily built forts and might land troops close to Richmond. Because this was apparent to all who knew anything about the geography of Virginia, the commanding officer at the mouth of the York River [2] became from the hour of his assignment a conspicuous figure. Indeed, he long had been that in the "old army," not because of rank but because of personality.

John Bankhead Magruder, No. 15 in the somewhat undistin-

[1] Soldiers of the War between the States adopted the Virginia usage and styled this Peninsula simply "*the* Peninsula." Whenever that term is used in these pages it refers always to the historic area between the James and the York. The retention of Fort Monroe by the Federals was recognized by Virginians from the very day of secession as a major obstacle to the achievement of Southern independence. (*Richmond Examiner*, April 26, p. 1, col. 6; May 1, p. 2, col. 6; May 8, p. 2, col. 5; June 12, p. 2, col. 1; Sept. 25, p. 2, col. 1; *Richmond Dispatch*, July 17, p. 2, col. 2; July 30, 1861, p. 2, col. 2). Oversanguine hopes of storming the fort (*Richmond Examiner*, April 17, 1861, p. 2, col. 3) gave place to many schemes for new forms of attack (*Richmond Examiner*, May 1, p. 2, col. 6; June 13, 1861, p. 2, col. 5). Among these was one for the organization of a stock company to manufacture a "rotary floating battery" to be used against the fort (*Richmond Dispatch*, June 20, p. 2, col. 2; *Richmond Examiner*, June 26, 1861, p. 2, col. 5). Plating the *Merrimac* with iron was ordered, according to one report, because the Confederate government intended to employ it to silence the guns of Fort Monroe, which, it was asserted, the Southern forces had to occupy "by September," 1861 (*Richmond Examiner*, June 13, 1861, p. 2, col. 5). Gradually Virginia had to reconcile herself to the continued occcupation of Fort Monroe by the Federals, but references to the activities there—arrivals, departures, sickness, discontent—were frequent in the Richmond press. Cf. *Richmond Dispatch*, May 31, p. 1, col. 2; June 8, p. 2, col. 5; June 20, p. 3, col. 2; June 27, p. 3, col. 2; July 3, p. 3, col. 3; July 18, p. 1, col. 6; *Richmond Examiner*, May 9, p. 2, col. 4; May 14, p. 2, col. 3; May 15, p. 2, col. 4, 6; May 17, p. 2, col. 5; May 23, p. 2, col. 6; May 31, p. 2, col. 3; June 3, p. 1, col. 4; June 4, p. 2, col. 4; June 7, p. 1, col. 6; June 19, p. 1, col. 3; p. 2, col. 5; June 20, p. 2, col. 6; p. 3, col. 2; June 24, p. 3, col. 2; July 3, p. 2, col. 5; July 4, p. 2, col. 5; July 12, p. 2, col. 3; July 18, p. 1, col. 6; p. 2, col. 6; July 19, p. 3, col. 2; July 23, p. 2, col. 6; July 29, p. 1, col. 3; Sept. 16, 1861, p. 2, col. 4.

[2] Yorktown and its environs were the principal defense. A small, co-operating force was placed at Gloucester Point on the north bank of the river, opposite Yorktown.

guished class of 1830 at West Point,[3] had procured transfer from the 7th Infantry to the 1st Artillery in 1831,[4] had earned his brevet as Lieutenant Colonel during the Mexican War, and thereafter had held some of the choicest posts in the Artillery. In particular he had served at Fort Adams, Newport, R. I., and had won a great name as a *bon vivant* and as an obliging host. Whenever celebrities were to be entertained, Colonel Magruder—"Prince John"—would tender a dress parade, with full trappings and gold-braided pomp, and this he would follow with a flawless dinner. From Fort Adams he had been transferred to far-off Fort Leavenworth, but there, too, he had held dress parades and reviews, though the spectators might be only Indians or frontiersmen; and when the troops had marched off the parade ground, he had entertained his brother officers, *mutatis mutandis,* no less lavishly than at Newport. In the serious work of his profession he had succeeded Colonel Dimick in direction of a new artillery school at Leavenworth and had convinced interested juniors that he knew his ranges as thoroughly as his vintages.[5]

The winter of 1860–61 found Magruder and his battery in Washington. When he resigned, rumor paid tribute to his personal popularity, if not to the historical verities, by spreading the report that he had galloped off to the defense of Virginia with his men and his guns.[6] Nothing would have delighted Magruder more than to have executed such a *coup,* for he loved the dramatic, and when occasion offered he would tread majestically the creaking boards of a garrison theatre. Nor did he make a casual entrance on the stage of Virginia's tragedy. Telegraphing his friend Judge James Lyons to meet him when the cars arrived,[7] he then revealed a prospect that led the Judge to seek for him an immediate audience with the Governor's Advisory Council. To that serious, burdened group of devoted men, Colonel Magruder said with frowning fervor: "I have just crossed the Long Bridge, which is guarded by my old Battery. The men recognized me by moonlight and would have cheered me but I repressed them.

---

[3] *Cullum,* No. 601. Magruder was born at Winchester, Va., Aug. 15, 1810.
[4] *Cullum, loc. cit.*
[5] A. L. Long in 12 *S. H. S. P.,* 105 ff.
[6] *Baltimore American,* Apr. 23; *Richmond Dispatch,* Apr. 26, 1861, p. 1, cols. 3, 7. Cullum gives the date of Magruder's resignation as Apr. 20.
[7] Occasionally, at this time in Virginia, if a "special train" was used, it was so described, but if it was a regular train one took or met, it was mentioned as "the cars."

Give me 5000 men and if I don't take Washington, you may take not only my sword but my life!" On so bold a proposal, the Council sought the judgment of General Lee. When Lee arrived, Magruder repeated his offer and made a speech to justify it. Lee shook his head. "We have not the men," said he—that and no more.[8]

"Prince John" was too well-disciplined a soldier to be disappointed at this. He was commissioned Colonel of Virginia Volunteers,[9] was assigned to direct the artillery around Richmond,[10] then was given control of all the troops there,[11] and, after a few days more with the artillery,[12] was sent on May 21 to command operations on the lower Peninsula, with headquarters at Yorktown.[13] There he found no cavalry,[14] little infantry and scant equipment. Naval officers scarcely had gear for mounting the guns that were to keep the enemy's fleet at a distance.[15] With furious energy Magruder went to work to improve his troops and his position, but, like Johnston at Harpers Ferry and Beauregard at Manassas, he felt that his first need was of larger force. To guard a line that extended from the James to the York, he must have, he said, 8000 to 10,000 men. Without them, he would be compelled to fall back.[16] In opening correspondence on this subject he was detailed and insistent. Like many another professional soldier who long had dealt with the War Department, he believed with all his heart that the importunate widow who wearied the unjust judge till he avenged her was the model to be followed by the commander in seeking what was required. Although the spirit was less Biblical than martial, he held that bombardment of the enemy might be infrequent but that bombardment of the Secretary of War should be incessant. His early dispatches doubtless were read with eagerness. Soon the sight of one of them was to evoke groans. At his station, from the first

---

[8] James Lyons, who was present, sent President Davis, in July, 1878, an account of this and other incidents. It appears in 8 Rowland, 213.

[9] April 25, 1861; O. R., 51, pt. 2, p. 36; cf. Richmond Examiner, Apr. 27, p. 2 col. 5; May 3, 1861, p. 3, col. 2.

[10] O. R., 51, pt. 2, p. 53; O. R., 2, 789–90.

[11] O. R., 2, 817; Richmond Examiner, May 9, 1861, p. 2, col. 4.

[12] O. R., 51, pt. 2, p. 95.

[13] O. R., 2, 865.

[14] O. R., 2, 884.

[15] O. R., 2, 887.

[16] Ibid.

hour, he was polite but impressive. The Confederacy—at York-town it was John Bankhead Magruder.

Fortune smiled on diligence. "Prince John" had opportunity of directing the South's first land "battle" and of winning the intoxicating first victory. At the very time of Magruder's arrival, one of the regiments needed to bring up his force to the required minimum had landed at Yorktown.[17] It was a remarkable organization cf 1100 enthusiastic young men, who by reason of their early enlistment and zeal in acquiring the elements of drill and discipline, had been awarded the proud title of the First North Carolina Volunteers. Their Colonel, Daniel Harvey Hill, and their Lieutenant Colonel, C. C. Lee, were West Pointers; their Major, James H. Lane, was a graduate of the Virginia Military Institute. Together, these three had been the ranking officers of the North Carolina Military Institute, a private school at Charlotte.

So well trained was the First North Carolina that Magruder sent it, with four guns and a few other troops on June 6, to an advanced position behind a bend in a branch of Back River at Big Bethel Church, thirteen miles below Yorktown and eight miles from Hampton. The enemy was then at Hampton and at New-port News and seemed to be inclined to advance. Colonel Hill accordingly strengthened his position at Big Bethel with a small enclosed work. To the South of the stream he placed a howitzer in battery. From this point, on June 8, he moved detachments to drive off two marauding parties which were within striking dis-tance. This task was performed with ease and soldierly dispatch.

Two days later, Hill received notice that the enemy was advanc-ing on him. The very prospect set every heart to beating fast. With confidence and delight, Hill moved out his troops, ascer-tained by what roads the Federals were moving, and then with-drew in the face of superior force to his prepared position. With Magruder directing a few changes in his dispositions, Hill met and repulsed at Big Bethel some feeble, poorly handled assaults by Federals who already had sustained casualties by firing wildly

[17] There was at this time no railroad down the Peninsula. Troops intended for the Yorktown front usually went via the Richmond and York River Railroad to West Point (at the junction of the Pamunkey and Mattapony) and there took steamer down the York. An alternative route that involved more marching was by steamer down the James to one of the wharves opposite Williamsburg and thence overland, past the old colonial capital, to Yorktown.

into one another.[18] When the enemy withdrew with more precipitancy than order, Hill pursued as far as he deemed possible. After the recall was sounded, Hill's troops returned triumphantly to the field of their battle.

It had been a small battle, to be sure. Not more than 300 of the 1400 Confederates had been engaged simultaneously and then for no longer than twenty minutes.[19] Three years later, such a clash would have been accounted a skirmish and, if reported at all, would have been the subject of a two-line dispatch. It was different on June 10, 1861. Green troops had stood, had fought, had sustained eleven casualties and had driven the enemy back to his starting point! Naturally, at Yorktown headquarters there was excitement, felicitation and exultation. Magruder sent off to Richmond successive dispatches by his aides in person.[20] Hill prepared an elaborate report, in which he distributed praise most generously. Of his own First North Carolina he said, "The men are influenced by high moral and religious sentiments, and their conduct has furnished another example of the great truth that he who fears God will ever do his duty to his country." Hill's superlative was reserved for a grandson of Thomas Jefferson, Major George W. Randolph, a Richmond lawyer who had commanded the guns: "He has," said Hill, "no superior as an artillerist in any country." [21] The Federal casualties Hill put at 300 and the strength of the attacking force at 5000, though actually the figures were, respectively, seventy-six and 4400.[22]

When news of this victory reached Richmond and spread to the South, there was immense satisfaction over what was proclaimed to be the demonstrated, indisputable superiority of the Confederate soldier in combat. With this were coupled gratitude and amazement. Big Bethel, said one Richmond paper, was one of the most extraordinary victories in the annals of war. Was not the hand of God manifest in such a triumph over such odds? [23]

18 *O. R.*, 2, 84, 95–96.
19 *O. R.*, 2, 97. Hill estimated the Confederate strength at 1200, but the later account in the *Histories of the Several Regiments and Battalions from North Carolina . . .* , edited by Walter Clark (cited hereafter as *N. C. Regts.*), vol. 1, p. 89, put the total at 1408.
20 *O. R.*, 2, 91 ff.   21 *O. R.*, 2, 97.
22 *O. R.*, 2, 82, 97; 1 *N. C. Regts.*, 88.
23 *Richmond Dispatch*, June 13. 1861, p. 2, col. 1; quoted in 19 *S. H. S. P.*, 222.

No detail of the engagement was too trivial for mention, none was incredible. Avidly the South read how Magruder had met a flag of truce, seeking the body of a slain Federal officer, had granted the removal of the corpse, and, in parting, had shaken hands with a Lieutenant and had said solemnly, "We part as friends, but on the field of battle we meet as enemies." [24] With keenest satisfaction Confederates learned that Magruder had declared the action as decisive as any in the Mexican War.[25] His every word was applauded; he himself was described as all that "fancy had pictured of the Virginia gentleman, the frank and manly representative of the chivalry of the dear Old Dominion." [26]

Swift promotion to the rank of Brigadier General in the Provisional Army of the Confederate States was demanded for Magruder and was granted. His commission bore date of June 17 —one week from that of his victory at Big Bethel. Forthwith he took his place among the foremost of Southern celebrities, a hero second only to Beauregard in the esteem of the Confederacy. Magruder accepted his new honors gratefully. In mien and dignity he lived up to his role. At 50 years of age, he was tall, erect, and handsome, and was impressive despite a curious lisp. Usually he dressed in full uniform—looking "every inch a King," one newspaper insisted [27]—and with his staff in attendance he daily made the rounds of his slowly mounting fortifications. He was a fighter, the South joyfully asserted, a personal fighter, too. Was it not rumored that he had challenged the Federal commander, Gen. Ben. Butler, to mortal combat? [28]

Harvey Hill, who had been in direct command at Big Bethel, did not appeal to the eye or to the imagination in the measure his chief did, but he had his full share of honor. He came of fighting stock. His paternal grandfather had made cannon for the Continental army and had been one of Sumter's colonels. On the maternal side, Harvey Hill had as grandparent that wily scout, Thomas Cabeen, who Sumter often had said was the bravest man he ever commanded. Not unnaturally, with that inheritance,

[24] *Richmond Dispatch*, June 24, 1861, p. 1, col. 4.
[25] *Ibid.*, June 15, 1861, p. 2, col. 4.   [26] *Ibid.*, June 26, 1861, p. 3, col. 1.
[27] *Richmond Dispatch*, July 10, 1861, p. 3, col. 2.
[28] *Baltimore Sun*, June 27; *Richmond Dispatch*, July 4, 1861, p. 2, col. 1. For the next detailed reference to Magruder, see *infra*, p. 152.

Harvey Hill had gone to West Point, where, despite poor health, he had been graduated No. 28 [29] in the excellent class of 1842.[30] Five years later, by the unhesitating display of the most reckless valor, he had won promotion from a first lieutenancy to a brevet majority during the Mexican War; but as he had found army life unstimulating in time of peace he had resigned in February, 1849, had taught mathematics for five years at Washington College, and then had become professor of Mathematics and Civil Engineering at Davidson College, North Carolina.

While there Hill had developed a marked interest in theology and, at the same time, a most vehement hatred of Northerners. His published work, *Consideration of the Sermon on the Mount* (1856) had been followed by a "Southern Series" of mathematical works in which he based many of his problems on "Yankee cunning." For example, "A Yankee mixes a certain quantity of wooden nutmegs, which cost him one-fourth cent apiece, with a quantity of real nutmegs, worth four cents apiece"; again, "the year in which the Governors of Massachusetts and Connecticut sent treasonable messages to their respective legislatures, is expressed by four digits," and, still again, "the field of Battle of Buena Vista is six and a half miles from Saltillo. Two Indiana volunteers ran away from the field of battle at the same time," etc.[31] In 1859, Hill decided that war with the fictitious masters of this alleged cunning and flight was probable, and, to prepare the State for defense, he accepted the superintendency of the North Carolina Military Institute.[32] From that post he was called in 1861 to command the Camp of Instruction for the North Carolina volunteers and, as a reward of diligent service, was elected Colonel of the First Regiment.[33] He then was nearing his fortieth birthday.

In person he was inconspicuous—five feet ten, thin, critical of eye, slightly bent from spinal affection and cursed with an odd humor; he was stiff and sharp when on duty and was wholly

29 *Cullum*, No. 1138.
30 It included Gens. John Newton, W. S. Rosecrans, Gustavus W. Smith, Mansfield Lovell, M. L. Smith, John Pope, Seth Williams, Abner Doubleday, George Sykes, R. H. Anderson, Lafayette McLaws, Earl van Dorn, James Longstreet and others almost as well known.
31 *Companions in Arms*, 450.
32 5 *N. C. Regts.*, 645.
33 1 *N. C. Regts.*, 125–26. The election was on May 11.

unpretending when not in command.[34] Hill observed the Sabbath as diligently as did his brother-in-law, Col. Thos. J. Jackson, then at Harpers Ferry,[35] and he always gave God the credit for victory.[36] There was both faith and feeling in his first letter to his wife after the battle at Big Bethel. "I have to thank God for a great and decided victory and that I have escaped with a slight contusion of the knee. . . . It is a little singular that my first battle in this war should be at Bethel where I was baptized and worshipped till I was sixteen years old, the church of my mother. Was she not a guardian spirit in the battle, averting ball and shell? Oh God, give me gratitude to Thee, and may we never dishonor Thee by weak faith!"[37]

Would Hill and Magruder work together in amity and comradeship? There were hints that Hill was perturbed because Magruder professed to rank him,[38] but outwardly there was no jealousy and no display of ill feeling between the two. If Magruder's first report mentioned the service of Major Randolph before that of Colonel Hill, there was the handsomest possible compliment for the infantryman: "Colonel Hill's judicious and determined action was worthy of his ancient glory";[39] and in Magruder's second report, the "valuable services and gallant conduct of the First North Carolina Regiment" were mentioned before those of "Major Randolph of the howitzer batteries."[40] When Magruder galloped off to make an inspection or to attend a dinner, Hill was put in command, and was duly credited by Magruder with diligence and efficiency.[41] Upon the expansion of the Confederate force on the Peninsula, after the fight at Big Bethel, Magruder gave Hill the post at Yorktown.[42] If Hill did not like the administrative detail, he could not complain that the

---

[34] Richmond Whig, July 26, 1861, p. 2, col. 3; G. Moxley Sorrel, Recollections of a Confederate Staff Officer (cited hereafter as Sorrel), 63. The best sketch of Hill is that of A. C. Avery in 21 S. H. S. P., 110 ff.

[35] They were brothers-in-law by Jackson's second marriage. Their wives were daughters of the first President of Davidson College, Robert Hall Morrison.

[36] Cf. the close of his report to Governor Ellis, in which he ascribed "all praise of our success to our Heavenly Father who had wonderfully interposed to shield our head in the day of battle. . . . Give unto His great name all the praise of our success." Richmond Examiner, June 15, 1861, p. 2, col. 6.

[37] 21 S. H. S. P., 120. Hill was born in York District, S. C., July 12, 1821.

[38] O. R., 2, 901. [39] O. R., 2, 91.

[40] O. R., 2, 92.

[41] O. R., 2, 913, 927, 939; O. R., 51, pt. 2, 123.

[42] O. R., 51, pt. 2, p. 144.

position lacked honorific distinction. Moreover, as of July 10, in response to an appeal by the Governor of North Carolina and in recognition of his achievements, Hill was commissioned Brigadier General.[43]

How fast and how far would he rise? What service would he render? Intense he was in his admiration, bitter in his antagonism. He could hate as hard as he could pray: would that make him a better soldier or a worse? An applauding country did not know enough about him to make the inquiry, nor would it have looked otherwise than with suspicion on any one who raised that or any other question about any Confederate leader. "Old Bory," "Prince John" Magruder, the pious Harvey Hill—these three at the beginning of the summer of 1861 were men to be trusted, to be followed. They were great soldiers. Of that the South was satisfied. No less were all Southerners convinced that new military genius would blaze on every battlefield.[44]

[43] Cf. *Richmond Dispatch*, June 17, 1861, p. 2, col. 2; M. J. Wright, *General Officers of the Confederate Army* (cited hereafter as *Wright*), 56.
[44] For the next references to Hill, see *infra*, pp. 169, 174 ff.

CHAPTER III

First Loss of a Leader

EXULTANT praise of Magruder, D. H. Hill and the other victors at Big Bethel was interrupted quickly by news of another sort from Western Virginia. There, from the very hour of secession, the Federals realized that the Baltimore and Ohio Railroad [1] between Washington and Parkersburg was at once the most important and the most exposed link in the iron chain that bound together the East and the Midwest. Not only must that railroad be held but also it must be free to operate without the threat of raids. To this end, the Federal administration had determined to organize around Grafton [2] an army that would protect the line in the surest manner—by clearing all organized Confederate troops from Northwestern Virginia.

Soon Richmond was aware of these formidable preparations. It had been on May 20 that the advance of a strong Union column had compelled a small Confederate force to evacuate Grafton.[3] Four days later, moving southward, the Federals surprised at Philippi, fifteen miles South of Grafton, the units that had withdrawn from Grafton.[4] The Confederate commander, Col. George A. Porterfield, a veteran of the Mexican War, thereupon had to call on his undisciplined, bewildered troops to carry their obsolete muskets and to drive their feeble wagon train thirty miles farther South to Beverly, and thence twelve miles in the same direction to Huttonsville.[5] Pursuing Federal cavalry reached Beverly but withdrew.

As Beverly was the junction of the Staunton-Parkersburg stage road with the turnpike to Grafton,[6] the Confederates could not

[1] Strictly speaking, the Northwestern Railroad, leased to the B. and O.
[2] See *supra*, p. 9.   [3] *O. R.*, 2, 49, 51 ff.
[4] *O. R.*, 2, 64 ff.
[5] These directions are approximate. Beverly is slightly East of the meridian between Philippi and Huttonsville.
[6] Hotchkiss in 3 *C. M. H.*, 45. This account by Major Hotchkiss, the brilliant topographical engineer of the Second Corps, who will appear later in these pages, deserves to be regarded almost as a primary source for this particular operation, both because of his participation and because of his complete familiarity with the terrain.

permit the enemy to penetrate farther. To do so would be to sacrifice all hope of recovering Northwestern Virginia. Further-more, southeast of Beverly the stage road made successive crossings of the ridges of the Alleghenies. If unopposed, the Federals might press on to Staunton, where, as explained already,[7] they would be in rear of all the forces in the lower Shenandoah Valley.

Such troops as were available must, then, be hurried to Staunton and over the mountains to reoccupy Beverly. If they were to suc-ceed, they must be under a commander of definite ability and experience. Because every other qualified officer already was assigned to field duty,[8] Col. Robert Selden Garnett, Adjutant General at Lee's headquarters, though he was irreplaceable, was detached and ordered to proceed to Western Virginia.[9] Garnett was then 42 years of age, the eldest son of R. S. Garnett, for twelve years [10] a member of Congress from Virginia, and a representative of one of the most intellectual families of the Old Dominion. On his maternal side, he was a descendant of Countess Olympe de Gouges, who was executed during the Reign of Terror [11] for counter-revolutionary writings. After Robert Garnett was gradu-ated midway the class of 1841 at West Point,[12] he was given virtu-ally every post a young officer in the Army could desire—assistant instructor of tactics at West Point, aide to General Wool and aide to General Taylor during the Mexican War. Garnett measured up to his extraordinary opportunities and won his brevet as Major for gallantry at Buena Vista. In Texas, he refused flatly to obey, in 1852, the orders of his superior, Gen. W. S. Harney, to seize the arms of some American citizens who were supposed to be partisans of the Mexican insurgent, Carbajal. For this he was tried by court-martial, was acquitted and was given the high post of commandant of cadets at the Military Academy.[13] In 1857, while on duty at Fort Simcoe, Washington Territory, he was sent with some 280 men in pursuit of hostile Indians. He covered 505 miles in thirty-one marching days and returned successfully—to

---

[7] See *supra,* p. 9.

[8] This may be an appropriate point at which readers interested in the resources of command and in the decision of the trained officer personnel may consult Appendix II.

[9] *O. R.,* 2, 910.

[10] 1817–29.

[11] Nov. 2, 1793.

[12] *Cullum,* No. 1085.

[13] See *Trial of Brevet Major R. S. Garnett, Captain 7th Regiment U. S. Infantry, by a General Court Martial at Ringgold Barracks, Texas, in May, 1852.* The text was pub-lished by Garnett himself.

find that both his wife and his child had died in his absence.[14] In his distress, he applied for leave and came East by steamer. When he arrived in New York, he was detailed on a board of officers to devise a more economical means of administering the service in the Indian country. "Considering our government sufficiently mean and niggardly in this respect already," Garnett subsequently wrote, "I got excused from this service." A year's absence in Europe brought him back to the United States just prior to the passage of the Virginia ordinance of secession.[15] He was at that time Major of the 9th Infantry,[16] but he resigned promptly [17] and received immediate appointment as Adjutant General to Lee with the rank of Colonel.[18] From the time he had lost his family, his entire interest had been fixed on his profession. It was his escape, his passion, his life. With his native austerity deepened by his grief, he seemed "frozen, stern and isolated." [19] Those who could profess to understand him said that he was professionally as ambitious as he was absorbed. He dreamed, men said, of high feats and fame. Now, promoted Brigadier General,[20] he had challenge, opportunity and—more than either—the difficulties of a strange country and a raw command.

Despite the thinness of his ranks, when Garnett reached the wild and beautiful mountains of Western Virginia, optimistic reports were spread.[21] The new General appreciated the urgency of his mission. With two regiments hastily thrown together as a van, Garnett left Huttonsville on June 15 and pushed straight for Rich Mountain, which runs roughly North and South through part of Randolph County. Over this mountain, by Buckhannon Pass, crossed the Staunton-Parkersburg turnpike. Around the north end of Rich Mountain, under Laurel Hill, was the Grafton-Beverly Road. Garnett reasoned that if he did not seize Rich Mountain and dominate both roads, the enemy might confine him to Cheat River Valley.[22] Not content with halfway measures, he

---

[14] *Mrs. Chesnut,* 119–20; R. S. Garnett's Military Record, prepared by himself and placed at the writer's disposal through the kindness of Miss Myrtle Cooper of Williamsburg, Va.; address of A. S. Garnett, June 20, 1898—*Garnett MSS.*
[15] Military Record, *loc. cit.* [16] *Army Register,* 1860.
[17] *Richmond Dispatch,* Apr. 23, p. 1, col. 5; May 18, 1861, p. 2, col. 2.
[18] *O. R.,* 51, pt. 2, p. 36; *Richmond Examiner,* May 3, 1861, p. 3, col. 2.
[19] *Mrs. Chesnut,* 19–20. [20] As of June 6, 1861; *Wright,* 52.
[21] *Richmond Dispatch,* June 25, 1861, p. 1, col. 6 (quoted from the *Staunton Vindicator*). See also *Richmond Dispatch,* June 29, 1861, p. 1. col. 6.
[22] *O. R.,* 2, 236–37.

occupied both Laurel Hill and Buckhannon Pass, and felt, as he put it, that he held the "gates to Northwestern Virginia." [23] He

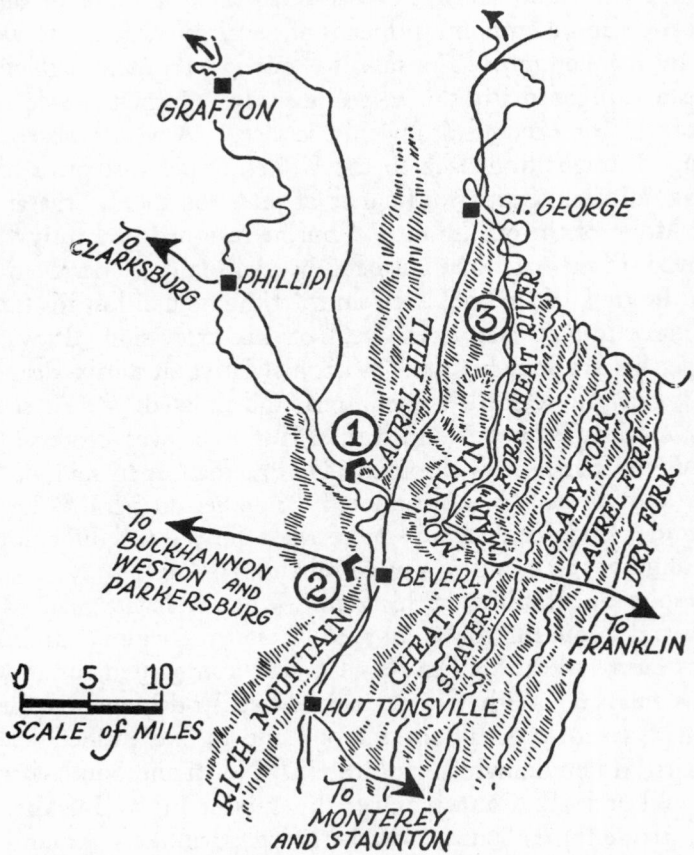

General Sketch of the Region of Gen. R. S. Garnett's Operations in Western Virginia. Positions are as follows: (1) Rough Approximation of Garnett's line on Laurel Hill, of which no detailed map is known; (2) Pegram's line on Rich Mountain, given in detail *infra*; (3) Carrick's Ford on Shaver's or "Main Fork" of Cheat River. This ford is about four miles South of the town of Parsons, Tucker County, and East of the present (1942) U. S. Route 219. Approached from the opposite direction, Carrick's Ford is about seventeen miles by air Northeast of the present city of Elkins. Contemporary maps of the region are scarce and unreliable. Perhaps the best of them is reproduced in 2 *C. M. H.* (W. Va.) 76. The sketch in *O. R. Atlas,* Plate CXVI-3 is grossly incorrect.

realized he could not dispossess with 4000 men the Federals, who were supposed to be twice as numerous, but, as he reported to Richmond, he would look for an opportunity to swoop down.

[23] *O. R.,* 2, 237.

Meantime, he said, "our presence here will necessarily occupy a considerable force of the enemy and, to that extent, relieve other points of the State where they might be employed against us." [24]

Most of his officers were as inexperienced as his troops, but some of them were unusual men. Most conspicuous among them was Lt. Col. John Pegram of the Twentieth Virginia, 29 years of age, a West Pointer of the class of 1854 [25] and a former Lieutenant of the 2nd Dragoons. Pegram had spent two years in Europe and had many fine social qualities, but he was a recent comer to Western Virginia and had scant acquaintance with the tangled country. On July 7, he went with his regiment to a post called Camp Garnett, which already had been established at Buckhannon Gap, eight miles West of Beverly. On arrival he displayed the spirit of the myopic type of professional soldier who never has realized in any war that the volunteer officer is sensitive, jealous even, almost in direct ratio to inexperience. Promptly, if politely, Pegram asserted command on the ground that he was Lieutenant Colonel in the Confederate Army, and that the senior officer at Camp Garnett, Lt. Col. J. M. Heck, had that rank in Virginia service only.[26] Pegram carried his point, but he rendered himself unpopular by his insistence.

A second interesting officer among Garnett's subordinates was Capt. Julius A. de Lagnel, a native of New Jersey but long a resident of Virginia and for fourteen years a Lieutenant in the United States Army. De Lagnel was made Chief of Artillery for Garnett's little command and was stationed with Pegram on the western flank of Rich Mountain.[27]

At that camp, also, reported for duty a man destined to have a place in Confederate service almost unique. Jedediah Hotchkiss, descendant of an old and distinguished Connecticut family, had been born at Windsor, New York, in 1828 and had been educated in academies there. When 19, he had come to Virginia on a walking tour. Soon he acquired so deep an attachment to the State that he decided to settle in Augusta County. After serving as a tutor there, he established Mossy Creek Academy, which soon was successful. Busy though he was as a teacher, and active in religion, he found time to learn, unhelped, the principles of

---

[24] *O. R.*, 2, 242.   [25] *Cullum*, No. 1640. Pegram was tenth in his class.
[26] *O. R.*, 2, 261.   [27] 3 *C. M. H.*, 691.

engineering, and as his avocation he made maps. "Professor Hotchkiss," as he first was called in the Army—he had no rank at the time—could sketch an area with substantial accuracy after riding over it once, and as he was a swift and indefatigable worker, he was to supply an incredible number of much-needed maps.[28]

Besides Hotchkiss, de Lagnel and Pegram, already with him, Garnett had word from Richmond that the Twelfth Georgia Regiment was being sent to Western Virginia under Col. Edward Johnson. The news of reinforcement probably meant more than the name of the commanding officer.

Garnett soon learned something of the men entrusted to him. City-dwellers he had, who never had seen mountains, and with them he had mountaineers who never had seen cities. Two things only did these soldiers possess in common—vast zeal and military inexperience. To them Garnett gave such slight instruction as time permitted. He also improved rapidly his position on Laurel Hill and felled trees to close all the lesser roads and trails by which he could be flanked.[29] Buckhannon Pass naturally was a strong position, but he prudently constructed below the pass various rough fortifications with which, he predicted, a regiment "will be able to hold five times their number in check for a sufficient time to admit of being reinforced, if they will stand to their work." [30]

Although supplies from the country were soon exhausted and those from Staunton were transported with great difficulty,[31] Garnett continued to occupy his fortifications, unassailed by the enemy, until July 6. Then skirmishing began. By July 8, the day Colonel Pegram took command at Buckhannon Pass, the enemy was active in that quarter. Pegram watched and wished to attack, because he did not think the Federals were in force. The 9th brought the enemy in sight from Camp Garnett at a distance of

[28] As an evidence of what Hotchkiss did in West Virginia, at the very beginning of his career as a topographical engineer, it might be of interest to record that his notes, sketches and tables of distances supplied virtually all the topographical data for this chapter and for much of what appears in later chapters on the operations of T. J. Jackson. The writer's thanks are extended most gratefully to Mrs. George Holmes of Charleston, S. C., and to Mrs. Ellen H. Christian of Deerfield, Va., for permitting him to have free access to the Hotchkiss papers, which are preserved perfectly.
[29] *O. R.,* 2, 237.
[30] *O. R.,* 2, 238.   [31] *O. R.,* 2, 242.

approximately two miles. That day and the next the Federals made reconnaissance in force but returned to camp.

On the morning of the 11th, from a captured Union sergeant, Pegram learned that the Federals were endeavoring to turn one of his flanks. He concluded that the attack was to be against his right and he sent back word to Col. William C. Scott, who was advancing to reinforce him with the Forty-fourth Virginia, to hold that regiment in position one and a half miles west of Beverly, where a minor road that ran down the eastern face of the mountain made a wide curve and entered the Parkersburg-Staunton stage road.[32] Although Pegram believed the approach to his left-rear almost impracticable for the enemy,[33] he sent back Captain de Lagnel with one gun and five thin companies of infantry to Hart's house at the highest point in the gap.

As of July 11, when the Confederates were waiting for the enemy to disclose his intentions, the situation, in summary, was this: At Laurel Hill, northeast of Pegram's position, there was no intimation of attack, though Union troops were known to be close at hand. In front of Camp Garnett, the Federals were visible but gave no evidence of any purpose to come directly up the mountain. At the camp, Pegram was on the alert and was expecting an attempt to turn his right. About one and a half miles in his rear, at the Hart House, were de Lagnel, his gun and a total of 310 men. Across the mountain to the eastward, more than four miles by road from de Lagnel, Colonel Scott was posting his Forty-fourth Virginia.[34]

At 11 o'clock or later,[35] there came an unhappy surprise: with a shout and a dash, the Federals drove in the Confederate pickets at the pass and swarmed from the thickets for an assault

---

[32] On one of Hotchkiss' sketch maps of the area, this Merritt road, so called, is figured as passing Caplinger's house and as entering another road which ran North and South, parallel to the Beverly-Philippi turnpike. On a later and more elaborate map, this north-and-south road does not appear. Instead, the Merritt road forms a half circle North of the Parkersburg-Staunton road and enters that highway about three-quarters of a mile West of Baker's Tavern, which was approximately one mile from Beverly. For the orders to Colonel Scott, see his report, O. R., 2, 275. Curiously enough, in Colonel Pegram's report, there is no mention of these instructions to Scott. He referred to that officer only when, in discussing possible lines of retreat, he said he thought it might be possible to reach Colonel Scott, who "was supposed to be with his regiment near Beverly."

[33] O. R., 2, 264.   [34] O. R., 2, 256, 264, 275.

[35] All the Confederate authorities say 11 A.M.; Rosecrans' report, O. R., 2, 2 3, gave 2 P.M. as the time of the final attack.

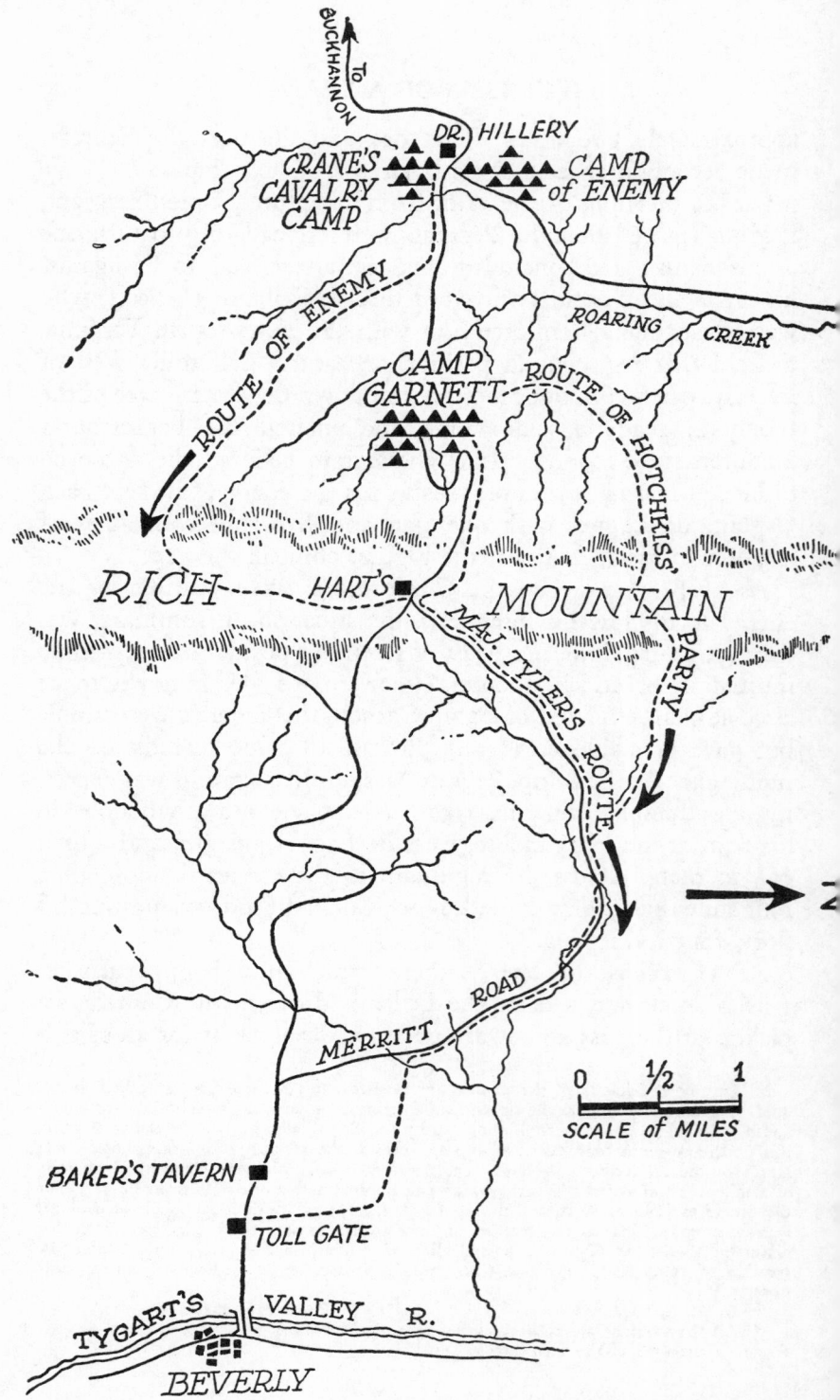

Rich Mountain and Pegram's position at Camp Garnett, after a contemporary sketch of Jed. Hotchkiss. Garnett's position at the southern end of Laurel Hill. North of Beverley, is approximately the preceding sketch.

on de Lagnel's little command. The enemy came from the left and not, as anticipated, from the right. Captain de Lagnel made the utmost of his scant numbers and of his single gun. When most of his artillerists had been shot down, he served the piece himself with the aid of one boy. Presently he fell with a serious wound.[36] His supporting infantry continued to fight, as best they knew how, but soon they began to waver. While they were hesitating, Colonel Pegram arrived from Camp Garnett. By example and plea, he tried to get his soldiers to drive off the enemy and to hold the road. His shouts and commands were in vain. The troops broke; the enemy seized the road and the gap. Pegram rode back down the hill to his camp. A grim plight was his. The Unionists were squarely across his only line of retreat.

What was to be done? Pegram decided to try the one expedient open to him: He would leave half his force to hold Camp Garnett and, with the other half, he would go back up the mountain and try to clear the enemy from the road and near-by thickets. His bewildered volunteers did not protest. They would do their utmost. They strained, they slipped, they struggled. Every step upward was a fight with stubborn, low-branching laurel. At last, after immense effort, they reached an elevation that appeared to be on a line with the flank of the enemy, but the pull up the mountain had exhausted them. Pegram looked at them and realized that if they were thrown forward, they would be slaughtered.[37]

There they were, in the maze of laurel, with no road open to them. Nothing could be gained by sending them back to Camp Garnett. The sole hope of escape was to go over the crest and to try to reach Beverly. Pegram entrusted this difficult mission to Maj. Nat Tyler of the Twentieth Virginia, who undertook a hard climb in good spirit. At 6.30 P.M. Colonel Pegram started once again to Camp Garnett—his second descent of the day.[38] He did not attempt to follow the lower stretches of the road, because he thought the Federals probably were swarming over them. Down the mountain he had to plunge in the darkness, through a spiteful rain, by any trails he could find. Several times he lost his way. The pain of a fall from his horse numbed him. It was 11.30 when he and his mount staggered into his camp. The 600 men who remained there were awake and miserable.

[36] O. R., 2, 257.   [37] O. R., 2, 265.   [38] O. R., 2, 260, 265.

All of them were wet; two thirds of them were hungry and without rations for the morrow. They had despaired of Pegram's
return, but they were attempting to carry out his previous orders,
which were that they should hold their position at all hazards.
To their nervous ears every sweep of the wind was a charge of
the enemy. The vaguest outline of a moving branch was a sharpshooter in the act of firing. Rain dripped terror.

Pegram brought the tired officers together in council and, with
their approval, decided that an effort should be made to cross the
mountain and to join Garnett at Laurel Hill. Pegram himself
was so close to exhaustion that he did not believe he could attempt
another ascent of the mountain. He would have to remain where
he was and take his chances, after he had rested, of eluding the
enemy. The command must be turned over to Lt. Col. J. M. Heck,
of the Twenty-fifth Virginia,[39] the man whom he had superseded.

Heck promptly formed a column, the head of which he assigned
to Professor Hotchkiss. With his singular sense of direction,
Hotchkiss started confidently upward. Behind him, though he
could see few soldiers, he could hear the laurel cracking where
the men forced their way through it. Pegram, by that time, had
decided that he would make the effort, come what might, to
conduct the men to General Garnett's camp. Up the mountain he
passed word for the troops to halt until he could reach the front.
This order never reached the front company, which continued
to follow Hotchkiss. About 1 A.M., Pegram was able to start with
the remaining troops.

The hours of this climbing and descent had been an anxious
time for General Garnett. At Laurel Hill, he had heard early on
the 11th of the impending threat to Pegram and he had sent
repeated instructions to Colonel Scott on the assumption that
Pegram was correct in predicting an attempt to turn the right of
the force that was defending the Buckhannon Pass.[40] On Garnett's own front, as the Federals were shelling his position, he
prepared to repel attack. His personal demeanor was one of complete unconcern. All day he watched, counselled Scott, and
waited for word from Pegram. As evening drew on, Garnett
started to eat his supper in front of his tent. With a greedy roar,

---

[39] O. R., 2, 257. This is Heck's account. Pegram, *ibid.*, 265–66, did not mention this
incident.
[40] For some of his orders, see Scott's report, O. R., 2, 276 ff.

a shell came as an unbidden guest and burst so near the General that dirt was thrown in his coffee. He quietly emptied the cup on the ground, called to his servant for more coffee, and went on with his meal.[41]

Sometime after nightfall, a startled, panting messenger brought news that Pegram was cut off and that the enemy commanded the road through the gap. This meant that Garnett's own line of retreat on Beverly was endangered. His rear, as surely as Pegram's, was open to the enemy. One of the "gates to North-western Virginia" had been stormed. The other would not hold. Laurel Hill was untenable. As Garnett did not know in what direction Pegram's troops would retire, if they succeeded in evading pursuit, he did what a man of his temper and training most regretted to do: he abandoned his detached force, left his tents in place to deceive the enemy, and marched eastward with his few regiments in the hope that he could escape across the mountains and reach Cheat Bridge.[42]

Daylight on the 12th of July found the army of Garnett in five retreating fragments. Colonel Scott had abandoned his futile watch on the eastern side of Rich Mountain, had passed through Beverly and was nearly seven miles South of the village on the road to Huttonsville.[43] Jed. Hotchkiss was two thirds of the way to the top of the mountain, on the western side, and was disgusted to find, for the first time, that only one company was following him. He did not know that the remainder of the troops had been halted by Pegram's order.[44] Maj. Nat Tyler with his Twentieth Virginia, having crossed the mountain, was at Beverly.[45] Pegram's wet and hungry men were on a high ridge whence, after sunrise, they could look down on Beverly and on a long stretch of Valley River.[46] Garnett's hurried march was under way without pursuit by the enemy.

The *dénouement* came quickly. Scott was joined by Tyler[47] at Huttonsville and was able to get away in safety. Hotchkiss followed him.[48] Pegram lost his opportunity of reaching Beverly before the arrival of the Federals and, after wandering all day in

[41] Jo. T. Derry to A. S. Garnett, Dec. 27, 1902. *Garnett MSS.*
[42] *O. R.*, 2, 283. The hour of his departure does not appear from the records, but it was after nightfall.
[43] *O. R.*, 2, 283.
[44] *O. R.*, 2, 262.
[45] *O. R.*, 2, 260.
[46] *O. R.*, 2, 258.
[47] *O. R.*, 2, 260.
[48] *O. R.*, 2, 262–63.

search of food, sent at midnight of the 12th–13th an offer to surrender the troops with him. They marched to Beverly, where on the 13th the 553 officers and men laid down their arms. Four days later, all of them except Pegram were paroled.[49] He was held as a prisoner of undetermined status because of his previous service in the United States Army.

Garnett's march on the 12th carried his van to Kaler's Ford on Cheat River, where the men bivouacked in a heavy rain. The next morning he continued his retreat over a heavy road and through a difficult country. Ford after ford lay ahead. Good soldier that Garnett was, mindful both of front and of rear, he proceeded with a squadron of cavalry, a section of artillery and a regiment in front. Next came his wagons and then his two other regiments, a couple of guns and a small cavalry rearguard. The entire force Garnett kept in close order.

Ere the wagon train had crossed the first ford above Kaler's, the cavalry brought the grim news that the enemy, with infantry and artillery in support of mounted troops, was near at hand. Immediately Garnett ordered the First Georgia, which was one of his rear regiments, to form across a meadow on the riverside and to hold the enemy in check till the wagons got away. The trains secured, the Georgia regiment was to retire and was to pass through the Twenty-third Virginia, which would be in position to repel attack. This was done under fire. By successive halts and withdrawals and with few casualties, the two regiments covered the wagon train until Carrick's Ford, three miles and a half from Kaler's, was reached. At that swift, deep crossing, some of the wagons stalled. Time was lost in trying vainly to extricate them. The Twenty-third Virginia then crossed and took up a defensive position. After the Georgians had passed through their line, the Virginians met the Federals with vigor and delayed them long enough for the wagons to get a good lead.

When the Twenty-third reached the third ford, which was not far distant, Garnett was waiting on the farther bank with a single junior aide. The General explained the ground to Col. William B. Taliaferro[50] and directed him to halt his regiment beyond a

---

49 O. R., 2, 258–59, 266–67.

50 This distinguished Virginia family pronounced its name as if it were spelled Tarl-iver, with the accent on the first syllable.

FIRST LOSS OF A LEADER

FIRST LOSS OF A LEADER   35

near turn in the road. "This is a good place behind this drift-wood," said Garnett, "to post skirmishers." Would Taliaferro send back ten good marksmen? The Colonel detached an entire company, but as the number was larger than could be concealed behind the logs, Garnett returned all except the desired ten. He posted them and prepared to direct in person their fire. A closer inspection of the ground showed Garnett possibilities of placing his entire rearguard where it could sweep the approaches to the ford. With appropriate orders, he dispatched his staff officers. As he waited for the troops to climb the bluff and for the enemy to appear, he and his aide, the youthful Sam M. Gaines, heard the cries of a wounded man who had been left on the other side of the ford. Gaines asked if he might ride across and succor him. Garnett consented. Gaines brought the bleeding soldier to safety.[51]

In a few minutes the Federals came in sight. They advanced cautiously, as if expecting a trap, and they soon encountered the fire of the hidden sharpshooters. As only Garnett and Gaines were visible, the Federals directed their fire at them. The missiles flew past. Young Gaines ducked. Garnett, erect and calm, reproved the youth. "When I told him I had felt on my face the wind from several bullets, and that I could not help but stoop," Gaines wrote years later, "he changed his tone and talked to me in a fatherly way as to the proper bearing of a soldier under fire." [52]

The enemy by this time was only fifty yards distant. Garnett turned his horse to see if his troops were coming up. At that instant, a bullet hit him in the back. He fell from his horse. Gaines dismounted and tried to lift the General to his own saddle. The younger man struggled at the task until the Federals were close to the ford. Then he caught Garnett's horse, jumped to the back of his own animal and galloped off unscathed. Soon he reached the rearguard.

[51] The heroic Gaines wrote this account, Jan. 29, 1903: "The man was terribly wounded, shot through the face; both jaws broken and his tongue almost cut off. . . . In June, 1862, I was sent to the hospital at Amelia courthouse, with a broken leg. A man was sent to nurse me who had horrible scars on his face, and he was unable to articulate, but communicated by writing on a slate. I asked him if he was wounded at Carrick's Ford, and if he remembered the boy who took him off the field, and he said 'Yes' on his slate and grabbed me in his arms." *Garnett MSS.*

[52] S. M. Gaines to A. S. Garnett, Dec. 29, 1902; *Garnett MSS.*

After long and wearing marches, the tattered and exhausted force escaped to Monterey.[53] The South was relieved that so many had escaped but was grieved and humiliated that more than 700 had been killed, wounded or taken prisoners.[54] Captain de Lagnel, central figure in the fight at the Hart house, escaped to the cabin of a mountaineer who, though a Union sympathizer, nursed him to recovery. When de Lagnel was well enough to walk, he disguised himself and passed several Union guards. At length one sharp-eyed Federal observed that the man in the garb of a mountain farmer had on boots that were much too fine for him. The soldier insisted that the boots be removed. In them was de Lagnel's name. As the circumstances of the Captain's fight and disappearance were well known, he was identified and imprisoned. After some hesitation, the Federals decided to hold Pegram as a prisoner of war and not as an army officer in rebellion. He was much criticized in the South for what the barroom strategists pronounced a poor deployment.

Garnett's fate and the abandonment of the western approaches to the Shenandoah Valley were lamented equally.[55] The General was dying when he fell and, as the Federals arrived, he drew his last breath. His body, with all his belongings, was returned to his family [56] by old friends in the Union Army. From the list

[53] Accounts of the operations of Garnett's force on and after July 11 are few. The principal source is Taliaferro's report, O. R., 2, 285 ff. In the Garnett MSS. are three modest letters from S. M. Gaines, Dec. 29, 1902, and Jan. n. d. and 29, 1903. These are supplemented by various newspaper clippings of 1861 ff. The most informative and accurate of these is one from the Louisville Courier-Journal, n. d. The Federal reports in O. R. are scant, but the Garnett MSS. include several letters from Union veterans who saw Garnett at the ford. There are contradictions in the accounts regarding the orders given Taliaferro for the movement of his troops just prior to the fall of Garnett, but these are not of material importance to the narrative.

[54] Besides the mention of 553 prisoners in Pegram's command, the only other detailed casualty list is that of the Twenty-third Virginia, which lost 32. The other units must have had at least 100 wounded and stragglers.

[55] "A true Panic Terror . . . seems to have seized on some unhappy persons," said the Examiner of July 18, 1861, p. 2, col. 4, which went on to appeal to "reasonable and resolute people" to put down with "stern and sharp means, if need be, all attempts to spread absurd and groundless fears among the ignorant and weak." The paper insisted that the effects of the disaster would be limited: "Officers of Gen. Garnett's command are the real sufferers in those disasters. Their reputation has been torn to pieces by the tongue of rumor." In a separate article on the 18th (p. 3, col. 3), the same journal reported that on the night of the 16th, groups of people on every corner discussed until midnight the bad news from Western Virginia: "We never knew this community more deeply stirred." The Richmond Dispatch (July 19, p. 2, col. 2) attributed the disaster "in greater part to faulty generalship" but believed the main reason was "treachery on the part of natives who guided the march of the invader."

[56] Cf. J. W. Gordon to "The relatives of the late General Robert S. Garnett," Aug. 14, 1861—Garnett MSS.

of those to whom the South looked hopefully, his high name had to be stricken—the first officer of his rank on either side to be killed in action. Of him Porter Alexander wrote, in the long perspective of years: ". . . the impression I formed of him as a soldier is not lower than that of any other officer I have ever known. In every one else I have seen some mere human traits, but in Garnett every trait was purely military. Had he lived, I am sure he would have been one of our great generals." [57]

Although his grim defeat humiliated the South, the troops opposed to him were numerically superior [58] and were far better equipped. Their leader was Maj. Gen. Geo. B. McClellan, who had moved from Ohio to Grafton and thence had advanced with vigor. The attack against Pegram at Rich Mountain was delivered by McClellan's ablest subordinate, Brig. Gen. W. S. Rosecrans. Good Federal management, the weakness of the Confederate force and McClellan's skillful presentation in brief telegraphic reports of his success in clearing Northwest Virginia of Southern troops [59] made the campaign appear on one side an example of incompetence and, on the other, of military brilliance. Garnett was buried and forgotten by the public; McClellan was the hope of the North.

[57] E. P. Alexander, *Military Memoirs of a Confederate* (cited hereafter as *Alexander*), 14. For the subsequent effort of Gen. R. E. Lee to halt the enemy in Western Virginia, and for the controversy between Gen. Henry A. Wise and Gen. John B. Floyd over the operations in the Kanawha Valley, see 1 *R. E. Lee*, pp. 541–602.

[58] It is almost impossible from existing records to compute McClellan's strength. The best basis of estimate is the narrative of the "Campaign in Western Virginia" with which he prefaced the edition of his *Report on the Organization and Campaign of the Army of the Potomac*, issued in 1864 by Sheldon & Co. If McClellan's regiments averaged 500 men, he had in Northwest Virginia about 9000 infantry. *Op. cit.*, 23–24.

[59] *Cf.* John G. Nicolay, *The Outbreak of Rebellion*, 153–54.

CHAPTER IV

BEAUREGARD ESSAYS GRAND STRATEGY

THE tragedy of Rich Mountain and of Carrick's Ford was effaced quickly by events around Manassas. Beauregard's little army increased steadily during the early summer. Most of the troops sent to him were of the very first type of volunteers, men of intelligence, courage and good physique. Their company officers varied much, but their field officers, though in some cases without previous military experience, had station and capacity that won the respect of the men in the ranks. Training proceeded without break. Although the Federals were believed to be receiving many new regiments, no offensive was undertaken. The same condition favored the preparations of General Johnston.

Within a few weeks Beauregard had a firm grip on the esteem of his troops. Because of the glamour of his success at Sumter, the men were ready to believe anything that was said of him— even the remarkable story that he had disguised himself as an Irish laborer, had gone to Washington and had inspected all the fortifications there.[1] With great pride, the South read how the North reported Beauregard in half a dozen places at the same moment, engaged in some daring and always fruitful enterprise. There was unquestioning faith in the fulfillment of a prediction in the *New York Times* that he would concentrate 70,000 men at Manassas, would make the place impregnable, would lure the Federals to exhaust themselves in attacks, and then would advance and overwhelm them.[2] Beauregard himself was much pleased with all this praise. "My troops," said he, "are in fine spirits and anxious for a fight." He added: "They seem to have the most unbounded confidence in me."[3]

[1] *Richmond Examiner*, June 21, p. 2, col. 6; *Richmond Dispatch*, June 22, 1861, p. 2, col. 3.
[2] *Richmond Dispatch*, June 15, p. 3, col. 4; June 22, 1861, p. 2, col. 3. For other comment on the popularity and prestige of Beauregard at this time, see *Richmond Examiner*, June 12, p. 1, col. 5; p. 2, col. 2 and p. 3, col. 1; July 12, p. 2, col. 5; July 20, p. 1, col. 6 (a quotation from the *New Orleans Picayune*); *Richmond Dispatch*, July 15, 1861, p. 3, col. 4 (reprint of an article from the *Charleston Mercury*): Mrs. Chesnut, 65.
[3] 1 *Roman*, 82.

Spurred by that confidence and by the prospect of an early advance, Beauregard prepared, about June 10, a plan of action which he sent to the President by one of the officers of his general staff.[4] Johnston, he assumed, was about to be attacked. If that commander, said Beauregard, "were ordered to abandon forthwith his present position and concentrate suddenly his forces with mine, guarding with small detachments, all the passes through which the enemy might follow him, we could by a bold and rapid movement forward, retake Arlington Heights and Alexandria, if not too strongly fortified and garrisoned, which would have the effect of recalling all the enemy's forces from Northern Virginia, for the protection of Washington." If this were not possible, Beauregard continued with reference to his superior officer, Johnston should retreat on Richmond. He himself and the other commanders of separate forces in Virginia would do the same thing. Beauregard proceeded to tell the President: Then, "acting on interior lines from Richmond as a center (our forces being increased by the reserves at that point) we could crush in rapid succession and in detail, the several columns of the enemy, which I have supposed would move on three or four different lines. With 35,000 men, properly handled, I have not the least doubt that we could annihilate 50,000 of the enemy." He closed with an appeal for a concerted plan of operations. "Otherwise, we will be assailed in detail by superior forces, and will be cut off, or destroyed entirely." [5]

The President replied to this promptly and moderately. He did not dwell on the uncertainty of the assumption that the Federals first would attack Johnston. Neither did Mr. Davis raise any question concerning the ability of an army that had little ordnance, poor ammunition and feeble transportation to storm the approaches to Washington. He contented himself with saying of the suggestion for a withdrawal by Johnston, that he trusted the commander at Harpers Ferry would be able to keep the enemy from marching up the Valley and from getting in rear of the position at Manassas. "We hope soon," Davis wrote Beauregard, "to reinforce you to an extent equal to the strength you require, by the junction of General Johnston, and I cannot doubt but that you would then be better circumstanced to advance upon

---

[4] Lt. Col., later Maj. Gen., Samuel Jones.   [5] 1 *Roman*, 77.

Alexandria than if General Johnston, by withdrawing from the valley, had left the enemy the power to pass to your rear, to cut your line of communication, and advance to attack you in reverse, while you were engaged with the enemy in front." Davis went on to say that while it was desirable to retake Arlington and Alexandria, provided Beauregard's rear were covered, "it is quite clear that if the case be otherwise, your possession, if acquired, would be both brief and fruitless." In the matter of a general withdrawal on Richmond, the President withheld the obvious criticism that the enemy might not be obliging enough to advance, as Beauregard assumed, "on three or four different lines." Mr. Davis stressed only the fact that the Confederacy did not have sufficient transportation for a simultaneous withdrawal. In case the armies in front of Washington had to retreat, Johnston, of course, would unite with Beauregard. Davis hastened to add: ". . . I have not anticipated the necessity of your retreat, and have struggled to increase your force, and look hopefully forward to see you enabled to assume the offensive."[6] There was not a hint in Davis's letter that he regarded Beauregard's plan as grandiose. Nor did rejection of this proposal, even with the strong arguments employed by the Chief Executive, discourage Beauregard from formulating another.

The General took some time to do this because he was busy over the organization of his quartermaster's and commissary service, both of which were rudimentary.[7] With the selection of higher officers for the daily arriving troops, he appears from his correspondence to have concerned himself little. Perhaps he knew that the President would choose the brigade commanders without asking or desiring advice. In Beauregard's published letters there is not a line of recommendation or so much as a hint that Generals of Brigade were needed.

The day "Prince John" Magruder got his promotion, June 17, Mr. Davis appointed ten other Brigadier Generals. Among them were two officers already at Manassas—Col. Richard S. Ewell of Virginia[8] and Col. David R. Jones, a South Carolinian. Included also were three officers with "Joe" Johnston in the Valley. These

[6] June 13, 1861; 1 *Roman*, 78.
[7] 1 *Roman*. ~1.   [8] Technically of the District of Columbia.

were Col. Barnard E. Bee of South Carolina, Col. E. Kirby Smith of Florida, and Col. Thos. J. Jackson of Virginia. All five were graduates of the United States Military Academy and all except Jackson had been in the regular army until approximately the time their States had seceded.[9]

Beauregard by this time had nineteen infantry regiments which, on June 20, he organized into six Brigades. Milledge Bonham, whom he had found at Manassas, formally received the First Brigade of South Carolina troops. To "Dick" Ewell were assigned two Alabama regiments and one from Louisiana. David Jones had one South Carolina and two Mississippi regiments. As these Brigades exhausted Beauregard's general officers, he had to place one Brigade of three Virginia regiments under Col. G. H. Terrett. A Brigade of like size and composition was entrusted to the great planter, Col. P. St. George Cocke. The sixth Brigade of two Virginia and one South Carolina regiments was placed under Col. Jubal A. Early, who, like Cocke, was a retired "West Pointer." Thus four of "Old Bory's" Brigades had one-time professional soldiers at their head. In addition, Terrett was an old officer of Marines; Bonham, as already noted, had held a commission in the Mexican War. The Colonels of the nineteen regiments swept a wide range of abilities—politicians, old militiamen, lawyers, teachers—but in most instances, they were men who had been among the first to raise regiments and to enter the service of their States.[10]

With these troops, Beauregard took an advanced position to cover Manassas and, if opportunity offered, to begin an offensive.[11] To fashion this blow he returned eagerly to his planning, but before he completed a new design he had discouragement. The North was as war-mad as the South and was arming furiously. Sumter was a spur, not a curb. Confidence in Washington did not fall below that in Richmond. Troops to drive Johnston up the Shenandoah Valley were being collected under Gen. Robert Patterson, a veteran of the war with Mexico. Gen. Irvin McDowell, who was commanding the front opposite Beauregard, was credited by the Confederates with 40,000 men and was believed to be ready to sound the advance. Beauregard, not unnaturally, lost

[9] The list is in *Wright*, 52 ff.   [10] *O. R.*, 2, 943–44.   [11] 1 *Roman*, 79.

some of his appetite for an offensive. He wrote an admiring member of Congress a letter full of complaints, set forth the smallness of his command, and appealed for reinforcements: "Oh, that I had the genius of a Napoleon, to be more worthy of our cause and of . . . [the] confidence [of the troops]! If I could only get the enemy to attack me, as I am trying to have him do, I would stake my reputation on the handsomest victory that could be hoped for." [12]

In writing the President, three days later, Beauregard put the strength of McDowell's army at 35,000, and credited the Federal commander with a reserve of 15,000. If the Unionists offered battle on Bull Run, he would accept it, he said, but he feared the Federals would move between him and Johnston and force a retreat in the direction of Fredericksburg. ". . . in view of the odds against me," he said, "and of the vital importance at this juncture of avoiding the hazard of a defeat, which would open to the enemy the way to Richmond, I shall act with extreme caution." [13] In short, his course was to be defensive. Then, almost overnight, he changed his mind again and sent one of his staff officers to Richmond with a new design for joint operations with Johnston. Before this officer could do more than get to the capital, General Beauregard revised his proposal and dispatched Col. James Chesnut to Mr. Davis with this plan, which was later the subject of much controversy: Johnston, with 20,000 men, was to join Beauregard. Together they were to advance and place themselves between the two lines of McDowell's army. They were to attack the Federals "separately with larger masses, and thus exterminate them or drive them into the Potomac." Johnston thereupon was to return to the Valley with his own army and 10,000 of Beauregard's troops, and was to destroy within a week the invading Union force under Gen. Robert Patterson, while Beauregard marched into the abandoned Washington defenses or else withdrew to Manassas. Johnston, having wiped out Patterson, was to send a part of his army to Gen. Robert Selden Garnett, who then was facing Gen. George B. McClellan and a Federal column in Western Virginia. Having disposed of McClellan,

[12] To L. T. Wigfall, July 8, 1861; 1 *Roman*, 81 ff.
[13] Beauregard to Davis, July 11, 1861; 1 *Roman*, 82–83.

Garnett would join Johnston and with him would move into Maryland and attack Washington from the rear. Beauregard himself simultaneously would attack the capital in front.[14]

In his enthusiasm for this extraordinary plan, Beauregard communicated it to Johnston with the observation: "I think this whole campaign could be completed brilliantly in from fifteen to twenty-five days. Oh, that we had but one good head to conduct all our operations!"[15] Johnston, who was not given to needless correspondence, apparently made no reply to this. In Richmond, where a junction between Johnston and Beauregard of course had suggested itself as an obvious defensive, the proposal presented by Colonel Chesnut was heard by President Davis, General Lee and the Adjutant General, Samuel Cooper, but, being verbal, it was considered merely a broad suggestion. As such, it was held to be hopelessly impractical for a multitude of reasons. The most obvious of these was that Johnston, who was expected to furnish Beauregard 20,000 troops, had only 11,000 effectives and was facing an enemy which the Confederate authorities estimated at 30,000.[16] The details of Beauregard's proposal, in fact, made so slight an impression that the members of Colonel Chesnut's little audience were to have difficulty, a few months later, in recalling what actually had been proposed.[17]

Action now was immediately in prospect. The battle which each side expected to end the conflict between North and South was about to be joined. By July 17, it became certain that McDowell was advancing toward Manassas. Beauregard urged that Johnston move to his support, but even when the march would have to be swift and direct, Beauregard could not refrain from suggesting at least a touch of grand strategy: Johnston, said Beauregard, should advance in two columns. One should travel by way of the Manassas Gap Railroad. The other should cross the mountains North of the railway, via Aldie, and should strike the enemy in flank and rear near Centreville at the moment Beauregard attacked in front. A staff officer rushed off with this

[14] James Chesnut to Beauregard, July 16, 1861; 1 *Roman*, 85–87.
[15] Letter of July 13, 1861: 1 *Roman*, 87.
[16] Actually, Patterson never had more than 18,200. See Robert Patterson, *A Narrative of the Campaign in the Valley of the Shenandoah in 1861*, p. 63.
[17] Vide *O. R.*, 2, 504 ff., for the statements made in October and November, 1861, by the participants in the conference.

proposal to General Johnston,[18] who, so far as position was concerned, was prepared for marching orders. He had evacuated Harpers Ferry on June 15[19] and had withdrawn to Winchester. There he was placed where he could meet Patterson, should that Federal commander advance up the Shenandoah Valley.[20] In the event General McClellan descended from the western mountains, Johnston could manœuvre to meet him; and if, finally, Johnston had to reinforce Beauregard, the troops at Winchester could march twenty miles to the Southeast and there could strike a direct railroad to Manassas Junction, thirty-five miles to the eastward. The one thing Johnston could not do at the time was to adopt Beauregard's suggestion and to move on Manassas in two widely separated colu ins. Johnston's 11,000 troops were inexperienced.[21] Any logis ics based on their movement over mountain roads would be uncertain. "I preferred," Johnston later explained, "the junction of the two armies at the earliest time possible, as the first measure to secure success." [22]

This was not the end of Beauregard's strategy. Other proposals, as dazzling in detail and holding out even richer prizes, were to be fashioned. The beginning was not promising. All Beauregard's plans from June 10 to July 17 had been rejected—all of them! He might not have even the command of the field. If the two Confederate forces were united at Manassas before McDowell attacked, Johnston would direct operations. He was the senior and might get the glory.

[18] See the map, *supra*, p. 11 and O. R., 2, 485–86. In his *Commentary on the Campaign and Battle of Manassas* (written, 1886, published, 1891, and cited hereafter as *Beauregard*), the General, p. 30, defended this proposal and insisted that the movement via Aldie was put forward as an alternative to a direct advance by the railroad, but he admitted that in July, 1861, he thought "the Shenandoah forces were somewhat greater than they really were."

[19] O. R., 2, 472.

[20] It should be noted here that as the Shenandoah River flows northward, a march "down the Valley" is northward and one "up the Valley" is southward, in reverse of the usual employment of the terms.

[21] R. M. Johnston in his excellent *Bull Run, Its Strategy and Tactics* (cited hereafter as *R. M. Johnston*), 110, computed Johnston's strength of all arms at 10,961.

[22] J. E. Johnston, *Narrative of Military Operations* (cited hereafter as *Johnston's Narrative*), 38; Johnston, in *Battles and Leaders of the Civil War* (cited hereafter as B. & L.), vol. 1, p. 250. Both times General Johnston narrated this incident, he overlooked the fact that Beauregard had proposed that the troops from the Shenandoah advance in two columns. Johnston wrote as though Beauregard intended all the forces from the Valley to move by Aldie.

CHAPTER V

BEAUREGARD PLANS A BATTLE

AGAINST the superior force marching to attack him, Beauregard did not know whether he could hold his own. He fell back to Bull Run, took position on the south bank, and advised the President that, if the Federals were overwhelming, "I shall retire to the Rappahannock railroad bridge, saving my command for defence there and future operations." Davis was requested to notify Johnston and Gen. Theophilus H. Holmes, an "old army" officer who had a small force on the Potomac about twenty-five miles South of Manassas. "Send forward any reinforcements," Beauregard concluded, "at the earliest possible instant, and by every possible means." [1]

A brush had occurred at the outposts before Beauregard forwarded this telegram. On the 18th the Federals undertook a long-range cannonade opposite one of the crossings of Bull Run and then felt out the Confederate position at Blackburn's Ford. There they were smartly repulsed by Virginia troops with some loss. The commander of the defending forces was a Georgian, James Longstreet, who had been a Paymaster in the United States Army and, in the extensive promotions of June 17, had been made a Confederate Brigadier General. Although he had not assumed command of the First, Eleventh and Seventeenth Virginia Volunteers until July 2, he had advanced their training remarkably in a fortnight. Longstreet's calm and soldierly bearing in this skirmish made him a reality to many officers who previously had known him as a name only. [2]

This affair at Blackburn's Ford, which Beauregard subsequently called the "Battle of Bull Run," [3] did much to restore his confi-

[1] 1 Roman, 90.
[2] O. R., 440 ff; 1 Roman, 92 ff; James Longstreet, From Manassas to Appomattox (cited hereafter as Longstreet), 33 ff.
[3] The contest of July 21 he and most Southerners styled the Battle of Manassas.

dence, but on the 19th misgivings and confusion troubled him again. From Richmond came a suggestion that if the Federals had retired and Johnston had not started for Manassas, it might be well for him to remain where he was. The Unionists, it was explained, knew of the Southern troop movements to Manassas and might change their plans. Beauregard paid no attention to this. The next day, July 20, Johnston and part of his troops arrived at Manassas Junction under authority received from Richmond at 1 A.M., July 18.[4] With some difficulty Johnston disposed of his 1700 sick in Winchester, and left militia to guard the town. His supposition was that the Federal army under Patterson would not attempt to march up the Valley but would parallel his movement and proceed to Manassas. Johnston then marched to Piedmont Station, whence railroad trains were to carry his entire force to a junction with Beauregard. The first troops to reach Manassas in this manner were a Brigade under T. J. Jackson. Behind him came two excellent Georgia regiments.[5]

Beauregard welcomed these troops and described to Johnston what had happened. The enemy, Beauregard said, in all probability was at Centreville, two miles and a half North of Bull Run. To cope with the Federals, Beauregard proposed to use Johnston's troops in an elaborate concentration. The new senior commander[6] had never been in Bull Run previously, and had he attempted to reconnoiter the ground after his arrival he would have found it too extensive to be covered in an afternoon and, perhaps, too complicated to be mastered quickly.[7] The only map

---

[4] The text of this message, O. R., 2, 478, which subsequently was a matter of some dispute (see infra, p. 103), was as follows:

Richmond, July 17, 1861

General J. E. Johnston, Winchester, Va.:
General Beauregard is attacked. To strike the enemy a decisive blow a junction of all your effective force will be needed. If practicable, make the movement, sending all your sick and baggage to Culpeper Court-House either by railroad or by Warrenton. In all the arrangements exercise your discretion.

S. Cooper
Adjutant and Inspector General

[5] O. R., 2, 473.

[6] Johnston had telegraphed the President to ask his status in relation to Beauregard and had received a tactful answer that as a General in Confederate service he had the power attached to that rank and would know how to avail himself of Beauregard's knowledge of the situation. "The zeal of both," said Davis, "assures me of harmonious action." O. R., 2, 985.

[7] Cf. Johnston's Narrative, 39. The student who visits Bull Run in the expectation of finding on its banks a compact battlefield that comes entirely within a single coup d'œil

that was shown him did not represent any of the elevations. It merely displayed the roads, villages and streams.[8] Moreover, Beauregard had ready for Johnston a specific plan: he would keep his forces "united within the lines of Bull Run, and thence

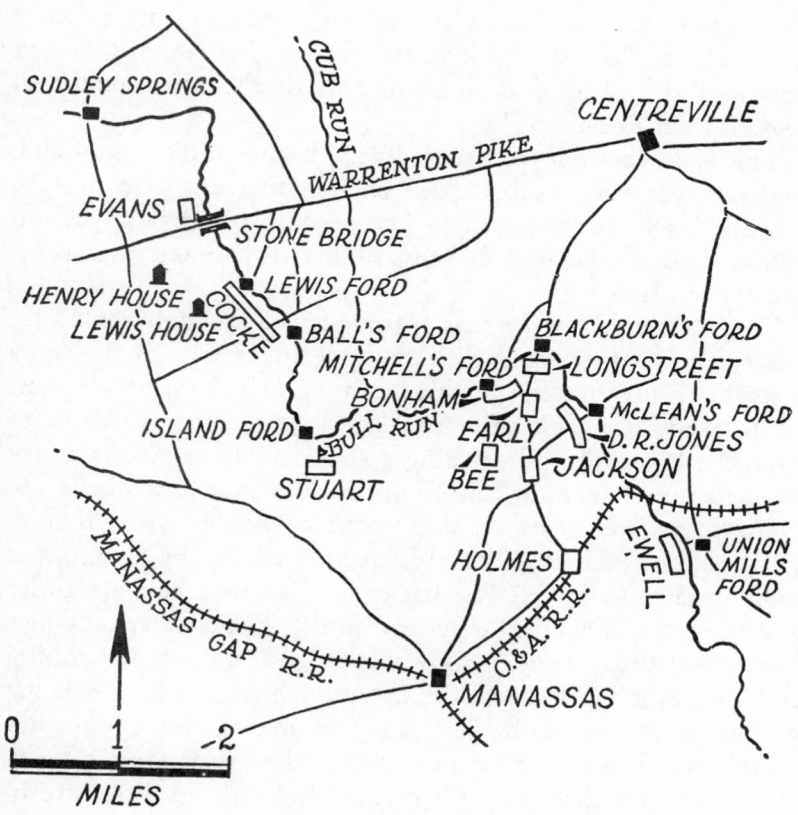

Position of Confederate Forces on Bull Run, July 21, 1861, sunrise.
After *R. M. Johnston*, 165.

advance, with all his forces," to the attack of the enemy at Centreville.[9] As Johnston was ignorant of the situation, he could interpret this proposal only in terms of the indicated movements of

will be surprised by its magnitude. The scene of the fighting around the Henry House is neither wide nor deep, but the entire Confederate position, from Stone Bridge to Union Mills Ford, is one of the largest of the War between the States.

[8] *Johnston's Narrative*, 39.   [9] *O. R.*, 2, 486.

General Patterson. It was prudent to continue to assume that when Patterson discovered the Confederate troops had left the vicinity of Winchester, he would move the Federal columns in the Shenandoah Valley to the support of McDowell. They would arrive, Johnston computed, on the 22d. For that reason, if McDowell was to be attacked before he was reinforced decisively, he must be struck on the 21st. Perforce, and without hesitation, Johnston approved the plan of Beauregard and directed that officer to undertake its execution.[10]

This was wholly in accordance with Beauregard's wishes and, perhaps, was what he had been angling to effect. He ordered Johnston's and Holmes's troops into position as they arrived, and before nightfall he had in prospect the dispositions shown on the appended sketch.

The nature of the terrain was described, though somewhat inadequately, by Beauregard himself to this effect: "Bull Run is a small stream, running in this locality nearly from west to east to its confluence with the Occoquan River, about twelve miles from the Potomac, and draining a considerable scope of country from its source in Bull Run Mountain to a short distance of the Potomac at Occoquan. At this season habitually low and sluggish, it is, however, rapidly and frequently swollen by the summer rains until unfordable. The banks for the most part are rocky and steep, but abound in long-used fords. The country on either side, much broken and thickly wooded, becomes gently rolling and open as it recedes from the stream. On the northern side the ground is much the highest, and commands the other bank completely. Roads traverse and intersect the surrounding country in almost every direction. Finally, at Mitchell's Ford the stream is about equidistant between Centreville and Manassas, some six miles apart." [11]

Beauregard's defended front, as the course of Bull Run twisted its way eastward, was approximately eight miles in length. For an advance by his right on Centreville, he placed his troops as advantageously as the roads permitted. On three miles of the right center, he concentrated one half the entire army.[12]

[10] O. R., 2, 473, 474; Johnston's Narrative, pp. 40–41. [11] O. R., 2, 441.
[12] Roughly 15,500 of 33,000. Kirby Smith's Brigade is not included in the total, inasmuch as his men had not arrived.

Offensively, he was ready; defensively, he was exposed to any movement other than a direct drive on his advanced base at Manassas Junction. He stated subsequently that, after the feeling-out action of the 18th, he did not believe the Federals would renew the attack on the right, where he was strong; but on two miles and a half of his left, where Beauregard later said he antici-pated attack,[13] he placed less than 5000 men.[14] These troops, as he subsequently stated, were "but slightly provided with artificial defensive appliances and artillery." [15] Their closest support was the general reserve, the nearer flank of which was almost four miles from the expected point of attack, namely, the vicinity of the Stone Bridge on the Warrenton turnpike. Such cavalry as the com-bined army possessed at the time was placed near the center. Most of the small artillery reserve was in the same general position.[16]

These dispositions, from the standpoint of a defensive, were the more remarkable because of certain minor peculiarities of the terrain, which Beauregard did not mention in his quoted descrip-tion. For most of the distance from the Stone Bridge eastward to Mitchell's Ford, the rolling ridges on the South lie at more than cannon shot from Bull Run and drop gradually toward it. Infantry could cross the stream at almost any point.[17] At Mitchell's Ford itself, an ugly and awkward position, a column probably could force its way across the Run, even in the face of strong artillery fire. For that reason troops in considerable num-ber might properly be stationed there. Downstream from Mitchell's Ford, the Run courses through a deep declivity, where the ridges entirely dominate every crossing. McLean's Ford was difficult; Blackburn's was almost impassable against infantry with

---

[13] O. R., 2, 486.

[14] Perhaps as few as 4376.

[15] O. R., 2, 486. For the arguments Beauregard advanced late in life, to justify his dispositions, see Beauregard, 52 ff.

[16] O. R., 2, 487. Johnston's troops had been styled the Army of the Shenandoah; Beauregard had called his the Army of the Potomac. After the junction of the two, the latter name prevailed until it was supplanted the next year by the one that became even more renowned. If, therefore, a date and a place were to be set for the birth of the force that later became the Army of Northern Virginia, it would be July 20, 1861, on the Plains of Manassas.

[17] The best description of this part of the terrain is given in the report of Brig. Gen. P. St. George Cocke, O. R., 51, pt. 1, p. 25. This document, printed in one of the last volumes of the Official Records, seems to have been overlooked by virtually all those who have written about the battle.

moderate artillery support; Union Mills Ford, on the Confederate side, virtually was impregnable. Beauregard, in short, was most heavily concentrated where his position was strongest, and was weakest numerically where the crossing was easiest.[18] The disproportion of force was startling.

Of all this, Beauregard must have been aware. He had studied the ground and had shaped the plan. As Johnston entrusted the drafting of the combat order to the man who had fashioned the design, Beauregard set about that task late in the night of July 20–21. His own exhausted Assistant Adjutant General had gone to bed, by medical command, under a narcotic. The General accordingly dictated the order to Johnston's engineer, Maj. W. H. C. Whiting,[19] who, of course, knew no more about the terrain or the dispositions than his chief did. At 4.30 A.M. on the 21st, Beauregard submitted the paper to General Johnston, who proceeded at once to examine it.

It was a confused document, and in retrospect it is a gloomy instance of the manner in which, during the first stage of hostilities, the ignorance of the commanding officer may be as gross as that of the men and infinitely more expensive in blood and misery. One of Beauregard's Brigades, for example, was instructed thus: It was to "march via McLean's Ford to place itself in position of attack upon the enemy on or about the Union Mills and Centreville road. It will be held in readiness either to support the attack upon Centreville or to move in the direction of Fairfax Station, according to circumstances, with its right flank toward the left of Ewell's command, more or less distant, according to the nature of the country and attack."

The other sections of the order were in language similarly

18 Whatever the testimony of the books, the evidence of the hills is that General Beauregard based all his dispositions on offensive strategy. It is inconceivable that an engineer of his experience, if he viewed carefully the three lower fords from the direction of the enemy's anticipated approach, could have massed so heavily there on any other assumption than that, besides guarding his depots, he could and would "jump off" there for a successful drive on Centreville. In *Beauregard*, 52–53, its author thus defended his dispositions: "A glance at the map will show that the limited forces at General Beauregard's disposal . . . must be mainly held along the lower fords, not only to cover the more direct approaches to [Camp Pickens, which guarded his depots] and his communications, but because a movement of the Federal army against or around the Stone Bridge involved a circuitous operation exposing its left flank and communications, upon which by a shorter and more rapid movement of attack from the lower fords General Beauregard could have thrown his readily concentrated forces."

19 *Beauregard*, 60.

vague. Each ended with the same sentence: "The order to advance will be given by the commander-in-chief." [20] It was not clear from the text whether this "order to advance" was to be sent before or after the various Brigades had crossed Bull Run. Participation in the forward movement was planned for one of Johnston's Brigades that had not arrived. The order provided, also, for the distribution of the cavalry and of the artillery among the infantry Brigades prior to the opening of an action expected to be fought that very day.

At the end of the paper, the various co-operating Brigades were divided into two groups. One of these was assigned to Gen. T. H. Holmes, though he was not so notified, and the other was assigned to an undesignated "second in command." [21] Whether these officers were to direct their forces throughout the operation or only during the pursuit of the enemy might have been subject to different interpretations. These obscurities were paralyzing. Regardless of them, execution of the plan called for much staff work, prompt and complicated, which Beauregard's inexperienced officers by no possibility could perform. Beauregard himself was so lacking in experience that he did not realize he was demanding more than his staff could give.

When this combat order was put before Johnston, he probably observed that it did not contemplate the employment against Centreville of so large a force as Beauregard had stated the previous evening he would use.[22] The order, moreover, was drawn as if it emanated from Beauregard. Instead of being offered for signature by Johnston, it was signed in Beauregard's name by his Assistant Adjutant General, Colonel Jordan, who had awakened from his narcotic. The commanding General was expected merely to approve in writing those copies of the order intended for the troops Johnston had brought from the Shenandoah Val-

---

[20] O. R., 2, 479. The defense made of these orders in 1886, after they had been criticized by General Johnston, will be found in Beauregard, 55 ff. It is not apt to convince students.

[21] O. R., 2, 480.

[22] This statement has to be qualified because Johnston did not mention in his contemporaneous report or in his Narrative (1874) the fact that the written plan varied from the verbal outline given on the 20th. Johnston's first published mention of this point was in 1 B. & L., 246, during the course of his controversy with Beauregard regarding the command of the army in the battle of July 21. It is possible, though scarcely probable, that Johnston did not perceive at the time that the force directed against Centreville was smaller than Beauregard had said he would use.

ley.[23] This was irregular, but as it was not immediately important, Johnston approved the entire paper rather than delay the movement of troops who already should have been on the march.[24]

A transcript of the order was made and was dispatched immediately to Brig. Gen. James Longstreet, who still was near Blackburn's Ford. Copies may have been sent to other brigade commanders.[25] Before anything could be done to execute the plan, the unanticipated realities of developing action began to upset strategical theory. The first contretemps was the discovery that Johnston's rear Brigade had not arrived from the Valley, though the President of the Manassas Gap Railroad had assured the commanding General it would reach Manassas on the 20th.[26] The absence of these troops might reduce the strength of the army to a point where a general offensive would be excessively hazardous.

[23] *Beauregard*, 61–62. The General explained, *loc. cit.*, that the order was "issued because of the express understanding that General Beauregard should be in command for execution of operations," and that Colonel Jordan "took to [Johnston] for his signature only such copies as were to be sent to the Army of the Shenandoah, in order, as [Jordan] stated to [Johnston] at the moment, to secure beyond the possibility of accident their complete recognition by the Shenandoah troops." Johnston, in his published statements, did not notice this explanation.

[24] *Johnston's Narrative*, 41.

[25] This is the first point to be remembered in approaching the complicated miscarriage of Beauregard's orders during the early morning of July 21. General Longstreet stated explicitly (*O. R.*, 2, 543) that he crossed Bull Run at an early hour "in obedience to the general's orders of the 20th. to assume the offensive." As the order described above bears date of July 20 and is the sole order issued for an offensive, there can be no mistaking the source of his instructions. He evidently interpreted the equivocal language of the order to mean that he was to proceed to the north side of the Run, without waiting for "the order to advance," which was to be "given by the commanding General." The moot question of the dispatch of the first instructions of the day to the other chiefs of Brigades is discussed in Appendix III, p. 726.

[26] The inefficient operation of this railroad created much indignant comment and aroused some suspicion of disloyalty. At least a part of Kirby Smith's Brigade reached Piedmont, where it was to entrain, at midnight July 19–20 but could not get aboard cars until 2 A.M. on the 21st. General Johnston in his *Narrative*, p. 56, said there was one minor collision in the movement of the Sixth North Carolina, but the contemporary account stated that a train left the track. The engine's water gave out. Soldiers had to use shovels to get water into the trough. Had it not been for the efforts of Col. C. F. Fisher of the Sixth North Carolina, former President of the North Carolina Railroad (1 *N. C. Regts.*, 294), it is improbable that Smith's Brigade could have reached Manassas in time to participate in the battle. See an important letter from a Maryland officer in the *Richmond Examiner*, Aug. 17, 1861, p. 1, cols. 2–3. That newspaper believed there had been "the vilest treachery" and it reported that the conductor of the train had received a bribe of $800 to delay the movement of his train (*ibid.*, July 31, p. 3, col. 3; cf. *ibid.*, July 27, p. 2, cols. 1–2). Apparently, the trouble was that the scanty personnel of the small railroad were exhausted by long hours of work. Moreover, on part of the line. there was only one locomotive. (19 *S. H. S. P.*, 87.)

Worse still, shortly after 5 o'clock on the morning of July 21,[27] a messenger arrived from General Bonham at Mitchell's Ford, with a disconcerting report that the Federals had appeared in force on his left front. Did this mean that the enemy had seized the initiative and was attacking, instead of waiting obligingly to be assailed? There certainly was no mistaking the direction of the sound of firing that now was audible. It was coming from the Confederate left, in the vicinity of the Stone Bridge,[28] the main crossing of Bull Run on the road that linked Alexandria and Warrenton. From that quarter, the firing spread toward the center, though not in heavy volume.[29] Ere long, Bonham sent a report to the effect that the Federals undoubtedly were moving down the Warrenton Pike in considerable force toward the Confederate left.[30]

Beauregard heard this bad news without evidence of chagrin. Unpleasant as was the prospect, he had to conclude that an attack was about to be made on Bonham and probably at the Stone Bridge. In that event, of course, an immediate general offensive by the Confederates would be impossible. The elaborate plan to which Johnston had just attached his signature could not be executed forthwith. That was clear. Even so, Beauregard's devotion to the Napoleonic strategy would not permit abandonment of all hope of a general offensive. An opening for that might yet be found. At the moment, Beauregard told himself, it was possible to undertake on his extreme right a diversion to confuse the enemy's attack on his center and left. At 5.30 Beauregard accordingly dispatched these instructions to Brig. Gen. R. S. Ewell, who commanded at Union Mills Ford, the crossing farthest downstream:

> Manassas Junction, Va., July 21, 1861.
> Sent at 5½ h. A.M.
>
> General,—You will hold yourself in readiness to take the offensive on Centreville at a moment's notice, to make a diversion against the

---

[27] *O. R.*, 2, 518. Bonham stated that Colonel Kirkland confirmed the presence of the enemy "before daylight." As sunrise was at 4.54 and as the distance from Bonham's headquarters to Manassas was about 2¾ miles, a swift rider would have reached G. H. Q. not long after 5 A.M.

[28] Evans said it began at 5.15. *O. R.*, 2, 559.

[29] *O. R.*, 2, 474.   [30] *O. R.*, 2, 518.

enemy's intended attack on Mitchell's Ford and, probably, Stone Bridge. You will protect well your right flank against any attack from the eastward.

General Holmes's brigade will support your movement.

If the enemy be prepared to attack in front of your left, leave it (said Brigade) in proper position, with orders to take the offensive when it hears your engagement on the other side of the Run. I intend to take the offensive throughout my front as soon as possible.

Respectfully, your obedient servant,

G. T. BEAUREGARD, Brig.-Genl. Comdg.

Genl. R. S. Ewell, Union Mills, Va.[31]

In the confusion at headquarters, a copy of this dispatch was not made out at once for General Holmes or else was entrusted to an incompetent courier.[32] Longstreet was not informed of this change of plan which, of course, cancelled his original instructions to cross Bull Run for an advance on Centreville. Beauregard's attention was divided; his aides were confused. Messengers were dispatched, about 5.30, to General Cocke and to Col. N. G. Evans, with instructions to hold to last extremity their positions on the left.[33] Colonel Early was directed to place himself where he could support either Longstreet at Blackburn's Ford or D. R. Jones at McLean's.[34]

As orders multiplied, Beauregard lost his grip on his widely spread Brigades. He may have forgotten momentarily that he had ordered Ewell merely to prepare to advance, rather than to begin his advance; or else some one who was signing for Beauregard may have had the same lapsus or may not have realized that the order of 4.30 for a general forward movement had ceased to be operative. In either event, at 6 o'clock or thereabouts, notice was sent D. R. Jones at McLean's Ford that Ewell had orders to take the offensive and that Jones should follow the movement by attacking in his front.[35]

---

[31] 1 *Roman*, 447–48.

[32] Although the dispatch to Ewell is marked as "sent" at 5.30, Holmes's copy was not received by him until "about 9 o'clock." *O. R.*, 2, 565. Holmes was less than two miles from G. H. Q. on a direct road.

[33] *O. R.*, 2, 487.

[34] *O. R.*, 2, 555.

[35] *O. R.*, 2, 537. The solution given in the text of this confusing point in the development of orders is based on (1) the fact that D. R. Jones received at 7.10 A.M. the direc-

A slow cannonade now was ranging the entire left wing; enemy forces were known to be moving down the Warrenton Pike toward Stone Bridge. That was all that actually had happened, but it had shaken to chaos the Confederate plan of action. As Beauregard's orders had been issued to that hour, or were interpreted by each of the affected officers, they provided:

1. That Longstreet should cross Bull Run and attack.[36]

2. That Ewell should await word to launch a diversion toward Centreville.

3. That Holmes should support Ewell, though orders had not reached Holmes.

4. That D. R. Jones should follow Ewell, in the understanding that Ewell had been instructed to attack.

5. That Cocke and Evans should stand to the last in defense of the left-center and left.

6. That Early should take position South of Bull Run to support either D. R. Jones or Longstreet.

Involved as all this was, it might have been simplified if it had been understood. It was not. At Beauregard's headquarters, nobody knew either the scope or the conflict of orders. About 7 o'clock, when the cannon fire seemed to be diminishing somewhat, Beauregard took his first step to reinforce his threatened left. From a reserve position South of Mitchell's Ford, Beauregard ordered a shift to Stone Bridge by the troops of Gen. Barnard E. Bee, who commanded one of the Brigades Johnston had brought from Winchester. With Bee, a Georgia contingent under Col. Francis S. Bartow was to hurry to the left. The joint com-

tions as stated; (2) the admission of Beauregard, July 26, 1861, *O. R.*, 51, pt. 2, p. 199, that he did not issue the orders for Ewell's advance until 8 or 8.30 A.M.; (3) the absence in Beauregard's report of any statement of the time at which he ordered the attack by Ewell. A first reading of the report of Beauregard, *O. R.*, 2, 488, may leave the impression that the orders to undertake the offensive were given earlier, but close scrutiny will show that Beauregard nowhere in his report contradicted the statement he made on July 26. Not until 1884–85, when Beauregard wrote his article on First Manassas for *B. & L.* (vol. 1, p. 209) did he place earlier than 8 A.M. his order for Ewell to advance. A statement from memory, almost twenty-four years after the event, is not, of course, comparable in value to one written five days after the happening. It may be proper to add that Johnston's report conforms to Beauregard's concerning the nature of this operation, but that, when Johnston reviewed the subject, about twenty-three years thereafter, in 1 *B. & L.*, 246, he confused the flanks and stated that Beauregard's plan was to move the Brigades from the right "rapidly to the left and assail the attacking Federal troops in flank."

[36] This, it should be remembered, was because of Longstreet's reading of the equivocal terms of the orders. See *supra*, p. 52, n. 25.

mand numbered about 2800 muskets.[37] Almost at the same hour, 7 A.M., Jackson was directed to take his Brigade and nine guns from a support position between Longstreet and D. R. Jones and to fill the gap between Cocke and Bonham. In this manner, before the enemy's point of attack was discovered, all Beauregard's reserves had been ordered to move from their first positions of the morning.

Eight o'clock found a desultory bombardment in progress opposite Bonham [38] and probably to his left. Nothing was known at General Headquarters of any infantry action. Scarcely any reports were arriving from the forces in contact with the enemy. To be nearer the front, Johnston and Beauregard left Colonel Jordan in charge of the office at Manassas Junction, and rode out to a high hill in rear of Bonham's position at Mitchell's Ford, where they established field headquarters.[39] No sooner had they arrived than Beauregard underwent another change of mind. He had strengthened his left; he had prepared a demonstration on the right; he would turn that demonstration into an offensive against Centreville. Although his forces on the right had diminished somewhat, he would hurl Ewell, Holmes, D. R. Jones, Longstreet and Bonham across Bull Run while the Federals were preoccupied with their developing attack on the Confederate left. Quickly and confidently, Beauregard explained this plan to Johnston. The commanding General approved. Whether he did so enthusiastically or after hesitation, the record does not show. Proper orders, Beauregard stated subsequently, were drawn and dispatched. This done, he listened with less concern to the fire on the left, because he expected ere long to hear the sound of his own attack on the right.[40]

For perhaps fifteen minutes Beauregard nursed this hope of a Napoleonic counterstroke. Then, about 9 o'clock, from a young Captain of Engineers, E. Porter Alexander by name, who was acting as signal officer, a courier placed in Beauregard's hands this message:

[37] O. R., 2, 489.
[38] O. R., 2, 519.
[39] The position was known as Lookout Hill. O. R., 2, 519. Johnston, ibid., 474, fixed the time of arrival there at 8 A.M.; Beauregard, ibid., 488, gave the hour as "about 8.30." For reference to the fact that Jordan remained at Manassas, see O. R., 2, 491.
[40] O. R., 2, 491.

"I see a body of troops crossing Bull Run about two miles above the Stone Bridge. The head of the column is in the woods on this side. The rear of the column is in the woods on the other side. About a half-mile of its length is visible in the open ground between. I can see both infantry and artillery." [41]

The enemy, in short, already had crossed Bull Run, far beyond the Confederate left and, if in force, was fast taking position to turn that flank! While Beauregard was moving to strike the Federals' left, they were playing precisely the same game, and were playing it more swiftly, from their side of the Run.

No need was there for argument over this alarming news. The demands of the new situation were clear. With all speed, the left must be strengthened further. Bee was marching for Stone Bridge—send him above it. Jackson was to take position below the Bridge—let him, too, advance to meet the Federals who had crossed the stream. Col. Wade Hampton of South Carolina had just arrived from Richmond with 600 infantry. They should be speeded to the exposed flank. In excitement over the imperilled left, nobody seems to have considered whether new instructions were needed for the Brigades on the right. At approximately 9.30, the contrast between the situation which headquarters assumed, and the situation that existed, from Ewell's right to Jackson's left, was as follows:

SITUATION ASSUMED AT HEADQUARTERS	ACTUAL SITUATION
Ewell: Moving beyond Union Mills Ford to advance on Centreville.	Ewell: Holding himself in readiness to make a diversion to relieve the pressure on the center and possibly on the left.
Holmes: Moving in support of Ewell.	Holmes: Orders as above.
D. R. Jones: Across Bull Run and supporting Ewell, in the belief that Ewell had received orders to cross.	D. R. Jones: Awaiting word of Ewell's advance.

[41] Alexander had reached Manassas July 2 and had received Beauregard's orders to install the "wigwag" system of flag-communication that Alexander in 1860 had helped to develop in the United States Army. See *Alexander*, 31.

Situation Assumed at Headquarters	Actual Situation
Longstreet: Perhaps not known; more probably, across the Run and sharing in the movement of Ewell and Jones.	Longstreet: Already across and lightly engaged under orders of 4.30 A.M., which had not been cancelled.
Bonham: Across the Run and participating in the movement of the Brigades to his right.	Bonham: No orders received; under artillery fire.
Early: In position to support either Longstreet or D. R. Jones.	Early: Situation as assumed at headquarters.
Cocke: Prepared to hold to the last extremity on the defensive.	Cocke: Situation as assumed at headquarters.
Jackson: Moving to Cocke's right.	Jackson: Situation as assumed at headquarters.

In other words, the columns of attack on the right were utterly at cross-purposes, Cocke was on the defensive, Jackson was marching to the left center, and Early alone, at a new position, was in reserve. On the left, beyond the Stone Bridge, Bee and Evans were engaged in an adventure, presently to be described, that had been neither ordered nor anticipated. Hampton was soon to share it. For the moment, the army was so scattered, so variously occupied, that orderly, united action of any sort was impossible.

Sound of firing, artillery and musketry, now rolled down the Run. In swelling volume, it seemed to come from the left of Stone Bridge. Worse still, Captain Alexander sent a courier to call to the attention of headquarters the rise of a cloud in the Northwest. It was raised by dust, apparently, and was judged to be distant about ten miles. Johnston concluded immediately that the dust cloud marked the advance from the Valley of Patterson's army,[42] which had learned of the disappearance of the Confederates from Winchester and had marched to join McDowell

42 *O. R.*, 2, 474.

in fighting the concentrated Southern forces. Patterson was believed by Johnston to have 30,000 men.[43]

If the van of that army was within three or four hours' march of the flank that already was being assailed, the afternoon might bring an overwhelming force against the Confederate left. Turning that flank and doubling it up, the Federals might seize Manassas Junction and cut off Johnston's army from its line of supply. Again, if Jackson, Bee, Evans and Hampton succeeded in concentrating to resist the enemy, they could count a bare 6650 muskets, or only a little more than 20 per cent of the effective strength of the Confederate forces. Although this would be an exceedingly thin line with which to confront a powerful adver- sary, Beauregard was so confident of the strategy of a counter- stroke delivered from his right that he did not attempt to change his confused dispositions, or to give further reinforcement to the left. Nor did he go there himself to see what was happening. An hour passed after the sound of the first volleys from the left.[44] Beauregard kept his station on Lookout Hill. With him, puzzled and increasingly concerned, waited Johnston.

Not long before 10.30, from the extreme right at Union Mills, a messenger of Gen. R. S. Ewell arrived at field headquarters: Ewell, he said, had been waiting since early morning for orders to advance; receiving none, he had sent his Assistant Adjutant General, Fitz Lee, to inquire of Gen. R. D. Jones, next on his left, if Jones had any news or orders; by the time of young Lee's arrival, Jones was North of the Run and was deployed; Jones said that he had understood Ewell also was to cross and attack; Ewell now wished Beauregard to know that he never had received such orders as Jones mentioned, but that he was proceeding at once to throw his troops over Bull Run and would advance on Centreville.[45]

---

[43] See *supra*, p. 43.

[44] Evans fixed the time at 9.15. *O. R.,* 2, 559.

[45] There is some conflict of evidence concerning the time of these various messages. Beauregard's watch stopped during the battle (see *infra*, p. 80). In his report, he stated. *O. R.,* 2, 491, that he received word from Ewell at 10.30; but as Beauregard's recall order, presently to be mentioned, was dated 10.30, *O. R.,* 2, 537, Ewell's courier must have arrived long enough before that time for the change of plan to be made. Fitz Lee said in 1885 that he visited Jones's headquarters "between 9 and 10 A.M.," 13 *S. H. S. P.,* 43; but Ewell in a letter of July 31, 1861, stated that he received Jones's answer "about 9 A.M." P. G. Hamlin, *The Making of a Soldier: Letters of General R. S. Ewell* (cited

That was the doom of hope for an offensive on the right! Beauregard understood little of what had been done by D. R. Jones, Holmes and Longstreet. He had received a message from Longstreet, which showed that officer was North of the Run,[46] and from Ewell's courier he knew that D. R. Jones also had crossed. For that reason he sent Jones an order which Jones later described as "somewhat discretionary." [47] Upon reflection and with the approval of Johnston, Beauregard next directed that the Brigades north of the Run recross to the south bank.[48] "I thus," Beauregard wrote in 1863, "had suddenly or on the spur of the moment to change my whole plan of battle, with troops which had never yet fought and could scarcely manœuvre. My heart for a moment failed me! I felt as though all was lost, and I wished I had fallen in the battle of the 18th; but I soon rallied, and I then solemnly pledged my life that I would that day conquer or die!" [49]

All the while, the fire from the Confederate left continued ominously to swell. By 11 o'clock it indicated that battle had been joined. Rising clouds of smoke from the Federal center, toward Stone Bridge and beyond, showed that more troops were being hurried there, but no reports whatever had come from that wing of the army.[50]

Johnston, who meticulously had respected his assignment to

hereafter as *Hamlin's Ewell*), 106. It would be difficult, moreover, to explain so long a lapse of time as occurred between the receipt of Ewell's information from Jones, "about 9 A.M.," and the arrival of Ewell's message at field headquarters, as late as 10.30. Taking into account the possibility that Ewell's courier may have gone first to Manassas Junction —for Ewell had not been notified of a change in the location of G. H. Q.—the nearest approach that can be made to timing the hour of arrival at Field Headquarters is to say "not long before 10.30." It is proper to add that the forthright Ewell wrote his family: "The reason I had not received the order was that it had not been sent." *Hamlin's Ewell*, 106. General Holmes did not receive his copy, either. *O. R.*, 51, pt. 2, p. 199. When Ewell inquired about the matter after the battle and asked for a transcript of the order, Beauregard said: "Unfortunately no copy, in the hurry of the moment, was kept of said orders, and so many guides—about a dozen or more—were sent off in different directions, that it is impossible to find out who was the bearer of the order referred to. Our guides and couriers were the worst set I ever employed, whether from ignorance or overanxiety to do well and quickly, I cannot say. . . ." *O. R.*, 51, pt. 2, p. 199. Campbell Brown, son-in-law and A. A. G. of Ewell, remarked in 1885 when he reviewed the whole episode in 13 *S. H. S. P.*, 41 ff: "[The disappearance of the courier] is mysterious. He was never heard of after receiving the order, yet his route lay wholly within our lines, over well-beaten roads and far out of reach of the enemy." *Ibid.*, 44.
[46] *O. R.*, 2, 543.   [47] *O. R.*, 2, 537.
[48] *O. R.*, 2, 536, 537, 543, 565; *Hamlin's Ewell*, 106.
[49] To Miss Augusta J. Evans, with copies of his reports, Mch. 24, 1863; *O. R.*, 51, pt. 2, p. 689.
[50] *Alexander*, 34.

Beauregard of the conduct of the battle, became more restless. He wanted information from the left. To satisfy him, Beauregard dispatched in that direction a staff officer and six couriers, who were to send back reports every ten minutes.[51] This did not allay Johnston's concern. He saw the dust clouds spread, he heard a louder fire, and he learned that the enemy was felling trees on the center and right as if for defense.[52] At length, after a new blast of cannon upstream, he broke over his self-imposed restraint and urged Beauregard to strengthen to the limit of the army's resources the troops on the left. "The battle is there," he said. "I am going!"[53]

[51] *Alexander*, 34.
[52] *Johnston's Narrative*, 47.   [53] *Alexander*, 34.

CHAPTER VI

Beauregard's Star At Zenith

BEAUREGARD hurriedly issued orders to carry out Johnston's wishes. Holmes, from support of Ewell, was directed to proceed to the sound of the firing. Early, still in reserve, was ordered to join his commanding General.[1] Bonham was told to send two of his regiments to the left.[2] On his own account, and still, perhaps, in the vague hope of launching an offensive, Beauregard instructed Ewell, Longstreet and D. R. Jones to ford Bull Run once more and to demonstrate jointly against some troublesome batteries.[3] After he dispatched these orders, Beauregard started to overtake Johnston, who had drawn rein only long enough to order two unengaged batteries to join in defense of the threatened flank.

As the two Generals together approached the scene of action, they encountered stragglers, wounded men and disorganized fragments of regiments. Most of these men still had their arms, but many of them were demoralized. Past these soldiers Johnston and Beauregard spurred until they came with their staffs, shortly before 12.30, to a ravine on the western side of which was a hillside dotted with pine thickets. The cavalcade quickly made its way upward and soon emerged on an eminence from which was

[1] *O. R.,* 2, 475. Johnston here stated that Early, like Holmes, was ordered to the sound of the firing, but Early, *ibid.,* 556, reported that he heard through D. R. Jones "that General Beauregard had directed that I should join him (General Beauregard) with my Brigade." This statement Early repeated and elaborated in his *Autobiographical Sketch and Narrative of the War between the States* (cited hereafter as *Early*), p. 19. Early explained that he saw at the end of a pencilled note from Beauregard to Jones substantially these words: "Send Early to me." The note, said Early, indicated Beauregard's "general purpose" to go to the left; but, Early added, "the note did not state to what point I was to go." *Ibid.,* 19. Beauregard doubtless assumed that Early would follow him from Lookout Hill. Early took two hours to reach the field of battle, but it is not probable that he was delayed materially by the vague language of his orders.

[2] *O. R.,* 2, 491.

[3] *O. R.,* 2, 543; cf. 536, 538. Beauregard stated in his report that these three Brigades, with the remainder of Bonham's, were "to make a demonstration to their several fronts, to retain and engross the enemy's reserves and any forces on their flank and at and around Centreville." *O. R.,* 2, 491. The officers who undertook the demonstration reported the simpler design stated in the text.

visible a wide range of smoke-covered landscape.[4] In front was a long, curving Federal front, ablaze at intervals with musketry fire and with artillery. To the right and North of Johnston and Beauregard, on an adjoining ridge, a short, thin line of Confederate infantry was in action. Behind this line, on the edge of a ravine that led to a little stream which skirted the hill, were other hundreds of confused Southern troops. To the left of the Generals, admirably placed behind the crest of the hill, was a waiting Confederate Brigade. Some of its men were lying down; others were in ranks. Near the center of this perfectly aligned Brigade, six field guns were barking viciously at the enemy. In rear of these troops and streaming backward over the shoulder of the ridge to the North, were broken units that evidently had been in the fight. Certain of them were as disordered as those through whom Johnston and Beauregard had passed, but one battered regiment without officers stood at order arms. Other regiments seemed to be endeavoring to re-form their lines.[5]

What had happened? How fared the battle? The answer was given the Generals in snatches and by different individuals, for no officer was in command of the field. Col. N. G. Evans, at Stone Bridge, had seen early in the morning the movement of the Federals to the left and had received from Captain Alexander a signal message that the enemy was crossing Bull Run beyond his flank. Without waiting for orders, Colonel Evans had notified his commanding officer, Colonel Cocke, who was to his right, that he would leave a guard at the bridge and, with the remainder, would march upstream to the left and would engage the enemy. Promptly Evans had moved; quickly he had thrown his 1100 men directly in front of an approaching Federal column. Gen. Barnard E. Bee, who had been started for Stone Bridge about 7 A.M., soon had learned that Evans was engaged with overwhelming force. Neither asking for instructions nor even sending back

[4] For reference to maps of this part of the battlefield, see Appendix IV, *infra*, p. 728. It is not possible to give the precise hour of the arrival of Johnston and Beauregard at Henry Hill. Beauregard undoubtedly was in error when he put the time at "about 12 M." (*O. R.*, 2, 491). The estimate here given is based on the knowledge that the two were at field headquarters as late as 11.30 and had more than four miles of poor road to cover. The published reports of Johnston and of Beauregard, written at a time when they were on a friendly footing, indicate (*O. R.*, 2, 475, 491) that they started together, but Johnston's statement in 1 *B. & L.*, 248, is that "Beauregard joined me without a word." Alexander's explicit language (*op. cit.*, 35) is that "Beauregard only paused to give a few brief orders."

[5] *O. R.*, 2, 475, 492.

to report what he was doing, Bee had taken his two regiments [6] and two from Col. Francis S. Bartow's force,[7] and had marched to Evans's support. These three commands had made a splendid fight. At a critical moment, they had been reinforced by Hampton's 600 South Carolinians, whom Beauregard had ordered to that wing. In the face of stiff odds and heavy fire, Evans, Bee, Bartow and Hampton had been compelled at length to withdraw to the hill where lived the widow Judith Henry.

While they were retiring, another Brigade had arrived in support. Its commander, T. J. Jackson, had been moving under Beauregard's orders to take position between Bonham and Cocke. When he had learned of the attack on the left, Jackson, like Bee, had marched in that direction at once and had reached Henry Hill scarcely an hour before the arrival of Johnston and Beauregard. In summary, then, the threat of a Federal turning movement far above the Stone Bridge had been met by the convergence of four small columns. Each of these had moved swiftly and to precisely the right point, but none had acted on specific orders or with the full knowledge of the Generals at field headquarters.[8]

Now that some of these troops had been driven back, they must be identified, reorganized, and put back into the fight. Those in the stubborn line on the next ridge to the North, Beauregard and Johnston soon learned, were Hampton's South Carolinians; those in the ravine and in confusion to the rear were the survivors of Evans's, Bee's and Bartow's commands—all of them shattered except for the regiment that stood, unofficered and waiting, a short distance beyond the crest of the hill. That was the Fourth

[6] The Second Mississippi and the Fourth Alabama, plus two companies of the Eleventh Mississippi. The remainder of the last-named regiment and the First Tennessee, which belonged to his Brigade, had not arrived from the Shenandoah Valley. Cf. O. R., 2, 487.
[7] The Seventh and Eighth Georgia.
[8] This statement is qualified because Johnston in his report (O. R., 2, 474), stated that Bee, Jackson and Hampton "were ordered to hasten to the left flank." The orders of Jackson as epitomized in his report (O. R., 2, 481), show that the position on "the left flank," to which he was assigned by Beauregard, was in support of Cocke and of Bonham. This would have placed him *below* the Stone Bridge. He started his march upstream, not at the instance of Beauregard or of Johnston, but at the request of Colonel Cocke, who asked him to "guard the Stone Bridge." (O. R., 2, 481.) Hampton stated in his report that his orders were "to take position in the direction of Stone Bridge, ready to support any of the troops engaged in that quarter." (O. R., 2, 566.) If, therefore, the immediate vicinity of Stone Bridge be regarded as the terminus of the left flank, General Johnston's statement implies that all these officers except Evans took their position in obedience to orders. In actual fact, the turning movement was launched from the Sudley Farm, nearly three miles upstream. In dealing with that unanticipated advance, the commanders of the Confederate columns assuredly acted on their own initiative.

Alabama. The waiting Brigade in a grim gray line to the left, almost opposite the head of the ravine, was Jackson's Virginians.[9]

Hastily but firmly Johnston, Beauregard and their staffs made their way among the scattered fugitives. At first, as rapidly as the officers formed one line and spurred on to rebuild another, the men would scatter. Presently, Johnston and Beauregard reached the Fourth Alabama. Johnston found its flag bearer, put the boy by his side, called to the soldiers and rode forward. With alacrity and ready cheers, the men followed. Johnston placed them in line with Jackson; Beauregard designated one of Bee's staff officers [10] to act as their Colonel; around these steady soldiers and the Virginians on their left, others quickly gathered. Soon the line was restored [11] in the face of Federals who were moving up the slope in front and on the right for another assault.

To await the development of this, the two Generals halted. No sooner had they done so than Beauregard, with polite firmness, made a startling request of Johnston: Would the commanding General please retire from the front and leave to him the direction of the fighting there? To Johnston's surprised ear he explained that one or the other of them had to supervise the entire field and, in particular, to see that reinforcements were hurried forward. If one must do this, Johnston as senior should. As the junior, said Beauregard, it was his right and his duty to handle the engaged wing of the army. Johnston at first refused. He would not turn his back on a battle. Beauregard persisted: it must be done. At length, with manifest reluctance, Johnston acquiesced and rode back a mile and more to Portici, the Lewis House. This proved to be a well-chosen post of command. Close

9 For the details of Jackson's battle before the arrival of the commanding Generals, see *infra*, p. 82.

10 S. R. Gist, later Brigadier General, killed at Franklin.

11 *O. R.*, 2, 475, 492; *Johnston's Narrative*, 48; 1 *B. & L.*, 210, 248. The account given by Beauregard and that by Johnston illustrate in a most interesting manner one of the temperamental differences between them. Said Beauregard in his report: "It was now that General Johnston impressively and gallantly charged to the front, with the colors of the Fourth Alabama by his side. . . ." *O. R.*, 2, 492. In 1 *B. & L.*, 210, he wrote: ". . . as General Johnston and myself rode forward . . . with the colors of the Fourth Alabama by our side, the line that had fought all morning, and had fled, routed and disordered, now advanced again into position as steadily as veterans." Johnston did not mention the incident in his formal report. Writing in 1 *B. & L.*, 248, he said, "I saw a regiment in line with ordered arms and facing to the front, but 200 or 300 yards in rear of its proper place. On inquiry I learned that it had lost all its field-officers; so, riding on the left flank, I easily moved it to its place. It was the Fourth Alabama, an excellent regiment; and I mention this because the circumstance has been greatly exaggerated."

by ran the roads that troops from the right or reinforcements from Manassas Junction would use. From the Lewis House, also, Johnston had a commanding view of a large part of the Federal position North of Bull Run. The approaches to Stone Bridge from Centreville were clearly visible.[12]

It was now after 1 P.M. Until that hour, the initiative and the advantage had been altogether on the side of the Federals. From the Confederate side, the Unionists did not appear to have made a single mistake or to have presented even one opening. Beauregard's elaborate plan of battle had been thrice changed and in each instance had been frustrated. Only the spirited fire of inexperienced Southern artillerists, the stubborn fighting of the infantry under Evans, Bee, Bartow and Hampton, and the fortunate arrival of Jackson had saved the army from disaster. Even now, if Patterson's army was sweeping forward from the Northwest, the left might be overwhelmed, though reinforced, and Manassas Junction might be lost.

To meet these uncertainties of the field, Beauregard continued to strengthen his line. Col. F. S. Bartow, who had rallied a remnant of the shattered Seventh Georgia, reported that it was ready to take position again. It was sent by Beauregard around the rear of Jackson to extend and protect his left.[13] Then three companies of the Forty-ninth Virginia, under Col. William Smith, arrived by Beauregard's order from Cocke's Brigade. Although these were raw recruits, who had been together only three days, Beauregard dispatched them to the left of the Seventh Georgia.[14]

12 O. R., 2, 475. Unless the height of intervening trees is much greater now than in 1861, only a small part of Henry Hill was visible from Portici at the time of the battle, but the site was the ideal point from which to direct troops to the Chinn farm, where the regiments that decided the action were placed. It is not known whether Beauregard realized this advantage, or even had in mind the possibility of a debouch from the vicinity of the Chinn house; but a study of the roads and terrain around Portici does much to explain the ease and speed with which Kirby Smith and Early were put in position. The old Lewis house itself has disappeared completely. In the near-by graveyard are the headstones of some of those who lived there. Among them were descendants of Robert Carter of Nomini Hall and of the Ball family to which the mother of George Washington belonged. Men of the Lewis stock, residing near by, explain the Italian name of the place by saying the house burned down so often that it reminded its owner of the oft-destroyed city beneath Vesuvius.

13 O. R., 2, 492.

14 O. R., 2, 492, 552; Cocke's report, ibid., 51, pt. 1, p. 29. With Smith, two companies of the Eleventh Mississippi went into the line. Smith (1796–1887) had been Governor and Congressman. He was entirely without military experience and made no pretense to it, but he accepted election as Colonel of the Forty-ninth Virginia and sought by courageous example and self-possession to compensate for his lack of professional knowledge. On a hot day's march, he always rode under a large umbrella (W. W.

Hampton's Legion, weakened but still full of fight, was placed in reserve on the right, as were seven companies of Col. Eppa Hunton's Eighth Virginia, who were hurried forward from Cocke's position by the pressing orders both of Johnston and of Beauregard.[15] The rallied Second Mississippi of Bee's Brigade thereupon was ordered to the left of Smith's Forty-ninth Virginia.[16]

In disposing these regiments on either side of Jackson's steadfast Brigade, Beauregard rode from left to right and, wherever he thought he could rally the men, he made them a brief speech. He summarized it afterward in his formal report: "I sought to infuse into the hearts of my officers and men the confidence and determined spirit of resistance to this wicked invasion of the homes of a free people which I felt. I informed them that reinforcements would rapidly come to their support, and that we must at all hazards hold our posts until reinforced. I reminded them that we fought for our homes, our firesides, and for the independence of our country. I urged them to the resolution of victory or death on that field." The General was satisfied with the effects of his eloquence. "These sentiments," said he, "were loudly, eagerly cheered wheresoever proclaimed, and I felt reassured of the unconquerable spirit of that army, which would enable us to wrench victory from the host then threatening us with destruction." [17]

Weak-hearted individuals were as deaf to Beauregard's oratory as they were blind to duty. They continued to seek the rear in the

Chamberlaine, *Memoirs of the Civil War*, cited hereafter as *W. W. Chamberlaine*, 134). His dealings with his troops and his openly avowed contempt for "those West P'int fellows" were the themes of many a tall tale in the Confederate camps. One yarn represented him as sitting on a rail fence, under his umbrella, as he drilled his regiment by reading the appropriate orders from a book on tactics. "Colonel," cried one of his men, "you've run us bang up against the fence!" Smith looked up from his book: "Well, then, boys, of course you'll have to turn around or climb the fence." A story current later in the war described his advance, by order, through abatis, where his men suffered heavily from sharpshooters, though they had been instructed to withhold their fire. "Colonel," the men cried out, "we can't stand this! These Yankees will kill us before we get in a shot!" Smith exploded: "Of course you can't stand it, boys; it's all this infernal tactics and West P'int tomfoolery. Damn it, fire, and flush the game!" (Robert Stiles, *Four Years under Marse Robert*, cited hereafter as *Stiles*, 111; *cf.* 8, *Confederate Veteran*, cited hereafter as C. V., 161–64.) Smith is mentioned many times in the pages that follow but is not the subject of a major sketch.

[15] *O. R.*, 2, 492, 545.

[16] *O. R.*, 2, 494. It appears from a later paragraph of Beauregard's report, *ibid.*, 495, that the Mississippians did not get into position for the advance ordered at 2 o'clock.

[17] *O. R.*, 2, 493.

belief that the army had been slaughtered and the day had been lost,[18] but the stalwart held their own. In the face of nervous, desultory attacks they prepared, at the word of command, to take the offensive.

At that moment, those traitorous war gods, Chance and Blunder, who had fought all morning against the Southerners, turned on the Federals. Through the smoke, there galloped boldly up the hill of the Henry House from the Federal position two magnificent batteries, eleven guns,[19] which opened fire immediately against the Confederate artillery.[20] The Union infantry support was slow in coming up. As it was forming on the right of the batteries, it was disorganized by a short cavalry charge, which Col. J. E. B. Stuart led.[21] About the same time, three of the Federal guns on the hill were moved to the right, as if to enfilade the Confederate batteries.[22] The Union artillerists sprang to these advanced pieces and fired two rounds,[23] but this time they had ventured too far.[24] Col. A. C. Cummings of the Thirty-third Virginia, a veteran of the Mexican War, saw the oppor-

[18] Early, 20-21.

[19] These, needless to say, were Battery I, 1st U. S. Artillery, Capt. J. B. Ricketts, and Battery D, 2nd U. S. Artillery, Capt. Charles Griffin. Both were six-gun batteries, but Griffin had one piece disabled before the advance to Henry Hill.

[20] Neither General McDowell in his report, O. R., 2, 320, nor Maj. William F. Barry, Chief of Artillery, ibid., 347, gave any reason why Ricketts and Griffin were placed in so exposed a position; but Col. S. P. Heintzelman, ibid., 402, said that Ricketts was ordered within 1000 feet of the Confederates because his previous range, which Lt. E. Kirby put at 1500 yards, ibid., 407, was too long to be effective. Kirby stated, loc. cit., that the battery was directed to advance about 100 yards. In that case, Ricketts carried his guns 166 yards beyond his prescribed position. That manifestly increased his exposure. Captain Griffin reported, ibid., 394, that his range was 800 yards when he was ordered forward. He did not estimate the distance from his final position to the Confederate lines.

[21] Stuart had received no orders from Beauregard, but, under Johnston's general instructions to "charge the enemy's flank," had crossed Bull Run to the Federal left. Finding no opening there, he had returned to the Confederate side of the stream and had ridden rapidly to the sound of the battle. It was at Jackson's instance that Stuart moved part of his small force to the extreme left of the Southern line. O. R., 2, 481, 483. The troops that Stuart assailed were the 11th New York Infantry, the so-called Fire Zouaves, of Willcox's 2nd Brigade of Heintzelman's 3rd Division. There is conflict of evidence whether Stuart's charge occurred before or after the attack of the Thirty-third Virginia on a section of Griffin's battery, but, as the point is not material, the facts need not be reviewed.

[22] That is, to the Federal right. O. R., 2, 494.

[23] O. R., 2, 394.

[24] For this advance, though it seemed suicidal, Captain Griffin perhaps was not so fairly subject to criticism as might appear. Immediately South of his position was a slight rise of ground, the highest on that part of the field. He may have reasoned that if he could place a section of his battery there, he could silence the guns on the Confederate left by a few rapid salvos. His judgment may have been at fault; his eye for position was not.

tunity. Without waiting to ask the approval of his brigade commander,[25] Cummings shouted to his men to charge. A roar and a volley—the Virginians were upon the Federals. Farther along the front, every one of Jackson's men who could bring a musket to bear on the Federal gunners was firing fast. The artillerists were cut down. Both batteries were silenced.[26] The Thirty-third Virginia reached the guns, the first captured that day, but soon the regiment had to abandon the coveted pieces and to fall back because of a concentrated fire from the Union infantry on the hillside.[27]

Beauregard was not discouraged. Cummings's men had shown dash. The most troublesome Federal batteries had been wrecked. A fresh regiment, Fisher's Sixth North Carolina, had just come on the field and had taken position on the left.[28] At 2 P.M., Beauregard boldly ordered an advance along the right of his line. Jackson and the other commanders took it up. Swiftly the plateau was swept clear of the enemy. The gain was momentary. Ere long, the enemy quickened his fire. Blue coats showed once again over the rim of the hill. Where one man fell, another appeared. A line soon was formed in strength too great for the Confederate musketry to shatter it. In succession, the Union flags were advanced. Men started up here and there, rushed a few steps, halted and fired. Soon, despite the exhortation of Southern officers, the defenders of the hill began to give ground. Once the line wavered, it yielded. In fifteen minutes the Federals had recovered nearly the whole of the advance positions they had lost.[29]

Five hours of fighting since Evans had challenged the Federal advance; five hours, and the question the same, though the theatre of action had shifted somewhat: would the Federals outflank the Confederate left? Steadily, if awkwardly, the Union line was being extended toward the Southwest until now it had become almost a crescent:[30] would that line bend still farther and envelop Fisher's Sixth North Carolina, which, except for a little fringe of cavalry, remained the flank element?

25 At least, Jackson, in reporting the incident, did not state that he authorized or directed the charge. O. R., 2, 481.

26 O. R., 2, 347, 394, 402, 406, 407, 481, 494.

27 Ibid., 481, 494.   28 Ibid., 495.

29 O. R., 2, 494–95.   30 O. R., 2, 406.

Beauregard asked the question and ordered another charge to drive the Federals from Henry Hill. Johnston, at Portici, already had seen the danger and had been hurrying forward all the troops within marching distance. With Johnston's concurrence, General Cocke had virtually abandoned his watch of the Stone Bridge and of the fords below it and was throwing all his troops into the line of battle. The Eighteenth Virginia of his Brigade was coming up on the right; the Twenty-eighth Virginia was moving toward the left.[31] Two regiments of South Carolinians were hastening in the same direction, with orders from Johnston to take position west of the road, parallel to which the Federals had been attacking.[32] Kemper's battery was rattling North along the same road and soon was to take an excellent position directly to the East of it.[33]

Together, these troops perhaps might suffice to hold the flank, but they could do no more than that. For a counterstroke, there must be strong Confederate reinforcements: would they arrive before the Federals threw their own reserves against the left? Beauregard believed the needed troops would come up. Without waiting for them, he renewed his attack from his center and his right. Again he swept across the plateau and cleared it, though at heavy cost. General Bee fell. Colonel Bartow went down. Johnston's chief ordnance officer, Col. F. J. Thomas, was killed. C. F. Fisher, who so opportunely had brought up the unattached Sixth North Carolina, died at its head. Losses were heavy in all the center regiments, but on the right, where Colonel Withers had the support of the Hampton Legion, the advance was easy. This time, also, the enemy was slower to form again. The ground recovered by the Confederates was held.[34]

Then, as it subsequently appeared to an amazed army, a miracle occurred. The two South Carolina regiments from Bonham's Brigade, panting through the dust across the July fields, were

---

[31] O. R., 2, 495, 496, 550; 51, pt. 1, pp. 29–30. R. E. Withers, *Autobiography of an Octogenarian* (cited hereafter as *Withers*), 147 ff.

[32] O. R., 2, 495, 547.

[33] This battery was said in Beauregard's report, O. R., 2, 495, to have taken position "on the open space . . . near where an enemy's battery had been captured," but the map in T. B. Warder and James M. Catlett, *Battle of Young's Branch*, gave the position as approximately 1000 feet from the southernmost point reached by Griffin's gunners. This unsatisfactory map probably is accurate in this instance. If so, it leads one to suspect that General Beauregard confused the first and second positions of Kemper's battery.

[34] O. R., 495; *Withers*, 148–49.

hurried on by one of Beauregard's staff officers[35] and were directed by Johnston to a point beyond the left of Fisher's men.[36] Preston's Twenty-eighth Virginia, sent by General Cocke, found its way to the position of the South Carolinians. At the suggestion of the senior South Carolina Colonel, a lawyer named J. B. Kershaw, the Virginia regiment moved beyond his flank and extended the Confederate left.

Scarcely had the Twenty-eighth come on the field than there arrived three good regiments of Johnston's army who had detrained that noon at Manassas and, under Johnston's orders, had moved straight to the sound of the firing with instructions to attack. Here again, Colonel Kershaw requested the newcomers to take ground beyond the Confederate left. Their brigade commander, E. Kirby Smith, was wounded almost as soon as he came within range, but his senior Colonel, Arnold Elzey, who had heard the whine of Mexican bullets in '47, quickly and with coolness took his place.[37] The left was long now and curved to the West. Opposite it the front of the enemy still was being extended for another attempt. Another Confederate Brigade on the flank was needed immediately—would it come up?

As Beauregard looked anxiously to the Southwest, he saw a marching column. At its head was its flag. Eagerly Beauregard turned his glass on the standard: was it the flag of the Union or of the South? For all his effort he could not tell. As he looked and waited for a breeze that would ripple the colors, a courier brought him a dispatch from the signal corps. A large force, the message stated, was approaching from the very quarter to which Beauregard was looking. The troops were believed by the signalmen to be Patterson's Federals, whose advance had been anticipated earlier in the day. Beauregard's heart sank. If Patterson was coming up on the left, with eager, fresh infantry, there was nothing to do but to draw in the flank, break off the action and pray for the coming of night so that the front could be reorganized.

Again Beauregard looked at the distant flag and the marching men. They defied identification. The General put down his glass

[35] O. R., 2, 522. This may be a convenient point at which to refer to the order of battle reviewed in Appendix IV, *infra*, p. 728.
[36] O. R., 2, 476, 522.
[37] O. R., 2, 476, 496, 522.

and turned to Colonel Evans, the only officer who happened to be at his side. If, said Beauregard, the approaching column was Federal, Johnston must be notified that the left would have to retreat. Then he paused and reflected. Yes, that was the bitter necessity. Would Evans be so good as to ride to Portici, acquaint Johnston with the dark news, and ask him to collect and form the reserves so that the left could fall back on them? Evans mounted and started off. Suddenly Beauregard called out to him to come back. "Let us wait a few minutes," he said, "to confirm our suspicions before finally resolving to yield the field!"

Once again he focused his glass on the approaching column, which now was nearer and in full view. There was an anxious heart-thumping delay. Then a breeze swept across the hill and set the summer leaves to rustling. It struck the column, it stirred the bunting, it spread the colors—Confederate. The needed Brigade had arrived to save the day! It was Early's.[38] As it deployed, Beauregard pointed it out to the near-by troops. They cheered its appearance. Up and down the front spread the news of reinforcement. Weary men were strengthened to speed their fire. The weird cry of the Southern foxhunters swelled at the prospect of such a chase as none of them had known before.[39] As Early's panting and excited men formed their line, they found the enemy in their front, ready to attack, but they saw no bluecoats farther to the West. Another pause, intolerable minutes of expectancy and confusion. Then, suddenly, all along the front, from Hunton to Early, the Confederates rushed forward. The Federal front of attack collapsed.[40] Before the fire of advancing Southerners, collapse soon became rout, the oft-described rout of Bull Run.

[38] Receiving his orders to join Beauregard, Early had marched to the General's post of command on Lookout Hill, and when he had failed to find his commander there, he had moved after him to the West. On the way, Johnston met and directed him to the extreme left, with orders to fall on the enemy's flank. *Early*, 20 ff.

[39] This account of an incident that seems to have escaped the eye of historians of the First Battle of Manassas, was given by Beauregard on Oct. 21, 1861, at an entertainment tendered him and other officers by Captain Gilman of the Crescent Rifles. The correspondent of the *New Orleans Delta*, who evidently was present, reported it to his paper "as nearly as possible in the General's own words." It was reprinted in the *Richmond Whig* of Nov. 20, 1861, p. 4, col. 3. While the incident may have been adorned extensively in the telling, it demonstrably is correct in its references to time, to terrain and to the individuals mentioned by Beauregard. It is not noted in any of the published reports or narratives, but it is not contrary to any of them. For these reasons the writer has accepted it as substantially authentic.

[40] *O. R.*, 2, 476, 496, 556–57.

CHAPTER VII

PURSUIT AND A CONFUSED COUNCIL

THE BATTLE was won—could there be pursuit? It was 4.40 P.M. by Johnston's watch.[1] Three full hours of daylight remained. Bonham had fresh regiments at Mitchell's Ford. Longstreet's Brigade was at Blackburn's. From these crossings the distance to Centreville was approximately three miles. The Federals, who were retreating madly toward the same village, had four miles to go. If Bonham and Longstreet moved quickly and did not encounter heavy resistance on their immediate front, they might cut off the Union Army from Centreville. Johnston issued immediately the necessary orders. Four companies of Confederate horse were directed to cross at Ball's Ford and to assail the fleeing enemy.[2]

From the left, meantime, Col. J. E. B. Stuart was spurring his small cavalry command in the direction of Sudley Ford. With the Nineteenth Virginia in support, Early's infantry were pursuing. Other regiments were following the enemy up the turnpike toward Stone Bridge.[3] Beauregard directed these dispositions and then galloped to the Lewis House for a brief, exultant meeting with Johnston. The senior ordered him to continue the chase from the scene of victory. Word was sent Jackson to take command of all the forces that remained around the Lewis House and to use them as circumstance required.[4]

---

[1] *Johnston's Narrative*, 52. [2] *O. R.*, 2, 476, 477.
[3] *O. R.*, 2, 497.
[4] *O. R.*, 2, 487. Roman, *op. cit.*, 108–9, and Beauregard, 1 *B. & L.*, 215, recounted twenty years later how Beauregard at Portici returned the command to Johnston. Roman's statement is: "With a proud and happy feeling of elation at the issue of the day, [Beauregard] then rode to the Lewis House to inform General Johnston of the glorious result, and, as had been agreed—the battle being now over—to commit to his hands the command of our united forces. The interview was a short one, and General Beauregard, anxious to reap the full benefit of the victory, hurried to the front to press the pursuit." Neither Johnston nor Beauregard mentioned this in official reports. Johnston did not refer to it in his *Narrative*, which was published in 1874, but as he did not deny the occurrence when he had his controversy with Beauregard ten years later, 1 *B. & L.*, 240 ff, there is no reason to question the truth of the accounts given by Beauregard and by Roman, though here again the details may have been touched up and the incident may have been made more theatrical than it actually was.

Little was accomplished. Stuart ere long was burdened with many prisoners and was deprived of virtually all power to strike, though he kept on for twelve miles until his force was reduced to one squad.[5] Early found his men so wearied by their march that he had to rest them for a time. He later cleared the ground on the extreme left but beyond that could do nothing.[6] Before the other pursuing regiments, the Federal infantry fled too rapidly for the Southerners to re-establish contact. The abandoned guns of the Union artillery, demoralized stragglers and the plunder of the field were the only additional rewards on the left.

On the right center, Bonham did not receive until after 5 o'clock Johnston's orders to advance on Centreville.[7] He had then to cross ford and fields with much effort and loss of time. General Longstreet advanced steadily along the Manassas-Centreville highway, but soon found Bonham's men coming into the road from the left. Bonham himself rode up, and as senior, insisted on marching his regiments ahead of Longstreet's. More minutes of waning daylight passed while Bonham formed his troops and took the lead. "Through the abandoned camps of the Federals," Longstreet wrote long afterward, "we found their pots and kettles over the fire, with food cooking; quarters of beef hanging on the trees, and wagons by the roadside loaded, some with bread and general provisions, others with ammunition." [8] Hungry Confederates could not stop to appropriate these treasures. They did not pause until there came from the North the challenge of artillery fire. This seemed to be directed at no target more definite than the dust cloud raised by the marching regiments, but it was, of course, a warning not wholly to be disregarded. Bonham called a halt and sent forward a member of his staff to reconnoiter. Soon the officer reported that the Federals had a line which was manned with artillery as well as with infantry. Bonham thereupon deployed Longstreet on the right, his own regiments on the left. The guns were put in battery. Then Bonham pondered. The sun was almost down. Should he risk an attack in gathering twilight against a foe that might or might not have rallied?

[5] O. R., 2, 483.   [6] Early, 25 ff.
[7] Bonham said that the orders reached him "between 5 and 6 o'clock." O. R., 2, 519.
[8] Longstreet, 51–52. For Bonham's and Longstreet's official reports, see O. R. 2. 519, 543.

At that moment Maj. W. H. C. Whiting, General Johnston's chief engineer, appeared. Whiting had heard rumors that the Federals were attacking at Union Mills and were striking for Manassas Junction. Some one had informed him, also, that orders had been issued or were to be issued for the return of Bonham and Longstreet to the right bank of Bull Run. Longstreet listened in amusement and ridiculed the possibility of a Federal counter-movement on the Confederate right. He knew a retreat when he saw one, he said; the Federals in his front were beaten and must be attacked at once. Let the batteries open!

Whiting rose in his stirrups. "In the name of General Johnston," said he, "I order that the batteries shall *not* open."

Longstreet snapped back: "Did General Johnston send you to communicate that order?"

"No, but I take the responsibility to give it!"

That was not enough. Longstreet maintained that he had the responsibility of the field and that he would engage the enemy. As Longstreet turned away to renew his order for the batteries to open fire, Bonham intervened with a request that action be not joined. That was tantamount to orders of a direct superior. Longstreet said no more and gave no command to his artillery. After half an hour, Bonham directed a withdrawal to the Confederate side of Bull Run. Longstreet reluctantly followed, though not until orders were repeated.[9] When the troops came back to familiar ground, they found that the rumor which had halted them in front of Centreville had spread widely and had prompted Beauregard to order a new concentration in the vicinity of Union Mills Ford. This movement had prevented Ewell and Holmes from striking at the enemy.[10]

The evil wrought in this manner by false report, and the opportunity lost on the other flank by the weakness of the cavalry, were forgotten amid rejoicing over the victory. In the first great test—the decisive test, many averred—the South had won. All that had

[9] *Longstreet*, 52; *O. R.*, 2, 519, 544. Johnston in his report merely said of Bonham's advance that his "progress was checked by the enemy's reserve and by night at Centreville." *O. R.*, 2, 476. Beauregard wrote: ". . . night and darkness intervening, General Bonham thought it proper to direct his own Brigade and that of Longstreet back to Bull Run." *O. R.*, 2, 498. For the next detailed reference to Longstreet, see *infra*, p. 164.

[10] *O. R.*, 2, 477, 497; 1 *Roman*, 109. The rumor, which seems to have reached every part of the field, originated with one of D. R. Jones's staff officers who mistook the blue uniforms of some of his own men, recrossing the Run, for those of the enemy.

been said of the individual superiority of the Confederate soldier seemed to be vindicated. Of the manner in which their adversaries had fought that morning, the victors had nothing to say. The Confederates who staggered back to their camps or stretched themselves out, exhausted, at their bivouacs, could talk only of the mad flight of their foe in the afternoon. Surely, after that experience, the Federals would not again attempt to invade the South. Independence was won; the war was over.[11]

The elation of the men in the ranks was shared by their officer and by Mr. Davis himself. The President had been unable to endure in Richmond the suspense of approaching battle. On the morning of the 21st, he had taken a special train for Manassas and had pushed on to the Junction in the cab of the locomotive when the conductor had refused to order the cars that far. At Beauregard's old headquarters in the village, the President had taken horse and had hurried to the field. Through the ranks of demoralized stragglers, who had recounted dark tales of overwhelming disaster to Confederate arms, he had made his way to Portici, where Johnston told him the day had been won. Not content with this assurance, the martial Davis spurred on to the vicinity of the Chinn House, where he caught a glimpse of the retreating Federals.[12] He joined the chase in the direction of Sudley Ford, spoke to the soldiers he met, ministered to a wounded officer, and then, in the darkness, rode back to Beauregard's headquarters at Manassas.[13] Because of this limited participation in the events of the afternoon, the President's knowledge of what had been done and what had been omitted in the battle was slight. He procured from Johnston such information as the General possessed and then, after supper, he sat down to enjoy the soldier's greatest delight, the writing of the first announcement of a victory.[14]

[11] See *infra,* p. 134, n. 131.
[12] Jefferson Davis, *The Rise and Fall of the Confederate Government* (cited hereafter as *Davis*), 1, 349. As Mr. Davis was unfamiliar with the ground, his description leaves some doubt concerning the exact part of the field he visited, but his references to meeting the troops of Kirby Smith and of Early indicate his general position. A chance remark of Col. John F. Lay that he found Mr. Davis in "the orchard" (*Ibid.,* 382), may mean that the President viewed the final operations from the excellent vantage ground of the Wheeler farm, about half a mile southeast of Chinn's Spring.
[13] A detailed description of Beauregard's office, etc., appears in *Richmond Whig,* July 22, 1861, p. 2, col. 6.
[14] For the dispatch. see *O. R.,* 2, 987.

While the President was engaged in drafting this dispatch to the War Department, General Beauregard came in. Jubilant congratulations were exchanged. New details of the triumph were explained. For the first time, apparently, Mr. Davis learned of the false alarm of a Union advance, which had led Beauregard to dispatch to Union Mills Ford some of the troops that might have been employed in pursuit. That news dampened joy. Was any part of the army following the enemy? the President asked. The answer was, None. Pursuit had ended for the night. Could it be renewed? The Generals, knowing the confusion and weariness of the troops, hesitated to answer.

Col. Thomas Jordan, Beauregard's chief of staff, who had just entered the room, broke in to say that Maj. R. C. Hill had come to headquarters and had reported that he had been to Centreville, where he had found the deserted street jammed with abandoned artillery and caissons. Immediately Mr. Davis observed that such a situation constituted the best of reasons for following the Federals furiously and in maximum force. Which troops were least exhausted and in the most favorable position to pursue? The Generals agreed that Bonham's Brigade could best advance. Davis urged that orders be issued accordingly.

Neither Beauregard nor Johnston made any move to prepare the paper. A pause ensued. Then, perhaps to relieve embarrassment, since Bonham was in Beauregard's force and the entire command was under Johnston, Colonel Jordan asked if the President would dictate the order. Mr. Davis, quite willing, undertook to say how and when Bonham should proceed. As the President was shaping the instructions, either Jordan or Capt. E. P. Alexander remarked that Major Hill, who had brought the sensational report concerning Centreville, had been known in the old army as "Crazy Hill" because of his manner, which always suggested excitability.[15]

Once the nickname was mentioned, Mr. Davis remembered Hill and stopped his dictation to consider whether, on such un-

---

[15] Maj. Robert C. Hill was born in Iredell County, N. C., and was graduated from the U. S. Military Academy in the class of 1855 (*Cullum*, No. 1709). At Manassas, he was serving on Johnston's staff and had participated with Maj. John Scott in a brief cavalry pursuit of the enemy (*O. R.*, 2, 524, 525). Subsequently, he became Colonel of the Forty-eighth North Carolina of Walker's, later Cooke's, brigade, and died in service, Dec., 1863. "Nothing that he had ever done," said Alexander (*op. cit.*, 49), "had ever justified his nickname."

sustained authority, a difficult night movement should be started. Further inquiry elicited the fact that Hill had been deceived concerning the ground: he had not penetrated to Centreville, as he thought, but only to Cub Run.[16]

This altered the outlook. Davis, Johnston and Beauregard agreed that an advance to Centreville in the darkness would be imprudent,[17] though Colonel Jordan believed that the enemy could be driven all the way to Washington. The decision was to issue no directions for pursuit that night, but to send Bonham forward the next morning. Mr. Davis understood that the order for the 22d was to cover pursuit; Beauregard, who promptly issued the instructions, provided only for a cautious reconnaissance in force and for the collection of the booty on the north side of Bull Run.[18]

Before dawn, rain began to fall and continued throughout Eastern Virginia all the 22d.[19] The numerous rivulets that flowed into Bull Run became swift creeks. Only the shallowest fords of the Run itself were passable. The spongy soil of camp and pasture made movement difficult even for infantry.[20] By none of the roads was mass pursuit possible. Loud was the lament, because everywhere the Confederate detachments penetrated that

[16] Alexander stated, op. cit., 49, that Hill was questioned by the President and his Generals; Colonel Jordan, 1 Davis, 354, wrote that Captain Alexander may have been the one who reminded him of Hill's alleged eccentricities. It is not quite clear from Alexander's narrative whether the council ascertained at the time or subsequently that Major Hill had not been beyond Cub Run, but the probability is that the range of his reconnaissance was established at once.

[17] The moon was full, but clouds, gathering heavily, made the night very dark.

[18] Virtually all the details of this conference on the night of July 21 have been in dispute. Most of the differences among the witnesses concern the order of events, but there was positive conflict of testimony over the scope of the order Mr. Davis gave. To the end of his life the President believed that he had instructed General Beauregard to begin pursuit of the Federals. General Beauregard affirmed that, after doubt had been raised regarding the accuracy of the information supplied by Major Hill, all idea of pursuit was abandoned. The preponderance of evidence is on the side of Beauregard except that he did not explain the reason for his instructions to General Bonham. Those orders were proper and, in a sense, were routine; but it is strange that none of the accounts of the conference refers in any manner to them. The testimony of General Beauregard will be found in 1 Roman, 114 ff; that of President Davis is in 8 Rowland, 175 ff; that of Colonel Jordan in 1 Davis, 354 ff, and that of Captain Alexander in his memoirs, op. cit., 49. Johnston, in his Narrative, 63, dismissed the matter with the statement that Davis gave no orders for pursuit.

[19] 1 Roman, 116. Miss Brock, op. cit., 64, noted the heaviness of this storm in Richmond and remarked that it seemed "especially sent for the relief of the wounded. . . ." McHenry Howard, Recollections of a Maryland Confederate Soldier (cited hereafter as McHenry Howard), 43, remembered the rain as a drizzle only.

[20] It is a singular fact that in a district as admirably drained as is the watershed of Bull Run, there is much soft ground not only in the meadows along the streams but also on some parts of the plateaus.

day, they found flattering evidence that many of the Federals had become panic-stricken and had abandoned all equipment that impeded flight. Small personal articles of a thousand sorts had been thrown away and now were picked up by Confederate soldiers for their own use or as souvenirs. Public property recovered in the field or in the wake of the retreating army included twenty-eight excellent field guns, thirty-seven caissons, half a million rounds of small-arms ammunition, 4500 sets of accouterments, 500 muskets and nine flags. The prisoners, wounded and unhurt, numbered approximately 1460, or only about 500 less than gross Confederate casualties.[21]

Credit for these captures and for the victory itself was given immediately, without stint or scrutiny, to General Beauregard. When General Johnston suggested before breakfast on the 22d that Beauregard's services be recognized by promotion, the President assured him that this already had been arranged.[22] While the three were eating, Mr. Davis handed Beauregard a note in his autograph. It read as follows:

Manassas, Va., July 21st, 1861.

Sir,—Appreciating your services in the battle of Manassas and on several other occasions during the existing war, as affording the highest evidence of your skill as a commander, your gallantry as a soldier, and your zeal as a patriot, you are appointed to be "General" in the army of the Confederate States of America, and, with the consent of the Congress, will be duly commissioned accordingly.

Yours, etc.

General G. T. Beauregard.   Jefferson Davis.[23]

The honor thus bestowed by the President and speedily confirmed by the Senate, without reference to committee,[24] was followed by public acclamation of Beauregard. Incidents of his valor on the field, some of them apocryphal, were read and repeated. All the South was told that he "came dashing up" to Elzey and hailed him as the "Blücher of the day," [25] that a six-

[21] O. R., 2, 502, 503. As Beauregard's casualty list of 1852 is incomplete, it is probable that his losses approximated 2000. Federal casualties, listed officially at 2603, were computed by R. M. Johnston, op. cit., 255, at 3000 to 3300.
[22] Johnston's Narrative, 59.
[23] 1 Roman, 119.
[24] Richmond Examiner, July 31, 1861, p. 3, col. 3.
[25] Richmond Dispatch, Aug. 5, 1861, p. 2, col. 3.

pounder solid shot had struck the flank of his horse "not quite a foot from the General's leg";[26] that when the standard of the Hampton Legion fell, Beauregard cried, "Hand it to me, let me bear the Palmetto Flag";[27] that Beauregard's watch had stopped during the battle and that the officer who returned it, after it had been repaired, observed aptly, "General, your watch, like yourself, cannot run under fire."[28] There was praise for Johnston, to be sure. His name, by reason of his seniority, was listed ahead of Beauregard's in the Congressional vote of thanks,[29] but the concentration of the two armies,[30] not less than the victory itself, was assumed to be the work of Beauregard.[31] The momentary, almost universal belief that the Battle of Manassas would end the war[32] gave place to a belief that Beauregard would invade the North for a desperate struggle. Then impatience was voiced that the advance was delayed.[33] Even the disorganization of the troops, their reckless firing in camp, and desertion by men who felt they no longer were needed in the army[34] were, in a sense, a tribute to their faith in the fullness of the victory won by Beauregard.

26 *Richmond Examiner*, Aug. 2, 1861, p. 3, col. 1.

27 *Richmond Whig*, July 25, 1861, p. 2, col. 2.

28 *Richmond Dispatch*, Aug. 8, 1861, p. 3, col. 4.

29 *O. R.*, 51, pt. 2, pp. 215–16; Aug. 6, 1861.

30 *Richmond Examiner*, Aug. 14, 1861, p. 3, col. 1.

31 Cf. *Richmond Dispatch*, July 23, p. 2, col. 1; 24, p. 2, col. 1; July 31, p. 1, cols. 4–6—the last issue quoting the correspondent of the *London Morning Herald;* and *Charleston Mercury*, July 23 ff, 1861.

32 *Richmond Examiner*, July 22, p. 2, col. 2; 25, p. 2, cols. 1–2; 31, p. 2, col. 2; *Louisville Courier*, July 23; *Richmond Dispatch*, July 25, 1861, p. 3, col. 4.

33 *Richmond Examiner*, July 23, p. 2, col. 1; 26, p. 2, cols. 1–2; 29, p. 2, cols. 1–2; *Richmond Dispatch*, July 25, p. 2, col. 1, and p. 3, col. 4; July 29, p. 2, col. 2; 30, p. 2, col. 1; Aug. 1, p. 2, col. 1; 10, p. 1. col. 5. These references, which might be multiplied indefinitely, show that many Southern newspapers, after the first exultation, realized that the war would be long and that the South could not afford to relax its efforts. The more intelligent element of the press apparently did not foster and in some cases discouraged the overconfidence that developed from the first successes in the field.

34 *Johnston's Narrative*, 60; Richard Taylor, *Destruction and Reconstruction* (cited hereafter as *R. Taylor*), 18.

CHAPTER VIII

SUBORDINATES OF PROMISE

So EXULTANT was the South after the Battle of Manassas that it had made no effort and, indeed, had no occasion to appraise critically the generalship of Beauregard. Amid the rejoicing, scarcely a voice was raised to ask if his strategy had been on a par with his tactics. Few inquired whether the victory might not have been due as much to chance and to the valor of his subordinates as to the design and the discernment of the commander. In those first intoxicating days of triumph, there was general praise for all, but little of specific commendation for any except for Beauregard himself, for Johnston and for the fallen officers. The bodies of Gen. Barnard S. Bee and Col. Francis S. Bartow, with that of Lt. Col. B. J. Johnson of the Hampton Legion,[1] were brought to Richmond and were laid in state, with a guard of honor, before they were returned for burial in native soil. All Richmond knew that Mrs. Jefferson Davis had assumed the task of breaking to Mrs. Bartow, as mercifully as might be, the news of her husband's death.[2] Eulogies echoed through three States.[3] Speedily where he fell, a shaft in Bartow's memory was erected.[4]

Through the circulation of stories of the death of General Bee, the South formed its first admiring estimate of Gen. T. J. Jackson. In the earliest detailed report of the conduct of the admired South Carolinian, the Richmond correspondent of the *Charleston Mercury* described how "Bee rode up and down his lines, encouraging his troops by everything that was dear to them to stand up and repel the tide which threatened them with destruc-

---

[1] For Johnson's death, see *O. R.*, 2, 566.

[2] *Mrs. Chesnut*, 87–88.

[3] *Richmond Dispatch*, July 24, 1861, p. 2, col. 5; p. 3, col. 1; obituaries of Bee and Johnson in the *Charleston Mercury*, reprinted in *ibid.*, July 27, p. 1, cols. 3–4; account of Bartow's death from oration by T. R. R. Cobb, *Richmond Whig*, July 25, 1861, p. 2, col. 6.

[4] *Richmond Dispatch*, Sept. 10, 1861, p. 1, col. 5. A correspondent of this paper wrote that the inscription on the shaft was incorrect. It quoted Bartow as calling to his men, "Never give up the field," whereas the dying Colonel actually said, "They have killed me, boys, but never give it up."

tion." The report continued: "At last his own brigade dwindled to a mere handful, with every field officer killed or disabled. He rode up to Gen. Jackson and said, 'General, they are beating us back.'

"The reply was, 'Sir, we'll give them the bayonet.'

"General Bee immediately rallied the remnant of his brigade, and his last words to them were: 'There is Jackson standing like a stone wall. Let us determine to die here, and we will conquer. Follow me.'

"His men obeyed the call; and, at the head of his column, the very moment when the battle was turning in our favor he fell, mortally wounded." [5]

This must have made instant appeal to the public imagination. The very next day a Charleston correspondent of *Punch* wrote that he drank, willingly or otherwise, "'two stone walls' and a 'General Jackson' before breakfast." [6] Although the sober Jackson would have disapproved the medium of its expression, he deserved this tribute. At a critical point of the battle, he had advanced straight to the point of danger, had held his ground through the hardest of the fighting and, as became an instructor in artillery, had massed his guns to play upon the enemy in front of his compact, unyielding line. Jackson's horse had been wounded under him; one bullet had made an ugly gash in his coat near the hip; another missile had broken the bone of the middle finger of his left hand. To reduce the bleeding and to ease the pain, he had carried his arm upraised through the remainder of the action. Observing this, some of his men thought he was invoking the blessing of Heaven. He believed that he had received that blessing. The day after the battle, he wrote his wife: "Whilst great credit is due to other parts of our gallant army, God made my brigade more instrumental than any other in repulsing the main attack. This is for your information only —say nothing about it. Let others speak praise, not myself."

When the young wife wrote that she saw very little in the press concerning the achievements of his troops, he bantered her: "And so you think the papers ought to say more about your husband! My brigade is not a brigade of newspaper correspondents. I know

---

[5] *Charleston Mercury*, July 25, 1861, p. 1, col. 1. For a review of the various versions of this famous incident, see Appendix V.

[6] Reprinted in *Richmond Examiner*, Sept. 6, 1861, p. 1, col. 3.

that the First Brigade was the first to meet and pass our retreating forces—to push on with no other aid than the smiles of God; to boldly take its position with the artillery that was under my command—to arrest the victorious foe in his onward progress —to hold him in check until reinforcements arrived—and finally to charge bayonets, and, thus advancing, pierce the enemy's center. I am well satisfied with what it did, and so are my generals, Johnston and Beauregard. It is not to be expected that I should receive the credit that Generals Beauregard and Johnston would, because I was under them; but I am thankful to my ever-kind Heavenly Father that He makes me content to await His own good time and pleasure for commendation—knowing that all things work together for my good." [7] He was "content to await," but not to be denied "commendation." Did he mean "fame"? Was ambition burning under the faded blue coat he had brought to Manassas from V. M. I.? Beneath his çadet cap, his large blue eyes had blazed with a strange light during the battle: what did that portend? [8] His soldiers did not know, but they confirmed the tribute implied in Bee's shouted words. From that day, Professor Jackson was "Stonewall" Jackson. [9]

With the service of Bee and of Jackson on the left, General Johnston ranked that of E. Kirby Smith. In fact, in his report, he was to list before the new "Stonewall" the Florida Brigadier, then 37, who had been his Chief of Staff at Harpers Ferry and had been left behind to bring up the rear Brigade. [10] The men detrained near the station, about 1 P.M., threw off their knapsacks, and formed a line. In front of them, behind Colonel Elzey, rode the magnificent Smith. With the back of his hand raised in front of his cap, he cried, "This is the signal, men; the watchword is 'Sumter.'" [11] Through dust so thick that one rank could not see the men immediately in front of them [12] Smith hurried

[7] Mary Anna Jackson, *Memoirs of Stonewall Jackson* (cited hereafter as *Mrs. Jackson*), 178, 180.

[8] For his apparel and appearance, see 19 *S. H. S. P.*, 83, 302.

[9] Public curiosity concerning Jackson grew with the weeks. The press obligingly described his career but had nothing to say of the peculiarities that subsequently were exaggerated *causerie de bivouac*. (*Richmond Enquirer*, reprinted in *Richmond Dispatch*, Aug. 9, 1861, p. 1, col. 5. The next references to Jackson will be found on p. 122 ff.)

[10] *Cullum*, No. 1255. Smith was graduated 25th in the class of 1845 at West Point, and when he resigned from the United States Army was third captain of the 2nd Cavalry, the regiment of Albert Sidney Johnston and R. E. Lee. For his early Confederate assignments, see *O. R.*, 2, 798; *O. R.*, 51, pt. 2, p. 82.

[11] *McHenry Howard*, 35.

[12] *Richmond Dispatch*, Aug. 5, 1861, p. 2, col. 3.

his troops to the battle. "I galloped ahead," Smith wrote in his diary, "with my staff, and found General Johnston who ordered me to halt my column and form a line in the rear."

Smith begged his commander to let him throw his men into the battle. "Take them to the front," Johnston said at length; "it is our left that is being driven back; but the ground is new to me, and I cannot direct you exactly." Smith rejoined the column, moved it at the double-quick and arrived on the left just as Kershaw was drawing his line.[13] Almost immediately, Smith received a minié ball which grazed his spinal column, plowed through the muscles of his neck and passed out near the collar-bone.[14]

As Smith fell, he turned over the command to his senior Colonel, a stout-hearted officer of the "old army," Arnold Elzey.[15] Listed in first reports as dead,[16] Smith was to recover speedily.[17] His future, all men saw, was to be large, nor did that of his second in command promise to be small. Elzey handled the troops admirably and gave a fine example of soldierly enthusiasm. As he approached the field, after assuming command, he rode ahead to reconnoiter and soon led his men within sight of a line drawn up between the Henry and the Chinn houses. For a few minutes he did not know whether he faced Confederates or Unionists. With his glass he studied the men in the distance. Then quickly —to quote an observer—"Elzey dropped his hand, his eye lighted up . . . and he hastily cried, 'Stars and Stripes! Stars and Stripes! Give it to them, boys.'"[18] The fire power he developed among his men and the judgment of his leading soon won for him a commission as Brigadier General.[19] Elzey had a bluff and hearty manner and on occasion did not disdain what the soldiers usually called "a dram." One evening, when he and some of his com-

13 Smith's diary in 7 C. V., 108.
14 Richmond Dispatch, Aug. 8, 1861, p. 2, col. 3; 7 C. V., 310.
15 O. R., 2, 476.
16 Richmond Examiner, July 22, 1861, p. 2, col. 1.
17 Richmond Dispatch, Aug. 8, 1861, p. 2, col. 3. O. R., 51, pt. 2, p. 222. He was sent from the field hospital to the home of Richard H. Cunningham in Culpeper. During September, he was married in Lynchburg to Miss Cassie Selden, daughter of Mr. and Mrs. Armistead Selden. His young wife immediately was styled "The Bride of the Confederacy." Savannah Republican, quoted in Richmond Dispatch, Sept. 26, 1861, p. 1, col. 4; T. C. De Leon, Belles, Beaux and Brains of the 60's (cited hereafter as De Leon, B. B. B.), 451. Smith is mentioned again on p. 130 infra, but he is not portrayed in any detail here because his service in Virginia was terminated before Lee took command.
18 McHenry Howard, 38.
19 Aug. 28, 1861, to rank from July 21, 1861. Wright, 58–59.

rades were in expansive mood, the General called in the sentinel on the post and gave him a drink, for which the man was pathetically grateful. Later in the night, when the party was over and Elzey was asleep, the same man was walking his post. Without abashment he put his head inside Elzey's tent and woke him with the loud query, "General, general, ain't it about time for us to take another drink?" The wrathful Elzey had the man put under arrest, but the soldier had the gratitude of the army for inspiring a question that echoed every day in all the camps.[20]

Col. Jubal A. Early, who had extended the left flank beyond the line of Smith and Elzey, received praise on the field and later in the reports, but in smaller measure than his comrades to the right. There were reasons for this, though they were not to his discredit. His march from his reserve position near the center had been somewhat confused by the equivocal nature of his orders.[21] Perhaps a close observer would have said that Early had exhibited a poor sense of direction. His arrival was decisive, because it showed the Federals they were outflanked; but his share in the actual fighting had been small.[22] The personality of the Colonel, even more, kept him from being a popular hero. Born in the Blue Ridge Mountains of Virginia, he went to West Point, where he was graduated No. 18 in the class of 1837,[23] but after two years in the army, he resigned to become an attorney in his native county. As lawyer, Whig legislator and prosecuting attorney, he labored until 1861, except for a period of uneventful service as a Major of volunteers during the Mexican War. While a member of the Virginia convention of 1861, he opposed secession with biting vehemence, but when his State left the Union, he at once tendered his services. He was sent first to Lynchburg, where he organized three regiments,[24] one of which, the Twenty-fourth Virginia, was assigned to him.[25] The day after his arrival

[20] John O. Casler, Four Years in the Stonewall Brigade (cited hereafter as Casler), 25. A more extended note on this classic of military realism will be found infra, Chapter XXI, p. 307.

[21] See supra, p. 62 n.

[22] Casualties, twelve killed and sixty-four wounded; O. R., 2, 558.

[23] Cullum, No. 908. This was the class of Henry W. Benham, Braxton Bragg, William H. French, John Sedgwick, John C. Pemberton, Joseph Hooker, Arnold Elzey, William H. T. Walker and R. H. Chilton. In the Academy with Early, though graduating in other years, were Beauregard, Ewell, Edward Johnson, McDowell and Meade. See Cullum, and Early, xviii.

[24] Early, 1; 22 S. H. S. P., 316; C. R., 2, 806, 851, 906; O. R., 51, pt. 2, pp 10, 76, 111; Richmond Examiner, May 29, 1861, p. 2, col. 4.

[25] Early, 2, 3; O R., 51, pt. 2, p. 123.

at Manassas, Beauregard appointed him, though he still ranked as Colonel, to the command of a small Brigade.[26] Early was then 44, about six feet tall and weighed under 170 pounds; but as a result of rheumatism contracted in Mexico, he stooped badly and seemed so much older than his years that his soldiers promptly dubbed him "Old Jube," with "Old Jubilee" as an occasional variant.[27] His long beard, his keen, flashing black eyes, his satirical smile, his avowed irreligion, his incisive but not unmusical voice, and his rasping, mordant wit made him appear almost saturnine to those who did not know how much of loyalty and of generosity he hid behind a forbidding front.[28] From the outset, he was stern in his discipline and was charged with a snarling harshness toward his subordinates. That he was able, many believed, and that he was coldly brave, all who saw him on the field admitted. What he would become as a commander, none knew and few cared. When the caustic Colonel was promoted Brigadier to rank from the day of the battle,[29] there probably was scant enthusiasm.

If praise in the penumbra of Beauregard's glory was accorded Jackson for holding the center and to Kirby Smith, Elzey and "Old Jube" for outflanking the Federals, applause was allotted also to Col. Nathan George Evans for his first challenge of the advancing enemy. It had been a picturesque exploit. As soon as Evans had learned that the Unionists were moving beyond his position, he had left the skirmish line in front of Stone Bridge with two companies in support, had sent word to his immediate superior that he was abandoning his position, and unhesitatingly, with his 1100 men and his two 6-pounder smooth-bore guns, had challenged the advance of the foe.[30] Then he had put up as stout resistance as could have been offered in the face of such odds. His casualties, 12 per cent of his engaged force, had been entailed in heavy fighting and not in a mere delaying action. The reports

[26] O. R., 2, 944; Early, 3.
[27] Companions in Arms, 477. Early made no pretense of being a martial dandy, but after writers described him as having "a rough, curly head," and as prone to negligence in dress, the General took pains to assert that his hair was straight and that he was his tailor's most exacting customer. Early, xxv, xxvi.
[28] The fullest, most affectionate appraisal of Early is that of John W. Daniel in 22 S. H. S. P., 285 ff; one of the most discriminating is that in Cooke's Wearing of the Gray, 110 ff; another good contemporary sketch is in Companions in Arms, 476-78.
[29] Wright, 59; commissioned Aug. 28, 1861. The next part of the sketch of Early will be found on p. 180 ff.
[30] O. R., 474, 499, 559.

were to commend his "skill and unshrinkable courage,"[31] his "dauntless conduct and imperturbable coolness,"[32] but promotion was not to follow immediately, for reasons as personal as those that denied popularity to Early. "Shank" Evans—his thinnest members receiving stoutest acclaim—had won some repute in the Indian fighting that had followed his graduation from West Point in the class of 1848.[33] Ere he resigned in February, 1861, his eleven years of service had made him a Captain of the 2nd Cavalry. He was 37, of medium height, slightly bald, with the fiercest of black mustachios, and small, restless eyes to match. His look was quick, cunning and contentious, as if he always were suspecting a Comanche ambush. It was only when a broad smile revealed glittering teeth that his martial mien softened.[34] There was no question of his capacity, but he was the "devil-may-care" type and was accused—falsely, it would appear—of excessive fondness of the bottle.

Much of the heaviest fighting under Evans had been done by a Louisiana battalion of Zouaves, one company of which, styled "The Tigers," had given its name and its evil reputation to the whole.[35] The original "Tigers" had been recruited along the levees and among the alleys of New Orleans, and had not been inhospitable to some volunteers whose names had adorned prison registers. In whatever cities these troops had halted on their way to the front, there had been undisciplined rioting and whispers, at the least, of theft and pillage.[36] Richmond had rejoiced at the Tigers' departure; no brigade commander had wanted them at Manassas. Their Major, fortunately, knew how to deal with them. Roberdeau C. Wheat he was, son of an Episcopal clergyman of Alexandria, Virginia, and inheritor of Huguenot tradition and Maryland blue blood. At 20 years of age,[37] after graduation from college, Rob Wheat was reading law in Memphis. Physically superb, over six feet in height, and with manners that bespoke his uprearing, he volunteered for service in Mexico, became a Captain and, on the conclusion of peace, went to

[31] Johnston, O. R., 2, 474.   [32] Beauregard, O. R., 2, 499.
[33] Cullum, No. 1404. Evans was thirty-sixth in a class of thirty-eight.
[34] "An English Combatant," Battlefields of the South . . . (cited hereafter as An English Combatant), 59.
[35] R. Taylor, 24.
[36] W. A. McClendon, Recollections of War Times, 36–37; Miss Brock, 35.
[37] Born Apr. 9. 1826.

New Orleans, entered politics and practiced his profession. He would have risen high, perhaps, as a criminal lawyer, had he not become absorbed in those Latin-American adventures of the 1850's in which Gulf State ideals of political freedom were combined paradoxically with the extension of slavery.

Rob Wheat shared in Lopez's first expedition and received a severe wound in the attack on Cardenas. He fought with Carravajal in Mexico, then with Walker in Nicaragua and again in Mexico with Alvarez. As head of that insurgent's artillery, he became a regular officer in the Mexican army on Alvarez's accession to the Presidency. When the old General retired, he took Wheat with him to his estate. There, for the second time, a career of peace and ease opened for the young Virginian. He cast it aside when he read of Garibaldi's rising in Sicily, and, joining some English volunteers, he shared the fortunes of the Red Shirts until threatened war in the United States prompted him to hurry home.

As Wheat had fought in four lands and with hard men of alien tongues, he had been wholly at ease when he led his "Tigers" into action at Manassas, and on the field he had given "Shanks" Evans counsel that officer gratefully acknowledged in his report.[38] Wheat was as reckless as brave. At the head of his battalion, in a charge, he had been shot down. The surgeon who examined him shook a sage professional head: a bullet wound of that nature, through both lungs, was necessarily fatal. "I don't feel like dying yet," Wheat avowed. The medical man held to his contention. "There is no instance on record," said he, "of recovery from such a wound." "Well, then," answered Wheat, in a phrase that became a lawyer, "I will put my case upon record." He was desperate; perhaps in battle he had been foolhardy, but he had accumulated more combat experience than any other Confederate officer at Manassas: would he survive his wound to use that experience?[39]

When Wheat had marched off with Evans on the morning of July 21 to meet the column that sought to turn the Confederate

[38] O. R., 2, 559: "I am also much indebted to him for his great experience and excellent advice."

[39] The best sketch of Wheat, paraphrased here, is that by his brilliant brother Leo, in 22 S. H. S. P., 47 ff. See also 19 C. V., 425 ff. Wheat is not treated in detail here, but he is mentioned several times in Chapter XXIV et seq.

left, their immediate superior, Col. Philip St. George Cocke, had hurried guns to protect the Stone Bridge.[40] Thereafter, from his brigade headquarters at Portici, he had repulsed Federal demonstrations along the Run and had directed forward the earliest reinforcements to reach the flank. He it was who informed first Bee and Bartow, then Hampton, and then Jackson of Evans's advance and of the progress of the action.[41] Without Cocke's guidance, based on his thorough knowledge of the terrain, the order of battle could not have been established so readily or so soon. What seemed in retrospect a marvel of distant control by Beauregard was, in reality, the work of Colonel Cocke. Later in the day, after he had changed the position of his battery and of Smith's regiment, both were ordered to Henry House Hill. Cocke boldly left vacant the gap created by the removal of Smith, because he was satisfied that the enemy, separated from his line by the Run and by a thicket of willows, would not observe the withdrawal.

After General Johnston established field headquarters at Portici, Cocke concluded that he should abandon the entire position and take the consequent risk of a Federal crossing, in order that he might use his four unengaged regiments to strengthen the swaying line of battle. With Johnston's approval, he sent off Hunton and then Withers and himself, with Preston and Strange, soon started at the double-quick for the extreme left flank. There he arrived with Strange's Nineteenth Virginia in rear of Early's line just as the pursuit began.[42]

Altogether, Cocke had met a succession of tests with clear judgment, decision and promptness. He was to be mentioned in Johnston's report for leading his "brigade into action . . . with alacrity and effect" and he was to be listed next after Evans among the Colonels whose "admirable conduct" sustained the "skill and resolution of General Beauregard." [43] In the long official account that Beauregard was to submit in October, Cocke was to be named among those who "also" deserved "high praise," [44] but he was not to be singled out for special commendation. As his report for

[40] One section of Rogers's Battery.
[41] Which then was between the Warrenton Turnpike and the bend in Bull Run opposite Sudley's Ford.
[42] Cocke's report, *O. R.,* 51, pt. 1, p. 29.
[43] *O. R.,* 2, 477.   [44] *O. R.,* 2, 500.

some reason was not forwarded to the War Department with those of the other brigade commanders,[45] his part in the battle has been underrated.

Cocke was ambitious for military rank and fame, but for neither did he have need. An interesting and exalted place in the life of Virginia already was his. Born in 1808 of one of the oldest and wealthiest families of the State, he had been schooled in arms at West Point,[46] but after less than two years' garrison duty, he resigned [47] to devote himself to the care of his estates. His career for the next two decades and more had combined distinct public service with rural life that approached the ideal. Belmead, his principal estate on the James River, was renowned. The system of management that Cocke expounded in his *Plantation and Farm Instruction,* published in 1852, he had exemplified on thousands of flourishing acres. As President of the Virginia Agricultural Society in 1853–56, he had preached responsibility for the soil and had advanced new methods. With the exception of Edmund Ruffin, who had found in the use of marl the cure for "sour land," Virginia had no planter more renowned than St. George Cocke. Through the years Cocke had kept his interest in military affairs and for a time he had held commission as an aide to Governor Henry A. Wise. His first assignment after secession had been the impossible one of commanding the "military operations of the State bounding on the Potomac River." [48] At Alexandria and later at Culpeper, he had combated a thousand difficulties with unequal success.[49]

When the Virginia Convention had changed his volunteer rank from that of Brigadier General to that of Colonel, Cocke suffered much distress of mind. The assignment of General Bonham to the frontier command likewise had been a humiliation; but Cocke's patriotism and General Lee's skillful treatment of bruised

[45] There is a tradition that Beauregard had a controversy with Cocke over this report, in which Cocke asserted a larger direction of early operations on the left than Beauregard thought justified. In the light of the other reports, Cocke seems to have claimed no credit he did not deserve, though the issue between him and Beauregard may have been confused by Cocke's subsequent illness.

[46] *Cullum,* No. 667; graduated sixth in the class of 1832.

[47] Apr. 1, 1834. Of the ten men who were graduated highest in the class of 1832, by Nov. 1, 1838, eight had resigned or had died.

[48] *O. R.,* 51, pt. 2, p. 21; *Richmond Examiner,* May 8, 1861, p. 1, col. 4.

[49] *O. R.,* 2, 786, 804, 823, 865; *Richmond Examiner,* May 1, 1861, p. 2, col. [1] *Cocke MSS.:* 1 *R. E. Lee,* 505–6.

sensibilities had removed the soreness.[50] It was after temporary service at the head of the Nineteenth Virginia Infantry [51] that Cocke had been given the Fifth Brigade in Beauregard's organization of the "First Corps" of the Army of the Potomac.[52] To this Brigade, Evans's command of a regiment and one battalion had been attached prior to the battle. Now that the first contest was over and Cocke had shown what he was capable of doing, the press had praise of him.[53] By brother officers he was recognized as "a high-minded and gallant soldier, a devoted patriot, and a gentleman of cultivation and refinement." [54] Would he and men like him, the middle-aged aristocrats and the proprietors of the great estates, measure up, as a class, to the requirements of command, and could they endure the hardships and exactions of prolonged field service?

A South Carolina Colonel, Wade Hampton, of a social station as high as that of General Cocke, gave on the field of Manassas a hopeful, if incomplete, answer to that question. He did more. In his antecedents and in his own career, he represented the rise and the attainments, the strength and the weakness, of the economic system which the war would vindicate or would destroy. Anthony Hampton, described as a "hemp-beater," left Virginia about the middle of the eighteenth century and established himself on the southwestern frontier, the Spartanburg area of South Carolina. There he recruited from his own loins the garrison that was to defend his farm against marauding savages. During the absence of five of his sons, the Cherokees attacked in July, 1776, and slew Anthony, his wife, one son and a grandchild. In the war that followed immediately, all the surviving boys espoused the colonial cause and became army officers.

One of them, Wade Hampton, seems to have maintained the old allegiance longer than his brothers did, but in 1781 he joined the Revolutionists and, at Eutaw Springs, highly distinguished himself. The close of hostilities found him with a Colonel's com-

[50] O. R., 2, 836–37, 865, 879; O. R., 51, pt. 2, p. 108.
[51] O. R., 51, pt. 2, p. 123.
[52] O. R., 2, 944. The War Department subsequently had to cancel this designation of "First Corps" because there was then no authorization in Confederate law for the organization of units larger than Divisions. See infra, pp. 101, 118.
[53] Richmond Whig, Aug. 3, 1861, p. 2, col. 2, a hint that Cocke deserved to be made a Major General. He was nominated Brigadier General Oct. 21, 1861, Wright, 63.
[54] E. P. Alexander, in 9 S. H. S. P., 515.

mission but with farmlands of such little value that neighbors with similar holdings were abandoning them and moving southward.[55] Wade Hampton held on. When green-seed cotton began to arouse interest, he must have been among the first to experiment with it on the Carolina midlands. By the season of 1799 he had so extended the culture that he produced 600 bales, which sold for $90,000. The foundation of a great fortune was thus laid. During the War of 1812, he interrupted his agricultural pursuits and served as brigade commander and then as Major General until a controversy with Gen. James Wilkinson prompted him to resign in disgust. Although he had neglected some of his properties while in the Army, he gained by his loss of time. While he was with Jackson around New Orleans, he sensed the possibilities of cane-growing and in 1811 he transferred part of his slaves to a sugar plantation in Louisiana. New cotton farms were so rapidly developed by him in Mississippi that when he died in 1835, he had 3000 slaves and ranked as the richest planter in the United States.[56]

The second Wade Hampton (1791–1858) left South Carolina College for a brief period of service in the War of 1812, but he was of a fortunate generation that could spend its maturity in an era of peace and plenitude. Without neglecting in the least the family estates, which prospered with expanding markets, this Hampton had leisure for horse breeding and for politics. He seldom held any office, but his mansion, Millwood, was almost as much the political capital of South Carolina as was near-by Columbia. In his great library, one of the best-stocked private collections in the United States,[57] he ruled as the "Great Warwick of South Carolina."[58]

[55] See the references cited in U. R. Phillips, *Life and Labor in the Old South*, 99.

[56] There is as yet (1942) no adequate history of the Hampton Family, though the long study by James E. Derieux approaches completion. The sketches in 8 *Dictionary of American Biography* (cited hereafter as *D. A. B.*), 212 ff are by J. Harold Easterby and, for their compass, are most admirable. Excellent bibliographies accompany them. Some intimate details are given in Edward L. Wells, *Hampton and His Cavalry in '64* (cited hereafter as *Wells*).

[57] Said to have contained, in 1861, in excess of 10,000 volumes, of which 1500 related to American history. *Richmond Dispatch*, July 15, 1861, p. 2, col. 6.

[58] Easterby, 8 *D. A. B.*, 213. Wells, *op. cit.*, 19–20, told a characteristic story of Wade Hampton II. A young friend of the family, a student at South Carolina, was in the habit of spending his week-ends at Millwood. Hampton observed that the boy rode a mount which he was keeping at a Columbia stable in calm defiance of the college rule that forbade students to have horses. As Hampton was a trustee of the institution, he did not feel that he should connive at this flouting of the regulations. Accordingly he said to the student, "I think you had better sell that horse." The boy obediently disposed

When he died, Millwood, a fortune and the leadership of the family passed to the third Wade Hampton,[59] who had been born in Charleston, March 28, 1818. After he was graduated from South Carolina College, he studied law, the better to handle his own affairs. By the time he was in his middle thirties, he came to doubt the economy of slave labor and on that account dissented from the politics of the dominant element of his State; but as a manager, he equalled his father and perhaps his grandfather.[60] In the legislature, which he entered in order that he might counteract some of the policies of the "fire eaters," he served diligently and without any shadow of selfish ambition.

Until 1861, in short, his was the ideal life of the society in which he was reared. As often as he might, he went hunting or climbed into the mountains to seek the elusive trout. Fabled as a sportsman and adept in all the arts of woodcraft, he was renowned no less for his physical strength. Just under six feet in height, he had the balance of the horseman and the smooth muscles of the athlete.[61] His courage, personal, moral and political, was in keeping with his physique. When the demand for secession arose, he admitted the right of withdrawal from the Union but disputed the policy. Once South Carolina acted, he put all doubt and argument behind·him and placed at the command of the State his wealth and his services. His cotton was tendered for export or as collateral for governmental credit; with the President's approval, he set about the enlistment of a "Legion," six companies of infantry, four of cavalry and a battery of artillery.[62] More than twice as many volunteers promptly answered his call as he was authorized to accept.[63] For them, at his own expense, he bought six field guns and much other equipment.[64]

of the animal and on the following Friday went to the stable to hire a mount to carry him to Millwood. The stableman immediately produced a fine thoroughbred. "Colonel Hampton," he explained, "sent this horse here and said he was to be kept for your use as long as you are in college."

[59] The Louisiana estates of Wade Hampton II were sold in 1857 for approximately $1,500,000. Phillips, op. cit., 98, n. 4.

[60] Despite the turmoil of the times, he produced in 1861 on his plantations in South Carolina and in Mississippi 5000 bales of cotton. Easterby in 8 D. A. B., 214.

[61] M. C. Butler in 5 Library Southern Literature, 2061 ff.

[62] Richmond Dispatch, May 29, 1861, p. 2, col. 1; IV O. R., 1, 303.

[63] IV O. R., 1, 296, 303. By May 28, according to the Charleston Courier (May 29, 1861) "over 30 companies of 75 men each" had offered for the Hampton Legion.

[64] IV O. R., 1, 296; Columbia South Carolinian, June 26, 1861. The artillery of the Hampton Legion subsequently was known in the Army of Northern Virginia as "Hart's South Carolina Battery."

Some of the best-born young men of the Palmetto State were proud to be privates in his "Legion." Its officers were of the élite. Every step toward complete organization of the command was reported in the press; the arrival of the "Legion" in Virginia and its encampment near Richmond were attended with much applause.[65] The personnel of the force and its admirable appearance drew compliments from the President. "It is," one of the officers confided to his mother, "by all odds the finest looking and best drilled body of men that has left the State." [66] The men needed their fiber and the discipline of their drill. Three weeks of camp life in an unattractive quarter of Richmond soon tested the morale of the Legion and provoked a noncommissioned officer to publish a newspaper advertisement in which he complained of cold, of hunger, of partiality and of restrictions on the freedom of speech.[67]

Through this, as through worse things to come, Colonel Hampton preserved a simple, grave imperturbability. He was then 43, older than many officers of like or higher rank, and he had the manner of one to whom war was not a frolic or an adventure but a grim, bitter business to be discharged as quickly as might be with determination and without relish. To strangers he was reserved though always courteous, the gentleman as surely as the aristocrat; with his friends he was candid, cordial and free of any suggestion of the Grand Seigneur.[68]

When, at last, marching orders for the Legion were received on July 19,[69] Hampton proceeded quickly and quietly to start his move. The overtaxed railroads took thirty hours to transport his 600 infantry to Manassas and did not detrain them at the Junction till the guns already were roaring.[70] Although Hampton had never been in action and never had been given even the rudimentary training of a militiaman before 1861, he led his men straight to the Robinson House [71] and thence to the stone wall

65 *Petersburg Express,* June 29; *Richmond Dispatch,* July 1, 1861, p. 1, col. 7. Hampton himself reached Richmond July 4. See *Richmond Dispatch,* July 8, 1861, p. 1, col. 3.

66 *Letters of General James Conner* . . . (cited hereafter as *Conner*), 27.

67 *Richmond Examiner,* July 18, 1861, p. 3, col. 3. "Camp Hampton," where the Legion had its quarters, was in Rocketts, which adjoined the present Fulton district in the eastern section of Richmond.

68 Butler, *loc. cit.; Southern Generals,* 472–73. The best character sketch of Hampton, one of the most admirable that John Esten Cooke ever wrote, appears in *Wearing* ʳ⁶ *the Gray,* 61 ff.

69 *Richmond Dispatch,* July 20, 1861, p. 2, col. 6.

70 *O. R.,* 2, 566.   71 NNE. of the Henry House.

that fronted the Warrenton Turnpike north of the farm buildings. There his second in command, Lt. Col. B. J. Johnson, was killed almost immediately.

Hampton was left with no field officer and with no company commanders of experience. He held his position until he was enfiladed, and then he led his men back over the brow of the hill. The enemy advanced again, to right and to left, and surrounded Hampton on three sides. Still his men fought furiously. In their pride they might have remained on the hillside till the last of them was killed, had not Bee and Bartow urged Hampton to retire. He sought the shelter of the near-by ravine, re-formed his thinned companies and, on word from Beauregard, awaited further orders.

As the final advance began, Hampton was told to join in it. He went forward—only to fall as he led a charge against two guns that the gallant Ricketts had hauled off. Capt. James Conner thereupon took command, captured the fieldpieces, and shared in a pursuit that did not end until the exhausted survivors were two miles East of Stone Bridge.[72]

Fortunately, Hampton's wound was slight, but among his 600 men the casualties reached 121, or 20 per cent.[73] Although in dispatches he merely was commended with two other Colonels in general terms for "soldierly ability," his soldiers had the highest praise for him.[74] Everything that was to have been expected of him, he had done. If he had carried his small command farther than prudence or experience would have counselled, he had contributed potently to check a dangerous advance and he had displayed inspiring courage and persistence.[75] When his report was filed, an appraising reader would have noticed, too, how quickly Hampton had grasped the details of the position and how accurately he had described the terrain. There was more of potential military excellence about him than his superiors at the moment realized.

---

[72] O. R., 2, 567.   [73] Ibid.

[74] One of the wounded told how, when Hampton's horse had been shot under him, the Colonel took a rifle and picked off one after another of the Federal officers who were leading the attack. Richmond Whig, July 25, 1861, p. 2, col. 2. This incident is not recorded elsewhere and may be apocryphal.

[75] Some interesting, little known material on Hampton's advance and engagement will be found in Mrs. Kate Virginia Cox Logan, My Confederate Girlhood, 120, 128–29. For the next detailed reference to Hampton, see infra, p. 195.

These, then, were the surviving officers who had most distinguished themselves in actual combat under Johnston and Beauregard: "Stonewall" Jackson, a former brevet Major in the regular army of the United States and then a professor in a State Military Institute; a tall young Floridian of 37, E. Kirby Smith, who only two months and a half previously had resigned a Major's commission; Jubal A. Early, one-time Lieutenant and for almost thirty years a lawyer and a politician; an Indian fighter, "Shanks" Evans; a young "soldier of fortune" who commanded a notoriously tough battalion, Rob Wheat; a successful planter and distinguished host, P. St. George Cocke, who had not borne arms for nearly thirty years; and a Carolina millionaire sportsman of no previous military training. Had Fate, blindfolded, drawn their names at random from a bag, they scarcely could have been those of men more diverse in temperament or in training.

Others had done well. The South Carolina lawyer-colonel, J. B. Kershaw, who had helped to put Preston and Elzey into position, was a man who seemed to have military aptitude. Arnold Elzey, as noted already, had handled his Brigade most intelligently after Kirby Smith fell. All three of Early's Colonels had behaved like veterans—James L. Kemper, Harry Hays and William Barksdale. Col. Eppa Hunton of the Eighth Virginia had borne himself gallantly. Brigadier General Holmes had marched fast from the right. On that same flank and in the center, each in accordance with his nature, those who had been denied a hand in the fray had chafed or had cursed. There was James Longstreet, who counted among his Colonels a restless man named Samuel Garland. The guardian of Union Mills Ford, Brig. Gen. "Dick" Ewell, had with him a young acting Assistant Adjutant General named Fitzhugh Lee, and also a stalwart Colonel of the fine Fifth Alabama, a soldierly figure with sandy mustache and penetrating eyes, Robert E. Rodes, who had been a teacher and a civil engineer in railway employ. In D. R. Jones's Brigade, ill content to play so small a role in so exciting a drama, was Micah Jenkins, Colonel of the Fifth South Carolina. Arriving late from the Shenandoah Valley, Col. A. P. Hill moved to the right with his Thirteenth Virginia, but could not fire a single shot.

The cavalry had been led with dash by Col. James E. B. Stuart, but the mounted men had been too few to sweep the field. Johnston was to admit that frankly in his report.[76] Many artillerists had won praise. Notable among them had been Rev. W. N. Pendleton, an old West Pointer and an Episcopal clergyman. With Jackson's guns, Capt. John D. Imboden had challenged every eye. A gigantic young Lieutenant, Thomas L. Rosser, had command of four howitzers of the Washington Artillery. After having been sent on a useless mission, he plunged across Union Mills Ford and rushed his men at the double-quick all the way to the scene of action—only to find the enemy gone.[77] Besides the artillerists, the staff officers had commendation. Beauregard saw to it that his Chief of Artillery and of Ordnance, Col. Samuel Jones, was promoted Brigadier General to rank from the date of the battle.[78] Johnston, in his report, was to mention first among staff officers his Chief Engineer, Maj. W. H. C. Whiting, who, said Johnston, "was invaluable to me for his signal ability in his profession and for his indefatigable activity before and in the battle." [79] Whiting, like Jones, was made a Brigadier as of July 21.[80] Young Capt. E. P. Alexander, signal officer, had praise but no immediate promotion.

That some of these men, when their opportunity came, would acquit themselves valiantly, any observer safely could predict; but none could foresee that from the small army of 30,000 were to come, in a long war, so large a number of general officers. Ten men held that rank at Manassas on the day of battle. One of them, Bee, was mortally wounded. Another, Bonham, resigned at the rank he then held. A third, Johnston, already had the highest grade in the army. Of the others, Beauregard and Kirby Smith became Generals; Longstreet, Jackson, Holmes and Ewell rose to be Lieutenant Generals, and D. R. Jones died as a Major General. Of the Colonels at Manassas, A. P. Hill, Early and Hampton ended their service as Lieutenant Generals. Seven other Colonels were to be Major Generals [81] and fourteen were to lead Brigades;[82] one Major, Whiting, and two Lieutenants,[83] became

---

[76] O. R., 2, 477.
[77] O. R., 2, 517.
[78] Wright, 59; O. R., 2, 501.
[79] O. R., 2, 477.
[80] Wright, 59.
[81] Stuart, Elzey, William Smith, Samuel Jones, Rodes, Kershaw and Kemper.
[82] M. Jenkins, Featherston, Garland, Corse, N. G. Evans, Harry Hays, Kirkland, Hunton, W. N. Pendleton, J. S. Preston, William Barksdale, J. C. Vaughn, P. St. George Cocke and Thomas Jordan.
[83] Fitz Lee and T. L. Rosser.

Generals of divisions; three Lieutenant Colonels,[84] eight Captains,[85] with one Lieutenant[86] and three State militia officers,[87] serving as aides, were to receive in time the three stars and the wreath of Brigadier General.

In short, to the nine general officers who survived Manassas, forty-two were to be added from men in the army along Bull Run that July day. Of the fifty-one, ten were doomed to lose their lives during the war. Eight, and no more than eight, were to prove plainly unqualified for the final grade they reached; nine were to show themselves of low capacity to command; seventeen could be regarded as average soldiers; the remaining seventeen were to be renowned.

[84] T. T. Munford, though his commission was never issued formally, Geo. H. Steuart and John Echols.

[85] Williams C. Wickham, E. P. Alexander, J. D. Imboden, R. L. Walker, James Conner, W. H. Stevens, W. H. Terry and G. M. Sorrel.

[86] James Dearing.

[87] Samuel McGowan, Johnson Hagood and S. R. Gist.

CHAPTER IX

The Star of Beauregard Is Beclouded

Before the star of any of these men of Manassas had been acclaimed, that of Beauregard was beclouded by a succession of controversies, the first of which arose over rations and wagons. During the days immediately following the battle of July 21, the poorly equipped commissaries and quartermasters were unable to supply promptly the larger army assembled at the Manassas railhead. Food ran low. Transportation was overtaxed.[1]

After some telegraphic exchanges, the scope of which was disputed later, General Beauregard appealed on July 29 directly to two Congressmen who temporarily had served as volunteer aides on his staff. He enclosed a *projet* drawn by one of his officers for a system of supply, and he revealed the fact that some of his regiments had been without food for more than twenty-four hours. "They have stood it . . . nobly," Beauregard wrote, "but if it happens again, I shall join one of their camps and share their wants with them; for I will never allow them to suppose that I feast while they suffer."

He then said: "The want of food and transportation has made us lose all the fruits of our victory. We ought at this moment to be in or about Washington, but we are perfectly anchored here, and God only knows when we will be able to advance; without these means we can neither advance nor retreat." Beauregard added: "From all accounts, Washington could have been taken up to the 24th instant by twenty thousand men! Only think of the brilliant results we have lost by the two causes referred to!" [2]

This startling letter was not marked "Confidential." Nothing indicated that it was designed solely for the eyes of its recipients. When they were told that the heroes of Manassas were hungry and that lack of food and of transportation had prevented the capture of Washington, they felt it their duty to read Beauregard's

[1] For the equipment of the Virginia railroads, on which Beauregard relied for the delivery of supplies, see *infra*, Appendix I, p. 683.
[2] 1 *Roman*, 121–22.

letter to Congress in secret session. The disclosure shocked the lawmakers. By resolution of August 1, Congress inquired of the President "whether or not he [had] received any authentic information going to show a want of sufficient and regular supply of food" for the Army. After hurried inquiry, Davis replied that he considered the condition of the commissariat "quite as good as was reasonable to expect" [3] and then, on August 4, he wrote Beauregard a friendly, well-reasoned letter. The substance of it was that the emergent needs of the Army had not been known, that they had been met when ascertained, and that Beauregard did himself injustice in "putting [the] failure to pursue the enemy to Washington to the account of short supplies of subsistence and transportation." Davis reviewed conditions at Manassas after the battle of July 21 and concluded: "Enough was done for glory, and the measure of duty was full; let us rather show the untaught that their desires are unreasonable, than, by dwelling on possibilities recently developed, give form and substance to the criticisms always easy to those who judge after the event." [4]

To this communication Beauregard made a somewhat apologetic reply. He had written, he said, "only for the purpose of expediting matters," and he regretted that his letter had been read to Congress. Davis, he was sure, had done more for the Army of the Potomac than could have been expected. As for the pursuit from the battlefield, Beauregard explained that he had never stated the Army could have followed the Federals on the 21st or the 22d, but "every news" confirmed him in the view that 20,000 men could have taken the city prior to the 24th of July. He answered with these words the closing appeal of Mr. Davis's letter: "We have, no doubt, by our success here achieved 'glory' for our country, but I am fighting for something more real and tangible, *i.e.,* to save our homes and firesides from our Northern invaders, and to maintain our freedom and independence as a nation. After that task shall have been accomplished, as I feel that I am only fit for private life, I shall retire to my home, if my means permit, never again to leave it, unless called upon to repel again the same or another foe." [5]

[3] 1 *Journal C. S. Congress,* 305, 306.
[4] *O. R.,* 2, 507–8. In 1 *Roman,* 122, the date of this letter is incorrectly given as August 10.
[5] Aug. 10, 1861; 1 *Roman,* 123–124.

That final sentence evidently was written to assure Mr. Davis that General Beauregard did not intend to heed those who were urging him to be a candidate in the election of November 5, 1861, for the office of President under the "permanent" constitution of the Confederacy.[6] Davis never had believed, so far as the records show, that Beauregard would oppose him or could defeat him by entering the political arena. In all probability Davis dropped the discussion after Beauregard's letter was received, not because of the General's disavowal of rival ambition but because of the statement "you have done more than could be expected of you for this army." Davis desired, apparently, nothing more in the matter than to clear his own skirts. He was not seeking to besmirch Beauregard's.

Had the facts been otherwise, the President could not have wished a sworn enemy to play more completely into his hands than Beauregard did by the blunders the General proceeded to make. In the first place, contrary to the plain limitations of existing military law, Beauregard did his utmost to have his troops regarded as a separate and autonomous Corps, which he was to handle in co-operation with Johnston, but with freedom of administrative control. His aim seems to have been to perpetuate the conditions that existed on the day of the Battle of Manassas. Correspondence and diplomacy alike failed to reconcile him to the fact that he was, as a new Secretary of War put it, second to Johnston "in command of the whole Army of the Potomac and not first in command of half the army." [7]

While controversy over this vexatious matter still was polite, Beauregard forwarded his report of the affair of July 18 at Black-

---

[6] Cf. 1 Roman, 135; 1 R. W. C. D., 88. It will be recalled that Davis was chosen by the Congress, under the constitution of Feb. 8, 1861, which stipulated (Art. II, sec. 1, par. 1) that he should "hold his office for one year, or until this provisional government shall be superseded by a permanent government, whichsoever shall first occur." The "permanent" constitution provided, in an article and section similarly numbered, that the President should hold office for six years and should not be re-eligible. Article VII, sec. 2, set forth that when five States had ratified the document, the Provisional Congress by law should decide when the election and the inauguration of the President should be held. (See James D. Richardson, A Compilation of the Messages and Papers of the Confederacy, vol. 1, pp. 8, 46, 53.) Congress provided that the election be held on the first Tuesday in November, 1861, and that the permanent government be inaugurated Feb. 22, 1862.

[7] O. R., 5, 904. For this controversy, see O. R., 5, 850, 877, 881, 903–4 ff, 913, 920, 921, 945, 990; O. R., 51, pt. 2, pp. 255, 272, 339, 345; 1 Roman, 157, 161–62, 187 ff; 1 R. W. C. D., 71, 88–89; Richmond Examiner, July 31, p. 3, col. 4; Aug. 7, 1861, p. 3, col. 1. Cf. infra, p. 118, n. 30.

burn's Ford.[8] It was a detailed document of nearly 4000 words
and it was received by most of his admirers with adulatory applause. "Nothing can be clearer or more forcible," said one Richmond journal, "than the style in which the General conveys his
thoughts. . . . In every respect, this is a model for all future
despatches, it is so intelligible, so impartial, so truthful, so unpretending, and so comprehensive." [9] From eulogium of this type
there was some dissent. The *Richmond Examiner* wrote: "One
of our contemporaries says that Gen. Beauregard writes like
Cæsar. Did Cæsar ever occupy all that space with accounts of a
battle in which fifteen men were killed? Some fifty officers were
mentioned for compliment in this report, and four private citizens.
At any rate, it is feared that the value of official compliment will
be cheapened." [10]

Undisturbed by this, General Beauregard revised the first draft
of his official account of the battle of July 21, and to it he added
such information as he had procured from the published Federal
reports of the engagement.[11] This document he forwarded to
the War Department about October 15. In the amplitude of 9000
words, he presented full details and occasional excursus.[12] At one
point, as he described the approaching climax of the battle, he
indulged himself in this sentence: "Oh, my country! I would
readily have sacrificed my life and those of all the brave men
around me to save your honor and to maintain your independence
from the degrading yoke which those ruthless invaders had come
to impose and render perpetual, and the day's issue has assured
me that such emotions must also have animated all under my
command." [13]

After the report reached the War Department, some one carelessly failed to forward it to the President. The first Mr. Davis
knew either of its arrival or of its content was on October 28,
when his attention was called to a Richmond paper of the 23d [14]
which contained a digest of parts of the document, introduced by
a reporter as follows: "I have been favored with a brief synopsis

---

[8] *O. R.*, 2, 440–47.
[9] *Richmond Dispatch*, Sept. 2, p. 2, col. 1; cf. *ibid.*, Sept. 12, 1861, p. 2, col. 1.
[10] *Richmond Examiner*, Sept 6, 1861, p. 2, col. 3.
[11] These had been printed in the *Richmond Examiner*, Aug. 14, p. 1, cols. 4–6; Aug.
16, 1861, p. 2, cols. 4–5.
[12] *O. R.*, 2, 484–504.   [13] *O. R.*, 2, 493.
[14] *Richmond Dispatch*, p. 3, col. 5.

of portions of General Beauregard's report of the battle of Manassa [*sic*] which has been forwarded to the War Department, and which will doubtless be published in a short time. General Beauregard opens with a statement of his position antecedent to the battle, and of the plan proposed by him to the Government of a junction of the armies of Shenandoah and Potomac, with a view to the relief of Maryland and the capture of the city of Washington, which plan was rejected by the President. Gen. B. states that he telegraphed the War Department on the 13th July of the contemplated attack of Gen. McDowell, urgently asking for a junction of General Johnston's force with his own, and continued to make urgent requests for the same until the 17th July, when the President consented to order General Johnston to his assistance." [15]

Mr. Davis sent at once for the report and read it. He found that the opening 600 words were an epitome of Beauregard's scheme of a great strategical combination, as communicated by Colonel Chesnut and rejected as impracticable.[16] Beauregard did not state officially that he had been "urgently asking" from July 13 for a junction of Johnston's forces with his own, but he referred to his belief, on that date, that a Federal advance was impending.[17] In concluding his sketch of his proposed grand strategy, Beauregard stated in his report: "This plan of operation . . . was not accepted at the time, from considerations which appeared so weighty as to more than counterbalance its proposed advantages."

That disclaimer, which had not been mentioned in the newspaper synopsis, manifestly changed the color of Beauregard's criticism, but another error darkened the report again. Beauregard said that, after he sent word on July 17 of the advance of Mc-Dowell, "General Johnston was immediately ordered to form a junction of his army corps with mine, should the movement be deemed advisable."[18] The exact language of the War Department's dispatch to Johnston had been: "If practicable, make the movement, sending your sick and baggage to Culpeper Court-House, either by railroad or by Warrenton. In all the arrangements exercise your discretion." [19]

[15] This was signed "A. M. G."
[16] See *supra*, pp. 42–43.
[17] O. R., 2, 485.
[18] *Ibid.*
[19] O. R., 2, 504.

Mr. Davis thought this difference material. The whole introduction to the report, in his opinion, was an effort on the part of
Beauregard to depreciate the work of others and to portray himself as the sole designer and executant of the Manassas triumph.
More specifically, the President thought that when Beauregard
styled the suggestions brought to Richmond on July 14 by Colonel
Chesnut "a plan of operations," the General created the impression
that the proposal had been formal and in writing.

Davis, accordingly, on October 30 sent a stiff protest to Beauregard. It began with a chilly "Sir" and ended "Very respectfully.
yours &c.," in pointed contrast to the "My dear General" and the
"Very truly, your friend" that had been employed in the letter
concerning the shortage of subsistence.[20] "With much surprise,"
the President wrote, after referring to the publication, "I found
that the newspaper statements were sustained by the text of your
report." Mr. Davis continued: "I was surprised, because if we did
differ in opinion as to the measures and purposes of contemplated
campaigns, such fact could have no appropriate place in the report
of a battle. Further, because it seemed to be an attempt to exalt
yourself at my expense, and especially because no such plan as
that described was submitted to me. It is true that sometime
before it was ordered you expressed a desire for the junction of
General Johnston's army with your own. The movement was
postponed until the operations of the enemy rendered it necessary,
and until it thereby became practicable to make it, with safety,[21]
to the valley of Virginia; hence I believe was secured the success
by which it was attended. If you have retained a copy of the plan
of campaign which, you say, was submitted to me through Colonel
Chesnut, allow me to request that you will furnish me with a
duplicate of it." [22]

The same day the President wrote to Colonel Chesnut for a
statement of what that gentleman had said when he came to
Richmond with Beauregard's plan. A little later, Mr. Davis asked
similar reports from General Lee and from General Cooper, who
had been present at the conference; and, as rumors were circulating in Richmond that the President had kept the army from

---

[20] Oct. 17, 1861; O. R., 5, 903.
[21] This comma was in the original, though it obscured the meaning.
[22] O. R., 2, 508.

following the Federals on the evening of July 21, Mr. Davis requested General Johnston "to say whether I obstructed the pursuit of the enemy after the victory at Manassas, or have ever objected to an advance or other active operations which it was feasible for the Army to undertake." [23]

Before answers to these inquiries were received, the whisper spread that Beauregard had resigned.[24] This was at once contradicted,[25] but denial was followed by the publication, through the *Richmond Whig,* of a letter in which the General acquainted the country with the fact that sharp differences had arisen between himself and the Administration. His communication read:

> Centreville, Va.
> Within hearing of the Enemy's Guns
> Nov. 3, 1861

To the Editors of the Whig:

Gentlemen:—My attention has just been called to an unfortunate controversy now going on relative to the publication of the synopsis of my report of the battle of Manassas. None can regret more than I do this publication, which was made without my knowledge or authority.

The President is the sole judge of when, and what parts of, the report of a commanding officer should be made public. I, individually, do not object to delaying its publication as long as the War Department shall think it proper and necessary for the success of our cause.

Meanwhile, I entreat my friends not to trouble themselves about refuting the slanders and calumnies aimed at me. Alcibiades, on a certain occasion, resorted to an extraordinary method to occupy the minds of his traducers: let then, "that synopsis" answer the same purpose for me in this instance.

If certain minds cannot understand the difference between *patriotism,* the highest civic virtue, and *office-seeking,* the lowest civic occupation, I pity them from the bottom of my heart. Suffice it to say, that I prefer the respect and esteem of my countrymen, to the admiration and envy of the world. I hope, for the sake of our cause and country, to be able, with the assistance of a kind Providence, to answer my calumniators with new victories over our national enemies; but I have nothing to ask of the country, the Government, or my friends, except to afford me all the aid they can, in the great struggle we are now engaged upon.

---

23 *O. R.,* 2, 509, 511, 512.
24 *Richmond Dispatch,* Nov. 4, 1861, p. 3, col. 1.
25 *Ibid.,* Nov. 5, 1861, p. 3, col. 1.

I am not, and never expect or desire to be, a candidate for any civil office in the gift of the people or of the Executive. The *acme* of my ambition is, after having cast my mite in defence of our sacred cause, and assisted, to the best of my ability, in securing our rights and independence as a nation, to retire into private life—my means then permitting—never again to leave my home, unless to fight anew the battles of my country.[26]

This letter was published two days after the Presidential election of November 5. For reasons that presently will appear, Beauregard's language probably was directed at Secretary Benjamin, of the War Department,[27] rather than at the Chief Executive; but the General's words could have been interpreted by the friends of Mr. Davis as an effort to becloud and to embarrass the beginning of the administration under the "permanent" constitution. Even the admirers of the "Hero of Sumter and Manassas" considered the letter ill-advised. "There was a theatrical circumstance and tone about it, that displeased many people." [28] It was, said *The Examiner,* a "very remarkable" document that would "hardly add to the General's reputation." The same paper asked bluntly: "What are we to infer from the *unique* heading—'within the sound of the enemy's guns'? [29] Are we expected to give special credit to the General's lucubrations by reason of a fact certainly not very unusual in military operations? or are we to consider it as merely thrown in to relieve the classical plea for the 'synopsis'? The whole letter is enigmatical in the extreme." [30]

Davis thought the communication worse than that. Letters from Colonel Chesnut, General Lee and General Cooper fortified the President in his contention that what General Beauregard had described as a "plan of operations," submitted on July 14,[31] was, in Davis's words, "a message from General Beauregard, but . . . no plan of battle or of campaign." [32] The Adjutant General, in his reply to the President, gave his recollection of what Colonel Chesnut had said of Beauregard's and of Johnston's need of rein-

[26] *Richmond Whig,* Nov. 7, reprinted in the *Richmond Dispatch,* Nov. 8, 1861, p. 3. col. 1. The newspaper text differs, though not materially, in punctuation and in one or two words, from that given in 1 *Roman,* 163–64.
[27] *Cf.* 1 R. W. C. D., 88–89.
[28] *Companions in Arms,* published in 1870, p. 248.
[29] The word in the original was not "sound" but "hearing."
[30] *Richmond Examiner,* Nov. 8, 1861, p. 2, cols. 1–2.
[31] *O. R.,* 2, 485.　　　　　[32] *O. R.,* 2, 513.

forcements. "Beyond these representations," said Cooper, "I am not sensible that any plan of operations was submitted, whether written or oral. . . ."[33] General Lee recalled more of the details of what Chesnut had stated, particularly of the benefits that might follow a junction of the forces of Beauregard and Johnston. "The advantages of the union of the armies on the Potomac had been more than once the subject of consideration by you," Lee wrote the President, "and I do not recollect that at the interview in question they were less apparent."[34]

As for the embarrassed Colonel Chesnut, a gentleman and a politician, he tried to reconcile the assertions of the President with those of Beauregard. In doing so, he disclosed the fact that, on his return to Manassas from Richmond, he had submitted to the General a written report on the conference. Davis took this up in a second letter to Chesnut. "I regret," said he, "as our conversation was to be reported and to be filed with the papers of General Beauregard, that the propositions were not reduced to writing and submitted for a written reply, or at least that I was not permitted to see the report of the interview before it became a public document."[35] Davis added: "My confidence and friendship for General Beauregard have been unmistakably manifested, and none can regret more than myself the error he has committed in bringing extraneous matter into his report of a battle, without any perceivable motive for doing so which is consistent with the good opinion I entertained of him."[36]

Beauregard himself did not reply until November 22 to the President's request of October 30 for a copy of the "plan of campaign" submitted through Colonel Chesnut.[37] When he did answer, Beauregard merely filed the text of Chesnut's report and other related papers as proof that he had offered on July 14 a definite "plan of operations for the defeat of the enemy."[38]

Of all these unhappy exchanges, nothing at the time was made public after the appearance of General Beauregard's letter to *The Whig*, but that communication itself had been sufficient to pique curiosity concerning his official account of the battle. On Novem-

33 *O. R.*, 2, 513.   34 *O. R.*, 2, 515.
35 *O. R.*, 2, 513.   36 *O. R.*, 2, 514.
37 Beauregard explained his long delay by saying that he had sent the original of the report to New Orleans for safekeeping.
38 The text of Beauregard's letter is in 1 *Roman*, 169; that of Chesnut's report of July 16 to Beauregard is in *ibid.*, 85-87.

ber 26, in secret session, Congress passed a resolution which requested the President to forward "the reports of all battles not heretofore communicated to Congress or published in full to the country." Mr. Davis replied at once that copies of all the reports had "been prepared to accompany the report of the Secretary of War, to which it was supposed proper to append them as documents." The report of the Secretary, he concluded, soon would be transmitted.[39] When, at length, in January 1362, this was laid before Congress, Beauregard's full report was attached, and was accompanied by Mr. Davis's letter of October 30 to Beauregard, by that of November 3 to General Johnston[40] and by the correspondence of Davis with Chesnut, Cooper and Lee. The President added, also, in direct endorsement on Beauregard's report, a correction of the General's statement concerning the discretionary orders given Johnston on July 17 to effect a junction of the two armies at Manassas.[41]

Discussion arose immediately in Congress over the printing of the report. The General's intimate admirers telegraphed to inquire whether he wished the document to appear and, if so, "must all, or a part, be published, omitting preliminary statement," which contained an outline of the "plan."[42] Beauregard answered: "Let Congress do for the best. We must think of the country before we think of ourselves." Then, as if his mind were fixed on other and larger concerns, he added: "I believe Burnside's expedition is intended for Wilmington, to cut off railroad to Charleston. Let government look to it."[43] This telegram was read to Congress by Roger Pryor. "The effect of its patriotic sentiment on Congress," Pryor wrote Beauregard, "would have been most grateful to your feelings had you witnessed it."[44]

Whatever the sentiment of individual members, their decision in secret session, after considering many motions during a two-day wrangle, was to publish the report without its strategical prologue or the correspondence Mr. Davis had attached to it.[45]

39 1 Journal C. S. Congress, 478, 486.   40 See supra, pp. 104–05.
41 For this endorsement, see O. R., 2, 504.   42 1 Roman, 173.
43 1 Roman, 173. The expedition was directed not against Wilmington but against Roanoke Island.
44 1 Roman, 173.
45 1 Journal C. S. Congress, 645, 646, 654, 655, 656. Cf. ibid., 658, 680, 691. See also Official Reports of Battles. Published by Order of Congress. Richmond. Enquirer Book & Job Press, 1862; see likewise Official Reports of Generals Johnston and Beauregard

This halted the controversy between Beauregard and the Administration.

Almost simultaneously, the command of General Beauregard in Northern Virginia was terminated. This was not solely—perhaps not even primarily—because of Beauregard's injudicious correspondence. As will be plain in the next chapter, his relations with General Johnston, marked on the surface by comradeship and due subordination, had a deeper aspect of jealousy that threatened the efficient handling of the army.[46] Nor was that all.

Differences between Beauregard and Secretary Benjamin had become irreconcilable. In November, 1861, during a dispute with the Secretary over the commission of officers for a proposed rocket battery, Beauregard told the President that his "motives must not be called into question" by Benjamin, and that he was being "put into the strait jackets of the law." Davis replied in the sternest terms: ". . . you surely did not intend to inform me that your army and yourself are outside of the limits of the law. It is my duty to see that the laws are faithfully executed, and I cannot recognize the pretension of any one that their restraint is too narrow for him." [47] There had been, also, revival of the dispute whether Beauregard commanded a semi-independent Corps or was second in command of the entire Army. On the last day of 1861, the General telegraphed the President: "Please state definitely what I am to command, if I do not command a corps, in consequence of latter being unauthorized." To this the President made no reply,[48] but the War Department ascertained that Beauregard was willing to accept service in Kentucky under Albert Sidney Johnston and, on January 26, 1862, ordered him thither.[49]

Very different was his departure from his arrival in Virginia. No less different was his place in the respect of the President and in the admiration of a large element of the South. His star had waned. Many still looked at Beauregard in the afterglow of Sumter and of Manassas, but the South, perplexed by his ego-

---

of the Battle of Manassas, July 21, 1861; also Official Reports of the Battle of 10th Sept. . . . Richmond, 1862. In both these books, Beauregard's report begins with what is the third paragraph on page 485 of O. R., 2: "The War Department having been informed by me by telegraph on the 17th of July," etc. Asterisks indicate the omission of reference to the rejected "plan of operations."

[46] See infra, p. 117.
[47] O. R., 5, 945.   [48] 1 Roman, 189.
[49] 1 Roman, 489, 491; O. R., 5, 1048; 1 R. W. C. D., 107.

tistical writings, no longer believed unanimously that in him it had found its Napoleon. The search for a leader had to be directed elsewhere and, naturally, first to Beauregard's colleague, "Joe" Johnston.

CHAPTER X

JOHNSTON PASSES A DARK WINTER

DURING THE WEEKS COVERED by Beauregard's controversy with the Administration, Joseph E. Johnston had been exercising uninterrupted, if not undisputed, command of the Army around Centreville. It had few skirmishes and no major battles to fight. There was a clash at Lewinsville on September 11, where "Jeb" Stuart showed some of the qualities of command;[1] on October 21 there was a handsome affair at Ball's Bluff, which ended in the rout by "Shanks" Evans's troops of a Federal force that had ventured across the Potomac.[2] Otherwise, except for an advance of the outposts to the hills overlooking Washington and a subsequent withdrawal of the Army from Fairfax Courthouse to Centreville,[3] little occurred to divert Johnston from what he considered his main task, that of "preparing our troops for active service by diligent instruction."[4]

As Johnston rode daily through their camps, his men, who were slowly increasing in number,[5] soon came to know a figure which, once seen, was recognized always. Johnston was of erect, trim figure and of middle height. His head was well moulded, his hair was grizzled; his short side whiskers of kindred color set off his florid complexion. In his glance there was more of questioning than of suspicion. Gray eyes that flashed often in quick resentment could gleam with a friendliness which seemed to play truant to his disciplined composure of countenance; his thin lips were as capable of smiling as of sneering. If Beauregard was likened by his admirers to an eagle, "Joe" Johnston seemed a gamecock.[6]

[1] *Johnston's Narrative*, 73; O. R., 5, 167 ff.

[2] O. R., 5, 289 ff; O. R., 51, pt. 2, pp. 352–53: *Richmond Dispatch*, Oct. 23, 1861, p. 3, col. 6; 34 S. H. S. P., 265; *Johnston's Narrative*, 80. Evans himself was in general command but was not on the scene of action.

[3] *Johnston's Narrative*, 74, 77; *Richmond Examiner*, Oct. 12, p. 2, col. 4 and p. 3, col. 2; Oct. 17, p. 2, col. 6; *Richmond Dispatch*, Oct. 21, 1861, p. 1, col. 4.

[4] *Johnston's Narrative*, 69.   [5] *Ibid.*, 70, 81.

[6] The best and fullest descriptions of his person are: *An English Combatant*, 305–6; *Companions in Arms*, 409; R. Taylor, 42–44; *Richmond Examiner*, July 22, 1861, p. 2, col. 3.

His reputation as a good soldier of the Mexican War had preceded him and found confirmation in his quick movement, his direct, brief answers, his strategic sense, his appearance of ready decision in matters of military routine.[7]

His essential quality, which was not disclosed at first, was contradiction. Had he lived and won renown in the Middle Ages, he might have been cited by physicians as proof that man is the creature of surging, ever-changing humors. Those of his subordinates who had demonstrated their faith in him and had won his confidence found him warm-hearted, affectionate, loyal, always the gentleman and quick to fight their battles. In his dealings with his military peers and his civil superiors Johnston was unpredictable. Today he was conciliatory and disposed to reason; tomorrow he might be sensitive and jealous of his powers. In one letter he was the chivalrous gentleman-soldier; in the next he would insist on every jot and tittle of authority conferred by army regulations. Ere long Jefferson Davis was to find that any letter from "Joe" Johnston might smoke with wrath as it lay on the executive desk. Love was not easily destroyed in his heart; hate once inflamed always was cherished.

When Johnston first had gone to Harpers Ferry, he had written amiably to Lee's Adjutant General that he begged "to receive the views and instructions of the Commander-in-Chief";[8] but he had not been at his post a month before he had become testy over the disapproval by Lee or by Letcher of his action in authorizing a militia officer of doubtful sobriety to raise two regiments.[9] After Manassas, Johnston flatly informed the Adjutant General that he could not "regard" orders from Lee, then in titular command in Virginia, "because they are illegal."[10] Toward Davis, at the outset, Johnston's manner had been friendly. In the case of an early misunderstanding over the evacuation of Harpers Ferry, he had said: "I know myself to be a careless writer, and will not, therefore, pretend to have expressed clearly the opinions I wished to put before the Government."[11] Davis had responded in kind. "May God bless and direct you," he had concluded one letter, "in

---

[7] For some of the early, favorable estimates of his ability, see *Richmond Examiner,* Apr. 26, p. 2, col. 5; June 21, p. 2, col. 5; *Richmond Dispatch,* July 26, 1861, p. 2, col. 2; 18 *S. H. S. P.,* 173.

[8] *O. R,,* 2, 881; cf. *ibid.,* 858.   [9] *O. R.,* 2, 948, 959; *O. R.,* 51, pt. 2, p. 145.

[10] *O. R.,* 2, 1007.   [11] *O. R.,* 2, 929.

this critical hour of our national history. Your friend . . ." [12] While Johnston's withdrawal from Harpers Ferry had been regretted, nothing occurred during the early summer to indicate any scorn on his part of fixed positions, any weakness as a military administrator, any neglect of public property. At the time Johnston had started to join Beauregard and had wished to know his rank in relation to that officer, the exchange of telegrams with the President had been both candid and tactful.[13] Scarcely a shadow, it will be remembered, had fallen across the council table when Johnston and Davis met at Manassas after the battle.

Until August 31, 1861, all went well between the two. On that date, Mr. Davis sent to the Senate for confirmation the names of the five officers who, under the act of May 16, 1861, were to be given the rank of full General, instead of that of Brigadier General, which previously had been the highest in Confederate service.[14] First on the submitted list, to rank from May 16, 1861, was the Adjutant General, Samuel Cooper; second was Albert Sidney Johnston, as of May 30; third came R. E. Lee, ranking as of June 14; fourth stood Joseph E. Johnston, with grade of General from July 4; fifth was P. G. T. Beauregard, whose commission was to date from July 21, Manassas Day.[15]

This order of nominations, which was confirmed at once by the Senate, outraged Joseph E. Johnston. From that day forward, he never was the same man in his dealing with the President. Vehemently, as if rank were the most important factor in his service to the South, Johnston argued his case. He held that he was the senior officer of the United States Army to resign and to join the Confederacy, that he was guaranteed this seniority under Confederate law, and that the act for the appointment of Generals of full rank was simply a measure to raise the grade of those who had been Brigadiers in the regular Army of the Confederacy, and not an act under which the President could change the relative seniority of those already made Brigadier General, C. S. A.[16] In Johnston's eyes, the correct order should have been: himself,

[12] O. R., 2, 974.
[13] O. R., 2, 985; Johnston's Narrative, 38–39.
[14] See Wright, 46; for the act, see IV O. R., 1, p. 326. The statute explicitly said that "appointments to the rank of general, after the Army is organized, shall be made by selection from the Army."
[15] Wright, 9–11.
[16] Johnston's Narrative, 71.

Samuel Cooper, Albert Sidney Johnston, R. E. Lee, and P. G. T. Beauregard.[17]

In his wrath at what he considered a violation both of law and of justice, Johnston wrote the President a protest, which for two days he refrained from mailing. At the end of forty-eight hours he still was so convinced of the correctness of his argument that he forwarded the letter without verbal change.[18] The communication, some 1800 words in length,[19] stated Johnston's contention clearly enough, but much that was intemperate it added. Said Johnston: "I will not affect to disguise the surprise and mortification produced in my mind by the action taken in this matter by the President and by Congress. . . . I now and here declare my claims, that notwithstanding these nominations by the President and their confirmation by Congress I still rightfully hold the rank of first general in the Armies of the Southern Confederacy. . . . Heretofore those who disputed my authority as general have done so because they denied the existence of the Government whose officer I claimed to be. Now that Government joins the hostile power in denying my authority. When I sent back the missives of the Government of the United States, because they ignored the Government which I served and acknowledged, I little thought that one of the acts of that Government would be to ignore me as its officer by trampling upon its own solemn legislative and executive action. . . . It seeks to tarnish my fair fame as a soldier and a man, earned by more than thirty years of laborious and perilous service. I had but this, the scars of many wounds, all honorably taken in my front and in the front of battle, and my father's Revolutionary sword. It was delivered to me from his venerated hand, without a stain of dishonor. Its blade is still unblemished as when it passed from his hand to mine. . . . If the action against which I have protested be legal, it is not for me to question the expediency of degrading one who has served laboriously from the commencement of the war on this frontier and borne a prominent part in the only great event of that war. for the benefit of persons neither of whom[20] has yet struck a blow for this Confederacy."

[17] Ibid., 72.
[19] IV O. R., 1, 605-8.
[18] Ibid., 72-73.
[20] That is, Albert Sidney Johnston and R. E. Lee.

This letter Davis read with rising wrath, not only as an insulting reflection on him but also as a display of ill temper, of unreason and—what was more personal—of ingratitude on the part of Johnston. For he felt that Johnston owed to him the appointment as Quartermaster General in the old army. "I as Chairman of the Committee on Military Affairs [of the United States Senate]," he wrote years afterward, "reported the nomination [of Johnston] with the recommendation that it be confirmed. . . . [It] met with serious opposition, and . . . all my power and influence were required to prevent its rejection." [21] Further, in Davis's eyes, Johnston's complaint was without basis in law or in fact;[22] but instead of engaging, after his habit, in a long verbal controversy, he decided to rebuke Johnston in a few sharp sentences. Accordingly he wrote this letter:

> Sir: I have just received and read your letter of the 12th. instant. Its language is, as you say, unusual; its arguments and statements utterly one sided, and its insinuations as unfounded as they are unbecoming.
> I am, &c.
>
> Jeff'n Davis [23]

Johnston made no reply to this. The issue passed, for the time, into the realm of those resentments that in private are remembered but in public are ignored. At the end of September, when Davis visited Johnston's headquarters to confer on the possibility of an offensive in Maryland,[24] the General showed him all courtesy and did not refer to disputed seniority. It might have remained, in Johnston's mind, an isolated if gross example of personal injustice had not a change of large consequences in the administration of

[21] Davis to James Lyons, Aug. 30, 1878; 8 *Rowland*, 257. Johnston's friends never admitted that Davis deserved credit for the confirmation of Johnston's appointment. They insisted that Davis gave his support to Albert Sidney Johnston and that Davis was much angered when John B. Floyd, Secretary of War, procured the place for Joseph E. Johnston, whose niece was Floyd's adopted daughter. Some of Johnston's friends believed that Davis took his revenge when he gave A. S. Johnston seniority above J. E. Johnston.

[22] For Davis's argument, see 8 *Rowland, loc. cit.* The substance of the contention by the President was that J. E. Johnston's rank of Brigadier General, in which Johnston asserted seniority, was a staff commission which prohibited assumption of command of troops. Seniority for line command, Davis insisted steadfastly, had to be based exclusively on line service.

[23] IV *O. R.*, 1, 611.

[24] This conference subsequently became the basis of another dispute. See *O. R.*, 5, 884; 8 *Rowland*, 506–12; 9 *ibid.*, 192–93, 196; 34 *S. H. S. P.*, 128 ff; G. W. Smith, *Confederate War Papers* (cited hereafter as *G. W. Smith*), 13 ff; 1 *Davis*, 449 ff.

the War Department brought into office a man with whom Johnston was doomed to clash ceaselessly.

L. Pope Walker of Alabama, Mr. Davis's first appointee to the secretaryship, was in every respect a gentleman of high sensibilities and devotion, but he was without administrative ability, was plagued with ill health, and was inclined to postpone a difficult decision. As Walker attempted, moreover, to handle many matters of detail that should have been delegated to subordinates, uncompleted public business accumulated in his office. Congress and the press complained; Walker on September 16 resigned; in his place Mr. Davis named the Attorney General, Judah P. Benjamin, as acting and then as regular Secretary of War.[25]

This brilliant son of English Jews had been born at St. Croix in 1811, while his parents were seeking to enter the United States. He had been reared in Louisiana and schooled at Yale. When a leader of the bar, though only 42, he had been elected to the United States Senate from the State of his adoption. Within two years he had become one of the most distinguished members of that body. His speeches had been as solid in content as they had been clear and powerful in argument. One of his sharpest passages had been with Davis, then Senator from Mississippi. Davis was convinced immediately that he was in the wrong and thereafter he was careful to be more than just to his legislative opponent. The urbanity that Benjamin displayed in that affair, without the quiver of anything that might have been mistaken for cowardice, was typical of his manner not less than of his character. Short, round, rosy and well groomed, he wore a smile that frowning disaster could dim for a moment only. He always looked as if he had just risen at the end of an enjoyed dinner to greet a friend with pleasant news.

His optimism was equalled by his industry. In his dispatch of business Benjamin exhibited a mind that was sure both of its penetration and of its quickness. Perhaps it was a mind too quick.

[25] IV O. R., 1, 600, 602–3, 957; De Leon, 50. The most intimate sketches of Walker appear in 1 R. W. C. D., 37, 38, 43–44, 62, 63, 63–64, 77. See also Richmond Examiner, Sept. 16, p. 3, col. 2; ibid., Sept. 19, p. 2, col. 5, Sept. 20, p. 2, col. 3; Richmond Whig, Sept. 19, p. 2, col. 1, Sept. 21, 1861, p. 2, col. 2; Ulrich B. Phillips, ed., The Correspondence of Robert Toombs, Alexander H. Stephens, and Howell Cobb (cited hereafter as Toombs, etc. Letters), 575–76; Mrs. Chesnut, 78. For Walker's subsequent activities, see Richmond Dispatch, Sept. 24, p. 3, col. 1, Sept. 28, 1861, p. 3, col. 1; 2 R. W. C. D., 171; 1 C. M. H., 605.

For within a few autumnal weeks, though he had no previous experience in military affairs, he came to believe that he had mastered the administration of the War Department. With this confidence in himself, he combined a large conception of the scope of his duties and a loyalty to the President so complete that no argument by the Generals in the field could weigh against the wishes of Mr. Davis, declared or anticipated. Always a strict constructionist, Benjamin saw the President as literally the Commander in Chief, and the Secretary of War as the agent both for executing the will and defending the action of his superior officer. So great were Benjamin's powers of verbal persuasion that, after a personal interview, he could carry all his subordinates with him even when they were unconvinced. In correspondence, he was not so successful. His written paragraphs bristled with a palisade of "I's."

So facile was the reasoning of Judah Benjamin, and so precise his logic that often he angered other men by making them seem clumsy. Most of all he maddened and baffled Joseph E. Johnston. After Davis's curt reply to Johnston's protest concerning his seniority, Benjamin's fealty to the President led the Secretary to deal with the General as if Johnston were an adversary at the bar.[26] It was not difficult to get the better of the General. Johnston's irascibility and his lack of skill in dialectics made him appear, for some months, generally in the wrong.

Until January, the situation was embarrassed, further, by the fact that Beauregard, though devoted to Johnston personally,[27] could not bring himself to regard his own command otherwise than as a separate Corps, over which Johnston's control was nominal. Beauregard's friends insisted that his relations with Johnston were perfect—that between them there was "no clashing of authority, no contention, no heart-burning." [28] Admirers of the two Generals lauded both;[29] but at the very time that Johnston was protesting against being overslaughed, he had to

---

[26] Mrs. Chesnut's *Diary* contains many illuminating references to Benjamin. See also 1 *R. W. C. D.*, 38, 71, 88, 89; *Richmond Dispatch*, Sept. 23, p. 3, col. 1; Oct. 26, p. 3, col. 1; Oct. 28, p. 3, col. 1; Nov. 22, 1861, p. 3, col. 2; *Toombs, etc. Letters*, 579. *Cf.* 8 *Rowland*, 180.

[27] *O. R.*, 5, 990; *O. R.*, 51, pt. 2, p. 379.

[28] *Richmond Examiner*, Sept. 6, 1861, p. 2, col. 6.

[29] *Conner*, 62; *Richmond Dispatch*, Oct. 21, 1861, p. 2, col. 5.

notify the President that Beauregard appeared to be dissatisfied with a subordinate relation.[30] Mr. Davis sought to uphold Johnston's authority, but he was not explicit and, a little later, in permitting Beauregard to correspond directly with him [31] on military matters, he displayed an excess of tact or of caution that may have encouraged momentarily Beauregard's ambitions for autonomous command. At that juncture, Secretary Benjamin took his fellow Louisianian in hand and by a succession of flawlessly reasoned letters he so routed Beauregard that the General, as already stated, became willing to accept command in the West.[32]

Johnston gained nothing by this, though his authority, in the main, was sustained. He had accumulating woes and humiliations of his own. By relying too much on untrained officers of the general staff, he neglected on occasion the care of public property and the service of the commissaries and the quartermasters. Whenever he erred in administration, he brought down on himself a sharp letter from the President or from the Secretary of War.[33] In particular, the commander's failure to undertake promptly a partial reorganization of the Army led to unpleasantness, deep and prolonged.

After the President visited the Army at the end of September,[34] he directed General Johnston to brigade together troops from the same State, in the belief that this would create wholesome rivalry. For transfer of the regiments Davis gave time and discretion to Johnston who, while not averse to the reorganization, considered it dangerous to undertake in the presence of the enemy.[35] He accordingly took no step to break up old Brigades, which had been formed casually as regiments from different States reported for duty at Manassas. Because of State pride, Davis impatiently desired the Mississippi troops to be brigaded together,[36] and when

---

[30] Johnston's letter is not in *O. R.*, but its content may be inferred from Davis to Johnston, Sept. 13, 1861, *O. R.*, 5, 850. Cf. *G. W. Smith*, 311: "Whether sanctioned by law and recognized by the Department or not, there were two separate General's commands in the Army of the Potomac at that time—and they were called and known as Corps. General Johnston commanded one, General Beauregard the other."

[31] Cf. *O. R.*, 5, 907-8.

[32] See *O. R.*, 5, 877, 881, 903, 904-5; for Davis's statement of the relationship of Beauregard to Johnston, see *O. R.*, 5, 906 ff.

[33] Cf. *O. R.*, 5, 883, 897, 905, 934, 941, 946-47, 948-49, 962, 1036-37, 1045. *Cf.* 8 *Rowland*, 146; *Toombs, etc. Letters*, 575-76, 577, 580.

[34] The date is in some doubt. It may have been Oct. 1 *et seq.*

[35] *Johnston's Narrative*, 78; *O. R.*, 5, 913.

[36] Cf. *O. R.*, 5, 913, 960.

he found early in December that they were scattered, he directed their "immediate assignment" to the Brigades of Generals Richard Griffith and W. H. C. Whiting, both of them natives of Mississippi.[37] Johnston protested against this, but received renewed orders. Again he expostulated to no purpose.[38]

At length, most imprudently, Whiting himself informed the War Department that he did not wish a Mississippi Brigade.[39] Whiting did this, as he wrote Gustavus Smith, both because he considered regimentation by States "a policy as suicidal as foolish" and also because he did not wish any of his regiments taken from him. "They are used to me," he explained, "and I to them, and accustomed to act together." Besides, Whiting was outraged that an ambitious Mississippian was trying to prevail upon two of Whiting's Colonels to ask transfer to the command of the gentleman from Mr. Davis's own State. "If they persist in Richmond," said Whiting, "they will be guilty of inconceivable folly."[40]

This was not the first time Whiting had made himself conspicuous. Son of an officer of the United States Army, he had been graduated No. 1 in the class of 1845 at West Point,[41] with marks which were said to have been the highest ever made at the Academy to that date.[42] A handsome man of intellectual countenance, he was not unmindful of his social position and professional standing and, at the time, was somewhat brusque in his dealings with the War Office. In November he had demanded of the Adjutant General, "What are they sending me unarmed new regiments for? Don't want them. They will only be in my way."[43]

This cavalier language apparently had been forgiven Whiting,[44] perhaps because of his high name and the excellent condition of his own command;[45] but now nothing could atone for unwillingness to accept a Brigade from his native Mississippi, whose earlier volunteers the President himself had led in the Mexican War. At the instance of the offended Davis, the Secretary of War in due time administered Whiting a stern rebuke. The President, Ben-

[37] O. R., 5, 979, 978; O. R., 51, pt. 2, p. 402.
[38] O. R., 5, 985, 978, 993.
[39] He wrote, evidently, on Dec. 19, 1861, but his letter seems to have been lost. Cf. O. R., 5, 1011.
[40] 26 S. H. S. P., 151.
[41] Cullum, No. 1231.
[42] 26 S. H. S. P., 135.
[43] O. R., 5, 961.
[44] O. R., 5, 963; O. R., 51, pt. 2, p. 381.
[45] Cf. O. R., 51, pt. 2, p. 1072.

jamin wrote Johnston, had no desire to give General Whiting a command that officer did not wish. Furthermore, as there was no other Brigade available for Whiting, would Johnston have the Brigadier report in the Valley District to serve at his rank of Major of Engineers in the regular Army? [46] This was, of course, undisguised and humiliating demotion for Whiting. It was coupled with a reminder to his commanding General: "The President," Benjamin concluded in his letter, "requests me to say that he trusts you will hereafter decline to forward to him communications of your subordinates having so obvious a tendency to excite a mutinous and disorganizing spirit in the Army." [47]

This language readily might have provoked Johnston's wrath, if not his resignation. Instead, it brought to light one of the most peculiar contradictions of his nature, a sudden cooling of his temper sometimes, though not always, when a controversy grew hot. Johnston assumed his blame for forwarding the letter from General Whiting, apologized, interceded and, after some rebuffs, saved Whiting's pride and service to the Army [48] by having that officer withdraw the offending letter for a "modification" that never was made.

Johnston's conduct in this episode perhaps was construed in Richmond as proof that he would eat humble pie when it was put before him by a stern cook, though there is no evidence on this point one way or the other. If such a conclusion was reached, Johnston soon shattered it by firing again in hot resentment. Negligently, during the autumn, some of his subordinates had failed to require that the weapons of sick, absent or discharged soldiers in certain commands be put in depot.[49] The arms were said to be in the possession of the commands and, inferentially, with no assurance of proper care. This state of affairs led to some correspondence with the War Department and quite naturally may have created the belief in Richmond that the surplus muskets of Johnston's troops, in a time of acute shortage, had better be placed in the hands of unarmed, waiting regiments than left where they might be lost or left behind during a sudden troop movement. On January 24, 1862, Johnston received from the Secretary of War an urgent order to send to Richmond 6000 stands of surplus

[46] *O. R.*, 5, 1011.   [47] *O. R.*, 5, 1012.
[48] *O. R.*, 5, 1015, 1016, 1020, 1028, 1035; *ibid.*, 11, pt. 3, p. 547.
[49] *O. R.*, 5, 807.

arms.[50] The General replied at once that this would deprive him of weapons for returned convalescents and of all arms for recruits. In the circumstances, he served notice that he would not countenance the expense of recruiting unless ordered to do so.[51] Fortunately, this defiant if natural answer came into the experienced hands of friendly Adjutant General Cooper, who knew how to reason with Johnston. A correspondence that might have produced much friction was handled tactfully;[52] but it left Johnston in a suspicious, if not a resentful, state of mind. "It will not do to send your arms to Richmond," he wrote Whiting in February. "You will never see them again if you do." [53]

Other tests of the temper of the commanding General were at hand, tests that must have seemed to him to threaten the life of the Army. In September, 1861,[54] Johnston had received as Major Generals, to direct Divisions then in the making, Gustavus W. Smith, former Street Commissioner of New York City, whose career was to form a singular chapter in the history of the Confederacy, and Earl Van Dorn, who had been junior Major of the 2nd United States Cavalry. The diminutive Van Dorn was a man of some reputation, whose arrival in Virginia had been chronicled with much applause.[55] Johnston had asked for him and had assigned him, on October 4, to Beauregard's unrecognized First Corps.[56] There had followed some protest by Van Dorn that his command had not been adequate to his rank. Then there had been commotion because Benjamin ignorantly had assigned all the cavalry of the Army to Van Dorn in order to make his command accord with his grade. Both Van Dorn and Johnston had pointed out the unwisdom of this and, in the end, had prevailed upon the Secretary to correct a bad blunder.[57] Now, on Jan. 10, 1862, Van Dorn was relieved and was ordered to the Trans-Mississippi.[58] As Beauregard was then about to leave the Army, Johnston felt that he would not have left with him a sufficient number of subordinates capable of handling large bodies of men.

While Johnston was attempting to adjust himself to the loss of

[50] O. R., 5, 1022, 1043. [51] O. R., 5, 1049.
[52] O. R., 5, 1049, 1050, 1064; O. R., 51, pt. 2, p. 459.
[53] O. R., 5, 1069. [54] O. R., 5, 866, 881.
[55] Richmond Dispatch, Sept. 18, p. 3, col. 1; Sept. 24, p. 3, col. 1; Sept. 30, p. 3, col. 1; Oct. 2, 1861, p. 3, col. 1.
[56] O. R., 5, 797, 829, 877, 889; O. R., 51, pt. 2, p. 325.
[57] O. R., 5, 922, 934–35, 950, 954, 960–61. [58] O. R., 5, 1027.

Van Dorn and was pleading for trained men, there came on February 3 a most disquieting paper from "Stonewall" Jackson. That officer had been made a Major General in the Provisional Army of the Confederacy on Oct. 7, 1861.[59] Two weeks later, when Johnston's department had been divided into three districts,[60] Jackson had been assigned to the Shenandoah Valley.[61] "Stonewall" had considered that "promotion among men is only a temptation and trouble," but, he said, "I am very thankful to that God who withholds no good thing from me (though I am so utterly unworthy and ungrateful) for making me a Major General." [62] After a moving farewell to his old Brigade,[63] which subsequently was sent to him against Johnston's wishes,[64] Jackson on November 5 [65] had established headquarters at Winchester. To the general satisfaction of the population of the Valley,[66] he had gone to work with great energy to improve his troops, who were few and poor.[67]

Within fifteen days, Jackson had developed a well-considered plan for an advance on Romney.[68] In acceptance of the maxims of Napoleon, he believed that "an active winter's campaign is less liable to produce disease than a sedentary life by camp-fires in winter-quarters." [69] Although this plan had seemed to Johnston to contemplate more than could easily be accomplished in a high, mountainous country during the winter,[70] it was approved. To aid the execution, Brig. Gen. W. W. Loring, who had been guarding the Staunton-Parkersburg road, was given discretion to leave a skeleton force on the crest of the Allegheny Mountains and to move with the remainder to Jackson.[71] Loring had started with alacrity and optimism [72] and by December 21 had his van in

---

59 Cf. *O. R.*, 5, 892, 896. Rank in the Provisional Army, indicated by the abbreviation P. A. C. S., corresponded roughly to that of United States Volunteers, as distinguished from permanent commission in the regular Army.

60 *O. R.*, 5, 913. This was done primarily, though in vain, to settle the question of Beauregard's relationship to Johnston.

61 *O. R.*, 5, 909, 925; *O. R.*, 51, pt. 2, p. 364.   62 *Mrs. Jackson*, 195, 199.

63 *Richmond Dispatch*, Nov. 8, 1861, p. 1, col. 4; Henry Kyd Douglas, *I Rode with Stonewall* (cited hereafter as *Douglas*), 15, 16.

64 *O. R.*, 5, 921, 940, 946, 959.   65 *O. R.*, 5, 389, 937.

66 *Richmond Dispatch*, Nov. 4, 1861, p. 2, col. 1; Jan. 9, 1862, p. 1, col. 1.

67 *O. R.*, 5, 389, 943.

68 *O. R.*, 5, 965 ff. This is an important paper, because it is the first of Jackson's written proposals for an independent operation.

69 *Mrs. Jackson*, 218.   70 *O. R.*, 5, 966.

71 *O. R.*, 5, 968–69.

72 *O. R.*, 5, 975, 983.

Winchester.[73] Perhaps because Loring, former Colonel of the United States Mounted Rifles, had shown much displeasure when Gen. R. E. Lee had assumed general charge of Western Virginia in August, 1861,[74] Jackson had suggested that Loring be continued in command of his troops but that they be designated the First Division of the Army of the Valley.[75] Jackson even had discussed that question directly with Loring. After Loring had expressed the belief that the War Department wished his force to remain separate as the Army of the Northwest, Jackson had acquiesced and had withdrawn the suggestion.[76]

On January 1, 1862, the march on Romney had begun. Jackson's own Brigade had been under Brig. Gen. Richard B. Garnett, one-time Captain of the 6th United States Infantry and a veteran Indian fighter.[77] Loring had commanded three Brigades. Two of militia had joined the column.[78] Jackson had advanced quickly, though he had complained of the frequency with which Loring had halted.[79] He had felt, also, that Loring had permitted some of his men to become demoralized.[80] When Jackson had cleared the Federals from a large area, he had left Loring at Romney, to go into winter quarters, and had returned Garnett to Winchester. This arrangement had been made for the reason that Garnett's experienced and fast-marching regiments could, in Jackson's opinion, have moved more quickly than Loring's troops to any threatened part of the district.[81]

In none of this had Jackson impressed Loring or the soldiers of the Army of the Northwest. On the contrary, some of the men under Loring had protested that Jackson was crazy, and they jeeringly had insisted that his Brigade was as mad as he because it had cheered him whenever it had seen him.[82] Left in wintry isolation at Romney, Loring and his subordinates had felt that Jackson had discriminated against them in favor of his former Brigade. Discontent had deepened demoralization; an eminent politician in Richmond had received a complaint from one of Loring's Colonels;[83] a round robin asking for the withdrawal of

[73] O. R., 5, 1003.   [74] 1 R. E. Lee, 550.
[75] O. R., 5, 1003.   [76] O. R., 5, 1005.
[77] Cullum, No. 1087. For his appointment, see O. R., 5, 967, 981.
[78] O. R., 5, 389–90. Three Brigades of militia had been called out, but apparently those employed on the expedition had been consolidated into two.
[79] O. R., 5, 390.   [80] O. R., 5, 393.   [81] O. R., 5, 393–94, 1034, 1039
[82] 23 S. H. S. P., 124.   [83] O. R., 5, 1040–41.

the command to Winchester had been signed by eleven officers, had been seconded by Loring and had been forwarded to Jackson.[84] Before this had reached Richmond, the Administration had become alarmed over the reported exposure of Loring's force and had called on Johnston to investigate,[85] but Mr. Davis had not waited for a report by the inspector whom Johnston had dispatched to the Valley.[86] On January 30, at the President's instance, Secretary Benjamin had telegraphed Jackson: "Our news indicates that a movement is being made to cut off General Loring's command. Order him back to Winchester immediately." [87]

The paper that lay before Johnston on February 3 was a letter from Jackson dated January 31, to be forwarded through channels to the Secretary of War. In this communication, Jackson acknowledged the receipt of orders from Benjamin and reported their execution. Then he wrote: "With such interference in my command I cannot expect to be of much service in the field and accordingly respectfully request to be ordered to report for duty to the superintendent of the Virginia Military Institute, as has been done in the case of other professors. Should this application not be granted, I respectfully request that the President will accept my resignation from the Army." [88]

[84] O. R., 5, 1048; cf. ibid., 1054.   [85] O. R., 5, 1049.
[86] O. R., 5, 1051, 1071.
[87] O. R., 5, 1050, 1051. Numerous quotations from Northern newspapers and some letters by Southern soldier-correspondents on the progress of Jackson's "Romney campaign" appear in the Richmond Dispatch, Jan. 11, p. 3, col. 2, Jan. 14, p. 3, col. 2, Jan. 15, p. 2, col. 4, Jan. 20, p. 1, col. 4, Jan. 21, 1862, p. 3, col. 2. In the Hotchkiss Papers is an undated clipping of 1884 from the Pittsburgh Weekly Chronicle Telegraph, with extracts from the diary of "C. A. R."
[88] O. R., 5, 1053. Jackson's request to be returned to his professorship at V. M. I. was based on interesting circumstances. The Institute had been closed on July 18, 1861, and had not been reopened in the autumn, but the Confederate Congress had directed that work be resumed Jan. 1, 1862, for the training of future officers (J. C. Wise's V. M. I., 172). In October, 1861, the Board of Visitors had directed that instructors then in the Army be recalled to their posts. Adj. Gen. W. H. Richardson had written Jackson confidentially that if he felt he should remain on duty in the field, the Institute doubtless would permit him to do so and to resume his professorship at the close of the war (W. H. Richardson to T. J. Jackson, Oct. 14, 1861, Jackson MSS.). Jackson had replied, Oct. 22, 1861, that he had an obligation to continue field service. "At the close of hostilities," he wrote, "I desire to resume the duties of my chair, and, accordingly, respectfully request that, if consistent with the interest of the Institute, the action of the Board of Visitors may be such as to admit of my return, upon the restoration of peace" (Wise's V. M. I., 172–73). Meanwhile, on or about October 10, Jackson had applied for commission in the regular Army of the Confederacy (T. J. Jackson to J. P. Benjamin, Oct. 10 [?], 1861, Jackson MSS.). On October 31, he had been commissioned Major of Artillery (Commission, ibid.). When, therefore, Jackson asked for a return to V. M. I. or the acceptance of his resignation, he was in the position where he stood to lose both regular and provisional rank in the Army were his resignation accepted, but, at the same time, he had reasonable assurance of return to the Institute.

Johnston read this with dismay. Beauregard and Van Dorn were gone; there was no assurance that Whiting would be retained in command; two Brigadier Generals were in Congress; one was absent sick.[89] Now Johnston was to lose Jackson as a result of mandatory orders from Benjamin that had not been communicated through army headquarters.[90] Johnston held his temper in the face of this disregard of his authority and, in a letter that showed his best qualities, urged Jackson to withdraw his resignation. He wrote: "Under ordinary circumstances, a due sense of one's own dignity, as well as care for professional character and official rights would demand such a course as yours, but the character of this war, the great energy exhibited by the Government of the United States, the danger in which our very existence as an independent people lies, requires sacrifices from us all who have been educated as soldiers. I receive my information of the order of which you have such cause to complain from your letter. Is not that as great an official wrong to me as the order itself to you? Let us dispassionately reason with the Government on this subject of command, and if we fail to influence its practice, then ask to be relieved from positions the authority of which is exercised by the War Department, while the responsibilities are left to us. I have taken the liberty to detain your letter to make this appeal to you, not merely from warm feelings of personal regard, but from the official opinion which makes me regard you as necessary to the country in your present position."[91]

Until February 4 or 5, no word on the subject came directly to Johnston from Benjamin. Then arrived a summary of the orders to General Jackson, which the Secretary prudently stated he had sent at the instance of the President. Benjamin adjoined some strategical reflections on the general outlook and concluded, humbly enough: "But these are mere suggestions, the decision being left to yourself."[92] Johnston did not reply to this immediately. Instead, on the 5th, he wrote his friend the Adjutant General and enclosed a letter which he requested General Cooper to lay before the President, to whom it was addressed. This was not a plea that Jackson be requested to withdraw the resignation but a formal application that Johnston himself be relieved of

[89] As of Feb. 7; *O. R.*, 5, 1053.   [90] *O. R.*, 5, 1059.
[91] *O. R.*, 5, 1059–61.   [92] *O. R.*, 5, 1059.

responsibility for the Valley District "on the ground that it is necessary for the public interest." Johnston explained: "A collision of the authority of the honorable Secretary of War with mine might occur at a critical moment. In such an event disaster would be inevitable. The responsibility of the command has been imposed upon me. Your excellency's known sense of justice will not hold me to that responsibility while the corresponding control is not in my hands." He added a request that Davis visit the Army and dropped a flattering hint that "the highest benefit would be your assuming the command." [93]

As Jackson made no reply to Johnston concerning withdrawal of the resignation, Johnston felt by February 7 that he should not hold the document longer. He accordingly sent it to Richmond with this endorsement: "Respectfully forwarded. I don't know how the loss of this officer can be supplied. General officers are much wanted in this department." [94] By the same mail he answered Benjamin and, after discussing various administrative matters, threw back on the Secretary all responsibility for the situation in the Valley. "Let me suggest," he said coldly, "that, having broken up the dispositions of the military commander, you give whatever other orders may be necessary." [95]

Fortunately, an impasse was avoided. On the day Jackson forwarded his formal resignation, he wrote his Lexington neighbor, Gov. John Letcher, a full account of what had happened. This read as follows:

Winchester, January 31st, 1862.
Governor—This morning I received an order from the Secretary of War to order General Loring and his command to fall back from Romney to this place immediately. The order was promptly complied with, but as the order was given without consulting me, and is abandoning to the enemy what has cost much preparation, expense and exposure to secure, and is in direct conflict with my military plans, and implies a want of confidence in my capacity to judge when General Loring's troops should fall back, and is an attempt to control military operations in detail from the Secretary's desk at a distance, I have for the reason set forth in the accompanying paper requested to be ordered back to the Institute, and if this is denied me, then to have my resigna·

93 O. R., 5, 1062.   94 O. R., 5, 1053.   95 O. R., 5, 1065.

tion accepted. I ask as a special favor that you will have me ordered back to the Institute.

As a single order like that of the Secretary's may destroy the entire fruits of a campaign, I cannot reasonably expect, if my operations are thus to be interfered with, to be of much service in the field. A sense of duty brought me into the field, and thus far has kept me. It now appears to be my duty to return to the Institute, and I hope that you will leave no stone unturned to get me there. If I have ever acquired through the blessing of Providence any influence over troops, this undoing of my work by the Secretary may greatly diminish that influence.

I regard the recent expedition as a great success. Before our troops left home on the 1st instant there was not, so far as I have been able to ascertain, a single loyal man in Morgan county who could remain at home in safety. In four days that county was entirely evacuated by the enemy. Romney and the most valuable portion of Hampshire county was recovered without firing a gun, and before we had even entered the county.

I desire to say nothing against the Secretary of War. I take it for granted that he has done what he believed to be best, but I regard such a policy as ruinous.

Very truly, your friend,

T. J. Jackson [96]

His Excellency John Letcher,
Governor of Virginia.

Jackson's actions conformed to his estimate of the situation in Western Virginia. While awaiting action on his resignation, he sought to have Loring returned to Romney.[97] Failing in that, Jackson preferred charges against Loring for neglect of duty and "conduct subversive of good order and military discipline."[98] "General Loring should be cashiered for his course," he subsequently wrote.[99] In the same spirit Jackson preferred charges of neglect of duty on the part of his colleague, the former commandant at V. M. I., Col. William Gilham of the Twenty-first Virginia.[100]

---

[96] This long-missing letter in the exchange over Jackson's resignation appears in the *Hotchkiss Papers* as a clipping from a letter of John Letcher in the *Richmond Whig* of Apr. 26, 1873, p. 2, col. 6.

[97] *O. R.*, 5, 1065.   [98] *Ibid.*, 1065–66.

[99] Feb. 12, 1862; letter quoted in *Douglas*, 26–27.

[100] *Jackson MSS*. For Gilham's invaluable service as general drill master at Camp Lee, see Wise's *V. M. I.*, 139 ff.

As it happened, Jackson's resignation reached Benjamin before the letter of January 31 came to Letcher's desk. The Governor went immediately to the War Department and found Benjamin entirely disposed to listen to reason. Agreement was reached at once that the resignation would be disregarded until Letcher had time to write Jackson and to receive an answer from him. Letcher communicated at once and instead of trusting the letter to the mail put it in the hands of his friend and Jackson's, Congressman A. R. Boteler.[101] Others heard quickly of the resignation and besought Jackson to withdraw it. J. M. Bennett, a man of much influence, wrote: ". . . I have been informed that the government will make the necessary advances to reconciliation." [102] John T. Harris [103] assured Jackson, probably on the basis of mistaken rumor, "I am happy to learn that the Secretary has met a most decided rebuff from the President." [104] Boteler wrote before he started from Richmond with Letcher's appeal.

In a determined answer to Boteler's early written plea that the resignation be withdrawn, Jackson said: "I hold to the opinion that a man should be in that position where he can be most useful. And I don't see how I can be of any service in the field so long as that principle which has been applied to me—of undoing at the War Department, what is done in the field—is adhered to." [105] To some of his friends, Jackson spoke with indignation of the action of Benjamin,[106] but to Rev. Dr. James R. Graham, a distinguished minister in whose manse the General and his wife were residing, Jackson, with modesty and excess of reasonableness, said: "The Department has indeed made a serious mistake, but, no doubt, they made it through inadvertence and with the best intentions. They have to consider the interests of the whole Confederacy, and no man should be allowed to stand in the way of its safety. If they have not confidence in my ability to admin-

101 Member U. S. Congress, 1859–61; member Provisional and regular Confederate Congress, Feb., 1862–Feb., 1864. Letcher's account of this part of the incident is in the *Richmond Whig*, Apr. 26, 1873, p. 2, col. 6.
102 J. M. Bennett to T. J. Jackson, Feb. 6, 1861, *Jackson MSS*. This J. M. Bennett may have been the one who was a member of the House of Delegates of Virginia in 1834–35 from Lewis County.
103 Harrisonburg lawyer, member U. S. Congress, 1859–61, member Va. House of Delegates, 1863–64, 1864–65.
104 Feb. 7, 1862, *Jackson MSS*.
105 Letter of Feb. 5, 1862; *Douglas*, 25–26.
106 See *infra*, p. 303.

ister wisely the affairs of this district, it is their privilege and duty to try and repair the damage they believe I am doing." [107]

At length Colonel Boteler arrived from Richmond and brought Jackson the letter from Letcher. To this Boteler added his own verbal appeal. Jackson listened but at first showed no inclination to yield. Boteler hung on and, searching about for all arguments, insisted that Virginia's defense called for the service of all her sons. Jackson, said he, had no right to withhold his. This argument made a manifest impression. Boteler pressed with a contention from Letcher that Jackson's abandonment of his post would have a discouraging effect on the country.

Shaken by this argument, Jackson yielded.[108] He sent Letcher a candid note in which he said: "If my retiring from the Army would produce the effect upon our country that you have named . . . I of course would not wish to leave the service, and if, upon receipt of this note, your opinion remains the same, you are authorized to withdraw my resignation, unless the Secretary of War desired that it should be accepted. My reasons for resigning were set forth in my letter . . . and my views remain unchanged, and if the Secretary persists in the ruinous policy complained of, I feel no officer can serve his country better than by making his strongest possible protest against it, which, in my opinion, is done by tendering his resignation, rather than be a wilful instrument in prosecuting the war upon a ruinous principle." [109] When this letter reached Governor Letcher, he took pains to see that it was read in the War Department.[110]

Jackson's letter of resignation was returned him, and Loring was transferred to another theatre of operations;[111] but neither Johnston nor Jackson escaped without rebuke. Jackson's charges against Loring were not entertained.[112] On the contrary, as of February 15, Loring was promoted to be Major General. Johnston's punishment was, in effect, a stiff reprimand from the President. Because Johnston had asked to be relieved of responsibility for the Valley District after Benjamin had sent orders directly to

[107] Graham, quoted in *Mrs. Jackson*, 496; cf. *infra*, Chapter XXI.
[108] *Douglas*, 26, supplemented by the clear inferences from Jackson's letter to Letcher.
[109] *O. R.*, 5, 1063.
[110] *O. R.*, 5, 1063. The letter was not in Letcher's hands until Feb. 15.
[111] *O. R.*, 5, 1066–67.
[112] See Loring's answer to the charges. *O. R.*, 5, 1070. See also *O. R.*, 51, pt. 2, pp. 468–69.

Jackson, Mr. Davis wrote Johnston: "While I admit the propriety in all cases of transmitting orders through you to those under your command, it is not surprising that the Secretary of War should, in a case requiring prompt action, have departed from this the usual method, in view of the fact that he had failed more than once in having his instructions carried out when forwarded to you in the proper manner."

Davis then recalled that Benjamin had suggested that Johnston send an inspector to Romney but that the inspector had gone only so far as Winchester: "Had you given your personal attention to the case, you may be assured that the confidence reposed in you would have prevented the Secretary from taking any action before your report had been received." With this rebuke was notice that the Valley District would not be separated from the Potomac command.[113] The very next day Johnston received word from the War Department, apologetically phrased, that Maj. Gen. E. Kirby Smith, one of Johnston's best officers, must be relieved from command with the Army in order that he might be assigned to duty elsewhere.[114] This transfer had no connection with the correspondence over Jackson, but it was ordered at a time when rumors were current that Maj. Gen. Gustavus W. Smith, whom Johnston much esteemed, also was to be detached.[115]

Serious at any time, the prospect of losing the two Smiths seemed to Johnston an invitation to disaster, when his Army, soon to meet the test of battle, was being disorganized by the "Furlough and Bounty Act." This extraordinary law had been passed in December[116] as a means of assuring the re-enlistment of the twelve-months' volunteers whose terms expired in the late winter or early spring. A bounty of fifty dollars and a furlough of sixty days were promised all enlisted men and noncommissioned officers who agreed to serve for the duration of the war to a maximum of three years. Soldiers desirous of changing company, or even their arm of service, were to be allowed to do so. When the reorganization of the Army was effected through re-enlistment on these terms, the men could elect their own company and field officers, regardless of previous law. Thereafter, all commissioned vacancies were to be filled by promotion. The statute even went so far as

[113] O. R., 5, 1071–72.
[115] O. R., 5, 1074.
[114] O. R., 5, 1073.
[116] It was signed on Dec. 11, 1861.

to provide that in future, new second Lieutenants had to be chosen from the company in which the vacancy existed.[117] Beauregard and Maj. Gen. James Longstreet had favored the act, even to the extent of approving the simultaneous furlough of one third of the soldiers in the ranks.[118] Johnston had considered that leaves of absence would stimulate re-enlistment, but he had insisted that the "practicability of granting them in this army must depend . . . upon the enemy's course during the winter." [119] He soon became convinced that the law, as passed, was unenforceable and ineffective. If furloughs were not given in large numbers, the twelve-months' volunteers would not re-enlist; should furloughs be granted with prompt liberality, the Army would be weakened dangerously in the face of the enemy.

Not unnaturally in these circumstances, Johnston sought to place on the War Department the responsibility of applying the act. At the end of a lengthy review of the statute, he wrote Benjamin on January 18, 1862: ". . . I find myself under the necessity of referring to you for instructions as to the government of my conduct. The law requires me to be guided by the Secretary of War, not only as to the 'time' of granting furloughs, but also as to the number of them to be granted." [120] To this, the suave Benjamin was ready with a prompt reply. He weighed the considerations on both sides, urged that Johnston go to the "extreme verge of prudence in tempting" the twelve-months' men to re-enlist and offered to send up a few regiments of unarmed men to drill with the arms of absentees, but he insisted that he "could not undertake to determine when and in what numbers the furloughs could be safely granted . . . the rest I must leave to your own judgment." [121] Johnston answered this with an intimation that the Secretary did not defer in the same manner to his judgment when it came to the issuance directly from the War

[117] 2 R. E. Lee, 26. For the Army's view of furloughs, see "Bohemian" in Richmond Dispatch, Dec. 13, 1861, p. 1, col. 3; Charleston Mercury, Feb. 20, 1862, p. 2, col. 1. The text of the act is in Richmond Dispatch, Dec. 12, 1861, p. 3, col. 3, and in IV O. R., 1, 825–26, 1016; cf. ibid., 903. For comment on antecedents and on the general effect of the Confederate law and the proposed Virginia re-enlistment bill, see IV O. R., 1, 635, 902, 951, 969; O. R. 12, pt. 3, p. 833; O. R., 51, pt. 2, pp. 336, 371, 454, 497; R. Taylor, 28; Letters of James Conner, 88; Richmond Examiner, Jan. 2, p. 2, col. 5; Richmond Dispatch, Jan. 2, p. 2, col. 1, Jan. 8, p. 3, col. 1, Jan. 11, p. 1, col. 3, Jan. 13, p. 3, col. 2, Jan. 16, p. 3, col. 2, Jan. 18, p. 3, cols. 1–2; Charleston Mercury, Jan. 11, p. 1, col. 3, Feb. 15, p. 4, col. 3, March 18, 1862, p. 1, col. 2.

[118] O. R., 5, 1001–02.   [119] O. R., 5, 974.

[120] O. R., 5, 1037.   [121] O. R., 5, 1045.

Department of orders for the furlough of individual soldiers or
for the assignment of men to noncombatant duty behind the lines.

These assignments, known technically as details, had been producing friction between the General and the Secretary, and had
been causing discontent among the soldiers who had to do the
drab, hard duty of the ranks. In deep concern over the situation,
Johnston appealed to the Secretary to cease direct details and
furloughs. He said: "I have been informed that you have already
granted furloughs to four entire companies, three belonging to
the same regiment, but have received but one of the orders. They
are, it is said, re-enlisted as artillery. We thus lose good infantry
and gain artillery having no other advantage over the recruits
than that of being inured to camp life. This increases the difficulty of inducing the re-enlistment of infantry as such. You will
readily perceive that while you are granting furloughs on such a
scale at Richmond I cannot grant them at all. . . . I have been
greatly surprised today to receive an order from the War Department detailing a private for a working party here. I hazard
nothing in saying that in time of war a Secretary of War never
before made such a detail."[122]

All this was politely put, "in order to remove any causes of
misunderstanding,"[123] and it was followed by a request to the
Adjutant General of the Confederacy for the dispatch to the Army
of recruits with which to fill out the companies depleted by
absentees. Johnston explained: "The Secretary of War proposed
to send unarmed Regiments to supply the places of the men fur-
loughed. Such Regiments would be of little value for some time,
but the men composing them, if distributed among our present
troops and mixed with them in companies, would be valuable at
once, and soon equal to the old soldiers."[124]

By adhering to this policy, while limiting the furloughs issued
in each command,[125] the perplexed and angry Johnston hoped to
maintain the Army at defensive strength. All the while, he had
to do battle with the Secretary to prevent additional furloughs,
details and transfers from one arm of the service to another. In
one case, when Benjamin referred to him the letter of a Captain of
infantry who had written directly to the Secretary of War for

[122] O. R., 5, 1057.
[124] O. R., 5, 1058–59.
[123] Ibid., 1058.
[125] Cf. O. R., 5, 1069.

permission to reorganize as a battery of artillery, Johnston had to make this request: "The rules of military correspondence require that letters addressed to you by members of this army should pass through my office. Let me ask, for the sake of distipline, that you have this rule enforced. It will save much time and trouble, and create the belief in the army that I am its commander, and, moreover, will enable you to see both sides of every case (the military and the personal at once)."

Thus did controversy shift, continue and accumulate. It was on Dec. 27, 1861, that Whiting had been threatened with stiff demotion; Earl Van Dorn had been ordered away Jan. 10, 1862; less than three weeks later, Beauregard had been sent to Kentucky; [126] the clash between Jackson and Loring reached its climax during the first week in February; at that very time Johnston was engaged in these exchanges with Benjamin over details and the enforcement of the Furlough and Bounty Act. The orders for the relief of Kirby Smith from command were sent from Richmond, February 15.[127] Another month, or six weeks at most, might bring sunshine that would dry the roads and start the march of the great Army which Maj. Gen. Geo. B. McClellan, successor to General McDowell, was known to be organizing for an offensive.

Against that amply equipped and numerically superior Army, Johnston believed it impossible to hold his lines in Northern Virginia. While he waited for an attack that might overwhelm him, furloughs had to be granted by the thousand. Re-enlistment was expedited, in order to prevent the disintegration of the Army; but there was no likelihood that all the regiments which had been organized in April and May, 1861, could be induced to enlist anew before the expiration of their original term of service. Daily, as the men agreed to continue in service, they would elect new officers. By relaxing discipline, designing men who sought to assure their continuation in command might curry favor. The ambitious would conduct electioneering campaigns. Any one from Lieutenant to Colonel who discharged his sworn duty might be humiliated by defeat at the hands of soldiers he disciplined and might be succeeded by some popular incompetent. All that had

[126] Jan. 30, 1862; *O. R.*, 5, 1051.
[127] *O. R.*, 5, 1073. They were announced to the Army on February 21. *Ibid.*, 1078.

been done in ten months to develop a competent corps of officers might be set at naught. The Southern cause might collapse.

This situation was at its blackest when, on February 19, Johnston was summoned to Richmond.[128] The city and the government he found in gloom. Disasters had swept the Confederacy. Fort Henry on the Tennessee River had been taken. On the 16th, near-by Fort Donelson, with 14,000 Southern soldiers, had been surrendered. Nashville was expected at any hour to fall into the hands of Gen. Don Carlos Buell. All Western Tennessee was overrun. Albert Sidney Johnston was in retreat to Murfreesboro. On the east coast of North Carolina, Gen. A. E. Burnside had occupied Roanoke Island, had captured more than 2500 men, had scattered the remnant of a small defending force under former Gov. Henry A. Wise of Virginia, and now held a position from which he might take Norfolk in reverse.[129] Secretary Benjamin was being charged with responsibility for the defeat at Roanoke Island and was being assailed for incompetency.[130] The tone of the press was nervous, critical or bitter.[131] Rumors of impending changes in the Cabinet were afloat. The shortage of arms and of powder, though widely known to exist, was worse than the government dared to admit.

In this atmosphere of a concern close to despair, Johnston at 10 A.M. called on the President and found him with the Cabinet.

[128] Johnston was addressed at his headquarters by the President in a letter of Feb. 19 (*O. R.*, 5, 1077), but as Johnston stated (*Narrative*, 96) that he was in Richmond early on the 20th, he must have received on the 19th a telegram or a messenger that supplemented the letter of that date.

[129] For Wise's assignment to the command of Roanoke Island, see *O. R.*, 4, 715; *O. R.*, 51, pt. 2, pp. 426, 432, 439; for the reports, see *O. R.*, 9, 116 ff (casualties, 79, 81, 82, 186); for Wise's defense see *ibid.* 118 ff, 190–91; *O. R.*, 51, pt. 2, pp. 519 ff; IV *O. R.*, 1, 1015; for comment, see Miss Brock, 96–97, 4 *N. C. Regts.*, 247. The Richmond newspapers from Feb. 10 to Feb. 27, 1862, contain daily references and numerous quotations from the *Norfolk Day Book* and *Wilmington Journal.* See also *Charleston Mercury*, Feb. 12, p. 1, col. 2, Feb. 15, p. 1, col. 3. In the *Richmond Dispatch*, Feb. 27, p. 1, cols. 4–6, Feb. 28, p. 2, cols. 4–5, March 3, 1862, p. 1, cols. 1–2, is the first-hand account by "Bohemian," Dr. William Shephardson, of the action at Roanoke Island. Shephardson was among those captured.

[130] See Debates in the C. S. House of Representatives, 44 *S. H. S. P.*, 27; *Richmond Examiner*, Feb. 15, p. 2, col. 5; Feb. 26, p. 2, col. 5; *Petersburg Express*, quoted in *Charleston Mercury*, Feb. 28, p. 1, col. 4. For Benjamin's defense, see *Richmond Dispatch*, Feb. 25, 1862, p. 3, cols. 1–2.

[131] The fullest and most hostile quotations from newspapers in every part of the South, far too numerous to be listed in a footnote, will be found in the *Charleston Mercury*, Feb. 20-March 18, 1862. Most of these relate to the fall of Fort Donelson, the causes and the consequences. It was in the newspapers of this period that full confession first was made of the overconfidence that followed the victory of First Manassas.

The General was ushered in. Greetings, apparently without restraint, were exchanged. The President stated that Johnston had been summoned to confer on the withdrawal of his Army from its exposed position: should it be done, and if so, when and how? The question was the most delicate before the government, but in the strict secrecy of the Cabinet meeting, it might and should be discussed.

Johnston stated his view. McClellan, he reasoned, could advance in such force on Richmond and by so many routes that the Confederate forces should not attempt to maintain themselves on Bull Run and Occoquan. The Army must take up a line farther South, but it was hampered by deep mud on the roads and it was embarrassed by much baggage. Withdrawals should not be undertaken until the end of the winter.[132] Begun sooner, any southward movement would entail the destruction or abandonment of a great deal of property, public and private.

President Davis subsequently stated that, at this point in the discussion, he asked Johnston to what line the retreat would be conducted, when it became practicable. The General, said Davis, "declared himself ignorant of the topography of the country in his rear." Davis commented: "This confession was a great shock to my confidence in him. That a General should have selected a line which he himself considered untenable, and should not have ascertained the topography of the country in his rear was inexplicable on any other theory than that he had neglected the primary duty of a commander." [133]

Of this Davis said nothing at the time. The council shifted to a long, long discussion of the removal of the guns, particularly of the heavy ordnance at Evansport Battery, which had been designed to fire across the channel of the Potomac. As cannon intended for the defenses of Richmond had been sent to advanced positions and could not be replaced, the President was most solicitous that those at Evansport, as well as those at Manassas, should be saved.[134] Nothing substantial developed from the wordy presentation of lay opinion. Johnston received no specific orders,

---

[132] It is not known whether Johnston stated the case precisely in these terms to the Cabinet, but his views at the time are set forth in his *Narrative*, 96.

[133] Davis, Feb. 18, 1865, in 6 *Rowland*, 494.

[134] 1 *Davis*, 462–63.

other than that he should lead the Army southward to a more secure position as soon as practicable.[135]

With this understanding, Johnston said good day to the departing Cabinet officers, but no sooner was he out of Mr. Davis's offices than he had one experience after another that startled and alarmed him. At his hotel he met Col. W. Dorsey Pender, of the Sixth North Carolina Infantry, a young officer who had been schooled at West Point and with the 1st United States Dragoons. Pender had just arrived in Richmond on his way back to the front. With a soldier's zest for news, he asked if Johnston had heard a report, then circulating in the lobby, that the Cabinet had been discussing during the day whether the Army should be withdrawn from Manassas. An accurate report of what had been considered in the utmost secrecy, behind guarded doors, had reached the hotel almost as soon as Johnston had!

The next morning, as Johnston was en route to Manassas, he had not gone twenty miles on the train before a friend from Northern Virginia confided that ominous news had been heard in Richmond the previous evening: the Cabinet was considering the removal of the Confederate forces from Manassas. As this friend was quite deaf, Johnston was sure he could not have overheard a conversation. The news must have been given him deliberately.[136] Arriving at headquarters, Johnston soon learned that an officer who had been in Richmond on the 21st had brought the same report to Dumfries.[137] It was enough to make a commander despair! What hope could there be of concealing from the enemy a movement vital to the very existence of the Army—if every one from Richmond knew all about it?[138]

---

[135] Johnston, in his *Narrative*, 96, stated the conference "terminated without the giving of orders, but with the understanding on my part that the army was to fall back as soon as practicable." In his dispatch of Feb. 23 to Davis, he mentioned "the orders you have given me" (*O. R.*, 5, 1079). On Feb. 28, he wrote the President of the "progress of our preparations to execute your plans" and also of "the movement you have ordered" (*O. R.*, 5, 1083). From the context, both "orders" and "plans" refer to the withdrawal.

[136] *Johnston's Narrative*, 97.   [137] *O. R.*, 5, 1079.

[138] It is wholly probable these experiences convinced Johnston that he could not trust Cabinet officers or other high functionaries of state to respect a military secret. This may have led Johnston to keep his own confidence even to the point of appearing arbitrarily secretive in dealing with the civil authorities. Perhaps it should be added that, while Johnston was the most uncommunicative of all the senior officers with whom the President and the Secretary of War had to deal, he explained freely to Whiting (cf. *O. R.*, 5, 1082) and perhaps to some of his other subordinates his purposes and his plans.

CHAPTER XI

JOHNSTON'S WITHDRAWAL FROM MANASSAS

ON THIS unhappy return from Richmond, Johnston found the roads of Northern Virginia even worse than when he left. Rain fell on the 22d—the day of Davis's somber inauguration as President under the permanent constitution.[1] So deep was the mud around Dumfries that men on good horses took six hours and a half to cover twelve miles.[2] Four animals could not pull a light field gun along a road. Removal of the heavy ordnance from fixed positions seemed impossible.

With all the adverse conditions that would attend his withdrawal, Johnston was determined that the government should be acquainted. His dispatches to Richmond, not altogether free of bewilderment, became a chronicle of calamities, impending and instant. He wrote on the 25th: "The Army is crippled and its discipline greatly impaired by the want of general officers . . . and, besides, a Division of five Brigades is without generals; and at least half the field officers are absent—generally sick. The accumulation of subsistence stores at Manassas is now a great evil. The Commissary General was requested more than once to suspend those supplies. A very extensive meat-packing establishment at Thoroughfare is also a great incumbrance. The great quantities of personal property in our camps is a still greater one."[3] A "trunk had come with every volunteer."[4] Although Johnston at once gave orders to remove all these surplus stores, he did not believe he could clear the depots before the enemy advanced. Either from candor or from apprehension he warned the President that much property "must be sacrificed."[5]

In the eyes of the depressed General, every movement of the enemy now was designed to manœuvre him out of his position before he was ready to retreat. No sooner had he learned of the

[1] *O. R.,* 5, 1079; 1 *R. W. D. C.,* 111; D. S. Freeman, "When War Came to Richmond" in *Richmond News Leader,* Bicentennial Supplement, Sept. 8, 1937, p. 64.
[2] *O. R.,* 5, 1079.   [3] *O. R.,* 5, 1081.
[4] *Johnston's Narrative,* 98.
[5] *O. R.,* 5, 1081: cf. *ibid.,* Feb. 28, 1862, p. 1083.

appearance of a Federal force at Harpers Ferry on February 24,[d] than he reasoned that the march of these troops to Winchester and the simultaneous movement of a column from the vicinity of Hancock[7] would so threaten his left as to compel without further delay the withdrawal which, he took pains to remind the President, "you have ordered."[8] Johnston's chief concern was for his right, which extended down the Bull Run-Occoquan to the Potomac and covered camps on that river as well as the terminus of the R. F. & P. Railroad on Aquia Creek. Federals in considerable number were known to be camped on the Maryland shore of the Potomac, opposite Dumfries. They could be reinforced by a secret march through Maryland, Johnston argued, and could be ferried quietly to the Virginia shore. This route, he told himself, assuredly would be that of the principal Union advance.[9] It would put McClellan's troops in rear of the Confederate line on the Occoquan, from which, of course, Johnston would be compelled to retire.

Davis, for his part, battled with hope and with alarm. Virginia officials, who were aroused at the prospect of a deep penetration of their territory, talked of a great recruitment that would make Johnston's Army as powerful as McClellan's. Half convinced by the promises of the Virginians, President Davis on February 28 told Johnston of the plan and dwelt on the possibilities of an offensive, if the troops were raised; but, at the same time, he admitted that Johnston's position might be turned. Then, as always thereafter, when a retreat was in prospect, Mr. Davis fought for its postponement. Equally was he insistent that Richmond be protected. The expression of these mingled feelings, in his letters to Johnston, was such as to leave any General doubtful of the wishes of the Executive.[10]

Johnston did not believe new Virginia regiments would be available in time to help him on the line he held. In the expectation that he might at any hour receive news of a Federal onmarch

---

[6] This was the 28th Pennsylvania, Col. John W. Geary, on reconnaissance (O. R., 5, 511), in advance of Gen. N. P. Banks's Division and two Brigades of Sedgwick's Division. O. R., 5, 548.

[7] Morgan County, Western Virginia, about twenty-two miles Northwest of Martinsburg.

[8] O. R., 5, 1083. For the military geography of the region, see infra, Appendix I, p. 688.

[9] Johnston's Narrative, 101–2.   [10] Cf. O. R., 5, 1084.

which would force his columns back to the Rappahannock and Rapidan, Johnston expedited the removal of supplies and fumed because the overloaded Orange and Alexandria Railroad did not haul them off more quickly.[11]

Serious as this task was, busy as Johnston should have been, he took time to pursue the controversy with Benjamin and to protest once more against that official's grant of furloughs, of details and of authorization to raise new companies from old regiments. "The course of the Secretary of War," he wrote the President, "has not only impaired discipline, but deprived me of the influence in the army, without which there can be little hope of success."[12]

To this, Davis coldly and promptly replied that he would safeguard Johnston's "proper authority," with which he did not believe the Secretary had any desire to interfere. "He has complained," the President said of Benjamin, "that his orders are not executed, and I regret that he was able to present to me so many instances to justify that complaint, which were in nowise the invasion of your prerogative as a commander in the field." Davis prefaced this rebuke with assurance that Johnston must have been the victim of some imposition: the Secretary had not granted any leaves of absence or furloughs in that Army for a month.[13] Said Johnston subsequently, in commenting on this assertion, "A large package of the orders in question had been received by the mail in which that letter had come."[14] This letter probably reached Johnston on March 5. That same day he had from President Davis a sharp telegram in which he was told that an order about which he had written the Adjutant General "did not admit of discussion and I hope will be obeyed with due promptitude." Davis added: "Military operations cannot be conducted otherwise."[15]

With relations at this unhappy pass, Johnston that same 5th

---

[11] The operation of this railway during the first days of March, 1862, was an early, classic example of the manner in which a single-tracked line that lacked adequate sidings could be overcrowded with trains. A brief but illuminating report by Quartermaster General Myers, dated March 7, 1862, will be found in *O. R.*, 5, 1093. Myers thought too many trains had been put on a railroad of limited turn-outs.

[12] *O. R.*, 5, 1087.   [13] *O. R.*, 5, 1089.

[14] *Johnston's Narrative*, 101.

[15] *O. R.*, 5, pt. 2, p. 487. There is, unfortunately, nothing in available records to show what this "order" was, but Davis's subsequent attitude toward withdrawal from Manassas would indicate that the order probably did not concern the major operation then in prospect.

of March was informed by General Whiting of "unusual activity" among the Federal troops opposite Dumfries.[16] This news was decisive with Johnston. He issued directions for all the forces east of the Blue Ridge to fall back to the line of the Rappahannock River.

The orders, which were issued piecemeal, were wretchedly drawn. In some instances, clarity was lacking. Marches were not precisely timed in relation to one another.[17] Gen. T. H. Holmes, commanding at the northern terminus of the R. F. & P. Railroad, actually was not informed of the withdrawal or told what to do with the troops or heavy guns on his sector.[18] Neither the President nor the Secretary of War was advised when the movement would begin or what the lines of retreat would be.

The flank columns got away promptly and plodded slowly southward through the mud. On the old Manassas line, Johnston held the central Divisions until the evening of March 9 to cover the last-minute removal of supplies. Cavalry remained in position until 10 o'clock on the following morning. Then they fired the depots and all the property left along the railroad track.[19] The loss was heavy. At Thoroughfare Gap, where the Commissary General rashly had established the oft-discussed plant for packing meat, more than 1,000,000 pounds were destroyed or given to farmers in the neighborhood.[20] As for personal baggage, "the pile of trunks along the railroad was appalling to behold." [21] Blankets and clothing sent by the States for the use of their troops dissolved in pungent smoke.[22] Whiskey by the barrel was poured on the ground. "The soldiers got rich with plunder," [23] much of which they threw away on the march. Virtually all the heavy ordnance in fixed position, except that close to Manassas, was left behind. Some of it was not even thrown from its carriages.[24]

---

16 *Johnston's Narrative*, 102. Whiting's message, despite its great historical importance, apparently was not preserved.

17 *O. R.*, 5, 1090 ff; *cf.* 1085; *ibid.*, 51, pt. 2, pp. 487 ff.

18 *O. R.*, 51, pt. 2, p. 497; *cf. O. R.*, 5, 1100.   19 *Johnston's Narrative*, 103.

20 *Johnston's Narrative*, 98 n., 103. In 1 *Davis*, 468, Gen. J. A. Early is quoted as saying that the loss of this meat "embarrassed us for the remainder of the war, as it put us at once on a running stock." It is not clear from the statement of Col. R. G. Cole, *Johnston's Narrative*, 98 n., whether the meat at Thoroughfare was included in the estimated total of 1,434,316 lbs. of supplies abandoned in the withdrawal. Johnston himself is authority for the statement, *O. R.*, 51, pt. 2, p. 1074, that "more than half the salt meat at Thoroughfare was left there."

21 Early, *loc. cit.*   22 *Ibid.*

23 25 *S. H. S. P.*, 154.   24 *O. R.*, 5, 525–26; *Ibid.*, 51, pt. 2, p. 497.

The destruction was rendered the more depressing to the South and the more provoking to Davis because the slowness of the Federals in moving forward led Johnston's critics to aver later that he would have had ample time to remove from the Manassas area the last pound of provisions and the newest trunk of the most recent volunteer. No advance from the Maryland shore was undertaken. A Union detachment sent across the Potomac to destroy the abandoned Confederate ordnance was recalled as soon as its work was done.[25] The main Federal army made a practice march to Centreville, but it did not start from Alexandria until sure that the Confederates had withdrawn,[26] and it did not reach Bull Run until March 11.[27]

Faced with these facts, Johnston would not have been without arguments to justify his action. He might reasonably have met the charge of premature retreat with the reminder that the presence of Banks's Army in the Shenandoah Valley made his position insecure; but he did not know—and could not have known—that an operation from across the Potomac, to turn his right, had been projected substantially as he had anticipated. It had been abandoned on March 8, while his withdrawal was in progress.[28]

Among officials who were acquainted with the facts of his retreat but not with the Federal plans, Johnston was put in the unhappy attitude of fleeing when no man pursued;[29] publicly, if any reference was made in the press to his withdrawal, his action was defended as strategically sound.[30] Fortunately, too, the mind of the Southern people, depressed by a succession of disasters, was diverted and stimulated by the exploits of the iron-clad *Virginia-Merrimac*. On March 8, this clumsy craft had steamed out from Norfolk and had disposed of two wooden men-of-war, *Congress* and *Cumberland*. Despite the challenge offered

[25] *O. R.*, 5, 525–26.   [26] *O. R.*, 5, 51, 537 ff.

[27] Frank Moore, *The Rebellion Record* (cited hereafter as *Moore's Rebellion Record*), 4, 286 ff.

[28] *O. R.*, 5, 49–50.   [29] See Davis in 8 *Rowland*, 187.

[30] *Richmond Examiner*, March 11, p. 2, cols. 2 and 5. As a commentary on the difference in the attitude of newspapers toward military secrets, it should be noted that the anti-administration *Examiner* announced on March 11 that Johnston had retreated, and it predicted that his defensive line would be from Gordonsville to Staunton. The *Richmond Dispatch*, on the other hand, made no direct reference to the withdrawal until March 24, 1862 (p. 2, col. 5) and then only in a quotation from the *Philadelphia Press* of March 11.

next day by the *Monitor,* the Confederate people believed that their ironclad would clear Virginia waters of the enemy.

Johnston did nothing to turn the mind of the rejoicing public from the Navy to his Army. On the contrary, he did not inform the Administration where he was or what he planned. From the time he left Manassas, without notifying the authorities in Richmond of his departure, he did not send a single report to the War Department or receive a dispatch from it until he was safely on the line of the Rappahannock. On March 13, from Rappahannock Bridge,[31] he forwarded to the President a brief report of his position. When he had finished clearing the reserve depot at Culpeper, he said, "I shall cross the Rapidan and take such a position as you may think best in connection with those of other troops." Then he reviewed the loss of property, which he blamed on the "wretched" management of the Orange and Alexandria Railroad, on the accumulation of supplies at Manassas, and on the vast quantity of private property there. "This Army," he concluded with disgust, "had accumulated a supply of baggage like that of Xerxes' myriads." [32]

Johnston's period of isolation, however welcome on other grounds, had deprived him for almost a week of contact with his right wing at Fredericksburg.[33] Deliberate silence concerning his position probably had cost him, also, receipt of a message which the President had sent him on March 10, in the belief that he still was on the Manassas line. Davis then had telegraphed: "Further assurance given to me this day that you shall be promptly and adequately re-enforced, so as to enable you to maintain your position and resume first policy when the roads will permit." [34]

This new reference to the raising of a larger Virginia force had behind it new State legislation and a firm purpose to resist invasion, but it ignored the element of time. Whatever was done to strengthen Johnston had to be done at once. Despite that obvious fact, the President cherished that telegram as another count in his indictment against Johnston for premature retreat.[35]

Whether the President was provoked because Johnston did not

---

[31] The subsequently famous crossing of the Orange and Alexandria Railroad over the Rappahannock; now styled Remington.

[32] *O. R.,* 51, pt. 2, pp. 1073–74.   [33] *O. R.,* 5, 1100, 1102.

[34] *O. R.,* 5, 1096.   [35] *Cf.* 6 *Rowland* 404.

await reinforcement, whether he was incensed by the burning of stores, or whether he was angered by the General's prolonged silence, the answer he made on receipt of Johnston's report from Rappahannock Bridge was stiffly discouraging: ". . . before the receipt of yours of the 13th," said the President, "I was as much in the dark as to your purposes, condition, and necessities as at the time of our conversation on the subject about a month since." Then he proceeded: " 'Tis true I have had many and alarming reports of great destruction of ammunition, camp equipage, and provisions, indicating precipitate retreat; but, having heard of no cause for such a sudden movement, I was at a loss to believe it. I have not the requisite topographical knowledge for the selection of your new position. I had intended that you should determine that question; and for this purpose a corps of topographical engineers was furnished to make a careful examination of the country to aid you in your decision."

That, with a few words on the military situation elsewhere, was all the President gave the General at the moment of comfort or of blame,[36] but Johnston was badgered even during his retreat by the two now familiar vexations—interference with his command and the threatened loss of trained officers. General Whiting, who had so deeply offended the President by his unwillingness to accept Mississippi troops, was deemed to have been particularly negligent in failing to bring off his equipment from the Occoquan and the Potomac. On March 20, at the instance of the President, Mr. Benjamin wrote Gen. T. H. Holmes of the alleged "great destruction of property" by Whiting's force, and asked that Whiting be required to file a detailed report.[37]

No copy of this demand seems to have been sent to Johnston, though Holmes and Whiting were under his command. Whiting, who had been despondent,[38] replied immediately and officially, in a calm report; but in a covering letter to Benjamin, he asked the name of his informant and wished to know whether his Division had been singled out for blame.[39] Nothing came of this request. Meantime, because of reverses in North Carolina and

---

[36] O. R., 5, 527–28.
[37] O. R., 5, 528.
[38] O. R., 5, 1092.
[39] O. R., 5, 528. Although a Brigadier General, he had command of the "Forces near Dumfries," which consisted of three Brigades of infantry, three batteries and two detachments of cavalry (O. R., 5, 1030). This mixed force was accounted a Division.

the evacuation of Newbern,[40] Johnston was asked if he could spare Major General Longstreet to take command there. As another of the Army's division commanders, Gustavus W. Smith, was of precarious health, the prospect of losing Longstreet, who had his troops well organized, alarmed Johnston. To retain Longstreet, he had to plead hard, even to the extent of saying that there should be left with the Army "at least one other" Major General besides Smith, "of courage and ability." [41]

The inquiry concerning Longstreet came not from Secretary Benjamin, but from Gen. R. E. Lee,[42] whom, to placate a discontented and alarmed Congress, the President had brought from command in South Carolina and had placed in general charge of military operations under his own direction.[43] This appointment, at a period of dangerous misunderstanding, gave Johnston the assurance, at the least, that military experience and admitted abilities were to be available in Richmond whenever the President chose to employ them in dealing with Johnston's Army.

As Johnston felt that he outranked Lee, it is possible that he did not relish the prospect of receiving his orders through that officer, but Lee could not be so objectionable as Benjamin had been—and Benjamin no longer was Secretary of War. The demand that Benjamin had made on Holmes for a report by Whiting had been signed "Acting Secretary" and probably was one of his final acts.[44] President Davis, who was as constant in his loyalties as in the maintenance of his prerogatives, had yielded at last to the clamor against Benjamin by the somewhat unusual expedient of promoting him from the War Office to the first position in the Cabinet, that of Secretary of State.[45]

No more was Johnston to receive irritating directions from a Secretary who had sprinkled his letters with too many an "I" and often had ignored official forms, but had been singularly successful in prevailing on a Congress which did not like him to accept his recommendations. "To do the Secretary justice," wrote Tucker de Leon, "he bore the universal attack with admirable good nature and *sang froid.*" More than that, "to all appearances, equally secure in his own views and indifferent to public odium, he

40 *O. R.,* 9, 240 ff; *O. R.,* 51. pt. 2, p. 503.
41 *O. R.,* 12, pt. 3, p. 832.   42 *O. R.,* 51, pt. 2, p. 512.
43 2 *R. E. Lee,* 4 ff.   44 *O. R.,* 5, 528.
45 As of March 17, 1862; IV *O. R.,* 1, 1005.

passed from reverse to reverse with perfectly bland manner and unwearying courtesy. . . ."[46] In Benjamin's stead, the President named George W. Randolph, 43 years of age, grandson of Thomas Jefferson, former midshipman in the United States Navy, lawyer and artillerist distinguished at Big Bethel.[47] This choice, Johnston subsequently said, in terse eulogium that was the more eloquent because of its restraint, "enabled the military officers to reestablish the discipline of the army."[48]

The effect of the change was immediate, and in nothing more remarkable than in the state of mind of Johnston. Secretary Randolph confined himself to administrative duties, utilized the machinery of the Department,[49] and employed General Lee substantially as Chief of Staff. Lee wrote Johnston on behalf of the President, as Benjamin had done, but in a tone so different and in a military knowledge so much wider that little friction was created. The question of a commander for North Carolina acceptably was determined at a conference of Davis, Lee and Johnston: the decision was to send General Holmes, a native of that State, and to replace him temporarily at Fredericksburg by Gustavus W. Smith.[50] No less amicably, under Lee's tactful influence, was settled an incipient controversy over a remark of Johnston's which Mr. Davis apparently took to be an insinuation that he, the Commander in Chief, was unwilling to assume responsibility for moving troops from the line of the Rapidan.[51]

Ample reason was at hand for a movement from the second line Johnston had occupied after he withdrew from Manassas. Evidence had accumulated rapidly on March 24 that a new

[46] De Leon, 165. See Richmond Examiner, March 20, 1862, p. 2, col. 3; "Mr. Davis has sacrificed to popular clamour without yielding to public opinion. . . . The Administration has now an opportunity of making some reputation, for, nothing being expected of it, of course every success will be clear gain." For other comment on Benjamin at this period, see Miss Brock, 99; 5 Rowland, 217; 44 S. H. S. P., 177; O. R., 51, pt. 2, p. 512. The last includes this pointed observation by D. H. Hill: "It seems to have been the policy of Mr. Benjamin (if he had any policy at all) to have a small detachment and a weak battery at every point where the enemy might land. The result is that we have been beaten in detail."

[47] IV O. R., 1, 1005; Richmond Dispatch, March 19, p. 3, col. 2; Richmond Examiner, March 31, 1862, p. 2, col. 2. Charleston Mercury, March 24, p. 1, col. 3; 1 R. W. C. D., 117, 174; De Leon, 91.

[48] Johnston's Narrative, 108.   [49] 1 R. W. C. D., 142.

[50] O. R., 11, pt. 3, p. 392; Toombs, etc. Letters, 591–92. Toombs stated that the conference which decided on this transfer was held at Gordonsville. Davis's letter, directing that Holmes be sent to North Carolina, was written March 22, 1862, from Fredericksburg (O. R., 11, pt. 3, p. 392).

[51] O. R., 11, pt. 3, pp. 405, 409. This episode is obscure and relatively unimportant.

Federal plan of advance was taking form. Enemy troops in large numbers were being concentrated around Fortress Monroe at the tip of the Peninsula between the York and the James Rivers.[52] Suspicion soon grew into certainty that General McClellan, instead of marching southward from Manassas to confront Johnston on the Rapidan, was to utilize the Federal sea power in overwhelming "Prince John" Magruder at Yorktown, or Benjamin Huger at Norfolk. If McClellan could accomplish this, the assumption was that he would advance on Richmond from the East. To confront him and to protect Richmond, would it not be essential to dispatch Johnston's army to the lower Peninsula or to the Norfolk area?[53]

In the decision of this cardinal question, Johnston had no part. The strategy and the manner of its execution were Lee's. With the approval of the President, he directed when and in what number troops should be sent from the Rapidan to Richmond and thence eastward. Johnston merely urged, and not insistently, that if the movement was to be made, it should include the whole army, except for a small force to mask it.[54] Even in advocating this, Johnston a few days later had doubts concerning the strength of the Federals in Northern Virginia, and wavered for a moment in his support of a general concentration in Eastern Virginia. Said he: "I cannot here compare the state of affairs in my front with that in front of others, and cannot, therefore, decide understandingly whether troops are less needed here than elsewhere. . . . He who directs military operations upon information from every department can."[55]

In the end, without discord, the movement was executed according to the logistics prescribed by General Lee. On April 12, while his strongest Divisions were on the march, Johnston reached Richmond and conferred again with the President. Nothing that had happened in the strained correspondence between the two, no dissatisfaction on the part of Davis over the loss of property in the withdrawal from Manassas, seems to have been revived at the meeting. As usual, when the General and the Chief Executive met face to face, the demands of common courtesy and of a common cause outbalanced personal differences. Immediately and

[52] See *supra*, Chapter I, p. 8.
[54] *O. R.*, 11, pt. 3, pp. 401, 405, 419.
[53] 2 *R. E. Lee*, 13 ff.
[55] April 6, 1862; *O. R.*, 11, pt. 3, p. 423.

as a matter of course, by order of the President, promulgated through Lee, the Departments of Norfolk and of the Peninsula were "embraced for the present within the limits of operations of the Army of Northern Virginia." Johnston was designated to "direct the military and naval preparations in those Departments." [56] Although he had not been recognized in his contention that he was the senior General of the Confederacy, he had now by far the most responsible command and the largest Army.

[56] *O. R.*, 11, pt. 3, p. 438.

CHAPTER XII

Johnston Retreats Again

As Johnston hastened, that same 12th of April, 1862, through the budding countryside and down the placid York to study the situation on the lower Peninsula, it might have seemed that the winter of his discontent was passing. It was not to be so. He was fated to pass from storm to storm, from one displeasing necessity to another unpopular decision.

After a rapid but critical inspection of the position held by Magruder, he hurried back to Richmond with a gloomy, grim report: the line was too long for the force that occupied it then or could assemble later to defend it. Engineering had been poor. Inundations from Warwick River, designed to protect a part of Magruder's front, barred offensive operations. Between these inundations and the entrenchments at Yorktown, a system of field fortifications run by Magruder was far from complete. Superior Federal ordnance, outranging the antiquated smoothbore guns of the Confederates, could destroy the works at Yorktown and across the river at Gloucester Point. That done, the Federals could escort their transports up the York and easily could land an army to operate in rear of Yorktown or to press on toward Richmond. Magruder had done well with the small number of men at his command, and he had bluffed superbly the superior force that threatened him, but his position was indefensible against such artillery and such a host as McClellan had.

This was the substance of Johnston's report on the conditions he had found. Davis heard it calmly and, when Johnston had finished, remarked that a situation of so much importance should be discussed fully: Would Johnston return at a later hour, when the Secretary of War and General Lee could be present? Johnston of course answered in the affirmative and asked if he might bring Gen. Gustavus W. Smith and Gen. James Longstreet with him. This was acceptable to the President. In the conversation,

Johnston had sketched a positive plan of operations, and, as he knew that Smith's views were in basic accord with that plan, he went in search of that officer in hope that Smith would advocate it at the council of war. Smith, when found, expressed entire willingness to do so. Besides possessing confidence in his own judgment, he had been schooled in disputation during his years as Street Commissioner of New York City and would be at his ease even with so renowned a debater as Mr. Davis.

Shortly before 11 A.M., April 14, the six men sat down in the President's office. Davis asked Johnston to report on his inspection of the Peninsular defenses. The General repeated what he had said earlier in the morning and concluded that McClellan undoubtedly could force a passage of the James, of the York, or of both, and thereby could turn the Yorktown-Warwick River line. That front had to be abandoned. Another plan of coping with the invasion had to be devised.[1] Then, instead of urging immediately the course of action he had proposed to the President at their meeting earlier that morning, Johnston produced a memorandum which, he explained, Smith had handed him a few minutes before the conference opened.[2]

The President took the paper and read it aloud: it endorsed Johnston's contention that the Yorktown line was indefensible and it proposed the early abandonment both of that position and of Norfolk. Forces from both places should be concentrated in front of Richmond and should be reinforced with all troops that could be drawn from the Carolinas and from Georgia. One of two courses then should be followed: either the enlarged Confederate Army should attack and seek to destroy McClellan where he could not utilize his sea power; or else Richmond should be garrisoned and, while McClellan laid siege to it, the greater part of the Confederate forces should march on Washington and Baltimore, perhaps on Philadelphia and New York. In such an operation, Jackson's Army of the Valley could co-operate.

[1] *Johnston's Narrative,* 112–14.
[2] At this point a minor conflict of testimony develops. Johnston, *op. cit.,* did not refer to any memorandum or to the submission by General Smith of two plans of campaign. He merely stated, p. 114, that "General Smith was then asked by the President to give his opinion and suggested the course we had agreed upon. . . ." G. W. Smith, *op. cit.,* 41, is followed here, except in respect to the sequence of some of the events, on the ground that he would be more apt than would Johnston to remember the presentation of a paper which he had himself written.

The entire offensive, asserted Smith, could be prepared and executed before McClellan could take Richmond.[3]

Johnston doubtless used Smith's paper to introduce his own plan, which was to draw the enemy inland, to concentrate all available forces at Richmond, and to give battle there. For such a course, Johnston now argued. Smith clung to his preference for an offensive across the Potomac. Longstreet, when asked for his opinion, expressed the view that McClellan would not attempt any movement until the beginning of May. On this premise, Longstreet subsequently wrote, he intended to base a plan somewhat akin to Smith's, namely, that Magruder occupy McClellan temporarily and that the main army march on Washington, by way of the Shenandoah Valley, in order that McClellan might be forced to forego the invasion of Virginia for the defense of the Federal capital. Before Longstreet had done more than state his premise, Davis admonished him against underrating McClellan's initiative. Longstreet then lapsed into silence and did not develop his project.[4]

With scant attention to Smith's proposal, the conference turned to a scrutiny of Johnston's plan to evacuate the lower Peninsula and Norfolk and to concentrate forces at Richmond for a decisive blow at McClellan there. Both the necessity of withdrawal and the practicability of collecting a large army around Richmond were challenged. Secretary Randolph insisted that the Confederacy could not afford to abandon the Norfolk navy yard, with its dry dock, its shipways, its shops and its materials for building war vessels. General Lee maintained quietly that the Peninsula offered numerous defensive positions which could and should be utilized. The Army, in his opinion, could not count on early reinforcements from South Carolina and from Georgia. His period of command there had led him to believe that, if those States were stripped immediately of troops, Charleston and Savannah might be captured.[5]

Johnston and Smith did not attempt so much to meet these

---

[3] *G. W. Smith*, 41–42.

[4] *Longstreet*, 66. Naturally, as Longstreet's proposal was not offered at the conference, the question arises, to what extent was it an afterthought? The doubt cannot be resolved, but such a plan, it is not unreasonable to assume, in April, 1862, a soldier of Longstreet's ability could have devised. As will appear in a later paragraph, other leaders were canvassing the possibilities of an offensive about the same time.

[5] *Johnston's Narrative*, 115.

objections as they did to prove the impossibility of standing on the Yorktown line. Nothing could be accomplished on the lower Peninsula by the entire Army, Johnston maintained, except to gain a few weeks. That much could be achieved by Magruder with the force he had. If the Divisions of Longstreet and of Smith were sent down the Peninsula, into a wet region of bad water and unhealthy swamp, and then were withdrawn in a short time—as they must be—they would suffer in morale. Meantime, Richmond would be in danger from a sudden Federal advance up the James or the York. There was scant prospect, Smith and Johnston thought, that the enemy could be engaged and beaten at any great distance East of the Confederate capital. Even if McClellan were defeated around Yorktown, he could take refuge under his permanent fortifications at Fortress Monroe.[6]

This argument continued all day. With the President sitting as if he were a judge, and with Longstreet as a silent observer, hampered by slightly defective hearing, Johnston and Smith assailed a concentration on the Peninsula. Randolph and Lee presented the reasons for it. At 6 o'clock, the President ordered a recess until 7 P.M., when the discussion was renewed at the Executive Mansion. Both sides had advanced virtually everything they had to say, but they continued to canvass the issues, with diminishing vigor, until 1 A.M.[7] Then the President announced that Johnston's entire Army would be united with Magruder's on the lower Peninsula and that both Yorktown and Norfolk would be held, with the aid of the Navy, as long as practicable. "Though Gen. J. E. Johnston did not agree with this decision," Davis subsequently wrote, "he did not ask to be relieved, and I had no wish to separate him from troops with whom he was so intimately acquainted, and whose confidence I believed he deservedly possessed."[8] Johnston's own later comment curiously and not creditably revealed the man: "The belief that events on the Peninsula would soon compel the Confederate government to adopt my method of opposing the Federal army, reconciled me somewhat to the necessity of obeying the President's order."[9]

In this mood, Johnston returned to Yorktown and took command on that front. This involved, of course, the relinquishment

[6] G. W. Smith, 43.   [7] Johnston's Narrative, 115.
[8] 2 Davis, 88.   [9] Johnston's Narrative, 116.

by Magruder of his leading role in the drama of the Peninsula. It meant, in fact, that from first place on that stage, Magruder, though now a Major General, fell back to fourth position, for not only Johnston but also Smith and Longstreet outranked him.[10] This was hard fate for an officer who had remained conspicuous in the news throughout the ten months that had elapsed since the action of Big Bethel. A public discussion of his alleged intemperance had produced formal evidence of a war-time sobriety that a Puritan might have envied.[11] All the South had chuckled over a hot exchange of letters with Gen. B. F. Butler,[12] whom Magruder had worsted verbally and, it still was currently believed, had challenged to mortal combat.[13] The Southern commander's faithful diligence,[14] his inexhaustible energy,[15] his magnificent appearance [16] and his ready human sympathy [17] had been as admiringly reported as his exhortation after Manassas—"the great command should be, 'There is the enemy, destroy him' "—had been applauded.[18] He had been in trouble with the War Department, to be sure, because of an overready exercise of his authority to call out the militia [19] and to impress slaves,[20] but in dealing with the civil authorities he usually had carried his point and had exercised command under few restraints save those he had himself imposed. If his engineering on the Yorktown-Warwick front

[10] Both Magruder and Longstreet had been nominated as Brigadier Generals on June 17, 1861, to rank from that date. On the list of nominations, later submitted to Congress, Magruder's name had then preceded Longstreet's (1 *Journal C. S. Congress*, 307; confirmed Aug. 28, 1861, *ibid.*, 433), but on Oct. 7, 1861, when both had been made Major Generals, as of even date, Longstreet's name had preceded Magruder's (*ibid.*, 473; confirmed, Dec. 13, 1861, *ibid.*, 568). Under Section 5 of the Confederate Army Regulations, this gave Longstreet seniority. In the "old army," Longstreet had ranked Magruder on the roster of the regular service. Magruder had a higher brevet rank. Cadmus Wilcox, then Brigadier and later Major General, said that, on his arrival at Yorktown, he found some who believed that Magruder ultimately would command the Army.

[11] *Richmond Dispatch*, Nov. 14, p. 1, cols. 5–6; *Richmond Whig*, Nov. 20, p. 4, cols. 1–2; *Richmond Examiner*, Nov. 22, p. 2, col. 6, Nov. 27, 1861, p. 2, col. 5; *O. R.*, 51, pt. 2. p. 251.

[12] *O. R.*, 2, 681, 686; *Richmond Examiner*, July 24, 1861, p. 1, col. 6.

[13] See *supra*, p. 19; *Richmond Dispatch*, June 29, p. 3, col. 1; July 4, 1861, p. 2, col. 1.

[14] *Richmond Whig*, Aug. 1, p. 2, col. 3; *Richmond Examiner*, Sept. 19, 1861, p. 1, col. 6, p. 2, col. 1.

[15] *Richmond Dispatch*, Nov. 2, 1861, p. 1, col. 4.

[16] *Richmond Dispatch*, July 10, 1861, p. 3, col. 2.

[17] *Richmond Dispatch*, Aug. 10, p. 2, col. 1; Nov. 29, 1861, p. 3, col. 2.

[18] *O. R.*, 51, pt. 2, pp. 352–53.

[19] *O. R.*, 9, 42; *O. R.*, 51, pt. 2, p. 431.

[20] *O. R.*, 9, 33, 34, 36, 49, 52; *O. R.*, 51, pt. 2, pp. 465 ff; cf. *Richmond Examiner*, Oct. 3, 1861, p. 3. col. 1.

had not been of the best, that generously was attributed to the inexperience of the officers under him and not to any shortcoming of his own. For that matter, only a few men knew that his frowning forts were not so formidable as they appeared to be. Magruder had become convinced in March that an attack on his lines was imminent and thereafter, almost daily, he had bombarded the War Department with requests for reinforcements and supplies. By reason of Randolph's special familiarity with the Yorktown line, Magruder had addressed most of his appeals to the Secretary. Randolph had turned them over to Lee, who had answered them conservatively.[21]

Now, outwardly, all this was changed. Magruder, if disappointed, was game. In a florid address of 800 words, he extolled his troops, welcomed Johnston and announced that "by the new arrangements which the exigencies of the service require the late major general commanding finds himself separated from a portion of the old Army of the Peninsula."[22] Then as new commander of the extensive right wing,[23] he retired to watch his restricted lines—and to employ his pen. The habit of reporting to headquarters had become so fixed that when he no longer could write long dispatches, half scolding and half hortatory, to Mr. Randolph in Richmond, he addressed himself to Johnston's Assistant Adjutant General, and if that did not suffice, to his old lieutenant, D. H. Hill. In calm disdain of the fact that he had drawn and had required others to hold the lines now entrusted to him, Magruder became instantly critical of their location and their armament.[24] It was almost as if he were quarrelling with himself.

Johnston probably did not see the humor of Magruder's correspondence. He certainly found no humor in the military situation. On the contrary, his every act of importance seemed to accord with his subsequent admission that he believed events soon would compel the government to adopt his plan of retiring from the lower Peninsula and of concentrating a large force at Richmond to attack McClellan. On April 20, Johnston reported

[21] O. R., 11, pt. 3, pp. 385, 390, 393, 395, 403, 404, 413, 422, 425, 426, 427, 430, 431, 433, 434, 436, 437, 438, 441, 447.

[22] O. R., 11, pt. 3, p. 449.

[23] Longstreet simultaneously was assigned the center, D. H. Hill the left, including Yorktown, and G. W. Smith the reserve. O. R., 11, pt. 3, p. 448.

[24] O. R., 11, pt. 3, pp. 450 ff.

formally to Lee what he had stated in Richmond, that the line was defective.[25] Two days later he protested: "Labor enough has been expended here to make a very strong position, but it has been wretchedly misapplied by the young engineer officers. No one but McClellan could have hesitated to attack. The defensive line is far better for him than for us." [26] The same day, dealing with the possibility of an attack on Richmond from the North, Johnston argued again for the plan of campaign that had been rejected at the conference with the President,[27] and urged that the bridges across the Chickahominy, more than twenty miles in his rear, should be repaired.[28] By the 24th, he was asking that supplies be sent to meet him on the road from Richmond "in the event of our being compelled to fall back from this point." [29] After the 27th, he interpreted the enemy's movements as an indication that he soon would be compelled to retreat, and he warned General Huger to prepare to evacuate Norfolk.[30] More explicitly on the 29th, he announced to Lee: "The fight for Yorktown, as I said in Richmond, must be one of artillery, in which we cannot win. The result is certain; the time only doubtful. Should the attack upon Yorktown be made earnestly, we cannot prevent its fall; nor can it hold out more than a few hours. We must abandon the Peninsula soon. As two or three days, more or less, can signify little, I think it best for the sake of the capital to do it now, to put the army in position to defend Richmond. I shall therefore move as soon as can be done conveniently, looking to the condition of the roads and the time necessary for the corresponding movement from Norfolk." [31]

The remainder was a matter of preparation and convenience— that and no more. Lee's suggestion for delay and a step-by-step defensive, even the President's warning that "enormous losses, including unfinished gunboats," would be sustained at Norfolk, did not deflect Johnston from his purpose. He was determined to abandon the Yorktown-Warwick line as soon as he could start his trains and get the troops ready for the march.[32] His one alter-

---

[25] His dispatch is not in *O. R.,* but its purport is clear from Lee's answer of April 21, *O. R.,* 11, pt. 3, p. 452.
[26] *O. R.,* 11, pt. 3, p. 456.   [27] *O. R.,* 11, pt. 3, p. 456.
[28] *Ibid.*   [29] *O. R.,* 11, pt. 3, p. 461.
[30] *O. R.,* 11, pt. 3, p. 469.   [31] *O. R.,* 11, pt. 3, p. 473.
[32] *O. R.,* 11, pt. 3, pp. 476, 477–78, 485, 486, 488. The telegram from Davis, May 1, appears in *ibid.,* 484–85.

native proposal was an adaptation of Smith's and was made on April 30. Said Johnston then: "We are engaged in a species of warfare in which we can never win. It is plain that General McClellan will adhere to the system adopted by him last summer, and depend for success upon artillery and engineering. We can compete with him in neither. We must therefore change our course, take the offensive, collect all the troops we have in the East and cross the Potomac with them, while Beauregard, with all we have in the West, invades Ohio. . . . We can have no success while McClellan is allowed, as he is by our defensive, to choose his mode of warfare." [33] These proposals did not elicit support in Richmond. An offensive from Northern Virginia had been under consideration. In the West, a general advance was deemed impracticable at the time. Lee so advised Johnston.[34]

Without regard to the development or rejection of this broad plan, early or late, Johnston gave the order for the retreat. On the night of May 3, after forty-eight hours of confusion and counter orders, the Army left its position.[35] The General effected the removal of the field pieces that had been in the works,[36] but he left all fifty-six of his heavy guns, fifty-three of them uninjured, with some ammunition and supplies.[37] In this respect, the withdrawal from Manassas was duplicated. So was the criticism of the commander. Johnston again was to be blamed for a premature retreat, but he had not miscalculated substantially the time of the impending Federal attack. In a document that Johnston was not to see for many months, General McClellan reported that he would have been ready to open with all his heavy artillery on the morning of May 6 at latest. Gen. William F. Barry, Federal Chief of Artillery, stated that all except two of the fourteen batteries were in condition for service when Johnston moved out, and that the remaining two could have gone into action six hours later. The fire of these guns, Barry was convinced, "would have compelled the enemy to surrender or abandon his works in less than twelve hours." [38]

[33] O. R., 11, pt. 3, p. 477.   [34] O. R., 11, pt. 3, p. 485.

[35] O. R., 11, pt. 3, pp. 486 ff. "I am continually finding something in the way never mentioned to me before," said Johnston, in explanation of a day's delay. Ibid., 486.

[36] There were barbettes for thirty-one field pieces. O. R., 11, pt. 1, p. 337. The records do not show how many were in place.

[37] O. R., 11, pt. 1, pp. 18, 337.   [38] O. R., 11, pt. 1, p. 348.

CHAPTER XIII

The Army That Left Yorktown

The army of 56,500 men that filed out of the Yorktown-Warwick lines on the night of May 3, 1862,[1] had sustained few battle casualties since Manassas, but already its command had suffered at the hands of the foe that was to pursue it to the end, the resistless foe of attrition. Besides Beauregard, who had won no new laurels at Shiloh, the Army had lost three of the early brigade commanders. Kirby Smith, as already noted, had taken command in East Tennessee.[2] On December 26, 1861, nervously shattered by eight months' anxious service, the chivalrous Philip St. George Cocke had ended his life.[3] Milledge Bonham had resigned January 29, 1862, because he felt himself overslaughed, probably by the promotion of "Dick" Ewell to the rank of Major General after the transfer of Van Dorn to the West.[4] "Shanks"

[1] The return of April 30, or approximate date, in O. R., 11, pt. 3, pp. 479–84, shows an effective strength of 54,344 infantry and attached artillery. Cavalry numbered 1289. The personnel of the artillery reserve of fifty-six pieces is not given, but on the basis of an average of sixty-five men per four-gun battery, was about 910. At this stage of the war, one or two batteries were assigned for continuous service with each Brigade and were carried on the trimonthly returns as part of the effective strength of that Brigade. For convenience, this is styled the "attached artillery," to distinguish it from the "reserve artillery," organized for use wherever needed.

[2] O. R., 7, 908.

[3] Richmond Dispatch, Dec. 28, p. 3, col. 1, Dec. 30, p. 3, col. 1; Richmond Examiner, Dec. 28, p. 3, col. 2, Dec. 31, p. 2, col. 6; Richmond Whig, Dec. 28, 1861, p. 2, col. 2. The resolutions passed by the officers of his Brigade on Dec. 30, 1861 thus reviewed his career: ". . . possessed of a princely estate, he freely expended his income in a liberal hospitality, and in acts of private charity and public munificence; and, above all, as a Christian gentleman, he illustrated by his deportment and works, the faith which he professed. [W]e who had the best opportunity of judging, give our testimony to the ardent zeal, which he displayed in this war, for republican freedom, against mobocratic despotism, and to the interest and energy with which he discharged the onerous duties of his responsible office" (Cocke MSS.). It was not until after his death that even a part of General Cocke's large gifts, particularly to the Virginia Military Institute and to the needy among its cadets, became known. Cf. extract from report of Supt. F. H. Smith, V. M. I., Feb. 4, 1862, Cocke MSS.

[4] Van Dorn's orders had been published January 10, 1862 (O. R., 5, 1027), Ewell had been promoted January 24 (Wright, 24), Bonham resigned January 29, (ibid., 49). As Bonham was the fourth general of Brigade on the list of the Provisional Army and was senior Brigadier of a Division that had no commander, overslaughing by the sixteenth brigade commander on the roster was of a sort to humiliate him. It was the greater blow because his promotion erroneously had been reported in the press (Richmond Dispatch, Oct. 29, 1861, p. 3, col. 1. The Richmond Examiner, Nov. 15, 1861, p. 2, col. 1, had quoted the Southern Presbyterian as stating that "even if the report

Evans also was gone from the Army. At the instance of Gov. F. W. Pickens, of South Carolina, he had been sent to that State.[5] Evans was a Brigadier General now. He had been commissioned as of the date of his victory at Ball's Bluff,[6] acclaimed by some newspapers,[7] applauded by the President and Secretary Benjamin,[8] and honored with the thanks of Congress.[9]

Not one of the Brigades that had fought at Manassas remained in its entirety under the man who had led it there.[10] Whiting, saved from Coventry, had Bee's old command; Colonel Kershaw, promoted Brigadier, had Bonham's; [11] D. R. Jones had been given Bartow's former regiments. The three Manassas Brigades that retained their regimental organization under new commanders were headed now by two former Captains and a former First Lieutenant of the United States Army who had resigned at secession. Oldest and most experienced of this trio was the commander of D. R. Jones's previous Brigade of South Carolina troops, Richard H. Anderson, aged 40, who had been graduated from West Point in the class of 1842.[12] "Dick" Anderson had served as a Lieutenant in the war with Mexico, and had spent most of his subsequent career with the Second Dragoons in the West. Temporarily he had taken over the defenses of Charleston after Beauregard had come to Virginia.[13] Then he had done a brief tour of duty at Pensacola,[14] and had not joined Johnston's Army until

is unfounded, he will soon be elected to Congress from our district"). J. B. Jones, in a belated entry, 1 *R. W. C. D.*, seems to have confused the case of Bonham with that of some one else. Bonham represented South Carolina in the first (Regular) Congress of the Confederacy from Feb. 18, 1862, until Jan. 17, 1863 (*Wright*, 171; 5 *Journal C. S. Congress*, 6; 6 *ibid.*, 29), when he resigned to become Governor of his State. That office he held during 1863–64. He was reappointed Brigadier General Feb. 20, 1865, to rank from Feb. 9, 1865 (*Wright*, 49). Adjutant General Cooper, according to 2 *R. W. C. D.*, 414, opposed the reappointment of Bonham.

    5 Nov. 24, 1861; *O. R.*, 6, 334; 5 *Rowland*, 175. Evans was assigned, Dec. 18, 1861, to command of the Third Military District of South Carolina. *Ibid.*, 347.

    6 See *supra*, p. 111; *Wright*, 62.

    7 Cf. *Richmond Examiner*, Aug. 16, p. 2, col. 3; Aug. 28, 1861, p. 3, col. 1.

    8 IV *O. R.*, 1, 796; 1 *R. W. C. D.*, 87.   9 *O. R.*, 51, pt. 2, p. 414.

    10 Early still had his Twenty-fourth Virginia; Hampton retained his Legion.

    11 Kershaw had come under some criticism for taking the wrong road in the advance on Lewinsville, Sept. 25, 1861 (*O. R.*, 51, pt. 2, p. 314; *Richmond Dispatch*, Sept. 30, 1861, p. 2, col. 3), but apparently he was not to blame. He was appointed Brigadier General Feb. 15, 1862 (*Wright*, 70). On Apr. 29, 1862, Magruder addressed Kershaw's Brigade and procured its complete re-enlistment. Although Magruder seemed to regard this as a tribute to his eloquence, it was a tribute no less to Kershaw's hold on the affection of his men. See *O. R.*, 11, pt. 3, p. 479.

    12 Fortieth in his class; *Cullum*, No. 1150.

    13 *Richmond Examiner*, May 31, 1861; IV *O. R.*, 1, 414.

    14 *O. R.*, 51, pt. 2, p. 245; *Richmond Dispatch*, Sept. 9, p. 3, col. 1; Sept. 10, p. 3, col. 1; *Richmond Examiner*. Sept. 19, 1861, p 1, cols. 5–6.

February.[15] As he had been a Captain for six years before his resignation, he could be regarded as a seasoned soldier by the standard that had to prevail in the Confederate Army. Tall, strong, and of fine background, Anderson never was disposed to quibble over authority or to indulge in any sort of boastfulness. Already he was beloved in the Army for his kindness, his amiability and his unselfishness. Whispers that he was overfond of a social glass seem to have had no foundation.[16]

One of Anderson's associates in Longstreet's Division, entrusted with the direction of Cocke's old Brigade, was Ex-Capt. George E. Pickett of the 9th United States Infantry. Although this young Virginian had been graduated at the absolute bottom of the class of 1846 at West Point, he had been a gallant figure in Scott's Mexican expedition, and after Chapultepec he had been awarded his brevet as Captain. Later orders had carried him to Texas and thence to Washington Territory, where he had won much praise for the firmness of his dealings with the British authorities in a dispute over the occupation of the Island of San Juan.[17] Pickett had entered the Military Academy from Illinois, but he had never questioned his allegiance to the Old Dominion and in 1861 he had crossed the continent to fight in her defense. His first assignment of importance in Virginia was as Colonel in command of the Confederate troops on both sides of the lower Rappahannock River.[18] In that district, he displayed much activity and won the warm good will of his superior, Gen. T. H. Holmes.[19] Probably through the efforts of Holmes, he was commissioned Brigadier General in February, 1862.[20]

Assignment to Longstreet's Division followed soon [21]—an association destined to be long and renowned. Pickett and Longstreet had served together in the 8th Infantry at Fort Bliss in 1854-55. Between them, the ties were close and binding. Many a time, in the battles that lay ahead, Longstreet was to remember Pickett and was to make certain that orders were understood.[22] At the moment, as Pickett's men moved from the Yorktown line, they

[15] O. R., 5, 1074. His commission as Brigadier General dated from July 19, 1861.
[16] D. S. Freeman, ed., Lee's Dispatches (cited hereafter as Lee's Dispatches), 10. For the next reference to Anderson, see infra, p. 176.
[17] Cullum, No. 1330.   [18] O. R., 5, 877.
[19] O. R., 5, 991, 994; O. R., 51, pt. 2, pp. 357, 359, 427 ff, 466-67.
[20] Wright, 69.
[21] O. R.. 5, 1085-86.   [22] Sorrel, 54.

knew little of him except that he was dapper and alert, that he looked all of his 37 years, and that he wore his dark hair in long, perfumed ringlets that fell to his shoulders. Even his curling beard was anointed.[23]

The third of the West Point Brigadiers in Longstreet's Division was a few months younger than Pickett and, like him, was a Virginian. His name was Ambrose Powell Hill, of stock long honored and influential in the State. Young Hill had been admitted to the United States Military Academy in 1842, but, because of bad health, had not been graduated until 1847,[24] just in time to have a small part in the closing operations of the Mexican War. Then he had played hide-and-seek with the Seminoles. In 1855, while ranking as First Lieutenant of Artillery, he had entered the office of the Superintendent of the Coast Survey. He had resigned before secession, had received early his commission as Colonel and soon trained one of the best of Johnston's regiments in the Valley.[25] A demonstration against Romney in June, 1861, had been conducted by Hill with so much skill [26] that his promotion had been expected.[27] Instead, he remained as Colonel and, when the movement to Manassas was made, he had the misfortune, as noted already, to be ordered to the confused right, instead of to the engaged left. Throughout the months that followed, his discipline had been good and his grasp of his duties manifest. In February, 1862, he had been advanced to the grade of Brigadier General.[28] His own men esteemed him as diligent and as mindful of their wants. Beyond that, he was, as yet, merely a figure.

This was true, also, of another West Point Brigadier, Cadmus M. Wilcox, who had entered the Academy with A. P. Hill and Pickett. He was a North Carolinian by birth, had received his appointment from Tennessee, and had served as aide to General Quitman in Mexico. After the battle of Manassas, he had joined Johnston with an excellent Alabama regiment. Perhaps some of the better-read officers of Longstreet's Division, to which he was attached on the withdrawal from Yorktown, were familiar with his published *Rifles and Rifle Practice* and his translation of

---

[23] *Sorrel*, 57–58.　　[24] Fifteenth in his class; *Cullum*, No. 1345.
[25] 20 *S. H. S. P.*, 378.　　[26] *O. R.*, 2, 471.
[27] 20 *S. H. S. P.*, 378.
[28] *Wright*, 71. For the next part of the sketch of A. P. Hill, see *infra*, pp. 178, 191.

Austrian Infantry Evolutions of the Line. This was the extent of the Army's acquaintance with his capabilities, though his commission as a Brigadier antedated that of Pickett and that of A. P. Hill.[29] Two other graduates of West Point, not already mentioned, rode with the long columns away from Yorktown and will appear in the hour of combat.[30]

The remaining commanders of the twenty-three retreating Brigades were, in the main, politicians whom the President, now mindful and now disdainful of professional training, had commissioned as general officers. Georgia had sent her two most eminent public men. One of these was Howell Cobb, 46 years of age, former Governor of Georgia, Secretary of the Treasury under Buchanan, ex-Speaker of the United States House of Representatives, and present Speaker of the House of the Provisional Congress—altogether one of the most distinguished of Southerners.[31] From the outset, Cobb had been as much pleased to be with Magruder as "Prince John" had been delighted to have so renowned a man among his subordinates. Within less than forty-eight hours after Cobb had arrived on the lower Peninsula, he was telegraphing back to a friend in the Cabinet that more troops should be sent to Yorktown. Said Cobb of Magruder: "You could not have a better man here. Rely fully upon his judgment."[32] By mid-February Cobb was a Brigadier General,[33] and

29 *Cullum,* No. 1325; *Wright,* 62–63. Wilcox appears again in Chap. XXXII *et seq.*
30 For Lafayette McLaws, see *infra,* p. 218, and for G. J. Rains, see *infra,* pp. 240 ff, 268.
31 Cobb had arrived in Richmond about June 13, 1861 (*Richmond Dispatch,* June 15, 1861, p. 2, col. 7), but he had gone almost immediately to Norfolk, where two of his three sons were serving. (*Richmond Dispatch,* May 28, 1861, p. 2, col. 3, stated that he had three sons in service—one in the Athens Guard and two in the Macon Volunteers. For his visit to Norfolk, see *Richmond Examiner,* June 20, 1861, p. 2, col. 6). Soon he was back in the Confederate capital, where seven companies of his regiment were encamped. Said *The Examiner,* July 31, 1861, p. 3, col. 3: "For over a month Col. Cobb has been industriously training himself in the duties and discipline of the soldier, and numerous are the attestations to his rapidly acquired proficiency in the art of war which come to us through educated officers. In a few days he exchanges for the second office in the Confederacy a Colonelcy and the camp." For a variety of reasons, departure was delayed. Cobb and his officers pursued their study. A visitor reported a finely disciplined camp, cheerful and happy men, and an absence of profanity (*Richmond Dispatch,* Sept. 25, 1861, p. 2, col. 4). Cobb's regiment was presented, October 17, with a stand of colors purchased by members of the Provisional Congress (IV *O. R.,* 1, 615; *Richmond Dispatch,* Oct. 18, 1861, p. 2, col. 2). A sword, in addition, was to be tendered Colonel Cobb as soon as a proper weapon could be found. For his orders to report to Magruder at Yorktown, see *O. R.,* 51, pt. 2, p. 288. Cobb left Richmond on the morning of Oct. 19 (*Richmond Dispatch,* Oct. 19, p. 2, col. 3; *Richmond Examiner,* Oct. 19, 1861, p. 3, col. 4).
32 *O. R.,* 4, 685.
33 Feb. 13, 1862; *Wright,* 70.

by the end of April he had one of the largest of Brigades—nearly 3800 men.[34]

The other noted Georgian of the rank of general officer was Robert Toombs, 51, former United States Senator and first Secretary of State in the new Confederacy, whose odd experiences will be related in a subsequent connection. While none of the other "political Generals" could compare in public reputation with him and his fellow Georgian, several had distinction. From Tennessee came former Congressman Robert Hatton, not yet a Brigadier, but a participant in the unhappy operations at Cheat Mountain and in the Romney expedition. The Treasurer of Mississippi, Richard Griffith, commanded a Brigade predominantly from that State; W. S. Featherston, for two terms a Federal Representative of Mississippi, had similar rank. Roger A. Pryor, of Virginia, editor, fire-eating secessionist and Congressman, wore the fresh stars and wreath of a Brigadier General. As in the case of the others, he had no military training, though he was perhaps the most notorious duellist of his day.

To recapitulate, command of the Brigades that marched from the Yorktown-Warwick line was in this status: Eleven of the twenty-three were under men who had been officers in the United States Army,[35] three were in charge of graduates of the Virginia Military Institute,[36] six were entrusted to politicians,[37] one had as its head the great patrician, Wade Hampton, and two were led by lawyers.[38]

None of these men, from the nature of army organization, theoretically meant so much in wise leadership as did Johnston's four division commanders. The most conspicuous of these, Magruder, moved from the "Right of Position" with a Division of six Brigades,[39] only two of which had belonged to his Army of

[34] O. R., 11, pt. 3, p. 480. This was the largest Brigade in Magruder's command at that time.

[35] R. H. Anderson, Jubal A. Early, A. P. Hill, John B. Hood, D. R. Jones, Lafayette McLaws, George E. Pickett, Gabriel J. Rains, J. E. B. Stuart, W. H. C. Whiting and Cadmus M. Wilcox.

[36] R. E. Colston, R. E. Rodes and C. A. Crump.

[37] Howell Cobb, W. S. Featherston, Richard Griffith, Robert Hatton, Roger A. Pryor and Robert Toombs.

[38] J. B. Kershaw and J. J. Pettigrew.

[39] Magruder, Nov. 10, 1861, had organized these troops, while in the field, as two Divisions, one under G. J. Rains and the other under Lafayette McLaws (O. R., 4, 697). After Robert Toombs arrived, he superseded Rains by reason of earlier commission, but neither Toombs nor McLaws had responsibility for a Division when the withdrawal from the Peninsula began.

162   LEE'S LIEUTENANTS

the Peninsula.[40] He was publicly the best known as he was in panoply the most dazzling of the Major Generals.

To the soldiers from Northern Virginia the most familiar of the divisional commanders was the senior, Gustavus W. Smith. This Kentuckian, 40 years of age, had unique position among Confederate officers in Virginia. He had been graduated No. 8 in the class of 1842 at West Point. With aptitude for construction engineering, he had erected batteries, built roads and discharged such a variety of other useful duties in Mexico that he had received brevet as Captain.[41] After the close of hostilities, he had served as Principal Assistant Professor of Engineering at the Military Academy for five years and had resigned in December, 1854, to undertake private practice.[42] It had been in 1858 that he had become Street Commissioner of New York City, with his West Point classmate, Mansfield Lovell, as his deputy. Smith had been in correspondence with Southern leaders after the establishment of the Confederacy[43] but had held his municipal office until he had been satisfied, in September, 1861, that a majority of the people of his native State were on the side of the South. Then he had left New York and had gone to Richmond,[44] where he had been nominated almost immediately as a Major General.[45]

No other man, with the exception of Albert Sidney Johnston and Leonidas Polk, previously had received so high a first commission.[46] Smith's prestige at that time had been extraordinary and, in a sense, puzzling, because his career had included nothing that justified great reputation as a field commander. The press of the Confederate capital had acclaimed him,[47] and perhaps had

40 Two, Kershaw's (Bonham's) and D. R. Jones's (Bartow's), were Manassas Brigades, and two, Toombs's and Griffith's, were post-Manassas Brigades from Johnston's Army.
41 Cullum, No. 1118.
42 The Richmond Examiner, Oct. 14, 1861, p. 3, col. 4, stated it as a "noteworthy fact" that Smith and Mansfield Lovell had resigned to assume command in Quitman's filibustering expedition to Cuba, which expedition was foiled by the "rash and untimely raid" of Narciso Lopez. Needless to say, Lopez was executed three years before Smith resigned.
43 Cf. O. R., 53, 129; IV O. R., 1, 107.
44 The date of his retirement as Street Commissioner is given by Cullum as Sept. 20, but Smith arrived in Richmond Sept. 11. Richmond Whig, Sept. 13, p. 2, col. 2; Richmond Dispatch, Sept. 14, 1861, p. 3, col. 1.
45 As of Sept. 19; Wright, 22; 1 Journal C. S. Congress, 473, 518, 568.
46 Mansfield Lovell was nominated later in the same way, to rank as of Oct. 7, 1861 See 1 Journal C. S. Congress, loc. cit.
47 Dispatch and Whig, as cited; Richmond Examiner, Sept. 19, 1861, p. 2, col. 5.

done so the more cordially, because the *New York Herald* [48] had denounced him as the fomenter of rebellion that "radiated forth into every corner of the city, and permeated the councils of the rotten leaders of the Regency party in the State."

Amid much applause, Smith had gone to Centreville, where he had been assigned to command of all the troops not then under Beauregard.[49] By Johnston the new commander had been appraised as one "of the best officers" the Confederacy could procure;[50] Robert Toombs thought the Army "a great gainer" by the appointment of Smith. Within a fortnight after the General's arrival, said the critical Georgian, "the administration of the Corps had been much improved."[51] If Toombs's judgment was influenced by the fact that he and Smith had the same political approach to military matters, neither of the men seems to have been aware of that fact.

Smith was altogether self-confident in camp and at council table. In the autumn, when Davis had gone to Manassas to discuss operations, Smith had broached, "with perhaps some abruptness"—to use his own words—the plan for an invasion of the North.[52] He had not thereby lost the goodwill or the good opinion of the President, nor had the rejection of the plan shaken his belief in its strategical wisdom. Although his command had been shifted from an unofficial Corps to a Division in October, and had been changed twice thereafter in composition,[53] Smith had been considered by Johnston as indispensable, the future "commander of the main body" of the forces.[54] Johnston was "Joe" to Smith;[55] their relations were cordial and intimate. Toward the other general officers, Smith's feeling was one of bluff camaraderie, touched, perhaps, with a shade of superiority. In appearance, he was tall and of powerful build, with massive, rough-hewn features. The line of his thin lips was proud, perhaps pompous. His manner was rapid and energetic and had the spirit of conscious command.[56] Despite his assured bearing, he never had commanded troops in his life. Except as an engineer and an administrator, he was wholly untried, he who was now

[48] Oct. 10, 1861.
[50] O. R., 5, 797.
[52] O. R., 5, 885.
[54] O. R., 5, 1074.
[49] O. R., 5, 866, 881.
[51] *Toombs, etc. Letters*, 579.
[53] O. R., 5, 911, 1061.
[55] Cf. O. R., 51, pt. 2, p. 593.
[56] *Nashville Patriot*, quoted in *Richmond Dispatch*, Sept. 25, 1861, p. 3, col. 5.

leading almost 15,000 men from Yorktown. His inexperience was not distrusted. There was doubt concerning his health.[57] For the rest, he had prevailed upon the Army and the country to take him at his own valuation of himself.

Next in seniority to Smith was Maj. Gen. James Longstreet, whose troops from the "Centre of Position" became a new and larger Division on the retreat from Yorktown. Many things had happened to Longstreet since Bonham had forbidden him to fire on the Federals in the twilight of Manassas Day.[58] Longstreet had obeyed the order that evening and had ridden off. In a grove of young pines he had dismounted—and had exploded in his wrath. ·He had pulled off his hat, had thrown it on the ground and, with bitter words for Bonham, had stamped in a white rage.[59] Frustrated as he had been in his pursuit of the enemy, he had not been "mentioned in dispatches" as one of those to whom belonged credit for the victory at Manassas,[60] though he had been praised for his handling of his Brigade in the affair at Blackburn's Ford.[61] In August, his excellent Virginia Brigade [62] had been pushed forward as the advance of the Army, and later, from its outposts on Munson's and Mason's Hills, had been within sight of Washington.[63]

There, Longstreet had discharged with soldierly diligence, but not with content, the duties of brigade command. Despite the fact that he had left the line in 1858, had become a paymaster [64] and had asked for a place in that department when he had joined the Confederates,[65] he placed no low estimate on what he described as the "hard service" he had rendered in Mexico and in the "old army." [66] Moreover, he considered himself the senior officer from Alabama who had left the United States service.[67] As such, he was determined that his rank should be respected and that none of

[57] O. R., 12, pt. 3, p. 832. For the next reference to Smith, see infra, p. 193.
[58] See supra, Chap. VII, p.* 75.   [59] Sorrel, 30.
[60] Cf. O. R., 2, 477, 543–44.
[61] Cf. O. R., 2, 445; for his report, see ibid., 461 ff.
[62] First, Seventh, Eleventh and Seventeenth Infantry; O. R., 2, 1000.
[63] Richmond Dispatch, Aug. 20, p. 3, col. 4, Aug. 27, p. 2, col. 3; Richmond Examiner, Aug. 31, 1861, p. 2, col. 4. Longstreet's headquarters had been established at Fairfax Courthouse and, about Sept. 9, had been advanced temporarily to Fall's Church (Richmond Dispatch, Sept. 30, 1861, p. 3, col. 3; cf. O. R., 51, pt. 2, pp. 296, 310).
[64] Cullum, No. 1164.   [65] Longstreet, 32.
[66] IV O. R., 1, 182.
[67] IV O. R., 1, 182, though on army lists, cf. 1 Journal C. S. Congress, 473, he was credited to South Carolina.

his juniors should be promoted over him except for valor.[68] When, therefore, Gustavus W. Smith had been made Major General, after no previous labors for the Confederacy, Longstreet had been outraged. He had written Beauregard's Assistant Adjutant General a vigorous protest, which had concluded with this unusual language: "When I returned to my home to take part in the cause of my people, I sacrificed everything except, as I thought, the hope of a proper recognition of my services. The placing of persons above me whom I have always ranked and who have just joined this service I regard as great injustice. I therefore request that an officer be detailed to relieve me of this command. I think I have done my share of this service, which is not altogether the most agreeable." [69] While this was a request to be relieved of advanced duty, and was not a direct threat of resignation, it had its effect. Longstreet, who probably had been slated already for promotion, had been made a Major General on October 7, to rank as of that date. This still had left him junior to Smith, but apparently it had satisfied him.[70] Longstreet then had been assigned a Division of two and soon of four Brigades of the best troops in the Army,[71] whom he quickly brought to a good standard of discipline.

The training of his men had not kept Longstreet from participation in the social life of winter quarters. Although his slight deafness probably contributed to make his slow and unimaginative conversation largely a laconic and reluctant succession of "Yes" and "No," [72] he had seemed to enjoy a social glass. In poker he had acquired some renown.[73] Occasionally, he had

[68] O. R., 51, pt. 2, p. 310.

[69] O. R., 51, pt. 2, p. 310. The reference to "persons" whom Longstreet had "always ranked and who have just joined this service" makes it reasonably clear that he was referring to Smith and perhaps to Mansfield Lovell. It is possible that he meant to include Earl Van Dorn also, but that would seem to be precluded because Van Dorn had not "just joined this service." If "this" meant the Confederate service and not merely that of Johnston's Army of the Potomac, Van Dorn could not have been in Longstreet's mind. Van Dorn had resigned Jan. 31, 1861; Longstreet, June 1 (Cullum, Nos. 1162 and 1164).

[70] T. H. Holmes was promoted to the same grade, October 7, and was listed ahead of Longstreet when the names were presented for confirmation (1 Journal C. S. Congress, 473), but as Holmes had outranked Longstreet in the "old army," Longstreet could not object.

[71] For his promotion see O. R.., 5, 892, 896. His first divisional command was of his own and Cocke's Brigade. O. R., 5, 897. This was enlarged, Oct. 22, O. R., 5, 913, and was changed Nov. 16, O. R., 5, 961, to include the Brigades of D. H. Hill, D. R. Jones, M. L. Bonham and L. T. Wigfall and the Hampton Legion.

[72] Memoirs of W. W. Blackford (cited hereafter as W. W. Blackford's MS. Memoirs), 06.　　[73] Sorrel. 41.

gone to Richmond, where Mrs. Longstreet was spending the winter,[74] and he had appeared at the President's levees [75]—a powerful figure, nearly six feet tall, broad of shoulder, with cold, gray-blue eyes, thin, sandy-brown hair and a heavy beard that almost concealed his mouth.[76] In January, Longstreet had answered a hurried summons from his wife, had rushed to the capital and had returned a changed, unhappy man. Scarlet fever had been raging in the city. Two of his children, who succumbed to it, had been buried the same day: a third, a boy of twelve, had died a week later.[77] There was for Longstreet no more gaiety, no more poker and, certainly for the time, no more liquor. Shaken by his grief, he had become less communicative than ever.[78] Essentially, from that tragic January, he was a soldier and little besides.[79]

Proud, martial ambition remained in Longstreet's heart, and grew with the larger responsibilities that had come after the withdrawal from Manassas. On that retreat Longstreet had been given temporary command over a second Division.[80] Perhaps, also, he had been told that, when the President had suggested that he be sent to take command in North Carolina, Johnston had mentioned Smith's precarious health and had insisted that Longstreet be not transferred. "Longstreet's value here," Johnston had written, "commanding troops devoted to him, and confident in his skill and courage, is far greater than it can be elsewhere." [81]

Still greater honor had come to Longstreet. About April 1, during the temporary absence of both Johnston and Smith, he had been ranking officer present with the Army on the Rapidan. Longstreet, not unnaturally, had construed this to give him control of the Department of Northern Virginia, and he had so dated some of his correspondence,[82] though he had no authorization to

---

[74] She arrived Dec. 3, 1861; *Richmond Examiner*, Dec. 4, 1861, p. 3, col. 5.
[75] *De Leon*, 154.
[76] In *An English Combatant*, 59, and in *Companions in Arms*, 420, are unpleasant descriptions of Longstreet's person. Sorrel, *op. cit.*, 27, presented him as more attractive: "a soldier every inch, and very handsome, tall and well proportioned . . . with an unsurpassed soldierly bearing. . . . The worst feature was the mouth, rather coarse."
[77] T. R. R. Cobb's letters to his wife, Jan. 27, Feb. 2, 1862; 28 *S. H. S. P.*, 290, 291. The pathetic monument to these children stands in Hollywood Cemetery, Richmond, Va.
[78] *Sorrel*, 41–42.
[79] F. W. Dawson, *Confederate Reminiscences*, 130.
[80] *O. R.*, 5, 1095–96.   [81] *O. R.*, 12, pt. 2. p. 832.
[82] Cf. *O. R.*, 51, pt. 2, pp. 527 ff.

assume command of the Valley District, which belonged to the department but was under the immediate direction of Maj. Gen. T. J. Jackson. As "Stonewall" then was in a situation that presented both danger and opportunity, he had asked on April 2 for reinforcements. In reporting this to his absent chief, Longstreet had said that he had informed Jackson the Army of the Valley should come closer to the Rapidan before he could undertake to reinforce it. Johnston had approved this answer and had stipulated that no troops should be sent to a distance greater than two days' march from the main position on the Rapidan.[83] This had been justified caution. Part of Johnston's Army was en route to the Peninsula. The remainder, in the judgment of its commander, should be moved there.[84] Desirable as it was for Jackson to be strengthened so that he could strike at the enemy, no risks could be taken in dealing with McClellan, the main adversary.

Longstreet had not accepted that view. The day he received Johnston's instructions, he had sent off one Brigade to Richmond, as directed, and had made ready another to follow. Then, without consulting further his commanding General, Longstreet had written Jackson that he conditionally would reinforce the Army of the Valley and would strike the Federals a swift, sudden blow. "I explained," Longstreet wrote afterward, "that the responsibility of the move could not be taken unless I was with the detachment to give it vigor and action to meet my views, or give time to get back behind the Rapidan in case the authorities discovered the move and ordered its recall."[85] In other words, he had been willing to reinforce Jackson and to launch an unauthorized offensive, provided he had command of it.[86]

Jackson had ignored this proposition. He had continued to address Longstreet at department headquarters; he had explained

---

[83] O. R., 11, pt. 3, p. 412.   [84] Cf. O. R., 11, pt. 3, pp. 405–6.

[85] Longstreet, 65. Unfortunately, the dispatch that contained this proposal has been lost.

[86] It must be remembered that the absence of Johnston was temporary. He was with the Army on the Rapidan as late as March 28, for on that date he forwarded papers to Lee in Richmond and did not intimate that he planned to go there (O. R., 11, pt. 3, p. 406). It would seem almost certain that Johnston did not decide to visit Richmond until the receipt of Lee's letter of March 28 (O. R., 11, pt. 3, p. 409). Johnston was at Fredericksburg on the evening of April 3 (O. R., 11, pt. 3, p. 419) and in communication with Longstreet via Richmond (ibid., 420). By April 6 the regular commander was back on the Rapidan (O. R., 12, pt. 3, p. 486). Longstreet's period of temporary command, therefore, could not have been longer than eight days. Neither R. W. C. D. nor the Richmond newspapers mention this visit of Johnston to Richmond.

his position, and he had presented the arguments for and against an advance, but he had spoken only of what he would endeavor to do with troops that might be sent him.[87] This had been construed by Longstreet to mean that Jackson would not accept his offer. "As the commander of the district did not care to have an officer there of higher rank," he explained in his memoirs, "the subject was discontinued."[88]

Upon Johnston's return, a day or two thereafter, Longstreet had reverted to divisional command and, except for his slight participation in the conference of April 14, had not again played a part in the larger strategy of the developing Virginia campaign. During the brief service of his troops on the lower Peninsula, his duties had been routine, but his soldierly worth had been appreciated. Almost on the eve of the retreat from Yorktown, President Davis had asked Johnston to send Longstreet or G. W. Smith to command the forces around Fredericksburg.[89] Johnston naturally had sought to defer any decision on this until he had completed the withdrawal from the front of the enemy. Now that the Army was on the move, he put six Brigades in Longstreet's care. These included the commands of A. P. Hill, G. E. Pickett and R. H. Anderson, all of them "Manassas Brigades,"[90] with Cadmus Wilcox's Alabama and Mississippi regiments from Smith's Division, R. E. Colston's small command from Huger's Division south of James River, and Roger A. Pryor's troops of Magruder's Army of the Peninsula.

The size and varied origin of this Division reflected the confidence of General Johnston in its commander. As Longstreet rode out for the long succession of battles that lay ahead, any appraisal of him would have taken into account the scantiness of his previous opportunities. He had done little and had proposed

---

[87] *O. R.,* 12, pt. 3, pp. 843–44.

[88] *Longstreet,* 65. No specific reference to this singular episode is to be found in *O. R.,* or in the *Hotchkiss Papers,* which contain a digest of Jackson's Letter Book. Nothing would have been known of the incident had not General Longstreet brought it to light in *op. cit.* Evidently he regarded it as a rejection of opportunity by Jackson, and not as a display of insubordination or ambition on his own part. In respect to seniority, apart from temporary departmental command, the facts were these: Longstreet's "higher rank," as compared with Jackson, rested on (1) the fact that Longstreet had been a Major on the active list of the Army and Jackson a resigned Major by brevet; and (2) the appearance of Longstreet's name ahead of Jackson's on the list of Major Generals appointed Oct. 7, 1861, to rank as of that date.

[89] *O. R.,* 11, pt. 3, p. 485.

[90] To repeat, Hill had Longstreet's old Brigade; Pickett had Cocke's; Anderson had D. R. Jones's.

nothing that had the stamp of genius. On the other hand, his administration had been excellent, and his discipline firm but not harsh. He never was tired.[91] Days and nights of exposure he might endure and, at the end, be the same clear-headed, imperturbable soldier. As Johnston had said, the troops who had served under Longstreet for any length of time believed in him. However deep his ambitions, irritating they were not. If he harbored jealousies at this period of the war, they were not obtrusive. His silence, his self-confidence and his success in creating manifest morale among his troops had given him a reputation that was solid. Had those who most thoroughly knew the Army been asked to describe in one word Longstreet and his command, in that fateful April, 1862, they probably would have agreed on the same soldierly term—*dependable*. Brilliance there might not be; reliability there undoubtedly was.[92]

As Longstreet marched that 3d of May up the Peninsula by the Hampton-Lee's Mill Road, the fourth and last Division of the Army followed the old route from Yorktown to Williamsburg. The commander of this Division was D. Harvey Hill, who had seen much service, of large interest and of small, after his days as Magruder's lieutenant on the Yorktown front.[93] In September, 1861, Hill had been transferred to North Carolina,[94] where he had shown great energy[95] in organizing the defenses between Fort Macon and the Virginia line.[96] With some difficulty he had acquired control of Roanoke Island as a part of his district[97] and had labored to put it in a proper state of defense.[98] Midway this task, while progress was being shown, he had been ordered, November 16, 1861, to report to Gen. Joseph E. Johnston.[99] The change had caused much regret in North Carolina,[100] but it had given Hill a North Carolina Brigade under Long-

91 "I remember one night General Longstreet rode into headquarters about 11 o'clock. He had been riding all day through Paris Gap and reconnoitering other passes of the Blue Ridge. I remarked to him that he must be very tired. He replied, 'No, I never felt fatigue in my life.' "—*MS. Journal of Maj. R. J. Moses*, 10.
92 The next part of the sketch of Longstreet is *infra*, Chap. XIV *et seq.*
93 For the account of D. H. Hill's first labors in Confederate service, see *supra*, Chap. II, p. 17 ff.
94 *O. R.*, 4, 656.   95 *O. R.*, 4, 705.
96 *O. R.*, 4, 662, 682; *O. R.*, 51, pt. 2, p. 329. His command technically was that of the District of the Pamlico, with headquarters at Newbern.
97 *O. R.*, 4, 683–84, 685; *O. R.*, 51, pt. 2, p. 352.
98 *O. R.*, 9, 188; *O. R.*, 51, pt. 2, p. 425.
99 *O. R.*, 4, 700.   100 *O. R.*, 51, pt. 2, pp. 396, 401, 425.

street.[101] Soon it had brought him semi-autonomous command at Leesburg,[102] with the assured confidence of his superiors [103] and the privilege of addressing directly the War Department.[104] His duty on the Potomac had been well performed,[105] so well, indeed, that after having led his troops back to the Rapidan, as a part of Longstreet's Division,[106] he received promotion [107] to the grade of Major General.

Assignment to a Division of his own [108] had come at a time when his spirits had been low. In writing to congratulate his friend and former subordinate, Geo. W. Randolph, on elevation to the Secretaryship of War, Hill had said: "I have mourned over these follies [of Benjamin's administration] until it has almost set me crazy. . . . It has been my misfortune to have been in command of a post since the breaking out of the war, and the sedentary life has been very injurious to one afflicted with a spinal disease. It was my hopes to have been a soldier in this war, but I have only been a passport clerk." [109] He suffered from chronic suspicion of Northern-born Confederates as well as from a weak spine. Incredible as it seems, he even doubted the loyalty of the brilliant and devoted chief of the Ordnance Bureau, Col. Josiah Gorgas.[110]

After Hill had been given command of the left at Yorktown,[111] pessimism had continued to possess him,[112] but he had labored vigorously to improve the works.[113] So deeply was he engrossed in this task that, when some of the units of Magruder's Army were put under his command, he scarcely had opportunity of learning their officers' names.[114] Now, as his Division was leaving Yorktown, he was to confront the enemy with troops that never had been in action together. Four permanent and one temporary Brigade (Crump's) were his, together with a mixed command (Ward's). One Brigade, Jubal Early's, included that General's original Twenty-fourth Virginia, which had fought at

---

101 O. R., 5, 914.
102 O. R., 5, 981.
103 O. R., 5, 995.
104 O. R., 5, 1027.
105 O. R., 51, pt. 2, p. 465.
106 O. R., 5, 1095.
107 As of March 26, 1862.
108 O. R., 12, pt. 3, p. 838.
109 O. R., 51, pt. 2, p. 512.
110 Ibid. and O. R., 11, pt. 3, pp. 461, 464.
111 O. R., 11, pt. 3, p. 448. Hill had arrived at Yorktown about April 10. O. R., 11, pt. 3, p. 436.
112 O. R., 11, pt. 3, pp. 439, 461.
113 O. R., 11, pt. 3, pp. 454, 461, 465.
114 O. R., 11, pt. 1, p. 605.

Manassas. In Robert Rodes's Brigade were two of Ewell's regiments of July, 1861, the Fifth and Sixth Alabama. D. H. Hill's third Brigade, Featherston's, was the former garrison of the works at Manassas. Rains's and Crump's Brigades, as well as Ward's command, were of Magruder's Army. It was a Division of unequal parts, to be sure, but it could be developed.

As much might have been said of the men in the ranks of all four of the Divisions, Magruder's, Smith's, Longstreet's, and D. H. Hill's. Although the troops came from every station of life and included the weak along with the healthy, the illiterate by the side of the educated, they were military material in which the South had full faith from the hour of enlistment. Although that faith persisted, alert officers and the War Department had to admit that the Army had been demoralized, perhaps dangerously, by the confused interpretation and vacillating amendment of the unwise "Furlough and Bounty Act." [115] Even when offered the bounty of $50, the furlough of sixty days, the privilege of changing from one arm of the service to another, and the opportunity of getting rid of unpopular officers by a new election, a majority of the men had declined to enter the service for three additional years.[116] After this became apparent,[117] the demand for general conscription grew.[118] The prospect of being compelled by law to remain in the ranks led the high-spirited to volunteer anew,[119] but the prediction of compulsory service created a rush for exemptions on the part of the cowardly and the war-weary.[120]

At length, under acts of April 16 and 23, conscription of all able-bodied white males between 18 and 35, with specified exceptions, was prescribed for three years or for the duration of the war if less than that term.[121] This meant, among other things,

[115] IV O. R., 1, 826. Cf. Letters of James Conner, 86: "It is a horribly poor bill and will lead to more electioneering jealousies and heart-burnings and discontent among officers and men than could be well devised."

[116] See supra, p. 133.

[117] Cf. IV O. R., 1, 1029, and sources cited in 2 R. E. Lee, 26.

[118] Charleston Mercury, Feb. 15, p. 1, col. 3; March 31, p. 1, col. 2; April 3, 1862, p. 1, col. 2; O. R., 11, pt. 3, p. 411; C. G. Chamberlayne, ed., Ham Chamberlayne— Virginian . . . (cited hereafter as Ham Chamberlayne), 72.

[119] Charleston Mercury, March 19, 1862, p. 1, col. 4.

[120] Charleston Mercury, March 15, p. 1, cols. 3 and 4, March 17, 1862, p. 1, col. 2 and p. 2, col. 2, with quotations from Richmond newspapers.

[121] IV O. R., 1, 1031, 1058, 1061, 1069, 1095 ff; 2 Journal C. S. Congress, 106, 129, 134, 137, 139–42, 145–49, 153–54, 166, 176, 181, 183, 191; 5 ibid., 156–57, 165, 217, 219–21, 224–27, 229, 232, 247, 258, 259, 261, 267, 281–82, 283, 287, 289, 291–94.

that if men of prescribed age who already were in the Army did not voluntarily re-enlist, they would be mustered out and then immediately conscripted.[122] While this created much grumbling [123] and provoked some reflections on the folly of the government in not providing for compulsory service from the outbreak of hostilities,[124] the act was, in the main, "bravely accepted." [125]

The chief concern in some quarters was that the law would not operate in time to supply recruits before the critical battles occurred,[126] but in actual outworking, the chief defect of conscription proved to be the scope of the exemptions. More immediately, the command of the Army was impaired by the inclusion in the new statute of the provision in the "Furlough and Bounty Act" which permitted companies and regiments, when re-enlisting, to elect their officers.[127] Objection to this principle had been voiced early in the war,[128] but President Davis held steadfastly to it.[129] The result was that many officers, including West Point graduates,[130] were rejected because of the strictness of their discipline, and, in their places, corporals or even men from the ranks were elected.[131] In Col. J. C. Haskell's discerning words: "Most of the men went home to visit their families. The majority soon enlisted but often in new commands. Many of the regiments reorganized with new officers, some did not re-enlist at all, others much later, but the general effect was very much to break up the organization of the army." [132]

Many were the exceptions. In some regiments, good men were promoted [133] and incompetents were displaced.[134] One North Carolina officer, Lt. William Quince, assured the desired outcome of an election with a directness that others dared not emulate but envied. He had the company fall in the line with arms; then he

[122] Cf. *O. R.*, 51, pt. 2, p. 548.
[123] See T. R. R. Cobb, in 28 *S. H. S. P.*, 291.
[124] *Letters of James Conner*, 101; De Leon, 174–88.
[125] Sec'y J. A. Seddon in IV *O. R.*, 2, 281.
[126] *O. R.*, 11, pt. 3, p. 461.
[127] IV *O. R.*, 1, 1069.
[128] *Richmond Dispatch*, June 15, 1861, p. 2, col. 2.
[129] 9 Rowland, 543.
[130] W. N. McDonald, *History of the Laurel Brigade* (cited hereafter as *Laurel Brigade*), 76.
[131] T. R. R. Cobb in 28 *S. H. S. P.*, 292; G. W. Randolph, IV *O. R.*, 2, 97; *Stiles*, 73, quoting D. H. Hill; E. P. Alexander in 10 *S. H. S. P.*, 37; *Charleston Mercury*, May 1, 1861, p. 1, col. 2.
[132] J. C. Haskell's *MS. Reminiscences*, p. 41.
[133] *Alexander*, loc. cit.   [134] 2 *N. C. Regts.*, 569.

read the order for the election of a Second Lieutenant, and said briskly: "Men, there are but two candidates for the office, and there is but one of them worth a damn. I nominate him. All who are in favor of electing Sergeant Blank, come to a shoulder. Company, Shoulder arms. . . . Sergeant, take charge of the company and dismiss them." [135] Leaders less positive permitted the men to conduct long elections, though none of the polls seems to have equalled the seven-day balloting of 1861 for the colonelcy of a North Carolina regiment.[136] Many of the regiments had new officers when they left Yorktown, many others were in the midst of their electoral campaigns, and in at least one case, a regiment chose its commanders while bivouacked on the retreat from the Peninsula.[137] "The troops," Johnston reported on May 9, "in addition to the lax discipline of volunteers, are partially discontented at the conscription act and demoralized by their recent elections." [138]

[135] 1 N. C. Regts., 221.
[136] 1 N. C. Regts., 654.
[137] 2 N. C. Regts., 201–2.
[138] O. R., 11, pt. 3, p. 503. Cf. the comment of D. H. Hill, O. R., 11, pt. 1, p. 605.

CHAPTER XIV

WILLIAMSBURG

IT WAS past midnight, May 3–4, 1862, when the last of D. H. Hill's men fired the final round from the batteries at Yorktown and, after spiking the nearest of the heavy guns, took the road to Williamsburg. Already Longstreet's Division from the center had moved off in the darkness, via the Hampton Road, toward the same destination. D. R. Jones, in the absence of Magruder, had led the right Division by the same route. Smith's reserve had marched by the Yorktown Road. Hill was to constitute the rearguard. Behind the last Division of infantry was to come the little force of cavalry under "Jeb" Stuart.[1]

To delay all these troops, deep mud, that ancestral foe and eternal concomitant of war, did its worst. Before the leading Divisions had passed, roads made heavy by recent rains [2] became almost impassable. Guns, wagons and marching men were rammed together like a charge in a musket. One stalled vehicle would halt the whole column till swearing teamsters and tugging soldiers got it moving again. Then the shivering troops would move on for a minute or two—to be stopped again and again in the darkness. The rear units did not cover more than a mile per hour.[3]

At length, during the late morning and early afternoon of the 4th,[4] the struggling columns reached and passed the line of works

---

1 *Johnston's Narrative*, 119.   2 *Early*, 67; 8 *S. H. S. P.*, 284.   3 *Alexander*, 66.

4 If any general order of march was issued for May 3–4, no copy seems to have been preserved, though the order prepared for the march of May 2–3, subsequently cancelled, appears in *O. R.*, 11, pt. 1, pp. 489–90. All that is known positively of the march is that Smith led on the Yorktown road, that one of Magruder's Divisions was entering Williamsburg at 1 P.M. on the 4th (*O. R.*, 11, pt. 1, p. 446), that the last of Longstreet's Brigades did not go into bivouac, one mile West of the town, till 5:30 P.M. (*O. R.*, 11, pt. 1, p. 590), and that, as indicated in the text, D. H. Hill formed the rearguard (8 *S. H. S. P.*, 287). To judge by the distances to be covered, the order of arrival in Williamsburg would have been Smith, Magruder, Longstreet and Hill. Col. Richard L. Maury (8 *S. H. S. P.*, 287) left the impression that Longstreet led, but this seems doubtful. Neither is it certain, as Maury intimated, that the order of march for May 4–5 followed the rule subsequently applied in the Army of Northern Virginia —that the leading Division halt at the end of a day and permit the other Divisions to pass in order that it might act the next day as rearguard. The employment of two

174

that Magruder had constructed across the low ridge that separated the watershed of James River from that of the York. It was a feeble line. At the junction of the Hampton and Yorktown roads was Fort Magruder, an earthwork of bastion front. On either side were small redoubts and epaulements, twelve in all.[5] At these entrenchments, as the infantry wormed their way to the old colonial capital, probably few of the weary officers and men cast more than a glance. What mattered the defenses of the second capital of the colony? The troops expected to rest at Williamsburg, not to fight there. Tired eyes were looking for camps and commissaries, not for forts and defenses that seemed to represent wasted labor only.

Little food the men found and no camps except sodden fields by the roadside, but rest of a sort the vanguard had during the late morning. The road to the West stretched out before the Army as a river of mud, but otherwise the situation was no more adverse than a retreat usually is. At noon, May 4, Johnston appeared to have a chance of getting away untouched. His withdrawal from Manassas might be duplicated. All the loss might be in what had been left behind.

Then, at 1 o'clock, the outlook changed. The Confederate cavalry were driven in. Federal infantry were believed to be in close support of their skirmishing mounted units. A strong column might fall upon the rear of Johnston's Army. To prevent that—and all its possible consequences—the obvious thing to do at the moment was to occupy and to hold Fort Magruder and the near-by line of redoubts. Johnston had expected to abandon them, in the belief that pursuit would not be close; but if the enemy was pressing close, the resistance that could be offered from the fortifications would permit Johnston to put more distance between the pursuers and the main Confederate force. As the nearest Brigade was that of Paul Semmes, Magruder's Divi-

Brigades of Magruder's Division to defend the line of Fort Magruder on the afternoon of May 4 seems to have been due to the fact that they chanced to be the troops nearest at hand. Their subsequent withdrawal and the substitution of two from Longstreet's Division may have been based on Johnston's adherence to a decision, reached during the day or possibly in advance, that Magruder should lead on the Richmond road. (Cf. *O. R.*, 11, pt. 1, p. 275). This, in turn, may have reflected Johnston's natural wish that the troops with which he was most familiar should be nearest the enemy in the event a rearguard action developed or a battle became necessary to protect the right flank from a Federal force which landed higher up York River.

[5] *O. R.*, 11, pt. 1, p. 19.

sion, Johnston personally led it into Fort Magruder. When General Lafayette McLaws rode up, Johnston ordered him to bring back another Brigade and to take charge of the defense. Fortunately, McLaws's service with Magruder had given him some familiarity with the ground. By a quick call for Kershaw's experienced South Carolinians and for two batteries of artillery, McLaws prepared to hold the line. There was momentary doubt whether the Confederates could man Fort Magruder in sufficient strength before the Federals overran the parapets, but after putting the artillery at a gallop, McLaws delivered a volume of fire that made the enemy recoil. An adequate, if temporary barrier seemed to have been placed between the Army and the pursuers. By erecting it promptly, McLaws received a credit in the mind of the commanding General. The Georgian could be trusted.[6]

Because Johnston had determined that Magruder's Division should head the retreat that evening,[7] the two Brigades under McLaws were recalled after sunset from the vicinity of the fort and were reunited with their Division.[8] Longstreet was ordered to put a Brigade in their place,[9] but, as his units were small, he decided to send two Brigades, R. H. Anderson's and Pryor's.[10] By the time those troops marched back from Williamsburg to the defenses, darkness had fallen.[11] At 8 o'clock,[12] before they had taken position for the night, a downpour came.[13] Anderson carefully advanced his pickets to the junction of the Hampton and Yorktown roads.[14] More than that, as the rain beat down in the black night,[15] he did not attempt.[16] His was an uncomfortable position, in more than one sense, for an officer who, while expe-

---

[6] For the reports, see O. R., 11, pt. 1, pp. 275, 441 ff; Johnston's Narrative, 119–20. As so often happened, there was conflict in the reports concerning the hour of the different incidents on the afternoon of May 4. Semmes's timing is accepted here on the theory that he, the officer most immediately involved, would be likely to remember when he was ordered to the line. His report, moreover, was written less than a fortnight after the action. Johnston's Narrative, which sets the hour at 4 P.M., was prepared about ten years later.

[7] O. R., 11, pt. 1, p. 275.
[8] Johnston's Narrative, 120.
[9] O. R., 11, pt. 1, p. 564.
[10] Longstreet, 72.
[11] Longstreet, 72.
[12] O. R., 11, pt. 1, p. 435.
[13] Longstreet, 72.
[14] Longstreet, 73.
[15] Alexander, 66.

[16] Johnston, op. cit., 120, seems definitely in error when he stated that on the night of May 4 Anderson occupied four redoubts to the right and two to the left of Fort Magruder. Longstreet specifically denied this (Longstreet, 73), and Anderson referred in his account (O. R., 11, pt. 1, p. 580) only to "the redoubt near Williamsburg." In writing of the operations of the following day he mentioned "the redoubts," though he did not state when he occupied them.

rienced, had never before occupied so responsible a field position or commanded so many men directly in the face of the enemy.[17]

After daylight on May 5 "Dick" Anderson could see that the immediate approaches to Fort Magruder, via the Yorktown and the Hampton roads, were from the South. The defenses were an obtuse angle that ran North to the redoubts West of Fort Magruder, and then passed the fort in a direction slightly North of East. Directly to the right of the fort, facing the enemy, several redoubts in an open field overlooked a little creek. On the opposite side of the stream, in the direction of the Federal advance, were newly felled trees and, beyond that, wide-spreading woodland. Immediately in front of the fort, as Anderson looked South, was a cleared area. Some trees had been cut to give protection on the Southwest. To the left [18] of the fort was boggy woodland in the northern background. Then came a stretch of growing wheat. South of that and Southeast of the fort was a branch of Queen's Creek, wooded on the side of the enemy's approach.[19] This much could be seen through the rain, which had diminished to a cold drizzle, but visibility was low. Of fortifications on the right, Anderson could discern only four redoubts, and on the left, two. These six he promptly occupied.[20]

About 6 A.M., the Federals in Anderson's front opened with their skirmishers and with their artillery.[21] As the Confederate forces were well covered, little damage resulted. Steadily, thereafter, the front of action widened. The fire became more intense. Evidently, the Federals either were making a strong demonstration or else they were seeking to storm the line of the rearguard and force a general engagement with the retreating main Army.

In this uncertainty, Longstreet felt it desirable to reinforce Anderson. As coolly as if he had fought a score of battles, Long-

---

[17] Anderson's only previous clash with Federal infantry had been in a raid on Santa Rosa Island, Florida, Oct. 8–9, 1861, when he had been wounded in the left elbow (O. R. 6, 459). See his report, ibid., 460 ff.

[18] East.

[19] Johnston's Narrative, 120; Longstreet, 72–73; McRae in 7 S. H. S. P., 368; Maury in 8 ibid., 285. Scarcely one of these descriptions of the ground is accurate. General Johnston overlooked one of the redoubts on the right and listed only four; Colonel McRae mistook East for North. The map in Johnston's Narrative, 119, is worthless; those in O. R., Atlas, Plate XX, Nos. 2, 3 and 4, were based on a hurried reconnaissance by a Federal engineer and are not good. The woodland has changed greatly since 1862, but careful examination of the ground will make plain the position. At present (1942) Fort Magruder is in fair condition. Six of the redoubts on the left can be located. Three on the right are preserved.

[20] Longstreet, 73.   [21] O. R., 11, pt. 1, p. 580.

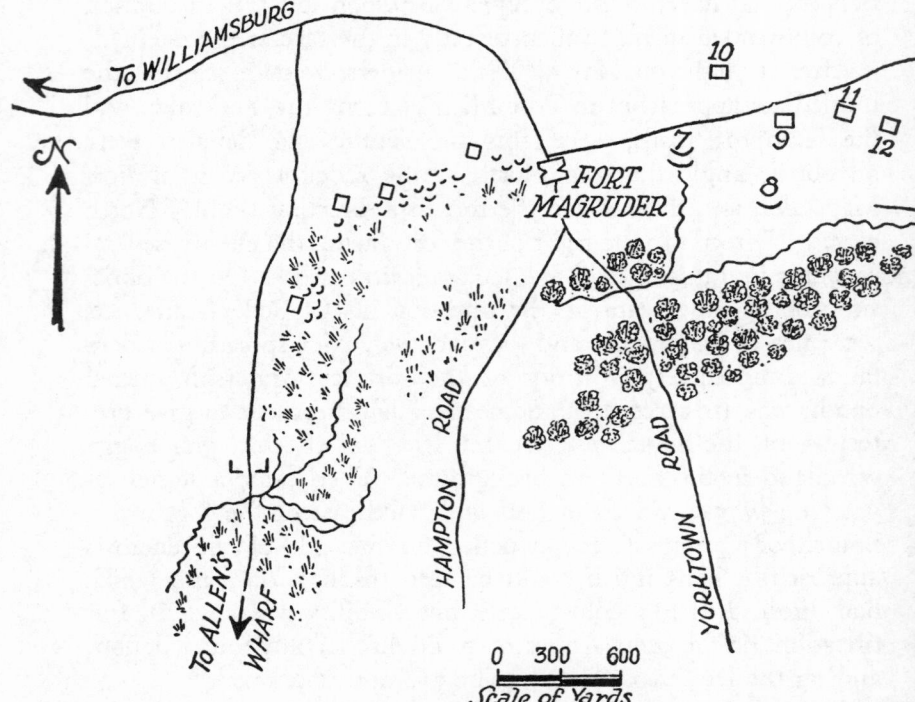

Fort Magruder and adjacent redoubts, woods, and abatis, May 4–5, 1862. For a critique of this sketch, see note 19.

street ordered first Cadmus Wilcox and then A. P. Hill to take their Brigades back to Fort Magruder.[22] A little later Longstreet went in person to the scene of Anderson's action. Thence, as he saw the fighting extended, he dispatched orders to the reserve of his Division, Pickett's and Colston's Brigades, to advance for employment in any emergency.[23] Anderson promptly placed these Brigades on his right, where the Federals were pressing forward with some vigor.

This reinforcement emboldened Anderson. He or Longstreet or both of them decided to take the offensive. Orders were given. The men soon realized what was to be attempted. Ardently they began to push forward and slowly to drive a stubborn, hard-hitting enemy back toward the woods. Guns, prisoners and flags

[22] Hill received his orders between 8 and 9 A.M. *O. R.*, 11. pt. 1, p. 575. The hour of the dispatch of the orders is not known.
[23] *Longstreet*, 74; *Johnston's Narrative*, 120.

were taken. Casualties were not excessive, though later in the day two Colonels of great promise were killed—C. H. Mott of the Nineteenth Mississippi and G. T. Ward of the Second Florida.[24] Untried soldiers bore themselves well. The field appeared to be theirs. All the general officers were confident that Johnston's wishes could be realized easily—that the enemy could be held without difficulty until nightfall, when the Army would take up the retreat.

The rearguard action was not to end so easily. Trouble was in the making. Anderson had posted Micah Jenkins's Palmetto Sharpshooters with six companies of the Fifth South Carolina in Fort Magruder and had placed a battalion of the Louisiana Foot Rifles in the first redoubt to the right of the Fort. In the corresponding redoubt on the left, he stationed the remaining four companies of the Fifth South Carolina. Farther to the left were two redoubts, one almost directly North and in rear of the other. In the southernmost of these works, Anderson placed three companies of the Sixth South Carolina. The remainder of that regiment, under Col. John Bratton, he held in reserve to the left and rear of Fort Magruder. As Anderson had charge of several Brigades, he then entrusted his own Brigade to the senior Colonel, Micah Jenkins.

Between 3 and 4 P.M., the Federals seized a redoubt far to the left, a redoubt that either had not been seen by Anderson or else had been assumed to be under the care of other troops. To this work, the enemy with much spirit quickly brought up guns, and from it he began to pour artillery fire into Fort Magruder. This created much confusion. The redoubt directly to the left of Fort Magruder was evacuated by its alarmed garrison, but the next redoubt to the left was held. This was the one behind which, to the North, was a similar work. If the bluecoats got the northern work, they could command the southern. As quickly as this fact was realized, yelling adversaries raced for the redoubt. Narrowly but jubilantly the reserve companies of the Sixth South Carolina occupied the parapet.[25] The Federals fell back but con-

---

[24] See Longstreet's tribute to them in 11 *O. R.*, pt. 1, p. 567. Had Mott lived, he probably would have been promoted speedily to the rank of Brigadier. He was a man of high ability. See *infra*, p. 195, n. 18.

[25] *O. R.*, 11, pt. 1, pp. 582–83; Col. John Bratton in 7 *S. H. S. P.*, 299. See the answer of Col. D. K. McRae to Colonel Bratton in *ibid.*, 360 ff.

tinued so heavy an artillery fire from the ground they had gained that they created some concern for the safety of Fort Magruder.

Even before this occurred, Longstreet had sensed danger on the left, and had dispatched to D. H. Hill a request to send back a Brigade to a point whence it could be moved quickly to strengthen the left wing in case of necessity. Johnston himself went to the vicinity of Fort Magruder, alarmed by the volume of fire, but, as he found the dispositions satisfactory and the troops gaining ground on the right, which was the only part of the front that he reconnoitered, he did not assume command [26] or give any instructions concerning the Brigade he had requested of D. H. Hill.

This Brigade was Jubal A. Early's. It had been the rearguard the previous night and had been put into camp two miles West of Williamsburg, where the men had bivouacked, hungry, in the rain. Now they splashed their way back through the mud and drizzle and halted on the campus of the College of William and Mary.[27] One of the four regiments of the Brigade, it will be recalled, was the Twenty-fourth Virginia, Early's original command, which had distinguished itself at Manassas. The others were the Fifth and Twenty-third North Carolina and the Thirty-eighth Virginia. None of these had any combat experience. The last-named regiment, which had been transferred to Early in exchange for the Twentieth Georgia, had joined him only two days previously.[28] The Second Florida Infantry and the Second Mississippi Battalion were operating temporarily with the Brigade.

The men waited, cold and dripping, till after 3 o'clock. Then a muddy courier arrived with a brief order: "Move quickly to the support of Longstreet."[29] As the fire from the front was plainly audible [30] and to inexperienced ears was heavy, the men formed quickly and, with vigorous step, marched eastward for about a mile from Williamsburg. They numbered close to 2300 rank and file—in size about an average Confederate Brigade for that period of the war.[31]

---

[26] Longstreet, 74; Johnston's Narrative, 120; O. R., 11, pt. 1, p. 275.
[27] O. R., 11, pt. 1, p. 606.
[28] Early, 67. The Thirty-eighth previously had belonged to Toombs's Brigade. O. R., 11, pt. 3, p. 480.
[29] Maury in 8 S. H. S. P., 285.   [30] Ibid.
[31] With the Twentieth Georgia and the Jeff. Davis Artillery, the Brigade, as of April 30, or thereabouts, numbered 2380 effectives, O. R., 11, pt. 3, p. 482. The Thirty-

As they pressed on, Early rode ahead and reported to "Jeb" Stuart, but Longstreet soon overtook Early and pointed out to him ground to the left and rear of Fort Magruder, where Early was to post his Brigade and await orders.[32] Almost before Early could start his men for this position, Longstreet sent word that two regiments of the Brigade must be dispatched to strengthen still further the Confederate right. Early accordingly detached the Mississippi Battalion and the Florida regiment. With his own four regiments, he hurried on across a plowed field [33] to the ground Longstreet had indicated. It was a ridge that ran almost East and West and overlooked a wheat field some 200 or 300 yards in depth. On the southern side of the grain were woods, with thick underbrush, that apparently ran down to a stream or a swamp. The position was not under fire. Neither to the green soldiers nor to their fiery-eyed, ambitious commander, would the situation have been more than vaguely exciting, but for one circumstance: from the South of the obscuring woods, furiously firing artillery was sending a loud echo up the ridge. The guns manifestly were near. Early felt sure they were Federal and were firing on Fort Magruder; but he could not ascertain their location, nor could he tell how deep the woods were.[34]

While Early was waiting here, listening to the fire of the guns and burning with a desire to storm the invisible battery, D. H. Hill rode up. He explained that after he had been directed to move one Brigade to the engaged rearguard, he had been ordered by Longstreet to bring back to the line of action the three remaining Brigades of his Division.[35] These he now was disposing in rear of Early,[36] but Hill was not content to do that and no more. He, like Early, was full of the confident ardor of attack. If only he could throw his men forward and storm those guns! That would be a better lesson than any he had given in his arithmetic with the enemy as his example.

Hill made a brief, partial reconnaissance of the woods and

eighth Virginia, *O. R.*, 11, pt. 3, p. 480, was slightly smaller. The Second Florida (530) and the Second Mississippi Battalion (360) are not included, because they were temporarily attached and did not act with the Brigade in the battle. For these two commands, see *O. R.*, 11, pt. 3, p. 482.

[32] *O. R.*, 11, pt. 1, p. 607.   [33] 8 *S. H. S. P.*, 289.
[34] *Early*, 69; *O. R.*, 11, pt. 1, p. 607.
[35] *O. R.*, 11, pt. 1, p. 565. The Brigades were (*O. R.*, 11. pt. 1, p. 602), Rains's, Featherston's and Rodes's.
[36] *O. R.*, 11, pt. 1, pp. 602-3.

found the ground swampy, as had been expected, and almost impenetrable by reason of the underbrush; but he agreed with Early that an attack could be made which would take the Federal artillery in rear.[37] For such an attack the consent of Johnston, who urged caution, was procured. Approval also was had from Longstreet, who directed Hill to accompany the column.[38] Hill thereupon posted guns to cover a retreat in case the attack failed, and he put Rains's Brigade where it could advance and take the place of Early's men when they went forward.[39] All the while, the enemy on the other side of the woods to the South did nothing to indicate that he intended either to push through the screen of trees and confront Hill, or to launch an attack against Fort Magruder. For all that could be seen or heard from the ridge where Hill and Early deployed the Brigade, the Federals merely were continuing their bombardment of the earthwork to the West of them.

Deployment of the excited Confederate troops then began. Eagerly, if nervously, the men took their places. Anxiously they speculated on the strength and position of the enemy. Hill directed that the advance, which was to be from North to South, should be in a single line on brigade front. The Twenty-fourth Virginia was placed on the left, farthest to the East. On its right was the Thirty-eighth Virginia, next was the Twenty-third North Carolina, and, on the right and West, was the Fifth North Carolina.[40] The two Carolina regiments were to be led by Hill in person; the Virginia units were to be under the brigade commander. Early took his station on horseback with his own former regiment, the Twenty-fourth, because he judged from the sound of the firing that this regiment would crash through the woods and into the open at the point where it would strike the battery. Although nothing was said of the subject, there undoubtedly was between Hill and Early a martial rivalry to have the troops from their respective States capture the Federal guns.

Presently, Hill ordered his two regiments forward. Early received no word but, when he saw the right advancing, he assumed

---

37 *O. R.*, 11, pt. 1, pp. 603, 607.
38 As it involves Early and Hill, this is stated impersonally because, as will appear, there is an irreconcilable conflict of testimony over the responsibility for the attack. See *infra*, p. 190
39 *Early*, 69   40 *Ibid.*

that the division commander intended the left to conform, and he gave the word.[41] The Twenty-fourth Virginia started off briskly across the wheat field and into the woods, but the less experienced Thirty-eighth, under a Lieutenant Colonel who had not been in action previously, was slow in getting under way. Soon it was fifty yards behind the regiment on its left. Early had to send back and order it to the double-quick.[42] By the time the Thirty-eighth reached the nearer edge of the woods, the Twenty-fourth was crashing downward through the underbrush in the direction of the ravine. Contact between the two regiments was lost almost immediately.

On the right, the units under the guidance of Hill started together and kept their formation until they reached and crossed the ravine. There they encountered a tangle so thick that Hill could see nothing of the regiments on his left. Uncertain whether the Virginians had reached the ravine, he halted the two Carolina regiments and directed his Assistant Adjutant General to go through the woods to find Early and to ascertain if the Twenty-fourth and the Thirty-eighth Virginia were ready to attack.[43]

It was a vain precaution. Early had not halted at the ravine or waited to see whether the troops on his right were aligned. Within less than five minutes after Hill had halted, Early was on the edge of the woods closest the enemy. "Follow me," he shouted and plunged into the open.[44]

Early still was facing southward, with his left to the East. Ahead of and parallel to the front of the Twenty-fourth Virginia was a fence on the edge of a field. Still farther to the South, beyond the field, was another wood. On the East were more woods. The ground to the right and West, in front, was clear all the way to Fort Magruder, distant half a mile.[45]

Several redoubts were visible, but Early did not observe the number with accuracy, nor determine which were in the hands of the Confederates or which the Federals had captured.[46] The

[41] *O. R.*, 11, pt. 1, p. 607.   [42] *O. R.*, 11, pt. 1, p. 613.   [43] *O. R.*, 11, pt. 1, p. 603.

[44] *O. R.*, 11, pt. 1, p. 603. Hill stated here that he heard "a voice which I took to be General Early's, above all the uproar, crying, 'Follow me.'" Early did not mention the incident, but as his voice had a singular carrying quality, it is virtually certain that Hill was correct in his identification.

[45] *O. R.*, 11, pt. 1, p. 603.

[46] *O. R.*, 11, pt. 1, p. 608. Gen. W. S. Hancock, who was commanding the Federal troops, actually held two redoubts at this time, *O. R.*, 11, pt. 1, p. 536, but one of these must have been out of sight of the Confederates.

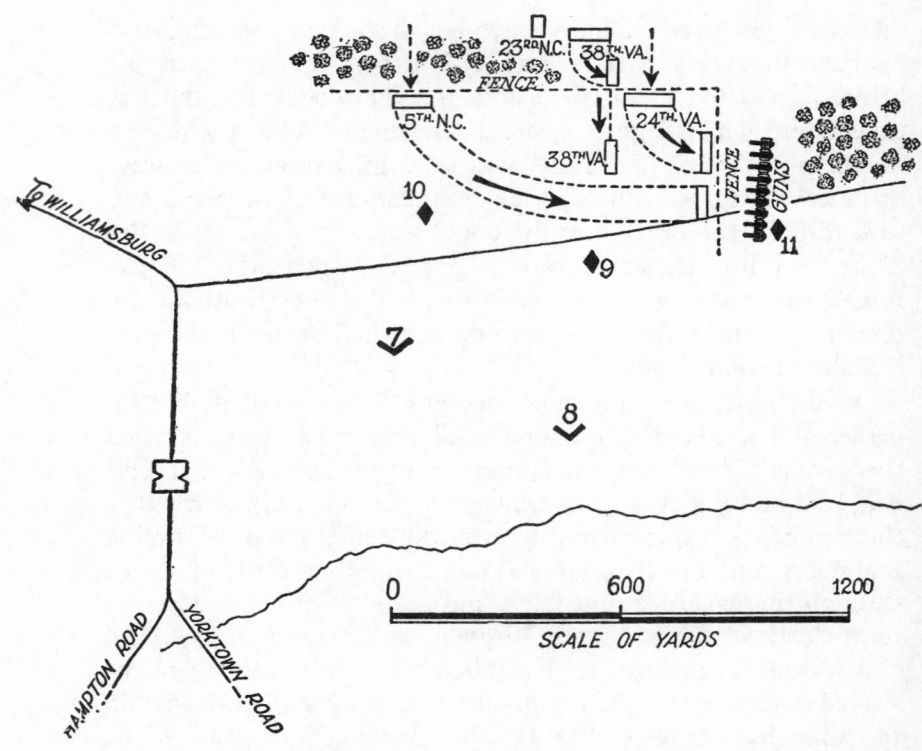

Advance of Early's Brigade in the Battle of Williamsburg (Fort Magruder), May 5, 1862, as reconstructed hypothetically from the reports of the battle.

General's eyes and those of the regiment were drawn instantly to a different spectacle: on a line roughly North and South, near some farm buildings, and almost perpendicular to the front of the Twenty-fourth, was the object of the Confederate advance— the battery that had been heard beyond the woods. Eight or nine Federal guns were in action. Infantry support was near at hand, around a captured redoubt which was to the East and in rear of the artillery. Other infantry apparently were waiting along a fence and in the edge of woods to the East.[47] As the Federals were deployed against Fort Magruder, their infantry and their guns were almost at a right angle with the left of Early's line.[48]

[47] *Early,* 70; *O. R.,* 11, pt. 1, p. 607.
[48] The accounts do not state that the enemy was opposite the left of the Twenty-fourth, but, of course, if he had been opposite the right, the Twenty-fourth could have charged his flank and rear.

This display of strength did not deter the Twenty-fourth or the General. Early pivoted the regiment roughly on its left. Quickly, furiously, it started for the artillery. The surprised Federals tried to turn their guns to meet the assault. A few rounds were fired almost at random. The attack did not falter. At the battery, orders were shouted. Next, gunners limbered up and dragged their pieces over the wet ground to the cover of the redoubt and the woods.[49] The Twenty-fourth began pursuit, but it found the field so heavy from the rain that the men were well-nigh bogged.[50] At this moment, Early received a minié ball in his shoulder. He tried to remain with the regiment, but the flow of blood and the wounding of his horse compelled him to turn back to one of the redoubts which was flying the Confederate flag.

As Early rode toward the earthwork, he met the Fifth North Carolina, which, it will be remembered, at the beginning of the advance had been on the extreme right of the Brigade. This regiment, under Col. D. K. McRae, had renewed its advance after Hill had stopped it near the ravine. When McRae had reached the southern edge of the woods and had found no Federals in his front, he had advanced about 100 yards into the open. There the regiment had come under fire from the battery which Early had chased back to the woods on the eastern side of the field. About this time, McRae had been joined by three [51] companies of the Sixth South Carolina, but he had not observed their arrival [52] because he was engrossed with the puzzling situation he had found. The Federal guns were distant some 800 or 900 yards, and were not in his front but were to the East, opposite his left. Were those guns the battery which Hill had told him, ere the advance began, he was to charge? In doubt. McRae had halted and had sent word to Hill, on the edge of the wood, to ask which battery he should assail. Hill had regretted that any of the troops had gone into the open, but now he had to tell McRae to attack the battery that was firing on the Fifth and to do it quickly.[53]

Execution of this movement, of course, had involved a wide oblique, which had been begun at the wrong angle. McRae had been compelled to halt the regiment a second time and to realign

[49] Early, 70.
[50] Longstreet, 71; O. R., 11, pt. 1, pp. 603, 610.
[51] McRae, 7 S. H. S. P., 371, thought the companies were only two in number.
[52] Ibid.   [53] O. R., 11, pt. 1, p. 610.

it before he had been able to commence his charge. Then, for a few minutes, he had the men lie down. Now, as Early met the Fifth, at the moment the Twenty-fourth was driving the Federals from the farm buildings, the Carolinians were advancing with great gallantry, but already were under a heavy fire.[54] Moreover, to form a continuous line with the Twenty-fourth, they had a long distance to go. The reason for this was that the Twenty-third North Carolina and the Thirty-eighth Virginia had not come out of the woods. From its position on the right of the Brigade, the Fifth had, in effect, to cross what should have been the front of two regiments.

As the Twenty-fourth and the Fifth continued to plow their way toward the enemy's position, D. H. Hill went to look for the two missing units of the Brigade. He found the Thirty-eighth Virginia, to use his own words, "huddled up and in considerable confusion." [55] Its commanding officer, Lt. Col. Powhatan B. Whittle, had lost contact with his three left companies and, apparently, had lost direction as well. Whittle thereupon had moved by his left flank toward the sound of the firing,[56] and had reached a point where the Federal missiles were falling.

Hill believed that the enemy's front, which Early now was assailing from the West, across the open field, extended northward into the eastern part of the woods through which the Brigade first had moved southward. If this was so, then the Thirty-eighth had presented its left flank to the Federals. That would explain the fire it was receiving. General Hill accordingly ordered Colonel Whittle to change direction from the South to the East, and to clear the Unionists from the woods. With some difficulty, this change of front was effected.

Hill then beat his way through the underbrush to find the Twenty-third North Carolina. At length he came upon it as it waited, idle, along a fence line. The regiment was ordered immediately to change position and to form on the left of the Thirty-eighth Virginia for a sweep through the woods, but the Twenty-third was poorly drilled and, in the tangle, was slow to get in line.[57]

54 Colonel McRae stated, O. R., 11, pt. 1, p. 610, that the Twenty-fourth was 300 yards to the left and front of the Fifth when the North Carolinians began their advance and before the halt and realignment. Obviously, these delays had increased the distance. 55 O. R., 11, pt. 1, p. 603. 56 O. R., 11, pt. 1, p. 613. 57 O. R., 11, pt. 1, pp. 603-4.

The confused tactical situation by this time was one that would have tested veteran regulars, but Hill mistakenly thought he had the entire Brigade in proper position to drive the Federals from the cover they had taken. That is to say, the brigade front, which had been facing southward as the men had been led into action, had been shifted so that the two regiments in the field and the two in the woods had been directed to the East.

Without waiting for the advance of the Twenty-third North Carolina and the Thirty-eighth Virginia to begin, Hill returned to the open field. There he found the Twenty-fourth Virginia and the Fifth North Carolina still struggling over the heavy ground toward the enemy. The men were falling fast. Unless they were reinforced, it did not seem possible that they could reach and dislodge the Federals. The only reinforcements near at hand were seven companies of the Sixth South Carolina, close to Fort Magruder. Col. John Bratton already had asked Early if these companies might join in the charge. With Early's consent, they were forming when Hill ordered them to reinforce the attacking column; but to Hill's impatient eye they seemed slow.[58] When the South Carolinians got under way and passed the edge of the woods opposite the point where the Thirty-eighth Virginia had formed, that regiment came out of the woods and joined them. This was contrary to Hill's instructions,[59] but apparently was done under orders from Early,[60] who did not know that his superior had told the Thirty-eighth to change front and to advance eastward through the woods.

By this time, the Federals, too, were in confusion. The infantry were leaving the field or were seeking shelter behind the redoubt they held. As far as the Confederates could see, a retreat was imminent.[61] Unhappily, the Twenty-fourth Virginia and the Fifth North Carolina came at that moment to a stout rail fence, where they paused to breathe a moment before they climbed over to a final grapple with the enemy. Perhaps Colonel McRae, as senior officer, then realized for the first time how many of his officers had fallen; perhaps he saw how scant was the force that lined the fence. In any event, he ordered his men to take such

---

58 7 S. H. S. P., 300–301; O. R., 11, pt. 1, p. 604.
59 O. R., 11, pt. 1, p. 604.
60 O. R., 11, pt. 1, p. 613.
61 8 S. H. S. P., 295.

cover as they could find behind the fence, and, as they were doing so, he got word from Hill to retire.[62]

On the left of McRae, the Twenty-fourth Virginia was in the act of mounting the fence when the order came to break off the attack.[63] The Virginians quickly obliqued into the woods on their left [64] with little further loss, but the North Carolinians had to recross the field under fire. In doing so, the regiment was shattered. No pursuit was attempted. The futile, bungling action ended. Early's men bivouacked where they had been when the engagement began.

Casualties in Early's Brigade were at least 600, and may have been higher.[65] Of 1560 Confederate losses that day in the whole participating force, this adventure on the left accounted for more than 38 per cent. For the troops engaged, that was excessive. There was much praise of the gallant attack, which was as fine as anything the war had witnessed, but there was no compensatory gain. Nor had there been any good reason for the costly assault of infantry on artillery. Although it was not known at the time, the Federals, who proved to be Hancock's Brigade, actually were retiring, for lack of reinforcements, when Early assailed them.[66] Even had that fact been realized, little would have been said of it by the Southerners. The repulse of the Unionists on the Confederate center and right had been so complete, and the Northern casualties there had been so heavy in comparison with those of Longstreet's command—approximately 2110 as against 1024—that the Confederates laid their emphasis on the success in front of Fort Magruder and to the southward.[67] Conversely, the Federals

---

[62] O. R., 11, pt. 1, p. 611.

[63] 8 S. H. S. P., 295. In this narrative, Colonel Maury said that the Confederates were within twenty yards of the Federals; Colonel McRae, O. R., 11, pt. 1, p. 611, gave the distance as 100 yards.

[64] 8 S. H. S. P., 295.

[65] Early reported 287, with no figures for the Fifth North Carolina, O. R., 11, pt. 1, p. 569. The difference between the summary, ibid., with the Fifth North Carolina unreported, and Longstreet's total, ibid., 568, which ostensibly included that regiment, is 309. If this covered all the loss of the Fifth, the sum is 596. In 1 N. C. Regts., 285, it is stated unofficially that the Fifth went into action with 415 and, the next morning, had 75. This would make the regimental casualties 340 and would raise the brigade total to 627. Colonel McRae, in 1879 (7 S. H. S. P., 360), gave his loss as 290, but did not state his authority. If he was correct, the killed, wounded and missing of the Brigade were 577. In his report of May 10, 1862 (O. R., 11, pt. 1, p. 611), Colonel McRae said: "My regiment is now so reduced as to be inefficient."

[66] See Hancock's report, O. R., 11, pt. 1, p. 538.

[67] Gross Federal casualties were 2239, O. R., 11, pt. 1, p. 450; those of Hancock he reported as 129, ibid., 542.

talked only of their accomplishments on the Confederate left, where Union losses were less than a fourth those sustained by Early.[68]

By May 25, all the Confederate reports save that of D. H. Hill [69] were written. Johnston, who treated the battle of Williamsburg in five brief paragraphs,[70] did not mention the fight on the left. He had praise for Magruder's "forethought" in constructing the "little works" across the Peninsula, and he commended two officers warmly. One was McLaws, who "made his dispositions with prompt courage and skill" on the 4th, "and quickly drove the Federal troops from the field." The other was Longstreet, whose "clear head and brave heart" made the commanding General "a mere spectator," with "no apology for interference." [71]

Longstreet wrote a casual, almost complacent report, in which he said: "My part in the battle was comparatively simple and easy, that of placing the troops in proper positions at proper times." [72] He distributed compliments broadly. D. H. Hill, presented as "hero of many battle-fields," was declared "conspicuous for the ability and courage exhibited in planning the left attack." [73] Anderson was applauded: ". . . his disposition of his forces and manner of leading them into action displayed great ability and signal gallantry and coolness." [74] A. P. Hill, Cadmus Wilcox, G. E. Pickett, Roger A. Pryor and R. E. Colston all were mentioned. Special tribute was paid to A. P. Hill's Brigade: "Its organization was perfect throughout the battle, and it was marched off the field in as good order as it entered it." [75] General Stuart was said by Longstreet to have been "exceedingly active and

[68] This assumes that the Confederate losses there, as explained in note *supra*, were about 600. General McClellan reported on the night of May 5 that Hancock's "conduct was brilliant in the extreme," *O. R.*, 11, pt. 1, p. 448. On the 6th, the commanding General telegraphed: "Every hour proves our victory more complete." *Ibid.*, 449. In his general report, McClellan said of Hancock's action: "This was one of the most brilliant engagements of the war, and General Hancock merits the highest praise for the soldierly qualities displayed and his perfect apperception of the vital importance of his position." *Ibid.*, 22–23.

[69] Hill's was not forwarded by Longstreet until Jan. 11, 1863, when he noted that it was "just received." *O. R.*, 11, pt. 1, p. 601.

[70] Three in *O. R.*, 11, pt. 1, p. 275, and two in *ibid.*, 276.

[71] *O. R.*, 11, pt. 1, p. 275. [72] *O. R.*, 11, pt. 1, p. 566.

[73] *O. R.*, 11, pt. 1, p. 567.

[74] *Ibid.*

[75] *Ibid.* General Longstreet subsequently had a controversy with A. P. Hill, as set forth in Chap. XLII; and when, about 1895, he described in his memoirs the action at Williamsburg, he barely mentioned the presence of Hill's Brigade on the field. *Op. cit.*, 7A.

zealous in conducting the different columns to their proper des-
tinations and in assisting them to get properly into action." [76]

General Early's part in the battle was handled with reticence
in the reports. Longstreet wrote: "D. H. Hill arranged his forces
for the attack with excellent judgment, but in the hurry of bringing the troops into action some of the officers failed to take due
advantage of the ground and exposed them to a fire which was
not absolutely necessary, and the effort to drive the enemy from
that part of his position failed. This mishap could have been
remedied by an extreme flank movement and complete victory
won; but . . . we were not in a condition to increase our responsibilities, and a great delay might have endangered other operations of the army." Longstreet explained, also, that when "a
diversion," as he styled Early's attack, was made against the left,
D. H. Hill was "ordered to watch it." [77] That was all Longstreet
had to say of Early, except that the General "was severely wounded
through the body, while leading an impetuous assault on the
enemy's position." [78]

While this language was considerate, the reports and subsequent publications showed a purpose on the part of both Early
and Hill to disclaim responsibility for ordering the attack on the
left. Early stated in his official account [79] that shortly after D. H.
Hill arrived on the field, that officer expressed a wish to capture
the Federal battery with Early's Brigade, "but before doing so, he
[Hill] must see General Longstreet upon the subject." Upon
completion of the reconnaissance, Early continued, Hill went to
the right, and Early announced to the troops that, when Hill
came back, they would advance. "General Hill returned," Early
wrote, "and, after informing me that the attack was to be made,
himself posted the artillery so as to cover the retreat of my
Brigade if it should be compelled to fall back." In Hill's delayed
report of January, 1863, he stated that Early went to Longstreet
in person, told of the battery in his front and "asked leave to
take it with his Brigade." Hill added: "General Longstreet approved of the movement, and directed me to accompany it. . . .
I have always regretted that General Early, carried away by his

76 *O. R.*, 11, pt. 1, p. 568.   77 *O. R.*, 11, pt. 1, p. 565.
78 *O. R.*, 11, pt. 1, pp. 565–66, 567.   79 *O. R.*, 11, pt. 1, p. 607.

impetuous and enthusiastic courage, advanced so far into the open field." [80]

To that account Hill adhered, though he subsequently wrote that he never thought of the attack "without horror." [81] Early modified his version only to the extent of saying that he suggested the attack to Hill, who went to Longstreet for approval.[82] Longstreet, late in life, maintained that the charge was suggested by Hill to Johnston who, in turn, referred Hill to him. "I said," Longstreet wrote, " 'the brigade you propose to use is not in safe hands.' " Longstreet related that he told Hill: "If you will go with it, and see that the troops are properly handled, you can make the attack, but don't involve us so as to delay the march after night." [83] Johnston's recollection, expressed in 1874, was that Early—not Hill—sent his request to Longstreet, who passed it on to the commanding General: "I authorized the attempt," Johnston wrote, "but enjoined caution in it." [84]

However this conflict of testimony may be resolved by present-day readers, contemporary opinion in the Army seems to have acquitted D. H. Hill of blame and to have raised concerning the brigade commander no question save one of impetuosity. There was humiliation because 400 wounded had to be left in Williamsburg,[85] inasmuch as Johnston was determined to continue his retreat on the morning of May 6, but there were few recriminations over the battle in which the men fell. Beyond doubt, the absence of detailed critique of the action around Fort Magruder was due in large part to the controversies over bloodier battles that soon were fought. Williamsburg dwindled, by comparison, to a small affair, a practice battle in which commanders learned what they should not do. Had there been an appraisal of those who had been most conspicuous in the largest action in Virginia after that of Manassas, the result would have been about as follows:

[80] *O. R.*, 11, pt. 1, pp. 603, 604–5.   [81] *Longstreet*, 78.

[82] *Early*, 69. For Early's return to the Army, see p. 588.

[83] *Longstreet*, 78. It should be noted that this was written after Longstreet had been engaged most bitterly with Early in the "Gettysburg controversy," for which see D. S. Freeman, *The South to Posterity*, 76 ff.

[84] *Johnston's Narrative*, 122. In 2 *N. C. Regts.*, 199, H. C. Wall stated that, after the war, General Johnston, in private conversation, placed on Hill the responsibility for the charge.

[85] Cf. *O. R.*, 11 pt. 1, p. 276.

Jos. E. Johnston—intent on his major plan, contemptuous of mere loss of ground, disposed to leave the tactical direction of combat to subordinates.

James Longstreet—composed, almost "jolly" in battle, subjected as yet to no test of strategical ability, but tactically master of his position and able to retain a grip on his Brigades.[86]

Lafayette McLaws—undeniably able to handle at least a small force with skill and with an accurate understanding of his mission.

R. H. Anderson—perhaps not altogether careful in reconnaissance, but steady and capable of handling more than one Brigade with none of a beginner's uncertainty; possibly a bit negligent in watching small details.

A. P. Hill—capable, hard-hitting and skillful in control of his men; by the capture of 160 prisoners, seven flags and, with the the Ninth Alabama assisting, of eight guns, the most conspicuous Brigadier, save Anderson, on the field.[87]

D. H. Hill—ambitious; tenacious and wholly master of himself in battle; perhaps too much disposed to the offensive and too little conscious of the tactical limitations of new troops.

Geo. E. Pickett—distinctly promising.

Cadmus M. Wilcox—definitely capable in brigade command.

J. A. Early—brave, ambitious to win renown, impetuous and possibly reckless.

J. E. B. Stuart—co-operative and useful, even when his own troops were not engaged.

In addition to these general officers, Col. Micah Jenkins of the "Palmetto Sharpshooters" had handled Anderson's Brigade and the artillery in Fort Magruder with a fiery zeal and a military judgment that won many plaudits. On the right, in an open field, a young captain of 23, with gunners who had been drilling only three weeks, had commanded a battery of mountain artillery with a gallant daring that made men ask his name. It was John Pelham.[88] He and Jenkins were men worth watching.

---

[86] The statement that Longstreet was "jolly today—in good spirits" was made by the Adjutant of the Twenty-eighth Virginia, Pickett's Brigade (O. R., 11, pt. 1, p. 455), to his Federal captors, but there seems to be no valid reason for subjecting this statement to the critique that usually should be applied to disclosures made by prisoners of war.

[87] For Hill's promotion, see p. 218; for Anderson, see pp. 242, 249.

[88] Longstreet, 74; Stuart in O. R., 11, pt. 1, p. 572.

CHAPTER XV

ELTHAM INTRODUCES JOHN B. HOOD

ARMY gossip subsequently had it that as Johnston rode away from the men who had charged across the fields around Williamsburg, he was so pleased with their performance that he hummed "I bet my money on the bob-tail horse" [1]; but if actually he felt elation, he did not show it in his correspondence or in his troop dispositions. He could be neither easy in mind nor leisurely in movement while the danger remained of an attack on his flank or rear by a force that might land from the York. On the evening of the 4th he had ordered Magruder to resume the withdrawal toward Richmond. Smith had been started in the same direction at dawn on the 5th, the day of the rearguard action. Within a few hours after Early's charge had failed, Magruder had reached Diascund Bridge, on the Chickahominy Road. Smith, following the New Kent Road, had camped that night at Barhamsville. [2]

Johnston had directed the separation of the two commands not only because they could march faster on different roads, but also because he wished Smith and his experienced troops to cover the flank nearer the York. [3] As Barhamsville was particularly vulnerable to attack from the river, Johnston reasoned that his wagon train would be exposed, even if the enemy did not get astride the line of retreat of Smith's troops. Consequently, he ordered Smith to remain at the village until the column was closed by the arrival of the rear Divisions. [4]

While Smith was waiting at Barhamsville, word came on the afternoon of May 6 that Federal transports, under the protection of gunboats, had arrived, precisely as Johnston had anticipated they might, at the head of York River [5] and were landing troops

[1] *Charleston Mercury*, May 20, 1862, p. 1, col. 1.

[2] *O. R.*, 11, pt. 1, pp. 275, 276. Magruder's turnout toward the Chickahominy was about two miles East of Barhamsville. See the map in *Johnston's Narrative*, 119.

[3] Cf. *O. R.*, 11, pt. 1, p. 275.

[4] This apparently is the meaning of the somewhat confused language of Smith's report, *O. R.*, 11, pt. 1, p. 627.

[5] At West Point, the York is formed by the confluence of the Mattapony and the Pamunkey.

on the south side of the river, below Eltham plantation and opposite Smith's flank.[6] On receipt of this information, Johnston prepared for the worst. He diverted Magruder's troops and placed
them under Smith in event they were needed. Similarly, he instructed Longstreet and D. H. Hill, who had left Williamsburg
on the 6th, to advance in close support of Smith.[7] By the morning
of May 7, the entire Army was concentrated around Barhamsville.[8]

Smith had refrained from contesting the debarkation of Federals, because the heavy ordnance of the gunboats cast its shadow
over the heads of the infantry. The wiser course for the Confederate commander on the 6th seemed to be to permit the
Federals to move inland, out of range of the naval support, and
then to assail them. To this mission Smith had assigned the
Division of Brig. Gen. W. H. C. Whiting, the same Whiting whose
official neck Johnston, with so much difficulty, had saved the previous winter. When the morning of the 7th brought no Federal
advance, other than of skirmishers in woods that faced the Confederate lines, Smith changed his plan. He decided to move
Whiting forward, to clear the woods, and then, if practicable, to
move up field artillery to a point where it could bombard the
landing place and the transports.[9]

In obedience to these orders, Whiting easily drove the skirmishers back a mile and a half through the woods, between 10 o'clock
and noon; but the officers whose guns were advanced to fire on
the transports reported the ships out of range.[10] The Federal
infantry meanwhile had taken shelter under a protecting bluff.[11]
With the loss of forty-eight of their own men, the capture of
forty-six prisoners, and the usual overestimate of Federal casualties, the Confederates returned in high satisfaction.[12]

Trivial as was this clash at Eltham's compared with the struggle
Johnston had anticipated when he had made plans at Yorktown
for his withdrawal, the steady, well-organized advance through

6 *O. R.*, 11, pt. 1, pp. 276, 627.   7 *O. R.*, 11, pt. 1, p. 627.
8 *O. R.*, 11, pt. 1, p. 276.   9 *O. R,.* 11, pt. 1, p. 627.
10 So read Confederate reports, *O. R.*, 11, pt. 1, pp. 627, 629–30. Capt. Josiah Porter,
Battery A, Mass. Artillery, reported that the Confederates fired only seven shells: "Most
of them . . . burst among the shipping in the river, a piece of one striking the smoke
stack of a steamer." *O. R.*, 11, pt. 1, p. 620.
11 *O. R.*, 11, pt. 1, pp. 627, 629–30.
12 Federal casualties, estimated by John B. Hood, *O. R.*, 11, pt. 1, p. 631, at not less
than 300, in reality numbered 186, prisoners included. *O. R.*, 11, pt. 1, p. 618.

the woods and the ease with which the enemy had been driven under the bluff confirmed Johnston's high opinion of Gustavus Smith and of Whiting. Smith appeared to be wholly qualified, indispensable indeed. Whiting seemed to Johnston to deserve promotion which the commanding General again urged the government to award.[13]

The action, moreover, brought anew to the attention of General Johnston the military qualifications of Col. Wade Hampton, who had led a part of Whiting's force. Colonel Hampton had spent the winter with Johnston's Army on Bull Run and Occoquan Creek.[14] By working zealously to recruit and to enlarge his command,[15] he had won the professional respect and the personal friendship of Johnston.[16] In January Johnston had given Hampton a provisional Brigade,[17] and the next month had advocated his commission at the appropriate rank, as one of six Colonels "fully qualified to command brigades." [18]

With his Legion, the Fourteenth and Nineteenth Georgia and the Sixteenth North Carolina,[19] Hampton had held on Occoquan Creek, at the beginning of March, a front of twelve miles, which he had evacuated when orders had come for the retreat to the line of the Rapidan and Rappahannock. As one of Whiting's brigade commanders, he had been involved in the charge that much public property had been abandoned on the retreat.[20] In a detailed report of March 21,[21] Hampton had defended himself against this accusation with candor and independence of mind. He had explained the paucity of his transportation, which had been late in arriving, and he had described the condition of the roads. All that had been destroyed, he said, was a small quantity

---

[13] *O. R.*, 11, pt. 3, p. 500. For the next detailed reference to Smith, see *infra*, p. 215 ff.

[14] IV *O. R.*, 1, 629; *O. R.*, 5, 913, 960; *Richmond Dispatch*, Nov. 26, 1861, p. 1, col. 1.

[15] IV *O. R.*, 1, 902, 907.

[16] Cf. *O. R.*, 5, 987.

[17] *O. R.*, 5, 1030. As early as Oct. 22, 1861, Hampton's Legion, under his command, had been listed as the Fourth Brigade of Van Dorn's First Division, *O. R.*, 5, 913; but in November, the Legion had been listed under its former name and had been supplementary to the four Brigades of Longstreet's Third Division. *O. R.*, 5, 961.

[18] *O. R.*, 5, 1058. These were, in order, A. P. Hill, John H. Forney, Wade Hampton, Charles S. Winder, Samuel Garland and Chris. H. Mott. All of these, except Colonel Mott, became general officers. Mott, as noted *supra*, p. 179, was killed at Williamsburg. Before the war ended, three of the remaining five had found soldiers' graves.

[19] *O. R.*, 5, 1030; *O. R.*, 11, pt. 3, p. 483.

[20] See *supra*, p. 143.

[21] *O. R.*, 5, 533.

of ammunition, fifty-nine tents and the personal baggage of the men. "... I think," he reported, "the loss of public property was remarkably small." Then he added forthrightly: "My greatest regret is that I cannot say the same as to private property, for it seems to be a hard case to make the soldier bear a loss which was caused by no fault of his own." [22] The spirit that had prompted his report made him more popular, rather than less. Now that he had led his men successfully through Eltham Forest, Whiting had official praise for Hampton's "conspicuous gallantry." [23] Johnston wrote Lee of Hampton's "high merit," in the same bracket with Whiting's, and asked his promotion.[24]

The distinction accorded Hampton, no less than that credited to Smith and to Whiting, had been anticipated in a measure by earlier performance than that of May 7. At Eltham, a fourth man, previously little known, made his first bid for fame. John B. Hood, son of a Kentucky physician,[25] had served in the 2nd United States Cavalry under Albert Sidney Johnston and R. E. Lee. As his sympathies had been wholly with the South, Hood had resigned in April, 1861, and, when he had found that his native State would not secede, he had gone to Montgomery, had received commission as First Lieutenant in the regular Army of the Confederate States, and had reported to General Lee in Richmond. Lee had assigned him to Magruder, who, in his first struggle to organize his extemporized force, had welcomed joyfully the young, well-trained trooper and, in a short time, had put him in command of the cavalry companies then on the lower Peninsula. "I was only a First Lieutenant," Hood subsequently wrote, "and the companies were of course under the direction of captains; a question eventually arose in respect to rank, and Magruder, unwilling to await action at Richmond, declared me Captain by his own order." [26] When jealous Captains then had proceeded to argue seniority, on the basis of the date of their respective commissions, Magruder had settled that question by promoting Hood a Major, and had left to the War Department the duty of acquiescing at its convenience.[27] As the temporary

[22] O. R., 1, pt. 1, pp. 533–34.	[23] O. R., 11, pt. 1, p. 630.
[24] O. R., 11, pt. 3, p. 500. For the next references to Hampton, see *infra*, pp. 218, 245.
[25] A West Pointer of the class of 1853, *Cullum*, No. 1622; forty-fourth in a class of fifty-two that included Jas. B. McPherson, John M. Schofield, and Philip H. Sheridan.
[26] In 21 *S. H. S. P.*, 118, this action erroneously is attributed to D. H. Hill.
[27] J. B. Hood, *Advance and Retreat* (cited hereafter as *Hood*), 17–18.

Rupert of "Prince John's" horse, Hood had one brush with the enemy [28] before a Colonel had been sent to form the cavalry into a regiment.[29]

Hood was not left long without like rank. Previously he had decided that he would make Texas his home, and, on that basis, perhaps, accounted himself a citizen of the Lone Star State. This had led the War Department, which could put its hand on few Texas officers so far away from home as Virginia, to select Hood to organize companies into the Fourth Texas Infantry. Hood had drilled these troops for some months around Richmond, and later had taken his regiment to Northern Virginia to join a Texas Brigade under ex-Senator Louis T. Wigfall.[30]

This had been precisely such a winter-quarters assignment as suited a vigorous, ambitious soldier whose experience in the United States Army had given him due knowledge of what might be expected in the campaign of 1862. He determined to instruct his regiment "in all its essential duties." His method, while in no sense original, deserves to be explained in his own words because it was one factor in creating superlative morale among men who ere long were a unit in the most renowned Brigade of the entire Army. Said Hood: "I lost no opportunity whenever the officers or men came to my quarters, or whenever I chanced to be in conversation with them, to arouse their pride, to impress upon them that no regiment in that Army should ever be allowed to go forth upon the battlefield and return with more trophies of war than the Fourth Texas—that the number of colors and guns captured, and prisoners taken, constituted the true test of the work done by any command in an engagement. Moreover, their conduct in camp should be such as not to require punishment and, when thrown near or within towns, should one of their comrades be led to commit some breach of military discipline they should, themselves, take him in charge, and not allow his misconduct to bring discredit upon the regiment; proper deportment was obligatory upon them at home, and, consequently, I should exact the same of them whilst in the Army." [31]

28 July 11, 1861; *O. R.*, 2, 297.   29 *Hood*, 18.
30 *Hood*, 18–19; *O. R.*, 5, 914, 961; for a complimentary reference to Wigfall as a man who had "too much good, hard sense to fail as a General in the field," see *Richmond Dispatch*, Nov. 27, 1861, p. 1, col. 5.
31 *Hood*, 19.

This discipline had received a certain glamour from the developing personality of Hood himself. Just 29 years of age,[32] he stood six feet, two inches and had a powerful chest and a giant's shoulders. His hair and beard were a light brown, almost blond; his penetrating, expressive and kindly eyes were blue. When he spoke it was with a booming, musical richness of tone.[33] On his arrival at Manassas, to visit his kinsman, Gustavus Smith, he had seemed to a cultured observer "a raw boned, country-looking man, with little of the soldierly appearance that West Point often gives its graduates." Hood looked then "like a raw backwoodsman, dressed up in an ill-fitting uniform," [34] but physically he filled out rapidly, and socially he learned fast. By the autumn of 1862, he was to be one of the most magnificent men in Confederate service. For the admiration of the lettered, he might have stepped out from the pages of Malory; to the untutored boy in the ranks, Hood was what every hero-worshiping lad wished his big brother to be.

So quickly had Hood brought his regiment to high efficiency that, on the eve of the retreat from Manassas, he had been made Brigadier General.[35] On March 7, by telegraphic orders of the War Department, he had been assigned to the leadership of Wigfall's Texas Brigade.[36] That command, which then consisted of the First, Fourth and Fifth Texas and the Eighteenth Georgia,[37] was a part of Whiting's Division, G. W. Smith's Reserve, during the last phase of the Yorktown operations,[38] and as such had no part in the action at Williamsburg; but now at Eltham's Landing, it showed its mettle.

Hood saw, ere the advance began, that there was danger of confused firing in the woods, and he determined not to permit his men to load their guns until they reached the Confederate cavalry picket. He then rode ahead of his column, which had been moving forward by the left flank. His own beloved Fourth Texas was in front. When Hood reached the sleepy cavalry picket, in rear of a little cabin, he ran squarely into a heavy Federal skirmish line. Behind the skirmishers was a heavy force. Instantly

[32] As of September, 1861.
[33] *Companions in Arms,* 673; *Southern Generals,* 385.
[34] *Col. J. C. Haskell's MS. Reminiscences,* 29.
[35] March 6, to rank from March 3, 1862; *Wright,* 74.
[36] *O. R.,* 5, 1097. [37] *O. R.,* 11, pt. 3, p. 483.
[38] Cf. *O. R.,* 51, pt. 2, p. 544.

Hood jumped from his horse and ran back to his own troops, who, fortunately, were not fifty feet from him.

"Forward into line," he cried. "Load!" At that moment some of the Federals fired, but their whole skirmish line halted at the sight of the Texans. One coolheaded Union corporal picked out the figure of Hood in front of the regiment and deliberately drew down his rifle on the General. A military career of high promise seemed at its end—because the muskets of the disciplined Fourth Texas obediently were unloaded. At that instant a single shot was fired, but it was the Federal corporal, not Hood, who was killed. One strong-minded individualist of the regiment, distrusting orders to approach with an empty gun an advancing enemy, surreptitiously had loaded his piece before starting and, by instant aim, saved Hood's life. The General scarcely knew whether to bless his deliverer or to reprimand him for violation of orders.[39] Naturally, after this experience, Hood's name was on many a lip. Smith mentioned him when reporting the action;[40] Whiting listed his "conspicuous gallantry" even before that of Hampton.[41]

Among other young officers mentioned casually in the reports on Eltham was Col. W. Dorsey Pender of the Sixth North Carolina. Whiting noted him as commander of the regiment that supported the battery which had attempted to shell the Union shipping. This regiment, said Whiting, "had been posted all the morning in advance of our extreme right"—that and no more.[42] There was nothing to suggest the picture of a rising professional soldier with high aptitude for combat.

Thus, in a brief action, scarcely more than a skirmish, did Smith vindicate Johnston's confidence in him, while Whiting and Hampton added to their reputation and Hood first held the gaze of admiring eyes. The aftermath was undramatic. Smith was content to be left alone, and was glad, without Federal interference, to pass the wagon train westward and, that night, to

---

[39] *Hood,* 21. This soldier was John Deal, Co. A, Fourth Texas, who survived the war and lived subsequently at Gonzales. A somewhat different account of this incident appears in J. B. Polley, *Hood's Texas Brigade* (cited hereafter as *Polley*), 24.

[40] *O. R.,* 11, pt. 1, p. 627.

[41] *O. R.,* 11, pt. 1, p. 630. For the next important incident in Hood's career see *infra,* p. 238 and Chap. XXXII.

[42] *O. R.,* 11, pt. 1, p. 629. Pender next appears, *infra,* p. 267, and many times thereafter.

continue his retreat as far as New Kent Court House.[43] Johnston approved this movement and decided to send the entire Army farther toward Richmond. "The want of provision," he wrote Gen. R. E. Lee, "and of any mode of obtaining it here, still more the dearth of forage, makes it impossible to wait to attack [the Federals] while landing. The sight of the iron-clads makes me apprehensive for Richmond, too. . . ."[44]

[43] Cf. *O. R.,* 11, pt. 1, p. 628.
[44] *O. R.,* 51, pt. 2, pp. 552–53. Johnston did not know that the Federal commander, whose movement against his flank he had regarded with so much apprehension, was convinced that the Union artillery had saved the landing Division from an overwhelming attack by superior numbers. See Brig. Gen. W. B. Franklin's report, *O. R.,* 11, pt. 1, p. 616, and Brig. Gen. John Newton's, *ibid.,* 625.

CHAPTER XVI

Twenty-four Unhappy Days

The safety of Richmond now became a concern in itself and the symbol of the multiplying vexations of the anxious mind of Johnston. He was fated to encounter and to display the carping and the crimination that always attend the gloom of a darkening cause. Between May 8 and May 31, more than at any other time in the Virginia campaign, were the strain and misunderstanding of retreat and inactive defense exhibited. In three distinct episodes, Johnston had, with President Davis, a clash of personality and a conflict over policy.

Johnston saw his problem in this form: an Army superior to his in numbers and in equipment was pursuing him. Hostile forces of undetermined size faced "Stonewall" Jackson, who was in the Shenandoah Valley with about 8400 infantry and perhaps 1000 cavalry.[1] "Dick" Ewell's Division, 6500, not immediately involved, was on the eastern slope of the Blue Ridge [2] and was being reinforced to the eastward by L. O'B. Branch's North Carolina Brigade.[3] Developments in that quarter were unpredictable.

Those at the opposite end of Johnston's large department were all too plainly forecast. Maj. Gen. Benjamin Huger, in charge of Norfolk, would be compelled to abandon his position immediately. Otherwise he might be cut off.[4] The troops with Huger, estimated at 9000 or 10,000 men, would have to move on Petersburg, by road or railway, unless they were lucky enough to stop their pursuers East of that city.[5] Quite apart from this unhappy

[1] O. R., 11, pt. 3, p. 879. The strength of the cavalry is an estimate.
[2] Cf. O. R., 12, pt. 3, p. 880.
[3] No figures for the exact strength of Branch's command at this time have been found, but the Brigade was one of the largest in the Army. It included five regiments, one of which is known, as of May 27, to have numbered 890 muskets. O. R., 11, pt. 1, p. 743.
[4] Cf. Huger in O. R., 11, pt. 3, p. 475; Lee in ibid., pp. 476–77.
[5] Singularly little is known of Huger's command. The Official Records contain no statement of his strength at the time of his withdrawal from Norfolk. As part of Colston's Brigade, 1750 men (O. R., 11, pt. 2, p. 487), was with Johnston, it would appear that Huger had with him only three Brigades, those of William Mahone, A. R. Wright (previously Blanchard's) and L. A. Armistead. If the fifteen regiments of these Brigades averaged 600 men, Huger's effective strength at the time of his withdrawal would have been 9000.

prospect, the evacuation of Norfolk would entail the loss of the invaluable Gosport navy yard. The ironclad *Virginia-Merrimac* would have no port. She drew too much water to ascend the James to Richmond.

To make a dark picture black, the 10,000 men under Brig. Gen. Joseph R. Anderson, who were defending the R. F. & P. Railroad South of the Rappahannock,[6] were far outnumbered by a Federal column under Gen. Irvin McDowell. This Union force probably would advance on Richmond from the North in an effort to form a junction with the Army of the Potomac, which enjoyed the mobility that sea power gave. McClellan could be stopped on or close to the York, because his gunboats and transports were near the head of navigation there, but he could not be prevented from landing troops for a march on Richmond from the East. Similarly, McClellan might attempt to send his fleet up James River. The only substantial barriers in his way were the homeless ironclad *Virginia-Merrimac* on guard at the mouth of the stream and, second, the uncompleted batteries and obstructions at Drewry's Bluff, seven miles downstream from Richmond. If the obstacles were passed, McClellan might get to Richmond before Johnston could.

What, then, should Johnston do? If the problem were correctly framed, what was the solution? Johnston never gave it in a single sentence, but he stated it consistently in the movements of his troops, and in the action he opposed as well as in that which he urged on the part of his government. Here was his solution: concentrate close to Richmond, in rear of his retreating Army, all the forces that could be gathered from other parts of the Confederacy; give to these forces unified command, and ample, competent leadership; regard no position in front of Richmond as fixed, in the sense that it had to be defended to the last at any cost; retreat and manœuvre as necessity and the movements of the enemy demanded; when opportunity offered itself at the proper stage of concentration—strike. The indeterminates were the route, the strength and the speed of the enemy's advance;

---

[6] Field's, Gregg's and J. R. Anderson's Brigades, with four additional regiments, the combined strength of which was about 3000. See *O. R.*, 12, pt. 1, p. 434; *O. R.*, 11, pt. 3, p. 458. General Anderson had been in command of the Wilmington, N. C., District, and on March 15, 1862, had assumed direction of the Department of North Carolina. *O. R.*, 9, 460.

the essentials were concentration, unity of command, proper leadership, freedom of action, and secrecy.

With the broad principles behind this policy, President Davis was in accord. The principles, in fact, were not debatable. He disagreed concerning details and application. These were not approached in cold detachment. They could not be. Too closely and too sensitively were they associated with all that had occurred between Davis and Johnston, and with the self-esteem of each of them. Although the lives of soldiers and the independence of the South were at stake, the peculiarities of two strange men weighed more heavily on the scales of decision. In the eyes of the Chief Executive, concentration was limited by the military requirements of other parts of the Confederacy, in particular of the Carolinas and of Georgia. Unity of command postulated a willingness on the part of Johnston to co-operate and to recognize the rights and the duties of the civil government. Trained leadership, while of course to be assured General Johnston, so far as available, did not call, in Davis's opinion, for the commission of an excessive number of officers of exalted rank, nor should it deprive smaller columns of good leadership in order that Johnston's task might be easier. Fixed positions were not essential, freedom of manœuvre was allowed; but Richmond must be held, the battle must be as far from the city as possible, and the first opportunity of striking the enemy must be taken. Secrecy should not be carried so far that the President and his responsible advisers were kept in the dark.

More fundamentally, though it never was set forth explicitly, Johnston was expected to demonstrate to a somewhat skeptical President, fully satisfied of his own military knowledge, that he was as competent to administer the Army as he was to command it, and that the plan of operations would be as well executed as it was soundly conceived. Johnston doubted Davis's confidence in him; Davis doubted whether Johnston was of a temperament to justify him in trusting to the General without reservation the entire conduct of a campaign on which the fate of the Confederacy manifestly depended.

Amid military movements of no great complexity, the President and the commanding General were first to have a bristling correspondence over unity of command, and then a sharp dif-

ference concerning what a General in the field should tell hi:
civil superior of pending operations. At length, with the battle
about to be joined, the question of subordinate leadership was,
after a fashion, to be settled.

Such were the circumstances and the prospects under which,
after the action at Eltham, Johnston attempted to direct his own
field army and, at the same time, to cover Richmond, to make
concentration of force a reality, and to supervise the operations of
Jackson, of Ewell, of Anderson and of Huger. All of this Johnston undertook with a small, mediocre staff. Distance, poor communications and, perhaps, Johnston's distaste for details soon
produced misunderstanding and confusion. In Richmond, Lee
sought as tactfully as he could to respect Johnston's authority and,
at the same time, to meet emergencies that confronted the minor
forces with which Johnston lost touch. Much of the pressing
correspondence with Jackson had to be conducted by Lee because
Johnston could not be reached.[7] Frequently, also, Lee had to
deal with Huger, and with Huger's subordinate, Maj. Gen. W. W.
Loring, in command at Suffolk.

The first of a long succession of unpleasant exchanges arose over
Loring. On the day of the action near Eltham's Landing, Loring
heard a rumor that the town of Smithfield and some of the Confederate batteries between Suffolk and Norfolk were being evacuated in obedience to Johnston's order. Mildly enough, Loring
reported that fact to Lee and added of Johnston, "I do not think
that it can be known to him that Huger has not moved away
from Norfolk." Obviously, if the Federals discovered that these
intermediate positions had been abandoned, the enemy might get
across the Confederates' line of retreat before the stores and men
were removed from Norfolk. In this emergency, Lee could not
wait on ceremony. He ordered that Confederate troops East of
Suffolk should not move until Loring had communicated with
Huger and had learned more of that officer's plans.[8] Lee at once [9]
wrote Johnston an account of this situation and prepared to send
it by messenger to Johnston's headquarters. Before the letter could
be copied, Lee was called out of his office. Lest he delay the
courier by waiting to sign this and two other communications

[7] Cf. 2 R. E. Lee, 50.   [8] O. R., 11, pt. 3, p. 407
[9] May 7.

addressed to Johnston,[10] Lee directed one of his aides to attach his signature.

Receipt the next day of these three papers, subscribed, "R. E. Lee, by W. H. Taylor, Aide-de-Camp," if it did not enrage General Johnston, ruffled him. In a bad-tempered reply he made an extraordinary request. After hinting at the impropriety of having "certain supposed orders of mine . . . countermanded by you or W. H. Taylor, A.A.G.," Johnston explained that he had issued only one direct order [11] for the troops on the south side of James River. Then he went on: "My authority does not extend beyond the troops immediately around me. I request therefore to be relieved of a merely nominal geographical command. The service will gain thereby the unity of command, which is essential in war." He intimated, in short, that Lee or Davis was the actual head of the forces, but in the very next paragraph, he asserted his wish to retain control of the troops that were defending the R. F. & P. Railroad: "I have had in the Peninsula no means of obtaining direct information from the other departments of my command nor has the Government furnished it. Please inform me without delay of the position and number of troops in the direction of Fredericksburg. I wish to place them so that they may not be cut off by an army landing at West Point. I have heard casually that you have caused the Pamunkey to be obstructed; if so, it is unfortunate that I was not apprised of the fact." [12]

Although Lee wrote a candid statement of how the offending letters were dispatched, he did not omit one positive reminder: "I do not recollect," he politely said, "your having requested information relating to the other departments of your command to be forwarded by any other means than the usual course of the mails, and supposed the commanders were in direct correspondence with you." [13] Johnston could not gainsay this. In his reply, he dropped all discussion of the offending orders to the troops south of the James, and argued the question of responsibility for the obstruction of the Pamunkey. The government, he said, should have directed and completed the work of closing that river.

[10] The contents of these two communications are not known. Cf. *O. R.*, 11, pt. 3, p. 499.
[11] With respect to the concentration of Colston's divided Brigade.
[12] *O. R.*, 11, pt. 3, pp. 499–500. [13] *O. R.*, 11, pt. 3, p. 500.

"I have been unable," he complained, "to find any one who can tell me what has been done or by whom or at what point, though it is thought in the neighborhood that such work was in progress, but interrupted by the Federal war vessels." [14]

Then Johnston turned to the request made by the President on May 1 for the assignment of Longstreet or Smith to command the force South of Fredericksburg. Mr. Davis had stated that it was "a necessity" to send one or the other of these men [15] to that district. Johnston had not ordered the transfer, nor did he feel that he could do so.[16] He said: "The two officers named are necessary to the preservation of anything like organization in this army. . . . Stragglers cover the country, and Richmond is no doubt filled with the absent without leave. It has been necessary to divide the army into two parts; one under General Smith on this [New Kent] road; the other under General Longstreet, on that by the Chickahominy. . . . This army cannot be commanded without these two officers; indeed, several more major-generals like them are required to make this an army. The men are full of spirit when near the enemy, but at other times to avoid restraint leave their regiments in crowds. To enable us to

[14] O. R., 11, pt. 3, p. 503. Lee had written Johnston on May 3 that the enemy might ascend the Pamunkey before the obstructions had been completed, and he had stated that the the President thought the dispatch of a light battery to the river "would have the effect of delaying the advance of the enemy, if not preventing him." Lee had added that he did not know whether this was practicable (O. R., 11, pt. 3, p. 493). In his letter of May 8, in answer to Johnston's protest against the dispatch of orders to Huger, Lee said: "In reference to the obstruction of the Pamunkey, before it was commenced, the subject was referred to you, and directions were given for the preparation of the material, procuring of pile-driver, etc." After explaining that he feared the work of closing the channel had been imperfectly done, he added, "all the transports . . . were carried above the obstructions, and their cargoes I understand are at present secure" (O. R., 11, pt. 3, p. 501). The obstructions proved an adequate barrier to the Federal gunboats when an attempt was made on May 17 to pass them, but the Confederates had no way of protecting the vessels that had been sent above the obstructions after those craft had been driven from the York. One propeller and one side-wheel steamer, together with seven schooners, had to be set afire and destroyed (O. R., 11, pt. 1, p. 637). At the instance of the writer, his friend J. Ambler Johnston, whose maternal ancestors lived for generations on or close to the Pamunkey River, made in 1938 an interesting study of the navigation of that stream. Mr. Johnston's conclusion was that, within the lifetime of men then of good memory, vessels of 75 to 100 feet occasionally had gone up the Pamunkey almost to Hanovertown, though New Castle usually was as high as vessels went. Navigation, Mr. Johnston found, was "so dependent on the tide that the river could not be used for troop movements or for supplies unless the authorities using the stream were quite sure the enemy would be unable to reach the river during a vessel's leisurely ascent."—Letter of Oct. 17, 1938.

[15] O. R., 11, pt. 3, p. 485.

[16] From Johnston's reference, O. R., 11, pt. 3, p. 503, to the receipt of a copy of the President's telegram of May 1, on this subject, it is possible to infer that the original had not reached him, but this scarcely is probable.

gather the whole army for battle would require a notice of several days."

Johnston proceeded: "The best mode of arranging this matter will be to unite the two armies, which, if I am in actual command, will be done. It is necessary to unite all our forces now. All that I can control shall be concentrated. If this command (mine) includes the Department of Northern Virginia still this Army of the North is a part of it; if not, my position should be defined anew. Nothing is more necessary to us than a distinct understanding of every officer's authority." [17] Not one further word did Johnston say at the moment regarding supervision of Huger's command. Apparently he had abandoned his concern in the light of an assurance Lee had given him in the letter of May 8—"I consider your authority to extend over the troops on both sides of James River." [18]

Thus Johnston was upheld in his insistence on one essential of his plan—unity of command. Only twice thereafter during the campaign, and then in respect to minor matters, was Johnston doubtful of his authority.[19] His second requirement, that of competent subordinate leadership, seemed to be supplied, in part, by word from Lee, in a few days, that the near approach of the Army to Richmond rendered the transfer of Longstreet or Smith to the Rappahannock less important than previously it had been.[20] In expressing the President's view, Lee spoke with his usual consideration for Johnston's sensibilities, but Mr. Davis himself, seldom dropping controversy, took this occasion for an inopportune return to his demand that troops from the same State be brigaded together. Although fourteen of Johnston's twenty-two Brigades still contained regiments from more than one State,[21] the President's insistence, as subsequently developed, primarily was for the separate organization of his beloved Mississippians.[22] In terms that might not unjustly be described as scolding, the President insisted on action and, regardless of the situation of the

---

[17] O. R., 11, pt. 3, p. 503.   [18] O. R., 11, pt. 3, p. 500.
[19] One of these was control over the Department of Henrico, for which see O. R., 11, pt. 3, p. 527. The other involved like control over the defenses at Drewry's Bluff. Lee assured Johnston that there was "no question as to the extent of your authority or command." O. R., 11, pt. 3, p. 534.
[20] O. R., 11, pt. 3, p. 505.
[21] O. R., 11, pt. 1, pp. 531–33. The Twenty-third Brigade, Crump's, was a temporary organization.
[22] Cf. O. R., 11, pt. 3, pp. 546–47.

Army at the time, asserted: "The reasons formerly offered [for delaying the reorganization] have one after another disappeared, and I hope you will, as you can, proceed to organize your troops as heretofore instructed." Davis added commendation for "the successes" Johnston had gained. Then he said: "I will not dwell on the lost opportunity afforded along the line of Northern Virginia, but must call your attention to the present condition of affairs and probable action of the enemy if not driven from his purpose to advance on the Fredericksburg route." Whatever that might mean, there was no concealing the fact that the President's temper was bad, that his nerves were raw, and that the whole communication was censorious.[23] Upon receipt of the letter, Johnston well might have asked, as he had of one of Benjamin's orders for a detail,[24] whether such an order ever had been given before—at least in such circumstances.

Those circumstances soon were of a character to call for a cessation of controversy. Apprehension for the security of Richmond, it will be recalled, coupled with the shortage of provisions and the lack of forage, had prompted Johnston on the 7th to order withdrawal from Barhamsville.[25] By the 8th, after the exchange with General Lee over the control of the troops near Fredericksburg, the position of the force under J. R. Anderson constituted another reason for bringing the main Army still closer to Richmond.[26] Longstreet was ordered to concentrate on the 9th near Long Bridge on the Chickahominy; Smith was moved to Baltimore Cross-roads, eight miles from New Kent Court House.[27] By these moves Johnston had the bridges of the Chickahominy conveniently to the rear. Moreover, his flanks could not be turned by the Federals unless they marched southward and threw their pontoons across the river below the point where any regular bridges existed. Supplies for Johnston now could be brought from Richmond by the York River Railroad.[28] A telegraph station was opened on that railway, five miles from Johnston's headquarters.[29]

Improved as was this position, Johnston could not breathe easily

---

[23] *O. R.*, 11, pt. 3, pp. 507–8.　　[24] See *supra*, p. 132.　　[25] *O. R.*, 51, pt. 2, p. 553.
[26] *O. R.*, 11, pt. 3, p. 500. Johnston's somewhat vague language was: "The impossibility of subsisting the army in the neighborhood and the supposed position of an army of ours near Fredericksburg render it impracticable to wait to oppose a landing opposite to West Point."
[27] *O. R.*, 11, pt. 3, p. 503.　　[28] *O. R.*, 11, pt. 3, p. 500.　　[29] *O. R.*, 11, pt. 3, p. 504.

there. The very day he took up his new line, he received from one of the ablest Confederate engineers the disconcerting information that only three guns were in position at Drewry's Bluff,[30] which was about fourteen miles West of his right flank. While work was progressing furiously to strengthen the defenses at the bluff,[31] it remained obvious that the presence of *Virginia-Merrimac* at the mouth of the James, as long as she could keep afloat without a base, was the only means of keeping the Federal fleet from ascending the river. Once the ironclad was scuttled or lost, it was more certainly apparent than ever that the enemy would be hammering at Drewry's Bluff. If those fortifications were passed, Richmond, seven miles upstream, would be at the mercy of the Federals before Johnston could arrive there.[32] Panic spread in the capital. The government packed up the archives.[33] Belief in the invincibility of Southern leaders was shaken where it was not destroyed.

One disaster precipitated another. On the 14th, Johnston learned [34] that the *Virginia-Merrimac* had been blown up on the 11th, to keep her from falling into Federal hands. In Richmond, on receipt of this news, there was bewilderment, consternation and resentment; [35] at Johnston's headquarters there was grave

[30] *O. R.,* 11, pt. 3, p. 503, but *cf.* Lee's comment, *ibid.,* 505. For references to the work on the defenses at Drewry's Bluff, see *ibid.,* 11, pt. 3, pp. 391, 476, 493, 505, 521, 523; *ibid.,* 51, pt. 2, pp. 445, 549. The best account of the armament and location of James River defenses, as of March 20, is A. L. Rives's report, *O. R.,* 51, pt. 2, p. 507. No reliance whatever had been placed by Johnston on the James River batteries below the mouth of the Chickahominy. He had himself ordered the evacuation of the works at Mulberry Point and the removal, if practicable, of their armament. *O. R.,* 11, pt. 3, pp. 500, 503; cf. *ibid.,* 504.

[31] See 2 *R. E. Lee,* 47–48, where the sources are cited.

[32] See Lee to Huger, May 8, 1862, *O. R.,* 11, pt. 3, p. 499; Johnston to Lee, May 9, *O. R.,* 11, pt. 3, p. 504. The relation of the *Virginia-Merrimac* to the defense of James River had been realized early. The *Richmond Examiner,* Nov. 4, 1861, p. 3, col. 2, had complained about the slowness of work on the vessel. A correspondent was quoted as saying that Governor Letcher, who had gone to Norfolk to study the situation, "had done nothing on arriving there but eat hog fish and drink whiskey." The *Examiner* had added: "It is certainly high time that the *Merrimac* was completed, if there had been a proper regard for our river defences."

[33] *O. R.,* 11, pt. 3, pp. 504, 513; cf. *ibid.,* 557; *Miss Brock,* 130; 1 *R. W. C. D.,* 126.

[34] *Johnston's Narrative,* 127.

[35] After all the newspapers had said about holding the seaboard, they had difficulty in building up a new theory of defense inland. Compare the *Richmond Examiner* of May 7, p. 2, cols. 1–2, with the *Richmond Dispatch,* May 12, 1862, p. 2, col. 1. Although Johnston stated that he did not learn until the 14th of the loss of the ironclad, the first reports reached Richmond May 12, the day after the vessel was destroyed. See *Richmond Dispatch,* May 13, p. 3, col. 2; *Richmond Examiner,* May 13, 1862, p. 1, col. 1 and p. 2, col. 2. Richmond papers from May 7 onward were filled with speculation over the fate of Norfolk. For typical comment on the loss of the ironclad, see E. A. Pollard, *Second Year of the War,* 26 ff. *Miss Brock,* 128.

fear that the enemy might pass the fortifications at Drewry's Bluff. Simultaneously, also, from the direction of West Point, General McClellan seemed to be preparing to advance against the Confederate left, but Johnston was not alarmed by this. He thought that the enemy would not risk a general engagement at a distance from the gunboats and the waterways when the easy river line was not contested below Drewry's Bluff.[36]

Of this Johnston spoke freely to Longstreet, but concerning it and all aspects of his defensive plan, he wrote nothing to the President or to General Lee. As a fixed rule, he virtually suspended correspondence when an engagement or a movement was impending. Perhaps, in addition, his memory of the quick spread of the report that Manassas was to be evacuated in March tightened his lips.[37]

Justified as was his reticence, Johnston carried it too far at this time in dealing with the President, and by his silence he now precipitated a succession of misunderstandings even more serious than those that had arisen over unity of command. Probably on the day that Johnston heard of the loss of the *Virginia-Merrimac*, the Chief Executive and General Lee rode out to confer with him.[38] The three talked so long that Lee and Davis could not return to Richmond that night, but the conversation did not satisfy the President. Johnston explained to the Chief Executive that he had drawn in his left to clear it of deep water, whence it could be turned, that he did not have strength to take the offensive, and that he would await attack.[39] That was all he confided.

On May 15 the Federal gunboats made the anticipated attempt to pass the fortifications at Drewry's. To the delight, and scarcely less to the surprise, of the Confederates, the obstructions proved impassable. Guns of the batteries bore down almost on the decks of the warships, which, in the narrow river, could not manœuvre

---

[36] *O. R.*, 11, pt. 3, p. 517.   [37] See *supra*, p. 136, n. 138.

[38] The fact of such a conference is given in 2 *Davis*, 101–2, but the date is not supplied. From Mr. Davis's reference to the fact that the destruction of the *Virginia-Merrimac* then was known, and from his casual mention that Johnston's headquarters were North of the Chickahominy, it would seem probable that the conference was on May 14. After that date, Johnston was South of the river. Reservation concerning the date has to be made because Mr. Davis's narrative, which contains the only account of the interview, was written long after the war. There is possibility of an error of one or two days in the date of the conference.

[39] 2 *B. & L.*, 206. Davis, writing years after, reported that Johnston said he intended to improve his position and to wait for the enemy to leave the gunboats, so that a chance would be offered for a land attack. 2 *Davis*, 101–2.

with any ease or speed. After three hours and twenty minutes of mauling from the heavy ordnance on the bluff, the Federals were glad to drop downstream out of range.[40]

While this repulse of the Federal gunboats was to Richmond a relief past reckoning, the enemy's attempt to force a passage showed the possibility of joint operations on James River by the Federal Army and Navy. Lee believed that the Unionists might undertake in front of the obstructions a campaign similar to that against Yorktown.[41] Johnston reasoned that he should draw still nearer Richmond and should put himself in position to cope with an attack from the river, from the Southside, and from the direction of West Point.[42] Accordingly, on the day of the attack on Drewry's Bluff, Johnston abandoned the middle and lower stretches of the Chickahominy and drew all his forces back to a line about seven miles below Richmond.[43] On the 17th, finding this line weak and the supply of water inadequate, he fell back again until he was, at some points, immediately in front of the earthworks that had been thrown up in 1861 within three miles of Richmond.[44]

Johnston's retreat almost to the suburbs of Richmond, and his continued silence regarding his defensive plans, brought to his headquarters Col. Custis Lee, son of the General and aide to the President. The Colonel delivered from Davis a carefully written letter that reviewed the supposed alternatives of the enemy and raised the question of how and where the enemy should be met outside Richmond. As if Davis were writing for a record, subsequently to be made public, he concluded: "As on all former occasions, my design is to suggest, not to direct, recognizing the impossibility of [sic] any one to decide in advance; and reposing

[40] In *O. R.*, 11, pt. 1, p. 636, the commanding officer of the *Wachusett* reported to General McClellan that "Commodore Rodgers, of the *Galena*, who commanded the expedition, is decidedly of the opinion that the works cannot be reduced without the assistance of land forces." For the Federal naval report, see *Official Records of the Union and Confederate Navies in the War of the Rebellion* (cited hereafter as *N. O. R.*), 7, 357 ff. Executive Officer Newman stated, *op. cit.*, 359, that the side of the leading vessel, the *Galena*, had been perforated by thirteen shot and shell. "The fire of the enemy," reported Lt. William N. Jeffers of the *Monitor*, "was remarkably well directed." *Ibid.*, 362. Apparently the Federals did not know that the C. S. S. *Patrick Henry* had participated in the defense and had put an eight-inch shell through the bow of the *Galena*. *Ibid.*, 370.
[41] *O. R.*, 11, pt. 3, p. 523.
[42] *O. R.*, 11, pt. 1, p. 276; *Johnston's Narrative*, 128.
[43] *Ibid.*
[44] *Johnston's Narrative*, 128; 2 *B. & L.*, 208.

confidently as well on your ability as your zeal, it is my wish to leave with you the fullest powers to exercise your judgment. Colonel Lee will communicate freely with you and bear to me any information and reply which you may intrust to him." [45] General Johnston confided nothing definite to young Lee. The Colonel left with no more knowledge of what was projected than he had when he arrived.[46]

On May 20, McClellan crossed troops over the Chickahominy at Bottom's Bridge and began a cautious advance.[47] Soon it was suspected that he was moving up the left bank of the river also, and was working his way to the North of Richmond. This was interpreted in the capital as preliminary to attempted junction with the Army under McDowell, which was known to be mustering in strength on the Rappahannock.[48] Vague whispers that Johnston intended to abandon the city without a fight [49] had not reached the President. He believed that Johnston would do battle for Richmond, but he felt dissatisfaction with Johnston's preparations,[50] and he redoubled his efforts to ascertain what plan the General proposed to follow. In the letter delivered by Custis Lee he had hinted politely that he desired information. Now, on the 21st, he directed Gen. R. E. Lee to write specifically and imperatively for it. Lee, as usual, did this with consideration. He said: ". . . your plan of operations, dependent upon circumstances perhaps yet to be developed, may not be easily explained, nor may it be prudent to commit it to paper. I would therefore respectfully suggest that you communicate your views on this subject personally to the President, which perhaps would be more convenient to you and satisfactory to him." [51]

Johnston readily enough supplied a desired statement of the strength of his forces,[52] but he made no immediate reply to the invitation. The next day, when Davis rode out with Lee beyond

[45] O. R., 11, pt. 3, p. 524.

[46] President Davis subsequently wrote, 2 Davis, 103, that he did not know Johnston had come nearer to Richmond until, riding out for another attempt at a conference, he ran into Confederate artillery almost within the eastern suburbs of Richmond. As Johnston pointed out, 2 B. & L., 207, if Custis Lee personally delivered a letter to him at his changed headquarters, the President certainly knew that the Army was West of the Chickahominy. Mr. Davis must have confused these events as he did those of a later ride to the front.

[47] O. R., 11, pt. 1, p. 25.

[48] Cf. O. R., 11, pt. 3, pp. 510–11.

[49] Cf. Hood, 153.

[50] 2 Davis, 120.

[51] O. R., 11, pt. 3, p. 530.

[52] Ibid., 530–51.

the left of Johnston's front to the hills overlooking Mechanics-ville,[53] where activity by the Federals was reported, the President thought he found evidence that, if Johnston had any plan, the organization for executing it was poor. Davis accordingly sent another of his staff officers to Johnston with information on the situation opposite Mechanicsville. In stiff terms the President wrote: "I saw General Stuart and General Cobb, but as neither of them communicated to me any plan of operations, or appeared to know what troops were in front as we approached, I suppose neither of them could have been commanding in chief in that locality. My conclusion was that if, as reported to be probable, General Franklin, with a division, was in that vicinity he might easily have advanced over the turnpike toward if not to Rich-mond." [54]

Still Johnston had nothing to say. It was the 24th, or about that date, before he came to Richmond for conference. Even then, if the General disclosed anything to the President, Davis did not regard it, apparently, as detailed or adequate.[55] Two days later,[56] in a renewed effort to procure information, General Lee appeared again at Johnston's headquarters. Johnston by that time had ascertained that the Federals were across the Chickahominy and were not more than ten miles East of Richmond.[57] He knew, also, that Federal cavalry had occupied Mechanicsville, five miles North of the city, and he had word that McDowell was moving southward from Fredericksburg.[58] McClellan and McDowell, then, evidently were planning an early junction. Furthermore, Johnston had summoned to him J. R. Anderson's force on the R. F. & P.; and from the vicinity of Gordonsville the commanding General had recalled Branch's Brigade, which had been in sup-port of Ewell. In addition, Huger, who had reached Petersburg about May 15,[59] had been ordered by Johnston to hold himself in readiness to repulse an attack on Drewry's Bluff or to move to Richmond by train.[60]

[53] For the front, as of May 22, see ibid., 533.   [54] O. R., 11, pt. 3, p. 536.
[55] No mention of this conference appears in Davis; but in O. R., 11, pt. 3, p. 541, Johnston wrote at 11.30 P.M., May 24, that he had "been to Richmond."
[56] This is not certain, though all the circumstantial evidence indicates that the date was the 26th.
[57] Johnston's Narrative, 130; G. W. Smith, 146.
[58] Johnston's Narrative, 130–31.   [59] Cf. O. R., 11, pt. 3, p. 520.
[60] O. R., 11, pt. 3, p. 534.

With these reinforcements at hand, Johnston felt that he could and must strike McClellan before McDowell joined the Army of the Potomac. In short, now that Johnston saw a possibility of doing more than defending himself, he could formulate a plan for an offensive. The details he promptly confided to Lee. The plan, commendably simple, was this: with part of his forces, Johnston would attack North of the Chickahominy and would clear that bank of Federals; then, while the Union forces were confused, he would strike hard with his right against the troops South of the Chickahominy and East of Richmond. As Mr. Davis subsequently recalled Lee's report, the operations were set for May 29.[61]

Statement of this plan of campaign temporarily satisfied President Davis. Although the official relations between him and Johnston continued cool and formal, their sharper differences were put aside, though not forgotten, in the excited preparations for the battle. The prospect of action did not have a like effect on all of Johnston's subordinates. On the contrary, the nervous strain and *amour-propre* that had jaundiced the relations of the President and the commanding General now showed in an unhappy if amusing clash between Magruder and G. W. Smith.

Despite Magruder's pride and peculiarities, he was not quarrelsome or caustic in speaking of his comrades in arms. An officer who saw much of Magruder remarked that, with the exception of D. H. Hill, he never heard "Prince John" abuse any man.[62] Insistence upon proper respect for his rank and abilities was another matter. By the division of the Army into two unofficial Corps, during the retreat from Williamsburg, Magruder had been subordinated to Smith. Whatever the judgment Magruder had of the capacities of Smith, the two had enough of similar pride

---

61 In 2 *Davis*, 120–21, the President gave a sketch of this plan but he confused details and geography and failed to remember that Johnston intended to attack South as well as North of the river. Johnston, in his *Narrative*, 131, outlined the first plan as here stated. The unusual and perhaps the defective aspect of the plan was that after battle had been joined North of the Chickahominy by Smith and A. P. Hill, the Divisions of Magruder and Huger were to cross by New Bridge and were to "form between the left wing" and the river. The attack to the South of the stream was to be made down the Williamsburg road by Longstreet and D. H. Hill. As if conscious of the lack of co-ordination that might be entailed by having the river between the attacking forces, Johnston wrote in his *Narrative*: "I supposed that the bridges and fords of the little river would furnish means of sufficient communication between the two parts of the Confederate army" (*loc. cit.*). For the evidence that Mr. Davis probably was in error concerning the choice of a specific date for these operations, see *infra*, p. 222, n. 95.
62 T. R. R. Cobb in 28 *S. H. S. P.*, 293.

and pomposity to make a disagreement certain and a quarrel probable. By nature and by the habits of semi-independent command, Magruder was insistent on the immediate consideration of whatever he had to refer to any one. He was a man who thought all his business so important that he would stop a galloping General, so to say, to compare watches.

Magruder did this metaphorically with Smith, during the days of waiting around Richmond, and received, for his pains, a letter from Smith's Assistant Adjutant General in which he was informed that Smith had "interrupted a very important conference in regard to the movements of the various armies in Virginia, in order to write over [Smith's] own signature . . . that the movements requisite to effect the dispositions in [Magruder's] front require time, and that [Smith] earnestly desires that time may patiently be given to it." The Assistant Adjutant General had added: "The Major General would be glad at any hour, day or night, to be informed whenever an attack in force upon [Magruder's] lines is clearly threatened, but he begs that information, unless of that nature, will be sent at such time as not to deprive him of his necessarily limited hours of rest." [63]

This did violence to the sensibilities of the General who had commanded at Big Bethel and had enjoyed access to the Secretary of War at all times. Magruder accordingly sat down and deliberately invoked his best style in an answer replete with an irony so insolently polite, so deliberately disciplined, so ostentatiously subordinate, that it could not be rebuked. After quoting Smith's Assistant Adjutant General and reviewing the specific military question at stake, Magruder said: "I sent this communication at 2 o'clock, and at [Smith's] particular request, made to me at my quarters, that I would communicate to him all important information at the Spotswood Hotel. . . . I regret to have disturbed the rest of the Major General commanding the reserve and my wing, but having had for nearly a year sentinels stationed at my headquarters with orders to pass every one to my bedroom with any communication in relation to the movements of the enemy or any other important character requiring action, and having in every case acted at once, I had become somewhat in the habit of disregarding hours, but do not remember to have ever

[63] O. R., 11, pt. 3, p. 528.

inflicted this inconvenience upon him except on the occasion here stated, and then at his specific request. I beg to assure the Major General that I shall be happy to carry out any instruction with which he may honor me, but believe it is the understanding that in all movements of troops I am to await his orders." [64]

This letter Magruder followed with one the next day to Johnston. He had been led to believe, Magruder said, that the arrangement which placed him under Smith had been temporary, and he therefore requested that now he be authorized to report directly to the commanding General. His command and Smith's, he went on, "are now acting separately, and there would seem to be no necessity that [sic] an inconvenience and delay, arising from the present arrangement, without mentioning other obvious reasons for my wishing a command independent of an officer of the same grade with myself." [65]

Instead of obliging compliance on the part of Johnston, there came the same day orders from the Adjutant General's Office. These assigned Magruder to the Trans-Mississippi District and directed that he report to Richmond for instructions. [66] While this was done after previous consultation with Magruder and was wholly agreeable to him, [67] the publication of the transfer that day probably was construed in some quarters as rebuke to Magruder. That was not all. Johnston apparently sided with Smith throughout this affair and, on May 25, without explanation or ado, he carried out his implied part of the orders. He assigned Lafayette McLaws "to the command of the troops heretofore commanded by Major General Magruder, the latter having been relieved by special orders. . . . Adjutant and Inspector General's Office." [68]

Magruder's friends, who were numerous and powerful, hotly resented this language. It seemed too much like kicking Magruder out of the Army without a word of thanks or any announcement of his promotion to departmental command. At best, Johnston's order seemed unceremoniously to speed the parting General. The Secretary of War, who had served under Magruder, at once wrote General Johnston and directed that the order be

---

[64] O. R., 11, pt. 3, pp. 528–29.   [65] O. R., 11, pt. 3, p. 537.
[36] O. R., 11, pt. 3, p. 540.
[67] For the negotiations concerning the assignment of Magruder to the Trans-Mississippi when the public thought Sterling Price should have been given the command, see O. R., 13, 829, 832, 837, 841, 845.
[68] O. R., 11, pt. 3, p. 551.

"modified." Whether Johnston was asked to explain Magruder's advancement, or to defer the order until the anticipated battle had been fought, the record does not show. Johnston felt, in any event, that Secretary Randolph was putting on him the blame for any misunderstanding the original order "relieving" Magruder had created. In a restrained but positive letter, Johnston reminded Randolph that if injustice had been done Magruder it was by the order that emanated from the Adjutant General's Office. Johnston concluded: "Obedience to the order contained in your letter would place me in a false position in relation to Major General Magruder and to the Army. I therefore respectfully ask you to recall it." So clearly was Johnston in the right that the Adjutant General's Office forthwith relieved Magruder of his new assignment and directed him to report for duty to Johnston.[69]

Smith, who had been silent until this time, now had his inning. At a time when he thought that a general engagement was immediately in prospect, he calmly asked to be relieved of command over Magruder.[70] Johnston on the 28th agreed to this but again displayed his confidence in Smith by putting under that officer the three Divisions that constituted the left wing.[71]

Simultaneously with this controversy between Smith and Magruder, the long-sought promotions were made. The only direct vacancy created by the battle of Williamsburg had been that due to the wounding of General Early. His injury, though it threatened no permanent invalidism, would keep him from service for weeks to come. To the command of his troops, Brig. Gen. Samuel Garland was assigned.[72] He had served as Colonel of the Eleventh Virginia, A. P. Hill's Brigade, had won praise at Dranesville in the minor action of December 20, 1861,[73] had the endorsement of Johnston as worthy of promotion,[74] and had distinguished himself in leading his fine regiment in the fighting on the right at Williamsburg. Wounded early in that battle, Garland had kept at the head of his troops.[75] He was a man who

[69] O. R., 11, pt. 3, p. 551.
[70] Smith explained this in 2 B. & L., 224, and stated in his War Papers, 147, that he retained temporarily command of D. R. Jones's Division of two Brigades. No specific orders on these points have been found, but on May 28 Magruder received direct instructions from Johnston, O. R., 11, pt. 3, p. 557, and on the 30th wrote to him without reference to Smith, O. R., 11, pt. 3, pp. 560–61.
[71] G. W. Smith, 168.   [72] O. R., 11, pt. 3, p. 543.
[73] O. R., 5, 493.   [74] O. R., 5, 1058.
[75] O. R., 11, pt. 1, pp. 567, 578; 5 C. V., 477.

could be trusted. Of that there was no doubt. Col. Wade Hampton likewise had tendered him a Brigadier's commission of the same date as Garland's,[76] but because of some unexplained controversy with the President, he at first declined it.[77] Like honor came to Robert Hatton, who already commanded the Tennessee regiments.[78]

Much more necessary than the promotion of these men was, in Johnston's opinion, the appointment of at least two additional Major Generals. He did not have sufficient officers of that grade to handle large bodies of troops. Davis's reluctance to increase the number of high-ranking Generals might confuse the coming battle and certainly would hamper Johnston in directing it. Whiting was at the head of a Division, though he still ranked as a Brigadier. Johnston had urged his promotion[79] but without success. The President had not forgotten and he now reminded Johnston that Whiting had rejected the command of a Mississippi Brigade "in an insubordinate letter, which was withdrawn by him for modification, but of which I have heard nothing further."[80] In addition, Davis may have been prejudiced, also, by an absurdly false report that Whiting had proposed while at Yorktown that the civil government be overthrown and that Johnston be made dictator.[81]

Whiting, in short, was persona non grata. Of men acceptable to the President, D. R. Jones of South Carolina already was slated to be Major General, but his nomination was pending before the Senate.[82] As Johnston continued earnestly to ask for additional officers to command Divisions,[83] Davis at last appointed two men who had distinguished themselves at Williamsburg—Lafayette McLaws and A. P. Hill.[84] To McLaws, after the flurry over the relief of Magruder, a Division of that officer's large force was assigned. A. P. Hill—"Powell" Hill to his intimates—was put in charge of Branch's Brigade and of Jos. R. Anderson's command, which was about to establish contact with Johnston's outposts.[85]

76 *Wright*, 82.   77 Cf. *O. R.*, 11, pt. 3, p. 543; *Conner*, 109.
78 *O. R.*, 11, pt. 3, p. 531; *Wright*, 82.
79 See *supra*, p. 195.   80 *O. R.*, 11, pt. 3, p. 547.
81 G. W. Smith, *op. cit.*, 328, stated that Davis subsequently repeated to him this rumor, which he at once denounced as false.
82 *Ibid.*
83 *O. R.*, 11, pt. 3, p. 543.
84 *Wright*, 27. For the next reference to McLaws, see p. 226.
85 Cf. *O. R.*, 11, pt. 3, p. 547. For Hill. see next Chap. XXX *et seq.*

All five of these promotions were made between May 23 and May 26, when a major battle was imminent. Inasmuch as four of the five general officers had seen some service in the command to which they were assigned, the delay in appointment might have no serious effect; but, in the case of Powell Hill, it might hamper. Except at Williamsburg, he had never commanded even a Brigade in action; now he must whip quickly into shape a Division with no Brigade of which he ever had been associated. It is doubtful if, when he opened headquarters, he even knew all his Brigadiers. For this condition, circumstance was in part responsible, because the troops had not been brought together until that time. On the other hand, Johnston's appeals for the assignment of Generals of Division had been frequent and pointed. As early as May 9, it will be remembered, he had protested against the proposed transfer of Longstreet or of Smith, and had gone so far as to tell the President, "several more Major Generals like them are required to make this an army." [86] Now, almost as the caissons began to rumble toward the battlefield, Johnston had six divisional commanders of appropriate rank and would have a seventh when Huger joined. This number, Davis economically calculated, "would cover Johnston's command very nearly." [87] Not one word did Davis say, then or thereafter, in explanation of his previous delay in supplying Major Generals. To an unfriendly mind, it might have appeared that the President had waited as long as he dared before yielding to Johnston in this, the last of their three current differences.

The day that A. P. Hill assumed command, May 27, 1862, was an important one in the preliminaries of the battle.[88] General Branch, brought down from Gordonsville, had been left by Johnston to choose his own positions to protect the Virginia Central Railroad and to establish liaison with J. R. Anderson. In the exercise of this discretion, Branch, on the 26th, moved his Brigade from Hanover Court House southward about four miles to Lebanon Church, near Peake's on the Virginia Central Railroad.[89]

---

86 *O. R.*, 11, pt. 3, p. 503.   87 *Ibid.*, 547
88 For Hill's assumption of command, see *O. R.*, 11, pt. 3, pp. 554-55.
89 Lebanon and Slash Churches often are confused. The writer's venerable friend, State Senator Henry T. Wickham, who in 1942 preserved full memory of the events of 1862, thus explained the locations: "Lebanon Church is about one-half mile South of Peake's Turnout on the C. & O. Slash Church is a mile away on the old Stage Road from Richmond to Hanover C. H."—*Letter of Oct. 18, 1938.*

This he did in order to make available a direct line of retreat to Ashland in event he were confronted by superior force. In this new position he was attacked on the 27th by a heavy Federal column.[90] Although his troops put up a stiff fight, they were driven back to Ashland, where, for the first time, he was ordered to report to his new commander, Hill.[91] The affair was in no sense discreditable to Branch,[92] but it was a somber induction of the new Division.

Even more serious than casualties and humiliation was the evidence offered by this clash that McClellan apparently was extending northward a strong hand of welcome to McDowell.[93] The "two Mc's" were not far from a junction of force—the one development above all others that Johnston had best reason to dread. Before the news of Branch's reverse reached him, Johnston wrote Smith, "We must get ready to fight." Smith hurried immediately to headquarters. On the afternoon of the 27th, battle plans were formulated. Circumstance, more than choice, shaped them. McClellan's troops North of the Chickahominy would be those who first united with McDowell. As soon as practicable, Smith with his three Divisions must attack and break the link the Federals were soon to weld.

By the evening of the 28th, Smith reported to a council of war at Army headquarters that his preparations were complete. The Federals, he told Johnston, had a strong position about a mile East of Mechanicsville, on the eastern bank of Beaver Dam Creek, but he had confidence that an assault by his three Divisions would clear the ground of Federals. Johnston listened and then announced—with more of inward relief than his manner disclosed —that an important change in the situation had occurred: "Jeb" Stuart, he said, had reported that McDowell had halted his

[90] One Division and one small Brigade of infantry, three regiments of cavalry and two batteries under Brig. Gen. Fitz-John Porter of the V Corps, O. R., 11, pt. 1, p. 681.
[91] Branch reported 243 killed and wounded, excluding those in J. H. Lane's Twenty-eighth North Carolina; O. R., 11, pt. 1, p. 742; but Porter asserted that he buried about 200 Confederate dead and had approximately 730 prisoners, wounded and unwounded, O. R., 11, pt. 1, p. 683. If this discrepancy is reconcilable at all, it must be by the inclusion among the prisoners of troops of other Confederate commands, picked up along the railroads. Porter's casualties were 355. See O. R., 11, pt. 1, p. 685. In this action, three of the four Robinett brothers of Co. G., Thirty-seventh North Carolina, were killed. This was one of the few instances, perhaps the only instance, where three brothers were slain in the same company on the same day. 2 N. C. Regts., 654.
[92] Lee made this plain in a commendatory note of June 3, 1862. See O. R., 11, pt. 1, p. 743.
[93] Cf. McClellan's comment in O. R., 11, pt. 1, p. 37.

advance to join McClellan. That seemed too good to be true, but it was not all. McDowell had returned to Fredericksburg, according to Stuart's information, and seemed to be planning to move even farther North.

If this information were correct, what had happened to McDowell? Johnston knew that "Stonewall" Jackson was on the move in the Shenandoah Valley. Perhaps, even probably, McDowell's countermarch was related to Jackson's advance, but, of the details, nothing was clear. The reality, not the reason for it, had to be considered by Johnston's council of war. If McDowell were withdrawing, should the Confederates attack McClellan, and if so, where? Smith did not believe that McDowell's column was permanently off the stage of the Richmond theatre of war, but he at once withdrew his plan for an attack North of the Chickahominy. It would be easier now, Smith said, to beat that part of the Federal Army South of the river, where the ground was less unfavorable for an offensive. Longstreet disagreed and expressed himself in favor of the execution of Smith's original plan.

A long discussion followed. Johnston at length got up, in weariness of mind, and walked to another part of the room. Longstreet followed after him and, in a brief, private conversation, continued to argue the point. When overruled by his chief, Longstreet urged that an attack be delivered the very next morning in the vicinity of Seven Pines, directly East of Richmond. Again Johnston shook his head. If it proved true, he said, that McDowell was not marching to reinforce McClellan, he would strike at the first large force of Federals that came within easy reach on the south side of the river; but the next day? No! Too many of his troops were concentrated on his left in anticipation of McDowell's advance. Moreover, Huger was soon to arrive The Army could afford to await him.[94]

---

[94] *G. W. Smith*, 148–50. Longstreet subsequently wrote that Johnston told him, as they talked privately together, that he agreed the plan for an attack North of the river was practicable, but said "that he had selected the wrong officer for the work." *Longstreet*, 86. This might suggest that, even before the events of May 31, Johnston had begun to doubt Smith's willingness to assume responsibility as a field commander, but that view seems to be debarred by Johnston's statement in his *Narrative*, p. 133, that the "accident of location"—and presumably that alone—deprived Smith of command on May 31 of the attacking column, "to which he was entitled by his rank." Furthermore, the day after this council of war, Johnston, as recorded on p. 217, placed Smith in general charge of the left wing. If Johnston then had misgivings of Smith's capability, would he have extended that officer's command?

This decision to defer and to shift the battle was made late in the night of the 28th, but no word of the change of plans was sent to Mr. Davis.[95] As events turned, Johnston, within a few hours, was not so sure an engagement would or could be delayed beyond the 29th. D. H. Hill reported that morning from the Williamsburg road that his skirmishers had encountered a Brigade of Federal infantry with cavalry and artillery support. Johnston communicated this news to Whiting, with jaunty indifference. He wrote: "Who knows but that in the course of the morning Longstreet's scheme may accomplish itself. If we get into a fight here you'll have to hurry to help us. I think it will be best for A. P. Hill's troops to watch the bridges and for yours to be well in this direction ready to act anywhere. Tell G. W."[96] Those were all the orders to Smith, who had three Divisions under him— "tell G. W."

The 29th passed without an opportunity for the execution of "Longstreet's scheme," but on May 30, D. H. Hill made a reconnaissance in force on the Williamsburg road and found the enemy had advanced farther to the West of Seven Pines.[97] No enemy was found near the western end of the Charles City road, which at Seven Pines is about two and half miles South of and approximately parallel to the Williamsburg road. The presence of the Federals on one of these roads and not on the other was somewhat puzzling. Either the Federal left flank, facing West, was refused, or else it was rested on the low, boggy ground between the roads.

[95] In 2 Davis, 121–22, the President stated that he went out the Mechanicsville Turnpike on the morning of May 29 in full expectation that the battle was to begin. He found no preparations for action, he said, and he met no officer who knew of any. A long letter from the President to his wife, of May 28, 1862, printed in 5 Rowland, 252, and attributed to Mrs. Davis's Jefferson Davis [v. 2], 275–79, would indicate an error in the date of Davis's ride but otherwise would seem, on casual reading, to confirm, by a contemporary document, what the President wrote years afterward. Actually, by a curious mistake in copying, the "letter" of May 28 in Rowland includes not only what Mr. Davis wrote his wife in 1862 but also an extract, plainly indicated by Mrs. Davis as such, from Mr. Davis's later book. General Smith, op. cit., 155, and General Johnston, 2 B. & L., 210, show that the President undoubtedly confused this ride with one of a different date or, perhaps, with several others. Davis's account of events of May 29 is so erroneous where it can be checked by other witnesses that it raises a question whether his memory could be trusted for the statement, 2 Davis, 120, that Lee, on or about May 26, was informed by Johnston (see supra, p. 214) that the attack would be made "the next Thursday," which was May 29. The sequence of the events given in the text, coupled with Johnston's known caution, renders it highly doubtful that Johnston, as early as the 26th, had set a specific date for the battle.
[96] G. W. Smith, 151.
[97] D. H. Hill in O. R., 11, pt. 1, p. 943. Johnston stated in his Narrative, 132, that the Federal outposts were two miles West of Seven Pines. Casey's report, O. R., 11, pt. 1, p. 913, indicated that the distance was a little more than one mile.

Furthermore, Hill's information was that the whole of the IV Corps, Keyes's, was South of the Chickahominy.[98] When this intelligence reached Johnston about noon, he knew that Huger was in the outskirts of Richmond and would be available the next day. Johnston accordingly decided to attack at Seven Pines on the 31st. In a long conference with Longstreet, he worked out the detailed plan. Longstreet was told to take command of the right—his own, Harvey Hill's and Huger's Divisions—and for his march and dispositions was given verbal orders.[99] Those of the other division commanders were in the form of letters from Johnston. Huger's instructions were dated 8.40 P.M. No copy of them was retained by Johnston.[100] Smith's orders, written at 9.15 P.M.,[101] were sent his headquarters, about six miles distant,[102] though they were duplicated to Whiting, who was somewhat nearer at hand. Again no word was sent to President Davis of the great events impending. General Lee ascertained little. When he sent a staff officer to Johnston, volunteering his services in any capacity during the action, he received the coldly polite, businesslike answer that Johnston would be glad to see him on the field and would be grateful for any reinforcements that could be dispatched.[103]

All these messages were sent, and all preparations for the battle were made in the midst of a deluge of rain.[104] The storm would slow the Confederate march and perhaps delay the action, but it would flood the Chickahominy and probably would prevent

98 O. R., 11, pt. 1, p. 943, cf. ibid., 933. Apparently the Confederates knew that Heintzelman's III Corps was in support of Keyes (cf. Johnston's Narrative, 133), though no references to Heintzelman's presence or position appear in Confederate correspondence of May 28–30 published in O. R.

99 Johnston, in his Narrative, 133–34, wrote: "Being confident Longstreet and Hill, with their forces united, would be successful in the earlier part of the action against an enemy formed in several lines, with wide intervals between them, I left the immediate control, on the Williamsburg road, to them, under general instructions, and placed myself on the left, where I could soonest learn the approach of Federal reenforcements from beyond the Chickahominy." Subsequently, in 2 B. & L., 212, Johnston elaborated: "Longstreet's command of the right was to end when the troops approached Seven Pines and I should be present to direct the movements, after which each Major General would command his own Division." If this was understood at the time by Longstreet, he did not record in any of his published writings that he knew his command of the right wing would terminate when he approached Seven Pines.

100 O. R., 11, pt. 1, p. 938.   101 O. R., 11, pt. 1, p. 563.

102 G W. Smith, op. cit., p. 161, stated that his headquarters were "on the Brook Turnpike, about four miles from Richmond." His orders were not received, he stated, op. cit., 168, until 12.30 A.M., May 31.

103 A. L. Long, Memoirs of Robert E. Lee (cited hereafter as Long), 158–59. This reply of Johnston's was verbal.

104 Longstreet, 88; Alexander, 75.

the movement or Federal troops from the North of that stream to strengthen the drenched Divisions that were to be assailed.[105] For the great day of Johnston's life, for the first major battle he was exclusively to direct, the prospect seemed as fair as the night was black.

[105] *Johnston's Narrative*, 133.

CHAPTER XVII

SEVEN PINES: A BATTLE OF STRANGE ERRORS

JOHNSTON's aim in the the battle of May 31, 1862, was to over-whelm the IV Federal Corps at Seven Pines before it could be reinforced.[1] His concentration and deployment were based on the direction of the three highways that led to the enemy's position. The first of these was the Nine Mile road.[2] This left the northeast suburbs of Richmond, near Oakwood Cemetery, and ran East and Southeast to Fair Oaks Station, on the York River Railroad, six miles from the corporate limits. After passing Fair Oaks Station, the Nine Mile road continued to the East for about 1600 yards and ended at Seven Pines.[3] Next, to the southward, was the Williamsburg road, which followed a course almost due East from Richmond to Seven Pines and thence to the Chicka-hominy River at Bottom's Bridge. At no point West of their convergence at Seven Pines were the Nine Mile and the Williams-burg roads more than 2.25 miles apart.[4] The third line of Johnston's advance was the Charles City road. This forked from the Williamsburg road 2.3 miles East of Richmond and ran there-after for several miles from Northwest to Southeast. For slightly more than two miles below the mouth of the Charles City road, communication between that highway and the Williamsburg road was easy in normal weather. Below that point, the upper stretches of troublesome White Oak Swamp separated the thoroughfares. Opposite Seven Pines,[5] much of the two and a half miles of

[1] O. R., 11, pt. 1, p. 933.

[2] Sometimes called the New Bridge road, though that name was applicable only to the turnout from Old Tavern northward to New Bridge over the Chickahominy. Several of the Confederate commanders styled this the Nine Miles road, but on A. H. Camp-bell's authoritative map of April 26, 1863, "Nine Mile" is used. That is the present (1942) name.

[3] A narrow farm road ran southward from Seven Pines to the edge of White Oak Swamp. This could not be considered, in a military sense, a continuance of the Nine Mile road.

[4] As they approached their meeting place, these roads formed, respectively, two sides of a triangle: the Nine Mile road was the northwestern-southeastern face; the Williams-burg road was the base, West to East. The third face of the triangle, Southeast to North-west, was represented only by a farm road, too remote from the scene of action to be of use.

[5] At White's Tavern on the Charles City road.

ground between the two roads was difficult in the best of conditions and impassable after heavy rains. Except for this fact, the location of the roads seemed ideal for a swift convergence on Seven Pines.

To facilitate that convergence, D. H. Hill already had three of the Brigades of his Division on the Williamsburg road: there seemed no reason why he could not bring his fourth Brigade, Rodes's, across from the Charles City road. Then, with his entire Division, Harvey Hill could lead the attack down the Williamsburg road. Longstreet was in camp on the Nine Mile road: simply by moving down that road, he could form on Hill's left and could attack the right flank of the Federals when Hill assailed their center and left. To reinforce Longstreet, in all contingencies, use could be made of Whiting's Division. That fine command, which had distinguished itself at Eltham's Landing, was Northwest of the Nine Mile road and within easy supporting distance. The remainder of Smith's command could guard the south bank of the upper Chickahominy against attack from the North of that stream.

Magruder, who held the advanced positions on the Nine Mile road, could be in general reserve. For that matter, McLaws's Division of Magruder's command, as the most advanced unit on that part of the front, might have led the attack down the Nine Mile road, but Johnston preferred to entrust that phase of the operation to Longstreet. If required, McLaws speedily could reinforce Longstreet.[6] As fourteen Brigades, without McLaws, thus would be available for the attack on the Federals, the concentration of force seemed more than adequate.

To complete a sound plan of operations, the only other essential requirement seemed to be to cover D. H. Hill's right flank in case it might be exposed to the Federal troops, whose exact position on McClellan's left, near the northern side of White Oak Swamp, was not known. For securing the Confederate right, Johnston could use Huger's Division of three Brigades,[7] which had reached Richmond and had gone into camp near Oakwood Cemetery. At first, Johnston had thought of employing Huger to attack the left flank of the Federals whom D. H. Hill was to assail in front,

---

[6] O. R., 11, pt. 3, p. 563. For McLaws's next battle, see Chap. XXXIII.
[7] Armistead's, Wright's, formerly Blanchard's, and Mahone's.

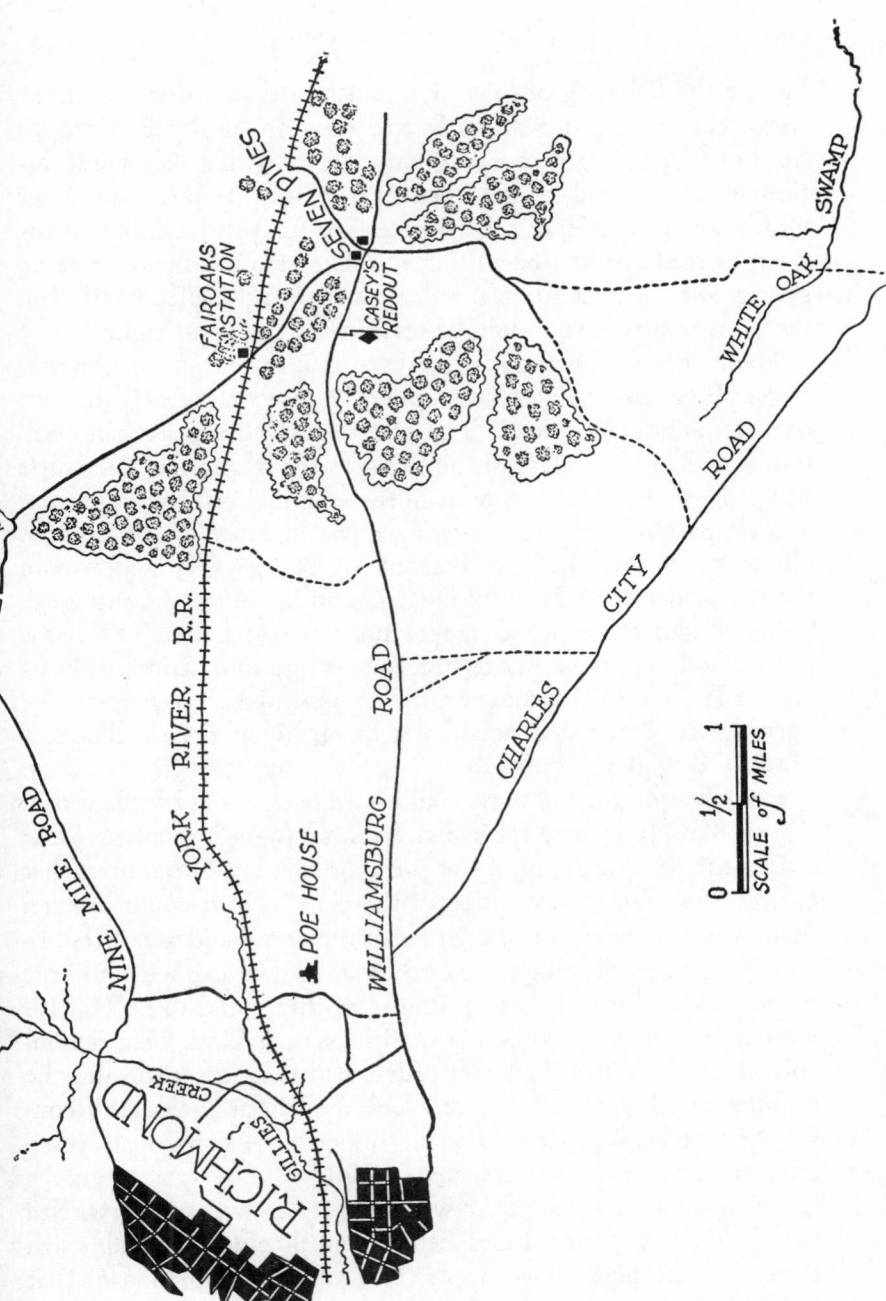

Lines of Advance eastward from Richmond to Seven Pines as used for the attempted concentration of May 31, 1862.

but, on the morning of May 31, Johnston decided that the uncertainty concerning the strength and position of the Federals in front of Huger might render a flank attack by that officer impracticable. He revised Huger's orders to read: "As our main force will be on your left, it will be necessary for your progress to the front to conform at first to that of General Hill. If you find no strong body in your front, it will be well to aid General Hill; but then a strong reserve should be retained to cover our right." [8]

These orders Johnston sent direct to Huger. No intimation was given Huger that he was to be under the direction of any one save the commanding General. The full plan of action was not communicated to him,[9] though the time for the opening of the battle was to be set by his movements in this essential respect: as soon as a corresponding unit of Huger's Division reached Rodes, that officer was to start his Brigade from the Charles City road to join the remainder of D. H. Hill's Division on the Williamsburg road. When Rodes came up, a signal gun was to be fired. Hill was immediately to attack. Longstreet was to go into action on hearing Hill's fire. In this manner, the complicated arrangements for opening the battle depended, first of all, upon the time one of Huger's Brigades reached Rodes.

Five questions, if no more, could have been asked on the morning of May 31 by any informed critic of Johnston's plan: First, would the deluging rain of the previous evening interfere in that flat country with the execution of the plan? None could be sure. Second, was the terrain known to all the commanders? Presumably yes, except to Huger. Third, were orders explicit and past misunderstanding? Those to Smith, to Huger and to D. H. Hill were in writing and, while not models of their kind, were reasonably clear. Longstreet's verbal orders had been given during the evening of May 30, while Longstreet had been in lengthy consultation at headquarters. Did he understand, beyond all possibility of error, what was expected of him?

Again, as the essence of the whole enterprise was to overwhelm the Federals at Seven Pines before reinforcements could reach them, did the plan allow ample time for the completion of that task? Slow advance would involve delayed concentration; a late attack that encountered stubborn resistance might not bring victory before nightfall. Under cover of darkness, the superior force of McClellan might be concentrated. Then the attackers might be assailed. That was the veriest A B C of battle: was it certain that Huger would arrive on the Charles City road and relieve Rodes at an hour that would permit Rodes to reach Hill early in the day?

The final question was the old one of convergence and coordination: would the commanders of the large, independent and poorly staffed Divisions be able to bring their troops together against the enemy? Those proud individualists at the head of some of the units—would they work in harness? What of Smith; what of the others? If the preliminaries of the battle had raised any doubts in Johnston's mind of Smith's willingness to assume responsibility or to endure physically the stress of action, there is no record of it. In the event Smith were sick, his troops could be led by Whiting, of whom Johnston had a high opinion. Again, if Magruder had sought to rid himself of Smith's control and had abused D. H. Hill—if Magruder, for these reasons perhaps, had impressed the commanding General as a reluctant subordinate, however he might shine as an independent commander, there now was no danger of immediate trouble. Magruder was not to participate in the battle. As for Hill and Longstreet, who were to be next each other, right to left, they had experience and they saw eye to eye.

The one participating divisional commander of whose cooperation in battle Johnston knew nothing was General Huger. After succeeding General Walter Gwynn in command at Norfolk, General Huger had remained there until the evacuation of the city. His high South Carolinian birth, the reputation he had won as Scott's Chief of Ordnance in the Mexican War, and his former position in the "old army" as fourth ranking major of the Ordnance Department [10] had raised high expectations,[11] which he had

[10] *U. S. Army Register,* 1860. His tender of service to Virginia is described in Appendix II, p. 719.

[11] For Huger, No. 8 in the class of 1825 at West Point, see *Cullum,* No. 399. The chronology of his service in Norfolk may be traced through the following references: *De Leon,* 98; *Richmond Dispatch,* April 19, p. 1, col. 2; May 23, p. 1, col. 4; May 27, p. 1, cols. 2, 3; June 17, p. 3, col. 5; July 4, p. 2, cols. 3, 5; July 8, p. 1, col. 2; *Richmond Examiner,* May 25, p. 2, col. 6; June 6, p. 2, col. 4; June 7, p. 2, col. 5; June 12, p. 2, col. 5; June 13, p. 2, col. 5; June 22, p. 2, col. 6; July 5, 1861, p. 2, col. 5; *O. R.,* 2, 867, 1001; *O. R.,* 4, 641, 659, 679; *O. R.,* 51, pt. 2, pp. 81, 102, 106, 110, 276, 347, 468, 482.

fulfilled by his administration at Norfolk, though somewhat slowly and in the face of many difficulties.[12] When rumor had reached Richmond of poor discipline among his troops in the late autumn of 1861, he had not pretended to have perfect morale, but he had reported improvement.[13] After the fall of Roanoke Island, he had been much abused by the protagonists of Gen. Henry A. Wise, and had been censured by an investigating committee of the Confederate House of Representatives for failure to reinforce and to supply the troops at Roanoke Island.[14] Despite assurances of Mr. Davis's continuing support, he had felt that his position at Norfolk was untenable and that evacuation was inevitable.[15] While he had not communicated frequently with his superiors,[16] there had been no indication that he had failed to remove ordnance and munitions as rapidly as his facilities allowed.[17]

Less than a fortnight before Huger had left the exposed city he had written: "I do not see what preparation I can make, if any, for the contingency but to repel every attack as promptly as possible and defend the position as long as I can. When they have the waters on both sides of me, you can calculate how long I can hold out as well as I can." [18] On his unopposed withdrawal, he had been under the close direction of General Lee.[19] With fair speed and probably with less straggling than later was charged against him,[20] Huger had reached Petersburg, to be met again with criticism. Some of the newspapers, unreasonably critical, spoke of him as if he, not Johnston, had decided on the abandonment of Norfolk. Now, with many questions raised and none answered, Huger waited West of Gillies Creek. At 56 years of age—medium in height, thick-set, stout, ruddy, with gray hair, gray eyes and heavy mustache, slow of speech and of motion,[21] but bearing unmistakably the stamp of the proud and martial

[12] *Richmond Dispatch,* July 8, p. 2, col. 3; Aug. 20, p. 1, col. 5; Sept. 28, p. 1, col. 6; Nov. 6, 1861, p. 2, col. 3.
[13] *O. R.,* 51, pt. 2, p. 391.
[14] *O. R.,* 6, 190–91; for the gravamen of Wise's charges against Huger, see *O. R.,* 51, pt. 2, pp. 519 ff; for the attacks made on Huger in Congress, see 44 *S. H. S. P.,* 176.
[15] *O. R.,* 9, 45, 59.
[16] Cf. *O. R.,* 11, pt. 3, pp. 426, 506.
[17] Cf. *O. R.,* 11, pt. 3, pp. 490 ff.   [18] *O. R.,* 11, pt. 3, pp. 474–75.
[19] *O. R.,* 11, pt. 3, pp. 524 ff.
[20] For the confusion over the size of Huger's command, put at 7000 by the General, see 2 *B. & L.,* 208.
[21] *An English Combatant,* 360.

aristocrat—he was to lead troops into action for the first time in his life. Would he have a chance; would he succeed? Did he know what was expected of him?

At dawn of the day that was to see a historic change in the organization of the Army that defended Richmond, Maj. Gen. G. W. Smith arrived at advanced headquarters on the Nine Mile road. Whiting's men, he said, had moved before daylight and would soon arrive at the Richmond end of the Nine Mile road, out which they would march. He had left A. P. Hill in charge of the remainder of the left wing, Smith went on, and he would not interfere with Whiting's direction of the advancing Division. His intention, Smith concluded, was to accompany the Division and to render what assistance he could. It was unusual in Confederate service for the commander of an entire wing of an army thus, in a sense, to abdicate his position and to become a mere observer of a battle; but on this point now there was no time for reflection or wonder. Smith might, in fact, have intended to do no more than to disencumber himself of detailed command in order to assure co-ordination of force.[22] Johnston must have assumed this. He made no objection, explained his plan in some detail to Smith, and expressed the belief that the rise in the waters of the Chickahominy, as a result of the heavy rain of the previous evening, would keep the enemy from sending troops from the north side of the river to reinforce those about to be attacked.[23]

By 6 o'clock, the leading Brigade of Whiting's Division was ready to start its march out Nine Mile road.[24] At the mouth of the road and moving across it, Whiting found a large part of Longstreet's Division, which had been encamped around the Fairfield

---

[22] *G. W. Smith*, 162.

[23] *G. W. Smith*, 163, 168–69.

[24] Some accounts of this advance, following the reference in *O. R.*, 11, pt. 3, p. 563, assert that Whiting was on the wrong road and had been directed to advance by the nonexistent "Gaines Road"; but the word "Gaines" is bracketed with a question-mark by the editors of *O. R.*, who were unable to decipher the word. A greater familiarity with the country and with the autograph of General Johnston would have made it plain that the words were "9 miles." The "9" was mistaken for "G" and "miles" for "aines." As Whiting had been in reserve on the Dill Farm, Meadow Bridge road (Froebel, in *G. W. Smith*, 178), in rear of D. R. Jones, who had been guarding the heights overlooking the Chickahominy (*G. W. Smith*, 159), the natural and shortest route for Whiting to follow would have been southward along the Meadow Bridge road to the vicinity of Battery 7, eastward and southeast across the Virginia Central Railroad, then to the Mechanicsville turnpike at the tollgate opposite the Jacobs House, and thence southward to the city limits and the Nine Mile road.

Race Course [25] and along the Nine Mile road to the eastward.[26] These troops were busily breaking camp and were loading wagons, as if they intended to take their trains with them.[27]

Whiting's orders required him to come "as early as possible" to the point where the New Bridge road turned off the Nine Mile road, more than four miles distant. The prospect of having to wait to execute these orders until Longstreet cleared the road made Whiting nervous and impatient. He was not entirely relieved when, after writing General Johnston that his route was obstructed, he received assurance from headquarters that Longstreet was to precede him.[28] Whiting waited for a time and then went to Johnston's headquarters, which were at the near-by Stubbs House,[29] whither Smith previously had ridden. Would Smith, he urged in effect, ask Longstreet to put an end to the delay? [30]

Smith was willing to make the request—but where could Longstreet be found? General Johnston, when asked for the information, said that Longstreet's Division was down the Nine Mile road and that its commander probably was with it. If Longstreet were not there, Johnston explained, he probably was on the Williamsburg road with that part of his command posted there.[31] Capt. R. F. Beckham of Smith's staff made off at once with a message to Longstreet. In about an hour Beckham sent back a courier to

[25] About midway between the Mechanicsville turnpike and the Nine Mile road, one and one half miles Northeast of the Capitol Square. The race track almost adjoined Battery 5, which was approximately one mile nearer Richmond than the Dabb House.
   [26] G. W. Smith, 159.   [27] Ibid., 164.
   [28] 2 B. & L., 241. The formal reply of Johnston, O. R., 11, pt. 1, p. 564, stated, "Longstreet will precede you." Whiting assumed that this of course referred to the march on the Nine Mile road.
   [29] S. B. French, in G. W. Smith, 247. Mrs. Fannie Gaines Talley informed the writer that the home of Robert Stubbs, probably the "Stubbs House" in question, was on the site later used as the Glenwood golf course.
   [30] The nature of Whiting's request, which might help to elucidate the puzzle of Longstreet's movements, cannot be stated with precision. In the suppressed part of his report, Smith said: "I directed Captain Beckham . . . to see General Longstreet on the Nine Miles road and learn from him the state of affairs, and communicate to me all the information he could obtain in regard to the probable movements of the troops under General Longstreet, in order that I might understandingly give instructions to General Whiting, who had arrived with the head of the division near General Johnston's head-quarters—having been for some time waiting for General Longstreet's troops to pass" (G. W. Smith, 169). In his formal narrative, published in 1884, Smith wrote: "General Smith then sent an aide-de-camp to General Longstreet, informing him of the cause of the delay, and requesting that it be remedied as soon as possible" (G. W. Smith, 164). In his final account of the battle, 2 B. & L., 241–42, Smith stated: "About 8 o'clock I sent my aide-de-camp, Captain Beckham, to see General Longstreet in regard to this matter."
   [31] 2 B. & L., 242. In his earlier review, Smith did not add that Johnston told him Longstreet might be over on the Williamsburg road.

report that Longstreet was not on the Nine Mile road. Beckham himself had ridden across country to see if he could find the General on the highway to the South.

Johnston was skeptical of this report that Longstreet was not on the designated road,[32] and probably he was confirmed in his doubt because those of Longstreet's troops who had been blocking the Nine Mile road had by this time disappeared.[33] Accordingly, Johnston gave the sensible precautionary orders: Whiting would remain where he was until the position of Longstreet's troops was established. One of Johnston's own staff officers would go down the Nine Mile road in search of Longstreet and, failing to find him, would ride over to the Williamsburg road, search out Longstreet and tell him to send three Brigades back to the Nine Mile road, unless they had moved so far that there would be a serious loss of time in returning them.[34]

Lt. J. B. Washington, the aide whom Johnston designated for this mission, did not return,[35] but the fast-riding Beckham, sometime after 10 o'clock, reported by courier that he had found Longstreet—and on the Williamsburg road opposite the point where the Charles City road forked.[36] There, Beckham wrote, Longstreet was waiting for D. H. Hill to pass down the Williamsburg road in order to open the action.

This meant that Longstreet was at the one point where congestion and resulting delay were most apt to occur. The plan had been for Longstreet to use the unobstructed Nine Mile road; D. H.

[32] 2 B. & L., 242.

[33] 2 G. W. Smith, 165. It is an ironical commentary on the inefficiency of staff work at this period of the war that apparently none of Smith's, Whiting's or Johnston's officers rode down to the troops in the road to seek out an officer of rank and to inquire what his orders were. Had this been done, the facts could have been established promptly.

[34] G. W. Smith, 165. Longstreet, op. cit., 90–91, maintained that Smith, failing to come by the "Gaines road," had set himself to work to make trouble "and induced General Johnston to so far modify the plans as to order three of my Brigades down the Nine Miles road to the New Bridge Fork." As it is beyond dispute that Johnston intended Longstreet to proceed by the Nine Mile road, the question arises, Why did he give Longstreet these discretionary orders—to continue to the Williamsburg road or to send back three Brigades? The most probable answer would seem to be that Johnston desired his original plan to be executed but that he reasoned he could use Smith's troops if Longstreet's were not available in time for an early attack.

[35] He unwittingly rode into the Federal picket line and had to surrender. Although Washington was silent under questioning, the presence of an officer of General Johnston's staff in an advanced position aroused Federal suspicions. O. R., 11, pt. 1, p. 914.

[36] Beckham, in G. W. Smith, 166, stated that he "found [Longstreet's] headquarters at a house on the side of the road, belonging, I think to a Mr. Poor." This evidently was the Poe House directly East of the intermediate line of 1864, and midway between the York River Railroad and the Williamsburg road.

Hill was to move early along the Williamsburg road; Huger, coming down from the vicinity of Oakwood, presumably was to follow D. H. Hill and was to turn to the right into the Charles City road. Now, by perverse misfortune, Longstreet was on Hill's road. Unless Huger previously had passed, his Division, too, might be on the Williamsburg road West of the turnout into the Charles City road. With three roads available for four Divisions, three of the four were, or might be, on a single mile of one road. Gone was all prospect of an early beginning of the battle!

How had such a mix-up occurred? One of two things had happened. Either Longstreet had understood that he should move down the Nine Mile road and then across [37] to the Williamsburg road in rear of D. H. Hill; or else Longstreet had concluded that, as he had been placed in command of the right wing, he could modify as he saw fit the lines of advance of that wing. Whatever the reason, he had confused the advance frightfully. As his Division had been spread some distance from the Fairfield Race Course down the Nine Mile road,[38] he had countermarched some of his troops up the Nine Mile road and then had turned southward. This had brought the whole Division down to a stream of several branches known as Gillies Creek. Even in normal weather, the passage of the steep valley by artillery and wagons would have been a slower task than would be assumed. After the storm of the previous evening, the creek was raging.[39]

Confronted with this barrier to his advance, Longstreet decided that he would save time by bridging the creek instead of seeking a different route along muddy, overflowed roads.[40] A wagon was placed in the stream bed for a trestle, and planks were extended to the banks, but this makeshift was a bridge so narrow that the men had to pass in single file.[41] Before the leading regiment had begun to walk the plank, another complication developed: Huger's Divi-

[37] In *Longstreet*, 88, he said "by the Nine Miles road and a lateral road leading across the rear of General Hill on the Williamsburg road." In *ibid.*, 91, he mentioned "the Nine Miles and lateral roads leading across to the Williamsburg road."

[38] G. W. Smith, in 2 *B. & L.*, 229, stated that Colston's Brigade of Longstreet's Division was three and one half miles down the Nine Mile road.

[39] It is remarkable that virtually all accounts of the preliminaries of the Battle of Seven Pines except G. W. Smith's (*op. cit.*, 228) minimize the obstacle presented by Gillies Creek in flood. North of the York River Railroad, the creek has a watershed of about twelve square miles. It drains an area that extends northward almost to the heights that overlook the Chickahominy. Above the site of Blakey's Mill, the hills are steep. The creek itself is scarped.

[40] *Longstreet*, 91.   [41] 2 *B. & L.*, 229.

sion came down the hillside to cross the rebellious creek at the same point in execution of his orders to march to the Charles City road. He had chosen the shortest way to the head of that road, and had no reason to assume that another Division would be following the same route.

The fact that the movement of Huger's front Brigade was to fix the time for opening the battle, by relieving Rodes, should have assured Huger the right of way at the creek, but apparently nobody at the crossing knew that the late comers should be the first over. At least, if any one on the creek bank understood the importance of speeding Huger, nothing was done. Longstreet's men insisted on the right of prior crossing because of earlier arrival.[42]

While this was happening, or soon thereafter, Longstreet and Huger met at D. H. Hill's headquarters.[43] Huger promptly inquired whether Longstreet knew which of them had earlier commission as Major General. Longstreet asserted that he had. If Longstreet were sure of the fact, Huger replied, that was sufficient.[44] In an atmosphere of some unpleasantness, the commanders waited for their respective troops to cross the creek. Longstreet's Division passed and by 9 o'clock reached the position opposite the mouth of the Charles City road where Beckham found the General.[45]

When Beckham's report of Longstreet's position was repeated by Smith to Johnston, after 10 A.M., the commanding General manfully told Smith that the misunderstanding over the line of advance might be his fault, not Longstreet's.[46] Without further

---

[42] *Longstreet,* 91; Huger in *O. R.,* 11, pt. 1, p. 942.

[43] *Richmond Examiner,* Aug. 25, 1862, p. 1, col. 3.

[44] *O. R.,* 11, pt. 1, p. 942. Longstreet did not discuss this question in any contemporary records now known to be in existence, but in *Longstreet,* 91, he stated: [discussion] "revealed that he [Huger] was the ranking officer, when I suggested that it was only necessary for him to take command and execute the orders. This he declined." Huger wrote explicitly, *loc. cit.:* "General Longstreet was not the senior officer present. We met on duty, and I inquired of him if he knew which was the senior, as I did not. He replied that he was. I told him if he knew it that was sufficient. But General Longstreet was mistaken, and the statement that he was senior was erroneous. I was the senior." The records bear out Huger: he and Longstreet were nominated as Major Generals on the same day, Oct. 7, 1861, to rank from that date, and both were confirmed Dec. 13, 1861 (*Wright,* 22, 24). This equality of footing threw back the question to their standing in the "old army." Huger's commission as Major, U. S. A., dated from Feb. 15, 1855, Longstreet's from July 19, 1859.

[45] This is the hour given by Longstreet, *op. cit.,* 91. Johnston, as will be noted in a subsequent paragraph, seemed to think the hour was earlier.

[46] *G. W. Smith,* 167.

discussion, Johnston proceeded to revise his dispositions on the left. He could employ either Whiting or McLaws to take the place assigned Longstreet on the Nine Mile road. McLaws was at the moment in advance, but Johnston chose to march Whiting forward. By 11 o'clock, Johnston knew that D. H. Hill had cleared Longstreet's columns and was making ready to attack;[47] by 1 o'clock, Whiting's line was across the Nine Mile road near the turnout of the road to New Bridge,[48] and close to Johnston's headquarters.

Now came a long period of suspense. From the direction of Longstreet's proposed attack, not a sound was audible.[49] No report arrived of progress or repulse. Although Johnston was distant only a little more than two miles from the point of anticipated contact with the Federals, he was so poorly served by his staff that he knew as little of Longstreet's dispositions on the Williamsburg road as he did of what "Stonewall" Jackson that day was attempting in the Shenandoah Valley. Perplexed by this silence, though outwardly calm, Johnston confided to S. B. French that he wished all the troops were back in their camps.[50] To General Lee, who had ridden quietly out to headquarters, Johnston had little to say.

As heavy minutes dragged to 2 o'clock, the commander waited. Thousands of troops were at hand, restless in the road. They should not be employed on the left, Johnston reasoned, until more was known of Longstreet's movements. What could be delaying Longstreet? Had anything gone amiss on the right? Smith, as anxious as Johnston, offered to dispatch another staff officer to the Williamsburg road. This was acceptable to Johnston. Swiftly Maj. Jasper Whiting galloped off.[51] In his absence, three o'clock came and went. Ten hours of daylight had been consumed; less than half as many remained for the execution of a plan the basic strategy of which had been to surprise and to destroy the IV Corps before it could be reinforced. Was it possible that the Federals still remained without information of troop movements in their front? Had the advantage of surprise been lost? What *had* happened to Longstreet? Why did he not report?

---

[47] G. W. Smith, 170. [48] G. W. Smith, 171.
[49] O. R., 11, pt. 1, p. 934. [50] French, in G. W. Smith, 248–49.
[51] G. W. Smith, 167. The time of Jasper Whiting's departure is not known.

At last, from the South, rolled the echo of artillery fire. It was not loud or frequent, but it was unmistakable. Lee thought he heard, also, as a vague undertone, the sound of distant musketry. Johnston would not allow it. An artillery duel was in progress, he said; that was all.[52] The irregular, broken growl of field guns, the mysterious accompaniment of something subdued and sinister, now caught by keen ears, now dismissed as imaginary, continued until 4 o'clock was drawing near. Then sensations, startling and sudden, came to headquarters. The mutter swelled definitely and unmistakably into furious small-arms fire—volleys and the grim rattle of engaged columns. Major Jasper Whiting rode up; Longstreet, he said, was in the midst of heavy fighting and was gaining ground.

On the heels of Whiting's horse dashed a courier with a note from Longstreet. This reported progress in driving the enemy, but may have voiced disappointment that no help had come from the left.[53] As Johnston had been waiting to attack ever since the

[52] 2 *Davis*, 122. On the basis of Johnston's reference to this "artillery duel," coupled with ignorance of the ground, there later was built up in the mind of Mr. Davis and apparently in that of Judah Benjamin, a belief that Johnston had been taken by surprise and that the enemy had built across the Chickahominy a bridge of which the commanding General knew nothing. The incident is obscure, 8 *Rowland*, 355, 382, but it serves to show how ill informed, through its own fault or through Johnston's, the Administration was of the actual situation.

[53] The text of this note is not believed to be in existence. The summary given by G. W. Smith, *op. cit.*, 170, reads as follows: ". . . between four and five o'clock a note was received from General Longstreet, stating that he had attacked and beaten the enemy after several hours' severe fighting; that he had been disappointed in not receiving assistance upon his left; and, although it was now nearly too late, that an attack, by the Nine Mile road, upon the right flank and rear of the enemy would probably yet enable him to drive them into the Chickahominy before dark." Twenty-one years later, when Smith was writing critically of Seven Pines, Johnston evidently asked for Longstreet's recollection of the note. Longstreet's answer, dated Oct. 18, 1883, is among the *Johnston MSS.* and was courteously placed at the writer's disposal by the late R. M. Hughes, the distinguished biographer of General Johnston. The note, Longstreet said, was written at 3 P.M., May 31, which timing virtually identifies it as the one Smith summarized. The pertinent paragraph is as follows: "As nearly as I can now recall the note of the 31st, it reported our successful advance[,] the capture of Casey's camp and position, the failure of Huger to cooperate on our right, and stated that in going forward we encountered also a flanking fire from the enemy in front of G. W. [Smith] which was exceedingly annoying, particularly with fresh troops, who were always 'as sensitive about the flanks as a virgin.' I think I can speak positively of the expression in quotation because I often felt mortified afterward at using it in official correspondence." The point Smith sought to make apparent was that his troops were put in action as soon as Longstreet needed them and because Longstreet asked for them. Johnston, for his part, evidently felt, when Smith's report was filed June 23, 1862, that Smith's summary of Longstreet's message was a reflection upon himself, or upon Longstreet, or upon both of them. In asking Smith to withdraw the reference (see *infra*, p. 257) Johnston stated that the question was one between him and Longstreet, but he did not question the accuracy of what Smith said. He made no public use, in 1883 or thereafter, of Longstreet's different version of the note.

receipt of the first message from Beckham in the forenoon—he did not delay a moment. He showed the note to Smith, who was at headquarters, and he at once ordered the commander of the left wing to send Whiting down the Nine Mile road with Smith's own Division to engage the right of the troops that confronted Longstreet. McLaws might be held in reserve to meet the improbable contingency of a Federal advance across the Chickahominy, which Johnston still believed to be impassable.[54] Thereupon, almost before Whiting's men could fall in, Johnston mounted and rode across the fields toward the Federal position. As the commanding General hurried away, Jefferson Davis came up the lane to headquarters. Some of those who saw the quick departure of Johnston thought that he hastened off to avoid a meeting with the President.[55]

Within an hour, two of Whiting's (Smith's) Brigades were attacking in the tangled forest around Fair Oaks Station. Two other Brigades of the same Division arrived shortly and fell afoul of an enemy that seemed fresh and vigorous, as if he had just come into action. The Fifth Brigade, Hood's, was placed by Johnston on the right to be in liaison with Longstreet's left. It was to no purpose. Strong Federal artillery and confident infantry easily repulsed Whiting's attacks. When night closed the confused action, 1283 of Smith's men had been killed, wounded or captured. The Division, gaining little ground anywhere, was back on the line from which the attack had been launched.[56] It was suspected, and soon established, that Whiting had encountered troops sent across the Chickahominy from the north bank to reinforce those whom Longstreet had assailed.

Not until late in the night of May 31–June 1 were the details of Longstreet's battle on the right known at headquarters. A strange story there was to tell. After Beckham had reported that D. H. Hill's column had cleared the intersection and that Longstreet was preparing to attack, Longstreet kept his Division waiting by the side of the Williamsburg road until Huger completed the crossing of Gillies Creek and came up. Then he directed

---

[54] *Johnston's Narrative*, 136–37; G. W. *Smith*, 167.
[55] 2 *Davis*, 122; *Alexander*, 92.
[56] For Johnston's report, see *O. R.*, 11, pt. 1, pp. 934–35; for Smith's, see *ibid.*, 989 ff. See also G. W. *Smith*, 174 and 2 *B. & L.*, 244 ff.

Huger to pass him.[57] Longstreet's orders to Huger, as subsequently reported by that officer,[58] were to march down the Charles City road with his Division and three of Longstreet's Brigades, to move to a "designated point," [59] and there to halt and await further instructions. The Brigades of Longstreet's Division that were sent with Huger, under the immediate command of Cadmus M. Wilcox, were Colston's, Pryor's and Wilcox's own. Orders to Wilcox, given directly by Longstreet, were that he should endeavor to keep abreast of the firing when it began on the Williamsburg road.[60] Pickett's Brigade then was detached by Longstreet from his own Division, and was instructed to march North to the near-by York River Railroad, to cover it, to repel any attack, and to hold itself ready to support the Confederate advance should occasion require.[61]

Having sent off four of his Brigades, Longstreet ordered the remaining two, Kemper's [62] and R. H. Anderson's, to move down the Williamsburg road and to be ready to join D. H. Hill's four in the main assault. That is to say, with thirteen Brigades at his disposal, Longstreet intended to open with only five of these the attack on the entrenched position of the enemy.

[57] Colston in 2 B. & L., 229. Colston was the only Confederate officer who made this direct statement, but he is confirmed, as respects at least two of Huger's three Brigades, by General Wilcox, who wrote that when he went down the Charles City road at 3.30 P.M., he was under orders to *follow* Blanchard's and Armistead's Brigades of Huger's Division. Manifestly, as Wilcox belonged to Longstreet's Division, Huger already had passed. See O. R., 11, pt. 1, p. 986. It seems virtually certain that Huger came South from Blakey's Mill past the Williams House and struck the Williamsburg road about one third of a mile East of the tollgate which stood almost opposite the entrance to the present National Cemetery.

[58] *Richmond Examiner*, Aug. 25, 1862, p. 1, col. 3.

[59] The records do not show where this was.

[60] This is the testimony of Huger and of Wilcox. General Longstreet wrote two conflicting statements on the subject. In his report, O. R., 11, pt. 1, p. 840, either misquoting or misunderstanding Huger's orders fom Johnston, Longstreet said: "The division of Major General Huger was intended to make a strong flank movement around the left of the enemy's position and attack him in rear of that flank. This division did not get into position, however, in time for any such attack, and I was obliged to send three of my small brigades on the Charles City road to support the one of Major General Huger's which had been ordered to protect my right flank." Wilcox, it will be observed from note 57, *supra*, stated that two—not one—of Huger's Brigades had preceded him. In *Longstreet*, 92, the author of that memoir explained that when he met Huger, he proposed that two of Huger's Brigades move across to extend the right of the column of attack, while Huger remained with the other Brigade, which was to relieve Rodes on the Charles City road. Longstreet then stated: "Though [Huger] expressed himself satisfied with this, his manner was eloquent of discontent. The better to harmonize, I proposed to reinforce his column by three of my own Brigades, to be sent under General Wilcox, to lead or follow his Division as he might order. Under this arrangement it seemed that concert of action was assured "

[61] O. R., 11, pt. 1, p. 982.   [62] Formerly A. P. Hill's.

The attack, indeed, already had opened. D. H. Hill, impatient and ardent, had sent an early message of unknown content to Rodes, on the Charles City road. By some error, the message was delivered as an order for Rodes to move at once to the Williams-burg road. Fortunately, the commander went ahead of his troops, reported to Hill, found that a mistake had occurred, and hurried back in time to save his men a premature march. A second order to Rodes for the movement of the Brigade across to the Williams-burg road was received and was put in execution promptly. The best effort of Rodes's men was not enough to satisfy Hill. While the Alabamians struggled through mud and water waist deep, messengers continued to arrive from Hill. Rodes sent word that he inevitably would be delayed, but this did not restrain Hill.[63] About 1 p.m., Hill ordered the signal gun fired for the opening of the attack.[64] The advance was begun while Rodes, who was to lead the assault on the right of the Williamsburg road, still was fifteen minutes' march behind the troops on the left of the high-way, Garland's [65] Brigade with Featherston's [66] in support.[67] On initial contact, these two Brigades received the full fire of the enemy, but Rodes soon caught up. In a short time his support, Rains's Brigade, cleverly flanked the main Federal earthwork, known as Casey's Redoubt, South of the Williamsburg road. Soon, by furious onrush, now here, now there, the Federal front line was swept back. Eight guns and all the equipment and supplies of a brigade camp were captured.

To the right of the road [68] at a distance of about 150 yards in rear of Casey's Redoubt, the enemy rallied in the woods behind a strong abatis.[69] From this position, Rodes determined to drive them. Around his martial figure—six feet tall, clear-eyed, thin, with a drooping tawny mustache—his men dressed their line for a second charge. Ere they could deliver it, a Federal column ap-peared at an angle across the road, as if to assail Rodes's left. The young General saw the danger at once and called on a company that had seen service as heavy artillery to man the guns in the captured redoubt and to beat off this attack.

[63] O. R., 11, pt. 1, p. 971.   [64] O. R., 11, pt. 1, p. 943.
[65] Formerly Early's.   [66] Under Col. G. B. Anderson.
[67] O. R., 11, pt. 1, p. 943.
[68] From the Confederate side.   [69] O. R., 11, pt. 1, p. 973.

While the willing Virginians were turning the pieces, up dashed Capt. Thomas H. Carter's King William Artillery at the gallop, unlimbered and opened fire at the very nick: It was done magnificently, with the precision of the manual and the dash of a field review. Under Carter's rapid and accurate fire, the Federals on the flank soon broke and retired. As if that were not enough, Carter dashed out into an open field and, at 400 yards, fought a duel with a Federal battery which occupied another redoubt. Hill saw all of this, thrilled with the joy of battle, and to the end of his days averred that war never had witnessed anything finer. Always Carter remained his ideal artillerist.

Rodes's left was safe. His center then plunged recklessly forward. The General knew that his right was exposed, but his expectation was that Rains would repeat the previous manœuvre and would turn the Federal left. For that reason, Rodes did not hesitate. His wild-eyed, panting men reached the open space in front of the woods. The Federals opened furiously. No pause, scarcely a wincing was there as the first volley was received. On went the writhing, uneven, but persistent line. Gaps were cut in it. Wounded men fell in water above their knees. Some drowned before they could be succored.

Soon it was apparent that General Rains was not advancing. Rodes had to shift his line and to refuse his right. Some of his troops broke. Others halted and, as soon as they did, began to lose ground. Two dauntless regiments and part of the Virginia battalion pushed into the farther woods and held firmly. They had few surviving officers. One after another of the Colonels had gone down while they had rallied the men or had urged them forward. In the heaviest of the fighting, the commander of the Sixth Alabama, John B. Gordon, saw his Lieutenant Colonel and his Major fall and his flank company torn to a bloody fragment. At length Kemper's Brigade [70] came up in support. Together, Kemper and Rodes untangled the line. In the midst of this valiant labor, Rodes received an ugly wound in the arm, but he kept the field until sunset. Then he turned over command to Colonel Gordon, who, under orders from D. H. Hill, drew his men out of the wood. Hill subsequently reported that Kemper's Brigade "did not engage

[70] Kemper, it will be remembered, was a veteran of the Mexican War.

the Yankees," and that "Rodes's men were badly cut up," but the Federals soon left the woods.[71]

On the other side of the Williamsburg road, Garland and G. B. Anderson[72] had, if possible, even worse conditions to face. Garland's men, in advance, started through a wood in which they found pools of water three or more feet deep, with bottoms so heavy that men often were mired.[73] The North Carolinians and the Virginians pushed furiously ahead with the dash they had displayed on the flank of Fort Magruder. Soon they reached the eastern edge of the wood—to find the enemy in strength behind an abatis and fence. The halt in sight of this obstacle brought G. B. Anderson's Brigade on the heels of Garland's. Regiments were confused. Lines overlapped. Officers fell and organization was lost, but by the volume of their fire, the Confederates steadily weakened the resistance of the enemy.[74]

Then, with a crash, R. H. Anderson's Brigade came forward and took the lead. Anderson displayed all the coolness that had marked his conduct on the right at Williamsburg. He divided his Brigade and, while he conducted one column, he entrusted the other to Col. Micah Jenkins of the Palmetto Sharpshooters, the officer who on May 5 had been in immediate command of Fort Magruder. The South Carolinians attacked like demons possessed and, though their lines overlapped, as those of Garland had, they swept through the abatis, passed a Federal camp, stormed two gun positions, and pursued with fury. At nightfall, they held probably the most advanced position on the entire field.[75] The other Brigades of Longstreet's Division, Wilcox's, Pryor's and Colston's, touched only the fringes of the battle or else did not arrive at the scene of action until after dark.[76] Pickett, by Longstreet's orders, continued his watch on the railroad to the left.

This, in incomplete outline, was the story that reached headquarters during the night of May 31–June 1. The next morning

---

[71] O. R., 11, pt. 1, pp. 970 ff. As Kemper filed no report, it is impossible to say what he did, or why he failed to do more than D. H. Hill credited to him. The probability is that he did not have his line drawn, in the confusion of the field, until night had fallen. Nothing happened to discredit Kemper. On the contrary, he was promoted immediately to command the troops he had led as senior Colonel.
[72] Commanding Featherston's Brigade.
[73] O. R., 11, pt. 1, p. 961.
[74] Ibid.   [75] O. R., 11, pt. 1, pp. 947 ff.
[76] Compare D. H. Hill's comment, O. R., 11, pt. 1, p. 944, with Wilcox's, ibid., 986–87.

an opportunity seemed to be offered on the Confederate right to drive the enemy farther, but because of vacillation, overcaution and conflicting orders on the part of G. W. Smith, the only results were more casualties, confusion, recrimination, and a gallant, futile fight in which Brig. Gen. George E. Pickett increased the reputation he had gained at Williamsburg.[77] That night the Confederate Army, unpursued, fell back to the position from which it had launched the attack.

[77] O. R., 11, pt. 1, pp. 945, 983, 987, 992–93; G. W. Smith, 204 ff.

CHAPTER XVIII

GRIM FRUITS OF ANNIVERSARY

WHAT, then, had been achieved by the attack at Seven Pines? The Confederate left had made little progress. Five Brigades on the right, despite confusion and difficult ground, had driven one Federal Brigade in rout [1] and had shaken Casey's Division but had not overwhelmed it, as had been hoped, before the arrival of reinforcements opposite Fair Oaks. In exchange for the temporary occupation of a square mile or so of woodland, two abandoned lines, ten guns, some 6000 small arms,[2] a handful of prisoners [3] and miscellaneous loot, Confederate losses had been excessive. The fine Brigade of Rodes had been shattered. He went into action with about 2000 men. Of these, 1094 were killed or wounded. Gordon's Sixth Alabama sacrificed 60 per cent of its effective strength. The right company of this regiment had forty-four casualties among its fifty-five officers and men.[4] Garland's Brigade lost 740.[5] R. H. Anderson's losses were not separately reported, but doubtless were as high as G. B. Anderson's 866.[6] For the entire army, the butcher's bill was 6134.[7]

Among the fallen was Brig. Gen. Robert Hatton, of Whiting's Division.[8] Johnston Pettigrew, a magnificent man who commanded another of Smith's Brigades, had been shot down far to the front. Because he believed his wourd mortal, he had refused to permit his men to leave the ranks and to carry him to the rear.

---

[1] O. R., 11, pt. 1, pp. 815–16, 838.
[2] Longstreet put them at 5000, O. R., 11, pt. 1, p. 941; Johnston reported them at 6000, ibid., 935; D. H. Hill, ibid., 945, gave the number as 6700.
[3] Three hundred forty-seven, according to Longstreet, ibid., 941.
[4] O. R., 11, pt. 1, p. 976.
[5] O. R., 11, pt. 1, p. 967.
[6] O. R., 11, pt. 1, p. 953.
[7] Alexander summarized these neatly, op. cit., 89. Federal losses, May 31–June 1, were 5031.
[8] O. R., 11, pt. 1, p. 91. Three days before his death, General Hatton wrote his wife: ". . . May the God of right and justice smile upon us in the hour of conflict! The struggle will no doubt be bloody. That we shall triumph, I am confident. Would that I might bind to my heart before the battle my wife and children! That pleasure may never again be granted me. If so, farewell; and may the God of all mercy be to you and ours a Guardian and Friend!" 7 C. V., 554.

Whether he lived or had died, none knew [9] until June 4, when he sent through the lines a letter to Whiting. "As I was in a state of insensibility," Pettigrew wrote, "I was picked up by the first party which came along, which proved to be the enemy." He went on: "I hope you know, General, that I never would have surrendered, under any circumstances, to save my own life, or anybody else's, and if Generals Smith or Johnston are under a different impression, I hope you will make a statement of the facts in the case." [10] Pettigrew's fellow brigade commander, Wade Hampton, also was wounded but kept the field and insisted that the bullet be extracted from his foot while he sat on his horse under fire.[11] Besides this toll on the right and the wounding of Rodes, three Colonels lost their lives—John R. R. Giles of the Fifth South Carolina, Tennent Lomax of the Third Alabama, and R. T. Jones of the Twelfth Alabama,[12] "one of the very best officers and purest men in the army," who had left his sick bed to lead his troops.[13]

Despite losses and failure to achieve any substantial result, Confederate victory was proclaimed in every key. The public was assured and apparently was persuaded that McClellan had been defeated with immense slaughter.[14] Exultant praise was given, first of all, to the men in the ranks. It was deserved. They were the real heroes of the battle. Most of D. H. Hill's troops had never been in action until May 31,[15] but where they were well led they acquitted themselves as admirably as did the regiments that had fought at Williamsburg and at Manassas.[16] Those of Longstreet's men who got into action sustained their reputation. No fault could be found with Whiting's Division. It had not beaten the enemy but it had not failed to try.

[9] O. R., 11, pt. 1, pp. 991–92.
[10] Pettigrew added: "I am extremely anxious to be exchanged into service again; I am not fit for field service, and will not be for some time, but I can be of service in any stationary position with heavy artillery." 26 S. H. S. P., 144.
[11] O. R., 11, pt. 1, p. 991. For the efforts of admiring women to lionize Hampton during his convalescence, see Mrs. Chesnut, pp. 181–82, 190, 193. She quoted this snatch of conversation: "How did General Hampton bear his honors?" "Well, to the last he looked as if he wished they would let him alone." Ibid., 193. See infra, p. 588.
[12] O. R., 11, pt. 1, p. 941.
[13] O. R., 11, pt. 1, p. 946. The quotation is from D. H. Hill.
[14] 1 R. W. C. D., 130–32. [15] O. R., 11, pt. 1, pp. 946, 960, 968.
[16] The Richmond newspapers of May 31, et seq., and those of Charleston contain tributes to the gallantry of the troops. In Richmond papers of this period, also, is much information on the mental state of a city after its first near-by battle. At no subsequent time did the press give so much space to reports of the wounded, the stragglers and the souvenir hunters.

A little later, when the reports were published, praise literally was poured on most of the high-ranking officers. General Johnston mentioned Longstreet first. "The skill, vigor and decision," said he, "with which these operations were conducted by General Longstreet are worthy of the highest praise." In the next sentence he commended Harvey Hill, "of whose conduct and courage [Longstreet] speaks in the highest terms." [17] Concerning the commander on the left, Johnston wrote, "The skill, energy and resolution with which Major General Smith directed his attack would have secured success if it could have been made an hour earlier." [18]

Longstreet, in his turn, said of D. H. Hill: "The conduct of the attack was left entirely to Major General Hill. The entire success of the affair is sufficient evidence of his ability, courage and skill." All the Brigadier Generals of his Division, together with the Colonels commanding Brigades, Longstreet wrote down as "distinguished for their usual gallantry and ability." [19]

Hill had high words for his Brigadiers, with the exception of General Rains. That officer was applauded for his first flank operation against Casey's Redoubt, but when Hill came to speak of the subsequent advance on the right to drive the Federals from the woods, he wrote of Rains, "I regret that that gallant and meritorious officer did not advance farther in that direction." [20] In sketching the operations of June 1, Hill reported that Armistead's Brigade of Huger's Division "fled early in the action, with the exception of a few heroic companies, with which that gallant officer [Armistead] maintained his ground against an entire Brigade." Mahone, said Hill bluntly, "withdrew his Brigade without any order." Colston was sent to replace him, "but he did not engage the Yankees, as I expected him to do." [21]

General Smith devoted his eulogies to Hampton, Hatton and Pettigrew and refrained from detailed praise of Whiting and of Hood because, as he said, they acted more immediately under Johnston. He added: "they were both equal on that occasion to their former well-earned high reputation for skill and gallantry." [22] The conduct neither of Hood nor of Whiting was

17 O. R., 11, pt. 1, p. 934. 18 Ibid., 935.
19 O. R., 11, pt. 1, p. 941. 20 O. R., 11, pt. 1, p. 944.
21 O. R., 11, pt. 1, p. 945. 22 O. R., 11, pt. 1, p. 993.

described *in extenso* by Johnston, but nothing in his report indicated that Hood made less than the utmost of the small opportunity given him. As for Whiting, it was common knowledge that, when Johnston proposed to push Whiting's Brigade across the York River Railroad, on the afternoon of May 31, Whiting expostulated that the Federals were in force in flank and rear. Johnston cried out impatiently, "Oh, General Whiting, you are too cautious!" Almost immediately the enemy opened with artillery from the direction Whiting had indicated.[23] Johnston, who was devoted to Whiting, probably remembered this. When the commanding General filed his report he made the *amende honorable* by renewing his familiar recommendation that Whiting be promoted.[24]

Some among those "mentioned in dispatches" did not deserve what was said of them; but when the account was balanced, the assets of army leadership, in terms of fulfillment or of promise, had been increased by the performance of seven men:

(1) D. H. Hill, though displaying the same impatience and precipitancy that had caused him to rush forward at Williamsburg, had conducted the operation in other particulars with cold calculation, vigor, and with sensitive feel of action. Nothing that was said of him was above the merit of his performance. He acted as if the command of a Division was an art he had mastered so long previously that he negligently could have disdained half he knew and still could have won.

(2) R. E. Rodes appeared as distinguished, when the battle was reviewed, as while it was being fought. He emerged with reputation as a hard-hitting Brigadier whom losses or difficult ground could not deter. A native of Lynchburg, Virginia, he had been graduated at the Virginia Military Institute in 1848. Thereafter he had served as civil engineer for various railroads, had married in Tuscaloosa, Alabama, and, just before the outbreak of the war had accepted the professorship of Applied Mathematics at his Alma Mater. He had left V. M. I. almost at once to organize a company in Alabama and soon had received in that State commission as Colonel of the Fifth Regiment. With this command he had come promptly to Virginia. At Blackburn's

---

[23] 2 *B. & L.*, 245.　　　　　　[24] *O. R.*, 11, pt. 1, p. 935.

Ford, which he regarded as no more than a skirmish,[25] he had won commendation.[26] On October 21, 1861,[27] he had been promoted Brigadier General and, after various shifts of commands,[28] had been assigned the Fifth, Sixth and Twelfth Alabama and the Twelfth Mississippi.[29] His standing in his profession had been so well recognized that he had been suggested to Johnston as one of the Army's two officers qualified to supervise the evacuation of Manassas,[30] but he had been retained with troops. Until that day at Seven Pines he never had opportunity of leading them into action. Once on the field, he had shone. "Coolness, ability and determination," the qualities that Longstreet praised, most justly characterized him. He was now 33. Given time, he would rise.[31]

(3) Samuel Garland had justified his promotion to the command of Early's Brigade. Like Rodes, he was a native of Lynchburg, Virginia, and a graduate of V. M. I.[32] His father was a lawyer of distinction, his great-grandmother a sister of President Madison. At the University of Virginia he had studied his father's profession and had practiced it in Lynchburg until the war, but not to the exclusion of other interests. He was one of the most studious and well-read men of his city, with a deep interest in the new Victorian literature and in the stage. From a captaincy in the Eleventh Virginia, he had been promoted speedily to the rank of Colonel and, at Williamsburg, it will be recalled, had been distinguished in A. P. Hill's Brigade and had been wounded. Now that he had fought his first battle as a brigade commander, he had shown the unmistakable qualities of the soldier. His leading had been excellent, his example all that could be asked. In the thickest of the struggle, his mount was so badly wounded that it had to be abandoned. Garland then took an artillery horse, which was twice struck. After R. H. Anderson assumed the lead on the left, Garland reported to D. H. Hill, with his aide and his adjutant, to assist the staff. The adjutant was killed and the

25 O. R., 2, 459.   26 Ibid., 446.
27 Wright, 63.   28 O. R., 5, 913, 936, 960.
29 Ibid., 1029.
30 O. R., 5, 1082. W. H. C. Whiting was the other.
31 For much material on General Rodes, the writer is indebted to Mrs. Pelham D. Brown of Tuscaloosa, Ala. The sketch of him in Charles D. Walker, Memorial, Virginia Military Institute, pp. 440 ff, is not adequate but is accurate. For the next detailed reference to Rodes, see infra, p. 532. He appears often in Vol. II.
32 Born Dec. 16, 1830.

aide wounded, but Garland, though much exposed, escaped unhurt.[33] Perhaps there was deliberate recklessness in his conspicuous disregard of fire: he was the last of his direct line. His wife and his only son had died since the war had begun.[34]

(4) Richard H. Anderson had confirmed all that had been said of him in his battle on the right at Williamsburg. Through abatis and forest, dripping and miry at Seven Pines, he had led part of his own command forward and had directed the operations of two other Brigades.[35] No performance on the field had been more difficult or more admirably executed. D. H. Hill and Longstreet praised him;[36] Johnston suggested [37] his promotion.

(5) Col. Micah Jenkins of the Palmetto Sharpshooters, a youngster of 26 years, had received command of one column when R. H. Anderson had divided the Brigade. In leading successively two regiments, then three and, for a time, four, his conduct had been above all praise. Often his men had fought at 100 yards and sometimes at a third of that distance. One of his companies, forty-seven strong, had bagged 139 armed prisoners,[38] or more than a third of all those taken South of the York River Railroad. Hill estimated that Jenkins had gone more than a mile beyond the main Federal works at Seven Pines.[39] Longstreet, perhaps with some partiality for his own Division, gave R. H. Anderson, Jenkins and James L. Kemper the credit for the decisive attack.[40] Johnston mentioned Jenkins with a hint that he deserved the promotion [41] which Longstreet six months before had urged for him.[42] The camps rang with praise, which was welcome to the young soldier. Jenkins had prepared himself for that day and for the honors that awaited him. Born of high blood on Edisto Island, South Carolina, in 1835, he had been graduated at the head of his class at the South Carolina Military College. While still under 25, he had organized his own military school. His regiment, which was one of the best, as well as one of the first to volunteer in South Carolina,[43] had aroused much admiration when, June

[33] O. R., 11, pt. 1, pp. 945–46; 963; 3 C. M. H., 595 ff; Memorial, Virginia Military Institute, 227 ff.
[34] Memorial, Virginia Military Institute, 231. Garland appears again, infra, p. 533.
[35] O. R., 11, pt. 1, p. 947.   [36] O. R., 11, pt. 1, pp. 940, 944.
[37] Ibid., 935. For the next reference to Anderson, see infra, pp. 652, 673.
[38] O. R., 11, pt. 1, p. 950.   [39] O. R., 11, pt. 1, p. 944.
[40] O R., 11, pt. 1, p. 940.   [41] Ibid., 935.
[42] O. R., 5, 1001.   [43] O. R., 51, pt. 2, p. 17.

8, 1861, it had arrived in Virginia.[44] During the operations of First Manassas and through the winter of 1861–62, Micah Jenkins had given every promise of the qualities he displayed at Williamsburg and at Seven Pines.[45] "The South Carolinians deserve praise," remarked an unknown observer after the battle, "and I am glad that Jenkins displayed himself to advantage. . . . He acted as Brigadier, and I do not see why the Secretary of War does not make him a General. He is highly educated in military matters, and far surpasses many of those political Generals who are incessantly blundering." [46]

(6) Brigadier General George E. Pickett, with his Virginia Brigade,[47] merited all that Harvey Hill said of his bearing. During the action of June 1, when Pickett detected Federal preparations for a heavy attack on his front, he quickly concluded that Smith would not use the troops on the left to stop the attack, and he rode rapidly to D. H. Hill to state his situation. Hill, who shared his feeling that the entire strength of the army would not be brought into action, asked Pickett if he could not retire. Pickett answered that he could, but that he did not desire to do so and that, if he did, he would have to leave his wounded behind him. Besides, he argued tersely, the enemy might then pour in upon the scattered and disorganized troops. Hill thereupon reinforced Pickett, who beat off the attack with some help from Mahone's Brigade, which Hill put back into line after it had withdrawn.[48] It was a staunch performance. "Pickett," said Hill in his report, "held his ground against the odds of ten to one for several hours longer and only retired when the Yankees had ceased to annoy him." [49] Here, evidently, was a stubborn fighter with a mind of his own. When he filed his account of the battle he did not hesitate to complain of the failure of Smith's troops to support him.[50]

(7) Col. John B. Gordon of the Sixth Alabama, Rodes's Brigade, had attracted attention for the first time by his daring leadership. He was a Georgian of 30, trained for the bar but engaged on the

---

[44] *Richmond Examiner*, May 28, p. 1, col. 6; May 29 (quoting *Columbia Guardian*), p. 3, col. 3; June 8, p. 3, col. 2; June 13, 1861, p. 1, col. 5. For his movement to Manassas, see *O. R.*, 51, pt. 2, p. 141.

[45] *O. R.*, 2, 538–39, 541, 944; *Richmond Dispatch*, July 5, 1861, p. 1, col. 4; *Richmond Examiner*, Sept. 6, 1861, p. 2, col. 6.

[46] *An English Combatant*, 254.

[47] Eighth, Eighteenth, Nineteenth and Twenty-eighth.

[48] *O. R.*, 11, pt. 1, pp. 945, 983.

[49] *Ibid.*, 945.   [50] *Ibid.*, 983.

outbreak of hostilities in the development of coal mines.[51] His whole inclination then had been to enlist at once. Only the care of his wife and two young children had troubled him. Mrs. Gordon had settled this by arranging to leave the children with Gordon's mother. She herself announced that she would go to the front with her husband, wherever he was sent. The admiring mountaineers of the coal district promptly chose Gordon their Captain, from which rank, though he had no previous military education, he rose quickly to be Colonel.

Although the combination was not demonstrated until that day in the woods East of Richmond, Gordon had the natural instincts of a soldier and the persuasive power of an orator who knew his auditors perfectly. By the honest exercise of these qualities, he had inculcated a superior and intelligent discipline. Before the battle of Seven Pines opened, he addressed his men and, as he stated in his report, "reminded them of the proclamation of the infamous Butler [52] and of the fate which awaited us if defeated." [53] The regiment then went swiftly forward as brigade skirmishers, and a little later formed the right element in the charge on the enemy's front line. Before their Colonel recalled them, the Alabamians pushed straight on into the Federal camp. When Gordon had them retrace their bloody steps, he marched them, of course, with their faces to the rear, where he obediently left them under cover.

After a breathing spell, Rodes's message was received for an attack on the second line. Gordon called, "Forward, march." His men, who had not been ordered about, at once rose and started to the rear again. The Colonel saw his blunder instantly. "I galloped about equidistant between my line and that of the enemy," Gordon reported, "and called to my men by word and gesture to move on the enemy." He continued: "Promptly facing about, and explaining from one end of the line to the other that the order was misunderstood, they moved at double-quick with such impetuosity that the enemy fled from his hiding-places before us." [54] As Gordon rode with them, all his field officers and his Adjutant were shot down. On the ground he saw his own brother lying half-dead but he could not stop to succor the young man. Bullets

[51] He was born in Upson County, Feb. 6, 1832.
[52] In New Orleans.   [53] O. R., 11, pt. 1, p. 979.
[54] O. R., 11, pt. 1, pp. 979–80.

pierced the Colonel's coat. His horse was killed. At the end of the action he was untouched, unshaken, and in charge of what was left of Rodes's Brigade. Because of his inexperience and his age, he hesitated to retain command of the Brigade during Rodes's convalescence, but his brother officers, sensing this, "did everything in their power," if Gordon's own words may be quoted, "to lessen my embarrassment and uphold my hands." [55]

To these seven most distinguished at Seven Pines—D. H. Hill, R. E. Rodes, Samuel Garland, R. H. Anderson, Micah Jenkins, George E. Pickett and John B. Gordon—three Captains of artillery might have been added. They were Thomas H. Carter,[56] J. W. Bondurant,[57] and James Dearing,[58] who had given the infantry such support as it had received in the tangle of forest-felled trees and water-covered fields.

The conduct of these officers, the indisputable valor of the troops and all the rejoicing of the public did not alter the stubborn fact that Johnston's plan had not been executed, and that the casualties were almost 50 per cent larger than publicly they were admitted to be.[59] President Davis had not been deceived. Before he left the field on the evening of May 31 he had asked whether it would not be possible to keep the troops in their positions, so that, if the enemy withdrew during the night, a victory might be asserted.[60] Others in high position knew that plans had miscarried and they proceeded immediately to place the blame.

In fairness, that blame scarcely could be put on Johnston. Failure to use Magruder, though remarkable and possibly open to

[55] John B. Gordon, *Reminiscences of the Civil War*, 3, 56, 58. Mrs. Gordon, whose remarkable war experiences should be retraced by some sympathetic writer, went out on the day of the Battle of Seven Pines to one of the hills near Richmond and there listened silently to the sounds of battle. An elderly uncle, her escort, wrote of her: "Pale and quiet, with clasped hands, she sat statuelike, with her face toward the field of battle. Her self-control was wonderful; only the quick-drawn sigh from the bottom of her heart revealed the depth of emotion that was struggling there. The news of her husband's safety afterward and the joy of meeting him later produced the inevitable reaction. The intensity of mental strain to which she had been subjected had overtaxed her strength, and when the excessive tension was relaxed, she was well-nigh prostrated; but a brief repose enabled her to bear up with a sublime fortitude through the protracted and trying experiences which followed the Seven Days' battle around Richmond." *Ibid.*, 59. For the next item in the sketch of Gordon, see *infra*, p. 533.
[56] *O. R.*, 11, pt. 1, pp. 941, 943, 971–73, 975, 976.
[57] *Ibid.*, 943, 966.
[58] *Ibid.*, 941, 973.
[59] Cf. *supra*, pp. 244 ff. Johnston in his report, dated June 24, 1862, *O. R.*, 11, pt. 1, p. 935, set them at 4283. In Richmond, June 2, the statement was that losses did not exceed 5000 (1 *R. W. C. D.*, 132). Actually, as noted *supra*, p. 244, they were 6134.
[60] *G. W. Smith*, 182.

criticism, might have been due as much to Johnston's regard for economy of force as to any feeling that Magruder would not co-operate. Johnston's orders had been drawn carelessly and had not been circulated promptly, but his general plan had been sound and his assumptions valid, except that the Federals had been able to send reinforcements from the north bank of the Chickahominy when he had hoped that high water would prevent. This error would not have deprived him of the advantage of surprise had the Confederate attack been delivered as early as Johnston's conservative logistics had led him to anticipate. The delay of two Divisions at Gillies Creek and the wait on the Williamsburg road had not been Johnston's fault, unless he were responsible for Longstreet's march. Even with that delay, he still might have won a victory had he been informed when Longstreet went into action. Good staff work and prompt reports would have offset failure to hear the sound of battle. Lacking notice from Longstreet, the "acoustic shadow" which disguised the rattle of Hill's muskets was the chief reason for the late launching of the attack by the Confederate left. It would be unjust to hold Johnston responsible for this phenomenon.

If Johnston was not to blame for failure, who was? As early as the evening of June 1, when the Confederate troops were moving back to their former position, it was alleged on the streets of Richmond that "the failure of General Huger to lead his division into action at the time appointed [was] the only reason . . . the left wing of the enemy was not completely destroyed." [61] By his report of June 10, General Longstreet, who continued to regard General Huger as his subordinate,[62] confirmed rumor. Longstreet

[61] 1 R. W. C. D., 132. It is possible, though from the internal evidence scarcely probable, that this entry was one of the interpolations that Jones, to the confusion of historical writers, made at a later time.

[62] By the evening of June 1, Longstreet had detached all Huger's troops from that divisional command and had put them under D. H. Hill. That fact Huger reported to Johnston on the 2d. ". . . finding myself on the field last evening without any command at all," he wrote, "I, with the permission of General Longstreet, returned to these headquarters." Huger stated the facts concerning the detachment of his troops and added: "I ask that all may be returned to my command. I hope the position I am placed in is merely an accidental one, and will be changed as soon as it can be done. I must demand the command and position my rank entitles me to. On no other condition will I hold it." That day, Longstreet sent for Huger to report to him. When Huger was not found at his quarters, Longstreet ordered "Jeb" Stuart to take command of the Division. In answer to Johnston, who asked for the facts after Huger complained of this supersession, Longstreet said tersely on the 3d: "He [Huger] has joined his Division this morning and taken command." O. R., 11, pt. 1, p. 570.

wrote: "I have reason to believe that the affair would have been a complete success had the troops upon the right been put in position within eight hours of the proper time. The want of promptness on that part of the field and the consequent severe struggle in my front so greatly reduced my supply of ammunition that at the late hour of the move on the left I was unable to make the rush necessary to relieve the attack." [63] General Johnston, reporting June 24, merely rephrased Longstreet's accusation: "Had General Huger's Division been in position and ready for action when those of Smith, Longstreet and Hill moved, I am satisfied that Keyes' corps would have been destroyed instead of being merely defeated. Had it gone into action even at 4 o'clock the victory would have been much more complete." [64]

Huger, in answer, admitted that time was consumed in crossing Gillies Creek, but he exposed the unreason of the charge that he was eight hours late. Such an allegation, he intimated, assumed that 8 A.M. was the time at which the battle was to be opened; but actually Longstreet himself, Huger pointed out, was not in position to commence operations at that hour.[65] The other criticisms in the reports Huger disputed, and subsequently he made efforts to have a court-martial or a court of inquiry investigate the circumstances, but in this he did not succeed.[66] When Johnston was asked to bring Huger to trial, he answered candidly, if coldly: "I have no desire to prefer charges against Major General Huger. The passage in my report of which he complains was written to show that the delay in commencing the action of May 31 was not my fault." [67]

Again, then, the question, whose *was* the fault? Huger's record has been as follows:

1. In his orders from Johnston on May 30, Huger had been told: "Be ready, if an action should be begun on your left, to fall upon the enemy's left flank"; [68] but in orders of the day of battle, as already noted,[69] he was told by Johnston: "I fear that in my note of last evening, of which there is no copy, I was too positive

[63] O. R., 11, pt. 1, p. 940. No reference to this shortage of ammunition appears in any other of the comparatively few reports on Seven Pines.
[64] O. R., 11, pt. 1, p. 935. [65] O. R., 11, pt. 1, p. 937.
[66] O. R., 11, pt. 1, pp. 935, 936, 937, 939.
[67] O. R., 11, pt. 1, p. 939. [68] O. R., 11, pt. 1, p. 938.
[69] See *supra*, p. 228.

on the subject of your attacking the enemy's left flank. It will, of course, be necessary for you to know what force is before you first. ... As our main force will be on your left, it will be necessary for your progress to the front to conform at first to that of General Hill. If you find no strong body in your front, it will be well to aid General Hill; but then a strong reserve should be retained to cover our right." [70] These were orders for a cautious action. Aid of Hill was not made mandatory.

2. Huger received no information concerning the general plan of action prior to the time he started from his bivouac, and he had no notice that Longstreet was in general command on the right.[71]

3. At 3 A.M., May 31, Huger notified D. H. Hill that he would start a Brigade for the Charles City road "as soon as possible," that he would inform Hill when this Brigade was in motion and that the commander of this Brigade would report to Rodes, whom he was to relieve. Huger added: "I fear delay may occur owing to the state of the roads." [72]

4. When Huger's troops reached Gillies Creek early on the morning of May 31,[73] they found Longstreet's Division there. Although Huger's leading Brigade had to reach Rodes on the Charles City road promptly, in order that Rodes might march over to the Williamsburg road in time for an early start of the attack, the relief Brigade was not allowed priority over Longstreet in crossing the creek. It is not known whether this was done in Longstreet's presence or Huger's, or with the immediate knowledge of either.

5. Huger's Division waited for Longstreet to cross. Then Huger moved, according to orders, to the mouth of the Charles City road. There Longstreet, who asserted seniority,[74] instructed Huger to march past Longstreet's Division and to go down the Charles City road.

6. As to objective, Huger stated: "[Longstreet] directed me to proceed down the Charles City road to a designated position, and

[70] *O. R.*, 11, pt. 1, p. 939.
[71] *Cf.* Huger, referring to his instructions: "No mention is made in them that General Longstreet had the direction of operations upon the right, and it will be seen from these letters that the plan of attack was not communicated to [me]." *O. R.*, 11, pt. 1. p. 937.
[72] *O. R.*, 11, pt. 3, p. 563.
[73] The hour is nowhere stated.
[74] See *supra*, p. 235, n. 44.

three Brigades of his division (Wilcox's, Colston's and Pryor's) with the three of my division, and there await his orders." [75]

7. The time of the arrival of Huger's column at the "designated position" on the Charles City road is stated by him to have been "before 4 o'clock." [76]

8. "Soon after getting into position," Huger wrote, "General Longstreet sent for the three Brigades of his Division, and a short time afterwards sent for General Armistead's brigade of my division. These troops were engaged on Saturday afternoon [May 31]. If these troops could be engaged, the rest of my Division could have been engaged also had I received orders." [77] In official protest, Huger said: ". . . if I did not go into action by 4 o'clock [78] it was because General Longstreet did not require it, as [my Division] was in position and awaiting his orders." [79]

What, in contrast, was Longstreet's record that day?

1. Whether the fault was his or his commander's, there was a misunderstanding of orders concerning his line of march. The plan undoubtedly was for Longstreet to advance down the Nine Mile road, but this was not stated in the official reports of Johnston or of Longstreet. When Smith filed his report on June 23 he gav'

[75] Huger in *Richmond Examiner*, Aug. 25, 1862, p. 1, col. 3. This defense, published over Huger's signature, seems to have been overlooked by students of the battle.
[76] *Ibid.* Wilcox, *O. R.*, 11, pt. 1, p. 986, made it plain that at 3.30 Armistead's and Blanchard's Brigades already were advanced on the Charles City road.
[77] Huger in *Richmond Examiner*, Aug. 25, 1862, p. 1, col. 3.
[78] Even at which hour Johnston said that Huger's participation would have made the "victory . . . much more complete."
[79] *O. R.*, 11, pt. 1, p. 938. Corroborative of this is a memoir in the *Hotchkiss Papers* by Rev. G. W. Finley, D.D., of Fishersville, Va. Because this is a late document (Mch. 17, 1897) it is not cited in the text, but it is worthy of note. Dr. Finley was Adjutant of the Fourteenth Virginia, which was leading Huger's Division. He wrote: "I rode with my Colonel just behind General Armistead and his staff, who were just behind General Huger and his staff. Thus I was so situated as to see almost all of General Huger's movements during that day. When the Division reached a point on the Charles City Road which seemed to have been designated, we took position in line of battle and waited for the signal guns to be fired on our right by troops who had marched by the Williamsburg Road. We waited a good while, but how long I cannot say. At the signal we moved down the Charles City Road meeting so far as I saw no troops of the enemy. What our advance guard saw I did not know. Moving cautiously but steadily we reached a point near which a road ran across from the Williamsburg to the Charles City Road. By this time the firing was pretty heavy on our right [left?] where the battle had opened. For some reason we were then put in column and occupied the Charles City Road now and were held there for several hours. Meanwhile every movement of General Huger and his staff indicated that he was looking and waiting for orders. For I noticed couriers coming and going and despite the manifest impatience at the delay, we got no orders to move until late in the afternoon. Then a courier came dashing up and handed a paper to General Huger. As soon as his eyes fell upon it, he at once put his Division in motion over this cross road and hurried to the sound of the firing. We got on the battlefield just a little before dusk and while the heavy firing of (as we were told afterwards) Whiting's men was raging to the left of the Nine Mile road."

the details of Whiting's delay, of the search for Longstreet and of Beckham's messages after finding Longstreet on the Williamsburg road. Smith related also the receipt by Johnston, about 4 P.M. on the 31st, of a message in which, as Smith alleged, Longstreet stated that he was disappointed in not receiving assistance from the left. General Johnston, on receiving Smith's report of June 23, sent it back with a request that Smith eliminate all reference to these incidents. Johnston stated that he never intended to make them generally known, that he considered them as essentially matters between Longstreet and himself, and that Longstreet's misunderstanding may have been his fault.[80]

2. Having started for the Williamsburg road on the morning of May 31, Longstreet chose the route that put Gillies Creek in his way. Had he moved by his left, instead of by his right,[81] he could have gone South from the vicinity of the Dabb House and could have come out near the entrance to the Charles City road. In doing so, though he might have been compelled to march for some distance by inundated roads, he would have had to cross only one small branch of Gillies Creek.[82]

3. At Gillies Creek, Longstreet's troops insisted on crossing before Huger, as stated already, despite the fact that the early opening of the battle depended on the relief of Rodes by Huger. It should be repeated that the records do not show whether Longstreet was then at the crossing. There is no evidence one way or the other that he sent any one to expedite the march of the relief Brigade.

4. After his troops reached the vicinity of the turn-out into the

<hr />

[80] G. W. Smith, 165 ff. Smith acquiesced in this request to strike these passages from his report and he did not make them public until twenty-two years later (ibid.) He was prompted in 1884 to publish the full text of the original report because, as one gathers from his long and labored explanation, he felt that he inferentially had been accused of unwillingness to participate fully in the battle. Smith's contention was that Johnston's orders were for Whiting's Division to support the attack of Longstreet, if necessary, but not to participate in the initial attack. It should be pointed out that when Smith mentioned this order in his official report he said: "I received a note from General Johnston, directing that my Division should take position as soon as practicable upon the Nine-mile road, near the New Bridge fork road, to support if necessary, the Divisions upon the right in an attack upon the enemy . . ." (O. R., 11, pt. 1, p. 989). When Smith reprinted this in his Confederate War Papers, he inserted the word "ready" in front of "to support" so that the sentence read "my Division should take position . . . ready to support if necessary, the Divisions" etc. See G. W. Smith, 168. The difference in meaning is substantial.

[81] Assuming him to be facing South.

[82] His route would have been almost directly in rear of what subsequently became the Intermediate Line of the Richmond defenses.

Charles City road, Longstreet delayed them at that point for the passage down the road of the Division that his own men had insisted on preceding at Gillies Creek.

5. Thereafter, for reasons that were not explained officially at the time,[83] Longstreet dispatched three of his Brigades down the Charles City road and left only three Brigades to reinforce D. H. Hill on the Williamsburg road and to maintain *liaison* with Smith on the left of Hill.

6. Longstreet's subsequent orders to Wilcox, who commanded the three Brigades sent down the Charles City road in support of Huger, were reported by General Wilcox as follows: ". . . this order [to follow Armistead and Blanchard] was soon modified and my three Brigades ordered to precede Huger's two. Having passed Huger's Brigades, the march was continued but a short time, when orders were again received, and this time to counter-march to the Williamsburg Road and follow on in rear of the troops then advancing. The Brigades had retraced their steps near one mile, and orders were again given to face about and march down the Charles City Road, and to keep abreast with the firing then heard raging furiously off to our left front, and known to be on the Williamsburg Road. Again orders were received in writing to move across to the Williamsburg Road, following country roads and paths through woods and fields, a guide being furnished to conduct the command. The intervening distance between the two roads was low and flat, and in many places covered with water and at one point waist deep." [84] All these orders, Wilcox explicitly stated, were given by Longstreet.[85] Why they were sent him, he did not know. Wilcox added, probably at a later time,[86] "When the head of my column reached the Williamsburg Road Longstreet said, 'You have taken a good deal of time to reach this road'; for that reason I reported the order and counter-orders, marches

[83] Attention again should be directed to the later explanation Longstreet gave in his memoirs. See *supra*, p. 239, n. 60.

[84] *O. R.*, 11, pt. 1, p. 986.

[85] *Ibid.*, 989.

[86] This is indicated by two facts: (1) The passage in question, *O. R.*, 11, pt. 1, p. 989, appears as a "Postscript" and contains some reflections that probably would not have been recorded at that time in a formal report by a soldier of Wilcox's familiarity with army usage; (2) examination by the writer of the MS. of Wilcox's report on Gettysburg (*cf.* 3 *R. E. Lee*, 554–55), confirmed the internal evidence that an addendum, similar to the "P. S." of the report on Seven Pines, was written at a considerable time after the original.

and countermarches he had given, and that I had made in obedi
ence to his orders."

7. Three decades later, when General Longstreet wrote his
memoirs, he quoted fully Johnston's orders of May 30 to Huger,
but Longstreet neither mentioned nor quoted the orders sent
Huger by Johnston on the morning of May 31, though these
appear in the *Official Records* immediately beneath those Longstreet cited with specific page reference. The orders of May 31, it
will be recalled, modified Huger's mission.[87]

The record speaks for itself, but as neither Huger nor any of his
Brigadiers filed any official reports, the facts were not known for
many years after the battle. Johnston prepared his report on the
basis of what Longstreet narrated and, as a result, he accepted the
charges against Huger without knowledge of all the circumstances.[88] At the same time, Johnston's sense of honor and his
affection for Longstreet led him to assume responsibility, in his
letter to Smith, for a possible misunderstanding over Longstreet's
line of advance. It is possible, also, though it cannot be stated as a
fact, that Johnston and the division commanders from the Manassas line had a *camaraderie* that made them defend one another
and assume a certain sense of superiority to the Army of the
Peninsula and to Huger's command from Norfolk. Perhaps it
was not solely by chance that, after General Johnston came to
Yorktown, he entrusted all major operations to his own troops.[89]
That may be a more considerate statement of the case than the
reverse, namely, that he did not employ either Magruder's troops
or Huger's in any major attack because he may not have had confidence in the high command of those forces.

Be that as it may, the Battle of Seven Pines left in widespread
distrust the abilities of Huger, who, it will be remembered, already was unpopular because of the affair at Roanoke Island and
the evacuation of Norfolk. On the other hand, Longstreet, whose
conduct at Seven Pines was most subject to question, emerged not
only without blame but also with prestige increased. A reading of

---

[87] See *Longstreet*, 90. For the specific difference between Huger's orders of May 30
and May 31, see *supra*, p. 254.

[88] As evidence of the extent to which Johnston was misled by the reports of some
of his subordinates, it may be noted that he stated, *O. R.*, 11, pt. 1, p. 934, "Smith, Hill
and Longstreet were in position . . . to be ready to commence operations at 8 A.M."

[89] The use of McLaws in front of Fort Magruder on May 4 was a minor affair.

the official reports of the action led the Southern people to put Longstreet's name ahead of any of those distinguished on that field of confusion. Now that after-discovered evidence suggests a reversal, there is danger that judgment of Longstreet, in all save one respect, may be too severe. It scarcely is reasonable to say that he marched over to the Williamsburg road to get rid of Johnston and of Smith, and to fight his own battle in his own way. The probability is that he moved southward through honest mistake in the issuance or interpretation of orders. Staff work at General Headquarters on May 30–31 was about as bad as it could have been. For this Johnston in large measure was responsible—witness his failure to have a copy made of the instructions he personally wrote for Huger the night before the battle. Longstreet has no culpability in this. If his orders were equivocal, his subsequent confusion was the result of inexperience in the logistics of a far larger command than ever he had handled in the field.

The inexcusable part of Longstreet's conduct was his successful effort to make Huger the scapegoat. All that Huger ever received, in the way of apology, was belated announcement, in general orders from Longstreet, that when congratulations had been published in earlier orders, "the extent of the service of Major General Huger's division was not understood." [90] Even then the few regiments of Huger's Division that were authorized to inscribe "Seven Pines" on their standards were not the troops on Longstreet's right, May 31, but those that on June 1 were engaged.

The main battle of Seven Pines was fought on the anniversary of Beauregard's official assignment to the command at Manassas.[91] One year of the Army's history was written. It was a story of preparation, rather than of action, a prologue to the red drama that was to begin in another month. From June, 1861, to the end of May, 1862, the Army had grown vastly in numbers but unequally in experience. Because there had been scant occasion for cavalry action in Northern Virginia, and little opportunity of using mounted troops in the wooded Peninsula, the cavalry was as yet an arm undeveloped. In the artillery service not one officer had risen to eminence. The infantry, on the other hand, had earned in marches, in charges, and in casualties the confidence of

[90] *Richmond Examiner*, Aug. 25, 1862, p. 1, col. 3, with reference to Longstreet's orders of June 12, 1862.
[91] *O. R.*, 2, 806.

every commander. So valiant, so willing was it that the tactics of the Army were based on infantry assaults. Some of the general officers were too readily disposed to employ the infantry in the discharge of tasks that should have devolved on the artillery.

Although there had been but two major battles, in neither of which the entire Army had been engaged, attrition and transfer had removed in twelve months many of the leaders to whom North and South, at the time of secession, had looked with confidence. Several of the Virginia-born senior officers who had adhered to the "old flag" in 1861 [92] no longer were on the active list. On Nov. 1, 1861, with multiplied honors and no diminution of his love of the Union, but after much bickering with General McClellan and others, Lt. Gen. Winfield Scott had retired.[93] Death had removed Col. John Garland. Five others—Col. Washington Seawell, Col. M. M. Payne, Maj. N. C. McRae, Maj. Campbell Brown, Maj. E. J. Steptoe—had been put in the background. Maj. John F. Lee was preparing to resign. At the end of May, 1862, two and only two of the Virginia Unionists of high rank were attaining distinction: George H. Thomas, already a Major General of Volunteers, was clearing Kentucky of Confederates; Col. P. St. George Cooke, now a Brigadier General, was in command of the regular cavalry under McClellan. Maj. L. P. Graham had received commission as a Brigadier General of Volunteers and had commanded under Keyes at Williamsburg, but he had gone to Maryland to be Chief of Cavalry of a new force being organized there.[94]

Fate had not spared those who had sided with the South. Colonel Fauntleroy, who had been quick to resign command of the 1st United States Dragoons in 1861, had been found too old for Confederate service or too proud to accept the assignment given him and, at his own request, had been relieved of command as a Virginia Brigadier General.[95] Brilliant Robert Selden Garnett, aggressive Barnard Bee, chivalrous Francis Bartow and courtly Philip St. George Cocke were dead. Bonham had resigned. Beauregard, Van Dorn, and Kirby Smith had been sent to other scenes

---

[92] In Appendix II, pp. 703 ff., will be found reference to all the officers mentioned in this paragraph.
[93] C. W. Elliott, in his *Winfield Scott*, pp. 729 ff., described admirably this period of Scott's life.
[94] *O. R.*, 12, pt. 3, p. 346.   [95] *O. R.*, 5, 807.

of action. Magruder was under orders to go to Texas. Huger had lost much of his reputation. "Shanks" Evans was in South Carolina. Jackson and Ewell were detached and were fighting a dramatic campaign in the Shenandoah Valley. Jubal Early, Wade Hampton and Robert Rodes were suffering from wounds. Johnston Pettigrew was a prisoner of war. Hatton was newly fallen. Seven Colonels of the line, some of them experienced and some of them promising, had been killed in action.[96] Of the twelve brigade commanders of the troops that Johnston and Beauregard had sought to concentrate at Manassas on July 21, 1861, two only were now with the Army in front of Richmond—Longstreet and D. R. Jones. If Jackson and Ewell were included, four of the twelve—and no more than four—remained in command of troops in Virginia on the anniversary of the first step in the organization of Beauregard's "Army of the Potomac."

Still more convulsionary changes had come. In the twilight of the battle of May 31 around Fair Oaks Station, Jos. E. Johnston had been twice wounded—once in the right shoulder by a musket ball and, a few minutes later, in the chest by a heavy fragment of shell.[97] The next day, G. W. Smith had made fumbling and over-cautious efforts to continue the battle[98] and, on June 2, had suffered an illness which he described as paralysis.[99] In action, he

[96] Bartow is, of course, technically to be added to this list, but popularly he was counted as a general officer.

[97] *Johnston's Narrative*, 138–39. The best account of the wounding of Johnston is that of his courier, Drury L. Armistead, in 18 *S. H. S. P.*, 186–87. Armistead stated that when Johnston recovered consciousness, after he had been removed from the spot where he was struck down, he found that his sword and pistols had been left where he fell. "That sword," he said, "was the one worn by my father in the Revolutionary war and I would not lose it for $10,000; will not some one please go back and get it and the pistols for me?" The weapons were recovered. There is no certainty concerning the spot where Johnston received his wounds. Armistead wrote that the General turned back when he reached the crossing of the Nine Mile road and the York River Railroad and found that intersection under fire: "General Johnston and staff rode back about 200 yards to an elevated position near a small house, which he occupied until he was wounded." The site cannot be identified from this description. General Johnston noted that President Davis rode to him "manifesting great concern, as he continued to do until I was out of danger." *Op. cit.*, 139.

[98] See *supra*, p. 243.

[99] 2 *B. & L.*, 261. Smith stated that no symptom of this malady manifested itself within eighteen hours of the time he was relieved of general command of the Army, but the record shows that his health had been bad in the early spring (see *supra*, p. 164), and that, on May 29, President Davis (2 *Davis*, 121), had heard that Smith was ill. The evidence unhappily is abundant that, on June 1, Smith could not bring himself to throw all his troops into action, or even to fight with vigor. General Smith's A.A.G., reporting his chief sick on June 2, wrote General Lee: ". . . General Smith finds himself utterly unable to endure the mental excitement incident to his actual presence with the army. Nothing but duty under fire could possibly keep him up, and there is danger of his

was one of the most unconcerned of soldiers and while under fire he did not even change the pitch of his voice.[100] Consequently, no question of his personal courage could be raised by any one who had seen him in battle. Responsibility it was that shattered his nerves, responsibility and, perhaps, the fear that if he failed his reputation was gone.

The commanding General indefinitely on the list of the wounded, if indeed he survived; the commander of the left wing, second in command, broken by excitement and responsibility. It was a grim price to add to all the toll of the mismanaged battle. A birthday present of ill omen to the Army, men might say it was, but there was another gift: To the command that Johnston laid down, to resume no more, the President on June 1 named Gen. R. E. Lee.

entire prostration. He goes to town today to gain a few days' respite. All business and all exciting questions must be kept from him for awhile. Major Melton will accompany him to prevent, while it is necessary, all such intrusion. Since writing the above I have again seen the general, and am pained to learn that partial paralysis has already commenced. The case is critical and the danger imminent" (O. R., 11, pt. 3, pp. 685–86).

[100] J. L. Brent, Memoirs of the War Between the States (cited hereafter as Brent), 147–48: "I was much struck by [Smith's] coolness, while shot and shell were falling about him. . . . I only recollect among the many I heard two voices of high officers in battle, which preserved their ordinary and usual tones. One was Gen. Gustavus Smith, and the other was Gen. Dick Taylor."

CHAPTER XIX

OLD SNARLS ARE UNTANGLED

THE LOSS to the Army of Johnston and of Gustavus Smith had results far less disconcerting than might have been anticipated. Johnston's admirers among the officers of the "Manassas troops" believed the South had and would have none like him in strategical ability,[1] but the commanders of the Army of the Peninsula and of the regiments from the Department of Norfolk had been with him for so brief a time that he was to them little more than a distinguished name. Smith was scarcely that. After his wounding, moreover, Johnston himself played a manful and honorable part in maintaining the morale of the corps of officers. He did not revive at the moment, by act or utterance, any of his controversies with the President, nor did he encourage any discontent with his successor. When a friend lamented the General's wounds as a calamity to the South, Johnston instantly objected. Said he: "No Sir! The shot that struck me down is the very best that has been fired for the Southern cause yet. For I possess in no degree the confidence of our government, and now they have in my place one who does possess it, and who can accomplish what I never could have done—the concentration of our armies for the defence of the capital of the Confederacy."[2]

This prediction by its old commander the Army soon saw its new chief realize. The men in the ranks were unacquainted with Lee and probably were curious only to know how he looked, how he would fight, and what he would do about furloughs and discipline. Although a few senior officers somewhat distrusted an "outsider" whose reputation primarily was that of an engineer,

---

[1] Longstreet for many years, and probably to the end of his life, believed Johnston the greatest soldier of the South. See *Philadelphia Times*, July 27, 1879, p. 8.

[2] D. H. Maury, *Recollections of a Virginian*, 161. General Maury, in 18 *S. H. S. P.*, 180, gave Dr. [A. M.] Fauntleroy, one of Johnston's surgeons, as authority for this statement. He leaves the impression that Dr. Fauntleroy was present when Johnston spoke. Mrs. Chesnut, *op. cit.*, 228, wrote later: "Joe Johnston can sulk. As he is sent west, he says 'They may give Lee the army Joe Johnston trained.'" This entry in Mrs. Chesnut's Diary apparently is misplaced in chronology.

thev soon began to drop their misgiving. They saw ere long that Lee had a sound knowledge of the Army and no previous entangling associations with it. As military adviser to the President, he had been informed but detached. When he came to headquarters, it was not as a "Manassas man" nor as a "Yorktown man" but as a new and unifying influence.

To one large and useful advantage that Lee enjoyed, observant Colonels and Generals learned in time to give proper valuation: Lee understood the President thoroughly, and from the day he assumed command he employed his knowledge to remove misunderstandings and to assure co-operation. The new leader's methods were as tactful as they were effective. He realized that much of the friction between Mr. Davis and General Johnston had been due to the unwillingness of the General to confide his plans to the Commander in Chief. In one of the first letters Lee wrote after he took the field, he told Davis of troubles in D. H. Hill's Division [3] and added: "I thought you ought to know it. Our position requires you should know everything and you must excuse my troubling you." [4]

That Lee was a diplomatist, many such letters were to show; that he was a most capable army administrator, the men soon and gratefully perceived. The condition in which he found the troops was at a later time a subject of some controversy. One of Lee's staff officers insisted that there was "considerable depression." [5] Another member of the staff, in retrospect, remembered the Army of June, 1862, as an "armed mob." He elaborated: "It was extremely wasteful, little observant of the relations which should exist between commanders and the commanded, and absenteeism without proper authority prevailed largely among both officers and soldiers, which greatly reduced effective strength. In a word, it was magnificent material, of undisciplined individuality, and as such correspondingly unreliable and disorganized." [6] Federal testimony was that the men, prior to Lee's coming, often were "sickly, half-fed and clothed, and had no heart for their work." [7] General Longstreet, in 1887, denied this *in toto*. "Experience at

---

[3] See *infra*, p. 268.   [4] *Lee's Dispatches*, 8.   [5] *Long*, 162.
[6] R. H. Chilton to Jefferson Davis, Dec. 7, 1874; 7 *Rowland*, 410. General Chilton attributed this state of affairs to the fact that the Army, in the midst of elections and reorganization, was at a stage of emergence.
[7] *Cf.* 2 *R. E. Lee*, 88, where the authorities are cited.

Seven Pines," he insisted, "so far from demoralizing the army, only gave the troops greater confidence in their valor."[8] Whether the impairment of good order was widespread or was limited to a few troops; whether it was the result of inefficient, changing organization and command, or merely the reaction to long retreat and indecisive combat, the Army was conscious of swift measures to correct much that was amiss.[9]

One complaint only the Army made against Lee: He made white men do Negroes' work—wield picks, throw up parapets, build fortifications. Lee acted as if Southern men should hide behind a pile of dirt to shoot at the enemy instead of going out in the open and whipping the invader in a fair fight.[10] The grumbling Army did not understand that the construction of earthworks was part of Lee's preparation for an offensive. He reasoned that if he permitted McClellan to remain in front of Richmond, the superior Federal artillery soon would blast its way into the city. A defensive behind temporary fortification was necessary until the Confederate Army could be disposed and, if possible, reinforced. Then it must assume the offensive. It was not to be the Army of Richmond, as President Davis somewhat infelicitously styled it,[11] nor even the Army of Virginia, but the Army of *Northern* Virginia.[12]

To fulfill its mission by carrying the war away from Richmond and into Northern Virginia, the Army at once must have proper organization and the best available leaders. Vacancies were the first of several immediate problems of command. A. P. Hill's fine Brigade of Longstreet's Division had gone into the action at Seven Pines under its senior Colonel, James L. Kemper. Because of Blanchard's resignation, his Brigade of Huger's Division had been led by Col. A. R. Wright. If the Brigade of Robert Hatton was to remain efficient, a successor to that fallen General must be selected. Until the fate of Johnston Pettigrew was known,[13] temporary provision, at the least, had to be made for the command of his fine North Carolina regiments.

---

[8] James Longstreet to Jefferson Davis, Sept. 2, 1887; 9 *Rowland*, 594.
[9] For the steps he took, see 2 *R. E. Lee*, 88 ff.
[10] Lee's surprised comment on the Army's resistance to "work" was set forth in a letter of June 5, 1862, to Davis. *Lee's Dispatches*, 8.
[11] *O. R.*, 51, pt. 2, p. 565.
[12] Discussion of the origin of the name will be found in 2 *R. E. Lee*, 77–78 n.
[13] It was not known, on June 1, that Pettigrew was a wounded prisoner of war. See *supra*, p. 244.

On June 2, Lee wrote the President of this situation and asked for immediate appointments. In contrast to the delay that so often had attended similar requests from General Johnston, came instant action by the President. Kemper and Wright were made Brigadiers; Col. J. J. Archer, a Marylander who had commanded the Fifth Texas in Hood's Brigade, received promotion. Although the President did not think he should fill Pettigrew's place, he authorized the assignment of Col. W. Dorsey Pender to the command of the troops with temporary rank as Brigadier General— an easy solution because Pender was an officer of the regular Confederate service and subject to any assignment. Davis reminded Lee of the connection of these men with particular Brigades, but, he added: "You will know how to dispose of these officers. I give you the material to be used at your discretion." More than that, he told Lee, "you can anticipate the receipt of orders by placing them on duty." [14] Three days after the battle ended, the promotions were announced formally.[15] Doubtless the good effect was doubled by celerity. In the cases of Kemper and Pender, quick advancement was almost equivalent to promotion on the field for valor.

General Huger presented a second problem. After the somewhat unpleasant experiences of June 1-2,[16] Huger returned to his headquarters and assumed direction of his troops. Lee doubtless had heard the charges against Huger for failure on May 31 and he had not seen any of the evidence that absolved that officer of blame. Not unnaturally, then, a doubt concerning Huger's diligence was raised in Lee's mind. Twice during the three weeks that followed, the commanding General suggested the possibility of transferring Huger to other stations. Huger's own conduct was not calculated to impress his chief. Although Huger knew he was not responsible for the delays of May 31, he gave color to the charges by his slow manner, by his adherence to army routine and by seeming negligence in the face of the enemy. Late in June, when Huger again was reported absent from his quarters during an attack on his outposts, Lee had to send him an order to take his position with his troops and to remain with them.[17] Huger

14 O. R., 11, pt. 3, pp. 569–70.
15 Ibid., 574. For Pender's next adventures, see 514, 523 and Vol. II.
16 See supra, p. 253, n. 62, and O. R., 11, pt. 3, p. 570.
17 Lee's Dispatches. 11. 14.

obeyed, as always, but always, too, he stood on his "rights" and claimed the full prerogatives of his rank. Soon the impression became general that he was of an "old army" type that could not adjust itself to new conditions—that he was living in the atmosphere of the Pikesville Arsenal, not of the Battle for Richmond.[18]

A third immediate problem of command was presented in the Division of D. H. Hill. That officer, though proud of the showing of his troops at Seven Pines, promptly reported to General Lee his dissatisfaction with two of his brigade commanders—Gen. G. J. Rains and Gen. W. S. Featherston. This was the most marked display Hill yet had given of his peculiar tendency to run to extremes of opinion. If he admired conduct on the field, no compliment was too extravagant; where he distrusted or disapproved, condemnation was complete. Hill's complaint against Rains apparently was the failure of that officer to deliver a second flank attack when the right of Rodes's Brigade was exposed after the assault on Casey's Redoubt. Hill believed that if Rains had opened fire against the flank and rear of the Federals, 500 casualties in Rodes's Brigade would have been avoided.[19]

The object of Hill's wrath was a North Carolinian, 59 years of age, a graduate of West Point in the class of 1827,[20] and former Lieutenant Colonel of the 4th United States Infantry. A man of fine appearance and of pronounced patriotism, Gabriel Rains was at heart a scientist, and was more interested in explosives than in field command. In 1840, while campaigning against the Seminole Indians, he first had experimented with booby-traps. On the retreat from Yorktown he had planted several of these in the way of the Federals and thereby had delayed somewhat the pursuit. He was gratified, but some of his superiors were convinced that these "land torpedoes" were not "a proper or effective method of war." Rains consequently was forbidden to use more of them. He protested vigorously that his device was permissible, and he asked, in effect, how its use differed from the employment of outranging

---

[18] In justice to Huger, it should be pointed out explicitly that no authority for this statement can be cited. The instance is one where a conclusion has to be drawn from negative evidence, but the conclusion itself seems inescapable. Perhaps the paucity of references to Huger is due to the fact that he left the Army of Northern Virginia immediately after the Seven Days and, except for his letter to *The Examiner* (see *supra* p. 256, n. 75), did not appear in any public controversy.

[19] *O. R.*, 11, pt. 1, p. 976; cf. *supra*, p. 241.

[20] *Cullum*, No. 482; graduated thirteenth in a somewhat undistinguished class.

naval guns. Missiles from such ordnance, he told D. H. Hill, had been "bursting with awful noise and scattering their death-dealing fragments among the innocent and unoffending, fiendish acts unknown among civilized nations, reversing the scriptural text that it is better for ninety-nine guilty persons to escape than for one innocent to suffer." [21] As this analogy was not allowed, a suggestion previously made by the Secretary of War [22] was adopted. Under orders of June 18, Rains was assigned to the river defenses, where the use of torpedoes was "clearly admissible." [23] A time was to come when his "subterra shells" were a welcome adjunct of the Richmond defenses.[24]

The ground of Hill's grievance against W. S. Featherston does not appear from the records.[25] Presumably, the reason was the frequent absence from his post of this officer, whose health was not of the best. Featherston was tall, clean-shaven and eagle-faced, blunt of manner and careless of dress, but with a reputation for hard drill. In his forty-first year, he was without formal military education, beyond that which he had acquired as a young volunteer in the Creek war. During the autumn of 1861, and particularly for his handling of his Seventeenth Mississippi at Ball's Bluff, he had won praise.[26] Despite Hill's criticism, there was nothing definitely adverse in Featherston's record. Against a man from his own State, President Davis was slow to credit vague charges. General Lee at the time knew nothing of Featherston [27] and would not judge him unheard. The course of justice to Featherston and of deference to D. H. Hill seemed to be to trans-

21 *O. R.*, 11, pt. 3, p. 517. The attribution to Holy Writ of a variant of Blackstone's maxim seems to have caused no comment on the part of the Biblical student, Hill.

22 *O. R.*, 11, pt. 3, p. 510.

23 *O. R.*, 11, pt. 3, p. 608. For Rains's experiments in Florida, during the operations against the Seminoles, see 10 *S. H. S. P.*, 39. His rank in the "old army" is given in *Army Register* of 1860. Confederate assignments to command, etc., are set forth in *O. R.*, 4, 697; *O. R.*, 11, pt. 3, pp. 482, 533; *O. R.*, 51, pt. 2, pp. 306, 325. On the employment of his booby-traps at Yorktown, consult M. C. Butler's Address of Apr. 26, 1895; for the controversy over the use of these devices, see *O. R.*, 11, pt. 3, pp. 509 ff.

24 Col. A. H. Colquitt assumed command of the Brigade.

25 Hill's letter to Lee, mentioned in Lee to Davis, June 5, 1862, *Lee's Dispatches*, 8, presumably was returned by Davis to Lee and by him destroyed. That was Lee's practice in disposing of documents that were derogatory and were not essential to the files of the Army.

26 Featherston's early part in the war was mentioned in *Richmond Examiner*, May 31, 1861; *O. R.*, 2, 944. His report on Manassas is in *O. R.*, 2, 539–40. Reference to him by the Secretary of War, in the annual report that included an account of Ball's Bluff, appears in IV *O. R.*, 1, 796. Later assignments to duty are noted in *O. R.*, 5, 979, and in *O. R.*, 11, pt. 3, pp. 425, 483.

27 *Lee's Dispatches*, 9.

fer Featherston to another Division and to give him troops from his own State.[28]

In providing these troops, the old, vexing question arose again of brigading units according to the States from which they came. The men themselves generally were favorable to this system. General Lee's view of the question was not materially different from that of General Johnston, but his approach was more conciliatory. Within a few days after he took command, he wrote the Chief Executive: "I have . . . sent a circular to division commanders to see what can be done as to reorganizing Brigades by States. I fear the result. Nor do I think it the best organization. I would rather command a Brigade composed of regiments from different States. I think it could be better controlled, more emulation would be excited, and there would be less combination against authority. I can understand why officers looking to political preferment would prefer it, and it may be more agreeable to the men. The latter consideration has much weight with me. But as it is your wish and may be in conformity to the spirit of the land, I will attempt what can be done. It must necessarily be slow and will require much time. All new Brigades I will endeavour so to arrange." As this was acceptable to the President, a controversy that had much vexed Johnston came to an end.[29]

Scarcely less serious than progressive reorganization by States, the strengthening of brigade command in D. H. Hill's Division and the promotion of competent men to fill vacancies, was the issue presented by Gustavus W. Smith's Division. What should be done about it? Smith's physical condition showed no improvement. Months might pass before he could return to the field, if ever he could. Of his five Brigades, only Hood's had at its head a man experienced in all his duties. Hampton was absent, wounded; Pettigrew was a prisoner of war; Archer had just succeeded Hatton; Whiting had to leave his Brigade in charge of its senior Colonel while he acted as divisional commander. Small

---

[28] He was assigned to Longstreet's Division.

[29] As rapidly as possible Lee carried out the President's wishes. For an early example, affecting the Louisiana troops, see *O. R.,* 12, pt. 3, p. 918. See also *O. R.,* 25, pt. 2, pp. 830, 838. One of the most troublesome cases, arising in December, 1863, concerned the Brigades of J. H. Lane and Geo H. Steuart. Lane thought that an effort was being made to weaken his Brigade in order to procure promotion for Col. C. M. Avery of the Thirty-third North Carolina. See *O. R.,* 29, pt. 2, pp. 867 ff. Under an act of Congress, made effective by regulations of Sept. 29, 1862 (IV *O. R.,* 2, 98), private soldiers were granted the right of transfer, upon request, to commands from their own States.

wonder was there, then, that part of the Division showed signs of disorganization, if not of demoralization, after its futile, costly part in the Battle of Seven Pines.[30] Logically, the restoration of the morale of these fine troops during Smith's invalidism seemed a proper assignment for Whiting. No fault had been found by Johnston with that officer's leadership on May 31. If there had been indecision and overcaution on June 1, the blame might have been placed more reasonably on Smith than on Whiting. The one weakness thus far disclosed in the brilliant Whiting was his extreme pessimism. This was irritating, if not demoralizing. Whiting did not believe that Richmond could be held or that the Army could maintain itself North of James River, and on this he expatiated. Lee replied that the same argument would carry the forces in retreat all the way to the Gulf of Mexico. More directly, Lee admonished, "If we go to ciphering we shall be whipped beforehand." [31] This was said with earnestness and almost with impatience, but it implied no distrust of Whiting's ability.

The new commanding General left to time the final decision in Whiting's case. No attempt was made to get Whiting promoted forthwith or to overcome Davis's antagonism to that officer, because of the controversy over Mississippi troops. Lee simply retained Whiting in the divisional command to which he had been assigned by Smith on May 28.[32] Longstreet was told that Whiting would prove a "good neighbor" in the line.[33] A little later, when Lee planned to reinforce Jackson, he assigned that task to Whiting with "eight veteran regiments." [34] As this detachment left Hampton's, Pender's[35] and Archer's[36] Brigades outside any Division, Lee assigned them to "the portion of General Smith's command under Gen. A. P. Hill." [37] It was to become an historic association.

---

[30] Longstreet to Davis, Sept. 2, 1887, 9 *Rowland*, 594, is authority for the statement that Lee considered Whiting's "demi-division" demoralized.
[31] 9 *Rowland*, 549; 10 *ibid.*, 83.
[32] *O. R.*, 11, pt. 3, p. 558. For Lee's continuance of Whiting in command, see *O. R.*, 11, pt. 3, p. 574.
[33] *O. R.*, 11, pt. 3, p. 577.   [34] *O. R.*, 11, pt. 3, pp. 589, 594. This was June 11.
[35] Formerly Pettigrew's.   [36] Previously Hatton's.
[37] *O. R.*, 11, pt. 3, p. 589. For the inclusion of Hampton, not mentioned in this order, see *ibid.*, Lee to A. P. Hill. In his long sketch of Whiting in 26 *S. H. S. P.*, C. B. Denson stated, p. 145, that Whiting proposed the detachment of troops to reinforce Jackson and, when Lee objected that he could not spare the whole of Whiting's Division, Whiting offered to go with two Brigades. The latter part of this statement may be correct, though it came to Mr. Denson second-hand. Plans to reinforce Jackson had been under consideration prior to the date of Whiting's suggestion.

If Smith's troops thus were divided temporarily between A. P. Hill and Whiting, what was to be done with the large command of Magruder, which was in some confusion?[38] Within less than a week after Lee established headquarters in the field, Magruder raised a question of the relationship between his command and that of Whiting, who was on his right, roughly between the Nine Mile road and the York River Railroad.[39] Four days later, Magruder wrote that as Longstreet continued to command the entire right, he wished to know whether he had control of Whiting as well as of his regular command.[40] Lee's Assistant Adjutant General replied promptly and unmistakably: ". . . the commanding general desires me to say that your command does not extend beyond those of Generals McLaws' and Jones'. He thinks by continuing the system of division commanders greater harmony may be preserved throughout the army, as all questions involving differences of opinion may be referred to a common superior and promptly settled. This arrangement may be changed during an engagement, if deemed expedient at the time."[41]

Magruder made haste to explain that he had not sought to press a claim of command over Whiting, and that differences of opinion between him and Whiting had not been "accompanied by anything unpleasant."[42] Relations with the adjoining command were not eased perceptibly by this assurance. Although Magruder displayed the most professional deference, he continued to send frequent protests to army headquarters concerning the relative duties of his own and of near-by troops.[43] Despite Magruder's bluster and his needless concern over his neighbors, his own organization improved. D. R. Jones had returned to duty, though his health was no better. He remained a Brigadier, because his nomination to higher grade had not yet been confirmed, but he was exercising divisional command acceptably. So was Magruder's new Major General, Lafayette McLaws.

Additional general officers, strangers to the Army, arrived during the first weeks of Lee's command. Every new Brigade raised hopes that the Army would become strong enough to assume the

[38] O. R., 11, pt. 3, p. 577.
[39] O. R., 11, pt. 3, p. 578. For Whiting's position, see *ibid.*, 577.
[40] O. R., 11, pt. 3, p. 586.   [41] *Ibid.*
[42] O. R., 11, pt. 3, p. 587.
[43] O. R., 11, pt. 3, pp. 593 ff, particularly p. 601.

offensive. Even before Seven Pines had been fought, one of Gen. T. H. Holmes's Brigades from North Carolina, under John G. Walker, had been brought to Petersburg, whence it soon was moved to Drewry's Bluff.[44] Robert Ransom's Brigade from the same department followed.[45] From South Carolina, early in June, came Roswell S. Ripley, who was assigned to D. H. Hill's Division.[46]

All three of these men had been professional soldiers. Walker, a Missourian, just 40, had been a Captain in the 1st Mounted Rifles;[47] Ransom, a West Pointer of the class of 1850,[48] had been a Captain of the 1st Cavalry and was an esteemed young soldier of 32, though cursed with ill health. Roswell S. Ripley, 39, had been graduated quite young from the Military Academy in 1843,[49] in the class with a man now beginning to win fame in the West on the other side of the line, U. S. Grant by name. In the Mexican War, Ripley had won his brevet as Major and had served on the staff of General Pillow, who figured prominently in a history the younger officer subsequently wrote of the campaigns below the Rio Grande. In 1853, Ripley had resigned from the Army to enter business. He had resided in Charleston, South Carolina, the home of his wife, and in the operations against Sumter he had displayed skill as an artillerist. His prime defect was his contentiousness. With Beauregard and with Pemberton he had quarrelled. For Lee, during the winter of 1861–62, he had acquired a contemptuous dislike. So bitterly had he denounced Lee, even before junior officers, that Governor Pickens had written in protest to President Davis.[50] Doubtless, in Virginia, Ripley would persist in backing his judgment against that of all men, but he cheerfully was accepted for the sake of the stout troops he brought to Richmond.

Might not others come as Ripley had? The Army of Northern Virginia believed it possible. "Chills and Fever" had risen from the marshes of the Carolina and Georgia coast to hold off the Federals and to guard the cities Lee had been unwilling in April to strip of their defenders. In the face of some muttering from poli-

---

[44] O. R., 11, pt. 3, pp. 553, 575, 579. The transfer was prior to June 5.
[45] O. R., 11, pt. 3, pp. 565, 613.   [46] O. R., 11, pt. 3, pp. 563, 573.
[47] 9 C. M. H., 224.   [48] Eighteenth in his class, Cullum, No. 1467.
[49] Cullum, No. 1173; graduated seventh.
[50] O. R., 6, 266.

ticians, who opposed its removal, the large Brigade of Gen. A. R. Lawton came to Petersburg whence, the whisper was, the willing Georgians were dispatched to reinforce "Stonewall" Jackson.[51] Finally, overflowing freight cars brought northward most of the remaining troops of Gen. T. H. Holmes, whose department was extended from Cape Fear River to the James. Holmes, under this arrangement, was entrusted with supervision of Drewry's Bluff.[52]

As a result of these arrivals and of the transfers and promotions after Seven Pines, the Army that defended Richmond had a command perceptibly different from that of the troops who had marched through the mud from Yorktown only six weeks previously. The infantry did not have an adequate corps of officers; but, when regarded as a revolutionary force organized hurriedly and under the direction of professional soldiers so few in number, it was remarkably well led. All Confederates had faith in mid-June, 1862, that the infantry would triumph. Now, overnight, by an adventure that made every chest swell, the cavalry were to test their leadership and to prove their quality.

[51] *O. R.*, 11, pt. 3, pp. 585, 589.   [52] *O. R.*, 11, pt. 3, pp. 610, 611.

CHAPTER XX

Stuart Justifies His Plume

The general strategic plan that rapidly was taking form in the mind of Lee contemplated an offensive against that part of McClellan's force North of the Chickahominy River. Little was known of the position of the right wing of the Army of the Potomac. Presumably, it had been placed where it was for the two fold purpose of forming a junction with McDowell and of protecting the line of supply from White House on the Pamunkey River. How far had the Federal flank been extended? Did it guard the ridge between the Chickahominy and the next stream to the Northeast, Totopotomoy Creek, an affluent of the Pamunkey? For a most particular reason, known only to a few, General Lee desired these questions answered. A reconnaissance in force was, of course, the means of ascertaining the facts. Cavalry would have to undertake the reconnaissance and, in doing so, they might drive some cattle into the Confederate lines. Should they find that the Federals were using the road that led to McClellan's right, an opportunity might offer of destroying Union wagon trains.

On June 10, Brig. Gen. J. E. B. Stuart, then 29 and in command of all the cavalry,[1] was called to Army headquarters at the Dabb House, High Meadows, on the Nine Mile road. Stuart had been with the Army through all its experiences since the day he had charged on the extreme left at Manassas. His zest, his vigilance, his skill in reconnaissance [2] soon increased the admiration that Johnston had formed for him in the Shenandoah Valley.[3] "He is a rare man," Johnston wrote of Stuart on August 10, 1861, "wonderfully endowed by nature with the qualities necessary for an officer of light cavalry." Johnston continued: "Calm, firm, acute, active and enterprising, I know of no one more competent than he to estimate the occurrences before him at their true value.

---

[1] Stuart was born in Patrick County, Virginia, Feb. 6, 1833.
[2] For an early instance of Stuart's aptitude for reconnaissance, see O. R., 2, 995.
[3] Cf. O. R., 1, 185; 2, 963, 969.

If you can add to this army a real brigade of cavalry, you can find no better brigadier-general to command it." [4] Newspaper correspondents with the Army shared Johnston's opinion and praised Stuart often.[5]

The conduct of the young Colonel in an affair at Lewinsville on September 11 brought further commendation from Johnston and a plea that he be advanced in rank.[6] After the President granted Stuart promotion on September 24,[7] the new Brigadier General soon became one of the shining figures at Manassas.[8] All the advanced outposts were placed under him.[9] In the projected reorganization of the Army, October 22, 1861, he was to command all the cavalry.[10] On December 20, he had a clash with the Federals at Dranesville, where he lost 194 men, foot and horse. Although he could not then bring himself to admit defeat—it was characteristic of him never to do so—he had distinctly the worse of the encounter.[11] Thereafter, his service was routine. He covered well the retreat from Manassas; at Williamsburg he aided in putting troops in position when his own forces were unoccupied; [12] in front of Seven Pines, where woods immobilized the cavalry, he acted virtually as an aide to Longstreet.[13] In none of these events had he gratified measurably his martial ambition or won the loud plaudits he craved.

He did not lack self-confidence or self-opinion. On the fourth day of Lee's command, Stuart felt that he should suggest a strategical plan to the commanding General. He prefaced it in this wise: "The present imperilled condition of the Nation, I presume, will be a sufficient apology for putting forth for your consideration, convictions derived from a close observation of the enemy's movements for months past, his system of war, and his conduct in Battle, as well as our own." The young cavalryman then argued that the Federals would not advance until they had perfected their works and armament on the south side of the

---

[4] O. R., 5, 777.
[5] Cf. Richmond Dispatch, Aug. 10, p. 3, col. 2; Oct. 3, p. 2, col. 3.
[6] O. R., 5, 182. For Longstreet's praise of Stuart in this clash, see O. R., 51, pt. 2, p. 291; Richmond Dispatch, Sept. 23, 1861, p. 2, col. 2.
[7] Wright, 61.
[8] Richmond Dispatch, Oct. 8, p. 2, col. 5; Nov. 7, p. 2, col. 3; Nov. 29, p. 1, col. 3; Dec. 10, p. 1, col. 2; Richmond Examiner, Oct. 10, 1861, p. 1, col. 4.
[9] O. R., 51, pt. 2, p. 349.
[10] O. R., 5, 913.
[11] O. R., 5, 489, 490, 494, 1008, 1063
[12] O. R., 11, pt. 1, pp. 568, 571, 585.
[13] O. R., 11, pt. 1, p. 491.

Chickahominy. As a result, said Stuart, "a pitched battle here, though a Victory, [would be] utterly fruitless to us." The proper course, Stuart went on, was to hold the Confederate left on the Chickahominy with a heavy concentration of artillery and to attack South of that stream. The youthful instructor of his chief concluded: "We have an army far better adapted to attack than defense. Let us fight at advantage before we are forced to fight at disadvantage. It may seem presumption in me to give these views, but I have not thus far mistaken the policy and practice of the enemy. At any rate, I would rather incur the charge of presumption than fold my arms in silence and indifference to the momentous crisis at hand. Be assured, however, General, that whatever course you pursue you will find nowhere a more zealous and determined cooperator and supporter than yours with the highest respect." [14]

The earnestness and naïveté of this had offset the defects of the strategy suggested, which essentially was that of throwing a numerically inferior force on a long front against an entrenched foe who had greatly superior artillery. Now, June 10, Stuart was not summoned to discuss strategy but execution. As he was ushered into the office of General Lee, he was introduced to the opportunity for which he had been waiting. Quietly he was told by General Lee of the design for an offensive North of the Chickahominy, and of the importance of ascertaining how far the enemy's outposts extended on the ridge. As the purpose of the reconnaissance was revealed, Stuart's imagination took fire: he could do more than ascertain the position of the Federal right; if the commanding General permitted, he would ride entirely around McClellan's army.[15] Lee probably shook his head at so rash a proposal, but Stuart would not dismiss it from mind. In high expectancy, he rode back to his own headquarters. What luck for a trooper who fifteen months previously had been a Captain! The color of the adventure was heightened that very evening: Lee sent Stuart the substance of intelligence reports which indicated that the Federals were stronger on their right than had been antici-

[14] J. E. B. Stuart to R. E. Lee, MS., June 4, 1862—*H. B. McClellan MSS.*

[15] It is singular that Stuart's statement on this point seems to have escaped observation. In his report, he said, *O. R.*, 11, pt. 1, p. 1038: "These circumstances [presented at Old Church] led me to look with more favor to my favorite scheme, disclosed to you before starting, of passing around."

pated.[16] There might lie ahead more than an exciting ride. A fight might be the reward of diligence and aggressiveness.

The next day, June 11, a courier handed Stuart his instructions in Lee's autograph. Caution was enjoined in these words: "You will return as soon as the object of your expedition is accomplished, and you must bear constantly in mind, while endeavoring to execute the general purpose of your mission, not to hazard unnecessarily your command or to attempt what your judgment may not approve; but be content to accomplish all the good you can without feeling it necessary to obtain all that might be desired. I recommend that you take only such men as can stand the expedition, and that you take every means in your power to save and cherish those you take. You must leave sufficient cavalry here for the service of this army, and remember that one of the chief objects of your expedition is to gain intelligence for the guidance of future operations. . . . Should you find upon investigation that the enemy is moving to his right, or is so strongly posted as to render your expedition inopportune—as its success, in my opinion, depends upon its secrecy—you will, after gaining all the information you can, resume your former position." [17]

Three times that important word "expedition" was to be read in these instructions! The affair was being lifted above the level of scouting, even of armed reconnaissance. Stuart read, pondered, and proceeded at once with his plans. Whom should he choose to go with him? Fitz Lee, the General's nephew—the same Fitz Lee who had been aide to Ewell at Manassas—was now Colonel of the First Virginia Cavalry.[18] He must lead his regiment on the "expedition," along with four companies of the Fourth, whose Colonel, Williams C. Wickham, had been wounded at Williamsburg. The second son of Gen. R. E. Lee, the quiet, handsome and capable "Rooney" Lee, who had celebrated his 25th birthday the day Seven Pines was fought, must take part of his Ninth Virginia Cavalry with him, and two squadrons of the Fourth.[19] Lt. Col. Will

16 O. R., 11, pt. 3, p. 590. Lee's reference on June 11 to this "information received last evening, the points of which I sent you" is the reason for. fixing June 10 as the date of the conference at Lee's headquarters.

17 O. R., 11, pt. 3, pp. 590–91.

18 Capt. W. E. ("Grumble") Jones had succeeded Stuart as Colonel of the First Virginia Cavalry (O. R., 51, pt. 2, pp. 316, 320), but had been displaced in the election of 1862, and had been assigned to the Seventh Virginia Cavalry (3 C. M. H., 617). Fitz Lee, former Lieutenant Colonel, then had become Colonel of the First.

19 O. R., 11, pt. 1, p. 1044.

Martin, of the Jeff Davis Legion,[20] must pick 250 of the best men of his command, and of the South Carolina Boykin Rangers. The Stuart Horse Artillery could supply a twelve-pound howitzer and a rifle gun,[21] under Lt. "Jim" Breathed. That young physician, just 22, had chanced to share the same train-seat with Stuart, as the two of them had come East to tender their services to Virginia, and after Breathed had volunteered as a private in Company B of the First Virginia Cavalry, he again met Stuart, then Colonel of that regiment. Stuart had urged him, in 1862, to transfer to Pelham's Horse Artillery and had arranged his election as First Lieutenant. The grateful young Breathed could be relied upon to requite kindness with valor.[22]

The members of Stuart's staff must go, of course, and with them Heros von Borcke, a Prussian officer on leave, who had joined headquarters as a volunteer aide and had shown joyous intrepidity on the field of Seven Pines. John S. Mosby likewise must accompany the expedition. He had volunteered in "Grumble" Jones's company from Southwest Virginia, a company that Jones deliberately had garbed in homespun. So apparelled, Mosby had not seemed different from any other mountaineer of the command. When named Adjutant of the regiment, he had taken especial delight in using a civilian saddle, and when at length he had procured a uniform, he had defied regulations by wearing the red facings of the artillery instead of the buff. Regimental gossip had it that he had found the uniform offered cheaply in Richmond and, as it had fitted him, he had bought it as a bargain.

Mosby had good social station and had attended the University of Virginia until arrested and imprisoned for wounding a fellow student. In jail, his prosecutor had taught him some law, which, after his term expired, Mosby had practiced in Bristol. Professional man though he was, it pleased him to affect the drawl and the vernacular of his clients. As a friend of "Grumble" Jones, who hated Stuart and was as cordially hated by the General, Mosby joyed in bedevilling Fitz Lee, Stuart's close friend. One day, when

---

[20] Two companies from Alabama, one from Georgia and three from Mississippi, O. R., 5, 1030.

[21] O. R., 11, pt. 1, p. 1045. For mention of the rifle, see Heros von Borcke, *Memoirs of the Confederate War* (cited hereafter as *von Borcke*), v. 1, p. 45.

[22] For a sketch of Breathed, see 30 *S. H. S. P.*, 346–48. His picture appears in J. C. Wise. *Long Arm of Lee*, 2, 608.

Jones was away and Lee was in command of the regiment, Mosby sauntered up as Adjutant and said: "Colonel, the horn has blowed for dress parade." The punctilious Lee was livid. He looked furiously at Mosby. "Sir," he burst out, "if I ever again hear you call that bugle a horn, I will put you under arrest!" [23] In the spring election of officers, Mosby had been defeated along with Jones, but Stuart by that time had sensed the daring and initiative of the former Adjutant, and had retained him at headquarters. Yes, there would be use on the expedition for that gaunt, thin-lipped Mosby with his satirical smile, his stooped neck and his strange, roving eyes.[24]

Another scout who must accompany the expedition was the alert and tireless Redmond Burke, who seemed to have been born for outpost service. Still a third scout who must accompany the expedition was William Downes Farley. This high-born South Carolina boy,[25] a former student of the University of Virginia, was a devotee of Shakespeare and of the early English poets. One of the handsomest young men in the Army, with hair a deep brown, and eyebrows and lashes so dark that they seemed to cast a shadow over his gray eyes, he had a soft voice, a quick smile and a quiet, modest grace. He would have made a perfect staff officer for a General on duty at the Confederate capital had there not flowed in his veins blood that fairly lusted for adventure. As a youth he had delighted to wander in forests of Arden, with his beloved Shakespeare in his pocket; but if he heard the sound of the horn and the cry of the pack, he was up and gone with the huntsmen. On the outbreak of the war, he had volunteered as a private in Gregg's Regiment, and soon had become a Lieutenant. Upon the disbandment of that command, Farley remained in Virginia as an aide to General Bonham, with rank of Captain.[26]

By that time, Farley's bold spirit had led him to undertake scouting in the enemy's country. Alone or with a few companions, armed, uniformed and mounted, he would spend days in the

---

[23] 6 C. V., 421; W. W. Blackford's MS. Memoirs, 319.
[24] J. E. Cooke, in Wearing of the Gray, 115 ff, gave an excellent sketch of Mosby.
[25] Dr. W. W. Ball, the distinguished editor of the Charleston News and Courier, informed the writer that William D. Farley's father was Samuel Farley, a native Virginian, lawyer and master in equity, who married a Miss Saxon, daughter of one of the oldest families of Laurens County. It is believed that Mrs. Samuel Farley's mother was a Lownes and a member of the most prominent Whig family of what is now Laurens County.
[26] O. R., 5, 449.

woods on the flank of the Federal columns, and, if opportunity offered, he would assail outposts or small detachments. On Nov. 27, 1861, he and two other South Carolinians were scouting in some timber beyond Dranesville when they sighted the 1st Pennsylvania Regiment, which had descended on the village and had captured the two pickets there. Without hesitation, Farley decided to attack the head of the column. At his word, the three scouts fired. Two men dropped; the horse of the Colonel of the regiment was killed. Immediately the Federals scattered, surrounded the woods and, closing in, captured the three Confederates.[27] For his daring, Farley spent some months in Old Capitol Prison, but at length won exchange and rejoined Johnston's Army as a scout.

His exploit made so great a sensation, despite his modest bearing, that he was a marked man. When he and Stuart met, an instant attachment was formed. "Farley the Scout," as every one styled him, soon was a fixture at Stuart's headquarters. To him were entrusted many dangerous duties. The more desperate they were, the more they pleased him. Nor did success spoil him, or create jealousies. Always in camp he was the quiet, self-effacing gentleman. For every one he had a smile and never a reference to his own feats. At Williamsburg he so distinguished himself that Stuart wrote in his report: "Captain W. D. Farley has always exhibited such admirable coolness, undaunted courage, and intelligent comprehension of military matters that he would be of invaluable service as a commanding officer assigned to outpost service." [28] Farley would not have it so: a scout he was, and a scout he would remain. It was enough to ride with Stuart on this daring, new expedition.[29]

These, then, were among the men Stuart selected—Fitz Lee, his cousin "Rooney," Will Martin, Jim Breathed, von Borcke,[30] John S. Mosby, Redmond Burke, William Farley—these and the best 1200 troopers that the cavalry had. Stuart chose them quietly on the 11th but apparently did not notify them. The secrecy which the commanding General enjoined on him was to be respected to

27 *O. R.*, 5, 448.
28 *O. R.*, 11, pt. 1, p. 573.
29 Apparently, the only sketch of Farley is that in *Wearing of the Gray*, 141 ff. Farley deserves a biography.
30 The Confederates never pronounced the final "e" of his name. He always was "von Borck," or to his intimates. "Von."

the letter. All the cavalry heard was a vague rumor that something was afoot.[31]

At 2 A.M. on the 12th, Stuart himself, in the cheeriest of moods, awakened his staff. "Gentlemen, in ten minutes," he announced, "every man must be in the saddle." [32] Soon the troopers were astir in the camps near Mordecai's and around Kilby's Station on the R. F. & P. Railroad.[33] Quietly and with no sounding of the bugle, the long column presently was in motion. Its route was toward Louisa Court House, as if it were bound for the Valley of Virginia, whence reports had come of a dazzling victory by Jackson. Reinforcement of "Stonewall" presumably was the mission of the cavalry, though nothing was confided by Stuart.

Along empty roads, past farms where the women waved handkerchiefs or aprons and the old men stared admiringly at the display of so much horse flesh, the troopers rode all day. Twenty-two miles they covered and then they went into camp on the Winston Farm near Taylorsville, close to the South Anna River.[34] Scouts were sent out; [35] troopers were left to their sleep. When everything was in order, Stuart mounted with "Rooney" Lee and rode to near-by Hickory Hill, the home of Mrs. Lee's family and of Col. Williams C. Wickham of the Fourth Cavalry. After his wound at Williamsburg, the Colonel had been paroled by his captors, and had been permitted to return to the gracious old plantation, where he was recovering. With him and with the other members of the household, "Rooney" Lee had high converse. Stuart, for his part, went to sleep in his chair.[36]

Back at camp before day, Stuart had a few rockets sent up as signal for the start, but again he permitted no reveille. He had, by that time, reports from his scouts that residents said the enemy was not in any of the country to the southeastward, as far as Old Church, twenty miles distant by the shortest road. Confidently, then, when men and beasts were fed, the column got under way again. The moment it turned toward the East, a stir went down

---

[31] R. L. T. Beale *History of the Ninth Virginia Cavalry* (cited hereafter as *Beale*, and to be distinguished from the narrative of his son, G. W. Beale, mentioned below), 11.

[32] I *von Borcke*, 37.

[33] G. W. Beale, *A Lieutenant of Cavalry in Lee's Army* (cited hereafter as *G. W. Beale*), 24; Stuart's report in *O. R.*, 11, pt. 1, p. 1036.

[34] *O. R.*, 11, pt. 1, p. 1036. *G. W. Beale*, 24.

[35] *O. R.*, 11, pt. 1, p. 1036

[36] A Confederate (pseudonym), *The Grayjackets*, 176.

the files: despite the ostentatious suggestion of a march to Louisa, the men had suspected that McClellan's flank was their objective, and now they knew it.[37] The day for which they had waited long had come at last. They were to measure swords with the enemy. Greatly must the leading squadron have been envied; deep must have been the resentment of Will Martin's Legion that it was designated as rearguard.[38]

Stuart ere long left the road and called the field officers in council. Every eye was fixed expectantly on him as he sat with careless rein on his horse. Not more than five feet ten in height, wide of shoulder and manifestly of great physical strength, he had a broad and lofty forehead, a large, prominent nose with conspicuous nostrils.[39] His face was florid; [40] his thick, curled mustache and his huge wide-spreading beard were a reddish brown. Brilliant and penetrating blue eyes, now calm, now burning, made one forget the homeliness of his other features and his "loud" apparel. The Army boasted nothing to excel that conspicuous uniform—a short gray jacket covered with buttons and braid, a gray cavalry cape over his shoulder, a broad hat looped with a gold star and adorned with a plume, high jack boots and gold spurs, an ornate and tasselled yellow sash, gauntlets that climbed almost to his elbows. His weapons were a light French saber and a pistol, which he carried in a black holster. On the pommel of his regulation saddle an oilcloth overall was strapped; behind the saddle was a red blanket wrapped in oilcloth. When he gave commands, it was in a clear voice that could reach the farthest squadron of a regiment in line.[41] On this particular morning of the 13th of June —a Friday at that—the information he had to confide to his field officers was not to be shouted on the battlefield: it was to be explained in an undertone. He gave his instructions for the next stage of the reconnaissance and aroused among his young companions no less enthusiasm than he exhibited.

The officers galloped off to take their places with their regi-

37 G. W. Beale, 25.

38 O. R., 11, pt. 1, p. 1045. While this reference establishes the fact that the Jeff Davis Legion constituted the rearguard, there is uncertainty whether the First or the Ninth Virginia led the route to Hanover Court House.

39 This description of Stuart's personality is based on Cooke's full account in *Wearing of the Gray*, 22 ff. Supplementary references are to characteristics that Cooke does not mention.

40 *Sorrel*, 29.

41 *Richmond Dispatch*, Nov. 7, 1861, p. 2, col. 3.

ments. On moved the column, through the woods and past fields where the young corn was showing itself. When the force came in sight of Hanover Court House, which straggled on either side of the road, horses and men were observed. Scouts reported that the enemy was there, but in what strength, nobody in the neighborhood knew.[42] Quickly it was decided that Fitz Lee should take his regiment and swing around on a detour to the right, which would bring him back into the Courthouse road, South of the village. When sufficient time had elapsed for Lee to reach that intersection, Stuart was to advance with the remainder of the column. The Federals would be cut off and would be forced either to surrender or else to scatter where they might be caught.

Fitz Lee and the First regiment slipped off; the Ninth Virginia and the Jeff Davis Legion waited impatiently. At length, fingering his watch, Stuart gave the word. Scouts near the Courthouse came out from their hiding places. The Southerners prepared to charge. Almost immediately a few shots rang out from the village. The game was flushed! Stuart shouted a command. The column dashed down the road. It was too late. The "blue birds," as the Confederates dubbed their enemy, had taken alarm and had fled under cover of the dust they raised. Stuart found nothing in the village except its few residents, the old Courthouse where Patrick Henry had won his first reputation as a lawyer, and the tavern where the great Revolutionary had worked for his father-in-law. Ill luck it was to lose the first covey! Fitz Lee made it worse by getting his regiment into a marsh, the passage of which was so slow that the enemy passed the crossroads before he arrived.[43]

"Rooney" Lee's Ninth Virginia was now in front. Its advance squadron, scouting ahead of the regiment, was under the eye of the regimental Adjutant, Lt. W. T. Robins, a daring man. As the Federals had escaped down the Courthouse road, that approach to the village of Old Church was certain to be guarded. Stuart accordingly left the highway about a mile below Hanover Courthouse and, turning South, followed the route via Taliaferro's Mill and Enon Church.[44] The march was hard and rapid. As

42 O. R., 11, pt. 1, p. 1036.
43 Wearing of the Gray, 176–77; O. R., 11, pt. 1, p. 1036.
44 O. R., 11, pt. 1, p. 1037.

the sun climbed toward noon, heat radiated from every field, but nobody heeded it. Only one thing mattered—to find and to drive the enemy.

Seven miles were covered from the turnout. Enon Church was passed. Then, near Haw's Shop, anxious eyes caught a glimpse of bluecoats. Some were ahead, some in a field on one flank. Before Stuart's leading squadron knew what was astir, the Federals came forward with a roar. They dashed almost to the head of the col-umn, fired a shot or two and veered off.

"Form fours! Draw saber! Charge!" Stuart commanded. Almost as uttered, his orders were obeyed. The Confederates swept forward—and again to no purpose. A few videttes were surprised and captured. Some dismounted men were bagged. The others escaped. All the satisfaction the Southerners had was in the behavior of their captives. Some of the prisoners stared at Col. Fitz Lee, then broke into grins of recognition and greeted him as "Lieutenant." They were of the 5th. United States Cav-alry, formerly the 2nd, with which Lee had served as a junior officer. He was as glad to see his former troopers as they were to hail him. Inquiries were made concerning old friends; familiar jests were revived. It was difficult to believe that the disarmed, laughing troopers and the smiling young Colonel represented opposing armies mustered to slaughter each other.[45]

Rumors, coming presumably from the prisoners, were that the 5th was in front and would make a stand,[46] but Stuart's column moved on at a trot and encountered no opposition. When the van approached Totopotomoy Creek, a difficult little stream, with its banks a maze of underbrush, there was every reason to assume that the Federals would contest the crossing. Perhaps the very fact that the bridge had not been destroyed was a reason for sus-pecting an ambush. Cautiously Stuart held back the main col-umn, dismounted half a squadron, and sent these men forward as skirmishers. Once again there was disappointment. The Fed-erals had left the barrier unguarded.[47]

It was now about 3 P.M. Old Church was distant only two and

[45] *Wearing of the Gray*, 177; G. W. Beale, 27. [46] *O. R.*, 11, pt. 1, p. 1037.
[47] *O. R.*, 11, pt. 1, p. 1037. H. B. McClellan, in *The Life and Campaigns of* . . .
J. E. B. Stuart (cited hereafter as H. B. McClellan), stated, p. 55, that there was brief opposition at the creek, but if there was any it was not sufficient for Stuart to mention it in his report.

a half miles. There, if anywhere, the enemy would offer resistance, because wagon trains from Piping Tree Ferry and from
New Castle Ferry would have to pass that point in order to supply
the right wing of the Federals North of the Chickahominy. Inasmuch as the Federal cavalry were known to be under Stuart's
own father-in-law, Brig. Gen. Philip St. George Cooke, a Virginian and a renowned trooper of the "old army," it could not
be that he had neglected that important and exposed crossroad.

For the first time that day, military logic was vindicated.
Word came back that the enemy was at a stand and apparently
was awaiting attack. Stuart did not hesitate. Straight up the
road, the only avenue of approach, he ordered the column to
charge. With a shout and a roar, the leading squadron, that of
Capt. William Latané, dashed forward and threw itself squarely
against the Federals. For a few minutes there was a mad mêlée,
sword against pistol; then the Federals made off. A brief second
stand, a short distance to the rear, ended in the same manner.
When the clash was over, Captain Latané was dead, pierced by
five bullets. The Federal Captain who had met him in combat
was said to have been wounded badly by a blow from Latané's
saber. A few Federals had been shot or slashed. Several bluecoats were killed; others were taken prisoner. Five guidons were
among the trophies—the first that had fallen into the hands of
the expedition.[48]

Fitz Lee was all entreaty to push on and to rout his old regiment. Stuart gave ready permission but admonished the Colonel
to return quickly. In a few moments the First Virginia rushed
on and soon reached the camp of the troops who had disputed
the advance. The tents were deserted, though supplies were
there in abundance. As there was no time to collect even what
the men most coveted, the place was fired; but an ambulance
that contained a keg of whiskey, a regal seizure in the eyes of
some, was rescued and made ready to move with the column.[49]
Of men, only a few near-by stragglers could be found. The Federals, strong or weak, had disappeared. Nothing was to be gained,

    [48] O. R., 11, pt. 1, p. 1038; Beale, 18; G. W. Beale, 27; 1 von Borcke. 39; H. B.
McClellan, 57.
    [49] Cf. Wearing of the Gray. 181

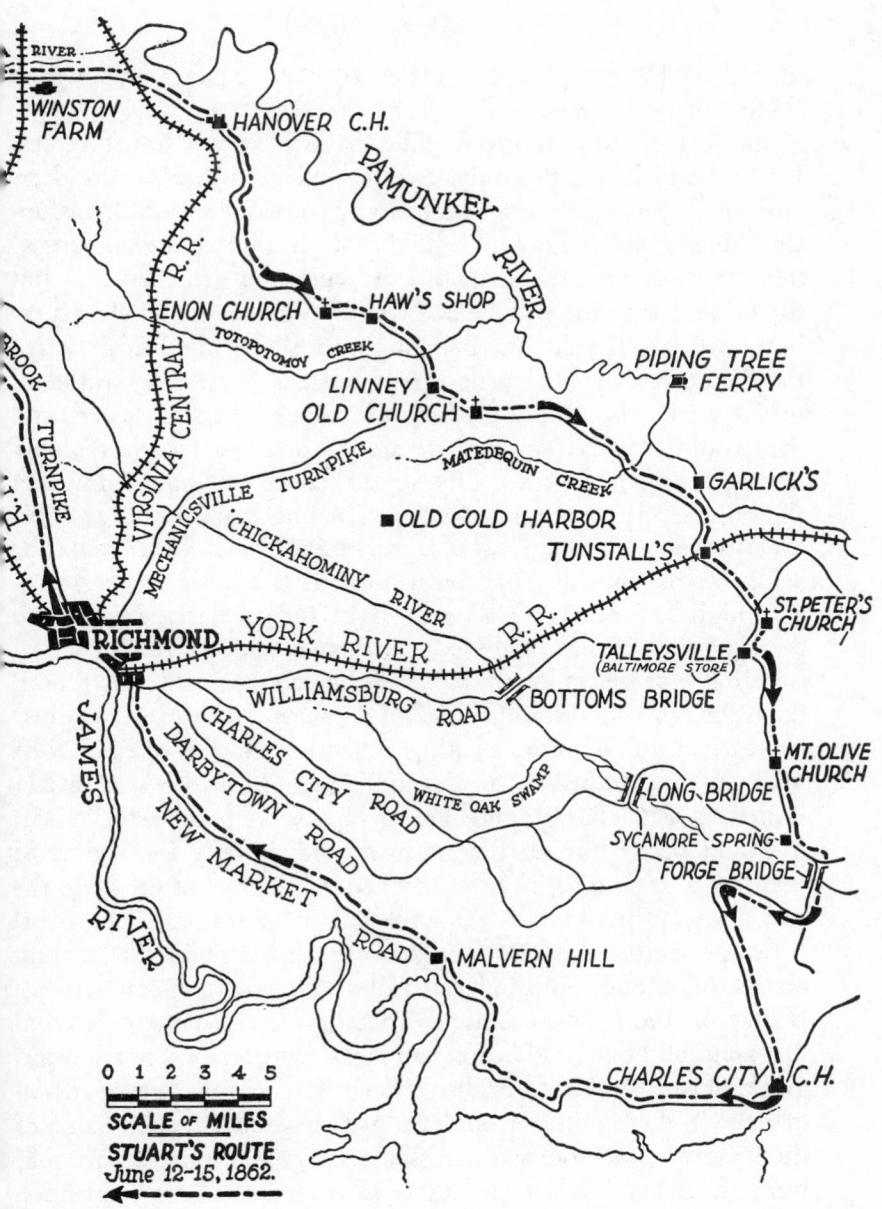

Route of Stuart's "Ride around McClellan" (Chickahominy Raid), June 12–15, 1862. After *H. B. McClellan.* The sketch that accompanied Stuart's report, as reproduced in *O. R. Atlas*, Plate XXI-9, is untrustworthy.

of course, by pursuing them toward their main force, which could not be far distant.[50]

Stuart was now fourteen miles from Hanover Court House He had established the main fact he had been directed to ascertain: there was no Federal force of any consequence on the watershed down which he had ridden. Of that he could be sure in the report he made General Lee when he returned . . . but should he return the way he had come? The enemy would expect him to do so. If alert, the Federals would burn the bridge across the Totopotomoy. In event they neglected that, they would of course watch the route by which the column had advanced, and they could waylay the Confederates at or near Hanover Court House, to which the most direct road led. Stuart could not skirt the village and strike for the South Anna, in an effort to cross that stream and swing back to Richmond on a wide arc. The bridge across the river had been burned; the fords were impassably high.[51] So Stuart reasoned. If he turned back, danger and perhaps disaster, he concluded speedily, would be his.

Perhaps, at the moment, or when he came to write his report, Stuart magnified the difficulties of a march to the rear, because he yearned for the more exciting adventure that lay ahead. Nine miles to the Southeast was Tunstall's Station on the York River Railroad, McClellan's main line of supply. A great achievement it would be to tear up that railway and, if only for a day, or even for a few hours, to have the Federal Army cut off from the base at the White House. How the public would praise that feat!

Escape from Tunstall's would not be impossible. By turning South there, and riding eleven miles, Stuart could reach Forge Bridge on the Chickahominy. That crossing, his troopers from the neighborhood told him, had been burned but not beyond quick repair. At Forge Bridge, moreover, there was every reason to believe the column would be well beyond the left flank of the enemy. Once he was across the Chickahominy, Stuart told himself, General Lee could make a diversion that would keep the enemy from dispatching a sufficient force to trap the returning column.

Was the whole plan feasible? Did it hang together? When

---

[50] *O. R.*, 11, pt. 1, p. 1038, for the condition of the camp.
[51] *H. B. McClellan.* 58; *O. R.*, 11. pt. 1, p. 1038.

the expedition had been planned, Stuart had suggested that the cavalry might ride entirely around the enemy: why not prove himself correct? Would the Federals have along the railroad sufficient infantry to destroy him? Could Union troops be sent down the railroad in time to intercept him? Cavalry he could beat off, but a heavy column of infantry . . . well, it was certain that the enemy would not expect him to do what he was contemplating. That was an excellent reason for doing it. Besides, whatever the risk, there was a chance of striking terror into the heart of "a boastful and insolent foe." [52] He would do it!

There was not a shadow of misgiving on his face.[53] Nor, when he found that his Colonels doubted the wisdom of his choice of routes,[54] was there any hesitation. Their misgiving hardened his resolution. He thanked them for their ready promise to go on, if he saw fit to do so, and he prepared to start forthwith. Ostentatiously he inquired of the farmers around Old Church which road he should take to Hanover Court House, and how far it was. Quietly he picked his guides from soldiers who resided in the country he was to enter. Over them he placed R. E. Frayser, who knew every bypath to Tunstall's.[55] Then, turning to John Esten Cooke, he said: "Tell Fitz Lee to come along. I'm going to move on with my column."

"I think," Cooke replied laughingly, "the quicker we move now the better."

"Right! Tell the column to move on with a trot." [56]

Stuart touched the flank of his horse and was off. He was relishing every moment of the drama he was shaping. "There was something of the sublime," he later wrote, "in the implicit confidence and unquestioning trust of the rank and file in a leader guiding them straight, apparently, into the very jaws of the enemy, every step appearing to them to diminish the faintest hope of extrication." [57]

The road of this adventure skirted the Pamunkey River. Southward, the country was populous. To the North and Northeast were great plantations that ran down to the meadows and swamps by the streamside. As the column passed, the women,

52 The words are Stuart's own. *O. R.*, 11, pt. 1, p. 1038.
53 *H. B. McClellan*, 58.
54 *O. R.*, 11, pt. 1, p. 1038.   55 *H. B. McClellan*, 62.
56 *Wearing of the Gray*. 179.   57 *O. R.*, 11, pt. 1, p. 1048.

the girls and the old men at every house came out to greet the first gray-clad soldiers they had seen in weeks. Now and again there would be a delighted scream of recognition, whereupon some dust-covered boy would break ranks, would leap from his horse and embrace mother or sister.[58]

None of these jubilant residents knew much concerning the enemy's strength or position. Vessels were known to be at Garlick's Landing; wagon trains passed frequently; a guard was on the railroad at Tunstall's. That was all the information Stuart could get.[59] Once, at a great distance to the Southwest, tents could be seen. It was surmised that they were McClellan's headquarters.[60] A strange and thrilling experience it was, surely, to look on the opposing commander's lodging place from his own rear!

At Tignor's house, two miles and a little more from Old Church, Frayser turned out of the road that led East to Piping Tree Ferry, and took the right fork toward Tunstall's Station. Weary though the men were, they straightened up expectantly: the New Kent boys explained that the column was getting closer to the point where the enemy must be waiting. Stuart turned ere long to Cooke: "Tell Colonel Martin," said he, "to have his artillery ready, and look out for an attack at any moment." The staff officer hurried back, delivered his message to the commander of the rearguard, and was returning to the front, when a cry was raised: "Yankees in the rear!" Swords instantly were gripped tightly. In a moment there was relieved laughter. Some one had attempted a joke. The men slumped back in their saddles, but not too comfortably. Next time the alarm might not be false.[61]

At length, the weary horses brought their tired riders to Wynne's Shop and Hopewell Church, whence a road led two miles East to Garlick's Landing. Satisfied that stores were there under scant guard, Stuart detached two squadrons to swoop down on the place, to bring off any horses they might find, and to apply the torch to what could not be moved off. The main column continued on its way. Its road now showed evidence of heavy travel and of vast alarm. Overturned wagons and booty

[58] G. W. Beale, 28; Wearing of the Gray, 181. [59] O. R., 11, pt. 1, p. 1038.
[60] 1 von Borcke, 40. [61] Wearing of the Gray, 180.

of all sorts lay temptingly at hand, where it had been left or thrown away by Federals who had been warned that "the rebels" were descending upon them. Perhaps, at Tunstall's, which now was distant only two miles, the enemy might be squarely across the front of advance.

Stuart accordingly sought to close the column and to bring the artillery to the front. Breathed was most willing, but, at the moment, he was engaged with a foe distinctly his own. Both the rifle and the howitzer were in mud from which all the lashing of the teams and all the tugging and swearing of the gunners could not extricate them. Ankle-deep in the hole, the fieldpieces seemed in fixed position. Further pulling at them settled them more deeply.

"Gott, Lieutenant," said a sergeant of German stock, "it can't be done!"

Then he eyed the ambulance which, with its treasured keg of liquor, had been captured in the camp at Old Church. "But," the sergeant added, "yust put dat keg on der gun, Lieutenant, und tell the men they can have it if only they vill pull through!"

Lt. William McGregor thought the experiment worth trying, so, with a laugh, he had the keg placed on the gun. In a moment, the gunners sprang into the knee-deep mud and, with one mighty effort, lifted the piece to dry ground.[62] The other gun the artillerists handled in the same way.

They had their reward, but they missed the excitement. While they were wrestling with the pieces, before the sergeant made his proposal, Frayser dashed up to Stuart from the direction of Tunstall's Station, which the head of the column was approaching. The scout reported that one or two companies of Federal infantry were guarding the station and that the commander of these troops had seen and greeted him, in broad Germanic accent, with the odd challenge, "Koom yay!" as if he hoped Frayser would ride into the lines and surrender. Stuart did not take time to laugh at this. Swiftly he advanced the head of the column within striking distance and then ordered: "Form platoons! Draw saber! Charge!"[63]

Down swept the cavalry at a thunderous gallop. The Federals, too few to resist, scattered almost instantly. Some were

---

62 *Wearing of the Gray*, 181–82.   63 *Wearing of the Gray*, 182.

captured. Others fled to the woods. Immediately, designated Confederates began to tear up the railroad in the delighted knowledge that, if they succeeded, they would separate the Federal Army from its base. Redmond Burke hurried off to set fire to the bridge across Black Creek. His fellow scouts proceeded to chop down the two telegraph poles nearest the station. The excited troopers who were ordered to remain in their saddles watched and yearned to search the countryside for prisoners and abandoned wagons for booty. It was a high moment—perhaps the most triumphant the cavalry had known since the time when the earliest volunteers had galloped across the fields that bordered Bull Run.

Now, above the chatter of the troopers and the sound of the axes on the telegraph poles, there came a shrill whistle from the westward. A train was approaching—did it bring infantry to oppose the raiders? From the boldness of the whistle blast, the engineer could not know that Tunstall's was in the hands of the Confederates. Derail the train, then; shoot or capture the troops on it. Quickly the orders were given. Lieutenant Robins ran to a near-by switch and tried to throw it, so that the train would run into the siding, but he had no success in hammering at the heavy lock.[64] Such obstructions as near-by men could find at the moment they hurled on the track. The troopers in ranks were hurried into ambush alongside the railway to open fire if the train stopped or left the track when it hit the obstructions.

All this was swift work, not well done. Before the slowest of the cavalrymen could get to cover, the train came in sight—a locomotive and a string of flatcars loaded with soldiers. Almost immediately, the brakes began to squeak. Was the engineer going to make a regular stop at the station or had he seen the obstructions? Slower still the train. A few of its passengers stepped off as if they knew it would remain at Tunstall long enough for them to stretch their legs or to find water.[65] Then, nervously, one excited trooper in ambush fired his pistol.[66] The engineer heard it, perhaps sensed danger and immediately put on full steam. All along the right of way, Southerners' pistols rang out. Startled Federals on the train dropped from wounds or threw

[64] O. R., 11, pt. 1, p. 1044.   [65] G. W. Beale, 28.   [66] G. W. Beale, 29.

themselves face down on the flatcars to escape the fire. Will Farley seized Heros von Borcke's rifle, spurred his horse till it caught up with the locomotive and, at a gallop, shot the engineer.[67] The train continued on its way, fast and faster. A moment more, and it was out of range.[68] Very different the story might have been if only the artillery had been near the head of the column. Now that the train had escaped them, there was nothing for the disappointed troopers to do except to round up the men who had fled from the station or had jumped from the train.[69]

Stuart, for his part, had to make another decision: should he continue on his way, cross the Chickahominy and make for his own lines, or should he rush down the railroad and attempt to capture the Federal base at the White House? A vast prize that was, distant a bare four miles. If it could be destroyed, McClellan would be compelled to retreat. The world would resound with praise for the leader of 1200 men who had forced 100,000 to break off an attempted siege of Richmond. Such a prospect was alluring, but was it not an enticement? A start could not be made until the arrival of the two squadrons that had been sent to Garlick's Landing. Billowing, high-mounting smoke from that direction[70] showed that those troopers had reached their objective. They probably had escaped, but some time might elapse before they rejoined. Every moment that passed after the arrival of the train at White House would be devoted to preparation for defense by a garrison that might be considerable. If it put up a good fight, reinforcements from McClellan's front might come down the railroad and close the Confederates' line of retreat. Regretfully, then, but decisively, Stuart shut his mind to this highest adventure of all.[71]

It was now close to nightfall, but not too dark to observe that

[67] I *von Borcke*, 42.

[68] *O. R.*, 11, pt. 1, p. 1039; *Wearing of the Gray*, 182.

[69] The Federals reported the casualties on the train as two killed and eight wounded. *O. R.*, 11, pt. 1, p. 1032. No estimate was made of those captured at the station.

[70] *Wearing of the Gray*, 181.

[71] H. B. *McClellan*, 61. Cooke, in *Wearing of the Gray*, 183, recorded that Stuart confided he "scarcely could resist" the temptation to attack the White House. Stuart's report, which was intended for early publication, prudently contained no reference to this aspect of the raid, doubtless because Stuart thought he subsequently might snatch the prize of the White House base.

many army wagons with deserted teams were standing around the station. Some of the vehicles had been in plain sight from the moment the column had arrived. A larger, tangled park was at a little distance. As rapidly as might be, the mules were unhitched. Then the wagons, which were loaded with grain and coffee, were set afire. While this was being done, something more than an hour after the train had passed, the squadrons from Garlick's Landing arrived. Their commander, Capt. O. M. Knight, reported that he had destroyed two schooners and many wagons loaded with fodder.[72] Not to be outdone by this feat, the rearguard, when it closed, presented the General with twenty-five prisoners who had surrendered in the belief that they were surrounded.[73]

As the bogged guns also had come up, without any evidence on the part of the gunners that the liquor in the keg had been too abundant, the column started at once for the Chickahominy. Stuart had no additional report of pursuit but he knew, of course, that the reflection of the fires and the report of the escaped trainmen and passengers would bring quickly toward Tunstall's Station a powerful force. He had reasoned at Old Church that the worst of his danger would be behind him after he passed Tunstall's.[74] Now it did not seem so probable that retreat and return would be unmolested.

As the column wound southeastward to the vicinity of old St. Peter's Church, and then turned southward to Talleysville,[75] the road grew worse.[76] When Talleysville was reached by the vanguard at 8.30, a Federal hospital of 150 patients was found. Stuart did not molest it or disturb the surgeons and attendants. Close by, a well-stocked sutler's store naturally did not fare so well—fared so ill, in fact, that its entire contents were taken and devoured, to the distress of some who ate too much as surely as to the grief of the sutler, who lost all.[77]

A bright moon now had risen, one day past the full, and lighted

[72] O. R., 11, pt. 1, p. 1038; G. W. Beale, 28. One schooner got off before the raiders could seize it. The Confederates estimated the number of burned wagons at seventy-five, the Federals at thirty. O. R., 11, pt. 1, pp. 1033, 1034.

[73] O. R., 11, pt. 1, pp. 1038, 1045.

[74] O. R., 11, pt. 1, p. 1038.

[75] Also known as Baltimore Store, distant by road from Tunstall's Station three miles.

[76] O. R., 11, pt. 1, p. 1039.

[77] G. W. Beale. 28–29; Wearing of the Gray, 184.

the bad road,[78] but the column was strung out almost back to Tunstall's. It had to be closed again. Midnight came before the exhausted artillery horses dragged the pieces to Talleysville.[79] From that point, the distance to Forge Bridge on the Chickahominy was less than seven miles. With good fortune, it could be negotiated before daylight. To expedite the march, which must be rapid if the column was to escape, the 165 prisoners were mounted on such of the captured animals[80] as were not required for the troopers whose horses had broken down. By putting two prisoners on each of the fresh Federal mules, Stuart saved the time that would have been lost had any of the captives been afoot.

Long as each minute seemed, the night was almost ended. If all went well, the winding, marshy river soon would lie between the Confederates and their pursuers. Lt. Jonas Christian, who lived at Sycamore Springs on the bank of the Chickahominy, told his commander that he knew a blind ford on the plantation that was nearer than Forge Bridge. The columns could slip across at that ford and would not waste precious hours putting timbers in place on the site of the destroyed bridge. Should the Federals be near, they scarcely would learn of this plantation crossing and would press on to Forge Bridge.[81]

Hopeful as was the outlook, the ride from Talleysville to the river was the hardest part of the long, long march. The Ninth Virginia, in advance, became separated from the First and made Stuart acutely anxious for a few minutes.[82] When he relaxed after finding that the Ninth was ahead, he became so sleepy that he, the tireless man who never knew exhaustion, put one knee over the pommel of the saddle and nodded often. Sometimes he lurched so far that John Esten Cooke had to ride closely by his side to keep him from falling off.[83] Like Stuart, the whole col-

---

[78] Stuart stated in his report, *O. R.*, 11, pt. 1, p. 1039, that the moon was visible on the ride from Tunstall's Station to Talleysville, but as the moon did not rise that evening until 8.56, he either was not near the head of the column or else he was in error when he fixed at 8.30 the hour of the arrival of the van at Talleysville.

[79] *O. R.*, 11, pt. 1, p. 1039.   [80] *O. R.*, 11, pt. 1, p. 1039.

[81] Cf. *H. B. McClellan*, 62.

[82] Cooke, *op. cit.*, 183–84, was almost certainly wrong in stating that this happened between Tunstall's and Talleysville, because, if Stuart is correct in saying that Talleysville was reached at 8.30, darkness scarcely had fallen at that time. The whole point of Cooke's incident is that Stuart thought "Rooney" Lee and his regiment might be lost in the darkness.

[83] *Wearing of the Gray*, 186.

umn dragged. Troopers snatched sleep, horses staggered. Fortunately, there was no alarm. If Federals were in pursuit, the rearguard caught no glimpse of them.

The moon was just being dimmed by a faint light in the East when Jonas Christian turned from the main road into the lane of Sycamore Springs, and led the head of the Ninth Regiment past the house and down toward the blind ford. An hour more and, with the stream behind the rearguard, a halt could be called and some rest could be given men and mounts. In a double sense, day was dawning. Presently young Christian halted in startled surprise. He was at the ford, but it had a different appearance from the easy crossing he had known all his life. In front of him was a wide, swift and evil-looking stream that extended far beyond its banks.[84] The placid Chickahominy was an angry torrent, the ford might be a death trap. Col. "Rooney" Lee, the first officer of rank to arrive at Sycamore Springs, stripped quickly and swam into the stream to test it. Strong and powerful though he was, he had to battle to escape being drowned or swept downstream.

"What do you think of the situation, Colonel?" John Esten Cooke asked when the Colonel pulled himself ashore.

"Well, Captain," replied the half-exhausted swimmer, with all the courtesy of his stock, "I think we are caught."

That was the feeling of the soldiers. The jig was up! Some of the boys, reconciled to the worst, merely stretched out on the ground. They were too weary to stand, but almost intuitively, they held their bridle reins over their arms, in order to be ready were an alarm sounded. Other exhausted cavalrymen[85] sat glumly on the ground and ate the remnants of what they had grabbed at Talleysville from the sutler's store. Gloom was written darkly on the face of all of them.[86]

At that moment Stuart rode down to the ford. He had little to say. Carefully he surveyed the stream from the vantage point of his horse's back. Then he stroked his beard with a peculiar twist that his staff officers noticed he never employed except when he was anxious.[87] He looked dangerous—just that. Silently

[84] H. B. McClellan, 63.

[85] It might be noted that the Confederates spelt and usually pronounced cavalryman as two distinct words.

[86] Wearing of the Gray, 186–87.   [87] Ibid.; H. B. McClellan, 64.

he observed while young George Beale, son of the Lieutenant Colonel of the Ninth, went into the water, and swam across with his father's steed, which he tied on the opposite bank. Then young Beale did the same thing with his own mount, an animal he had caught the previous day after his horse had run off. The boy was an excellent swimmer and he got over, as did the captured animal, but when Beale started back to the shore where the troopers were waiting, the horse insisted on coming back with him.[88]

Encouraged by this success, the most experienced swimmers began in the same way to cross the river with their horses, but only a few of the men had enough skill in the water to breast so wrathful a stream. Stuart continued silently to watch. Presently the General summoned Turner Doswell and asked that daring courier if he thought he could reach the other side. When Doswell said he could, Stuart gave him a dispatch for General Lee. Doswell must ride hard, because the dispatch was a request to the commanding General to make a diversion that would keep the Federals from attempting to intercept the column on its return. It would return. Of that Stuart was certain; of the means, he was not.

Axes were sent for. Trees were felled in the hope that the men might clamber over them. The trees crashed in the desired direction, but they were too short to bridge the swollen stream. Thereupon, mustering their ingenuity, some of the men tried to made a crude ferry. They strung bridle reins and halters together to serve in place of a rope and, from fence rails, they made a raft. This floated so promisingly that some of the men put their belongings on it and ventured with it into the water. It tipped promptly and dropped its cargo.[89]

Time was passing. The summer sun was up. A rumor was afloat that Federal infantry in large force were close at hand. Stuart decided that his one hope of escaping was to patch together a crude bridge. He directed the men who already had swum to the right bank—some thirty-five they were—to make their way downstream under Lt. Col. R. L. Beale. The main body, with a brief command, he ordered to the site of Forge Bridge.[90] This

---

[88] G. W. Beale, 30.   [89] G. W. Beale, 30.
[90] Beale, 20–21; G. W. Beale, 30; H. B. McClellan, 64.

familiar crossing of the Chickahominy, one mile below Sycamore Springs, was on the road from Providence Forge to Charles
City Court House. From the north bank, a narrow stream of
considerable depth led to an island. Beyond this island was the
south channel, spanned in normal times by a second bridge. At
the western end of the island, above this bridge, was a swampy
ford which could be used in emergency.

All Stuart's information had been that the main bridge across
the north channel was destroyed but that enough remained to
make possible a reconstruction of the span.[91] He found conditions precisely as described. The stream was swift but the channel was narrower than at the Sycamore Springs ford. Stone
abutments on either side were intact. Stuart at once threw out
videttes, posted his artillery and entrusted to Redmond Burke, as
resourceful as dauntless, the task of building a bridge. Burke
went instantly to work in the knowledge that delay might mean
disaster, perhaps the destruction of the whole force. A skiff was
found on the bank and was moored unsteadily in midstream by
a rope tied to a tree. From a large abandoned warehouse near
at hand, boards were stripped. Troopers and prisoners hustled
several of these to the bank, placed the ends aboard the skiff, as
if it were a pontoon, and in that way made a narrow if treacher-
ously unstable bridge. Across this, one by one, troopers made
their way. With their right arms they carried their saddles and
with the left they held the rein of horses that swam on the
downstream side of the bridge.

This soon proved too slow a procedure, and, besides, it would
not permit of the passage of the guns. Burke accordingly decided
to try the one expedient left him—to secure the main timbers
of the warehouse and to see if they were long enough to span
the river from the abutments. Battering-rams knocked down the
frame of the structure. Tired men shouldered the old uprights
and brought them to the streamside. From the skiff, with much
effort, they were pushed across and then were lifted up toward
the abutments. Stuart watched all the while and counselled with
calm cheer. Ere long, the dangerous look faded from his face.
He began to hum a tune. His eye told him the timbers were
long enough, but even he must have held his breath when, with

[91] O. R., 11, pt. 1, p. 1039.

a final "pull together" the long beam was set. It rested safely on both banks, but with few inches to spare.

A shout went up from the men. They could save the guns! Quickly the bridge was floored. Over it, in renewed strength, the men made their way. Undamaged, the rifle and the howitzer lumbered across. The rearguard was drawn in. Fitz Lee, listening and watching the road, left five men to fire the bridge and then he, too, crossed to the island. By the time the rear of the column had passed out of sight, the flames were crackling. Then —as if to add the perfect dramatic touch to the climax—a little knot of Federal lancers appeared on the north bank and opened fire. The margin of escape from a clash with this contingent was ten minutes.[92] Time consumed in building the bridge was three hours.[93]

Now on the island, the Confederate cavalry found that the ford from the western end to the south bank of the Chickahominy was difficult but not impracticable. Horses might flounder through the successive swamps but, with luck, they and even the guns could pass. The prisoners went across first, and a most unhappy time they had. Again and again a mule, with two bluecoats astride him, would lose his footing and, in scrambling to recover it, would jettison his riders. The Confederate guard would laugh; the prisoners would swear. One of them, entangled in a third swamp, exploded violently: "How many damned Chicken-hominies are there, I wonder, in this infernal country!" [94]

Downstream, meantime, Lieutenant Colonel Beale, early on the ground, had rebuilt a bridge, but the column did not know of this easy crossing until one of the limbers had been caught hopelessly in the swampy ford above. Had the artillery been sent down the island to Beale's bridge, Stuart might have been able to report that, except for the death of Captain Latané, and the runaway of a few horses which he had replaced five for one, he had sustained no casualties and had lost nothing entrusted to him.[95]

When on the right bank of the Chickahominy at last, Stuart was thirty-five miles from Richmond. Twenty miles of this dis-

92 O. R., 11, pt. 1, pp. 1017, 1039; H. B. McClellan, 65; Wearing of the Gray, 187.
93 O. R., 11, pt. 1, p. 1039.
94 Wearing of the Gray, 188–89.
95 Beale, 21; Wearing of the Gray, 189; G. W. Beale, 31; O. R., 11, pt. 1, p. 1039.

tance was East of the left flank of the enemy.[96] The return meant tedious riding for the troopers and more suffering for their worn horses, but it was nothing compared with what had been endured on the other side of the river. Stuart himself turned over the command to Fitz Lee, and hurried on to report. He rested for two hours at Thomas Christian's, then rode on to Judge Isaac Christian's plantation near Charles City Court House, stopped again for a cup of coffee at Rowland's Mill and, on the morning of June 15, forty-eight hours from the time he had left the Winston Farm at the beginning of the ride, reported to General Lee.[97] The column moved more slowly from the river to Buckland, the seat of Col. J. M. Wilcox, and arrived in Richmond on the 16th, to receive a conqueror's welcome.[98]

In the eyes of a jubilant city and an applauding South, the glamour of Stuart's exploit was not dimmed by the enemy's incredible slowness and lack of organization in pursuit. First news of the raid had been received at Federal cavalry headquarters in rumors of a direct attack on the camps. Countermoves were complicated by the insistence of a cavalry Lieutenant that he had seen not less than seven regiments of infantry with Stuart. The commander of the cavalry reserve, Gen. Philip St. George Cooke, whose service Virginia had coveted a year previously, proved himself utterly incapable of grasping his military problem or of acting promptly.[99] There was no pursuit directly from Old Church. The first Federals to reach Tunstall's were infantry who arrived at midnight on the 13th–14th, when Stuart was leaving Talleysville. Union cavalry did not get to Tunstall's until 2 A.M.[100] The party that pushed on to Forge Bridge, ten minutes after the crossing of the Confederate rearguard, consisted of only eight men under Maj. Robert Morris of the 6th Pennsylvania Cavalry.[101]

Although none of these circumstances was known, the Confederacy rejoiced that Stuart the son-in-law had outwitted Cooke the father-in-law. Honors were heaped upon the man who had "ridden around McClellan." Governor Letcher, to whom Stuart

96 H. B. McClellan, 65.　　　　　　　97 H. B. McClellan, 66.
98 G. W. Beale, 31.
99 Cf. O. R., 11, pt. 1, pp. 1006, 1008, 1010 ff.
100 O. R., 11. pt. 1, pp. 1014, 1024.　　　101 O. R., 11, pt. 1, p. 1017.

had sent a verbal report while he hastened personally to General Lee, rewarded him with a sword.[102] A few days after the expedition, when Stuart rode in to see the Governor, a crowd gathered in front of the Executive Mansion and demanded a speech. Stuart duly appeared "and acknowledged the compliment paid him in a few remarks full of spirit and good cheer." He told the crowd that "he had been to the Chickahominy to visit some of his old friends of the United States Army, but they, very uncivilly, turned their backs upon him." The early chronicler of this incident added: "Seeing a manifest desire on the part of the people to make for him an ovation, the General then mounted his charger and galloped off amid the shouts of the crowd, which by this time had increased to more than a thousand persons." [103] In his own congratulatory order to the command, Stuart spoke of himself as "the general of cavalry," [104] and in his formal report, written two days after his return, he minimized nothing of his own achievement; but, in an accompanying letter to Lee, he listed those of his subordinates who had most distinguished themselves and he urged their promotion.[105] The immediate reply of the commanding General was an order in which he took "great pleasure in expressing his admiration of the courage and skill so conspicuously exhibited throughout by the general and the officers and men under his command." [106] Stuart's satisfaction was as boyish as his feat had been extraordinary. Whether the raid was well conceived by Lee--whether it did or did not put McClellan on guard for the security of his right flank—is a question much disputed.[107] That the whole was flawlessly executed, none would dispute. Stuart became the hero of his troopers and one of the idols of the public. Lee's confidence in him and his confidence in himself were confirmed. What was not less important, the cavalry was shown to be as trustworthy as the infantry.[108]

"That was a tight place at the river, General," John Esten

102 H. B. McClellan, 67.   103 Southern Generals, 363.
104 O. R., 11, pt. 1, p. 1041.   105 O. R., 11, pt. 1, p. 1041.
106 O. R., 11, pt. 1, p. 1042.
107 See Alexander, 113–14; Thomason, 153–55.
108 Cf. H. B. McClellan, 67: "Aside from these strategic considerations the influence of this expedition on the morale not only of the cavalry but of the whole army was most important."

Cooke said to Stuart when it was all over. "If the enemy had come down on us, you would have been compelled to have surrendered."

"No," answered Stuart, "one other course was left."

"What was that?"

"To die game." [109]

[109] *Wearing of the Gray*, 180. For the continuance of the sketch of Stuart, see *intra* p. 633.

CHAPTER XXI

GENERAL AND DEACON JACKSON AT ODDS

"JACKSON is coming!" [1] Within a few days after Stuart had returned from his ride around McClellan, that was the rumor. "Jackson is coming to reinforce Lee." The possibility, credited by some and by others disputed, was itself enough to raise public hope and to restore to the threatened capital some of the lost confidence of 1861. Magic had become associated with the name of Jackson during the four months since his threatened resignation—magic and the victory that fervent Southerners had argued so often would follow a daring offensive. Through successive revaluations he had passed. In February, a few had appraised him as an able soldier, but some of his officers and many of his troops thought him eccentric, if not insane. Ministers and zealous church members had been those, and those only, who held him up as a model. Now, after a dazzling campaign, "Stonewall" was the new hero of the war. His rise had been as rapid as that of Beauregard the previous year, and it promised to be more enduring.

General Jackson had not lacked resentment of Benjamin's orders for the recall of Loring from Romney, nor had he yielded with meekness to those who urged him to make sacrifices of pride for his country's good. Once, at least, he had answered those friends with vehemence: "Sacrifices! Have I not made them? What is my life here but a daily sacrifice? Nor shall I ever withhold sacrifices for my country where they avail anything. I intend to serve her anywhere, in any way in which I am permitted to do it with effect, even if it be as a private soldier. But if this method of making war is to prevail, which they seek to establish in my case, the country is ruined. My duty to her requires that I shall utter my protest against it in the most energetic form in my power, and that is to resign." Only

[1] 1 *R. W. C. D.*, 135; T. R. R. Cobb in 28 *S. H. S. P.*, 293; J. D. McCabe, Jr., *Life and Campaigns of General Robert E. Lee* (cited hereafter as *McCabe*), 122 and n; *Richmond Dispatch*, July 9, 1862, p. 2, col. 1.

when he was told that he personally was invaluable did his Christian humility of spirit show itself: "No, no, you greatly overestimate my capacity for usefulness. A better man will soon be sent to take my place. The government have no confidence in my capacity, or they would not thus countermand my orders, and throw away the fruits of victory that have been secured at such a sacrifice of the comfort of my noble troops in their hurried march through the storm of snow and sleet. No, sir, I must resign and give my place to someone in whom they have more confidence." [2]

Among some of his officers there had been little doubt that he would adhere to this decision. Regret at losing him was coupled with resentment against Loring. Said the redoubtable Maj. John A. Harman: "Loring is like a scared turkey and so is his command." Again, on February 6, Harman noted, "Loring's command has been dropping in [to Winchester] all day, a terribly disorganized band," and, still again, "Loring's advent into the Valley broke up the efficiency of the whole army." [3]

After Jackson at length had agreed to permit his resignation to be withdrawn, he talked no more about the episode [4] and from his headquarters in Winchester discharged his duties as if there had been no friction with the War Department. Drill and discipline remained his military gospel. Daily he was at his desk in his office; daily he insisted that the officers of the general staff report to him. [5] He rode and inspected and studied ground, and then, when every task of the day had been performed, he joined his wife, who had come to Winchester to spend the winter. Her visit to him at Manassas the previous summer scarcely could have been a success. He had been able at that time to arrange for entertainment sermons only, and a tour of the battlefield, where the dead horses still were unburied. [6] Now everything was agreeable. He had a place for her in the home of an able minister whose sympathetic, intelligent wife had pleasant patrician friends, with handsome homes and good cooks.

[2] *Mrs. Jackson,* 232, 233. It is possible that this is a variant of the remark of Jackson to Graham cited *supra,* Chapter X, p. 128.

[3] MS. letters of Maj. J. A. Harman, Feb. 2, 3, 6, 9 and 28, 1861: copies in the *Hotchkiss Papers* (cited hereafter as *Harman MSS.*).

[4] R. L. Dabney, *Life and Campaigns of Lieut. Gen. Thomas J. Jackson* (cited hereafter as *Dabney*), 282.

[5] 19 *S. H. S. P.,* 155; 43 *ibid.,* 61.   [6] *Mrs. Jackson,* 190.

In this company, there was little except his old uniform coat and his bronzed face to identify Jackson as the flaming "Stone-wall" of Manassas. His blue eyes, always direct and penetrating in gaze,[7] seemed to soften; his voice was gentler than ever. Per-haps, in the light of a shaded lamp, his martial beard and his thin lips were less pronounced features than his tall forehead—a poet's forehead, one keen observer said.[8] He delighted in the company of gentle old ladies and of serious ministers.[9] Spiritual more than martial discourse seemed to delight him. That evening at Manassas, whither his own pastor had come to conduct a revival, had he not risen from his knees after the delivery of a fervent prayer, to inquire, "Doctor, I would be glad to learn more fully than I have yet done what your views are of the prayer of faith?"[10] At Winchester, when military duty permitted, did he not bear his full share in the exchange of religious experience and in the discussion of theology? He was not reserved of speech, either, or stumbling in expression. Skillful he was in dialectic and resourceful, too. If the argument over religion grew complicated, he would "recur to some premise which others had overlooked," and from it proceed "by a short and convincing direction, to his own conclusion."[11] Occasionally at such times he aimed a keen question, but usually his manner was one of calm dignity. In repose or in social conversation, his expression was tender,[12] and mild his manner. The pleasure he found in domestic life was almost pathetic. High among his joys was that of bringing downstairs on his back every morning the small-est son of the house.[13] Such a man scarcely seemed capable of doing battle. His delight was in the law of the Lord.

So pleasant a life—in a manse and among devout Presbyterians —could not last long for the commander of what was, in reality, an outpost town. Jackson's little force of 4600 men covered the left flank of the Confederate Army at Manassas and confronted directly a foe who gradually had assembled almost 38,000 troops north of the Potomac.[14] Of Johnston's prospective withdrawal from Manassas, Jackson was kept informed, but he was loath to leave the lower Valley. In soldierly tone, as he acknowledged

[7] 19 *S. H. S. P.*, 302.
[9] *Ibid.*
[11] 1 *Land We Love*, 310.
[13] *Mrs. Jackson*, 237.
[8] *Wearing of the Gray*, 48.
[10] *Mrs. Jackson*, 199.
[12] *Ibid.*, and *Mrs. Jackson*, 199.
[14] 1 *Henderson*, 214.

orders to conform to Johnston's movement, he did not minimize the task of interposing between the main Confederate Army and the Federals who would be certain to follow him up the Valley. "If," he wrote Johnston, "you will examine the roads leading from the valley across the Blue Ridge you will see the difficulty of keeping between you and the enemy and at the same time opposing his advance along the valley." [15] Jackson's hope was that Johnston would reinforce him and relieve him of the responsibility of guarding the passes of the mountains. He wished above all to be free to manœuvre. "If," he explained to Johnston, "we cannot be successful in defeating the enemy should he advance, a kind Providence may enable us to inflict a terrible wound and effect a safe retreat in the event of having to fall back." [16] That was to be the basis of Jackson's offensive-defensive strategy.

Unwillingly, on March 11, he left Winchester and started southward. With his troops went every item of equipment and every pound of their supplies.[17] In the first confused stage of the advance of the Federals, then under Maj. Gen. Nathaniel P. Banks, the plan of Jackson was to turn on his pursuer and to deliver a swift night attack. When Jackson discovered that a blunder in logistics had been made and that his columns had been sent farther than he had intended they should go that first day, he was furious. For some reason he blamed the mistake on a conference he had called to prepare for the night attack: "That is the last council of war I will ever hold!" It was.[18]

Falling back first to Strasburg and then to Mount Jackson, forty-two miles South of Winchester, "Stonewall" established his camps and, as he watched the enemy, vigilantly prepared his men for the coming test. For the first time, some of the new recruits saw him at close range. A different man he was, in some respects, from the church-going Deacon of the winter, different in apparent interest but still profoundly religious. His life in Winchester had been a New Testament sermon. In the field, he was an Old Testament Joshua. God was Love, but He also was Lord of Hosts and, as such, was to be followed. The Sermon

<hr/>

[15] *O. R.,* 5, 1088, letter of Mch. 3, 1862. Cf. *infra,* p. 332, n. 50.
[16] *O. R.,* 5, 1095.
[17] Commissary General Northrop, supplementing a report on the heavy loss of provisions in the retreat from Manassas (IV *O. R.,* 1, 1038), reported Apr. 11, 1862, that in the withdrawal of Jackson "no stores whatever were lost." (*O. R.,* 51, pt. 2, p. 534.)
[18] Dr. H. H. McGuire, in 1 *Henderson,* 230.

on the Mount did not cancel the Book of Judges or of Kings. Soldiers began to call Jackson "Old Blue Light." Those who had read Thomas Carlyle's *Cromwell* came to wonder, perhaps, if Jackson had in him the qualities of "Old Noll."

Jackson lived in simple quarters. His fare was plain. Corn bread, milk and butter sufficed him. Tobacco he never used. Whiskey he avoided because he thought he might come to like it.[19] Although he was no more than 38 years of age, his men agreed that he was "set in his ways." When he was attending to business in his tent, he was bolt upright on a stool and kept the toes of his boot directly in front of his legs as if that were a disciplinary exercise of mathematical precision.[20] Sometimes he would talk freely, though never brilliantly, of general topics. Again he would remain almost wholly silent. One of his men wrote: "I . . . have seen couriers bring dispatches to him which he would read, write out something, hand it back to them and not open his mouth to speak during the time. I have seen some of his aides and staff officers ride up to him, when he was sitting on the 'Old Sorrel' viewing the country, and tell him something about the lines, or about something of importance, and he would calmly sit there for a few moments, then turn his horse and ride slowly away, his staff following, without his uttering a single word." [21] If he was to answer a military question in the field or at headquarters, he first half-shut his eyes; [22] and when he indulged in a rare laugh, he threw back his head, opened widely his thin-lipped mouth and emitted little or no sound.[23] His reticent conversation in camp was in his habitual soft and restrained voice. If he walked, it was with the long stride of the

[19] 19 *S. H. S. P.*, 315. For reference to Jackson as "Old Blue Light," see Casler, 83, in description of events of March, 1862. The first recorded parallel between Jackson and Cromwell that has come to the writer's eye is that of Sandie Pendleton, *infra*, Vol II.

[20] *Cf.* 9 *S. H. S. P.*, 41.

[21] *Casler*, 128. This may be a suitable point at which to call attention to the unusual value historically of John O. Casler's *Four Years in the Stonewall Brigade* (Guthrie, Okla., 1893). Casler was a private in Co. A, Thirty-third Virginia. He made no pretense to learning or to superlative patriotism, but in an era when old soldiers were writing about the war through the glamour of the years, he was most distinctly a realist. Although his memoirs have no literary merit, they are a corrective of the excessive romanticism that mars the accuracy of most of the books about Jackson's "New Model Army." Without intending to muckrake, and with no proclamation *J'expose*, Casler makes it plain that the Stonewall Brigade had its full contingent of rogues, wreckers and shirkers.

[22] 19 *S. H. S. P.*, 83.

[23] *Ibid.*, 312. Kyd Douglas, *op. cit.*, inferentially disputed this by mentioning several instances when Jackson laughed aloud.

farmer who seeks to cover ground swiftly.[24] When he rode, his stirrups were short [25] and his seat, though secure, was awkward.[26] In the saddle, he held his head high and his chin up, for full vision ahead, though he kept the brim of his weather-beaten cap down over his eyes.[27] Always he wore the same ill-fitting, single-breasted Major's uniform coat that had been a jest to his cadets at V. M. I.[28] In the sun, his brown hair and beard, which showed some curl, took on a shade of auburn. His deep-blue eyes kept their direct gaze. In height he stood close to six feet and was strong and angular, without any surplus flesh.[29] He was slightly deaf in one ear and for that reason sometimes could not determine the direction of distant artillery fire.[30]

The commanding General was in sharp physical contrast to the next man in the esteem of the Army of the Valley—Col. Turner Ashby, head of the cavalry. Ashby, then 38, was the grandson of Capt. "Jack" Ashby, whose fame as a daring soldier of the Revolution had survived in Northern Virginia. After the early death of his father, Turner Ashby and his brothers managed the family farm, Rose Hill, in Fauquier County. Turner sensed in 1859 the approach of war and organized a volunteer cavalry company, to which his reputation as a horseman attracted adventurous young men. When the crisis came, Ashby helped to plan the seizure of Harpers Ferry and immediately took the field. His troop and others from near-by counties speedily were formed into a regiment under Col. Angus W. McDonald, a picturesque old lawyer, capitalist, graduate of West Point and one-time Indian trader.[31] Colonel McDonald knew a fighting man when he saw one and he promptly asked that Ashby be made Lieutenant Colonel. He wrote the Secretary of War: "As to Captain Ashby, I need not speak of his qualities, for already he is known as one of the best partisan leaders in the service. Himself a thorough soldier, he is eminently qualified to com-

[24] Ibid., 302.   [25] 1 N. C. Regts., 763.
[26] So asserted most of those who saw him, though some considered him a good horseman. Cf. An English Combatant, 140–41; D. H. Maury in 25 S. H. S. P., 315.
[27] Cf. An English Combatant, loc. cit.
[28] 19 S. H. S. P., 83; 38 ibid., 283.
[29] Perhaps the best description of Jackson's appearance is that in 19 S. H. S. P., 302.
[30] McHenry Howard, 80.
[31] Colonel McDonald's remarkable career is sketched by Hunter McDonald in Mrs. Cornelia McDonald, A Diary with Reminiscences of the War and Refugee Life in the Shenandoah Valley, 1860–65 (cited hereafter as Mrs. McDonald), 340 ff.

mand." [32] This was on June 25, 1861. The next day, on the Potomac, Turner Ashby's younger brother Richard, while searching for a Northern sympathizer, was ambushed by a hostile patrol and was left for dead. When Turner arrived on the scene, Richard was still alive but bore wounds which indicated that he had been stabbed after he had fallen. From the hour of Richard's death, Turner had one interest only- to make the enemy pay. [33]

In appearance, Turner Ashby was dark, almost swarthy, suggested the popular conception of an Arab. [34] To romantic Southerners he looked as if he had stepped out of a Waverley novel. With fierce mustachios and a beard that a brigand would have envied, he was of middle height and of a frame not apparently robust, though wiry and of astonishing strength. His eyes were dark, deep-set, sad and earnest; [35] and when he spoke it was in a voice as soft as Jackson's. Away from bugles and battle smoke, Turner Ashby's mien was that of a mild, affable and modest gentleman, to whom men and women were equally attracted. Like Stuart, he was rigid though not ostentatious in morals and in speech similarly clean; but, unlike Stuart, he had no banter and probably little humor. Those admirers who always remembered how he looked never recalled anything he said. He spoke best with his sword. His personality and his reputation for successful adventure attracted recruits; [36] he fired the enthusiasm of war correspondents without catering to them. [37] When rheumatism forced the stout-hearted old McDonald to retire, Ashby became Colonel of the cavalry and exercised virtually independent command in the country West of Harpers Ferry.

On Oct. 16, 1861, Ashby determined to attack Federal troops who, as he tersely explained, had "been committing depredations in the vicinity of their camp" [38] on Bolivar Heights in rear

[32] O. R., 2, 954.
[33] Of the numerous and varying accounts of the death of Richard Ashby, the one that bears most of the stamp of accuracy is that in Laurel Brigade, 22 ff.
[34] McHenry Howard, 78.
[35] Mrs. Jackson, op. cit., 216, said they were gray; Cooke, Wearing of the Gray, 71, stated they were of a "deep rich brown"; Colonel McDonald, Laurel Brigade, 30, remembered them as black. McHenry Howard, op. cit., 78, described them as "a dark hazel, perhaps some would call them brown."
[36] O. R., 5, 919.
[37] Richmond Dispatch, Aug. 21, p. 3, col. 1; Aug. 31, p. 1, col. 5; Sept. 24, p. 1, col. 4; Nov. 13, 1861, p. 9, col. 1.
[38] O. R., 5, 247.

of Harpers Ferry. Ashby had a force of not more than 550 men, 300 of whom were militia. Only two guns were at his disposal. One of these was a rifled four-pounder; the other was a twenty-four-pounder, mounted on wagon wheels. The heavy gun broke down early in the action, but employment of the light piece gave Ashby a new conception of the value of highly mobile artillery in co-ordination with cavalry.

After he had driven the enemy from the Heights and had beaten off a counterattack, he sent the Secretary of War a report in which he said: "I cannot impress too forcibly the necessity of perfect organization of my artillery and the forwarding at a very early day of the other guns promised. These guns are drawn by horses obtained for the occasion, and are worked by volunteers. We are in want of cavalry arms and long-range guns, and would be glad to have an arrangement made to mount my men." [39] Secretary Benjamin already had authorized Ashby to muster into service for local defense "a sufficient number of men to serve the pieces of artillery now with his command and thus form a company of artillery." [40] Soon the War Department supplied the ordnance for this battery—one long-range English Blakely gun, a smooth-bore twelve-pounder howitzer, and a three-inch rifle gun. [41]

When Ashby received these pieces, [42] he had no experience in gunnery beyond that acquired in a few brushes with the enemy. Jackson, who by that time had assumed command in the Valley, doubtless knew Ashby's inexperience, but he knew also the quality of the graduates of Virginia Military Institute, his own

[39] O. R., 5, 248; Richmond Dispatch, Oct. 19, 1861, p. 3, col. 1.
[40] O. R., 5, 892–93; ibid., 51, pt. 2, p. 336.
[41] 1 J. C. Wise, Long Arm of Lee, 163. According to A. W. Starke, Instruction for Field Artillery, 243–44, the twelve-pounder howitzer, bore 4.62 inches, with a charge of 1 lb. of powder had an extreme range of 1072 yards with shell, and with spherical case and a charge of 1¼ lbs. of powder, a maximum range of 1050 yards. The three-inch rifle gun of this period had an extreme range of 2300 yards, with a charge of 1 lb. Joseph Roberts, Handbook of Artillery, asserted that the three-inch Federal wrought-iron gun of 1863 could be used to 4180 yards at 16 degrees elevation. Ashby's three-inch iron gun probably was ineffective beyond 2000 yards. The Blakely gun must have been a 3.1", mentioned by typographical error in 1 J. C. Wise, Long Arm of Lee, 55, as a 2.1". The range of this gun does not appear in available records, but an investigation graciously made for the writer by Lt. Gen. J. L. DeWitt, when commandant of the Army War College, indicated that the 3.1" Blakely had approximately the range of the rival Armstrong, viz., 1200 yards at 3 degrees elevation, 1820 yards at 5 degrees, and 3030 yards at 10 degrees. "The short and light Blakely guns," McHenry Howard noted in his Recollections, p. 168 n., "kicked like a mule, and for this and other reasons they gradually disappeared."
[42] Probably in November, 1861, though the date is not certain.

former students, who were to command the battery. There was challenge, rather than sarcasm, in the question he put them: "Young men, now that you have your company, what are you going to do with it?"[43] The three addressed in this manner were Robert Preston Chew, 19, Captain; Milton Rouse, 17, First Lieutenant, and James Thomson, 18, Second Lieutenant. These lads had no answer at the moment to give their teacher; but Ashby was preparing one. He proposed that the thirty-three gunners who were to serve in Chew's Battery should be mounted instead of being required to plod along afoot or to ride the caissons when they could. Where the cavalry went, the guns were to go. That was the substance of Ashby's proposed tactics, which were to be an all-sufficient answer to Jackson.

The battery and the troopers would have desperate work to do. This was made plainer every hour. When the withdrawal of the Army from Winchester to Mount Jackson began, Ashby remained in the town until the Federals arrived. Even after their columns were visible, he sat defiantly on his conspicuous white stallion.[44] Two Federal cavalrymen determined to gallop down side streets and to cut off his retreat. Ashby either did not see them or else, for a time, disregarded them, but he contrived to elude them and, before overtaking his rearguard, had time enough to draw rein and to accept a biscuit a lady offered him. That was not enough for the romancers. They insisted that Ashby wheeled, rode straight at his pursuers, shot one with his pistol, reached over, grabbed the other man by the neck, unseated him and dragged him off to the Confederate outpost.[45] A commander who was credited, even fictitiously, with that exploit was a man to be followed eagerly by boys. As General Banks advanced Shields's Division[46] to Strasburg, almost halfway from Winchester to Mount Jackson, Ashby had no difficulty in keeping his troopers where they could report and could challenge every Federal move.

The first serious test came quickly. On Friday, March 21, ten

[43] 1 J. C. Wise, Long Arm of Lee, 162, 163.
[44] Said to have been by Talbrim; Companions in Arms, 578.
[45] Cooke, Wearing of the Gray, 74, affirmed: "This scene, which some readers may set down for romance, was witnessed by hundreds both of the Confederate and Federal army." For Avirett's account and the development of this myth, see D. S. Freeman, The South to Posterity, 52–53.
[46] Eleven thousand men, twenty-seven guns, 1 Henderson, 220.

days after the Confederates evacuated Winchester, Ashby found that the Federals were retiring northward from Strasburg.[47] He had at the moment only one company of cavalry in condition to move, but he sent word to Jackson of the enemy's withdrawal and, with his few horsemen and Chew's Battery, started immediately in pursuit.[48] Jackson quickly prepared to follow. Some of his troops marched twenty-one miles the next day. The rear regiments covered twenty-seven.[49] Another rapid march, averaging sixteen miles, brought Jackson's column by 2 P.M. on Sunday the 23d to Kernstown, four miles South of Winchester.

There Jackson found Ashby in artillery skirmish with the Unionists.[50] The commander of the cavalry had important news: he had pressed close to Winchester on the evening of the 22d and had heard from friendly sources that only four regiments of Federal infantry, with some cavalry and artillery, remained in the town. Even these, Ashby was informed by trusted residents, had orders to move to Harpers Ferry.[51] Ashby's information was that the Federal troops visible on open ground to the East of the Valley Turnpike, when Jackson reached Kernstown, were merely a rearguard.

Jackson probably received this intelligence with more excitement than he showed. For the first time in his career, he was about to make his own decision to give battle. He hoped for the guidance of the Almighty but he must discharge his responsibility. Not one of his subordinates did he consult; to none of them did he give any indication of what he was thinking. The hurried marches of the 21st–22d had left so many stragglers by the road that he could count only a few more than 3000 infantry, with twenty-seven field guns.[52] Ashby's strength, not precisely known to Jackson at the moment, was 290 cavalry and the three-piece battery.[53] This force seemed ample for the task in hand, which now and always, in Jackson's military code, was to smite the Northern invader and to drive him from Virginia. The opportunity seemed to be offered; the enemy was there by the road, to be slain or routed. There was one obstacle only: the day was

47 O. R., 12, pt. 1, p. 380. 48 O. R., 12, pt. 1, p. 386.
49 J. H. Worsham, One of Jackson's Foot Cavalry (cited hereafter as Worsham), 66.
50 O. R., 12, pt. 1, p. 385. 51 O. R., 12, pt. 1, p. 385.
52 O. R., 12, pt. 1, p. 383. 53 Ibid.. 383, 386.

the Lord's. Was it a sin against the Heavenly Father to order an attack on Sunday? Was not the commandment plain—the Lord had blessed the day and had hallowed it. That was the Law, but the fact was grim: Jackson's columns were in plain sight of the enemy. To delay until the Sabbath was past might be a worse sin and one against his own men, because the Philistines might bring up new hosts.[54] If the decision were wrong, might the Lord forgive an humble sinner—but the enemy must be attacked that day, aye, that hour.

As Jackson saw it, his best opening was on his left. The right was too open and was commanded by Federal artillery. Swiftly, sharply, unhesitatingly, the orders were issued: Ashby must hold the Valley Pike, with the second of the three small infantry Brigades, that of Col. Jesse S. Burks, in support. This Brigade was to serve also as a general reserve. The greater part of the artillery was to remain near the center until the attack was developed. Four companies of cavalry were ordered off beyond the left to deal with any flanking movement. The Third Brigade, Col. Samuel V. Fulkerson, and Jackson's own veterans of the First, under Brig. Gen. Richard B. Garnett, were to deliver on the left the attack designed to turn the enemy's right.

Inasmuch as the front was narrow, with most of the units already in position, the deployment did not take long. When it was complete, Jackson gave the order for the advance. Garnett moved up to support Fulkerson. The infantry pushed steadily forward. Batteries came up quickly on call. Ashby held his own. At least one Federal reserve unit was seen in slow withdrawal. Ere long, the rain of shell was diminishing. A thrust against the Confederate right was beaten off. As Jackson fed in his reserves, few though they were, they seemed to assure victory.

Then, on the center, where the "Stonewall Brigade" was fighting, the enemy's fire swelled ominously. That of the Confederates diminished. Word passed that ammunition was giving out. Disheartened men, with empty cartridge boxes, began to slip to the rear. Jackson was startled but not dismayed. His eyes began to glare. He rode toward the front. On the way he met a man with back to the enemy.

54 *O. R.*, 12, pt. 1, p. 381.

"Where are you going?" the General demanded.

The soldier explained that he had fired all his cartridges and did not know where to get more.

Jackson's face flamed. He rose in his stirrups. "Then go back and give them the bayonet!" he snapped.[55]

It was too late. Federals seemed literally to pour through the woods on the Confederate left. Instead of a retiring rearguard, the Confederates now faced onrushing regiments. Pressure was heavy. Soon "Dick" Garnett, though as brave as the bravest, realized that the odds against him were hopeless. Before he could communicate with Jackson, he might be overwhelmed. Reluctantly, Garnett ordered a withdrawal. Some of his overstrained men lost their heads and broke for the rear. Fulkerson's right was exposed. He, too, had to give ground.

Quickly Jackson met the fugitives. At the sight of his own Brigade in retreat, he put his horse at a gallop and rode to Garnett. In hoarse, commanding tones he bade the Brigadier halt the withdrawal. The men must stand to their work! A moment later, Jackson saw a drummer close at hand. Instantly the General pounced on the lad, seized him by the shoulder and dragged him to higher ground. "Beat the rally!" he cried.

The drum rolled, but it scarcely was audible. In the confusion of the field, none could tell whether the retreat was continuing or whether the First Brigade was beginning to rally. Jackson was intensely excited but he was not despairing. Two regiments he still had in reserve. They were supposed to be advancing. With them, he would remake his line and hurl back the attack. Eagerly he scanned the field for the reserves. They did not come up. Where were they? What delayed them? Who knew their position? Jackson asked and soon heard the answer: The two regiments were in line of battle a short distance to the rear. General Garnett had told the senior Colonel to halt there and to cover the retreat of the infantry and the artillery.

That settled it! Nothing now could be done except to break off the action and to get the little army out of range; but, at that, the troops must maintain their ground until every man and every musket that could be retrieved from the field was carried to the

[55] *Worsham,* 68.

rear. First must go the wounded. Send back every man who could be removed without endangering his life.

"But that requires time," said Dr. Hunter McGuire, Medical Director.

"Make yourself easy about that," Jackson grimly answered, "this Army stays here until the last wounded man is removed." Then he added: "Before I will leave them to the enemy I will lose many more men." [56] This was repeated, remembered and elaborated. Thenceforward, it was part of the Army's creed. Wrote "Dick" Taylor of Jackson: "In advance, his trains were left far behind. In retreat, he would fight for a wheelbarrow." [57] Tom Munford confirmed: "If a tire came off a wagon, he would stop the whole train and wait for it to be fixed, and let the rearguard hold its position." [58]

The halt that 23d of March was made at Newtown, four miles and a half South of Kernstown. Ashby, as zealous as ever, stopped at Bartonsville, only a mile and a half from Kernstown.[59] The enemy made no immediate attempt at pursuit beyond Bartonsville.

At the infantry camp, as Jackson stood silently by the fire, an excessively "fresh" young trooper addressed him: "The Yankees don't seem willing to quit Winchester, General."

"Winchester is a very pleasant place to stay in, sir."

"It was reported that they were retreating," said the boy, "but I guess they're retreating after us."

"I think I may say I am satisfied, sir." [60]

In one sense, he had a right to be. The fault was not with his troops or his tactics but with his information and reconnaissance. Ashby had been misled by Winchester friends who themselves had been deceived. Jackson had not faced merely a rearguard at Kernstown, which had been strengthened by the four regiments known to be in town. Shields's Division of 9000 men had

[56] *Mrs. Jackson*, 246–47.   [57] *R. Taylor*, 56.
[58] 7 *S. H. S. P.*, 528.
[59] So stated Henderson, *op. cit.*, 1, 246. Col. William Allan wrote that Jackson "fell back five or six miles slowly and sullenly to the trains, which had been parked a short distance south of Newtown." The admirable work of Colonel Allan, *History of the Campaign of Gen. T. J. (Stonewall) Jackson in the Shenandoah Valley of Virginia . . .*, is hereafter cited as *William Allan*, with page references (in this instance, p. 162) to the reprint in 43 *S. H. S. P.*
[60] 1 *Henderson*. 247.

been near Winchester on the 22d and had been led back quietly toward Kernstown. Part of it had been in concealment at the time of Jackson's approach. Reconnaissance, which had been hasty and inexperienced, had failed to disclose them. The assault that had driven back Garnett's men had been reinforced by a Brigade which had been moved from the Federal left in the sound belief that the Confederate right was too weak to attack. Although Jackson had lost 700 men, killed, wounded and missing,[61] he thought that the Federal casualties had been larger.[62] He reasoned that if he had done that well with the odds three to one against him, he could afford to be satisfied with his troops and with his cavalry and artillery no less than with his infantry.

Ashby, to be sure, had erred grievously in his intelligence report, but he had been magnificent on the field. Some of his men thought that his daring saved Jackson from defeat.[63] On the left, the cavalry contingent had not been equally successful. Jackson considered that the officer on that flank had "neglected his duty." [64] Chew's Battery had distinguished itself. Carpenter's artillerists had used their antiquated guns for the first time, and had done so well on their initial shot that Jackson cried, "Good, good!" [65] He might have echoed those words when the battle was done.

Tactics apart, there was a large strategical consideration. Jackson possibly reasoned, even at this early stage of the operations,

61 *William Allan*, 163.

62 In writing Mrs. Jackson, Mch. 24, 1862, he said the Unionist loss "was probablv superior to ours" (*Mrs. Jackson*, 247); and in his official report of Apr. 9 on the basis of a Federal officer's reported statement that the Union dead numbered 418, he surmised that the enemy had sustained casualties three times as great as his (*O. R.*, 12, pt. 1, p. 383). Actually the total of Federal killed, wounded and missing, Mch. 22–23, was 590 (*O. R.*, 11, pt. 1, pp. 346–47).

63 J. B. Avirett, *The Memoirs of General Turner Ashby and His Compeers* (cited hereafter as *Avirett*), 256–57, 272.

64 *Ibid.*, 501.

65 C. A. Fonderon, *A Brief History of the Military Career of Carpenter's Battery* . . . (New Market, Va., 1911), p. 20. This famous battery originally was the "Alleghany Roughs," Co. A, Twenty-seventh Virginia Infantry, and as such fought at First Manassas. Joseph Carpenter, First Lieutenant of the Company, had been a cadet at V. M. I. of the class of 1858. Upon the retirement of Thompson McAllister as Captain of the company, because of ill health, Jackson made Company A into a battery, whicn was styled Carpenter's, after the young soldier promoted to command it. The battery began with four crude six-pounder iron, smooth-bore guns made by the Tredegar Iron Works in the earliest stages of work at that plant for the Confederacy. These guns were "much laughed at" but they were employed successfully at Kernstown. The shot that won Jackson's praise crashed through the door of an old barn that was crowded with Federals. They scattered precipitately.

that after so hard a blow, General Banks would hesitate to withdraw from the Shenandoah Valley and to join the Army operating against Johnston. Such a withdrawal had been considered probable, because the Confederates assumed McClellan would call to him every available man. If the fight at Kernstown held Banks's troops West of the Blue Ridge, Jackson's satisfaction would be doubled. How better could he serve the South at the moment, than by keeping Banks from sharing in a Federal concentration that might overwhelm Johnston? [66]

The possible effect of the battle and the stout defense against odds did not prevent soreness. Specifically, it did not alter the fact that General Richard Garnett had ordered the Stonewall Brigade to retire from the front of action. Jackson could not forgive that. It did not matter that Garnett belonged to one of the ablest families of Tidewater Virginia, that he was a cousin of Gen. Robert Garnett who had fallen at Carrick's Ford, that he had been graduated at West Point the year before Jackson entered the Academy,[67] that he had been for six years a Captain in the "old army" prior to secession,[68] or that he had kept the Stonewall Brigade well in hand during the Romney campaign.[69] In the conviction that Garnett had withdrawn unnecessarily at Kernstown, Jackson, on April 1, relieved the General of command, put him under arrest [70] and drew up charges and specifi-

[66] It cannot be suggested, otherwise than as a possibility, that Jackson perceived at this time how success against Banks might affect McClellan's campaign, the direction of which, on March 23, he did not know. Jackson's first recorded observation on the subject is in a letter of April 5 to Longstreet: "If Banks is defeated it may greatly retard McClellan's movements" (O. R., 11, pt. 1, p. 844). There is no evidence whatsoever to justify the intimation of 1 Henderson, 247, that at the period of Kernstown, Jackson foresaw that his movements would induce President Lincoln to retain large forces in Northern Virginia for the defense of Washington. By the time Jackson wrote his report on Kernstown, April 9 (O. R., 12, pt. 1, p. 380), the effect of the battle in detaining Federals who might have formed a junction "with other forces" began to be apparent. See infra, p. 344 n. 102, and p. 485.

[67] Cullum, No. 1087; graduated twenty-ninth in the class of 1841.

[68] U. S. Army Register, 1860.

[69] O. R., 5, 394. Garnett had been commissioned Major of Artillery in the regular Army of the Confederate States, 3 C. M. H., 597, and on Nov. 14, 1861, Wright, 66, had been made Brigadier General in the Provisional Army. He was sent at once to Manassas for assignment to command, because of the shortage of brigade commanders, O. R., 5, 954; O. R., 51, pt. 2, p. 399, and, after brief service there, O. R., 5, 961, was ordered to Winchester to take Iackson's old Brigade, O R., 5, 981. Garnett was then 42 years of age.

[70] Jackson's MS. Order Book, p. 3. For the nature and history of this Order Book, see Bibliography, Vol. III. The abstract of the order merely states that Garnett was relieved, but as Jackson noted on April 29 that Garnett was in arrest, it is probable that the original order covered arrest also.

cations for a court-martial.[71] Garnett was charged with neglect of duty under seven specifications—that he had not put his Brigade into position properly, that he had separated himself from his command, that he had not been with his leading unit, that he had no troops within supporting distance of his front regiment, that regiments had become intermingled, that he had absented himself from his command, that he had given the order to fall back "when he should have encouraged his command to hold its position," and that he had sent an order to reserve forces to withdraw.[72]

Besides the determination Jackson thus exhibited for the maintenance of discipline and the precise execution of the letter of orders, something personally rigid was involved: Jackson was resolved that affection for his old Brigade should not induce him to spare it. "We had to pay dearly for our reputation . . .", one private wrote years afterward, "for whenever there was any extra hard duty to be performed, General Jackson always sent his old brigade to that post of duty for fear the other brigades under his command would think and say that he favored his old command." [73]

At the moment, feeling in the Army of the Valley, particularly in the Stonewall Brigade, was that Garnett did not deserve arrest and court-martial.[74] Some sense of this must have reached Richmond, because ere long there came a suggestion from the Adjutant General that Garnett should be released from arrest and assigned to command. "I have only to say," Jackson replied, "that I have no desire to see the case pressed any further; but that I regard Gen. Garnett as so incompetent a Brigade commander, that, instead of building up a Brigade, a good one, if turned over to him, would actually deteriorate under the command." [75] Jackson never consented to have Garnett again in his Army and prepared to testify against him if a court-martial were held.

[71] These bore date of April 1, but, according to *Jackson's MS. Letter Book*, they were sent to General Johnston April 7.

[72] *R. B. Garnett Court-martial Papers* (cited hereafter as *R. B. Garnett MSS.*), Confederate Museum, Richmond, Va.

[73] *Casler*, 66. That writer thought Jackson took this view after First Manassas and held to it throughout the operations he directed.

[74] Cf. *R. Taylor*, 79: "I have never seen an officer or soldier, present at Kernstown, who failed to condemn the harsh treatment of Garnett after that action." *Cf.* also *McHenry Howard*, 81 and *Douglas*, 37.

[75] *Jackson's MS. Letter Book*, Apr. 29, 1862.

Of all this, Jackson was convinced: the battle had been worth waging: his stand concerning Garnett was correct. Regarding one aspect of the contest he was not quite so certain. That was the violation of the Sabbath by fighting that day. His original misgiving had been relieved by what he told himself was a victory. He was sure that the Lord had been on his side. The day after the battle, he wrote his wife: "Our God was my shield. His protecting care is an additional cause for gratitude." Sunday, March 30, he spent in quietness that seemed the more precious by reason of the contrast with the 23d. Of course, he could not write Mrs. Jackson that day, for such an act would be a desecration, but on the 31st he could say: "Yesterday was a lovely Sabbath day. Although I had not the privilege of hearing the word of life, yet it felt like a holy Sabbath day, beautiful, serene, and lovely. All it wanted was the church-bell and God's services in the sanctuary to make it complete."

In answer to this, the General received a letter wherein his beloved expressed distress and a measure of spiritual alarm that he had attacked on the Lord's Day, though apparently she had drawn a distinction between offense and defense on the Sabbath. Deacon Jackson of the Presbyterian Church of Lexington, Virginia, had now to square his conduct with that of Maj. Gen. T. J. Jackson in command of the Valley District. It was the Deacon who wrote the apologia the General dictated: "You appear much concerned at my attacking *on Sunday*. I was greatly concerned, too; but I felt it my duty to do it, in consideration of the ruinous effects that might result from postponing the battle until the morning. So far as I can see, my course was a wise one; the best that I could do under the circumstances, though very distasteful to my feelings; and I hope and pray to our Heavenly Father that I may never again be circumstanced as on that day. I believed that so far as our troops were concerned, necessity and mercy both called for the battle. I do hope the war will soon be over, and that I shall never again have to take the field."

Then the General had the Deacon come to the point: "Arms is a profession that, if its principles are adhered to for success, requires an officer to do what he fears may be wrong, and yet, according to military experience, must be done, if success is to be attained. And this fact of its being necessary to success, and being accompanied with success, and that a departure from it is accompanied with disaster, suggests that it must be right. Had I fought the battle on Monday instead of Sunday, I fear our cause would have suffered; whereas, as things turned out, I consider our cause gained much from the engagement." [76]

The military argument and the religious were reconciled as well as might be: If a battle had to be fought on the Sabbath, for strategical or tactical reasons, then success was evidence of the favor of the Lord. Less clear but not to be disdained was the implication of the converse—that if a soldier unwisely delayed a Sunday battle and by so doing sustained defeat on Monday, then that was proof that the Lord disapproved poor military judgment.

In that argument, the General triumphed over the Deacon.

[76] *Mrs. Jackson,* 247–49.

CHAPTER XXII

The Building of a "New Model" Army

"Stonewall's" apologia on Sunday fighting was written from Rude's Hill, two and a half miles south of Mount Jackson. He defended his action at length in his letter to Mrs. Jackson and he took abundant time in preparing his dispatch. For other correspondence he had few hours. His thought was centered on making ready his troops for the next move of adversaries who had followed at a discreet distance; nor was his thought unavailing. The manner in which he went about the recruitment, training, discipline and organization of his men brought to light, moreover, some interesting personal characteristics not observed previously by his comrades. Tested also was his aptitude for army administration, in which soldierly art his earlier experience had been limited by the small size of his command.

The first man he put in training was himself; his initial lessons were in geography. He was confused in his mind concerning the names and location of certain of the passes or "gaps" of the Blue Ridge Mountains,[1] and he was unacquainted with some of the roads. As it happened, Jed. Hotchkiss, whose skill in topographical engineering had been demonstrated in Robert Garnett's tragic expedition, had reported at Mount Airy, the Meems estate, on March 20 as acting Adjutant of the Militia Regiment from Augusta County.[2] Jackson sent for him on the 26th and asked him about his work in Northwest Virginia. Then the General said: "I want you to make me a map of the Valley from Harpers Ferry to Lexington, showing all the points of offense and defense between those points. Mr. Pendleton will give you orders for whatever outfit you want. Good morning,

---

[1] As late as April 12, he thought Fisher's Gap, which leads from the Luray Valley to Madison Courthouse and thence to Gordonsville, was Swift Run Gap, which links the southern end of Luray Valley and Stannardsville, Orange Courthouse and Gordonsville. Cf. *O. R.*, 12, pt. 3, p. 848. Even on April 21, Jackson sent Jed. Hotchkiss to Swift Run when he intended him to go to Fisher's Gap. *Hotchkiss' MS. Diary*, Apr. 21, 1862.

[2] Some 380 men of this regiment, Hotchkiss among them, were mustered into service on March 23 as a battalion of volunteers. *Hotchkiss' MS. Diary*, Mch. 20, 23, 1862.

Sir." Thus, in three sentences, began the making of the maps which were to contribute to the sureness, and thereby to the speed and the boldness of all Jackson's future operations in the Valley.[3] Simultaneously, and perhaps earlier, Jackson must have prepared the tables from which, at a glance, he could tell precisely the distance between any two points in his military district.[4]

Recruitment was advanced by similarly direct methods. The Conscription Act, which at the moment was coming into operation, had created much discontent among the peace-loving residents of the Shenandoah. In Rockingham County, numerous Dunkards, who were an offshoot of the Mennonites, murmured much at the performance of military duty, and sought to arrange for the enlistment of Indians as substitutes.[5] Jackson consented to delay for ten days the embodiment of the County Militia and, in the end, agreed to employ conscientious objectors as teamsters.

He already had applied this policy to other Dunkards who had been called out in Virginia's levy en masse. Jackson had written: "Those who do not desert, to some extent, hire substitutes; others will turn out in obedience to the Governor's call, but I understand some of them say they will not 'shoot.' They can be made to fire, but they can very easily take bad aim. So, for the purpose of giving to the command the highest degree of efficiency and securing loyal feelings and cooperation, I have, as those non-combatants are said to be good teamsters and faithful to their promise, determined to organize them into companies of 100 each, rank and file, and after mustering them with the legal number of company officers into service assign them to the various staff departments without issuing arms to them; but if at any time they have insufficient labor, to have them drilled, so that in case circumstances should justify it arms may be given them. If these men are, as represented to me, faithful laborers and careful of property, this arrangement not only will enable many volunteers to return to the ranks, but will also save many valuable horses and other public property in addition to arms."

[3] *Hotchkiss' MS. Diary,* Mch. 26, 1862.
[4] Part of one such table Jackson sent Johnston March 25, *O. R.,* 12, pt. 3, p. 837, and another Apr. 5, 1862, *O. R.,* 12, pt. 3, p. 844. Numerous copies and abstracts of similar tables are preserved in the *Hotchkiss Papers.* The writer has not found comparably so many in the papers of any other Confederate officer whose records he has examined.
[5] *Hotchkiss' MS. Diary,* Mch. 18, 1862.
[6] *O. R.,* 12, pt. 3, p. 835; Mch. 21, 1862.

Although this arrangement perforce was accepted by the Dunkards, some of the Rockingham militia openly rebelled against conscription and fled to the mountains. Jackson did not hesitate for an hour. He sent four companies of infantry, some cavalry and two guns after the insurrectionists. When the commander of the expedition found that the men had hidden in the woods, he calmly put his guns on high ground and shelled the woods. One man was killed; twenty-four came out and surrendered. A leader of the movement later was captured while attempting to escape to the enemy. That was the end of the insurrection.[7] As for absence without leave, Jackson tersely instructed his quartermaster: "Arrest every man whom you possibly can find absent from this District, unless he produces proper permission to be absent[,] and send all such delinquents to their posts in irons as deserters."[8]

To supply arms for chastened conscripts, returned A.W.O.L.'s, and new recruits seemed at the moment almost impossible. Jackson had asked in March for 3000 muskets with which to make the militia effective.[9] On the somber assurance that no muskets could be provided, he urged modification of a proposal by Governor Letcher's aide that the bayonet be used. "Let me," wrote Jackson, "have a substitute, so to make the arm six or more inches longer than the musket with the bayonet, so that when we teach our troops to rely upon the bayonet, they may feel that they have the superiority of arm resulting from its length."[10] These pikes were duly ordered, but before they were ready, Jackson was to find a new source of supply for muskets—the enemy.[11]

The military reorganization that brought into the ranks more recruits than Jackson could arm immediately involved, also, an attempt by many men to transfer from the infantry to the cavalry. Jackson flatly prohibited this type of re-enlistment[12] but he could not prevent the selection of cavalry service by new

7 *William Allan*, 171; Jackson's report to Lee, Apr. 15, 1862; *Jackson's MS. Letter Book*. Casler, *op. cit.*, 90, quoted an army yarn to this effect: "An old lady living near remarked that 'the deserters had mortified in the Blue Ridge, but that General Jackson had sent a foot company and a critter company to ramshag the Blue Ridge and capture them.'" In this, "ramshag" doubtless was meant for "ramshack," which was a corruption of "ransack."

8 *Jackson's MS. Letter Book*, Apr. 21, 1862.

9 *O. R.*, 12, pt. 3, p. 835.
10 *O. R.*, 12, pt. 3, p. 842.
11 *O. R.*, 12, pt. 3, pp. 844–45.
12 *O. R.*, 12, pt. 3, p. 880.

volunteers. Colonel Ashby maintained that he had the right, under authority from the Secretary of War, to recruit infantry, artillery and cavalry independent of Jackson, and he speedily built up his mounted force to twenty-one companies.[13] Reports soon began to circulate that these scattered forces, often operating separately and under no field officers but Ashby and his second in command, Maj. O. R. Funsten, had poor discipline or none at all. Great as was Ashby's prowess in action and skillful as he was on outpost duty, was he lacking in ability to maintain discipline or to direct administration? If this were as serious as some officers believed, Jackson's model Army sooner or later must suffer.

Infantry or cavalry, willing or unwilling recruits, armed with musket or expected to carry pikes, Jackson's men had a spiritual life that was not to be overlooked. On that he was intent. In spite of the lapse at Kernstown, he held most rigidly to Sunday observance. His staff officers discovered that he not only would not write a letter on Sunday but also would not mail one to be transported that day, unless the emergency was clear to his conscience.[14] Of course he would not drill or march his troops on the Sabbath otherwise than when he thought the Lord would recognize the necessity or the mercy of it. Quiet and preaching were the normal order of the day. At least one Sunday in April, when religious service was not adequate, the General rode to a near-by brigade camp and personally distributed tracts to the soldiers,[15] who soon were to decide—according to the unique and paradoxical reasoning of the man in the ranks—that Jackson actually preferred to fight on the Lord's Day.[16]

During this training period, the troops of Jackson's command had to elect their officers. In accordance with the rashly unwise re-enlistment acts, the troops of any regiment or company could displace any man who had offended the majority. This process was democratic but it was not military. In the Stonewall Brigade, it was complicated by the discontent of the Colonels over the treatment of Garnett and over the general severity of Jackson's attitude toward them. One Colonel was so embittered that he had sworn he never would go again to Jackson's headquarters

13 Ibid.   14 Wearing of the Gray, 48
15 Hotchkiss' MS. Diary, Apr. 12, 1862, p. 25.   16 McHenry Howard, 122 n

unless summoned. His grievance was that, on one visit, he had made some polite remark unrelated to military affairs, whereupon Jackson had replied that he had no time to talk on any subject except army business.[17] With more of dignity but perhaps with no less of resentment, Col. A. C. Cummings of the Thirty-third Virginia, who largely had been responsible for the most brilliant achievement of Jackson's Brigade at Manassas, refused to stand for election. Cummings made no explanation, but he was supposed to have made up his mind that he would not serve under Jackson.[18] Col. James W. Allen of the Second Virginia, though consenting to re-election, was equally bitter toward Jackson. So determined was he to be away from his taskmaster that his resignation was expected.[19] In some of the other regiments, officers who had been willing to remain in the service were defeated for re-election. Among them was Jackson's fellow townsman, E. Franklin Paxton, Major of the Twenty-seventh Virginia.[20] Of those elevated by the suffrage of a regiment of the Stonewall Brigade, the most promising, perhaps, was Adjutant John F. Neff of the Thirty-third, who was chosen Colonel in succession to Cummings. The outcome of the elections as a whole was much the same as among Joseph E. Johnston's troops: organization was disrupted in the very presence of the enemy, but the transfer of command to new men was attended by less demoralization than might have been anticipated.

Brigade reorganization was at least as serious a matter. Jackson now had 6000 infantry and he no longer could keep his entire command under his own eye. To Garnett's place, Brig. Gen. Charles S. Winder already had been assigned by Johnston's orders.[21] This young Marylander, 33 years of age, had the usual West Point career,[22] and in 1854 started for California with his

---

[17] McHenry Howard, 81.

[18] After the First Manassas, Cummings's men had burned all the rails of a fence around a field in which the regiment was camped. Knowing that he could not identify the offenders, Cummings adopted the course of direct mass discipline, sent the whole regiment into the woods, made the men cut trees and maul rails, and then had them replace the fence. (Casler, 61. Cf. ibid., 89.)

[19] McHenry Howard, 87, 88.

[20] For Paxton's later service, see Vol. II.

[21] O. R., 12, pt. 3, p. 587. From the evidence now available, it does not seem possible to say whether the choice was made directly by Johnston, on notice from Jackson of Garnett's arrest, or whether Winder was assigned at the request of Jackson, who doubtless had known Winder at Manassas.

[22] Cullum, No. 1471; graduated twenty-second in the class of 1850.

command aboard the *San Francisco*. The vessel encountered a hurricane which blew her far off her course and almost caused her to founder. Winder's behavior at that time and during the weeks that passed before the rescued ship was carried into Liverpool, won for him promotion at 26 to a captaincy in the 9th Infantry. Rough Indian fighting in Washington Territory confirmed his reputation for cold courage and leadership and made him a figure of some importance when he resigned in 1861 and entered Confederate service.[23] He soon was named Colonel of the Sixth South Carolina,[24] which he brought to high excellence. At the time Johnston was complaining in February, 1862, of the shortage of brigade commanders, he had listed Colonel Winder as one of six officers of that grade qualified for promotion.[25] In Winder's case, Johnston had procured earlier action than in some instances of like character.[26] The garrison of the Manassas defenses [27] had been given the new Brigadier only a few days [28] before he had been sent to the Valley.

Confederate service had few young Generals of a personality more military. Winder's thin, waving hair was combed back from a wide and towering forehead. A curling beard seemed to lengthen his sensitive, intelligent face. Restless, alert eyes, deepset, reflected both daring and ill health. In the field, he was flawlessly uniformed, even to immaculate gauntlets, and always he had the finest of mounts,[29] but he did not create the impression of being a mere dress-parade officer. His reception by his Brigade was distinctly cold. Because of their resentment over the arrest of Garnett, the Colonels had agreed quietly that they would not call on the new commander. The men openly were hostile. As Winder was riding through the camp of one of the regiments, he was greeted with faint hissing. He gave no indication that he heard it, but after he got back to his headquarters he called in the Colonel and pointed out that the hissing indicated a bad state of discipline. If it were repeated, said Winder, he would hold the

---

23 The *Richmond Dispatch*, July 11, 1861, p. 2, col. 5, noted his arrival in Richmond.
24 *O. R.*, 2, 1000; IV *O. R.*, 1, 629.   25 *O. R.*, 5, 1058.
26 Winder was commissioned as of Mch. 1, 1862. *Wright*, 74.
27 Previously under Col. G. B. Anderson.
28 Mch. 25, 1862; *O. R.*, 12, pt. 3, p. 837.
29 4 *N. C. Regts.*, 446.

commanding officer responsible.[30] This was the course of a determined soldier, but the incident suggested that Winder was to have a difficult assignment as head of the First Brigade.

Col. J. S. Burks, who had commanded the Second Brigade at Kernstown, was absent on an indefinite sick leave.[31] A qualified Brigadier was much wanted in his place. Col. S. V. Fulkerson, who soon would be ripe for promotion, could be continued safely to direct the Third Brigade, formerly under Brig. Gen. William B. Taliaferro. On the 13th of April, Taliaferro returned by General Johnston's order for assignment, not to the command of Burks's Brigade, which might have used him, but of his old Brigade, now Fulkerson's, which did not need him. General Taliaferro, who shared the retreat from Carrick's Ford after the death of Gen. Robert Garnett, subsequently had come to the Valley with General Loring. In the squabble over the alleged exposure of Loring's command at Romney, Taliaferro had sided with Loring. For that reason, it was surmised immediately that Jackson did not welcome him to the command of one of the Valley Brigades,[32] but Jackson himself said nothing to his staff. His protest went to the Adjutant General of the Confederate Army— and at once. Jackson wrote: "Through God's blessing my command, though small, is efficient, and I respectfully request its efficiency may not be injured by assigning to it inefficient Officers. Last winter Gen. Taliaferro had charge of a Brigade and he permitted it to become so demoralized that I had to abandon an important enterprise in consequence of the inefficient condition in which he reported his Brigade. Notwithstanding the demoralized condition of his Brigade he left and visited Richmond, thus making a second visit there within two months. His Brigade since he left it, has, under other hands, become efficient, and it, as well as the others bids fair to render good service if not placed under incompetent Officers. I attach so much importance to this matter as to induce me to send this communication direct. The same statement will be forwarded through Gen. Johnston." [33] Jackson wrote in vain. General Taliaferro remained. Nothing

---

30 *McHenry Howard,* 83.   31 *Jackson's MS. Letter Book,* Apr. 28, 1862.
32 *Hotchkiss' MS. Diary,* p. 25, Apr. 13, 1862.
33 *Jackson's MS. Letter Book,* Apr. 14, 1862.

was done in Richmond concerning a general officer for Burks's Brigade.

By approximately the middle of April, the reorganization and refit of the little Army of the Valley were as far advanced as Jackson could carry them. Difficulties considered, he had been swift, decisive and efficient in making good the losses and deficiencies of Kernstown. He had found time, also, to write his report of that engagement. To do this he had remained alone for many hours in his room [34] and personally had penned the document. Unless he was more facile than he usually was at such a task, he revised heavily in an effort to obtain accuracy and to eliminate verbiage. In the final draft of the report, Garnett was blamed for withdrawing and for ordering the reserve to take a defensive position, but the reference, which might be made public, was far milder than that employed in the letter of April 29 to General Cooper. In closing the official account of the action, Jackson wrote: "Though Winchester was not recovered, yet the more important object for the present, that of calling back troops that were leaving the valley, and thus preventing a junction of Banks' command with other forces, was accomplished, in addition to his heavy loss in killed and wounded. Under these circumstances I feel justified in saying that, though the field is in possession of the enemy, yet the most essential fruits of the battle are ours." [35]

Jackson doubtless felt that the thanks of the Confederate Congress, published by General Johnston before the completion of the report,[36] were deserved by his officers and men. As for Congressional praise of himself, he gave the glory to God. His military ambition might be far greater than any of his friends knew —greater than even he realized; but always he purposed to shape it to the will of the Almighty. Pride was the tool of the Evil One and was to be shunned. Perhaps Jackson soberly reproached himself one day that April because he showed pleasure when an old woman inquired of him, "Gineral, are you any relation of Old Gineral Jackson, who used to stop here?" The Confederate was quick to say that he did not know of any kinship to "Old Hickory," but, Democrat and admirer of Andrew Jackson though

[34] *Hotchkiss' MS. Diary*, p. 24, Apr. 4, 1862.
[35] *O. R.*, 12, pt. 1, pp. 383–84. See *supra*, p. 315. [36] *Ibid.*, 384.

he was, had he not shown a vain, worldly spirit in feeling satisfaction that the question had been asked? [37]

The day of this little colloquy, April 17, was an historic one. General Banks started down the Valley that day and forced the crossing of Stony Creek, which, from the beginning of the month, Jackson had held in front of Rude's Hill. The Federal commander was not a professional soldier, but in his rise from youthful hard labor in a Massachusetts cotton mill, he had shown intelligence and persistence. A man who had been Speaker of the Federal House of Representatives, and thrice Governor of Massachusetts, had a reputation he would do his utmost to preserve, and to increase, in campaigning against the former professor of V. M. I. All the theories Jackson had formulated of the Federal plans and all the strategy he had pondered, he now would have to put to the test.

Johnston, it will be remembered, had instructed Jackson, ere the retreat from Manassas began, to keep himself between Banks and the main Army of the Confederacy, to withdraw southward as that Army did so, and to delay Banks as long as he could without risking the destruction of his force.[38] Jackson had interpreted these orders realistically, not as injunction to a strict defensive. The battle of Kernstown had demonstrated that. Johnston immediately after that action had promised Jackson reinforcements [39] in the event the enemy assailed him heavily.[40] Thereupon, the first thought of "Stonewall" had been to use the combined forces offensively should opportunity be offered him.[41] Subsequent instructions from Johnston to leave the Valley in case of pursuit, and to join the main Army at Orange Court-

[37] Hotchkiss, who recorded this incident in his diary, Apr. 17, 1862, noted that the old lady who made this inquiry was the wife of Abe Lincoln of Lacy's, or Big Spring, "a distant relative of President Lincoln."

[38] Few of Johnston's letters of this period to Jackson have been preserved, but from Jackson's replies, O. R., 5, 1088, 1095, it is possible to reconstruct this much of Johnston's orders. Writing some ten years subsequent to the events, Johnston stated: "After it had become evident that the Valley was to be invaded by an enemy too strong to be encountered by Jackson's division, that officer was instructed to endeavor to employ the invaders in the Valley, but without exposing himself to the danger of defeat, oy keeping so near the enemy as to prevent him from making any considerable detachment to reenforce McClellan, but not so near that he might be compelled to fight." (Johnston's Narrative, 106). Although this was as accurate a statement as could be expected from memory, after a decade, it did not embrace the obligation imposed on Jackson to remain between Banks and Johnston. Until Johnston's Army left the Rapidan, Jackson was circumscribed in his movements by reason of his instructions.

[39] O. R., 12, pt. 3, p. 837.

[40] Ibid., 838.   [41] Ibid., 837.

house,[42] had come about the time Longstreet had proposed to march to Jackson's relief and to take command.[43] In ignoring that proposal, Jackson had not abandoned his hopes of attacking Banks, though he had not been sanguine that the Federal commander would pursue him far.[44]

When Johnston had quit the line of the Rapidan for his march to Richmond, or a few days thereafter, he sent new, written instructions to Jackson, and also to Maj. Gen. R. S. Ewell, whom he had left on the Rappahannock [45] with a Division of 6500 infantry and some 500 cavalry. Jackson was known to be facing numerically superior forces which Banks might push up the Valley to Staunton. There he would be close to a main line of supply to Richmond and, at the same time, he would be master of the rich Shenandoah. General Banks must be held at a distance from Staunton and, if possible, must be driven out of the Valley. In the event General Jackson had to fall back much farther, Ewell was to retire behind the Rapidan and was to march by way of Madison Court House to Swift Run Gap. Jackson was to withdraw to the same position. The two forces were then to unite and were to give battle to Banks's Army near the crest of the Blue Ridge.[46]

Some discussion had followed between Jackson and Ewell concerning the route that Johnston intended Ewell to take. This ended in the belief on Jackson's part that Johnston had confused Swift Run Gap with Fisher's Gap, and that the commanding General meant for the two forces to unite at Fisher's Gap.[47] Jackson accordingly had prepared on April 13, while still near New Market, to concentrate, if necessity required, at the point indicated by Johnston.

Strategically, because of the peculiar terrain, this became a matter of large importance in relation to all that followed.[48] Between Strasburg on the North and Harrisonburg on the South, a distance of forty-five miles, the Massanutton Mountains divide

---

[42] O. R., 11, pt. 3, p. 419.   [43] See *supra*, p. 166 ff.

[44] O. R., 12, pt. 3, pp. 843, 848.   [45] Headquarters near Brandy Station.

[46] These instructions, which seem to have been overlooked by Henderson, were contained in a lost letter from Johnston, dated April 8. The contents of the letter can be reconstructed from Jackson's and Ewell's references to them in O. R., 12, pt. 3, pp. 845, 848, 863.

[47] O. R., 12, pt. 3, pp. 846, 848.

[48] If the ground be understood, the campaign can be. For the general relationship of the Massanuttons to the Shenandoah area, see *infra*, Appendix I.

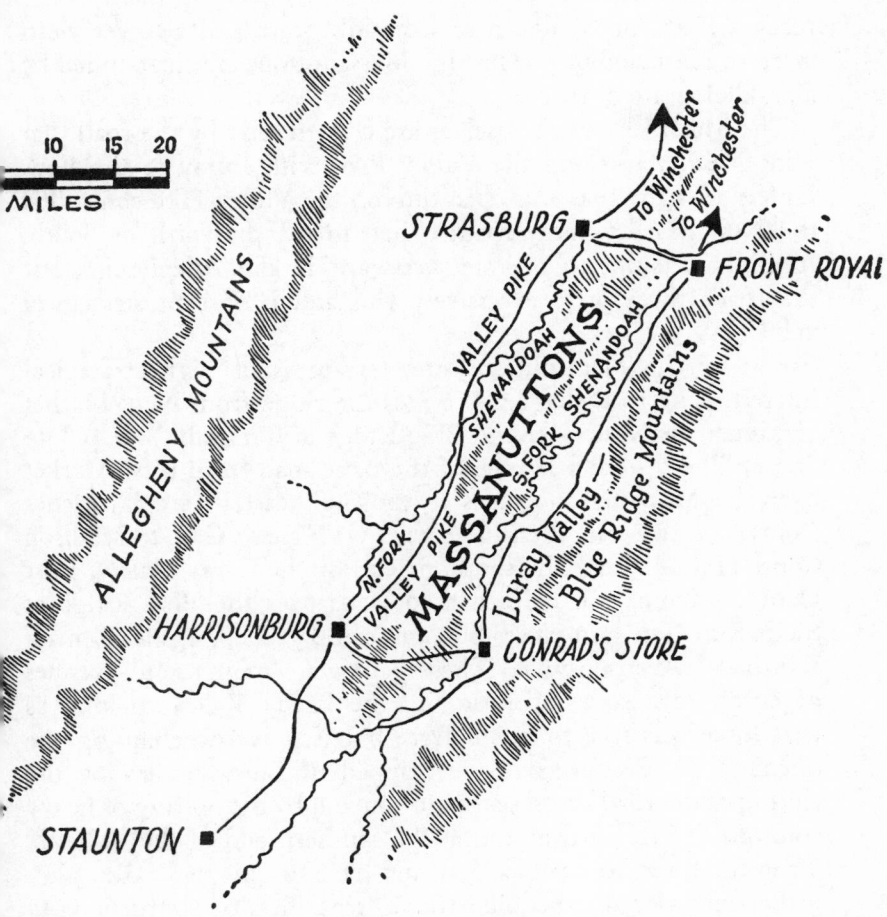

The Parallelogram of the Massanuttons. This sketch is elaborated in the one that follows, but the course of the roads should be examined carefully in order that the importance of the New Market-Luray road and of the various mountain passes or "gaps" may be understood from the more detailed sketch *infra*.

the Shenandoah Valley in twain. West of the Massanuttons, through a wide, open country, run the North Fork of the Shenandoah and the Valley turnpike. East of the Massanuttons is the wooded Luray Valley, which is narrowed by the Blue Ridge. Down this eastern Valley courses the South Fork of the Shenandoah. An inferior road leads northward to Front Royal. Thence a road to the West links Front Royal with Strasburg. At the southern end of the Luray Valley, the road from Front Royal reaches Elk Run Valley near Conrad's Store and swerves westward to Harrisonburg. Thus the Massanuttons are surrounded by a parallelogram of roads.

The Massanuttons themselves are crossed only by the road that joins New Market on the Valley Pike with Luray to the East. Unless an army that was operating on the Valley Pike controlled the New Market-Luray road, it had to march North or South. It might attempt to operate westward in the Alleghenies, but the roads there were excessively bad and had scant strategical value.

East of the Massanuttons, the terrain is of high strategical interest. The road that leads across the ridge from New Market continues eastward over the Blue Ridge at Thornton's Gap [49] to Sperryville. Another branch of the same road from New Market over the Massanuttons turns to the Southeast before it reaches Luray, and traverses the Blue Ridge, via Fisher's Gap, to Madison Court House. From the southern end of the Luray Valley, near Conrad's Store, still a third road leads over the Blue Ridge at Swift Run Gap, and passes Stannardsville to the Virginia Central Railroad at Gordonsville. These gaps were most useful avenues of egress to a force operating in the Luray Valley so long as that force was free to manœuvre; but if it were defending the Shenandoah area, it could be trapped in Luray Valley by the closing of the road across Massanutton and by the posting of heavy columns at Front Royal and at the southern end of the Valley.[50] Then the force, to save itself, would have to quit the Valley altogether and to cross the Blue Ridge, regardless of instructions to defend the Shenandoah region.

That was not all. Still a third strategical value attached to the Luray Valley. If an enemy, on the west side of the Massanuttons, moved up the Valley Pike, with his line of communications extending northward past Strasburg, was not the Luray Valley a perfect covered way for an attack on the rear of such an adver-

---

[49] It must be noted that the large map of Virginia and Maryland, in all editions of Henderson's *Jackson*, marks this as Fisher's Gap and has no legend for Fisher's Gap proper. The smaller map of the Valley, in the same work, distinguishes the two gaps.

[50] This had been the reason Jackson had told Johnston, early in March, that if he was to keep between Banks and Johnston, he either should be free to cross the Blue Ridge North of the Luray Valley, or else should go up the North Fork of the Shenandoah to New Market. See *supra*. p. 306.

ary? Moreover, while an enemy was marching South, to the West of the Massanuttons, Confederates might hurry down Luray Valley and strike across from Front Royal to Strasburg. If the Federals put the Manassas Gap Railroad in operation, and used it as a line of supply in the direction of Mount Jackson, the Confederates would not even have to go around the northern end of the Massanuttons to strike this supply line. Inasmuch as he railroad from Manassas ran past Front Royal, at the northern end of the Luray Valley, to take Front Royal was to break the line of supply of an enemy in the main Valley. Once that line were lost to an invader, he would be compelled to get his supplies from Winchester by wagon. If that long and tenuous line were broken, the enemy would be compelled to retreat toward Winchester or westward over the Alleghenies.

These strategic possibilities of the Massanuttons were doubled for Jackson because he wisely had pitched his camps close to New Market. There he commanded the indispensable road over the mountains to Luray. So long as that road was in Jackson's hands, he could oppose the Federals in front as they advanced up the Valley toward New Market. Then, should the pressure be heavy, the Confederates could move over the mountain from New Market to Luray. If Banks pursued, he either could be met in the Massanuttons or he could be lured into the Blue Ridge. Should Banks decline to pursue over the Massanuttons and attempt instead to press on up the Valley pike, his rear would be exposed dangerously to troops descending the Luray-New Market road.

Much of this, Jackson had reasoned to a sound conclusion ere Banks's troops renewed their march. "Stonewall's" basic strategy, assuming an approximate parity of force, had been explained on April 5 to Longstreet: "With such a force," he had said, ". . . my opinion is that I could so threaten the enemy's rear as to induce him to fall back and thus enable me to attack him whilst retreating. . . ." [51] On the 14th, as Jackson had pondered a junction at Fisher's Gap, he had doubted whether Banks could be drawn into the Blue Ridge. "My desire," he had written, "is, as far as practicable to hold the Valley, and if I fall back from New Market

[51] *O. R.*, 12, pt. 3. p. 844.

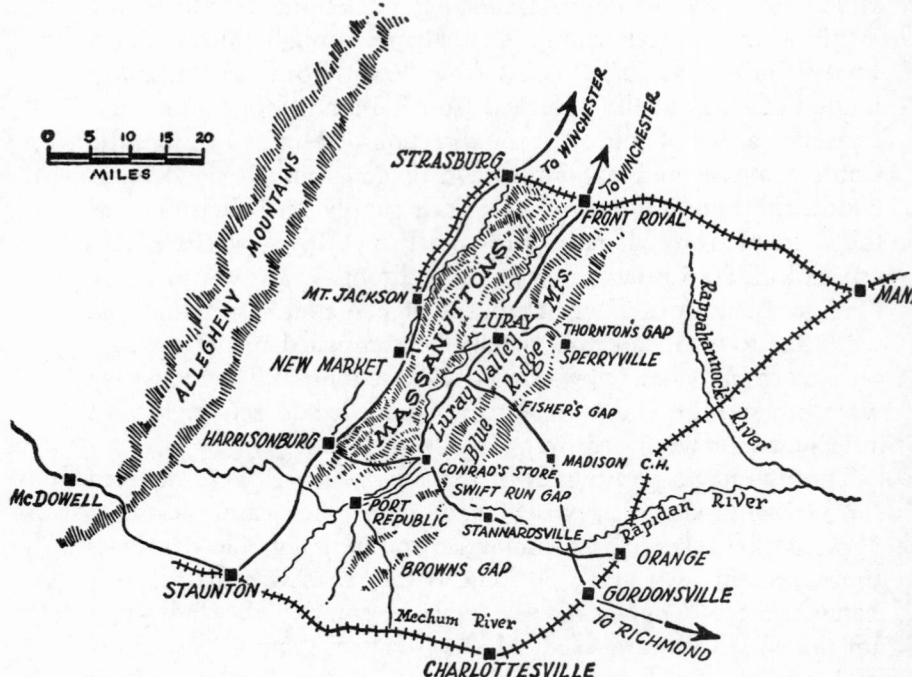

The Central Shenandoah Valley in relation to the passes of the Blue Ridge and the railroads of Midland Virginia. Particularly to be noted is the New Market-Luray road across the Massanuttons.

toward Madison Court House [*i.e.*, by Fisher's Gap], I hope that Banks will be deterred from advancing much further toward Staunton by the apprehension of my returning to New Market and thus getting in his rear." [52]

Initiative and its dynamic, which is imagination, are not for long the exclusive possession of one belligerent. What would happen if Banks should realize the importance of the New Market-Luray road, should seize it and then should press on toward Staunton? Jackson had considered that question prior to April 15 and had decided that, if the roads on the eastern side of the Blue Ridge were practicable, the vicinity of Swift Run Gap was a desirable point of concentration. On the 15th he had written to Ewell to ascertain whether there was a good road from Madison Court House to Stannardsville. Between Stannardsville

52 *O. R.*, 12, pt. 3, p. 848.

and the Gap, he had the road examined by his own officers.[53] If this route were practicable, Swift Run Gap had much the same strategic relationship to Harrisonburg that Luray had to New Market. That was still another geographical fact of the greatest importance that now became apparent to Jackson: by placing his troops at Conrad's Store, just West of the Gap, he would be in position to meet any force coming South down Luray Valley. If the Federals moved toward Staunton from Harrisonburg, he would be standing on their flank and could threaten their rear.

Were Conrad's Store and Swift Run Gap a position preferable to Fisher's Gap, seventeen miles farther North? The choice between them depended in large measure on how far Banks ventured, and on how heavily, after he reached New Market, he guarded the road to Luray. On the 17th, Jackson thought the junction with Ewell should be at Swift Run Gap, and he ordered Ewell to march toward that pass; [54] the next morning he thought Fisher's should be the point of concentration; [55] before evening he decided that Ewell would do better to march to Swift Run and thence toward Harrisonburg; [56] on the 20th, Jackson concluded that Ewell should halt East of the Blue Ridge, at an intersection from which an advance could be made either to Fisher's Gap or to Swift Run.[57] Ewell obediently and uncomplainingly made successive starts and stops,[58] and he corresponded on the friendliest terms, but in bewilderment he began seriously to doubt whether his brother officer over the mountains, who seemed so often to change his mind, was altogether sane.

Each day brought complications that justified the caution which Ewell mistook for vacillation or for aberration. Jackson established himself on April 19 at Conrad's Store; Banks moved slowly but confidently up the Valley, encamped his main force at New Market, advanced his outposts on the road to Harrisonburg, and showed no concern whatsoever about his adversary.[59] The Fed-

---

53 *O. R.*, 12, pt. 3, p. 849. A dispatch from Jackson to Ewell, dated April 12 and published in *ibid.*, 846, may have led some writers to assert that Jackson on the 12th ordered Ewell to join him at Swift Run Gap, but the dispatch patently was dated April 17, not April 12. Essentially the same paper, correctly dated, appears in *ibid.*, 853.

54 *O. R.*, 12, pt. 3, p. 853.   55 *O. R.*, 12, pt. 3, p. 854.
56 *O. R.*, 12, pt. 3, p. 857.   57 *O. R.*, 12, pt. 3, p. 857.
58 *Ibid.*, 857, 860.

59 It has been assumed by most Confederate historians of this campaign, and even by Henderson, that Banks's movements were paralyzed by the presence of Jackson at Conrad's Store, which Jackson reached on the 19th. The fact is, Banks was satisfied Jackson had left the Valley. *O. R.*, 12, pt. 1, pp. 445–46.

eral commander, moreover, was alive to the danger of an attack
via the Luray-New Market road. Not content with guarding
the western declivity, Banks promptly dispatched toward Luray
a covering force, which Jackson estimated at 1000 men.[60] These
troops reached the principal bridge across the South Fork of the
Shenandoah before Jackson could burn it.[61] "Stonewall" readily
enough could fall on the new guardians of this important crossing, but he felt that they had the advantage of ground and probably could hold out until reinforcements arrived from New
Market, which was distant only twelve miles.[62] Banks, for his
part, did not seem disposed to adventure farther eastward. He
had closed, at least temporarily, the road of attack on his rear
at New Market; he would not approach the Blue Ridge, whence
the Confederates could pour their fire on him.[63] Altogether,
Banks appeared to be checkmating Jackson.

Still further discouragement was presented Jackson by the
situation West of Staunton. Throughout the winter of 1861–62,
Brig. Gen. Edward Johnson had held the crest of the Allegheny
Mountains with a small contingent and had beaten off one attack
with so much success that he had received the *nom de guerre*
"Allegheny" Johnson. Rumor had it in the early spring that
heavy Federal columns under Maj. Gen. John C. Frémont were
marching against Johnson. They were said to be determined
not only to drive him from his high eyrie at Buffalo Gap,
west of Staunton, but also to descend on Staunton itself and
to cut Jackson's rail communications with Richmond. On April
15, Jackson had heard this rumor in some detail. There were
indications, also, that Banks might attempt to turn Johnson's
rear by a movement from Harrisonburg. Jackson doubted whether
the condition of the roads would permit this,[64] but he sent for
Johnson. When "Allegheny" reached camp—"a large and rather
rough-looking man on horseback"[65]—he was greeted with jeers
by the troops, who did not identify him; but he was welcomed

---

[60] Apr. 23. *O. R.*, 12, pt. 3, p. 863. On the 21st, Jackson thought this force 3000.
Ibid., 861.
[61] Columbia Bridge; *Hotchkiss' MS. Diary*, Apr. 19, 1862.
[62] *O. R.*, 12, pt. 3, p. 863.
[63] Jackson had doubted as early as April 14 whether Banks would pursue him to the
Blue Ridge (cf. *O. R.*, 12, pt. 3, p. 848), and he never cherished much hope of such
good fortune, unless Banks thought him in rout. (Cf. *ibid.*, 863.)
[64] *O. R.*, 12, pt. 3, p. 849.
[65] *McHenry Howard*, 86.

with much interest by Jackson. Their long discussion [66] led Jackson to conclude that Banks could so threaten Staunton, without exposing the Federal rear, that Johnson's small force would be compelled to fall back lest it be caught between one column from the North and another from the mountains. If Johnson had to withdraw from Buffalo Gap to a position East or South of Staunton, two things might happen: Johnson would be cut off from Jackson; the Federals who were marching against Johnson from the West could pass the barrier of the Alleghenies without opposition and would have no difficulty in reaching Staunton.[67] In short, it was altogether probable that Banks could assure the fall of Staunton without placing his own Army in material danger of attack by Jackson and Ewell. This probability was increased on April 21, when the van of the Federals occupied Harrisonburg. That same day, unknown to Jackson, a Federal force in considerable strength debarked at Aquia Creek to strengthen the troops already at Fredericksburg.

The outlook for the Confederates was gloomy—so gloomy that Jackson halted Ewell East of the Blue Ridge on the 22d.[68] The next day, in writing to General Lee in Richmond, "Stonewall" explained that he could not hope to attack Banks without Ewell. He could hold out no prospect, he said, better than that of assailing Banks's flank if the Federals advanced on Staunton, or of attacking some exposed point in the event Banks kept his main force at New Market.[69] It might be, Jackson admitted somewhat reluctantly, that Ewell would be of more use if sent to reinforce near Fredericksburg the Confederates, who were facing a steadily increasing Federal Army.[70]

To add to all Jackson's difficulties, part of Ashby's cavalry had become demoralized. The twenty-one companies were scattered over a wide area. Those on detached duty were directed solely by their own Captains, some of whom were incompetent. On the 16th, at Columbia Furnace, seven miles from Woodstock, an entire company of sixty men had been captured with their mounts.[71] Three days later, when Jackson had sent Jed. Hotchkiss to burn the bridges across the South Fork of the Shenan-

[66] *Hotchkiss' MS. Diary*, Apr. 20, 1862.
[67] *O. R.*, 12, pt. 3, p. 863.
[68] *O. R.*, 12, pt. 3, p. 861.
[69] *Ibid.*
[70] *O. R.*, 12, pt. 3, p. 863.
[71] *O. R.*, 12, pt. 1, p. 426.

doah, the engineer had found many men on outpost *hors de combat* because of overindulgence in a favorite regional beverage, to wit, applejack. In a clash that had followed, a drunken Captain and some of his men had run from charging Federals. Many of the gray-coated troopers took to the woods during a pursuit of three miles. A few of them actually crossed the Blue Ridge, to be seen no more for ten days.[72]

Such disgraceful conditions, of course, were contagious and were a threat to all future operations. Jackson had received a hint from Richmond that he would do well to regiment the twenty-one companies of cavalry,[73] and he undertook now to divide them for disciplinary training. He assigned Ashby to the command of the advance, with authority to apply for such forces as he required. Eight other companies were divided equally between the First and Third infantry Brigades.[74] The result was a rumor that the resignations of Colonel Ashby and Major Funsten would be tendered immediately if, indeed, they were not actually placed before Jackson.[75]

What should Jackson do? Major Funsten was a gallant and useful officer, but he probably could be replaced. Ashby could not be. That is to say, no known individual could hope to command the admiration of the troopers as he did, or, perhaps, even to hold together their loose and undisciplined units. Ashby's every act had made the eyes of his men brighten. Hour after hour, his guns had barked in front of Rude's Hill when the Federals had shown themselves. Within a month, his soldiers boasted, he had engaged the enemy twenty-eight times.[76]

On the day following the disgraceful affair at Columbia Furnace, Ashby had set an example of cold courage. He had reported to Jackson the advance of the enemy and had sent back his artillery. Then, with a few men, he had taken position on the

---

[72] *Hotchkiss' MS. Diary,* Apr. 19, 1862.

[73] As of Apr. 16, 1862, Walter H. Taylor had written that Lee desired to know whether the companies had been organized into regiments, and whether the election of officers, as required by law, had been held. It was necessary, Lee admonished, in order that the men be well drilled and disciplined, to provide the requisite number of officers. —*Jackson MSS.* At this time, it will be recalled, the twenty-one companies, which must have numbered at least 1200 sabers, had one Colonel and one Major, and no other officers above the grade of Captain.

[74] *Laurel Brigade,* 51; *Hotchkiss' MS. Diary,* Apr. 25, 1862; *Jackson's MS. Order Book,* G. O. 41; *Jackson's MS. Letter Book,* Apr. 25, 1862.

[75] On this point there is a conflict of testimony. See *infra,* n. 79.

[76] *Laurel Brigade,* 50.

hill overlooking Stony Creek to observe the Federal approach and, at the last minute, to fire the bridge. He lighted the combustibles in ample time, but they burned so slowly that a Federal patrol dashed up, crossed the bridge and drove Ashby and his escort down the pike. Ashby was intent on reaching his rearguard so that he could turn, challenge his pursuers, run them back across the bridge and set it aflame. He scarcely gave a glance at the enemy and none, apparently, at one Federal who dashed after him, ahead of the others, in a gallant attempt to overtake him. Just as the Federal fired on Ashby, one of the small Confederate escort, Harry Hatcher of Loudoun, wheeled in the road and killed the bluecoat. Ashby rode calmly on. He was more concerned, by far, at the fatal wounding of his famous white horse than at the danger to himself.[77]

Of this and a score of other daring ventures, Jackson had full knowledge. To lose Ashby might be to anger and demoralize the cavalry; but to leave the cavalry undisciplined would be to lose its service. Earlier fears were confirmed: manifestly, for all his prowess and brilliance in combat, Ashby was neither a disciplinarian nor an army administrator.

Again the question: what should be done? In suggesting an answer, Charles Winder rendered his first substantial service to the Army. He had survived the prediction of some army malcontents who believed Jackson crazy and felt that Winder would be arrested within a few weeks after assuming command.[78] Not only was Winder still head of the Stonewall Brigade, but he also had begun to make friends. Among them was Ashby. The two seemed to understand and to appreciate each other from the outset. As soon as Winder heard of the controversy, he went to Ashby, talked with him, and then boldly rode to Jackson's headquarters and undertook to mediate. After some conferences, Jackson decided on a personal meeting with the cavalryman.[79]

[77] *Laurel Brigade*, 49–50; *Hotchkiss' MS. Diary*, April 17, 1862; *McHenry Howard*, 84 n., *Douglas*, 41. Ashby's rearguard had moved so far that he did not reach it in time to muster his men and to return to burn the bridge.

[78] *McHenry Howard*, 82.

[79] *McHenry Howard*, 90. Howard is authority for the statement that Ashby gave a written resignation to Winder "and trusted the forwarding of it to [Winder's] judgment." Other officers state that the resignation was sent to Jackson. As Howard's relations with Winder put him in a position to know the facts, his testimony seems of sufficient weight to justify the doubt expressed in the text concerning the majority opinion and the traditional view that the resignation actually was tendered.

Ashby came on the evening of April 24. For hours the two were alone. Precisely what was said, neither explained afterward. The next morning, Jackson issued a new order whereby, in few words, all the cavalry companies assigned the previous day to the two Brigades were "detailed from those Brigades" and "placed under the command of Col. Turner Ashby." [80]

"The difficulty . . . has been settled for the present by General Jackson backing square down," wrote Maj. J. A. Harman, who the preceding day had thought the Army "in great danger from our crack-brained General." [81] More friendly observers explained that Jackson had restored the whole of the cavalry to Ashby on that officer's promise to discipline his troopers,[82] though left to dispose them as he saw fit.

Neither of these statements was precisely correct. Jackson had made the best compromise he could without direct reversal of his former stand. Ashby remained in titular command of the advance and of the advance only; the cavalry previously taken from him were "detailed," not assigned, to his continued direction.

Ashby was satisfied; Jackson technically maintained control of the companies, but he did not deceive himself. His report of the incident, made to General Lee, faced the facts with candor. Ashby, said Jackson, "claimed that I could not interfere with his organization, as he was acting under the instructions of the late Secretary of War, Mr. Benjamin," who had authorized Ashby to "raise cavalry, infantry and heavy artillery." Jackson went on: ". . . such was Colonel Ashby's influence over his command that I became well satisfied that if I persisted in my attempt to increase the efficiency of the cavalry it would produce the contrary effect, as Colonel Ashby's influence, who is very popular with his men, would be thrown against me." [83] This was a new aspect of Jackson's character, a contradiction of the prevalent belief among his men that he never yielded. He had taken, for the country's sake, a realistic view of a situation he could not change immediately, and he buttressed his position by an official letter to Ashby, in which he requested that officer to continue

80 *Jackson's MS. Order Book*, G. O. 42.
81 *Harman MSS.*, Apr. 25, 26, 1862.
82 *Hotchkiss' MS. Diary*, Apr. 25, 1862.
83 May 5, 1862; *O. R.*, 12, pt. 3, p. 880.

in command of the advance, to make such disposition of his force as he saw fit, and to report it in writing to headquarters. In another letter, requesting a copy of Benjamin's authorization to raise troops, he directed Ashby not to permit "any instruc- tions from these headquarters to interfere with those received from the War Department." [84] None of this changed Jackson's conviction that "the cavalry should be organized into regiments at the earliest practicable moment." [85]

While the camps were agog on the 26th with discussion of this clash, the cavalry commander, who had not relaxed his vigilance in asserting his authority, reported that the enemy was advancing on him and was within six miles of Jackson's posi- tion at Conrad's Store.[86] It was apparent that Banks was moving his main Army from New Market to Harrisonburg.[87] Although still guarding the road across the Massanuttons to New Market, he was reducing force in the Luray Valley.[88]

What did this indicate and what did it require Jackson to do? He held to his belief that Banks would not venture farther toward the Blue Ridge,[89] but, of course, either defensive or offensive demanded that all the Confederate forces be concen- trated. Orders consequently were dispatched to Ewell that same day, April 26, to move to Stannardsville.[90] On the 27th, as Banks made no farther advance, Jackson directed Ewell not to wear out his men by forced marches but to bring them in good fighting order, on the 28th, as close as possible to Swift Run Gap.[91]

Beyond that, what was practicable? Lee's injunctions from Richmond conformed wholly to Jackson's inclination to assume the offensive. If Banks could not be attacked, Lee suggested, Jackson might consider the possibility of a rapid drive against Warrenton, where a small Federal force was reported. Such a

[84] Jackson's MS. Letter Book, Apr. 25, 1862.
[85] O. R., 12, pt. 3, p. 880. It should be said, in justice to those who have misstated the details of this famous controversy, that the facts could not be established until the Hotchkiss Papers were accessible.
[86] O. R., 12, pt. 3, p. 868.   [87] O. R., 12, pt. 3, p. 871.
[88] O. R., 12, pt. 3, p. 870. Banks reported to the War Department on the 26th that he had two Brigades of infantry, 600 cavalry and two batteries at Harrisonburg, and that his advance was at Mount Crawford, "eight miles from Staunton." O. R., 12, pt. 3, p. 106. The General was in error concerning the distance, or else there was an error in transmission. Mount Crawford is eighteen miles from Staunton.
[89] O. R., 12, pt. 3, p. 871.
[90] O. R., 12, pt. 3, p. 869.   [91] O. R., 12, pt. 3, p. 870.

move might relieve the pressure on Fredericksburg and, indirectly, the threat of an advance on Richmond from the North.[92] Jackson knew nothing of the strength of this force at Warrenton,[93] which Ewell had not taken seriously,[94] and he promptly discarded the idea of attacking it unless the general strategic situation in Virginia made such a step necessary.[95] His flaming desire was to attack Banks, whose sprawling column seemed, in Jackson's words, to present "the golden opportunity for striking a blow." [96] With 5000 men to reinforce his own and Ewell's Divisions, Jackson believed he could assail Banks in front and drive the Federals. Until Jackson heard whether Lee could supply the reinforcements, he would seek an exposed point and attack it.[97]

Such was Jackson's state of mind on April 28. That night must have been one of prayer and reflection. He had to consider the probability that Lee would not be able speedily to send him reinforcements. What should he do if the answer came from Richmond that he must conduct his campaign for the time with the forces he had? Should he remain potentially on the flank of Banks and hope, as he had written Lee, to strike some isolated force, while the enemy elsewhere moved without hindrance? Must Jackson be content to hold Banks inactive and to permit his adversary so to threaten Staunton that Edward Johnson would have to retreat and let the town fall into the hands of Frémont who was now advancing from the West? Jackson had sent Jed. Hotchkiss to ascertain the exact situation on Johnson's front. Would it be possible to reinforce Johnson, to rout the Federals west of Staunton, and then . . .

As Jackson debated these questions, alone at his headquarters, three alternative answers shaped themselves in his mind:

First, he might go to Johnson's relief and assail Frémont's van, which was under Brig. Gen. Robert Milroy.

Second, he might go northward down the Luray Valley, attack the Federals there and, if he beat them, start across the Massanuttons toward New Market—a move that would force Banks to retreat.

Third, he might sweep down the Luray Valley, pass Thorn-

92 *O. R.*, 12, pt. 3, p. 866.   93 *O. R.*, 12, pt. 3, p. 870.
94 *O. R.*, 12, pt. 3, p. 846–47, 851, 858, 868.
95 *O. R.*, 12, pt. 3, p. 871.
96 Apr. 28, 1862, *O. R.*, 12, pt. 3, p. 871.   97 *Ibid.*

ton's Gap, move to Sperryville and so threaten the Federals' long line of communications that Banks would retire.

This last possibility had something to commend it. No great difficulty would be encountered in reaching Thornton's Gap,

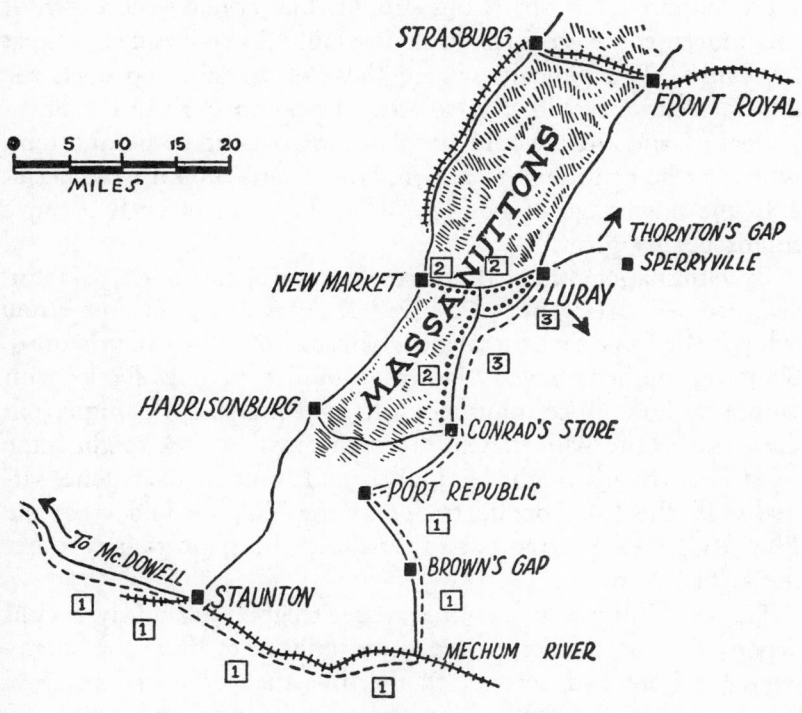

Jackson's Alternative Lines of Advance, end of April, 1862.

once the small, reduced Federal force around Luray were swept aside. The Confederates could concentrate safely at Sperryville on the eastern side of the Gap and could threaten Winchester, by way of Front Royal, or could move against the force at Warrenton. If the Federals collected around Sperryville a force he could not whip, Jackson reasoned that he could slip off via Culpeper Court House. The obvious defects of this course were three: it would not protect Staunton against an attack from the West; it would not involve the destruction of a single Army of the Federals; and it would not prevent the junction of the Union forces scattered North of the Rappahannock. No aspect of the plan conformed to Jackson's idea of the strategy his situation required, the strategy of "concentrating our forces on the enemy in his exposed positions." [98]

An attack on the Federals spread out from Luray to New Market was an operation that involved shorter marches than those required for operations around Sperryville. Moreover, if the movement were successful, it would force a quick retreat by Banks. The difficulties were those of terrain. To open the attack, Jackson would have to cross the South Fork of the Shenandoah,[99] and then would have to pass over the Massanuttons, where, as he continued to reason, "the enemy would have decidedly the advantage of position." [100] The risks of such a move might be too great.[101]

By elimination, then, the first alternative, the relief of Johnson, seemed preferable. Positive advantage was on the same side. If the force that threatened Johnson could be overwhelmed, Staunton might be saved. Jackson would have only Banks with whom to deal. Once Johnson was free of pressure, he might join the Army of the Valley. Reinforcements by that time might come from Lee. Banks might be assailed and routed. That done, virtually all the Confederate troops in the Valley could cross the Blue Ridge to Warrenton, to Fredericksburg or to any other threatened point.[102]

The possibility was exciting; the execution obviously would depend first on the force needed by Johnson to drive the enemy from his front and, second, on the time that would be required for the operation. Neither too protracted nor too great a diversion of force would be safe. If no more troops than Jackson had under his own command would be necessary for a swift, brief attack West of Staunton, might not the movement be undertaken? Banks, of course, would need watching, lest he march on Staun-

[98] For Jackson's advocacy of this course, in the words quoted, see his letter of Apr. 28, 1862, to Lee. *O. R.*, 12, pt. 3, p. 871.

[99] It should be noted that in his explanation of these alternatives Jackson spoke of the Federal "detached force between New Market and the Shenandoah" (*O. R.*, 12, pt. 3, p. 872), whereas, for clarity, the river has been described in these pages as the South Fork. The context makes plain that this and not the North Fork, which is a short distance West of New Market, was the stream to which Jackson referred.

[100] *O. R.*, 12, pt. 3, p. 872.   [101] *Ibid.*

[102] This sentence, which is almost in Jackson's own words, is of itself a sufficient refutation of the view that Jackson, at this period of the Valley campaign, already contemplated the offensive use of his Army of the Valley to threaten Washington and thereby to relieve pressure on Richmond. It will be noted that Jackson's conception of the possible use of his forces, after Banks had been driven from the Valley, was that they would bolster the defensive.

ton, but could not that be accomplished by bringing Ewell across the Blue Ridge and placing him in the strategic flank position at Conrad's Store? Carefully, in a letter to Lee on the 29th, Jackson canvassed this and the alternative plans. The Valley commander ended thus: "I have written to General Edward Johnson to know what force, in addition to his command, would be required for a successful blow in his vicinity. If I receive an answer justifying a move in that direction I may leave here tomorrow via Port Republic." [103]

That afternoon of the 29th, at 4 o'clock, in misty weather, Jed. Hotchkiss reached headquarters and reported the results of his conference with General Johnson. The engineer described also the condition of the roads over which he had passed and furnished much topographical information of the sort his sharp eyes always observed.[104] Jackson listened and questioned, but gave no intimation of what he intended to do. All he said was that Hotchkiss the next morning should go to a designated lookout at the southern end of the Massanuttons and, if he observed any movements of the Federals, should signal to Colonel Ashby, whose troops were to advance up the road toward Harrisonburg.

From the opening of operations Jackson had kept his own counsel. Although he had changed troops at the front every three days [105] and had met his general staff officers daily,[106] he had said nothing of his plans. "I think General Jackson is entirely too close about everything," Maj. John A. Harman, as early as April 23, had grumbled.[107] Even Ewell had been admonished to keep from people in the neighborhood of Madison Courthouse any hint of an advance to that point.[108] This secrecy on Jackson's part now was redoubled. When Ashby went out on the

---

[103] O. R., 12, pt. 3, p. 872.

[104] Hotchkiss in his MS. Diary mentioned no letter to Johnson or one from him. It is impossible to say whether he made verbal report on the number of troops Johnson would require to rout the enemy, but in his entry of Apr. 28, he noted that he discussed with Johnson "the enemy's position . . . and the feasibility of capturing it." Probabilities are that Jackson received a written answer from Johnson, and that Hotchkiss, who had been going to Staunton on private business, had been instructed to report solely on the terrain and the strength of the Federals. This statement postulates no distrust of the loyal Hotchkiss, but the procedure would have accorded with Jackson's sound practice that military secrets should be confided to the smallest possible number of persons. If Hotchkiss brought no letter from Edward Johnson, then Jackson must have received a communication from Johnson by some other hand prior to 4 P.M. and subsequent to the hour at which Jackson had written General Lee.

[105] Hotchkiss' MS. Diary, Apr. 7, 1862.   [106] See supra, p. 304.

[107] Harman MSS.   [108] O. R., 12, pt. 3, p. 861.

morning of April 30, to make the demonstration on the Harrisonburg road, he doubtless thought he was to "feel out" the Federals, but actually he was screening a move. Later in the day, Jackson gave terse orders and started his columns on the road to Port Republic. Only one man beside himself at Conrad's Store had any inkling of the plan. That man was Major General Ewell. Briskly that morning, Ewell had come through Swift Run Gap and had placed his 8000 men in the camps Jackson evacuated.[109] Ewell himself had scant information. All he knew was that Jackson was setting out for Staunton to aid Johnson, and that he, Ewell, was to hold Banks in check until Jackson returned.

109 Cf. *Hotchkiss' MS. Diary*, Apr. 30. 1862; Ewell to Lee, *O. R.*, 12, pt. 3, p. 876.

CHAPTER XXIII

"DICK" EWELL STICKS BY A "CRAZY MAN"

RICHARD STODDERT EWELL, to whom Jackson assigned the task of keeping Banks occupied during the mysterious absence of the Army of the Valley, had been 44 years of age in 1861. After he had resigned his Captain's commission in the 1st Dragoons and had tendered his service to Virginia, he modestly asserted that in two decades of service in the cavalry, he had learned all about commanding fifty dragoons and had forgotten everything else.[1] Actually, he had been a good soldier all his life—had been graduated well at West Point,[2] had been awarded his Captain's brevet in Mexico, and in the West had been daring and diligent. Tall tales were told of his pursuit of two deserters who went off with a pair of his horses;[3] tales scarcely less tall he himself related of a steed he had owned in Texas, Tangent by name, who always was going to win a race and always lost his master's bets but never his confidence.[4] Ewell was an excellent cook,[5] though a chronic dyspeptic[6] and, despite a lisp,[7] was voluble. Completely bald, and with bulging, bright eyes, he was likened by some to an eagle, by some to a woodcock. When he spoke, he put his head to one side, and as likely as not he swore.

It was averred of him that in a skirmish at Fairfax Courthouse, May 31, 1861, he had rushed out partially clad to rally some green troops; but his own forthright version was that he had been wounded and had been prompted to throw off his uniform coat, lest the enemy observe that he was an officer and make a special effort to capture him.[8] Ewell's subordinates insisted, further, that when they had complained of a shortage of beef, he had affirmed that he could find cattle, had gone off in person,

---

[1] R. Taylor, 37.
[2] Cullum, No. 1029; thirteenth in the class of 1840. George H. Thomas had been twelfth.
[3] Hamlin's Ewell, 92.   [4] Sorrel, 56–57.   [5] Hamlin's Ewell, 143.
[6] R. Taylor, 37–38. Dr. Percy Hamlin thinks Ewell had ulcer of the stomach.
[7] Sorrel, loc. cit.
[8] Companions in Arms, 458; 10 S. H. S. P., 374; O. R., 1, 63.

and had returned triumphantly with a solitary, bewildered and time-battered bull. A moment later Ewell had been crestfallen at the reminder that this venerable animal would not feed 8000 soldiers. "Ah," he had said humbly, "I was thinking of my fifty dragoons!" [9] His peculiarities had endeared him to the Army and had not stood in the way of his rapid promotion. A Lieutenant Colonel of the Virginia service in April, 1861, he was a Major General, P. A. C. S., before the end of January, 1862.[10] Now he occupied at Conrad's Store, on the flank of Banks's Army at Harrisonburg, a position of instant strategic importance.[11]

With Ewell were three Brigades of infantry. At the head of one of these was Arnold Elzey, who gallantly had handled Kirby Smith's troops at Manassas after that officer had been wounded. Another of Ewell's Brigades was under Isaac R. Trimble, a Virginian whose family had moved to Kentucky, from which State he had gone to West Point. Graduated there in 1822, he had served ten years in the artillery and then had resigned to embark on what proved to be a distinguished career as a railroad construction engineer and superintendent. Fifty-nine when the war began, Trimble did his utmost to block the railroad north of Baltimore, in order to delay the arrival in Washington of Union volunteers. Later, when convinced that the secession of Maryland would be prevented, he had come to Virginia. At first there had been complaints that he did not know how to manage or to manœuvre troops,[12] but he had persisted and in November had received formal assignment to Crittenden's Brigade.[13] During the withdrawal from Manassas, he had charge of train movement, which was an assignment that would have overtaxed the ingenuity of any railroad man.[14] He had survived that strain, had rejoined his Brigade, and had endured the minor hardships of the long wait on the Rappahannock. In the eyes of his fellow officers, he seemed old and perhaps fussy. The plainly dressed Jackson was on a memorable day to joke at Trimble's

[9] R. Taylor, 38.

[10] Nominated and confirmed January 24; Wright, 24–25.

[11] For Ewell's previous assignments in Confederate service, see O. R., 2, 944; 5, 913, 935, 939, 1029, 1056, 1079; 51, pt. 2, pp. 36, 95; Richmond Examiner, April 27, p. 1, col. 5; Richmond Dispatch, Nov. 12, 1861, p. 1, col. 5. The last reference quoted resolutions of the Sixth Alabama on his transfer to a different brigade.

[12] O. R., 5, 949, 959, 960; ibid., 51, pt. 2, pp. 357, 372, 375; Richmond Dispatch, Nov. 25, 1861, p. 2, col. 3.

[13] O. R., 5, 967.   [14] O. R., 5, 1089.

black army hat, with its cord and its sweeping feathers,[15] but Trimble was to have a gallant revenge.

Ewell's third Brigadier was Richard Taylor, brilliant only son of President Zachary Taylor. Schooled at Harvard and at Yale, widely travelled and even more widely read, "Dick" Taylor had operated a fine sugar plantation in Louisiana and had played a gentleman's part in politics. Although he had received no formal military training, he had studied enthusiastically the campaigns of great captains. Early in the war he had been elected Colonel of the Ninth Louisiana Infantry, which he had brought to Virginia just too late for it to participate in the Battle of Manassas. In October he had been promoted Brigadier General, and had been assigned five regiments from his State in Johnston's Army.[16] Army gossip had it that he received at that time a tender of the post of Quartermaster General,[17] but he remained with his troops and brought them to a high state of discipline. At 32, he was absolutely self-reliant. With a "total irreverence," as a tactful comrade put it, "for any man's opinion," [18] he combined deep affection for those he admired. His antipathy was no less marked toward those whose conduct he thought unworthy. He believed Ewell as queer as his division commander considered him odd,[19] but the two were the staunchest of friends. When the Confederacy was no more than a memory, Taylor in his published reminiscences [20]—among the most fascinating of military memoirs—was to present pictures of Ewell that Thackeray would not have disowned.

With Taylor, and much chastened by his stern discipline, which was based on a discerning knowledge of them, served the Louisiana Tigers. They had taken all the praise lavished on them for their conduct at Manassas, and along with it they had taken virtually everything else on which they could lay hands.[21] Now they were as ready to fight as to loot, and again they were under the eye of their daring Major. "Rob" Wheat had survived his

15 5 C. V., 613; see infra, p. 444, n. 33.

16 Richmond Dispatch, July 11, 1861, p. 2, col. 3; O. R., 2, 1000; O. R., 5, 913, 936, 960, 1030; IV O. R., 1, 144.

17 Richmond Dispatch, Oct. 26, 1861, p. 3, col. 2.

18 D. H. Maury in 7 S. H. S. P., 345.   19 20 S. H. S. P., 33.

20 Destruction and Reconstruction.

21 Two or three of them had been court-martialled and executed during the winter for forcing a guard that had arrested some of the battalion. R. Taylor, 25; McHenry Howard, 59.

wound of July 21, as if to spite the surgeons. For adventures as amazing as any he had known in Mexico or in Italy, he waited in the rain of the dripping camp that Jackson had vacated and Ewell had occupied.

Ewell's instructions from Jackson were of the meagerest and most embarrassing: he was to watch Banks and, presumably, was authorized to assail an exposed force in Jackson's absence, if he could do so without too great risks; but how was Ewell to determine the risks? He was a stranger to Ashby and had no intelligence system for operating within the enemy's lines. The first plan that occurred to Ewell, after he studied the ground, was to attack Banks's communications by way of the road from Luray to New Market. Jackson had said something of this before his departure. Accordingly, Ewell on May 2 or 3 wrote Jackson to ask his judgment of such an advance and to inquire how Jackson had ascertained what the enemy was doing. The answer, which came back promptly, was neither encouraging nor illuminating. Jackson barred the attack as too hazardous. For the rest, he wrote: "I have been relying on spies for my information from the enemy." [22] This did not have a good effect on Ewell's temper. When rumor reached him, about the same time, that Banks was moving on him, he fairly seethed. Col. James A. Walker of the Thirteenth Virginia, who called at headquarters, was admonished by a staff officer that he would do well not to broach his business. Consequently, Walker was about to ride off when Ewell called him. "Colonel Walker," he began abruptly, "did it ever occur to you that General Jackson is crazy?"

Walker, who had been one of Jackson's cadets, answered, "I don't know, General. We used to call him 'Fool Tom Jackson' at the Virginia Military Institute, but I do not suppose that he is really crazy."

"I tell you, sir," Ewell stormed, "he is as crazy as a March hare. He has gone away, I don't know where, and left me here with instructions to stay until he returns. But Banks's whole army is advancing on me, and I have not the most remote idea where to communicate with General Jackson. I tell you, sir, he is crazy,

---

[22] *O. R.*, 12, pt. 3, p. 878. As Ewell's letter to Jackson does not seem to be in existence, the nature of his inquiry has to be reconstructed from Jackson's answer and may not be altogether accurate, though the inferential evidence seems adequate.

and I will just march my Division away from here. I do not mean to have it cut to pieces at the behest of a crazy man." With that Ewell began furiously to pace the yard.

Glad enough to get away, Colonel Walker rode down to see his own brigade commander, Gen. Arnold Elzey. He, too, was in a rage over some order he had received from Ewell. "I tell you, sir," he roared to Walker, "General Ewell is crazy, and I have a serious notion of marching my Brigade back to Gordonsville."

At that moment, a raw conscript rushed into the room with a paper which he thrust before Elzey: "I want you, sir, to sign that paper at once, and give me my discharge. You have no right to keep me here, and I mean to go home!"

Elzey gasped. He stared at the man, then looked hastily around until his eyes lit on his pistols. With a bound he seized them, though not before the conscript sensed his purpose and sought safety in flight. Elzey tore open the holster as the man ran, and fired two shots while he pursued heavily. Missing his mark, he returned and glared at Walker: "I should like to know, Colonel Walker, what sort of men you keep over at the Thirteenth Regiment? The idea of the rascal's demanding of me, a Brigadier General, to sign a paper! Oh, if I only could have gotten hold of my pistols sooner."

Walker was perfectly self-contained and had withal a sharp sense of humor. He was equal to the occasion: "Well, I don't know what to do myself. I was up to see General Ewell just now, and he said that General Jackson was crazy; I come down to see you, and you say that General Ewell is crazy; and I have not the slightest doubt that my conscript, who ran from you just now, will report it all over camp that General Elzey is crazy; so it seems to me I have fallen into evil hands, and I reckon the best thing for me to do is to turn the conscripts loose, and march the rest of my Regiment back to Richmond." [23]

Elzey's loud laugh ended the incident, but, if the tale were told to Ewell, he could have rejoined with new evidence to support

[23] 9 *S. H. S. P.*, 364–65. This delicious story was told by Walker to J. William Jones, who published it in the form here given. Of course, in the telling, the tale was much adorned, but the conversation is so amusing that it deserves to be quoted as Jones set it down.

his contention that "Jackson was crazy." With his jesting liberality in crediting his superior with insanity, Ewell might have asserted that the whole military establishment of the Confederacy had gone mad. Conflicting orders rolled in. From White Hall, East of Brown's Gap, Jackson wrote on May 4 that Gen. Edward Johnson reported a Federal advance and urged Jackson to come to his support. Jackson added: "I accordingly press forward. Do what you can consistently with the safety of your command to prevent Banks giving assistance to the forces in front of Johnson." [24] The next day from Staunton, Jackson told Ewell that the enemy was reported to have left Harrisonburg. "If," said he, "the enemy has advanced in the direction of the Warm Springs it must be for the purpose of effecting a junction with Milroy,[25] and if you can do anything to call him back I hope that you will do so." [26]

Before Ewell could canvass this possibility, Jackson wrote again that his information pointed to a withdrawal by the Federals from Harrisonburg to Strasburg. "Should they move back there," Jackson directed, "I hope that you will follow as far as may be consistent with your safety, so that they may know that their movements are being watched." [27] Following this, Jackson sent a second dispatch on the 6th: "Has the enemy left Columbia Bridge yet? Do not leave the Valley so long as Banks is in it and I am on the expedition of which I spoke to you. If you will follow Banks down the Valley you will soon ascertain whether he designs going [sic] to cross the Blue Ridge." [28]

That was explicit enough, even though it set a difficult task before a single Division of 8000 men; but Jackson's orders were confused by proposals that General Lee made from Richmond by telegraph: "If enemy have withdrawn from Harrisonburg, I see no necessity for your division at Swift Run Gap. Object may be concentration at Fredericksburg. Try and ascertain. Can you cut off party at Culpeper Courthouse?" [29] Ewell pondered once more—to be interrupted by another courier from Jackson: "If

24 O. R., 12, pt. 3, p. 879.
25 Brig. Gen. R. H. Milroy, who had just been identified as commander of the advance of the army of Maj. Gen. J. C. Frémont, who was moving against Johnson. General Frémont at the time was head of the "Mountain Department."
26 O. R., 12, pt. 3, p. 881.   27 O. R., 12, pt. 3, p. 881.
28 O. R., 12, pt. 3, p. 882.   29 O. R., 12, pt. 3, p. 881.

the enemy go down the Valley beyond the neighborhood of Mount Jackson or New Market you should follow him but not compromise your safety." [30]

Ewell's temper was inflamed by these vexing suggestions, but it was relieved slightly that 7th of May by a skirmish near Somerville Heights, where the Seventh Louisiana lured into a trap the cavalry that was covering a bridge-burning expedition of the Thirteenth Indiana.[31] Satisfaction scarcely outlasted the day. To the exasperated General there came on the 9th and 10th a reiteration of orders from Jackson to watch Banks [32] and new suggestions from Lee that Banks might be preparing to move to Fredericksburg. Were that established, Ewell should attack him en route.[33] Ewell's respect for Lee did not cool his wrath over these endless changes of plan. He wrote Ashby, who had been sick: "When you are able to move, I should like to see you very much, as I am tired of waiting here. Gen. Jackson has stayed much longer than I anticipated. If I hear nothing definite from him in a few days I expect to be obliged to go back." [34] Ashby came promptly—to be greeted with this cheerful assurance: "I've been in hell for three days, been in hell for three days, Colonel Ashby! What's the news from Jackson?" [35]

[30] *O. R.,* 12, pt. 3, p. 882.

[31] For the reports, all Federal, see *O. R.,* 12, pt. 1, pp. 458 ff.

[32] *O. R.,* 12, pt. 3, p. 884.

[33] *O. R.,* 12, pt. 3, p. 885. Dabney, *op. cit.,* 340–41, left the impression, which Henderson, *op. cit.,* 1, 289, did not dispel as fully as he might, that Banks's withdrawal from Harrisonburg to New Market was due to the appearance of Ewell at Swift Run Gap and to the disappearance of Jackson. The facts are that Banks until May 1 thought Jackson in demoralization had quit the Valley. After that date, Banks's information was not seriously at fault, nor were his proposals unwise. A careful reading of the correspondence between him and the War Department, in *O. R.,* 12, pt. 3, pp. 118–80, will show that he thought Harrisonburg a needlessly advanced position and that the War Department, somewhat at his instance and somewhat because it deemed his line of communications too extended, ordered him back to Strasburg. As early as May 2, Banks presented as a possibility a movement by Jackson to reinforce Johnson (*O. R.,* 12, pt. 3, p. 126). His statement on May 3, "I do not think it possible to divide our force at this time with safety" (*O. R.,* 12, pt. 3, p. 129) was not the statement of a man whose bluff of an offensive had been called by the order to retire to Strasburg and to detach Shields's Division for co-operation with McDowell. On the contrary, Banks's warning was based on the knowledge that Ewell had brought "a very material increase" to Jackson's Army. The evidence does not show that Banks felt himself paralyzed by the presence of Jackson at Conrad's Store late in April, or that he was guilty of any serious strategical blunder from the time he reached Harrisonburg until he returned on May 13 to Strasburg. His failure after that date to appreciate fully the strategical importance of Front Royal may be another matter.

[34] Letter of May 11; *Avirett,* 402.

[35] F. M. Myers, *The Comanches,* 37–38. Ashby is there addressed as General, but he still was a Colonel.

Either from Ashby, then, or from the absent commander, in a few hours,[36] Ewell learned that Jackson had joined Johnson and, on May 8, had given battle to Brig. Gen. R. H. Milroy at McDowell, twenty-five miles west of Staunton. The advance had been more spectacular than the engagement. Jackson had turned off at Port Republic and after one of the muddiest, most difficult marches of the entire war,[37] had crossed the Blue Ridge at Brown's Gap. By way of White Hall, he had reached Mechum River Station on the Virginia Central Railroad and had moved his little Army by train to Staunton. Thence he had marched out the Parkersburg Turnpike, had joined Johnson and had repulsed a Federal attack. Milroy had retreated after the action, though he had sustained only 256 casualties for the 498 he had inflicted on the Confederates.[38] Jackson had started in pursuit but had been able to accomplish little. The roads were incredibly bad; his transport was feeble.

During the march and the pursuit, two of Jackson's subordinates were conspicuous. In the opening action, Edward Johnson was wounded in a manner that was to render him *hors de combat* for many months. Winder had different fortune. He felt himself humiliated by Jackson in some trivial matter, and he spoke sharply, perhaps insubordinately, to Jackson. Contrary to the expectation of bystanders, Jackson had refrained from putting the Brigadier under arrest. That was not all. Ere the movement began, Winder had been ordered to reduce baggage and he had done so relentlessly. Some of his troops, who were sore already because of the displacement of Garnett, grew angry over this order and, as Winder passed, they yelled, "More baggage, more baggage." He ordered the offenders arrested, but he could not identify them. His abilities achieved what his attempt at punishment could not. Before the Army turned back toward the Shenandoah Valley, Winder had displayed so much enterprise and so clearly had established himself as a leader that when he rode onto the field where a service of thanksgiving was to be held, men in all the regiments of his Brigade cheered him. From

---

[36] Myers, *loc. cit.*, said Ashby made the announcement, but this may be an error.

[37] *Douglas*, 47–48; *McHenry Howard*, 92.

[38] 1 *Henderson*, 298–99. As Henderson wrote of this action in fullest detail, it is not deemed necessary to review here an engagement that tactically was not important.

that time, there was lessened coldness on the part of officers and of men toward Winder.[39]

All the while, Jackson had been intent on following Milroy, but he had not forgotten Banks. On the 10th of May, Jackson wrote Ewell: "Should circumstances justify it, I will try, through God's blessing, to get in Banks' rear; and if I succeed in this I desire you to press him back as far as may be consistent with your own safety should he fall back." [40] This was coupled with an inquiry whether Ewell could not use his own cavalry in the Valley and let Jackson have the whole of Ashby's command. Inasmuch as there was as yet no hint of the probable time of Jackson's return to the Valley, an inquiry concerning the withdrawal of Ashby's cavalry was not apt to improve Ewell's temper. When General Trimble later, on the 11th, from his camp in Swift Run Gap,[41] sent for cavalry to serve as couriers, Ewell transferred his resentment. To Col. "Tom" Munford he snapped: "Look here, send that old man Trimble a mounted man or two. Nobody is going to hurt him behind me, yet he wants some cavalry to keep him posted; and he has a fellow named Kirkland over on the mountain, on picket, who wants horsemen. I expect if a fellow in the woods would say *boo,* the whole crew would get away!" [42]

In a family letter, Ewell voiced his complete disgust with the situation: "I have spent two weeks of the most unhappy I ever remember. I was ordered here to support General Jackson, pressed by Banks. But he [Jackson], immediately upon my arrival, started on a long chase after a body of the enemy far above Staunton. I have been keeping one eye on Banks, one on Jackson, all the time jogged up from Richmond, until I am sick and worn down. Jackson wants me to watch Banks. At Richmond, they want me everywhere and call me off, when, at the same time, I am compelled to remain until that enthusiastic fanatic comes to some conclusion. Now I ought to be en route

[39] McHenry Howard, *op. cit.*, 99, 104, was of opinion that all the hostility to Winder was ended, but Dabney was of different mind. See *infra*, p. 398, n. 15.

[40] *O. R.*, 12, pt. 3, p. 886.

[41] *O. R.*, 12, pt. 3, p. 885.

[42] Munford in 7 *S. H. S. P.*, 526. That "fellow named Kirkland" was Colonel of the Twenty-first (originally the Eleventh) North Carolina. For Ewell's revised opinion of him and of Trimble, see *infra*, pp. 487–88.

to Gordonsville, at this place, and going to Jackson, all at the same time. That is, there is reason for all these movements and which one is taken makes it bad for the others. The fact is there seems no head here at all, though there is room for one or two. I have a bad headache, what with the bother and folly of things. I never suffered as much with dyspepsia in my life. As an Irishman would say, 'I'm kilt entirely.' " [43]

Ewell had heard from a deserter on the 11th that Maj. Gen. James Shields's Division of Banks's Army was preparing to march out of the Valley to reinforce McDowell, and the same day Ewell learned that two captured prisoners had three days' cooked rations on their persons.[44] Ewell at once sent this news to Jackson and ordered Col. T. T. Munford to take a regiment and more of cavalry, with two guns, and to do what he could to hamper Shields's movement. Munford was to start at midnight and was to report in person ere he departed.

At the designated hour, Munford knocked at Ewell's door. The General was abed, but he told Munford to enter and, with the aid of a map, attempted to explain to the Colonel the position of the various opposing forces. Munford wrote later: "Before I knew what [Ewell] was after, he sprang out of bed, with only a night-shirt on—no carpet on the floor—and spreading the map open . . . down on his knees he went; his bones fairly rattled; his bald head and long beard made him look more like a witch than a Major General. He became much excited, pointed out Jackson's position, General Shields' and General McDowell's, who was then at Warrenton [45] to act as McClellan's right wing." [46]

Then Ewell delivered himself: "This great wagon hunter is after a Dutchman, an old fool! General Lee at Richmond will have little use for wagons if all of these people close in around him; we are left out here in the cold. Why, I could crush Shields before night if I could move from here. This man Jackson is certainly a crazy fool, an idiot. Now look at this"—whereupon he handed the Colonel a dispatch in which Jackson announced his victory at McDowell, told of the capture of Milroy's wagon

[43] To Miss Lizzie Ewell, May 13, 1862; *Hamlin's Ewell*, 108.
[44] 7 *S. H. S. P.*, 526. Jackson's reference on the 12th to the receipt of Ewell's note concerning the cooking of three days' rations makes possible the dating of this incident and of the observations of Ewell on Trimble and Kirkland.
[45] Colonel Munford was mistaken in this: General McDowell was at Fredericksburg.
[46] 7 *S. H. S. P.*, 526.

train through the assistance of God, and admonished Ewell to hold his position.[47]

"What has Providence to do with Milroy's wagon train? Mark my words, if this old fool keeps this thing up, and Shields joins McDowell, we will go up at Richmond! I'll stay here, but you go and do all you can to keep these people from getting together, and keep me posted—follow Shields as long as it is safe, and send me a courier to let me know the hour you get off!"[48]

Munford hurried away. Ewell went back to bed and to sleep, but not for long. In a short time a courier came thumping noisily up the stairs and asked if Colonel Munford were there. Ewell barked at him: "Look under the bed—do you see him there? Do you know how many steps you came up?"

"No, sir," the boy answered.

"Well, I do, by every lick you gave them with that thing you have hanging about your feet, which should be hooked up when you come to my quarters. Do you know how many ears you have? You will go out of here less one, and maybe both if you ever wake me up this time anight looking for your Colonel."[49]

If the wrathful General enjoyed sleep after that, the next day found him in no happier state of mind. The news that Banks was cooking three days' rations was repeated.[50] Beyond that, nothing of a positive nature reached Ewell's headquarters. On the 13th, Ewell had information that some Federal units which had been at New Market were withdrawing across Massanutton to Luray and were marching toward Front Royal. This news seemed to be confirmed on the 14th.[51]

The detachment of this Federal force from New Market

---

47 This dispatch, which Colonel Munford quoted from memory, does not appear in the *O. R.*, but from the internal evidence was written late in the night of May 8 or early on the morning of May 9.

48 7 *S. H. S. P.*, 527.   49 *Ibid.*

50 Cf. *O. R.*, 12, pt. 3, p. 888, where Jackson mentioned receipt of a dispatch of the 12th on this subject. It may be observed here that the course of events during this interesting period of the Valley Campaign has been confused by failure to take into account the time required for the transmission of orders. Existing documents indicate that letters from the War Department to Ewell took two or two and a half days to reach him; that communications from Johnston, so long as he was East of Richmond, required four days; and that the time for the ride of a courier from Ewell to Jackson varied from one day to a day and a half. This condition, needless to say, has necessitated redating various events and some of the major decisions.

51 Ewell to Jackson, May 13, 1862 (two dispatches), *Jackson MSS.; O. R.*, 12, pt. 3, pp. 889, 893. Curiously enough, Federal dispatches do not show the route of Shields's march from New Market, but Ewell's letters and *Hotchkiss' MS. Diary*, May 19, 1862, make it plain that the march was via Luray.

naturally heightened Ewell's desire to strike a blow. More than ever he chafed under orders to remain where he was, though he realized the supreme importance of concentrating at Richmond. He consequently must have emitted a whoop of joy when a courier, later in the day of the 14th, delivered him a letter [52] in which Jackson expressed the view that Banks was not leaving the Valley but was manœuvring to cover Winchester and probably to co-operate with Frémont for a march on Staunton. Jackson continued: "If Banks goes down the valley I wish you to follow him, so that he may feel that if he leaves the valley, not only will we reoccupy it, but that he will be liable to be attacked as soon as he shall have sufficiently weakened his forces on this side the Shenandoah." [53]

"Follow him"—that long-sought permission was conditional on Banks's movement northward, but in it, at the least, was the hope of an end to the maddening delay at the foot of Swift Run Gap. Ewell resolved immediately but shrewdly to make the most of the order. Because he feared that Jackson might undergo another change of mind "at any minute," [54] Ewell did not project an advance that would carry him too far down the Valley or away from the gaps through which he might have to hasten toward Fredericksburg. Quickly he decided that he would march down the Luray Valley, not farther than Thornton's Gap, and that he would have part of the force at Gordonsville march by way of Fisher's Gap to meet him at Luray. This would assure a concentration in considerable force with minimum delay and at a strategic point whence he could move toward New Market, toward Front Royal or across the Blue Ridge. Orders to this effect were dispatched forthwith to General Branch at Gordonsville. The necessity of moving with a small wagon train was impressed on Branch. "The road to glory," wrote Ewell, "cannot be followed with much baggage." [55]

No sooner did Ewell formulate this plan and prepare to move

[52] Dated May 13; O. R., 12, pt. 3, pp. 888–89.

[53] In this letter Jackson observed: "If [Banks] leaves the Valley at this time, not only Winchester but the Baltimore and Ohio Railroad would be exposed, both of which it is important to the enemy to hold." O. R., 12, pt. 3, p. 888. Jackson, it will be observed, said nothing of the exposure of Washington by such a move. This is another and an important bit of evidence to show that Jackson at this time had not developed his strategic plan to the point where he contemplated a threat against Washington that would induce President Lincoln to withdraw troops from Virginia to protect the capital.

[54] O. R., 12, pt. 3, p. 890.   [55] O. R., 12, pt. 3, p. 890.

than another succession of contradictory orders began to arrive. Jackson instructed him to push forward the cavalry and to delay Banks until the Army of the Valley could return,[56] but that evening or the next morning, May 14 or 15, Ewell received from General Lee a telegram in which he was told to stay where he was, pending further orders, until Jackson's safe return was assured, unless Banks meantime quit the Valley altogether.[57]

"Dick" Ewell no longer was willing to swear over the conflict of counsel and then to wait for his superior officers to reach agreement. War was insistent. It would not wait on argument. A choice of action was imperative. Whatever the consequences to himself personally, Ewell had to disregard the instructions of Lee or of Jackson. The decision had to be made on the realities, not on the personalities. Ewell reasoned that one proviso had been met: Jackson already was secure. Besides, Ewell's information was that Ashby would reoccupy New Market on the night of the 15th,[58] and that no enemy remained on the Valley pike west of the Massanuttons and south of the New Market-Luray road. Sound strategy dictated an advance by Ewell on Luray and the movement to that town of Branch's force, except for such a guard as might be necessary to cover Gordonsville.[59] That was Ewell's decision. Jackson's instructions, not Lee's, must be followed. Orders followed decision. "You will take possession of what transportation is to be had at the post. . . . We can get along without anything but food and ammunition"—thus Ewell spurred Branch.[60] From Johnston, under date of May 13, came a letter in which the commanding General favored an offensive against the Federals in the Valley but said more imperatively than subjunctively: "Should [Banks] cross the Blue Ridge to join General McDowell at Fredericksburg, General Jackson and yourself should move eastward. . . ."[61]

New complications came on the 16th of May. Ashby had rumors of the dispatch of reinforcements from Banks to Frémont; Jackson consequently determined to retain the mounted forces

[56] O. R., 12, pt. 3, p. 889.
[57] O. R., 12, pt. 3, p. 889. This telegram was received at Gordonsville on the 14th. The hour is not known.
[58] O. R., 12, pt. 3, p. 892.   [59] O. R., 12, pt. 3, pp. 891–92.
[60] Ibid., 892.
[61] Ibid., 888. The receipt of this letter on the 15th is mentioned in Ewell to Jackson, May 16, infra.

in the western Valley and to use Ashby as a screen for his own advance. Ewell was told that if he struck at Banks's rail communications he must do so without Ashby. The one thing that sustained Ewell's hope of an offensive was this final sentence of a dispatch from Jackson: "The high water, I fear, will delay me some but I design moving, via Harrisonburg, down the Valley, and it may be that a kind Providence will enable us to unite and strike a successful blow." Ewell answered this by quoting his instructions of the 13th from Johnston and by reiterating his own willingness to move wherever he might strike a blow. "On your course," Ewell wrote Jackson, "may depend the fate of Richmond." Such hope as Ewell cherished that day was for the offensive.[62]

Even this hope was dashed for Ewell on the 17th by new dispatches. Lee wrote that Jackson was safe and was returning to the Valley—a fact that Ewell of course knew already—that Johnston had sent orders to Jackson, and that, if the two forces in the Valley could attack Banks, "it would make a happy diversion in our favor in other directions."[63] Jackson in his turn[64] ordered Ewell to move on New Market if Banks was not leaving the Valley. In the event the Federals were crossing the Blue Ridge, Ewell was to threaten them and, if he could, to detain them. There followed a hint from the cautious Jackson of a plan of attack which Ewell was admonished not "to breathe . . . to any one."[65]

What were the differences the harassed Ewell had now to contrast? Lee favored an offensive subject to such orders as Johnston had sent Jackson; the commander of the Valley District wanted to hold Banks and to attack him according to a plan that was taking definite form; Johnston was agreeable to this but was insistent that *if* Banks left the Valley, Ewell must follow him.

That "if," on which hung many potentialities, was no sooner stated than it seemed to be resolved for Ewell in the manner most distasteful to him: news came from two sources that 6000 of Banks's troops, under Shields, already were East of the Blue

---

[62] Ewell to Jackson, MS., May 16, 1862. *Jackson MSS.* Jackson's letter to Ewell is printed in *O. R.,* 12, pt. 3, p. 893.
[63] Letter of May 15, received at 2.55 P.M.. May 17. *O. R.,* 12, pt. 3, p. 891.
[64] From Lebanon White Sulphur Springs.
[65] *O. R.,* 12, pt. 3, p. 895.

Ridge.[66] That fact gave precedence to Johnston's orders. In the state of affairs that had arisen, Ewell had no discretion. No course seemed open to him other than to abandon all hope of a joint attack with Jackson on Banks and to climb over the mountains in pursuit of Shields.

Ewell regretfully advised Jackson by courier of his orders from Johnston and began preparations to cross Swift Run Gap, but he could not convince himself that the move, though mandatory, was wise. What if Shields *had* left the Valley? For a few days, at least, that officer was where he could do little harm to the Confederacy, and he had left Banks less able to beat off an attack. Jackson planned such an attack. Doubtless he was crazy, but the plan of which he had given Ewell a momentary glimpse in his dispatch of the 17th was one that might rout Banks. Must that plan of offensive action be abandoned and the forces in the Valley divided? Had Johnston, when he had written on the 13th, been aware of the full possibilities of smashing Banks?

These questions Ewell debated. He answered them with a sharp order: bring him his horse. He was going to ride to Jackson's headquarters.

[66] *O. R.,* 12, pt. 3, p. 894.

CHAPTER XXIV

JACKSON LAUNCHES HIS OFFENSIVE

WHEN Ewell reached Jackson's field headquarters at Mount Solon [1] on Sunday, May 18, [2] he saw "Stonewall" for the first time in the gray uniform of a Confederate Major General. Jackson had laid aside at Staunton on May 5 his rusty blue and had put on the coat and trousers required by Army regulations. [3] Not so easily had he met the requirements of Army administration. The efficiency of Edward Johnson's command was crippled by the bullet that struck down its leader. Adjustment of relations between Winder and his Brigade must have imposed some strain on Jackson. A reprimand of Major Harman had nearly cost Jackson the service of that unique Quartermaster. [4] Worse, far, than all of this had been a near mutiny in the Twenty-seventh Virginia of his own old Brigade. Several companies of the regiment, while at McDowell, had laid down their arms. The promised twelve months of service, the men asserted, they had performed. To conscript them after the expiration of their term of enlistment was a breach of faith. When their Colonel had failed to persuade them to return to duty, he reported the situation to the commanding General. With flashing eye and stern manner, Jackson had demanded: "What is this but mutiny?

[1] Ten miles Southwest of Harrisonburg.

[2] Henderson unfortunately gave this date as May 17, *op. cit.*, 1, 303, and thereby threw out of sequence some of the most important preliminaries of the campaign. Hotchkiss, in his MS. Diary, and Dabney, 359, state the date to have been the 18th. Douglas, *op. cit.*, 93, stated that Ewell reached Jackson on the 20th, and he quoted an alleged conversation between them that seems distinctly out of character. Jackson scarcely would have inquired, "What—are the Yankees after you?" nor would Ewell have blurted out, even if none save staff officers were present, "Worse than that, I am ordered to join General Johnston." Some exchange between the two officers doubtless occurred, but it probably was in form less dramatic, and it was on the 18th, not on the 20th.

[3] *Hotchkiss' MS. Diary*, May 5, 1862.

[4] Maj. J. A. Harman was told by Jackson on May 15 that he did not show his former "driving disposition" and that he pried too much into military matters. Indignant at this, Harman immediately asked to be relieved and told Jackson he intended to resign. Jackson's manner seemed to Harman more friendly after this clash, but the quartermaster insisted later that "Jackson's mysterious ways are unbearable," that the commander was "a hard master and that nothing but a mean spirited man remain [*sic*] long with him." *Harman MSS.*, May 15, June 13, 1862.

Why does Colonel Grigsby refer to me, to know what to do with a mutiny? He should shoot them where they stand." Jackson then had ordered the Colonel to parade his regiment instantly with loaded muskets, to place the mutineers, unarmed, before the rest of the regiment and to give the men the alternative of accepting service or of being killed in their tracks. The mutinous companies had yielded at once. Soon they could not be distinguished "from the rest of the regiment in their soldierly behavior." [5]

Despite this affair and a score of minor vexations, Jackson had kept his force together, had closed all the roads by which Banks might communicate with Frémont,[6] and had marched hard to get within striking distance of Banks. The plan of Jackson's attack was formulated and his ardor fired anew by a letter just received from Lee. Writing on the 16th, Lee had discussed the movement of troops from Banks toward Front Royal and had speculated on their probable destination. Lee had said: "Whatever may be Banks' intention it is very desirable to prevent him from going either to Fredericksburg or the Peninsula, and also to destroy the Manassas road. A successful blow struck at him would delay, if it does not prevent, his moving to either place, and might also lead to the recall of the reenforcements sent to Frémont from Winchester, as reported by you." In the same letter, Lee had endorsed the employment in the Valley of the troops at Gordonsville.

After cautioning Jackson that Johnston might call all Confederate forces from the Shenandoah to Eastern Virginia, Lee had written: "Whatever movement you make against Banks do it speedily, and if successful drive him back toward the Potomac, and create the impression, as far as practicable, that you design threatening that line." [7] This was more than an elaboration of the plan for the offensive that Jackson long had wished. It was a suggestion of new strategic possibilities by advancing all the way to the Potomac. The proposal had set every nerve in Jackson's lank body atingle.

Now, at Mount Solon headquarters on May 18, Ewell interrupted the Sabbath calm. Sorrowfully he laid before Jackson

---

[5] *Dabney*, 354.
[6] All the details of this road obstruction are given in *Hotchkiss' MS. Diary*, May 9–11, 1862.
[7] *O. R.*, 12, pt. 3, pp. 892–93.

the instructions from Johnston and the report that Shields had moved East of the Blue Ridge. Was it imperative that Ewell conform? Must the whole exciting plan of an offensive against Banks be abandoned? That was the question put to Jackson. His judgment had been expressed clearly on the 17th. In a letter to Johnston he had stated: "I will move on toward Harrisonburg, and if you desire me to cross the Blue Ridge, please let me know by telegraph. My design was to try and defeat Banks, and then, by threatening Frémont's rear, prevent him from moving up the South Branch [of the Potomac] . . .[8] If I do not hear from you soon I will continue my march until I get within striking distance of him."

That was as much as Jackson could say to his superior, but, when he wrote, he had no assurance, and perhaps scant hope, that this statement would bring permission from Johnston to remain in the Valley and to attack Banks. Now, as Ewell reviewed the correspondence with Lee and with Johnston, the little hope that had remained to Jackson dwindled and died. Orders were orders! They were issued by authority and they must be obeyed—even though they cost the South such an opportunity as war rarely would offer. When Ewell had finished, Jackson spoke with resignation but in deep depression: "Then Providence denies me the privilege of striking a decisive blow for my country; and I must be satisfied with the humble task of hiding my little army about these mountains, to watch a superior force." [9]

Ewell might have repeated his question to Colonel Munford concerning the improbable relationship of Providence to the capture of Milroy's wagon train, but this time Ewell's sympathies were so entirely with Jackson that he did not protest against the association of the Almighty with military affairs. Earnestly, with his bulging eyes, Ewell stared at his commander and pondered: Although Jackson probably was insane, he was correct in thinking a unique opportunity was being thrown away. It was a shame to lose the chance of defeating the weakened Banks.

[8] Frémont's headquarters were at Franklin, high up that river, and twenty-one miles NNE. of Monterey on the road to Staunton.

[9] Dabney, 359. It is more than probable that the Rev. Dr. Dabney, an eloquent minister, unintentionally charged Jackson with more adjectives than the General actually used in this remark; but Jackson's declarations at such moments always were formal and often were tinged with some of the color of ministerial deliverance.

At length Ewell broke out with a bold proposal: He belonged to Johnston's Army; he was subject to Johnston's order; but so long as he was in the Valley District, Jackson was his immediate superior. If Jackson would say the word, he would disregard Johnston's orders and would remain in the Valley until Jackson received an answer to the letter he had written Johnston the previous day.[10]

Jackson accepted this gallant offer with eagerness and with gratitude. His own most recent instructions from Richmond had been contained in Lee's letter of May 16, which had urged him to drive Banks toward the Potomac. Regardless of the relative authority of Johnston and of Lee, the letter from the Military Adviser to the President was of date three days subsequent to Johnston's of May 13 to Ewell. On this fact, Jackson decided to base orders which Ewell could cite, if necessary, as justification for delay in crossing the Blue Ridge to pursue Shields. The final text read as follows:

> Headquarters Valley District,
> Mount Solon, May 18, 1862

Maj. Gen. R. S. Ewell,

Commanding Third Division, Army of the Peninsula:

General: Your letter of this date, in which you state that you have received letters from Generals Lee, Johnston, and myself requiring somewhat different movements, and desiring my views respecting your position, has been received. In reply I would state that as you are in the Valley District you constitute part of my command. Should you receive orders different from those sent from these headquarters, please advise me of the same at as early a period as practicable.

You will please move your command so as to encamp between New Market and Mount Jackson on next Wednesday night, unless you receive orders from a superior officer and of a date subsequent to the 16th instant.

> I am, general, your obedient servant,
>
> T. J. JACKSON,
> Major General.[11]

---

10 *Dabney*, 359. That author wrote without knowledge of the full correspondence and stated that the contingency "under which General Johnston had authorized [Ewell] to leave the Valley had not yet occurred." The *Official Records* make Ewell's action even more courageous than it appeared to Dabney.

11 *O. R.*, 12, pt. 3, p. 897.

Nothing was said in this letter of Branch's command which, under Ewell's orders of the 14th–15th, was to move from Gordonsville to Luray. Ewell did not direct otherwise now. Perhaps he reasoned that he would use Branch if he could; perhaps he told himself that if Johnston or Lee had any new instructions for Branch, they would be sent direct. Back, then, and in soldierly cheer, Ewell rode to Conrad's Store. This time he did not complain because he had once more to reverse all his preparations and to start troops, not for Stannardsville, East of the mountains, but for the strategic position at New Market. Preparation now meant action.

On the 19th, when the columns got in motion, Jackson sent orders that Ewell should camp beyond New Market the next day and, on the 21st, should proceed beyond Mount Jackson.[12] Ewell understood. It was not his entire force but Taylor's Brigade only that was to proceed down the western side of the Massanuttons. Under the vigilant eye of Taylor himself, the Louisianians made the long march to New Market on the 20th. As the Brigade approached, the veterans of Jackson's own command flocked to see the men from the far South. "Over 3000 strong," Taylor recalled, "neat in fresh clothing of gray with white gaiters, bands playing at the head of their regiments, not a straggler, but every man in his place, stepping jauntily as on parade . . . in open columns with arms at 'right shoulder shift,' and rays of the declining sun flaming on polished bayonets, the brigade moved down the broad, smooth pike and wheeled on to its camping ground." [13]

Taylor rode off to report to Jackson, whom, apparently, he never had met. To quote Taylor's own delightful narrative: "The mounted officer who had been sent on in advance pointed out a figure perched on the topmost rail of a fence overlooking the road and field, and said it was Jackson. Approaching, I saluted and declared my name and rank, then waited for a response. Before this came I had time to see a pair of cavalry boots covering feet of a gigantic size, a mangy cap with visor drawn low, a heavy, dark beard, and weary eyes—eyes I afterward saw filled with intense but never brilliant light. A low, gentle voice inquired the road and distance marched that day." [14]

12 O. R.. 12, pt. 3, p. 898.   13 R. Taylor, 49.   14 R. Taylor, 49–50.

"Keezletown road, six and twenty miles," answered Taylor.

"You seem to have no stragglers," Jackson observed.

"Never allow straggling," answered the confident young Brigadier.

"You must teach my people," said the senior, without a touch of satire; "they straggle badly."

At that moment, one of Taylor's bands struck up a gay air. Jackson, with no ear for music, listened attentively and took a suck at a lemon he held in his hand: "Thoughtless fellows for serious work," he concluded.[15]

It looked ere night, that 20th of May, that there would be no serious offensive work for thoughtless or for thoughtful fellows. Early in the day, Ewell had heard that Branch was moving toward Fisher's Gap and he had notified Jackson with the reminder, "I have given no order in the premises." Jackson had answered, "Let the troops come on. I wish they were at New Market."[16] Then Ewell received, like a bolt, a dispatch in which Branch announced that on the road to join Ewell he had been recalled by Johnston's order and had been directed to proceed at once to Hanover Court House, on the Richmond front.[17] Directly from Johnston there was, also, a letter to Ewell. Based on information that reflected conditions existing in the Valley about May 12,[18] this letter stated that if Banks were fortifying near Strasburg, it would be hazardous for Jackson and Ewell to attack him. Jackson must watch the enemy; Ewell must come East. Should the two find that Shields was on the Orange and Alexandria Railroad near the Rapidan, they might attack him jointly, after which Jackson might return to the Valley and Ewell might proceed eastward. Johnston ordered this on the principle that he should call to Richmond "all the troops who do not keep away from McClellan greatly superior forces."[19]

These were precisely such "orders from a superior officer" as Jackson had mentioned two days previously in the letter that had been written to give Ewell justification for remaining in the Valley. Now superior authority had intervened. There was no apparent alternative to direct and immediate compliance. All

15 *Ibid.*   16 *O. R.*, 51, pt. 2, p. 560.   17 *O. R.*, 12, pt. 3, p. 898.
18 *Cf.* Jackson's references to the fortification of Strasburg, which Ewell apparently had reported May 12; *O. R.*, 12, pt. 3, p 889.
19 *O. R.*, 12, pt. 3, pp. 896-97.

Ewell could do, pending execution of the orders, was to send the letter to Jackson, as Johnston requested in a postscript.

Jackson received promptly this new veto on an offensive against Banks. He knew that Johnston's information was days old and he felt that the course which Lee had urged was the proper one —to drive Banks toward the Potomac. Every hour was precious. A long delay in communicating with Johnston might give Banks time to carry out his own plans unhindered. The attack should be and, if possible, must be delivered, but it had to be authorized. The sole way of procuring permission promptly was to appeal to Lee. Accordingly, Jackson sat down and wrote this telegram:

> Camp Near New Market, Va.,
> May 20, 1862
>
> General R. E. Lee:
> I am of opinion that an attempt should be made to defeat Banks, but under instructions just received from General Johnston I do not feel at liberty to make an attack. Please answer by telegraph at once.
> T. J. JACKSON,
> Major General.[20]

Then he wrote across the bottom of Johnston's letter: "Major General Ewell: Suspend the execution of the order for returning to the east until I receive an answer to my telegram." [21] Ewell, on the 18th, had assumed the responsibility of delaying his movement from the Valley. Jackson now had a corresponding duty. If consent were given, he would attack as soon as he could bring his troops into position. The great opportunity was at its peak. It must not be lost. Shields was separated from Banks; Frémont and Banks had not formed a junction. With Lee's approval—or Johnston's or the President's—Jackson purposed to throw the whole Confederate force against the weakened Banks and to do even more than "drive him toward the Potomac."

The Army that Jackson concentrated while he awaited an answer from Richmond was large enough for the task he was fashioning for it. By hurling back the van of Frémont's column, he had added Johnson's 2500 to his own and Ewell's forces. Part of the troops from the Alleghenies he had placed under

---

[20] O. R., 12, pt. 3, p. 898.   [21] O. R., 12, pt. 3, p. 897.

the competent direction of Arnold Elzey.[22] The others, three Virginia regiments, were left with Col. W. C. Scott of the Forty-fourth Virginia, who had figured the previous summer in the unhappy affair at Rich Mountain.[23] Both these Brigades Jackson attached to Ewell's Division and thereby raised its effective strength to 10,000 muskets.[24] Ewell's cavalry, the Second and the Sixth Virginia, about 500 sabers, temporarily were under Col. Thos. S. Flournoy of the Sixth; but they were entrusted, ere the fighting ended, to Brig. Gen. George H. Steuart, a Marylander and formerly a Captain of the 1st United States Cavalry.[25] Steuart was known to be an experienced regular: there had been nothing to suggest that he was an excessively "strict constructionist" of Army regulations.

[22] Elzey's Brigade, as of Jan. 14, 1862, O. R., 5, 1030, had consisted of the First Maryland, the Third Tennessee and the Thirteenth and Sixteenth Virginia. The Third Tennessee had been transferred before the withdrawal from Manassas. O. R., 5, 1030. The Sixteenth Virginia, left to guard the Rapidan when Ewell moved West of the Blue Ridge, O. R., 12, pt. 3, p. 899, became a part of Mahone's Brigade, which was ordered temporarily to Gordonsville. Ibid. This left Elzey only the First Maryland and the Thirteenth Virginia, a command that Ewell thought too small for his senior Brigadier. O. R., 12, pt. 3, p. 890. After the First Maryland was detached to be made the nucleus of the Maryland Line under Geo. H. Steuart, as noted infra, Elzey received the Twelfth Georgia and the Twenty-fifth and Thirty-first Virginia. Together, these regiments had formed one of the two provisional Brigades into which on Apr. 21, 1862, Edward Johnson had divided his command. O. R., 12, pt. 1, p. 487. The Thirteenth Virginia remained in Elzey's Brigade.

[23] See supra, p. 29. From Scott's note in O. R., 12, pt. 1, p. 487, a question seems to have been raised concerning his title to brigade command, but he exercised that command in the Army of the Valley until the battle of Winchester had been fought, and again on June 8–9, after General Steuart was wounded. O. R., 12, pt. 1, pp. 788–89. Scott's regiments were the Forty-fourth, Fifty-second and Fifty-eighth Virginia.

[24] William Allan, S. H. S. ed., 206–207 n.

[25] Steuart, born Aug. 24, 1828 (2 C. M. H., 167) and graduated No. 37 in the class of 1848 at West Point (Cullum, No. 1405), had served in the West, and after vigorous but futile efforts to bring Maryland into the Confederacy (Mrs. McDonald, 16; O. R., 51, pt. 2, pp. 34 ff), had been commissioned Captain in the regular Army of the Confederacy (2 C. M. H., 168), and then Lieutenant Colonel of the First Maryland Infantry, with which he had fought in Elzey's (Kirby Smith's) Brigade at Manassas. Commended for valor on that field (O. R., 2, 477), he wrongly had been reported among those captured (Richmond Whig, July 30, 1861, p. 2, col. 6, with quotation from the New York World). Steuart suffered from the habitual misspelling of his name as Stuart and as Stewart. To distinguish him later from the more renowned "Jeb" Stuart, the Army always styled him "Maryland Steuart" (35 S. H. S. P., p. 360). Upon the promotion of Elzey, he had been made Colonel of the First Maryland (2 C. M. H., 168), and had been elevated Mch. 18, 1862 (Wright, 76), to the grade of Brigadier General. On assignment to the Army of the Valley, Jackson had given him the First Maryland of Elzey's Brigade and, on May 17, had announced that he would organize the "Maryland Line" (O. R., 12, pt. 3, p. 897). As this was a slow work, Steuart might be available temporarily for other duty, but whether Jackson had in mind, as early as Apr. 21, the assignment of Steuart to the command of Ewell's cavalry, it is impossible to say. Col. T. T. Munford of the Second Virginia Cavalry had gone to Richmond to seek arms. Both Munford's Second and Flournoy's Sixth Cavalry had been reorganized not long previously, under the Conscription Act.

With Ewell's two cavalry regiments to support Ashby, and Ewell's 10,000 infantry to co-operate with his own 6000 men, Jackson was ready to set a swift pace in the offensive that hung on word from Richmond. Taylor's Louisiana Brigade had shown how Ewell's Division could cover ground. Jackson simultaneously had been training his own men for the road. On May 13, he had distributed a circular in which he had summarized standard regulations for the march and had incorporated some special requirements. The men were to leave camp and each resting place as if on drill; they were to proceed 200 or 300 yards and then, on command, were to use route step. No soldier was to leave ranks without permission; none was to ride except when a surgeon, on examination, found him unable to walk. The companies not only must proceed in ranks but also must maintain the proper distances, "and thus convert a march, as it should be, into an important drill, that of habituating the men to keep in ranks."

Fifty minutes of the hour they were to march, no more, no less, and when they approached the point where they were to halt, they were to come to attention, and, on command, were to stack arms. After ten minutes' rest, the men were to start again. In the middle of the day, at 12 or 1 o'clock, they were to have an hour for lunch. Finally: "Brigade commanders will see that the foregoing rules are strictly adhered to, and for this purpose will, from time to time, allow his [sic] command to move by him, so as to verify its condition. He will also designate one of his staff officers to do the same at such times as he may deem necessary." [26]

These were to prove historic orders, not so much in any novelty of terms as in the unrelenting rigor of enforcement. More than once, slight infraction was to evoke a stern order for the arrest of a shining officer. When Jackson's voice no more was to say, "Close up, men, close up; push on, push on," a subordinate who had marched many days after him was to describe, half in admiration and half in awe, how Jackson had performed incredible marches: "He had . . . small sympathy with human infirmity. He was a one-idea-ed men. He looked upon the broken down men and stragglers as the same thing. He classed all who

[26] *Jackson's MS. Letter Book,* May 13, 1862.

were weak and weary, who fainted by the wayside, as men wanting in patriotism. If a man's face was as white as cotton and his pulse so low you scarce could feel it, he looked upon him merely as an inefficient soldier and rode off impatiently. He was the true type of all great soldiers. Like the successful warriors of the world, he did not value human life when he had an object to accomplish. He could order men to their death as a matter of course." [27]

This time just such an order came. Probably on the evening of the day Jackson telegraphed Lee, authorization was received from Richmond for him to retain Ewell's troops and to use them with his own against Banks.[28] Not a word of this did Jackson confide to any one. His sole order was that, with Taylor's Brigade in front, his Division and the troops of Johnson's command should march at dawn. Ere the darkness had begun to thin on the western side of the Massanuttons, May 21, he was at Taylor's camp. The column would head North, he said. That was all. Probably about the same time, unknown to the infantry commanders, he dispatched orders to the cavalry: Ashby was to hold position in front of Strasburg that day; on the 22d, leaving

[27] Gen. A. R. Lawton, quoted in *Mrs. Chesnut*, 261–62.

[28] As noted in 2 *R. E. Lee*, 57, there is nothing to show whether Lee communicated with Johnston after the receipt of the telegram from Jackson, or whether he put the question before the President. From the promptness with which the answer was dispatched to Jackson, it is possible to assume that Lee consulted only the President. Other correspondence in *O. R.*, 11, pt. 3, p. 527, dated May 20, would indicate that Johnston and Lee were at their respective headquarters that day and did not see each other. Since the appearance of *R. E. Lee*, two previously unknown dispatches from Johnston to Ewell have come to light in the *Jackson MSS*. These letters, both dated May 18, increase the honorable part of Johnston in plans for Jackson's Valley campaign. In the earlier of the letters, Johnston said that the mission of Jackson and of Ewell was to prevent the junction of Banks's troops with McDowell's. If it was too late to do this by attacking Banks, then Ewell must move East if Banks did. Jackson and Ewell, said Johnston, could conform to circumstance. He had full confidence in their judgment and in their courage. In the second dispatch, 2 P.M., May 18, Johnston was even more in accord with Lee's proposals. Said Johnston: "The whole question is, whether or not General Jackson and yourself are too late to attack Banks. If so the march eastward should be made. If not (supposing your strength sufficient) the attack."—*Jackson MSS*. It is possible, though it seems improbable, in view of the slowness of communications between Johnston's headquarters and Jackson's, that these dispatches may have reached New Market on the night of the 20th. Be that as it may, these two documents are of importance in the biography of Joseph E. Johnston. They show that Johnston was not inclined to withdraw Ewell toward Richmond at the sacrifice of any substantial opportunity of striking Banks in the Valley. In the light of this new information there would seem to be no material difference between the final instructions of Johnston and the advice of Lee to Jackson, unless there was a somewhat greater emphasis by Lee on the desirability of striking Banks. Even if these instructions from Johnston did not reach Jackson before the start of the march for Front Royal, they must have been read with satisfaction by Ewell and by Jackson as evidence of accord among the authorities in Richmond.

a strong guard to watch Banks at Strasburg and to cut all com-munication up and down the Shenandoah, Ashby was to follow the route of the Army.[29]

In these last-minute preparations, Jackson appears to have shown no concern over his batteries, though a few days previously he had replaced his former Chief of Artillery with Colonel Stapleton Crutchfield, a young graduate of Virginia Military Institute. Crutchfield's ability was known to be high. The fact that he was entirely unfamiliar with Ewell's guns and gunners does not seem to have been regarded as of importance. Nor did the inexperience of some of Jackson's staff officers appear to him or to any one else a serious matter. Perhaps it was regarded as a disadvantage inherent in the Southern cause and one that time would cancel. Most of the officers of the general staff had been tested. The personal staff included several young men of military aptitude and high promise.

There was one curious exception. As Assistant Adjutant General with rank of Major, Jackson had named Rev. Dr. Robert Lewis Dabney, 42 years of age, a distinguished Presbyterian divine, a man of powerful intellect, and a professor in Union Theological Seminary, Hampden Sydney, Virginia. Somewhat reluctantly, Dabney had joined Jackson's staff by the General's invitation about the middle of April, but he had scant liking for his hours or his duties and even less for martial appearances. For a time, he had worn his long, black Prince Albert coat and his beaver hat. In preference to a sword, the Major had carried an umbrella. Thus armed and apparelled, the reverend Chief of Staff had followed Jackson. One day, as the General and his staff were on the march in the rain, the sight of the Major under his umbrella had provoked jeers and jests and cheers and sar-casms: "Come out from under that umbrella!" ... "Come out! I know you're under there, I see your feet a-shaking" ... " 'Fraid you're going to get your beegum spoiled?" The banter had aroused Jackson from his meditation. When he had ascertained the reason for the shouts, he had turned off from the road and had trotted with his cavalcade through the near-by wood. He doubtless had done this to get Dr. Dabney away from the col-umn of mocking men; but had he desired to mar that gentle-

[29] *R. Taylor*, 50; *Dabney*, 364; Jackson, in *O. R.*, 12, pt. 1, p. 701.

man's clerical garb, he could not have found an easier way. The umbrella was a skeleton, the beaver hat a wreck.[30] Major Dabney had to borrow a cap and, later, to buy a uniform.

Well staffed or ill, the Army began early on the morning of May 21 to move down the Valley Pike. Jackson rode with Taylor in the van; but they had not proceeded far when Jackson quietly turned the head of the column to the right and began to climb toward Massanutton Gap. He was going over the mountains into the Luray Valley—that was apparent; but why he should be moving Taylor's Brigade to a position it could have reached in one day's march from Conrad's Store, Jackson did not explain. As troops and teams toiled up the winding road to the crest and then began the descent to the South Fork of the Shenandoah, Jackson spoke scarcely at all.[31] Toward evening the Army crossed the river and headed North. "I began to think," said Taylor in later years, "that Jackson was an unconscious poet and, as an ardent lover of nature, desired to give strangers an opportunity to admire the beauties of the Valley." [32]

When at length the troops halted in the vicinity of the Church beyond White House Bridge,[33] Ewell and his Division were found near by. While Jackson's old command and Taylor's Brigade had been moving over Massanutton, Ewell had been marching from Conrad's Store up the Luray Valley. For the first time, Jackson now had every regiment of his infantry concentrated. All his guns, save those of Chew, were with him. His officers realized what he never would have told them—that he had undertaken an offensive which, from the line of march, had to be in one or the other of two directions: either Jackson was going East of the Blue Ridge, or else he was moving against Front Royal, where the railroad comes through the Gap from Manassas and the two branches of the Shenandoah form their junction.

The alternatives soon were resolved by the march of the 22nd. Front Royal, now the manifest objective, had been chosen by Jackson not later than the night of May 16–17, as the point where he could strike swiftly, surely and hard. It was of a march on Front Royal that he had admonished Ewell on the 17th, "Do

[30] T. C. Johnson, *Robert Lewis Dabney*, 262, 270.
[31] *R. Taylor*, 50.
[32] *Ibid.*
[33] *Hotchkiss' MS. Diary.*

not breathe this plan to any one." [34] Now that Jackson was embarked on the movement, any one who knew the country could see the three advantages his strategy offered. First, when Jackson entered the Luray Valley and commanded the passes to the East, he was between Banks and Eastern Virginia, whither Lee suspected that Banks might move. Second, on the eastern side of the Massanuttons, Jackson was in a great covered way, where he was secure from observation by the enemy and in position to move secretly on Front Royal. Finally, if Jackson could sweep aside the small force that his scouts and spies told him was in that village, he could cut Banks's communications and probably could compel his adversary to leave the fortifications the Federals were believed to be erecting at Strasburg.[35] The rest, in Jackson's eyes, depended on God, and on his own soldiers' legs and bayonets.

In the sunshine of a fine, warm day,[36] the Army on the 22d continued its march down the Luray Valley. Taylor's fast-moving Louisianians set the pace. The remainder of Ewell's Division followed. Then came Jackson's own road-weary men, dauntless if footsore. No remembered incident marred the steady advance. Through the woods that bordered the South Fork of the river and often under the shadow of the enclosing mountains, the column moved on in strict compliance with Jackson's new orders of march. Nightfall found headquarters at Cedar Point,[37] and the advance of the Army within ten miles of Front Royal.[38]

The next day would bring battle. Carefully Jackson planned the details. He knew, of course, that Front Royal was as indefensible as Harpers Ferry. High ground looked down upon it from every side. The problem was not to take it but to do so with such speed that the small garrison could not escape, or receive aid from Strasburg, or even send warning to Banks.

How was this problem to be solved? First, Jackson knew that the main road into the village, along the defile of the river, could be swept by the Union artillery, which would delay the Confederate onrush. Obviously, the way to meet that situation

34 *O. R.*, 12, pt. 3, p. 895. See *supra*, p. 360.
35 *Dabney*, 364. In explanation of the term "scouts and spies," it will be recalled that a soldier engaged in espionage was styled a "scout" in Confederate service, and that a civilian so employed was called a "spy."
36 *Hotchkiss' MS. Diary.*
37 *Hotchkiss' MS. Diary.*   38 *O. R.*, 12, pt. 1, p. 702.

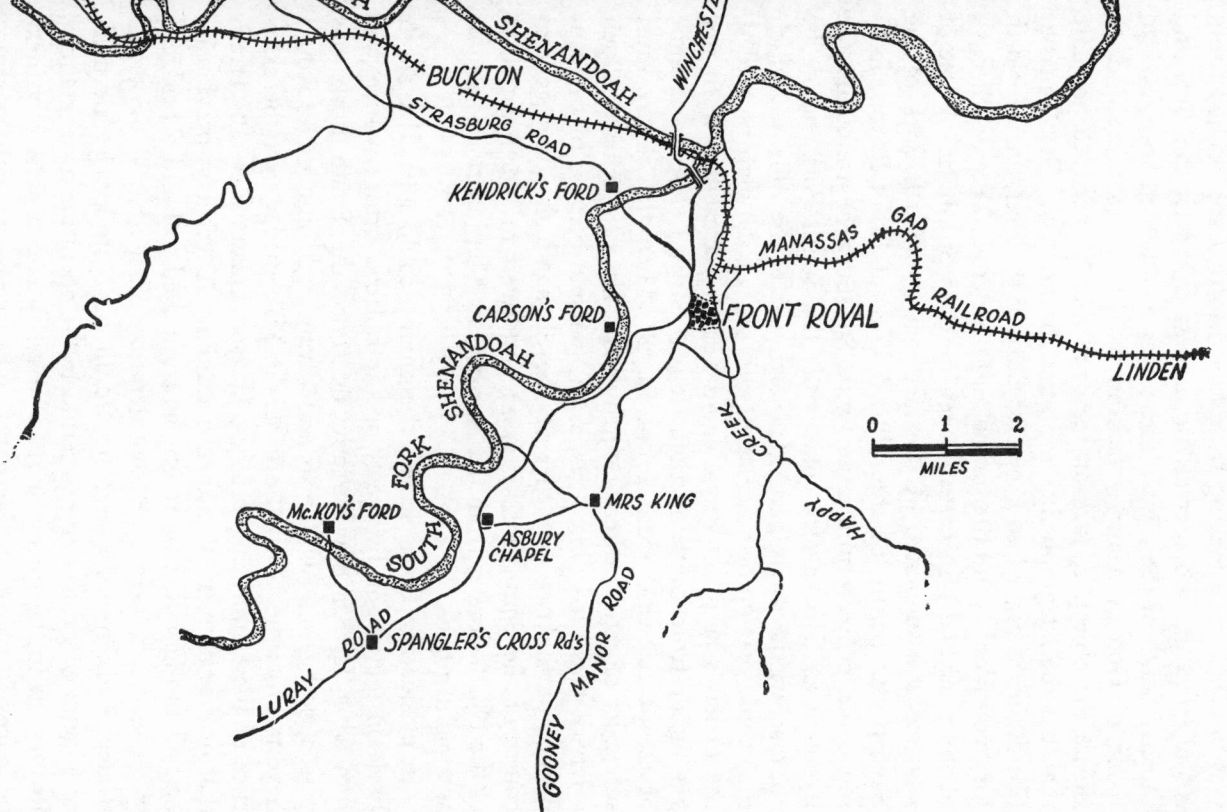

The Environs of Front Royal, to illustrate the action of May 23, 1862. Neither in the Hotchkiss Papers nor in the Atlas of the Official Records is there any large-scale map of Front Royal. This sketch has been prepared from Hotchkiss' general map of the Valley, which is incomplete for the vicinity of Front Royal, and from the Luray Sheet of the Topographical Survey, itself in this instance a reconnaissance. The map may not be accurate for the route Wheat pursued after he left the Gooney Manor road.

was to divert the attacking force to a road that approached Front Royal from the shoulder of the mountain East of the river and directly South of the town. There was such a road with the odd name of Gooney Manor. Jackson would use that. Second, to isolate the objective, Jackson reasoned that he need do no more than cut the telegraph line and seize the railway. The Manassas Gap Railroad came into Front Royal from the East, turned North for two miles beyond the station and then crossed the South Fork of the river and ran westward ten miles to Strasburg. A line of advance was suggested by the fact that the North Fork of the Shenandoah paralleled the railroad West of Front Royal. Jackson could cut communication with Strasburg by following the hypotenuse. His cavalry could cross the South Fork, before he approached the town, and ride Northwest to the railroad, which they could tear up or obstruct. If this part of the plan succeeded, the Federals at Front Royal could neither retreat westward nor get succor from that direction. It was easy to close the avenue of escape eastward from Front Royal. Then the enemy must surrender or retreat directly northward toward Winchester. Such a retreat presented difficulties, as did pursuit, because of the confluence of the two branches of the Shenandoah. The general course of the South Fork is from Southwest to Northeast; that of the North Fork is from the Northwest. The junction is almost at a right angle.

In evacuating Front Royal, the enemy could cross the South Fork on the wagon bridge or on the railroad bridge, which was somewhat farther downstream; but once the South Fork was passed, both fleeing Unionists and advancing Confederates would have to cross the North Fork on the Pike Bridge. Of the existence of these confusing bridges, Jackson knew. It is not certain that he was familiar with their condition. A few days previously, he had thought that he might be compelled to build a bridge.[39]

These, then, were the considerations that shaped Jackson's strategy. Six months later he would have smiled in his half-apologetic way for taking so seriously the operation against Front Royal; but in the spring of 1862 he still was comparatively inexperienced in planning. He had fought two battles only as senior

[39] Cf. Jackson to Ewell, May 17: "See whether you can get enough boats, &c., to build a bridge at Front Royal." O. R., 12, pt. 3, p. 895.

in command. One of these, Kernstown, had not been a success. The other, McDowell, had been more Johnson's fight than his. It was prudent always to be exact in military arrangements. Besides, in this instance, full success at Front Royal would open the way to greater things.

The principal work of Jackson had been in getting permission to attack; his second task had been the strategical planning. Tactically, with such odds as Jackson assumed himself to command, the remainder was simple. Wherefore, on the morning of May 23, when Ashby arrived with most of his cavalry to reinforce the two regiments under Flournoy of the Sixth Virginia, Jackson issued these simple orders:

1. The cavalry, except for outposts, was to turn to the left at Spangler's Ford, was to cross the South Fork of the Shenandoah, and then was to make for the Manassas Gap Railroad to cut the telegraph line, to capture any force along the railroad and to prevent either a retreat from Front Royal along the railroad or the dispatch of reinforcements from Strasburg to Front Royal.[40]

2. The infantry, with Ewell's fresh Division in front, was to move forward on the main road till it reached the Asbury Chapel, four miles Southwest of Front Royal. Then it was to turn to the right, to advance to the Gooney Manor road and to move on Front Royal from the South. The enemy was to be driven and pursued.

That was all: Let the march begin. Ewell's Division, with the First Maryland regiment of Steuart in the lead and then Taylor's Brigade, promptly took the road. Jackson and his staff rode with the advance. After the troops turned toward the Gooney Manor road, their progress was slow because there was a climb of 500 feet. The road itself, when reached, was a succession of grades. In places, the mire from the recent rains was deep.[41] Past mudholes and through the far-spreading woods Jackson kept ahead. He was alert and eager but composed. His battle blood had not risen. Quietly he rode until, when he was close to the edge of the forest that overlooked the town, Jackson was called from the front to settle some question or to make observation. He

---

[40] Reports do not indicate whether Jackson assigned to Ashby and to Flournoy the separate missions they subsequently discharged.

[41] R. Taylor, 51.

attended to it and then started for the front at the gallop. A troop
of horse accompanied him. As he came in sight of the Louisiana
Brigade, he saw that it was moving at the double-quick. What
had happened? Had contact been established? Quickly he was
told that a woman spy had come out of the woods and had
reported the position of the enemy with so much clarity that the
ambitious Taylor had determined to rush forward at once.[42]

Jackson immediately took direction of the advance. The First
Maryland and Rob Wheat's Tigers were diverted to the right,
so that they would sweep down on the streets of Front Royal
from the East.[43] Taylor's Sixth Louisiana was placed in immediate support. Orders were given for the remainder of the
Brigade to deploy and to press forward when the attack from the
East cleared the way.

Everything went according to plan, and to the indescribable
surprise and joy of the natives of Front Royal. One girl wrote
in her diary: ". . . There was . . . the quick, sharp report of a
rifle and another and another in rapid succession. Going to the
door we saw the Yankees scampering over the meadow below
our house and [we] were at a loss to account for such evident
excitement on their part until presently Miss B. White rushed in
with purple face and dishevelled hair crying, 'Oh, my God! The
Hill above town is black with our boys. . . .' Ma and I did not
wait . . . but started for home in double quick time, all the
[while] hearing the firing exchanged more and more rapidly.
Found all the family upstairs at the windows. Nellie, spy-glass
in hand, clapping her hand exclaiming, 'Oh, there they are. I
see our dear brave fellows just in the edge of the woods on the
hill over the town! There they are, bless them!' I looked in
the same direction and surely enough some of our cavalry
emerged from the little skirt of woods above the court house.
As long as I live, I think I cannot forget that sight, the first
glimpse caught of a grey figure upon horseback seemingly in
command, until then I could not believe our deliverers had

---

[42] This spy was the renowned Belle Boyd, one of the most active and most reliable
of the many secret women agents of the Confederacy. In this instance, if General Taylor
remembered correctly her report, she was mistaken in some of the information she gave.
R. Taylor, 51, Douglas, 51 (sic). The latter is perhaps a somewhat theatrical account
of the episode.

[43] Dabney, 365.

really come, but seeing was believing and I could only sink on my knees with my face in my hands and sob for joy. Presently some one called out, 'Only see! The Yankees run!' Leaning out the back window we saw them, contrabands and Yankees together, tearing wildly by." [44]

It was about 2 o'clock, a mile and a half from town, that the weak Federal picket was driven in. Behind it pressed the Marylanders and the Tigers. They quickly cleared the town itself, but they soon discovered that the Federals were making a stand on a good position North of Front Royal, on the east side of the Winchester turnpike.[45] There the Union artillery opened gallantly. Although its infantry support was small, apparently about one regiment,[46] the resistance was firm. Stapleton Crutch·field, Jackson's new Chief of Artillery, instantly ordered up Ewell's guns—only to find that the nearest battery was armed with six-pounder smooth bores and twelve-pounder howitzers, which were quite outranged. In the whole of Ewell's Division, it developed, there were only three rifled guns.[47]

The infantry had, in consequence, to retain the initiative until rifled pieces could be brought up. Steuart's Marylanders pushed forward against the Federal front; the Sixth Louisiana worked its way around the enemy's left by the railroad bridge over Happy Creek; [48] Taylor's other regiments advanced on the Union right, West of Front Royal. This movement was developed steadily. After much effort, Ewell's rifles were brought into action. By that time, Confederate horsemen were galloping over the fields on the west side of the South Fork opposite the town.

For a moment it looked as if these troops might reach the Pike Bridge across the North Fork and might cut off the enemy's line of retreat. The Federals sensed their danger. Quickly the Union guns were limbered up and were dashed away through dust and smoke toward the bridge over the South Fork. As rapidly as they could close in, the Confederates started in pursuit. Past the Federal camp, through which flames were sweeping, the gray-coats pressed toward the crossing. Jackson dashed up, his eyes ablaze now. He galloped over the South Fork Bridge and made

[44] *Diary of Lucy R. Buck*, May 23, 1862, p. 58.
[45] *O. R.*, 12, pt. 1, pp. 556, 702.   [46] *O. R.*, 12, pt. 1, p. 725.
[47] *Ibid.*   [48] *O. R.*, 12, pt. 1, p. 565.

toward the Pike Bridge; but on commanding ground, he drew rein and gazed ahead: It was too late! In plain view, the well-ordered blue column was climbing up the road that led toward Winchester.

"Oh," cried Jackson, "what an opportunity for artillery; oh, that my guns were here!"

He looked about him. One staff officer was by his side. "Hurry to the rear," he said. "Order up every rifled gun and every Brigade of the Army." [49]

Slow the guns were in coming; slower still the infantry.[50] Meantime, smoke was rising from the bridge over the North Fork. If that were burned, pursuit must wait on repairs or on slow fording of the river. The first skirmishers to reach the south end of the span were rushed on it to beat out the fire. Jackson, dim but commanding amid the smoke, fought this new enemy. At length the flames were extinguished, but not until part of the bridge had been so damaged that the passage of horsemen was hazardous.[51]

The Federals, meantime, had disappeared over the ridge. A lone Confederate battery arrived in time to drive off a Union gun that sought to sweep the crossing.[52] Jackson would not be balked. Colonel Flournoy, having cut the wire to Strasburg while Ashby had pushed on to capture a Federal post at Buckton, was at hand with his cavalry. He must cross; he must throw himself against the Federals ere they could rally. By keeping in single file on the less-damaged side, four companies of cavalry had contrived to get over the North Fork on the half-burned planks. No sooner were these men across the river than Jackson ordered Colonel Flournoy to start after the enemy with the troops he had and not to wait for more.

Flournoy shouted the command, the bugle rang out, the troopers pressed up the ridge and out of sight. Jackson, too, disappeared. Later in the afternoon, as the third company on the road

---

[49] *Dabney*, 365–66.

[50] Dabney noted, *op. cit.*, 366, that the untrained boy courier, sent with the orders, became frightened and ran away. The rear Brigades, receiving no instructions that the direct road was clear of the enemy, pursued the circuitous route that Taylor's Brigade had followed. Some of them did not reach Front Royal till 9 P.M. and after. *Cf.* Winder's report, *O. R.*, 12, pt. 1, p. 734.

[51] *Dabney*, 366; *O. R.*, 12, pt. 1, p. 702.

[52] *O. R.*, 12, pt. 1, p. 725.

was hurrying forward in column of fours, its Captain, George Baxter, became annoyed at two horsemen who were riding ahead of him but not with the company he was following. "Get out of the way of my men!" he yelled. The younger of the two riders turned and motioned toward his companion. "This is General Jackson," he said.

In confusion, Baxter could think of nothing better to do than to order three cheers for the General; but Jackson wheeled about for more important business:[53] the little column was nearing Cedarville;[54] the enemy had made a stand; the cavalry must deploy for a charge. In a few brisk words he gave his orders to the men, who did not number more than 250. Again the bugle sounded—this time the thrilling notes of the charge. With wild abandon, the men rushed on. The Federals gave their assailants a volley, then broke and escaped to an orchard by the roadside, where some of them rallied. Again Jackson ordered the charge; again Flournoy's men dashed straight at the infantry and the guns. This time the rout was complete. Off galloped the few Federal cavalry; the artillerists left one piece; the infantry sought cover. When the First Maryland Confederate Infantry arrived in support of the cavalry, it had the pleasure of rounding up the Union 1st Maryland, the identification of which at Front Royal had speeded its march.[55]

Jackson, overjoyed, climbed to the rare state of mind in which he employed a superlative. Never, he told his staff officers, had he seen such a charge of cavalry.[56] By the time Taylor brought up the infantry who had fought the entire action at Front Royal, Jackson was back to his normal restraint. He said nothing more than that the Brigade would move in the morning, but, said Taylor, "I fancied he looked at me kindly."[57] Jackson was satisfied. It developed that the Federals at Front Royal had numbered no more than 1063—one regiment and two companies of infantry,[58] about ninety cavalrymen, a few pioneers and one section of artillery[59]—fewer men than should have been left at so

[53] 24 *S. H. S. P.*, 133.
[54] Two and a half miles North of the bridge.
[55] *O. R.*, 12, pt. 1, pp. 557–58, 702, 733–37; *William Allan*, 210–11; *Dabney*, 367–68; *Laurel Brigade*, 57–58; 24 *S. H. S. P.*, 133–34.
[56] *Dabney*, 368.   [57] *R. Taylor*, 54.
[58] The latter of the 29th Pennsylvania.   [59] *O. R.*, 12, pt. 1, p. 559.

important an outpost. Against them Jackson had been in position to throw 16,000. No fault could be found with the defense the Federals had made in the town; but of the whole number 904 were killed, wounded or missing.[60] Opulent supplies had been captured; the Union wagon train was in Jackson's hands; two locomotives had been taken by Ashby; besides the gun captured at Cedarville, another was found by a couple of daring soldiers who pressed on within four miles of Winchester. They requisitioned two plow-horses and, under the eyes of Federal pickets, brought the piece—a fine, 10-pounder Parrott—back to Front Royal.[61] The price Jackson had paid for all this was less than fifty casualties.[62] Gain was great, loss was small, but the reckoning was not final. That night, by Taylor's campfire, Jackson sat long and silently. His eyes were on the flames. "I took up the idea," said Taylor, "that he was inwardly praying." [63] Perhaps Jackson was. He certainly was planning.

[60] According to the report of the Surgeon General; *William Allan*, 211.
[61] *O. R.*, 12, pt. 1, p. 779. These gallant men were Privates Fontaine and Moore, Co. I, Sixth Virginia Cavalry.
[62] The cavalry lost twenty-six men, of whom eleven were killed. Taylor had two killed and seven wounded. *O. R.*, 12, pt. 1, p. 734. Casualties in the First Maryland are not listed but were not large.
[63] *R. Taylor*, 54.

CHAPTER XXV

CEDARVILLE TO WINCHESTER—A DREADFUL NIGHT

FIRST of all, that night of May 23–24, at Cedarville, Jackson picketed all the roads along which the Federals could advance. Thereby he hoped to assure for himself one essential of surprise operations, prompt and accurate information of the enemy's movements.

Until he knew the realities, he had to weigh the probabilities: what was the Federal commander most apt to do? With rail communications severed at Front Royal, Banks could not remain at Strasburg longer than his supplies sufficed. As Frémont might march over the Alleghenies to join him, while other troops were hurried to him from the East, there was a possibility that Banks might take a chance of a shortage of food and might invite attack in the fortifications he had erected at Strasburg. This Jackson considered improbable, but he could not disregard it.

What alternatives had Banks? Jackson knew too well the difficulties of the mountain roads to believe that Banks would attempt to cross the Allegheny Range, and join Frémont on the South Fork of the Potomac.[1] If this were ruled out, Banks had to undertake one or another of two things: either he must push East to Front Royal and cut his way through Chester Gap, or else he must move northward to Winchester, which was eighteen miles from Strasburg.

As between these alternative avenues of escape, Front Royal and Winchester, Banks scarcely would attempt to move by Front Royal unless the Confederates cleared that point. Banks was ignorant of the strength of the Confederate force at Front Royal, but he doubtless was familiar with the difficulty of crossing the Blue Ridge. Was he not, therefore, much more apt to

1 Banks considered this, but, as he reported, *O. R.*, 12, pt. 1, p. 546, "to move over the mountains was to abandon our train at the outset and subject my command to flank attacks without possibility of succor . . ."

take the easy straight line of the Valley Pike from Strasburg to Winchester? If so, he must be struck en route. He also should be outfooted to the town, so that his retreat to the Potomac could be prevented. It was as desirable, in short, for the Confederates to press on to Winchester as it was for them not to leave open to Banks a road of escape across their rear, by way of Front Royal.

Jackson's problem, then, as he shaped it in the flames of Taylor's campfire, was this: how could he dispose his troops in such a manner that he could (1) attack Strasburg if Banks stayed there, (2) thwart an attempt by Banks to slip past the rear and pass over the Blue Ridge, (3) strike in force any Federal column moving on Winchester and (4) advance his own troops to that town swiftly? The immediate essential was to watch both lines of possible retreat and, whether Banks retreated or not, to be in position to attack him at once.

The roads, which Jackson knew well, offered an opportunity of doing this. Passing Strasburg, the Valley Pike ran slightly East of North to Winchester. From Front Royal, the road on which Jackson was advancing his army stretched almost due North to Winchester. Between these converging highways, a cross road ran from Cedarville seven miles to Middletown, which was five miles North of Strasburg. If the cavalry and part of the Army were sent the next morning from Cedarville to Middletown, they might be able to strike a Federal column while it was in motion along the Valley Pike toward Winchester. In the event that Banks remained at Strasburg, the Confederate column that reached the Valley Pike at Middletown could turn South instead of North and could march on Strasburg. Meantime, the remainder of the Confederate Army could start the advance from Cedarville directly on Winchester. If Banks stayed at Strasburg, this Confederate column from Front Royal could take Winchester, which was not believed to be held in force. Should Banks decide to strike eastward from Strasburg to Front Royal, instead of remaining at Strasburg or retreating to Winchester, then either the column sent to Middletown or that directed against Winchester could be recalled to attack Banks in rear. His left flank, of course, would be protected by the North Fork, behind which he would move eastward.

So Jackson reasoned.[2] Before daybreak he conferred with Ewell[3] and explained the details of their co-operation. Then he arranged for the use of the cavalry. Ashby had come to the front, though apparently no check was made to ascertain how many of his widely scattered troopers were with him. Ewell's two cavalry regiments, unshaken by their activities on the 23d, were in camp. To make certain that every saber would count, Jackson decided he would place these regiments under Gen. George H. Steuart.[4] With Ewell's cavalrymen, in the first move of the day, Steuart was directed to strike for Newtown, four miles North of Middletown, on the Valley Pike.[5] After Steuart got under way, Ashby was to start via the Chapel road[6] for Middletown. With him were to proceed his cavalry, Chew's Battery, and the fine Parrott-gun section of the Rockbridge Artillery. Taylor was to supply skirmishers to support the artillery and was to follow with his fast-moving Brigade. Ashby was to make Middletown his first objective, but he was to keep his scouts well to the South in order to make sure that Banks did not march unobserved toward Front Royal.[7] Ewell was to retain Trimble's

2 It was characteristic of Jackson that, when he came to write his report of this campaign, nearly eleven months after the operation had closed, his soldierly reticence led him to state in two sentences a plan he spent much of the night of May 23-24 in developing. He said: "In the event of Banks leaving Strasburg he might escape toward the Potomac, or if we moved directly to Winchester he might move via Front Royal toward Washington City. In order to watch both directions, and at the same time advance upon him if he remained at Strasburg, I determined, with the main body of the Army to strike the turnpike near Middletown . . ." O. R., 12, pt. 1, p. 703. For the preparation of this report, see infra, Vol. II.

3 Avirett, 199.

4 Cf. O. R., 12, pt. 1, pp. 703, 734. Detailed reasons for the change of command nowhere appear. The natural surmise is that Jackson was dissatisfied with Lieutenant Colonel Flournoy's inexperienced handling of the cavalry on the 23rd, but Jackson in his report, ibid., 707, commended the manner in which the four companies had fought near Cedarville. In all probability, Jackson reasoned that, for such extensive operations as were opening, a professional soldier, with eleven years' experience in the cavalry, was better qualified than a young Lieutenant Colonel.

5 Jackson's references to the operations of Steuart on the 24th are so brief in O. R., 12, pt. 1, p. 703, that it is impossible to reconstruct Steuart's orders. Undoubtedly, some of the cavalry whom Federal officers reported on their flank North of Middletown were Steuart's men, but the reports of General Banks, ibid., 595, and Col. Dudley Donnally, ibid., 603, disagree concerning the point where the Confederate cavalry skirmished with Banks's First Brigade. Consequently, there is doubt how far South Steuart operated and how far North went Funsten, whose operations are mentioned in a later paragraph of the text. The report of Col. J. F. Knipe, 46th Penn., ibid., 613, shows that he encountered opposition early in the day at Newtown. The cavalry he met there were almost certainly Steuart's. Because Jackson scarcely would have sent off two regiments of cavalry simply as an observation force, the presumption of course is that Steuart's orders were to reconnoiter, to harass and, if opportunity offered, to attack; but as this cannot be asserted positively, the vague statement in the text has to stand.

6 Avirett, 193.   7 O. R., 12, pt. 1, p. 703.

Brigade, the First Maryland and two batteries, with which he was to advance on Winchester by the Front Royal road. The remainder of the Army, as it came up, was to march in Taylor's rear for the Valley Pike.

At an hour not determinable,[8] the march of the infantry began. The men of Wheat's Battalion, whom Taylor designated as skirmishers for the artillery, gaily trotted along beside the guns and soon outdistanced the remainder of the Brigade.[9] Ahead of the Tigers and of the artillery rode Jackson. He had not proceeded far before a courier brought word from "Maryland" Steuart that all circumstances indicated Banks was preparing to leave Strasburg.[10] Good news that! In whatever direction Banks was moving, it was far better to hit him on the march than to assault him in his works at Strasburg. The odds still were that he was starting for Winchester. What was more to be desired than to strike him in the open country on his road?

The Confederate column kept on its way. If Jackson spoke at all, it was to give the command that soon was to epitomize his generalship in the minds of his soldiers, "Press on, men; press on!" Ere long—firing in front. Eyes swept the green horizon; glasses were focused. Soon were visible Federal cavalrymen who had halted in the road at the unexpected encounter.[11] Jackson surveyed them a moment only, and then he ordered the artillerists, as if they, too, were cavalry, to drive straight at the blue-coated horsemen.[12] At the first lunge forward of the pieces, the Federals wheeled and started off. Jackson delayed only long enough to be sure of the ground and of the position of the enemy. Then he pressed forward. Again there was a brief halt and an exchange of fire. The column moved on; once more the Unionists paused uncertainly; another fusillade and another advance. It was not a rapid march but it was steady. At length, the van came in sight of Middletown—in startled sight. Over the village

[8] For a full discussion of this march, see Appendix VI.

[9] R. Taylor, 54.

[10] So wrote Jackson, O. R., 12, pt. 1, p. 703. Dabney, op. cit., 371, stated erroneously that Steuart reported the enemy in retreat on Winchester.

[11] This was the 1st Maine and two companies of the 1st Vermont. They reported that they met the Confederates four and a half miles East of Middletown, O. R., 12, pt. 1, p. 574. Dabney, op. cit., 371, placed the brush halfway, that is about three miles, from Cedarville.

[12] Dabney, 371.

and as far as vision reached to North and to South, was a dust cloud raised by the hurrying feet and horses' hoofs of Banks's Army. Jackson had reasoned soundly; the enemy was in full retreat down the Valley.[13]

The artillery with its stout-limbed support was now a mile or more ahead of the infantry. What mattered that? The thing to do was to strike at once. Chew and Poague were directed to rising ground. The Tigers formed behind one of the rough stone fences in which the country abounded.[14] Ashby hurried off Major Funsten to the right, with most of the cavalry, but he kept a few horsemen under his own eye.[15] A glance along the fence, a sharp order, the bark of the guns and, in a few minutes, the Federal wagon train was in chaos. Colonel Crutchfield, who commanded the artillery, was on the point of pushing his guns into the pike itself, to sweep it with fire, when a considerable force of Federal cavalry was seen to the South in the road. Whence these troopers had come, and why they had ridden almost into the wagons, nobody paused to ask. Bugles sounded. Artillerists fairly leaped. Crutchfield advanced his guns within canister range, opened furiously and scattered the bluecoats in panic.[16]

At that moment Jackson rode up—to witness a sight he never forgot. "The road," in his words, "was literally obstructed with the mingled and confused mass of struggling and dying horses and riders."[17] When the artillery no longer could see a target, in rushed the Tigers. Soon other parts of Taylor's Brigade arrived at the double-quick, formed on a wide front and dashed through the village. Some 200 Federals, hopelessly trapped and blinded by the dust, were rounded up. Those who escaped capture galloped wildly off in every direction.[18]

13 For a discussion of the curious errors in print concerning the march to Middletown, see Appendix VI.

14 *O. R.*, 12, pt. 1, p. 574.

15 *O. R.*, 12, pt. 1, p. 703; *Dabney*, 371; *Avirett*, 194, 270; Edward A. Moore, *The Story of a Cannoneer under Stonewall Jackson* (cited hereafter as E. A. Moore), 54.

16 *O. R.*, 12, pt. 1, pp. 725–26.

17 *O. R.*, 12, pt. 1, p. 703. Col. Calvin S. Douty of the 1st Maine Cavalry noted in his report, *ibid.*, 576, that at one point, "the bodies of men and horses [were] so piled up that it was impossible to proceed."

18 *O. R.*, 12, pt. 1, p. 703; *Dabney*, 372; *Douglas*, 53–54. On Mch. 31, 1863, when Col. Charles J. Faulkner was writing Jackson's report of what happened at Middletown, some dispute arose concerning the identity of the infantry who fell on the Unionists. Faulkner attributed the exploit to Wheat's Tigers; Jed. Hotchkiss said the

Banks's column was pierced! His march was interrupted. "Good, good," Jackson might have said. What next? How many of Banks's troops already had passed toward Winchester? Did many remain between Middletown and Strasburg? Jackson could not determine immediately. All that was clear at the moment, amid the slaughter and confusion, was that wagons were disappearing to the northward as fast as frantic drivers could force their teams down the Valley Pike. They must be captured: was not Jackson the "wagon hunter"? After the enemy! Press on! Ashby must pursue with the same troopers that had led the advance from Cedarville.

Jackson gave the order but probably did not wait to see the execution. He did not observe that, as Funsten already was detached, Ashby gathered only a thin detachment when assembly was sounded. With these, Ashby dashed away. Eagerly, then, Jackson and his staff officers sought out the residents of the bewildered village to ascertain how long the Federals had been moving through Middletown. The answer was instant and unanimous: Since early morning, wagons and infantry had been pouring down the highway.[19] Jackson's conclusion was clear: most of the Federal column probably was between Middletown and Winchester, not between Middletown and Strasburg.

It was now 4 o'clock.[20] The distance to Winchester was thirteen miles. For Banks's army with all its trains, to reach the hills that protected the town, seven or eight hours would be required. The head of the column might get there sooner, but—calculations were interrupted suddenly by the opening of artillery fire South of Middletown. Were Federals still there in force? and bound for Winchester? Had fewer infantry passed through Middletown than the residents thought?

Jackson could not be sure, but he took no chances. Although

attacking troops were two companies of the Seventh and one of the Ninth Louisiana, under Maj. David B. Penn. The matter was settled by Jackson, who decided that the expedient term would be, "Some of Taylor's Brigade." *Hotchkiss' MS. Diary*, 155. In the final, published text, the language was, "The batteries of Poague and Chew, with Taylor's infantry." *O. R.*, 12, pt. 1, p. 703.

[19] *Dabney*, 372.

[20] According to Col. G. H. Gordon, who was North of Middletown, word of the attack on the Federals reached him at 2 P.M. (*O. R.*, 12, pt. 1, p. 614). A dispatch from Jackson to Ewell (*O. R.*, 51, pt. 2, p. 562), announcing from Middletown that the enemy had retreated "en masse toward Winchester," is marked "4 P.M." A second dispatch, mentioned in the text and written after the Federal artillery opened, was sent at 4.30 P.M. (*O. R.*, 12, pt. 3, p. 899).

his own infantry were now coming up in strength from Cedarville, he might need more men. It would be wise, he concluded, to halt Ewell on the Front Royal road for the time being, and to send part of his command over to the Valley Pike. Orders were dispatched accordingly at 4.30 for Elzey's Brigade.[21] For dealing immediately with the Federal artillery and its support, Taylor was directed to turn South from Middletown and to attack.[22] At least two Brigades, Jackson's First[23] and the Second,[24] were ordered to follow Taylor. The batteries that now had come up from Cedarville with the other Brigades were moved into position to answer the Federal fire and to cover Taylor's advance.

Quickly enough, considering the chaos in Middletown, Taylor got his regiments under way. After a brief cannonade, the Federals withdrew southward and then turned off to the West. On a good position, they formed as if to invite attack. When Taylor rode forward to reconnoiter, he was greeted with a shell which exploded squarely under his horse. The edges of his saddle blanket were torn away, and he and his Adjutant were deluged with flying dirt; but neither of the men nor of the mounts had so much as a scratch.[25] Luck was with the Brigade as with its commander. After a brief, brisk action the Federals retreated. Whether they went back toward Strasburg and then journeyed across the mountains to Frémont, or whether they followed side roads and rejoined Banks, the Confederates did not know for months.[26]

As soon as Jackson saw that the force South of Middletown

21 *O. R.*, 12, pt. 1, p. 899. The Second Brigade of Edward Johnson's Army, Col. W. C. Scott, was operating on the 24th, under command of General Elzey, *O. R.*, 51, pt. 2, p. 563, but Ewell's report, *O. R.*, 12, pt. 1, p. 779, would indicate that only the First Brigade of Johnson, formally assigned Elzey, was covered by Jackson's order to reinforce the column on the Valley Pike.

22 *O. R.*, 12, pt. 1, p. 704.   23 *O. R.*, 12, pt. 1, p. 735.
24 *Worsham*, 84.   25 *R. Taylor*, 55.
26 This Union force, much smaller than the Confederates thought it, consisted of six companies of the 5th New York Cavalry, five companies of the 1st Vermont Cavalry, General Banks's bodyguard of Pennsylvania Zouaves, Hampton's Battery of four 10-pdr. Parrotts, and a few men detached for rearguard service. The units scattered after the clash with the Louisiana Brigade. Capt. C. H. T. Collis, commander of the Zouaves, who finally rejoined General Banks via Hancock, asserted that his men marched 141 miles in forty-seven hours (*O. R.*, 12, pt. 1, p. 573). For details of the engagement and the march of the various units, see *ibid.*, 568, 572, 582, 600. Dabney (*op. cit.*, 372), noted that the Confederates thought the bridge over Cedar Creek had been burned by the Federal rearguard, but the report of Capt. James W. Abert (*O. R.*, 12, pt. 1, p. 568), shows that a fire was started near by but that the crossing was not destroyed.

was not formidable, he started down the pike toward Winchester and ordered the troops at Middletown to follow him. Because Taylor, who had led the van, still was South of the town, Jackson's old Brigade, under the vigilant eye of Winder, was countermarched and placed in advance.[27] Ewell, at 5.45, was ordered to resume on the Front Royal-Winchester road.

Jackson, riding ahead, was as taciturn as ever, but inwardly he was confident and exultant. "From the attack at Front Royal up to the present moment," he said later, "every opposition had been borne down, and there was reason to believe, if Banks reached Winchester, it would be without a train, if not without an army." [28] All along the road were abandoned wagons, loaded with supplies of every description. If Ashby found as much property farther down the road, at Newtown and beyond, Banks would be stripped indeed and the Confederate government would be richer for that day's fighting!

As Jackson approached Newtown, four miles North of Middletown and nine miles South of Winchester, the sound of a minor artillery duel was heard. What did it signify? Had the enemy rallied? The General pushed on with his staff to the edge of the village. There to his amazement, he found Poague's two Parrott guns hammering away, with scarcely any supporting infantry or cavalry in sight.

Col. Stapleton Crutchfield, Chief of Artillery, was at the front and in flaming rage. When Poague's men had reached the vicinity of Newtown, Crutchfield explained, after a running fight from Middletown, no other troops had been at hand to serve as a support. He had halted the guns and had ridden back to hurry up the infantry. On the road he had found more than 100 members of the Seventh Louisiana, the leading regiment of Taylor's Brigade, who, from weariness and exhaustion, had been moving slowly. Having urged them to better speed, Crutchfield had returned to the southern edge of Newtown, where he had come upon numbers of Louisiana infantrymen and some of Ashby's cavalry. Instead of taking position to support the artillery, these men were plundering Federal wagons. Crutchfield's pleas and orders to desist had been in vain. Turning wrathfully

[27] *Dabney.* 373.   [28] *O. R.*, 12, pt. 1, p. 704.

from the looters, he had ridden into the town and there, after 3 P.M.,[29] he had found Ashby and Funsten, but their command had so dwindled that they had only some fifty troopers in ranks! The others had scattered either to pursue the enemy or, as Crutchfield thought, to pilfer. He and Ashby reluctantly had agreed that they must halt the pursuit until infantry support arrived. After they had been waiting two hours for help, four Federal guns had been planted just North of the town and had been loosed on the Confederates. Poague answered immediately and was now in action against adversaries who held stubbornly to their ground.[30]

Jackson was outraged at the looting and still more at the delay in the pursuit, but, as he was far ahead of his infantry and of the other batteries, there was nothing he could do until the Federal guns were silenced by Poague or were withdrawn. It was nearly night when the Federal battery ceased its fire.[31] No sooner had it moved off than Jackson ordered the pursuit resumed. Knowing well the ground ahead, he believed that Banks would seek to rally on the hills Southwest of Winchester, and, regardless of hunger and weariness, he determined to press on through the night in order to wrest that dominating position from the Federals before they could get a firm grip on it.

A hideous march it proved to be. One veteran artillerist pronounced it the worst he experienced during the entire war. Said Ned Moore: "From dark till daylight we did not advance more than four miles. Step by step we moved along, halting for five minutes; then a few steps and halt again. . . . Occasionally we were startled by the sharp report of a rifle, followed in quick

29 This estimate of the hour is based on Poague's statement that the Federal artillery took position about 5 o'clock, O. R., 12, pt. 1, p. 761, and on Crutchfield's report that this occurred about two hours after the halt of the Confederate advance. Ibid., 726. The time spent in Crutchfield's ride to the rear must be taken into account.

30 O. R., 12, pt. 1, p. 726. The absence of all reference to Chew's Battery in Crutchfield's report is puzzling. In Avirett, 271, Colonel Chew wrote as if his guns remained in action until nightfall, when he went into camp, North of Newtown, to feed his exhausted horses. It is possible that Crutchfield did not feel that Ashby's artillery was under his orders and consequently was not to be covered by his report, but he commended Chew's men for the "skill in perseverance" displayed in the pursuit. The Blakely gun under Chew had as long range as Poague's rifles and could not have been silent because it was outranged. For the facts concerning the looting at Newtown, see O. R., 12, pt. 1, p. 704 and infra, p. 477.

31 Dabney, op. cit., 374, said the enemy was driven off at sunset, which was at 7.07; Jackson fixed the time at dusk; Col. Geo. H. Gordon, commanding Banks's Third Brigade, gave 8 o'clock. See O. R., 12, pt. 1, pp. 615, 704.

succession by others; then all as quiet as the grave. Sometimes, when a longer halt was made, we would endeavor to steal a few moments' sleep, for want of which it was hard to stand up. By the time a blanket was unrolled, the column was astir again, and so it continued throughout the long, dreary hours. . . ." [32] At first, the march was past burned or smoldering wagons, the sight of which gave Jackson acute distress. "Wagon-hunter" that he was, in Ewell's crisp phrase, he reported dolefully, "the same profusion of abandoned Federal wagons loaded with stores met the eye; but we derived no benefit from this property, as the time lost during the disorder and pillage . . . and the consequent delay of our advance at Newtown, enabled the enemy to make arrangements for burning them." [33]

Not far beyond these lost treasures, the head of the column ran into an ambuscade, which was cleared by the Thirty-third Virginia of Manassas fame. Again at Bartonsville and still again at Kernstown the column was delayed by skillful resistance.[34] The tactics of this night fighting Jackson left to Charles Winder, who handled his men with a skill that accorded with his rising reputation. In the first of the encounters, Jackson was at the front, and when the cavalry advance drew rein at the first fusillade he cried fiercely, "Charge them; charge them!" The troopers obediently rode forward but, at a second volley, wheeled and almost ran over the General and his staff. Jackson broke out furiously: "Shameful! Did you see anybody struck, Sir? Did you see anybody struck? Surely they need not have run, at least until they were hurt!" [35] Shamefaced, the cavalrymen rallied ere long and plodded on in the darkness.

Down almost every stone wall, now, a line of disputing fire would dance through the darkness. Then the Federals would stumble away to the next field.[36] More frequently, from behind a tree, a single soldier of the rearguard would send a shot in the direction of the noise and the moving shadows. Jackson apparently did not notice the bullets. "I quite remember thinking at the time," wrote Taylor, "that Jackson was invulnerable, and that persons near him shared that quality." [37] Agonizingly

---

[32] E. A. Moore, 56.   [33] O. R., 12, pt. 1, p. 704.
[34] Chiefly from the excellent 2nd Massachusetts, which Geo. H. Gordon had trained and Geo. L. Andrews was leading that night. Cf. O. R., 12, pt. 1, p. 620.
[35] Dabney, 375.   [36] Worsham, 84–85.   [37] R. Taylor, 56.

for men and mounts benumbed, the persecuting minutes dragged out. At intervals a courier would ride up and whisper a message, or would deliver a dispatch which Jackson, by a moment's light, would read in silence. One rider, following fast, proved to be Major Harman, the Army Quartermaster, who not long previously had been writing that Jackson undoubtedly was "cracked." Now he had a breathless tale to tell: the mud of Luray Valley had most vexatiously delayed the commissary train, which could not arrive for hours.

"But the ammunition wagons?" Jackson broke in sternly.

"All right, sir. They were in advance, and I doubled teams on them and brought them through."

"Ah!" That was the only answer, but in it Taylor was sure he heard relief.

"Never mind the wagons," said Taylor to the weary quartermaster. "There are quantities of stores in Winchester, and the General has invited me to breakfast there tomorrow."

Swiftly Jackson reached out to touch him on the arm. Although every pair of feet in the Army was pointed straight toward Winchester, Jackson's secrecy was so ingrained that he could not endure to have an officer mention the objective. As for rations, Taylor reflected: "Without physical wants himself," Jackson "forgot that others were differently constituted, and paid little attention to commissariat; but woe to the man who failed to bring up ammunition!" Then Taylor bestowed on Jackson the compliment already quoted: "In advance, his trains were left far behind. In retreat, he would fight for a wheelbarrow." [38]

After 1 o'clock, Colonel Fulkerson came up to Jackson. "General," said he, "if I may be permitted to make a suggestion, I think the troops had better be rested for an hour or so; my men are falling by the roadside from fatigue and loss of sleep. Unless they are rested, I shall be able to present but a thin line tomorrow."

Jackson reflected and then answered steadily: "Colonel, I yield to no man in sympathy for the gallant men under my command; but I am obliged to sweat them tonight, that I may save their blood tomorrow. The line of hills southwest of Winchester must not be occupied by the enemy's artillery. My own must be there

[38] R. Taylor, 56; cf. supra, p. 315

and in position by daylight. You shall, however, have two hours'
rest." [39]

The column was halted. Thousands slumped in their tracks
and fell asleep on the road.[40]

[39] *Avirett*, 196–97. Douglas, *op. cit.*, 57, gave a slighly different version.

[40] Douglas, *loc. cit.*, and Col. A. G. Taliaferro's report, *O. R.*, 12, pt. 1, p. 776.
bear out Avirett's statement that the Third Brigade got at least two hours' rest. It was
halted about midnight. The First Brigade, which was ahead of the Third, was pushed
on until about 3 A.M. Jackson said in his report that "the advance continued to move
forward till morning. . . . The other troops were permitted to halt for about an hour
during the night" (*O. R.*, 12, pt. 1, p. 704); but he could have used the word
"advance" only in respect to the skirmishers, viz., two companies of the Fifth Virginia,
raised in Winchester, and one company of the Second Virginia, three members of
which were familiar with the terrain (*O. R.*, 12, pt. 1, pp. 735; 748). Winder stated
that the remainder of the First Brigade (*ibid.*, 735), "halted for an hour and slept
previous to daylight."

CHAPTER XXVI

A Victory Ends at a Manse

At the very front of his old Brigade [1] Jackson kept watch and, about 4 o'clock on the morning of May 25, passed word down the column for the men to be aroused and started toward Winchester. He had received no news from Ewell during the later hours of the night, but about 2.30 A.M. he had sent Col. Stapleton Crutchfield across country to the commander on the Front Royal-Winchester road,[2] and he had every reason to believe that Ewell would be on his right when he formed for battle. Brief instructions Jackson gave Ashby, who disappeared quickly to the left.[3]

The weather was favorable. Above, as the stars began to dim, the skies were cloudless, though there was a touch of moisture in the air. If the column were closed and the cavalry at hand, there was promise of victory that Sabbath morning. It might even be an easy triumph. The Federals might have been pushed so hard that they had not halted on the high ridge which shielded Winchester on the South and Southwest. Beyond that elevation, at a distance of about 400 yards, as Jackson well knew, there was a second, but it was commanded in part by the heights nearer the Confederates.

Soon the vanguard was approaching Abraham's Creek, which ran from Northwest to Southeast almost perpendicular to the Valley Pike. As the First Brigade began to deploy in the glowing dawn, a report came back from the companies in advance that the Federals had a skirmish line, but apparently no more, on the nearer ridge. At the word, Jackson pushed forward to reconnoiter and to confirm the report. Soon he saw for himself the shadowy figures against the high horizon. The sight must

---

[1] *Dabney*, 375.
[2] *Cf.* Crutchfield's report, *O. R.*, 12, pt. 1, p. 726. Crutchfield did not state what his message was. To reach Ewell, Crutchfield had to travel far back down the Valley Pike, had to cross to Nineveh and had to follow Ewell down the Front Royal road, a distance of twenty-nine miles. *Ibid.* Despite the long ride, Crutchfield reached Ewell in time to direct the fire of the batteries on the right.
[3] *Avirett*, 199.

have revived him. Although he had not slept for twenty-four
hours, he was lithe with energy. Confident in command he was.
also. He was not the novice, the amateur, or the cautious prac-
titioner of an ill-learned art. Master of that field he was from
the moment he beheld the enemy.

In a few moments, as Jackson watched, Winder, dapper and
alert, arrived and asked for orders. Jackson gave them in five
words—"You must occupy that hill."[4] Winder touched his
horse and was off. Swiftly, as dawn grew to day, his veterans
deployed under the edge of the hill. Jackson rode back to Carpenter's Battery, which was waiting in the road, and he pointed
out a position on the ridge which he told the Captain to take as
soon as the infantry had cleared the ridge.[5] Already the skirmishers were quarrelling in front. From the right, also, there rolled
the cheerful sound of fire, a welcome indication that Ewell was
in position and was ready to do his part. Winder previously had
thrown out the Fifth Virginia on a long skirmish line. He now
put three regiments in order of battle [6] and held one [7] in reserve.
On the left of Winder, the Second Brigade, Campbell's, was
deployed.[8]

Jackson did not have to wait long for these dispositions to be
made. Then, up the hill from Abraham's Creek came the Second
Virginia. From some woodland on the left emerged the Twenty-
seventh. Jackson held rein till he saw the regiments start. The
moment they began to mount the ridge, he rode after them.
With him he took Col. John A. Campbell, commanding the
Second Brigade, in the event that command had to be employed
quickly in support.

Up the hill went the two officers. By the time the Federal
skirmishers had withdrawn in the face of the advancing line,
Jackson was on the crest. Bullets screamed past him from a Union
line 400 yards in front, on the ridge near the town. Federal
artillery was plastering the position. Evidently Banks was antici-

---

[4] O. R., 12, pt. 1, p. 735.

[5] O. R., 12, pt. 1, p. 758. There is a possibility that this order to Carpenter came a
little later, but the probability is as stated. Cf. O. R., 12, pt. 1, p. 736, where Winder
noted that his order for Carpenter's advance had been anticipated by Jackson.

[6] Grigsby's Twenty-seventh Virginia on the left, Allen's Second on the center and
Ronald's Fourth in a wheat field on the right. The map in O. R., Atlas, Plate LXXXV-2,
is at fault in not showing the extension of Winder's line to the right of the Valley
Pike. See O. R., 12, pt. 1, pp. 736, 746.

[7] The Thirty-third Virginia.   [8] O. R., 12, pt. 1, p. 764.

pating the assault and was determined to make the crest of the hill too hot for occupancy. Jackson paid no heed to the fire. Eagerly he studied the ground before him. Swiftly his eye ran to the left, where a stone wall ran obliquely from a crossroad and

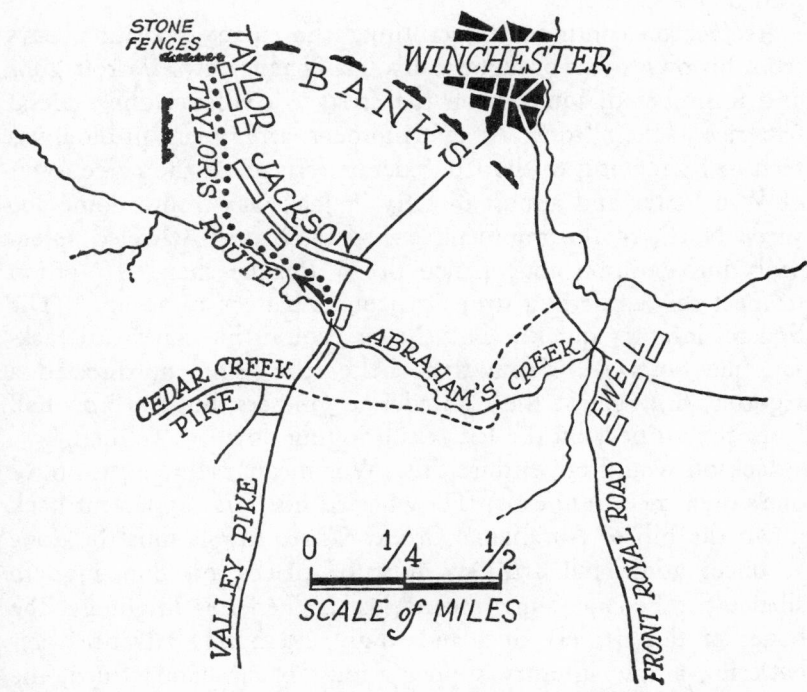

Battle of Winchester, May 25, 1862, after Jed. Hotchkiss' Contemporary Map

almost at right angles to the line the Confederates were taking. Dangerous cover that was, if the Federals should throw a force behind it!

Now the Second Virginia was crowding the hilltop. To the left was the Twenty-seventh. Both were resolute, but the plunging fire directed at them was too heavy to be faced while merely awaiting orders for another advance. Wisely and promptly, Colonel Allen recalled his men and placed them on the southern slope of the hills. They were still exposed there to the shells of the enemy, but they were out of the direct line of infantry fire.[9] The Twenty-seventh, better sheltered from musketry, was equally

9 *Cf.* Col. J. W. Allen's report, *O. R.*, 12, pt. 1, p. 743.

galled by grape and shell.[10] At Jackson's side, Colonel Campbell received an ugly wound. Colonel Grigsby of the Twenty-seventh, coming up on foot, had the sleeve of his coat cut by a bullet.[11] The General seemed to wear magic armor. Not a bullet touched him or his garments.

As Jackson continued to scrutinize the enemy's position, boys from his own town brought to his left Poague's two Parrott guns and unlimbered, squarely on the crest, to challenge the Federal batteries in their front. At that moment, a regiment in blue was seen to be moving to the Confederate left across the ridge West of Winchester and almost directly in Jackson's front. Some 200 yards North of the regiment, a Federal battery wheeled splendidly into position and opened fire.[12] Poague changed position to meet this enfilading fire; Carpenter's battery came up.[13] The Federal infantry quickly took shelter behind the stone wall Jackson had observed. From that shelter the regiment directed a vigorous fire against the Confederate gunners, but the iron hail from the artillery on the left was bringing down more men.[14]

Jackson would not endure this. War meant killing, but not of one's own men needlessly. He wheeled his horse and went back down the hill to Abraham's Creek. Three things must be done at once: additional artillery must be placed on the ridge to silence the Federal guns; second, as the Federals might get the better of the artillery duel and might attempt to advance their batteries, ample infantry supports must be at hand; third, the Confederate left must be extended to drive off the infantry and the two guns that were enfilading Poague. To the first of these movements, the vigilant Winder already was attending, and of the third, as he now met Jackson again, he spoke. The enemy, said Winder, should be attacked from the left. "Very well," answered Jackson, "I will send you up Taylor," and he started toward the rear.[15]

[10] O. R., 12, pt. 1, p. 753.
[11] Worsham, 86. Colonel Patton of the Twenty-first also came afoot to Jackson's side, but was unwounded.
[12] The somewhat inadequate Federal reports indicate that this "battery" was a two-gun section of Lt. F. W. Peabody's six-gun, Co. M., 1st New York Artillery, known as Cothran's Battery, equipped with six-pounder Parrotts. Cf. O. R., 12, pt. 1, pp. 596, 602, 758.
[13] O. R., 12, pt. 1, pp. 758, 76:.   [14] Ibid.
[15] McHenry Howard, 110. Dabney observed, op. cit., 498–99, that Winder's behavior in this action destroyed the antagonism to him that had existed in the Stonewall Brigade

Cutshaw's Battery was mounting the hill to take position between Poague and Carpenter, who was on Poague's right. Straining upgrade, also, were the four remaining guns of Poague, which were to find a position, none too good, on the left of the two Parrotts.[16] Orders were for Poague to fire solid shot directly at the stone wall and to knock it down.[17] This easy task he neatly performed. The Federals who had taken position there moved off. That simplified Taylor's task.

To speed the movement of the Louisiana Brigade, which already was moving forward from its reserve position, "Old Jack" rode in the direction of Taylor's advance, and in doing so came upon the Thirty-third Virginia, which Winder had placed under the ridge.

"Colonel," he said to John Neff, the new commanding officer, "where is your regiment posted?"

"Here," Neff answered, "the right masked in this depression of ground, and the left behind that fence."

"What are your orders?"

Colonel Neff pointed to Cutshaw's guns, which were just getting into position: "To support that battery."

Jackson clenched his fist; his voice was sharp: "I expect the enemy to bring artillery to this hill, and they must not do it! Do you understand me, sir? They must not do it! Keep a good lookout, and your men well in hand; and if they attempt to come, charge them with the bayonet, and seize their guns. Clamp them, sir, on the spot!"

"Very well, General," Neff replied calmly, "but my regiment is rather small!"

"Take it!" Jackson said and went swiftly off.[18]

Jackson's watch gave the time as 6 and a little more. An early fight was at a difficult stage. Poague's Battery was being over-

because of resentment over Jackson's treatment of Garnett. As noted *supra*, pp. 354–55, McHenry Howard set an earlier date for the moderation of the Brigade's hostile attitude toward Winder.

[16] The batteries in order, from left to right, thus were: Four guns of Poague, then the two Parrotts, then Cutshaw's four and, on the extreme right, Carpenter's four. Cf. *O. R.*, 12, pt. 1, p. 736. Carpenter and Cutshaw had long-range rifles. Poague's four were two brass smooth-bore six-pounders and two howitzers.

[17] Nearly all the stone walls of the district around Winchester were made by piling the flat stones one on another without mortar.

[18] Dabney's account of this colloquy, *loc. cit.*, 378, and Neff's, *O. R.*, 12, pt. 1, p. 755, complement each other perfectly.

whelmed. Carpenter was getting all he could stand. The infantry West of the Valley Pike was idle, unable to advance over the crest of the ridge. On the right, Ewell had opened at 5.40,[19] but, as yet, seemed to be making no progress. From the field, and particularly on Ewell's front, a morning mist as heavy as fog was rising.[20] If victory was to be won quickly, Taylor must get beyond the enemy's right and turn it. Jackson continued to spur toward Taylor's oncoming Brigade. It must hasten! Past his Virginians Jackson rode. Inquiringly they looked at him. As they had been told not to cheer, they did not greet him in their usual manner, but as he rushed by, with the battle light flaming in his eyes, they took off their hats. He removed his cap in acknowledgment,[21] but not a word did he say. Soon he found the Louisiana Brigadier, who was riding ahead of his troops.

One gesture and one sentence covered orders. Jackson pointed to the ridge on the left: "You must carry it." [22]

Taylor was more than willing. His Brigade, he said, would be at hand by the time he had examined the ground, and, with no more ado, he turned to the left.

Jackson waited a few moments until the column arrived. Leading it in person, he soon overtook Taylor and rode on with him under a fire that now was quickening. It was in vain that Taylor insisted the commanding General of the Army should not expose himself. Jackson paid no heed whatever and rode straight on to a point where the enemy's artillery could be brought to bear directly on the column. As some men fell, the Louisianians began to duck.

"What the hell are you dodging for?" Taylor yelled. "If there is any more of it, you will be halted under this fire for an hour!"

Taylor remembered afterward that a look of "reproachful surprise" came over Jackson's face. "He placed his hand on my shoulder, said in a gentle voice, 'I am afraid you are a wicked fellow,' turned and rode back to the Pike." [23]

---

[19] O. R., 12, pt. 1, p. 779.   [20] O. R., 12, pt. 1, pp. 606, 779, 794; Dabney, 377.
[21] Douglas, 57–58.

[22] Douglas, op. cit., 58, gave the conversation as follows: Jackson: "General, can your Brigade charge a battery?" Taylor: "It can try." Jackson: "Very good. It must do it then. Move it forward." Taylor's account, earlier and more authoritative, is followed here.

[23] R. Taylor, 58. Moore, op. cit., 56, noted that when one of the Louisiana Colonels chided his men for dodging, the soldier replied, "Colonel, lead us up to where we can get at them and then we won't dodge."

As Jackson went back toward the center, he ordered the Tenth Virginia to extend Taylor's left and the Twenty-third to strengthen the Louisianians' right; [24] and everywhere, as he spurred on, he directed all the regiments to be ready to charge when Taylor advanced. Apparently Jackson did not attempt to send word to Ewell to share in this movement, but that officer was manœuvring. Having seen the Twenty-first North Carolina and the Twenty-first Georgia repulsed in an initial attack, Ewell had taken a line of advance suggested by General Trimble. From that flank, the mist had begun to lift. Directions and positions were less obscure. Ewell was moving around to the Federal left precisely as Taylor was to the right.

The outlook was brightening. In half an hour, at most, Taylor would charge. Then the test would come! To be ready for it, Jackson headed his horse back up the hill down which he had come after the Federal artillery first had opened. This time he did not mount to the crest, but stopped where he could peer over the eminence.[25] Carpenter's Battery was gone from its position; [26] so were the Federal guns in front of Carpenter on the opposite ridge.[27] Poague, after a duel in which seventeen of his men had been killed and wounded, had withdrawn behind cover, and had left his two Parrott guns as a deserted target for the enemy.[28] Only Cutshaw's Battery remained in the position to which Jackson had seen it climbing, and it had a borrowed Lieutenant in command. All its commissioned officers had been killed or wounded.[29] The loss of such gallant gunners was grievous, but now . . . when would Taylor start?

Looking over the brow of the hill, Jackson waited while the Louisiana Tigers under the daring Rob Wheat slipped around to a point almost directly opposite the end of the shattered and abandoned wall from which the Federals had been firing on Poague. The regiments of the Louisiana Brigade formed in a

[24] Hotchkiss, in 3 *C. M. H.*, 241.
[25] *Dabney*, 379.
[26] He had been ordered, he did not state by whom, to follow Taylor and to take position on the extreme left. *O. R.*, 12, pt. 1, p. 759.
[27] *Ibid.*, 758.
[28] Poague, in his report, *O. R.*, 12, pt. 1, p. 762, did not mention that he left his guns on the ridge when he had to take cover; but as Moore, who was near at hand, stated, *op. cit.*, 86, that he saw them standing unattended, safe within the line, there is no reason for not accepting his statement.
[29] *O. R.*, 12, pt. 1, pp. 758-59.

long line to the South of Wheat. Then, about 7.30 o'clock,[30] as
Taylor emerged, there was staged such a spectacle as the Army
of the Valley never had witnessed before: "The enemy poured
grape and musketry into Taylor's line as soon as it came in sight.
Gen. Taylor rode in front of his brigade, drawn sword in hand,
occasionally turning his horse, at other times merely turning in
his saddle to see that his line was up. They marched up the hill
in perfect order, not firing a shot! About half way . . . he gave
in a loud and commanding voice . . . the order to charge!"[31]
Jackson could restrain himself no longer. "Forward after the
enemy," he cried, and bounded in full pursuit over the crest of
the hill.[32]

From the door of a house close to the Union front, the wife of
a Confederate Colonel was watching: "I could see . . . the hill
side covered with Federal troops, a long line of blue forms lying
down just behind its crest, on the top of which just in their front
a battery spouted flame at the lines which were slowly advancing
to the top. Suddenly I saw a long, even line of gray caps above
the crest of the hill, then appeared the gray forms that wore them,
with the battleflag floating over their heads! The cannon ceased
suddenly, and as the crouching forms that had been lying behind
the cannon rose to their feet they were greeted by a volley from
their assailants. . . ."[33]

The whole Confederate Army seemed now to be pouring over
the ridge and into the streets of Winchester—Ewell from the right
and, from the ridge, the First and Second Brigades of Jackson.
Taylor's men were in front of them all. Jackson was among them.
"Order forward the whole line," he shouted, "the battle's won";
and soon, as Taylor's men swept on, he cried, "Very good; let's
holler!" His cap was off and in his hand; he cheered as wildly
as any private. When an officer remonstrated with him, he disdained answer and commanded: "Go back and tell the whole
Army to press forward to the Potomac!"[34]

Near the outskirts of the town, he met Taylor. Without a word,
he reached over from his saddle, silently wrung the younger

---

[30] *O. R.*, 12, pt. 1, p. 769. William Allan, *op. cit.*, 231, put it between 8 and 9.
Gordon, *O. R.*, 12, pt. 1, p. 616, said that Taylor moved to the Confederate left between
6.30 and 7 A.M.
[31] *Worsham*, 87.   [32] *Dabney*, 379.
[33] *Mrs. McDonald*, 67.
[34] Hotchkiss in 3 *C. M. H.*, 242; *Douglas*, 59.

officer's hand, and hurried on.[35] He found that the enemy had kept good formation for the first few hundred yards of withdrawal,[36] but that, in the streets of the rejoicing, liberated city, the Union columns had been broken and the regiments confused. Then, as the Federal units had crowded the approaches to the northern roads, rout had begun. When Jackson and his shouting infantry pressed after the hurrying foe and reached the open country, before them to the horizon the enemy seemed to be spread in hopeless disorder. Quickly, and almost without orders, the panting gray regiments formed an irregular line and opened fire. Instead of mowing down the Unionists, the minié balls seemed to speed their flight.[37]

It was futile for Jackson to attempt swift, organized pursuit with his scattered infantry; but the situation was the traditional one for cavalry to sweep forward with pistol and saber. Jackson sensed the opportunity on the instant and looked about for his squadrons. None was in sight. Ashby, it will be remembered, had been with Jackson in the early morning, but he and his handful of men had gone off to the left, beyond Taylor's flank. Nothing had been seen of him after that time.[38] "Maryland" Steuart had the Second and the Sixth Virginia on Ewell's right when the battle commenced—where was Steuart now ? "Never," cried Jackson as he looked vainly about him, "was there such a chance for cavalry! Oh, that my cavalry were in place!"[39]

If the troopers were not at hand, then, as some one suggested at the moment to Jackson, the alternative was to advance the artillery and to have the infantry follow in support. "Yes," said the General tersely, "go back and order up the nearest batteries you find!"[40] Soon the artillery was advanced to the front, though it was plain the exhausted horses scarcely could drag the guns. Forward the drivers lashed the horses. Behind them staggered some of the infantry, like sick men fired to strength by some wild delirium. Jackson seemed oblivious of their plight. "Order every battery and every Brigade forward to the Potomac,"

[35] R. Taylor, 59.   [36] O. R., 12, pt. 1, p. 706.
[37] The minié bullet was not, strictly speaking, a "ball," but was conical with a hollowed bottom designed to expand and to force the bullet into the rifling. In the Confederacy, the term "minié ball" was of general use. The name of the inventor was pronounced by the soldiers as if it had been the feminine "Minnie."
[38] Avirett, 271; Hotchkiss, in 3 C. M. H., 243.
[39] Dabney, 381.   [40] Ibid., 381.

he cried hoarsely, and himself spurred on.[41] It did not matter that the Potomac at Williamsport was full thirty-six miles from Winchester, and at Harpers Ferry twenty-five. The enemy was routed and must be pursued.

Again and again, as he pressed forward, Jackson looked back for the cavalry. Not one troop did he see. When he was three miles North of Winchester, still determined to follow the fast-disappearing enemy, he sent Lt. "Sandie" Pendleton back with instructions to find "Maryland" Steuart and to order him instantly to the front.[42] Meantime, the infantry and the artillery must keep on! They did their utmost, but men and horses were failing fast. Only a shadow of a column kept the road, which now traversed a wooded country that lent itself to ambuscades.[43] By the time the foremost battery had reached the vicinity of Stephenson's Depot, about five miles North of Winchester, the guns were without infantry support.

Reluctantly Jackson had to call a halt, but he could not bring himself to abandon the field. He would glean if he might not reap. Capt. William H. Caskie, commanding the Hampden Artillery, was directed to unhitch the lead horses of his caissons and to call for volunteers to mount and chase. Although the gunners were willing, no sooner were they astride the harness-burdened, half-dead animals than it was manifest that they could do little. Jackson countermanded the order and, with bitter regret, ended the chase.[44]

An hour later,[45] Steuart came thundering up with his two regiments and went after the vanished foe. The reason for Steuart's delay "Sandie" Pendleton reported indignantly on his return to field headquarters. He had found the cavalry about two and a half miles East of Winchester. The men were dismounted and idle; the horses were grazing in a clover field. As Pendleton did not see Steuart, he delivered Jackson's orders to the regimental commanders. Their senior, Lieutenant Colonel

---

[41] *Ibid.*, 381. Dabney is much the best authority on this phase of the Battle of Winchester. Apparently he remained with Jackson through most of the pursuit.

[42] *O. R.*, 12, pt. 1, p. 709.

[43] *O. R.*, 12, pt. 3, p. 901.

[44] *O. R.*, 12, pt. 1, pp. 706, 771–72. Worsham, *op. cit.*, 87, stated that some of the other artillerymen, being unable to make their way through Winchester, unhitched the lead horses of guns and caissons, threw the traces over the backs of the animals, charged into the town and captured numerous prisoners.

[45] *O. R.*, 12, pt. 1, p. 706.

Flournoy, tactfully suggested that Pendleton should see Steuart, who had told the regiments to await him where they were. Pendleton galloped on and at length overtook Steuart. When informed of Jackson's orders, Steuart showed himself a stickler: he was under Ewell, he said; orders to him must come through the division commander. In vain Pendleton explained the peremptory nature of the order and offered to see Ewell and to square the matter with him. Steuart was adamant. Regulations were regulations, channels were channels. Pendleton was compelled to ride two miles farther to the headquarters of Ewell, who, in the restrained language of Pendleton's report, "seemed surprised that General Steuart had not gone immediately on receipt of the order." [46] Again Jackson's aide wheeled his horse and galloped back—only to find that Steuart had followed him toward Ewell's camp. In the road, Pendleton stopped the Marylander and explained that Ewell directed Steuart to do as Jackson told him. Satisfied with this, Steuart returned to the clover field and sounded assembly. [47]

Once in pursuit, Steuart pressed vigorously, [48] but the two hours that had been lost in bringing him up [49] had sufficed for the enemy to get beyond the range of effective pursuit. [50] Ashby, who joined Steuart at Bunker Hill, was powerless to follow the Federals. When asked by Jackson why he had not reached the front sooner, Ashby explained that, after leaving Taylor's flank, he had swept around to the right to cut off the Federals who moved in that direction. [51] Jackson was not satisfied with Steuart's performance or Ashby's explanation, but there was nothing he could do. The battle was over. He gave his exhausted troops such rest as they could find, and himself rode back to Winchester—to count his prisoners and to survey the field? No; it was the Sabbath evening. He would reward himself with the luxury of a visit to the manse where Mrs. Jackson had spent the winter. [52]

On Monday, May 26, in gratitude for a victory on the Sabbath, he directed that religious services be held for the entire Army. [53] His formal published order combined a brief review of the opera-

46 O. R., 12, pt. 1, p. 710.   47 Ibid.
48 O. R., 12, pt. 1, p. 706.   49 Dabney, 382.
50 O. R., 12, pt. 1, p. 706.   51 Ibid., 706–7.
52 Mrs. Jackson, 265.   53 Ibid., 707.

tions, his thanks to the troops, and his appeal that the men "make the oblation of our thanks to God for his mercies to us and our country. . . ." [54] He worshiped in person with the Thirty-seventh Virginia and, wrote Rev.-Maj. R. L. Dabney, D.D., "presented an edifying example of devotion to the men." The General's letter to his wife was not penned, of course, till the Sabbath was past, but when written it was not such an apology as he had made after the Battle of Kernstown for fighting on Sunday. In fact, he did not mention the day by its familiar and cherished name. "My precious darling," he said, "an ever-kind Providence blessed us with success at Front Royal on Friday, between Strasburg and Winchester on Saturday and here with a successful engagement on yesterday." He went on: "Our entrance into Winchester was one of the most stirring scenes of my life. The town is much improved in loyalty to our cause. Your friends greatly desired to see you with me. . . . Time forbids my writing a longer letter, but it does not forbid my loving my *esposita*." [55]

Nor did circumstance or letter-writing forbid his vigorous compliance with Lee's admonition "to press the enemy toward the Potomac." Steuart, on the 25th, had pushed within half a mile of Martinsburg, which lies eight miles from the Potomac. [56] The next day, finding that the enemy had evacuated the town, Steuart entered it and captured many military stores. [57] From Martinsburg, the advance went almost to the crossing of the Potomac at Williamsport and destroyed the bridge of the B. & O. Railroad at North Mountain Depot. [58] On the 28th, the infantry moved on Charlestown, and on the 29th, made a demonstration against Harpers Ferry. [59]

These operations completed the execution of Jackson's orders. The enemy was driven to and not merely toward the Potomac, but, after the blood-stirring events at Front Royal, Middletown and Winchester, the advance to the river was an anticlimax. Despite the reports Banks sent to Washington of his "safe

---

[54] *Jackson's MS. Letter Book*, 58; *Dabney*, 384.
[55] *Mrs. Jackson*, 265.
[56] *O. R.*, 12, pt. 3, p. 901.
[57] *O. R.*, 12, pt. 1, pp. 707, 730. From May 27 to the end of the campaign, Col. T. T. Munford's report, *ibid.*, 729 ff, supplies an account of the operations of the Second and Sixth Virginia Cavalry, concerning which there are no other official narratives, except those of Col. T. S. Flournoy for May 23–24, and, in a brief, unsatisfactory sketch, for May 25–26.
[58] *O. R.*, 12, pt. 1, p. 730.　　　　[59] *O. R.*, 12, pt. 1, pp. 639, 707, 738

arrival" at Williamsport "with comparatively little loss," [60] Jackson's Army had taken an estimated 3030 prisoners, wounded and unwounded, 9300 small arms, two field guns, many wagons and rich commissary supplies. Of quartermasters' stores, the captures most precisely were valued for the thrifty Jackson at $125,185, "besides an immense amount destroyed."

Confederate casualties in the entire operation had been sixty-eight killed, 329 wounded and three missing, a total of 400.[61] Banks subsequently maintained that his combat force around Strasburg, at the beginning of the operations, was less than 4000, or, with the troops at Winchester, about 5000,[62] but on May 21, he had given the figure for the troops at Strasburg as 6076, exclusive of artillery.[63] He estimated that his loss was 904, and he reasoned that when stragglers returned, the total would not exceed 700.[64] More realistically, the tabulation showed casualties of 2019,[65] which did not include 750 sick and previously wounded men in the hospitals at Strasburg and Winchester.[66] If, as seems probable, Banks's participating force on May 23–25 was about 8500,[67] his losses were between 2769 and 3030, or from 31 to 34 per cent.[68] Loss of equipment, of fighting spirit, and perhaps of confidence in the command was serious, also. Not until June 9 were any of Banks's infantry re-equipped and ready for active operations.[69]

This was done by Jackson in three days of fighting, but the strategical results went far beyond the impairment of a Federal Corps, misstyled an Army. On May 28, as noted in Chapter

60 *O. R.*, 12, pt. 1, p. 530   61 *O. R.*, 12, pt. 1, p. 708.
62 *O. R.*, 12, pt. 1, p. 550.
63 *O. R.*, 12, pt. 1, p. 523. Actually he had given the figures as 7076, but the editors of the *O. R.* assumed an error of 1000 in the strength of the cavalry and bracketed "1600" where he wrote "2600." This total did not include 2500 infantry on the railroad between Manassas and Strasburg, and thereby excluded the force of about 1000 at Front Royal. Cf. *O. R.*, 12, pt. 1, p. 536.
64 *Ibid.*, 551.
65 *Ibid.*, 554.
66 *O. R.*, 12, pt. 1, p. 708.
67 That is, 6000 at Strasburg, 1000 at Winchester, 1000 at and near Front Royal and 250 cavalry sent by Col. T. F. Brodhead from Williamsport, *O. R.*, 12, pt. 1, pp. 580, 581, and 292 men of the 8th N. Y. Cavalry from Harpers Ferry, *O. R.*, 12, pt. 1, p. 585.
68 William Allan, always careful, estimated Banks's total force on May 23 in the district from Loudoun to Strasburg and North to Winchester at 10,252, but he did not have the revised figures for Hatch's cavalry. These would reduce the total to 9252. He put the participating force around Winchester on the 25th at 6408. *Op. cit.*, *S. H. S.* ed., 208, 225.
69 *O. R.*, 12, pt. 1, p. 542.

XVI,[70] Jeb Stuart had reported to General Johnston that the advance of McDowell's Army, which had been marching southward from Fredericksburg, had turned back to that city.[71] Confederate leaders had reasoned immediately that McDowell's return to Fredericksburg gave them at least a chance of defeating the Army of the Potomac before he could reinforce the right of the Federal lines that threatened Richmond. Both for the withdrawal of McDowell and for the resultant improvement in the prospect of holding Richmond, the credit belonged primarily to Jackson and his men.

Behind the scenes in Washington, at 5 o'clock on the afternoon of the 24th, when Jackson had been pursuing Banks from Middletown, Secretary Stanton had telegraphed McDowell to suspend his advance on Richmond and to send 20,000 of his troops to the Shenandoah Valley.[72] As a report had come, also, that the Confederates were moving northward from Richmond, the Secretary had telegraphed the Governors of all the Northern States to prepare the whole of their armed forces for a sudden call.[73] General Frémont, at Franklin in Pendleton County, Western Virginia, was told to advance immediately to Harrisonburg in order to relieve the pressure on Banks.[74] It was a mission more readily ordered than fulfilled.

The next day, the War Department took possession of the railroads[75] and sent this startling message to the executives of the States: "Intelligence from various quarters leaves no doubt that the enemy in great force are advancing on Washington. You will please organize and forward immediately all the volunteer and militia force in your State."[76] By the time Jackson was fighting at Winchester, McDowell had issued orders for two Divisions and one regiment to start for the Shenandoah Valley;[77] on the afternoon of the 26th, President Lincoln was questioning whether the troops left with McDowell—less than half the original force of 40,000[78]—should not be recalled to the defense of

---

70 See *supra*, p. 221; 2 *R. E. Lee*, 65.

71 The last southward march of McDowell was, in reality, nothing more than a reconnaissance. He had abandoned by that time his attempt to form a junction with McClellan. *O. R.*, 12, pt. 3, pp. 253, 258.

72 *O. R.*, 12, pt. 3, p. 219.

73 III *O. R.*, 2, 68.

74 *O. R.*, 12, pt. 1, p. 643.

75 *Ibid.*, 69-70.

76 III *O. R.*, 2, 70.

77 *O. R.*, 12, pt. 2, p. 222.

78 *O. R.*, 12, pt. 1, p. 282.

Washington.[79] From the east side of the Blue Ridge, Gen. J. W. Geary was sending alarming dispatches that Jackson with at least 20,000 men was coming through the mountains.[80] Despite these reports, it became apparent in Washington on the 27th that the situation was not desperate. Although Gen. Rufus Saxton at Harpers Ferry pronounced the retreat a rout,[81] Banks himself recovered his sang-froid and wrote almost as if he had won a victory.[82] Gen. James Shields, who had met Jackson at Kernstown, hastened from the vicinity of Fredericksburg [83] with a clear understanding of the situation.[84] After Shields arrived at Catlett's Station on the 26th, he realized quickly that all the direful warnings to Washington of a Confederate advance East of the Blue Ridge had originated with the panic-stricken cavalry command of Brig. Gen. J. W. Geary.[85]

By wrathful denunciation of this "shameful panic," which involved the hasty burning of arms, accouterments and even of cooking utensils,[86] Shields allayed the concern of President Lincoln and of Secretary Stanton. Bold assurances by Shields that "the enemy will fly before us," and that he would "intercept the force against Banks," which "was very inconsiderable," [87] restored in the War Department a measure of confidence. Mr. Stanton began to hope, early on the 26th, that a quick concentration by Frémont and part of McDowell's Army would "bag the enemy that attacked Banks." [88] The Secretary had another attack of nerves on the 29th, lest Jackson advance on Washington,[89] but Stanton soon turned the call for troops into a general recruiting campaign.[90] President Lincoln was relieved in spirit immediately.

The improved outlook in the Valley and exaggerated reports of Fitz-John Porter's success at Hanover Court House [91] led the President to inquire of McDowell on the 28th whether the sus-

---

[79] *Ibid,* 243.
[80] *O. R., 12,* pt. 3, p. 242.
[81] *O. R.,* 12, pt. 1, pp. 628 ff.
[82] Cf. *ibid.,* 530.
[83] His Division, road-worn, had arrived there May 22. *O. R.,* 12, pt. 1, p. 281.
[84] Cf. *O. R.,* 12, pt. 3, p. 243.
[85] *O. R.,* 12, pt. 3, p. 248. For Geary's dispatches, which are a classic example of the mischief that can be wrought by the uncritical transmission of rumor, see *ibid.,* 234, 240, 242, 247, 255, 256, 257, 259, 260–61, 277.
[86] *Ibid.,* 257, 259, 277.
[87] *Ibid.,* 259.
[88] *O. R.,* 12, pt. 3, p. 246.
[89] *Ibid.,* 276, 279.
[90] III *O. R.,* 2, 101.
[91] See *supra,* pp. 210–20.

pended advance from Fredericksburg southward should not be renewed.⁹² Quickly came McDowell's answer: ". . . I do not think, in the present state of affairs, it would be well to attempt to put through a part of that force, or to leave Fredericksburg otherwise than strongly held, which could not be done as the troops are now posted." ⁹³ McDowell was immobilized. That was Jackson's reward.⁹⁴

⁹² *O. R.,* 12, pt. 3, p. 266.   ⁹³ *O. R.,* 12, pt. 3, p. 268.
⁹⁴ The magnitude of the panic in Washington has not been exaggerated by biographers of Jackson, but the duration of the panic and the extent to which it was reflected in the press have been overstated. The *National Intelligencer,* as early as May 26 (p. 3, col. 1), denounced "the absurd rumors which find currency among idlers, quid nuncs, and 'secession sympathizers.'" In its reports, that paper (May 28, p. 3, cols. 2 and 3) presented the North as confident and maintained that Banks was safe. In Philadelphia, *The Inquirer* narrated events with no evidence of concern (May 27, p. 1, col. 1; May 28, p. 4, col. 1). The same view was expressed in New York by *The Tribune* (May 26, p. 1, cols. 5 and 6). Reports somewhat more excited found publication in the *New York Herald* (May 26, p. 1, col. 1; May 27, p. 3, col. 1; p. 6, col. 1; May 29, p. 4, col. 3). To that paper is attributable the oft-printed but unfounded assertion that "the call of the President for additional troops . . . was responded to by nearly half a million of men who offered their services within twenty-four hours after the proclamations were issued." The *New York Times* reported the panic but denied justification for it (May 26, p. 4, col. 3), and as early as May 27 (p. 1, col. 1) insisted that Banks was across the Potomac in safety (cf. *ibid.,* p. 1, col. 4; May 28, p. 1, col. 6; May 29, p. 1, col. 5). In Boston, the *Daily Advertiser* had fairly accurate news reports (May 26, p. 1, col. 8; May 27, p. 1, col. 8) and, while denouncing Secretary Stanton (May 27, p. 2, col. 1), reproved the people of the city (May 28, p. 2, col. 1) for yielding to excitement. *The Advertiser* said editorially: "Such of the good people of this State as were led, in their anxiety for the capital of the nation on Monday, to suppose that the rest of the United States were in as great a panic, made a great mistake. In fact it is almost provoking to observe the equanimity with which in other cities the public received that news, which created such a ferment here. Orders were given in State street on that day to buy United States stocks at par, upon the supposition that there was really some ground for all the alarm which has been excited. Stocks, however, did not fall even so much as one per cent., not coming within sight of the quotation expected by those who had anticipated a fall. The stock exchange, of course, received its tone from New York, thus illustrating the coolness with which an alleged menace to the safety of Washington was there received. . . . The news of what is still erroneously termed 'the repulse of General Banks,' will no doubt be eagerly seized upon by the foreign foes of our government, as a proof of the uncertain struggle which is kept up with the rebellion. We shall no doubt hear that this is another proof of the enterprise and skill of the rebel generals, of the inefficiency of our own, and of the helpless character of that vast force which the government has collected. And yet what especial display of ability did the rebel leaders make in walking in at the door which the Secretary of War so temptingly opened for them, by weakening and withdrawing General Banks? . . ." In the Middle West, the Cincinnati *Daily Gazette* had an alarming report on the 26th (p. 3, col. 3), but on the 27th (p. 1, col. 7), its tone was calmer. An editorial on May 29 (p. 2, col. 1) insisted that "nothing of a permanently injurious character has been suffered and that fears for an advance on Washington and into Maryland and Pennsylvania were greatly exaggerated."

CHAPTER XXVII

"From the Snare of the Fowler"

By the morning of May 30, Jackson's demonstration to the line of the Potomac was developed fully. He had pressed it to the utmost because he wanted to give his quartermaster time in which to remove all the supplies and equipment that had been captured. These were prizes worth some risks. In addition to the 9300 small arms, virtually all of them new,[1] he had taken in Winchester a rich storehouse of surgical instruments and dressings and an incredible quantity of medicines of every sort. As the Federal blockade had included medicine and anæsthetics with contraband of war, the South needed sorely what Banks's medical director lavishly had provided for the Union troops. Jackson was determined that every dram of drugs should be saved,[2] though he did not interfere with the Union surgeons, the stores or the sick and wounded in two large army hospitals in Winchester. All else that had been taken from the enemy, Maj. John A. Harman was hauling toward Staunton by every conveyance he could hire, borrow or requisition.

Jackson did more than strain to carry up the Valley all the contents of the Federal warehouses. The soldiers were admonished in general orders that captured property belonged to the Confederate government and that its conversion to private use was theft.[3] Ragged privates who had dressed themselves in articles of Federal uniform were warned that they were subject to arrest and to close custody until they proved they were not Union soldiers. Thereupon, read the orders, the Confederates would "be released upon leaving the prohibited article with the officer making the arrest." [4] A sorrowful and well-nigh universal shedding of blue jackets, new trousers, U. S. belts and comfortable caps followed.[5] In addition, to keep the men out of mischief

[1] See *supra*, p. 407.
[2] *Dabney*, 389–90.
[3] *O. R.*, 12, pt. 3, p. 902.
[4] *Ibid.*, 900.
[5] *Dabney*, 385.

and to prepare them for future struggles, Jackson on the 28th ordered the resumption of four hours of drill daily.[6]

Not even with these measures was Jackson content. Harpers Ferry, where once he had commanded, lay under Bolivar Heights, which Winder was threatening. Might it not be possible, ere the demonstration ended, to recover the town and to add it to the list of Confederate prizes? Jackson knew every eminence of that vast rift where the Shenandoah joins the Potomac and both break through the mountains. He felt that he must press advantage to the limit of the attainable and he reasoned that if he sent a force across the Shenandoah and occupied Loudoun Heights East of that river, he might alarm the enemy and induce a retreat across the Potomac;[7] but he did not wish to make any large detachment for this purpose lest his troops be cut off from the main Army in the event he had to retreat hurriedly. The Second Virginia, and only that regiment, had been sent on the 29th to Loudoun Heights.[8]

His officers were puzzled by this advance. Winder had received from two friendly sources a detailed statement of the strength of the Federals at Harpers Ferry. He had learned, also, that the Unionists had planted on Maryland Heights heavy guns which gave protection to the town from all attack in the direction of Jackson's movement. What could "Old Jack" be planning? His lieutenants asked but scarcely could shape an hypothesis. Stapleton Crutchfield, Chief of Artillery, in despair shook his head and quoted grimly, "Quem Deus vult perdere, prius dementat."[9]

Jackson paid no heed to the questioning looks of his subordinates; but in making the long gamble of this demonstration, he realized that the time in which he could manœuvre on the Potomac was being reduced from days to hours. On the night of May 27–28, an intelligent gentleman of advanced age had brought to Winchester a detailed report that General Shields, who had moved from the Valley to join General McDowell, was hurrying back toward Front Royal, and was within a day's march of that town.[10] This report had been relayed to Jackson on the morning

6 Jackson's MS. Order Book, p. 58.
7 O. R., 12, pt. 1, p. 707.
8 Ibid.
9 Douglas, 66; McHenry Howard, 114–15.
10 Douglas, 62–63.

of the 28th. Now, on the 30th, it was confirmed. Some of Ashby's scouts from the Blue Ridge galloped up to headquarters with definite information of Shields's approach to Front Royal. McDowell himself was believed to be marching on Berryville. Spies from across the Potomac reported, also, that Banks was reorganizing his defeated force at Williamsport.[11]

Jackson at Charlestown said not a word to indicate either surprise or dismay on the receipt of this news. Daily his composure was more nearly flawless. His reserve, as always, was impenetrable. Quietly he dispatched his couriers with orders. Then he received some ladies who called "to pay their respects." Upon their departure, he rode to the front,[12] where he watched an artillery duel [13] and some lively skirmishing by the Fifth Virginia.[14] Presently rain began to fall.[15] Jackson went to the shelter of a large tree, seated himself and ere long stretched out and fell asleep. When he opened his eyes again, Col. A. R. Boteler was busily sketching him.

"Let me see what you have been doing there," said the General.

Boteler submitted the sketch, which Jackson examined without a word of praise or of criticism. "My hardest tasks at West Point," he confessed, "were the drawing lessons, and I never could do anything in that line to satisfy myself, or indeed, any one else." He paused for a moment and changed the subject. "But, Colonel, I have some harder work than this for you to do, and, if you'll sit down here, now, I'll tell you what it is."

Boteler, a former Congressman and a trusted friend of proven discretion, took a place by Jackson's side. The General began: "I want you to go to Richmond for me. I must have reinforcements. You can explain to them down there what the situation is here. Get as many men as can be spared, and I'd like you, if you please, to go as soon as you can."

The Colonel expressed readiness to start at once, but he said, "You must first tell me, General, what is the situation here."

11 *Hotchkiss' MS. Diary*, 41.
12 *Ibid*.
13 A. R. Boteler, in 40 *S. H. S. P.*, 164. It probably was during the preliminaries of this exchange of fire that Jackson humiliated Arnold Elzey. The Marylander remarked that he had heard of the planting of heavy guns on Maryland Heights. "General Elzey," Jackson answered, "are you afraid of heavy guns?" Elzey's face reddened, but he held his tongue (*McHenry Howard*, 115).
14 Hotchkiss. *loc. cit.*   15 *Ibid*.

Jackson answered with none of the reticence he usually exhibited. He told Boteler of the reports he had received that day of Federal forces marching toward the Valley. Frémont, he coolly said, would move against him also. Once the Confederates withdrew, the garrison at Harpers Ferry of course would join Banks in pursuit. Jackson proceeded: "McDowell and Frémont are probably aiming to effect a junction at Strasburg, so as to head me off from the upper Valley, and are both nearer to it now than we are; consequently, no time is to be lost. You can say to them in Richmond that I'll send on the prisoners, secure most if not all the captured property, and with God's blessing will be able to baffle the enemy's plans here with my present force, but that it will have to be increased as soon thereafter as possible." Without any show of bravado or any gesture to indicate that he was proposing a bold stroke, Jackson then uncovered a plan which he must have pondered long: "You may tell them, too, that if my command can be gotten up to 40,000 men a movement may be made beyond the Potomac, which will soon raise the siege of Richmond and transfer this campaign from the banks of the Potomac to those of the Susquehanna." [16]

Boteler left at once for Charlestown, where Jackson told him he would find a train that would carry him to Winchester, whence he must take horse to Staunton. A few minutes later Jackson left Winder to make a final thrust at Harpers Ferry, and himself mounted and started back to Charlestown with his staff. By this time, troops filled the road. The wagons were on the move. All were headed South. A retreat was on. How far it was to extend, only those could surmise who knew what information Jackson had received of the threat to his rear.

---

[16] Boteler, in 40 S. H. S. P., 165. The usual caveat, of course, must be entered here concerning the literal accuracy of this quotation. Colonel Boteler's paper was not published, so far as the writer has ascertained, until 1915, but as early as 1866, or thereabouts, Boteler related the substance of a part of this conversation to John Esten Cooke. Moreover, though the date of the composition of the article in 40 S. H. S. P., 162 ff, is not given, the paper bears none of the marks of old-age reminiscence. Internal evidence suggests (p. 169) that Boteler wrote subsequently to November, 1878, and prior to the publication in book form of William Allan's fine study of the Valley Campaign, which appeared in 1880. Boteler's precision of detail and the references to his notebook create confidence in the substantial correctness of what he narrated. The confidence is increased by the fact that his account is much less theatrical than the version Cooke gave of the one incident described on the authority of Boteler. At the time of the interview of which he wrote, Boteler was 46 years of age. He died in Shepherdstown, W. Va., May 8, 1892. Incidentally, in the published text in 40 S. H. S. P., a paragraph beginning on p. 176 with the words "The movement proposed" belongs at the bottom of p. 174 after the asterisks. A corrected text was printed. without explanation, in 42 S. H. S. P., 174 ff

"General," asked a young Lieutenant of cavalry, as he rode up to Jackson, "are the troops going back?"

"Don't you see them going?" Jackson answered bluntly.

"Are they all going?" the inquisitive Lieutenant pressed.

Jackson eyed him narrowly, and then turned to Col. Abner Smead. "Colonel," said he sharply, "arrest that man as a spy."

The Lieutenant almost fell off his horse in dismay, but, records Hotchkiss, Colonel Ashby "soon coming up, got him off by say-ing that he had not much sense." [17]

Back in Charlestown, Jackson had dinner in the home of his capable commissary, Maj. W. J. Hawks, and there he received a dispatch that had been rushed with the utmost speed from Joseph E. Johnston's headquarters. Writing under date of the 27th, his superior officer congratulated Jackson and said: "If you can threaten Baltimore and Washington, do so. It may produce an important diversion. McClellan is near and McDowell reported advancing from Fredericksburg. Your movements depend, of course, upon the enemy's strength remaining in your neighbor-hood. Upon that depends the practicability of your advancing to the Potomac and even crossing it. I know of no hostile force to prevent either." [18]

All that was attainable in these orders, Jackson had to his credit. Johnston's wishes had been anticipated. Now there was nothing Jackson could do except to get back up the Valley ere the Federals closed on him. Gratefully he thanked his host for his dinner and unhurriedly he climbed aboard the train where Colonel Boteler already was waiting. Most of the staff went with the General, but Jed. Hotchkiss preferred to go on horseback [19] in order that he might have his mount at hand for immediate use in Winchester. After the train started through the rain, which now was falling heavily, Jackson put his arm on the seat in front of him, leaned over and quickly went to sleep. He was as composed as if he were returning home from a pleasant vaca-

[17] *Hotchkiss' MS. Diary*, 41.

[18] Letter of May 27, 1862, printed in *Douglas*, 65. Johnston added as a postscript: "Time will be gained and saved by addressing me always instead of the government." Douglas stated that this letter was received "on the 29th or 30th of May, while General Jackson was in Charlestown at the house of one of his staff, Major Wells J. Hawks." The date of receipt almost certainly was the 30th.

[19] *Hotchkiss' MS. Diary*, 41.

tion. Nothing indicated that he felt any concern over the task of extricating his Army from the net the enemy was spreading.

Near Summit Point, as Colonel Boteler looked across the storm-swept fields, he observed a horseman who was waving to the train to stop. Boteler took out his field glass, scrutinized the figure and identified a Confederate uniform. Sensing that the man might be a courier with an important dispatch, Boteler awakened Jackson, who ordered the train halted. Presently through a window, the courier handed a paper to Jackson. The General read it, tore it up and then said to the conductor, "Go on, sir, if you please." Without a word or even the quiver of an eye-lash, he resumed his position and dropped to sleep again.

After the train reached Winchester, the character of the news that had reached Jackson en route was for any man's reading. The Twelfth Georgia Regiment, a fine unit of Edward Johnson's command, had been left at Front Royal to guard the prisoners and the captured stores. On the 30th, Federals under General Shields had come swiftly through the Blue Ridge and had moved against the regiment. Its commander, Col. Z. T. Conner, had lost his head and had started precipitately for Winchester to report. The bewildered Major of the regiment had thought that escape was impossible and had so said, but the men of the Twelfth had refused to surrender. A stout-hearted Captain, William F. Brown, who was nearly 60 years of age, had then assumed command and had marched the regiment to Winchester. Colonel Conner had arrived there about 6 P.M. and had written Ewell, "Unless you can throw reenforcements here by morning all will be gone." [20] Hotchkiss had heard of the loss of Front Royal when he had reached Winchester ahead of Jackson's railway train, and he had sent a courier to deliver the news to Jackson.[21]

Grim news it was! All the captured supplies and stores at Front Royal, to the value of $300,000, had been destroyed by the retreating Confederates.[22] Shields, moreover, had reached the

[20] O. R., 12, pt. 1, p. 793.
[21] Hotchkiss' MS. Diary. The account of Jackson's train journey from Charlestown to Winchester, given in J. E. Cooke's Stonewall Jackson, 158, and reprinted in 1 Henderson, 347–48, was attributed to Boteler but was confused in the sequence of events. At least one part of the conversation credited to Jackson on May 30 actually dated from June 13. See Boteler, in 40 S. H. S. P., 173, and infra.
[22] O. R., 12, pt. 1, pp. 707–8.

town before noon, and at that point had closed one of Jackson's two lines of retreat up the Shenandoah Valley. If Shields pressed rapidly westward, a march of eleven miles would bring him to Strasburg. In the event that Frémont from the Alleghenies joined Shields there, the two might block the Valley Pike while Banks and Saxton followed Jackson's retreat. What might not happen then? From Halltown, near which most of Jackson's troops had been encamped that morning, there was a long, long stretch of forty-four miles of road to Strasburg. Forty-four for the gray-coats, eleven for the blue—the odds were stiff; but if Jackson had any doubt of his ability of reaching Strasburg before the enemy closed on him, he gave no indication of it. In Winchester, he went to the hotel to prepare some papers which he wished Colonel Boteler to carry to Richmond, and to his room, it was whispered soon after, Jackson called Colonel Conner.

"Colonel," he asked the crestfallen officer, according to the story, "how many men did you have killed?"

"None."

"How many wounded?"

"None, sir," replied Conner.

"Do you call that much of a fight?" the General retorted, and with no more ado he ordered Conner put in arrest.[23]

Late in the evening, while the long columns were tramping through Winchester in the rain, the papers that Boteler was to take to Richmond were copied and signed. Jackson summoned the Colonel, who, ere he went to the General's room, ordered two whiskey toddies sent up. When he offered one to Jackson, the General drew back: "No, no, Colonel, you must excuse me; I never drink intoxicating liquors."

"I know that, General," answered Boteler soothingly, "but though you habitually abstain, as I do myself, from everything of the sort, there are occasions, and this is one of them, when a stimulant will do us both good, otherwise I would neither take it myself nor offer it to you. So you must make an exception to your general rule and join me in a toddy tonight."

Jackson shook his head but, at Boteler's urging, finally lifted

---

[23] *Hotchkiss' MS Diary*, 41. Shields stated, *O. R.*, 12, pt. 1, p. 682, that he captured six officers and 150 men at Front Royal. He reported, also, the recovery that day of ighteen and the next day of six Federals taken at Front Royal on May 23. *Ibid.*, 683.

the glass and took several sips. Then he put it down again: "Colonel, do you know why I habitually abstain from intoxicating drinks?"

"No."

"Why, sir, because I like the taste of them, and when I discovered that to be the case I made up my mind to do without them altogether." [24]

Boteler remembered the conversation as an evidence of Jackson's temperance and process of reasoning. The Colonel might as readily have instanced it to show the composure of Jackson in an hour of desperate danger to his Army, a composure so absolute that the man and the soldier seemed to be separate personalities.

At 3 o'clock on the morning of the 31st, Jackson was knocking at Jed. Hotchkiss' door. "I want you," said he, "to go to Charlestown and bring up the First Brigade." He added, "I will stay in Winchester until you get here if I can, but if I cannot, and the enemy gets here first, you must bring it around through the mountains." [25] When Hotchkiss wrote this down in his diary he noted: Jackson "feared that the converging columns of Frémont, Shields, McDowell and Banks might compel him to go out and fight one of them, but he was in fine spirits." [26]

After Hotchkiss hurried away, Jackson saw to it that the last of the wagons with captured stores started. Next the prisoners, some 2300 in number, who had been kept in Winchester, were put on the Valley Pike to tramp to Staunton. As a guard, Jackson designated the Twenty-first Virginia, under the vigilant command of Lt. Col. R. H. Cunningham. [27]

With his prizes and his captives ahead of him, Jackson ordered the infantry to begin the march on which the very life of the Army and perhaps of the Confederacy depended. If he and his troops escaped, they might be able to go to Richmond and to share the effort to drive McClellan off; but if Jackson were trapped by the converging columns and were overwhelmed, what would prevent McDowell from joining McClellan and defeating Johnston's defending forces which, at that very hour, were deploying for the unsuccessful Battle of Seven Pines?

[24] 40 S. H. S. P., 168.
[26] Ibid.
[25] Hotchkiss' MS. Diary, 41–42.
[27] O. R., 12, pt. 1, p. 708.

Swiftly and steadily, to the unspeakable regret of the people of Winchester,[28] Jackson's troops passed southward through the streets they had entered with shouts six days before. Some of the men suspected the enemy was closing on them, but they appeared as confident as their commander was. At 2.30 P.M., when all the infantry except Winder's Brigade had cleared the town, and only the cavalry remained to guard against a dash by the enemy, Jackson took horse and rode past his toiling men.

The march proved uneventful. Regulations were followed strictly. The men rested ten minutes of every hour. Officers saw to it that the column was closed. Stragglers received no mercy. Jackson watched closely the progress of the retreat, but as he neared his objective and heard no sound of firing, he could not resist the impulse to ride ahead and see for himself whether Frémont or Shields or both of them had intercepted him. At last, he came in sight of Strasburg. After the first careful gaze, he must have felt immeasurable relief. Not a Federal was in the village. A clash had occurred during the day between a Confederate outpost and a Federal Brigade about halfway between Strasburg and Front Royal; [29] Frémont was known to be close at hand to the West of Strasburg; but the Valley Pike itself still was open! If it could be held until the main body of Confederate troops reached there that evening and Winder's Brigade arrived the next day, the Army was safe.[30]

Jackson halted at Hupp's, just North of the village and issued his orders. The trains were to continue up the Valley. At nightfall the infantry Brigades were to go into camp as near as possible to Strasburg and were to prepare to remain at the town the next day. Ewell's troops, who would be the last to reach the vicinity of Strasburg that night, were to move again at daylight. Their wagons were to proceed straight ahead toward New Market, but the infantry were to turn westward at Strasburg and were to move out on the road by which Frémont was advancing eastward from Wardensburg.[31]

After issuing these orders, Jackson went to the campfire of Gen. "Dick" Taylor and sat for some time. Taylor subsequently wrote: "Jackson was more communicative than I remember him

28 Cf. *Mrs. McDonald*, 71.   29 *O. R.*, 12, pt. 1, p. 314.
30 *O. R.*, 12, pt. 1, p. 708; *Hotchkiss' MS. Diary*, 42.   31 *O. R.*, 12, pt. 3, p. 904.

before or after. He said Frémont, with a large force, was three miles west of our present camp, and must be defeated in the morning. Shields was moving up Luray Valley, and might cross Massanutton to New Market, or continue South until he turned the mountain to fall on our trains near Harrisonburg. The importance of preserving the immense trains, filled with captured stores, was great and would engage much of his personal attention; while he relied on the Army, under Ewell's direction, to deal promptly with Frémont. This he told in a low, gentle voice, and with many interruptions to afford time, as I thought and believe, for inward prayer." [32]

Reliance on Ewell was not in vain. When that officer received his orders to march to Strasburg and to take the road to meet Frémont, he endorsed the paper heartily and sent it to his brigade commanders: "As we ought to be in front instead of in rear," he wrote, "it is hoped the within order will be carried out, so as to be in motion by the earliest dawn." [33] That phrase, "the earliest dawn," might well have been Jackson's own. Ewell was beginning to think in the very terms of the man whom, a fortnight previously, he had styled crazy.

The brigade commanders, on the morning of June 1, were as diligent as Ewell desired. By a rapid march, they established early contact with Frémont's vanguard several miles West of Strasburg. A lively exchange of artillery and of musketry followed. When Jackson heard the sound of the guns, he rode out and joined Ewell,[34] but as Winder had not yet arrived from the vicinity of Harpers Ferry, Jackson enjoined caution and hurried back to look after the progress of the trains toward Harrisonburg. Ewell watched and wondered. After "Dick" Taylor came up, Ewell left him in charge of the line and went out to the skirmishers. Said he: "I can't make out what these people are about, for my skirmish line has stopped them." He piped on: "They won't advance, but stay out there in the wood, making a great fuss with their guns; and I do not wish to commit myself to much advance in Jackson's absence." With that, Ewell galloped off and sent out his skirmishers, but ere long he returned to his front. His state of mind was the same: "I am completely puzzled. I have just driven everything back to the main body,

[32] R. Taylor, 61.   [33] O. R., 12, pt. 3, p. 904.   [34] Hotchkiss' MS. Diary, 41

which is large. Dense wood everywhere. Jackson told me not to commit myself too far. At this rate my attentions are not serious enough to commit any one. I wish Jackson was here himself."

Taylor suggested that if he moved his Brigade and placed it at right angles to the enemy's front, he might discover what the Federals had afoot. "Do so," said Ewell, "that may stir them up, and I am sick of this fiddling about!" In a short time, Taylor reached the Union flank, swept down it easily and threw it back. He advanced until he came under the enfilading fire of Ewell's skirmishers, who then were East of him. Thereupon Taylor halted and sent for new instructions. Ewell was itching to press the advantage, as was Taylor, but Jackson's orders were not to be disregarded. The enemy was to be held; the risks of a general engagement were not to be taken.[35] About noon, the fire died away.[36]

Ewell maintained his position for some hours until, finally, Frémont put his infantry in camp, though the Federal cavalry continued to feel out the Confederates. On the other flank, facing Front Royal, there was no evidence that any of Shields's infantry were close at hand. All the intelligence reports that reached Jackson continued to indicate that, in an effort to get in rear of the Southern force, Shields was marching up the Luray Valley.

During the late afternoon of that same 1st of June,[37] down the road from Winchester came the head of Winder's gallant Brigade. The men were fairly staggering from weariness, for the Second Virginia, from Loudoun Heights, had covered thirty-six miles in a single day,[38] and the other regiments had marched about thirty miles; but there they were, unscathed and undemoralized. Behind them now was Ashby's rearguard only. The trap might snap; the Army was beyond its jaws. Jackson's gratitude to

---

[35] R. Taylor, 64–65.   [36] O. R., 12, pt. 1, p. 14.

[37] The hour is not certain. McHenry Howard, op. cit., 116–17, stated that he rode in advance of Winder's leading regiment, and that near Middletown he met Ashby, who inquired, "Is that General Winder coming up?" When assured that Winder was near, Ashby answered: "Thank God for that." On Winder's arrival, Ashby shook his hand and said: "General, I never was so relieved in my life. I thought that you would be cut off and had made up my mind to join you and advise you to make your escape over the mountain to Gordonsville." The circumstances show that all this happened before nightfall, but there is no mention of the time of afternoon.

[38] O. R., 12, pt. 1, p. 708.

God was as great as was his relief. He wrote his wife: "[The Federals] endeavored to get in my rear by moving on both flanks of my gallant army, but our God has been my guide and saved me from their grasp." Then the husband gained a hearing over the Old Testament warrior, and he added tenderly: "You must not expect long letters from me in such busy times as these, but always believe that your husband never forgets his little darling." [39]

Amid his prayers of gratitude, Jackson issued further orders. The moment all of Winder's Brigade was up, the other infantry commanders were to resume their march toward New Market; Taylor's Brigade was to deploy West of the turnpike to prevent a possible surprise attack from that quarter; [40] the cavalry were to guard the rear and to delay Frémont; the wagon train was to press on ahead of all. These were hard orders for tired men and they were issued in the midst of a bewildering storm,[41] but they were necessary.

To one commander, Jackson had to address a biting question: "Colonel, why do you not get your Brigade together, keep it together, and move on?"

"It's impossible, General; I can't do it!"

Jackson shot back: "Don't say it's impossible! Turn your command over to the next officer. If he can't do it, I'll find some one who can, if I have to take him from the ranks." [42]

This was not the full measure of Jackson's resolution. He was determined that he would not be caught West of the Massanuttons. Some of Ashby's men he hurried off to burn the Columbia and White House bridges across the South Fork near Luray, so that the Federals moving on the east side of Massanutton could not head him by marching westward over that mountain to New Market. Meantime, Jackson would make the best time he could toward that village.

While some of the infantrymen plodded southward and others sought such sleep as they could find in drenched camps, there came firing from the rear and then a wild stampede. The

[39] Mrs. Jackson, 269; letter of June 2, 1862.   [40] R. Taylor, 66.
[41] O. R., 12, pt. 1, p. 650. Frémont reported that the hailstones were "as large as hen's eggs."
[42] Douglas, 71.

Sixth Virginia Cavalry broke and ran through the Second. When these troops burst upon the Seventh Louisiana, which was cooking rations, the startled infantrymen mistook them for the enemy and gave them a volley. It was some time before the Second rallied and drove back the Federals, who, it developed, had been permitted to approach close to the outposts by pretending that they were Ashby's men.[43] Thereafter, for the remainder of a long and bitter night, "Dick" Taylor in person, with the Irish of the Sixth Louisiana, kept the Union cavalry at bay.[44]

Leaden clouds brought heavy rain the next day, June 2.[45] The wagon train, moving in two columns along the Valley Pike, fell into such confusion that Jackson sent Jed. Hotchkiss to untangle it.[46] Although the Army subsequently had a tradition that Jackson's retreats were far less hard than his advances,[47] there was much straggling by exhausted soldiers. Numbers of disheartened men threw away their arms and their accouterments.[48] Taylor had a running fight, with some close escapes, until first Winder and then Ashby relieved him.[49]

Under vigorous pressure by a large mounted force,[50] the cavalry defense in the rear weakened. Near Woodstock, both Steuart and Ashby drew up their commands to halt the enemy, but Steuart mismanaged his part of the affair and saw some of his men break again in panic. Mistaken for the enemy, the Second Virginia Cavalry, borne ahead of the rearguard, was fired upon by the Twenty-seventh Virginia.

This fusillade was too much for Colonels Flournoy and Munford. They apparently had registered no complaint over Steuart's delay in beginning the pursuit after the Battle of Winchester;

43 *O. R.*, 12, pt. 1, pp. 650, 730–31.
44 *R. Taylor*, 67–68.
45 General McDowell dated from June 2 the "heavy rain storm which lasted several days and flooded the country from the Lehigh to Richmond, carrying away millions of property in Pennsylvania and sweeping off all the bridges on the Shenandoah and the Rappahannock" (*O. R.*, 12, pt. 1, p. 283). This storm, though adding much to the difficulties of Jackson's retreat, was a godsend to the Confederates in front of Richmond, because it gave General Lee, the new commander, time in which to organize his defense of the city (see 2 *R. E. Lee*, 80–81).
46 *Hotchkiss' MS. Diary*, 43.
47 *Dabney*, 396. This, it will be noted, implied a contradiction of Taylor's dictum that Jackson would stop to fight for a wheelbarrow.
48 *O. R.*, 12, pt. 1, p. 651.
49 *R. Taylor*, 68–69.
50 Frémont gave its strength at 1600. Included were two batteries, *O. R.*, 12, pt. 1, p. 651.

but now they went to Ewell and besought him to have their regiments transferred to Ashby's command. [51] Ewell was too devoted a soldier to insist on retaining troops, simply that he might have an imposing command. He approved his Colonels' proposal and carried it at once to Jackson, who had kept near the rear all the morning to observe the skirmishing. Without hesitation, Jackson assented and put Ashby in charge of all the cavalry. Even before the order reached him, Ashby had rallied a few stragglers and had beaten off the attack. [52]

If this was an unpleasant incident, it was offset by one bit of good news: the White House and Columbia bridges, across the South Fork, had been burned. Jackson had taken the precaution to send the vigilant Stapleton Crutchfield over the Massanuttons to make certain that the orders of the previous day for the destruction of the crossing had been executed. Crutchfield came back in due time to report that the work had been done. [53]

Assured of this, Jackson, with an easy mind, spent the night at Israel Allen's, near Hawkinsville. [54] There Col. J. M. Patton came to report that, in the final mêlée with the Federal cavalry that had broken the rearguard, all except one of the attacking force had been killed or captured. He regretted, said Patton, to see the bluecoats shot down. Jackson at the moment made no answer to this, but continued to question the Colonel on all the details of the affair.

At the end, Jackson asked quietly, "Colonel, why do you say that you saw those Federal soldiers fall with regret?"

In surprise, Patton answered that the Union troopers had shown so much more courage and valor than the enemy usually had that he had sympathy with the brave men and wished that their lives might be spared.

"No," said Jackson in a dry tone, "shoot them all; I do not wish them to be brave." [55]

The head of the wagon train was now near New Market. [56] As the destruction of the bridges on the other side of the mountain

[51] R. H. McKim, *A Soldier's Recollections*, 84, remarked that Steuart's discipline, for some reason, became less strict in the spring of 1862. That Jackson must have regarded this as a temporary lapse is shown by his action, June 4, in placing under Steuart's command the Brigade temporarily headed by Col. W. C. Scott (*Avirett*, 403–4).

[52] *O. R.*, 12, pt. 1, p. 731.

[53] *Hotchkiss' MS. Diary*, 43.   [54] *Ibid.*

[55] *Dabney*, 397.   [56] *Ibid.*

made it certain that Shields, who had no pontoons, could not cross the Massanuttons, it was manifest that the Federals in Luray Valley would continue their advance to the southern end of the range. Then, almost certainly, Shields would turn West toward Harrisonburg and get in Jackson's front, while Frémont assailed the rear.

How could Shields be kept from doing this or, as an alternative, forming a junction with Frémont? Was there a chance that one of the Federal Armies could be beaten before the other came up? In the event that this was possible, where should Jackson give battle? He probably had decided the question by the evening of June 2, if not earlier, but he did not hint to any one whither he would move.

The immediate danger, Jackson felt, already was past. He had escaped, first, because of the speed of his march and, second, because of the continuance of heavy rains in a region where high water favored his defensive. Although the Valley Pike ran close to the North Fork of the Shenandoah from New Market all the way to Strasburg, the road crossed the stream only once. That was at "Meem's Bottom," South of Mount Jackson. When the last of the infantry had passed over the bridge there, during the forenoon of June 3, Ashby brought the cavalry rearguard to the south side and then carefully set the structure afire.[57] With the stream already high and still rising, the destruction of the bridge would stop Frémont. He was known to have a pontoon train, but there was slight chance he could use it. Jackson consequently gave the Army a rest for the day and pitched his tents in a field of Doctor Rice's below New Market. Afternoon rain turned into an evening deluge, and almost set the camp afloat.[58] Early on the morning of the 4th, Jackson left his camp and went up the road to higher ground.[59]

For a few hours it appeared that Jackson had miscalculated: information reached headquarters that Frémont had brought up his pontoon bridge and was throwing it across the North Fork at Mount Jackson. Immediate resumption of the Confederate retreat might be necessary. Orders consequently were issued for

[57] *Hotchkiss' MS. Diary*, 43.   [58] *Ibid.*

[59] Hotchkiss, *loc. cit.*, 44, stated that Jackson went to Strayer's. This may have been a mistake in transcription. No such name appears in the vicinity on Hotchkiss' detailed MS. map, though Strayer is a "Valley name."

the wagons to be packed and for two days' rations to be cooked. Ammunition for active service was issued.[60] When a report came, later in the day, that Frémont had crossed the river and was trying a turning movement from the West, troops were placed on the commanding ridge in rear of Williamson's;[61] but once again the rain was Southern. Before General Frémont succeeded in getting any considerable force over the river, the North Fork rose, as a result of a widespread downpour, twelve feet in four hours. To save his pontoons, the Federal commander had to cut them loose from the south shore and swing them around to the north bank.[62] That was a boon. The Confederate Army was free to pursue its march in the assurance that at least twenty-four hours would elapse before the main body of Frémont's force could take up the pursuit.

Jackson was thinking more intently now of the situation that would develop when his Divisions, Frémont's Army, and Shields's column would be beyond the dividing ridge of the Massanuttons. As always, Jackson's first care was of his sick and ambulant wounded. He wanted to send them directly to Staunton where they could enter a hospital or, if the town was threatened, could take train to Richmond. Capt. J. K. Boswell, chief topographical engineer, was dispatched to Mount Crawford to see if he could reconstruct quickly at that point the bridge across the North River. The report came back promptly that the river was higher than it had been in twenty years and that no bridge could be erected. Jackson then directed—or Boswell with his usual fine initiative undertook—the building of crude boats on which the sick could be ferried over the stream.[63]

If Boswell succeeded, the safety of the sick was assured. What of the Army—whither should it move? Its aim, of course, should be to prevent a junction of Shields and Frémont.[64] How was that to be achieved? Jackson's plan, maturing for several days, was based on the terrain. The prime barrier to the junction of the two forces, once they reached the southern end of the Massanuttons, was the South Fork of the Shenandoah. This was bridged at Conrad's Store. Fifteen miles farther South, at the

[60] O. R., 12, pt. 3, p. 905.
[61] Hotchkiss' MS. Diary, 44.
[62] O. R., 12, pt. 1, p. 14.
[63] O. R., 12, pt. 1, p. 719.
[64] Cf. O. R., 12, pt. 1, p. 712.

village of Port Republic, the South River normally could be forded with ease, but the North River, which there joins the South River to form the South Fork, could be crossed only by a bridge, beyond which the main road ran to Harrisonburg.[65]

Inasmuch as Shields might get to Conrad's Store before the Confederate infantry could do so, Jackson decided [66] to send a force to burn the crossing there. If this could be done, Jackson reasoned that Shields would be reduced to two alternatives: first, Shields could go back toward Luray, rebuild the bridge near there and cross to New Market—a slow and difficult undertaking; second, Shields could advance up the South Fork and try to get over the stream at one of the ten fords between Conrad's Store and Port Republic, or attempt to seize the bridge at Port Republic.[67] The river was high; which of the fords were passable, if any, Jackson did not know, but he did not gamble on the probability that none was. On June 4, he twice quizzed Jed. Hotchkiss on the terrain and at 10 o'clock that night sent for him again and directed him to go with a signalman to the Peaked Mountain at the southern end of the Massanuttons and to observe Shields's movements.[68]

The van of the Army Jackson decided to send toward Port Republic to hold the bridge there and to prevent a crossing by Shields. Then, it would appear, Jackson decided on dispositions which might prove equally important in the event that Shields got across the South Fork at one of the fords between Conrad's Store and Port Republic. The south end of the Massanuttons came within a few miles of all the narrow roads that led from the fords toward Harrisonburg. If part of Jackson's Army were North of Port Republic and relatively close to the Massanuttons, then Shields would be compelled to pass so close to the Confederate front that he would be observed and could be struck.[69]

Besides these advantages from a march to Port Republic, Jackson at that point would be potentially on Frémont's flank, in

<hr />

65 The crossings at Port Republic are described somewhat more at length in Chapter XXVIII.

66 Presumably on June 4.

67 The locations of the ten fords are given on the original of Hotchkiss' large-scale map of the Shenandoah Valley.

68 *Hotchkiss' MS. Diary*, 44; *O. R.*, 12, pt. 1, p. 719.

69 The evidence regarding these dispositions is in part inferential. *Cf.* Jackson to J. E. Johnston, June 6, 1862; *O. R.*, 12. pt. 3, pp. 906-7.

the event of a Federal advance on Staunton, precisely as, at Conrad's Store in April, he had paralyzed Banks's march toward the same city. Still again, from Port Republic through Brown's Gap led the shortest road over the mountains to the Virginia Central Railroad, which was the line that would be employed to transport Jackson to Richmond. Near the gap was a great natural fortress to which Jackson, if need be, could retreat and be safe.[70]

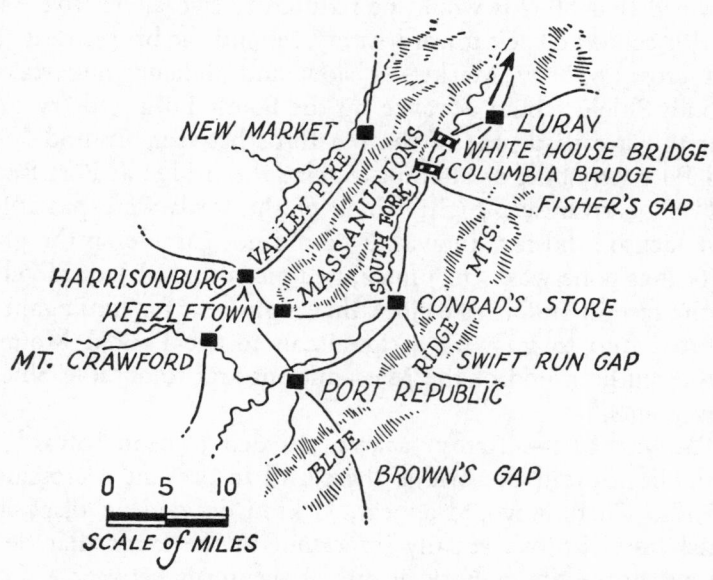

Southern End of the Massanuttons to Illustrate Jackson's Choice of Position on his Retreat before Frémont and Shields

Thus did Jackson's strategic sense and his eye for terrain lead him to choose a position that (1) would interpose his forces between Shields and Frémont; (2) would give him the one bridge that Shields could cross for an early junction with Frémont; (3) would limit Shields to a narrow and observed front of advance; (4) would delay any attempted advance on Staunton; (5) would afford access to the railroad which would carry the Confederate force to Richmond; (6) would at the same time leave open a safe avenue of retreat were unexpected disaster to come; and (7) would make it possible for him to parallel Shields's

[70] Cf. *Dabney*, 403–4.

march, were that officer to pass, via Swift Run Gap, to the eastern side of the Blue Ridge.

The march on the morning of June 5 brought Jackson early to Harrisonburg.[71] There he left the macadamized Valley Pike and turned into the road that led Southeast toward Port Republic. Captain Boswell went ahead to build a bridge across Cook's Creek.[72] Later in the day, to assist the wagons through the deep mud that was immediately encountered, Jackson directed that forty men under a commissioned officer be designated as pioneers for each brigade train,[73] but, even with this aid, the wagons were stalled often.

At nightfall, some of the trains and all of the prisoners were close to Port Republic and the advance units were near Cross Keys, but the rear Brigades had been held up so long that Jackson went into camp one mile from Harrisonburg and decided to delay the march the next day until the road was clear.[74] There was at least a promise that this would be possible, because the weather was mild. The rain, though still falling, had slackened noticeably.[75] Of developments more definite there was one, and a cheering one: the force sent to burn the bridge near Conrad's Store had succeeded, somewhat narrowly, in doing so.[76]

It probably was this evening, June 5, by Taylor's fireside, that Jackson showed a side of his nature seldom observed in the Army.[77] As the two officers talked, Tom Strother, the swarthy and indispensable body servant of Taylor, came up to the fire to bring his master some coffee. Tom never spoke unless addressed and consequently did not greet the guest by Taylor's side. No sooner did Jackson see Tom than he got up, shook the Negro's hand and, without a word, sat down again.

Taylor, of course, asked why Jackson paid this special honor

---

71 O. R., 12, pt. 1, p. 712. 72 O. R., 12, pt. 1, p. 719.
73 O. R., 12, pt. 3, p. 906.
74 O. R., 12, pt. 3, p. 906; Hotchkiss' MS. Diary, 45. 75 Hotchkiss, loc. cit.
76 Hotchkiss, in 3 C. M. H., 253, fixed the date as June 5. Dabney, op. cit., 404–6, cited as a special Providence the fact that Federals reached the bridge at Conrad's Store before the Confederates did, but, hearing that an outpost was guarding some stores a few miles distant, the Unionists rushed off to capture this prize before posting a guard at the crossing. When they returned they found that the Confederates had arrived in their absence and had fired the structure.
77 The reason for selecting this as the date for the incident is that it was, apparently, the first time Jackson was bivouacked near Taylor after June 1. Hotchkiss noted, loc. cit., that Ewell's Division, on the 5th, was in camp near Jackson's headquarters.

to Tom, whom he had seen many times previously. The General explained. On June 1, he said, when Taylor was fighting West of Strasburg, he had come upon Tom in an exposed position and had told the Negro he should go to a place of safety. Tom had thanked him but had said that General Taylor had directed him to stay there and, if the General pleased, he would do so. Jackson did not intend that this act of fidelity should go unnoticed. Even before that time, Taylor recorded in an affectionate tribute to the loyal Negro, "I used to fancy that there was a mute sympathy between General Jackson and Tom, as they sat silent by a camp fire, the latter respectfully withdrawn." [78] This little incident of June 5 confirmed Taylor's belief, but if he had known of the afternoons, years on end, when Jackson had taught Negroes at Sabbath School in Lexington, the Southern officer would not have been surprised. Every Negro whose association with Jackson is recorded at all was devoted to the General.

After Tom had gone off with the coffeepot and with new admiration for the General, Jed. Hotchkiss came to report. He had additional good news: from the Peaked Mountain, he had been able to look across the South Fork to Shields's line of march. About 4 P.M., the van of the Federal Army had encamped at the Big Spring, two miles North of Conrad's Store.[79] The roads East of the South Fork were as bad as the one Jackson was following. Consequently, it was apparent that Shields could not reach the bridge at Port Republic before Jackson arrived there. If a battle impended, which Jackson now began to doubt, there was scant prospect that it would be waged against Shields and Frémont combined.

Although the progress of the rear Brigades was delayed on the 6th, Jackson marched easily with the van of his Army to Port Republic and encamped on the heights between North River and the Massanuttons. There doubtless he received dispatches and newspapers from Richmond and learned of the immense sensation his operations had created. Johnston in general orders, issued on May 29, ere the Battle of Seven Pines, had announced Jackson's and Ewell's victories.[80] The *Charleston Mercury* had acclaimed Jackson a "true general" and had predicted that the

---

[78] R. Taylor, 63.   [79] Hotchkiss' MS. Diary, 45.
[80] Richmond Examiner, June 5, 1862, p. 1, col. 1: O. R., 12, pt. 1, p. 710.

next news would be that he was "leading his unconquerable battalions through Maryland into Pennsylvania." [81] In Richmond, the *Whig* had insisted, "This man Jackson must be suppressed, or else he will change the humane and Christian policy of the war, and demoralize the Government." [82] Depressing articles in the Northern press were jubilantly republished.[83] All this had a noticeable effect on Jackson. Ambitious as he was for military distinction, his conscience told him that the South was giving him glory that belonged to God. Those close to him observed that he ceased to read the newspapers.[84]

The communications from Richmond were, of course, a different matter. By his own hand, President Davis wrote to congratulate Jackson on his "brilliant campaign" and to express regret that no reinforcements could be sent.[85] This letter was based on the information Colonel Boteler had given the President upon arrival in Richmond from Winchester. Consequently the argument of the Chief Executive was outdated in part, but if denial of reinforcements dampened satisfaction over the President's approval, Jackson was too disciplined a soldier to complain. Apparently unaware that Johnston's wound had forced him to relinquish command of the forces defending the capital, Jackson promptly described his situation for the review of the General and told him that if the Army of the Valley were required at Richmond, it could march to Mechum River Station.[86] "At present," Jackson went on, "I do not see that I can do much more than rest my command and devote its time to drilling." He added an inquiry whether, if Shields crossed the Blue Ridge again, he should follow his adversary.[87]

The day of June 6 was not to end on that key. Late in the afternoon, while Jackson was in Port Republic, awaiting the

---

[81] *Charleston Mercury,* May 29, 1862, p. 2, col. 1.   [82] Quoted in *ibid.*

[83] Cf. *Richmond Examiner,* June 2, 1862, p. 1, cols. 3, 5; *Richmond Enquirer,* June 5, 1862, p. 2, col. 5. This praise of Jackson continued for days and shaped itself quickly into a general demand by the press for offensive operations in the North. Cf. *Richmond Examiner,* June 6, p. 2, col. 2, June 17, p. 2, col. 2; *Richmond Whig,* June 7, p. 1, col. 1, June 12, p. 2, col. 1; *Richmond Dispatch,* June 13, p. 2, cols. 1–2; *Charleston Mercury,* June 3, p. 1, col. 2. In this latest article the *Mercury* declared that "but two men in the Confederate service had proved themselves to be Generals—Price and Jackson."

[84] Douglas, in *Annals of the War,* 649. That author did not state the time when this occurred; but as it was after Winchester that the praise of Jackson began on a large scale, there would seem no doubt that this was the period to which Douglas referred.

[85] *O. R.,* 12, pt. 3, p. 905.

[86] Via Brown's Gap.   [87] *O. R.,* 12, pt. 3, pp. 906–7.

arrival of Ewell's Division, word came that the cavalry rearguard
had been attacked. Ashby, it developed, had been two miles
South of Harrisonburg, where his men had been resting and
grazing their horses, when he had seen a Federal cavalry column approaching. Quickly Ashby had given the order, "Mount
and form," and then, employing his usual tactics of meeting a
charge with a countercharge, he had driven straight at the
enemy.[88] In a brief clash, sixty-four Federals had been captured
and the remainder had been driven back. Among the prisoners,
who belonged to the 1st New Jersey, was their leader, "a stalwart
man with huge mustaches, cavalry boots adorned with spurs
worthy of a caballero, slouched hat and plume." He was coming
into the Confederate lines "with the nonchalant air of one who
had wooed Dame Fortune too long to be cast down by her
frowns."[89] Presently, when Maj. "Rob" Wheat of the Louisiana
Tigers saw the captive Colonel, he sprang from his horse with
a loud cry, "Percy, old boy." The stranger, recognizing him
instantly, answered, "Why, Bob." After they had embraced,
Wheat explained that the prisoner was his friend Sir Percy Wyndham, a Britisher by whose side he had fought under Garibaldi
in Italy.[90]

In a short time, Wyndham was brought to Jackson. Probably
word was passed simultaneously that Federal infantry were coming along the same road the prisoner had taken, and that Ashby
had sent for part of Ewell's command. Jackson knew that the
situation was entirely safe in the hands of Ewell and he sat down
to chat in his quiet way with his British prisoner.[91]

About 9 o'clock an officer came to the door of the room and
asked Jackson to step into the hall. Jackson excused himself from
his prisoner and went out—to receive the worst news that had
come to him in the entire campaign. After beating off the cavalry
attack and sending for infantry support, Ashby had waited some
time for its arrival. His request for help had gone to Gen. "Maryland" Steuart, who had resumed command of his infantry Brigade.
Steuart had refused, as at Winchester, to move without orders
from Ewell.[92] When this was reported to Ewell, he not only

[88] Avirett, 219.　　　　　　　[89] R. Taylor, 26.
[90] Ibid., though Taylor was a bit hazy concerning the country where the two had
met while "the pleasant business of killing was going on."
[91] Avirett, 226.　　　　　　　[92] Ibid., 220; Chew, ibid., 273.

sent word to Steuart to move at once, but also went in person to the rear. It was then nearly dusk. Ashby immediately told Ewell that he thought it would be wise to leave his cavalry where it was, to move the infantry through the woods to the right, to take the Federals in flank and then, when they were driven from the wood, to ride them down with the full force of his cavalry. Ewell had approved. Ashby had started out with two companies of the First Maryland as skirmishers and with the Fifty-ninth Virginia and the remainder of the First Maryland behind him.[93] Instead of framing an ambush for his cavalry to exploit, he soon had run into a heavy Federal fire,[94] before which the Fifty-ninth had recoiled quickly. Ewell had been compelled to bring up the First Maryland and to throw it furiously against the Federals.[95] In the end, the bluecoats had been driven back and, while retiring, had exposed themselves to Chew's Battery. The affair was over,[96] all danger was past; but, in the first clash in the woods . . . well, Ashby's horse had been shot, Ashby himself had gone forward on foot with the cry, "Forward, my brave men" . . . and had fallen dead with a bullet through his body.

Ashby dead? It took all Jackson's self-mastery to receive that news without paralyzing emotion. As soon as he could control himself, he told one of his staff officers to get rid of Wyndham— "I cannot see him further tonight"[97]—and then he went back into his room and paced the floor for a long, long time. Ashby dead, the idol of his troopers, the modest gentleman, the leader whose daring seemed instinctive! Jackson had sought to discipline the troopers; Ashby had been angry and defiant; but he had been reconciled to his chief and, if possible, he had fought harder after the controversy than before. His humiliation at looting by his men during the advance to Winchester had been pathetic;[98] the simplicity with which he had received his commission as Brigadier General at Winchester on May 27 had been characteristic of him. "Sandie" Pendleton of Jackson's staff had handed him the document and had said, "I do this with great pleasure, General Ashby, hoping that as you are soon to command a Brigade, the country may expect less exposure of your

---

[93] Goldsborough, in *Avirett*, 222.   [94] Munford in *O. R.*, 12, pt. 1, p. 732.
[95] Jackson, *O. R.*, 12, pt. 1, p. 712.
[96] For Frémont's account, see *O. R.*, 12, pt. 1, pp. 8, 652.
[97] *Avirett*, 226; *Douglas*, 80–81.   [98] Cf. *R. Taylor*, 72.

life." Ashby had smiled, had taken the paper, and soon had ridden off to the front.[99]

"Less exposure of his life," Pendleton had said, but now they were bringing Ashby's body to the town. His troopers were gathered about the body. Scout Brown, bravest of the brave, was delivering the soldiers' eulogy: "We shall miss you mightily, General," he was saying, "we shall miss you in camp; we shall miss you as we go out to scout. But we shall miss you most of all when we go out to—" There he stopped. He could say no more.[100]

[99] *Avirett*, 206.   [100] *Avirett*, 226.

CHAPTER XXVIII

A Crowning Double Victory

On the morning of June 7, though the South mourned the fallen Ashby, the skies smiled. The roads around Port Republic still were heavy, and the streams were high, but the rain had ceased. In the splendor of early summer, the terrain was cheeringly reminiscent of Front Royal, scene of victory. From the West flowed North River to meet, Northeast of Port Republic, the South River. Together, the two passed Luray Valley as the South Fork of the Shenandoah. The village of Port Republic lay in the angle formed by the North and the South Rivers. Back of the village, to the South and Southwest, was a high ridge, whence ran a road to the village of Mount Meridian and thence sixteen miles to Staunton: Strategically, the important area was that on the left bank of the North River near the confluence. There, commanding ground overlooked the village. Eastward and southeastward were the long, open meadows on the right bank of the South River, beyond which, still farther eastward, at a distance of from one to two miles, was a heavy forest that ran up to the spurs of the Blue Ridge. Between the woods and the river, the whole of the meadows could be swept by artillery fire.

The crossings were as important as the high ground that overlooked them. From the village, the traveller on the road to Harrisonburg traversed the North River on a long wooden structure; but there was no bridge over the South River or over the South Fork of the Shenandoah near the junction of the two streams. Only fords were available there, and these were now dangerously high and swift.

As Hotchkiss had reported that Shields still was East of the South Fork, in the vicinity of Conrad's Store, and was moving southward, Jackson consequently could hope, not unreasonably, to prevent a junction between Frémont and Shields. So long as the Confederates held off Frémont to the West, Shields could continue to the South only along the road that led up the South Fork and under the dominating ridge. On the other hand, if Shields should venture up the east bank of the South Fork and should offer battle opposite Port Republic, Jackson could not afford to disregard Frémont altogether and to cross the entire Army to the left bank of South River. Were Jackson to do that, Frémont could advance to the height near the bridge and, with his batteries, could sweep the Confederate Army engaged with Shields East of the river.

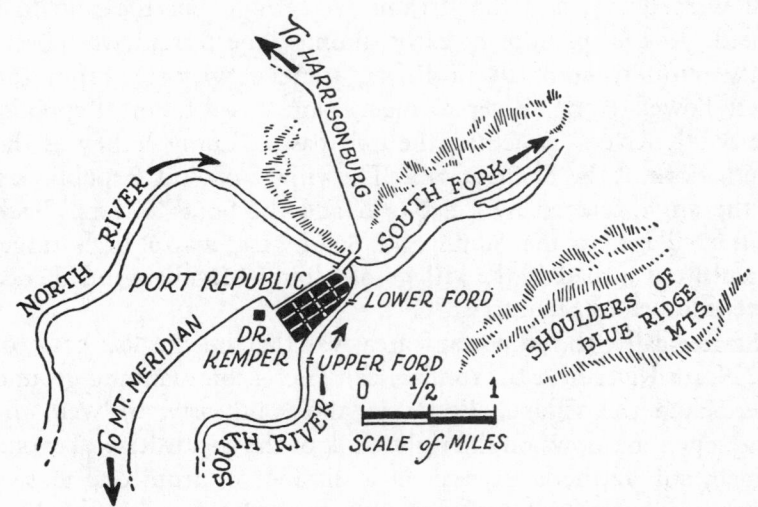

Port Republic and Environs

Besides, if Jackson moved all his forces to the eastern side of South River and burned the one bridge behind him, he would have no means of dealing later with Frémont. It was reasonable to suppose that if either Frémont or Shields were defeated, the other would not venture a march on Staunton or toward the railroad that linked Staunton with Eastern Virginia; but Jackson was anxious not to limit his own ability to move in any direction. Much as he feared he might not be able to strike his adversaries, he did not intend to throw away any of his opportunities. His decision consequently was to tempt Frémont to battle and, meantime, to hold the ridge opposite Port Republic and the bridge that linked the two positions. This course seemed the more expedient, because all Jackson's information was that

rémont had passed Harrisonburg and was moving toward Port
epublic. Shields was not known to have advanced many miles
outh of Conrad's Store.[1]

It was in vain, on the 7th, that Jackson rode to Ewell's lines
ear Cross Keys, and there manœuvred in the hope of inducing
rémont to fight. The Federal commander, though he had pur-
ied with much vigor, seemed in no mood to force events.[2] At
ngth Jackson returned to Port Republic, and by nightfall,
:viewed his infantry dispositions as follows:

Ewell was on good ground near Cross Keys with three Brigades,
oout 5000 effectives.[3]

Jackson on the ridge North of Port Republic had his own
•ivision and Edward Johnson's command. Taylor's Brigade of
well's Division was to come up the next morning. With it,
ickson would have a total of not more than 8000 bayonets.[4]

At the upper ford of South River, on the southeastern edge of
ort Republic, was a picket of three officers and twenty-two men
nder Capt. Samuel J. C. Moore, Company I, Second Virginia.
South of Port Republic and on the road to Mount Meridian,
"as extended the Army wagon train.[5]

While the batteries were with the infantry units, the cavalry
"as much scattered. Most of the companies of the Sixth and
ie Seventh Virginia [6] were guarding the wagon train, and were
oread far down the road toward Mount Meridian. The Second
'irginia was covering Ewell's right and rear on the road that
ın from Conrad's Store via McGaheysville to the Valley Pike
t Harrisonburg—a necessary protection of the entire flank.[7]
nmediately around Port Republic were a few cavalry scouting
arties; in the town was J. J. Chipley's troop.

---

[1] O. R., 12, pt. 1, p. 712. The guiding considerations with Jackson are outlined in
abney, 407–8.

[2] R. Taylor, 72. Actually, there was in front of Ewell, on the 7th, only the Brigade
Milroy, which Frémont had sent down the Port Republic road to make a recon-
iissance in force. O. R., 12, pt. 1, p. 18.

[3] O. R., 12, pt. 1, p. 781.

[4] William Allan, ed. cit., 266 n., maintained that Jackson did not have of all arms,
cluding Ewell, a force in excess of 13,000. It is true, as Allan asserted, that many of
ckson's regiments were very small, but 13,000 infantry, plus 1000 cavalry and 500 or
•o artillery seems a reasonable estimate. The difference between Allan's figures and the
riter's estimate is 1500 to 1600, or only a little more than 11 per cent.

[5] Hotchkiss' MS. Diary, 49.

[6] Ashby's command now was styled the Seventh Virginia.

[7] These were the dispositions reported by Col. T. T. Munford as of the early mOrning
June 8.

It was possible on the evening of June 7 to relate these dispositions one to another, because Jackson now had for the first
time a map of substantial accuracy which Hotchkiss quickly had
prepared.[8] With this map and the scouts' reports before him,
Jackson could assume reasonably enough that all was well—too
well, in fact, to promise an early battle with either of his opponents. There may have been both hope and skepticism, late in
the evening, when an outpost sent word that Shields was advancing from Conrad's Store. To ascertain the truth, Jackson no
longer had a tireless and vigilant Ashby to ride off on the instant;
but Capt. Emanuel Sipe was at hand and was dispatched down
the east side of the South Fork to reconnoiter and to ascertain
if the enemy was astir. Later in the night, one of Ashby's best
Captains, G. W. Myers, a man who had bluffed Banks at Strasburg while Jackson was moving on Front Royal, was sent after
Captain Sipe with similar orders.[9]

Early on the morning of Sunday, June 8, a fine, cool day,[10]
news of unexpected character arrived from Captain Sipe. He
said that during the early morning the Federals had sent a scouting party of about twenty close to the North River bridge at
Port Republic. These men had learned of Sipe's approach and
had made off. "We pursued them," Sipe wrote, "but did not see
the scout at all." Sipe had gone on to Lewiston, the estate of
General Lewis, a little more than two miles East of Port Republic, and then he had proceeded two miles farther down the
road toward Conrad's Store. There he had run into an advancing
regiment of Federal cavalry. As he wrote, the Union troopers
were just below General Lewis's.[11]

This, of course, might mean much or little, but if Shields were
advancing, Ewell would do well to defer action until the situation was clear. Jackson, who was at the Kemper House in Port
Republic, so advised Ewell, and himself prepared to go over to
the high ground on the other side of the bridge in order to see
from that point of vantage what was afoot on the right side of
the South Fork.[12] He felt no concern and, when Major Dabney

[8] Hotchkiss' MS. Diary, 49; O. R., 12, pt. 1, p. 719.   [9] O. R., 12, pt. 1, p. 712.
[10] Hotchkiss' MS. Diary, 49. Douglas, op. cit., 85, considered the temperature warm.
[11] O. R., 12, pt. 3, p. 908. The dispatch does not carry the hour.
[12] O. R., 12. pt. 3, pp. 907–8.

reported for orders and asked if there would be any military operations that day, the General answered: "No, you know I always try to keep the Sabbath if the enemy will let me." [13] The General went about his routine duties; the Adjutant returned to his camp to prepare his sermon; the Sabbath calm continued.

About 9 o'clock or later,[14] Jackson was ready to go to the ridge where the Stonewall Brigade was encamped. While his officers were gathering, to await their horses, a single cavalryman rode up at a gallop and went directly to the General: The Federals, he said, had crossed the lower ford of South River, with cavalry and artillery, and already were in the town.[15]

Jackson received the news quietly: "Go back and fight them," he said—that and no more. Scarcely had he spoken than firing broke out to the right and North—it was difficult to say whether in the town or on the east bank of the South River opposite the lower ford. Jackson did not wait for horse or escort. With long strides he started from Doctor Kemper's house toward the scene of the fusillade. His staff officers followed him. In a few moments, he saw down the street a column of Federal cavalrymen. Had they observed the Confederates on foot? Did they recognize officers in gray? Would they dash on and capture the General? Breathless the questions, doubtful the issue, but, at that moment, Jackson's servant brought up his horse. The General mounted quickly and galloped off toward the bridge across the North River. Several of his staff contrived to follow, but Col. Stapleton Crutchfield and Lt. Edward Willis, who were behind the others, fell into the hands of the blue troopers.

In deep humiliation, Crutchfield handed his sword to a Union Colonel. That officer did not make the Colonel dismount. He was too busy, he said, to attend to him. Crutchfield must stay

---

[13] Dabney's narrative of May 7, 1896. That year, for some reason, Maj. Jed. Hotchkiss became much interested in the events of June 8, 1862, and corresponded with various participants. A controversy developed between Major Dabney and Maj. Samuel J. C. Moore and, at one period, waxed hot and personal. Through the efforts of Major Hotchkiss and Dr. Hunter McGuire, the controversy was settled substantially to the satisfaction of the participants. The whole of the correspondence, which is much the fullest in existence on this dramatic incident, is in the *Hotchkiss Papers*.

[14] Hotchkiss, in his *Diary*, said "about 10"; Winder, *O. R.*, 12, pt. 1, p. 739, gave the hour as between 8 and 9, in which timing McHenry Howard, *op. cit.*, 112, inferentially concurred. Douglas, *op. cit.*, 85, fixed the time between 7 and 8.

[15] This soldier was Henry D. Kerfoot, later a physician at Berryville. V.

near him, under the charge of a single guard. With no more wasted words, the Union officer began to form his dragoons in column in the main street. He was at this when one of his men galloped jubilantly up from the direction of the Kemper House.

"Colonel," he yelled, "you have just got Jackson's whole wagon train!"

"Where is it?" the Colonel asked eagerly.

"Just up yonder, in full sight across that old farm—hundreds of wagons and no troops."

The Federal turned to Crutchfield, "Is that so, Colonel?"

"You must find that out for yourself," answered the Confederate.

The despair in his heart must have made his statement a confession. "Captain," the Federal commander said to one of his officers, "you take that front squadron and go up and see after that baggage train in short order!" [16]

Crutchfield knew that some wagons might have gone to Mount Meridian, but that his entire ordnance train was in the field beyond Doctor Kemper's and was hopelessly conspicuous because new, white wagon sheets had just been issued. Whether Jackson himself had escaped or not, how could the Army continue its struggle if the whole ordnance train were captured?

The Federals formed confidently in the street and started at a slow trot toward the Kemper House. Crutchfield could only watch in mute misery. Soon the Union troopers reached the end of the street and turned toward Doctor Kemper's lawn. As they did so, a brisk little volley of rifle fire greeted them. The Union troopers recoiled. Their Colonel re-formed them and sent them forward again. This time, when they made the turn, "bang! bang!" went two cannon. Again the Federals galloped back; again their commander sent them forward—to be met with the same artillery fire and another infantry volley. Crutchfield straightened himself in his saddle and scarcely could believe that the Confederate artillery had fired into the head of the column. "Where on earth did those guns come from?" he asked himself.

[16] Dabney's statement, and that of Maj. James McDowell Carrington, June 17, 1896, *Hotchkiss Papers,* present different snatches of this conversation, which the writers had from Crutchfield, but the two accounts conform.

"Am I not chief of artillery? Did I not post all the batteries? Don't I know they are all on the north side of the river?"[17]

Viciously the two guns continued to bark; the Federal troopers galloped off the street. In the alleys and behind the houses the bluecoats gathered. Nor could their Colonel induce them to face a fire that swept the street from end to end. They had no ordnance at hand and had to stand idle till they knew more of the situation; but by this time, Federal artillery was in action at a distance and was, for Jackson, the center of as startling a drama as that which Crutchfield had been unable to fathom.

Jackson had galloped across the bridge just as the Federals were closing on him. No sooner was he on the ridge than he hurried to the nearest batteries and ordered three of them to open on Federals who were plainly visible on the east side of South River and below the confluence. Taliaferro and Winder were directed to put their Brigades under arms and to take possession of the bridge. Taylor's Brigade was called up in support.[18]

Before these troops could be assembled, some of Jackson's fieldpieces challenged a Federal battery that had gone into action East of South River. After a few long shots at the bridge, two of the Federal guns were limbered up and were hurried to the ford. Crossing with some difficulty, they disappeared in the village. Were they heading for the south end of the town, to answer the mysterious battery that was holding up the Federal cavalry who sought to capture the wagon train? Or were the Federal artillerists seeking to get within closer range of the bridge?

Presently, at a quiet pace, a single gun came in sight at the lower end of the village, wheeled to the right and approached the bridge.[19] Jackson saw that the cannoneers wore blue, and he turned to Captain Poague, who had one of his Parrott guns near the crest above the bridge, whence he had been firing across South River.[20]

"Fire on that gun!" Jackson said to the Captain.

"General," Poague's young soldiers cried, "General, those are our men!"

---

[17] This is Crutchfield's own statement of his thoughts at the moment, as given by him to Major Dabney—*Hotchkiss Papers*.

[18] *O. R.*, 12, pt. 1, p. 713; *R. Taylor*, 72.

[19] *E. A. Moore*, 71.   [20] *ibid*.

"Fire on that gun," Jackson repeated.

"General," said Captain Poague, "I know those are our men," [21] and he went on quickly to explain that he had been at headquarters and had seen, near the Kemper House, a new and partially equipped battery, Carrington's, which recently had been sent to the Army but had not been assigned. Carrington's men, said Poague, had uniforms similar to those of the gunners on whom Jackson wished him to fire.[22]

That made Jackson pause. He rode a little to the left and front and, in a loud voice, cried to the men opposite the bridge, "Bring that gun up here!"

He got no answer, no action. Rising in his stirrups, he shouted again in angry tones, "Bring that gun up here, I say!"

The soldiers at the other end of the bridge moved this time, but it was not to cross the bridge. It was to trail their gun so that it would bear on the party on the height. Jackson did not mistake that movement. He knew it was hostile. "Let 'em have it," said he—and the Parrott sent its charge toward the bluecoats,[23] though the piece could not be depressed enough for a good shot.[24] The answering projectile of the Federal rifle went over the Confederate battery, but struck in the Thirty-seventh Virginia Infantry, Taliaferro's Brigade, which was now coming up. Jackson rode to the head of the infantry column, ordered it to keep to the right of the road, to descend to the bridge, to give a volley and then to rush the crossing with the bayonet.[25]

This said, Jackson dropped the reins on the neck of his horse and lifted both hands on high.[26] The reply was a roar from the

---

[21] *E. A. Moore.*   [22] See Poague's statement in *William Allan*, 271 n.
[23] Poague, in *William Allan, loc. cit.; Douglas,* 85–86.
[24] *E. A. Moore,* 71. This is the incident which was wrongly related to John Esten Cooke and was represented by him as an instance in which Jackson impersonated a Federal officer. Col. William Allan spoiled part of that charming story as long ago as 1880 (*ed. cit.,* p. 271). Among the *Hotchkiss Papers* is a letter that robs the remainder of much of its interest. Under date of Apr. 18, 1894, James Gildea, former Lieutenant of Battery L, Ohio Artillery, wrote Major Hotchkiss that he was with the detachment that served the piece brought close to the bridge. He stated that he heard some one shouting from the other side of the river, but that he could not understand what was said.
[25] *Dabney,* 413; *William Allan,* 270. In *O. R.,* 12, pt. 1, p. 713, a typographical error, duly noted in the "Additions and Corrections," made the leading regiment the Fifty-seventh Virginia, instead of the Thirty-seventh. Both Taliaferro, *ibid.,* 773, and Boswell, *ibid.,* 719, give the regimental number correctly. There can be no doubt of the identity of the regiment, because Jackson himself lists its commander as Colonel [Samuel V.] Fulkerson.
[26] *Dabney,* 413. The Major, who was not present, thought Jackson was invoking the blessing of Heaven.

men, an overwhelming volley and, in another moment or two, a dash across the bridge, from which by this time all the cannoneers had fled.[27]

In a few minutes, the village was cleared. As the retreating Federals crossed the river and fled northward in the direction from which they had come, they were a target for the artillery on the ridge.[28] Crutchfield, Willis and other captured officers were recovered. Then, in rejoicing and relief, the mystery of the first attack on the Federals in the village was explained: most members of Chipley's cavalry troop, which was guarding the place, had fled shamefully.[29] Myers's troop had rushed into Port Republic and through it without stopping to dispute the enemy's advance. Captain Moore's infantry picket at the ford had been scattered at the moment the Federals appeared, but it had been assembled quickly and had been placed in a good position. The volleys that had met the Federals as they had approached the Kemper House had been delivered by this small force of less than twenty-five men. Those artillery salvoes—veritable blasts from Heaven they had seemed to Colonel Crutchfield—had been the work of Carrington's Battery, the Charlottesville Artillery whose Captain, James McDowell Carrington, with Lieutenant Timberlake, had displayed rare judgment. Major Dabney, aroused from meditation on his sermon, had a hand in this defense.[30] Thanks to those men, none of the wagons or men had been lost. The Confederacy, in fact, was richer by two guns.

The narrowness of the escape of Jackson and his staff would have been a day-long theme of wonderment and congratulation,[31] had not there drifted across the fields at that very hour

27 O. R., 12, pt. 1, pp. 713, 773.

28 O. R., 12, pt. 1, pp. 713, 739, 740; Dabney, 407.

29 O. R., 12, pt. 1, p. 713.

30 The controversy recorded in the Hotchkiss Papers concerned the extent of Dr. Dabney's control of the defense in the village. Dabney asserted a measure of direction that Moore denied.

31 In General Shields's report on the battle of Port Republic he vigorously assailed Col. S. S. Carroll for failing to fire the bridge across North River while it was virtually in his grip (O. R., 12, pt. 1, pp. 684, 687). Colonel Carroll made no formal reply and in his report (ibid., 698 ff), simply related the circumstances and recounted his efforts to seize the bridge, which he feared the Confederates would burn. In 5 Moore's Rebellion Record, 112–13, an anonymous defense of Carroll was reprinted from the National Intelligencer. This asserted that Carroll's instructions were to preserve rather than to burn the bridge. Instead of being in Port Republic three quarters of an hour as Shields alleged (O. R., 12, pt. 1, p. 684), Carroll is said to have held the village less than twenty minutes. The Official Records bear out the main assertion concerning the instructions under which Carroll operated. On June 4, Shields ordered Carroll to burn the

the sound of battle to the westward. Ewell was engaged with Frémont. Shields, of course, heard the same rumble—would he launch his attack? Was the Army to be compelled to fight two actions simultaneously? Jackson did not wish his officers to believe it. "No, sir! No!" he replied with a sweep of the hand toward the batteries on the ridge. "He cannot do it; I should tear him to pieces!" [32] Actually, in anticipation of a possible renewal of the attack by Shields he decided to remain at Port Republic and to leave to Ewell the handling of the action at Cross Keys. [33]

Ewell had encamped the previous night seven miles from Port Republic [34] and two miles Southeast of the village of Cross Keys. The Eighteenth Alabama of Trimble's Brigade had been placed one mile in advance at Union Church. [35] On the morning of June 8, the Federals struck the Alabama troops and drove them in, but proceeded so slowly that Ewell had abundant time in which to take up a position recommended to him by Arnold Elzey. [36] The line rested on a ridge, in front of which was a branch of Mill Creek and several hundred acres of open fields. Woods protected both flanks; beyond the right remained the Second Virginia Cavalry, to patrol the roads by which the Federals might attempt a turning movement. [37] In Ewell's judgment, the center, which was pierced by a road, was decidedly weak. He did not expect an attack there but, as a precaution, he posted his four batteries to command the road and he put Elzey's Brigade in reserve behind the center, whence it could move in either direction. [38]

bridge at Conrad's Store (O. R., 12, pt. 3, p. 316), but on June 4 he wrote Carroll, "You must go forward at once with cavalry and guns to save the bridge at Port Republic" (O. R., 12, pt. 3, p. 335). In the face of this, Shields wrote the War Department that Carroll's report "that the bridge was burned five days ago deceived me." A critique of the conduct of Sprigg Carroll was written later by Kyd Douglas, op. cit., 87–88, who knew him well in Maryland after the war.

[32] Dabney, 415.
[33] O. R., 12, pt. 1, p. 714. In 5 C. V., 613, M. Warner Hewes related that, while Jackson was waiting near the bridge, which by a lapsus pennæ Mr. Hewes located at Cross Keys, some one spoke of "fancy soldiers." Jackson pointed to General Trimble, "sitting on the fence, with black army hat, cord and feathers, [and said] 'There is the only fancy soldier in my command.'" This anecdote may contain some error of time or place, though there is nothing in Trimble's report (O. R., 12, pt. 1, p. 795) to preclude the possibility that he was at the bridge as late as, say, 9 A.M.
[34] O. R., 12, pt. 1, p. 785.   [35] O. R., 12, pt. 1, p. 795.
[36] O. R., 12, pt. 1, p. 781.   [37] See supra, pp. 436–37.
[38] O. R., 12, pt. 1, pp. 712, 732, 781, 796. Later in the day, Ewell had five batteries on his center and two in reserve. Ibid., 728.

About 10 A.M., the Federals threw out their skirmishers again and in a short time advanced their artillery opposite the Confederate center. A duel then began that continued steadily but without decisive result of any sort. General Elzey directed the Confederate fire with admirable judgment and rode among the gunners with fine contempt for the enemy's sharpshooters and their shell. When his horse was wounded, he paid no heed to the suggestion that the next shot might be his.

As Frémont made no move to follow up his cannonade on the center, it became apparent that he intended to direct his infantry attack against the Confederate right. Trimble's Brigade was there, admirably placed. Its commander had the fullest confidence that he could repulse any attack, and, to inflict the heaviest casualties, he gave orders that all fire be withheld until the enemy was close at hand. The bluecoats seemed unaware of what was awaiting them. Slowly, conspicuously and in good order they mounted the hill, as if they were on a practice manœuvre. Scarcely a shot greeted them until they were near the crest. Then, as if they had a single trigger, all the muskets along the Confederate line were loosed. The Federals staggered, attempted to rally, recoiled in the face of a second volley and, in a short time, retired.[39]

Back, now, the action shifted to the artillery. Elzey shrewdly directed the fire for a few minutes until his horse was killed and he himself was wounded.[40] Thereafter, as the Confederates saw their ammunition dwindling fast, they reduced the rate of fire to that of the Federals.[41] Within fifteen minutes [42] the battle became so dull an affair that it irked General Trimble. If the enemy would not attack him, he would take the offensive! With supports from Elzey's Brigade, he would storm a battery which had just been brought up on the Federal left, half a mile in front. Carefully he made all his preparations [43] and at length threw his troops forward—only to see the battery trot off before he could reach it.[44]

Trimble's front now had been advanced more than a mile beyond its first position. There, when Jackson reached the field

---

39 O. R., 12, pt. 1, pp. 713, 796.   40 O. R., 12, pt. 1, p. 782.
41 Ibid., 728.   42 Ibid., 796.
43 Ibid., 796.   44 Ibid., 713, 792, 796.

about noon, it was resting, and there Ewell reluctantly decided he must leave it. Both he and Jackson wished to make the most of so easy a repulse, but neither of them considered it wise to extend the front too far. Besides, there were reports from a Lieutenant of Topographical Engineers, who had gone out to reconnoiter, that the enemy seemed to be moving two miles to the Confederate left, as if to envelop that flank.[45] With Taylor's Brigade, which Jackson had recalled halfway on its march to Port Republic, Ewell proceeded to strengthen his left and center. To that part of the line, also, he brought those of Elzey's regiments previously in reserve.[46] If Frémont designed to attack the left, he should have a vigorous reception.

Nothing happened. The artillery fire died away; the enemy scarcely showed himself within range. Ewell's day-long impatience was heightened now by the fact that his cavalry was beyond the right wing of the Division and could render no assistance on the left.[47] Finally, after it seemed certain that no attack would develop on the left, Ewell slowly moved up his skirmishers and. at nightfall, occupied the position from which the enemy had advanced in the morning.[48]

Trimble was not content to have the Battle of Cross Keys end thus. He already had insisted on a further attack and had boiled with indignation when Taylor had declined to participate on the ground that no good would be accomplished.[49] After night, Trimble devised a new attack and rode first to Ewell and then to Jackson for approval. Jackson had gone back to Port Republic and merely said, "Consult General Ewell and be guided by him." Ewell shook his head and declined to permit the venture. "You have done well enough for one day," he said, "and even a partial reverse would interfere with General Jackson's plans for the next day." Trimble answered hotly that if Frémont were not driven that night, he would press the Army in the morning. It was better, he argued, to fight one army at a time. Ewell would not yield.[50] In unconcealed disgust, Trimble went back to his camp, nor would he concede when he came to write his report that Ewell was correct. He underestimated the difficulty of

---

[45] O. R., 12, pt. 1, pp. 714, 782.
[47] O. R., 12, pt. 1, p. 782.
[49] Ibid., 797.

[46] Ibid., 714.
[48] Ibid., 714.
[50] O. R., 12 pt. 1, p. 798.

delivering a night attack, and he did not seem to reflect that it was one thing to hold a good position with an inferior force and quite another to use that small force in an attack on Frémont.[51] At Port Republic, ere Trimble had come, Jackson had appeared at his strangest. Not long after noon, he remarked to R. H. Dabney, his Chief of Staff, "Major, wouldn't it be a blessed thing if God would give us a glorious victory today?" He spoke in an undertone but, said a Lieutenant who overheard him, Jackson's "expression [was] . . . that of a child hoping to receive some favor."[52] Most of the time "Old Jack" stood in silent thought with his eyes on the ground. A courier came from Ewell and, following him, an eccentric chaplain. Neither had news of any decision. After some hours, confident of victory, Jackson dispatched orders to Ewell to press with his cavalry and, if need be, with artillery and with Wheat's Louisianians.[53] While some of his subordinates whispered that this was prescience, Jackson was shaping his plans for the morrow in the knowledge that the day's losses had been light. General Steuart had been wounded in the shoulder;[54] General Elzey would be out of action for a fortnight or more; but the other casualties in Ewell's Division

---

[51] Accounts of this action at Cross Keys are few and inadequate. As seen by a Captain in Trimble's Brigade, the battle is described in W. C. Oates, *The War between the Union and the Confederacy* (cited hereafter as *Oates*), 102 ff. General Frémont's explanation of his cautious handling of his troops (*O. R.*, 12, pt. 1, p. 20) was that the Confederates occupied a "position of uncommon strength" and that, after the repulse, he "judged it best . . . to re-establish my whole line in conformity to the changes on the left preparatory to a renewal of the battle" (*ibid.*, 21). His casualties were 684 (*ibid.*, 665), in a force which he reckoned at 10,500 (*ibid.*, 19).

[52] *McHenry Howard*, 124.

[53] *McHenry Howard*, 124. Howard affirmed often in later years that Jackson said to Pendleton, "Write a note to General Ewell. Say that the enemy are defeated at all points, and to press them with cavalry, and, if necessary, with artillery and Wheat's battalion." This, according to Howard, was at a time when Jackson had no news of what was happening at Cross Keys and could not have told from the sound of the firing whether Ewell was advancing or retreating. Said Howard: ". . . about the time I calculated the message would reach General Ewell the firing certainly began to abate and after a while intelligence came, substantially, that the enemy had been driven back." As Major Howard was a witness careful to qualify what he could not affirm positively, the only possible explanation of this incident is that he missed some word Jackson spoke. Jackson well may have instructed Pendleton to say that, "if the enemy are defeated," etc. The whole incident may have been confused. In the spring of 1863, Jed. Hotchkiss heard that Jackson at one stage of the fight sent "Sandie" Pendleton to Ewell with the message, "I will keep Shields back if you will hold Frémont in check." Ewell is said to have answered: "The worst is over now; I can manage him" (*Hotchkiss' MS. Diary*, 163). As the time of this cannot be stated, the exchange of messages is not mentioned in the text, but, if these messages passed, they seem to cast in doubt the view that Jackson urged Ewell to press the enemy. For that task, in 1862, Ewell never required any urging.

[54] *O. R.*, 12, pt. 1, p. 818.

had not been more than 288, of whom only forty-one had been killed.[55] The Army, unimpaired, was ready for whatever might give it the largest promise of victory.

How best could it be employed? Jackson's reasoning was prompt and decisive: He was nearer Shields than Frémont; he had reason to believe Shields commanded the smaller of the two Union forces; in the vicinity of Port Republic Jackson was closer to his base of supplies and to a road over the mountains in the event of defeat. Finally, if he beat Frémont, that officer would have an easy line of retreat down the Valley Pike, while Shields had a bad road to follow back to Luray. All the weight of advantage was on the side of dealing first with Shields.[56] He should be attacked heavily and should be driven back. If that were done early, while Frémont was being held at Cross Keys, might it not be possible to return to Port Republic, cross the bridge and assail Frémont? It was worth trying! Should events preclude a battle against Frémont, after Shields had been beaten, then the destruction of the bridge across the North River would leave Frémont powerless to force action or even to attempt quick pursuit.[57]

For the execution of the more difficult part of this daring design, Jackson issued explicit instructions. Ewell was told to send forward his trains from Port Republic to Cross Keys, in order to feed and supply his troops, and then to bring back the wagons and to start them for Brown's Gap, where they would be out of all danger. At daybreak on the 9th, Ewell was to march for Port Republic,[58] but was to leave in front of Frémont the Brigade of Trimble and Patton's Forty-second Virginia and First Virginia Battalion. These troops were to put up a bold front and were to delay Frémont as long as possible. Should they be pressed hard, they were to retire toward Port Republic and were to burn behind them the bridge on North River.[59] Taliaferro,

---

[55] O. R., 12, pt. 1, p. 784.

[56] O. R., 12, pt. 1, p. 714. For a full statement of the factors that led Jackson to an important decision, history is indebted to Jed. Hotchkiss. On Apr. 4, 1863, Col. Charles J. Faulkner, who was then preparing Jackson's reports of the battles of 1862, asked the General why Shields, instead of Frémont, was attacked. Jackson, as appears *infra*, Vol. II, was disinclined to put into his reports the reasoning that led him to conclusions, but he was frank in answering Faulkner's inquiry. Hotchkiss promptly wrote down what Faulkner repeated to him (*MS. Diary*, 155).

[57] *Dabney*, 419; *William Allan*, 278.

[58] Cf. O. R., 12, pt. 1, p. 785.   [59] O. R., 12, pt. 1, p. 714.

at Port Republic, was to send part of his Brigade to the ridge above the crossing, in order to deal with any force that might attempt to make a dash for the bridge and to destroy it before Trimble got there.[60]

To make sure that these orders to the rearguard were understood, Jackson then sent for Colonel Patton and instructed him in detail. Said the General in his quiet, positive manner, "I wish you to throw out all your men, if necessary, as skirmishers, and to make a great show, so as to cause the enemy to think the whole army are behind you. Hold your position as well as you can; then fall back, when obliged; take a new position; hold it in the same way; and I will be back to join you in the morning."

Patton answered, reasonably enough, that as he had a small command and had to withdraw through a country that offered few good positions, he would like to know how long Jackson expected him to delay Frémont. Jackson's answer was explicit: "By the blessing of Providence, I hope to be back by 10 o'clock." [61]

After moonrise, Jackson went down to the ford of South River and there directed the construction of a crude bridge on the running gear of some army wagons.[62] That done, he returned to headquarters and stretched himself out on his bed without unbelting his sword, or taking off his boots, or even putting out the candle. He probably had not fallen asleep when there was a slight stir in the room.

"Who is that?" he inquired.

It was Col. John D. Imboden, who had come to report for orders. He apologized and explained that he had been looking for "Sandie" Pendleton's room.

"That's all right. It's time to be up. I am glad to see you. Were all the men up as you came through camp?"

"Yes, General, and cooking," Imboden answered.

"That's right. We move at daybreak. Sit down. I want to talk to you." Then, as he had not seen Imboden since the death of Ashby, he spoke of the Army's loss.

"General," said Imboden, perhaps to turn Jackson's thoughts from so gloomy a theme, "you made a glorious winding-up of your four weeks' work yesterday."

[60] O. R., 12, pt. 1, p. 715.   [61] Dabney, 420–21.   [62] Dabney, 419.

"Yes, God blessed our army again yesterday, and I hope with His protection and blessing we shall do still better today." [63]

Orders to Imboden were given in a few clear words. When Jackson came down and mounted, the wagon train was on the way to Brown's Gap to the accompaniment of many protests among officers and men that Jackson was "crazy again." [64] Why should he be going over the mountains? Was he starting for McDowell or some equally remote destination? As the silent General rode from his headquarters, he soon encountered General Winder, who asked for instructions. The commander was cautious in his reply. General Winder would take his Brigade across the South Fork of the Shenandoah. Jackson would himself go with them. He said no more but touched his horse and, under a sky that gave promise of a clear day, he proceeded through a haze that, farther down the river, was a fog. [65] When the leading regiment was on the eastern bank of the stream, Jackson directed Winder to march northeastward along the line of the enemy's retreat the previous day. [66]

In the open country that lay between the river and the rising, wooded ridges of the mountains, the column moved slowly for nearly an hour. Madison's Run was passed; [67] on the right ahead, the plantation buildings of Lewiston, home of General Lewis, were visible. About 7 o'clock, a cavalry officer came back to Winder from the advance with the news that always stirs and sickens: the enemy's picket line had been reached. [68]

Winder referred the officer to Jackson, who had ridden close behind the cavalry. Jackson stopped and studied the position. Open ground to the Northeast rose gradually from the river to the wooded shoulder of the Blue Ridge. The profile below the mountain seemed in the form of two terraces, on the upper of which stood Lewiston. Almost directly in rear of the house, [69]

---

[63] Imboden, in 2 *B. & L.*, 293. General Imboden's account of Jackson's orders, following this exchange, must be read with some caution. The General's memory must have confused what Jackson then told him of his plans with what subsequently occurred in the battle, because there is no reason to believe that Jackson anticipated early that morning the maneuver Taylor's Brigade was called upon to make later.

[64] *Douglas*, 88–89.

[65] *O. R.*, 12, pt. 1, p. 692.

[66] *Ibid.*, 740.

[67] Sometimes known as White Oak Run.

[68] The distance from the extemporized bridge, according to Jackson, *ibid.*, 714, and Poague, *ibid.*, 762, was 1½ miles; according to Winder, *ibid.*, 740, it was 1 mile.

[69] That is to say, East of the house.

as seen from the point where Jackson stood, was a large "coaling," so called, a clear space on which charcoal was prepared. In this clearing were indications of the presence of artillery, though no guns were visible.[70] From the coaling down toward the river, in a general direction slightly West of North, the Federal infantry could be glimpsed. The force, of unknown strength, apparently was along a small stream and behind a double fence which bordered a lane that ran almost at right angles to the main road.[71] Between the Confederates and the enemy the ground was entirely open and, except for an orchard, was covered with a field of ripening wheat.

A strong position the enemy held, but Jackson impetuously determined to take it at a single blow in order not to delay his proposed march on Frémont. Without waiting for any supports to come up,[72] he ordered Winder to drive in the pickets and to attack the enemy.[73] Execution of the first part of these orders was simple. A dash by Winder's skirmishers and a few whiffs of shell sent the Union pickets back to the main line. No sooner was this done and the advance of the Confederate infantry started, than smoke billowed over the coaling near the Lewis House. Federal shell from unseen guns there screamed down the road and burst among the Confederate infantrymen who were too far distant to reply with their muskets. The cannon fire was fast, accurate and continuous. Along the road and on either side of it, man after man went down.

To permit this to continue was, of course, to consent to the slaughter of the Stonewall Brigade. Quickly Jackson directed Winder to send a force to the right through the woods to take the Federal guns; a Confederate battery was to follow and was to find a position above that of the enemy. Winder assigned this soldierly task to the Second Virginia, with the Fourth in support, and he designated Carpenter's Battery to climb the ridge to a

70 O. R., 12, pt. 1, p. 740.

71 For descriptions of the terrain, see Hotchkiss in 3 C. M. H., 261; William Allan, 280; Dabney, 422; R. Taylor, 74. In reading Taylor's fine paragraph, it must be remembered that, when he viewed the battlefield, the Federals had left their first position and were advancing.

72 O. R., 12, pt. 1, p. 740. "Had [Jackson] waited to get his troops up and into formation, his victory would have been easier and his loss less," Douglas, 90.

73 Reference to woods "immediately in front" is made in some of the reports, but is omitted here because it may confuse. The woods were "ahead" when the column faced East but were on the right flank when the column moved Northeast.

point whence it could pour down its fire on the Union artillerists. The other two regiments of his Brigade, Winder disposed on the center and left. Poague's Battery he sent into the wheat field, on the left of the road. Gallantly Poague opened; valiantly he was answered; but only the fire of his two Parrott guns could reach the Federal fieldpieces at the coaling. The remaining Confederate guns had to be held in idleness under cover.

It must have been about this time,[74] as the artillery duel opened and the Second and Fourth Virginia started up the ridge to turn the Federal left, that Jackson observed the nonarrival of supports. The Thirty-third Virginia of Winder's Brigade had not come up, though Winder had taken its presence for granted and had assigned it a place in the line, which was struggling vainly to advance.[75] Taylor's Louisianians, those sure, swift marchers, were not at hand. Jackson sent back his chief of artillery to hurry them forward,[76] only to learn that the temporary bridge, laid across the South Fork on the running gear of wagons, had proved so unsteady that the men would not venture over it except in single file.[77] The brunt of the infantry action and that killing fire from the vicinity of the Lewis House must be borne by the Stonewall Brigade alone.

Nor was this the full measure of disadvantage. When Carpenter's Battery and Allen's Second Virginia entered the woods on the right, they soon ran into a tangle of mountain laurel that proved almost impenetrable. The infantrymen crashed and cut and dodged their way slowly forward, step by step; the battery had to give up the attempt. Captain Carpenter brought the guns back to the open ground and put them into play near Poague's two Parrotts.[78] Colonel Crutchfield sought to add weight to their fire by calling up other batteries which had forded the river, but he found these short of ammunition because, after the fight of the previous day, their commanders had been slow in locating the ordnance train.[79]

The situation began to look serious. Valiant as was the effort of the artillery officers to find good positions and to silence those vicious guns at the coaling, the Confederate fire remained defen-

[74] Cf. Crutchfield, in O. R., 12, pt. 1, p. 728.
[75] O. R., 12, pt. 1, pp. 740–41.
[76] Ibid., 728.   [77] Dabney, 419.
[78] O. R.. 12, pt. 1, pp. 714, 760.   [79] Ibid., 728.

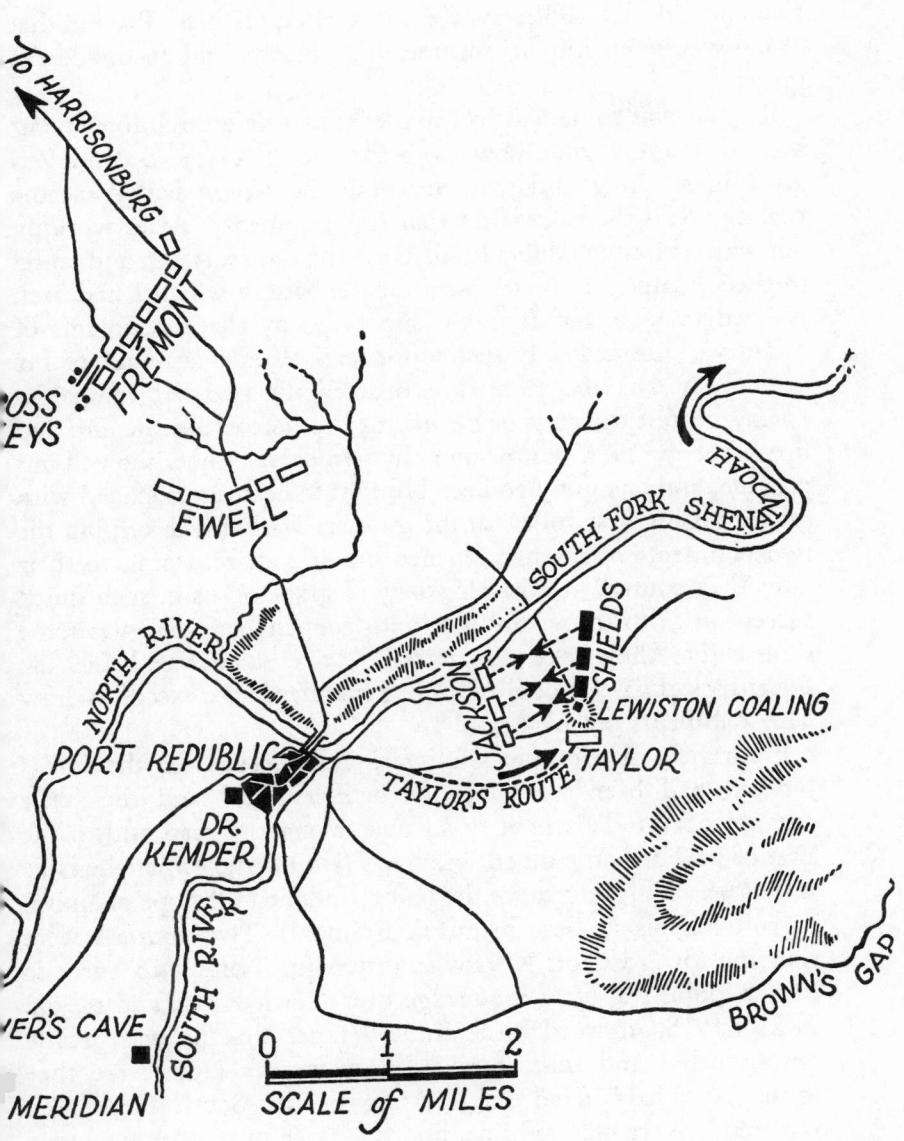

Battle of Port Republic, June 9, 1862

sive and inferior. So heavily did the Federals blast Poague that Winder ordered him to separate his Parrotts and to divide the target.[80]

If relief was to be had by Winder's men before reinforcements arrived, it must come now from the success of the Second Virginia in reaching and overwhelming the Union battery at the coaling. Said the Colonel of that fine regiment: "After working our way with much difficulty through the undergrowth and laurel thickets I came within 100 yards of the battery which I had been ordered to take, but found it supported by three regiments of infantry. I immediately sent to General Winder a report of my position, and at the same time ordered the two left companies (being nearest the guns of the enemy) to take deliberate aim and fire at the gunners. Unfortunately, two chance shots showed our position, and one gun had been brought to bear on us loaded with grape. At my first volley all the gunners were driven off, but the two regiments of infantry opened on us, and returning to their guns they poured volley after volley of grape on us in such quick succession as to throw my men into confusion, and it was some time before they were reformed." [81] The same fate befell the Fourth Virginia. Colonel Allen had no alternative except to draw both regiments out of action.[82]

From field headquarters in rear of the center of the line,[83] Jackson had been watching the artillery duel and the futile attempt of Winder's men to advance along the road and to the East of it. His battle blood was up. He knew now that the issue was close. With reluctance, he had abandoned all hope of finishing off Shields in time to attack Frémont. Two couriers were spurring toward Cross Keys with orders for Trimble to hurry to Port Republic, to burn the bridge over North River, and to join Jackson.[84] Soon word came from Winder that he was greatly outnumbered and must have reinforcements. How were they to be provided? Had the crossing of the South Fork been repaired? Were officers hastening the march of troops that surely were strong enough to overwhelm Shields?

In direct answer to the question appeared Hays's Seventh Louis-

[80] O. R., 12, pt. 1, p. 741.
[81] O. R., 12, pt. 1, p. 745.   [82] Ibid., 745, 747.
[83] 3 C. M. H., 261.   [84] O. R., 12, pt. 1, p. 798.

iana, which was coming up at the head of Taylor's Brigade. Jackson immediately dispatched Hays to Winder, and in a few minutes saw Taylor riding toward him at the head of his other regiments. Jackson, with eyes aflame, had only two words for him, and those two in his usual quiet tones: "Delightful excitement!"

Taylor replied, somewhat grimly, that it was pleasant to learn the General was enjoying himself, but that, if the battery on the coal hearth were not silenced, there might be indigestion of such fun.[35] Jackson turned instantly to Jed. Hotchkiss, who by fortunate chance, had arrived at field headquarters only a few minutes before Taylor. Pointing to the smoke from the coaling, Jackson said tersely: "Take General Taylor around and take those batteries." [36] Hotchkiss and Taylor returned at once to the head of the approaching Brigade and started it up the ridge and into the laurel thickets.

Could Winder hold his position on the plain until Taylor stormed the battery? Already the Federal skirmishers were creeping forward to attack the depleted Stonewall Brigade. The whole line of the enemy might advance at any moment and drive the few, wavering troops on Winder's center. Winder saw that his best prospect of preventing an assault was to deliver one. He threw the Seventh Louisiana to the right of the Fifth Virginia, brought up the Twenty-seventh Virginia from support of the artillery, and placed that regiment on the right of the Louisianians. Then he ordered the line forward and told the artillery to follow to more advanced positions.[87]

With a cheer, the fine Louisiana troops rushed forward. The Virginians kept pace. Poague's short-range guns and a section of Carpenter's Battery strained through the wheat field in rear of the infantry. The troops reached a fence and there they had to halt in the face of a combined artillery and rifle fire. Stubbornly

---

[85] R. Taylor, 74.

[86] Hotchkiss' MS. Diary, 49. Taylor, in his memoirs, p. 77, stated that he was guided by "Lieutenant English," who lived "near Harpers Ferry," but Lt. R. M. English of the Second Virginia, who was killed in an advanced position, could not have acted as guide until Taylor reached the front of the Second Virginia. The responsibility for leading Taylor up the ridge and along it toward the battery at the coaling rested on Jed. Hotchkiss. He was credited in Capt. J. K. Boswell's report, O. R., 12, pt. 1, p. 719, with that fine feat.

[87] O. R., 12, pt. 1, p. 741.

the graycoats along the fence answered this fire, but without reducing it. All they could do was precariously to hold on. Even that soon seemed to be rendered impossible by the receipt of orders for Winder to send the Seventh Louisiana after its Brigade and to replace it with the Thirty-first Virginia,[88] which had reached the field a few minutes previously. Winder knew that any attempt to draw the Louisianians out of the line would be fatal. Consequently, he held them steadily along the fence, and prudently he placed the fresh regiment in support of the artillery which, at the moment, had no infantry behind it.[89]

A second appeal was sent to Jackson by Winder, but no more reinforcements came. Ammunition was low in the cartridge boxes of the men huddled under the fence.[90] Unless Taylor attacked soon, Winder would be compelled to give ground. Warning to that effect Winder sent directly to Taylor.[91] Minutes passed. The Federal battery at the coaling kept blasting away. Unchallenged it was by infantry and undisturbed by the feeble Confederate artillery. Evidently, Taylor was delayed in his advance—if he was advancing at all. Soon some of Winder's men began to crawl away from the fence. He saw that the whole line was wavering, and he ordered the artillery back to safety—just in time. There was a swift break. The Seventh Louisiana and the two Virginia regiments streamed back through the wheat. Their organization disappeared. They were fugitives. Winder and the regimental officers rode across the field, again and again. They wheeled and veered; they pleaded and shouted, they cut and commanded—all was futile. To the left and front, pursuing Federals now were visible.[92] They came on so fast and so persistently that Winder ordered one of Poague's pieces halted. It must be turned on the Unionists. They must be held off till the scattered infantry could be rallied. The gunners stopped in perfect order; they loaded; they sent their charge where the pursuing Federal most threatened.[93]

Dangerous the situation was, but if it could be preserved for a few moments, it could be redeemed. The second Brigade of

[88] Elzey's Brigade, Ewell's Division; cf. *William Allan*, 224 n.
[89] *O. R.*, 12, pt. 1, p. 741.   [90] *O. R.*, 12, pt. 1, pp. 741, 750.
[91] 3 *C. M. H.*, 262.   [92] *O. R.*, 12, pt. 1, pp. 714, 729, 741.
[93] *O. R.*, 12, pt. 1, pp. 715, 741, 763, 789.

Ewell's Division[94] already had reached the scene of action. Jackson had ordered one of its regiments[95] to support the left. The other two regiments of the Brigade, Ewell had started in support of Taylor. At the moment, Ewell had them on an extended front in the wood on the Confederate right, but he had always an eye for danger and a heart for a comrade in difficulties. The instant Ewell saw the Federals pushing forward in pursuit of Winder's broken line, he did the wise and soldierly thing: he unhesitatingly threw the two regiments against the Federal flank. With a cheer and a volley, the Forty-fourth and the Fifty-eighth Virginia dashed out of the wood. They took the advancing enemy by surprise, they halted him, they hurled him back. Poague's lone gun joyfully added its iron to their lead.

Not for long did Ewell's Division hold this advantage. Formation had not been lost in the Union withdrawal. The line quickly was dressed to face Ewell. With steadiness and a hot fire, the Union regiments advanced again and drove Ewell's men back into the wood. So vigorous and gallant was the onrush that it soon approached the ground where Poague had his gun. As a wounded horse had fallen across the pole, the artillerists had to leave the piece and scamper to cover.[96]

A gun abandoned, a famous Brigade worsted—was the battle to be lost also? The cheers of the advancing Federals, rolling all along their line,[97] showed that they believed the victory was theirs. Winder was beginning to rally his men, and Ewell in the woods on the right was doing all that an officer could to get his two regiments into line again; but if the Federals continued to press on, and Taylor did not attack their flank, then, as the least of possible calamities, the Stonewall Brigade would be routed shamefully. Even Jackson had to admit to himself that the plight of Winder was critical.[98]

At that moment, a mile to the eastward, Taylor was on the edge of the tangled woodland not far from the Federal battery. The difficult scramble through the undergrowth had scattered and exhausted his men, who could hear the triumphant cheers of the

94 Under Col. W. C. Scott of the Fifty-eighth Virginia.
95 The Fifty-second Virginia; O. R., 12, pt. 1, p. 790.
96 O. R., 12, pt. 1, pp. 763, 786.
97 Cf. O. R., 12, pt. 1, p. 715.   98 O. R., 12, pt. 1, p. 715.

enemy.[99] To his disappointment, when he looked out from the laurel, Taylor saw that he had not progressed far enough to take the Federal guns from the rear. Union infantry still were on his flank. A charge would bring bloody losses, but his military instinct told him he could not afford to wait long enough to work around to the rear of the Federals. He was South of and above them, across a ravine where the woods came down close to the battery.[100] Reckless as the venture might be, he would take the most stalwart of his troops and make a dash for the guns on the coal hearth.

Out the Louisianians went, more in a spring than at a dash—due North and over the ravine. Before the enemy realized that a column was near, the still-smoking field pieces were seized. Turn them! was the order. Give the enemy his own medicine! Ready hands pulled, the wheels moved slowly, but now the Federals were surging back. The Louisiana boys, unable to load, had to run. With few hurts, they got to cover. Unshaken in purpose, Taylor rallied them. Two companies he detached and sent clambering up the ridge still higher to drive out some Federal riflemen who were pouring a destructive fire on the panting Louisianians. These bluecoats dislodged, Taylor led his men in a second rush for the guns. This time the opposing troops came to grips with bayonet, with clubbed musket and even with the ramrods of the pieces. Desperate the struggle was, but brief. The Federals were too strong to worst. Swearing and bloody, the Confederates dropped back to the woods.

Casualties now had so reduced the three regiments that Taylor needed every man who could fire a musket. Even the musicians laid down their instruments and prepared to join in the assault. Once more, with a wild shout, the thin line rushed down the grade, over the ravine and on to the coal hearth, where writhing horses and wounded men covered some of the dead. The Confederates stormed the guns and then drew a line to face the woods from which the enemy twice had rushed out to repulse them. Anxious seconds of tense waiting dragged into minutes. No countercharge came. The guns were Taylor's!

Then, ere the wounded could be extricated or the infantrymen could find the gear to use the weapons, a ripping Union fire from

[99] *O. R.*, 12, pt. 1, p. 803.   [100] *Ibid.*, 693.

the West swept the left flank of the graycoats on the hearth. The Federals between Lewiston and the river had seen Taylor's maneuver and were moving eastward against him. A gun was rolled out within plain view, not more than 350 yards away,[101] and was opened on the coaling. Exposed as Taylor's men were, they could not face this fire. For the third time they tumbled over the ravine and up the hillside South of the coaling. Despite this, Taylor continued to fight. If he could not hold the battery position, he would give the new force on his flank so hot a reception that it could not recover the guns. He adjusted his line slightly to face the attack from the West, against his left,[102] and opened a vigorous fire. The Federals replied in kind. Canister from their gun winged with a flight of minié balls. Bold Union soldiers slipped up to the coaling and carried off one of the guns. The remaining five pieces, for lack of horses, they could not take away.[103]

Taylor's position in the skirt of the woods was entirely defensible; his men were putting up a good fight; but, if his thinned regiments were left to receive the attack of the entire Federal force that had driven off Winder, they must in time be overwhelmed. Taylor's fellow commanders were resolved that it should not be so. Winder already had felt the relief that Taylor's attack had brought. Not only was the battery silenced that had torn Winder's ranks, but also the Federal pursuit of the Stonewall Brigade had been halted.[104] In pushing across the open ground, in the direction of Taylor's attack, the Federals had an exposed flank to the South. Winder had seen this, and was massing his artillery to assail that flank.[105] Ewell was re-forming Scott's two regiments, which had been repulsed in the first effort to relieve the pressure on Winder.

Against Taylor, now, the Federals skillfully threw all the strength they could muster. The flag of the Union was flying bravely; the approaching line appeared to Taylor's men as a solid wall. "There seemed," said Taylor afterward, "nothing left but

[101] Col. Philip Daum, Federal chief of artillery, O. R., 12, pt. 1, p. 692, gave the distance as 200 yards and spoke of employing the "guns of the right wing," but if more than one piece was brought to bear, the Confederates were not aware of the fact.
[102] The reports mention no such tactical disposition, but it was demanded by the terrain, and could not have been overlooked by a competent soldier such as Taylor had shown himself to be.
[103] O. R., 12, pt. 1, pp. 715, 802; R. Taylor, 75.
[104] O. R., 12, pt. 1, pp. 715, 802.
[105] O. R., 12, pt. 1, pp. 715, 763.

to set our backs to the mountain and die hard." [106] Nearer the Federals came, though their supports were not yet within rifle range. A few moments, and the final grapple would begin. Just when a hand-to-hand struggle seemed certain, with a fatal result equally certain, "Dick" Ewell came crashing on his horse through the woods. Behind him were Scott's Forty-fourth and Fifty-eighth Virginia. [107]

With this reinforcement, Taylor quickly determined not to await attack but to deliver it. As soon as the command could be given, his men sprang up, dashed out of the woods and started for the enemy. By happy chance, the assault was delivered precisely when Winder's fire and that of his artillery began to blast the blue flank. The Federals halted uncertainly and then fell back before the Confederates. Quickly Taylor's men and Scott's reached the coal hearth. They gripped the wheels, they turned the guns, they found charges and ramrods and, in a few minutes, they were firing on the retreating enemy. Ewell himself, his beak shining with joy, got off his horse and served one of the field-pieces. [108] Farther the Federals withdrew, and swiftly, but in creditable order. Neither the Southern shells nor a roaring volley from Taliaferro's Brigade, which had arrived at the moment, [109] could do more than hasten the retreat. As the Federals disappeared, Jackson rode up to Taylor, shook his hand as at Winchester, and promised that the captured guns should be attached to the Louisiana Brigade. [110]

Now at 11 A.M. or about that time, [111] the pursuit was begun. Wherever the batteries could find a field of fire, they halted, fired on the retiring column, and then moved on to a new position. [112] In this manner, with Jackson always at the front, the gunners and the infantry pushed northward for four miles, until they found the woods so thick on both sides of the roads that farther progress was almost impossible. [113] The cavalry kept up the chase for another four miles. [114] About 450 prisoners, some wagons, one

[106] R. Taylor, 75, probably a rhetorical flourish.
[107] O. R., 12, pt. I, pp. 715, 786; R. Taylor, 75.
[108] R. Taylor, 76.
[109] O. R., 12, pt. I, p. 715.
[110] R. Taylor, 76.
[111] Crutchfield, O. R., 12, pt. I, p. 728, stated that the action opened at 7 A.M.; Shields, ibid., 684, reported that it lasted four hours.
[112] O. R., 12, pt. I, p. 742.
[113] O. R., 12, pt. I, p. 742; Dabney, 425.   [114] O. R., 12, pt. I, p. 732.

field gun and approximately 800 muskets were the army's reward for the pursuit.[115] "General," said Jackson to Ewell, as he put a hand gently on Ewell's arm, "he who does not see the hand of God in this is blind, sir, blind!" [116]

Carefully Jackson collected this booty and marched back to the battlefield of Port Republic, where he found Trimble's and Patton's men. Obedient to Jackson's orders, they had left their line near Cross Keys between 8.30 and 9.00 A.M.,[117] had crossed the North River bridge at 10 o'clock [118] and had burned it fifteen minutes later.[119] Frémont, following fast, had found no way of crossing or of giving help to Shields, and had opened from the ridge a fire that had no other effect than to drive off the ambulances and the stretcher-bearers who were searching for the wounded.[120]

A close action this Battle of Port Republic had been, and a costly! The Federals, it developed, comprised two small Brigades that numbered no more than 3000 men,[121] and sixteen guns.[122] The infantry, under Brig. Gen. E. B. Tyler and Col. S. S. Carroll, acting Brigadier, were from Pennsylvania, Ohio, West Virginia and Indiana, and they had fought admirably. Those fine guns on the coaling had been three of Clark's regulars, 4th U. S. Artillery, three of Huntington's and one of Robinson's Ohio Batteries. The combined force of eight infantry regiments, three batteries and 150 cavalry [123] had been hurried forward by General Shields in an attempt to reach Waynesboro,[124] where he thought there were a depot and a bridge, the destruction of which would be fatal to Jackson.[125] It had been the advanced units of this column, led by Colonel Carroll, that had entered Port Republic on the 8th. Upon his retirement, Carroll had reached the van of General Tyler, who had pushed forward to his support.[126] Tyler, perhaps injudiciously, had decided to remain in his advanced position overnight. Early in the morning of the 9th, he had received orders

---

115 *O. R.*, 12, pt. 1, p. 715. 116 *Douglas,* 91.
117 *O. R.*, 12, pt. 1, pp. 771, 798. 118 *O. R.*, 12, pt. 1, p. 766.
119 *Ibid.,* 771.
120 *O. R.*, 12, pt. 1, pp. 716, 771. Frémont reached the ridge about 11.45. *Ibid.*, 771.
121 So Gen. E. B. Tyler, who was in direct command, *O. R.*, 12, pt. 1, p. 697. General Shields, *ibid.*, 688, put the effective strength at 2500.
122 *O. R.*, 12, pt. 1, p. 691.
123 *O. R.*, 12, pt. 1, p. 698.
124 Eighteen miles from Shields's outposts, according to his estimate, *O. R.*, 12, pt. 1, p. 686.
125 *Ibid.*
126 *O. R.*, 12, pt. 1, p. 695.

from Shields to retire to Conrad's Store,[127] but before he could do so, Jackson had been upon him. In the battle itself, Tyler's killed and wounded were few. On his retreat he had lost about 20 per cent of his force as prisoners. His total casualties were 1018.[128] The remnant that made its way back to Luray was in sad plight.[129] Jackson, for his part, had suffered in excess of 800 casualties, which were more than he had sustained in any other action of the campaign.[130]

Jackson did not stop to count all his losses. He believed that Shields was defeated, but he did not wish the Army to be exposed simultaneously to a possible attack from the direction of Conrad's Store and a turning movement by Frémont. The wagon train already was high up the Blue Ridge in Brown's Gap. Without any longer delay than was necessary to get the weary but exultant troops together, Jackson started the infantry and the artillery up the mountain. Before daylight on June 10, he was fairly astride the Gap and was fully protected, except for supplies, against any movement from either side of the Blue Ridge.[131]

In that position the Army was resting when, on the 10th, word came that Frémont had not attempted to cross North River at Port Republic or to turn it by a countermarch, but, instead, had started a retreat down the Valley.[132] Jackson at once sent out his cavalry who, on the 12th, occupied Harrisonburg and advanced their outposts to New Market. Some loot, 200 of Frémont's sick and wounded, and 200 small arms were found in Harrisonburg.[133] To be near at hand in event Frémont was attempting to deceive him, Jackson that same day came down the mountain, crossed

[127] Cf. O. R., 12, pt. 1, p. 687, with ibid., 696.

[128] Killed, sixty-seven; wounded, 393; captured or missing, 558; O. R., 12, pt. 1, p. 690.

[129] Cf. O. R., 12, pt. 3, pp. 367–68.

[130] O. R., 12, pt. 1, pp. 712, 717, 718, 742, 784, 787; William Allan, 284 n. It is not possible to segregate all the losses of all the commands. Some of the reports give the casualties of June 9 along with those of June 8.

[131] Hotchkiss' MS. Diary, 49, 161; O. R., 12, pt. 1, p. 742.

[132] O. R., 12, pt. 1, p. 716. In his report, O. R., 12, pt. 1, p. 24, Frémont thus explained his retreat to Harrisonburg: "The withdrawal of Shields had left my command an isolated body far in advance of all other troops, and all expectation of aid or concert of action with others was now cut off. My troops had been long without proper food or shelter; their march had been exhausting, and I had expended their last effort in reaching Port Republic." At Harrisonburg Frémont received orders from President Lincoln to "halt [there], pursuing Jackson no farther" and to "stand on the defensive" until new orders were sent him. As Frémont considered Harrisonburg a weak position, he withdrew on June 11–12 to Mount Jackson (ibid.; cf. Carl Schurz's comment, O. R., 12, pt. 3, pp. 379–80).

[133] O. R., 12, pt. 1, pp. 716, 732.

South River again and established his camps between that stream and Middle River, near Weyer's Cave and Mount Meridian.[134] Another consideration in making this movement may have been the comfort of his Army.

In a lush and beautiful country, Jackson rested his men, held a day of thanksgiving, and with the humblest of privates participated in brigade communion.[135] He had telegraphed Mrs. Jackson on the 9th that he was safe and on the 10th he had written her a brief account of the victories. This had concluded: "God has been our shield, and to His name be all the glory. . . . How I do wish for peace, but only upon the condition of our national independence." Now, from the communion, he turned to write her again. "When I look at the locality of the cave," he said, "I take additional interest in it from the fact that my *esposita* was once there." There followed, as became the day and the Christian, an expression of his gratitude to God for deliverance and for victory, and, at the end, one wistful sentence: "Wouldn't you like to get home again?"[136]

For a few days he had time to indulge a mood that was almost emotional. When the father of one of his young officers came to solicit a furlough for the son, Jackson did not dismiss him with a simple "No." He took the parent into his tent and exhorted him so eloquently that the visitor shed tears. In leaving, the father accepted uncomplainingly the rejection of his plea and added fervently: "May God bless you, General Jackson. If it only pleased Him that the weight of fewer years were resting on these old shoulders, I should be with you myself, to aid in fighting this quarrel through, under your banner!"[137]

Not all of Jackson's expressions in the aftermath of the battles were at this pitch. The day after the Battle of Port Republic, Jackson told his exhaustless quartermaster, "Old John" Harman, to collect the small arms that were scattered over the field. When Harman reported, he said, "General, a good many of them look like our own arms." Jackson exploded instantly. Shields, he said, had many similar weapons; he wanted to hear no more of such talk! Harman angrily replied that he would not be addressed in such manner. He would tender his resignation at once. Jackson

[134] *O. R.*, 12, pt. 1, p. 716; *Dabney*, 429–30.
[135] *Dabney*, 430.
[136] *Mrs. Jackson*, 283–84.
[137] 1 *Land We Love*, 311–12.

protested against such a step, but Harman went angrily away and soon sent in the paper. Thereupon Jackson summoned the quartermaster again and explained that he had been annoyed by frequent references to the arms his men had thrown away. He would not, he said, approve Harman's resignation. Harman was willing, for the moment, to leave the matter there.[138]

Less violent though no less indicative of Jackson's fighting spirit was a conversation with Ewell. At Port Republic, Ewell had seen on a white horse a Federal officer who gave a magnificent example of gallant behavior. So much did Ewell admire this bravery that he rode along the line, under fire himself, and told his men not to kill so fine a foe. Despite Ewell's plea, the Federal and the white horse soon went down. When word of this incident came to Jackson's ears he sent for Ewell, verified the facts and then told Ewell not to do such a thing again. Said Jackson: "This is no ordinary war. The brave and gallant Federal officers are the very kind that must be killed. Shoot the brave officers and the cowards will run away and take the men with them." [139]

Still a third unpleasant incident concerned Charles Winder. That officer, who had distinguished himself highly during the campaign, asked leave to go to Richmond for a few days on private business. Jackson brusquely refused. His reason doubtless was that he did not wish one of his best Brigades to be without its able commander while the movements of the enemy still were uncertain, but he did not explain that. Winder became offended and tendered his resignation.

Through regard for Taylor, with whom his relations during the campaign had been finely chivalrous,[140] Winder rode over to the headquarters of the Louisiana Brigade to say farewell. Taylor perceived that the rejection of Winder's request for leave was not all that rankled. Behind it was unexpressed resentment over interference, presumably by Jackson, with Winder's discharge of command. In the conviction that so capable an officer should not be allowed to leave the Army, Taylor went to Jackson, dwelt on the plenitude of the glory won during the campaign, and appealed to Jackson's magnanimity: "Observing him closely, I caught a

[138] *Hotchkiss' MS. Diary*, Apr. 15, 1863, p. 161.
[139] *Stiles*, 245–46, on the authority of Medical Director Hunter McGuire.
[140] Cf. *R. Taylor*, 68.

glimpse of the man's inner nature. It was but a glimpse. The curtain closed, and he was absorbed in prayer. Yet in that moment I saw an ambition boundless as Cromwell's or as merciless. . . . No reply was made to my effort for Winder, and I rose to take my leave, when Jackson said he would ride with me. We passed silently along the way to my camp where he left me. That night a few lines came from Winder, to inform me that Jackson had called on him, and his resignation was withdrawn." [141]

This incident and others of the week that followed the Battle of Port Republic were put in the shadow by the concentration of all the light of Jackson's mind on the possibilities General Lee now suggested of employing the victorious Army of the Valley in front of Richmond. Johnston's successor had received Jackson's unpromising letter of June 6[142] on the day the Battle of Cross Keys had been fought. Lee had concluded from what Jackson had said that no offensive operations were practicable in the Valley and that such reinforcements as he would be able to send Jackson would be useless.[143] In that belief he wrote on the 8th to suggest that the troops on the Shenandoah be prepared for a movement to Richmond. Lee had added: "Make your arrangements accordingly, but should an opportunity occur for striking the enemy a successful blow do not let it escape you." [144]

Before this letter reached Jackson, the actions at Cross Keys and Port Republic had been won and had been reported to Richmond in brief dispatches.[145] Lee reasoned immediately that this double victory would permit Jackson to take the offensive again and that the Army of the Valley would need reinforcement.[146] To make the most of what seemed to be an opening, Lee decided that he should send Jackson at least two good Brigades in addition to Lawton's Georgia Brigade and a North Carolina battalion previously ordered to the Valley. On the 10th, Lee submitted this proposal for the President's approval and urged immediate action

[141] R. Taylor, 79.
[142] See supra, p. 431.
[143] O. R., 12, pt. 3, p. 906.
[144] O. R., 12, pt. 3, p. 908.
[145] The originals, in two telegrams from Port Republic, via Staunton, are among the Chilton MSS., Confederate Museum. One report, dated June 9, addressed to General Lee, and received in Richmond the same day, read as follows: "Yesterday God crowned our arms with success by repulsing the attacks of Frémont & Shields at Port Republic." The other, dated June 9 but not received until June 10, was to General Cooper: "Through God's blessing the Enemy near Port Republic was this day routed with the loss of Six (6) pieces of his artillery."
[146] Cf. O. R., 11, pt. 3, p. 584.

both because Jackson must strike soon and also because the Confederate Army in front of Richmond could not hope to hold off
McClellan for any length of time.[147] With the approval of Mr.
Davis, a troop movement under W. H. C. Whiting began on the
11th.[148]

Information of this reinforcement did not reach Jackson immediately. It was not until the 13th that he received Lee's letter of
the 8th, in which he was told to prepare, if practicable, to bring
his Army to Richmond. Jackson knew, as he read the letter of
the 8th, that Shields, at last reports, was near Luray and that Frémont had retreated as far as Mount Jackson.[149] For these reasons,
Jackson concluded that if he was to reinforce Lee at all, the time
for doing so was near at hand. He could drive Frémont and
Shields down the Valley as he had driven Banks; but he asked
himself what would be gained thereby unless he could hold the
lower Valley after he had cleared it of the enemy.

Jackson saw one useful alternative, one only, to transferring his
Army to Richmond, and that was to relieve the capital by a heavy
counter-offensive that would carry him into the enemy's country.
He had been pondering that possibility in terms of troops. If he
could procure sufficient reinforcements to raise his total strength
to 40,000 men, he would cross the Blue Ridge in order to deceive

[147] *O. R.*, 51, pt. 2, p. 1094.
[148] *O. R.*, 11, pt. 3, pp. 590, 594. This famous movement of Whiting's command
mistakenly was assumed to be altogether a ruse on the part of Lee. To the witnesses
cited in 2 *R. E. Lee*, 96 n., should be added J. L. Brent, *op. cit.*, 154–55, published in
1940. After Whiting had reached the Valley and had started back toward Richmond
with Jackson, publication was made of the reinforcement of the Confederate forces in
the Valley. (See *Richmond Dispatch*, June 18, p. 1, col. 1; *Richmond Examiner*, June
19, p. 1, col. 1; *Richmond Whig*, June 19, 1862, p. 2, col. 2). The evidence does not show
whether this publication was based on mistaken reports or whether it was inspired by
General Lee, who sought then to make a ruse of a reality. W. P. Scobey, U. S. A., then
Major of Infantry, made in 1938 a study of the movement and concluded that Lee
"saw the opportunity of developing a reality into a ruse . . ."
[149] See note 132, *supra*. Confederate reports on Shields's movements and on the condition of his troops were meager. Apparently Jackson felt that the defeat of two Brigades
put Shields *hors de combat*. It is not certain how soon Jackson learned that Shields had
received orders to leave the Valley altogether and, with the remainder of McDowell's
force, to resume via Fredericksburg, the movement to support McClellan (cf. *O. R.*, 12,
pt. 1, p. 689). Although General Shields later protested that this order deprived him of
an opportunity of defeating Jackson with the assistance of General Frémont, he reported
on the 12th, as he was marching on Luray, that he would require a few days' rest
before starting for Catlett's. "I find," said he, "that about half my command are barefoot
and foot-sore" (*ibid.*, 683). In an endorsement on Shields's final report, General
McDowell justified the President's order for the recall of the force and added: "Both the
condition of General Shields' division and that of the roads and rivers, as represented
by him, indicated anything than the success he anticipated" from continued operations
in the Valley (*O. R.*, 12, pt. 1, p. 689).

the Federals, and then would proceed northward until he found a convenient gap that would put him in rear of General Banks's army, which presumably was marching slowly up the Shenandoah. Having disposed of Banks, Jackson planned to invade Western Maryland and Pennsylvania.[150] This, it will be observed, was essentially the same plan, strategically, that he had sent Boteler to Richmond to advocate after the Battle of Winchester.[151] Jackson decided now that he would transmit by the same messenger a report on his situation and, in so doing, would suggest informally the bolder, more magnificent but necessarily secret design.

To that end, on the 13th of June, after Jackson had received Lee's letter of June 8, he asked Boteler to make another journey to Richmond, explain Jackson's alternative, and to solicit troops in sufficient number to make possible the invasion of the North. "By that means," Jackson told his emissary, "Richmond can be relieved and the campaign transferred to Pennsylvania." [152] The formal report entrusted to Boteler for personal delivery to Lee read as follows:

General,
Your letter of the 8th instant was not received until this morning. From a letter received from Shields on the 11th, he was about ten miles above Luray in Page County. From a letter received this morning from Frémont he was at Mount Jackson yesterday. Our cavalry have been upwards of (12) twelve miles beyond Harrisonburg. So circumstances greatly favor my moving to Richmond in accordance with your plan.

I will remain if practicable in this neighborhood until I hear from you and rest the troops who are greatly fatigued.

You can halt the reenforcements coming here if you so desire, without interfering with my plans provided the movement to Richmond takes place. So far as I am concerned my opinion is that we should not attempt another march down the valley to Winchester until we are in a condition under the blessing of Providence to hold the country.

Gratefully appreciating your kind expressions I remain General your obdt. servt.[153]

[150] See A. R. Boteler, in 40 S. H. S. P., 173.
[151] See *supra*, p. 414.
[152] Boteler, *loc. cit.*, 172.
[153] MS. Duke University; printed in full for the first time in *The Centennial Exhibit of the Duke University Library*, 1939, pp. 15–16. "Frémont" appears in the printed text as "Fairmont."

Whatever the decision of the government, Jackson reasoned that he would move ere long, and he accordingly ordered his cavalry to set up a screen of secrecy. All communication by civilians with the area of Federal occupation was prohibited.[154] Guards were posted on the roads. For the next step, Jackson had to wait on Richmond. By the 16th, the first of the reinforcements promised in Lee's letter of June 11 reported—and splendid troops they manifestly were.[155] The next day, regiments began to arrive from the Richmond front. Whiting had been left free by General Lee to select eight regiments from Smith's Division, and he had been quick to choose his own Brigade, temporarily under Col. E. M. Law, and Hood's Brigade, to which the Hampton Legion was attached.[156] These were as good soldiers as the Army of Northern Virginia had.

Jackson welcomed Whiting and these veterans,[157] but, before the day was out, a decision on the proposals sent Lee by Colonel Boteler was received. In a letter written on the 16th,[158] Lee expressed the opinion that it would be difficult for Jackson to strike Frémont and Shields where they then were, to defeat them, to break off pursuit, to move eastward and to join the Army of Northern Virginia in time for the attack that soon must be made on McClellan. If, Lee went on, Jackson was of this opinion, the course to pursue was to conceal all movement and to start for Richmond as soon as practicable. The commanding General concluded with this explanation of the reasons for haste: "Unless McClellan can be driven out of his intrenchments he will move by positions under cover of his heavy guns within shelling distance of Richmond. I know of no surer way of thwarting him than that proposed. I should like to have the

154 O. R., 12, pt. 3, p. 912.
155 Hotchkiss' MS. Diary, p. 51.
156 Cf. O. R., 11, pt. 2, p. 552; Hood, 24.   157 O. R., 12, pt. 3, p. 913.
158 The text is given this form because there is a possibility that Lee communicated his decision to Jackson by telegraph on the 17th, and that the letter of the 16th was not received until later, but the probabilities are that it was in Jackson's hands on the evening of the 17th. Lee had forwarded to the President the letter Jackson had written on the 13th. This was Lee's endorsement: "Respt. referred for the information of the President. I think the sooner Jackson can move this way the better—The first object now is to defeat McClellan. The enemy in the Valley seem at a pause—We may strike them here before they are ready there to move up the valley. They will naturally be cautious and we must be secret & quick. Will you ask the Sec. to make arrangements for moving Jackson down if you agree with me, as soon as his troops are refreshed a little—They must rest in the journy (sic)—Please return me this letter that I may reply." Davis endorsed, in turn, "Views concurred in." MS. Duke University, supra.

advantage of your views and be able to confer with you." [159]
Nothing was said in the letter about the proposal to invade Pennsylvania. Colonel Boteler was left to state verbally to Jackson
that the pressure on Richmond prevented the detachment of
enough troops to make possible a large-scale offensive.

Jackson lost no time in obeying this discretionary order. With
precautions to keep all early information of his withdrawal from
reaching the enemy,[160] he set the columns in motion for the Virginia Central Railroad. On the morning of the 18th, he was in
Staunton, and after arranging a multitude of details he set out
for Waynesboro, where he arrived at 5 P.M.

Then began an interesting experience, which Jed. Hotchkiss
thus recorded: ". . . we went on up the Blue Ridge, as Maj.
Dabney had said to Rev. Richardson, 'Following our noses.' The
whole western slope of the mountains on both sides of the road,
for over three miles, was covered with troops with camp fires
burning. It was a very fine sight. We saw Gen. Whiting at the
foot of the mountain and then rode on, in the darkness, looking
for our Hd. Qrs. camp by inquiring at every camp fire, but
could not find it. I saw Gen. C. S. Winder at the Mountain Top
House, Rockfish Gap,[161] where I went to look for our Hd. Qrs.
On my return I said [to Jackson], 'General, I fear we will not
find our wagons tonight.' He replied, earnestly, 'Never take
counsel of your fears. . . .' " [162]

---

[159] O. R., 12, pt. 3, p. 913.

[160] As set forth at length in Cooke's *Jackson* (ed. 1866), 202 ff., and in *Dabney*, 432
ff., some of the stories of the ruses employed to deceive the enemy have to be dismissed
as apocryphal. One of the most familiar stories concerns Jackson's instructions to Col.
T. T. Munford to meet him, if convenient, at Mount Sidney about 10 P.M. on the 17th.
Jackson added: "I will be on my horse at north end of the town, so you need not
inquire after me. I do not desire it to be known that I am absent" from the camp near
Weyer's Cave (O. R., 12, pt. 3, p. 914). Cooke, op. cit., 202–3, gave the date as the
16th, the place as Mount Crawford, and then repeated the conversation between Munford and Jackson at this odd meeting. Unfortunately for the yarn, Hotchkiss noted in
his *Diary*, p. 51, that Jackson sent *him* to meet Munford and to tell that officer Jackson
had attended to the matter set for discussion at the rendezvous. Munford did not appear
at the meeting place, doubtless because he had accepted Jackson's alternative proposal
to meet the next morning at 5 A.M. in Staunton (cf. 7 S. H. S. P., 534).

[161] From the western approach, this was the name given the pass which, on the
eastern side of the mountains, is known at present as Afton Gap.

[162] *Hotchkiss' MS. Diary*, p. 53.

CHAPTER XXIX

"The Hero of the South"

"Never take counsel of your fears"—that was Jackson's statement of a principle. The immediate application, there in Rockfish Gap on the evening of June 18, 1862, was homely: "Go," Jackson continued, "and see if you can find some place where we can stay; at least find some place where we can sleep. Get something to eat if you can."

Hotchkiss wrote later in his diary: "As my horse had been rested, I pushed on, over the rough and rocky road, and found a place for us at Mr. James McCue's, at the foot of the Blue Ridge, on the eastern side, where we got a good supper and nice lodgings, our party being Gen. Jackson, Col. Jackson, a courier and myself. The day had been quite warm and the roads are very dusty. Our whole army is moving; some of it has reached Mechum River today. No one knows where the army is going; but some hard blow is to be struck. The General was long at his devotions after we retired to our chamber, he, Col. Jackson and myself having each a bed in the same large room. After we had retired, I amused him by telling him of the various opinions I had heard during the day, from the citizens, in reference to our destination. When I got through, he asked in his own quick, sharp way, 'Do any of them say I am going to Washington?' " [1]

The next morning, in high spirits,[2] Jackson rode on to Mechum River, nine miles West of Charlottesville, and there climbed aboard the postal car of a troop train bound eastward. By the time he reached Charlottesville, he was deep in the details of preparation for the next great adventure.[3] As the wheels of the train wailed on their way toward Richmond, a candid student who wished to learn the lessons that every campaign teaches of the art of war might well have asked five questions of the silent

[1] *Hotchkiss' MS. Diary*, p. 53.
[2] *Ibid.*

[3] *Cf.* Boteler, in 42 *S. H. S. P.*, 174-76.

General in the postal car. The student would not have received an answer, but he would have been prepared, in a measure, for what was soon to happen in the woods and swamps of the Chickahominy.

First among the questions raised by the Valley Campaign was one asked already in these pages [4] and, in part, answered adversely: Was Jackson's artillery well handled on May 23 at Front Royal? Jackson's Chief of Artillery, Col. Stapleton Crutchfield, had not made a proper study of the Army's equipment. Crutchfield did not know, as he ordered forward the artillery, that in the whole of Ewell's Division there were, of rifled guns, three only. The first battery that arrived at Front Royal in answer to Crutchfield's summons had none of these pieces; the next battery had one. Before long-range fire in any volume could be opened, the retreating Federals were gone completely. Colonel Crutchfield, frankly admitting that the Confederate guns were "badly served and did no execution," excused his lack of familiarity with Ewell's batteries on the ground that they had not joined until "a day or so" previously. He might have added that he himself had not assumed his duties until May 16. On that date Jackson had placed under arrest his previous Chief of Artillery, who had been accused of "drunkenness on duty and extreme insubordination." [5] Crutchfield had commanded the guns temporarily during a brief previous period of like difficulty for his predecessor,[6] but he was not permanently in charge until a week before the attack on Front Royal. Although that fact extenuates, it does not excuse. The indictment has to stand: in a situation where rifled guns might be required, no effort had been made to see that equipment of this type was close to the head of the column. To this bit of negligence was due, in large part, the escape of the small Federal garrison at Front Royal.[7] Who was to blame—Jackson, or Crutchfield, or both?

A second question arises over the delay in the movement of Jackson's Army on May 24 from Cedarville to Middletown. The statement has been made that the advance began early but encountered resistance which prolonged for hours a march of

[4] See *supra*, p. 379.
[5] *Jackson's MS. Letter Book*, May 16, 1862, p. 38.
[6] G. O., 38, series of 1862, Valley District, *Jackson's MS. Order Book*.
[7] For Crutchfield's statement, see *O. R.*, 12, pt. 1, p. 725.

seven miles. Available evidence does not sustain this assertion.[8] Jackson did not make an early start for Middletown, but when he got under way, he did not take more time for the march than was to be expected on a narrow road through a rolling country. Early that morning, Jackson had no definite information concerning the movement of the Federals. Apparently, Jackson thought the probabilities favored a retreat by Banks on Winchester. For that reason he sent "Maryland" Steuart and two regiments of cavalry to reconnoiter in force the Valley Pike around Newtown.

Pending report from Steuart or from some of Ashby's outposts, Jackson could do one of three things: he could remain at Cedarville; he could march straight up the Front Royal road toward Winchester in an effort to get there before Banks did; or he could attempt to strike Banks on the march. Jackson seems to have decided, at the outset, on the second of these courses, but after he reached Nineveh he appears to have reasoned that, if he continued to move directly on Winchester, Banks might discover that he had uncovered Front Royal and might then strike out, across his rear, for Chester Gap and Manassas. Accordingly, Jackson left Ewell himself at Nineveh and, with part of Ewell's Division, countermarched to Cedarville.

As the road was poor,[9] and both rain and hail were falling,[10] the return to Cedarville must have been slow. When Jackson arrived there, probably about 9 A.M., he still had no news of

[8] Henderson wrote, op. cit., I, 329, that the 29th Pennsylvania Infantry and then the 1st Maine Cavalry and a squadron of the 1st Vermont opposed Taylor's advance in terrain which, said Henderson, "was almost a continuous forest; and wood-fighting is very slow fighting." On the contrary, Capt. S. M. Zulich, commanding the 29th Pennsylvania, after mentioning his orders to hold the road from Front Royal to Middletown, merely reported: "We advanced along that road . . . a distance of 4 miles. Ascertaining that the enemy were in force in that direction we turned back, and were stationed in the vicinity of Middletown" (O. R., 12, pt. 1, p. 623). The regiment manifestly was not engaged with the Confederates who were advancing from Cedarville. Reports of Lt. Col. C. S. Douty, 1st Maine Cav. (O. R., 12, pt. 1, pp. 575–77), and Maj. W. D. Collins, 1st Vt. Cav. (ibid., 587 ff.), show that these two commands did no more than maintain hesitant, long-range contact with the advancing Confederates. Dabney, op. cit., 371, mentioned no material delay on the march and dwelt, with satisfaction, on a charge by field artillery, which of course would have been impossible in the face of substantial opposition. Avirett, op. cit., 193, referred to nothing more than "some skirmishing."

[9] Hotchkiss noted in his MS. Sketchbook, p. 42, that on part of this road the planking was "used up" and that what was left was "merely a dirt road—badly cut up—clayey and sandy." While Hotchkiss' sketch ended at the junction of the Newtown road and did not cover the section between Nineveh and Cedarville, there is no reason to assume that stretch better than those North of it.

[10] Hotchkiss' MS. Diary, p. 37.

Banks's movements, and he sent out his topographer, Jed. Hotchkiss, to ascertain, if possible, where the enemy was. Hotchkiss soon reported that the Federals were operating close to Cedarville. On the basis of that information, Jackson dispatched Ashby toward Middletown with artillery and infantry support and ordered the greater part of the Army to follow. After this movement along the Chapel road to Middletown had begun, a report was received by Jackson from "Maryland" Steuart, but it was not specific. The indications, said the cavalry commander, were that Banks was preparing to leave Strasburg—that and no more.[11] Ere this, the forces that Hotchkiss had seen on his scout had disappeared. Jackson continued "in the dark." Except for the fact that Federal forces in small number were observed on the Chapel road, he did not know precisely what the Union Army was doing until he struck the wagon train at Middletown.

If this is a correct statement of a situation concerning which information is far from adequate,[12] then criticism of Jackson's own generalship on the morning of May 24 must rest on whether his start for Winchester up the Front Royal road, and his halt for fear Banks might cross his rear, was a movement based on poor judgment. The answer may be wholly a matter of opinion, but when the paucity and vagueness of his information are taken into account, Jackson's initial movement of the day is defensible. Perhaps there is some justification for saying that a march across his rear was a move more daring than Jackson should have credited to an adversary of Banks's temperament. In framing such an opinion, there is danger that Banks will be judged by what the entire campaign revealed concerning his temperament, rather than by what Jackson could have known of him at this stage of operations.

The question, then, may take a different form. Banks's wagon train had started northward "before daylight,"[13] that is to say, by 4.30.[14] None of the infantry left Strasburg until after 9

---

[11] Jackson, in *O. R.*, 12, pt. 1, p. 703. Dabney, *loc. cit.*, 371, erroneously said that Steuart "found evident signs of a general retreat upon Winchester." This statement seems to have misled several writers on the campaign.

[12] The evidence in support of the views here expressed, which are contrary to those of Dabney and Henderson, is set forth in Appendix VI.

[13] *O. R.*, 12, pt. 1, p. 594.

[14] Sunrise on May 24 was at 4.53.

o'clock.[15] Admitting that Jackson could not have hoped to hear of this infantry movement until nearly noon, should he have been given earlier notice of the wagon train? Were his outposts negligent? Here, again, informed opinion may differ. The country between Strasburg and Cedarville is one of many confusing small roads that had not been mapped.[16] Ashby himself, the inspiration of his force, was not on reconnaissance duty but was at Army headquarters. Some of his best company commanders were on remote detached service; two of the best of them had been killed the previous day.[17] At the time, Ashby's limited force may have been disorganized and incapable of average service.

Could the same excuse be made for "Maryland" Steuart? The evidence seems to indicate, though it is not conclusive, that his march for the Valley Pike was begun early in the morning. From Nineveh to Newtown he had an unmistakable road, and he had troops sufficient not only for scouting but also for reconnaissance in force. If he reached Newtown as soon as there is reason to believe he did, and if he found no enemy there and no report from the natives of any movement along the road, would it not have been reasonable for him to reconnoiter southward? Had he done so, would he not speedily have established contact with Banks's wagon train? It seldom is safe to pass judgment on military officers when their reports cannot be studied. Nor is it ever proper to assume perfect performance by raw cavalrymen operating in strange country. The doubt persists whether Jackson was as well served by Steuart as he should have been.

To sum up the question raised by Jackson's march of May 24, every critic will admit, as a matter of course, that the Confederate commander lost an opportunity by not reaching Middletown sooner. Had he caught Banks's infantry on the march, he might have destroyed his adversary. At the least Jackson would have had more time for the pursuit. Beyond that, all one may say

15 Gen. A. S. Williams, who was in immediate command of the infantry Division, stated that the march began "about 10 A.M." (*O. R.*, 12, pt. 1, p. 595). General Banks (*ibid.*, 547) gave the time as "soon after 9." Col. Geo. H. Gordon, whose Brigade was second in the column, reported (*ibid.*, 614) that he left at 10 o'clock.

16 On Hotchkiss' original large map of the Valley, 1–80,000, made during the war and subsequently revised, part of the area between the Valley Pike and the Winchester-Front Royal highway carries the legend "Unexplored." The only road depicted is that from Cedarville to Middletown.

17 John Fletcher and Geo. F. Sheetz. *O. R.*, 12, pt. 1, p. 703.

with certainty is that Jackson had to deal with several contingencies at a time when, for reasons adequate or inadequate, he could not procure prompt and accurate information of the enemy's movements. Perhaps the situation was such that Banks inevitably could steal half a day's march on Jackson. Unsatisfactory as is this conclusion, any other carries the critic into the realm of speculation where the evidence is and probably will remain obscure.

Whatever the restraints that justice imposes in reviewing the operations of Jackson's cavalry in the early morning of May 24, the third question is more inclusive: was or was not the cavalry efficient during the campaign? Recapitulation of the facts must precede the answer. On the 24th, there were charges that some of the cavalry abandoned the pursuit in order to plunder wagons. Apart from all question of intelligence reports, "Maryland" Steuart certainly made a poor showing that day for the number of sabers he had at his command. The next day he refused to obey verbal orders direct from headquarters to drive the defeated enemy, and he would not move till Ewell approved. On June 1 and 2, stampedes and mismanagement so outraged the commanders of the Second and Sixth Virginia Cavalry that they went to the extreme of pleading that they be taken from Steuart and placed under Ashby. The conduct of outposts on several occasions was shameful. More fundamentally, the campaign was marred by failure to employ in strength a force which, if united and well led, could have capitalized all the gains the infantry made by much hard marching and gallant fighting.

Against all this may be set down many admirable achievements. Ashby was invaluable in covering the Confederate right at Kernstown. His handling of the cavalry on the afternoon of May 23, aflank the Massanuttons, left nothing to be desired; the charges near Cedarville that afternoon were vigorous; in all the retreats, those rearguard actions fought under Ashby's own eyes were models of what a few hundred courageous cavalry, supported by horse artillery, could do to delay a pursuer. Wherever Ashby himself was engaged, there was brilliance; elsewhere, the handling of the mounted forces during the campaign leaves the critic convinced that something was wrong.

What was it? For one thing, of course, many of the soldiers

of the Second and Sixth Virginia were green; for another, the system that required cavalrymen to supply their own mounts tempted many of Ashby's troopers who lived near the scenes of action to slip off and to take captured horses home so that they would have reserve animals. These conditions could have been corrected or controlled, in large part, had the cavalry been organized properly. It was not. Ashby lacked nothing in devotion but, it must be repeated,[18] he was essentially a combat officer and not an administrator. The evidence does not show how highly he cherished the authorization given him by the War Department to organize a separate and, as he believed, an independent force. If he insisted on his "rights" in this respect, the basic mistake was in the grant of special privileges that became "rights." Here, probably, as in the order to recall Loring from Romney, and in the ceaseless irritation to which "Joe" Johnston was subjected, the first fault must be laid at the door of Secretary Benjamin. He it was who permitted Ashby to build up a separate force.

How far was Jackson to be blamed for permitting this organization to become so highly personal to Ashby that it was unwieldy and ineffective? Jackson realized in April, and perhaps earlier, that the cavalry was undisciplined and could not be handled as if it were a single regiment. He sought to change this, but, when faeed with Ashby's resignation, he cancelled the orders. In Major Harman's words, he "backed down." Had the situation been one in which the personality of Ashby had not counted so heavily, Jackson of course would have followed his disciplinary training and would have placed the cavalry under some one else. As it was, the explanation he gave to headquarters was as comprehensive as it was candid: he believed that if he relieved Ashby the "influence" of that officer "would be thrown against" him and that the cavalry would be even less efficient. Where Jackson had to deal with hundreds of vigorous individualists who almost worshiped Ashby, the commanding General may have been prudent in avoiding an immediate test of strength, but the price he had to pay was a heavy one. At no time during the campaign, if Ashby chanced to be absent, was Jackson able to count on the cavalry as he could, for example, on Taylor's or on Winder's infantry. When he cried at Winchester, "Oh, that

18 See *supra*, p. 324.

my cavalry were in place!" he was admitting a failure that was not confined to one field.

What were the specific shortcomings of the cavalry on the critical days of the campaign, especially May 24 and 25, when Jackson had a reasonable chance of destroying Banks's little army? In general, the men close to Ashby denied the charge that he was a poor administrator. Preston Chew, who commanded Ashby's famous battery and later headed all the horse artillery of the Army of Northern Virginia, said deliberately: "[Ashby] could always command more men for duty from the same musterrolls than any other cavalry commander under whom I have since served." [19] Chaplain Avirett insisted, in effect, that the weakness of the cavalry on May 24–25 was the result of detachments and not poor organization or of negligent administration. Ten companies, he explained, had been sent to watch Frémont, and most of them had been left at the gaps of the Alleghenies. Captain Myers, with from two to four companies, had been advanced down the Valley Pike toward Strasburg for what was admitted to have been a successful demonstration against Banks. One other of Ashby's companies had been detached East of Front Royal, two had been held at that town to help in guarding stores and prisoners; still another company was on a scout in the direction of Strasburg. As a result, Ashby had a much reduced force for co-operation with Jackson. One estimate [20] puts the number available for service on the Valley Pike, during the pursuit on the afternoon of the 24th, as low as 100. Chew stated that the attack at Newtown was made with not more than forty sabers. [21]

If these estimates even approximate the reality, the criticism obviously ceases to be one of what Ashby's cavalry achieved and becomes the more serious one of an imprudent dispersal of force on the eve of an important action. The only possible excuse for scattering Ashby's men would be the presence with Jackson of the two cavalry regiments under Steuart.

The personality of "Maryland" Steuart thus has much bearing on the events of May 24–25. Steuart was not, like Ashby, a Vir-

---

[19] *Avirett*, 272. [20] That of Lt. J. H. Williams, Chew's Battery, *Avirett*, 198.
[21] *Avirett*, 198, 270. For Myers's activities South of Strasburg, see *ibid.*, 364, where the statement is made that he had two companies there. Avirett himself, *ibid.*, 198, put the number of Myers's companies as four.

ginian of the Valley, reared to follow his own code of independence; he was a professional soldier who for thirteen years had been in the cavalry of the United States Army and, for the greater part of that time, had served against the Indians on the frontier. Previously, for two years he had been with Jackson at West Point. Between them, so far as the records show, there had been no bad blood. Certainly there had been no protest on Jackson's part when Steuart had been assigned to duty with him. On the contrary, Steuart had been introduced to the Army with something of a flourish as "one of Maryland's gifted sons" to whom the men of that State should rally.[22]

Of the reasons for Steuart's refusal to advance on the 25th, until he received direct orders from Ewell, existing records give no hint. The natural assumption, of course, is that he was the type of soldier, trained to the absolute letter of printed regulations, who insists, no matter how dire the emergency, that every order come "through channels." When Steuart's scant achievement on the 24th is judged alongside his poor handling of his troopers on the retreat from Strasburg, June 1–2, it is difficult to escape the conclusion that his experience as a Captain of cavalry had not qualified him for higher command of that arm. As head of two regiments, plus part of Ashby's force, he still was a Captain. He will appear again, and in circumstances which leave no doubt that, whatever the explanation of his failure with Jackson, it was not lack of courage.[23]

This long review prepares the way for an answer to the underlying third question of campaign: was the cavalry efficient during the operations from Front Royal to Port Republic? No. With the fullest credit for the many daring and dazzling acts of Ashby and a few of his men, the cavalry failed to achieve maximum results because it was organized in a manner that Jackson knew to be defective but did not feel himself justified at the moment in revising. The cavalry did less than it should because, in the second place, Ashby scattered his command too widely at the critical juncture, and thereby left to Steuart a task which this officer did not discharge with competence and co-operation.

Jackson promptly transferred the cavalry to Ashby after the

[22] O. R.. 12, pt. 3, p. 897; cf. *supra*, p. 369, n. 25.   [23] See *infra*, Vol. III.

Colonels of two regiments protested that the troops had been mismanaged by Steuart, but in his official report on the Battle of Winchester, Jackson contented himself with appending to his own narrative his staff officer's account of Steuart's refusal to accept orders. No charges were preferred against Steuart. Why was that so? Was it because he had been wounded at Cross Keys? So many instances were there of sternest discipline on Jackson's part that a fourth broad question arises: as an autonomous army commander, was Jackson wise and successful in his handling of his officers? Here, again, the answer must be in the negative. Jackson sought to bring Loring to court-martial; he followed a similar course with Colonel Gilham, one of his colleagues at Virginia Military Institute; he protested against the return of Taliaferro to command; he put his Chief of Artillery under arrest; he visited like punishment on "Dick" Garnett after Kernstown; he provoked the tender of Winder's resignation; he forced Colonel Conner to resign; as will appear in due course, he was to prefer charges against the first Major General, Ewell excepted, who was to be assigned to him when, in July, he was to resume semi-independent command. That was a bad record, an indictment of many counts. Along with these examples of sternness, not to say of severity, the outcome of the clash with Ashby and Jackson's failure to take any action against Steuart appear in curious contrast.

Although the explanation must not be stated as more than a theory, it would seem to be simple: Jackson was a stiff disciplinarian, and he always followed that bent unless he believed the Southern cause would suffer worse by the imposition of discipline than by the neglect of it. This tacit policy accounts, by his own admission, for his treatment of Ashby, and probably for his leniency toward Steuart. To the fullest, Jackson shared in the desire of his government to enlist Marylanders and to bring their State into the Confederacy. As a Maryland soldier of standing, Steuart was expected to have large influence. Recruitment was to be one of his principal duties. Manifestly, if Steuart were arrested as a failure, or were censured publicly for his refusal to obey orders, there was danger that Marylanders of Southern sympathy would be disillusioned and perhaps would be resentful.

Considerations of policy outweighed personalities. Where these considerations did not appear, Jackson's rule was to hold his officers to the most rigid standards of military conduct.

In the employment of these officers and of their commands, did Jackson display in the Valley Campaign any eminent tactical ability? That is the fifth question to be answered. In his first independent battle, that of Kernstown, his aim was to demonstrate on his right, to hold on the center and, on his left, to turn the enemy's flank. The action at McDowell was, tactically, simple repulse and pursuit. On May 23, at Front Royal, Jackson's superiority of force was so overwhelming that his principal task was that of expediting the chase. In the Battle of Winchester, he advanced his center and then turned the Federal flank as he vainly had attempted to do at Kernstown. When the Army stood at Cross Keys, where Ewell rather than Jackson directed the battle, the Confederate position was so strong and the Federal advance so feeble that some observers were inclined to regard the affair as no more than a skirmish.[24] Finally, in the action of the 9th at Port Republic, Jackson's ambition to achieve a double victory led him to attack before he had sufficient force on the field. When Jackson discovered the strength of the Federal position on the coaling—a position that completely dominated his field of advance—he repeated his flank tactics and, by Taylor's successful attack, drove the enemy northward. This was, on Jackson's part, a poorly managed battle. To lose approximately 815 men in driving an enemy who had 3000 muskets, when Jackson himself had at least 8000 troops close at hand, was not a distinguished achievement.

Taken as a whole, Jackson's infantry tactics in the Valley Campaign have, for these reasons, to be written down as commonplace. Tactically, the battles were lifted above the level of mediocrity by nothing save an intelligent effort to co-ordinate the three arms of the service. That effort did not always succeed. As respects the cavalry, in the advance, it twice failed—at Middletown and at Winchester. Despite these failures, Jackson cannot be denied credit for a sound theory of co-ordination. At a time when many other commanders were fumbling with their artil-

[24] While Col. Charles J. Faulkner was preparing Jackson's reports in April, 1863, this was much discussed. The conclusion was that the action at Cross Keys was more important than it had appeared to be (*Hotchkiss' MS. Diary*, 163).

lery and were using their cavalry for little more than outpost duty, Jackson was striving to weld all three arms into an effective machine. To illustrate this would be to repeat the narrative of virtually all the actions of the campaign. It is no more than justice to add that the admirable tactical combination of horse artillery and of cavalry, displayed so often during May, was the conception of Ashby and not of Jackson.

If then, the answers be summarized to the five major questions that arise of the generalship in the Valley of the quiet man who was riding in the postal car on the way to Richmond, he or his Chief of Artillery could be charged undeniably with failure to provide in advance for the proper concentration of his batteries at Front Royal. Less certainly, Jackson may be blamable for a slow decision on the difficult military problem presented him on the morning of May 24. It should be said of him, in the third place, that, for reasons which he deemed compelling, he had not organized his cavalry properly. Fourth, he had encountered more than the average tactful commander's due difficulties with his subordinates. Finally, while laboring to co-ordinate his infantry, his artillery and his cavalry, he had not risen above routine infantry tactics.

Left at this, appraisal of Jackson the soldier, as he was in mid-June, 1862, would be negative and unfair. It would ignore three superior qualities which, though perhaps not discernible at the moment or even developed, were the marks of a great captain.

The first of these was Jackson's quick and sure sense of position. For military geography, in its larger aspects, or even for fashioning an accurate mental picture of ground he had not seen, Jackson had shown no special aptitude. In planning to bring Ewell across the Blue Ridge, he had been slow to get a grasp of the passes. He had confused Swift Run Gap with Fisher's. Instead of reaching a swift, inspired decision, as has been assumed, that Conrad's Store was his strategic point of concentration in the retreat before Banks after Kernstown, he had reached that conclusion with much awkwardness and at the expense of the legs of Ewell's men. Similarly, though Jackson had passed Port Republic at the end of April, on his way to join Edward Johnson, his memory of the rivers and roads seems to have been so confused that Hotchkiss had to give him three lessons in a single day before he convinced himself that he knew the terrain. Jackson's insistent demand for maps may have indicated a consciousness of special personal need as surely as it reflected the thorough, professional study of the trained soldier.

Once Jackson learned the geography of an area, his interpretation of it was strategical; and when he came to a field of battle, his sense of position was sure, unhesitating and quickly displayed. The miserable night march of May 24 he imposed on exhausted troops because he knew the ground around Winchester and had determined that Banks should not be allowed to hold the ridge North of Abraham's Creek. After the battle opened there, one glance at the Federal column moving for the stone wall on his left seems to have sufficed: that position must be taken immediately. On the retreat up the Valley, though Jackson seldom had to deploy his infantry, he chose excellent positions. At Port Republic, where the military value of the Lewiston coal hearth was manifest to every eye, he saw swiftly how it could be turned. His orders to Taylor and to Hotchkiss [25] were as assured as they were terse.

Jackson demonstrated, secondly, a pronounced strategic sense, the components of which were secrecy and consequent surprise, superiority of force and sound logistics. The interworking of the three was fascinating. First of all, Jackson reasoned that his adversaries must not know what he intended to do. In order to make sure that his opponents did not discover his plans, nobody must be aware of them. During the Romney campaign he did not even tell his bedfellow and fellow townsman, Col. J. L. T. Preston, what he was undertaking, though the two were bound by the closest ties.[26] Major Harman and others might grumble that Jackson was secretive; but the results justified all the precautions the General took. Never did he begin an important march until he had stopped, as far as practicable, all communication between his lines and those of the Federals. When he started for Front Royal on May 21, Ewell across the mountain was the only human beside himself who knew his objective. The march from Cedarville to Middletown was unannounced; Jackson's plan of striking Shields and Frémont the same day was not revealed until

[25] See *supra*, p. 455. [26] *Hotchkiss' MS. Diary*, 155.

the night before the Battle of Port Republic and then, apparently, to none except the commander who immediately faced Frémont. Even Winder did not know whither he was bound on the morning of June 9 until after his van had forded South River.

Secrecy made surprise possible. In capitalizing surprise or in the development of plans that could not be concealed, Jackson sought always to employ superior force. No suggestion was there at any stage of the campaign that he relied primarily on the much-vaunted individual superiority of the Southern soldier, though he believed his men much the better fighters. The superiority that Jackson sought always was that of numbers. He attacked at Kernstown primarily because he believed he had to deal with little more than a rearguard. Admonished by his repulse there, he labored for weeks to raise his Army to an effective strength equal to that which he credited to his opponent. When he took the offensive, it was in the determination that he would throw against Banks every man he could bring up. At the end of May, when he had to face the prospect that he might lose superiority of force because two Federal armies were closing in on him and a third was making ready to pursue, he did not hesitate to make the most rapid retreat his men could endure. In the last phase of the operations, his manœuvres were designed, of course, to prevent the junction of Frémont and Shields in order that he might assail them separately with numbers they could not resist.

In order to strike with more men than his adversary could assemble to oppose him on a given field at a given moment, Jackson relied in large part on logistics. Although he never so phrased it, he applied the maxim soon to be associated with Nathan Bedford Forrest—"to get there first with most men." Jackson's appreciation of swift, well-timed movement was shown before the campaign opened. His regulations for the march [27] were familiar in content but novel in rigid application. "Close up, men, close up" was almost the epitome of his system. He saw to it that officers rode ceaselessly up and down the column to keep it in steady motion.

At the outset, this practice did not seem to have especial effect. If Taylor was correct in saying he covered twenty-six miles on

27 See *supra*, p. 370.

May 20,[28] then he, and not the Stonewall Brigade, first set the pace. Thereafter, no march of special distinction was recorded until June 1. That day, when Winder had to press his men to the absolute limit in order to reach Strasburg, he fortunately could use the macadamized Valley Pike for nearly the whole of his march. The Second Virginia made thirty-six miles;[29] the other regiments probably averaged thirty miles. In a single participial phrase of a two-sentence paragraph of his report, Jackson noted this fine feat,[30] but he probably never forgot the distance. What once had been done by his men, under immense strain, he regarded as attainable again. Although on his later marches Jackson seldom had a Valley Pike, he always marched as if the worst road presented no more difficulties than did the thoroughfare along the Shenandoah.

Exacting as were some of Jackson's marches in March–June, 1862, all except two of them were admirably timed. On March 23 he had to open the fight at Kernstown late in the day because bad marching had brought him during the afternoon to a position where he was visible to the enemy. Jackson's only other bad logistics were those of May 24, which necessitated the hideous night march toward Winchester. In every other movement, his marches brought him into action with sufficient daylight to exploit any advantage he gained. Similarly, though the calculation was close, every regiment passed Strasburg on June 1.

This soldierly combination of secrecy, superiority of force and excellent logistics contributed to the third notable characteristic of the campaign, namely, the employment of the initiative in such a fashion as to strip his adversary of alternatives. In the forenoon of the unhappy 24th of May, as has been explained, it was impossible for Jackson to limit Banks to a single course that could be foreseen and countered. At every other stage of the campaign, Jackson's strategic system so completely gave him the initiative that he could impose his will and dictate his opponent's action. In the little engagement at Front Royal, the Federals of course could do nothing but offer their best resistance to a surprise attack in great force. After Banks made his choice the next day and decided he would retreat on Winchester, Jackson

---

[28] See *supra*, pp. 366–67.   [29] *O. R.*, 12, pt. 1, p. 708.

[30] "Toward evening, Winder arrived, part of his Brigade (the Second Virginia Regiment) having in one day marched 36 miles." *Ibid.*

left him no alternative. Banks had to continue his retreat and then, closely pursued, to give battle at Winchester.

Even after advantage shifted and Jackson himself had to retreat, he interposed where he could compel Frémont to attack. Shields's choice, which was fight or run, was forced upon the Federal commander. When the battle of June 9 had been concluded, Jackson left Frémont on the hill overlooking the confluence of North and South Rivers—as helpless as if the action of the morning had been a hundred miles away. Jackson may have known—as he subsequently demonstrated—that he was not particularly apt in guessing what his antagonist would do. He used his strategic weapons to carry the problem beyond the realm of guesswork and to leave his opponent only one course of action, the course for which he was prepared.

For these three reasons—judgment of ground, a sound balance of strategy, and the employment of that strategy to impose his will on his adversary—the Valley campaign of "Stonewall" Jackson marked him as a soldier of the highest promise.

Immediately, the basis of his success was less considered than the results. With a force that never had exceeded, if indeed it reached, 17,000 men of all arms, he had cleared the enemy from the greater part of the Shenandoah. What was far more important, he had used this small force so effectively that he had forced President Lincoln to change the entire plan for the capture of Richmond. At a time when the junction of McDowell with McClellan would have rendered the defense of the Confederate capital almost hopeless, Jackson temporarily had paralyzed the advance of close to 40,000 Federal troops. Rarely in war had so few infantry achieved such dazzling strategic results.

"Stonewall's" victories had come, moreover, when they inspirited a discouraged Confederacy. Press and people did not know, and would not have responded differently had they known, that the larger strategic plan was Lee's, not Jackson's. What the South saw of the outcome was enough. Through a long and losing defensive, the Confederacy had seen its leaders killed and its territory overrun. Albert Sidney Johnston was dead; Beauregard's star was low in the West; "Joe" Johnston lay wounded in Richmond after a battle that many knew to have been mismanaged; Lee was in the public eye an administrator, a theorist, an engineer and not a field commander. None of these had undertaken the offensive for which editors and politicians had been pleading until Jackson had struck. Now men's eyes lighted and their hearts beat up when they mentioned him. He was a mystery, a phenomenon, perhaps a genius, but he was the living vindication of the argument for the offensive; he was the hope of the South.

So, according to their literacy and knowledge, each shaping his tribute in his own vernacular, thought the men who crowded the trains that were rumbling down the Virginia Central toward Richmond. Jackson had marched them till their legs ached; Jackson had shown them no mercy; but Jackson had won battles! The soldiers did not cease to regard him as crazy, but they looked at him with wondering eye. He no longer was "Old Blue Light"; he was not often "Stonewall." They called him "Old Jack" in a strange, affectionate awe. His ranking officers were less warm toward him, though some of them shared, after a fashion, the soldiers' awe of him. In colder estimation and larger knowledge of what had been done and what omitted, most of his Brigadiers thought him, above all, lucky. The night before the Army started for Richmond, four of Jackson's general officers were talking of the campaign. Their conclusion McHenry Howard thus reported: ". . . all were of the opinion that Jackson could not continue to take such risks without at some time meeting with a great disaster. They dwelt particularly on the situation in which he put himself when near Harpers Ferry with two armies closing in forty miles in his rear and his wonderful escape." [31]

Some of the men who thus criticized the pursuit to the Potomac were winning the right to speak with a measure of authority. In all the battles he had shared, Winder had been conspicuous for sound judgment and swift, courageous leading. His daring after the occupation of Winchester, in the opinion of at least one of his staff officers, had disposed Jackson favorably to him for the first time. At Port Republic, Winder masterfully had handled his Brigade. His advancement in the Army seemed certain, and appeared to be acceptable to all the officers of Jackson's Division, though "Stonewall" himself made no move to procure the nomination of another Major General. [32] If Winder felt any

[31] McHenry Howard, 130.   [32] McHenry Howard, 114, 128, 134.

soreness over this, or over Jackson's refusal to grant him leave after Port Republic, this did not interfere with his performance. Taylor's record in the campaign fully equalled Winder's. There was, moreover, a certain emotional quality in Taylor's personal affection for Jackson and in his admitted superstition concerning "Old Jack." When his chief was concerned, Taylor put aside his own self-confidence and his critical intellectuality.

The performances of Trimble and of Elzey at Cross Keys spoke for themselves. The action of June 8 was unique in that the three Brigades most conspicuous on the field—and Winder's which had held the rear against Shields—were commanded by Marylanders.[33] For the Maryland troops and especially for Trimble and Elzey, the generous Ewell had high praise in his report. Of Elzey, this was said: ". . . the credit of selecting the position is due to General Elzey. I availed myself frequently during the action of that officer's counsel, profiting largely by his known military skill and judgment."[34]

He who thus bestowed praise was of all Jackson's subordinates the man who most deserved it. Next to Jackson himself, Ewell stood out. He had co-operated wholeheartedly with the "wagon-hunter" he had denounced as "an old fool." Every act of "Dick" Ewell's in the campaign had been at the standard of a competent, alert and courageous lieutenant. At Port Republic, he thus appeared in the eyes of a youthful Confederate: "He is a gallant officer. I could but notice his coolness in leading us in a charge against the batteries. A shell exploding under his horse he did not even look to see the effect but with his eyes fixed . . . on the piece before him moved steadily on. The men are willing to follow him. His horse being killed he mounted a wagon horse with a blind bridle and followed the retreating enemy."[35]

Nor was Ewell above acknowledging his previous errors in appraising his comrades in arms. What his eyes had seen, his lips would confess. The night after Port Republic, he had made the *amende honorable* in his own piping voice.

"Look here, Munford," he had said to the cavalry commander,

---

33 The other Brigade, besides Trimble's and Elzey's, was George H. Steuart's.
34 *O. R.*, 12, pt. 1, p. 782.
35 Diary of Captain H. W. Wingfield, in *Bulletin of Virginia State Library*, July, 1927 (cited hereafter as *Wingfield*). 12.

"do you remember a conversation we had one day at Conrad's Store?"

"To what do you allude?"

"Why, to old Trimble, to General Jackson and that other fellow, Colonel Kirkland of North Carolina."

"Very well," Munford admitted.

"I take it all back," said Ewell, "and will never prejudge another man. Old Jackson is no fool; he knows how to keep his own counsel, and does curious things; but he has method in his madness; he has disappointed me entirely." [36]

"Disappointed me entirely" . . . those were terms of high praise as Ewell jestingly used them; but, as Richmond whispered "Jackson's coming" and waited expectantly for his lightning attack to flash, there was something ominous in Ewell's choice of the word "disappointed."

[36] Munford, in 7 *S. H. S. P.*, 530. Ewell continued: "And old Trimble is a real trump; instead of being overcautious, he is as bold as any man, and, in fact, is the hero of yesterday's fight. Jackson was not on the field. They will call it mine, but Trimble won the fight; and I believe now if I had followed his views we would have destroyed Frémont's army. And Colonel Kirkland, of North Carolina, behaved as handsomely near Winchester as any man in our army, leading his regiment and taking a stone wall from the Yankees; he is a splendid fellow."

CHAPTER XXX

Jackson Marches to a Confusing Field

Jackson had done his utmost to keep his destination a complete secret. When Whiting, who had been his brilliant senior at West Point, had ridden to Port Republic and had asked for orders, Jackson merely had told him to go back to Staunton—twenty miles!—where a dispatch would be sent him the next day. Whiting had been furious: "I believe," he stormed, "[Jackson] has no more sense than my horse!" After Whiting got instructions to retrace his steps to Gordonsville, he broke out: "Didn't I tell you [Jackson] was a fool, and doesn't this prove it? Why, I just came through Gordonsville day before yesterday!" [1] Ewell had shown the utmost discretion throughout the operations along the Shenandoah and had kept the few secrets Jackson had entrusted to him; but at the beginning of the movement from the Valley, even "Old Bald Head" had received no directions except for a march to Charlottesville.[2] Major Harman, always curious to know whither the Army was going, had been given, in the utmost confidence, and as a special evidence of Jackson's regard, notice that the Army was going to that town. Dabney himself had not been informed of the General's plan until the head of the column reached Mechum River. Then Jackson took the Major into a room in the hotel, locked the door and explained that he intended to go on to Richmond and that Dabney must march the Army down the Virginia Central toward that city. Thereupon Jackson boarded the train and started eastward. Later that day, when Ewell and Dabney were dining together, Ewell complained with bitterness: "Here, now, the General has gone off on the railroad without intrusting to me, his senior Major General, any order, or any hint whither we are going; but Harman, his Quartermaster, enjoys his full confidence, I suppose, for I hear he is telling the troops that we are going to Richmond to fight McClellan."

Dabney had a soothing answer: "You may be certain, General Ewell, that you stand higher in General Jackson's confidence than

[1] 2 B. & L., 296–97.　　　　　[2] Dabney, 434.

any one else, as your rank and services entitle you to. As for
Major Harman, he has not heard a word more than others. If he
thinks that we are going to Richmond, it is only his surmise,
which I suppose every intelligent private is now making." [3]

In this atmosphere of curiosity and speculation, the march got
under way. The difficulties that attended the first stage did not
seem to be more than the normal vexations of a journey that had
to be made in part by road and in part by railway. Because the
Virginia Central Railroad had been cut by the destruction of the
long bridge over the South Anna River, Jackson had at his disposal only the rolling stock that chanced to be West of the stream
when Federal raiders had burned the crossing.[4]

Less than 200 small cars, most of them for freight, were available.[5] Jackson used these to handle his heaviest stores, as well as
his men; and after he unloaded a train, he sent it back to pick up
the troops farthest in rear.[6] This expedited the march, of course,
but, as the sidings of the single-tracked railway were few and
short,[7] congestion was serious. The wagons, the artillery and the
few cavalrymen whom Jackson had thought it safe to detach at
the outset from service in the Valley had to make the best of the
bad roads they traversed.

Vehicles made fair time in Albemarle County and into Orange,
though Jackson's staff officers had to contend with much carelessness on the part of the troops that were supposed to protect the
trains. Before Charlottesville was reached, Major Dabney met a
brigade wagon train far in advance of its guards, and, when he
rebuked the officer in command, he received the naïve reply: "I
just came along; I had no orders; I had no orders from anybody."
The outraged Assistant Adjutant General, hurrying on to Gordonsville, unexpectedly found Jackson there, and indignantly
reported what had occurred.

"General," he warned, "if this is the way officers are allowed to
behave, your army is going to sticks."

[3] 2 B. & L., 348–49.
[4] R. L. Dabney's Memorandum of Mch. 31, 1896, prepared for Col. G. F. R. Henderson. This document, of which Henderson used a small part only, will be cited hereafter as Dabney Memo. to distinguish it from the same author's life of Jackson. The
memorandum is in the Hotchkiss Papers.
[5] C. S. Anderson: "Train Running for the Confederacy." Locomotive Engineering,
August, 1892, p. 287.
[6] Dabney, 435.   [7] Cf. Appendix I, p. 683.

Jackson was more philosophical and actually smiled at Dabney's excitement: "Well, yes, these things are bad, of course, and my corps is not disciplined as I wish, but in the urgency of the campaign I have not had time to straighten out such people. My object now must be to get the corps at the place at the time for striking the blow, in such order as I may." [8]

Jackson might have added that already he was losing time in accomplishing that object. Instead of proceeding directly to Richmond, he had to wait at Gordonsville all of Saturday, June 21, because of a rumor that a Federal force was advancing from the Rapidan. Whiting's Division and Lawton's Brigade were moved on from Gordonsville late that day and during the night, but Ewell remained until the falsity of the rumor was established.[9] Jackson's Division closed on Ewell.

In the ranks of these troops, arrival and detrainment at Gordonsville fanned anew the curiosity concerning their objective. From Gordonsville led the railway and the road to Rapidan, to Culpeper and to Manassas: Did Jackson intend to follow that route and to launch a movement against Washington? Was the journey to continue down the Virginia Central Railroad till the Divisions were in easy marching distance of Fredericksburg? In spite of Major Harman's prediction, as quoted by Ewell, Richmond often in conversation was ruled out as a possible objective, on the ground that there would have been no sense in dispatching Whiting to the Valley if the Army were going to Richmond.[10] Jackson, of course, knew of this chatter. Now that he was starting eastward, with Richmond or Fredericksburg as his only possible objectives, he redoubled all his precautions to conceal his movement from the enemy. The cavalry were ordered toward the little station of Frederickshall on the Virginia Central, and were told that when they reached that part of Louisa, they must stop all travel by citizens.[11]

His personal movements Jackson guarded with superlative care,

[8] *Dabney Memo.*

[9] *Dabney,* 435. The Major stated that the whole Army was held at Gordonsville on June 21, but as he met Whiting's Division and Lawton's Brigade at Frederickshall the next morning, the facts must have been as stated in the text.

[10] *Worsham,* 97.

[11] *Dabney,* 435. This order may have been given on the 22d. There is no positive evidence in favor of either date.

and when he prepared to leave Gordonsville, just before sunset on the 21st, he decided to take only Major Dabney with him. All he said was: "Will you take a railroad ride with me? We will leave our horses and so forth, with the staff." Then he had a yard engine attached to a postal car and climbed aboard. Soon he was asleep in the mail clerk's bunk.[12]

After all these precautions, Jackson reasonably enough might have told himself that he had done all that a commanding General could to mystify both foe and friend; but he had failed. Not long after he left Gordonsville a private soldier slipped away also, a soldier who had a very definite suspicion of what Jackson intended to do.

Sunday morning, June 22, found Jackson at Frederickshall, twenty-six miles by rail East of Gordonsville. Whiting's Division and Lawton's Brigade were camped there or farther down the railroad toward Beaver Dam. To Jackson, it seemed proper that they and the Divisions to the rear should remain where they were until the Sabbath was ended. He intended to apply, as he always did when circumstance permitted, the principle he had explained at another time to Major Dabney: "The Sabbath is written in the constitution of man and horses as really as in the Bible: I can march my men farther in a week, marching six days and resting the seventh, and get through with my men and horses in better condition than if I marched them all seven days." [13]

At Nathaniel Harris's home the General himself spent a quiet, meditative Sunday morning. During the afternoon he attended religious service in Hood's Brigade. Dr. Dabney preached. The only known military business Jackson transacted that day was to arrange for a guide in the unfamiliar country ahead. A messenger was sent for Major Dabney's brother, Capt. C. W. Dabney, who had been Commonwealth's Attorney of Hanover and knew all the roads of the county.[14]

That evening, when Mrs. Harris asked Jackson when he wished breakfast the next morning, the General mildly told her to have the meal at her usual time and to call him when it was ready. By that hour he and Major Harman, with Mr. Harris and another native as guides, were far on the way to Richmond.[15] Hard riding

---

[12] Dabney Memo.   [13] Dabney Memo.   [14] Dabney Memo.

[15] 1 Henderson, 396; 2 R. E. Lee, 108, where the sources of this familiar incident in Jackson's career are cited in detail. As that of an eyewitness, Major Harman's

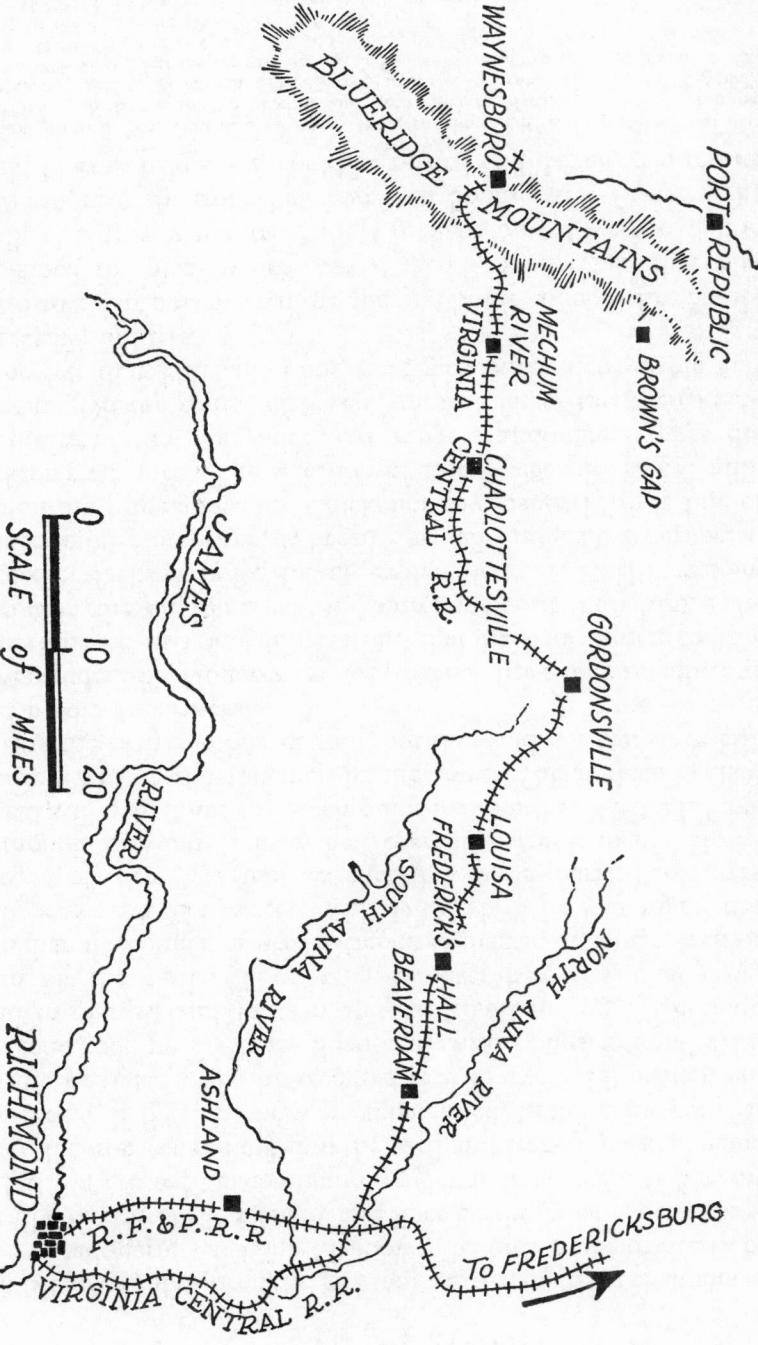

General Line of Jackson's Advance from the Shenandoah Valley to the Richmond Front, June, 1862

for fifty-two miles brought Jackson wearily in fourteen hours to Lee's headquarters at High Meadows, the little home of the Dabb family, in rear of the Confederate lines on the Nine Mile road.

Jackson greeted the commanding General and then, as Lee was busy, Jackson walked out into the yard and leaned heavily against the fence. If he felt lonely or embarrassed, nothing indicated it, but he was glad when he recognized as Harvey Hill a man who ere long rode up the lane. Soon came also Longstreet and A. P. Hill to discuss with Jackson and the commanding General the plan for the battle. The five men never before had sat down together at a council of war. Often at Manassas, of course, Jackson had been with Longstreet; with D. H. Hill he had many ties. Closest of them was the fact that they were married to sisters. Although Lee and Jackson had been in correspondence almost weekly, they had not seen each other for months. A. P. Hill and Jackson had served together in the lower Shenandoah Valley, during the early summer of 1861, but they had not met since Hill had become a General.

Magruder and Huger were not present. Lee's only reference to their absence was the indirect one that he had chosen for the operation the Divisions whose commanders sat with him. The choice of Jackson called for no explanation. A. P. Hill was included in the plan primarily because he had a large Division spread out on the ridge above the Chickahominy, parallel to the line of Jackson's advance. The selection of Longstreet and D. H. Hill, in preference to Magruder and Huger, undoubtedly was deliberate. On the record of Seven Pines, as far as Lee then knew it, he felt that Hill and Longstreet were alert, dependable and aggressive fighters.

No awkwardness marred the opening of the council. Lee briefly explained his plan, which was shaped [16] by the fact that McClellan's Army was astride the Chickahominy River on a line that ran roughly from Northwest to Southeast.[17] If the right flank, North of the river, could be turned and driven, two results

account, given to Jed. Hotchkiss in April, 1863, is followed here, in preference to that of Dabney, which was used by Henderson. According to Harman, he bought a horse for Jackson's ride to Richmond. The General instructed Harman to call him "Colonel" and not "General," lest his identity be revealed. Jackson came to the city, Harman said, via the Three Chopt road (*Hotchkiss' MS. Diary*, p. 161).

[16] All the details are given in 2 *R. E. Lee*, 110 ff.

[17] McClellan had taken that position, it will be recalled, to cover his line of supply, and to prepare for the long-expected, long-deferred junction with McDowell, who was to march down from Fredericksburg.

could be expected: First, McClellan's line of rail supply with the White House on the Pamunkey could be threatened and perhaps broken. It crossed the Chickahominy at Dispatch Station and had no near defense except that afforded by the Federal troops North of that stream. Second, if McClellan's right were hurled back, the Federal divisions South of the river would be compelled either to retreat or to come out of their entrenchments and to give battle.

The rough outlines of this general plan had been under discussion for some weeks between Davis and Lee. All the misgiving of the President was summarized in one question: Might not McClellan launch a counterattack on Richmond from the front South of the Chickahominy as soon as Lee assailed the Federals North of that river? Lee answered that he did not believe McClellan would attempt this. In the event that his adversary did, Lee reasoned that the Confederate forces which he intended to leave on the south side of the river could resist long enough for him to send troops back from the north side and to get in rear of the Unionists who were driving on Richmond.[18] D. H. Hill also had criticized the plan in conversation with Longstreet, who independently had proposed to Lee substantially the same idea Lee had submitted to Davis. In the judgment of Hill, an attack on McClellan's left, near White Oak Swamp, might serve a better purpose in that it would prevent McClellan from changing his base to James River.[19] If McClellan were assailed North of the Chickahominy, Hill reasoned, loss of communications with the White House simply would mean a transfer of base to the James.

Because all the members of the council, except Jackson, were familiar with the plan in general terms, Lee did not review it *in extenso*. He explained the dispatch of Whiting to the Valley, announced the approach of Jackson's command, and told how it would be employed to clear the bridges of the Chickahominy. This could be done in such a manner that, when the other troops moved to the attack on the north side of the river, they would not have to force a crossing under fire.[20] With this statement, Lee excused himself temporarily to transact some army business, and left his four subordinates to agree on the details.

Longstreet, as the senior, seems to have directed the discussion

[18] 2 *R. E. Lee*, 106, 110.   [19] *Longstreet*, 120; 2 *R. E. Lee*, 106, n. 10.
[20] D. H. Hill, in 2 *B. and L.*, 347.

that followed, a discussion of which regrettably little is known.[21] There is no record that Jackson ventured an opinion on a problem that concerned terrain and troop dispositions of which he knew nothing. If any question was raised, it was by D. H. Hill, who may have renewed his argument that an attack on McClellan's left might be more fruitful than the proposed movement against the Federal right.[22]

More in detail, the four Generals discussed how the attack should be made. Their conclusion was that Jackson should proceed from Frederickshall and take position Southeast of Ashland on the road to Hanover Court House.[23] Jackson was then to communicate to A. P. Hill his position. When Jackson moved south-

[21] The only first-hand accounts are those of Longstreet and of D. H. Hill, already cited. Both are brief and unsatisfactory.

[22] In 1 *Shotwell Papers*, 233–35, the author, R. A. Shotwell, stated that "one of the participants" in the conference—he could have meant only his later editorial associate, D. H. Hill—told him that Hill argued: "To my mind, the Yankee should be assailed on his left wing—striking in somewhere between Bottom's Bridge and Savage Station—where I am confident he has no fortifications that our men will not leap over, as they did the other day at Seven Pines. If we attack on this [south] side we can cut him off from his gunboats, and from the Peninsula[;] then where will he run? We shall take the whole of his camps and artillery, and destroy him entirely; whereas if we succeed in driving him from his heavy earth works across yonder on the heights, he will swing around on his gunboats or to the Pamunkey." In appraising this statement, it must be noted, first of all, that Shotwell often was inaccurate in his hastily written military narrative. Moreover, there was, in June, 1862, no Federal position "between Bottom's Bridge and Savage Station." The two places were more nearly perpendicular than parallel to the line of Confederate attack. Still again, except for the few gun emplacements visible from the south side of the Chickahominy, the Confederates on June 24 had no information of "heavy earth works across yonder on the heights." While these objections invalidate Shotwell's statement, the known independent thinking of D. H. Hill made it not improbable that he questioned the wisdom of the plan proposed on June 24 at the council of war. He must have been satisfied, in the end, because his published account of the conference on June 23 included no reference to any alternative proposal. (2 *B. & L.*, 347 ff) In a second article (*ibid.*, 383 ff), he praised Lee's decision on June 28 to return Longstreet and A. P. Hill to the south side of the Chickahominy and he explained: "McClellan could have retreated to Yorktown with as little loss as Johnston sustained on his retreat from it. The roads from Richmond to Yorktown lead through a wooded and swampy country, on which strong rearguards could have afforded perfect protection to a retreating column without bringing on a general engagement." This scarcely would have been written, even twenty years after the event, by a man who himself had argued that if McClellan were defeated on the south side of the Chickahominy, he could be destroyed. Finally, Gen. D. H. Hill's son, of the same name, in 2 *North Carolina in the War Between the States*, 101, described the conference of June 23 but did not intimate that Hill had made any objection to Lee's plan.

[23] Modern students of this campaign should remember that in 1862 the "Ashcake Road" was known also as the "Courthouse Road." It crossed the R. F. & P. Railroad about one mile South of Ashland, ran on a wide arc, via Peakes on the Virginia Central Railroad, to Dr. Price's and then turned Northwest again to the courthouse. That stretch of the road from Dr. Price's to Hanover Court House was, in reality, part of the road from Hanover Court House to New Castle Ferry. The other road from Ashland to Hanover Court House ran roughly Northeast to Wickham's Station and thence

ward early on the morning of the day after he passed Ashland, he was to notify General Branch. That officer was to be stationed at Half Sink on the Chickahominy, in liaison between Jackson and the remainder of A. P. Hill's Division, to which Branch belonged. On the arrival of messengers from Jackson, Branch was to start South. He was to take the nearest road parallel to the Chickahominy and East of it; Jackson was to be on the next road to the East, the second from the river. As soon as A. P. Hill saw that Jackson and Branch were moving southward on these roads, he was to cross the Chickahominy at Meadow Bridge and, turning to the right, was to proceed Southeast to Mechanicsville, near which the Federal right flank was supposed to rest. Jackson was to come in on Hill's left, East of Mechanicsville. The two Divisions then were to unite but were to take different roads to the Southeast and were to make for Cold Harbor, whence the way was open to McClellan's line of supply. Longstreet's Division was to cross the Chickahominy at Mechanicsville Bridge, which the march of Jackson and of A. P. Hill would clear of the enemy. Then Longstreet was to support A. P. Hill. By the same route and in the same manner, D. H. Hill was to support Jackson. If practicable, Longstreet and D. H. Hill were to follow different roads from those pursued by Jackson and A. P. Hill, but they were to remain close to the main columns of attack.[24] All of this was clear to the officers who had been around Richmond long enough to understand directions and routes. The plan readily may have been confusing to Jackson, who was not quick to grasp the geography of country he had not seen.

If the details were acceptable, when should the attack be delivered? That was the next question. Inasmuch as the other Divisions were within striking distance, the answer depended on Jackson. Perhaps in pride over the record of his troops for long, swift marches, but certainly in ignorance of the difference between the Valley Pike and Hanover roads, Jackson made a reckless answer: He could reach his destination on the Courthouse road the next day, June 24. The battle could be opened June 25. Longstreet had good reason to know the resistance that the roads of eastern Virginia offered to marching columns, and he suggested that Jackson well might allow himself another day. Jackson acqui-

[24] See note 34, *infra*

esced.[25] Soon thereafter, Lee re-entered the room. His lieutenants told him of their decision, which he approved. Written orders, he said, would be dispatched to each of them. About nightfall, the conference adjourned.[26]

Jackson left promptly and spent a second long and sleepless night on the road. When he reached the vicinity of Beaver Dam during the morning of June 24,[27] he found conditions far from satisfactory. Rain was falling steadily. The previous day there had been some precipitation along part of the watershed. Might a freshet be on the way? Would the streams rise past fording? That was not all. Jackson's faith in the versatility of ministers had not been vindicated in the case of Dr. Dabney. That gentleman had been successful as a staff officer in camp and, no doubt for that reason, had been left in general charge of the march; but he had been green at that work and now had been stricken with a violent intestinal malady,[28] which had forced him to go to bed. In Jackson's absence, the march had slowed down. Most of the wagons and artillery of the rear Divisions, in particular, had been delayed by reason of rains and consequent mud on the poor roads of Louisa County.[29] The column was extended over many miles. Jed. Hotchkiss was not at hand to ascertain the shortest and the least bad route. Jackson had sent the topographer back to the Valley to work on the detailed map of that region. With Hotchkiss away, Jackson was not blinded, but his vision was dimmed.

Prudence consequently dictated a halt on the 24th until the column could be closed. This meant a loss of hours, perhaps of an entire day. Until Major Harman got some sleep, he could not push the march. After two long nights in the saddle, Jackson himself did not possess his normal energy and probably failed to realize that he lacked drive and grasp of the situation. So far as is known, he did not explain to any of his subordinates the imperative necessity of haste. In the few records of the day, there is not a hint that a single commander, Jackson included, regarded

25 *Longstreet*, 121–22. While there seems no valid reason to doubt Longstreet's explicit statement concerning the selection of a date, it is proper to note that D. H. Hill, in 2 *B. & L.*, 347, stated that Jackson set the 26th.

26 For other sources on the conference, see 2 *R. E. Lee*, 113, n. 10.

27 The hour of his arrival is not known, but, if he left around 8 P.M. and took 13 hours on the road, as against 14 hours for the somewhat longer ride the previous night from Frederickshall, he should have reached Beaver Dam about 9 A.M.

28 *Dabney Memo.*

29 *E. A. Moore*, 83.

the delay as serious. To the men on the road, June 24 seemed "just another day," and a provoking day at that. Once the whole of Winder's Brigade, finding a bridge down, had to cross precariously on the trunks of two trees cut from opposite sides of the stream.[30]

In these circumstances, the appearance of Captain Dabney must have been most welcome. If longer marches lay ahead, the brother of Major Dabney could not supply substitutes for Hotchkiss' quick sketches, but he had a knowledge of the immediate terrain and he knew all the short cuts. With this new guide, Jackson went over to the plantation of Henry Carter to wait for the slow-moving rear units. He must have felt the need of some diversion, because he undertook something he rarely allowed himself to do: He sat down to read a novel. After an hour he gave that up [31] and, without abashment, went to bed. There some of his staff officers found him. Said Kyd Douglas facetiously in his memoirs: ". . . not a very refreshing or creditable sight met us. The General must have been on a rollicking frolic. His wet and muddy uniform was being dried by the fire and the appearance of his ponderous boots indicated that he might have been wading all night through mud and mire. No one seemed to know where he had been or what doing." [32]

Doubtless when he at length awakened, with mind less weary, Jackson pondered the part he was to play in the coming battle for the deliverance of Richmond. Of the contemplated movement, he had a memorandum which read as follows:

"Maj Gen Jackson to be in position on Wednesday night on the Hanover Ct. Ho. road, or near that road, about half way between Half Sink Bridge, and Hanover Ct. Ho. He will communicate to Maj Gen A. P. Hill, through Brig Gen Branch at Half Sink Bridge his position.

"Gen Jackson will commence his movement, precisely at 3 o'clock Thursday morning, and the moment he moves, send messengers to Gen Branch in duplicate, to inform Gen Branch, who will immediately move himself.

"Gen Jackson to move from his position down the second road from the Chickahominy, parallel to the first road, and near to it. Major Gen A. P. Hill, as soon as the movement of Jackson or Branch is

[30] McHenry Howard, 135.   [31] Dabney Memo.   [32] Douglas, 99.

shown on the other side of the Chickahominy, will push his columns across the Chickahominy at Meadow Bridge, turn to the right and move on Mechanicsville. Maj Gen Jackson will endeavor to come into the Mechanicsville Turnpike in rear of Mechanicsville.

"Maj Gen Jackson [33] and Hill will unite here, and taking different roads bear down towards Coal Harbor, and on to York R. R. Maj Gen Longstreet to support Maj Gen A. P. Hill, and Maj Gen D. H. Hill to support Maj Gen Jackson. If practicable, it will be best for the supporting columns to take different roads from, but near to the main columns." [34]

If Jackson reread this document at Beaver Dam, he could not have failed to reason that the time allotted him to get into position was running fast. No substantial progress could be expected on the 24th. For the 25th he had approximately twenty miles to Ashland and five or six beyond that point. It was a long but not an impossible march. That it was an indispensable march became more apparent late in the night of the 24th–25th, when a courier arrived from Lee's headquarters with the full text of the order for the impending battle.[35] This order changed somewhat Jackson's part in the battle. He was directed to proceed on the 25th from Ashland and to encamp for the night "at some convenient point

[33] The MS. reads Jacksons.

[34] MS. This document is undated, but from a notation "Mrs. Jackson," in the handwriting of Jed. Hotchkiss, it probably was one of numerous personal papers sent her after Jackson's death. Evidently Jackson had kept it among his effects as a record he wished to preserve. Whether it is in Jackson's autograph is uncertain. Jackson's formal "copying hand" differed so much from his "running hand" that, in several instances besides this, it is almost impossible to identify papers as his own. The internal evidence renders the question of autograph relatively unimportant. Manifestly the paper was not one submitted to the council of war when it first assembled. Had it been such a draft, it would not have mentioned "Wednesday" and "Thursday" because, as we know, those days were not selected until nearly the close of the council. Moreover, the insistent use of the term "Maj Gen" suggests that the paper may have been drawn in a council of officers of that rank. An officer of that grade, acting as secretary, may have been carefully deferential. So meticulous a use of the title of divisional command would seem, also, to reduce the probability that this was a memorandum submitted to the council by General Lee. When he drew up the final order the next day, he nowhere used "Brig." or "Maj." in listing the Generals who were to participate. Aside from this, the preliminary plan as here set forth was more at variance with the final text of Lee's order than overnight reflection on the part of a common author of both documents would render likely. The conclusion must be that this memorandum was prepared during the council at the Dabb House or that it was written later by Jackson for his own use.

[35] Jackson's copy of the order, in the autograph of Walter H. Taylor and signed for Lee by R. H. Chilton, A.A.G., is among the *Jackson MSS*. This proves its delivery, which heretofore has been assumed on circumstantial evidence, but never has been established positively. The hour of receipt is not given on the MS., but the date of the order is June 24. Lee usually wrote important papers early in the day. On the 24th, it is known that he was absent from headquarters during the afternoon, when he went over to the Williamsburg road to observe some heavy skirmishing. That evening he

west of the Central Railroad." This was a less specific requirement than that in the earlier memorandum, though it fixed his
camp in the same locality. Thence, at the hour set in the memorandum, 3 A.M. on the 26th, he was to begin his march and was to
communicate with General Branch as previously understood; but,
instead of following the second road East of the Chickahominy
to the rear of Mechanicsville, he was to move farther to the eastward by a longer march. Then, *en échelon* with the Divisions that
were by that time to have crossed the Chickahominy, he was to
turn Beaver Dam Creek and was to proceed, as agreed at the conference on the 23rd, toward Cold Harbor. No attempt was made
in the orders to set a time for turning the creek or for the advance
beyond it.

When Jackson had been at headquarters he may or may not
have learned enough about the terrain to realize that the change
in orders reflected a purpose on the part of Lee to avoid a direct
attack on Beaver Dam Creek, which was known to be a difficult
position. That phase of the operation naturally was not covered
by the orders themselves. The point of the orders, as they related
to Jackson, was that he had a longer and perhaps more difficult
march set for him on the day the battle was to open,[36] and that
his troops were to be the spearhead of the attack.

Delay, change of orders, the prospect of long marches and hard
fighting—to all these, on the 24th, treachery was added. The name-
less soldier who had left his command at Gordonsville, about the
time Jackson had entrained there on the 21st, had proceeded eastward and then had headed straight for the Federal lines. During
the afternoon of the 24th, he ran into Union scouts near Hanover

wrote President Davis, "I have determined to make no change in the plan," which
would indicate that the plan had been drafted and, inferentially, that the order had
been issued (*Lee's Dispatches*, 12–13). If the text was finished and copied by noon, a
fresh courier with a relay of good horses could have delivered Jackson's copy by midnight or by 1 A.M.

[36] It is natural to interpret the opening sentence of Lee's orders of June 24, *O. R.*,
I, pt. 2, pp. 500–501, reprinted in 2 *R. E. Lee*, 565–66, as indicating that Lee expected
Jackson to reach Ashland on the 24th. The order reads, "General Jackson's command
will proceed tomorrow [June 25] from Ashland toward the Slash Church and encamp,"
etc. In view of Jackson's confident statement on the 23d, that he could be in position
for battle on the 25th, this interpretation may be correct. On the other hand, in a note
of June 26 to the President, Lee wrote: ". . . Jackson . . . states that . . . his command only reached Ashland last night." The use of the word "only" may be awkward
—as it usually is—but the meaning of the sentence would seem to be that Jackson did
not get beyond Ashland on the 25th. If Lee had meant that Jackson did not reach
Ashland until the evening of the 25th, with the inference that he had been expected
sooner, he was enough of a literary precisian to have said so.

Court House. They questioned him. At first he insisted that he was a member of Kenly's 1st Maryland Infantry, that he had been captured at Front Royal, and that he had escaped from Jackson's Army. When he found that story would not hold water, he finally professed himself a deserter and told how he had left Gordonsville. Then, in detail, he described Jackson's Army as consisting of Ewell's, Whiting's and Jackson's Divisions, the strength of which he put at fifteen Brigades.[37] Jackson, said the deserter, had been moving for Frederickshall, whence he intended on June 28 to attack McClellan's rear.

The appearance of the professed deserter was suspicious, though he manifestly was intelligent. Naturally, the Federal scouts carried him to their station, whence, apparently, either he was taken to G.H.Q. or else a full report of his statement was forwarded in haste. By midnight on the 24th–25th—about the time Jackson got his combat order—General McClellan was telegraphing to Washington all the deserter had reported and was asking that it be compared with the Army's intelligence reports of Jackson's movements.[38] Secrecy was lost. Jackson could not hope for another Front Royal.

[37] Actually, as reorganized, Jackson had nine Brigades and the Maryland Line, but one of these Brigades, Lawton's, was as large as two usually were.

[38] O. R., 11, pt. 1, p. 49. The name of this deserter is not given, nor is there any note of the regiment to which he belonged.

CHAPTER XXXI

The New Organization Fails

JACKSON's march on the 25th was begun without an inkling that his approach had been revealed to the enemy. Maj. Jasper Whiting, who had served on Gustavus Smith's staff, reported to serve as guide and supplemented with sound military knowledge the lore of Captain Dabney.[1] Every assurance there was that the day's tramp would be directed where the legs of the men least would be strained; but the start was slow and without spirit. "The brigade commanders," Major Dabney indignantly wrote years afterward, "would not or could not get rations cooked, their own breakfasts, and their men under order earlier than an hour after sunrise, probably because their supply-trains were rarely in place, by reason of the indolence and carelessness of julep-drinking officers."[2] The "New Model" Army of the Valley, in a word, had not shaken off the habits of Old Virginia.

From the "Forward, march," mud and high water were encountered. The rains of the preceding days upcountry had reached the edge of the coastal plain into which Jackson was moving. The roads were heavy; the streams roared. Where bridges had been destroyed, there was no pioneer corps to replace them. No tools were available except the battery axes. Halts were frequent and long. Captain Dabney knew all the fords and took the nearest and best, but progress was slow. At last, when nightfall approached, the tired, mud-covered troops had not passed Ashland, but they were so weary that Jackson had to stop and let them go into camp. He then was about five miles short of the crossing of the Virginia Central Railroad, West of which, "at some convenient point," Lee had ordered him to camp that evening. The march of the day had been about twenty miles, perhaps twenty-two.[3]

[1] "He was of invaluable service and soon gained the General's confidence and personal regard." *Douglas,* 100.

[2] *Dabney Memo.*

[3] Dabney, in the oft-cited *Memo.,* insisted that the distance was twenty-four miles, plus the detours, but Hotchkiss, in revising the *Memo.* for Henderson, added a note "19 by rail" as the distance between Beaver Dam and Ashland. Neither of these

Although, in the circumstances, this was an excellent day's advance, Jackson was in manifest distress that he had not reached
the objective assigned him for the day. He was concerned, also,
over reports that cavalry pickets had been driven in below Ashland, and that the telegraph wire had been cut near the town.[4]
When the brigade commanders came to report, he said to Winder:
"You must have your men cook their rations and be ready to start
tomorrow morning at dawn."

Winder objected. "That is impossible," said he, "because of the
position of my baggage-train."

Jackson snapped back, "General Winder, it must be done." The
tone was so sharp and severe, to an officer of Winder's known zeal,
that even Major Dabney, for all his devotion to Jackson, had to
admit his chief "scarcely courteous." [5]

Besides having the morrow's rations cooked overnight, Jackson
decided that he would start his march at 2.30 A.M., instead of 3
o'clock. In order that Lee might be informed, he wrote a note
concerning the delay on account of mud and high water, told of
the hour of expected march, and reported the cutting of the telegraph wire and the attack on the pickets. This dispatch he had to
send by a courier,[6] who may have passed a fellow messenger with
a letter from Lee. Eagerly, carefully, Jackson read this document.
If the map was correct, said Lee, the columns of the Army of the

officers was on the march. Dabney, writing late, apparently assumed that Jackson
marched down the Virginia Central R. R. to a point about one mile below Verdon
and then moved Southeast to the Telegraph road, from which he had again to deflect
his march to the westward to avoid the destroyed railroad bridges. This is highly
improbable, and even as a possibility is well-nigh ruled out by Dabney's manifest mistakes in describing the rivers and the crossing. All subsequent accounts were based on
Dabney or else seem to have been written without access to any reliable war-time map
of the area immediately East and South of Beaver Dam. There is such a map in the
Hotchkiss Papers. This and local tradition indicate that the route of the Army was as
follows: From Beaver Dam Station South along the railroad for about a mile; then
Southwest by Mitchell's across Beaver Dam Creek to Trinity Church; down the Fork
Church road by Fulcher's; across Little River at Honeyman's Bridge, on by Fontain's
(Pinhook, now Coatesville), Lowry's, Berkley's, Oliver's, Fork Church and Coleman's to
the intersection of the Winston's Mill Road; thence right to Blunt's Bridge, on into the
Independence Church road and to Ashland. In Hanover, it is thought also that part of
the Army, which camped for a night at the intersection of the Fork Church and Negrofoot roads (Pinhook), took the road to Negrofoot; whence, via Anthony's, it crossed
the South Anna at Horseshoe, came into the Independence Church road below the Blunt's
Bridge intersection, and proceeded to Ashland. For this information the writer is indebted to Messrs. Robert and Rosewell Page, Jr.

[4] See note 6, *infra*. This information doubtless came from "Jeb" Stuart. Cf. *O. R.*,
11, pt. 2, p. 514.

[5] *Dabney Memo*.

[6] The text is lost, but the content was given the next morning by Lee to Davis;
see *Lee' Dispatches*, 15–16.

'alley could march from the vicinity of the Central Railroad by
vo roads, instead of by one. The westerly column would unite
vith Branch's Brigade and, when Meadow Bridges were passed,
vith the remainder of A. P. Hill's Division. A column moving
outhward, farther to the East, would [7] have a clear road.

This information, which might facilitate the march, was sup-
lemented by the arrival of an officer who, from that hour, was
o become an unfailing admirer of the victor in the Valley cam-
aign. "Jeb" Stuart had been assigned to cover Jackson's left
ank the next day, and he had been prompted to ride out to Ash-
ind in the hope that he might assist Jackson in an unfamiliar
ountry. After Jackson had conferred with Stuart, the confident
rooper went off to make ready for the morning of the battle.
ackson was left alone to pray and to ponder. Past midnight
Ewell and Whiting came to his quarters to ask whether they
night not advance by different routes. Jackson may not have
een sure that the roads named by the two officers were those
hat Lee suggested. For that or for some other reason, he told
Whiting and Ewell that he would think over the proposal and
vould communicate with them later. The officers left.

Said Ewell, when they were out of earshot: "Don't you know
vhy 'Old Jack' would not decide at once? He is going to pray
ver it first!"

Noting, in a short time, that he had left his sword, Ewell went
ack to Jackson's quarters to get it; and there, as he had expected,
e found the General on his knees.[8]

If Jackson slept at all after that, it could not have been for long,
ecause, as the Army was ordered to march at 2.30, he would set
n example of promptness. He always did. His men were beginning to say that when he fixed a march for early dawn, he moved
the night before." [9] It was a soldierly habit, no doubt, but for

[7] Unfortunately, the last page of Lee's dispatch to Jackson is missing from the *Jack-
on MSS*. No member of the family knows what became of it. From the mutilated
orm of other MSS., clipped of their signatures, it seems likely that the lost page was
iven by Mrs. Jackson to some admirer of her husband. The existing pages end with
n unfinished reference to the route of the second column. "Have a clear road" is all
hat can be supplied with any assurance.

[8] *Dabney*, 440; the language quoted in the text is from Dabney to Hotchkiss,
ept. 12, 1896, and while it is much later than that in Dabney's biography of Jackson,
t is less formal and has more of the real savor of Ewell's speech.

[9] Dabney, *op. cit.*, 440, stated that Jackson got no sleep on the night of June 25–26,
ut apparently he based his statement on Ewell's anecdote, which related to an inter-
iew after midnight. If Imboden's observation in the Valley was of any value, see

a man who had spent two of the three preceding nights in the saddle, it was poor preparation for the coming conflict. When he rose and made his brief toilet, he could not have counted for himself more than ten hours' sleep in ninety-six of anxious activity, hard riding, and vexatious administration of an army on the march. Those vigils would have exhausted mentally any man, and especially one who notoriously was dependent on abundant sleep.[10]

Now, as if on two stages, both visible to the spectator but separated impenetrably the one from the other, began a grim drama. On the eastern stage, across the Chickahominy from Richmond, the gaunt figure of Jackson was to stand out as if the 18,500 men of his Army were mere supernumeraries for the day. West of the Chickahominy were many actors—Lee, Longstreet, D. H. Hill and others capable but not yet sprung to fame. In all that shining company, Fate was to have it that the most conspicuous in the drama, half hero, half marplot, was to be the youngest and the most recently risen of the Major Generals—A. P. Hill.

Jackson's camps scarcely were astir at daylight, despite his orders for the march to begin at 2.30. The "julep-drinking" officers of whom Dabney made complaint may not have had the commissary wagons in position for rations to be cooked overnight. Besides, drinking water was not abundant around Ashland. The men lost time in seeking wells where they could fill their canteens. Some of the troops left for the long summer day's march with no water.[14]

Longstreet's and D. H. Hill's camps were astir most of the night while the men cooked their rations. At 2 A.M. D. H. Hill started; at 3, Longstreet. To the Mechanicsville Turnpike, they moved in the darkness.[11] Branch, at 4 A.M., marched his Brigade into the open fields near the west bank of the Chickahominy, to be ready to cross when the expected message came from Jackson.[12] A. P. Hill, his troops fully hidden, was concentrated opposite the Meadow Bridges.[13]

supra, p. 449, Jackson may have thrown himself on his bed, fully dressed, and may have slept for a short time.
[10] The fullest account of Jackson's habits of sleep is given by Maj. H. K. Douglas in Annals of the War, 646–47. See also the references cited in 2 R. E. Lee, 579.
[11] O. R., 11, pt. 2, p. 756.
[12] O. R., 11, pt. 2, pp. 881–82.
[13] Ibid., 834–35.
[14] Dabney Memo.

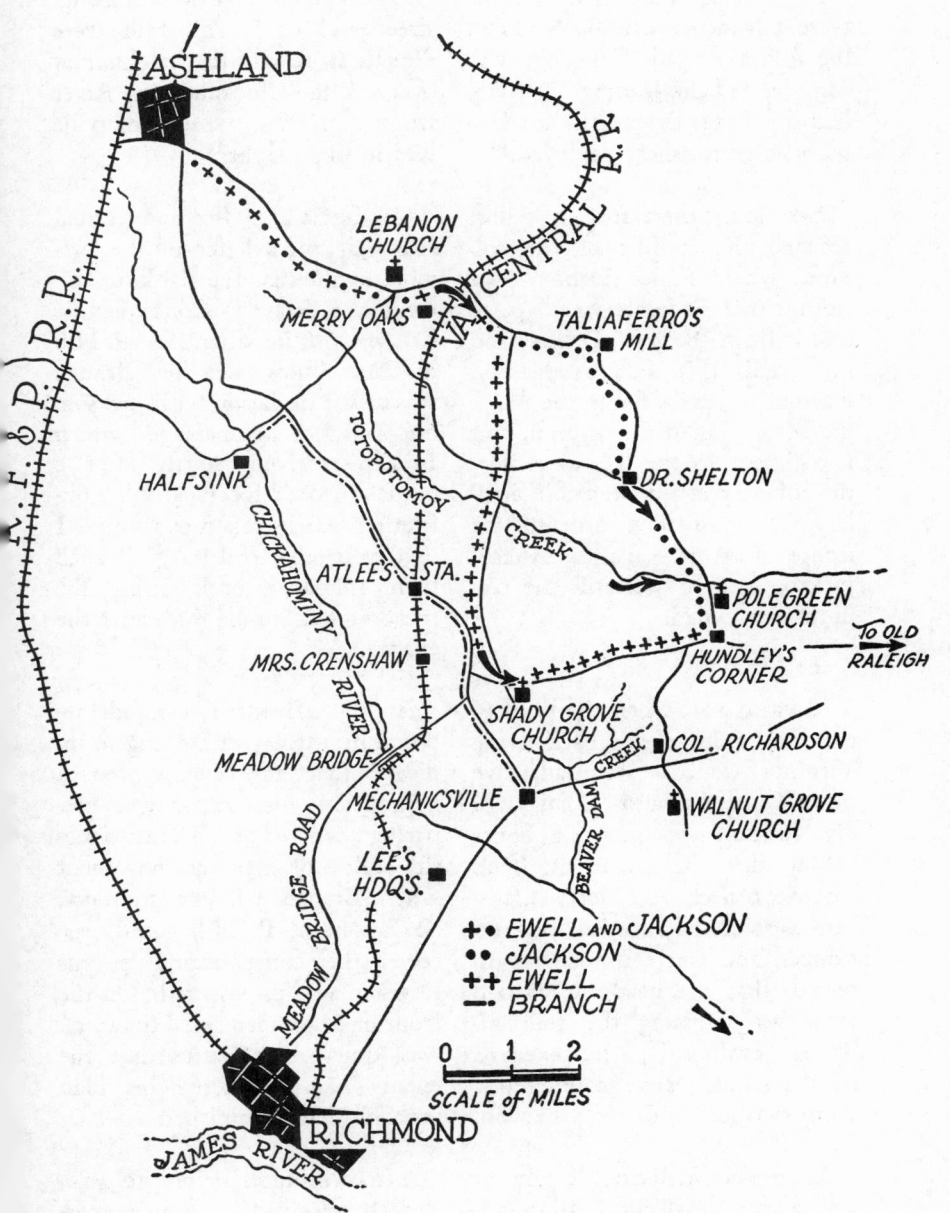

Route of Jackson, Ewell and Branch, June 26, 1862

At 8 A.M., Jackson's columns were advancing cautiously down the Ashcake road. Whiting, who commanded the leading Division, had the Texas Brigade in advance with its skirmishers deployed.[16]

Not long thereafter, a report reached the middle of the column, where Major Dabney was riding, that Federals were apt to attack from the left. Dabney did not credit this, but, as Jackson was out of reach, far to the front, the Major halted the column, sent a regiment to the left to protect the infantry against possible artillery fire, and then ordered the troops forward again. Ahead, Jackson had to wait till the column was closed.

It was 9 A.M. when the head of the long column approached the Virginia Central Railroad, five miles from Ashland. That is to say, Jackson was now six hours behind the schedule set in Lee's combat order. At Merry Oaks, just west of the railroad, Jackson stopped and wrote Branch, as directed, that the head of his column was crossing the railroad. There, ominously, the enemy's cavalry scouts were encountered.[18] Time was lost in driving them in.

At 10 o'clock, Jackson's column was across the Central Railroad.

By 8 A.M., the Divisions of Longstreet and of D. H. Hill were directly in rear of the heights that overlook the Chickahominy River from the East. Mechanicsville was in plain sight.[15]

On the heights, Lee had learned from Jackson's letter of the previous night that the flanking column was delayed. Consequently, Lee was not impatient. A. P. Hill did not know whether Branch was as yet in liaison with Jackson, but he sent a message, which Branch received shortly after 8 o'clock: "Wait for Jackson's notification before you move unless I send you other orders."[17] Branch then marched back from the meadow half a mile to deceive the enemy.

At the advanced Confederate positions, there was nothing to indicate that the enemy sensed approaching danger or was preparing for it. The Federals opposite Half Sink made no movement when Branch left the meadow. So far as A. P. Hill could perceive, the concentration of his Division was unobserved. On the front of Magruder and Huger, all was quiet. Lee's fear that the enemy had discovered his plan probably had diminished.

A few minutes before 10 A.M., Branch received Jackson's mes-

[15] *O. R.*, 11, pt. 2, p. 756. [16] *O. R.*, 11, pt. 2, p. 562. [17] *O. R.*, 11, pt. 2, p. 881.
[18] In *O. R.*, 11, pt. 2, p. 552, Jackson set the time of the actual crossing at 10 A.M. His note to Branch from Merry Oaks was dated 9 A.M.

Ewell turned to the right, about three quarters of a mile East of the railroad and moved South toward Shady Grove Church. Jackson went about 1200 yards farther and made a similar turn on his march in the direction of Pole Green Church.[20]

By 11 A.M., the sun was hot, the sky cloudless. The men were thirsty in a district where streams were few. When the column passed a house which had a well, some of the soldiers would break ranks and run to fill their canteens and those of their comrades. As many had procured no water since they had crossed at Blount's Ford the previous day, their officers did not have the heart to forbid them going to the wells; but this slowed down the march of Jackson's column.[22] Ewell, on his road, was making good time.

At noon, as usual, Jackson doubtless halted for an hour and rested his men. Ewell probably did the same thing.

Not long after Jackson resumed his march at 1 P.M., he reached Dr. Shelton's house, where his road turned from South to Southeast. Jackson there found Jeb

sage of 9 o'clock and started at once for the Chickahominy. He crossed without opposition and took the road that ran slightly East of South, parallel to the river. The Federal pickets retired before him, but his advance was slow.[19]

The Divisions East of the Chickahominy remained in position and out of sight of the Federals. Branch's message from Jackson at 9 A.M. doubtless was relayed to A. P. Hill and by him sent to Lee on the Mechanicsville Pike, but of this there is no record. Branch was continuing his march on the road to Atlee's and, a few miles from his starting point, encountered about 200 Federals. The Seventh North Carolina, the leading regiment, attacked and, after a short clash drove the enemy, who disappeared.[21]

Branch, whether marching or halted at noon, had no further report from Jackson and did not know that officer's position.

About 1 o'clock, Branch's skirmishers approached Atlee's Station, on the Virginia Central Railroad. Their coming was at once reported to the Union out-

[19] O. R., 11, pt. 2, pp. 835, 882.
[20] In O. R., 11, pt. 3, p. 620, is a message from Jackson to Branch dated "10 P.M.," to the effect that the head of his column was "nearly 2 miles from where it crossed the Central Railroad." If the hour was a mistake for "10 A.M.," the first hour's march after crossing the railroad was rapid; but there is no assurance that the error simply was of "P.M." for "A.M."
[21] O. R., 11, pt. 2, p. 886.   [22] *Dabney Memo.*

Stuart, who had been covering the front of advance and had seen no enemy in strength. Stuart explained to Jackson the disposition of the cavalry, but he had no report, apparently, of conditions on Jackson's right, in the area between Jackson and Ewell. The nature of the country ahead, in its relation to Jackson's advance and to Lee's plan, also was described by Stuart on the basis of his previous "ride around McClellan" and of his reconnaissance during the day. Stuart, of course, as well as Jackson, had a copy of Lee's combat orders. There is no record of any discussion between Jackson and Stuart of any ambiguity in those orders.[25]

post, which prepared for resistance. First Federal reports were that the advance included an infantry battalion and a squadron of cavalry.[23] At this time, when contact was about to be established, Branch was out of touch with his Division, which was distant about two miles by air but, because of intervening swamp and the presence of the enemy, almost twelve miles by the only open road. No signalmen were with Branch; no provision had been made for signal guns. Ewell was not more than one mile East of Branch, but was not in liaison with him or with Jackson, who was two and one half miles Northeast of Ewell by air, and about four and a half miles by road.[24]

From 2 to 3 P.M., Jackson continued his march from the vicinity of Dr. Shelton's toward Totopotomoy Creek. Stuart sent a contingent ahead to seize the bridge across the creek.[27]

The hour between 2 and 3, or thereabouts, Branch spent in a stiff skirmish at Atlee's, when he drove the Federals back toward Mechanicsville, his objective.[26]

At 3 P.M., which was to prove the decisive hour in the day's operations, Jackson drove in a Federal cavalry outpost from the left bank of Totopotomoy Creek. The retreating Unionists fled southward and set fire to the

By 3 P.M., A. P. Hill's thin patience was worn out. He had received no dispatch from Branch for several hours and he had heard none of the firing. Not a word had come to Hill directly from Jackson. Impetuously Hill determined

[23] O. R., 11, pt. 2, p. 414.
[24] According to A. H. Campbell's excellent map of April, 1864.
[25] O. R., 11, pt. 2, p. 514.
[26] O. R., 11, pt. 2, pp. 882, 886. The time estimate is based on the distance and on the fact that Branch is known not to have reached Meadow Bridge until well after Hill had crossed at 3 P.M.
[27] O. R., 11, pt. 2, p. 514.

bridge. Through the ingenuity of engineer officers, the crossing was soon repaired;[28] but before Jackson moved his column forward, he carefully deployed the skirmishers of Hood's Texas Brigade. Then, with Reilly's Battery, he shelled the woods on the opposite bank to drive out any Federals who might be lurking there.[30] As no enemy was visible at the time of this brief cannonade, Major Dabney believed that Jackson merely was firing signal guns to indicate to Lee that he was approaching his objective.[31]

While Jackson, between 3.30 and 4 P.M., was preparing to cross Totopotomoy Creek, Ewell was a mile or a little more to the North of Shady Grove Church. At that point, opposite the Crenshaw plantation, Ewell discovered that a Confederate column was moving in the same direction on a road parallel to his and only a quarter of a mile distant. Soon, from that road, Branch rode over to meet him. Branch had continued to move cautiously forward, in the face of a succession of ambushes,[33] but he still was out of touch with Hill. After a brief exchange, Ewell and Branch resumed their march by routes that slowly diverged.[34] So far as is known, Ewell did not notify

to cross, as he later reported, "rather than hazard the failure of the whole plan by longer deferring it." [29] Without sending word to Lee, who was distant less than two miles down the same side of the Chickahominy, Hill easily forced a crossing and started down the river for Mechanicsville. Until Hill subsequently emerged in sight opposite Lee's field headquarters, the only information Lee had of any new development was the sight of distant smoke in the line of Jackson's advance—probably the burning bridge.[32]

By 3.30, the head of Hill's Division was across the Chickahominy, but it had no road close to the left bank of the stream. Part of the infantry formed for an advance across the open fields in the direction of Mechanicsville; the artillery and the wagons had to move nearly a mile and a half to the Northeast before they struck the road from Atlee's to Mechanicsville, the road down which Branch was to advance. When Hill's leading battery reached this road and turned almost South, Branch was then scarcely more than one mile farther up that road in the direction of Atlee's. Ewell was about the same distance to the Northeast. No effort was made by Hill to send couriers

---

28 *Dabney Memo.*
30 *O. R.*, 11, pt. 2, pp. 552, 562.
32 Col. Charles Marshall, *An Aide-de-Camp of Lee*, ed. by Major General Sir Frederick Maurice (cited hereafter as *Marshall*), 93.
33 *O. R.*, 11, pt. 2, p. 882.

29 *O. R.*, 11, pt. 2, p. 835.
31 *Dabney Memo.*

34 *Ibid*

Jackson that liaison had been established with Branch.

Jackson's column, crossing the Totopotomoy, heard artillery fire about 4 o'clock and, according to General Trimble, musketry as well;[36] but of the significance of this, nothing was known. Removing felled trees easily from the road,[38] Jackson passed Pole Green Church and advanced southward toward the road from Shady Grove Church to Old Raleigh, as directed in Lee's letter of the preceding day. Ewell pressed steadily on, during midafternoon, reached Shady Grove Church and turned eastward. Even if Jackson had told Ewell of Lee's letter of June 25, which spoke of a union of Ewell's column with Hill's on the Meadow Bridge Road, the fact that Branch had not reached Hill precluded any such junction by Ewell. Naturally, Ewell moved, according to the main plan, to rejoin Jackson.

Around 5 o'clock the van of Jackson's column reached Hundley's Corner, on the road Lee had mentioned.[39] Ewell, marching

to Branch. The proximity of Ewell was not known to Hill.[35]

About 4 P.M., the advance of Hill's Division came within artillery range of Mechanicsville. Hill ordered McIntosh's Battery to open on the enemy's guns in rear of the village.[37] This fire and the appearance of the van of Hill's infantry on the opposite ridge led Longstreet and D. H. Hill to prepare their Divisions to cross the Mechanicsville Bridge as soon as A. P. Hill had cleared it of the enemy. Lee, who was on the ground, did not know that A. P. Hill had crossed at Meadow Bridges without having ascertained the position either of Jackson or of Branch. The assumption of Lee was that A. P. Hill had "discovered" the movement of Branch and of Jackson opposite his front, as required by orders, and that A. P. Hill was advancing in liaison with them.

By 5 o'clock, A. P. Hill was under heavy fire on the high ground adjacent to Mechanicsville. He posted his batteries as

---

[35] The general combat order, it will be remembered, did not specify different routes for Ewell and the remainder of Jackson's force. There is no reason to assume that Hill had been notified of Lee's suggestion to Jackson, on June 25, that Ewell might use the road designated for Hill.

[36] *O. R.*, 11, pt. 2, p. 614.   [37] *O. R.*, 11, pt. 2, p. 860.

[38] *O. R.*, 11, pt. 2, p. 552.

[39] Henderson, *op. cit.*, 2, 16, without stating his authority, fixed the hour of Jackson's arrival at 4.30, but Dabney, who may have remained near the middle of the column, gave the time as one and a half hours by sun, that is, approximately 5.45 (*Memo.*). In a later letter, Dabney put the time half an hour later. The conflict of testimony concerning the hour doubtless was due to the difference in the time at which various witnesses reached Hundley's. The hour given by Henderson must have been that of the arrival of the cavalry skirmishers.

rom Shady Grove Church, soon ame into position on Jackson's ight, but Ewell had no information of what was happening in he direction of Mechanicsville. Although the sound of a heavy engagement was audible, Ewell could report only that he had met Branch near Crenshaw's and that Branch knew nothing of the movements of A. P. Hill. What was to be done? Jackson's face showed that he was deeply disturbed over the answer.[41] Late he was, lamentably late, but he was where Lee had told him A. P. Hill would be on his right and D. H. Hill in support, for a general advance en échelon. Neither of the Hills was there; no notice of any change of plan—no directions of any sort—had come. Should Jackson press on toward Beaver Dam Creek, unsupported and ignorant of the situation on his right; or should he wait for more information? Jackson decided that he should move no farther. While the battle to the South still raged, he bivouacked for the night.[43]

they arrived, but for a time could not ascertain whence the fire was coming. As his infantry regiments arrived, he used them to drive the Federals from the village, and one Brigade he sent to his left to try to take a battery in reverse. The confusion was great. Not more than half his troops were up.[40] Branch had not reached Meadow Bridge Road until Hill already had passed that point and had turned southward. Following the artillery, Branch did not get to Mechanicsville until about 6 P.M.[42] Longstreet and D. H. Hill were delayed at Mechanicsville Bridge because no pioneer troops were at hand to repair the crossing. All the while, A. P. Hill deferred assault on the Federal position along Beaver Dam Creek because he knew this would entail heavy losses. He waited for the sound of Jackson's guns in the belief that "Stonewall" would attack at any moment and, turning the creek, would force the Federals to retreat from in front of Hill's Brigades.[44]

Hill sought, meanwhile, to establish his line of battle as prescribed by orders and, ere twilight came, he succeeded in doing so, but he continued to suffer heavily from the artillery fire of the enemy. Although he got some of his infantry to the fringe of Beaver Dam Creek, he could advance them no farther.

[40] The excellent First South Carolina Rifles, of Gregg's Brigade, did not cross Meadow Bridges till 6 P.M. O. R., 11, pt. 2, p. 872.
[41] Dabney Memo.
[42] Branch, O. R., 11, pt. 2, p. 882, put the time at about one hour before sunset, which was at 7.18.
[43] O. R., 11, pt. 2, pp. 553, 562.   [44] O. R., 11, pt. 2, p. 835.

The leading Brigade of D. H. Hill's Division now had come up; Longstreet's men were crowding behind D. H. Hill. In the confusion of the struggle, there was little that any of these troops could do. General Lee had ridden out and had posted himself in Binford's field,[45] where, if anywhere, he could see what was happening. The previous evening he had been told by T. W. Sydnor, a Lieutenant of cavalry, who lived in the neighborhood and knew every foot of the ground, that the bottom along Beaver Dam Creek, at the crossing of the Old Church road, was of quicksand, through which troops could not hope to cross. As the battle shifted in that direction, Lee sent for the young officer, confirmed his impression of the terrain and dispatched Sydnor to A. P. Hill with orders not to advance but to hold the position already occupied. Hill must have thought these orders gave him discretion to attack on his opposite flank. In any event, he hurled Ripley's Brigade of D. H. Hill's Division in support of Pender's North Carolinians, against the Federal right. There the two Brigades attacked, most gallantly and in vain. The repulse was complete.[46] Infantry fire continued aimlessly till 9 o'clock; the artillery disputed vainly for an hour or more thereafter.[47]

When the action was over, Lee brought his division commanders together at the Lumpkin House and reviewed the situation. There was, as yet, no report of any sort from Jackson. No effort had been made to have a courier or staff officer find him; neither Jackson nor Stuart had sent any one from Hundley's Corner to ascertain how close was the flank of Lee's troops, the sound of whose battle they heard plainly. On the field of combat, it was manifest that, at the time of A. P. Hill's arrival, the Federals had withdrawn from Mechanicsville to the East of Beaver Dam Creek, where they had excellent artillery positions and good cover for the infantry.

---

[45] Southeast of the junction of the Mechanicsville Turnpike and the Cold Harbor road.
[46] O. R., 11, pt. 2, pp. 835–36. The only account of Lee's orders to A. P. Hill to halt his advance is given in a letter of T. W. Sydnor to Jed. Hotchkiss, Dec. 27, 1897 (Hotchkiss Papers). This was cited in 2 Henderson, 16, but in such a manner that doubt was left concerning the time the order was sent. A full copy of Lieutenant Sydnor's letter shows some confusion in the mind of its writer over the part General Branch had in the action, but it makes clear the fact that the quicksand against which Sydnor warned General Lee was opposite the crossing of Old Church road at Beaver Dam Creek, and not at Ellerson's Mill, or South of the Mill. That is to say, the dangerous ground was on the left of Archer and the right of J. R. Anderson, rather than on the front of Pender, though the last-named officer, as he came down to the declivity at Ellerson's Mill, faced a hayfield and a millrace.
[47] The reports are cited in 2 R. E. Lee. 134.

All the Federals had been called upon to do was to wait for the Confederates to come into range and then to mow them down. Casualties, of course, could not be ascertained in the midst of so much confusion, but they were known to be heavy. The Forty-fourth Georgia of Ripley's Brigade had virtually been wiped out; the First North Carolina had lost 142 men.[48]

Responsibility for this slaughter appeared to be divided. A. P. Hill was the conspicuous offender. Without waiting for Branch or for Jackson, he had crossed Meadow Bridges in violation of orders. The defense of Hill was that he moved when he did because he believed further delay would jeopardize the whole plan. Lee did not pass judgment on this point, but he did question both Hill and Branch concerning the receipt of orders, sent through Lieutenant Sydnor, to hold the position at Mechanicsville and not to attack. Sydnor was called to headquarters and was asked to repeat what Lee had told him and what he had said to the division and the brigade commanders. No denial was made of the accuracy of his statement.[49]

Perhaps there was, at the time, no way of establishing exactly what had happened. Too many men had given orders. Instructions to D. H. Hill to send a Brigade in support of A. P. Hill had been issued both by General Lee and by President Davis, who had ridden out to see the battle; but D. H. Hill had put Ripley into action at the request of Pender.[50] When A. P. Hill wrote his official report, he either had forgotten what the other Hill had done, or else he thought he should assume the odium of sending Ripley's Brigade to the butcher's pen on Beaver Dam Creek.[51]

Conspicuous feats of valor there had been on the part of regimental and company officers, feats that had in some instances cost the lives of rising men. In the ranks, the soldiers had done everything that could reasonably have been demanded of them. It was the high command that had failed. None could deny that. Except for the disposition of the cavalry and the arrival of Longstreet and D. H. Hill on the right bank of the Chickahominy, no detail of the plan of action had been executed on time and in accordance

---

[48] Gross casualties probably were about 1400. Those of the Forty-fourth Georgia were 335 in a total of 514. See 2 R. E. Lee, 135, n. 51.
[49] Sydnor letter, supra.
[50] O. R., 11, pt. 2, p. 625; for Davis's presence on the field, see 2 R. E. Lee, 131-32
[51] Ibid., 835-36.

with the plan. A costly attack had been directed against a position the strength of which had been so well known that a turning movement upstream had been regarded as the *sine qua non*. Concentration for an advance *en échelon* down the Chickahominy had not been effected. Worst of all, Jackson, the hero of the South, the unfailing Jackson who had dazzled the continent by his swift marches—Jackson had not arrived in time to have any share in the attack that was to save Richmond!

CHAPTER XXXII

First Battle of the Army of Northern Virginia

When the front Brigade of A. P. Hill's Division renewed its attack on the line of Beaver Dam Creek in the early morning of June 27, 1862, it encountered feeble resistance. The Federals had learned during the night of the proximity of Jackson to the headwaters of the stream and, quietly and skillfully, they had drawn out their guns. Their infantry had followed. Only a sufficient force had remained to delay the Confederates.[1]

Soon the entire Southern Army was across the stream and in pursuit. Its general direction was eastward in four columns. Nearest the Chickahominy, and using farm roads, was Longstreet's Division. On his left, A. P. Hill followed the county road toward Gaines' Mill and Cold Harbor. North of that Division marched D. H. Hill.[2] By the same route, Jackson followed.

The command seemed in good condition. All the Brigadier Generals were present for duty except two. Jubal A. Early had not returned from his home, to which he had gone after he had been wounded at Williamsburg, but, in the belief that a battle was imminent, he was on his way.[3] "Dick" Taylor, the second absentee, had been taken ill on the 25th, and on the 26th had been put to bed. He, too, was chafing, and was about to start for the front in an ambulance. His Louisianians, decimated and weary, were moving forward with Ewell and under the temporary command of gallant old Isaac Seymour, Colonel of the Sixth.[4] Of the ardor of all the troops, and of their determination, there could be no dispute. Whether General Lee could co-ordinate the attack of 56,000 men; whether the division commanders were equal to their duty; whether some of the new regimental and company officers

[1] See 2 R. E. Lee, 136 ff. As that work describes in detail the strategy and the major engagements of the Army after Lee assumed command, this book, from the present chapter, will omit details that are not essential to the history of the command. Where facts are stated, concerning engagements or movements, with no citation of authority, the corresponding chapters in R. E. Lee give the references.

[2] From the Old Church road past Colonel Richardson's, and then to a point just East of Walnut Grove Church.

[3] Early, 75. [4] R. Taylor, 83 ff.

chosen under the elective system were competent [5]—these were the doubtful questions added to the usual uncertainties of battle.

All the hazards, all the hopes and all the prowess of the thirty-five Brigades of infantry seemed to be dramatized when, at Walnut Grove Church, two miles East of Beaver Dam Creek, Lee met Jackson. Officers of each staff looked with curiosity at the General of the other. Scores of eyes were fixed at decent distance on Lee, who sat on a stump. As many gazed in admiration at the mysterious, bearded man from the Valley. Cap in hand, he stood by his horse opposite Lee and said little. About 11 o'clock, after a short conference, Jackson mounted and resumed the march toward Cold Harbor.

A. P. Hill's "Light Division," as its commander had decided to call it, already had contact with the retreating Federals. It expected soon to bring the enemy to a stand. Battle was in the air. The leading Brigade of the Division, as it happened, was that of Maxcy Gregg. Forty-eight years of age was Gregg, a South Carolina lawyer, a bachelor and culturally one of the best-furnished men of the Confederacy. Few knew the Greek dramatists or the philosophers so thoroughly. Perhaps none combined so precise a knowledge of botany, of ornithology, and of astronomy. The equipment of his private observatory in Columbia would have been the envy of many a college. A scholar he was, a scientist and a gentleman. Was he a soldier? That day would show. He would open the battle.[6] His service in the Army dated from the beginning of the war but, save for a little affair at Vienna, in June,

---

[5] Cf. D. H. Hill in O. R., 11, pt. 1, pp. 605–6.

[6] Gregg was the son of James Gregg of Columbia, and of Cornelia Manning Maxcy, daughter of Jonathan Maxcy, first President of South Carolina College. Mrs. Jonathan Maxcy was a daughter of Commodore Esek Hopkins. During the Mexican War Maxcy Gregg had been a Major of South Carolina Volunteers, but he had not been engaged. He long was a leading secessionist and an avowed advocate of the reopening of the slave trade. Immediately after the withdrawal of South Carolina, Maxcy Gregg had organized hastily the First South Carolina Volunteers to forestall a possible attempt to recapture Fort Moultrie (Richmond Dispatch, Apr. 11, 1861, p. 1, col. 3). In his command, at the outset, had been twenty-seven physicians, thirty members of the bar and many of the most eminent young business men of Carolina. (See letter of L. W. Spratt in Richmond Dispatch, July 13, 1861, p. 1, col. 3.) This regiment had received an overwhelming reception when it had come to Virginia Apr. 24, 1861 (see Richmond Dispatch, Apr. 24, p. 1, cols. 4, 6; Apr. 25, p. 1, col. 6; May 1, p. 2, col. 4; May 24, p. 2, col. 5; Richmond Examiner, Apr. 25, p. 3, col. 1; May 6, p. 3, col. 3; May 24, p. 3, col. 1; May 28, 1861, p. 1, col. 6); but after the six months' enlistment ended, a majority of the men insisted on returning home before they entered the service again. Gregg soon had re-enlisted the greater part of the regiment (ibid., July 11, p. 2, col. 3; July 23, 1861, p. 2, col. 3) and had returned to Virginia (Richmond Dispatch, Aug. 29, p. 2, col. 7; Sept. 23, p. 1, col. 4; Richmond Examiner, Sept. 16, 1861, p. 3, col. 4).

1861,[7] he had not been in action, though, as part of the reserve on the 26th, his command had been under fire at Mechanicsville.[8]

Gregg was stopped by General Lee near Selwyn, where temporary headquarters had been established, and there he was given orders concerning the advance.[9] A little later, Gregg was recalled to Selwyn to explain his route to Longstreet and to learn from that officer where, on the right, the Georgian's Division was advancing. Back Gregg rode to his command. Through deserted Union camps he galloped and past a fine pontoon train the enemy had set afire.

Ere long Gregg's skirmishers sighted Federals behind the trees on a hill that overlooked a little north-and-south stream known as Powhite Creek. Dropping to the ground, the Confederate skirmishers loaded and fired. Soon they had the better of the exchange, but not to their commander's full satisfaction. He felt that he was losing time and he ordered the skirmishers to go forward at the double-quick. A yell swept the field. Gray figures sprang up. A scattered volley rattled down the front. Then, as the Federal rearguard slipped away, Gregg's men piled down the hill to the creek.

There, at Gaines' Mill—a cool and pleasant place on a drowsy day—they found themselves exposed. On the eastern side of the creek was a hill as high as that to the West. It was a strong position, and the one where General Lee had expected the Federal commander to give battle. A few good Union regiments, over the brow of the hill, could have made the environs of the mill too hot for the South Carolinians.

When the Confederates found the bridge over the creek and that over the millrace gone, they expected a contest. Abundant evidence there was, also, of the recent presence of the Federals in strength, but from the opposite hill came no fire. Gregg did not hesitate. He had his engineers repair the bridges quickly; he hurried his men over the crossing and up the hill. No Federals

where, on Dec. 12, 1861 (*Wright*, p. 67; *Richmond Dispatch*, Dec. 16, 1861, p. 2, col. 1), he had been made Brigadier General. (For his civil career, see references in *D. A. B. Cf.* also, 8 *C. V.*, 429; *De Leon*, 95; *Miss Brock*, 29; *Mrs. Chesnut*, 31; *O. R.*, 1, 306; *O. R.*, 51, pt. 2, p. 17; *O. R.*, 53, 140. An account of his body servant will be found in 2 *C. V.*, 233.)

[7] *Richmond Dispatch*, June 19, p. 3, col. 1; June 24, p. 3, col. 1; *Richmond Examiner*, July 1, 1861, p. 3, col. 1; *O. R.*, 1, 128.

[8] *O. R.*, 11, pt. 2, p. 853.

[9] Selwyn was the "Hogan House." See *O. R.*, 11, pt. 2, p. 853.

there, but enough and to spare in the distance! Two regiments of his Brigade Gregg hastily put in line. As many more he placed in support. "Forward," he called, and started across the flat, open fields.[10] A. P. Hill looked and admired. "It was," said he, "the handsomest charge in line I have seen during the war." [11]

On Gregg pressed, his direction a little South of East, until he came to the crossroads of New Cold Harbor. There on his right was the Parsons farm and, in front, thick woods and two narrow farm roads, one South, one Southeast. Gregg followed the one to the Southeast. Soon he was in the woods, which widened as he advanced. The ground, by this time, was falling away to the southward. Evidently a stream of some sort was on the right front. Gregg changed direction more to the South. His eager van hurled the Union skirmishers back and moved down the hill.

Suddenly and with a crash, the enemy delivered a powerful volley. Before its echo died, Union artillery opened. The enemy was flushed, was ready, was awaiting attack. Here, it became apparent, in the woods and not on Powhite Creek, was the position General McClellan had chosen to defend. All the cleared ground visible to the Confederates led down to a boggy little stream, which natives styled Boatswain's Swamp. This was bordered widely by almost impenetrable underbrush and by large trees and small. South of the swamp, at a good elevation, most of it open farm land, the Federals had their infantry and their artillery. For a mile and more, as the Confederates soon discovered, the course of the stream and the forest maze was from Northeast to Southwest. Then Boatswain's Swamp turned South, parallel to Powhite Creek, and emptied into the Chickahominy. In a word, the Federals had a perfectly protected position, of which they had made the most. At some points, the enemy had three lines of temporary works in front of his commanding artillery. He could have searched the countryside and could not have found a position easier to defend or more difficult to assail.

Gregg, as it chanced, had entered the woods opposite the point where they climbed farthest up the ridge on the Federal side of the swamp. Perhaps for that reason Gregg thought he could break the enemy's front. When he notified Hill that he had

[10] O. R., 11, pt. 2, pp. 853–54. [11] O. R., 11, pt. 2, p. 836.

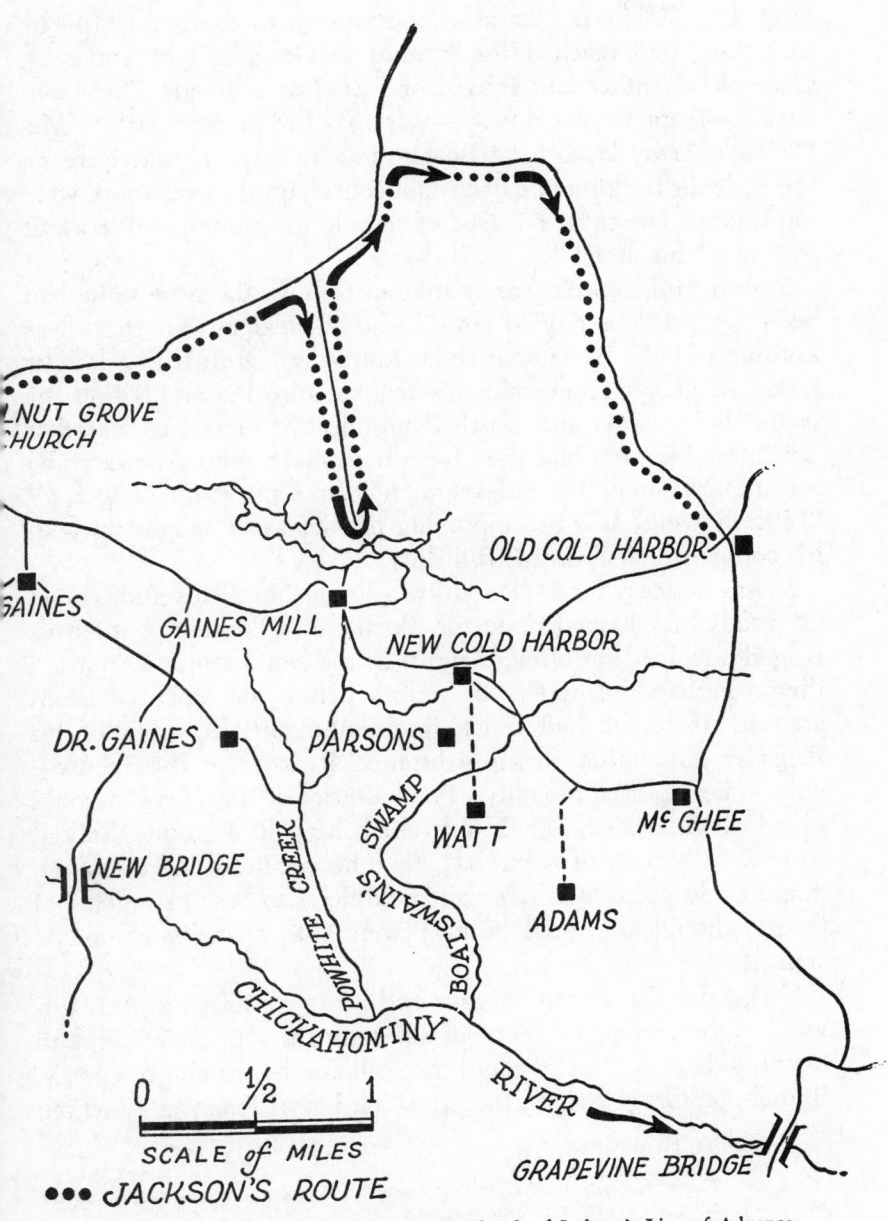

WALNUT GROVE CHURCH

OLD COLD HARBOR

GAINES

GAINES MILL

NEW COLD HARBOR

DR. GAINES

PARSONS

WATT

McGHEE

NEW BRIDGE

SWAMP

SWAIN'S

BOAT

ADAMS

POWHITE CREEK

CHICKAHOMINY

RIVER

GRAPEVINE BRIDGE

0 ½ 1

SCALE of MILES

●●● JACKSON'S ROUTE

Battlefield of Gaines' Mill, June 27, 1862, with Sketch of Jackson's Line of Advance

located the Unionists, he asked permission to charge.[12] Hill, by that time, had reached the ground to Gregg's right and rear. General Lee either had arrived or was close at hand. Their conclusion—from scant evidence—was that the greater part of McClellan's Army lay behind Boatswain's Swamp. If that were so, the Federals could not be driven, of course, until more troops were in position. Gregg was instructed to hold his ground and to await the signal for attack.[13]

Powell Hill himself was as anxious to press the issue as he had been the previous day to cross Meadow Bridges, but there was nothing of wild excitement about him now. Dressed in a fatigue jacket of gray flannel, with his felt hat down over his eyes, he sat his horse easily and watched proudly the arrival of his other Brigades. He even had time for a handshake with a private and for inquiry about his old regiment, the Thirteenth Virginia.[14] "Little Powell," said the approving private. as he caught up with his company, "will do his full duty today." [15]

It was not easy for Hill to draw a line in the fields and fringes of woods that looked down on Boatswain's Swamp; but as his Brigades formed on Gregg's right, he did not attempt to restrain them. Perhaps he hoped for victory before the other Divisions arrived. If so, he had quick disappointment. As each of his Brigades got within striking distance, it drove at the enemy— only to be repulsed bloodily. The batteries of the Division could give little assistance. Their able chief, Maj. R. Lindsay Walker, was absent because of sickness.[16] No other artillerist in Hill's command could get more than eight fieldpieces to bear in support of Gregg, though an equal number went into action later on the right.[17]

Gregg did his utmost. Again and again he tried to press forward. Once, even, he sent out six companies in an attempt to storm a battery.[18] He could not shake the stubborn enemy. Branch, on Gregg's right, fought as hard as at Hanover Junction.

---

[12] O. R., 11, pt. 2, p. 854.	[13] O. R., 12, pt. 1, p. 854
[14] 9 S. H. S. P., 558.
[15] Ibid. The private was the "Fighting Parson," J. William Jones, to whose zeal the preservation of much Confederate history is due.
[16] 3 C. M. H., 681.
[17] Exclusive of Maurin, who was near Dr. Gaines's house.
[18] O. R., 11, pt. 2, p. 855.

Dorsey Pender, supporting Branch, easily could lead his men to a certain point where the miniés began to whine. Then even the stout North Carolinians would recoil. J. R. Anderson, Archer and Field, in that order to the right, all had the same experience. Their men could get to the swamp; they could not penetrate it. The fire was too heavy.

A. P. Hill could not break the front. That was manifest. What, then, was to be done? Longstreet, now in position on Hill's right, was as calm and as cheerfully observant as if he had been watching a sham battle. His powerful command was at an angle of almost ninety degrees to the "Light Division"; but he had a difficult position from which to assault. In Longstreet's front was a wide-open space, a quarter of a mile in depth. Two streams had to be crossed. Behind the farther of these were Federal sharpshooters. Strong infantry, with improvised works, supported the sharpshooters. Still farther to the rear was Union artillery. Across the Chickahominy, McClellan's long-range batteries might enfilade the front of attack. "I was, in fact," said Longstreet, "in the position from which the enemy wished us to attack him." [19] Lee felt it prudent, in these circumstances, to defer Longstreet's attack until the arrival of Jackson on the extreme Confederate left forced the Federals to extend their line eastward. Then, when the force in front of Longstreet had been diminished, he could assail the Federal left.

That was a prudent and a logical plan, but its success depended on the arrival of Jackson before A. P. Hill's Division was wrecked. Where was Jackson? What delayed him? Including D. H. Hill, he had under his command the largest force he ever had directed. Fourteen Brigades were his, compared with the twelve of Longstreet and of A. P. Hill. When would Jackson's men be thrown against the Federal right? Anxiously the question was asked, but there was not the staff organization to answer it. From the time Jackson had left Walnut Grove Church, no word had been heard of him.

The explanation was one of circumstance, of the trivial, unforeseen circumstance that so often wrecks battle plans. D. H. Hill had taken the road ahead of Jackson and had advanced promptly

[19] *O. R.*, 11, pt. 1, p. 757.

He had reached Old Cold Harbor about the time Gregg had struck. With little trouble, D. H. Hill had taken position on the northern fringe of the upper end of Boatswain's Swamp, but there he had found the Federals. They were facing North and were strongly posted. Behind them were ten guns to sweep the road that led southward from Old Cold Harbor, the only road by which D. H. Hill could advance his own artillery.[20] Hill decided that he would remain where he was until Jackson arrived.

Jackson was late because his soldierly reticence, which perhaps was deepened in a strange country, had got him into trouble. He had been furnished with a competent guide to whom he had said only, in effect, Take me to Old Cold Harbor. Naturally the guide had chosen the shortest route which struck the Cold Harbor road near Gaines' Mill.

As Jackson approached the millpond, he heard the sound of A. P. Hill's action.

"Where is that firing?" he demanded.

The guide answered that it seemed to come from the direction of Gaines' Mill.

"Does this road lead there?"

He was told that the road went by Gaines' Mill to Cold Harbor.

"But," Jackson broke out, "I do not wish to go to Gaines' Mill; I wish to go to Cold Harbor, leaving that place on the right."

"Then," said the guide, "the left-hand road was the one which should have been taken, and had you let me know what you desired, I could have directed you aright at first."[21]

This meant reversing the column and marching it about four miles to Old Cold Harbor.[22] On this stage of the advance, Ewell proceeded at the head of the column until he met Maj. Walter H. Taylor of Lee's staff, who had been sent to look for the troops. How far Jackson and Whiting were behind him, Ewell did not know, but he had his own troops at hand—"Dick" Taylor's, Trimble's and Elzey's Brigades—and he could use them as Lee wished. They at once were put in support of the left half of A. P. Hill's Division, and ere long were thrown forward toward

[20] O. R., 11, pt. 2, p. 624.
[21] So Dabney, 443, with perhaps some furbishing of the guide's language.
[22] That is, northward to the vicinity of Carlton's Farm and thence via Beulah Church to Old Cold Harbor.

the swamp.[23] Soon they reached the ground to which some of Hill's men were clinging. At several points Ewell's veterans of the Valley passed beyond that broken and irregular front. As old Isaac Trimble led part of his Brigade down the slope, his regiments were greeted with cries: "You need not go in; we are whipped; you can't do anything." The answer of the soldiers who had fought at Winchester and at Cross Keys was confident: "Get out of our way; we will show you how to do it!" [24]

Ewell's seasoned troops found a task to test their staunchness. Through the swamp, from the opposite hillside, crashed the enemy's fire. Its fierceness shook the Louisianians. Gallant Colonel Seymour was killed. As Rob Wheat, commanding the Tigers, cheered on his men, he fell of a mortal wound. Field officers went down fast. Taylor was not there to calm by his presence and to inspire with his firm words. For the first time in its history, the Louisiana Brigade broke. Ewell had to withdraw it.[25]

Of Trimble's Brigade, one regiment only and part of another got to the front on the first advance. As they headed for the very center of the fight, Ewell himself could not resist the impulse to join them. When the Louisianians fell back, exposing the right of Trimble's men, Ewell quickly sensed the added danger: If his thin line broke, the enemy might take the offensive. Trimble hurried back to bring up his other regiments; Ewell remained near the front. Regardless of losses, he must hold off the Federals. To that end, Ewell decided to renew the offensive.

Fortunately, in John F. Trentlen, the Lieutenant Colonel of the Fifteenth Alabama, Ewell found a man of high mettle. Some of the soldiers of that regiment had exhausted their ammunition. The muskets of others were too hot to handle. Trentlen, in complete disregard of fire, simply held the men where they were by his words and example. Up and down the line rode, also, a young man of fiery exhortation. Where there was wavering, he appeared. Those who stood to their bloody work or crept forward for a

[23] Col. H. L. Landers, who studied the ground with great care, concluded that the right of Taylor's Brigade was slightly less than a quarter of a mile West of the road from New Cold Harbor to the Watt house and that the direction of his advance was Southeast. That part of Elzey's Brigade on Ewell's left was directly to the East of the road from New Cold Harbor to the McGhee house.

[24] O. R., 11, pt. 2, p. 615.

[25] O. R., 11, pt. 2, p. 605.

better shot, he commended loudly. As the soldiers saw him riding about, untroubled by the rain of bullets, most of them took him to be an officer of rank. Few recognized him as Private Frank Champion, who, in the frenzy of the battle, had caught a runaway horse, had mounted, and had undertaken to help in rallying the regiment.[26] The Fifteenth Alabama held. No less gallantly, the Twenty-first Georgia plugged the gap in the line.

It was now past 4 o'clock. Over the field hung the smoke. Dim and red shone the June sun.[27] Close was the issue. The battle, on the Confederate side, clumsily had been one of Divisions—first A. P. Hill's and, later, part of Ewell's. To the left, D. H. Hill merely had occupied the enemy in his front. On the right, Longstreet was ready, but still was being held for the arrival of Jackson to lead the other wing.

Now that Ewell had met such a fire that he could not hope to advance, Longstreet got orders to make a diversion that would take some of the pressure off Hill and Ewell. Promptly and calmly, Longstreet began the deployment on his right of three Brigades. On his left, next Hill's weakened right, he advanced Pickett. Unhesitatingly the Virginia regiments went forward in a vigorous demonstration. Volleys from the swamp and from the ridge rocked them. Soon it was apparent that, if Pickett's men kept on, they would be destroyed. The position was too strong. A diversion would be futile. The enemy would not for a moment be deceived by it. If anything at all was done, a general assault had to be delivered. So reasoned Longstreet. Notifying Lee, he began to arrange his forces for a direct thrust at the hillside in front of him. It was a soldierly decision in the face of an enemy who held firmly to every foot of his ground. Union artillery was being employed with fine persistence. To the Confederates across the swamp, the Federals seemed to have exhaustless reserves to replace those wearied in the fray.

On the Confederate left, the situation was no better. Jackson had arrived on D. H. Hill's front,[28] but he knew nothing of the terrain. Nor was Jackson sure of the position of the Southern forces whose battle was raging to the West. His assumption was that A. P. Hill and Longstreet were attacking and soon would

---

[26] *O. R.*, 11, pt. 2, p. 606.   [27] *McHenry Howard*, 140.
[28] The hour is not certain. It probably was about 3 o'clock.

drive the enemy; but in his confusion he was afraid that if D. H. Hill's Division were advanced it might be mistaken for a Federal command by Longstreet and A. P. Hill and might be assailed by their fire.

To obviate this risk, Jackson made D. H. Hill form a line under cover of some woods and at angle to the front Hill previously had held. In this way Jackson sought to get open ground in advance of Hill so that, if the enemy were driven eastward, a clear field of fire would be offered. Then, when Jackson learned that Ewell's Division already was engaged, he directed the only staff officer at hand, Major Harman, to carry orders back to Whiting and to Winder, who were on the road that led to Old Cold Harbor from the North. The two commanders were to move up at once *en échelon* on the left of Ewell, and were to fill the gap between Ewell and D. H. Hill.

Major Harman knew all about horses and wagons and little about military terms. When he reached General Whiting, he gave a muddled version of his instructions to that officer, who, by ill chance, was in no humor for any orders from Jackson. Earlier in the day, Whiting had mistaken D. H. Hill's column for a force of the enemy and had received a snub from Jackson because of his error. In the opinion of one observer, Whiting had been trying all the morning to tell Jackson what to do and had taken offense because Jackson had paid no heed. Now, as Whiting sharply quizzed Harman, he confused the quartermaster still more.

When the colloquy was ended, Whiting was left in the belief that Jackson merely wished him to remain where he was and to await further instructions. Winder was behind Whiting and, as senior brigade officer, was commanding Jackson's Division. It is not certain whether Harman reached Winder. If he did, and correctly repeated Jackson's orders, Winder could not advance to execute them: the road was blocked.[29] For an hour and more, then, the two Divisions, together with Lawton's Brigade, waited along the road while Ewell was wearing away his strength in the swamp. Still the battle remained one of futile divisional attack. The Confederate Army as a whole had not been employed.

The hot June sun was dropping toward the West. McClellan's

---

[29] *Dabney Memo., Hotchkiss Papers.* In reporting Major Harman's error, Major Dabney himself appears to have confused the flanks of the *échelon* movement.

troops were unshaken. From their strong position behind Boatswain's Swamp, they still beat off easily all attacks. Nothing less than an assault by the entire Army, driven home at any cost, could rout the bluecoats. Longstreet was preparing to attack; D. H. Hill was ready; Ewell was still putting up a good fight; Gregg's men and parts of other Brigades of A. P. Hill were hanging on. The outcome of the entire action might depend on Jackson. He did not realize it. Still less did Whiting and Winder. Because none of the three had any clear understanding of what was happening on the right, all of them might remain idle till the hour was too late for a strong, united blow.

Fortunately, Major Dabney had heard Jackson dispatch the orders that Harman had carried to Whiting. Perhaps because of his general dissatisfaction with the quartermaster's service, the Assistant Adjutant General doubted whether Harman would deliver correctly the commanding General's instructions. Dabney still was so ill that Jackson had ordered him to stay out of the sun, but he determined to ride back up the road to the division commanders and to make certain they understood orders. Without difficulty or long search he found Whiting.

"General," he began, "has Major Harman delivered you General Jackson's instructions?"

"Yes," answered Whiting, in tones that Dabney regarded as surly, "that man has been here with a farrago of which I could understand nothing."

"Did he tell you that it was the General's wish you should engage the enemy immediately?"

Dabney then explained what Jackson wished. Whiting was disposed to argue,[30] but he was prompt in moving. For some reason, as he advanced, he drifted to the right. With Hood's Brigade in front, he came ere long to the rear of the action at New Cold Harbor. Hood, vigilant and full of fight, soon found and questioned one of Ewell's staff officers: How fared the battle? The answer was that Ewell was hard pressed and needed help. That was enough for Hood. Waiting neither to report nor to ask instructions, he began to deploy his Brigade. While his right was forming, he sent to Ewell's support the Fifth Texas and part of the Hampton Legion.[31]

[30] *Dabney Memo.*   [31] *O. R.* 11, pt. 2, pp. 568, 606.

The remainder of Whiting's Division its commander placed on ground indicated by Lee. Behind Whiting's troops, Lawton now was coming up. He found nobody to direct him, but he observed on either flank of his line of advance a regiment that had drawn out of the fight, and he reasoned that the open space between them might be exposed.[32] His judgment was correct. Almost directly in front of him was Gregg. The South Carolinian still was holding his ground and had received a timely reinforcement in the arrival of his Fourteenth Regiment, which its vigilant Colonel, Samuel McGowan, had brought across the Chickahominy from the post where it had been left on picket duty.[33] Behind Gregg's thin but stubborn line, Lawton formed his 3500 men, the largest Brigade in the entire Army, and soon he crashed downward toward the swamp. "Dick" Ewell, in the heaviest of the fighting, saw Lawton's men coming forward and, waving his sword, he cried, "Hurrah for Georgia!"[34]

Whiting now was deployed. Hood's left was fighting independently; his right was taking position; Lawton was engaging; far to the eastward, Harvey Hill was waiting to go forward. That left only Winder to complete Jackson's line. For all his zeal, Winder had some difficulty in reaching the front because of unfamiliarity with the ground; but when he received a call from Ewell to move up rapidly, he directed his advance to the sound of the heaviest fire from the swamp[35] and fortunately hit the road between Old and New Cold Harbor. Soon he found A. P. Hill, to whom he reported for orders. They were given prudently: Winder was to remain where he was until it could be ascertained where he could be used most effectively.

Five o'clock it now was. Only three hours of the long summer daylight remained. Then would come confusing darkness. Would it be possible ere nightfall to put all those tangled Brigades into position and to throw them, as one man, against that fiery front on the long hill? Or must this battle end, as had that at Mechanicsville, with the enemy unshaken? There was as much of doubt as of promise on the field. Although Longstreet's deployment was complete, Pickett's first advance had shown that success was possible only if the entire Division went forward.

[32] Ibid.
[34] Ibid., 595.
[33] Ibid., 853, 856, 869.
[35] O. R., 11, pt 2, p. 570.

A. P. Hill's weary men could be expected to do little more than to follow a strong, fresh line. Ewell still was capable of hard fighting and, with Lawton's stout Brigade, might share in the final gamble. Winder, rightly placed, had good fire power. D. H. Hill, almost unscathed, could sweep forward at the word of command. He would be compelled, after he passed the heavy swamp, to cross 400 yards of open ground that were swept by musketry and field artillery and perhaps were enfiladed by batteries on his extreme left. Was the gamble an even one? Could Jackson decide it?

Jackson knew of Ewell's dispositions and of Harvey Hill's, and perhaps he had learned by this time that Winder, Whiting and Lawton were advancing on the right. The long day in a bewildering country had wearied Jackson. He needed refreshment. Out of his haversack he pulled, not a bottle but a lemon, which he rolled in his hands. He began to suck it and, so engaged, started down the sun-scorched road that linked Old Cold Harbor with the New. Dust covered him; his old cap was pulled down to his nose to shade his weak eyes from the glare. Not a word, not a gesture indicated his thought. Earlier in the afternoon he had been calm, and mindful even of so small a thing as the exposure of a sick staff officer to the sun. Had the uncertain combat changed him; was strange companionship embarrassing to him? Ahead he saw Lee; straight to the commander he rode.

"Ah, General," said Lee, as Jackson rode up, "I am very glad to see you. I had hoped to be with you before."

There was a mumbled answer, a jerk of the head—no more.

"That fire is very heavy. Do you think your men can stand it?"

"They can stand almost anything," came the proud answer. "They can stand that!" [36]

Jackson listened then as Lee explained how he was organizing the line. There was nothing unfriendly or unsympathetic in Jackson's manner, but neither was there any waste of words or any display of suave manners. As soon as he was sure he understood the plan, he was off to the left to prepare for its execution.

Later, when men looked back on the battle, they read into this brief scene a display of confidence on the part of Jackson and of

[36] 2 R. F. Lee, 153–54.

wise, comprehensive planning by Lee. At the moment, there seemed neither confidence nor plan in what was happening. Immeasurably different the realities were from what those civilian soldiers in the swamp and in the woods and along the road had thought a battle would be. They had been reared on stories of Napoleon's great victories; but instead of an assured march, with flapping flags, to a described position, they had seen that day on Boatswain's Swamp groping, floundering, halts, confusion, uncertainty. Every field seemed to be hedged about with blinding woodland. No fiery panorama was this, visible in all its parts, but a narrow strip of debris-strewn ground in front, or a bit of smoke-covered forest, from which the wounded were emerging or skulkers were slipping back, pale-faced. Who saw or could describe a plan? Officers knew only that the fighting was bitter, the outcome uncertain. In the place of swift movement, there was, even now, delay that seemed endless to those who waited for the command to advance. Through it all, maddening and ceaseless, was the ear-splitting din of conflict.[37]

Slowly, almost imperceptibly, some of the reinforcements felt their way across the fields. The greater part of Whiting's two Brigades got in rear of A. P. Hill's broken right; Cunningham and Fulkerson, senior Colonels of Brigades in Jackson's Division under Winder, were sent, very late, to support the left of Longstreet's line, which was creeping forward toward Powhite Creek. Lawton scarcely had halted from the moment he had moved to the relief of Ewell. At A. P. Hill's order [38] Winder now put the Stonewall Brigade on the left of Lawton and next to D. H. Hill's right Brigade, which was that of Ripley. At last, close to 7 o'clock, as the battle in the swamp spread more actively to Longstreet's Division, the front was complete. Five hours it had taken to get all the Brigades in position—five hours of hell for the men

---

[37] Remarkable stories were circulated concerning the distance at which the sound of the Seven Days' Battles could be heard. The action at Gaines' Mill was the noisiest of them all and, many veterans said, the most appalling in its din of any combat of the war. A "highly respectable gentleman" was authority for the statement that the rumble was distinct at the Peaks of Otter, computed to be 130 miles away (*Richmond Examiner*, July 2, 1862, p. 2, col. 2). One writer affirmed that the sound of battle could be heard at Staunton, and that the artillery fire was audible at McDowell, thirty miles farther West, but that it did not reach Beaver Dam, in Hanover County, about twenty-five miles away (*Richmond Dispatch*, Aug. 13, 1862, p. 1, col. 5).

[38] Doubtless issued after consultation with Lee.

already engaged—but the task was done. The Army of Northern Virginia was almost ready for its first general assault on an enemy whose defense of his position thus far had been superb.

Hood and A. P. Hill, at the moment, were examining the Federal position in their front, across the Parsons Farm and beyond the very thickest of the swamp.

Could Hood take that position? Hill asked.

Intently Hood looked. "I don't know whether I can or not," he said with blazing eyes, "but I will try!"

He touched his horse and started across the front of his waiting troops. About that time word was passed that General Lee had ordered a general advance by all the troops. To Hood it was a challenge as stirring as a bugle call. Drop your knapsacks and blankets, he told his men; we are going to take that line. I am going to lead you.[39] Whiting, too, rode along the front, and when the men cheered him he raised his hat. "Boys," he cried, as he pointed toward the enemy's position, "you can take it!" [40]

The Texans and their comrades started forward across the field and toward the swamp. On their right, Longstreet already was at grips with the Federal infantry.[41] His right flank was being enfiladed by Federal batteries across the Chickahominy, but this was not serious. Ewell was down in the swamp and in person was directing his men, who were getting support from Gregg and from other of A. P. Hill's Brigades. Lawton's men, most of them armed with Enfield rifles, kept an unbroken front; [42] Trimble was everywhere among his troops with the same cry, "Charge, men, charge!" [43] Winder, on Ewell's left, went forward in all the experience of the Valley Campaign.

So sure of themselves were the men of the Stonewall Brigade that the Second and the Fifth Virginia pushed ahead of the troops to right and to left. Ere long they found themselves exposed and in advance. Winder halted them, to wait for the other regiments to catch up. They stood, but they fell fast under the vicious fire.[44] Back of the line, a little farther to the left, Jackson was in the exaltation of conflict. His face was crimson; under his cap-brim

[39] Gen. H. T. Douglas, an eyewitness, in 19 *C. V.*, 78. The language of Hood's words to his men probably is verbatim, but, as General Douglas did not use quotation marks, they are omitted here.

[40] 1 *N. C. Regts.*, 304.

[41] *O. R.*, 11, pt. 2, p. 757.

[42] *Ibid.*, 595.

[43] *Ibid.*

[44] *O. R.*, 11, pt. 2, p. 570.

ıis eyes were burning. To each division commander he sent the ame message: "Tell them this affair must hang in suspense no onger; sweep the field with the bayonet!" [45]

D. H. Hill, on the extreme left, moved forward swiftly to the :dge of the swamp. In ignorance of the ground, some of his ›rigade commanders overlapped their lines. Whole regiments, on ıdvancing, found other Confederate units in their front. Vainly ǂill sought to correct the alignment. Robert Rodes, still weak 'rom his wounds at Seven Pines, strove to untangle his men. His ǂifth and his Twenty-sixth Alabama soon captured an advanced ›attery. They reached the maze of underbrush and crashed hrough it, but they did not venture into the open ground to the ;outh. The perfectly disciplined Sixth Alabama, under Col. John ɜ. Gordon, rushed on until it found itself beyond the swamp and n front of the other regiments of Rodes's Brigade. Opposing Gorlon were Federal infantry who seemed well covered and conident. From the left, Federal gunners were tearing the flank. ᴧs calmly as at Seven Pines on May 31, Gordon made his men ie down in line and, a little later, when the fire slackened momenarily, he led them back to the shelter of the swamp.[46] G. B. ᴧnderson—tall, erect, composed—found Federal infantry in the naze, but at the word of command in his magnificent voice his nen drove out the enemy.[47] Garland kept pace with Anderson.

All along the left, the swamp was cleared of the enemy. More han half the men of Harvey Hill's Division were on the southern 'ringe of the boggy stream. Ahead was a shell-swept open field, ı quarter of a mile to the crest. On the right, Lawton's troops and Ʌinder's could be seen in their steady advance toward the Federal ›osition on the ridge. G. B. Anderson and Garland crept out ·ogether from the swamp to study the ground. They were exɔosed but were as unconcerned as if no battle were raging. Could ⵂey strike in flank the Federals who were fighting Lawton and Ʌinder? Was such a movement possible in the face of the Federal ›attery that was enfilading the line of D. H. Hill's advance? Hill ıimself came up coolly and joined Garland and Anderson as they ısked the question. Eying the battery, Garland declared, "I don'ᵗ hink it can do much harm, and I am willing to risk it." Anderson

---

[45] *Dabney*, 455.
[46] For the next reference to Gordon, see *infra.* ɒ. 602. [47] 4 *N. C. Regts.*, 445.

agreed. Hill was willing but thought he could devise a better plan: while the advance was getting under way, he would have an effort made to take the troublesome battery from front and from rear.

Quickly Hill sent off two unemployed regiments of Elzey's Brigade, under a capable guide, to work around the left and to close in from the South on the barking Federal guns. Three other regiments he directed to dash straight for the battery. The division drew its line and waited. To the flank moved the troops who were to thrust at the Federal artillery. Swiftly, unhesitatingly, two of the regiments rushed forward, but, because of bad leading, they failed quickly and fell back panting. The Twentieth North Carolina, under a former regular, Col. Alfred Iverson, manœuvred separately into position to deliver an independent assault. As this regiment came into the open, the Division held its breath. Iverson fell, but Lt. Col. Franklin J. Faison took his place. A few minutes more, and the Carolinians were in full cry; a little longer and they were upon the guns. The instant Hill saw his men struggling with the Federal artillerists, he unloosed every regiment on the southern edge of the swamp. In a long, cheering line, they mounted the ridge. Soon the Federals were wavering, were breaking.[48]

Far from the West, almost at that moment, rolled the triumphant yells of Whiting's men. Hood's and Law's Brigades, leaving a thousand dead and wounded behind them, had cracked the Unionist front and were clambering over the batteries that for five hours had defied A. P. Hill's attack. Longstreet was on the crest of the hill within a few minutes; Lawton and Winder and Ewell swept up. Their fire covered the ridge and mowed down almost as many men as had fallen on the Federal side since the beginning of the battle. For half an hour there was spasmodic fighting, a futile Union cavalry charge, a rally here and there, a halt in the face of threatened attack by Federal reinforcements, and then darkness and a field of victory.

Because the battle might be renewed at dawn, there was no time that night to appraise divisional leadership or to ask whether the late co-ordination of attack was the best the Army could have expected of inexperienced officers who handled 56,000 men in that

48 O. R., 11, pt. 2, pp. 625-26.

bewildering country. Of brigade achievements, there had been many. In the praise of the camps, highest honors went to Hood and his fine regiments. They first had broken the line in a charge that had thrilled every observer. Said Jackson the next day, as he rode over the ground of Hood's advance, "These men are soldiers indeed!" It was noticed that in front of the position where Hood had broken through, all the Confederate dead were on the side of the swamp from which the attack had been delivered. Scarcely any had fallen South of the stream. Evidently, the Federals had abandoned all resistance on that part of the line as soon as those fierce soldiers were upon them.[49] The same condition prevailed on the line of Pickett's advance, immediately to the Southwest of Hood. The other Brigade of Whiting, composed of his own troops led by Col. E. M. Law, had shared fully the advance of Hood. For his general direction of these two Brigades, Whiting received at least as much credit as he deserved.

Among the other general officers, Maxcy Gregg, lawyer and savant, had given an unequivocal answer to the question whether he would make a soldier. Trimble had merited new apologies from Ewell for the aspersions made in that bitter monologue at Conrad's Store. Winder had added new honors to those won at Winchester and at Port Republic. Jackson, in his report, was to refer to him, with unusual warmth, as "that gallant officer, whose conduct here was marked by the coolness and courage which distinguished him on the battlefields of the Valley." [50] Garland had justified everything that had been said of him after Seven Pines. Lt. Col. Trentlen and Private Frank Champion were to have mention in dispatches. D. H. Hill was to commend Col. Alfred Iverson for his attack on the battery. In reporting the mortal wound of Lt. Col. Franklin Faison, who had succeeded Iverson at the head of the Twentieth North Carolina, the critical Hill was to assert that while Faison's troops had been able to hold the captured guns only ten minutes, and at a loss of 272 men, "no doubt a greater loss was saved to the Division in its advance by this gallant attack." [51] Maj. J. C. Haskell was praised by Whiting, by

---

[49] *Dabney,* 454.
[50] *O. R.,* 11, pt. 2, p. 555. Lest this tribute be regarded as the *amende honorable* for the slight Winder felt he had received at Jackson's hands, it should be noted that the report was not written until after Winder's death.
[51] *O. R.,* 11, pt. 2, p. 626.

D. R. Jones and by Longstreet, for his conspicuously gallant service as voluntary aide to Longstreet and, in particular, for carrying the flag of a regiment that had suffered heavily.[52]

The gunners had been given small opportunity. Even on Jackson's front, where the former instructor in artillery at the Virginia Military Institute had some open ground, only about thirty field-pieces, first and last, had been employed.[53] Capt. John Pelham alone had been afforded a chance of performing any spectacular service. He had gone forward with two guns, by Stuart's permission, to meet an artillery advance. Although his rifled Blakely then had been disabled at the first fire, Pelham used his single Napoleon so furiously and with so much skill that he occupied the full attention of two Federal batteries. When Stuart later brought Pelham up and presented him to Jackson, who gravely shook his hand, the young artillerist bowed deeply and blushed crimson.[54] Both Jackson and Stuart praised him in their reports.[55] Scores of others had deserved commendation almost as warm. "There was," said Longstreet, "more individual gallantry displayed upon this field than any I have ever seen." [56]

But the casualties! Some 8000 Confederates had fallen. Among them were men whom the South had taken generations to breed. No general officers had been killed, but Arnold Elzey had received a horrible wound of the face and neck. Pickett had been wounded somewhat seriously. The most gruesome loss had been among the regimental commanders. Besides Col. Isaac G. Seymour, acting head of the Louisiana Brigade, the battle had claimed Col. R. P. Campbell of the Seventh North Carolina,[57] Col. J. J. Woodward of the Tenth Alabama,[58] Col. C. C. Pegues of the Fifth Alabama,[59] and Col. John Marshall of the Fourth Texas,[60] which lost all of its field officers, killed or wounded. Fallen also were Col. J. W. Allen of the Second Virginia, who had led a regiment of the Stonewall Brigade throughout the Valley Campaign,[61] and, perhaps most serious of all, Col. S. V. Fulkerson, acting Brigadier

---

[52] *Ibid.*, 564, 693, 758.
[53] *O. R.*, 11, pt. 2, p. 556.
[54] Philip Mercer, *The Gallant Pelham*, 64.
[55] *O. R.*, 11, pt. 2, pp. 515, 556.   [56] *Ibid.*, 758.
[57] Branch's Brigade, *O. R.*, 11, pt. 2, pp. 883, 886.
[58] Wilcox's Brigade, *ibid.*, 758, 774.
[59] Rodes' Brigade, *ibid.*, 625, 632.
[60] Hood's Brigade, *ibid.*, 564.
[61] *Ibid.*, 555, 575. Winder's fine tribute to Allen appears *ibid.*, 570.

f the Third Brigade of Jackson's Division,[62] an officer of great romise. "Had he lived," said Dr. Dabney, "the highest distinc- ion must have crowned his merits; for his judgment, diligence nd talent for command were equal to his heroic courage."[63] Across the Chickahominy that same day, in an action at Garnett's 'arm, Col. W. M. McIntosh of the Fifteenth Georgia received a atal wound.[64] Besides these eight killed or mortally wounded, Col. R. E. Withers of the Eighteenth Virginia, Pickett's Brigade, ad been shot so badly that there was little hope he ever could eturn to field duty.[65] As Col. M. S. Stokes of the First North Carolina and Col. R. A. Smith of the Forty-fourth Georgia had een killed the previous day at Mechanicsville,[66] the offensive thus ad taken ten Colonels, besides those wounded. Many other field fficers had fallen, but none so picturesque or so well known as Rob Wheat. Time was to show that, without him, the Irish Battalion from Louisiana could not be kept in hand.

Costly, then, the victory was . . . and it was only the sec- nd engagement in what might prove a long struggle to save Richmond.

[62] *Ibid.*, 555.
[63] *Dabney*, 452.
[64] *O. R.*, 11, pt. 2, p. 690.
[65] *O. R.*, 11, pt. 2, p. 758. He survived to great age and to a seat in the United tates Senate, but never headed his regiment again.
[66] *O. R.*, 11, pt. 2, p. 623. A lofty tribute to Colonel Smith appears in W. W. Bennett *Narrative of the Great Revival*, 164.

CHAPTER XXXIII

MAGRUDER STAYS UP TOO LONG

BENEATH the "fog of war" and beyond the impenetrable woods, much had been happening to the Federals since A. P. Hill had opened the battle at Mechanicsville. In advance of that fight, General McClellan had been convinced by a shamefully incompetent company of civilian spies that his Army was outnumbered almost two to one. The approach of Jackson had decided him that he could not retain North of the Chickahominy any part of his Army, which numbered about 105,000 officers and men.[1] Accordingly, on the night of June 26, following the action on Beaver Dam Creek, he had concluded to retreat and to establish a new base on James River, where he would have the protection of the Federal gunboats.[2] He had accepted battle at Gaines' Mill because he feared a general withdrawal on the 27th would have exposed the rear of the Army and, as he phrased it, would have "enabled Jackson's fresh troops to interrupt the movement to James River."[3]

To delay the Confederate attack, he left behind Boatswain's Swamp the V Provisional Corps of Fitz-John Porter, which he reinforced to a fighting strength of about 35,000 before the close of the action.[4] Porter's defense, costing 6837 casualties,[5] won McClellan's praise, but the outcome confirmed his purpose to retreat or, more euphemistically, to "change his base." A counterthrust on the south side of the river against Huger and Magruder he ruled out. In his full report, he thus stated his reasons: ". . . the enemy was in our rear, and there was every reason to believe that he would sever our communications with the supply depot at the White House. We had on hand but a limited amount of rations, and if we had advanced directly on Richmond we would have required considerable time to carry the strong works around that place, during which our men would have been destitute of food,

---

[1] Classified as "present for duty." From the total force, 115,102, have been deducted the 9277 stationed at Fort Monroe (*O. R.*, 11, pt. 3, p. 238).
[2] *O. R.*, 11, pt. 1, p. 53. [3] *O. R.*, 11, pt. 1, p. 55.
[4] *Ibid.*, p. 56. [5] *Alexander*, 131.

nd even if Richmond had fallen before our arms the enemy could
till have occupied our supply communications between that place
nd the gunboats and turned the disaster into victory. If, on the
ther hand, the enemy had concentrated all his forces at Rich-
nond during the progress of our attack, and we had been de-
eated, we must in all probability have lost our trains before reach-
ng the flotilla." [6] This faulty reasoning, of course, had its origin
n the Federal commander's gross overestimate of the forces
pposing him, and even led him to apprehend an attack on the
outh as well as on the north bank of the river.[7]

On the night of the 27th, after the Battle of Gaines' Mill, Mc-
Clellan met his corps commanders and announced his plans of
vithdrawal.[8] Keyes's IV Corps was to cross White Oak Swamp
n the 28th, and was to cover the flank against the Confederate
ttack from the direction of Richmond. Porter was to follow.[9]
As soon as the wagon trains had passed, Franklin, Sumner and
Heintzelman, commanding the other Corps, were to withdraw
on the 28th–29th from their lines South of the Chickahominy.
These troops were to hold the rear against attack and were then
o head for James River.

To this retreat the little stream known as White Oak Swamp
presented both obstacle and cover. Beginning in the flat lands
around Seven Pines, and fed by several branches, White Oak
Swamp forms almost a half circle of about ten miles in total
length, with its arc to the South, ere it empties into the Chickahominy River near Fisher's Bridge.[10] On its upper stretches, the
creek or "swamp" presented no material difficulty in dry weather,
but after heavy rains it overflowed swiftly and transformed all
approaches into a bog. Access to it was easy enough from McClellan's position. Numbers of roads ran down to it from the North,
through thick woods. Just before the swamp was reached from
that direction, a lateral "New" road, paralleling the stream, gave
troops a choice of crossings—at Jordan's, at Fisher's and at Brackett's Fords—where crude bridges led to high ground. Beyond
this, on the south side of the swamp, was the Charles City road.
The principal crossing was at White Oak Swamp Bridge, about

6 O. R., 11, pt. 1, p. 60.
7 Cf. ibid., pp. 51, 271.
8 Ibid., p. 59.   9 O. R., 11, pt. 1, p. 62; ibid., pt. 2, p. 192.
10 One and three quarter miles Southeast of Bottom's Bridge.

five miles Southeast of Savage Station. From this crossing a decent road ascended to Long Bridge Road. Once this highway was passed, there was a slow descent to the James, which was distant slightly less than five miles on a straight line, though nearer seven by road. McClellan's problem was to get quickly across the swamp without overcrowding the approaches. Once he was on the south side, he could hope to hold the swamp against an attack on his rear. Stated differently, as he progressed toward James River, he probably would have to guard his column against attack from the West only. From no other quarter did it seem likely he could be assailed.

None of this was known, on the morning of June 28, to the Confederates around Cold Harbor or to those who faced the enemy between New Bridge and White Oak Swamp. McClellan's forces were South of the Chickahominy, in the vicinity of the battlefield of the previous day; but would the Federals stay there? Might not McClellan move down the south bank of the Chicka- hominy, take advantage of the southeasterly course of that river and recross to the north bank in order to re-establish his line of supply down the Peninsula? Not until the early morning of the 29th was the answer clearly "No." Then, but not until then, was it established that McClellan was heading for James River.[11] A full concentration by the Confederates that day on the Federal rear North of White Oak Swamp was impracticable. Even if the entire Confederate army could have been brought to the south side of the Chickahominy before night, McClellan could give battle and then, under cover of darkness, could pass over the swamp as Porter had over the Chickahominy after the action at Gaines' Mill. The distances were too great for Lee to move the whole of his Army West of the head of the swamp and to get in position on the south bank in time to dispute a crossing. Besides, if McClellan preserved his lines of supply, this would have exposed Richmond to attack from the direction of Seven Pines.

For these reasons, Lee did not undertake to prevent a crossing of White Oak Swamp. He planned, instead, to press the Federal rear North of the morass on the 29th, and to move the remainder of his troops, by the roads nearer Richmond, until they could

11 This move had been suspected late in the afternoon of the 28th, but had not been confirmed. See 2 R. E. Lee, 162–63.

strike the Federals the next day, June 30, on the march from White Oak Swamp toward James River. This involved a difficult convergence, but in a country so cut by small streams and covered by tangled woodland that an opponent could steal a day's march, there was no alternative.

Early on the morning of the 29th, the division commanders got their orders. Jackson was to reconstruct and cross Grapevine Bridge. Then he was to sweep down between the Chickahominy and the swamp, with his own, Ewell's, Whiting's and D. H. Hill's Divisions. As he went, Jackson was to clear the country of Federals and was to assail their rear. Magruder was instructed, as will be explained later in more detail, to push down the Williamsburg road. When Jackson came up, Magruder was to have that officer's support in attacking the enemy. Huger's orders were to proceed eastward on the Charles City road, South of the swamp, and on the 30th to take the Federals in flank. Longstreet and A. P. Hill were to recross the Chickahominy close to Richmond, and were to march down the Darbytown road to a position on Huger's right, where they, also, were to assail the flank of McClellan as he moved toward James River. Gen. T. H. Holmes, who had crossed from the south bank of the James, was to be on the right of Longstreet and A. P. Hill, in order to head off McClellan.

Which were the more difficult tasks in this convergence? Who had the largest opportunity? How well suited for their missions were the divisional commanders? Longstreet, who ranked A. P. Hill, was given direction of their joint operations. He would have a long march, but he would encounter no natural obstacle. Holmes had a clear road. Huger had to cover approximately eight and a half miles. So far as was known, none of these columns would be in contact with the enemy until its march had been completed. Magruder would have rearguard action and might have to pass through some fortified positions. To Jackson, as in the opening of the campaign, the most arduous task was assigned. After the engagement of the 27th, he had been required to send Ewell down the Chickahominy to guard against a possible return of McClellan to the north bank. Consequently, before Jackson could employ his full force, he had to recall Ewell. Meantime, the rebuilding of Grapevine Bridge might prove a troublesome task. Thereafter, Jackson's work was of the sort in which

he was proficient. Troops enough he had: Was his mission too
large for the time allowed him?

Magruder was to open the third act of the drama and probably
was to have the largest opportunity. His immediate preparation
had not been happy. Many vexations and embarrassments had
been his during the period covered by the operations North of the
Chickahominy. Magruder had not felt that he was slighted by
being denied a part in the initial attack. One of his staff officers,
writing thirty years later, doubtless remembered correctly the feelings of the time: "When we considered and discussed the plan,
we all thought that the position of holding our front lines against
McClellan and thereby protecting Richmond, was the post of
honor as well as of danger, because it never occurred to us that
McClellan with his superior numbers could fail to attack and seek
to break through . . ." [12]

The instructions of Magruder and of Huger had been to demonstrate on the 26th, in order to ascertain what the Federals were
doing. If opportunity offered, the two commanders were to convert their demonstration into an attack. Once the battle was
joined across the stream, they were to hold their positions at all
hazards. They understood that McClellan must not be permitted
to crash his way into Richmond with his left on the 27th while he
was warding off Lee with his right. That was imperative. If the
enemy abandoned his entrenchments on the south side, he was to
be pursued closely.[13] So, in plain, explicit terms, the two Generals
were admonished. Huger ranked Magruder;[14] but on receipt of
the combat order, Magruder apparently made his preparations
independently of the senior. "Prince John" was determined that
everything be done under his own eyes and that nothing go
wrong. He moved his headquarters up to the front line, which
was close to that of the enemy; he stirred the pickets; at frequent
intervals he had his batteries challenge those of the Unionists to
be sure no withdrawal was in progress.

After the Federals were brought to bay on the 27th behind
Boatswain's Swamp, Magruder's anxiety mounted. The contest

---

[12] *Brent*, 158–59.   [13] *O. R.*, 11, pt. 2, p. 660.
[14] His name appeared ahead of the Virginian's on the list of promotions of Oct. 7,
1861. He had outranked Magruder in the "Old Army" as respected both regular and
brevet commissions.

was raging a mile and a half to the Southeast. Some of the fighting was visible from high points. All that Magruder was able to do was to watch, to wonder and, with his long-range artillery, to attempt to reach the Federals in front of Longstreet.[15] Later in the afternoon Magruder grew restless and apprehensive. What if the Federals should attack; what if they were about to do so? He decided to feel them out opposite the points where their lines were closest to the Chickahominy. Through D. R. Jones, commander of one of his three half-divisions, he directed that a demonstration be made by G. T. Anderson's Brigade. Fiery Robert Toombs, who had a contempt for the caution of professional soldiers, was ordered—in writing, lest there be misunderstanding—to move forward when Anderson made his feint. If any advantage was gained, it was to be exploited. On the right, the demonstration then was started by Anderson, but was stifled quickly. Wisely, Anderson stopped his men and abandoned the demonstration. Toombs would not have it so. He pushed on pugnaciously, threw six companies forward, supported them with a regiment and, in a short time, lost heavily and to no purpose.[16]

This, of course, was not a pleasing incident on the 27th, but it was to Magruder a small concern in comparison with the responsibility he felt during the night. Then he learned that the Federals on the north side of the Chickahominy had given up the battle there and had returned to the lines South of that stream. His information, moreover, was that McClellan had destroyed all the bridges and thereby had isolated Huger's and Magruder's troops. Lee could not reinforce him, Magruder reasoned, otherwise than by sending troops back to Mechanicsville and having them march down the heights on the south side—a matter of ten miles, or more than half a day on the road. His troops and Huger's, a total of 25,000 men, Magruder told himself, had opposite them perhaps 100,000. What was there to keep the Federal commander from forming his Army in column and repeating the great maneuver of Napoleon at Austerlitz? Although the head of this column of attack "would have suffered greatly," Magruder concluded, "its momentum would have insured him success, and

15 *O. R.*, 11, pt. 2, p. 689. Many details are given in *Brent*, 169 ff.
16 *O. R.*, 11, pt. 2, pp. 689–90.

the occupation of our works about Richmond, and consequently of the city, might have been his reward." [17] Magruder's apprehension was deepened still further because Lee, across the river, had considered that the two wings of his Army had been united when his advance had passed New Bridge, which D. R. Jones's Brigade had repaired promptly in Magruder's rear. Magruder could not take that confident view: New Bridge, he maintained, was under Federal fire and of little use.[18] The situation, in his judgment, was "extremely critical and perilous." [19]

Morning of the 28th brought no relief to "Prince John." His worry was producing a bad attack of indigestion.[20] It was manifest, as he had suspected the previous night, that the Federals had abandoned the north side of the Chickahominy. He believed the whole Federal Army was in front of him and of Huger and might break through at any time and at almost any point. He had been enjoined by new orders, which Lee issued after Toombs's fiasco the previous day, to continue on the alert and to resist attack at any cost, but not to assume the offensive, except in co-operation with Lee, unless he was absolutely sure of success.[21] What should he do? Magruder asked himself. If an attack were delivered by the overwhelming adversary, how should he meet it?

Early on the 28th, Magruder left his headquarters.[22] Where he went and why he left, the records do not show. When he returned, a little after 11 A.M., he found some of his artillery playing heavily on the strong Federal work at Golding's Farm in his front. D. R. Jones had been looking for him.

Had he ordered an attack by Toombs's Brigade? Jones inquired.

Magruder replied that he had not.

Toombs was preparing a charge, Jones explained.

Thereupon Jones hastened to give an account of what had happened while Magruder was absent from headquarters. He himself had concluded, Jones said, that the Federals were about to retreat: and, when he had not been able to find General Magruder, he had sent a staff officer across the Chickahominy to inform General

---

[17] Magruder included his reflections in his report, O. R., 11, pt. 2, p. 662. It is reasonable to assume that they occurred to him at the time.
[18] O. R., 11, pt. 2, pp. 661, 662.
[19] Ibid., 662.
[20] Brent, 192.
[21] O. R., 11, pt. 2, p. 661.
[22] O. R., 11, pt. 2, p. 690.

ee and to request an artillery enfilade that would help to cover
1 assault by Magruder's troops. Next, Jones went on, he had
moved up some of his own guns to test the volume of answering
re. Then he had notified General Toombs that, if the enemy
ithdrew, Toombs was to advance, was to seize the strong redoubt
Golding's Farm and was to open on the retreating foe. The
tillery, Jones continued, had forced the Federals to leave their
utworks; Toombs had been so advised and had been told to put
is batteries into action. On receipt of these instructions, Jones
id, Toombs had told the staff officer who carried the message to
de on to G. T. Anderson and to instruct him to attack with the
ssurance of Toombs's support.[23]

That, Jones now told his chief, was the reason he asked if
Magruder had ordered the attack by Toombs. At that moment,
apt. Osman Latrobe spoke up. He was the officer whom Jones
ad sent to Lee's headquarters with the request for artillery
ssistance, and he was back with a message. General Lee, said
aptain Latrobe, renewed his instructions that no attack, other
an one made in co-operation with him, be made on the south
de of the river unless success was absolutely certain.

Instantly Magruder's excitement mounted. The positive orders
f the commanding General were being disobeyed. If Toombs
nade an attack and failed, the enemy might follow Toombs back
the Confederate position, might turn the left of the Confederate
ne next the river, and might march into Richmond. Stop
oombs, then! That was imperative.

Off galloped one of Jones's staff with countermanding orders.
He had not gone far before a report came that Toombs already
ad attacked and had carried the rifle pits in front of the strong
oint of the Federal line. That, of course, changed everything:
nstead of admitting a violation of orders, Magruder could report
success. Let a swift rider carry the good news to General Lee;
end another to get further details; Magruder himself would pro-
eed to the front to follow up the advantage.

Forward went Magruder, as gloriously as on the day of Big
Bethel—only to meet his crestfallen Assistant Adjutant General
with news of another mishap. Col. G. T. Anderson, the staff
officer reported, duly had delivered the attack Toombs had or-

[23] O. R., 11, pt. 2, p. 690.

dered, but the countermand from Magruder had been received by Anderson before Toombs had come up in support. Anderson already was withdrawing his troops; Toombs had been halted before he got into action. The whole affair had been abortive, except for losses in the attacking regiments.[24] Magruder had, consequently, the humiliation of dispatching to Lee another messenger to announce what had happened. Lee's only reply was to direct that Toombs file a report of his reasons for attacking without orders.[25]

This affair was eclipsed by the greater events that followed and in a few weeks it almost was forgotten, but it was a somber forecast of failure in co-ordination. Magruder had disregarded Huger; when Jones had not found Magruder at headquarters, he had acted as if he were exercising independent command; Toombs was told to advance under certain conditions, but he proceeded to issue orders to G. T. Anderson, though Jones, who had direction of both Brigades, was near at hand.

All this occurred before midday on the 28th.[26] When it ended, quiet had fallen on Magruder's front. Efforts to ascertain the movements of the Federals came to nothing. Where the earthworks were visible, they appeared to be fully manned; the woods were impenetrable; every road was well guarded. Magruder still remained in the deepest concern lest he be attacked.[27] Lee's renewed instructions were for Huger and Magruder to be vigilant that night and to pursue promptly if they found the enemy in retreat.[28]

Direct and simple as were these orders, they increased Magruder's excitement still more. Both risk and obligation he magnified. When subsequently he wrote of the events of the night, he said: "I received repeated instructions during Saturday night from General Lee's headquarters enjoining upon my command the utmost vigilance, directing the men to sleep on their

[24] O. R., 11, pt. 2, pp. 661, 690. The attack was delivered by the Seventh and Eighth Georgia. The only detailed account of the repulse is that given by Capt. James D. Campbell, who commanded the 49th Pennsylvania (O. R., 11, pt. 2, pp. 473–74).

[25] Apparently, Magruder did not ask for such a report. When Toombs sent in his account of operations during the campaign, he omitted all reference to the occurrences of June 27 (O. R., 11, pt. 2, pp. 661, 695–96).

[26] O. R., 11, pt. 2, p. 473.

[27] Lee's description of conditions on the south side of the Chickahominy on the 28th, O. R., 11, pt. 2, p. 494, made it clear that he did not consider Magruder or Huger negligent because they were unable to discover what was happening in their front.

[28] O. R., 11, pt. 2, p. 494.

rms, and to be prepared for whatever might occur." [29] Magruder
was not content to communicate these orders to his division commanders and to Huger. To be sure that the entire force was on
he alert, he decided to supervise personally the transmission of
orders and to check their proper execution. To this task he devoted the entire night.[30]

So much for the background. It was now 3.30 on the morning
of the 29th. Magruder's indigestion was persisting. Medicine
given by the surgeon was having an exciting effect. The General
was not physically at his best for what might prove his day of
days. In none of the dramas he had played as an amateur Thes-
pian, had he assumed so great a role as the one that now was his,
that of pursuing a vast army. His information before daylight
was that the enemy was still in the works opposite him, though,
in actual fact, only the thinnest rearguard was there. Soon after
dawn, word came from the pickets that the Federals had evacuated. Immediately Magruder dispatched the news to General Lee
and added that he was preparing to attack. Almost simultaneously, word came from G. H. Q. of the enemy's withdrawal.
When the messenger sent to Lee's headquarters returned to
Magruder, he brought thanks from the commanding General
and the request, half-facetious and half-rebuking, that when the
Federal works were attacked, Lee hoped Magruder would not
injure the two engineers of Longstreet's Division who already
had crossed the river and had entered the fortifications.

Magruder's relief was immense when he heard that the Federals were withdrawing from his front,[31] but before he made his
dispositions to pursue, Col. R. H. Chilton of Lee's staff rode up.
The commanding General, said Chilton, had crossed to the south
side of the Chickahominy and was on the Nine Mile road, where
he wished to see Magruder and to give him instructions for the
day.[32] Magruder started off with Chilton and, as he rode, dis-

29 O. R., 11, pt. 2, p. 662.
30 Ibid.
31 O. R., 11, pt. 2, p. 662.
32 Ibid. Magruder did not state the hour of Chilton's arrival. Consequently, it is
impossible to say whether Magruder had reasonable time to organize pursuit before he
left his quarters. Failure on Magruder's part to specify the time naturally suggests that
it was not early. Had it been so, Magruder probably would have recorded that fact to
explain why he had not issued orders. His statement that Chilton "hurried me off to
see General Lee" carries, of course, the implication that Magruder felt he should have
been allowed more time.

patched orders to his subordinates to move forward.[33] After the
two officers overtook General Lee and his staff, the cavalcade
followed the line of the Federal retreat toward Fair Oaks. Magruder listened, perhaps abstractedly, while Lee explained the
plan for the reconcentration:[34] Longstreet and A. P. Hill were
to cross in rear of Magruder's position and were to move to the
extreme right, so that they could intercept McClellan en route to
James River; Huger was to proceed down the Charles City road;
Jackson was to cross—perhaps already had crossed—at Grapevine
Bridge and was to operate against the enemy's flank nearest the
Chickahominy. Magruder's mission was explicit: He was to press
directly on the Federal rear and was to attack.

When the riders reached Fair Oaks Station, Lee went over the
plan again, in order that there might be no possible misunderstanding. Then, as Lee found the Federal line already occupied
by J. B. Kershaw's South Carolina Brigade of McLaws's Division, he rode off toward the Charles City road to give full verbal
instructions to General Huger.[35]

Magruder was now in charge of the field and of the pursuit of
the rearguard. He knew the country well, because he had traversed it on the retreat up the Peninsula. Around him was all the
debris of the abandoned Federal line and the encumbering, with-
ered abatis that had been cut before the battle of Seven Pines.
Eastward, the track of the York River Railroad disappeared in a
long, scarcely perceptible curve between woodland on either side.
Less than a mile to the Southeast, hidden by forest, was the Williamsburg road, which roughly paralleled the railway at an average distance to the South of half a mile. Down that road, as
Magruder knew, was a continuance of the same flat country.
With one or two small streams to break them, alternating woods
and open fields ran all the way to the Chickahominy. South of
the Williamsburg road, the woods thickened and the fields narrowed till the sodden jungle of White Oak Swamp was reached.

From the nature of the terrain, the Federal retreat had to be
eastward and southeastward across the swamp toward James
River. Ready to follow the enemy, D. R. Jones was coming up on
the left, and North of the railroad, though as yet perhaps a mile

---

[33] O. R., 11, pt. 2, p. 662.　　　[34] Given in slightly more detail. *supra*, p. 545.
[35] O. R., 11, pt. 2, p. 662.

off. Kershaw was prepared to go forward at the word of command. McLaws's other Brigade, that of Paul Semmes, had not yet arrived from the line of fortifications. Magruder's own Division was approaching, under Howell Cobb and Richard Griffith.

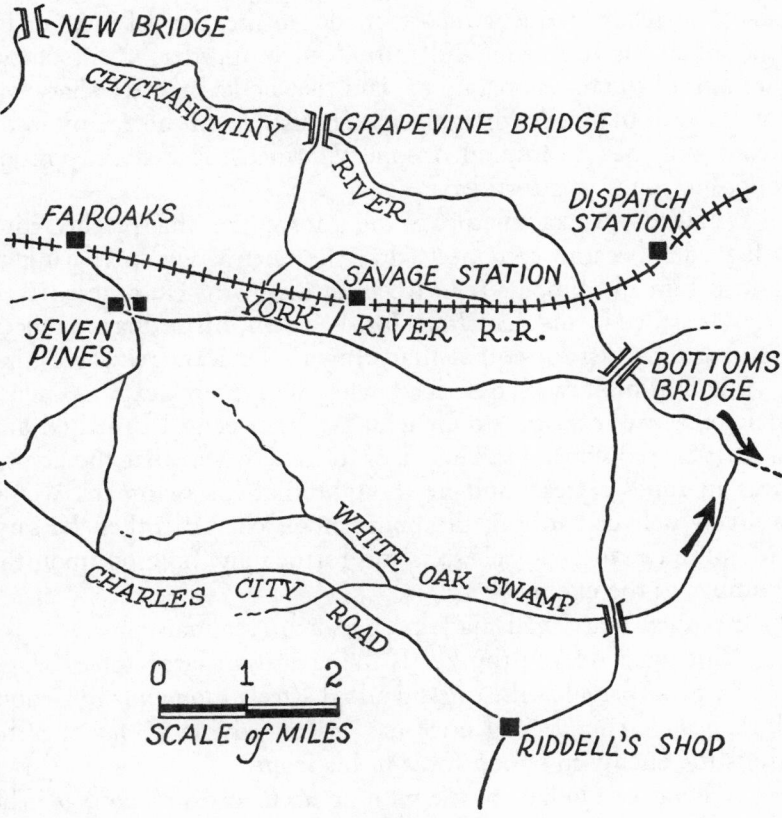

The Environs of Savage Station

Six Brigades, then, approximately 11,000 infantry, could be concentrated against an enemy who, as yet, had shown no more than a skirmish line and had not halted anywhere for a stand.

Slowly Magruder began to make his dispositions North and South of the railroad and, when they seemed adequate, he permitted Kershaw to advance warily along the railway and to the right of it.[36] Kershaw soon saw troops crossing the tracks at some

[36] O. R., 11, pt. 2, pp. 716, 726.

distance ahead of him and, as he had received cautions that he might have a collision with Jackson, coming up from the left, he halted after an advance of about one mile. By reason of this halt, D. R. Jones, moving up, found himself ahead of the troops directly North of the railroad. He, too, stopped his advance. Kershaw, in his subsequent report, made no mention of any fortifications in his front, nor did Jones; but Magruder, in his official account of the day's operations, said that he learned Kershaw was facing well-manned works, that Jones discovered the enemy in his front and that a captured prisoner affirmed the Federal position opposite Jones was fortified.[37]

Whatever the exact nature of the information that reached him, Magruder became convinced that the enemy was preparing to attack him in numbers far exceeding his own. He ordered Kershaw recalled[38] and sent Maj. Jos. L. Brent, his ordnance officer, posthaste to Lee to request that Huger's Division reinforce him.

Brent himself well described what happened next: "When I delivered my message [to General Lee] he seemed surprised and a little incredulous. He said his information was that the enemy was in rapid retreat, and he thought that his rearguard would scarcely deliver battle at the point indicated. And then he said, 'Major, have you yourself seen and formed any opinion upon the number of the enemy?'

"I replied that I had made no personal reconnaissance.

" 'But what do you think? Is the enemy in large force?'

"I was surprised at the question, and after a moment's reflection, I replied, 'General Magruder has instructed me to say that he finds the enemy in strong force in his front.'

"General Lee looked at me with an amused expression, as if he appreciated the loyalty that declined to express an opinion contrary to the message that I bore.

"After some consideration and reflection, he said, 'Tell General Magruder that General Huger is much needed to carry out an important duty, from which he cannot be spared, but I will order him to detach two of his Brigades to report to General Magruder.

[37] Magruder's report, *O. R.,* 11, pt. 2, p. 663.
[38] *O. R.,* 11, pt. 2, p. 726.

But if they are not actually engaged by 2 o'clock, he must order them to resume their march and rejoin General Huger on the Charles City Road.' " [39]

Huger, at that moment, was marching down the Charles City road, but he started two Brigades back up the road in accordance with Lee's order.[40] Magruder had forgotten at the time, or else he forgot when he came to prepare his official narrative, that Lee had sent Huger forward by that route. According to his report, Magruder thought that Huger was to march down the Williamsburg road, not down the Charles City road on the south side of White Oak Swamp. He relied on Huger, he said, to cover his right.

Not content with assurance of help in that quarter, Magruder sent to the left to ascertain where Jackson was and what co-operation could be given on that flank. Magruder was told, in reply, that Jackson was rebuilding Grapevine Bridge and would not be ready to cross for two hours.[41] Thereupon, still in the belief that he was about to be attacked, Magruder decided that he would delay his advance until Huger came up on his right and Jackson on his left. When they arrived, he explained in his report, he intended to envelop the entire Federal rearguard.[42]

Forgotten, apparently, were Magruder's orders to pursue vigorously. With six good Brigades at hand, ready for advance and supported by artillery, he waited out of range. An hour, perhaps two hours, passed until, at last, Huger rode over through the blistering heat to Magruder's field headquarters and stated that his two Brigades were arriving. There was, at the time, some firing in front of Kershaw, [43] though no evidence that the enemy intended to take the offensive; but Magruder insisted to Huger that the Federals were advancing in great force. Would Huger see to it that his Brigades formed line of battle with their left on

---

[39] *Brent*, 181. It is possible that while Brent remained for a "very pleasant conversation" with some of Lee's staff officers (*ibid.*), Magruder sent directly to Huger for help. Huger so stated (*O. R.*, 11, pt. 2, p. 789).

[40] *O. R.*, 11, pt. 2, pp. 680, 789. Nowhere in his report did Magruder record the fact that he requested the two Brigades. He left the implication that these troops properly should have been on the Williamsburg road under Lee's plan of advance.

[41] *O. R.*, 11, pt. 2, p. 663. [42] *Ibid.*

[43] *O. R.*, 11, pt. 2, p. 726.

the railroad and their right at Seven Pines? Then Magruder rode off.

Huger was puzzled. Was there any indication of a Federal advance? He could see none. The works around Seven Pines were abandoned. If the Unionists had intended to fight, Huger reasoned, they would not have left their fortifications. What they were doing bore every sign of a mere demonstration to delay pursuit. Still, Magruder had been on the ground all morning. If Magruder were convinced of an impending attack, Huger reluctantly concluded that he should put his troops in the desired position.[44]

Magruder thereafter busied himself for some time in moving his troops to a better defensive position. Several of his regiments he advanced to more commanding ground on the edge of a wood, whence they would have a better field of fire on an approaching foe.[45] When the bluecoats attacked him, he would give them the best battle he could! While Magruder was thus engaged, a messenger arrived from General Huger: the division commander on the right, said the messenger, presented his compliments and begged to advise that under his orders he did not think it necessary to stay where he was. He consequently was withdrawing his two Brigades for other service.

When Magruder prepared his report, he wrote somewhat hazily concerning the reason Huger gave for leaving the Williamsburg road and he insisted that this, and a development that came a short time afterward, robbed him of the opportunity of capturing "a large portion of the enemy's forces." [46] The fact was that while Huger was drawing his line, as requested by Magruder, he saw a Confederate force in his front and, upon inquiry, he learned that the two Brigades of McLaws had taken that ground. Just at that moment there arrived a dispatch from headquarters. In it Lee stated that if Huger were not needed in support of Magruder, he

[44] *O. R.*, 11, pt. 2, p. 789.   [45] *Ibid.*, 664.

[46] *O. R.*, 11, pt. 2, p. 664. Magruder did not state in his report that Huger's withdrawal was in accordance with Lee's instructions, but Huger, *ibid.*, 789, said: "I . . . sent a message to General Magruder that under my orders I had decided it was not necessary for me to stay." By the time Huger had arrived with the van of his troops, Brent was back with Magruder (*op. cit.*, 181–82) and, of course, was careful to report what had happened at Lee's headquarters. Magruder, therefore, could not have been unprepared for the announcement that Huger was leaving, but later Magruder may have forgotten this.

should resume down the Charles City road his march, which was most important for the plan of operations. Huger considered that he was in a second-line position where, so far as he could see, there was no prospect of a Federal attack. Accordingly, Huger did not hesitate to start his troops back toward the Charles City road.[47]

That was not the end of troubles for the tired and excited Magruder. While he still hesitated to undertake pursuit, in the belief that he was about to be attacked, D. R. Jones sent from the left a dispatch. This concerned the position and movements of the enemy there. Jones said: "I do not think it will be prudent for me to attack with my small force, unless there be a simultaneous attack all along our lines. I will keep a good lookout on my left." Then Jones added a sentence that shook Magruder to his boot heels: "I had hoped that Jackson would have cooperated with me on my left, but he sends me word that he cannot, as he has other important duty to perform." [48]

Huger withdrawing; Jackson unable to co-operate—what was Magruder to do? What could he do except to obey orders that had contemplated his pursuit of the enemy in the forenoon? There was no chance now of a great coup and, at that hour of the afternoon, little prospect of pressing far. Did he reason, too, that there was small risk of defeat? "I ordered the whole [force] to move to the front," he subsequently reported, "and each commander to attack the enemy in whatever force or works he might be found." [49]

Rhetorically, the statement was fine; tactically, the performance was timid. The "whole" was not sent forward. Instead, Magruder advanced Kershaw on a narrow front [50] and supported him with the other Brigade of McLaws's small Division. When these troops came to grips with the enemy, Magruder threw in two regiments of Griffith's Brigade. On the railroad, he used a piece of heavy ordnance on a truck, and he employed a few guns from his left, but he confined his attack on his right. Out of six Brigades present, he used only two and a half. Although D. R. Jones was advantageously placed on the left, he was not given the

---

47 *O. R.,* 11, pt. 2, p. 789.   48 *O. R.,* 11, pt. 2, p. 675.
49 *O. R.,* 11, pt. 2, p. 664.   50 *O. R.,* 11, pt. 2, p. 726.

order to advance. Instead, about nightfall he, too, was called to support the right. Darkness and a terrific thunderstorm halted him before he reached that position.[51]

The advance of Kershaw and of Semmes, gallantly led and well handled, was resisted stoutly but was met with no counterattack. When the two Brigades stopped in the blackness of the storm, after sustaining 354 casualties,[52] they were close to the farthest point they had gained.[53] A confident enemy, beating off the advance with manifest strength, ceased fire. The Battle of Savage Station was over, but Magruder was not satisfied that this meant an end to the attack of which he had been apprehensive all day. He continued to feel that he was vastly outnumbered and in danger. During the evening he received notice from Lee that there was some mistake about the report that Jackson had other "important duty" that would prevent co-operation. To be reassured on this point, Magruder sent to ascertain what Jackson was doing —whether he was near at hand or had gone on some other mission. As the messenger was slow in returning through the rain, Magruder hurried off to Lee a request for reinforcements in the event that Jackson could not aid him.[54]

At last, about 3.30 A.M. on the 30th, to which hour Magruder had remained anxiously awake, Jackson arrived at Magruder's post and announced that the Valley troops probably would be up by daylight. Magruder breathed freely once again. "I then slept an hour," he observed in his report, "—the first in forty-eight."[55] His brief rest could not have been sweetened by the last note he had received from Lee. The commanding General had written: "I regret very much that you have made so little progress today in the pursuit of the enemy. In order to reap the fruits of our victory the pursuit must be most vigorous. I must urge you, then, again to press on his rear rapidly and steadily. We must lose no more time or he will escape us entirely."[56]

The past tense might have been employed. So far as Magruder was involved, the enemy *had* escaped already. Publication of the Federal reports was to show that Magruder was mistaken in expecting he would be attacked. Lee was in error in assuming

[51] O. R., 11, pt. 2, p. 691.
[53] O. R., 11, pt. 2, pp. 665, 717.
[55] Ibid.
[52] Ibid., 717.
[54] O. R., 11, pt. 2, p. 665.
[56] O. R., 11, pt. 2, p. 687.

Magruder could have progressed if he had attempted to do so. In front of Magruder, in the vicinity of Savage Station, had been three Corps—Sumner's, Heintzelman's, and Franklin's—but they had been under orders simply to hold their ground until darkness and then to continue their retreat.[57] General Heintzelman had not halted that long. During the afternoon, he found "the whole open space near Savage's . . . crowded with troops—more than I supposed could be brought into action judiciously." Instead of waiting to participate in such an attack as Magruder apprehended, Heintzelman put his column in motion and crossed White Oak Swamp.[58] Manifestly, even after Heintzelman left, an attack by Magruder on two fresh Corps probably would have led to a bloody repulse. When the Confederates did attack, a single Brigade stopped them.[59]

Ironically, the operations of June 27, for which Magruder received no criticism, were in reality more censurable than those of the 29th. Before the action of Gaines' Mill grew serious, McClellan expected a simultaneous attack on the south side of the Chickahominy;[60] but while the battle was being fought North of the river, one of the two Divisions opposite Magruder was taken out of the line, was started for the north side, was recalled to camp and then was hurried across the Chickahominy to reinforce the troops behind Boatswain's Swamp.[61] Magruder discovered none of these movements.[62]

When all of this was brought to light, months later, Magruder was in a different theatre of war, where men did not know the fine and disputable points of the battles around Richmond. More immediately, early on the morning of June 30, Magruder received orders that might have been construed as indicating that his performance on the 29th was not rated highly at G. H. Q.: he was to leave to Jackson the pursuit of the enemy, was to retrace his steps to a cross road above the head of White Oak Swamp and was to move down the Darbytown road.[63] That is to say, he was

[57] O. R., 11, pt. 2, p. 61.
[58] O. R., 11, pt. 2, p. 99.
[59] O. R., 11, pt. 2, pp. 431, 464, 477. The Brigade was Brooks's (2nd Brigade) of Smith's (2nd) Division of Franklin's (VI) Corps. Hancock was brought up, but was not engaged.
[60] O. R., 11, pt. 3, p. 264.
[61] O. R., 11, pt. 2, pp. 429, 432.
[62] O. R., 11, pt. 2, pp. 429–30.   [63] O. R., 11, pt. 2, p. 666.

to be taken from the rear of the enemy and was to be placed in support of the Confederate right.[64] The post of danger and of opportunity—if of responsibility—was taken from him and given that strange man Jackson.

[64] Lee, in his official report, *O. R.,* 11, pt. 2, p. 495, gave no explanation of this shift of Magruder. The commanding General may have been prompted to make the change in the belief that he was concentrating too heavily on the Federal rear and was not confronting the enemy's flank with sufficient force. If this consideration were in Lee's mind, he may have reasoned that better results could be had by leaving the pursuit to Jackson's strong and unified command, and moving Magruder to the right, than by sending part of Jackson's force to the south side of the swamp and entrusting the pursuit to Magruder's command and to the remainder of Jackson's troops. Lee simply may have concluded, on the other hand, that Magruder's timid pursuit and slow progress showed him unfitted for the mission assigned him.

CHAPTER XXXIV

THE DELAY IN THE RECONCENTRATION

WHILE Magruder was hesitating on the afternoon of June 29, because he feared a Federal onslaught, the preparations of General Lee to attack McClellan the next morning were being developed unevenly. Longstreet and A. P. Hill, with all their trains, were moving from the north to the south side of the Chickahominy and were advancing at satisfactory speed to the Darbytown road. There was every reason to believe they would be in position, early on the 30th, to assail the flank of the Federals, who then would be en route to James River. Full convergence of the Southern columns would depend, first, on the ability of Huger to come up promptly on Longstreet's left; second, on the success of Jackson in crossing White Oak Swamp to strike the rear of McClellan; and, third, though less importantly, on the arrival of Holmes to the right of Longstreet.

Huger left Magruder, it will be remembered,[1] after 2 P.M. on the 29th, and returned with two of his four Brigades[2] to the Charles City road, down which his other troops were marching. As it happened, Huger's leading Brigade was that of William Mahone, a most unusual man. Virginian born, he physically was so short of stature and so frail that he seemed insignificant, but he had been graduated from the Virginia Military Institute in 1847 and, within a few years, had been established as a resourceful construction engineer for railroads. When the war began, he was in his 35th year, was President of the Petersburg and Norfolk Railroad, was full of a restless, driving energy and was dreaming already of railway consolidations by which he was to link the Virginia coast with the Mississippi and ultimately with the Pacific.[3] He put these dreams aside temporarily, volunteered with promptness and received rapid promotion. His reputation as a swift builder had led, in the spring of 1862, to his assignment to Drewry's Bluff, where the immediate strengthening of the river

[1] See *supra*, p. 552.   [2] Ransom's and Wright's.   [3] 3 *C. M. H.*, 634.

defenses had been considered essential to the safety of Richmond. This work done, Mahone resumed command as the senior Briga-dier of Huger's Division,[4] and, in the absence of Huger, occa-sionally acted as its head.

During the early afternoon of the 29th, while Huger was near Seven Pines and later was riding back to the front of his Division, Mahone continued the march down the Charles City road. When the column reached the Brightwell Farm, about five miles from its starting point, the advance encountered a small cavalry out-post, which quickly disappeared. Mahone halted the troops and examined the ground. It was terrain to make an inexperienced soldier hesitate. Save for the clearing at Brightwell's, the country-side was heavily wooded and offered hiding place for an army of almost any size. To the North, a road ran through the forest to Jordan's Ford in White Oak Swamp.[5] Beyond the swamp, Mahone knew, of course, that the Federals had been encamped. As there was a byway southward from Brightwell's to the Darby-town road, might not the enemy be planning to cross at Jordan's Ford and to take this route via Brightwell's toward the James? There were other fords farther down the swamp, Mahone learned, but what assurance had he that the Federals would choose one of those instead of passing at Jordan's?

The obvious precaution was to ascertain if the Unionists had left their camps in the vicinity of Jordan's Ford. A reconnoitering party was dispatched toward the swamp; the two Brigades re-mained at the crossroads. Soon word came back that the enemy was at Jordan's Ford and was in the very act of crossing south-ward. Mahone immediately changed front to meet the expected attack from the North, and threw out a heavy skirmish line. A collision followed—a spat of fire and a quick, somewhat suspi-cious withdrawal by the bluecoats. Would they return? Had their plans been upset? Mahone did not know, but in a determi-nation to hold the position he pushed forward two regiments to the ford.[6]

By this time, General Huger had reached Brightwell's and had

[4] His commission dated from November, 1861, Wright, 66; Robert Ransom's from March, 1862, *ibid.*, 74; Lewis A. Armistead's from April, 1862, *ibid.*, 78; and A. R. Wright's from June, 1862, *ibid.*, 83.
[5] Federal reports always refer to this as Jordon's Ford, but from the occurrence of the name Jordan in the locality, the "a" seems the proper vowel.
[6] *O. R.*, 11, pt. 2, p. 797.

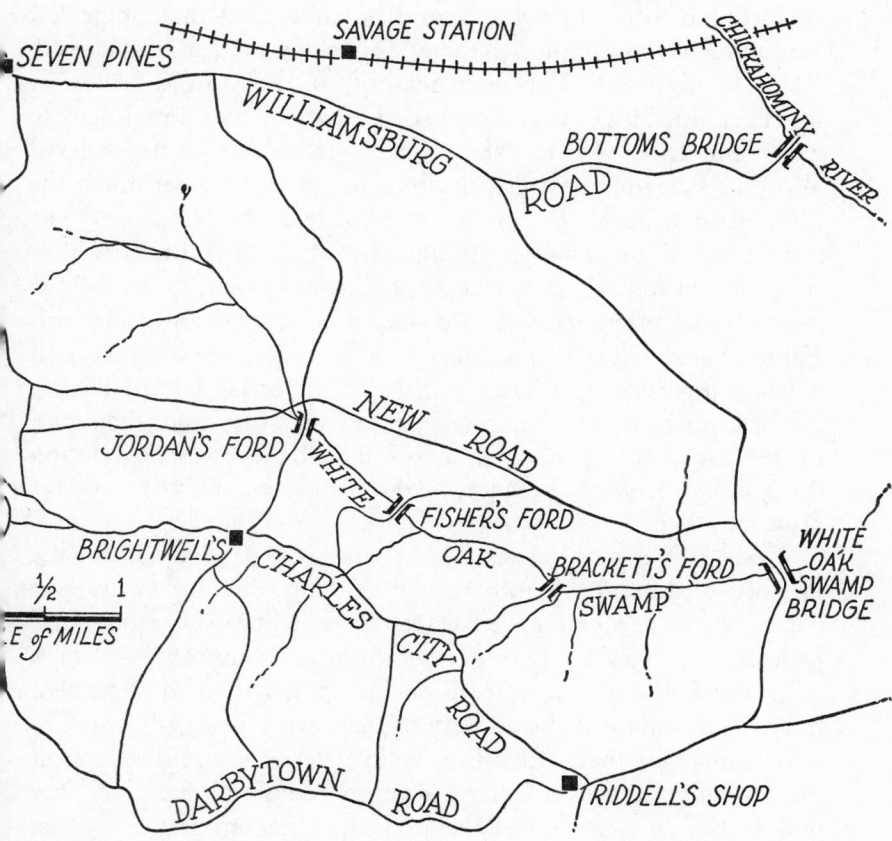

White Oak Swamp, New Road and Charles City Road to Illustrate Huger's Advance
of June 29–30, 1862

resumed command. He was far from satisfied with the prospect.
A boy who had been across the swamp that day said the Federals
still were on the north side. Prisoners confirmed the boy's report
and stated that they belonged to Phil. Kearny's Division of
Heintzelman's III Corps. Huger learned also—apparently for the
first time—of the New Road that ran North of and parallel to the
swamp.[7] This road gave the Federals freedom of action. They
could move from one ford to another and, if they so desired, they
could demonstrate at one crossing to cover the passage of another.

Huger accepted as final the evidence that Union troops re-

[7] See *supra*, p. 539.

mained North of the swamp, and he concluded that, if he left Jordan's Ford unguarded, Kearny might cross in his rear as readily as in his front. For these reasons, and because it was now nearly night, Huger decided to send a battery and a regiment to cover the exits of the New Road.[8] In addition, he ordered Wright's Brigade to start at daylight the next morning down the New Road to locate the enemy and to cover the left flank. The remainder of the Division, Huger bivouacked at Brightwell's.[9] It seemed a logical or, at the least, a cautious course to follow. Actually, as often happens in war, the information on which Huger based these dispositions was outdated almost before it reached him. Kearny had gone down to Jordan's Ford during the afternoon, but had decided against crossing there, had proceeded eastward on the New Road and already was negotiating the swamp between Huger's bivouac and the objective set for Huger by Lee.[10]

While Huger was debating his proper course of action on the evening of June 29, at the very time Magruder hesitantly was engaging the Federal rearguard at Savage Station, "Stonewall" Jackson was ending two exasperating and unprofitable days. After the Battle of Gaines' Mill on the 27th, he had moved down the next morning to the vicinity of Grapevine Bridge but had to remain inactive there until Lee could determine the direction of the Unionists' retreat. Federal artillery, South of the river, not only forbade a crossing but also prevented reconnaissance on that bank.[11]

When, on the 29th, Lee became convinced that the Federal Army was moving for James River, he directed Jackson immediately to repair Grapevine Bridge, which McClellan prudently had destroyed. Jackson's further orders, as Major Dabney remembered them in later years, were "to march eastward by the Savage Station road, parallel to and not far distant from the Chickahominy; to guard all the northward so as to prevent any [Federal] attack, thus forming a line of protection on that side for the

---

[8] Huger said, vaguely, "the junction of the New road with the Charles City road," O. R., 11, pt. 2, p. 789, without specifying which of several junctions. The reports do not show when the two regiments were recalled from Jordan's Ford.
[9] O. R., 11, pt. 2, p. 789.
[10] O. R., 11, pt. 2, pp. 181, 185.
[11] Ewell, it will be remembered, was detached and sent to Bottom's Bridge to prevent a possible recrossing of the Chickahominy by McClellan.

movement of Lee's other columns South of him; and not to leave that eastbound road until he had passed the extreme northern flank of McClellan's force and [had] gotten in [the Federal] rear." [12]

These seemed to be clear and simple orders. To obey them, Jackson, on the morning of the 29th, directed Major Dabney to take a detail of soldiers and to reconstruct the bridge immediately. The Major scarcely could have been given that troublesome assignment because of Jackson's faith in the omniscience of the clergy. Dabney must have been chosen for the task because none of the engineers was at hand. He soon demonstrated that he was not so good a builder as he was a preacher. The men at his disposal were inexperienced and, in his disgusted term, were "shilly-shally" besides.[13] Progress was discouragingly slow. During the forenoon, fortunately, Capt. C. R. Mason arrived with his Negro navvies. This remarkable man, ranking as an acting quartermaster,[14] was one of Jackson's "finds." He was not an educated engineer, but he had a knack for the rapid construction of rough, stout bridges with the labor of his Negroes who understood perfectly the execution of his orders. He promptly relieved Dabney's detachment and began to give form to the structure.[15]

It must have been after Captain Mason's men went to work that Maj. Henry Bryan, Magruder's Assistant Adjutant General, arrived with an inquiry from his chief concerning Jackson's position. Jackson answered that the bridge probably would be finished in about two hours and that his troops then would cross. In adherence to his rule of reticence, Jackson did not tell Bryan the nature of his orders for movement after the passage of the Chickahominy; but for some reason—probably to procure information about the roads on the south side of the river—he sent his engineer, Capt. J. K. Boswell, back with Major Bryan.[16] It was when these two officers arrived at his field headquarters that Magruder determined he would await the arrival of Jackson on his left before launching his attack on the Federal rearguard.[17]

Jackson was so sure of the speedy completion of the bridge that, in the early afternoon, he sent back word to his brigade com-

[12] R. L. Dabney to Jed. Hotchkiss, MS., Apr. 22, 1896—*Hotchkiss Papers.*
[13] *Ibid.*
[14] *O. R.,* 11, pt. 1, p. 718; the initials are supplied from *Hotchkiss' MS. Diary.*
[15] Dabney to Hotchkiss, *loc. cit.*   [16] *O. R.,* 11, pt. 2, p. 663.   [17] *Ibid.*

manders to bring their columns down to the Chickahominy for the crossing.[18] They duly moved; but, for once, Captain Mason took longer than had been anticipated.[19] Jackson's infantry found the bridge incomplete when they arrived. As soon as it was pass-- able at all, though still unfinished, Jackson himself went over and rode about three quarters of a mile southward to the Trent House. This building and the field adjacent to it had been General McClellan's headquarters. Even after the retreat of the Federal army, the premises still were so comfortably furnished that they aroused the envy of the Confederates.[20]

While Jackson was examining the grounds, there rolled up from the South the bark of artillery and the sound of Kershaw's attack on the right of the Williamsburg road. Jackson knew little or nothing of the magnitude and course of the action, but doubtless he asked himself whether he should undertake to co-operate with Magruder. This could not be done, in any event, until the bridge was complete and the troops had come up on Magruder's left, after a march of approximately three miles; but should it be attempted then? Did Jackson's orders contemplate such a move? He decided that they did not, and, probably in answer to an inquiry from D. R. Jones, he sent word—with characteristic reserve—that he had other important duty to perform.[21] Orders were sent to the troops then waiting at the bridge to return to their bivouacs.[22]

[18] *O. R.*, 11, pt. 2, pp. 571, 591.

[19] Prior to May, 1862, there had been no bridge here. All crossing had been at a wide, marshy ford. Gen. E. V. Sumner had built the structure, which was known as "Sumner's Upper Bridge." It had been rendered impracticable by the rise of the Chickahominy on the night of May 31 and thereafter had been put "in condition to be used in emergency by all arms," but apparently it had not been used with regularity by the Federals in June (*O. R.*, 11, pt. 1, pp. 111, 114, 115).

[20] *Dabney*, 459.

[21] *O. R.*, 11, pt. 2, p. 675.

[22] It is much to be regretted that this is the fullest explanation that can be given at present concerning the "other important business" that Jackson assigned as his reason for not co-operating with Magruder on the afternoon of June 29. Those who have studied the campaign will observe that, if Dr. Dabney correctly remembered Jackson's orders for the operations of June 29, the citations given in the text explode the myth that religious services on the Sabbath were the "other important duty" that Jackson had to perform. (For reference to this myth, see *Alexander*, 145.) Beyond this, little can be established positively. Something more than the usual difficulty is encountered in fixing the time of the various events of the day. There is no way of ascertaining whether Jones sent to Jackson for help or whether Jackson on his own motion sent notice to Jones of his delay in completing Grapevine Bridge. The most baffling of the many perplexities of the day is presented by the statement of Major Dabney to Dr. Hunter McGuire that Jackson had a conference with Lee on the 29th, after he crossed Grapevine Bridge. Such a meeting is not mentioned in any of the reports or in the memoirs of Lee's staff officers, but two

How, then, stood the Army command at the end of the first day of the pursuit of McClellan? Four Confederate chiefs of division had been tested.

Down on the Darbytown road, Longstreet, who was responsible that day for A. P. Hill, had marched unhindered and had reached a point within striking distance of his objective.

Magruder had displayed alarming excitement, had hesitated and had made poor progress in pursuit.

Huger, covering little ground, had been deceived by the movements of the enemy on the north side of White Oak Swamp, but he had a short march ahead of him and, with vigor on the morning of the 30th, should be able to take his place in the order of battle.

As for Jackson—how was his day to be appraised? Had the delay in the rebuilding of Grapevine Bridge been unreasonable? Could it be said that his utmost effort had been exerted to complete the work? Was he blamable for entrusting the reconstruction of the bridge to Dr. Dabney? Should Jackson have brought his troops across the Chickahominy late in the afternoon of the 30th, and should he have thrown them against the Federal flank in extension of D. R. Jones's front? Jackson's orders probably were explicit, in that they held him to the Savage Station road; but, if he had advanced his infantry during the afternoon of the 29th, his eastward movement on that road would have put his

such witnesses as Drs. McGuire and Dabney are not to be disregarded. Actually the two witnesses may be one. Some parts of Dr. McGuire's MS. in the Confederate Museum, Richmond, indicate that he drew on Dabney's life of Jackson for details of the day's events. Dr. Dabney is a witness as respected as indispensable, but his account of happenings on the 29th of June must be accepted with some reservation because he made at least one demonstrable error. The Stonewall Brigade, said Dr. Dabney, advanced to the Trent Farm on the afternoon of June 29 (op. cit., 459). On the contrary, General Winder stated explicitly in his contemporary report: "On the 29th it [the Brigade] was ordered to take the advance and move to the Chickahominy river, which it did. The bridge being incomplete, shortly before sunset it was ordered to its former bivouac" (O. R., 11, pt. 2, p. 571). McHenry Howard (op. cit., 147), bore out this statement. Dr. Dabney, then, may not be an accurate witness for the incidents of a crowded day, but, fundamentally, the two reasons for not accepting the story of a conference between Lee and Jackson on the afternoon of June 29 are these: First, it is most improbable that Lee would have been so close to the headquarters of Magruder without visiting that officer, and, second, it is similarly improbable that any misunderstanding could have arisen over Jackson's duty to co-operate with Magruder if Lee had been with Jackson at a later hour of the afternoon when the nature of Magruder's situation would have been known. In the circumstances, it has seemed prudent to assume that Jackson received his orders early on the 29th, and that the meeting with Lee was on the morning of the 30th; but if the evidence should be forthcoming later to prove that Jackson and Lee did have a conference on the afternoon of the 29th, then Jackson's statement of "other important duty" may be found to refer to orders given him at that time.

column within half a mile of Magruder's left at the point of deployment. When opposite the Federal position, Jackson would have been only three quarters of a mile North of Savage Station. Did he know that; and if, in an unfamiliar country, he was ignorant of that fact, had he been diligent in reconnaissance? Would he measure up to the requirements of his large command in co-operation with divisional commanders who seemed to regard themselves as independent? Was the strain of hard days and sleepless nights sapping his initiative? The driving power of the Valley Campaign—was it being lost?

CHAPTER XXXV

Two Columns Are Halted

GENERAL LEE correctly assumed that after General McClellan crossed White Oak Swamp, the direction of the Federal retreat on June 30 would be toward James River by the shortest route. This almost certainly would carry the Federals to a little settlement known as Glendale or Riddell's Shop, two and a quarter miles Southwest of White Oak Swamp Bridge, and at the junction of the Charles City and Darbytown roads. From Riddell's Shop, McClellan would head South, but what roads he would find available and how rapidly he would progress over them, the Confederates did not know.

The plan of the Army of Northern Virginia called for a general concentration all the way southward from the fringe of the swamp to the river, and parallel to the north-and-south roads by which McClellan was moving. This would make the direction of the Confederate attack eastward, except for Jackson, who would close in on the Federal rear from the North and attempt to roll it up to the southward. Simultaneous convergence of four columns was undeniably a difficult matter, but in the situation that existed, it was the only practicable maneuver, and it did not seem complicated beyond attainment. It met, at the least, one of the absolute essentials of such a movement in this: each of the major columns of attack was to advance by a separate road; none of the four had to cross the route of any of the others.

Here were the specific missions of the columns:

1. Gen. T. H. Holmes was to proceed down the New Market road from Cornelius Creek [1] and to engage the enemy where found. The length of his march obviously was not computable, but it probably would be about nine miles with no material obstruction.[2]

[1] O. R., 11, pt. 2, p. 906. For sketches of the proposed convergence and of the actual advance of June 29, see 2 R. E. Lee, 170, 175. Cornelius Creek, entering the James opposite Drewry's Bluff, appears on some maps as Wilton Creek.

[2] Neither Holmes nor Lee, in official reports, stated the exact nature of Holmes's orders. The safe assumption is that Holmes was advanced in general support of the left. Possibly Lee hoped that Holmes might be able to damage the Federal column, but he could not have expected any great accomplishment by 6000 troops, most of them raw, even though Holmes had six field batteries.

2. General Magruder was to turn from Savage Station to the rear, then to cross over to the Darbytown road and to support Longstreet. The distance to Longstreet's bivouac of the night of June 29–30 was approximately eleven miles.[3]

3. General Longstreet, with his own and A. P. Hill's Divisions, was to continue along the Darbytown road from Atlee's Farm until he encountered the Federals. His march was of uncertain stretch, because of doubt concerning the enemy's lines of retreat, but it probably would not be more than six miles, through partly forested country.

4. General Huger was to proceed from Brightwell's Farm for about three miles down the Charles City road, through woodland, to the junction of the Darbytown road and was to attack the enemy when found.

5. General Jackson, as already indicated, was to advance from Grapevine Bridge and was to clear the enemy from the woods next the Chickahominy. Then he was to turn South when opposite McClellan's rear, was to pass White Oak Swamp Bridge and was to press the Unionists. He had approximately eight and a half miles to go and had to cross a stream that might be troublesome.

If all went well, the order of battle would be: extreme right, Holmes; right center and center, Longstreet and A. P. Hill, with Magruder in support; left, Huger; rear of the enemy, Jackson. Except for the cavalry, which Stuart was bringing back from a raid to the White House, the entire Army would be thrown against the foe.

Such was the plan of convergence as seen from Army Headquarters. Appropriate orders were dispatched to the division commanders. Although maps were few,[4] each of the Generals in charge of columns knew what he and the others were expected to do. Because all were well instructed, the story of the day should have been one of a driving march and of a straining effort by every column to reach its assigned place at the earliest moment. Instead, the events of June 30 fall into a succession of delays, of

[3] Magruder (O. R., 11, pt. 2, p. 666) stated that he covered "some twelve miles" to Timberlake's Store, which was one mile East of Atlee's Farm, where Longstreet had halted the previous evening (2 R. E. Lee, 172).

[4] "I never saw a map of the country in which we operated, except the one General Lee used . . . and that map contained the gross error . . ." (Brent, 206. Cf. infra, p. 591).

groping marches, of separate decisions, as if some of the divisional commanders had no regard for time and felt more concern for their reputation and independent position than for the outcome of the battle.

Soon after daybreak, June 30, with Mahone in front, Huger started his advance from Brightwell's. The uncertainty of the previous evening seemed to pervade the woods that bordered both sides of the Charles City road. Mahone proceeded with great caution. He still believed that Kearny's Brigade the previous night had gone northward from Jordan's Ford—"had recrossed the swamp" as he phrased it [5]—and he thought his adversary might attempt to turn southward again at Fisher's, the next ford on the left of Huger's advance. The same care, Mahone reasoned, that had been exercised at Jordan's Ford was required now.[6] Otherwise Kearny might wait in the swamp and get in rear of the Confederates after they had passed down the road.

Huger seems to have left dispositions to his subordinate. Both he and Mahone were mystified early in the day by a dispatch found on the body of a courier whom the skirmishers killed. By this paper Kearny was ordered to retire and to keep a strong battery with his rearguard.[7] What did that mean? Whence was Kearny to retire? Not knowing, Mahone proceeded carefully to cover with his Brigade the approaches opposite Fisher's Ford—only to be told in a short time by residents that an uncomputed number of Union troops had crossed southward at that point the previous evening.[8]

Was Kearny, then, now in front of Huger, down the Charles City road? Could the Confederate advance be pushed without further thought for the security of the left flank? Huger and Mahone concluded that this could be done. Mahone's Brigade was called in from the direction of the ford, and was started down the road once more. The other Brigades followed; but no sooner was the clearing at Fisher's passed, than fire was opened from the enveloping woods. Ahead, on the road, as far as vision carried, newly felled trees lay in grim obstruction.

What was to be done now? Huger, it would appear, again left the decision to Mahone, either because that officer was in imme-

5 *O. R.*, 11, pt. 2, p. 789.   6 *Ibid.*, 797.
7 *Ibid.*, 789.   8 *Ibid.*, 797.

diate command of the leading Brigade or else because the younger man had the reputation of a specialist in dealing with swamp and forests. When Mahone reported that it would be easier to make a new road through the woods for the artillery than to clear the old one, Huger sent word to Lee that his march was obstructed, but he did not send any estimate of the hour at which his way would be cleared.[9]

Mahone put his men to work felling trees so that the artillery could advance. Tools were few; progress was slow. There were some indications that, as the Confederates cut away, the enemy continued to deepen the obstruction. The strange spectacle was presented of a battle of rival axemen. Apparently, Huger never considered the possibility of leaving his guns in the rear, of keeping up an active skirmish and of offering to move his troops through the woods in support of Longstreet and Hill. He played safe, and played a lone hand. As he chopped, the Divisions on his right withheld their advance. Beyond their front, McClellan's wagon train and reserve artillery, covered by deployed infantry, rumbled toward the river where gunboats waited to protect them with long-range fire.[10] It was a curious episode. In a metaphor of the woods, while the hunter fumbled, the quarry was escaping.

Jackson was having adventures of a different sort in the discharge of his orders to close in on the rear of the Federal Army. The drowning rain of the night of June 29–30 routed him from his bivouac and sent him to the shelter of a wagon, but he got so uncomfortably wet that he abandoned at 1 A.M. all attempt to sleep. Tersely he ordered Major Dabney to start the columns from Grapevine Bridge at earliest dawn. Through the night and mud he rode over to Magruder's headquarters and, as already noted, at 3.30 o'clock, he relieved the concern of that excited officer.

Soon after sunrise, Lee came up and gave Magruder his orders to start for the Darbytown road. Once more Major Brent is a

---

[9] *O. R.,* 11, pt. 2, p. 495. Lee did not state in his report that Huger failed to indicate when the obstruction would be removed, but Lee's delay in opening the action and all the known circumstances of the long wait show plainly that Lee had no intimation whether Huger expected to be detained an hour or half a day. It is fair to add that nothing short of a reconnaissance in force by Huger would have shown that the obstruction was deep. Huger did not order such a reconnaissance.

[10] *O. R.,* 11, pt. 1, p. 66; pt. 2, pp. 789–90, 797. The obstruction of the Charles City road was ordered by Gen. S. P. Heintzelman and was undertaken by men of Gen. H. W. Slocum's Division.

andid witness concerning his chief: "As our troops were bivouac-
ig upon each side of the railway, it took a considerable time to
1arch them up and get ready for the route. General Magruder
/as on horseback, galloping here and there with great rapidity.
Ie seemed to me to be under a nervous excitement that strangely
ffected him. He frequently interposed in minor matters, re-
ersing previous arrangements and delaying the movement he
/as so anxious to hasten. I looked on with great sadness at what
eemed to me a loss of equilibrium in a man I knew to be earnest
nd indefatigable in the discharge of duty." Other staff officers
oticed Magruder's excitement and urged Brent, who had much
nfluence with the General, to speak to him.

At length, while their horses stopped to drink at a stream, soon
fter the march got under way, Brent spoke up: "General, I am
orry to see you are not feeling well this morning."

"Why do you think so?"

"Because I have never seen you act as you have this morning."

"What have you seen me do," Magruder inquired, "different
rom my usual habit?"

"Well, General," said the ordnance officer, "I hope you will
ardon me, but I have never seen your usual calmness so much lost
y an extreme irritability, sometimes exhibited without any
pparent cause, and hence I inferred that you must be feeling
adly."

Magruder answered as an honest man would: "Well, Major,
ou are right. I am feeling horribly. For two days I have been
listurbed about my digestion, and the doctor has been giving me
nedicine, and I fear he has given me some morphine in his
nixture, and the smallest quantity of it acts upon me as an irritant.
And besides that, I have lost so much sleep that it affects me
trangely; but I fully appreciate your kindness in speaking to me,
and I will endeavor to regain my self control." Magruder made
he effort, but his excitement continued.[11]

Ere Magruder started, Lee reviewed with Jackson the part that

11 *Brent*, 191–92. It will not be necessary to point out to students of the campaign
hat Major (later Brigadier General) Brent's statement is the first intelligible explanation
iven of Magruder's physical condition June 29–July 1. As will appear *infra*, p. 608,
Magruder's surgeon denied the prevalent report that the General was drunk, but he did
ot explain what was wrong with Magruder.

officer was to have in the operations of the day. Jackson seemed all energy.[12] His troops now were at hand but they found no organized force to oppose them. The Federals manifestly had evacuated the area. Booty was found everywhere. At Savage Station were some 2500 sick and wounded in a tented hospital, "remarkable," said Jackson, "for the extent and convenience of its accommodations."[13] The "wagon-hunter," of course, could not fail to gather, while he might, at least something from the abundance the Federals had left. This took time. So did the collection of the hundreds of Federal stragglers found in the woods. When one of Jackson's companions began to grumble at the expense to which the government would be put in providing for the prisoners, Jackson shook his head. As a sound military economist, he reasoned: "It is cheaper to feed them than to fight them."[14]

As D. H. Hill was exemplifying diligently this law of Confederate economy and was corralling the prisoners, Jackson himself had little to do. He rode nearer the swamp and, while waiting, he turned his thoughts homeward. Presently he sat down and wrote Mrs. Jackson this letter.

Near White Oak Swamp Bridge.

An ever-kind Providence has greatly blessed our efforts and given us great reason for thankfulness in having defended Richmond. Today the enemy is retreating down the Chickahominy toward the James River. Many prisoners are falling into our hands. General D. H. Hill and I are together. I had a wet bed last night, as the rain fell in torrents. I got up about midnight, and haven't seen much rest since. I do trust that our God will soon bless us with an honorable peace, and permit us to be together at home again in the enjoyment of domestic happiness.

[12] One young witness described him thus: "Jackson began talking in a jerky, impetuous way, meanwhile drawing a diamond on the ground with the toe of his right boot. He traced two sides of a triangle with promptness and decision; then starting at the end of the second line, began to draw a third projected toward the first. This third line he traced slowly and with hesitation, alternately looking up at Lee's face and down at his diagram, meanwhile talking earnestly; and when at last the third line crossed the first and the triangle was complete, he raised his foot, and stamped it down with emphasis, saying, 'We've got him'; then signalled for his horse, and when he came, vaulted awkwardly into the saddle and was off." (*Stiles*, 99). Major Stiles wrote about 1902 and may have confused some details of this meeting with a later. Jackson, for instance, after his night's drenching, scarcely would have had "hair, skin, eyes and clothes . . . all one neutral dust tint." Nor is it clear what Jackson could have been triangulating. The essential facts of a conference, at which Jackson appeared alert and aggressive, do not seem open to question.

[13] *O. R.*, 11, pt. 2, p. 556.   [14] *Mrs. Jackson*, 298.

You must give fifty dollars for church purposes, and more should you be disposed. Keep an account of the amount, as we must give at least one tenth of our income. I would like very much to see my darling, but hope that God will enable me to remain at the post of duty until, in his own good time, He blesses us with independence. This going home has injured the army immensely.[15]

About noon, the General reached the fringe of White Oak Swamp, close to the bridge over which the Federals had retreated. He found Colonel Crutchfield, his Chief of Artillery, already there.[16] Hampton's Brigade of infantry and Munford's Second Virginia Cavalry, which were in front,[17] had approached the swamp down a north-and-south road to the edge of a cleared farm on the right. Thence, as the road descended to the swamp, the vanguard had followed to the Southeast across miry land for about a quarter of a mile to the vicinity of White Oak Bridge. As Hampton and Munford had attempted to explore this part of the road, they had come under a vigorous fire from Federal sharpshooters in the swamp.

A forbidding place the swamp was. Like the Chickahominy, the stream itself was shallow and little scarped. In dry weather, the sole difficulty in crossing it was offered by the underbrush and briers along the banks. Deciduous trees and pine so shaded the lower growth that it had lush, entangling thickness. This guardian forest varied in depth. At intervals, the native could approach within a hundred yards of the swamp before he had to combat the defiant jungle. Elsewhere, the forest and the wide-spreading brambles baffled the adventurer half a mile, even a mile, from the little stream. Of sound and of beauty there was little. The kildee and the mockingbird shunned the confinement of crossed boughs that shut out the sun. Voiceless the stream flowed over its soft bottom. Only the moccasin splashed the tawny waters. No vistas opened on the variant greens. Shadows dulled the colors.

Such was White Oak Swamp at its best. At its worst, the stream spread swiftly from its bed and set a barrier almost impassable. The stains on the vegetation showed how far the stream might

<hr />

[15] *Mrs. Jackson*, 297.   [16] *O. R.*, 11, pt. 2, p. 561.
[17] Hampton, in *Alexander*, 151. Munford, following Jackson from the Valley, rejoined the column on the 24th above Ashland—*Munford MSS.*

swell. Long, low fields that should have been rich pastures had so often been inundated that only the hardiest bumps of deep crab grass and the most defiant mullen survived. To this condition the torrential downpour of the night of the 29th had brought the swamp. The Federals, apparently, had passed before the floodwaters had swept down to the bridge. It was the fate of the Confederates to find the bottom water-soaked, spongy and tenacious. Where now they ventured close, the ring of the sharpshooter's rifle warned them that man's weapons reinforced the swamp's resistance.

Contact was established: what was ahead? Were the Unionists contesting strongly the passage of the stream? From an elevation on the right, Jackson could see across the swamp to the enemy's position on the left of the road.[18] The bridge itself manifestly was broken, though its exact condition could not be observed. Beyond it the road passed directly over a hill and disappeared. Opposite the Confederate left was open ground [19] North and South of a little dwelling house.[20] On the level crest stood a large hospital tent.[21] Near the hospital, and at a distance of about 1000 yards from Jackson's observation post,[22] the guns of about three field batteries were visible.[23] Two hundred yards behind these guns,[24] a long line of infantry, lying down and apparently asleep,[25] could be seen. Still farther to the rear, discernible perhaps from the highest point only of the Confederate position, the field was covered with wagon and ambulance trains, which were slowly moving off.[26] To this extent, the situation on the left was clear, but a heavy fringe of tall timber along the edge of the swamp opposite the Confederate right provokingly cut off all observation.[27] There was no way of telling in what strength the Federals

[18] In this description, left and right will be from the Confederate side.
[19] *Dabney*, 464; 2 *B. & L.*, 387.   [20] Munford, in *Alexander*, 148.
[21] Hampton, in *ibid.*, 150.   [22] *O. R.*, 11, pt. 2, p. 561.
[23] Hampton (*loc. cit.*), stated that he saw four guns; Dabney (*op. cit.*, 464), put the number at "fifteen to twenty"; Maj. H. P. Jones of the artillery counted twelve (*O. R.*, 11, pt. 2, p. 653). Federal reports show that four batteries were on the hill but that one of them, badly weakened, had been put in park, and that another was somewhat in rear of the two advanced units, Mott's and Ayres's (*O. R.*, 11, pt. 2, pp. 465–66). This arrangement of the guns doubtless accounted for the contradictions in the Southern estimates.
[24] *O. R.*, 11, pt. 2, p. 561.   [25] 2 *B. & L.*, 387.
[26] *O. R.*, 11, pt. 2, p. 465.
[27] *Dabney*, 464. Dabney's description would leave the impression that the ground in front of the Confederate right was clear all the way to the rim of the swamp, but actually, North of the stream, a tangle of timber and of underbrush spread back more than a quarter of a mile. See Michler's map of 1867.

occupied the elevation on that side of the road, or how high the ground was.

Such a situation, of course, called for the employment of Jackson's artillery. A dominating ridge on the Confederate right had the desired elevation, but it was cleared ground and was so much

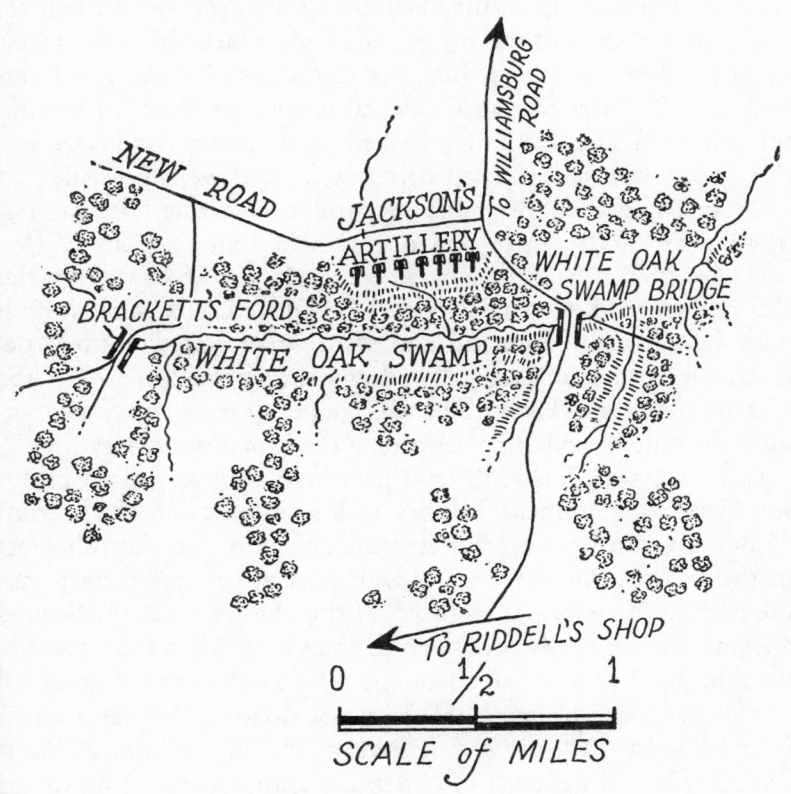

The Vicinity of White Oak Swamp Bridge

exposed that batteries placed there might be destroyed before they could get into action. Fortunately, examination showed to the North of the ridge a ravine that led up almost to the rear of the very best artillery position on the front.[28] Capt. Burnet Rhett quickly cut a road up this incline.[29] Thereupon Colonel Crutchfield advanced twenty-eight guns and had them shotted under cover.[30] At 1.45 P.M.,[31] with a rush, he brought out these

[28] Dabney, 465.
[30] Dabney, loc. cit.

[29] O. R., 11, pt. 2, p. 655.
[31] O. R., 11, pt. 2, p. 561.

field pieces to the ridge and opened on the Federal batteries across the swamp.

The effect must have warmed the heart of the General who as a young man first had caught the eyes of his superiors by his handling of a gun section under the shadow of Chapultepec.[32]

As the hot salvo from the Confederate artillery swept the field, visible to the South of the swamp, the Federal artillerists fired four shots in return and then limbered up some of their pieces and hurried off. Three damaged rifles were left. At the same instant, the startled Federal infantry dashed for the rear. So heavy was the fire of Jackson's massed batteries, and so well directed, that one candid Federal Brigadier General later wrote, "it was impossible for the troops to remain in [their camp] a minute." [33]

It was now 2 o'clock or a bit after. In the woods along the Darbytown road, General Lee and President Davis were waiting with Longstreet's command and were wondering what had delayed for hours the attack by Huger and by Jackson. On the Charles City road, Huger still was chopping trees and was dragging the trunks aside to clear a new road for his artillery.

Late as it was, Jackson's own part in the convergence did not seem beyond attainment. His first task was done. Directly in front of the advance of the column remained only the sharpshooters in the swamp. Orders were passed quietly: bring a battery into the road near the bridge to drive off the bluecoats; let the Second Virginia Cavalry cross the swamp, charge up the hill and secure the guns the Federals had abandoned.[34] Jackson himself mounted to ride with the troopers. Had he not done so the day he had forced his way over the North Fork of the Shenandoah at Front Royal? He had galloped to Cedarville with Flournoy; he would pursue with Munford.

A rumble of the battery, the clatter of the cavalry, a splash through the ford and then—up the hill! The column deployed as it reached the open ground. Jackson was close in rear. Quickly on the left, from behind the house that overlooked the ford, a detachment of sharpshooters opened fire. Almost on the instant, seconding them, a field battery roared. Jackson turned to see whence came this challenge. One glance was enough: the Federals who had

[32] Cf. 1 Henderson, 41–42.
[33] W. T. H. Brooks, in O. R., 11, pt. 2, p. 477.
[34] Munford, in Alexander, 148; O. R., 11, pt. 2, pp. 561, 594.

been driven from the ground opposite the Confederate left had gone over the crest of the hill and then, screened by the forest, swiftly had descended again on their own left, opposite Jackson's right. There the blue infantrymen were now, thousands of them, apparently, across the road and in full possession of a fine position, the strength of which had been hidden by the trees that had cut off vision from the north side of the swamp. As Jackson looked, more of the Union batteries dashed up. Regiments were forming in line of battle.

Jackson's quick eye must have seen that the ground taken by the Federals was stronger than to the East of the road. Not only was there cover from the Confederate artillery but also, through the woods, there was an enfilade of the approaches to the bridge. In the face of this Federal force, what could Munford's men do? Nothing except quit the field or subject themselves to futile slaughter! Quickly and skillfully the Colonel veered off to the East to escape the fire. Jackson turned back swiftly the way he had come and returned to the north side of the swamp.[35] In passing the ford, he may have observed more closely the condition of the bridge. It had been a trestle structure[36] which had been broken up and burned.[37] Around the uprights, charred stringers were floating in a tangle.[38]

This incident was a definite repulse. Those Federals on the high ground could prevent a crossing at the bridge. None could deny that. It was manifest; it was indisputable. The Confederate battery that had been sent into the road to sweep the approaches to the bridge would be smashed sooner or later. It might as well be withdrawn.[39] D. H. Hill's and Whiting's infantry, who were waiting in the open, could be given the shelter of a pine wood on the left of the road.[40] The artillery to the right and rear could turn its attention to the Federal batteries in their new position, though the Union guns were so well sheltered that even the smoke

[35] Munford, in *Alexander*, 149; *Dabney*, 465; Hampton, in *Alexander*, 151; *O. R.*, 11, pt. 2, pp. 627, 655.
[36] *O. R.*, 11, pt. 2, p. 561.
[37] About 10 A.M., by Richardson's Division; *O. R.*, 11, pt. 2, pp. 55, 561.
[38] *Dabney*, 465. When General Hampton, late in life, described the bridge for General Alexander (*loc. cit.*), he remembered it as simply a structure of poles; but the contemporary reports of other officers naturally are preferred. The bridge was not then or for years thereafter a formidable structure, but reconstruction of it, in the best working conditions, would have been a task of several hours.
[39] *O. R.*, 11, pt. 2, p. 561.   [40] *Dabney* 465–66.

from their fire could not be seen from the hill where the Confederate ordnance had been placed.[41] An attempt could be made to repair the bridge.

These were the four obvious things to do—and they were all that Jackson undertook. Incredibly, almost mysteriously, and for the first time in his martial career, he quit. His initiative died almost in the moment of his return from the south side of the swamp. The alert, vigorous Jackson of the early morning grew weary, taciturn and drowsy. Marshy approaches, destruction of the bridge, and the fire from the new Federal position made a crossing impossible.[42] This he concluded and then, exhausted, went to sleep under a tree.[43]

D. H. Hill was not willing to admit that nothing more could be done. Without asking orders, he threw his skirmishers into the fringe of the swamp West of the crossing, pushed some of them across the stream [44] and kept them there. By threats and scoldings, he got a fatigue party forward to the site of the broken bridge. When the men came back and complained that they could not work under the random shellfire of the Federals, he vainly sought to find soldiers who would.[45] At length in desperation Hill sent his engineer officer, Capt. W. F. Lee, through the swamp to find General Huger and to ask if the force on the Charles City road could not attack the Federals and drive them from the hill above the broken bridge.[46]

Hill's sole diversion in the swamp, where the flies bit as viciously as the mosquitoes stung, was with a drunken Union Sergeant. This man, who belonged to Company C, 7th Maine Volunteers, was captured early in the day, but refused to surrender. When a Confederate soldier asked Hill whether he should kill the prisoner or let him go, the General ironically remarked that the Sergeant should be spared to be a comfort to his family. Then the Sergeant went back to the Federal side of the swamp, beyond the Confederate skirmishers, and stretched out under the shelter of his gum coat, which he hung on his stick. Rev. L. W. Allen, one of D. H. Hill's chaplains and an excellent marksman, shot

[41] O. R., 11, pt. 2, pp. 557, 561, 655.
[42] Cf. his explanation in O. R., 11, pt. 2, p. 557.
[43] McHenry Howard, 148.   [44] O. R., 11, pt. 2, p. 627.
[45] O. R., 11, pt. 2, p. 566; Dabney, 466.
[46] 2 B. & L., 388.

four times at the prone Sergeant, from a distance of not more than fifty yards, but could not hit him. Said Hill afterward: ". . . the only recognition that I could see the man make was to raise his hand as if to brush away a fly." At length the skirmishers decided to let the Federal enjoy unhindered his drunken siesta. That evening he slipped away, rejoined his command at Malvern Hill and boasted that he had been repeatedly within the Confederate lines. If he had had one more canteen of whiskey, he asserted, he could have held the position at the bridge all day.[47]

The exploit of this Irish Horatius did not interest Jackson. Nothing stirred him. For once, he seemed to have given up. When he awakened, he sat on a tree trunk, gazing at the ground, and said little. Ere long Brig. Gen. "Rans" Wright came up the New Road, in rear of the Confederate artillery position, and reported that he had completed the task assigned him the previous evening by General Huger.[48] He had traversed the whole length of the road and had not found any Federals North of the swamp, except for the stragglers he had gathered. Numerous deserted camps had been passed. Did Jackson have any orders for him? None, Jackson answered. The enemy was in large force and was disputing obstinately the crossing of the swamp. Wright would do well to retrace his steps and, if he could, to get back over the swamp and rejoin his Division.[49]

Obediently and without debate, Wright marched back up New Road and, with the assistance of a guide, found Brackett's Ford at a distance of about one mile. Wright advanced his skirmishers but soon discovered the south side of the swamp heavily obstructed and well covered by artillery. He marched three miles farther upstream and crossed without difficulty at Fisher's.[50] Jackson did not detail an officer to see how Wright fared and he did not direct that any report be made him.

While Wright marched, a messenger reached Jackson from Munford. The cavalryman announced that after he had come under fire on the south side of the swamp, he had swung to the left and proceeded eastward for some 400 yards. On the way he had passed a post where many Federal troops must have been resting earlier in the day, because knapsacks covered the ground.

[47] *Ibid.*
[49] *O. R.*, 11, pt. 2, p. 810.
[48] See *supra*, p. 560.
[50] *Ibid.*

In easy distance he had found a cowpath that led back to the Confederate side. He had left videttes South of the swamp and he begged to send the General some captured newspapers. Further orders were awaited. Jackson took the newspapers but he sent back no instructions.[51]

Three o'clock had passed. From the South, plainly audible to Jackson, was the swelling sound of artillery fire. Longstreet had heard about 2.30 a gun which he had taken to be the signal of Huger's approach and he had ordered some of his own batteries to open. As the Federals had replied in kind, a noisy duel had begun, though the infantry as yet were not engaged. Huger, in actual fact, was testing cautiously a Federal position which he had reached near the Williams house, after a mile's wasted exercise in cutting and clearing for his new road.[52] Longstreet had no knowledge of what the column on his left was doing, but he dispatched one of his staff officers, Capt. J. W. Fairfax, across the swamp to apprise Jackson of his situation and, presumably, to inquire when Jackson could attack.

Neither the message nor the answer is recorded. Doubtless Jackson made the same reply he had, in effect, given Wright—that his passage of the swamp was obstructed by a heavy force.[53] When Huger sent back the engineer whom D. H. Hill had dispatched with a request for an attack on the flank of the Federals opposite White Oak Swamp Bridge, Huger's statement to Hill was to the same effect: his road was obstructed.[54] Jackson was acquainted, therefore, with the condition of affairs on the other side of the swamp, and, though he later stated that he was eager to cooperate,[55] he remained listlessly inactive.

At length, Gen. Wade Hampton emerged from the pine thicket on the left of the road and reported. True woodsman that he was, he had examined the strange, intriguing country. With his son and another aide he had ridden to the edge of the stream and, at a short distance, had found a good crossing, which was not more than ten or fifteen feet wide. The bottom was sandy, the approaches firm. Over this, Hampton had ridden and soon had come in sight of the open ground on the Union side. There,

[51] Munford, in *Alexander*, 149.
[52] *O. R.*, 11, pt. 2, pp. 789, 797–98.
[53] Hampton, in *Alexander*, 151; *Marshall*, 111.
[54] 2 *B. & L.*, 388.   [55] *O. R.*, 11, pt. 2, p. 557.

Hampton proceeded now to tell Jackson, he had observed at a distance a Federal line of infantry in a deep ravine that commanded the hill up which the Confederates would have to advance from the bridge.

Jackson showed somewhat more interest in this than in Wright's or in Munford's report. Could Hampton, asked Jackson, make a bridge across the stream at the point he had described?

It would be easy, Hampton answered, to erect a bridge for infantry, but if trees had to be felled to open a road for the artillery, the sound would give the enemy notice of what was afoot.

Build the bridge, Jackson ordered.

Hampton went off at once. When he returned from his mission, he found Jackson seated on a log, silent and motionless. Poles had been cut, Hampton reported, from that part of the wood where his Brigade was waiting. These poles had been carried downstream to the selected point. A simple bridge was ready. To make sure that the work had not attracted the attention of the Federals, Hampton said, he had crossed again to the south side and had found the Federals as quiet and as unsuspecting as when he first had observed them.

Jackson pulled down his cap over his closed eyes and listened attentively till Hampton had finished. Then, without a word of thanks or of instruction to the Brigadier, Jackson got up and walked away.[56]

Louder roared the battle from the South, but the futile fire of Jackson's own artillery against the unseen target behind the high trees opposite the Confederate left slackened.[57] Efforts to repair the White Oak Swamp Bridge virtually had been abandoned before this time, because the men would not work where the enemy's shells came crashing through the woods.[58] Eighteen thousand infantry, as good troops as wore the Confederate gray, loitered in the thickets and listened to the cannonade till the shadows fell.

Night found Jackson so weary, so confused, after almost twenty hours of profitless marching and waiting in unfamiliar country,

---

[56] Hampton, in *Alexander,* 150–51. The exact sequence of events at the time of these two interviews with Hampton is difficult to establish. Neither can the moment of Captain Fairfax's arrival be fixed. As given in the text, the order of these happenings seems the most logical that can be inferred from Hampton's statement, but a *caveat* is in order.

[57] *O. R.,* 11, pt. 2, p. 655.   [58] Cf. *O. R.,* 11, pt. 2, p. 566.

that he was stupefied. When he sat down to eat by the side of some of his staff officers, he nodded with food in his mouth. "Now, gentlemen," he said, arousing himself, "let us at once to bed, and see if tomorrow we cannot do something." [59]

[59] *Dabney,* 467.

CHAPTER XXXVI

Holmes Advances and Magruder Gallops in Vain

Jackson's words, at the end of a futile and fateful day, might well have been echoed on the extreme Confederate right, that 30th of June, by Maj. Gen. Theophilus H. Holmes, a stiff and deaf representative of the "Old Army." After his service on Aquia Creek, in the winter of 1861–62, General Holmes, 57 years of age and a close friend of the President, had been sent to North Carolina.[1] On this tour of duty he gave no evidence of particular aloofness or professional pride. As far as the records show, he did creditably in reorganizing the defenses of his State, though he may not have been aggressive. Federal pressure in Virginia compelled Lee early in June to call for troops from Holmes's Department and led him, June 21, to extend the northern boundary of that Department to James River.[2] On the 26th, Lee ordered Holmes to join him[3] and, as already noted, directed that after Holmes's forces crossed James River they should proceed down the Henrico side to co-operate with the Confederate Divisions that were converging on McClellan's line of retreat.

From his camp, Holmes moved down the New Market road to the heights of the same name. These constituted a position of great natural strength and of strategic value. From New Market Heights a Federal column advancing on Richmond, nine miles to the West, could be hurled back easily. Moreover, directly East of the Heights, the highway forked. The New Market or River road continued to parallel the James, but the diverging Long Bridge road turned to the left and put Holmes within easy supporting distance of Longstreet and A. P. Hill, who had marched down the Darbytown road.

Even with the voluntary addition of the force of Brig. Gen. Henry A. Wise, who commanded at Chaffin's Bluff, Holmes

---

[1] O. R., 11, pt. 3, p. 392; O. R., 9, 450–51. His assignment to the Department of North Carolina bore date of Mch. 24, 1862.
[2] O. R., 9, 475.   [3] O R., 11, pt. 3, p. 617.

could muster not more than 6000 infantry, most of whom had never been under fire; but, as noted already, he had six batteries of approximately thirty guns.[4] This column manifestly was not strong enough to engage in heavy infantry action. At the same time, if it could bring its gun into play, it might be able to confuse the Federal retreat.

For the coming of this or of any other opportunity, Holmes waited on New Market Heights through the forenoon of June 30 and until about 4 o'clock. Then Maj. R. K. Meade of the Engineers galloped up to the General's field headquarters and reported exciting news: the enemy was retreating in some confusion over Malvern Hill, a strong ridge about two and a half miles East of Holmes's position. This foe could be assailed. There was, Major Meade explained, a thick wood on either side of the River road about 800 yards from the Federal column. If Holmes would advance some of his batteries into this wood, he could sweep the line of the retreating enemy. Maj. W. H. Stevens, Chief Engineer of the Army, who happened to be on that part of the front, agreed with Meade that this movement was practicable.

Holmes approved. His Chief of Artillery, Col. James Deshler, a gallant and energetic officer, was directed to select from the various batteries three sections of two rifled guns each and to advance them to the ground indicated by Major Meade. A strong regiment of Virginia infantry was ordered to support the artillery.[5] All these arrangements appear to have been unhurried. While they were being made without any recorded urgency, Maj. J. L. Brent arrived at Holmes's headquarters and stated that his chief, General Magruder, had sent him to say that Magruder's troops were under orders to move over in support of Holmes: did that officer have any suggestion to make concerning their position? Holmes answered "very brusquely"—to quote Brent—that he had no suggestion.

The Major tried again: Could the General inform him where the enemy was and in what probable strength?

"No," said Holmes.

[4] The return of July 15, 1862, O. R., 11, pt. 2, p. 912, shows thirty-one, but there is some uncertainty regarding the exact strength of the various batteries on June 30. Four of the batteries were of six guns, a form of organization that was reduced later in 1862. Experience showed that four-gun batteries were, as a rule, more efficiently managed.

[5] O. R., 11, pt. 2, p. 907.

Once more: Brent was returning to Magruder; did Holmes have any message?

"No"—that was all.

Said Brent, years later: "The impression produced upon me was that General Holmes found in some way a cause of resentment at receiving a message from General Magruder. His bearing was the most singular I have ever seen, and was marked by the absence of even a simulation of ordinary courtesy." [6]

After Holmes dismissed Brent and started his troops forward, he became apprehensive lest the infantry line would prove too weak in the event of a Federal attack on the artillery. He decided to reconnoiter in person and then to advance the whole of his Division within striking distance. As he neared Malvern Hill, he met the commanding General. Lee had been informed by a young cavalry Colonel [7] that a Union column was moving South, and he naturally had asked himself whether this might not indicate that McClellan was seeking to get off while Longstreet and A. P. Hill waited on Huger and Jackson. To ascertain the situation and the strength of the escaping column, Lee had ridden down from the vicinity of Frayser's Farm. Personally he may not have seen any wagons and infantry crossing the hill, [8] but he satisfied himself of the enemy's presence, and now he learned of Holmes's advance. Lee approved this and urged that Holmes should open fire with the rifled guns the moment the infantry were at hand. [9]

Holmes promptly moved his Division down the River road, but the hurrying feet of the men raised so much dust [10] that it gave the Union troops a warning of the Confederates' approach. Soon, over the head of the men in line, there burst a heavy shell. "We could form no idea whence it came," wrote a member of the Fiftieth North Carolina, "but [we] were not long kept in doubt, for in a few minutes there was a perfect shower of shells of tremendous proportion and hideous sound hurled from the heavy naval guns of the Federal fleet on the James river, just opposite

[6] *Brent*, 193–94.
[7] This was Thomas L. Rosser, concerning whom see *infra*, p. 647.
[8] See *infra*, note 18.
[9] *O. R.*, 11, pt. 2, p. 907. It is possible that Holmes was told by Lee that Magruder would move up on the left in support, but, from Holmes's attitude when Major Brent reported to him later, it would appear that Holmes then learned for the first time of the plan. Holmes scarcely would have been uncooperative if he had been informed by the commanding General that Magruder would take position on the left.
[10] *O. R.*, 11. pt. 2, p. 907; 3 *N. C. Regts.*, 39.

and about 900 yards distant, with a perfectly open field intervening."[11]

The raw troops were startled and confused by this fire. Their cavalry stampeded, ran into a plank fence and crushed some of the infantrymen who had taken shelter behind it. A flag bearer, more daring than experienced, rushed into the field on the right of the road and planted his colors there, a veritable target for the enemy.[12] The Forty-fifth North Carolina broke.[13] Part of a reserve battery, sent up to support the rifled guns, was caught in a tangle of timber. The excited artillerists cut the traces, left two guns and three caissons and galloped off.[14] Everywhere, for a moment, there was chaos. General Holmes alone was calm, and he by reason of his deafness. During the advance, he had gone into a little house by the roadside to transact some army business. When he emerged quietly amid the din, he stopped abruptly and cupped his ear suspiciously. "I thought," said he, "I heard firing."[15]

As soon as order was restored in the ranks, Holmes directed the waiting artillery in his front to open on the Federals who still were crossing Malvern Hill. Colonel Deshler obeyed with a roaring challenge; but almost on the instant he was answered with a salvo. Case shot and shell crashed into the woods on so wide an arc that they presented almost a cross fire. Horses and men went down. The hostile bombardment became a tornado. Although the smoke from the Federal guns billowed so heavily that Deshler could not count the opposing pieces, he estimated that twenty-five or thirty were blasting him.[16]

It was a hopeless duel against an overpowering adversary. After an hour, as night fell, Deshler's batteries, badly mauled, were withdrawn. Holmes, meantime, had concluded that an infantry attack by his small Division would, in his own words, have been

[11] 3 N. C. Regts., 163–64. For the mistake concerning the origin of these shells, which came principally from the Union heavy artillery, see 2 R. E. Lee, 207, infra, Chap. XL.

[12] 3 N. C. Regts., 163–64. [13] N. C. Regts., 39.

[14] O. R., 11, pt. 2, p. 911. [15] 2 B. & L., 390.

[16] O. R., 11, pt. 2, p. 910. The actual number seems to have been thirty-six though four and perhaps others were poorly served by inexperienced officers. They employed canister which, at the range of 1500 to 1800 yards, did no execution (cf. 2 B. & L., 409–10; O. R., 11, pt. 2, p. 355). Most of the Federal guns belonged to the reserve artillery under Col. Henry J. Hunt. Included were eight 20-pdr. Parrotts. Later the siege guns of the 1st Conn. Arty. were added (2 B. & L., loc. cit.: O. R., 11, pt. 2, p. 238).

"perfect madness," because "it would have required a march of over three-quarters of a mile up a steep hill destitute of cover." [17] At 9 P.M. he sent back his infantry to a position slightly in advance of New Market Heights, whence he had marched that afternoon.[18]

"Prince John" Magruder, who during the afternoon received orders to support Holmes, had suffered irritating mishaps all day. After a morning march that was confused at the outset by want of guides,[19] Magruder halted between 1 and 2 P.M.[20] at Timberlake's Store, where he found the Darbytown road blocked by the rear of A. P. Hill's Division.[21] While waiting, Magruder received from Lee a notice of the location of general field headquarters and a request for information concerning his progress.[22] On the arrival of Magruder's answer, Lee may have assumed Magruder was then on the march, East of the store, because Lee then sent back word for Magruder to halt and to rest his men, but to be ready to move at any minute. As it was, Magruder had not started from Timberlake's Store when these instructions arrived. He consequently remained there, though Lee thought him nearer.[23] At 4.30, Longstreet, who was ranking officer during Lee's reconnaissance on the right, directed Magruder to go to the support of Holmes. This order, it appears, was not intended by its author to strengthen Holmes for an attack, but was de-

[17] O. R., 11, pt. 2, p. 908.

[18] Ibid. Perhaps because he knew more than he said of Holmes's singular mood on the 30th, D. H. Hill, describing these movements (2 B. & L., 391), was most critical of his fellow Carolinian. That was permissible and perhaps was justified. Hill's inaccuracy was not excusable and scarcely is understandable. He wrote that Holmes reached Malvern Hill at 10.30 A.M. on June 30, when actually Holmes reached New Market Heights that morning; Hill affirmed, further, that Holmes asked for reinforcements, a statement not confirmed by the records; he gave Holmes's position on the night of June 30 as that which Holmes actually occupied on the evening of July 1 (cf. 2 B. & L., 390–391 and O. R., 11, pt. 2, p. 908). The implication is that Holmes should have seized Malvern Hill on the 30th and, failing that, should have attacked again on the 1st. Suffice it to say that Porter's Corps reached Malvern Hill at 9 A.M. on the 30th (O. R., 11, pt. 2, p. 228), that the flow of wagons and reserve artillery over the hill ended about 4 P.M. (ibid.), and that Porter had at hand to oppose Holmes, not the thin Brigade of Warren only, as Hill intimated, but virtually all that was left of his Corps, close to 20,000 men. As for position, Gen. Geo. Sykes, commanding a Division of Porter's Corps, wrote in his report: "Nothing could be more commanding than the line I held" (O. R., 11, pt. 2, p. 350).

[19] O. R., 11, pt. 2, p. 718.

[20] McLaws, loc. cit., said 1 o'clock; Magruder, ibid., 666, fixed the time at 2.

[21] Ibid., 718.

[22] O. R., 11, pt. 2, pp. 666, 675.

[23] Cf. Lee, in O. R., 11, pt. 2, p. 495: "Magruder . . . was ordered to reenforce Holmes, but being at a greater distance than had been supposed . . ."

signed to cover Longstreet's own flank in the event that the enemy should drive Holmes.[24]

Magruder, the ever-galloping, started immediately by a short route a local guide showed him, and he left his artillery to follow by the road.[25] While he was on his way through the woods, another summons came. Col. R. H. Chilton sent word that he wished to show Magruder where to take position. Without waiting to see what Chilton intended to do, Magruder hurried off Major Brent to Holmes on the unpleasant mission that already has been described. Then "Prince John" dashed off and met the Chief of Staff, who conducted him to a position in the forest on the right of Holmes. There, Chilton explained, Lee wished Magruder to place his troops. Magruder did not wait for more details. He dispatched officers to find his Brigades and to bring them up. In person he spurred away to locate Holmes.

Failing in that, Magruder ordered one of his staff to continue the search, while he galloped back to the woods where his troops were to form. By that time, the exhaustion, lack of sleep and indigestion probably had brought Magruder to a state of mental confusion. When he met in the woods one of his Brigadiers, Paul Semmes, he ordered the Georgian to move forward his troops. Semmes protested, justly enough, that in the gathering darkness of the forest, he would be certain to have his command disorganized and scattered if he attempted to advance, but Magruder would not heed: The effort must be made! [26]

Off once more rode Magruder, this time to hasten the advance of the remainder of his troops. On the way, he received orders to abandon the movement on the right of Holmes and to return to the support of Longstreet. Most of Magruder's troops by this time had reached New Market, much farther to the rear than he should have directed them. He sent an officer to recall them, and himself waited for them at the junction of the Long Bridge and Darbytown roads. As soon as the head of his column arrived, he put spurs to his mount again and hurried to report to Lee. At headquarters, he was told that, when his troops were at hand, he was to relieve Longstreet. To supervising this transfer of front-

[24] *Longstreet*, 139. It is not clear from Longstreet's narrative whether he sent these orders to Magruder on his own initiative or at the instance of Lee.
[25] *O. R.*, 11, pt. 2, p. 666.
[26] *O. R.*, 11, pt. 2, pp. 667, 718.

line position, Magruder devoted himself until 3 A.M. and then he slept an hour. It was his second hour of repose in seventy-two.[27] His men, of course, were exhausted. Most of them had marched twenty miles that day and had kept the road for eighteen hours,[28] but not one of them had been privileged to draw trigger.

This, then, was the result of the attempted convergence of all the infantry opposite the line of McClellan's retreat: Holmes had been stopped by superior artillery; the reserve Divisions of Magruder had been worn out to no purpose; Huger had spent the day cutting a road; Jackson had not crossed White Oak Swamp; almost 50,000 Confederate troops, for one reason or another, had done virtually nothing on the day when Lee had hoped to overwhelm his adversary.

To complete the tragedy of the Army's failure, Lee had felt compelled to attack in the late afternoon, opposite Frayser's Farm, with the Divisions of Longstreet and of A. P. Hill. The ground was confusing and the prospect of substantial results was small; but a vigorous onslaught with the troops at hand seemed the one alternative to permitting McClellan to march, unhindered and undisturbed, past the Confederate front. The two Confederate Divisions fought magnificently. Slowly the fluctuating lines pressed through the woods and charged with ghastly losses across clearings where the Federals had planted artillery. At one point and then at another the Federals were forced back until, when blackness covered the field and stopped the battle, the Unionists held one small part only of their previous line.

Tactically this Battle of Frayser's Farm was of encouragement solely because Longstreet and Hill showed themselves capable of maintaining touch with all their troops through a maze of woodland. To Longstreet went first honors, but Hill, who commanded the field for an hour, while "Old Pete" was posting a Brigade, showed admirable judgment. The gain was small. All the Army had to show for its effort was a causeway of dead bodies, some hard-won Federal ordnance and a bit of shell-torn woods.[29]

[27] No sleep on the night of June 28–29; an hour on the night of June 29–30. *O. R.*, 11, pt. 2, pp. 662, 665, 667.

[28] *O. R.*, 11, pt. 2, pp. 705, 707.

[29] Because a full account of the Battle of Frayser's Farm is to be found in 2 *R. E. Lee*, 184 ff., the details of the action are not reviewed here. For reference to some conspicuous performances, see *infra*, Chap. XLI.

CHAPTER XXXVII

MALVERN HILL: A TRAGEDY OF STAFF

THE ARMY that bestirred itself in the clear dawn of July 1 was weaker by 10,000 men than it had been at the beginning of the campaign. Nine of its thirty-eight infantry Brigades [1] had changed command. After the wounding of Pickett at Gaines' Mill, Col. Eppa Hunton had directed the Brigade until he had fallen of exhaustion at Frayser's Farm. Col. John B. Strange of the Nineteenth Virginia had concluded that tangled action and now led the five regiments.[2] To the command of Arnold Elzey was assigned Jubal A. Early,[3] who, despite his wound, had succeeded in reaching the front, though unable to mount a horse without assistance.[4] The Mississippians of the fallen Griffith were under their senior Colonel, William Barksdale of the Thirteenth Regiment,[5] a picturesque veteran of the Mexican War and a former Congressman.[6] Wade Hampton had been assigned on the 28th to temporary command of Taliaferro's Third Brigade of Jackson's Division.[7] Named at the instance of "Stonewall" himself, Brig. Gen. John R. Jones now led the Second Brigade, which had been Campbell's.[8] Taylor's Louisianians, during his continued disability and after the death of Colonel Seymour, passed to Col. L. A. Stafford of the Ninth.[9] As Featherstone had been wounded severely on the 30th, his Brigade was in the care of a Colonel,[10] as was that of Jos. R. Anderson, who had been injured at Frayser's

1 Holmes's command included.
2 *O. R.*, 11, pt. 2, p. 769.
3 As of July 1.
4 *O. R.*, 11, pt. 2, pp. 607, 611; Early, 77–78.
5 *O. R.*, 11, pt. 2, p. 750.
6 Cf. *O. R.*, 2, 556, 1000; 5, 354, 979; 11, pt. 2, pp. 666, 750; 7 *C. M. H.*, Miss., 239. For a sketch of his Brigade, see 32 *S. H. S. P.*, 250.
7 *O. R.*, 11, pt. 2, p. 593.
8 *Ibid.*, 587. Jones, Lieutenant Colonel of the Thirty-third Virginia, Jackson's old Brigade, was appointed Brigadier General, June 25, and was assigned to the Second Brigade, Jackson's Division, which for some weeks had been under its senior Colonel. At Gaines' Mill it had been led by Lt. Col. R. H. Cunningham, Jr. Cf. *O. R.*, 12, pt. 2, pp. 586–87. According to Wright, *op. cit.*, 84, the Senate never confirmed the appointment of Jones. For his career, see 3 *C. M. H.*, 614–15.
9 *Ibid.*, 620.
10 *Ibid.*, 786.

Farm.[11] Finally, because Robert E. Rodes found himself too weak to keep the field, Col. John B. Gordon of the Sixth Alabama led a Brigade that already had twice distinguished itself.[12]

Thus under new or unfamiliar brigade commanders, more than a fifth of the Army faced the next uncertain stage of the campaign; but all the Divisions remained in the charge of the Generals who had commenced the operations. When these men came up, one after another, on the 1st of July, to Lee's field headquarters near the battlefield of the previous day, they showed in varying degree the strain of five days of march and combat. Lee was tired and somewhat unwell. His disappointment over the failure of his plan was manifest; his curb on his temper was not at its perfection, but he was calm and clear in mind. Longstreet showed no weariness. If A. P. Hill did, there is no record of it, though his physical fiber was by no means so stout as that of Longstreet. The night's rest which Jackson had commended to his staff officers seemed to have benefited him: he was alert and ready.

Huger was absent from the early conferences. He had not discovered, till Longstreet sent him word, that the enemy had disappeared from his front; and now he was waiting, while other troops passed on the road. Another delay awaited him because, as he subsequently said: "I had no one to show us what road to take." [13] Physically, Huger had no complaint. Magruder's nervous condition must have been worse than ever, but, as happens in many such cases, he was unaware of his condition and apparently that day did not question his capacity of sound decision and intelligent action. Holmes was down on the River road and did not report in person at field headquarters.

D. H. Hill was fit for the tests of the day, but, when he met General Lee, he had a warning: Rev. L. W. Allen—the same chaplain who had shot vainly at the drunken Irish Sergeant the previous day—had been reared in the country through which the Army was passing. He had described, Hill said, a strong position known as Malvern Hill, ahead of the line of advance. Hill repeated Allen's description of the ground, and added: "If General McClellan is there in force, we had better let him alone."

<hr />

11 *Ibid.*, 800. His sucessor was Col. E. L. Thomas of the Thirty-fifth Georgia, who, though wounded June 26, continued on duty. *Ibid.*, 878.

12 *Ibid.*, 622.   13 *O. R.*, 11, pt. 2, p. 790.

Longstreet broke in, half-banteringly: "Don't get scared, now that we have got him licked!"

Hill did not like this, though he and Longstreet were on a friendly footing, and he said no more.[14]

Lee himself, ignorant of the ground and having no alternative. ordered an advance toward James River on the road of McClellan's retreat, the road that led over the eminence Hill mentioned. Jackson and Magruder were to press after the enemy. Huger was to receive orders on arrival. Longstreet and A. P. Hill, who had borne the brunt of the fighting on June 30, were to be in reserve.

Magruder had his command close at hand and he offered to take the lead; but, when Jackson insisted that his troops were fresher, Lee directed him to advance. To Magruder, Lee gave instructions to proceed by the Quaker road and to form on the right of Jackson.[15] It was Lee's intention to have Huger follow substantially the same line of march.[16]

These orders seemed simple enough, but from the time they were put in execution co-ordinated effort virtually ended. Although the divisional leaders were not to be far apart at any hour, most of them lost touch. This was due, in the first place, to the nature of the ground and to lack of information concerning it. Most of the Divisions had to move down the narrow Quaker or Willis Church road. After a march of a mile and a quarter, they came to a little creek known as Western Run.

This stream ran West of and parallel to the road, before it made the eastward turn perpendicular to the highway. Dammed at one point, Western Run constituted near Malvern Hill a swamp almost as difficult as White Oak itself. To the right of the road, thick woodland led directly into this swamp and afforded no open ground for deployment. Through the forest, which thick underbrush rendered almost impassable, a few obscure farm trails could be followed. Along a stretch of more than a mile, the Run could not be crossed save at favored spots and then with much effort. Agriculture had despaired of conquering the land along the creek. Jungle possessed it and defied every adventurer except the native woodsman. From the road, the forest and the fern-covered ground to the westward may have seemed intriguing, but a regiment

[14] 2 B. & L., 391.   [15] O. R., 11, pt. 2, pp. 496, 667.
[16] Huger's movements during the forenoon of July 1 are reviewed *infra*, pp. 611-12.

ᴸould be lost within 200 yards of the only thoroughfare. The task of organizing a line there was beyond the resources of any except a soldier of large experience. As will appear, it had to be undertaken by Brigadier Generals, newly commissioned, for the reason that General Huger was slow in getting to the front. To the left, East of the road, beyond a shallow woodland lay the open ground of the Poindexter farm, a decent position of some strength; but for Jackson to get his three Divisions there and to deploy them consumed all the morning hours until 11 o'clock.[17]

Co-ordination was lost, in the second place, through a singular mistake on the part of General Magruder. The Quaker road, he was told by Lee, was to be his line of advance into position on the right of Jackson. Apparently the galloping Magruder did not ask to examine Lee's map—the only one available[18]—nor does he seem to have inquired of the commanding General where the road ran. If the Quaker road was his route, he would find it for himself. He had three guides from the neighborhood and, still without explanation, he bade them conduct him to the Quaker road.

After these men had started Magruder's Division to the West, almost at a right angle to the line of Jackson's march southward, Longstreet became concerned: was not Magruder going in the wrong direction; could that route lead to the Quaker road? When Longstreet raised the question Magruder recalled his guides and catechized them. They insisted that they were correct, nor did any of them know that the road from Glendale past Willis Church to Malvern Hill also was styled the Quaker road, though often given the name of the church.

Thus reassured by his guides, Magruder elaborately informed Longstreet that, if that officer still thought he was in error, he would take any other road his senior designated. Longstreet still believed Magruder was on the wrong road, but as he was not familiar with the ground he refrained from giving an order for a change of route. Magruder moved on—back from the battlefield of Frayser's Farm, into the Long Bridge road, up that road to a point beyond the gate to Nathan Enroughty's house, and then southwestward into an obscure, little-used byway which his guides told him was the veritable Quaker road.[19]

[17] *O. R.*, 11, pt. 2, p. 566.   [18] Cf. *supra*, p. 566, n. 4.
[19] *O. R.*, 11, pt. 2, pp. 608, 675–77.

Longstreet, meantime, must have become convinced that Magruder was following a divergent line of advance and he probably so reported to Lee. In order to prevent further loss of time, Longstreet rode after Magruder. When he overtook "Prince John," Longstreet said more firmly than before that the virtually abandoned lane could not possibly be the Quaker road. Magruder held to his opinion that it was the designated route. Argument was ended by the arrival of one of Lee's staff officers with orders for Magruder to retrace his steps and then to use a forest trail nearer the right of Jackson.[20] In the end, as D. R. Jones wrote in his official report, part of Magruder's command "marched back on the Darbytown road some 3 or 4 miles, counter-marched and finally halted some two miles in rear of the position occupied in the morning."[21]

While Magruder was marching and counter-marching, an incomplete order of battle had been drawn with much fumbling and difficulty in the tangle along Western Run. Jackson's Division and all of Ewell's, except Trimble, were held in reserve on the left.[22] Whiting, under Jackson's command, formed the active Confederate left of a front that faced South. Next on his right, toward the West, Trimble's Brigade of Ewell's Division later was put in position. Astride the Quaker or Willis Church road, was D. H. Hill's Division. Magruder was to have been immediately on Jackson's right, but Armistead had reached the front with his and Wright's Brigades of Huger's Division and, in the absence of Magruder, had occupied part of the ground assigned "Prince John."[23] These two Brigades did not extend the right as far as the opposing line ran, and they had no reserve closer than the battle-weary Divisions of Longstreet and A. P. Hill.

From every point along this front, Malvern Hill in times of peace would have been a pleasant site. Its locust trees were breeze-swept, its grass abundant. From the elevation, the verdant

[20] *O. R.*, 11, pt. 2, p. 668. "Magruder's Quaker Road" appears on Col. H. L. Lander's Map No. 10 of the Seven Days' Battles.
[21] *O. R.*, 11, pt. 2, p. 691. General Brent, *op. cit.*, 207, expressed the opinion that "no injury resulted from the two or three hours' delay caused by the misunderstanding of the names of the roads, except extra fatigue to the men." The author went so far as to add: "In fact, considering the results it was very beneficial that our attack suffered the delay."
[22] *O. R.*, 11, pt. 2, p. 557.
[23] *O. R.*, 11, pt. 2, pp. 496, 566, 811, 818. The circumstances of Armistead's advance are described *infra*, p. 600.

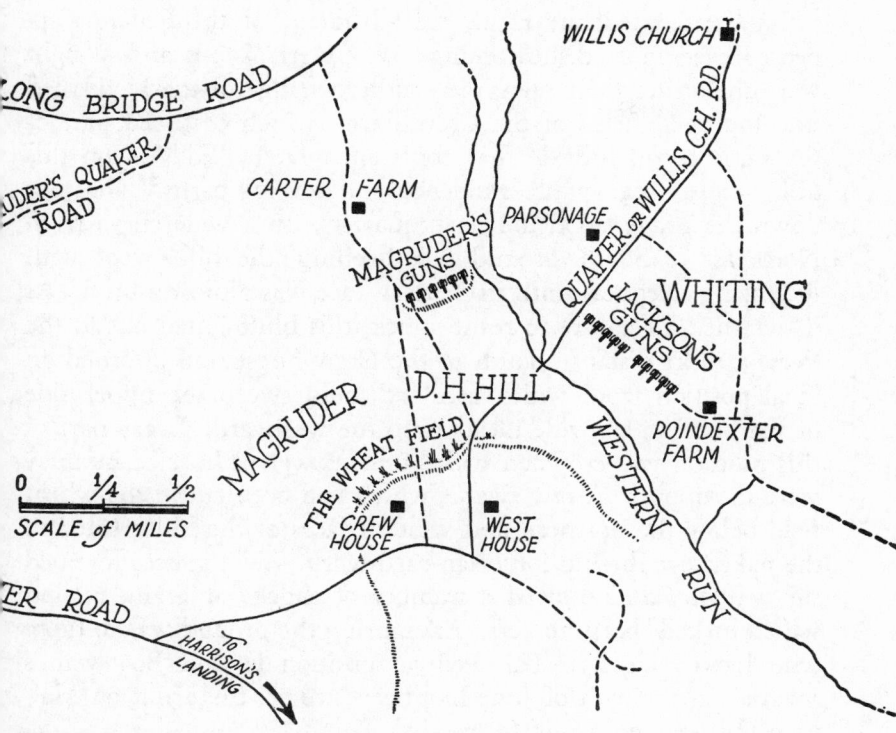

Terrain, Artillery Positions and General Troop Dispositions at Malvern Hill, July 1, 1862

forests on the south side of James River spread alluringly. Now, where the enemy was visible at all, his position was one of discouraging strength, if not of impregnability. Opposite Jackson, the ground South of the Run and in front of the Federals was cleared farmland that led up to the West house, a middle-class country residence with the usual outbuildings. The hill did not appear too steep to be mounted, but its length concealed the full grade. It offered the Federals a perfect field of fire for 300 or 400 yards. A level crest afforded space for many batteries, which were defiantly exposed as if inviting attack. "If [the] first line was carried," D. H. Hill subsequently wrote, "another and another still more difficult remained in the rear." [24] Hill looked all this over and shook his head. Fighter though he was, he had to conclude that no attempt should be made to storm the hill.[25]

[24] O. R., 11, pt. 2, p. 628.   [25] Ibid.

On the Confederate right, the advantage of the Federals appeared even more disheartening. Where Armistead and Wright were sheltering their men, the southern fringe of the woods led into the open fields of the Crew Farm, which occupied part of the same broad hillside that confronted D. H. Hill. Atop this hill were a large white residence and several barns.[26] Farther down the grade stood the slave quarters. In a wide curve from Northeast to South, around the dwelling, the hill swept with increasing steepness until its western face was almost a bluff. As if designed by nature to resist attack, this bluff jutted out to the West a short distance South of the Crew house and afforded an ideal position from which artillery could sweep the upper side of the bluff and a wide meadow to the westward. Every part of this position was crowned with guns. Powerful lines of infantry were in support. A few swaths which had been cut in the wheat field below the northern and western faces of the hill created to the naked eye the illusion of an earthwork. Field glasses revealed the actuality and showed a number of shocks of grain, behind which lurked sharpshooters. Affrighting the ground was to those who looked closely. The Federal position behind Boatswain's Swamp on the 27th of June had been strong; this front on Malvern Hill seemed a field fortress! [27]

From the swamp and the forest few of these aspects of the terrain on the right were visible immediately. No high-ranking officer was at hand to assume responsibility for a careful examination of all the ground in advance of that wing. Brigadier General Armistead, with the assistance of General Wright, made a reconnaissance of his own front, but apparently he did not know that he was the senior officer on that flank and consequently he made no effort to extend his observation westward or to inform General Lee of what he had seen. With care and good judgment, Armistead found ground where his own and Wright's men could be protected. Then he soundly decided that no advance could be made until Confederate artillery, which he promptly ordered up,

---

[26] *O. R.,* 11, pt. 2, pp. 274, 811–12. The residence, though styled the "Crew House" in reports, was owned by Dr. J. H. Mellert.

[27] Much the fullest contemporary description of the ground is that in Gen. A. R. Wright's report, *O. R.,* 11, pt. 2, pp. 811–12. A detailed account will be found in 2 *R. E. Lee,* 582–84. Since the publication of that work, a few additional facts have come to light in *Brent,* 209–10.

could cope with the Union batteries on the hill.[28] The same conclusion had been reached on Jackson's part of the line.[29]

At length, after midday, when confused reports could be put
together, it appeared that two tenable artillery positions had been
found on the Confederate front. One was to the left, in a large
wheat field on the Poindexter Farm. The other was on the southern, wooded rim of a hill in rear of Armistead.[30] If these two
positions could be occupied and held by powerful batteries, a
converging fire might be opened on the Federal array. Then, if
the Union guns were silenced, or even were thrown into confusion, a general infantry assault might rout Federal troops who
were believed to be demoralized by their previous defeats.[31] As
Armistead had the most favorable position from which to launch
the assault, the initial plan was that he should start his advance
when he saw the Federal line broken by the artillery, and that,
when he went forward with a cheer, the whole line should sweep
up the hill. Orders to this effect were given all the division commanders who could be reached.[32]

To bring up the guns was the first task. On Jackson's front,
this did not seem difficult. The approaches were passable, the
ground not wholly unfavorable. Shelter could be found for at
least some of the ordnance that was to play on the Federal massed
artillery.[33] Unfortunately, Stapleton Crutchfield, Chief of Artillery to Jackson and a wholly competent officer, was sick that day
and was not able to keep the field.[34] No acting chief had been
appointed in his stead. Jackson himself consequently had to order
the batteries up. In at least one case, when an artillery Captain
could not find Whiting, to whom he was directed to report, "Old
Jack" put him in position.[35] Available field pieces were not
abundant. On order, D. H. Hill had sent all his artillery back to

---

[28] O. R., 11, pt. 2, pp. 818–19.   [29] Ibid., 566.

[30] The Crew house is at an elevation of about 130 feet. North-northwest, at a
distance of 1500 yards, the 140-foot contour passes about 400 yards South of the Carter
house. The artillery position almost certainly was in and to the East of the lane on the
southern edge of the belt of woods South of the "Carter field," later the Garthright
Farm. To the Crew house, the range was 1200 yards.

[31] Cf. D. H. Hill, in 2 B. & L., 391: "It was this belief in the demoralization of the
Federal army that made our leader risk the attack."

[32] O. R., 11, pt. 2, pp. 496, 628, 669, 677.

[33] The range from the 120-foot contour in the Poindexter wheat field to the corresponding opposite elevation, where the artillery was in battery near the West house,
was about 1400 yards. Direction was nearly Southwest.

[34] O. R., 11, pt. 2, p. 562.   [35] Ibid., 572.

Seven Pines to refit, and had no guns to add to the fire.[36] He should have been supplied from the reserve, but General Pendleton, with more than twenty batteries at his disposal, was not to be found. One of the few batteries at hand, Wooding's, could bring up a single section only.[37]

Armistead, who still was without a division commander on the field, did not have to wait long before a battery arrived, but its commander made many excuses and seemed unwilling to face the Federal fire. In red wrath, Armistead ordered him off the field.[38] In his place soon arrived Capt. C. F. Grimes, though he had only two guns of sufficient range to reach the enemy.[39] After Grimes came Capt. William J. Pegram, who already had distinguished himself at Mechanicsville.[40] These gallant officers and their courageous gunners unhesitatingly took their assigned station. To reduce the odds they faced, Armistead asked for more artillery, but no divisional officer was at hand to supply it. About 3 P.M., when Longstreet rode to that part of the field, Armistead requested him to send needed batteries. Longstreet rode off to find the pieces.

The Federal artillerists had opened about 1 P.M., as if anticipating the Confederate bombardment,[41] and they soon commanded the entire front.[42] Around the infantry in woods fell shattered branches and fragments of shells. As the Southern batteries came up, one after another, they received a concentrated, powerful and well-directed fire.[43] Gun after gun was put out of action. Jackson, first and last, got eighteen only into action. Some of these an unidentified officer ordered to take shelter. Although the bolder of the Captains held to their ground, confusion among the batteries resulted.[44]

The few that kept up their fire, though they were blanketed every minute of the uneven bombardment, contrived to make their charges count. One Federal commander later admitted that he had been subjected to a "severe converging fire";[45] opposite the veteran artillerists from the Valley, the Union reserve infantry

[36] *Ibid.*, 653.
[37] *Ibid.*, 594.
[38] O. R., 11, pt. 2, p. 802.
[39] *Ibid.*, 812.
[40] *Ibid.*, 819, 835, 839. See *infra*, p. 649.
[41] O. R., 11, pt. 2, p. 818.
[42] O. R., 11, pt. 2, p. 496.
[43] *Cf.* Gen. D. N. Couch, O. R., 11, pt. 2, p 204: "[The artillery] did brilliant service. It could not have been excelled."
[44] O. R., 11, pt. 2, pp. 572, 574.
[45] O. R., 11, pt. 2, p. 319.

had to be called up.[46] About 2.30 o'clock, when the Confederate fire was hottest, the situation was serious in the opinion of some of the Northern gunners, but the Confederates realized they were losing the duel. Harvey Hill complained to Jackson that the bombardment from the Poindexter Farm was of the "most farcical character." General Lee himself concluded that the Southern batteries would fail to break the Federal front, and he rode out with Longstreet, beyond Jackson's extreme left, to see if he could turn the Union right from that quarter.[47]

At 3 P.M., some crippled Confederate batteries were banging away with stubbornness; half an hour later a few guns still were in action, though almost overwhelmed by the blasting fire from the hill. The infantry watched, listened, and wondered whether, as at Gaines' Mill, they would be commanded to charge the artillery position. D. H. Hill, for his part, virtually had decided that no assault would be delivered, but in answer to his complaint over the ineffective fire of the artillery, he received from Jackson renewal of his orders to charge when Armistead's men raised a shout. Prudently, after this message, Hill kept his Brigadiers near him and directed them to have their men ready to move.[48]

Beyond D. H. Hill's right, the situation remained one of confusion. Armistead's troops and those of Wright were all the infantry definitely in position there, but other Brigades were approaching. Mahone and Ransom, both of Huger's command,[49] had spent half a day in marching about five miles, but they now were floundering through the woods toward the front. Huger himself was on the lane that led from the Darbytown road through the Carter Farm to the Willis Church road. He had heard that Armistead and Wright had taken position at the front, but where they were and what he himself was to do, he did not know. By the road he waited for orders that had not come.[50]

Armistead did not have any information regarding Huger's movement and now, uncounselled, he had to act. Federal skirmishers were creeping forward and were threatening the front. Half of his command, which comprised five regiments and a

---

[46] *Ibid.*, 351.   [47] *Longstreet*, 144.
[48] *O. R.*, 11, pt. 2, p. 628.
[49] Ransom had been assigned temporarily to Huger from Holmes; cf. *O. R., 11*, pt 2, p. 791.
[50] *Cf.* Brent's statement, *infra*, p. 612.

battalion, Armistead promptly advanced. Glad of a chance to meet infantry, after having endured artillery fire for hours, the three Virginia regiments drove back the Union skirmishers and pursued them to the hillside below the Crew house. There, in an advanced position but covered by the roll of the land, Armistead had to leave this part of his Brigade.[51]

By this time, it was 4 o'clock. Disappointment was general among the commanding officers who were scattered through the woods and over the fields. Five hours the Army had waited. Nothing had happened except the uneven artillery duel, which now was drawing to a humiliating end. On left and on right, the last of the Confederate batteries that had attempted to break the Federal line had virtually exhausted their ammunition and were preparing to withdraw. None of the guns that Longstreet had sought to collect for Armistead had arrived.[52]

The fire of the Union artillery, still steady and accurate, had a note of triumph. D. H. Hill waited at his post with his Brigadiers, though he was more convinced than ever that Armistead would not give the signal and that no infantry action would occur. Armistead and Wright held to their ground. Mahone now was moving to their support. In rear of the right, Cobb and Barksdale were advancing. D. R. Jones's Division, which had followed these two Brigades in the advance of Magruder's forces, had been formed by Longstreet.[53] McLaws's Division, which brought up Magruder's rear, similarly was given direction by Longstreet, who unfortunately sent the command too far toward the center.[54]

Now, suddenly, everything changed. Galloping Magruder came on the scene after his long, wasted march.[55] He was all ardor, all excitement, and altogether ignorant of the situation on his immediate front. Lee's orders were that Magruder was to form on the right of Huger, who would be on the right of Jackson. Quickly Magruder dispatched Major Brent to find Huger and to ascertain where the flank of Huger rested.[56] Then Ma-

---

[51] *O. R.*, 11, pt. 2, p. 819.   [52] *Ibid.*, 819.

[53] It is impossible to say whether Longstreet did this before or after his ride to the left with Lee. Cf. *O. R.*, 11, pt. 2, pp. 691–92.

[54] *O. R.*, 11, pt. 2, p. 719.

[55] He arrived about 4 o'clock or a little later. *Cf.* Armistead's account, *O. R.*, 11, pt. 2, p. 819: "About this time (somewhat between 4 and 5 P.M.) General Magruder came to where I was . . ." Wright, slightly in rear of Armistead, said, *ibid.*, 814: "Major General Magruder came on the field about 4 o'clock."

[56] *Brent*, 211.

gruder undertook a reconnaissance with officers supplied him by General Armistead. When Armistead told him of the request made Longstreet for more guns, Magruder sent word to his Chief of Artillery to bring up, if possible, thirty rifled pieces. Wheeling then, before any of his troops were in position, he dashed back to the rear to hurry forward D. R. Jones's Division.

While Magruder was attempting to speed the advance, he received for the first time the circular Lee had dispatched to the division commanders, some three hours previously, for a general advance when Armistead raised a shout. In a short time, there also was handed Magruder a note from a staff officer he had sent Lee.[57] This was brief and perhaps mystifying, but behind it was a new situation.

Lee had ridden far to the left, after he had concluded the bombardment would be a failure, and beyond Jackson's flank he had found favorable ground for launching an attack. He had discussed with Longstreet how the reserve Divisions could be moved up for this assault. That determined, Lee had started back toward the center. On the way, he had word from Whiting that the enemy in front of Jackson had ceased artillery fire, that heavy infantry columns were moving to the Union left, and that wagons and troops in retreat could be seen in the Federal rear.[58] Atop this news from Whiting, Lee may have heard from Magruder's staff officer that Armistead had won advantage. Lee, in any event, had abandoned his design for an attack on the left and had reverted to his earlier plan for a general assault when Armistead went forward.

The note sent Magruder by his staff officer was to the effect that, as the Federals were said to be getting off, Lee expected him to advance rapidly and to follow up Armistead's success. Assurance was given by the staff officer that two Brigades of Huger's Division, Ransom's and Mahone's, would aid Magruder.[59] Once more, "Prince John" put spurs to his horse and galloped to the front. Again he reconnoitered briefly, this time with Wright and Armistead, and then he directed them to prepare for the assault.

[57] This officer was Capt. A. G. Dickinson, whose note to Magruder appears in O. R., 11, pt. 2, pp. 677–78. Dickinson said, among other things, "Press forward your whole line and follow up Armistead's successes," which admonition suggests that Dickinson had been sent to Lee to announce Armistead's advance in the skirmish, but there is no positive proof that Dickinson's mission had been to inform Lee of this affair.
[58] O. R., 11, pt. 2, p. 566.   [59] O. R., 11, pt. 2, pp. 677–78.

He did not know, at the moment, precisely how far D. R. Jones's Division had advanced, nor had Ransom reported. As Mahone was said to be coming up, Magruder assumed that Ransom would file in on the left and D. R. Jones on the center, but, to make sure that Ransom would join them, he dispatched Major Brent to that officer with a request for assistance.[60] Magruder's plan, as he subsequently stated in his report, was "to hurl about 15,000 men against the enemy's batteries and supporting infantry; to follow up any successes they might obtain, and if unable to drive the enemy from his strong position, to continue the fight in front by pouring in fresh troops; and in case they were repulsed to hold strongly the line of battle where I stood, to prevent serious disaster to our own arms."[61]

Because Magruder acted on assumption and did not get in touch with his support, execution fell murderously short of the plan. Ransom sent word that he could not move without orders from Huger, to whom he was transmitting Magruder's request.[62] When Wright was ordered to begin his advance,[63] no other troops were in position to go forward with him. Less than 1000 men stepped out into the open to storm the hill.[64] Not long afterward, Mahone got in position, but he suffered further delay because Magruder took time, as he said, to "address a few words" to the Brigade.[65] Armistead then was told to move up his three rear regiments. To this, Armistead replied that the best of his troops already were on the hillside and that the others were raw. About that time, probably, the appearance of Federal skirmishers on the

[60] On these details, it is impossible fully to reconcile the report of Magruder (O. R., 11, pt. 2, pp. 669–70) with the account written by General Brent in 1903 (op. cit., 215–16; for the date when this part of the narrative was composed, see ibid., 208). General Brent stated that he returned to Magruder after interviewing Huger and D. H. Hill and reported that a long gap existed in the line between the right of Hill and the left of Magruder. It was General Brent's recollection that Magruder sent him to get Ransom from a reserve position to fill this gap along with Mahone. Both Ransom and Mahone, though entirely willing to comply, stated that they were under orders from Huger not to heed orders which did not come through him. Of this reported gap in the line, Magruder said nothing in his contemporary report. Nor did D. H. Hill, in his sharp and critical official account, mention it, though he admitted (O. R., 11, pt. 2, p. 628) that he knew little about the order of battle on his right. General Brent, also, timed differently from his chief the arrival of the note from Lee.
[61] O. R., 11, pt. 2, p. 669.   [62] Ibid., 794; Brent, 216.
[63] Magruder fixed the time as about 5.30 P.M., O. R., 11, pt. 2, p. 670; Wright gave it as 4.45. Ibid., 814.
[64] Ibid., 814.
[65] Ibid., 670.

left of Wright's Brigade led the excited Magruder to conclude that the enemy was advancing on him. Hurriedly, he appealed to Lee for reinforcements.[66]

In place of Armistead's inexperienced men, Magruder now sent in three regiments of Cobb's Brigade, which previously had been divided and posted in three different positions.[67] Ransom again was summoned from Magruder's left, and was told to charge the battery. His reply was that he did not know the location of the battery he was asked to charge, and that orders to him must come through Huger,[68] who by that time had joined him. Magruder thereupon rode back to Barksdale's Brigade, undertook personally to deploy it, and told its commander to move forward in support of the attacking column.[69]

The result of all these orders, messages and gallops forward and back was that now, by 6 o'clock,[70] Magruder had put into action two of Huger's Brigades, besides the three regiments of Armistead on the hillside. Of the six Brigades of his three demi-Divisions, only one Brigade and three regiments of another had been brought to the front. Even these were in support, rather than in the front line of attack. Not more than 5000 men were challenging the stronghold of the Crew House Hill, and they had little artillery behind them. The batteries that began to revive in obedience to Magruder's order had to advance along a single, narrow lane under a blasting fire. As they came up, they were disabled.[71]

Hopeless and ill-handled as was Magruder's partial attack, it precipitated a slaughter of D. H. Hill's troops, who had been waiting for the shout and the charge of Armistead's men. Samuel Garland reported later: "We were returning to our posts under the impression that no movement of infantry would be ordered, when suddenly one or two Brigades . . . charged out of the woods to the right with a shout Major General Hill at once ex-

[66] This call for reinforcements, mentioned somewhat casually by Magruder (O. R., 11, pt. 2, p. 671), was noted by Lee (ibid., 680). It can be given its proper place in the sequence of events by Cobb's remark (ibid., 749), that a second advance was made by the Georgians after Magruder was informed that the enemy was moving against him. The movement which Magruder mistook for an advance against him almost certainly was the attempt, mentioned by Wright (ibid., 814), of a Federal force, probably skirmishers, to turn his left soon after he emerged from the woods.

[67] O. R., 11, pt. 2, p. 749.   [68] Ibid., 670, 795.
[69] Ibid., 670.   [70] Ibid., 751.
[71] O. R., 11, pt. 2, p. 729.

claimed, 'That must be the general advance! Bring up your Brigades as soon as possible and join in it.' " [72]

The well-trained officers of Hill's Division hurried back to their commands and, between 6.30 and 7,[73] led them, cheering, straight up the low, cleared hill on either side of the Willis Church road. Wright and Mahone, meantime, were working around the western end of the hill and were clambering up the bluff.[74] Ransom, who had been given discretion by Huger, on Magruder's third plea for reinforcements,[75] doubled across the rear of Wright and Mahone, came in on their right and attempted to mount the steep hill from the West.

It was not war; it was mass murder. As in every action of the campaign, the men in the ranks did all they could to make good the blunders and delays of their leaders; but this time they were sent to achieve the impossible. Valor could not conquer those perfectly served batteries on the crest, nor could fortitude long endure the fire that seemed to sweep every foot of the open ground. Some of Rodes's regiments under Col. John B. Gordon got within 200 yards of the Federal guns, though they lost half their numbers;[76] Ripley's troops rushed on until they reached level ground, where they were mown by canister.[77] In the end, the shattered, bloody wreckage of D. H. Hill's Division slipped back down the hill. Ewell gallantly attempted to lend support, but it was futile.

Magruder ere this completely had lost his grip on his troops. Mahone and Wright, too far advanced to retreat and too weak to press over the rim of the bluff, decided to remain where they were and to fight on in the growing darkness. Ransom crouched defiantly almost under the mouth of guns.[78] Cobb and Barksdale, first in support, were beaten back with heavy casualties. As D. R. Jones advanced, Toombs's Brigade drifted to the left and came under D. H. Hill's direction.[79] The small Division split into three parts [80] and had little power to strike. As for McLaws's Division, Magruder rode back vainly in search of it,[81] but finally one of

[72] O. R., 11, pt. 2, p. 643.
[73] O. R., 11, pt. 2, pp. 628, 650.   [74] Ibid., 800, 815.
[75] Ibid., 794. Brent stated, op. cit., 215–16, it was the fourth request.
[76] O. R., 11, pt. 2, p. 634.   [77] Ibid., 650.
[78] O. R., 11, pt. 2, p. 795.   [79] Ibid., 628, 692, 698.
[80] Ibid., 692.   [81] Ibid.

Magruder's staff officers, without the authorization of either commander, got the troops to the front, though he put the two Brigades so far apart that one Brigade could not see the other.[82] They then were employed in support of D. H. Hill's right and of Magruder's left. A blood-stirring effort they made, but, in the utter confusion of the twilight, both Kershaw and Semmes were fired on from the rear.[83] As night fell, the opposing forces could be distinguished only by their lines of musketry.[84] "The men in the fight," Magruder wrote Lee, in a final call for reinforcements, "are so entirely disorganized, arising principally from the darkness, that not an organized body exists."[85] On the field and in the woods, as he wrote, lay 5000 dead and wounded boys.

Old Isaac Trimble alone remained unwilling to let the battle end without one more effort. While the red glare of the guns spread weird, intermittent light through the forest, he formed his Brigade for an assault. Just then Jackson came along.

"What are you going to do, General Trimble?" he inquired.

Said Trimble stoutly: "I am going to charge those batteries, sir.'

"I guess you had better not try it. General D. H. Hill has just tried it with his whole Division and been repulsed; I guess you had better not try it, sir," and he rode off.[86]

During the night, General McClellan retreated, as he had after every battle of the campaign. This time he took a position at Harrison's Landing, near Westover, where he was sheltered by the fire of gunboats in James River. His weary men left more rifles and equipment along their route than on any previous march of the retreat. That fact led both D. H. Hill and Magruder to maintain in their reports that the charge on Malvern Hill had shaken and demoralized the foe.[87] The frailty of that basis for an assertion of victory was in itself an admission of failure.

No pursuit was attempted. Although Jackson was anxious to follow, a heavy downpour on the morning of July 2 and uncertainty regarding McClellan's position prompted the commanding General, after some preliminary moves, to remain in the vicinity

---

[82] *Ibid.*, 719, where "A.M." should read "P.M."
[83] *Ibid.*, 724, 728. Cf. *ibid.*, 753.   [84] *Ibid.*, 204.
[85] *Ibid.*, 686.   [86] *Oates*, 143.
[87] *O. R.*, 11, pt. 2, pp. 629, 671.

of Malvern Hill until July 3.[88] When the Army at length was assembled in front of McClellan's new position, an act of bravado on the part of "Jeb" Stuart, presently to be described, threw away the one chance—and that remote—of routing the Federals from their refuge.

The strategic aim of the campaign had been achieved despite bad co-ordination, worse tactics and the worst imaginable staff work: Richmond had been relieved. McClellan no longer was at the city's gates. In the brief period of rest that followed, the command of the Army could be appraised, the men who had failed in action could be relieved, and a reorganization, historic in all its aspects, could be effected.

[88] 2 *R. E. Lee,* 220 ff. In a memorandum of May 7, 1896, prepared for Col. G. F. R. Henderson and used in part by him (*cf.* 2 *Henderson,* 68 ff.), Major Dabney condemned Lee's decision not to pursue on July 2, and argued, in effect, that a great opportunity was lost. The condition of the Federal forces at that time, as set forth in 2 *R. E. Lee,* 224, n. 23, leaves little doubt that, if pursuit in force had been feasible, much loss could have been inflicted on the Union army; but the available roads were few and those were in wretched condition. Any rapid movement to the enemy's rear was impracticable. The poor march of July 3 demonstrated that.

CHAPTER XXXVIII

The End of Magruder and of Huger

First to be reckoned were the casualties. Including those of Huger's affair of June 25, the final computation was 20,141 killed, wounded and missing,[1] but these were most unevenly divided. Those of thirteen Brigades, one third of the Army, were 10,506, or more than half the total. Eight of these thirteen Brigades were in Longstreet's and A. P. Hill's Divisions.[2] In Jackson's and Ewell's Divisions, which included nine Brigades and the Maryland Line, or roughly 23 per cent of the Brigades, gross casualties numbered 1195, or less than 6 per cent of the whole. The three Brigades of the old "Army of the Valley," Jackson's own Division, accounted for only 208 of these. Magruder's three Divisions, six Brigades, lost 2491.[3] Heaviest losses in a single Brigade were those of Cadmus Wilcox, Longstreet's Division—1055. Of regiments, the worst toll in a single battle was the 335 paid at Mechanicsville, during the first assault of the campaign, by the Forty-fourth Georgia of Ripley's Brigade.[4] Whatever the explanation of these figures, they showed that the Army of the Valley had not contributed heavily in blood to the direct defense of Richmond. Lee's men, not Jackson's, had borne the brunt.

Fatalities in the high command had not been numerous. Only one Brigadier General, Richard Griffith, had been killed. Of the seven who had been wounded or injured,[5] Arnold Elzey alone was disabled permanently for field duty, though Pickett and Featherston were listed as "severely wounded."[6] Far more numerous,

---

[1] *Alexander*, 171, 174. His totals evidently were struck from brigade returns, *O. R.*, 11, pt. 2, pp. 973–84. Federal losses were: Killed, 1734, wounded, 8062, missing 6053; total, 15,849. As the Confederate missing numbered only 946, the comparative figures of killed and wounded—Confederate, 19,195, Union, 9796—are a grim illustration of the costliness of the offensive. The ratio is 1.9 to 1.
[2] In Longstreet's Division: R. H. Anderson, 787; Wilcox, 1055; Pryor, 862; Featherston, 666; Pickett, 654. In A. P. Hill's Division: Gregg, 939; Branch, 839; Pender, approximately 800. The other heaviest losers were: Hood of Whiting, 623; Garland, 844, G. B. Anderson, 863, and Ripley, 908, of D. H. Hill; and Wright of Huger, 666.
[3] Jones's Division, 852; McLaws's, 672; Magruder's, 940; Artillery, 27.
[4] D. H. Hill's Division.
[5] G. B. Anderson, July 1; J. R. Anderson, June 30; Arnold Elzey, June 27; W. S. Featherston, June 30; J. R. Jones, July 1; W. D. Pender, July 1; G. E. Pickett, June 27.
[6] *O. R.*, 11, pt. 2, pp. 758, 759.

naturally, had been the fatalities among regimental commanders. Fourteen Colonels had been killed or mortally wounded. Two others had received hurts that were to keep them from ever serving again with their regiments.[7] Besides those slain North of the Chickahominy and mentioned already, two Colonels of particular promise had been lost in the closing battles, Gaston Meares of the Third North Carolina and C. C. Lee, a young West Pointer who commanded the Thirty-seventh North Carolina. Both these men almost certainly would have risen to the rank of general officers.

Some of the Brigades had been crippled by the loss of officers.[8] A. P. Hill had two Colonels killed, and two Brigadier Generals, eleven Colonels and six Lieutenant Colonels wounded.[9] Hood lost eighteen officers in his Brigade;[10] at Frayser's Farm, all of Wilcox's regimental commanders were wounded;[11] in the fighting around Malvern Hill, Ransom had three Colonels wounded and one Lieutenant Colonel killed;[12] Ripley, in the same way, had to report three of his four Colonels killed during the campaign.[13] In some instances, the heavy casualties among both officers and enlisted men were due to bad positions, to unavoidable assaults or to circumstance unpreventable. Other casualty lists, laden with hundreds of names, could be explained in terms of poor leading only.

All the division commanders had escaped physical injury, but several of them had suffered in reputation. Magruder was the most conspicuous of these men and, in the aftermath, figured in a curious dispute. He had been irked for weeks by his loss of

[7] These two were Col. T. P. August of the Fifteenth Virginia, *O. R.*, 11, pt. 2, p. 720, and Col. R. E. Withers of the Eighteenth Virginia, a veteran of First Manassas, *ibid.*, 758. Those killed or mortally wounded, and listed in part, *supra*, p. 536, were: J. W. Allen, Second Virginia, June 27, *ibid.*, 570; R. P. Campbell, Seventh North Carolina, June 27, *ibid.*, 839, 888; S. V. Fulkerson, commanding Jackson's Third Brigade, June 27, *ibid.*, 555; C. C. Lee, Thirty-seventh North Carolina, June 30, *ibid.*, 683, 839, 896; W. M. McIntosh, Fifteenth Georgia, June 27, *ibid.*, 696; John Marshall, Fourth Texas, June 27, *ibid.*, 564; Gaston Meares, Third North Carolina, July 1, *ibid.*, 628, 629, 650; J. T. Norwood, Second Louisiana, July 1, *ibid.*, 672; C. C. Pegues, Fifth Alabama, June 27, *ibid.*, 625; I. G. Seymour, Sixth Louisiana, June 27, *ibid.*, 620; Robert A. Smith, Forty-fourth Georgia, June 26, *ibid.*, 629; M. S. Stokes, First North Carolina, June 26, *ibid.*, 629; T. J. Warthen, Twenty-eighth Georgia, probably July 1, *ibid.*, 629; J. J. Woodward, Tenth Alabama, June 27, *ibid.*, 758, 774.

[8] Certain of the commands had not received new officers after their losses of May 31–June 1. For example, the Twenty-third North Carolina had begun the campaign of the Seven Days with no field officer except its Colonel and with one Captain only. (*O. R.*, 11, pt. 2, p. 647.)

[9] *Ibid.*, 839.

[10] *Ibid.*, 569.

[11] *Ibid.*, 778.

[12] *Ibid.*, 795.

[13] *Ibid.*, 648, 652.

independent command [14] and had been most anxious to go to the Department of the Trans-Mississippi, whither, it will be remembered, he had been transferred on May 23. The day after the Battle of Malvern Hill he applied for orders. Without hesitation, Lee relieved him on July 3 and broke up his cumbersome command: Jones's half Division was put under Longstreet; Magruder's own Division, made up of Toombs's and Barksdale's Brigades, was consolidated with McLaws's.[15]

As soon as these arrangements were made, Magruder ceremoniously bade farewell to his troops through the publication of a general order,[16] and in strict accordance with his practice at Yorktown, he began forthwith to bedevil the Secretary of War for small arms and artillery to be used in the West.[17] With commendation from a friendly newspaper [18] and in the midst of some talk of sending him to South Carolina,[19] he started about July 12 for his new post.[20]

Rumor, by that time, was wagging a vicious tongue concerning him. He was accused of gross recklessness, of wild excitement and intoxication at Malvern Hill.[21] "Old Magruder," wrote Col. T. R. R. Cobb to his wife, "made no reputation in this battle." The Georgian added: "He lost rather than gained. He was depressed, and I fear was drinking." [22] Still darker, in the eyes of many, was the wholly unjust charge that the General had shown the white feather and had sought to screen himself from the enemy's fire.[23] Some or all of these allegations were put forward by an officer of rank who cannot now be identified positively,[24]

---

14 *Cf.* A. L. Long, in 12 *S. H. S. P.,* 105 ff.
15 *O. R.,* 11, pt. 3, p. 630.
16 *Richmond Whig,* July 8, 1862, p. 2, col. 2.
17 *O. R.,* 13, 851.
18 *Richmond Dispatch,* July 8, 1862: "Nothing could be more complimentary . . . or more justly deserved [than the change of command]."
19 *O. R.,* 14, 560, 567, 568, 570.
20 *O. R.,* 11, pt. 3, p. 641; *Charleston Mercury,* July 16, 1862.
21 *English Combatant,* 373; *Miss Brock,* 148; *Charleston Mercury,* June 28, 1862.
22 28 *S. H. S. P.,* 293.   23 Cf. *O. R.,* 11, pt. 2, p. 682.
24 *Ibid.,* 674. The writer's opinion is that this officer was D. H. Hill, but the evidence is circumstantial and does not justify a direct assertion in the text. Magruder spoke of his critic as an "officer of inferior rank" (*ibid.*). Although Hill was a Major General, this would not exclude him. His commission bore date of March 26, 1862; Magruder's was dated Oct. 7, 1861 (*Wright,* 23, 26). In strictest accord with regulations, it was Magruder's practice always to refer to Major Generals of prior commission as his superiors (*vide* his mention of Jackson and of Holmes, *O. R.,* 11, pt. 2, p. 674). Those of later commission at his grade were his inferiors. The reasons for thinking that Hill was Magruder's critic are: (1) The known dislike of Magruder for Hill, *supra* p. 214; (2) Hill's assertion in his report (*O. R.,* 11, pt. 2, p. 629): "So far as I can

and, of course, they were not long in reaching the ears of the President. To ignore them was unjust alike to the Army and to Magruder. The General, while en route to his new post, was recalled to Richmond for an explanation.[25] In his place, General Holmes temporarily was assigned to the Trans-Mississippi.[26]

Back in the capital, where he found at least one defender in the press,[27] Magruder did not challenge to a duel the officer who had criticized him, nor did he bluster publicly. He took the charges seriously and undertook to meet them with meticulous regard for military usage. Two days after the Battle of Malvern Hill, he had written a report of some 200 words. This he proceeded to elaborate into a document of forty times that length.[28] In addition, he assiduously collected affidavits from his guides to prove that the road he had taken on the morning of July 1 was the true and only Quaker road.[29] Miscellaneous field dispatches, some of doubtful relevancy, he put in an appendix. To clinch his case, he included a statement by the Surgeon of the Sixteenth Georgia, who duly denied that the General was excited or drunk or showed "disposition to screen himself from the enemy's fire." [30]

Magruder's report itself was not altogether frank. It passed lightly over his various calls for reinforcements, and it insisted that Huger on June 29 had orders to move down the Williamsburg road.[31] Although the hunger and exhaustion of Magruder's men on July 1 were mentioned more than once, Magruder appeared to feel no responsibility for wearing out the general reserve

learn none of our troops drew trigger, except McLaws's division, mine, and a portion of Huger's"; (3) the omission from Magruder's report of any reference to Hill's support on his left; (4) and, most significantly, the inclusion in the appendix to Magruder's report of a letter from Hill to Magruder's A. A. G., June 19, 1862, in which Hill spoke of "the kind and gentlemanly character" of a communication from Magruder (O. R., 11, pt. 2, p. 685). As this was apropos of nothing whatever in the report itself, the letter seems logically to have been published by Magruder to show that, prior to the campaign, Hill had praised him. Hill's own report, which bears no date, was not forwarded until July 3, 1863. From this fact it may be argued that Magruder would not have known soon after the battle of possible strictures by Hill; but this objection is overruled by the fact that Hill's resentment over lack of support on his right was voiced immediately after the battle in a wrathful colloquy with General Toombs (see *infra*, p. 627). If Hill boldly accused Toombs of cowardice, he may have been equally unsparing of Toombs's responsible chief. It is in order to add that, while there is no evidence to show that Hill ever modified his hostile judgment of Magruder, he later paid the highest tribute to those of Magruder's Brigades that participated in the assault on the right (2 B. & L., 394).

[25] O. R., 11, pt. 2, p. 674; pt. 3, p. 641.
[26] O. R., 13, 855, 860.
[27] *Richmond Whig*, Aug. 25, p. 1, col. 5; Aug. 28, 1862, p. 1, cois. 3–4.
[28] O. R., 11, pt. 2, pp. 660–7ə.   [29] *Ibid.*, 675–77, 684.
[30] *Ibid.*. 682.   [31] *Ibid.*. 662. 66ʌ.

of the Army.[32] In describing his arrival in front of Malvern Hill, Magruder omitted all reference to the lateness of the hour.[33] Not a word was there of the vigorous assault by D. H. Hill's troops. At least inferentially, the retreat of the enemy on the night of July 1 was attributed to the attack Magruder delivered. He was the hero of his narrative and, apparently in his own mind, of the Battle of Malvern Hill.

When the report was finished, about August 13, Magruder transmitted it to Lee. The commanding General was requested to forward the paper to the President "at the very earliest moment, with such remarks as justice to the service and to me may dictate." This was desired, Magruder explained, "in order to obtain, with as little delay as possible, if [the] report be satisfactory, my restoration to the command of the Trans-Mississippi Department." [34] Lee held the document long enough only to point out what he termed the obvious "misapprehensions" of Magruder concerning numerous events of the campaign. These matters Lee set right in seven "remarks" on the report and, on August 14, he sent it to the Secretary of War. Lee's covering letter was at once candid and reserved. After stating that his examination of the paper had been cursory, he summed up: "General Magruder appears to have greatly exerted himself to accomplish the duty devolved on him, and I can bear testimony to the uniform alacrity he displayed in its execution. He had many difficulties to contend with, I know. I regretted at the time, and still regret, that they could not have been more readily overcome. I feel assured, however, that General Magruder intentionally omitted nothing that he could do to insure success." [35] That was both just and generous to Magruder. With it was coupled neither commendation of

[32] For the state of his troops, July 1, see *O. R.*, 11, pt. 2, pp. 708, 719, 723, 749–50. Some of the men had no rations served them for forty-eight hours.

[33] In the last paragraph of the report itself (*O. R.*, 11, pt. 2, p. 674), Magruder wrote: "As to the time when the attack on the enemy's batteries in front were made, Brigadier General Armistead, whose advanced troops led in the attack from the center, states in his report that in the charge the brigades of Mahone and Wright came up immediately on his right, Cobb's brigade closely following his advance." It is doubtful from Armistead's report (*ibid.*, 819), whether he justified the use by Magruder of the word "immediately" with respect either to time or to position. Of Cobb, Armistead wrote: "Following my regiments came General Cobb's Brigade," without reference to the time of arrival, though he added that "soon after" two more of his regiments went forward. Wright, in his report (*ibid.*, 814), did not suggest close timing or co-ordination of attack. He stated that when he was ordered at 4.45 to attack, "No other troops had yet come upon the field." Cobb's report showed him (*ibid.*, 749) under the impression that his advance to immediate support of Armistead was to repel an attack.

[34] *Ibid.*, 660.   [35] *Ibid.*, 679.

Magruder's handling of his force, nor a hint, even the faintest, that Lee desired Magruder to remain in the Army of Northern Virginia.

Two days after Lee forwarded the report, Magruder became convinced, upon further conversation with Huger, that he had been mistaken in stating that Huger had been ordered on the 29th of June to proceed via the Williamsburg road. Magruder so advised the President, though he did not ask the privilege of correcting the text of his report.[36] Mr. Davis read the document and endorsed it with the commonplace remark that "the objections to the report of General Magruder indicate that General Lee will give a different aspect to the affairs noted . . .";[37] but beyond that the President did not go. Magruder's assignment to the West meantime had become involved in a controversy over the command of Sterling Price, whom Magruder was credited with placating.[38] It was not until October 10 that "Prince John" received orders, and then he did not get the entire Trans-Mississippi command. Instead he was given the District of Texas, New Mexico and Arizona.[39]

From his new headquarters, Magruder arranged at his own cost for the early and separate printing of his report. This course, he said in a general postscript, "was rendered desirable to meet strictures which had been made by an officer of inferior rank on my military operations near Richmond." He reiterated that his attack on Malvern Hill had been delivered after "repeated orders from my superiors, and that it could have been made by me in no other way, having officers of superior rank to me both on my left and right—Jackson and Holmes . . ." The reader was not informed that Magruder had no contact whatever that fateful first day of July with Holmes, and none with Jackson after their meeting, early in the morning, near Willis Church. Magruder reasserted, in his final apologia, that the "enemy was routed" and that "our loss in killed and wounded was less than 2900 men, less in proportion than that sustained in most of the previous battles." Here, again, there was no reference to the share of other Divisions in the assaults on Malvern Hill.

Magruder went on: "This report General Lee has forwarded

[36] Ibid., 687–88.
[38] Charleston Mercury, July 28, 1862.
[37] Ibid., 680.
[39] O. R., 15, 826, 880

to the President with his testimony as to the uniform alacrity with which I discharged the difficult duty devolved upon me and the great exertions made by me in its performance. Every officer and every soldier engaged in the battles of Savage Station and Malvern Hill can point with pride to the results on both sides of these victories [*sic*] as the best evidence that these great exertions were crowned with triumphant success." He sounded a final flourish over the "independent and important commands in the Southwest," thrice tendered him by the President, and announced that his explanation of his part in the battles had been made "to the satisfaction of the War Department as well as of General Lee." That done, "I proceeded immediately to the command in the Southwest, to which the President had assigned me, reserving to myself the right, as well as satisfaction, of attending at a more appropriate time to matters purely personal." [40] New and curious adventures awaited him in Texas, but with these words he verbally galloped off for the last time from the Army of Northern Virginia.

General Benjamin Huger, next to General Magruder, was the officer most criticized for his part in the Seven Days. To his slow march on the 30th of June, more than to any other miscarriage of the day, was attributed the failure of Lee's plan. [41] Against Huger personally, no feeling is discoverable, but in extenuation of his delays not a voice seems to have been raised. When Lee wrote his report of the campaign, he distinguished between Huger's failure and that of Jackson by a delicate choice of words: "Huger not coming up, and Jackson having been unable to force the passage of White Oak Swamp," Longstreet and A. P. Hill lacked support at Frayser's Farm. [42]

Huger's own report, which was dated July 21, failed to change the impression that he was what press and Army styled a "do-nothing General." He described at some length the minor affair of June 25 at King's School House, which had been fought while he was absent from his headquarters. [43] Of the events of June 30 Huger wrote briefly, and concerning those of July 1 he did not report because, as he said, "I was not in command during this battle."

40 *O. R.*, 11, pt. 2, p. 674.   41 Cf. *Miss Brock,* 148.
42 *O. R.*, 11, pt. 2, p. 495.   43 *Lee's Dispatches,* 14.

What he recorded and what others remarked of him then and thereafter constitute a singular exhibit of the opportunities of good and of evil—by doing foolish things and of doing nothing— that an "independent" division commander may have in battle. Huger evidently intended on the night of June 30 to continue at dawn his advance down the Charles City road,[44] but before morning, apparently without orders from Lee, he elected to move Armistead's and Wright's Brigades from his left to the opposite flank and to send them off at a right angle to his line of advance in order, as Armistead stated, to "take the enemy in flank." [45] Of this move, so far as the records show, Huger did not so much as notify the commanding General.

At 3 A.M. Huger saw Armistead start and Wright follow,[46] but he did not join them or attempt to direct their movements after they began their march. The division commander remained with Mahone and Ransom until he was informed by Longstreet that the enemy had disappeared from his front. Ransom and Mahone then prepared to move. Meantime, Armistead and Wright, advancing aimlessly, had come out on the Long Bridge road, where Armistead, reporting to Lee, was directed to enter the Quaker road near Willis Church.[47] One of Lee's staff officers subsequently met the two Brigadiers and gave them information of the proximity of the Federals. Thereupon Armistead advanced and took advantageous position.[48] Huger, at his leisure, ere that had directed Mahone and Ransom to advance, but he found other troops on the road and—to repeat—"no one to show [him] what road to take." [49]

In the afternoon, Major Brent found Huger by the side of a lane on the Carter Farm. When asked where his flank was, Huger replied with much feeling: "I do not know where my Brigades are, and I hear that at least some of them have been moved without my knowledge by orders independent of me, and I have no information enabling me to answer to your inquiries." To that he stuck, though Brent explained that Lee had informed Magruder that Huger was to fill the gap between Jackson's right and Magruder's left.[50] Later one of Lee's aides conducted Huger

44 O. R., 11, pt. 2, p. 811.   45 Ibid., 818.
46 Ibid., 790.   47 Ibid., 818.
48 Ibid.   49 Ibid., 790; see supra, p. 589.
50 Brent, 212.

to the front where, at an hour unstated but late in the afternoon, he reported to Lee. For the first time he found where Armistead and Wright were, and he expressed pride, in his report, that they were "exactly opposite the enemy." [51] Mahone, according to his own official account of the battle, subsequently was told by Huger to report to Magruder, but Huger himself stated that Mahone, at Lee's request, was sent to support Cobb.[52] It will be remembered that Ransom repeatedly was asked by Magruder to assist him and, in the end, did so under discretionary orders. Although Huger, in effect, had lost his Brigades during the morning, he insisted in his report that his troops had been taken from him. "As I was treated in the same manner at Seven Pines," he said, "I can only hope this course was accidental and required by the necessities of the service." [53]

Circumstance and developments shattered other hope. Previously Lee had suggested that Huger, if acceptable, might be sent to South Carolina.[54] Now, quietly and without an explanatory word in newspapers or in army orders, General Huger was relieved of duty with his Division and was assigned as Inspector of Artillery and Ordnance, the type of work that had been his before the war.[55] There is no record of any protest by Huger. He sought to vindicate himself from the unjustified criticism of his conduct at Seven Pines, and he asked permission to publish correspondence which would show that the evacuation of Norfolk had not been at his instance.[56] Beyond that he did not go. He undertook his changed duties, discharged them loyally and, in 1863, went to the Trans-Mississippi as Chief of the Bureau of Ordnance in Kirby Smith's semi-autonomous command.[57] A singular, silent and proud figure he dimly appears through the years. He had been too long habituated to the slow, peace-time routine of the ordnance service to adjust himself to field command, for which he had no aptitude. If his photographs portray him accurately, one reason for his slowness must have been physical. Although he was no more than 56, he had the look of a man prematurely aged by hardened arteries.

51 *O. R.,* 11, pt. 2, p. 790.   52 *Ibid.,* 790, 800.
53 *O. R.,* 11, pt. 2, p. 790.   54 *Lee's Dispatches,* 14.
55 As of July 12, *O. R.,* 11, pt. 3, p. 640, but he did not leave his troops until after July 21.
56 *O. R.,* 11, pt. 3, pp. 643–44.   57 5 *C. M. H.,* 403–4.

General Holmes, in the judgment of some critics of the campaign, had been as remiss as either Magruder or Huger. Both D. H. Hill [58] and Magruder [59] noted that Holmes gave them no support. In Lee's report of the operations of June 30, Holmes was exculpated, at least by inference;[60] and in the commanding General's account of the battle of July 1, he was not mentioned. The probability is that those who criticized him knew neither the weakness of his troops nor the strength of the position against which he was sent. At the moment, resentfully they wrote him down as a failure, but they soon forgot him. He was the commander of a separate Department, he did not associate long with the Army of Northern Virginia, and within a few weeks he went West, as already noted, to command the Department previously assigned Magruder.

If Holmes be regarded as scarcely an active participant in the campaign and consequently be not adjudged responsible for serious failure, there was a question concerning the performance of a fourth prominent officer—the Chief of Lee's Artillery, Brig. Gen. W. N. Pendleton, who will appear often and curiously in these pages.

At 21 Pendleton had been graduated at West Point, No. 8 in the class of 1830, the class immediately junior to that in which Robert E. Lee had been No. 2.[61] After three years in the artillery, Pendleton had resigned, and had taught in Pennsylvania and at Delaware College. Having entered the ministry in 1837, he subsequently had accepted the rectorate of the small Episcopal church at Lexington, Virginia. He had been in charge of the parish when, in 1860, some of the young men of the community had organized as a battery and had asked him to drill them. This he undertook. After secession the command had enlisted as the Rockridge Artillery and had elected Pendleton, then 51, as its Captain. The company of seventy-eight, rank and file, had included twenty-three students and professional men.[62] As some of the eight lawyers and six teachers were young men of local prominence, the battery from the outset had been conspicuous.

During the early months of the war, Captain Pendleton had come into the news through a report of a singular order he had

58 O. R., 11, pt. 2, p. 629.   59 Ibid., 672.
60 O. R., 11, pt. 2, p. 495.   61 Cullum, No. 591.
62 See Pendleton, in 8 Rowland, 561.

given his battery. In a brush with the Federals in the Shenandoah Valley [63]—so ran the story—he had loaded and aimed his gun and then had raised his hand in prayer: "May the Lord have mercy on their poor souls—fire!" The ball was said to have "struck the head of a column, and when the smoke cleared away its path was still visible." This, wrote an admiring newspaper correspondent, "shows clearly what stuff he is made of." [64]

At Manassas, on July 21, 1861, the gunners under Pendleton had done such fine service that he had been commended by Jackson [65] and had been mentioned in Joseph E. Johnston's report as the Army's "one educated artillerist . . . that model of a Christian soldier." [66] Pendleton had been promoted Colonel without delay and again had been lauded in a Richmond paper: "The inquiry among the prisoners was general 'who the devil commanded that battery on the left, that killed so many of our men?' Our reply was that it was commanded by a saint, named Pendleton." [67] In some way, also, the incident of his prayer in the Valley for the victims of his fire had been transferred to Manassas.[68]

Pendleton had acted during part of the autumn as Johnston's Chief of Artillery and, on March 26, 1862, had been made a Brigadier General.[69] Picturesque in person, he somewhat resembled General Lee. With gray beard and with mien half martial, half clerical, he had preached fervently when he was not drilling and, all in all, had kept in the public eye. At the end of April, 1862, he had been listed as in command of the reserve artillery,[70] but by the middle of June he had begun to date his orders from "Headquarters Artillery Corps." [71] He wrote letters as long, though not so numerous, as those of Magruder, and he had definite aptitude for organization.

On June 21, he had submitted to General Lee the first of many proposals for the regrouping of the batteries under an "army chief of artillery." [72] This plan Lee promptly approved,[73] but in the

---

63 Falling Waters, July 2, 1861, O. R., 2, 185.
64 *Richmond Dispatch*, July 18, 1861, p. 2, col. 4.
65 O. R., 2, 481.
66 *Ibid.*, 476.
67 *Richmond Dispatch*, July 29, 1861, p. 3, cols. 1-2.
68 *Cf* 3 C. M. H., 650.   69 *Wright*, 78.
70 O. R., 11, pt. 3, p. 484.   71 O. R., 51, pt. 2, p. 575.
72 O. R., 51, pt. 2, pp. 577–78. The draft order that he presented for Lee's approval began with this flourish: "Extensively diffused as is necessarily the artillery of this army," etc. (*ibid.*).
73 O. R., 11, pt. 3, pp. 612–13.

haste of preparation for battle, he could not make it operative in its entirety. The result was that General Pendleton did not enter the campaign with all his guns wisely apportioned, nor could he or any other single officer exercise authority over all the batteries then scattered among the various Brigades and Divisions. There were Chiefs of Artillery for most of the Divisions, but there was no standard organization. Pendleton's specific charge was the Reserve Artillery of more than twenty batteries of approximately ninety guns.[74] With part of this substantial force, more than a fourth of all the artillery of the Army, General Pendleton had co-operated on the south side of the Chickahominy, June 26–27, while Lee was fighting at Mechanicsville and at Gaines' Mill. On the 28th, Pendleton had worked to put heavy guns in position to cover Magruder's position. That evening President Davis had employed him to take a message to General Lee.

Thereafter, Pendleton's own curious account of his movements, as set forth in his official report and in his letters home, is a sufficient commentary on his conduct. Officially he wrote: "Fever supervening disabled me on the 29th, so that the day was necessarily passed by me as a quiet Sabbath. Portions of my command were, however, quite actively engaged, under arrangements already described, in pursuing with other forces, the retreating enemy." Privately, in a long letter that day, he told his wife of his "immense labor and exposure" and of the manner in which he had been "exposed to cannon-shot and shells again and again." Said he: "I have done my duty to the utmost of my power. No man in the service, General Lee excepted, has had more work to do, and I thank God that help has been given for its discharge thus far. You need not be uneasy about me. I am lying on a lounge under a shady tree in the yard of my headquarters. . . . I feel better already, and hope a day's rest, a blue pill, etc., may have me quite well again tomorrow." [75]

[74] Owing to the paucity of reports on artillery operations during the Seven Days, the editors of *O. R.* list eighteen known batteries as the Artillery Reserve of the Army of Northern Virginia and under the heading "Miscellaneous" name five batteries "mentioned in the reports and not otherwise accounted for." (*O. R.*, 11, pt. 2, p. 489.) It is certain that one of these batteries, Grimes's, was attached to Huger's Division (cf. *O. R.*, 11, pt. 2, p. 487), and it is probable that some of the others similarly were associated with particular commands.

[75] Susan P. Lee, *Memoirs of William Nelson Pendleton* (cited hereafter as *Pendleton*), 194–95.

The next day, as he predicted, he was well enough for field duty. His report proceeded: "On Monday, 30th, I was again able to be in the field, and employed the forenoon in ascertaining movements in progress and adjusting to them the arrangements of my own command. The afternoon was given to making sure of three large guns for use in the field on Tuesday, if needed and practicable.

"Tuesday morning, July 1"—the day of the Battle of Malvern Hill—"was spent by me in seeking for some time the commanding general, that I might get orders, and by reason of the intricacy of routes failing in this, in examining positions near the two armies, toward ascertaining what could be best done with a large artillery force, and especially whether any position could be reached whence our large guns might be used to good purpose. These endeavors had of course to be made again and again under the enemy's shells, yet no site was found from which the large guns could play upon the enemy without endangering our own troops, and no occasion was presented for bringing up the reserve artillery—indeed, it seemed that not one-half of the division batteries were brought into action on either Monday or Tuesday. To remain near by, therefore, and await events and orders, in readiness for whatever service might be called for, was all that I could do. Here again it was my privilege to be thrown with the President, he having arrived some time after nightfall at the house near the battle field, where I had just before sought a resting place." [76]

There was somber, costly truth in what Pendleton said about the non-employment of brigade and divisional artillery. The tragic losses of the infantry attested the failure of the Confederates to bring up their guns through the woods that faced the elevated, cleared positions General McClellan had chosen. Where any part of the reserve artillery had been used, as at White Oak Swamp, [77] it had done admirably.

This did not alter the fact that the Chief of Artillery, on the final day of the operations, did not even reach the general headquarters of the Army. For this, Lee himself made no criticism

[76] *O. R.*, 11, pt. 2, p. 536.

[77] Where Maj. H. P. Jones of the Reserve had supplemented Jackson's artillery with Clark's, Peyton's and Rhett's batteries.

of Pendleton in his report. He listed the artillerist among the staff officers who "attended unceasingly to their several departments," [78] and apparently he did not consider the replacement of Pendleton or any change in that officer's authority. Had the commanding General been dissatisfied, with whom would he have succeeded Pendleton? Many promising young artillerists there were, but none who could boast even Pendleton's limited experience in directing a large number of guns.

Some of the younger artillery officers were not so philosophical. Already certain of them were laughing at Pendleton behind his back. More mature men felt that the reserve batteries had not been handled well. A devoted battalion commander, Col. Thompson Brown, lamented the lack of "opportunity to do anything amid the great superabundance of artillery and the scant use that was made of it." [79] More sharply, in describing the day at Malvern Hill, Lt. Col. A. S. Cutts reported: ". . . although I am sure that more artillery could have been used . . . and also that my command [80] could have done good service, yet I received no orders . . ." [81] Had Brown and Cutts been privileged to read the report that Col. Henry J. Hunt, commander of McClellan's artillery reserve, wrote at approximately the time they were preparing their accounts of the campaign, they would have had stronger reason to lament the fact that ninety Confederate guns had remained idle in the woods North of Malvern Hill. Hunt's artillery, which was handled with skill and courage, was the rock of the Federal defense.[82]

Would Pendleton learn, as his adversary in blue already had? Outranged, the Confederate artillery was served with ammunition less good: was it now to be outfought or better handled? Pendleton had not fulfilled his opportunities. That was the most charitable judgment that could be passed on him. Would he justify Lee's confidence, or would he at some new crisis follow Magruder and Huger into obscurity? Of stout fabric was the patience of Lee, but it might wear thin. Sharply, on the 5th of July, his Assistant Adjutant General wrote young Porter Alexander: "General Lee directs me to say that General Pendleton is

[78] O. R., 11, pt. 2, p. 498.   [79] O. R., 11, pt. 2, p. 551.
[80] Four batteries, fifteen guns. O. R., 11, pt. 2, p. 547.
[81] Ibid.
[82] Hunt's report is in O. R., 11, pt. 2, pp. 236 ff.

absent, and he [does] not know who is in charge of the Reserve Artillery; he therefore desires that you will go at once and ascertain the condition of the Reserve Artillery, and have it put in condition to move to Malvern Hill . . ." [83] That was unpromising.

[83] *O. R.*, 11, pt. 3, p. 634.

CHAPTER XXXIX

DISCONTENT AND DYSPEPSIA AS PROBLEMS OF COMMAND

IF PENDLETON had not purged himself on June 29, he might have had the energy to reach headquarters on July 1. In Magruder's case, his excitement and confusion, his reckless galloping to and fro and his attempts to perform the duties of half a dozen general officers undoubtedly were attributable, in part, to his lack of sleep. Huger's slowness, as already indicated, may be explained by the despairing term arteriosclerosis. Other officers exhibited during the campaign a discontent, an arrogant or disdainful individualism, or an insubordinate spirit of criticism that raises a question: were they physically ill or were they unsuited temperamentally for command? Because this question has to be asked in every war regarding some men in high position, it is regrettable that the evidence does not justify an answer in one or more of the instances now to be cited. All that can be done is to state the known facts and to show how a wise and patient Commander in Chief dealt with each man.

Unhappily on this list of the disgruntled was Brig. Gen. W. H. C. Whiting. He was given amplest credit for leading his Division to the post of opportunity at Gaines' Mill. On the surface, his record shone. Beneath there were ugly rumors—that he was jealous of Jackson,[1] that he had been overcritical of the dispositions made by his superior, that he had been tipsy at Gaines' Mill, that he had not personally shared there in the charge of his Division, and that he had done less than his part at Malvern Hill.[2]

Of none of these alleged derelictions was there a hint in reports, but neither was there praise for the division commander. Jackson

---

[1] It has been stated that his feeling was aggravated because Whiting had been brilliant and Jackson mediocre in the same class at West Point. Actually, Whiting, as noted *supra*, p. 119, had been graduated No. 1 in the class of 1845, *Cullum*, No. 1231. Jackson, who had been graduated No. 17, belonged to the class of 1846, *Cullum*, No. 1288.

[2] *Dabney Memo.* It would appear that Dr. Dabney was prejudiced against Whiting, and that the suggestion of any lack of courage on Whiting's part was wholly false. Col. J. C. Haskell, who observed Whiting on the field of Gaines' Mill, spoke of him as "very ambitious and very brave." *MS. Rem.*, 47.

accurately described Whiting's movement to the right on the 27th, but when he came to recount the advance across Boatswain's Swamp, he had nothing to say of Whiting, though he noted that "General Hood and Colonel Law, at the heads of their respective Brigades, rushed to the charge with a yell." [3] Lee merely stated Whiting's place in the order of battle at Gaines' Mill and on July 1.[4] D. H. Hill, in his report, affirmed with choler that, at Malvern Hill, "Whiting's division did not engage at all." [5]

Whiting's own account of Gaines' Mill was full of pride in the performance of his men, and of commendation for their regimental and brigade leaders, but it made only the most casual reference to Jackson. In narrating separately the events of June 30, Whiting included one brief sentence that he may or may not have designed as a criticism of his temporary chief: "Our delay at White Oak Swamp," he said, "was unfortunate"—that and no more. Concerning Jackson's order of march on July 1 he spoke bluntly, and on it he blamed the plunge of a Confederate cavalry command through his column in the Willis Church road. In relating the disappointing events of the day, Whiting made it conspicuously plain that he was acting under Jackson's direct orders.[6] Common report had it that Whiting cried bitterly: "Great God! Won't some ranking officer come, and save us from this fool?" [7]

Although, in short, the campaign developed nothing tangibly to the discredit of Whiting, he did not distinguish himself either in leadership or in co-operation. Doubtless at headquarters there was speculation over the reason. Perhaps, too, there was disappointment that a man of his intellectual endowment should not have risen in reputation. What was amiss? Was it a permanent defect, enslaving habit, or temporary eclipse? General Lee apparently did not attempt an answer. He left Whiting at the head of the Division in a semi-autonomous command, as if he did not know under whom the abilities of Whiting effectively could be employed.

In a far lower bracket of military knowledge than Whiting, but enjoying a political reputation that made his discontent a subject of much gossip, was Brig. Gen. Robert Toombs. When his native

[3] O. R., 11, pt. 2, p. 555.
[4] Ibid., 492, 496.
[5] Ibid., 629.
[6] O. R., 11, pt. 2, pp. 566–67.   [7] R. H. McKim, A Soldier's Recollections, 92.

Georgia seceded, Senator Toombs was in his fifty-first year[8] and was in general estimation among the half-dozen leading public men of the South. His most enthusiastic admirers would have acclaimed him *primus inter pares*. Portly but pale, with a face half-studious, half-contemptuous,[9] he had a frowning Senatorial air. Limitless confidence in the rightness of his own views, skill in dramatic phrase-making and a plausible if superficial logic made his oratorical deliverances as convincing to his followers as they were provoking to his opponents. Had he been less surely entrenched as a member of the ruling class, he would have been a demagogue. If he had been more patiently tolerant, he would have been a statesman. As he was, he was neither. Nor was he politically consistent. "Bob Toombs," it was said, "disagrees with himself between meals."[10] Howell Cobb remarked of him, "Toombs had altogether the best mind of any statesman in the United States but lacked balance." Wrote Major Raphael J. Moses, who saw him at close range, "[Toombs's] impulses were generous and noble, his faults were bluster and a vivid imagination not always hampered by facts."[11]

When the Confederate government was organized, Toombs was disappointed in not being elected to the Presidency,[12] and he was not placated by the tender of the first position in the Cabinet. He accepted and labored, furiously if sullenly, for about five months. Then he resigned to accept command of a Georgia Brigade of infantry.[13] He did not believe that the war would be long, and he did not intend that it should stop his political career, but, for the time, he felt that more of service was to be rendered and more of honor won in the field than in the forum.

During the winter of 1861–62, in northern Virginia, Toombs served first under Kirby Smith and then under Gustavus W. Smith,[14] and indulged all the while in a correspondence that was

---

[8] Born in Wilkes Co., Ga., July 2, 1810.

[9] *Cf.* 1 *R. W. C. D.*, 38–39.

[10] *De Leon*, 83.

[11] *Journal of Major Raphael J. Moses*, p. 9. That writer is responsible for the quotation from Cobb.

[12] See Burton Hendrick, *Statesmen of the Lost Cause*, 96 ff., for a review of the circumstances that, in the opinion of Toombs's friends, were responsible for the election of Davis instead of Toombs.

[13] *Mrs. Chesnut*, 108; 1 *R. W. C. D.*, 40; *Richmond Dispatch*, July 24, p. 2, col. 7; July 26, p. 2, col. 1; *Richmond Whig*, July 29, 1861, p. 2, col. 2.

[14] *Richmond Examiner*, Aug. 28, 1861, p. 3, col. 1; *Richmond Dispatch*, Sept. 12, 1861, p. 1, col. 3; *O. R.*, 5, 961, 1061.

a succession of growls. "Johnston," he wrote Vice President Stephens on September 22, 1861, "is a poor devil, small, arbitrary and inefficient." [15] Again of Johnston he wrote: "I never knew as incompetent [an] executive officer. As he has been at West Point, tho', I suppose he necessarily knows everything about it. . . . The army is dying . . . and it will not survive the winter. Set this down in your book, and set down opposite to it its epitaph, 'died of West Point.' We have patched a new government with old cloth, we have tied the living to the dead." [16] Apparently the only one of his superior officers on the Manassas front who enjoyed Toombs's good opinion was Gustavus W. Smith.[17]

Toombs's sharpest controversy arose with a Colonel of his own Brigade. It was a petty and unseemly quarrel, which Johnston had settled—only to discover that Toombs defiantly refused to obey the order he issued. Johnston accordingly sent Capt. J. C. Haskell, one of his aides, to put Toombs under arrest. Haskell admirably told what followed: "When I got to [Toombs's] quarters, which were in a small farm house, I presented the order, which he received with a perfect torrent of blasphemous abuse. At the first pause, I resented it very decidedly and he stopped a moment and at once said I was right and made the most ample and manly apology. A violent storm which suddenly broke, kept me for hours at his quarters, and I never spent a more interesting night. He went on with his apology, saying 'Captain, I should not have given away, but it does gall me when I am oppressed by a little man like Johnston, who a few months ago I could have made or ruined by a word and who as soon as this little war is over and I go back to the Senate, will be so much below me that my sense of magnanimity will forbid my ever getting even with him. Now, I don't mind Davis. We will be on the same ground and, damn him, I can make him smart for what he does, but it will be like hitting a child to go at Johnston.' " [18]

The reputation of Toombs did not suffer because of quarrels at

[15] Toombs, etc., Letters, 575.
[16] Ibid., 577–78.
[17] Ibid., 579, 592.
[18] J. C. Haskell's MS. Rem., 30–32. Haskell continued: "After [Toombs] cooled down he talked for hours of Washington life and men and gave a most vivid, brilliant picture of it. . . . I saw a good deal of him afterwards and always liked him greatly. He was no soldier and had no business in the Army, but he took good care of his men and did the best he could and was deserving much more credit than some who have a higher name in history for their war record."

Manassas. In the dark days of February, 1862, when the young Confederacy seemed close to collapse, a member of the House of Representatives boldly asserted that if he were to suggest men to form a plan of action, he would name Beauregard and Toombs. The merits of Beauregard, he said, were known. Toombs, he insisted, had "the requisite military genius and the true revolutionary spirit." [19] Toombs must have enjoyed that, and no less did he enjoy martial pomp. The march of the Army through Richmond, on its way to the Peninsula, offered him an opportunity of exhibiting himself that was as welcome as a "full-dress" debate in the Senate had been in other days. One observer laughed in retrospect at the memory of Toombs's performance: "He marched his troops down Main Street, past the crowds at Spotswood Hotel, with childlike delight. He put himself at the head of one Regiment and moved it out of sight amid hurrahs, then galloping back he brought on another, ready himself for cheers, until the Brigade was down the street and near the embarkation." [20]

After Toombs reached Yorktown, Magruder put him in temporary command of an informal Division.[21] This force participated in a minor action of April 16, 1862, at Dam No. 1, and won Magruder's commendation. Of Toombs himself, "Prince John" wrote in his report: "Brigadier General Toombs . . . late in the evening, when ordered forward by me, promptly and energetically led the remainder of his command, under fire, arriving just before the enemy ceased the vigor of his attack and in time to share its dangers." [22]

<hr>

[19] Boyce, in 44 S. H. S. P., 35.
[20] *Sorrel*, 63.
[21] Cf. O. R., 11, pt. 3, pp. 480 ff.
[22] O. R., 11, pt. 1, p. 408. Major Moses, *op. cit.*, described how he heard the firing at Dam No. 1 and rode forward. Soon Toombs was encountered: "He was a very poor horseman, and as a shell whistled near him his mare, Alice Gray, who had never before been under fire, pranced about a good deal more than Toombs bargained for. However, after a bit she went on, and our men made a most successful fight. The next day at Cobb's headquarters Toombs commenced talking about the fight at Dam No. 1—how his men fought, how he passed to the front, the opening of the line for him to pass through, the antics of his mare. . . . 'By God, Cobb, she trembled like an aspen leaf and seemed to think all the shell were meant for her. Moses, you were there. Did you ever see a horse so scared in all your life?' I replied that she seemed to be badly scared, but that I was reminded of a French barber of New Orleans. This barber, who had never ridden horseback, decided to join the fashionable riders on the shell road. On his very first attempt his mount, frightened by a snake crossing the road, shied. The barber clamped his knees, his spurs stuck the horse, the horse jumped—and threw the Frenchman right on top of the snake. Returning to New Orleans and relating his adventure, the barber climaxed his tale by exclaiming, 'Mon Dieu gentlemen, if you ever see one snake scare, she was zat snake.' I left them to

On the retreat from Yorktown, Toombs lost his temporary rating as a divisional chief and reached Richmond in deep discontent. Another letter to his friend the Vice President of the Confederacy thus expressed his opinion of the campaign and of the men who had conducted it: "We had a rough time in the Peninsula, lost about 1/3 of my men by exposure mainly, having only some 10 or 12 killed and thirty or forty wounded. The most of them I suppose will come back some time or another. We were kept in the trenches, often times a foot deep in water, for eighteen days, without any necessity or object that I could [learn except] the stupidity and cowardice of our officers. McClellan was there with his whole army, a good deal less I think than ours, and we could have whipped as easily there as anywhere else. But as usual we burnt up everything and fled, were attacked in the retreat, and left in the hands of the enemy some ten or twelve hundred of our killed, wounded and sick, and that *after a decided victory*. This is called generalship!! . . . This army will not fight until McClellan attacks it. Science will do anything but fight. It will burn, retreat, curse, swear, get drunk, strip soldiers—anything but fight. Davis's capacity is lamentable, and the very thought of the baseness of Congress in the impressment act makes me sick. I feel but little like fighting for a people base enough to submit to such despotism from such contemptible sources." [23]

Nor was his wrath confined to West Pointers, President, and Congressmen. In his own Georgia, local committees were undertaking to divert acreage from cotton-growing to the raising of food crops. The committees from the county of Randolph and from Eufaula, across the line in Alabama, telegraphed to know whether he would not employ some of his slaves in this movement. Toombs almost raved in his answer: "I refuse a single hand. My property, as long as I live, shall never be subject to those cowardly miscreants, the Committees of Public Safety of Randolph County, Ga., and Eufaula. You may rob me in my absence, but you cannot intimidate me." His overseer he promptly and imperatively ordered to plant a full crop of cotton.[24]

In that mood, a fortnight later, Toombs entered the battles of

make the application to Toombs, his mare Alice Gray and the shells that were flying at Dam No. 1. Did Cobb laugh! He and all his staff! And, in fairness be it said, Toombs most uproariously of all."

[23] *Toombs, etc., Letters,* 594–95.   [24] *Toombs. etc., Letters,* 595 and n.

the Seven Days. He cheerfully promised his surgeon that during the operations he would not indulge in strong liquor, "a practice" said one of his early biographers, "that had grown somewhat upon General Toombs during his service in the field and . . . at times deprived him of his best powers." [25] There is no evidence that he failed to keep his pledge, but neither is there any evidence that he progressed toward the military fame he coveted. How Magruder viewed Toombs's action at Golding's Farm on June 27–28 has been described. In Toombs's eyes, the fault was not his but his chief's. To Alexander H. Stephens, in another characteristic letter, Toombs protested: ". . . Near night [I] was ordered [to] advance and attack the enemy to prevent his sending reinforcements over [to] the other side [of Chickahominy]. I had but 2000 men for duty and was in 400 yards of the enemy's entrenchments whom I knew to be in heavy force. I objected to the order and required it in writing and peremptory. It was given me, and I made the attack. The battle raged with terrific fury for about two hours, the [enemy] trying to drive me from a position I was ordered to hold at every hazard by that old ass Magruder. I finally repulsed him with loss on my part of 200 in killed and wounded and on his, from his official report which we found in his camp two days after, of 253 killed and 700 or 800 wounded. . . . My men fought like lions this unnecessary battle, and the thanks we got for it was a lie sent out from Magruder's head quarters before the action was over that I had attacked without orders and ·was repulsed." [26]

Toombs was not engaged on the 29th, except under casual artillery fire, and on the 30th was marched and countermarched with the rest of Magruder's command. So worn were Toombs's men by hunger and exhaustion that when they moved forward at Malvern Hill, they scarcely counted more than 1200 muskets.[27] This force, though resolute, was mishandled inexcusably. Toombs virtually lost control of it. In the twilight, part of the Brigade

[25] Pleasant A. Stovall, *Robert Toombs*, 243.

[26] *Toombs, etc., Letters*, 600. The report Toombs found in the Federal camp must have covered larger operations than those of June 27 on his front. That day Slocum's Division of Franklin's VI Corps was engaged heavily at Gaines' Mill and lost 1972 men, as computed from O. R., 11, pt. 2, pp. 39–40. Toombs's attack on the south side of the river was repulsed by Hancock's Division of the same Corps, with casualties of 118 (*ibid.*, 468).

[27] O. R., 11, pt. 2. p. 698.

lined up behind a fence, where D. H. Hill found it and ordered it to charge. "The brigade advanced handsomely to the brow of the hill," the North Carolinian wrote, "but soon retreated in disorder."[28] During the confusion, D. H. Hill came upon the bewildered Toombs and hotly demanded to know why, after pretending to want to fight, Toombs had not done so, though the enemy was in plain sight.

"For shame," stormed Hill. "Rally your troops," and he added: "Where were you when I was riding up and down your line, rallying your troops?"

Toombs's instant reply is not of record, but after the battle he demanded an explanation and, when it proved "unsatisfactory," he challenged Hill. In answer Hill wrote: "In regard to your demand for satisfaction, I construe it to mean either that I must apologize to you for the language used by me on the battlefield, or that I must grant you a hostile meeting. If the first interpretation be correct, I will state that I will make full, public and ample concessions when satisfied that I did you injustice; and this I would do without any demand. I certainly thought that you had taken the field too late, and that you left it too early. You may, however, have done your whole duty and held your ground as long as it was possible for a brave and skillful officer to hold it. If the facts prove this to be so, no one will be more gratified than myself, and my acknowledgment of error will be cordial and complete. But if your demand means a challenge, its acceptance, when we have a country to defend and enemies to fight, would be highly improper and contrary to the dictates of plain duty, without reference to higher grounds of action. I would not make myself a party to a course of conduct forbidden alike by the plainest principles of duty, and the laws which we have mutually sworn to serve."

Toombs must have replied[29] with a renewal of his demand for the "satisfaction due a gentleman." Hill rejected this flatly as contrary to his religion and his duty and in so doing terminated the correspondence. All of this might have led to animosities of the sort that end in "shooting on sight," but the Confederacy was

---

[28] *O. R.*, 11, pt. 2, p. 628. Part of Toombs's Brigade advanced with Kershaw. See *ibid.*, 697, 703, 705.
[29] His answer is believed not to be extant

not made ridiculous by a battle behind a battle line. Apparently, in short order, Hill and Toombs were reconciled.[30]

Of this episode, Toombs does not seem to have written his confidant, the Vice President, but, in appraising the outcome of the Battle of Malvern Hill and the conduct of the campaign, he was violent: ". . . our loss has been terrible, and of many of our best men. They were fought without skill or judgment and were victorious by dint of dead hard fighting, thousands and thousands of them never receiving an order except from brigade or regimental commanders for whole hours upon hours in battle. Longstreet has won more reputation, and I think deservedly, than all of our Major Generals put together. Stonewall Jackson and his troops did little or nothing in these battles of the Chickahominy and Lee was far below the occasion. If we had had a general in command we could easily have taken McClellan's whole command and baggage, whereas he saved all his wagons and stores except what he burned, and far the greater part of his valuable outfit. After the fight of Friday the 27th he was not pursued with the least vigour and never was attacked except when he wanted to be, at his rearguard which of course he made as strong as possible. Then while we have gained so much I cannot but feel sad and disheartened at what we lost. It was Manassas and Shiloh over again, barren victories without results when everything was in our power. McClellan will reorganize his yet powerful army, get reinforcements, and we shall have all this blood and toil to shed over again, and worst of all the poor people cannot see it, and all who will not sing peans to such blunderers and imbeciles will probably be crushed and dishonored."

Toombs did not seem to have considered that he had failed in any particular, but he was disgusted. He told Stephens: "I shall leave the army the instant I can do so without dishonor. Davis and his Janissaries (the regular army) conspire for the destruction of all who will not bend to them, and avail themselves of the public danger to aid them in their selfish and infamous schemes." [31]

These opinions on the part of a man habitually outspoken

---

[30] For the correspondence regarding the challenge, see Stovall, *op. cit.*, 254 ff. See also T. R. R. Cobb to his wife, July 18, 1862, in 28 *S. H. S. P.*, 294; *Gordon*, 75.
[31] *Toombs, etc., Letters*, 601.

doubtless were known in the Army, but nothing was done to silence or to discipline Toombs. If a reason might be hazarded, in the absence of any contemporary explanation, it would be that Davis and Lee did not wish to arouse resentments among Toombs's supporters. Probably the feeling was that Toombs would do less harm if kept closely under the eye of a vigilant division commander than he would if he became an anti-Administration leader in Georgia or in the Confederate Congress.

In a category different from that of Toombs, save in one troublesome particular, stood D. H. Hill at the close of the campaign. His leadership had been courageous and skillful. General Lee, who abhorred adjectives and used adverbs sparingly, employed both in that paragraph of his report which described Harvey Hill's advance at Gaines' Mill.[32] Jackson, himself scoring obstacles, was at pains to explain those Hill had overcome on June 27.[33] No division commander that day had done better. Had all the facts been known at the time, it could have been said also that Hill showed vigor at White Oak Swamp on the 30th, when Jackson not unreasonably could have been charged with lack of initiative. For failure to drive home his attack on July 1, Hill was not and could not have been blamed by his superiors.[34] "D. H. Hill," wrote Lee, "pressed forward across the open field and engaged the enemy gallantly, breaking and driving back his first line, but a simultaneous advance of the other troops not taking place, he found himself unable to maintain the ground he had gained against the overwhelming numbers and numerous batteries of the enemy."

Personally, too, Hill had been recklessly and obstinately contemptuous of danger. Col. John B. Gordon, at Malvern Hill, found the divisional commander busy over the drafting of his orders on the exposed side of a large tree. In vain the Georgian urged him to put the trunk between him and the Federal bullets "Don't worry about me," Hill replied, "look after the men," and he added as became a predestinarian: "I am not going to be killed until my time comes." Almost at the sound of the word, a shell crashed close by. The concussion rolled Hill over on the ground; a fragment of the iron tore the breast of his coat. He got up with-

[32] *O. R.*, 11, pt. 2, p. 493.
[33] *Ibid.*, 554.
[34] *Ibid.*, 496, 558–59.

out a word, shook the dirt from his uniform and sat down again—on the far side of the tree. That was the maximum he would concede in self-protection.[35]

Hill's strategic sense had been excellent, his tactics sound. No complaints of clumsiness or of negligence in administration are in the records. Professionally, then, at the close of the Seven Days, D. H. Hill was among the first of Lee's lieutenants, but he was not generally popular. "I don't like Hill, much to my surprise," confided Howell Cobb's intelligent brother Thomas, then a Colonel of cavalry, "for I was ready to love him for his Christian character." Cobb went on regretfully: "There is much bad blood among these high officers, jealousies and backbitings." [36]

Backbiting was not the word to describe Hill's habit of mind, but critical he was, ceaselessly critical. For his dead officers, he usually had laudation; the living, high or low, he seldom spared when he thought them derelict. If one of Lee's divisional commanders failed, the rebuke of the General in Chief usually was omission from his report of all unnecessary reference to the offender. Jackson, as a rule, would put a delinquent in arrest, but when he came to draft his report he would state the facts of nonperformance or retreat and would let them speak for themselves. Hill, in contrast, was almost certain to condemn the man who failed as well as the failure itself. Nor would he stop at the line of his own Division. Adjoining units and their commanders, if they did what he considered to be less than their part, would receive the arrows of his wrath. "We advanced alone," he wrote of his Division at Malvern Hill, "neither Whiting, on the left, nor Magruder and Huger, on the right, moved forward an inch." [37]

Lee himself was not exempt from Hill's criticism. En route to White Oak Swamp, the North Carolinian had regaled Maj. R. L. Dabney with a review of the defects of the plan of operations; [38] before the attack on July 1, as already noted, Hill had expressed disapproval of further pursuit; [39] in his report he was to affirm that "the battle of Malvern Hill might have been a complete and glorious success had not our artillery and infantry been fought in detail." [40]

[35] *Gordon*, 67.
[36] June 10, 1862; 28 *S. H. S. P.*, 292.
[38] *Dabney Memo.*
[37] *O. R.*, 11, pt. 2, p. 628.
[39] *O. R.*, 11, pt. 2, p. 628.
[40] *Ibid.*, 629. For further examples of D. H. Hill's critical attitude toward his superiors, see *O. R.*, 11, pt. 3, pp. 587–88; *ibid.*, 51, pt. 2, p. 574.

More often than not, Hill was sound in his adverse military judgment, though apt to disregard practical difficulties; but his insistence on pointing out the errors of others, at the same time that he dwelt on the accomplishments of his own men,[41] irritated some of his comrades.

There is every reason to believe that Harvey Hill's criticisms sprang from his chronic dyspepsia and not from jealousy or any sense of superiority. Whether this was recognized at the time, none can be sure, but at Army headquarters there was no disposition to overlook the abilities of the man because his tongue was sharp. Hill in his most dyspeptic criticism better could be entrusted with the lives of boys than could many a commander who never knew digestive ills. Beyond question, Hill would have remained with the Army of Northern Virginia after the Seven Days had not the transfer of Holmes to the Department of the Trans-Mississippi created a vacancy in North Carolina that seemed to demand the appointment of Hill. He had been under consideration for the post at Charleston, South Carolina, where some dissatisfaction prevailed;[42] but, as he was at the time the outstanding North Carolinian in Confederate service, it seemed better to name him to command in his own State, which had been stripped of troops.[43]

He was assigned accordingly.[44] On July 21, he bade farewell to his soldiers in orders that reviewed their achievements and revealed something more of the character of their chief: "The Division . . . has been endeared to its commander by its uniform good conduct in the camp as well as in the field. The troops have ever shown by their quiet and conservative character, their orderly behavior, and prompt obedience that they do not believe whiskey, bluster and profanity and rowdyism to be necessary adjuncts to the soldier. May you ever maintain your present proud position. May you ever rebuke with proper scorn the wretches who desert your colors in battle or straggle from your ranks on the march or in camp. May your future deeds be such that when your name is

---

41 *Cf.* his account of his advance on the left at Gaines' Mill: "The statements of the Yankees themselves and of the French princes on McClellan's staff fully concur with General Garland that it was this final charge upon their right flank which decided the fortunes of the day." (*O. R.*, 11, pt. 2, p. 626.)

42 *O. R.*, 53, 247, 251.

43 2 D. H. Hill, Jr., *op. cit.*, 197 ff. Cf. *O. R.*, 9, 478.

44 *O. R.*, 9, 496; orders as of July 17, 1862.

mentioned it may send a thrill of joy through the heart of him who once had the honor of commanding you." [45] In Hill's place, because of uncertainty regarding the permissible number and seniority of Major Generals, no successor was named.[46] His troops continued to be known as "D. H. Hill's Division" and, in some minor operations undertaken by him on the south side of the James after the Seven Days, were under his direction. Strange and unpredicted was the fate that awaited him.

[45] *O. R.,* 11, pt. 3, p. 646.
[46] *O. R.,* 12, pt. 3, p. 917.

CHAPTER XL

Stuart Makes a Second "Raid"

When reports of the Seven Days were filed and the service of the different arms was given its proper valuation, how stood the cavalry? Had "Jeb" Stuart added to the reputation he had won in the ride around McClellan? Stuart's father-in-law and immedate adversary, Brig. Gen. Philip St. George Cooke of the Union Army, had disappointed expectations and, in the reorganization of the Federal cavalry, soon lost command.[1] Was the star of the son-in-law rising as that of Cooke waned?

In covering the left of Jackson's advance on June 26, Stuart executed his orders literally, but without imagination. Like Jackson, he failed to see the importance of liaison on the right. On the 27th, at Gaines' Mill, he gained no new laurels. One of his gunners, as will hereafter appear, distinguished himself, but his troopers were well-nigh helpless in the blinding underbrush and enveloping forests of the Chickahominy. On the 28th, Stuart was sent to cut the York River Railroad and thereby to sever McClellan's communications with the shipping on the Pamunkey River. The task was performed easily in the face of trivial opposition.

Ere the end of the day, Stuart observed immense clouds of smoke billowing upward from the direction of the Federal base at the White House and he concluded that the enemy was destroying the supplies there. He would have been delighted to push on forthwith to the base he had been forced to skirt on his raid earlier in the month, but he faced a stiff obstacle in the high banks of Black Creek, behind which he suspected the Federal cavalry were awaiting him. Accordingly he camped for the night near Tunstall's Station, where the bivouac of his tired boys was lighted by the reflection of the distant fire. Their slumber was broken, too, by the explosion of shells the advancing flames had reached.

[1] He was on court-martial duty from July, 1862, to August, 1863, and in command of the Baton Rouge District, Department of the Gulf, from Oct. 13, 1863, to May 2, 1864. Thereafter he was General Superintendent of the Recruiting Service of the Army, May 24, 1864, to March 19, 1866 (*Cullum*, No. 492).

Dawn of the 29th found Stuart and his men moving forward. Every step was cautious, because residents warned him that the enemy had full 5000 troops on guard at the base. When he came within a quarter of a mile of the White House, he saw the smoking ruins of the residence that had been reared on the site of the old home where the ardent Washington had wooed the widow Custis.[2] What held Stuart's gaze far longer was a Federal gunboat at the landing. Cavalry against a navy—there was a chance for an encounter that would make the entire Army talk!

One of General Lee's sons, Col. "Rooney" Lee, was in command of the Ninth Virginia and, after glancing at the desolation of the White House, which was his own property, he pointed out to Stuart where troopers could take best advantage of the ground in dealing with the gunboat. Stuart then advanced seventy-five of his men with rifled carbines and stationed them at intervals of forty paces along the bank to pepper the deck of the vessel. With an amusing compound of gusto and of nonchalance, Stuart later wrote of what happened: "the troopers carrying carbines advanced boldly on this monster, so terrible to our fancy, and a body of sharpshooters were sent ashore from the boat to meet them. Quite a determined engagement of skirmishers ensued, but our gallant men never faltered in their determination to expose this Yankee bugaboo called gunboat. To save time, however, I ordered up the howitzer, a few shells from which, fired with great accuracy and bursting directly over her decks, caused an instantaneous withdrawal of sharpshooters and precipitate flight under full headway of steam down the river. The howitzer gave chase at a gallop, the more to cause the apprehension of being cut off below than of really effecting anything. The gunboat never returned." [3]

To the deserted base the cavalrymen trotted and found evidences of prodigal destruction that made them marvel at the resources of their foe. "The accumulation of commissary supplies," wrote one officer, "seemed endless." He gave the incredible de-

---

[2] It usually is assumed that the building burned at this time was the original "White House," but B. J. Lossing was correct in saying, 2 *Pictorial History of the Civil War*, 386, that it was "only a modern structure bearing the ancient title." The original White House had been destroyed by fire, Lossing said, about thirty years before the war.

[3] *O. R.*, 11, pt. 2, pp. 516–17. This vessel was U.S.S. *Marblehead*, which had aboard three companies of the 17th New York. Only one man on the gunboat was struck (7 *N. O. R.*, 718).

tails: "We saw a small lake of vinegar which, bursting from huge piles of barrels, had extinguished the fire, and covered the ground for some feet beyond the charred mass of staves and hoops. The houghs of hams and shoulders were still discernible over a surface of a thousand feet of charred bacon and smouldering ashes. . . . Many barrels of salted fish remained unscathed by the fire. . . . Immense piles of muskets were found burned, and many wagons had been backed over the bank into the river. . . . The hospital tents remained intact, and in the distance resembled a village of painted cottages." [4] Nine large barges, filled with supplies, were aflame.[5] Sutlers' stores, the prize most desired by hungry soldiers, had been set out, as if a Union column had been expected. "Provisions and delicacies of every description lay in heaps," Stuart reported with a smack of his lips, "and the men regaled themselves on the fruits of the tropics as well as the substantials of the land." [6]

To feasting and to the destruction of what could not be removed, Stuart devoted the day. He dared not leave, he subsequently explained, until he had completed the wreck the departing Federals had begun. They might return, he reasoned, and carry off anything he left. In this connection, of course, he may have been seeking to justify a frolic, but he rendered that day one service of a sort soon to be recognized as his forte.

From Lee came a courier with a note that asked a question on which the strategy of the campaign hung: What movements of the enemy had Stuart observed; what did he think McClellan intended to do? The answer in this instance was not difficult, but it involved sound military reasoning from such evidence as a cavalry commander on outpost duty always should seek to collect. Promptly Stuart sent back word to Lee that he saw no indications of any retreat down the Peninsula, and that he had no doubt McClellan, having lost communication with the York, was moving toward the James.[7] Many a time thereafter, when the military situation was well-nigh baffling, Lee was to ask similar questions and was to receive from his young cavalry commander answers no less explicit and soundly buttressed by meticulous reconnaissance and by intelligent observation.

4 *Beale*, 26.   5 *O. R.*, 11, pt. 2, p. 517.
6 *Ibid*. Cf. *Beale, loc. cit.*   7 *O. R.*, 11, pt. 2, p. 517.

Ere sunset, perhaps, all Stuart's troopers might have been put in the road for a swift return to the Army, but the General contented himself with sending the First Virginia Cavalry to watch the lower crossings of the Chickahominy. The other regiments were given the evening in which to complete their plundering and their surfeit. While Magruder at Savage Station was awaiting Jackson's arrival, and Lee was planning to catch McClellan on the march to the James, Stuart and his cavalrymen, full-stomached and content, bivouacked amid the savors of burned bacon.

Reveille on the morning of June 30 presented Stuart with the cavalryman's usual problem—what next? His orders of the 28th had been to strike the York River Railroad, in order to cut the Federals' communications with their base and to intercept their retreat. The first part of these orders he had executed. For the rest, he had no more reason than on the previous evening to believe that the Union Army was moving down the Peninsula, but he scarcely could have overlooked the possibility that McClellan had suffered delay on his retreat and might be marching eastward. Whether or not Stuart reasoned the case in these terms, his report does not show, but it records a prudent if simple decision: the column must proceed to the bridges of the Chickahominy, which he had put under observation the previous day. If McClellan intended to recross the Chickahominy, Stuart would be in position to ascertain the fact; and if the Federals were making for the James, Stuart could pass over the Chickahominy and close on them.

The march of Stuart's men on June 30 was at good speed. By 11 A.M., part of the troopers drew rein on the wooded hills above Forge Bridge [8] nearly thirteen miles from their starting point.[9] At the bridge was a Union force which seemed to be of all arms of the service,[10] though not of great strength. From Long Bridge, six miles upstream,[11] Col. Fitz Lee reported that enemy pickets could be seen.

Were these troops awaiting the arrival of McClellan's Army, or had they been placed at the bridges simply to protect the Federal

[8] O. R., 11, pt. 2, p. 201.
[9] Assuming that the route was via St. Peter's Church, Baltimore Store (Talleysville) and Mt. Olivet Church.
[10] O. R., 11, pt. 2, pp. 529–30.   [11] As the river winds.

flank? Stuart still believed McClellan was retreating toward the James, but he could not tell what support might be in rear of the forces at the crossings. "Jeb" determined to find out, though two hours were lost before guns could be brought up by the horse artillery. After these guns were run out, within 400 yards of the bridge, the Federal pieces, equal in number, soon were driven back to the hills beyond the stream.

A Confederate reconnoitering party then crossed and enjoyed a brush with Federal cavalry. To clear the road for a longer distance, Stuart had Captain Pelham carry his two howitzers out on the bridge itself. Quick fire in a hot exchange ere long sent the Federals scampering out of range.[12] As the day ended, uncertainty still prevailed regarding the force behind the hill. Fitz Lee, at Long Bridge, scoured near-by country and quizzed the numerous prisoners his men brought in. None of the Federals knew what his Army was doing or, if he knew, would tell. "I tried in vain," Stuart later reported, "to ascertain by scouts the force beyond, and it being now nearly dark we had to bivouac again." [13]

It was not a bivouac so satisfying as that of the previous evening, because there had come from the direction of White Oak Swamp the disturbing sound of heavy fire. A battle manifestly was on— and Stuart was not there to share its dangers and its honors! While others were winning fame, he could do nothing but wait and sleep.

At 3.30 he waked—quickly and as always, in his full senses. By his pallet stood a courier with a dispatch from Lee's Chief of Staff: the enemy, wrote Colonel Chilton, had been headed off at the intersection of the Long Bridge and Charles City roads; Stuart should recross the Chickahominy to co-operate with Jackson. Grapevine probably would be the best bridge for him to use.[14] Stuart scrutinized the note: it bore date of June 30, but no hour. When, Stuart demanded of the courier, had the dispatch been written? "Nine P.M." answered the man.

Stuart did not stop to question the statement or to inquire how a courier could have found him so quickly in the confusing hours of a dark night.[15] He reasoned that if the enemy had been found and had been halted at the designated point, the quickest way to

---

12 *O. R.*, 11, pt. 2, pp. 529–30.   13 *O. R.*, 11, pt. 2, p. 518.
14 *O. R.*, 11. pt. 2, pp. 497, 518.   15 The moon, three days old, had set at 9.30 P.M.

reach Jackson would be to move by Bottom's Bridge, not by Grape-vine. Time might be saved, also, if he rode ahead of his troops and ascertained for himself what the situation was. Quickly he mounted and galloped off. The orders left for the men were that they should follow him via the bridge he had chosen.

To Bottom's, Stuart rode at his dashing speed. No enemy re-mained at that point. Up the Williamsburg road he went, then turned abruptly to his left and hurried southward to White Oak Swamp. There the rear Brigades of Jackson's command were moving swiftly over the swamp unopposed. No sound of firing was audible. The Federals evidently were not "headed off" at the crossroads as Chilton had written. Jackson was advancing—and rapidly. If "Stonewall" was to be overtaken and supported, with the least delay, the march of the cavalry should be shifted. The Chickahominy should be crossed below Bottom's Bridge. Then the column could come up on the left of Jackson.[16]

Back Stuart hurried by the same roads. Fortunately, when he reached Bottom's Bridge, he found that his troopers had not passed there and, consequently, would not have to make a double cross-ing of the river.[17] He soon came upon his men East of the Chicka-hominy, but he brought them disappointment, because rumor had spread among them that they were en route to witness the sur-render of McClellan's Army.[18] It was an unpleasantly different matter to turn the horses and the guns around and to head South toward another battle!

The weary road was covered once more; Forge Bridge was reached and passed.[19] Beyond it was found a detachment of

[16] O. R., 11, pt. 2, p. 518.
[17] Ibid.   [18] Beale, 27; G. W. Beale, 38–39.
[19] It is difficult to ascertain from the reports the condition of all the lower bridges of the Chickahominy during the Seven Days. The Federals effectually had destroyed the railroad bridge, opposite Dispatch Station, on the evening of June 29, and certainly believed they had done as much for Bottom's (O. R., 11, pt. 2, p. 192), though Stuart in his report (loc. cit.) wrote as if that structure could be used. This was not of par-ticular importance because, at low water, the Chickahominy near Bottom's Bridge could be forded easily by mounted troops. Of Long Bridge, little had been left after June 28. Troops of Peck's Federal Division, at 2 P.M. that day, had been directed to proceed to Long Bridge and "to destroy what remained of it" (ibid., 216). Col. D. M. Gregg, who made reconnaissance East of the Chickahominy on the 28th, "rejoined the IV Corps by swimming the river at Long Bridge and rafting over his arms" (ibid., 192). The main crossing at Forge Bridge, over the north channel, was standing on June 29-July 1, though it may have lacked planking. Pelham, on June 30, as already noted, took position on the bridge, which, Col. W. T. Martin mistakenly reported, an enemy force had been sent to "reopen" (ibid., 529). Stuart wrote of fording on July 1 at that point (ibid., 518), instead of using the bridge, but he perhaps referred to the small span across the north channel. The Federals were of the impression that Forg

Jackson's Second Virginia Cavalry, Munford's regiment, which had been at White Oak Swamp the previous day.[20] From these troops, Stuart learned of the movement of the Army toward the James. Already Stuart had decided—evidently from his map— that the point toward which he should direct the last stage of his march was Haxall's Landing, South of Malvern Hill; but distance, darkness and manifest proximity of the Federals compelled him to halt before he could join Jackson. About an hour after Stuart bivouacked, the roar of the battle of Malvern Hill died out. His men were then about a mile and a half East of the Confederate left flank, and had covered forty-two miles that day.[21]

When Stuart later reported this march and the position he had taken, he did not withhold praise from himself. Said he: "My arrival could not have been more fortunately timed, for, arriving after dark, its ponderous march, with the rolling artillery, must have impressed the enemy's cavalry, watching the approaches to their rear, with the idea of an immense army about to cut off their retreat, and contributed to cause that sudden collapse and stampede that soon occurred, leaving us in possession of Malvern Hill, which the enemy might have held next day much to our detriment. It is a remarkable fact worthy of the commanding general's notice that in taking the position I did in rear of Turkey Creek I acted entirely from my own judgment, but was much gratified the next day, on receiving his note, to find that his orders were to the same effect, though failing to reach me till the next morning, after its execution." [22] Unfortunately for Stuart's proud boast of contribution to the "sudden collapse and stampede" of the Unionists, there is not one line in Federal reports to show that his arrival on the Confederate left was observed, much less that it was a cause of concern.

The 2d of July was spent by Stuart in reconnoitering, in rounding up Federal stragglers, in collecting abandoned arms and in intermittent skirmishing. If any opportunity was lost that day,

---

Bridge had not been burned (*ibid.*, 217). It should be added that confusion may be caused in the study of the campaign by Federal reference to Forge Bridge as Jones's Bridge. They sometimes styled it Charles City Bridge. For the identification of the two as the same structure, see *O. R.*, 11, pt. 1, p. 1045; *ibid.*, pt. 2, p. 1034.

20 *O. R.*, 11, pt. 2, p. 518.

21 *O. R.*, 11, pt. 2, p. 518. Stuart's bivouac was slightly South of J. Rock's house, which was approximately one and one half miles South and somewhat West of Smith's Store, on the road from Nance's Shop to the main River road.

22 *O. R.*, 11, pt. 2, pp. 518–10.

the fault was not "Jeb's," because he was directly under Jackson's orders and was in close touch with Lee.

At night, when reports from troopers sent to Charles City Court House made it clear that the enemy was not extending his lines northward, Stuart reasoned that the Federals were close to James River and that a bit of artillery fire might keep McClellan's tired army where it was. Young Captain Pelham, of the horse artillery, who had one serviceable gun only, a howitzer, was sent off through the darkness to see if he could find a position from which he could sweep the River road. It was a difficult mission, but it was brilliantly performed. Before morning, Pelham had in Stuart's hands a report that the enemy was near the famous old Byrd mansion of Westover, on low ground dominated by a long ridge known as Evelington Heights. Much might be gained, Captain Pelham suggested, by planting artillery on those heights.

It was a prospect that appealed to Stuart. Off went the Ninth Virginia Cavalry to cover the rear against possible attack by Federal mounted troops from beyond the Chickahominy. The remainder of Stuart's force, save for a few outposts, hurried eastward, then southward. The march was swift and easy. Evelington Heights were reached, a Federal squadron on guard there was sent ascampering. No time was lost in reconnoitering; below the heights, the enemy's camps and wagon trains could be seen. Pelham, who had been waiting quietly near by, was told to "let 'em have it." Soon the bark of his little howitzer was heard. The fall of his shell on the flats set teamsters to running and horses to rearing, but did no other damage.

While the gun kept up its fire, Stuart collected stragglers and questioned residents. Their information was all to the same effect— that virtually the whole of the Federal Army was in far-spreading camps under the heights and adjacent to the river. This important news Stuart sent forthwith to General Lee and, in reply, learned that Jackson and Longstreet were on the march eastward.[23] In the hope that the infantry would arrive ere long, Stuart continued to bang away with his howitzer. Gray-coated sharpshooters were

---

[23] Stuart, in his report, said that Lee informed him that Longstreet and Jackson were "en route to my support" (O. R., 11, pt. 2, p. 520); but it is manifest that the advance of the infantry toward Harrison's Landing, in general pursuit of the enemy, had been ordered and put under way several hours before Stuart's message had reached G. H. Q. (cf. ibid., 558–59, 760–61).

scattered along the edge of the plateau to contest a Federal advance that was beginning to take form on his flank.[24] Soon the enemy's pressure forced Pelham to take a new position, about half a mile to the rear.[25] A Federal battery, appearing East of Herring Creek, began to throw its iron among the Confederate ranks.[26]

This fire Pelham could not stop, because he virtually had exhausted his ammunition. By 2 P.M., Stuart learned that Longstreet, whose troops were leading the advance, was on the Charles City Road at Nance's Shop, six or seven miles distant.[27] The heights could not be held, by any possibility, long enough for the infantry to arrive. Stuart's game was up. Reluctantly, he fell back two miles to the northward and went into camp. The next morning, July 4, when both Longstreet and Jackson were near enough to strike, the Federal grip on the heights was too strong to be challenged. Dramatically enough, as Jackson's advance felt out the Union pickets, it encountered part of Shields's Division, which had been brought from the Shenandoah after the Battle of Port Republic to strengthen McClellan.[28]

In this manner ended Stuart's part in the campaign of the Seven Days. Had it been a full part, the maximum that could have been expected of the cavalry commander in an offensive on which the life of the Confederacy depended? Stuart himself thought so. In a letter to his wife he wrote, almost gleefully: "I have been marching and fighting for one solid week. Generally on my own hook, with the cavalry detached from the main body. I ran a gunboat from the White House and took possession. What do you think of that? We have been everywhere victorious and

24 This was Kimball's Brigade (O. R., 11, pt. 2, p. 922) which then was approaching Stuart's right (ibid., 520). Evelington Heights stretch from Roland's mill pond to Westover Church. The deployment of the infantry the following day was on both sides of Herring Creek (ibid., 520, 531, 761).

25 O. R., 11, pt. 2, p. 922.

26 This was Tidball's Co. A, 2nd (regular) Artillery. See O. R., 11, pt. 2, p. 246.

27 Stuart, in writing of this (O. R., 11, pt. 2, p. 520), said Longstreet's guide had led him by the wrong road. This is probably inaccurate. The road from Riddell's Shop by Nance's Shop, Samaria and Shiloh Churches to Evelington Heights was as direct as any other and was on high ground.

28 The route had been by transport from Alexandria to Fort Monroe and up James River. Kimball's Brigade, with the other units of Shields's Division, the whole under the temporary command of Brig. Gen. O. S. Ferry, had been attached, on arrival at Harrison's Landing, to Smith's Division of Franklin's VI Corps. It was Kimball's Brigade, as observed in note 24, that had marched to confront Stuart on July 3. The fact that this Brigade had so recently joined McClellan doubtless accounts for mistakes made in identifying it by some writers on this campaign. For the composition and advance of Shields's Division, see O. R., 12, pt. 3, pp. 309, 361, 414, 431, 436, 439.

on the 3rd I had the infinite satisfaction of slipping around to the enemy's rear and shelling his camp at Westover. If the army had been up with me we could have finished this business." [29]

Most of all, then, it would appear, Stuart was pleased with his performance on Evelington Heights and, next to that, with the dash down the banks of the Pamunkey after the *Marblehead*. There were no misgivings in his mind—certainly he admitted none —concerning the duration of his absence from the immediate flank of the Army. He seems never to have asked whether the time spent at the White House on the afternoon of the 29th might not have been utilized more profitably in hurrying back to share in the pursuit of McClellan. For the wasted day of the 30th, Stuart made no apologies.

Was he justified in his self-satisfaction? At least one Federal cavalry officer felt that the whole expedition to the White House had been a Confederate blunder and that Stuart should have been sent directly from Gaines' Mill to obstruct the crossings of White Oak Swamp.[30] To the same adversary it seemed that the absence of the Confederate cavalry on July 1 prevented the exploitation of the opportunity that Lee had found on the Federal right.[31] Among Stuart's own companions in arms, there were some who felt that his operations had been to no good purpose,[32] and, in particular, that from sheer bravado he had flushed the game at Evelington Heights. It was argued that his futile bombardment had disclosed to the Federals the unrealized strength of a position which, in another eighteen hours, the Confederate infantry would have occupied. If Stuart, said his critics, had kept to the woods, after he reached the high ground North of the sprawling Federal camp, exhausted Union commanders would have neglected to seize the heights that day. Then Lee, coming up, could have used his artillery to slaughter the Federals and perhaps to compel their surrender.

The question was long debated by the Confederates. Cavalry-men, in the main, defended Stuart; artillerists and infantrymen held against him.[33] In long retrospect, Stuart's action was proof,

[29] July 5, 1862; *Thomason*, 206.   [30] Gen. W. W. Averell, in 2 *B. & L.*, 433.
[31] *Ibid.*   [32] Cf. *Dabney*, 480.
[33] For the defense, see H. B. *McClellan*, 84–85, *Thomason*, 204. The other side is presented in W. H. Taylor's *Four Years with General Lee*, 41, and in *Alexander*, 168–70. Alexander condemned Stuart for opening fire on the 3d, but he thought Jackson and Longstreet should have attacked on the 4th.

as Alexander put it, that "dangers lurk in excess of enterprise as well as in its deficiency." [34] Beyond that, in specific application of the sound principle, it is by no means certain that the half-exhausted Confederate artillery could have conducted from Evelington Heights a successful bombardment of McClellan's camp in the face of a covering fire from the gunboats in James River. On June 30, Holmes's men had broken quickly under similar fire. Veteran troops, on the following day, had shown no relish for the "lamp-posts," as they styled the large-caliber shell, though, actually, the projectiles that fell among them did not come from the gunboats but from Tyler's siege guns on Malvern Hill. [35]

General Lee himself did not sit in judgment on the action of Stuart. In his report he did not praise the young cavalryman, but when he came to recount briefly the events of July 2-4, he omitted all reference to the affair on Evelington Heights. Stuart might be theatrical and loud, might be avid of praise, and might be inclined to prolong his raids at a distance from the Army; but he was alert, he was intelligent, he was possessed of many essentials of sound military judgment, and he was beginning to show uncommon aptitude in fathoming the intentions of the enemy. Lee had faith in Stuart, and now that the cavalry had increased to two Brigades and required divisional command, Lee recommended Stuart for promotion. As of July 28, "Jeb" became a Major General. [36]

His assigned senior Brigadier, in a wise settlement of obscure differences with President Davis, was Wade Hampton who, at Malvern Hill, had commanded Fulkerson's Third Brigade of Jackson's Division, though he had not been engaged actively. [37] The second cavalry Brigadier was named on Stuart's recommendation. After the raid to the rear of the Federal Army, he had filed a list of the men who, in that operation, had rendered particularly distinguished service. First of all, Stuart named Col. Fitz Lee of the First Virginia Cavalry. "In my estimation," Stuart had written, "no one in the Confederacy possesses more of the elements of what a brigadier of cavalry ought to be." [38] Next Stuart recommended Col. W. H. F. ("Rooney") Lee, who, he asserted, had rivalled "his

[34] *Op. cit.*, 169.
[35] Cf. *O. R.*, 11, pt. 2, pp. 971-72.
[36] *Wright*, 28.
[37] *O. R.*, 11, pt. 2, p. 566. As noted on p. 588, Hampton had taken this Brigade on June 28. *Ibid.*, 593.
[38] *O. R.*, 11, pt. 1, p. 1041.

cousin in the daring exploits of the expedition" and had "established a like claim to promotion to the same grade." [39] Naturally,
on the basis of this document, the promotion went to Fitz Lee.[40]
The cavalry was organized—and ready.

[39] *Ibid.*

[40] As of July 25, to rank from July 24 (*Wright*, 86). For the order of July 28,
assigning the new cavalry commanders, see *O. R.*, 11, pt. 3, p. 657.

CHAPTER XLI

The Juniors Who Vied with Veterans

As ready as Stuart were many others of less renown. If some reports were black with failure or were dark with disappointment, many glowed with honest tributes to junior officers and to men in the ranks. Private Frank Champion's behavior at Gaines' Mill [1] was rivalled by that of the brothers Christian, Robert and Eli, at Frayser's Farm. Col. W. E. Starke of the Sixtieth Virginia wrote proudly: "[Robert] Christian, in the bayonet charge of the 30th, was assailed by no less than four of the enemy at the same instant. He succeeded in killing three of them with his own hands, though wounded in several places by bayonet-thrusts, and his brother, Eli W. Christian, going to his aid, dispatched the fourth." [2] In that same battle, the struggle of the Alabama Brigade of Cadmus Wilcox for two six-gun batteries had shed honor on the entire command.[3]

At Malvern Hill, when every flag was a target for hundreds of marksmen, case after case was cited of unhesitating valor in carrying the colors. Here is the statement of Col. E. C. Edmonds, Thirty-eighth Virginia, of what happened in his regiment of Armistead's Brigade: "I have the painful duty to announce the loss of my color-sergeant (L. P. H. Tarpley), first color-corporal (Cornelius Gilbert) and Private Parker, of Company F, who fell upon the field while bearing the colors in advance of the regiment during the charges made. Color-Corporals Watkins, Burlington, and Gregory were severely wounded each in turn as they grasped the colors. They were then seized by Lieutenant-Colonel [Powhatan B.] Whittle, who was badly wounded and compelled to retire. Captain [R. T.] Daniel (volunteer officer, commanding Company F) then took them, and he, too, fell severely wounded in three places, and was borne from the field. I then took them for a while, and when in the act of handing them over to the only

---

[1] *Supra*, p. 526. [2] *O. R.*, 11, pt. 2, p. 851.
[3] *O. R.*, 11, pt. 2, p. 777; 2 *R. E. Lee*, 187 ff.

remaining color guard, who claimed the right to carry them, the staff was shattered, the flag falling, but not upon the ground; it was caught by Color Corpl. William M. Bohannon, who stuck it upon his bayonet and gallantly bore it the remainder of the fight." [4]

Destined to a larger renown than any of these gallant boys was a private of the Fourth Virginia Cavalry, mentioned for the first time in a single sentence of "Jeb" Stuart's report: "Private Frank Stringfellow, Fourth Virginia Cavalry, was particularly conspicuous for gallantry and efficiency at Cold Harbor." [5] That was all. At the time, Stringfellow was unknown, outside his own company. He probably had been detailed as a courier at the headquarters of Stuart, whose infectious courage brought out the fighting qualities of the boy. Stuart had observed the unhesitating bravery of the trooper and, as always, he remembered its display; but even the penetrating blue eyes of "Jeb" could not have foreseen the incredible adventures that lay ahead of Franklin Stringfellow.

In young John Pelham, who had attracted attention by the manner in which he had used his green company of horse artillery at Williamsburg, the trial of the Seven Days had developed leadership unmistakable. Far to the left at Gaines' Mill, late on the afternoon of June 27, vedettes had reported to the cavalry commander the approach of Federal artillery.

Stuart himself gave in his report the best account of what followed: "The only artillery under my command being Pelham's Stuart Horse Artillery, the 12-pounder Blakely and Napoleon were ordered forward to meet this bold effort to damage our left flank. The Blakely was disabled at the first fire, the enemy opening simultaneously eight pieces, proving afterward to be Weed's and Tidball's batteries. Then ensued one of the most gallant and heroic feats of the war. The Napoleon gun, solitary and alone, received the fire of these batteries, concealed in the pines on a ridge commanding its ground, yet not a man quailed, and the noble captain directing the fire himself with a coolness and intrepidity only equalled by his previous brilliant career. The enemy's fire sensibly slackened under the determined fire of this Napoleon, which clung to its ground with unflinching tenacity.

[4] *O. R.*, 11, pt. 2, p. 824.   [5] *O. R.*, 11, pt. 2. p. 522.

I had an opportunity of calling General Jackson's attention to the heroic conduct of the officers and men of this piece, and later he, by his personal efforts, re-enforced it with several batteries of rifled pieces which, firing, advanced *en échelon* about dark and drove the enemy from his last foothold on the right." [6] "Old Jack" remembered the incident and, near the end of his days, when he wrote his report of the Seven Days, he had a sentence for Pelham, who, he said, "bravely dashed forward" [7]—few words but, from the laconic Jackson, high praise.

Pelham it was who cleared the way for Stuart's advance to the White House, Pelham who chased the *Marblehead* down the Pamunkey, Pelham who challenged the Federals across the Chickahominy, and Pelham who, at Stuart's order, opened from Evelington Heights. In Stuart's report, the Alabamian, as handsome in his clear blond youth as he was modest and valiant, won perhaps the highest commendation accorded any officer: "Captain John Pelham, of the Horse Artillery, displayed such signal ability as an artillerist, such heroic example and devotion in danger, and indomitable energy under difficulties in the movement of his battery, that, reluctant as I am at the chance of losing such a valuable limb from the brigade, I feel bound to ask for his promotion, with the remark that in either cavalry or artillery no field grade is too high for his merit and capacity." [8]

Among Pelham's classmates at West Point had been a young Virginian, a year and a half his senior, Thomas L. Rosser. As soon as Alabama had seceded, Pelham had resigned, but Rosser had remained as long as Virginia had held to the Union. Upon her secession and the call of the graduating class to field duty, Rosser had sent in his resignation and had hurried to Montgomery. He was physically a superb young man, well over six feet, Indian in erectness, broad-shouldered and muscular, black-haired and brown-eyed, with a strong jaw and the indescribable quality of the soldier in his bearing and direct gaze. [9] His personality and training won him promptly a commission as First Lieutenant in the regular Army of the Confederacy and an assignment to the Washington Artillery of New Orleans. He had commanded one

---

[6] *O. R.*, 11, pt. 2, p. 515.
[8] *O. R.*, 11, pt. 2, p. 522.
[7] *Ibid.*, 556.
[9] *Laurel Brigade*, 196.

of its batteries at First Manassas, but he had no part in the fighting at Henry Hill.[10]

Although Rosser shared in Stuart's minor foray at Lewinsville in September, 1861,[11] and later won the praise of the Army for shooting down one of McClellan's observation balloons,[12] he had no large opportunity until the Seven Days. Two days prior to the opening of the campaign,[13] he had been promoted Colonel and had been given command of the Fifth Virginia Cavalry, a newly organized unit. This advancement was at the instance of "Jeb" Stuart, who wrote that he had "pushed through" the commission. Exuberantly Stuart bade him "Come a-runnin'." [14]

Rosser found his regiment was one of three[15] designated to guard the Confederate right, while Stuart with the greater part of the mounted troops operated on the left. The command was entirely green. Few of the men even had been under fire. Scarcely any of them had been drilled. The young Colonel had by his own vigilance to compensate for the inexperience of his troopers Gallantly he had measured up, and with the display of exceptional judgment. On June 30, while he was picketing Malvern Hill, he had discovered the enemy crossing hurriedly to the river. This movement he had reported to Longstreet and to Holmes, neither of whom, so far as Rosser could see at the time, paid any attention to it. The youthful Rosser was not to be balked. In the sound belief that the retreat of the enemy might affect the plan of the commanding General, he sent the information directly to Lee. His reward was the early appearance of the General himself at his outpost, first to observe the movement of the enemy and then to order Holmes forward.[16]

This notable service Rosser followed, the next week, by a stubborn defensive on the River road below Westover. Stuart, who previously had not had Rosser under his direct command, watched and applauded. "Colonel Rosser," reported Stuart, ". . . inspired his men with such determined resistance—arrang-

[10] O. R., 2, 517, 537. He was assigned as First Lieutenant of Artillery, June 7, 1861. and on Sept. 27 was appointed temporary Captain for service with volunteers. Rosser MSS.
[11] O. R., 5, 183–84.   [12] C. M. H., 658.
[13] Lieutenant Colonel of Artillery, P. A. C. S., June 10, 1862; Colonel, June 24 Rosser MSS.
[14] Stuart to Rosser, June 23, 1862. Rosser MSS.
[15] Plus the cavalry of the Hampton Legion. O. R., 11, pt. 2, p. 499.
[16] O. R., 11, pt. 2, p. 532. Cf. supra, p. 583.

ing them so as to resist to best advantage—that the enemy failed . . ."[17] From that day, in a service that boasted many daring and ambitious officers, Rosser was a marked man. Within a week, he had earned among cavalrymen as high a reputation as he had enjoyed in the artillery.

That red arm of the service had not failed to show during the Seven Days that it included other young men as gallant as Rosser and Pelham. Admittedly, the opportunities for the guns had been few, because of the absences,[18] defective organization, poor leadership and unfavorable terrain already described; but where battery commanders had a fair field of fire, some of them shone.

First among them in performance had been Capt. William J. Pegram, a younger brother of Col. John Pegram, who had shared in the tragedy of Rich Mountain.[19] "Willie" Pegram, small of stature, spectacled,[20] retiring, had been a quiet listener at the University of Virginia while fiery fellow students had debated during the winter of 1860–61 the burning question of secession. His classmates had respected him for his unpretending Christian character and for his modest dependability,[21] but they probably had not observed in him anything to suggest the soldier. When the hour of decision came, he left the University and reported as a member of "Company F," a *corps d'élite* of his native Richmond.[22] In a short time he had been elected Lieutenant of the Purcell Battery, another Richmond command.[23] With this he had participated in the repulse of the Federals from Lewis's Ford during the First Battle of Manassas.[24]

Eleven months later, when Lee opened the offensive at Mechanicsville, "Willie" Pegram was Captain of the Purcell Battery and was sent forward with Field's Brigade, the van of A. P. Hill's Division. Almost as soon as Pegram reached the field, he came under the converging fire of the Federal artillery across Beaver Dam Creek. His six guns coped for a time with close to thirty of superior accuracy. Man after man went down. One piece and then another was damaged or fouled. His was the advanced

---

17 *O. R.*, 11, pt. 2, p. 521. For Rosser's later career, see Vols. II and III.
18 Notably of Lindsay Walker and, at Malvern Hill, of Stapleton Crutchfield.
19 See *supra*, p. 27.
20 35 *S. H. S. P.*, 57.
21 *Cf.* W. Gordon McCabe, in 14 *S. H. S. P.*, 11.   22 6 *C. V.*, 270.
23 *Richmond Examiner*, June 4, 1861.
24 McCabe, *loc. cit.*; *O. R.*, 2, 476, 491.

artillery position, the nearest target of the Federals.[25] When night mercifully came to cover him, Pegram had lost forty-seven of his command, with many of his horses, and had four of his guns out of action;[26] but with the help of valiant boys as exhausted but as determined as he was, he got his battery in condition to fight the next day.[27] At Gaines' Mill, though he engaged gallantly,[28] he was spared losses. With the limping remnant of his company, he followed Hill on the 29th to the Darbytown road.

Denied any conspicuous rôle in the battle of Frayser's Farm, "Willie" Pegram diligently had his men at their station with the reserve North of Malvern Hill, and he answered the desperate call of Armistead for artillery support on the right of the Confederate line in front of the Crew Farm. Behind the fine Portsmouth battery of Carey F. Grimes, the youthful Pegram crashed through the woods, unlimbered and defied the blast from the ordnance that crowded the lane on the crest of the hill on the Carter Farm. "No men," wrote Armistead, "could have behaved better than Captains Pegram and Grimes; they worked their guns after their men were cut down, and only retired when entirely disabled." [29]

After the last hot fieldpiece was hauled out, and the casualties of the campaign could be reckoned, the roll showed that Pegram had lost seven killed and fifty-three wounded, a total of sixty, in a battery of about eighty men.[30] A gruesome toll it was, and due in part to Pegram's belief that the largest service was to be rendered at the short range;[31] but the Division rang with praise of the battery. "Always eager, always alert," was General Field's characterization of Pegram.[32] Commendation came also from A. P. Hill [33] to second that of Field and of Armistead. Said one comrade of Pegram after thirty years: "He had always been such a modest, self-contained and almost shrinking youth that his most intimate friends were astonished at his rapid development and

[25] Col. H. L. Landers, who has made the closest study of troop positions on the field of the Seven Days, placed that of Pegram as on the south side of the road from Mechanicsville to Ellerson's Mill and almost directly opposite the entrance to the Brooks House. See his Map No. 2.

[26] O. R., 11, pt. 2, p. 837; 14 S. H. S. P., 12.

[27] O. R., loc. cit.

[28] Ibid.

[29] O. R., 11, pt. 2, pp. 818–19.

[30] These were the final figures, O. R., 11, pt. 2, p. 983. The total given in ibid., 503, doubtless was computed prior to the death of some of the wounded.

[31] Stiles, 110.

[32] O. R., 11, pt. 2, p. 843.   [33] Ibid., 835.

promotion; but it was one of those strongly-marked cases where war seemed to be the needed and almost the native air of a young man. He was, in some respects, of the type of Stonewall Jackson, and like him combined the stoutest faith and the deepest spirituality with the most intense spirit of fight." [34]

If artillerists and Stuart of the cavalry could point to many individuals who had distinguished themselves during the Seven Days, the roll of those conspicuous in the hard service of the infantry was so long that division commanders did not try to call it. Even Brigadiers had to explain in their reports that, with few exceptions, they could not attempt to name those below the rank of field officer who had shown valor and sound military judgment. For the first time appeared prominently in reports the names of Robert F. Hoke,[35] S. Dodson Ramseur,[36] Samuel McGowan,[37] E. L. Thomas,[38] all of whom, then Colonels or Lieutenant Colonels, soon were to be promoted. Col. John B. Gordon, distinguished at Seven Pines, won new admiration for his gallant leading of Rodes's Brigades at Malvern Hill,[39] where more than 400 of his Alabamians fell.[40]

Of the Brigadier Generals it could be said that most of them had shown intelligence, that some of them had done admirably in view of their inexperience or lack of military training, and that those who had failed outright had been few. Charges that Micah Jenkins had neglected to support Kemper at Frayser's Farm, and that Branch did not help Longstreet had no other basis than that both Jenkins and Branch probably had all they could do on their own fronts.[41] Reports that advanced Brigades had been fired on from the rear at Malvern Hill undoubtedly were true, but the explanation was the confusion of officers in the maddening maze of swamp and forest.[42]

The disposition of some of the brigade commanders, as always in war, was to blame their non-success on the lack of co-operation beyond their own flanks. In the main, where conduct actually was

[34] Stiles, 110.
[35] O. R., 11, pt. 2, p. 884.
[36] Ibid., 793–95.
[37] Ibid., 838, 839, 852, 856, 865.
[38] Ibid., 878.
[39] Ibid., 628. For Gordon's report, see ibid., 633 ff.
[40] In ibid., 635, Gordon gave his casualties as 1027, but a subsequent return, prepared from the nominal lists, ibid., 975–76, put Malvern Hill casualties at 425 and those of the campaign at 570.
[41] Cf. O. R., 11, pt. 2, pp. 764, 769
[42] O. R., 11, pt. 2, pp. 724, 728.

discreditable, it wrathfully was exposed. To cite one instance, "Rans" Wright indignantly rebuked in his report the Colonel of one of his own regiments. At Malvern Hill, he explained, he was unable to find the officer or the troops. He wrote: "After a long search and considerable delay I discovered [the Colonel] approaching from the rear, where he had been some mile or more, without my assent, knowledge, or approval. He had received a slight scratch in the face from a fragment of shell, left his command, and retired to the rear. I ordered him to collect his regiment and form on the left. . . . This he failed to do." [43]

Of all the Brigadiers, R. H. Anderson, in his modest way, probably had been the most definitely marked throughout the campaign by soldierly competence. At Frayser's Farm, he had been in charge of Longstreet's Division while "Old Pete" had directed the field.[44] In Longstreet's bestowal of praise on his subordinates, both for Gaines' Mill and for the action of June 30, Anderson's name headed all.[45] Jackson, too, had observed the "gallant style" of the South Carolinian's advance on the 27th in support of Whiting.[46] It was plain that Anderson soon was to be promoted.[47]

George Pickett, he of the curling locks, had been wounded in the charge that added to "Dick" Anderson's reputation at Gaines' Mill.[48] But he was not forgotten in reports. Cadmus Wilcox, another of Longstreet's Brigadiers, had acquitted himself admirably in that same battle and had added, besides, to the Army's store of humor. Early in the action, before the position of the enemy had been plain to him, he had dismounted on the farm of Dr. Gaines and had asked a soldier whether from the ground

[43] O. R., 11, pt. 2, p. 814.
[44] Cf. O. R., 11, pt. 2, pp. 763, 776.
[45] Ibid., 758, 759.
[46] Ibid., 556. Unfortunately, Anderson filed no report of the campaign. C. Irvine Walker, in his Life of Lt. Gen. Richard Heron Anderson, 85 ff, quoted a brief account of the Brigade's action at Gaines' Mill. This was by Capt. James A. Hoyt and appeared originally in the Greenville Mountaineer, Apr. 26, 1899. In the Anderson Papers is a letter "Dick" Anderson, on May 9, 1862, wrote his father, Dr. W. W. Anderson. It records tenderly but with manly affection and religious spirit the death, May 5, in the action around Fort Magruder, of "Dick's" brother, McKenzie.
[47] See infra, p. 673.
[48] Gen. Eppa Hunton noted in his Autobiography, p. 70, that Pickett was wounded before the Brigade crossed Powhite. A somewhat more detailed account by General Hunton will be found in 7 C. V., 223–24. J. C. Haskell wrote in his MS. Rem., 47: "On the way in [to the lines at the request of General Whiting to rally scattered men], I passed Gen. Pickett who was standing by his horse in a deep small hollow, almost like a well, bewailing himself. He called to me to send him a litter, as he was mortally wounded. I had none and was too busy with my men. He was very slightly wounded and perfectly able to take care of himself."

where the man was standing, on an elevation under a tree, the Federals could be seen. Assured that they could, Wilcox climbed up, only to be greeted on the instant by a cannon shot that hit the tree. Down clambered Wilcox quickly.

"Did you get a good view?" asked the soldier.

"Too good for me," Wilcox answered and spurred forward.[49]

Wilcox reached Longstreet's side at the moment the division commander was being told by Roger A. Pryor that between the Confederates and the enemy was an impossible ravine.

"My people can cross it," said Wilcox in his nervous manner.

Longstreet bade him try. He did—and carried the position.[50] At Frayser's Farm, Wilcox had perhaps the hardest fighting of the day, in the face of two valiantly defended Federal batteries. Once, when his orders conflicted, he halted his advance, but, when the day was over, his record was as good as that of any Brigadier, though his loss had been ghastly.[51]

In A. P. Hill's Division, Pender's attack at Mechanicsville, Gregg's at Gaines' Mill and the final, well-organized advance of Jos. R. Anderson at Frayser's Farm [52] probably had been the outstanding accomplishments. On the 30th, Field impetuously had carried his Brigade too far.[53] For a Division of which three Brigades had never been previously under fire,[54] the showing of all the units was creditable and more.

D. H. Hill had felt that Colquitt and Ripley had done less than their part at Gaines' Mill and in his report he was to say so in plain terms.[55] For Samuel Garland and George B. Anderson he had nothing but praise.[56] Rodes, it will be remembered, had been too much enfeebled by his wound to keep the field on June 27 and had not attempted to accompany his Brigade to Malvern Hill.

Of all the Brigadiers of Jackson's command, including those of Whiting's Division, the most shining figure had been Hood, whose attack at Gaines' Mill was regarded as the most brilliant single achievement in the Seven Days. Winder had been given no opportunity, save in the same battle, but he was credited with excellent leadership.[57] Lawton, too, had done splendidly. Trimble

49 C. Irvine Walker, op. cit., 88.   50 8 C. V., 443.
51 Cf. O. R., 11, pt. 2, pp. 776, 980, and supra, p. 605.
52 Cf. O. R., 11, pt. 2, pp. 838–39.
53 Ibid., 838.   54 Ibid., 839.
55 O. R., 11, pt. 2, p. 626.   56 Ibid.
57 O. R., 11, pt. 2, p. 555.

at Malvern Hill, had justified the record he had made in the later battles on the Shenandoah and at Gaines' Mill. On July 1, all ardor, he had shown the spirit he had exhibited at Cross Keys and vainly had pleaded with Jackson to be permitted to launch a surprise attack against the extreme right of the Federals. Later, it will be remembered, he had asked to be allowed to make a night assault.[58]

Magruder's command had been so overmarched and so mis-handled that the competent men had not been revealed, though the worst misfits had been exposed. As for Huger's Division, the commander had better reason to be proud of Armistead, Mahone and Wright than they had to applaud his direction. If, of this trio, Mahone had shown poor judgment on June 30, he had redeemed himself at Malvern Hill.

Tactical mistakes there had been, wasteful exposure under fire, and assaults that more experienced leading might have rendered unnecessary; but had all the reports been bundled together, and one word written across the jacket, that one word would have been *Promising*.

[58] *O. R.*, 11, pt. 2, p. 618.

CHAPTER XLII

The Enigma of Jackson's State of Mind

More important than the promise of any of the Brigadier Generals during the Seven Days was the performance of those divisional commanders who, despite tactical bungling and in the face of delays by others, had carried the strategical plan to success.

"Dick" Ewell was to be reckoned high among those who had contributed unmistakably to the defeat of the Federals. He had been denied full play of his abilities because of the circumstances of the field, but in every essential, to the limits allowed, he had met the test. His marches had been well-ordered and prompt. At Gaines' Mill, he not only had led his men admirably, but he also had given all possible aid to the adjoining units. Whether it was to direct Winder in the choice of a route[1] or to halt and to counsel a regiment about to enter action,[2] Ewell was at hand. When he was sent down the Chickahominy on June 28 to guard against a possible return of McClellan to the north bank, he had been restrained only by Jackson's direct orders from pushing across the river to assail McClellan on the march to White Oak Swamp.[3] At Malvern Hill, he had been held in reserve until late in the action. Then he had advanced valiantly.[4] As at Gaines' Mill, he seemed to be everywhere on his part of the field. No officer was mentioned more often or more gratefully by others. The picture of him that takes form, in a score of reports, is that of an intelligent, trained, self-contained and daring man, unique in personality, who had cheer and help for every fellow soldier who needed either.

In the final hours of the Seven Days' Battles, Jackson had been as diligent as his lieutenant, Ewell. Late in the evening of July 1, when Stuart's engineer came to report that the cavalry were close at hand, Jackson was in good humor and was disposed to joke: "That's good, that's good," he said in his usual formula of ap-

[1] O. R., 11, pt. 2, p. 570.　　[2] Ibid., 584.
[3] O. R., 11, pt. 2, pp. 617-18.　　[4] Cf. O. R., 11, pt. 2, pp. 629, 729.

proval, "'changing his base,' is he? Ha-ha." [5] During the night, after some of his officers awakened Jackson from a hard sleep, with a request for orders, he answered only, "Please let me sleep; there will be no enemy here in the morning." [6] On the 2nd, he awakened early. Non-fulfillment of his prediction that the enemy would disappear before daylight did not disturb him. Promptly he sent a fatigue party to clean up the battlefield in his front. When asked his reason for this, he said simply, "Why, I am going to attack here presently, as soon as the fog rises, and it won't do to march the troops over their own dead, you know; that's what I am doing it for." [7] His complete dissent a little later from Lee's decision not to pursue McClellan that day was silent but apparent to observers.

All this was in keeping with the reputation Jackson had acquired in the Valley; but what of the march on June 26, of the delay at Grapevine Bridge, and of the day-long wait on the north side of White Oak Swamp? How were these things to be explained? Were they the performance of a man who could be trusted to lead larger forces under a ranking General in a new campaign?

Many Confederates in and out of the Army had unfriendly answers. Robert Toombs already has been quoted. [8] Longstreet, perhaps at the time and publicly in later years, maintained that

---

[5] *W. W. Blackford's MS. Memoirs*, p. 109. Blackford explained a propos of this joke, that McClellan's announcement of the retreat to the James as a "Change of base" immediately became a "catch word among our fun loving troops, to signify discomfiture or defeat; if two dogs fought and one ran, the men cheered and shouted, 'Look at him changing his base'; if a man fell in the mud, his comrades would laugh and ask him what he was changing his base for, or if the rain flooded the place where they were sleeping they would say, 'Come, fellows, let's change our base'" (*ibid.*, p. 105).

[6] 19 *S. H. S. P.*, 311 ff. Dr. Hunter McGuire, authority for this statement, remarked *passim:* "When [Jackson] went to sleep he was the most difficult man to arouse I ever saw. I have seen his servant pull his boots off and remove his clothes without waking him up, and so here at Malvern Hill . . . it was almost impossible to arouse him. At last some one got him up into a sitting posture, and another yelled into his ear something about the condition of our army. . . . Many a night I have kept him on his horse by holding on to his coat-tail. He always promised to do as much for me when he finished his nap. He meant to do it, I am sure, but my turn never came." Again, a correspondent of the *Richmond Dispatch* (Aug. 13, 1862, p. 1, col. 5), remarked that Jackson, who was inclined to take short naps, had little sleep during the battles around Richmond. One evening, at the time while Jackson was nodding in his saddle, a soldier from the roadside asked, "Hillow, where did that man get that liquor?" Jackson roused himself and said, "Well, I think I had better keep awake now." Cooke, in his *Jackson*, 460, quoted Dr. McGuire to this effect: "If [Jackson's] rest was broken for one night, he was almost certain to go to sleep upon his horse if riding the next day."

[7] Blackford *op. cit.*, 109.   [8] See *supra*, p. 628.

"Jackson was a very skillful man against such men as Shields, Banks and Frémont, but when pitted against the best of the Federal commanders he did not appear so well." [9] Among staff officers it was whispered that "Old Jack" had said "he did not intend that *his* men should do all the fighting." His light casualties gave some color to the rumor. Even D. H. Hill, with all his admiration for his brother-in-law, thought that "an important factor" in Jackson's lost day at White Oak Swamp was the General's "pity for his own corps, worn out by long and exhausting marches, and reduced in numbers by its numerous sanguinary battles." Hill echoed the gossip of staff officers that Jackson thought the "garrison of Richmond ought now to bear the brunt of the fighting." [10] Dr. Dabney believed Jackson mentally exhausted on the critical day.[11] William Allan, who was not second even to Dabney in his admiration for his chief, could say only, when most of the evidence had been sifted, that "Jackson's comparative inaction" was "one of the few great mistakes of his marvellous career." [12] President Davis had no comment in 1862, though he said in later years that he thought a careful study of the ground would show that "Franklin's position was the real obstacle to Jackson's crossing." [13]

Jackson himself never indicated that he thought he had failed during the Seven Days. His report, which was written in February, 1863, described his marches of June 26–27 as though they had been made precisely in accordance with the plan. He recounted with pride the action of his men at Gaines' Mill. Ever the artillerist, he did not fail to mention that he had massed about thirty guns there and twenty-eight at White Oak Swamp.[14] For his failure to advance on June 30, the marshy character of the soil, the destruction of the bridge and the strong position of the enemy were set down as the reasons.[15] He concluded: "Undying gratitude is due to God for this great victory, by which despondency increased in the North, hope brightened in the South, and the capital of Virginia and of the Confederacy was saved." [16]

[9] 2 *B & L.*, 405.　　　　　　　　　[10] 2 *B. & L.*, 389.
[11] *Dabney*, 466–67.
[12] William Alian, *The Army of Northern Virginia in 1862* (cited hereafter as *Allan's Army*), p. 121.
[13] 14 *S. H. S. P.*, 451.　　　　　　[14] *O. R.*, 11, pt. 2, pp. 556, 557.
[15] *Ibid.*, 557.　　　　　　　　　　　[16] *Ibid.*, 559.

Once only, in all his known conversations with his staff, did Jackson ever speak of White Oak Swamp. A fortnight after the battle, he chanced to overhear some of his assistants arguing whether troops from his command should not have been sent across the swamp to Longstreet's assistance. "If General Lee had wanted me," Jackson said curtly, "he could have sent for me."[17] What made him give that answer? On the 30th, had he been striving to hold rigidly to soldierly subordination in the large Army to which he was a stranger; or had he been so weary that he had not exerted himself beyond the letter of his orders? Did he voice justification or excuse? He gave no hint.

Lee never understood why the delay occurred at White Oak Swamp,[18] but he did not lose his high opinion of Jackson as a soldier. The commanding General may have reasoned that Jackson in an unfamiliar country, co-operating with distant columns through inexperienced staff officers, faced difficulties that could not be overcome. Chance and not lack of ability or of effort may have seemed to Lee the reason for Jackson's failure.

In the general report on the campaign, though it was not compiled until Jackson had vindicated himself on other fields, Lee gave the leader of the Army of the Valley the maximum benefit of every permissible doubt. Regarding the preliminaries, Lee wrote: "In consequence of unavoidable delays the whole of Jackson's command did not arrive at Ashland in time to enable him to reach the point designated on the 25th. His march on the 26th was consequently longer than had been anticipated, and his progress being also retarded by the enemy, A. P. Hill did not begin his movement until 3 P.M." The only other references to Jackson's operations on the opening day of the campaign were made to explain the attack on Beaver Dam Creek.[19] No criticism was expressed of the slow bridging of the Chickahominy. All Lee said on that score was: "Jackson's route led to the flank and rear of Savage Station, but he was delayed by the necessity of reconstructing Grapevine Bridge."[20] As for White Oak Swamp, the difference between Huger's "not coming up" and Jackson's "having been unable to force the passage" has been cited already.[21]

[17] 2 Henderson, 57.
[18] Wade Hampton, in Alexander, 151.
[19] O. R., 11, pt. 2, p. 491.
[20] Ibid., 494.
[21] See supra, p. 611.

This was not praise, but it was not condemnation. Although Jackson had not accomplished what was expected of him, Lee was content to believe he could not have done it.

Physical exhaustion and the resulting benumbment of a mind that depended much on sleep probably are the basic explanation of Jackson's inability to meet the demands of the campaign. In addition, every other circumstance was adverse: Jackson had no skill in quick mastery of terrain, though his eye for tactical use of a position was admirable. The man who could have helped him most, his topographer Jed. Hotchkiss, was not with him. Jackson's troops were in a hot country, away from their usual "hard" water. Whiting may have been sulking. Major Dabney, an excellent administrator in camp, was inexperienced in transportation. On the critical days' marches, the Chief Quartermaster was absent or, like his chief, was weary. Jackson was attempting, also, to handle a much larger force than ever had been under his charge.[22]

Most of this, Lee took into account. If, at the end of the campaign, he had any doubts concerning Jackson, they probably were two—whether the victor of the Valley could display his full capacity in a subordinate position, and whether he could use the abilities of other men sufficiently to direct a large force.[23] Was he or was he not an abler man of the type of Magruder—useful only when exercising independent command of no more troops than he personally could handle?

Circumstance curiously deferred the answer. On June 26, the Federal forces left in the area of the Shenandoah, those under General McDowell and the troops designated for the defense of the approaches to Washington, had been consolidated as the Army of Virginia. To the direction of this Army was assigned Maj. Gen. John Pope, who had displayed much vigor in successful operations on the upper Mississippi. Pope had assumed command immediately, and after spending two weeks in acquainting him-

[22] In 2 R. E. Lee, 581–82, the writer inclined to the opinion that Jackson's physical exhaustion, itself the result of an excess of zeal, accounted for his apparent lethargy on June 30. Evidence that has come to light since 1934 has changed that opinion to the extent, only, that other factors appear somewhat more important. There is no single, all-inclusive explanation of Jackson's poor performance.

[23] For the former of these considerations, see *infra*, Vol. II. As respects Lee's possible concern that Jackson might not be able to direct a large command by giving discretion to his subordinates, there is no direct evidence, but the letter of Lee to Jackson regarding the employment of A. P. Hill lends itself to this interpretation. See Vol. II.

self with his troops and his problems, had begun an advance toward the Rapidan River.[24]

Mirth was aroused among Confederates and resentment among Federal veterans of the Virginia campaigns by Pope's haughty boast in his first address to his soldiers. "I have come to you," he said, "from the West, where we have always seen the backs of our enemies; from an army whose business it has been to seek the adversary and to beat him where found; whose policy has been attack and not defense." He went on: "I presume I have been called here to pursue the same system and to lead you against the enemy. It is my purpose to do so, and that speedily. . . . Meantime I desire you to dismiss from your minds certain phrases which I am sorry to find so much in vogue amongst you. I hear constantly of 'taking strong positions and holding them,' of 'lines of retreat,' and of 'bases of supplies.' Let us discard such ideas. The strongest position a soldier should desire to occupy is one from which he can most easily advance against the enemy. . . . Let us look before us, and not behind." [25]

These tactless words did not seem likely to achieve their object, but behind them was arrayed a large force, precisely how large the Confederate high command did not know.[26] Pope's Army was capable, at the least, of advancing quickly to the Virginia Central Railroad at "the Gordonsville loop" and thereby of severing communications between Richmond and the Shenandoah Valley. That done, Pope, if strong, might march toward Rich-

---

[24] O. R., 12, pt. 3, pp. 435, 436–37, 473–74. Pope himself did not leave Washington until July 29 or 30 (ibid., 519, 520).

[25] O. R., 12, pt. 3, p. 474.

[26] Pope testified on July 8 that he had 43,000 mobile troops and 12,000 in the garrison of Washington (Report of the [U. S.] Joint Committee on the Conduct of the War, vol. I, p. 277). His morning report of July 31 showed 53,358 in his three field Corps. He deducted 6500 at Winchester and elsewhere as in fixed positions or unfit for duty, and he credited himself with net 46,858 (O. R., 12, pt. 1, p. 53). The abstract of return of the Army, that same date, gave him an aggregate present of 77,779. He reported the reserve—Sturgis's Corps for the defense of Washington—at 9226, and his detached forces at Winchester and in Western Virginia at 12,460. If the Washington garrison and the troops in Western Virginia be deducted as unavailable for field service, and the Winchester garrison (White's Brigade, 2958) be accounted a mobile reserve, Pope's net aggregate present would be 59,051. "Those present for duty" in the three Corps at hand numbered 51,801 officers and men (O. R., 12, pt. 3, p. 523). In round numbers, then, his field force was 50,000 of all arms. In all computations of the strength of forces during the War between the States, it is well to remember that "effective" was the term used in the tabulation to cover all privates and non-commissioned officers present for duty; "total" embraced the above, plus all present in camp who were sick, in arrest and on extra duty; "aggregate" embraced all officers and men present. Combat strength most readily is calculated by adding to the "effective" summary the number of "officers present for duty." See 43 S. H. S. P., 206 n.

mond and renew the threat McDowell had made in May of a junction with McClellan.

Jackson would not state the case in defensive terms. He went to Lee and argued with vigor that the best means of dealing with Mc-Clellan and with Pope was through an offensive into the enemy's own country. When Lee reserved judgment, Jackson determined on a bold step: he would appeal over the head of the commanding General to the President. In doing this, of course, he would be proceeding close to the farthest line of military subordination and he must, in consequence, be careful.

After some reflection he sent one evening for his aid and political champion, Col. A. R. Boteler. "Do you know," he began, in a tone of some excitement, "we are losing valuable time here?"

"How so?" asked Boteler.

"Why, by repeating the blunder we made after the battle of Manassas, in allowing the enemy leisure to recover from his defeat and ourselves to suffer by inaction." He became more excited as he voiced his conviction. "Yes—we are wasting precious time and energies in this malarious region that can be much better employed elsewhere, and I want to talk with you about it."

Jackson proceeded with his appraisal: the Army of the Potomac was beaten; the Federals would not resume the offensive until they were reinforced; Richmond was safe; the offensive proposed by him in May should be launched.[27]

At this point, Jackson's caution and military training prompted a disclaimer: when telling the President all this, Boteler must make it plain that Jackson was not prompted by self-seeking in urging persistently this offensive. He was willing to follow any leader Davis might designate.

Boteler interposed: "What is the use of my going to Mr. Davis, as he'll probably refer me again to General Lee? So, why don't you yourself speak to General Lee upon the subject?"

"I have already done so," Jackson admitted.

"Well, what does he say?"

"He says nothing. Don't think I complain of his silence; he doubtless has good reasons for it."

[27] Boteler, in 40 S. H. S. P., 180–81. Some caution must be exercised in accepting the full letter of Boteler's summary of the argument Jackson presented, for the reason that Boteler, while earnestly seeking to be accurate, readily might have confused, in retrospect, what Jackson said in July, 1862, with what came to light subsequently.

"Then," asked Boteler—more to draw out Jackson than to express his own opinion—"you don't think that General Lee is slow
in making up his mind?"

"Slow? By no means, Colonel! On the contrary, his perception
is as quick and unerring as his judgment is infallible. But with
the vast responsibilities resting on him, he is perfectly right in
withholding a hasty expresson of his opinions and purposes."

Broad as was this statement, it did not quite satisfy Jackson.
He paused, pondered, and reiterated: "So great is my confidence
in General Lee that I am willing to follow him blindfolded. But
I fear he is unable to give me a definite answer now because of
influences at Richmond, where, perhaps, the matter has been
mentioned by him and may be under consideration. I therefore
want you to see the President and urge the importance of prompt
action." [28]

The Congressman went to the President and repeated Jackson's
argument. Davis was no more prepared than was Lee to say that
the Confederacy could muster immediately in Northern Virginia
a sufficient force to assume the offensive. That might come later.
At the moment, the task was to halt Pope. If he was to be defeated, it must be by heavy detachments from the Richmond
front. What part of Lee's forces could perform that mission so
readily as the Army of the Valley? Ewell knew intimately the
ground of Pope's advance; Jackson had some acquaintance with
that terrain. The two officers were accustomed to joint operations
in which they admirably had exemplified the doctrine of economy
of force. Jackson could not be allowed sufficient troops for the
early invasion of the North, but he could be given again the semi-
independent status in which he had shone. His aptitude fitted
the strategical necessities.

Orders were issued on July 13 for entraining Jackson's and
Ewell's Divisions, less Taylor's Brigade.[29] Six days later, Jackson
reached Gordonsville [30] and saw again the Blue Ridge. Who may
say with what emotions he viewed the mountains that screened
the theatre of his independent campaign? Was he glad for other
reasons than those of health to be away from a "malarious region"? Had he learned while in front of Richmond to co-operate

28 Boteler, *loc. cit.*
29 *O. R.,* 12, pt. 3, p. 915.   30 *O. R.,* 12, pt. 2, p. 191.

willingly, or had he chafed? Not one line did he write, not a word did he speak that disclosed his mind. Curious posterity will never know whether, in his heart of hearts, a battle was raging between ambition for independent command and a purpose to discipline his own spirit for labor with Lee and Lee's other lieutenants in the achievement of Southern independence.

With one of the division commanders of Lee's Army Jackson again became associated before the end of July. The circumstances that led to this connection were as curious as its results were to prove. A. P. Hill's impetuosity in crossing the Chickahominy and in opening the Battle of Mechanicsville had been forgotten overnight in admiration of his boldness and persistence at Gaines' Mill. In fact, when Lee came to write his report of the engagement of June 27, he employed in praise the very word that might have been used to condemn Hill on the 26th. Hill and his Division, said Lee, "met this large [Federal] force with the impetuous courage for which that officer and his troops are distinguished." [31] Impetuous Hill had been in assailing the Federals behind Boatswain's Swamp, but stubbornly determined he had shown himself to be, and capable of directing men on a long, confused front. At Frayser's Farm, Hill had handled his troops easily and with indisputable effectiveness. All his marches had been prompt and orderly. He could not be credited with forcing a decision, but he had shown clear competence.

That and more could be said of Longstreet. Among the division commanders of Lee's Army, "Old Pete"—as his men had begun to call him—now stood pre-eminent. His attack on the right at Gaines' Mill had been shrewd and not unduly expensive of life. In the woods West of Frayser's Farm, while Lee had been reconnoitering on the River road, Longstreet had directed his own and A. P. Hill's Division with sure confidence and entire calm. The next day, though his own troops were in reserve, he had been useful to Lee in many ways. Although no direct evidence can be cited in proof, there can be little doubt that, when the campaign ended, Lee was leaning more heavily on Longstreet than on any other of his subordinates. All Longstreet's actions had been well-reasoned and free, apparently, of any grasping after authority. Not a suggestion was there of the spirit he had shown

[31] O. R., 11, pt. 2, p. 492.

at Seven Pines. Had he been conscious that he should redeem a record which he knew to be less creditable than the official reports of the action of May 31 would indicate? His new effort—had it been aroused by a new commander? Was he, like Lee, learning the art of war? Or had he determined that in a campaign where divisional leadership was shared by the hero of the Valley, he would not be outdone? History cannot answer.

The fine record of co-operation between the Divisions of A. P. Hill and Longstreet was marred almost as soon as it was made. Among Hill's volunteer aides during the first days of the campaign had been John M. Daniel, editor of the *Richmond Examiner*. This strange, ambitious man of 36, half genius, half misanthrope, had served as United States Minister to the Court of Sardinia but had hurried back to Richmond after the secession of South Carolina and had resumed the direction of his paper. His slashing, dogmatic editorial style was coupled with a sense of news that made his journal much the most interesting of Richmond war-time papers. Although Daniel had as his goal the acquisition of a fortune that would permit him to exemplify his ideals of the life of a country gentleman, he pictured himself also as an editorial Warwick, to make and unmake Presidents and Cabinet-members. Not content with that, he sought like Warwick the honors of a St. Albans or a Towton, though he shunned a Barnet. The rough realities of war, which disgusted him, he softened when he took the field. Two servants attended him. His equipment and uniform outshone those of Magruder or of Trimble.[32] At Gaines' Mill, Daniel had received in the arm the wound he sought, a trifling wound, to be sure, but one that served both to attest his valor and to give him a sense of disability for further duty as a soldier.[33]

He retired forthwith to Richmond and, through the columns of *The Examiner,* glorified the General under whom he had served. A. P. Hill was credited with the "investment of Mechanicsville" and with throwing his 12,000 men against four times as many entrenched Federals.[34] The Battle of Frayser's Farm, the same paper proclaimed, was fought under "the immediate and sole

---

[32] *Dabney Memo;* G. W. Bagby, *John M. Daniel's Latch-Key.*
[33] *Cf.* John D. Wade, in 5 *D. A. B.,* 68.
[34] *Richmond Examiner.* June 28, 1862, p. 1. col. 1.

command" of Hill. According to Daniel, of Hill's 14,000 gallant men—the number being raised slightly—not more than 6000 effectives remained.[35] In a subsequent editorial review, Daniel affirmed that Hill's command, consisting of his own and "one of Longstreet's two divisions" had achieved on June 30 a "success which broke the spirit of the enemy and completed the circuit of our victories." [36]

As *The Examiner* was read in all the camps, the laudation of A. P. Hill, with implied disparagement of others, stirred many jealousies and aroused no little wrath. Longstreet, in particular, was incensed. The day after the appearance of Daniel's summation of Hill's achievements, Longstreet wrote the editor a brief, stiff note, in which he stated that the articles in *The Examiner* were calculated to alarm the public. There was, Longstreet went on, no objection to notoriety for Hill, provided no injustice was done others; but the statement by Daniel that Hill had command of the field at Frayser's Farm for a short time suggested indirectly that other officers improperly were absent. The fact was, said Longstreet, that General Lee and he rode upon the field together, some hours before A. P. Hill, and that both remained there through the day and night. Longstreet was absent from his "usual position" for perhaps an hour, while he was putting Gregg's Brigade of Hill's Division into action. As for the statement that Hill alone had lost 8000 men, that figure, Longstreet maintained, would cover the casualties of the entire Army, except for trifling wounds. Exaggerated statements, he concluded, might do great injury to the Army both at home and abroad.

Longstreet did not overlook the fact that A. P. Hill was not associated directly with the adulation voiced by *The Examiner*. Consequently, "Old Pete" did not propose to publish this answer over his own signature. Hill's volunteer aide had exalted the divisional commander; one of Longstreet's military family should sponsor the reply. Maj. Moxley Sorrel was summoned to the General's tent. Would he, the Assistant Adjutant General of the Division, attach his name to the letter? With the request, Longstreet coupled assurance that he would support Sorrel in any controversy that might arise from criticism of a superior officer.

[35] *Ibid.*, July 2, 1862, p. 1, col. 1.   [36] *Ibid.*, July 8, 1862, p. 1, cols. 2-3.

The Major already was in a fighting mood because of the articles in Daniel's paper, and he was entirely agreeable to Longstreet's proposal.

Two days later, in the rival *Richmond Whig*, the "card" appeared.[37] It created much satisfaction among those who had resented the manner in which one Division had been credited with winning the campaign, but the publication aroused wrath at Hill's headquarters. Formally, the next day Hill wrote Lee: "I have the honor to request that I may be relieved from the command of Major-General Longstreet." When this reached Longstreet's office, for transmission through channels, "Old Pete" endorsed the paper with deliberate unconcern: "Respectfully forwarded. If it is convenient to exchange the troops, or to exchange the commanders, I see no particular reason why Maj. Gen. A. P. Hill should not be gratified."[38] Of this, at the moment, Lee took no notice.

The next time Major Sorrel had occasion to call for a routine report from Hill, the note was returned with the terse endorsement: "Maj. Gen. Hill declines to hold further communication with Major Sorrel."

"Write him again," Longstreet said, when Sorrel showed him this endorsement, "and say that note was written by my command, and must be answered satisfactorily."

Sorrel so wrote. Again Hill sent back the letter. Longstreet thereupon took up the correspondence. Hill refused to budge. After another exchange or two, Longstreet sent for Sorrel once more. "Major," he ordered stiffly, "you will be good enough to put on your sword and sash, mount, and place Major General Hill in arrest with orders to confine himself to limits of his camp and vicinity."

When Sorrel, full-panoplied, arrived at Hill's headquarters, the General was seated in his tent. He arose, coldly returned Sorrel's salute, listened in silence to the order, saluted again and let the Major depart without a word.[39] The command of Hill's Division passed temporarily to his senior Brigadier General, Jos. R. Anderson.[40]

[37] *Richmond Whig*, July 11, 1862, p. 1, col. 3; *Sorrel*, 88.
[38] *O. R.*, 11, pt. 3, pp. 639–40.   [39] *Sorrel*, 89.
[40] *O. R.*, 51, pt. 2, p. 590. The date of the instructions to Anderson to assume command, July 13, was that of orders for Jackson to entrain and almost certainly was that of Hill's arrest

A furious correspondence between A. P. Hill and Longstreet followed. One of its points of contention was whether Longstreet had left his "usual position" to discharge what should have been Hill's own task—that of putting Gregg's Brigade into line.[41] No adjustment could be reached. Friends were called in. All the indications pointed to a duel, though arrangements were made with so much secrecy that even Sorrel did not know what was afoot.[42]

Could the perplexities of the reorganization of the Army of Northern Virginia after the Seven Days have been illustrated more dramatically than by the threat of this duel? Huger had proved "too slow"; Magruder was to leave Virginia with the assurance that, when opportunity offered, he would deal with his critics; Jackson, in the eyes of many, had not fulfilled expectations; Whiting's conduct had raised a question; D. H. Hill was overcritical, though competent, and had been sent a challenge by Toombs. Of the division commanders only Ewell, A. P. Hill and Longstreet had come through the campaign with a record for meeting creditably, and without quarrel or cavil, all the opportunities that had come to them; and now two of these three might seek to kill each other!

Until the quarrel between Longstreet and Hill reached this dangerous pass, Lee had continued to ignore Hill's application to be relieved from Longstreet's direction. Lee himself had never ordered the arrest of an officer, but he respected the traditional army reasoning that, when a General was responsible for another, the power of arrest should not be denied. Precisely what happened when Lee learned that a duel was imminent, the records do not show explicitly. Sorrel, who admitted his lack of first-hand information, wrote long afterward: "General Lee heard of the [impending duel] . . . and acted quickly and effectively, using his unvarying tact and great influence. He brought matters, through other friends, to an adjustment honorable to both." [43]

41 Cf. O. R., 51, pt. 2, p. 590.
42 Sorrel stated, op. cit., 89, that D. H. Hill and Toombs acted for Longstreet. The relations of these two men with Longstreet would have made his choice of them logical, but they scarcely could have consulted together in Longstreet's interest until their own differences had been settled. That had not been done by July 15 (Stovall, op. cit., 257–58). Besides, Hill scarcely could have consented to act as Longstreet's second in a duel while himself refusing to be a principal.
43 Sorrel, 89.

The "adjustment," in all probability, was effected by Lee on the plea, among others, of urgent military necessity. Jackson, at Gordonsville, already had found himself too weak to attack Pope, whom Lee thought too strong to be left within striking distance of the Virginia Central Railroad.[44] At least another Division had to be sent Jackson from the Richmond front, and it must be under a competent leader. Lee may have reasoned that, if A. P. Hill were selected for this mission, Hill would be satisfied to drop his demand for a duel and Longstreet to release Hill from arrest. In a letter to Jackson, Lee explained somewhat elaborately that he wished to send him Hill's Division, but that Hill was in arrest and the senior Brigadier of A. P. Hill's Division was not of sufficient experience to be entrusted with the entire command.[45] Somewhat the same thing may have been said both to Longstreet and to Hill. Be the details as they may, Hill was returned to duty by July 26,[46] and the next day was ordered to move his Division by rail to reinforce Jackson.[47]

With the Division, a Louisiana Brigade went back to Jackson, but it was not in its entirety the famous force that Taylor brilliantly had led in the Valley campaign, nor was Taylor with it. His illness had proved serious and had produced temporary paralysis of his lower limbs. From his Brigade, the Ninth Louisiana, Stafford's Regiment was now removed. To the Brigade were added the Fifth Louisiana from Paul Semmes and the Fourteenth Louisiana from Roger A. Pryor. The remnants of Wheat's Battalion remained temporarily with the Brigade, though early disbandment was contemplated.[48] To command this Brigade, Col. Harry T. Hays of the Seventh was promoted Brigadier General. He was a good soldier, distinguished alike for courage and for promptness, but at the outset he could not hope for the estimation

[44] *Lee's Dispatches,* 39.
[45] *Lee's Dispatches,* 39.
[46] In *O. R.,* 51, pt. 2, p. 598, he is addressed by Longstreet's A.A.G. on July 26 as "commanding Light Division." Lee spoke of Hill on the 25th as still in arrest, *O. R.,* 12, pt. 3, p. 917. Release, therefore, was late on the 25th or on the 26th.
[47] *O. R.,* 12, pt. 3, p. 919.
[48] *O. R.,* 11, pt. 3, pp. 655, 656; *ibid.,* 51, pt. 2, p. 597; *Lee's Dispatches,* 35. As reconstituted, the Brigade consisted of the Fifth, Sixth, Seventh, Eighth and Fourteenth Louisiana Regiments and the First Special Louisiana Battalion. The Ninth Louisiana was united with the First (Wright's Brigade), the Second, the Tenth, the Fifteenth (formerly the Third Louisiana Battalion of J. R. Anderson's Brigade) and Coppen's Zouave Chasseurs (Pryor's Brigade) to form a Brigade. This originally was intended to be part of McLaws's Division, but later was Starke's Brigade of Jackson's Division.

his predecessor enjoyed. Taylor was sent home to rest and to recruit his old regiments, and was given the well-won rank of Major General. This was done, Taylor always thought, on Jackson's recommendation and as a reward for service in the Valley.[49] The Army was the poorer for Taylor's departure.

[49] *R. Taylor*, 93. His appointment was dated July 28, 1862; *Wright*, 28.

CHAPTER XLIII

A New Organization for New Battles

By the date of Powell Hill's departure, the first major reorganization of the Army of Northern Virginia had been completed. It had been necessitated by the failure of some of the leaders and, no less, by the defects of the old organization. Among a multitude of lessons in command taught by the Seven Days, the most impressive of all was this: under a system that placed the direction of operations largely in the hands of division commanders too numerous to be controlled directly by the General in Chief, the Divisions were, in effect, distinct little armies. In a wooded country of confusing, bad roads, the Major General of a column operating even a few miles from army headquarters virtually was independent. If reckless, he could not be restrained; if he was determined to preserve his command and to take no risks, he could not be brought to action. Every battle had demonstrated this. In the operations from the beginning of Jackson's march on June 25 to Harvey Hill's assault in the twilight of Malvern Hill, there had been one instance where two Divisions had cooperated for the whole of a battle. That had been by Longstreet and Powell Hill on June 30 at Frayser's Farm. Elsewhere, how tragic had been the record, how complete the indictment of the organization! At Mechanicsville, Powell Hill had acted as if he had been afraid the other Divisions might snatch glory from his hands. The next day at Gaines' Mill, he had plunged in eagerly and had exhausted his Division on the right before any help was at hand; Harvey Hill had outmarched Jackson that day as if determined to seize the honors of battle from his senior. Savage Station, the futile marches and long halts of June 30, the failure of Lee to get the full force of any Division employed against Malvern Hill while any other Division was attacking with all its Brigades—had war ever offered worse examples of dissipated strength, of might ill-used?

Along with the leaders, the law was to blame. The Confederate military acts provided no formal organization larger than a Division. Legally, there was no such military body as a Corps, no grade between that of Major General and that of General. The first of these facts had been pointed out rather sharply to Beauregard by Secretary Benjamin.[1] Subsequently, for convenience, Johnston had permitted Gustavus Smith to administer what was, in effect, a Corps; but even when Smith was anxious to exalt the importance of the post he had held, he had to admit that the Corps was "informal." [2]

Now, after the disappointments and lapses of the Seven Days, a means had to be found of co-ordinating the independent Divisions. The Confederacy could not hope to win if it had six armies, six independent commanders on one field. No lawful device could prevent and correct this so readily as the one Johnston had employed. Scarcely a reference appears in extant correspondence to any decision to establish Corps; but, by the time A. P. Hill reinforced Jackson at Gordonsville, the remainder of the infantry had been placed under the general direction of Longstreet. Few written orders were issued, no new titles were conferred. Neither "Corps" nor "Wing" was mentioned. The infantry around Richmond simply became "Longstreet's Command," and the troops near the Rapidan "Jackson's Command." Necessity forced Lee to anticipate the amendment of the law. That this was being done, Jackson may not have realized. If he did, he preferred to consider, for reasons of sentiment or of ambition, that when he left Lee he resumed command of the Army of the Valley.

The organization now was as follows:

JACKSON'S COMMAND

Jackson's Division was under the immediate command of Charles S. Winder, of the First Brigade, who, next to Jackson, was the senior general officer. John R. Jones had the Second Brigade;[3] William B. Taliaferro was back in command of his (the Third) Brigade; A. R. Lawton and his large force of Georgians, who had won fame at Gaines' Mill, constituted the Fourth Brigade.

Ewell's Division had substantially the same organization as in

---

[1] See *supra*, pp. 109, 118.   [2] See *G. W. Smith*, 311.
[3] See *supra*, p. 588.

the Valley campaign, but Jubal Early had Elzey's Brigade, and Harry Hays the reconstructed Louisiana Brigade. Trimble continued at the head of his troops.

A. P. Hill's Division was unchanged in organization or command, except that Jos. R. Anderson had resigned in order to resume direction of the important Tredegar Iron Works in Richmond. No successor to him had been named, but the Brigade was safe in the hands of the senior Colonel, E. L. Thomas of the Thirty-fifth Georgia.[4]

LONGSTREET'S COMMAND

Longstreet's Division remained intact otherwise than for the transfer of R. H. Anderson's Brigade to Micah Jenkins, who was promoted Brigadier General. His name had been presented by Lee to President Davis with the statement that Jenkins had "been repeatedly recommended for promotion by officers with whom he served, and his conduct at Seven Pines was worthy of all commendation." Lee added: "He has also in the recent battles, shown great skill." [5]

D. R. Jones's Division of two Brigades, including that of the tempestuous Toombs,[6] retained its organization but passed from the disbanded general command of Magruder to that of Longstreet.

McLaws's Division of Semmes's and Kershaw's Brigades was enlarged to regulation size by the inclusion of Howell Cobb's and Paul Semmes's commands, which two previously had been Magruder's own Division.[7] McLaws had not displayed brilliance in any of the actions of the Seven Days, but he had shown himself sturdy and dependable.

D. H. Hill's Division was increased by the addition of a Brigade that now was assigned Henry A. Wise.[8] To this Division, it will

---

[4] The Cavalry of Jackson's command is described in Vol. II.

[5] *Lee's Dispatches,* 33. It had been the hope of Lee that Jenkins's commission would date from the action at Seven Pines, but it was issued as of July 22. *Wright,* 86.

[6] The other was G. T. Anderson's.

[7] Strictly speaking, from the numbering of the Brigades in *O. R.,* 11, pt. 2, pp 485–86, McLaws's command of two Brigades, the First and the Fourth, and Magruder's of two, the Second and Third, might have been regarded all the while as one Division, but the combat organization had been as here set forth.

[8] Fourth Virginia Heavy Artillery, later the Thirty-fourth Virginia, the Twenty-sixth, Forty-sixth and Fifty-ninth Virginia, with which temporarily was included the Twentieth Virginia.

be remembered, no commander had been appointed in succession to Harvey Hill because of uncertainty over the status of the Major Generals.[9]

R. H. Anderson's Division was Huger's old command—Mahone's, Armistead's and Wright's Brigades. Anderson was given this Division on Lee's and doubtless on Longstreet's recommendation as a reward for consistent soldierly service in every engagement from Williamsburg to Frayser's Farm. So manifestly was the promotion deserved that it created little comment.[10]

WHITING'S DIVISION

Whiting's Division, for reasons not disclosed by the records, was kept under the direct control of Lee and was not a part of Longstreet's command.[11]

THE CAVALRY

The Cavalry now constituted a Division of two Brigades, or seven regiments and four battalions [12] under Maj. Gen. J. E. B. Stuart. One of these Brigades was under Wade Hampton, the other was commanded by Fitz Lee.

THE ARTILLERY

Artillery organization was not improved. As stated already,[13] each Brigade had a battery assigned to it substantially as its own. This battery might assist another of the same Division or, at least in theory, another Division commanded by the same general officer. In actual test, during the Seven Days, Jackson had been the only commander who had been able to mass the guns of more than one Division.

To summarize the reorganization, it involved two promotions only to the grade of Major General, those, namely, of "Jeb"

[9] *O. R.,* 12, pt. 3, p. 897; see *supra,* p. 621.

[10] *Lee's Dispatches,* 33; *Wright,* 28. The commission bore date of July 14, 1862.

[11] *O. R.,* 12, pt. 3, p. 915. Efforts were being made at this time to detach two Mississippi Regiments from Whiting's own Brigade, under the acting command of Col. E. M. Law. Against this transfer Lee protested, July 25, on the ground that it would "break up a veteran brigade, distinguished for good service from the beginning of the war in Virginia, and [would] leave General Whiting . . . without a brigade" (*O. R.* 11, pt. 3, p. 654).

[12] Three of these battalions were styled Legions.

[13] See *supra,* p. 156, n. 1.

Stuart and of "Dick" Anderson. As Brigadiers, Fitz Lee, Micah Jenkins and Harry Hays were commissioned. To the infantry returned "Jube" Early as a Brigadier under Ewell; to the cavalry went Hampton—historic assignments both. These promotions and transfers and the selection, far more important, of Longstreet and of Jackson to direct all the infantry, were quiet but rapid moves. So tactfully were the changes made and with such manifest regard for merit that few realized how far the Army had been revolutionized.

The list already has been given [14] of the "Manassas men" who had disappeared from the Army by the first anniversary, June 1, 1862, of Beauregard's arrival on Bull Run. A long list it was. Dead were Bartow, Bee and Cocke; wounded, transferred or resigned were Johnston, Beauregard, Kirby Smith, Bonham and "Shanks" Evans. In Western Virginia, Robert Selden Garnett had fallen. At McDowell, "Allegheny" Johnson had been wounded. To this list, during the period between the fight at Front Royal and the completion of the new organization, Richard Griffith and Turner Ashby had been added. Arnold Elzey had been wounded again and grievously. "Maryland" Steuart had a broken bone that would not knit. Johnston had begun to recover, but he certainly would not replace Lee. Wherever Johnston's abilities might be utilized, it would not be in the Army of Northern Virginia. That was assured. Besides the commanding General, the Army had lost the long-esteemed Gustavus Smith, whose nervous condition still was puzzling. Magruder, Huger, and D. H. Hill had been transferred. These five, with Longstreet and Whiting, ere the arrival of Jackson, had been the most conspicuous figures in the Army that had faced McClellan between White Oak Swamp and the Chickahominy. Now, of the seven, three remained!

The explanation of all this was in the one grim word, combat. In particular, those forty days of bloody action from Front Royal to Malvern Hill had shattered the command. Many had fallen, but more had failed. The battle deaths the South had expected, the failures it had not. In 1861, as in the first period of every war, appearance had shaped appraisal. A confident people had accepted promise before performance. Then, under test of fire, high reputations quickly had been destroyed, pretense had been shattered,

14 See *supra*, p. 261.

nerves that had seemed strong had been as wax, excitement had cost some men their self-mastery and others it had bewildered. That same fire of battle, burning to the soul of man, had shown valor beneath a cover of uncouthness, heroic composure under a commonplace mien, steel where the surface seemed soft, ability as dazzling as unsuspected.

All the capacities of the new Army would be required now. "Fire-eating" politicians and editors were beginning to doubt the "recognition" of the Confederacy by England and France and the intervention of those powers against the North. The bloody way of battle, whether it led across the Potomac or back again to the James, was lengthening, though it was promising. Past belief was the transformation in the Southern cause since the dreadful days of February. Bragg was at Tupelo in Mississippi, farther South than was welcome, but he was planning an offensive. Halleck's Federal army, though powerful, was scattered. Down to Vicksburg, incredibly, the ram *Arkansas* had made its struggling voyage and had cheered a valiant garrison. Kirby Smith in East Tennessee and T. C. Hindman in Arkansas were doing admirably with small resources. All was well, but . . . but . . . John Pope was threatening to advance down the Orange and Alexandria Railroad against Jackson. At Harrison's Landing, McClellan's Army still outnumbered Lee's. A force of unknown destination was being mustered at Fort Monroe. Could the reorganized Army of Northern Virginia cope with all these troops? Was it well led now, or had it merely been fortunate in the operations against McClellan? After a year, how much more capable, if any, would Lee show himself than Johnston? That strange man Jackson, was he a mad genius, unable, unwilling to co-operate, or would he prove himself the right arm, perhaps the successor of the new commanding General? Longstreet the impassive, was he qualified, or was he another Huger, imperturbable, to be sure, but wellnigh immovable? Would the new leaders, like the old, find battle a traitor to reputation, a betrayer of the fame it brought?

APPENDIX I

The Military Geography of Virginia

Prior to the mad spring of 1861, whenever Virginians had occasion to mention the geography of their State, it had been to boast of wide streams, to extol blue mountains or to praise valleys of abundance. Overnight, geography had a new meaning. The Potomac and the Ohio had become frontier rivers: were they defensible? The insistent mountains: would they bar an enemy? That "Pan-handle" which extended on the western flank of Pennsylvania as far North as the latitude of New York City, that western border of Virginia which lay beyond the longitude of Detroit, could these be protected? Virginia's area of 67,230 square miles made her the largest State of the South, except for Texas and for Missouri: would her population of 1,596,000, only 1,047,000 of them white, supply man power proportionate to the military needs of wide borders?

A large part of Virginia was flanked by deep water which was accessible to the Federals. That was the first major fact in the military geography of the Commonwealth. The Ohio was navigable for steamboats upward from the northern end of the Virginia-Kentucky border all the way to Wheeling and beyond. At its nearest point, the Ohio was a bare eighty miles from the Potomac. Two hundred and eighty-five miles downstream, as the dividing Potomac wound its way, was Washington. Below the Federal capital, the Potomac was navigable for transports and for all warships except the largest. From the mouth of the river, southward to the district around Norfolk, the Chesapeake Bay washed Virginia. Two counties, not so richly fruitful as they are today, lay between the Bay and the ocean. In short, the waterways that had been the routes of easy settlement in the era prior to the locomotive suddenly had become highways for an enemy.

Into these frontier waters of Virginia flowed the numerous navigable streams that were the second natural characteristic of the military geography of the State. In Western Virginia, which then was a domain of few decent roads, the Kanawha was open upstream to light craft from Point Pleasant, past Charleston, to Loop Creek Shoals. Along the northern boundary of the State no rivers that emptied into the Potomac would carry vessels. On the eastern watershed, the Rappahannock admitted steamships as far as Fredericksburg, the York was passable to

West Point, and the Pamunkey, one of the two streams that formed the York, could be ascended from West Point past the White House,[1] famous as the home of the Widow Custis when George Washington was her suitor. James River and its affluent, the Appomattox, brought tide and trade inland for 100 miles to the fall line at Richmond and at Petersburg. No State of the Atlantic seaboard, indeed no State of the entire Union, could be rendered so vulnerable in case its rivers should prove indefensible.

The mountains that sent half the rainfall of Virginia into the Ohio and half into the Chesapeake constituted the third natural characteristic of the military geography of the State. This long range, part of the Appalachian system, ran from the upper waters of the Potomac to Cumberland Gap in the far Southwest, a distance of about 390 miles, roughly on an axis NE. by N.-SW. by S. The elevation varied greatly. For miles the crest of the main ridge, the Allegheny Mountains, was not more than 2500 feet above sea level. At its highest point it mounted almost to 4500 feet. So stout a barrier had a profound effect on the early settlement of the country West of it. The Valley of the Kanawha had tempted pioneers to cross the mountains from the older sections of Virginia, but the Shenandoah and the Ohio had afforded easier access to other parts of Western Virginia. More of the immigration had been from the North than from the East, by those who had few slaves, not by those who had many. This was a condition that had shaped political sympathies and might have a ponderable influence on military operations.

The most unusual aspect of the great mountain range in Virginia is presented on its eastern face. There, by easy steps, Midland Virginia climbs to picturesque Piedmont, literally the "foot of the mountains." From Piedmont westward rises the Blue Ridge, which has an average elevation of approximately 2500 feet. It is a ridge as rambling as it is blue, with coves and spurs and long, buttressing shoulders. Instead of blending itself into the higher Alleghenies, the western side of the Blue Ridge dips down into the Valley of the Shenandoah River. This stream, rising eighteen miles South of Staunton, flows northward through a limestone country and empties at Harpers Ferry into the Potomac. The average width of the Valley is about forty miles.[2] In military value, offensive and defensive, it was as remarkable in 1861 as agriculturally it was opulent.[3]

[1] For J. Ambler Johnston's statement on the navigation of the Pamunkey, see *supra* p. 206, n. 14.
[2] M. F. Maury, in his *Physical Survey of Virginia, Preliminary Report No. 2*, pp 97–98, gave the maximum width as *c.* 60 miles and the minimum as 30–35.
[3] See *infra*, p. 691.

Land in the Shenandoah was too valuable to be left in timber, though the mountains were heavily wooded. East of the Blue Ridge, it was the singular characteristic of Virginia, from the standpoint of military geography, to offer more cover as one went back, so to say, from the newer settlements to the older. Exhausted land had been abandoned and had been returned to Nature. "From the Potomac to the James River, and from the Blue Ridge to the Chesapeake," in the words of a topographical engineer, spread "a region whose characteristic [was] a dense forest of oak or pine, with occasional clearings, rarely extensive enough to prevent the rifleman concealed in one border from shooting across to the other side; a forest which, with but few exceptions, required the axemen to precede the artillery. . . ." [4] The timber ranged in diversity from virgin pine and hardwood to thickets of worthless, coniferous second-growth and gnarled scrub oak. In Piedmont and in the Shenandoah Valley, the undergrowth was scant and rarely would obstruct troops, but nearer the Chesapeake it grew thick and thicker until it became almost impenetrable. Often in midsummer a man might be lost in these woods and would be unable to see 100 yards in any direction. This prevalence of cover, which was the fifth natural major characteristic of the military terrain of Virginia, made it ideal for unobservable concentration, for surprise, for fighting at close quarters and for swift, secret flank marches. Only when telltale dust clouds rose from dragging feet or from pounding hoofs could troop movements be discovered.

Man's work, his sympathies and his neglect added conditions that modified or emphasized the natural characteristics of Virginia as a battleground. Immeasurably the most important of these conditions developed almost in the hour of secession and before a startled people realized what it meant. Ten ships of war had been at the Norfolk or Gosport Navy Yard, ten prizes so much to be desired that Norfolk volunteers sank hulks in Elizabeth River and then prepared to storm the yard.

Before they could do so, the commander of the gunboat *Pawnee* forced his way upstream through the obstructions, landed a detachment at Gosport, set fire to buildings, scuttled or burned most of the vessels, and successfully towed into Hampton Roads the powerful *Cumberland*. When the Virginians at length entered Gosport, they found an immense store of naval guns, but no warships above the water. The best they could hope to accomplish would be to raise the frigate *Merrimac* and perhaps one or two other vessels.[5] So well

[4] *O. R.*, 25, pt. 1, p. 193.
[5] 1 *R. E Lee*, 473–74.

equipped was the yard and so little damaged by the fire that it could be repaired speedily and used for ship construction.

Experienced naval designers and engineers would be available. They could be relied upon to do their utmost, but they could not be expected soon to offset the immense advantage the Union navy enjoyed. Few passenger vessels or freighters in other "territorial waters" were captured by the Virginians. It became apparent that sea power, at least for a time, would be in Northern hands. Unless the State were able promptly to establish land batteries which the enemy could not pass or take in reverse, the navigable streams of Virginia would be open to the enemy, for landings, for raids, for inland bases and for easy lines of supply.

The railroads of Virginia, the second artificial factor in the military geography of the State, manifestly would have a definite if untested offensive and defensive value. Successively, they had been under construction after 1831 and they had been extended, with large State subscription, into most parts of Virginia where raw materials were produced in bulk or new markets were anticipated. By the spring of 1861, the railroads of the Commonwealth were as follows:

	Mileage in Virginia
Alexandria, Loudoun and Hampshire (Alexandria to Clarke's Gap)	37.50
Baltimore and Ohio (Harpers Ferry to Wheeling, via Grafton)	188
Manassas Gap (Manassas Junction to Mt. Jackson)	77.77
Norfolk and Petersburg	80
Northwestern Virginia (Grafton to Parkersburg)	103.50
Orange and Alexandria (Alexandria to Lynchburg, via Gordonsville and Charlottesville)[6]	143
Petersburg and Roanoke (Petersburg to North Carolina line, thence to Weldon, N. C., and by branch from Hicksford to North Carolina line and thence to Gaston, N. C.)	65
Richmond, Fredericksburg and Potomac (Richmond, via Fredericksburg to Aquia Creek, an estuary of the Potomac River)	75
Richmond and Petersburg	22.14
Richmond and Danville (which crossed the South Side at Burkeville)	140.50

[6] This railroad used between Gordonsville and Charlottesville the tracks of the Virginia Central, which are not included in this mileage of 143.

Richmond and York River (Richmond eastward to West
Point) 38.30
Roanoke Valley (Clarksville to North Carolina line, thence
to Junction, N. C.) 8
Seaboard and Roanoke (Portsmouth to North Carolina line,
thence to Weldon, N. C.).............................. 59
South Side (City Point, on James River, via Petersburg, to
Lynchburg) 132
Virginia Central (Richmond via Hanover Junction, Louisa,
Gordonsville, Charlottesville and Staunton to Jackson's
River near Covington) 195.39
Virginia and Tennessee (Lynchburg to Bristol)............ 204.24
Winchester and Potomac (Harpers Ferry to Winchester).... 32

_____

1601.34 [7]

For strategic use, this mileage of 1601 was unevenly divided. The Tidewater district,[8] apart from the areas around the cities, had few railways and still relied upon water transportation. From the fall line at the head of Tidewater, westward to the crest of the Allegheny Mountains, railroads were numerous and not far apart. In this entire area, there were only five small districts in as many counties that were more than three days' march from a railroad.[9]

Beyond this well-served section, within the confines of what is now the State of West Virginia, the Baltimore and Ohio ran from Harpers Ferry to Grafton and thence northward to Wheeling. From Grafton West to Parkersburg was the track of the Northwestern Virginia Railroad, a branch of the B. & O. If this, the sole railroad of this great area, together with the navigable waters, could be retained in the hands of the secessionists, then Western Virginia was safe. Should the B. & O. Railroad and the Ohio and Kanawha Rivers be lost, then nearly the whole of Western Virginia would be isolated. Only a few of the counties that fringed the Allegheny Mountains [10] were within easy

[7] See statements by these railroads in the *Report of the Board of Public Works* of Virginia, 1859–60.
[8] Tidewater, for convenient reference, may be defined as that section of Virginia East of the Richmond, Fredericksburg and Potomac Railroad, thence southward via the Richmond and Petersburg and the Petersburg and Roanoke railroads; in short, the region East of the present Richmond-Washington and A. C. L. systems.
[9] Pendleton, Buchanan, Wise, Lee, and Patrick counties.
[10] Mercer, Monroe, Greenbrier, Pocahontas, Pendleton, Hardy, and Hampshire.

distance of any railroad which a force defending Midland Virginia might hope to command.

Besides this concentration in the area West of Tidewater and East of the Alleghenies, the railroads of Virginia presented another condition that was certain to have strategic importance. This was the lack of easy connection with the railroads of other States. Travelling northward from Richmond, one could go by R. F. & P. to Aquia Creek, above Fredericksburg; but to proceed farther with speed, one had to leave the railroad at Aquia Creek and take steamer to Washington. The alternative was a roundabout rail journey via the Virginia Central from Richmond to Gordonsville, thence to Alexandria by way of the Orange and Alexandria and, from the last-named town, by steamer to the capital.

Thin, also, was the iron thread that bound Virginia to the Southern States. From the lower terminus of the Richmond-Petersburg Railroad, the next link was the Petersburg and Roanoke. At Weldon, N. C., that road met the Wilmington and Weldon, by which it was joined to South Carolina and to Georgia. Together, these railways formed the only line along the coastal plain. There was no other contact by Virginia railroads with those of the South except via Bristol, which was almost 270 miles West of the Petersburg and Roanoke. To reach Bristol, one had to travel from Richmond about 300 miles by a trio of railroads. The last of these, the Virginia and Tennessee Railroad, crossed the State line at Bristol and ran to Knoxville, where it met the Tennessee and Georgia. If the Petersburg and Roanoke were destroyed, troops and supplies dispatched to Virginia from the South by rail must be routed via Bristol, thence by Lynchburg and on to the defensive area of Richmond. Tenuous, surely, was the line on which the life of the new Southern republic might hang!

Still another feature of the Virginia railroads that might have an influence on military operations was the absence of any continuous line down the Shenandoah Valley. From the East, the Virginia Central penetrated that region and, passing Staunton, turned southwestward to the Alleghenies. By way of the pass at Thoroughfare, the Manassas Gap Railroad led into the Valley at Strasburg and thence southward to Mount Jackson. Still a third railway ran from Harpers Ferry to Winchester. The B. & O. crossed the lower Valley via Martinsburg. All these lines strategically were useful, but, even in the worst emergency, they could do little to expedite the movement of troops from Staunton to Harpers Ferry. For that grim business, reliance had to be placed on the legs of youth. If war were waged North of Harpers

Ferry, and the Valley were used as a line of supply, then wagon trains must groan over more than 110 miles of highway.

Would the rails of the Virginia roads stand the strain of war; would the equipment suffice? The much-abused Board of Public Works of Virginia answered many questions in the statistical tables of its annual reports, but it never had interpreted the carrying power and endurance of Virginia railways in these terms. Broadly speaking, the rails were standard for the period—50 to 60 lbs. per yard. The principal exception of any importance was the Richmond and Danville, a part of which had rails as light as 22.75 lbs. per yard. On the short Winchester and Potomac, rails of 16½ lbs. were laid on sleepers which rested on cross ties. This was the only instance of the kind in Virginia.

The equipment of the railways was somewhat larger than might have been supposed. Twenty-seven locomotives, for example, were ready for service on the Virginia and Tennessee. Together, the railroads of the State [11] had 136 locomotives in good order and a reserve of forty-four in need of repair. Their passenger cars numbered only 142, but their freight cars of all classes [12] reached a total of 2078. With this equipment, the trains made an average of about 25 miles per hour, or slightly under 20 miles when stops were taken into account.

Lack of co-operation among the railroads might present a definite, even a dangerous, obstacle to the swift movement of troop trains. Union stations were rare. Often there was no physical connection between railways that served the same city. Where tracks were joined, the interchange of equipment usually was opposed with much bitterness. It was proverbial in Virginia that a railroad would make great effort to ascertain when a competitor's train would arrive at the junction—in order that it might be sure to have its own cars leave before that hour.

As the railroads of Virginia were single-tracked, trains often had to wait long on sidings for the passing of traffic from the opposite direction. In the entire State, these sidings and turnouts, including the main terminals, had a gross mileage of only sixty-eight. The R. F. & P. had no more than four and one-half miles of second track of all descriptions and locations, the Manassas Gap barely three and one-quarter, and the Orange and Alexandria a scant four miles. These three railroads, in case of invasion from the North, would be those subjected to the heaviest strain and the greatest congestion.

Still another weakness of the Virginia railways was the large number

[11] Excluding the B. & O. and its affiliate, the Northwestern Virginia.
[12] Other than gravel cars.

of bridges. Eighteen of these were of stone [13] and five were of iron. All the others, to the surprising total of 432, were of wood, and some of these were long.[14] The destruction of any one of a dozen bridges would halt for at least a month through traffic on a railroad that might be an army's main line of supply. Widespread military operations within the State would make necessary the detachment of numerous guards for bridges.

Efficient or feeble, well or ill equipped, these railroads were to be the first ever employed in war. Prior to 1861, commanders never had calculated logistics according to the speed and carrying capacity of railroads, and never had tested the effect of steam transportation on strategical combinations, on concentration and on the service of supply. Would the opposing Generals know how to use the railroads adequately and not to expect the impossible of them? Difficult to balance a new weapon might be in old hands.

The roads of the Commonwealth were as interesting as the railways and were as surely destined to play an important part in any general war. Some of these roads were almost as old as the colony of Virginia. Their badness was a joke when they were at their best and a calamity when they were at their worst. In almost every section of Virginia, during the optimistic era of "internal improvements," a turnpike company had been chartered. New roads had been graded and opened on the assumption that tolls would cover the cost of maintenance. For a few seasons expectations had been realized, but in many instances a false economy had located the roads where they were washed away by overflowing streams or buried under landslides. Repair cost so much more than tolls yielded that the roads soon declined to the state where wagoners no longer would pay to drive over them.[15] Then, in many instances, disappointed stockholders were glad to present the turnpikes to the counties—to be "worked" or neglected according to the usage of the powers that were. A few, a very few, of the longer roads had strategic value. The Valley Turnpike, for example, which ran from Staunton to Martinsburg, was in large part macadamized and was a most excellent line of advance along the Shenandoah. In Western Virginia were several highways the control of which was militarily decisive.

From late November until April, most of the roads were not passable for large bodies of men and for wagon trains unless the mire was

[13] Long arches included.

[14] Truss, trestle and lattice bridging is included in this total, which is compiled from the annual reports of the Board of Public Works, but bridges with a span of less than twenty feet, and all overhead crossings, are excluded.

[15] The Staunton and Parkersburg road, chartered Mch. 16, 1838, was perhaps the most disastrous of these investments.

frozen. Often, too, during the rainy period known as the "Long Spell in May," many roads were serpentine, tenacious mud trails. After a heavy thunderstorm in summer, twenty-four hours must elapse before a road was passable. In the average year, from mid-April until the oaks dropped their leaves, Virginia roads were dusty but endurable. Not least among their deficiencies was, paradoxically, their abundance. Secondary roads ran in all directions to no apparent purpose and confused the traveller by the number of approaches their frequent crossings offered. As Gen. R. E. Lee subsequently said of the routes to Lexington, it scarcely mattered which road one selected between two points. Whatever one's choice, one was certain to wish one had gone another way.

The plank roads occasionally defied the seasons. These roads could not have been built except in a country of much timber, because every stage of their construction was wasteful. After the right of way was determined—or a decision was made to plank an existing road—large trees were cut at intervals and were split in half. The logs so formed then were placed on the ground as sills, parallel to the course of the road and about eight feet apart. Transversely across the sills, squared timbers were laid. Whether hewn or sawed, these cross boards were 6 x 6 or 8 x 8 and were placed so as to offer a continuous surface. At intervals, the cross boards were extended outward several feet as a shoulder, alternately to the right and to the left. This was done in order that a vehicle could enter the road at any point or could get back on the road if its right wheel had been run on the shoulder in passing another wagon. The planking was intended for heavy traffic. By the side of the plank road there often was a dirt track for horsemen and passenger vehicles. This second track frequently was muddy when the other was rough. On the assumption, perhaps, that a plank road would require few repairs, it generally received none and, in a surprisingly short time, was dangerously full of holes.

Had Virginians made orderly analysis, in that excited April, 1861, of the part their lack of sea power, their 1600 miles of railways and their bad roads were to play in war, they might have asked whether there was not a fourth factor, most distinctly of man's making, in their military geography. The roads that ran through the woods and over the hills not only were confusingly numerous but also were unmapped.[16] No stranger could find his way among them. If natives

[16] When Matthew Fontaine Maury was writing his *Physical Survey of Virginia,* in 1867–71, he took the standard nine-sheet map, prepared by authority of the General Assembly of Virginia, and from sections of this he asked the county judges to draw the lines of the magisterial districts. The reply often came back, wrote Maury, "to the effect that the map section was so inaccurate that the townships could not be projected thereon." The great oceanographer continued: "This induced a special examination of the nine-sheet map. It was found so erroneous that I decided to abandon all the work" that had been based on it (*Physical Survey of Virginia,* Part II, p. 142).

ventured ten miles from their own neighborhood, they often were lost. In war, therefore, until maps could be prepared, opposing armies would be compelled to rely on local guides. The sympathies of these guides—whether with the South or with the Union—would determine the willingness, the speed and even the accuracy with which they showed a commander the shortest route or the readiest ford. To a degree unforeseen and often when the stake was the lives of hundreds, the sure adherence of the people of Eastern Virginia to the Southern cause was destined to facilitate the march of the defending troops and to delay the advance of the invaders. Across the Potomac and in the counties West of the Alleghenies, the case was to be different.

These, then, were the characteristics by which Nature gave depth, range and variety to the stage that was being set for war in Virginia:

1. The Old Dominion had frontier waters that might be employed as readily for her isolation as for her protection.

2. Into these frontier waters flowed navigable rivers, up which, if defense failed, hostile men-of-war could ascend to the interior.

3. Across the State from North to South ran a major mountain barrier, the Appalachian range, which divided Virginia strategically and in sympathy.

4. On the eastern flank of this range, protected both from the East and from the West, was the Shenandoah Valley, an excellent avenue of penetration.

5. Despite the long settlement of Virginia, the widespreading forests gave ample cover, particularly in many eastern districts, for concealed operations.

To these five natural characteristics, four others, man-made, were properly to be added:

1. The seceding Virginians had scant prospect of naval command of the frontier waters and could protect their navigable rivers in no other way than by shore batteries.

2. The State possessed a railroad system of approximately 1600 miles, most unevenly divided. Western Virginia was without railways except on the northern border; Midland Virginia did not include many districts more than three days' march from a railroad. Tidewater had few lines. As a whole, the system was lacking in adequate connection with the South and had scant sidings and turnouts.

3. Virginia roads were numberless, seasonally bad and, with few exceptions, of small strategic value.

4. The State was so nearly without maps that troops in unfamiliar

country would be compelled to rely on local guides. Sympathy on the part of these guides varied geographically.

The manner in which these factors of military geography were to operate in the strategic areas of Virginia was in April, 1861, a part of the unplayed drama. Almost before the first shouts for secession had died in men's throats, one geographic influence after another began to make itself felt, but what did not come quickly was an understanding

The Northeastern Frontier District of Virginia

of their relationship. Great districts were overrun, humiliating retreats were experienced, and the calls of loyal districts for help had to be denied before even those high in authority realized the fundamentals which the military geography of Virginia permitted, imposed or prohibited. As the war progressed each campaign brought to light some condition that few persons had sensed and none previously had studied. The armies rediscovered Virginia. In following troop movements, through this or any other work on the military annals of Virginia, the reader will save much time by acquainting himself with the distinctive

features of the more important of the twelve strategic areas into which
the course of the rivers, the strength of the hills and the labor of man
divided Virginia.[17]

The Northeastern Frontier District as shown on the map, p. 687, was
a crude triangle with depth and extreme width of about sixty-five miles.
It lay between the Blue Ridge, the Potomac and the Rappahannock-
Rapidan as far downstream as Fredericksburg, and it had high strategical importance. The Federals of course would seek to protect Washington, and when they were ready for the offensive they probably
would utilize the Orange and Alexandria Railroad, which was the
simplest, easiest overland line of advance from Washington as a general
base.[18] To accomplish those two objects, the enemy might be expected
to occupy the Northeastern area.

Defensively, that area had certain advantages. It offered a fair line
along Bull Run and Occoquan River, which form the boundary between Fairfax and Prince William Counties. As the southern end of
the area, and delimiting it, was the line of the Rappahannock and
Rapidan. All these streams were readily fordable at various points,
but they were sufficiently strong to make an enemy hesitate. In relation
to Maryland and to Washington, a strategic advantage still greater
was afforded this Northeastern area by the proximity of the Shenandoah Valley. So long as a defending force held both the line of Bull
Run-Occoquan and the lower Shenandoah Valley, each of these positions covered the other.

The chief defensive weaknesses of the Northeastern area were four.
In the event that the control of the Potomac were lost, as it probably
would be, only one rail line of supply would be available, the Orange
and Alexandria. Second, in the same contingency of the loss of the
Potomac to the enemy, the line of Bull Run-Occoquan could be turned
from Aquia Creek. If, third, an enemy in the Shenandoah Valley
advanced twenty-five miles southward from Harpers Ferry and seized
the passes or "gaps" of the Blue Ridge with its spurs, the position along
Bull Run would be untenable. Finally, South of that stream, until the
Rappahannock was reached, there was no natural defensive position of
strength.

[17] Needless to say, this first attempt to define the strategic areas of Virginia in terms
of weapons and transport of 1861 is made in the knowledge that it must be tentative
and subject always to dispute and to revision. The last thing the writer would do in so
complicated a field would be to pretend to finality or even to aver that the present
sketch of the strategic divisions of Virginia is the best or the most logical. The reader
will understand, of course, that tanks, long-range guns, other modern weapons, aircraft
and transport have changed substantially the strategic problems presented by the terrain
of Virginia.
[18] For the relation of this line of advance to the severance of rail communication
with Staunton and the upper valley of the Shenandoah, see *infra*, p. 691.

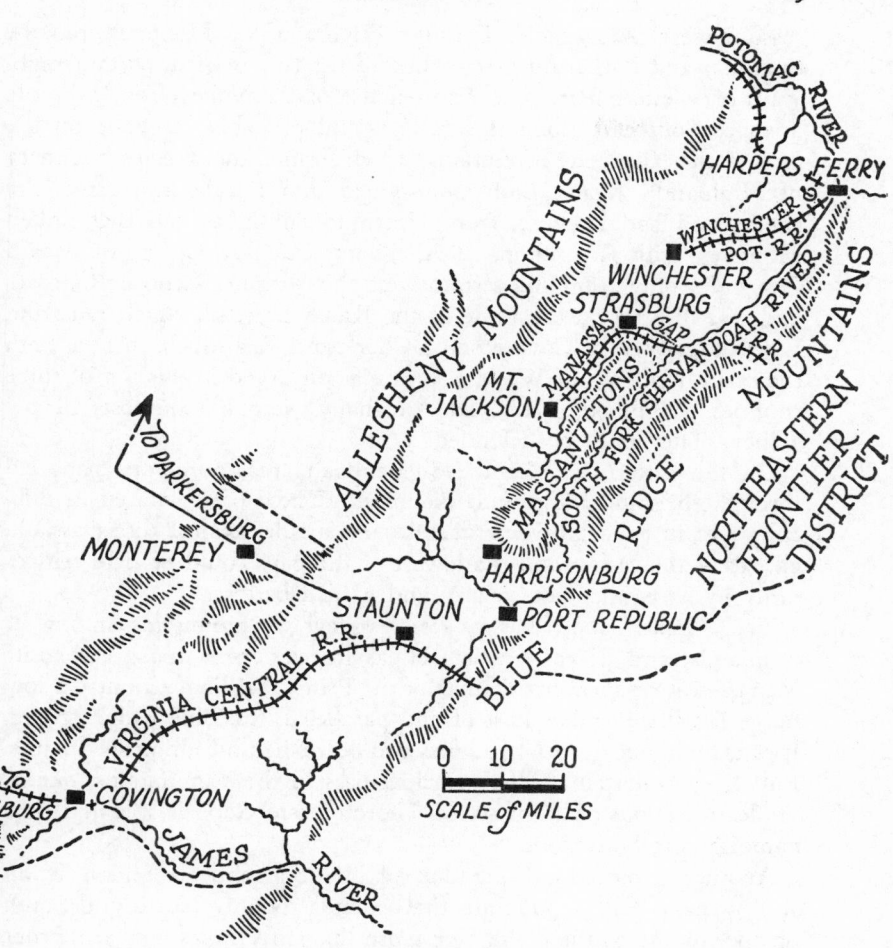

The Shenandoah Defensive Area

Soon to become renowned in military parlance as the Valley District
was the Shenandoah Defensive Area, the second of the State. This
lovely section between the Blue Ridge and the Allegheny Mountains
traditionally sets its southern boundary where the James River crosses
it near the line of Botetourt County, but the country South of Botetourt
is almost identical in geology with that to the North. Despite cross
ranges and divergent watersheds, the "Great Valley," as some of the early
geographers styled it, runs southwestward into Tennessee.

With the Shenandoah area, three mountain counties to the westward,
Highland, Bath and Alleghany, had strategically to be included. The

reasons were unescapable. Through Highland, via Monterey, ran the Staunton and Parkersburg road, one of the two most important highways of Western Virginia. The defense of the Valley from a hostile advance Southeast along this road would probably be made on the crest of the Allegheny Mountains, which formed the western boundary of Highland. Again, Bath County led into Pocahontas, across the range, and had likewise, from North to South, a road that linked Monterey with Covington, in Alleghany County. Covington was a few miles only from the terminus of the Virginia Central Railroad, and was directly on the route of the Kanawha road, which ran from Lewisburg, West of Covington, to Charleston. Inasmuch, then, as both the main highways of Western Virginia converged in this tier of three counties, Highland, Bath and Alleghany were the outposts of the Valley. They must be defended.

On the eastern side of the Shenandoah area, numerous gaps led through the Blue Ridge into Piedmont. These passes varied in difficulty and in availability for defense. As a rule, against direct assault, all except the easiest and the lowest of the gaps could be held temporarily by a regiment of cavalry and a field battery.

The "Great Valley" has its lesser valleys, its mountains among its farmlands, and its eastern as well as its western outposts. Opposite Manassas, a small railroad junction in Prince William County, a low range lies fifteen miles East of and parallel to the Blue Ridge proper. It runs for about twenty-five miles and bears the undistinguished name, Bull Run Mountains. The principal pass in these mountains, one of the least arduous of all, is styled Thoroughfare Gap. It was in 1861 a name soon to be famous.

Another geographical paradox of the Shenandoah region is an abrupt mass of low mountain that extends roughly North and South up the middle of the Valley for more than fifty miles between Front Royal and Harrisonburg.[19] The South Fork, or main stream of the Shenandoah, runs to the East of these mountains; the North Fork rises to the West. Thus there are two valleys with mountains on both sides of each of them. The fine country along the South Fork, nearest the Blue Ridge, was called the Luray Valley; to the West, the name Shenandoah prevailed. "Massanutton" was the odd appellation of the mid-Valley mountains. If Virginia were fortunate enough to find a great strategist to operate in that area, the hide-and-seek terrain around the Massanutton Mountains would be a perfect chessboard for him.

Immediately, the northern end of the Valley, often called the "Lower Valley," had far greater strategic value than the Massanutton could

19 For a sketch of the Massanuttons and the adjacent country, see *supra*, pp. 331–32.

possess. The reason was this: If a line were drawn directly West from Washington, it would pass through Woodstock and the northern end of the Massanutton. All the Lower Valley, from Woodstock to the Potomac,[20] a distance of sixty miles, was, so to speak, on the flank of the Federal capital. If a Southern army could hold the passes of the Blue Ridge, it would be in a vast covered way. It could cross the Potomac with security to its line of supply, and perhaps could threaten Washington from the Northwest. Such an army would be forty miles closer to Baltimore than a Federal force in Washington would be to Richmond. Again, if Union troops marched down the Orange and Alexandria Railroad, Southern soldiers in the Lower Valley would be on their flank and might get in their rear. Thanks to the Manassas Gap Railway, it would be easy to move troops from the Valley to the Northeastern district and vice versa. At the same time, Southern forces in the Lower Valley could interrupt communication on the Baltimore and Ohio Railroad. That indispensable link between East and West ran on an exposed right of way along the Potomac.

Besides presenting these possibilities for an offensive, the Lower Valley had to be held by the Confederates for defensive reasons. If it were abandoned at the outset, Virginia could not hope to remove to safety the valuable rifle machinery in the United States Arsenal at Harpers Ferry, situated where the Shenandoah enters the Potomac. The Valley, moreover, was the most productive area in Virginia both for cattle and for grain. To evacuate those fruitful counties would be to lose tens of thousands of rations. Still again, if the Valley constituted a covered way for an army moving to invade the North or to threaten Washington, so, in reverse, to an enemy who seized and held the gaps, the Valley offered an easy route to the geographical center of Virginia.

Defense of the Valley was not so simple as it was desirable. The frontier from Leesburg to Williamsport was open. Harpers Ferry could not be held against an enemy who commanded any of the heights that on three sides overlook the town. Loss of the Northeastern District would make the occupation of the Lower Valley entirely dependent upon ability to retain control of the mountain gaps. The moment a powerful force of the enemy commanded the passes, a Confederate army anywhere North of Winchester would be compelled to retreat southward up the Valley. Besides, such an army, North of Winchester, would be difficult to supply. Unless both the Orange and Alexandria and the Manassas railroads were in Southern hands, ammunition and stores must be forwarded by the long wagon journey down the Valley from Staunton. Even Staunton could not be regarded as altogether a

[20] At Williamsport.

safe base, because it was exposed to raids from the Northwest. To secure Staunton, it was necessary to command Western Virginia or, at the least, as already noted, to hold the crest of the Alleghenies.[21]

East of the Valley and directly South of the defensive area facing Washington was a succession of river lines destined to bloody fame. The largest and most advanced of these are the Rappahannock and the Rapidan, which meet nine and a quarter miles Northwest of Fredericksburg and three and a half miles North of a settlement known as Chancellorsville. The North Anna constituted the southern strategic boundary of these river lines and was itself the outpost of the Richmond-Petersburg district.[22]

As the Blue Ridge was the natural western boundary and Tidewater the eastern, the width of this third strategic area of Virginia was about fifty miles. The depth, North and South, varied from nine miles on the West to about thirty miles on the East. For convenience this may be styled the Rappahannock-North Anna Area, though a more descriptive name would be the Gordonsville-Fredericksburg-Hanover Junction Triangle. Through it, the course of the numerous small rivers was generally East or Southeast. They were neither wide nor deep, but most of them had high, difficult banks and marshy bottoms. Quite often, the watercourses were fringed heavily with trees.

Because of these streams and even more because of the railways, the triangle was of great military importance. The Orange and Alexandria Railroad traversed the Rappahannock on a high bridge, served Culpeper Court House, passed the Rapidan River and ran, via Orange, to Gordonsville. There it met the Virginia Central. This line, starting at Richmond, ran on an arc to the North, crossed the Richmond, Fredericksburg Railroad at Hanover Junction and went on to Gordonsville and thence to Charlottesville, Staunton and beyond. As the Richmond, Fredericksburg and Potomac ran almost due North from Richmond to Fredericksburg and thence to Aquia Creek, the Rappahannock-North Anna Area presented the combination of two perpendicular lines of advance by railways to a third, lateral railroad. This will be apparent from the facing sketch:

21 See *supra*, pp. 336, 690.
22 General Lee, in the years that lay ahead, was to refer to "the Annas" and not to the North Anna as a defensive line that covered Richmond. For this reason, it may be questioned whether the North Anna should be chosen as the boundary between two strategic areas. In explanation it should be said that, while Little River and the South Anna were to prove most useful as a part of the defenses of the North Anna, the Virginia Central Railroad and Hanover Junction were between the North and the South Annas. As that railroad and the junction had to be protected, the natural line was the North Anna. Further, though the South Anna helped to protect it, the North Anna offered the stronger position. If the North Anna were lost, the South Anna could not be held.

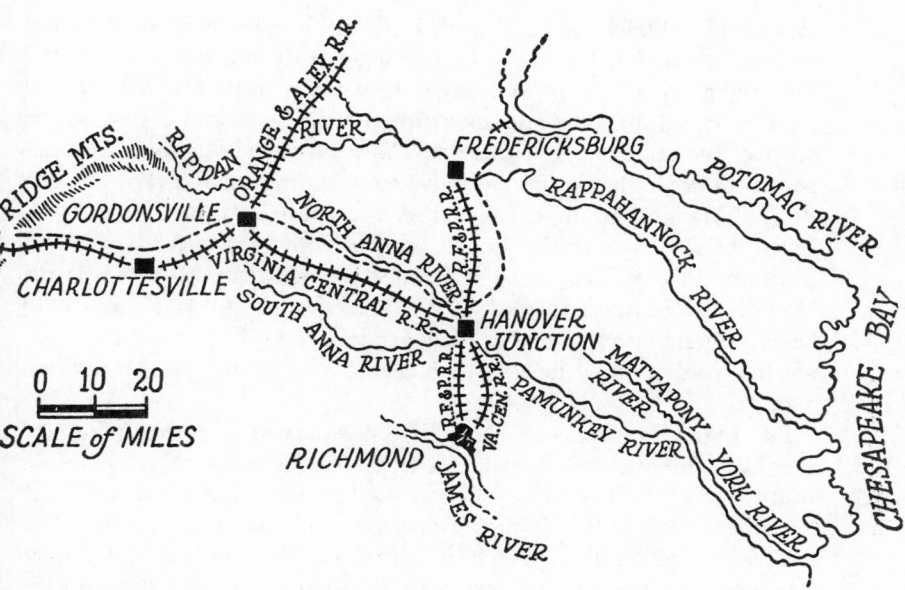

The Rappahannock-North Anna Area and the Mid-Tidewater District

Obviously, the forty-five miles of the Virginia Central from Hanover Junction to Gordonsville would be a long line to defend and, consequently, would be a tempting military objective for an army of invasion. An advance on Gordonsville would have much to commend it to Northern strategists. The Orange and Alexandria, as already indicated,[23] would form a direct line of supply. Gordonsville itself was farther North than any other point on the Virginia Central and was at the extreme of what railroad men called the "Gordonsville Loop." If an army could take Gordonsville and press on to Charlottesville, it could deprive the Shenandoah Valley of all rail communication.

The first objection to this line of advance and, consequently, the prime defensive strength of the area, was the difficulty of crossing the Rappahannock and the Rapidan. In event an enemy passed the Rappahannock and could not force the Rapidan, he might find himself in a trap between the two rivers. A second objection was the proximity of the mountains to the West of the Orange and Alexandria. The roughness of the country there would necessitate a march directly along and to the East of the railway. An advance restricted in this manner could, of course, be opposed more readily.

If an enemy chose, instead, to approach the lateral Virginia Central

23 See *supra*, p. 688.

by marching down the R. F. & P. Railroad, he would have proximity to deep water and he would be moving hourly nearer to Richmond. He might hope, with good fortune, to make a successful cavalry raid on Hanover Junction or to interrupt traffic elsewhere on one or the other of the railroads. For these possible advantages he would be compelled to pay by having to cross five troublesome small rivers, the Ny, Po, Ta, Mat and South, between Fredericksburg and the North Anna. From the Rappahannock, also, an army moving southward by the best fords would have to traverse a gloomy, tangled district known as the "Wilderness of Spotsylvania." Many other forests, not so large, would be encountered on the way to Hanover Junction. The rivers, the roads and the fords seemed to have been placed as if to lure an invader into a maze.

East of the Rappahannock-North Anna Area was what may be termed the Mid-Tidewater or Fourth District. This ran from the Potomac southward to the York and westward to the approaches of the R. F. & P. Railroad almost at the head of Tidewater. Included were the peninsula known as the Northern Neck, between the Potomac and the Rappahannock, and the next peninsula to the southward—that between the Rappahannock and the York. This section was valuable to the South for the provisions it could supply. It would be useful to the North, perhaps, as a *point d'appui* for raids against bridges or for larger operations against the R. F. & P. Railroad.

No part of the area was more than twenty-eight miles from water deep enough for gunboats to cover a troop landing. Northeast of the Pamunkey River, the most remote part of the district was within seventeen miles of water navigable by light naval vessels. In war, therefore, the control of this region depended entirely on the success or failure of land batteries in preventing the ascent of the rivers. Along the Potomac, the most promising location for a powerful battery seemed to be at Mathias Point, in King George County, twenty-two miles ENE. of Fredericksburg. On the Rappahannock were numerous sites for heavy guns, but none that was commanding.

Directly South of this Mid-Tidewater District was the peninsula between the York and the James, which constituted a fifth strategic area. Above West Point on the York and Barrets Point on the James, the inland boundaries of "the Peninsula" area,[24] both geographically and strategically, are a matter of dispute. Perhaps the most logical limits are the Pamunkey on the North, and, on the West, a line that would cover the Virginia Central Railroad and then run South to

[24] For reference to the Virginia usage which terms the region between the James and the York "The" Peninsula—as if it were the only one—see *supra*, p. 14.

James River. These are the confines marked on the accompanying map. They include the "Cradle of the Republic," the old church tower that marked the site of Jamestown, the second colonial capital ι ι Williamsburg, and the grass-covered redoubts around Yorktown. At the tip of the Peninsula stood Fortress Monroe, so nearly impregnable that no land attack on it was worth the planning. From Fortress Monroe, an army might advance directly up the Peninsula toward Richmond, distant eighty-five miles by road. If the invader commanded the James, he could move transports directly to the capital; and if he could pass the York, he might put troops ashore at West Point, whence for thirty-eight miles ran a new, single-track railway to Richmond.

Although there was no railroad down the Peninsula, the defense of that area was simple, so long as the James and the York were closed to the enemy. Troops could be moved by steamer down the James, or sent by rail to West Point and embarked there for employment on the shores of the York. Every crossroads on the Peninsula was within eleven miles of deep water or else was not farther than that from the Richmond and York River Railroad. On the other hand, defense of the Peninsula, East of the mouth of the Chickahominy—if that far— scarcely was possible when the two flanking rivers were open to the enemy. He easily could land troops in rear of an army fighting on the lower Peninsula and might even cut off its retreat.

One of the first questions of war in Virginia, then, probably would be: Can the James and the York be held? The lower James, broad and sluggish, had a few promontories or low-lying "points" from which guns of long range and heavy weight of metal perhaps might sweep the channel. A battle between these shore batteries and the powerful Federal warships would be of doubtful outcome. On the York, at the narrows between Yorktown and Gloucester Point, the prospect of closing the river to hostile ships was favorable, but success there would not avail, of course, if the enemy ascended the James and landed troops where they could march to the rear of the Yorktown line.

Besides the Mid-Tidewater section and the doubtful Peninsula District, there was another deep-water strategic area, the sixth and in one respect the most vital of all. This was the Norfolk Zone, which included Hampton Roads, Norfolk and the district eastward to the Atlantic and westward from Norfolk to the Blackwater. This river rises a few miles South of Petersburg, flows southeastward and then turns sharply southward to serve as the boundary between Isle of Wight and Southampton counties. It crosses into North Carolina at a point twenty-one miles Southwest of Suffolk and there joins the Nottoway.

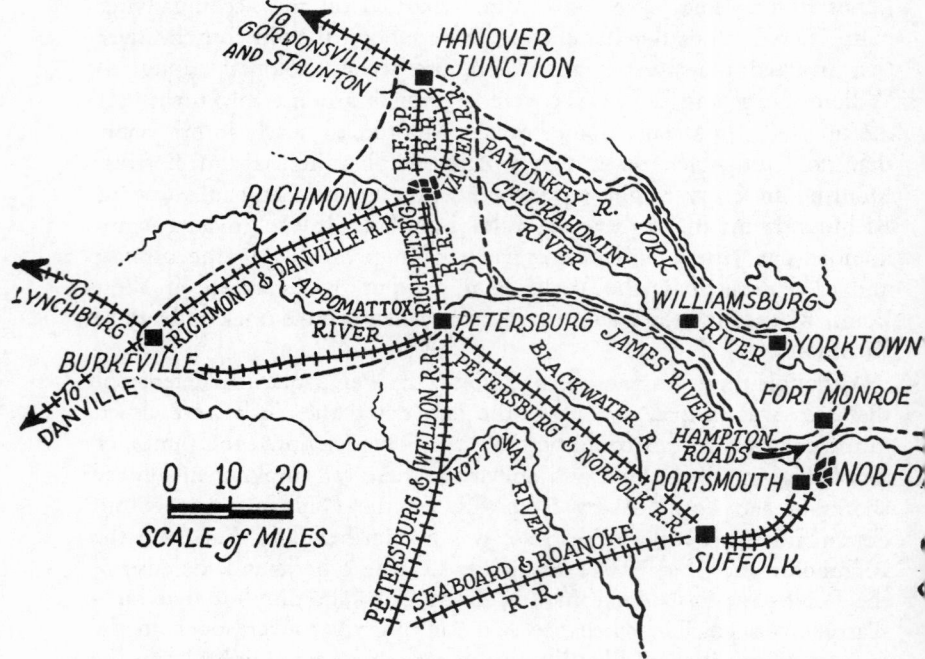

The Peninsula, the Norfolk Zone, and the Richmond-Petersburg Area

These two streams, with the Meherrin, form the Chowan, which merges into Albemarle Sound, which formed the defensive southern border of the Norfolk Zone.

Valuable as Norfolk would be to the South because of its shipyard,[25] it would be equally desirable to the Federals as a naval base. The recovery of the city might be considered one of the probable early objectives of the enemy. Against his heavy attack the defense of Norfolk or of any part of the district East of the Blackwater would be difficult. Around Norfolk were many inlets where a powerful enemy could effect a landing. From North Carolina, the city might be taken in reverse. Moreover, Norfolk was located at a rail end and might be isolated' by an expedition which would ascend the Nansemond River and seize Suffolk. In these circumstances, all hope of defending the Norfolk Zone hung on the rapid development of Southern sea power, on the wise location and skillful use of powerful land batteries, or on the retention in that area of a force large enough to cope with any invasion.

[25] See *supra*, p. 154.

Much the same conclusion, then, concerning the Mid-Tidewater District, the Peninsula, and the Norfolk Zone would have been reached in April, 1861, by any trained soldier who studied the military geography: in each of these three areas, the strongest and perhaps the decisive influence would be that of sea power. If the Unionists had sufficient vessels and used them wisely, then the whole of Tidewater from Aquia Creek above Fredericksburg to the Blackwater River would be open to incursion, to formal invasion or even to occupation for the entire war. This was a serious outlook because it would put perhaps 5300 square miles of Virginia, much of it productive, in the hands of the enemy. Homes of thousands of potential soldiers would be within hostile lines. The approaches to the Richmond-Petersburg Area, the industrial center of the State, would be most conveniently at the end of a gangplank.

That Richmond-Petersburg Area, the seventh strategic district of the State, was an obtuse triangle [26] of about forty-five miles from North to South and seventy miles from East to West. It owed its singular form as much to railroads which supplied the cities as to the rivers which flowed by them. On the North, as already explained, the natural defensive barrier was the North Anna River, which also covered the Virginia Central Railroad. From Hanover Junction, any line for the defense of Richmond had to run southward and East of the Virginia Central and R. F. & P. Railroads and thence still southward to James River. On the right bank of that stream, from City Point, where the Appomattox entered the James, the line to defend the Petersburg district must protect the South Side Railroad to its junction at Burkeville with the Richmond and Danville. The third side of the triangle, having no natural barrier to shape it, would have to run across country to shield the R. & D. Completion of the triangle by carrying the third side back to Hanover Junction would be hypothetical. Strategically, defense of this area would not cover the Petersburg and Roanoke Railroad. South of Petersburg, that carrier would not be protected from the line of the James but from that of the Blackwater.

In the Richmond-Petersburg Area were numerous establishments for the manufacture and storage of tobacco. Richmond had, in addition, iron works, rolling mills, boiler factories, cannon and gun works, small shipyards, flour mills and woolen mills.[27] For these reasons and because of their railroad connections, Richmond and Petersburg were certain to be the general base of any war for the defense of Virginia. If, as

[26] Compare the Northeastern area, *supra*, p. 688.
[27] The best report on the industries of Richmond at this time prefaced the report of the James River and Kanawha Canal Co. in that of the Board of Public Works of Virginia for 1859–60, pp. 228–31.

some expected, Richmond should become the capital of the Confederacy, the city would have a moral value. In any war of position, Richmond was almost as certain to be one of the enemy's two major objectives as Norfolk was to be the other. If the war proved to be one of communications, then, too, Richmond and Petersburg would be assailed, because they were directly on the only railroads that traversed the coastal plain for its entire distance from Southern Georgia to the estuaries of the Potomac.

How vulnerable were the two cities? The insecurity of the river line was admitted. James River might be open all the way to the narrows known as Drewry's Bluff, seven miles below Richmond. There, with diligence, it might be possible to stop the enemy. Were the attack made, not from the James but overland from Fortress Monroe, the defensive problems of the Richmond-Petersburg district were those of the Peninsula. Against a blow from the East and Northeast, Richmond was not well shielded. At the points where the two protecting rivers, the Mattapony and the Pamunkey, were not fordable, they easily could be bridged. Finally, the Richmond and Petersburg Railroad, which linked the two cities, was itself exposed to attack from James River. If it were seized or destroyed, the co-ordination of defense would be most difficult.

While nothing could remove these dangers, especially that of attack from the James River, Richmond and Petersburg were not without defensive advantages. An enemy moving on Richmond from the North could be delayed and might be halted on one or another of the rivers in the Rappahannock-North Anna Area. If, by an improbable repetition of the strategy of the American Revolution, the enemy should advance on Petersburg from the South, other river lines could be defended. Was there a prospect that the approach to the Richmond-Petersburg Area would be from the Southeast, by way of the Blackwater? In that contingency, destruction of the Petersburg and Norfolk Railroad would impose a long, difficult march on the enemy. Should the attack come from the direction of the Richmond and York River Railroad, then an upper stretch of the Chickahominy River, though it was inconveniently close to Richmond, formed an almost impenetrable swamp.

Above all defensive advantages was this: Richmond and Petersburg were so well served by railroads, by routes so divergent, that the actual investment of either town, in the literal sense of cutting off reinforcements and destroying communication with the outside world, was exceedingly difficult.

South and West of the Richmond-Petersburg area were three other strategic districts, which need not be described here, because they never were occupied by the armies. These areas owed their outline to the railroads that had to be defended with or without the aid of river lines. Most of these inland districts were so located that, if exposed at all, they had nothing more serious to fear than cavalry raids.

The strategic area of Southwest Virginia, the eleventh in the State, was on a somewhat different footing. Traditionally, Southwest Virginia is the country beyond New River, as one approaches from the Northeast; strategically, the whole line of the Virginia and Tennessee Railroad, from its passage through the Blue Ridge to its terminus at Knoxville, had to be guarded as a unit. This of necessity extended the Southwestern district to the line of James River in Botetourt County. Moreover, this area included the large salt works on the border of Smyth and Washington counties, about six miles North of the railroad. All the southwestern counties of Virginia, about half of Tennessee and parts of North Carolina, Georgia and Alabama depended on these wells, or on those of the Upper Kanawha for their salt. Conditions might arise in which the protection of these works and their continuous operation to meet a larger demand would be a military obligation.[28]

The final or twelfth strategic area was that of Virginia beyond the mountains—West Virginia from the Alleghenies to the Ohio. If, to repeat,[29] the secessionists would be able to control the Baltimore and Ohio Railroad, and to navigate the Kanawha, Western Virginia might be divided into a number of districts where contest might be expected. Should the Baltimore and Ohio be lost—as seemed in every way probable—then the Confederates in Virginia would not command a single mile of railway beyond the mountains. Whatever was undertaken to hold or to regain Western Virginia must be done by man and horse over difficult roads and treacherous streams.

In the passion and the enthusiasm of secession, no leader, so far as is known, considered in their just relationship the natural characteristics of the military geography of Virginia, the ponderables of man's own making, and the defensive strength and weakness of the twelve strategic areas into which the State might have been divided. Having determined to withdraw from the Union, the people of Virginia were engrossed in the act and, as yet, gave little thought to the consequences. The political chieftains realized that Harpers Ferry and the Norfolk Navy Yard were prizes worth possessing, and they seized immediately

[28] As a matter of fact, Maury, *op. cit.*, 106, subsequently estimated that the production of the wells in Southwest Virginia during 1864 was raised to approximately 3,000,000 bushels. In his *Resources of the Coal Field of the Upper Kanawha* (1873), p. 25, Maury credited to the Kanawha area before the war a like annual production.

[29] See *supra*, p. 681.

the arsenal as well as the shipways. One of the ablest naval officers of his generation, Matthew Fontaine Maury, a member of the Governor's Advisory Council, probably was the man responsible for following up these first steps with prompt action for the defense of the rivers. He perceived that among all the factors, adverse and favorable, in the complicated equation of the State's defense, the one that might force an immediate decision was sea power. If the Federal navy could be frustrated, then but only then, might Virginia have opportunity of employing the wits of her sons to overcome the other weaknesses of her frontiers.

APPENDIX II

Southern Resources of Command

When Virginia seceded, April 17, 1861, she already had the *cadre* of a substantial volunteer military organization. The Adjutant General of the Commonwealth reported armed units to an estimated total of 12,150 men—118 companies of light infantry, forty-two of riflemen, sixty-seven troops of cavalry and twelve companies of artillery. Volunteer infantry, riflemen and cavalry without weapons were half as numerous as those that were armed.[1] Twelve additional companies of artillery awaited the issue of ordnance.

On the roster of the militia were carried 187 regiments of infantry in twenty-eight Brigades, 138,310 officers and men. In theory, Virginia also had five regiments of artillery, 1066 men, seventy-two companies of riflemen, and five regiments of cavalry, 3779. This, a "paper reserve" of 143,155, was the largest enrolled strength in the South and the seventh in the old Union.[2] In the hands of the militia were supposed to be 300 cannon of all ages and sizes, and some 70,000 small arms. Most of these were obsolete muskets.[3] As the militia were established on the basis of a levy *en masse*, they were without organization except in name. Thousands of men physically unfit for field duty were counted as effectives. Ultimately, of course, East of the Alleghenies, the militia would yield many good recruits. West of the mountains, none could say at the time of secession what percentage of the militia would put allegiance to the Union above loyalty to the State. As for the volunteers, who were the ardent spirits of Virginia, the task was not that of bringing them into service, but that of restraining them until camps, arms or equipment could be provided.

The volunteers had elected their company officers. Under an ordinance of the convention, when the companies were organized into regiments, the field officers were to be appointed by the Governor and Council.[4] How were competent field officers to be provided? Whence

[1] 14 *S. H. S. P.*, 179–81.
[2] Exceeded, in the order named, by New York, Pennsylvania, Ohio, Illinois, California and Massachusetts, *Exec. Doc. No. 58, 2nd Sess., 36th Congress.* The enlisted strength of the riflemen was not given in the table, nor carried in the total.
[3] *Ibid.*
[4] *O. R.*, 2, 777. The Confederate government already had a different rule: if volunteers were offered as battalions or as regiments, they could elect their field officers. where State law permitted. Only when unattached companies or other units, which

were to come the brigade, divisional and army commanders? These two questions, vital to the defense of Virginia, did not cause concern comparable to that aroused by the manifest shortage of arms. Although admission subsequently was made in the press that the South could not expect immediately to provide a full corps of qualified officers,[5] it was assumed in the first hour of Virginia's secession that all sons of the State in the "old army" would follow the example set by most of their comrades of the Far South in resigning and in tendering their military service. The superiority of these officers to those of the North was asserted as a matter of course.[6] They were younger[7] as well as abler. Only one or perhaps two, among all Northern soldiers, were adjudged capable of "wielding large masses of men."[8]

The number of Virginia officers who could be expected to resign from the United States Army was small, because the regular military establishment was limited to two regiments of dragoons, two of cavalry, one of mounted riflemen, four of artillery and ten of infantry. On the roster of these forces were the names of nineteen Colonels, a like number of Lieutenant Colonels and twice as many Majors—in round figures, seventy-five field officers. The staff[9] listed ten Colonels, ten Lieutenant Colonels and fifty-one Majors.[10] Altogether, there were four Generals and 146 other officers above the rank of Captain.

This number, tragically scant to be divided between the sections, was subject to deduction. In the absence of any retirement law, many of the senior officers had held to their commissions far beyond the age when they could stand the strain of field operations. The average age of the Generals of the line was 68. Excluding the staff, the average

offered their services directly to the government, were formed into regiments after being mustered into Confederate service, could their Majors, Lieutenant Colonels and Colonels be named by the President. Thereafter all vacancies in battalion and regimental, as well as in company command, were filled by election (see the Act of Mch. 6, 1861, IV O. R.; 1, 126, as interpreted Sept. 12, 1861, by Secretary L. P. Walker, ibid., 608; cf. ibid., 766). The political doctrine behind this unwise system was that the volunteers constituted, in effect, militia mustered into Confederate service. Under the permanent constitution, Art. 1, Sec. 8, par. 16, the appointment of militia officers was reserved to the States (ibid., 140). All commissions in the small regular Army of the Confederacy were by Presidential appointment, though vacancies in the established regiments, below the rank of Brigadier General, were to be "filled by promotion according to seniority" (IV O. R., 1, 128).

5 Richmond Examiner, Sept. 10, 1861, p. 2, col. 2; Richmond Dispatch, Nov. 5, 1861, p. 2, col. 1.

6 Richmond Examiner, May 3, p. 2, col. 6; June 27, p. 2, col. 1; July 1, p. 1, col. 4; p. 2, col. 2; July 5, p. 2, col. 6. Richmond Dispatch, June 17, 1861, p. 1, col. 4.

7 Richmond Dispatch, June·17, 1861, p. 2, col. 1.

8 Richmond Examiner, July 12, 1861, p. 2, col. 5.

9 Exclusive of the Medical Department. Inspector General Sylvester Churchill, Commissary General George Gibson and Surgeon General Thomas Lawson were general officers by brevet, but their regular rank was that of Colonel.

10 Twenty-six of these Majors were in the Pay Department.

Colonel was about 67. After the first clash of war, the burden of com-manding the large armies of North and of South was certain to pass to the younger field officers and, perhaps, even to some of the 29c Captains of staff and of line.[11] Incidentally, none of the four Generals of the line was a graduate of the United States Military Academy, and eleven of the nineteen Colonels of the line [12] were not, but nearly the whole corps of younger officers had received that professional training. Increasingly, then, as the older soldiers were broken by the hardships of war, high command would test the methods by which West Pointers had been selected and trained.

How many of this small corps of officers, young and old, distin-guished or promising, were Virginians? It is probable that two mem-bers of the Governor's Council, Capt. Matthew Fontaine Maury, of the Navy, who had resided long in Washington, and Col. Francis H. Smith, Superintendent of the Virginia Military Institute, listed those of their acquaintances who might join in the defense of their State. No formal roster was prepared then or thereafter.[13] If, from the rec-ord, those were omitted who had been born in Virginia and had entered the Army from other States, or were natives of other States and had been appointed from Virginia, the native Virginians credited on the *Army Register* to the Old Dominion were the following:[14]

The Brevet Lieutenant General commanding the Army, Winfield Scott, who was not a graduate of the Military Academy but, needless to say, was the most distinguished of living American soldiers.

The Quartermaster General, Joseph E. Johnston, with staff rank of Brigadier General, who had been graduated No. 13 in the class of 1829 at West Point.

Six Colonels of the line:[15] John Garland of the Eighth Infantry, 1849;[16] Thomas T. Fauntleroy of the First Dragoons, 1850; Matthew

[11] These figures are compiled from the *Army Register* of 1860. In three instances, where no record of the age of the Colonels of 1861 is available, it has been necessary to estimate the date of their respective births from that of their first commission.

[12] As shown by the *Army Register* of 1860. The promotion of Col. E. V. Sumner, Mch., 1861, to be Brigadier General, and the promotion of Lt. Col. R. E. Lee to full regimental rank increased to twelve the number of Colonels who were graduates of the Military Academy.

[13] From all these calculations of the resources of trained army personnel, the follow-ing have been excluded: medical officers, military storekeepers, graduates of the class of 1861 at West Point and graduates of that institution who presumably were dead, though the date of death cannot be established.

[14] Exclusive of the Medical Corps and of army storekeepers. In this list, officers who had brevet rank (*e.g.,* J. B. Magruder) and acted at that grade are entered by that rank. Those who had brevet rank but acted at their regular rank (*e.g.,* John Garland) are entered at their regular grade.

[15] These and all other officers on this list are named according to seniority. The numerals after the name indicate the year of commission at the grade here mentioned.

[16] Brevet Brigadier General, 1847, but serving as Colonel.

M. Payne [17] of the Second Artillery, 1856; Philip St. George Cooke of the Second Dragoons, 1858; Washington Seawell of the Sixth Infantry, 1860; and Robert E. Lee, 1861, of the First Cavalry. Of these, Cooke and Lee only were graduates of the United States Military Academy.

Two Lieutenant Colonels: John Bankhead Magruder, who held this rank by brevet of 1847, and discharged corresponding duties, though he was carried on the army register as a Captain of the First Artillery, 1846; and George W. Lay, 1855, who had served as aide-de-camp to General Scott and already had resigned. Both had passed through the Military Academy.

Ten Majors, staff and line, seven of them West Pointers: Henry Hill, Paymaster, 1847; Albert J. Smith, Paymaster, 1849; Brevet Major John F. Lee, Judge Advocate General, 1849; R. H. Chilton, Paymaster, 1854; E. J. Steptoe, Ninth Infantry, 1855; Robert S. Garnett, Ninth Infantry, 1855; George H. Thomas, Second Cavalry, 1855; N. C. Macrae, Third Infantry, 1857; Campbell Graham, Topographical Engineers, 1857; and Lawrence P. Graham, Second Dragoons, 1858.

Twenty-three Captains: William H. Gordon,[18] Third Infantry, 1846; Larkin Smith,[19] Eighth Infantry, 1846; Thomas Jordan, Asst. Quartermaster, 1847; C. L. Stevenson, Fifth Infantry, 1847; A. W. Reynolds, Asst. Quartermaster, 1847; Joseph Selden,[20] Eighth Infantry, 1848; W. B. Blair, Commissary, 1850; Samuel Jones, First Artillery, 1853; John W. Davidson, First Dragoons, 1855; Harry Heth, Tenth Infantry, 1855; John M. Jones, Seventh Infantry, 1855; S. S. Anderson,[21] Second Artillery, 1855; Richard B. Garnett, Sixth Infantry, 1855; T. T. S. Laidley, Jr.,[22] Ordnance, 1856; John Newton, Engineers, 1856; Seth M. Barton, First Infantry, 1857; W. L. Cabell, Asst. Quartermaster, 1858; Louis H. Marshall, Tenth Infantry, 1860; Henry E. Maynadier, Tenth Infantry, 1861; C. H. Tyler, Second Dragoons, 1861; John C. Bonnycastle, Asst. Quartermaster, 1861; B. H. Robertson, Second Dragoons, 1861; J. E. B. Stuart, First Cavalry, 1861. All except three of these were graduates of West Point.

Thirty-one First Lieutenants: Caleb Smith, Second Infantry, 1851; Ambrose P. Hill, First Artillery, 1851; James E. Slaughter, First Artillery, 1852; Dabney H. Maury,[23] Mounted Rifles, 1853; A. L. Long, Second Artillery, 1854; John Mullan, Second Artillery, 1855; George W. Carr, Ninth Infantry, 1855; Andrew Jackson, Third Infantry, 1855;

---

[17] The *Army Register* of 1860 gave his middle initial as *W*. In Heitman's *Historical Register and Dictionary of the United States Army, 1789–1903,* the name is printed correctly as Matthew Mountjoy Payne.

[18] Bvt. Major.   [19] Bvt. Major.
[20] Bvt. Major.   [21] Bvt. Major.
[22] Bvt. Major.   [23] Brevet Captain, A. A. G., 1860.

Robert Johnston, First Dragoons, 1855; Robert Williams, First Dragoons, 1855; T. G. Williams, First Infantry, 1855; R. G. Cole, Eighth Infantry, 1855; S. H. Reynolds, First Infantry, 1855; T. A. Washington, First Infantry, 1855; W. R. Terrill, Fourth Artillery, 1856; John Pegram, Second Dragoons, 1857; H. H. Walker, Sixth Infantry, 1857; J. Thomas Goode, Fourth Artillery, 1857; M. T. Carr, First Dragoons, 1857; Edwin J. Harvie, Ninth Infantry, 1857; G. A. Gordon, Second Dragoons, 1858; T. M. Jones, Eighth Infantry, 1858; T. M. Saunders, Third Artillery, 1858; W. P. Craighill, Engineers, 1859; G. W. C. Lee, Engineers, 1859; E. C. Bainbridge, Fourth Artillery, 1859; T. G. Baylor, Ordnance, 1861; John R. Waddy, Fourth Artillery, 1861; F. S. Armistead, Tenth Infantry, 1861; Fitz Lee, Second Cavalry, 1861; George Jackson, Second Dragoons, 1861. Twenty-three of these had been graduated at the Military Academy.

Ten Second Lieutenants: W. H. F. Lee, Second Infantry, 1855;[24] Francis Mallory, Fourth Infantry, 1856; A. S. Cunningham, Tenth Infantry, 1857; W. P. Smith,[25] Topographical Engineers, 1857; R. K. Meade, Engineers, 1858; R. F. Beckham,[26] Topographical Engineers, 1859; H. A. F. Worth, Sixth Infantry, 1860; W. W. McCreery, Fourth Artillery, 1861; Frank Huger, Tenth Infantry, 1861; John S. Saunders, Ordnance, 1861—eight of them West Pointers.

A second source from which experienced officers could be drawn for the training and command of troops consisted of those Virginia graduates of West Point who had served in the regular Army and had resigned prior to 1861. There were twenty-two such men, natives of Virginia and appointed to the Academy from the State or "at large." Thomas B. Randolph had attended the school in 1808–12 and had risen to be a Captain in the War of 1812. During the Mexican campaigns he served as Lieutenant Colonel of the First Virginia Volunteers, but he was now 69 and was residing in Missouri.[27] Walter Gwynn, an experienced engineer who had constructed many of the railroads and bridges in Virginia and North Carolina, had been commissioned back in 1822 and had been ten years a Lieutenant. In Lexington was an Episcopal clergyman, Rev. W. N. Pendleton, who had belonged to the class of 1830 and had resigned his Second Lieutenant's commission three years later.

One of the great planters of the State, Philip St. George Cocke, also had been a West Pointer thirty years before and had remained two years in the Army. The Superintendent of the Virginia Military In-

[24] *Army Register* of 1860. Heitman credits Lee with commission as Second Lieutenant, Sixth Infantry, 1857.
[25] Brevet.   [26] Brevet.
[27] *Cullum*, No. 79.

stitute, Francis H. Smith, had been graduated one year after Cocke. At the head of the Tredegar Iron Works in Richmond was Joseph R. Anderson, who had been a Second Lieutenant twenty-five years before. A lawyer in Franklin County, with the odd name of Jubal A. Early, had been graduated at West Point in 1837 and had been a Lieutenant one year only before resigning; but had re-entered the volunteer service at the time of the Mexican War and had become a Major. He, by the way, was a member of the Virginia Convention and voted against secession. Capt. R. C. W. Radford had eleven years in the Army to his credit before he retired to his rich plantation in Bedford County, and he had borne an excellent name in the war with Mexico. In Washington resided Staff Lt. Col. W. G. Freeman, former aide to General Scott, and in the House of Representatives was Bvt. Maj. Henry S. Turner, who had removed to Missouri. One former Second Lieutenant, Fisher A. Lewis, was a farmer in Western Virginia; another, William B. Magruder, was head of a girls' school in Kentucky; a resigned First Lieutenant of the class of 1846, H. L. Shields, who had been aide to General Wool, was farming in Vermont. Among these and others,[28] perhaps the best known in Virginia, though they had seen no service in wartime, were Walter Gwynn and Philip St. George Cocke.

The retired officer with the most distinguished record in the Mexican War was Professor Thomas Jonathan Jackson. As a Lieutenant of artillery, Jackson had been sent, on the stirring day of the storming of Chapultepec, to support with a section of artillery a column of infantry that was connecting two attacks. The young subaltern of 22 could not move the ordnance out of a road that was swept by the Mexican fire, but he got one gun over a cross ditch and, when his men no longer would stand to the piece, he served it himself with the aid of an unflinching Sergeant. It was a brilliant feat on a field where valor was prodigal, and it brought to Lieutenant Jackson much admiring praise. Had he been scared? his friends asked him later. "No," he said honestly, "the only anxiety of which I was conscious during the engagements was a fear lest I should not meet danger enough to make my conduct conspicuous." [29] He need have had no concern. Already brevetted Captain for his conduct at Contreras and Churu-

[28] H. W. Mercer, First Lieutenant, class of 1822, resigned 1832; Sec. Lt. D. B. Harris, c. 1833, r. 1835; Sec. Lt. J. Lucius Davis, c. 1833, r. 1836; Capt. Christopher Q. Tompkins, c. 1836, r. 1847; Fst. Lt. R. T. Jones, c. 1836, r. 1837; Sec. Lt. A. T. M, Rust, c. 1842, r. 1845; Fst. Lt. W. E. Jones, c. 1848, r. 1857, and Bvt. Sec. Lt. J. R. Chambliss, c. 1853, r. 1854.
[29] 2 *Henderson*, 46. Bishop Collins Denny notes (1942): "Major Murfee of Marion, Alabama, a V. M. I. student under Jackson, told me that Jackson said, in answer to an inquiry how he felt that day at Chapultepec: 'Very much afraid, Mr. Murfee, very much afraid.' "

busco, he was made Brevet Major for gallantry at Chapultepec, within a little more than fifteen months from the time he had been graduated from West Point.[30]

Peace put an end to promotion. Three dull years of garrison duty, broken only by a tedious expedition against the Seminole Indians, had ended in his resignation from the Army to become Professor of Physics [31] and Instructor of Artillery at the Virginia Military Institute, at Lexington. There he had submerged himself in the work of the school and of the Presbyterian church, and there he was when secession came.

Besides looking to these officers, Virginia might hope to have the services of others who had participated in the war with Mexico. In that contest, among the officers of the regular Army, 130, and perhaps more, who held commissions, were Virginians.[32] Thirty-eight of these officers had died prior to 1861. Of the remaining ninety-two, a total of forty-eight already have been taken into account as active or retired West Point graduates, or as active Army officers who had not attended the Military Academy. These deductions left forty-four who had held commissions in the regular Army during the war with Mexico, without graduation from West Point, and subsequently had retired. In addition, an unascertainable number of Virginians had served as officers of volunteers in the course of the Mexican hostilities. Sixty-seven of these natives had belonged to the First Virginia Volunteers.[33] With allowance for deaths among these men in 1847–60,[34] about fifty of them were alive at the time of secession. Thus the total of veteran Mexican officers, of all ages and ranks, not included on other lists, was ninety-four at a minimum.

Several of these were men of distinction. Arthur C. Cummings, a graduate of the Virginia Military Institute, had been accepted in the service as a Captain in the Eleventh Infantry, and had been brevetted Major for gallantry in Mexico. In April, 1861, he was practicing law and was a Colonel in the State militia.[35] Still another Brevet Major of the Mexican War was William B. Taliaferro of Gloucester, a rich planter who, in April, 1847, had been made a Captain in the Eleventh Infantry.[36] Jas. L. Kemper, a lawyer of Charleston, Kanawha County, and a graduate of V. M. I., had been a Captain in Mexico. D. A.

[30] *Cullum*, No. 1288.
[31] The official title was Professor of Natural and Experimental Philosophy.
[32] Besides fifty-eight born in Virginia and commissioned from other States, and ten born in other States and commissioned from Virginia.
[33] Exclusive of medical officers.
[34] As these officers were younger, on the average, than the commissioned Virginia personnel as a whole, the death rate has been assumed 10 per cent lower.
[35] Wise's *V. M. I.*, 515.   [36] 1 Heitman, *ov. cit.*, 944.

Weisiger, a Petersburg merchant, had served as a Second Lieutenant during that contest. Montgomery D. Corse, a private banker of Alexandria and a Forty-niner in California, had won his Captain's commission in the earlier war.

A fourth reservoir of officers was represented by the graduates of the Virginia Military Institute. This school had been opened in Lexington in 1839, and had been continuously under the direction of the remarkable Superintendent already mentioned as a member of the Governor's Advisory Council, Francis H. Smith. He was a native of Norfolk, born October 18, 1812, and had been graduated No. 5 in the class of 1833 at West Point.[37] After nearly three years in the First Artillery, he had resigned to become Professor of Mathematics in Hampden-Sydney College.[38] In 1839, he had been called to be "Principal Professor" at the Military Institute the Commonwealth was then preparing to open. The immediate argument for the establishment of the school had been "to supply the place" of the regular, paid guard of the State Arsenal at Lexington [39] "by another, composed of young men, from seventeen to twenty-four years, to perform the necessary duties of a guard, who would receive no pay, but, in lieu, have afforded to them the opportunities of a liberal education." [40]

From the first, West Point had been regarded as the ideal of V. M. I.,[41] and had been made a practical model through the experience of Col. Claude Crozet, President of the Board of Visitors and a former Professor at West Point.[42] In the outworking, the Institute had combined much of the work of a college with the full discipline and a large part of the professional training of the United States Military Academy. It provided, in the words of one of its historians, "a liberal education, coupled with a military training, in the belief that its graduates would prove valuable citizens, all the more useful because capable of bearing arms efficiently in the hour of their country's need." [43] That hour had struck. The Virginia Military Institute in 1861 had 433 living graduates and 654 non-graduates. The greater percentage of these were in Virginia [44] and constituted a large, immediate and indispensable officers reserve corps.

Besides these four sources of officer personnel, Virginia's adherence

37 *Cullum*, No. 711. In the edition of 1891, Smith was listed as No. 17 in his class, but as his name appears between Nos. 4 and 6, and as Edmund Schriver appears as No. 17, Smith's proper number must have been 5.

38 Wise's *V. M. I.*, 38.

39 Established in 1816 to guard 30,000 stand of arms.

40 F. H. Smith, *The Virginia Military Institute*, p. 15.

41 *Ibid.*, 13, 60.

42 Crozet had been an officer of Engineers in the French Army under Napoleon and had been captured by the Russians on the retreat from Moscow (Wise's *V. M. I.*, 29).

43 Wise's *V. M. I.*, 36–37.   44 Wise's *V. M. I.*, 146.

to the Confederacy would give her the service of some of its officers. Their number would not be large. One hundred and eighty-four living graduates of West Point were credited at that time to Southern States outside Virginia,[45] a total only eighty larger than that of the Old Dominion.[46] There were on the *Army Register*, also, thirty-six officers, not West Pointers, who were natives of States South of Virginia.

In these two classes of Southern-born officers were men of achievement and men of promise. Brig. Gen. D. E. Twiggs, who had been dismissed from the United States Army on March 1 for surrendering the military posts in Texas [47] was, of course, a national figure, familiar for a generation; but Twiggs was 71 and manifestly was incapable of hard service in the field. Albert Sidney Johnston, Colonel of the Second Cavalry and Brevet Brigadier General for his conduct of the Utah campaign,[48] represented all President Davis's ideals of a soldier; but Johnston, surely, would command in his native Kentucky, not in Virginia. Brig. Gen. W. S. Harney of Louisiana already had declared for the Union. Col. Samuel Cooper, a native New Yorker [49] bound by the ties of marriage to the South, had resigned in March to join the Confederacy. Despite his 66 years, Colonel Cooper was vigorous, but manifestly would be most valuable in the post corresponding to the one he had renounced, that of Adjutant and Inspector General. Maj. Braxton Bragg, Brevet Lieutenant Colonel, had won a name in the Mexican War; Capt. P. G. T. Beauregard, now a Confederate Brigadier General of the regular Army, already was acclaimed as the "hero of Fort Sumter"; W. W. Loring, former Colonel of the United States Mounted Rifles, was an esteemed soldier, though not a West Point graduate; Lt. Col. W. J. Hardee, who had resigned from the First Cavalry, was a recognized tactician. Majors Earl Van Dorn and E. Kirby Smith of the Second Cavalry were men of military reputation. A resigned paymaster, Maj. James Longstreet, had won that brevet of the line by conspicuously fine conduct with the Eighth Infantry, at Molino del Rey.[50] Apart from these ten men, the other Southern officers at the command of the President were one or two Colonels long resigned, a few Majors, relatively unknown, and a considerable number of Captains who, because of the smallness of the military establishment of the United States, were old for their grade. Still more former Lieutenants there were, of a quality discovered, if at all, only by their former commanding officers at scattered Army posts. Virginia might find some

45 Exclusive of the class of 1861.
46 From the three border States of Maryland, Kentucky and Missouri, with Indian Territory and the District of Columbia added, had come a total of 152 living West Point graduates. These included natives appointed at large or from other border States.
47 O. R., 1, 597.   48 Cullum, No. 436.
49 Cullum, No. 156.   50 Cullum. No. 1164.

of these men valuable comrades in arms, but most of them already were training recruits in the Far South. Few, if any, would be available to assist in organizing and leading Virginia troops.[51]

Neither could Virginia expect to get officers from graduates of existing or defunct military schools in other Southern States. The only one of these that had large distinction was the South Carolina Military Academy, which, by act of January 28, 1861, had become the legal successor to The Arsenal Academy at Columbia and The Citadel Academy at Charleston. Those two institutions, created under a law of Dec. 20, 1842, had been operated by a single board. After 1845, cadets had their first year's instruction at The Arsenal and spent their remaining three years at The Citadel. Although graduates living in 1861 probably numbered less than 225, they were well trained and, with few exceptions, were quick to enlist. They rendered for South Carolina a service similar to that performed for the Old Dominion by the Virginia Military Institute,[52] but, of course, they were needed in their own State.

Were there any other sources, then, on which Virginia might draw? There scarcely seemed to be. She might have the support of a few Northern soldiers who sympathized with the stand the Old Dominion had taken. Perhaps a few foreigners would rally to her. So might one or another of the regular army officers of Virginia antecedents who had been appointed from other States, but these included only one Colonel and four Majors.[53]

In summary, then, the trained personnel available for commission, if the individuals sided with Virginia in the struggle, was as follows:

[51] In his admirable work, The United States Army in War and Peace, p. 244, Gen. O. L. Spaulding makes the point that while the corps of resigning officers available to the South was small, it had this great advantage: Confederate officers could be sent wherever they were needed, and without regard to post or regimental duty, which for a time cost the Union service in the field of many of its most experienced officers.

[52] See J. P. Thomas, The History of the South Carolina Military Academy, pp. 33, 37–38, 108; O. J. Bond, The Story of the Citadel, 42. In a copy of Thomas now in The Citadel Library and graciously lent the writer by Gen. C. P. Summerall is a typed summary by Colonel Bond of the record of Citadel graduates in the War between the States. This shows that of the 224 living graduates, prior to the class of 1864, a total of 193 served in the Confederate Army as follows: Brigadier Generals, 4; Colonels, 17; Lieutenant Colonels, 10; Majors, 22; Captains, 58; Lieutenants, 62; not commissioned, 20; total, 193. Of this number, thirty-nine were killed in battle. Four died in service. It is much to be regretted that similar statistics are not available for other Southern military schools, the very names of which seem, in some instances, to have been forgotten. In Cullum's Register, various West Point graduates are listed as instructors in short-lived schools the history of which cannot be traced in the Library of Congress or in the Library of the War College.

[53] These officers, with their rank, their number in Cullum's Register and the State from which they were named to West Point, were as follows: Col. Edmund B. Alexander, Tenth Infantry, No. 358, Kentucky; Bvt. Maj. Geo. D. Ramsay, Ordnance, No. 257, District of Columbia; Maj. B. W. Brice, Staff, No. 580, Ohio; Maj. T. L. Alexander, Eighth Infantry, No. 615, Kentucky; Bvt. Maj. William Hays, Second Artillery, No. 1034, Tennessee.

On the active list of the Army: One Brevet Lieutenant General of the line, one Brigadier General of the staff, six Colonels of the line, two Lieutenant Colonels, ten Majors, line and staff, twenty-three Captains, thirty-one First Lieutenants and ten Second Lieutenants. Sixty-three of these eighty-four were West Point graduates.

Retired Virginia graduates of West Point: Twenty-one, of whom only two had been regular field officers, one a Brevet Major and one a Major of Volunteers.

Former officers of the Mexican War, not included in the above classes: A minimum of ninety-four, none of them above the rank of Major by brevet.

Graduates of the Virginia Military Institute: About 425,[54] an undetermined majority of whom were Virginians.

Northern sympathizers, foreigners, native Virginians who had been commissioned from other States: Unpredictable.

The computable total was 625. Exclusive of V. M. I. graduates, the number did not exceed 200. If the full personnel of all the known categories joined Virginia, there would be sufficient officers for not more than fourteen regiments; but could even that many trained leaders be assured? Would the 625, or a strong majority of them, support Virginia? That was the pressing issue. In particular, would those regular army officers of known capacity and experience side with their own State in its withdrawal from the Union?

Hope was high that Lt. Gen. Winfield Scott would lead all eighty-four of the Virginia officers of the regular Army to share in the defense of the Old Dominion. Reports circulated that the commanding General had resigned, but as these were confirmed by no word or hint from Scott, even after the secession of his State, his lifelong friend and fellow student of college days, Judge John Robertson of Petersburg, was sent to Washington on April 19 to interview him and other Virginians of distinction in the Army. Judge Robertson did not reach the Federal capital until the 21st, and then found Scott in attendance upon a Cabinet meeting. About 3 o'clock, the Judge saw the General crossing the street and intercepted him. Would Scott give him a few minutes? Old "Fuss and Feathers" hesitated and complained that his engagements were heavy, but at length he agreed to listen. Robertson at once appealed to him to join Virginia. Scott was instant in refusal. He was determined, in all circumstances, he said, to defend the Stars and Stripes and to maintain his allegiance to the Union. In doing this,

---

[54] Actually, 433, less those who, as officers in the Mexican War, have been counted already.

he went on, it was not his intention to invade the South, but to act on the defensive.

"I have so far addressed you as a private citizen," Robertson answered. "I now inform you that I am officially charged with a communication to you from the Governor of Virginia and under the direction of the State Convention. I shall not make that communication unless you answer me that it will be received without offense."

Scott was as unyielding as before: If the communication was intended to turn him from his allegiance to the Union, he would not hear it.

"I shall say nothing more," the Judge replied, "than that I am satisfied it was not so intended or considered by the Convention or the Governor, and I would not have borne it to you, had I not thought it honorable to you and indispensable to your good name." [55]

There the conversation ended. Perhaps it never would have begun had Robertson and the authorities realized that, in addition to his devotion to the Union, General Scott had for the President of the Confederacy a hatred deeper in 1861 than that which he had exhibited in a long, fiery correspondence when Davis was Secretary of War. [56] On the day following the election of Mr. Davis to head the government of the seceding States, General Scott was reported to have said: "I am amazed that any man of judgment should hope for the success of any cause in which Jefferson Davis is a leader. There is contamination in his touch. If secession was 'the holiest cause that tongue or sword of mortal ever lost or gained,' he would ruin it! He will bear a great deal of watching. . . . He is not a cheap Judas. I do not think he would have sold the Saviour for thirty shillings, but for the successorship of Pontius Pilate he would have betrayed Christ and the apostles and the whole Christian Church." [57] Although this remark was not quoted at the time, the disappointment of Virginia at the failure of General Scott to support her cause was, no doubt, greater than that felt by the Southern President against whom the General's savage words were directed. Davis must have reflected that, had General Scott resigned and joined the South, there would have been a war within a war.

[55] John Robertson to John Letcher, Richmond, Apr. 23, 1861, MS., *Exec. Papers of John Letcher*, Va. State Library. Major Elliott, *op. cit.*, 714, on the authority of Gen. E. D. Townsend's *Anecdotes of the American Civil War*, 4–5, quotes General Scott as saying to the Judge: "Friend Robertson, go no further! It is best that we part here, before you compel me to resent a mortal insult! I have served my country, under the flag of the Union, for more than fifty years, and so long as God permits me to live, I will defend that flag with my sword, even if my native State assails it." These remarks are quite in character, but as they came at second-hand through Townsend, whose memory was not flawless, it seems better to quote the less dramatic official version given at the time by one of the participants in the conversation.

[56] Elliott, *op. cit.*, 647 ff.

[57] Elliott, *op. cit.*, 712, who quoted Chittenden, *Recollections of President Lincoln*, 95–96.

Virginians saw only that their most distinguished soldier was unwilling to bear arms for his native State.

If Scott were lost, what of R. E. Lee, then 54 years old, whom the commanding General regarded as the ablest officer of the Army? The answer came quickly through Robertson: Lee deplored secession and agonized over the dissolution of the Union, but, without hesitation, he had resigned from the Army after the secession of his State, and he would defend Virginia. By the evening of April 22, on call from the Governor, he was in Richmond.[58]

Would George H. Thomas, a Major of Lee's former regiment, the Second Cavalry, go with Lee or remain with Scott—was he for Virginia first or for the Union? An able soldier he was admitted to be. At Monterey and at Buena Vista he had distinguished himself: few of the younger field officers had seer more service. His native county of Southampton had given him a sword; all Virginia was proud of him. Not yet 45 years of age, physically powerful and commanding, mentally strong, he was of the stuff of great commanders.

Everything had indicated that, when Virginia seceded, he would resign. On January 18, 1861, at a time when he was fearful that an injury received in a railroad accident would incapacitate him for active military duty, he had made inquiry concerning a prospective vacancy in the office of Commandant at the Virginia Military Institute. He had written then: "If not already filled, I will be under obligations if you will inform me what salary and perquisites pertain to the situation, as from present appearances I fear it will soon be necessary for me to be looking up some means of support." This had been construed to mean that Thomas anticipated the obligation, as a Virginian, of resigning from the Army, and not merely the necessity, as an invalid, of retiring from it.[59]

Major Thomas's letter of inquiry may have been inspired by his friend Maj. William Gilham, then Commandant of the Institute, who was hoping to have some one named to that post so that he might devote himself more largely to academic duties. Early in 1861, it became apparent that a new Commandant would not be elected immediately and that the choice of the board ultimately would be another than Thomas. Accordingly, in March, Major Gilham mentioned to Governor Letcher the possibility of procuring Thomas's services for the State. The Governor was interested, because he was seeking a Chief of Ord-

[58] See 1 R. E. Lee, 435 ff.

[59] For Thomas's letter, see Donn Piatt, General George H. Thomas, 82. Mr. Piatt made some singular mistakes, p. 81, concerning the ratification of the ordinance of secession and, p. 83, he curiously affirmed that the Virginia Military Institute was "a private school, differing from others only in the fact that the pupils were called cadets instead of students, and were subject to the drill and discipline of private soldiers."

nance. Letcher accordingly asked Gilham to address Thomas and to inquire whether that officer intended to resign from the Army and, if so, whether he cared for the position. Gilham wrote on March 8 to Thomas, who was then in New York.

The Major replied on March 12, directly to Letcher. After noting that Gilham had communicated with him, he said: "I have the honor to state, after expressing my most sincere thanks for your very kind offer, that it is not my wish to leave the service of the United States as long as it is honorable for me to remain in, and, therefore, as long as my native state (Virginia) remains in the Union, it is my purpose to remain in the army, unless requested to perform duties alike repulsive to my honor and humanity." [60] To officials of the State, this appeared to be the maximum assurance a soldier who held a United States commission could give that, if Virginia did leave the Union, or he were called upon to perform duty repugnant to him, he would resign.

In mid-April, 1861, Thomas rejoined his regiment at Carlisle Barracks. There, on the 21st, he received an order to take four troops of cavalry and to disperse Marylanders who were threatening to tear up the railroad track in order to prevent the movement of troops to Washington. Thomas is said to have hesitated before obeying this order but to have been persuaded by Fitz-John Porter that it was his duty to adhere to the Union.[61] From the hour of his decision, whether made then or previously, Thomas gave himself to the Union cause with full and inflexible resolution.

Would Thomas's decision be that of an even more distinguished Virginian——Brig. Gen. Joseph E. Johnston, who, at 54, was Quartermaster General of the Army? Johnston, like Thomas, had been born in Southside Virginia. Of long, Revolutionary lineage, he had been graduated No. 13 in the West Point class of 1829, when his friend Robert E. Lee had been No. 2. Many opportunities had come to Johnston during thirty years' service as a soldier. Of all of them he had made the most. In 1838, while with a small detachment in Florida, he had been ambushed and, after almost all the other officers had been wounded, he had been forced to retreat for seven miles. Although a bullet struck his forehead and coursed around his skull, and six other missiles cut his uniform, he escaped with the remnant of the command.

[60] Piatt, op. cit., 82–83; Wise's V. M. I., 122–24; D. H. Maury in 10 S. H. S. P., 524–25.
[61] The authority for this is Senator Simon Cameron, then Secretary of War, who subsequently related the circumstances at length as one reason for the restoration of Fitz John Porter to the Army. Mr. Cameron, whose remarks are given in 12 S. H. S. P., 569–70, was present at the conversation between Thomas and Porter, but as his account was given in his old age, at a time when his memory may have been defective, it has been necessary to qualify the statement of what occurred.

By display of the same reckless valor, at Cerro Gordo, during the Mexican War, he had sustained a dangerous wound, but he had recovered in time to get another at Chapultepec and to win recognition by General Scott as the first to plant a regimental flag on the parapet of the fortress. From a campaign which he had entered as a Captain, Johnston emerged a Brevet Colonel of Infantry and Brevet Lieutenant Colonel of Engineers.[62] When two new regiments of cavalry had been organized in 1855, he had been made second in command of one, as his friend Lee had been of the other. A little more than five years thereafter, Johnston outclimbed all his classmates and won the staff rank of Brigadier General as head of the quartermaster service of the Army.

Something almost magical had attended his rise through grades where promotion was slow. No less was there about him the romance of gallant daring that appealed to the Southern heart: Would he give of his high reputation and his acknowledged abilities to the cause of Virginia? He did not delay. "The passage of the ordinance of secession," Johnston wrote years after, without the tinge of regret, "on the 17th of April was not known in Washington . . . until the 19th." He continued: "I believed, like most others, that the division of the country would be permanent; and that, apart from any right of secession, the revolution begun was justified by the maxims so often repeated by Americans, that free government is founded on the consent of the governed, and that every community strong enough to establish and maintain its independence has a right to assert it. Having been educated in such opinions, I naturally determined to return to the State of which I was a native, join the people among whom I was born, and live with my kindred, and, if necessary, fight in their defense. Accordingly, the resignation of my commission, written on Saturday [63] was offered to the Secretary of War Monday morning. That gentleman was requested, at the same time, to instruct the Adjutant General, who had kindly accompanied me, to write the order announcing its acceptance, immediately." [64] Thus, without reserve, was Johnston's sword at the command of his State.

Scott and Thomas for the Union; Lee and Johnston for Virginia—how would the choice of Philip St. George Cooke fall? He was from the Leesburg district of northern Virginia, member of a family with a taste for letters and himself author of a volume of memoirs based on his long and picturesque service in the West as an Indian fighter. Not yet 52, he was at the head of the Second Dragoons in the Depart-

---

[62] *Cullum*, No. 553.   [63] April 20.
[64] *Johnston's Narrative*. 10.

ment of Utah, and was among the best-known men in the Army. If he joined Virginia he would be invaluable in the training of those boys who wished to carry their horses with them into the Army. He had prepared the new system of cavalry tactics which the government was soon to adopt,[65] and perhaps as commander of a dashing Virginia cavalry corps he might . . . but he would not. The newspapers brought no news of his resignation. It was June before they carried anything from him. Then came a letter in which he declared that his first allegiance was to the Union and not to Virginia. That meant the division of the family. Already his son, John R. Cooke, 28, and a Harvard man, had resigned his commission as First Lieutenant. Colonel Cooke's daughter, Flora, had married a young Virginia trooper, a First Lieutenant,[66] whose whole heart was with his State. When he decided to hurry home, she and her two children went with him. He was a breakneck youngster of 28, with a head full of plans for the organization of a "legion of cavalry—200 men—myself as commander, or a battery of light artillery, 100 men or less." His name was James E. B. Stuart.[67]

The commander of the First Dragoons answered the call the leader of the Second disregarded. Col. Thomas T. Fauntleroy, a native of Richmond County on the Northern Neck of Virginia, had been a Lieutenant at 17 years of age during the second war with Britain and then had followed the law. Returning to the Army in 1836 as Major of Dragoons, he had risen steadily. In front of Mexico City he had commanded Scott's little force of cavalry and then, for a decade in the West, he had galloped after Indians. From Santa Fe, as early as March 25, 1861, he had tendered his services to Virginia in the event of war, and by May 12 he was in Richmond.[68] He was experienced, he was courageous, but he was no longer young. In October, 1861, he would be 65.

Of the thirteen other field officers from Virginia,[69] five supported Virginia—Magruder, Chilton, Robert S. Garnett, Henry Hill and Albert J. Smith. Seven of the remaining eight, Colonel Garland, Colonel Seawell, Maj. John F. Lee, Major Steptoe, Major Macrae, Maj. Lawrence P. Graham, and Maj. Campbell Graham, adhered to the Union. Colonel Payne, who was 77, resigned in July, but did not attempt to fight for the South.[70] His comrade, Colonel Garland, was

---

[65] *Cullum,* No. 492.
[66] Captain, April 21, 1861; *Cullum,* No. 1643.
[67] *Thomason,* 60 ff.
[68] 11 *Cal. Va. State Papers,* 106, 127.
[69] Geo. W. Lay, already resigned, was the fourteenth.
[70] Heitman, *op. cit.,* gave the date of Colonel Payne's resignation as July 23, 1861, and the date of his death as Aug. 1, 1862. The end came in Goochland County, Virginia, within the Confederate lines. Payne had received a sword of honor from Virginia in 1848 for his gallantry at Palo Alto and Resaca de la Palma (11 *Cal. Va. State Papers,* 23). The *Richmond Dispatch* (Aug. 7, 1862, p. 2, col. 2) said of him: "It is well known

69 and close to death.[71] Colonel Seawell was 59. Major Steptoe and Maj. Campbell Graham had been on sick leave for years and were near their end.[72]

When the balance was struck, then, of the twenty active general and field officers born in Virginia and appointed to the Army from that State or at large, the Old Dominion could count on nine, Lee, Johnston, Fauntleroy, Magruder, Lay, Garnett, Chilton, Henry Hill and Albert J. Smith. The Union held Scott, Thomas and Cooke, and four other active field officers.

How would the company officers divide; what would be the decision of those who, before 1861, had retired? On the active list were sixty-four native sons appointed to the United States Army from Virginia; resigned officers of the same category numbered at least seventeen.[73] Would they be as little disposed as the seniors to accept the decision of the Old Dominion and to drill and train the volunteers? Professor Jackson, Maj. Jubal A. Early and most of the former officers who resided in the Commonwealth unhesitatingly espoused the cause of Virginia. Inasmuch as numerous officers were in the Far West when the State seceded, weeks elapsed before some of those who "decided for the South" could report and tender their service. In the end, of the sixty-four who held current commissions in the regular Army, forty-seven rallied to Virginia, sixteen adhered to the Union[74] and one apparently resigned from the Army but took no part in the war.[75] Thirteen of the seventeen who had resigned prior to 1861 fought for the Confederacy, one for the Union,[76] and three, so far as the records show, did not participate on either side.[77]

that he encountered severe censure on account of the pertinacity with which he held to the shadow of the old Union . . . We will not undertake to justify his course, but we *will* venture to say that he acted from a conviction of what he considered to be right. We will further say, that during the last twelve months of his life, after the designs of the North had become apparent, no man was more ardent in his wishes for the prosperity of the Confederacy, or exulted more sincerely in the victories of the Southern troops."

[71] He died June 5, 1861.

[72] Steptoe was promoted Lieutenant Colonel of the Tenth Infantry, Sept. 9, 1861, but he resigned Nov. 1, 1861, and died near Lynchburg, Va., Apr. 1, 1865, aged 49. (*Cullum,* No. 924). Graham was on sick leave from 1855 onward, was retired Sept. 9, 1861, and was not employed thereafter. He died in Baltimore, Nov. 8, 1866, aged 67 (*Cullum,* No. 294).

[73] To recapitulate the summary list, *supra,* p. 705, these were: Captains R. C. W. Radford and C. Q. Tompkins; Lieutenants Walter Gwynn, R. T. Jones, W. E. Jones, H. W. Mercer, J. R. Anderson, J. R. Chamoliss, P. St. George Cocke, J. Lucius Davis, D. B. Harris, W. N. Pendleton, A. T. M. Rust, F. H. Smith, H. L. Shields, Fisher A. Lewis and W. B. Magruder.

[74] Namely, Captains J. W. Davidson, T. S. S. Laidley, L. H. Marshall, H. E. Maynadier, John Newton, W. H. Gordon, and Lieutenants E. C. Bainbridge, M. T. Carr, W. P. Craighill, Geo. A. Gordon, John Mullan, W. R. Terrill, Robt. Williams, T. S. Baylor, Thomas M. Saunders and H. A. F. Worth.

[75] Capt. J. C. Bonnycastle.   [76] Capt. E. H. Carrington.

[77] H. L. Shields, Fisher A. Lewis and W. B. Magruder.

Because of their age, the response of veteran officers of Mexican War Volunteers, not of other classification, was disappointing, but some excellent officers were forthcoming. Kemper and Taliaferro, Corse and Weisiger immediately volunteered and received commissions. At least twenty-one others did likewise. From an estimated total of ninety-four in this category there were to be listed, ere the sun set on Appomattox, two Major Generals, two Brigadiers, eight Colonels,[78] six Lieutenant Colonels, three Majors and four Captains.

Nothing could exceed the response that came from the next source of potential officers, the graduates of the Virginia Military Institute. Within less than three months from the day Virginia seceded, one third of the field officers of Virginia volunteer regiments, and two thirds of like officers of the "provisional" regiments of the State, were men who had been trained at V. M. I.[79] The end of 1861 was to find fifty-six Virginia regiments of infantry and of heavy artillery organized. Twenty of these, as well as two of the eight regiments of Virginia cavalry, were to be commanded by V. M. I. graduates. That is to say, the Institute, within nine months, was to furnish almost exactly one third of the regimental leaders.[80] The number of commissioned officers from V. M. I.[81] exceeded by 82 per cent the total of graduates.[82] Seventeen hundred and eighty-one, of the 1902 matriculates from 1839 to 1865, served in the Confederate Army.[83]

Of the higher-ranking native Virginians in the regular Army who had been appointed to West Point from other States, not one placed himself at the command of the Governor, but several company officers did so. Among them was a Captain of 36, born in Richmond and appointed to West Point from Illinois.[84] His name, Geo. E. Pickett, had appeared in the news because of his defiance of the British at San Juan Island, Washington Territory, but he was little known in Virginia.

Besides these men there soon came three welcome officers of some distinction. The first of them was Maj. Daniel Ruggles of Massachusetts, a West Pointer of the Class of 1833,[85] who had married Richardetta

---

[78] O. E. Edwards of the Thirteenth South Carolina and I. W. Patton of the Twenty-second Louisiana are not counted in this list because their regiments were not from Virginia.

[79] Superintendent's report, July 15, 1861, cited in Wise's *V. M. I.*, 146. For the "provisional" regiments, an abortive attempt to create a small regular Army for Virginia, see *infra*, p. 722. A full account of this interesting period will be found in William Cooper, *One Hundred Years at V. M. I.*, vol. II, pp. 88 ff.

[80] Wise's *V. M. I.*, 149–50.

[81] Including officers who served with troops from other States. Counted also in this total are those V. M. I. graduates who participated in the Mexican War.

[82] *Cf.* Wise's *V. M. I.*, 485. The figures were, respectively, 790 and 433.

[83] Wise's *V. M. I.*, 461.

[84] *Cullum*, No. 1330.

[85] *Cullum*, No. 740.

Hooe of Friedland, King George County, Virginia.[86] He was on sick leave in the Old Dominion. He immediately resigned his United States commission and, on April 17, offered his services to Virginia.[87] A second Northern officer whose devotion to Southern principles led him to make great sacrifice was Bvt. Maj. John C. Pemberton, Captain of the Fourth Artillery, a Pennsylvanian born and reared. He resigned and hurried to Richmond.[88] The third unexpected volunteer was a Southerner, Maj. Benjamin Huger of South Carolina. This officer, 56 years of age, had been Chief of Ordnance and commander of the siege train in Scott's Mexican campaign and had received brevet as Colonel for his conduct at Chapultepec. Huger subsequently had risen high in the Ordnance Department, and had served as a member of the board to prepare a "complete system of instruction" for the artillery. The climax of secession found him in command of the arsenal at Pikesville, Maryland. He resigned after the withdrawal of Virginia from the Union and, without waiting to enlist in Confederate service, offered his sword to Virginia.

Although there was acclaim for these three men and for every native who resigned a Federal commission, there was humiliation and resentment that so many Virginia officers in the United States Army refused to recognize the secession of their State. Had comparative figures for the remainder of the South been compiled at the time, the distress of Virginia would have been deepened. Among living West Point graduates from other Southern States,[89] slightly less than 10 per cent sided with the North. Of the Virginia graduates, almost 30 per cent held to the Union.[90] Again, of the Virginians who. held regular army com-

[86] For this information the writer is indebted to the late Mrs. Vivian M. Fleming, of Fredericksburg, Va.

[87] 11 *Cal. Va. State Papers,* 107.

[88] *Cullum,* No. 917. Pemberton was graduated No. 27 in the class of 1837. The date of his resignation is given by Cullum as Apr. 29, 1861. It should be explained that in this, as in all other cases of the period, the date is that of the *acceptance,* not of the *tender* of the resignation. Officers who availed themselves of the right to resign at pleasure felt that they were free, from the hour of resignation, to fight for the South. The War Department never accepted a resignation until the paper had been sent through the bureaux and had been endorsed with notes on the status of the officer's accounts. Lack of familiarity with this procedure has led some writers to conclude that Confederate leaders, in some instances, actually were bearing arms against the United States before they had resigned.

[89] These were natives of a Southern State appointed to the Military Academy from their own or from some other Southern State, or at large. Natives of a Southern State, sent to West Point from a Northern or Western State, and natives of Northern or Western States appointed to the Academy from the South are excluded from this count because their allegiance in most instances naturally was with the Union.

[90] To be exact, 28.8 per cent. For the entire South, Virginia included, the division of all West Point graduates was as follows: One hundred and ninety-nine, or 62.5 per cent, bore arms for the South; seventy-eight, or 24.5 per cent, remained in the United States Army; and forty-one, or 12.8 per cent, did not serve as soldiers on either side; total ascertained graduates, 318. The class of 1861 at West Point is not included. Of the 152

missions, without graduation from West Point, eighteen sided with the South, and eleven with the Union. Among those from the other Southern States, the Confederacy commanded the support of twenty-seven, and the Union of seven.[91]

The two reasons for this disparity were obvious: Virginia was in some sense a border State, where the cleavage over secession was deeper than in the Far South. Second, as one of the oldest and most populous States, Virginia early had supplied to the Army a large quota of officers, many of whom had grown up, so to say, with the Union. Some of these men had been associated so long with the Federal Army and had been absent from Virginia for so many years that they had lost touch with her. Most of the professional soldiers who had retained close ties sided with her in the hour of separation. For example, of the twenty-six senior officers from Virginia who were to take any active part in the war, only half declared for the South. Among approximately

West Point graduates from the border—Maryland, District of Columbia, Kentucky, Missouri and Indian Territory—those who championed the Southern cause numbered fifty-five (36.1 per cent), those who adhered to the Union were seventy-six (50 per cent), and those who did not fight under either flag were twenty-one (13.8 per cent). If any significance attached to figures that included among potential officers of the Confederacy all graduates of West Point born in the South, in the border States, in the District of Columbia, or born in one of these and appointed to the Academy from another of them, the final totals would be: total graduates, active and resigned, 440; served in the Confederate army, 254 (57.7 per cent); served in the Union Army, 124 (28.1 per cent); did not serve, 62 (14 per cent).

[91] One Virginian and two other Southerners are not known to have participated on either side. For the entire South, the figures were: with the Confederacy, forty-five (68.1 per cent); with the Union, eighteen (27.1 per cent); inactive, three (4.5 per cent). The forty-six border-State officers, not graduates of West Point (i.e., those from Kentucky, Maryland, Missouri and the District of Columbia, as Indian Territory had none), divided in this wise: Confederates, fifteen (32.6 per cent); Unionists, thirty (65.2 per cent); non-participants, one (2 per cent). Were this group of officers—Southerners, border-State men and appointees from the District of Columbia—considered as a whole, the figures would be: joined the Southern Army, sixty, or 53.5 per cent; remained in the Union Army, forty-eight, or 42.8 per cent; neutral, 3.5 per cent. When the last active officer had made his choice, and all those who once had worn the epaulets of the United States had reached their decision, the Southern graduates of the Military Academy and those Southern officers of the "old army" who had not received diplomas at West Point were arrayed tragically thus: for the new Confederacy, 244 (68.7 per cent); for the Union, sixty-seven (18.8 per cent); fighting on neither side, forty-five (12.3 per cent). Among like officers of the border States, the District of Columbia and the Indian Territory, the division was: with the South, seventy (35.3 per cent); with the Union, 106 (53.5 per cent); non-participating, twenty-two (11.1 per cent). For the entire South, the border States and the District of Columbia, this was the decision of all active and resigned officers, whether graduates of West Point or not: to bear arms in behalf of the South, 314 (56.8 per cent); to adhere to the Union, 172 (31.1 per cent); to have no part in fratricidal strife, sixty-six (11.9 per cent). To the 314 Southern and border-State officers, active and resigned, of the "old army" who cast in their lot with the Confederacy, were added other Northern men besides Pemberton and Ruggles. The total number of West Point graduates who made this sacrifice, greater far than that of native Southerners, was forty. From the regular army came four officers Northern-born, not West Point graduates, who had been appointed to the United States Army from Southern or border States, and one officer, the inimitable George Deas, born in Pennsylvania and appointed from that State. These raised to 359 the total corps of professional soldiers, formerly of the United States Army, who were ready for Southern service.

eighty-seven junior officers, sixty-six, or about 75 per cent, supported Virginia. Those graduates of West Point who had resigned from the United States Army prior to 1861 and had resided in Virginia were three to one for the cause of the Confederacy.[92]

Before it was known what most of these men would do, the Virginia Convention, on the day of secession, authorized the Governor to muster into service as many volunteer companies as might be necessary to repel invasion, and to appoint their general, field and staff officers. By the same ordinance he was directed immediately to "invite all efficient and worthy Virginians and residents of Virginia in the Army and Navy of the United States to retire therefrom and to enter the service of Virginia, assigning to them such rank as will not reverse the relative rank held by them in the United States service, and will at least be equal thereto." [93]

Under the first authorization of this ordinance, Governor Letcher immediately called on W. B. Taliaferro, Major of Volunteers in the Mexican War and now a Major General of Militia, to take temporary command at Norfolk,[94] and to Harpers Ferry the Governor sent Kenton Harper, another Major General of Militia, and a former Captain of the Mexican War.[95] Philip St. George Cocke was commissioned Brigadier General of Volunteers and was ordered to assume direction of affairs at Alexandria.[96] Maj. Daniel Ruggles of Massachusetts was named Brigadier General of Volunteers and was assigned to the Fredericksburg area.

The Convention decided further that Virginia must have a commanding officer for all her armed forces and, on April 19, it passed an ordinance to that effect.[97] In execution of this measure, on April 22,

[92] The careers of several native Virginians, who received appointment to the United States Military Academy from other States and served in the Union Army in 1861–65, were full of interest. Some of these officers have been mentioned *supra*, p. 710. In the appended list, the State of appointment, the number in *Cullum*, and the highest rank attained in Federal service are given: Edmund B. Alexander, Ky., No. 358, Bvt. Brig. General; Thomas L. Alexander, Ky., No. 615, Lieutenant Colonel; Jacob Ammen, Ohio, No. 640, Brigadier General; Benj. W. Brice, Ohio, No. 580, Paymaster General, Bvt. Maj. General; Alexander B. Dyer, Mo., No. 896, Chief of Ordnance after Sept. 12, 1864, Bvt. Maj. General; William Hays, Tenn., No. 1034, in command of the II Corps, July 3–Sept. 13, 1863, Bvt. Maj. General; John Love, Tenn., No. 1072, Maj. General Indiana Legion; George D. Ramsay, D. C., No. 257, Chief of Ordnance, Sept. 15, 1863–Sept. 12, 1864, Bvt. Maj. General; Jesse L. Reno, Pa., No. 1279, Maj. General Vols., killed at South Mountain; John C. Tidball, Ohio, No. 1379, Bvt. Maj. General. Of this number, it scarcely is necessary to say, the most brilliant was General Reno, a native of Wheeling who was affiliated from childhood with Pennsylvania. Bvt. Col. Gurden Chapin, No. 1518, a native of the District of Columbia, Maj. Jas. P. Roy, No. 1444, born in England, and Bvt. Brig. General James Totten, No. 1083, of Pennsylvania, received their appointments to West Point from Virginia and served in the Union Army.
[93] Ordinances, Virginia Convention, 1861, No. 9.
[94] *O. R.*, 2, 771.   [95] *Ibid.*, 772.
[96] *Ibid.*, 775.
[97] Ordinance No. 11, Virginia Convention, 1861.

the Governor nominated Col. R. E. Lee, with the rank of Major General. After unanimous confirmation and a formal reception by the Convention on April 23, Lee took command. The Governor, meantime, continued to commission officers. Joseph E. Johnston was nominated as Major General of Volunteers and was placed by Lee in command of the forces in and around Richmond.[98] Similar rank was given Walter Gwynn. A little later, when the Convention authorized the establishment of a small "provisional army" to supplement the volunteers,[99] Governor Letcher issued many commissions for its command.

Although the Convention was prompt, in most instances, to confirm Letcher's nominations, it rebelled against the grant of exalted rank. It held up the nominations of Johnston and Gwynn until the Governor and the Advisory Council withdrew the names and offered to renominate the two as Brigadier Generals.[100] By similar compromise, Ruggles and Cocke were commissioned as Colonels, instead of as Brigadier Generals. These and other appointments were divided between the provisional and the volunteer service.

By June 9, the resigned and retired field officers of the United States Army who had tendered their services to Virginia had been commissioned as follows:

R. E. Lee, commanding, Major General;

J. E. Johnston, Brigadier General, Provisional Army, which commission he declined, May 8, 1861, to accept like rank in the Confederate Army; [101]

T. T. Fauntleroy, Brigadier General, Provisional Army;

Benjamin Huger, Brigadier General of Volunteers; [102]

J. B. Magruder, Colonel, Provisional Army; [103]

G. W. Lay, Aide to the Governor, Colonel of Cavalry,[104] and, subsequently, Lieutenant Colonel of Light Infantry, Provisional Army; [105]

Robert S. Garnett, Adjutant General to the Commanding General; Colonel of Cavalry, Provisional Army; [106]

R. H. Chilton, Colonel of Cavalry, Provisional Army, a position he

[98] O. R., 2, 873.

[99] Ordinance No. 13, Apr. 27, 1861, loc. cit. This army was to be enlisted for a term of three years, but as volunteers were accepted for twelve months (Ordinance No. 23, Apr. 30, 1861, loc. cit.) scant progress was made in procuring men for the "provisional" force. That organization served only as a convenient means of commissioning qualified company or recruiting officers who, for one reason or another, were not elected by volunteer units.

[100] O. R., 51, pt. 2, p. 60.

[101] Governor's MS. Minute Book, June 10, 1861.

[102] Ibid., May 22, 1861.

[103] Magruder's services were tendered April 23 (Governor's MS. Minute Book). For his assigned rank, see Journal of Virginia Convention, May 1, 1861.

[104] As of April 24; Governor's MS. Minute Book, April 27.

[105] Document 24, p. 10, Virginia Convention.

[106] Document No. 24, p. 10, Virginia Convention.

resigned, May 29, to become Lieutenant Colonel, Adjutant General's Department, C. S. A.; [107]

T. J. Jackson, Colonel of Volunteers; [108]

Henry Hill, Colonel of Infantry, Provisional Army; [109]

Jubal A. Early, Colonel of Volunteers; [110]

Daniel Ruggles, Colonel of Light Infantry, Provisional Army; [111]

Arthur C. Cummings, Colonel of Volunteers; [112]

William B. Taliaferro, Colonel of Volunteers; [113]

John C. Pemberton, Lieutenant Colonel of Artillery, Provisional Army.[114]

This organization was known to be temporary. On April 24, Virginia completed a "Military Convention" [115] and agreed formally to join the Confederate States, provided the voters, in an election on May 23, ratified the ordinance of secession.[116] It was understood that the transfer of Virginia's troops to the Confederacy would be made when ratification was effected and that most, if not all, the State commissions would be vacated. This was the reason Johnston declined and Chilton resigned the commands offered them. Because organization had to be effected immediately for the defense of the State, other officers took the risk of losing their commissions, of receiving lower Confederate rank, or of having to serve under a Confederate officer of a grade below their own. In the case of Lee, Vice President Stephens explained the evening after Lee accepted the Virginia command as a Major General that, when Virginia entered the Confederacy, Lee might be commanded by a Brigadier General because the law then authorized no Confederate general officers above that rank. Lee put this consideration aside as of no importance in determining the necessary adherence of Virginia to the Confederacy.[117]

---

[107] *Governor's MS. Minute Book*, June 10, 1861; 1 *Journal Confederate Congress* (edition of 1904), 422, 567–68.

[108] *Ibid.*, Apr. 27, 1861.

[109] Document No. 24, p. 5, Virginia Convention.

[110] *Governor's MS. Minute Book*, May 2, 1861.

[111] May 9, 1861; Document No. 24, p. 10, Virginia Convention.

[112] Wise's *V. M. I.*, 515.

[113] *O. R.*, 2, 800. Albert J. Smith apparently had not entered Virginia by June 9. He appears on the records of the United States Army as "dismissed June 20, 1861." Subsequently he became Lieutenant Colonel and Paymaster, C. S. A.

[114] Document 24, p. 5, Virginia Convention. On April 28 Letcher had planned to commission Pemberton as Lieutenant Colonel of Volunteers (*Governor's MS. Minute Book*, April 29, 1861).

[115] IV *O. R.*, 1, 390.

[116] See the excellent study of H. T. Shanks, *The Secession Movement in Virginia*, 204.

[117] 1 *R. E. Lee*, 470. Stephens had been apprehensive that the prospect of subordinating their ranking officer to a Confederate Brigadier might lead the members of the Virginia Convention to decline to enter into the military convention. He entirely misjudged the temper of the State.

Within two days after the military convention was signed, the Confederate Secretary of War began to press for information concerning the strength and disposition of the Virginia forces.[118] By May 1, eight regiments from other States were ordered to concentrate at Lynchburg, under a native of Florida, a former Major of the Second United States Cavalry, now Lt. Col. E. Kirby Smith of the Confederate Army.[119] He knew how to adapt himself to the unusual conditions of dual sovereignty. This unhappily was not true of the commander of Confederate troops from Louisiana, who reached Richmond before the end of the first week in May. This officer was Col. Albert G. Blanchard, a Massachusetts classmate of General Lee at West Point,[120] a Major of the Twelfth Infantry in the Mexican War and, in 1861, Treasurer of two Louisiana Railroads. Colonel Blanchard was not disposed to take crders from the Governor of Virginia. Friction between the Confederate and State authorities arose almost immediately,[121] but this was relieved momentarily by a simple and sensible expedient: the Secretary of War, in formal orders, gave General Lee, as Virginia commander, temporary control of the Confederate forces in the State.[122]

Tactful and patient Lee was, but his best effort could not control the complex emotions, rivalries and ambition of all the officers from the South who came to Virginia with troops. Because the task of assigning these officers and troops was a long one, there was impatience and bickering. Lee was accused of inefficiency or worse.[123] Although he organized the State's defense with fine speed and judgment, difficulties multiplied. Northwestern Virginia was stirred by open antagonism to secession and to the Confederate government.[124] Scarcely was the Norfolk area established as a military command than it became evident that General Gwynn was not the man for that station. He had to be relieved by General Huger—the first warning to the South that those of high name and professional station might not always prove equal to the bewildering duties of preparation, much less of combat.[125]

In other respects, as the date for the referendum on secession approached, there was endless excitement and confusion but little military action. Except for the harmless exchange of a few shots between Federal warships, and the hastily constructed batteries at Gloucester Point on the York, and at Sewell's Point near Norfolk,[126] no hostilities occurred even after the end of the twenty days Mr. Lincoln on April 15 had allowed for the dispersal of the "combinations" in the Southern

---

[118] O. R., 2, 783, 792.
[119] O. R., 2, 792.
[120] Cullum, No. 566.
[121] O. R., 2, 813.
[122] O. R., 2, 837.
[123] 1 R. E. Lee, 501.
[124] Ibid., 503-4. This confused period is treated at length in the work here cited.
[125] 1 R. E. Lee, 507-8; See supra, p. 23 ff.
[126] O. R., 2, 27 ff., 33 ff.

States.[127] Then, on May 23, as the voters of Virginia were registering overwhelmingly at the polls their approval of the ordinance of secession, there was a brief, polite Federal reconnaissance from Fortress Monroe to Hampton.[128] The next day strong Union forces crossed the Potomac and occupied Alexandria, Virginia. It was to cope with this invasion that Beauregard, as set forth in Chapter I, was summoned from South Carolina.

[127] III *O. R.*, 1, 60.   [128] *O. R.*, 2, 35–36.

APPENDIX III

The Distribution of Beauregard's Combat Order of July 20, 1861

In his *Responsibilities of the First Bull Run*,[1] General Johnston wrote concerning Beauregard's combat order of the night of July 20–21, 1861: "This offensive movement [of the Federals down the Warrenton Turnpike] would have frustrated our plan of the day before, if the orders for it had been delivered to the troops. It appears from the reports of the commanders of the six brigades on the right that but one of them, General Longstreet, received it."

To this, in his *Battle of Manassas*,[2] General Beauregard replied: "That the order of march and battle was received by all the commanders immediately concerned in the offensive is too apparent from the action in conformity with it, not only of Longstreet, but of Jones and Ewell, as well as Holmes, to warrant General Johnston in his extraordinary assumption. Their receipt of this never was questioned for a moment. It was only the order to Ewell to begin the movement that miscarried."

Printed reports of the various brigade commanders, with the exception of Longstreet, do not mention the receipt of the combat order. The failure of these men to refer to the document does not necessarily mean, of course, that it did not reach them. On the other hand, the scope and form of the report of D. R. Jones indicates that if he had received the order he would have mentioned it. He spoke specifically of a different one received at 7.10 A.M., as if it were the first of the day.[3] The inference from Holmes's report [4] is almost as strong.

In support of General Johnston's statement that the order did not reach most of the commanders of Brigades, three items of evidence not available at the time of his controversy with Beauregard are now of record:

(1) Early specifically stated in his *Autobiography*,[5] that the order was not communicated to him;

(2) Cocke's report not only is without mention of the order but also is so worded as virtually to preclude the possibility of receipt;[6]

(3) Dr. Hamlin [7] quoted a letter of July 31, 1861, in which Ewell

---

[1] 2 *B. & L.*, 246.
[2] Page 51.
[3] *O. R.*, 2, 537.
[4] *Ibid.*, 565.
[5] Page 16.
[6] *O. R.*, 51, pt. 1, p. 28.
[7] *The Making of a Soldier*, 106.

stated: "On the 21st we were roused before daylight with orders to hold ourselves in readiness at a moment's warning. . . ." Manifestly, Ewell was mistaken concerning the hour, but as he quoted almost the exact language of the dispatch of 5.30 A.M., he must have referred to that and not to the long, earlier combat order. The next information Ewell had from Beauregard came "about 9 A.M." through Jones.[8]

It thus would appear that Ewell and Early did not receive the combat order, and it is almost certain that Cocke did not. The other commanders, it may be repeated, in their contemporary reports, are silent. They cannot be called as witnesses in support or in denial of the assertion General Beauregard made about twenty-five years after the event.

[8] *Ibid.*

APPENDIX IV

SOME of the inexperienced Confederate commanders in the action on the plateau around the Henry house had never seen the terrain before they took position and apparently, in some instances, never examined it during the preparation of their reports. Other officers filed no reports. For these reasons, the usual difficulties of determining an order of battle are increased.

The maps, which are listed fully in R. M. Johnston, *op. cit.*, 282 ff, are far from satisfactory. Much the best of them is that prepared by Lt. W. G. Atkinson, C. S. A. Engineers, and reproduced in *O. R. Atlas,* Plate III-2. This shows the topography with reasonable accuracy and gives the roads of advance, but in its present form it does not show troop positions. Sundry unexplained numerals and letters on the map indicate that a key at one time may have been attached to it. If this key ever is found, the map may show where some of the units were located. The map printed in Warder and Catlett, *Battle of Young's Branch,*[1] is the most convenient large-scale topographical base, but it is incomplete and, with the exception noted on p. 70, is altogether untrustworthy as respects troop positions. Numerals given in the key do not always appear on the map; some numerals are duplicated; to other positions there is no reference in the key; the artillery positions do not appear in the key, though it is easy to interpret them by the initials of the commanders' names; finally, in some instances, as that of Elzey, the position assigned by Warder and Catlett demonstrably is erroneous. The map made by Capt. Saml. P. Mitchell of the First Virginia and published by W. Margrave White of Richmond is of small value. In these circumstances, though nothing better than a reasonable approximation is attainable, it seemed to the writer desirable to start *de novo* and to reconstruct from the reports the order of battle of the Confederate infantry. The artillery changed position so often that it is futile to attempt to locate the batteries on a small sketch.

When the survivors of the composite Brigade of Bee and Bartow, together with those of Evans's command, retreated to Henry Hill, most of them undoubtedly took refuge in the first ravine to the East

[1] Richmond, 1862. For the preparation of this map, see *Richmond Dispatch,* Dec. 30, 1861, p. 1, col. 1.

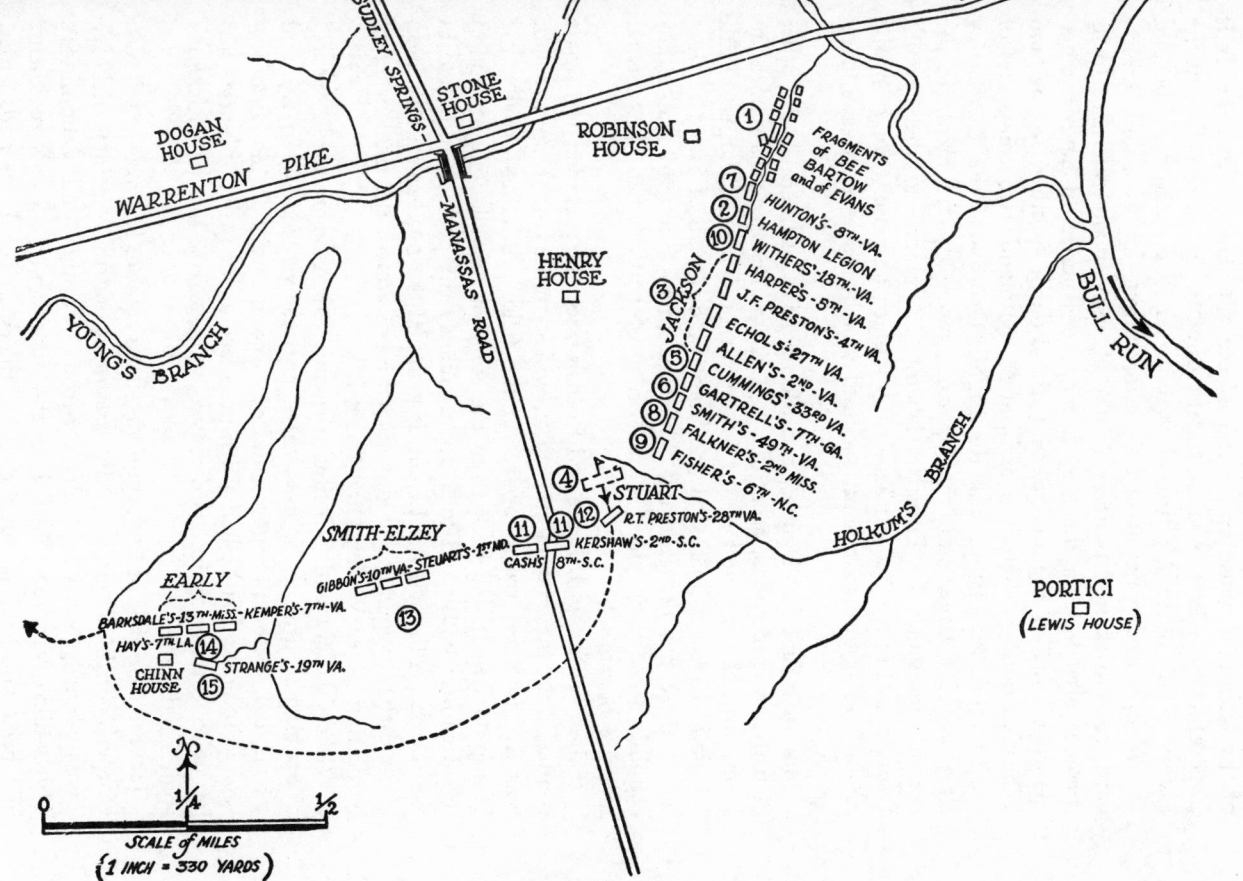

The Order of Battle of the Confederate Infantry on the left, First Manassas, July 21, 1861. Numerals indicate the order in which the various units took position.

of the Robinson house and South of the Warrenton Turnpike. It is impossible to say how many of them crossed to the eastern slope of the ravine. The Fourth Alabama drew out completely and went beyond the ridge, where it maintained some formation. Johnston and Beauregard led it back into position. In the absence of any reference to its presence elsewhere in the line, it may be assumed to have rejoined the fragments in the ravine, viz., the Fourth South Carolina and Wheat's Louisiana Battalion of Evans's command, two companies of the Eleventh Mississippi, and the Eighth Georgia of the Bee-Bartow Brigade. The larger unit that appears among the fragments in the sketch represents the Fourth Alabama. Reference to the Seventh Georgia and to the Second Mississippi, which also drew out from the ravine and re-formed behind Jackson, will be made in a later paragraph.

Hunton's Eighth Virginia,[2] the effective right element in the order of battle, was intended, according to General Beauregard's report,[3] to form, with the remnant of the Hampton Legion and Harper's Fifth Virginia, a reserve against attack from the direction of Stone Bridge; but if these regiments at any time constituted a refused flank, they certainly took their place in the order of battle when the general advance began.

If the Bee-Bartow Brigade and Evans's troops be regarded as a single combat unit, the Hampton Legion, which formed on Hunton's left, was the second force to arrive on the field. Suffering heavily, the Hampton Legion fell back from the scene of its valiant fight around the Robinson house and took approximately the position indicated in the sketch. Although the Legion is assigned the numeral 2, by reason of its early engagement, it did not take position in the final order of battle until after Withers had formed.

Withers's Eighteenth Virginia is mentioned in Beauregard's report[4] as arriving in time to "follow" the charge delivered between 2.30 and 3 P.M.; but Withers's report[5] and the account given in his *Autobiography*[6] indicate that he had a definite place in the order of battle. His left oblique, under Beauregard's instructions, carried him past Ricketts's abandoned guns.[7]

Jackson's Brigade of five regiments, from right to left, was as follows: Harper's Fifth Virginia, J. F. Preston's Fourth Virginia, Echols's Twenty-fourth Virginia, Allen's Second Virginia and Cummings's Thirty-third Virginia. Earlier in the afternoon, Jackson's regiments had been arranged to support the artillery in his front and center.

[2] Seven companies.   [3] *O. R.*, 2, 492.
[4] *Ibid.*, 495.   [5] *Ibid.*, 547.
[6] Pages 148–49   [7] *Withers*, 149.

As a result of the charges and the shift of the guns, it seems probable that Jackson was in full line of battle when the final advance was made. There can be no certainty regarding the exact distance of Jackson's front from the Henry house at any time after he came over the edge of the plateau to cover Bee's withdrawal. At different crises in the afternoon the front may have been as much as 200 yards on either side of the line given in the sketch.

Gartrell's Seventh Georgia, the first infantry to extend Jackson's left, belonged to Bartow's command. The regiment probably passed over the ravine East of the Robinson house, re-formed in Jackson's rear and then gallantly entered the action again. This movement may account for the statement in Jackson's report,[8] "I continued to advance with the understanding that Bee would form in my rear." Only a part of the Bee-Bartow Brigade reached the rear of Jackson.

Smith's Forty-ninth Virginia,[9] which formed on Gartrell's left, had marched from Cocke's position.

Falkner's Second Mississippi, on the left of Smith, belonged to Bee's Brigade and doubtless took its final place in much the same manner as the Seventh Georgia.

Fisher's Sixth North Carolina, the next regiment on the left, arrived at Manassas Junction on the 21st and marched to the sound of the firing. It is not listed in the Army of the Shenandoah;[10] but it is mentioned by the A. A. G. of Johnston on Aug. 23 as belonging to Bee's Brigade.[11]

Stuart's cavalry, which reached the field after Jackson and covered his left flank until infantry took its place, held ground that cannot be identified with any certainty from the report of its commander. The reference by Stuart to his attack on the 11th New York indicates that his front was parallel to the advance of that regiment in column of twos. As he would have been too far away from Jackson had he been on the West side of the Sudley road, the probabilities are that the "skirt of woods" he mentioned was that North of Holkum Branch. Stuart shifted from this position soon after Kershaw and Cash had formed. He was to the left of the Chinn house when Early arrived there,[12] and then he moved still farther to the West.

R. T. Preston's Twenty-eighth Virginia, from his report,[13] was not in contact with the Confederate troops on his right. He stated, further, that Kershaw was "beyond" him. While it is not quite certain in which direction Kershaw's guide subsequently led him, after Preston had wandered into the Sudley road, it seems probable that Preston turned

8 O. R., 2, 481.
10 O. R., 2, 470.
12 O. R., 2, 557.
9 Three companies.
11 O. R., 2, 569.
13 O. R., 2, 550.

back to the right. This would place him about midway between Fisher and Kershaw.

Kershaw's Second and Cash's Eighth South Carolina regiments can be located with a closer approach to certainty than almost any other regiments on the field. This is because it is easy to establish, from the contours, where Kemper's battery had its guns.

Elzey's Brigade, which consisted of Steuart's First Maryland, Gibbon's Tenth Virginia and Vaughn's Third Texas, was between Cash and Early in the final order of battle. Elevation and cover fix its position with fair accuracy. The arrangement of the three regiments, left to right, is determinable from a letter in the *Richmond Whig*.[14]

Early's Brigade, the left element, can be placed with some assurance because of its known proximity to the Chinn house.

Strange's Nineteenth Virginia, Cocke's Brigade, was the last infantry force to reach the ground before the beginning of the Federal rout. Apparently it followed Early's charge.

[14] Aug. 17, 1861, p. 1, cols. 2–3.

APPENDIX V

Origin of the Name "Stonewall"

R. M. Johnston[1] rejected the entire story of Bee's apostrophe, and concluded only that "something was said by somebody, during or immediately after the battle that likened Jackson or his men or both to a stone wall."

It seems to the present writer that the onus was on Johnston to disprove and not merely to disallow the story as it related to Bee. In favor of general probability, as distinguished from the precise language that Bee may have used, these specific circumstances should be noted: first: the story was circulating in Richmond within three days after the battle; second, there was no reason why a correspondent of a South Carolina newspaper should have quoted a hero of that State in praise of a little-known Virginian, unless the correspondent regarded the episode as authentic biography; third, General Jackson himself believed that Bee had spoken of a "stone wall"; fourth, as some Southern soldiers were equally prone with politicians to indulge in eloquent exhortation, especially during the early days of the war, there is nothing intrinsically improbable in the remark. It is of record, finally, that during the battle Jackson planned to "give them the bayonet," precisely as he was quoted in his terse dialogue with Bee. In his report Jackson said: "At 3.30 P.M. the advance of the enemy having reached a position which called for the use of the bayonet . . ."[2]

The only historical difficulty the incident presents, in the judgment of the author, is that of ascertaining when Bee made the appeal to his men. This difficulty does not concern the essential verities. Henderson[3] fixed the time at approximately 11.30 A.M., when Bee fell back on Jackson. This reasonable conclusion doubtless was based on the language of Jackson's report: ". . . before arriving within cannon range of the enemy, I met General Bee's forces falling back. I continued to advance with the understanding that he would form in my rear . . . General Bee, with his rallied troops, soon marched to my support."[4] That statement discredits no part of the *Mercury's* report except the inference that Bee was killed almost immediately after he spoke of Jackson's "stone wall." As none of Bee's subordinates filed any reports

[1] *Op. cit.*, 202, n. 1. [2] *O. R.*, 2, 482.
[3] *Op. cit.*, 1, 145. [4] *O. R.*, 2, 481.

on the battle, it is not possible to reconstruct in any detail the precise movements of the different units.

Concerning the term "Stonewall," the late R. M. Hughes of Norfolk, Virginia, biographer of Gen. Jos. E. Johnston, pointed out to the writer the interesting fact attested by Alexander,[5] that later, on the 21st, Johnston, who probably had not heard of Bee's remark, said of the Fourth Virginia, "Preston's regiment stood there like a stone wall." Mr. Hughes noted, also, that at Marengo, where two battalions of the Old Grenadiers and two squadrons of the Consular Guard had beaten off Elsnitz's repeated attacks, the admiring Berthier had said that the small French force had been "une redoute de granit, contre laquelle tous les efforts devenaient impuissants."

An entirely different theory of the Bee-Jackson incident appears in the *Reminiscences of Col. J. C. Haskell*,[6] as follows: "Almost universally, it is believed that Bee, in exhorting his Brigade, called to them admiringly to look at Jackson's men standing like a stone wall. Major Rhett, who was Gen. Johnston's Chief of Staff and a classmate of Bee and Jackson at West Point, was with Bee from soon after he was shot till he died. He has told me often, as did Gen. W. H. C. Whiting, that the fact was that Bee said that his and Bartow's brigades were hard pressed and that Jackson refused to move to their relief and in a passionate expression of anger he denounced him for standing, like a stone wall and allowing them to be sacrificed. This was confirmed to me repeatedly during the war and after it by Jas. Hill, Bee's brother-in-law and Aide de Camp, who was with him when he fell and said Bee was angry and excited when the fight was going on and bitterly denounced Jackson for refusing to move. That this is the true history of Bee's connection, I have no doubt as I heard it confirmed by more than one who was present at Bee's deathbed (he died in a house at Manassas Junction, four miles from the battlefield), but I am equally confident that Jackson acted from no unworthy motive. He was not only a great man, but one of the sternest Puritan natures, who would come as near as any man could to doing what he thought best absolutely regardless of whom it helped or hurt and he did what he thought best from a military point of view. He certainly never doubted he was right and the man who differed was wrong, and I have no doubt that this was the reason of the difference between him and Bee."

[5] *Op. cit.*, 36 n.   [6] MS., page 37.

APPENDIX VI

JACKSON'S PLANS AND MARCHES OF MAY 24, 1862

DABNEY, *op. cit.,* 369-71, and Henderson, *op. cit.,* 1, 328–330, assume that Jackson's plan for an advance from Cedarville to Middletown was the first and only one formulated by him for May 24. No suggestion of a late start was made by Major Dabney. Henderson mentioned that possibility, but in the belief that Taylor began his march for Middletown at 6 A.M. In this, Henderson manifestly mistook the start of Ewell for Nineveh as the time of Taylor's "Fall in" for Middletown.[1] Apparently no particular attention was paid Ewell's reference [2] to his eight-mile march and to the recall of Taylor and, later, of Elzey. Furthermore, Jackson's statement of his plan, as given in his official report,[3] naturally if unintentionally created the impression that the plan for the march on Middletown was formulated in advance of any movements on the morning of May 24.

First doubts concerning the validity of this general assumption were raised by this passage from the Diary of Jed. Hotchkiss:

"Saturday, May 24th. It rained and hailed some in the morning and was quite cool. The army was all marched up until the rear rested at Cedarville, while Gen. Ewell and his troops, the advance, went on beyond Nineveh, where we stopped, at Mr. Mason's, and got some breakfast; then Gen. Jackson had a consultation with Gen. Ewell after which we went back to Cedarville, going by the troops which were halted. General Ewell went on, by the turnpike, to within some four miles of Winchester. When we got back to Cedarville, the Gen. went a short distance with me on the road to Middletown; then directed me to take 16 cavalry and go and find where Banks was, and to report to him every half hour. I started and at about a mile and a half was fired on by the enemy's picket, some 60 in number, in the woods the rain falling. . . ."

Unfortunately, at this point, a leaf is missing from *Hotchkiss' MS. Diary.* In the typescript, he left space for it, doubtless in the hope that he would find it, but it is not among his papers. In 3 *C. M. H.,* 239, written many years later, Majoi Hotchkiss modestly hinted that his discovery of the Federals led to the dispatch of troops to the Valley Pike and that Jackson followed with the main force.

[1] For Ewell's departure, see *O. R.,* 12, pt. 1, p. 779.
[2] *Ibid.*   [3] *O. R.,* 12, pt. 1, p. 702.

There is no reason to doubt the accuracy of the quoted passage. It is guaranteed by the character of Major Hotchkiss and it is confirmed, in part, by this passage in Ewell's report:

"At 6 o'clock the next morning my division was again moving toward Winchester. The head of the column had marched about eight miles, when it was halted by Major-General Jackson. The brigades of Generals Elzey and Taylor were detached from my position on the Front Royal and Winchester turnpike and carried by the major-general commanding with his division of the army to the road leading from Strasburg to Winchester. . . . The Seventh Brigade (General Trimble commanding) remained until 5 P.M. where halted by Major-General Jackson, about eight miles from Front Royal. Seeing that the enemy were retreating before General Jackson from Strasburg, I immediately ordered Generals Trimble and Steuart to move forward, and reported to the general commanding what I was doing. . . . The Twenty-first North Carolina, under Colonel Kirkland, drove in the enemy's pickets that evening and held the position 2 miles from Winchester. . . . The rest of the command slept on their arms about 3 miles from Winchester." [4]

From these quotations, it is evident that, on the morning of May 24, at an hour when "Before-Dawn" Jackson usually was moving his troops toward their objective, he had his whole column headed not for Middletown via the Chapel road, but for Winchester by the Front Royal road. According to Hotchkiss, Jackson closed the column as rapidly as the Brigades came up.[5] There is no evidence here, or in any of the reports of the commanders of the rear Brigades,[6] that Jackson delayed the march in order to cover Front Royal against attack by Banks, though the Twelfth Georgia Infantry and two companies of Ashby's cavalry were left at Front Royal to guard the prisoners and supplies.[7]

These dispositions do not prove conclusively that Jackson's plan early on the 24th was to move directly on Winchester by the Front Royal road, and to ignore the remote possibility that Banks might attempt to cross his rear and to make for Chester Gap. At the same time, it is difficult to explain the closing of the column and Jackson's presence with the van otherwise than on the ground that Winchester, by that route, was his objective. Had Jackson desired merely to confer with

[4] O. R., 12, pt. 1, p. 779. The orders for Elzey to move over to the Valley Pike were dispatched from Middletown at 4.30 P.M. and therefore were not simultaneous with those for Taylor. O. R., 12, pt. 3, p. 899.
[5] "The army was all marched up until the rear rested at Cedarville."
[6] O. R., 12, pt. 1, pp. 734, 764, 772.
[7] For the cavalry, see Avirett, 198. The Twelfth Georgia was there on May 30. O. R., 12, pt. 1, p. 793, and was not mentioned in any of the reports of actions elsewhere May 24–29.

Ewell, why would he not have done so before Ewell left Cedarville, which was not until 6 o'clock? Certainly there was no point in marching with Ewell to see that the Division got a prompt start: Taylor had demonstrated, to Jackson's admiration, that Ewell's troops knew how to cover ground. Still again, if Jackson early in the day intended that Ewell should advance on Winchester with a small force and that Taylor should cross over with the remainder of the Army to the Valley Pike at Middletown, why did Jackson permit Taylor to march past Cedarville toward Nineveh?

That Taylor did go North of Cedarville seems almost certain from Ewell's report. The distance from Cedarville to Nineveh was two miles and a half.[8] Not more than 6000 men, without their wagons, were on the road. If one assumes that Taylor was the rear Brigade—which is not established from available records—and even if one goes farther and disregards Hotchkiss' assertion that the rear of the entire Army was at Cedarville, Taylor must be placed North of that village when the column was halted. Why should he have been there if his mission was in the direction of Middletown? There is no hint anywhere that he was advanced beyond Cedarville, in the direction of Nineveh, with an eye to sending him to the Valley Pike, via the road from Nineveh to Newtown. Nor can Taylor's silence on the subject in his published memoirs be cited as evidence that he did not go beyond Cedarville. He wrote charmingly but sketchily of the operations. If his evidence is to be used at all, it well may be on the side of the probability here advanced. Taylor mentioned that, on the night of May 23, Jackson said that Louisianians would march with him the next morning.[9] If Jackson then had intended to go to Middletown from Cedarville, he would have left Taylor at or South of Cedarville on the 24th.

What conclusion, then, is to be reached; what happened during the hours after 6 A.M., when Ewell put his column in motion for Winchester? Jackson had breakfast and then conferred with Ewell. In all probability, Steuart already had been sent out to reconnoiter in the direction of the Valley Pike, but no report had been received from him. None of Ashby's outposts had notified headquarters that Banks's wagon train had headed North from Strasburg. Jackson was in the dark. As a result of his conference with Ewell, he decided that if the entire column left Front Royal too far in its rear, as it pressed on toward Winchester, Banks, after all, might decide to march for Chester Gap. Jackson consequently halted Ewell's advance.

[8] It should be noted that when Ewell spoke in his report of an advance of eight miles, he meant eight miles from Front Royal, not from Cedarville. He explained that in the latter part of the passage quoted from his report.
[9] R. Taylor, 54.

What besides that could he do? If he marched back down the road to Front Royal and found Banks there, he knew that Banks had only to burn the bridge across the North Fork in order to stop him. It seemed reasonable to suppose that Banks had not started for Front Royal, else word of that certainly would have been sent from the two companies of cavalry left there.[10] Besides, the sensible thing for Banks to do was to make for the Potomac by way of Winchester and the Valley Pike.[11] How, then, could Jackson deal with that probability and, at the same time, be ready to attack Banks if the Federal com-mander started for Front Royal and availed himself of the cover offered by the North Fork of the Shenandoah, which the Confederates might not be able to recross by marching directly South from Cedar-ville? Jackson's decision was that he should go back from Nineveh to Cedarville and take the Chapel road to the Valley Pike at Middletown. Once there, he could do any one of three things: he could intercept a retreat to Winchester; he could move back to the vicinity of Strasburg and get in Banks's rear if the Federals retreated toward Front Royal and Chester Gap; or, if Banks remained at Strasburg, he could attack that town without having to cross the North Fork.

This explanation fits in with the newly ascertained fact of Jackson's presence at Nineveh; it suggests that the northward advance of Ewell made Jackson take seriously the possibility, otherwise remote, that Banks might move on Front Royal; it accounts for the long delay in starting the march for Middletown; and it accords with the statement of plan in Jackson's report: "In the event of Banks' leaving Strasburg he might escape toward the Potomac, or if we moved directly to Win-chester he might move via Front Royal toward Washington City. In order to watch both directions, and at the same time advance upon him if he remained at Strasburg, I determined, with the main body of the army, to strike the turnpike near Middletown, a village 5 miles north of Strasburg and 13 south of Winchester."[12]

The only objection to stating as a fact that Jackson made this deci-sion on the morning of May 24, after the march to Nineveh, is that, in the published text of his report, he began the next paragraph with the words: "Accordingly, the next morning, General Ashby advanced from Cedarville toward Middletown, supported by skirmishers from Taylor's

[10] *Avirett,* 198.
[11] Although the *caveat* may not be necessary, it is to be remembered that, when Banks spoke in his report of a "retreat to the Potomac," he meant a march across Little North Mountain to the Potomac in what is now West Virginia (*O. R.,* 12, pt. 1, p. 546); Jackson, in his appraisal of Banks's alternatives, seems to have considered an "escape toward the Potomac" (*ibid.,* 703) only in the sense of a retreat up the Valley Pike toward Winchester.
[12] *O. R.,* 12, pt. 1, p. 703.

brigade . . . followed by the whole command, except the troops left under the command of General Ewell near Cedarville." [13] It is natural on first reading, at least, to conclude from the language "Accordingly, the next morning" that the decision to move to Middletown was reached on the evening of the 23d, but this interpretation does not weigh heavily against the contrary evidence. "Accordingly" may be no more than a transitional flourish at the beginning of a new paragraph.

Besides all this, if the decision had been made on the 23d to start directly for Middletown on the 24th, then the march was begun with a tardiness and was conducted at a slow pace for which the Valley campaign offers no parallel. An early Federal reconnaissance from Middletown almost to Cedarville showed no Confederates on the road.[14] It was 11 A.M. before Steuart's advance from Newtown was reported to Federals, who then were in undisturbed possession of the vicinity of Middletown.[15] A Federal Brigade which left Strasburg at 10 o'clock had passed Middletown—five miles—without any alarm over the nearness of Confederates on the road from Cedarville.[16] Not until 2 o'clock did this Brigade, then past Newtown, hear of the attack on the wagon train at Middletown. This would put the attack by Ashby and the Tigers after 1 o'clock, at earliest.[17] Taylor obviously came up well in the rear of Ashby. At 4.30 P.M., Jackson had not left Middletown for Newtown. In ordering Elzey to reinforce him and in directing Ewell not to advance farther toward Winchester, Jackson wrote, through his A. A. G.: "There seems to be still a considerable body of the enemy advancing on us from Strasburg." [18] This evidently was the force that Taylor went out to meet not long after he reached Middletown. At the most cautious estimate, then, it would not seem that Taylor arrived at Middletown before 3 P.M. Is it conceivable that he would have spent on seven miles of road all the time that this late arrival would indicate, unless his start from Cedarville was much delayed? On the other hand, that delay is entirely understandable if Jackson first ordered the Army up the Front Royal road toward Winchester, then changed his mind and countermarched.

[13] Ibid.
[14] O. R., 12, pt. 1, pp. 579, 594–95, 623.
[15] Ibid., 623.
[16] Ibid., 614. Col. Geo. H. Gordon reported, in fact, that no Confederates were within four miles, but he probably based his information on the early reconnaissance.
[17] Ibid., 614–15. The reason for asserting that this was Ashby's attack with Chew's Battery and part of Poague's, and not an earlier skirmish reported by some Federal authorities, is that Colonel Gordon mentioned that he heard artillery. The Confederates who first reached the road—whether Steuart's or Funsten's men—had no artillery.
[18] O. R., 12, pt. 3, p. 899.

PRINCIPAL MANUSCRIPT SOURCES

This list covers manuscript sources of importance used or cited in this volume. A few additional items for the period July 15, 1862–May 30, 1863, appear at the end of Volume II. In the manuscript section of the general bibliography, in the final volume, an inclusive list is printed. Many hundred letters of prominent Confederate officers of the Army of Northern Virginia are deposited in libraries or are preserved in autograph albums, etc. Usually, where such scattered papers are quoted in the present work, the location of the original is given in the footnotes.

Lt. Gen. Richard H. Anderson—A small but valuable collection of this officer's papers is in the possession of his granddaughter, Mrs. Walter C. White, of Gates Mills, Ohio.

Maj. W. N. Berkeley—Fine domestic letters of this one of the renowned "Berkeley brothers" are owned by Francis L. Berkeley, Jr., and are deposited at the University of Virginia.

Lt. Col. W. W. Blackford—The reminiscences of W. W. Blackford, who served on Jeb Stuart's staff and later was Lt. Colonel of the First Virginia Engineers, were written after the war, but they are among the most interesting and valuable of the unpublished memoirs of the Confederacy. They are the cherished possession of his grandsons, Messrs. Pelham Baylor and Frank Blackford, Richmond, Virginia.

Maj. J. K. Boswell—The extant commissions, memorabilia and souvenirs of Jackson's first topographical engineer are in the *Hotchkiss Papers, infra.*

Col. J. Thompson Brown—Official papers and orders of the Colonel of the First Virginia Artillery are in the Confederate Museum, Richmond, Virginia.

Lucy R. Buck—A long wartime diary of this Valley girl, with a thrilling account of the Battle of Front Royal, is owned by William R. Buck of Baltimore, Maryland.

Brig. Gen. R. H. Chilton—Some personal letters and historical papers preserved by Lee's Chief of Staff are in the Confederate Museum.

Brig. Gen. R. E. Colston—A large collection of his papers, not yet assorted fully, has been acquired by the University of North Carolina.

Brig. Gen. John R. Cooke—Interesting papers, which include some of "Jeb" Stuart's and cover a long period, are in the possession of P. St. George Cooke and of Stuart Cooke, Sr. and Jr., Richmond, Virginia.

Maj. John Esten Cooke—Journals and miscellaneous items of "Jeb" Stuart's ordnance officer, the well-known novelist, are in the library of Duke University and were described by Prof. Jay B. Hubbell in the *Journal of Southern History,* vol. 7, No. 4.

Brig. Gen. P. St. George Cocke—His reports and memorabilia are extant and are in the keeping of Miss Betty Cocke, University, Virginia.

Maj. R. L. Dabney—Various post-bellum papers are among the *Hotchkiss Papers, infra.*

BRIG. GEN. N. G. ("SHANKS") EVANS—A large collection, principally of official papers, was owned by his son, the late ex-Gov. John Gary Evans of South Carolina.

LT. GEN. R. S. EWELL—Two series of letters, deposited by Maj. and Mrs. P. G. Hamlin, are in the Library of Congress.

COL. J. W. FAIRFAX—Some illuminating papers of this staff officer of Lt. Gen. James Longstreet are owned by Mrs. Henry Fairfax, daughter-in-law of Colonel Fairfax.

BRIG. GEN. R. B. GARNETT—Papers relating to the court-martial of Garnett, on charges preferred by Lt. Gen. T. J. Jackson, have been given the Confederate Museum.

BRIG. GEN. R. S. GARNETT—Many interesting papers relating to this officer are owned by Mrs. Myrtle Cooper-Schwarz of Williamsburg, Va.

D. H. GORDON—A long series of his letters on conditions in Fredericksburg, Virginia, is owned by Douglas G. Lovell and made available through the kindness of R. E. L. Russell of Baltimore, Maryland.

MAJ. J. A. HARMAN—Copies of forthright letters by Jackson's renowned quartermaster, covering part of the Valley campaign, are in the *Hotchkiss Papers, infra.*

COL. J. C. HASKELL—The charming memoirs of this distinguished South Carolinian are in the possession of Mrs. Preston H. Haskell, Jr., of Birmingham, Ala.

MAJ. GEN. HENRY HETH—His unpublished memoirs, written late in life, are owned by Mrs. Emlyn H. Marsteller, Manassas, Virginia. Other Heth papers belong to Mrs. Douglas Vander Hoof, Richmond, Virginia. Still others have been deposited in the Confederate Museum.

LT. GEN. D. H. HILL—His miscellaneous papers are in the archives of the North Carolina Historical Commission, Raleigh.

MAJ. JED. HOTCHKISS—This distinguished topographical engineer of the Second Corps devoted much of his life to preserving material on Jackson and Jackson's troops, and he assembled a vast and varied collection. Included are his diary, his letters to his wife and brother, his maps, and hundred of clippings, memoranda and documents. The most important items relating to Stonewall Jackson are listed *infra* under the name of that officer. The *Hotchkiss Papers* have been deposited in the Confederate Memorial Institute, Richmond, by their owners, Mrs. George Holmes, Charleston, S. C., and Mrs. Ellen H. Christian, Deerfield, Va.

LT. GEN. T. J. JACKSON—Certain papers of controversial, historical, or of special associational interest to Jackson were turned over, presumably after his death, to Mrs. Jackson. Some of them were presented by her to admirers of the General. From other papers, autographs were clipped. Those manuscripts that remained in the family's hands and photostats of some that have disappeared, are owned by the Confederate Memorial Institute, Richmond, to which they were given by an anonymous friend.

LT. GEN. T. J. JACKSON—His Order Book while commanding at Harpers Ferry in 1861 is in the Confederate Museum.

LT. GEN. T. J. JACKSON—The official Order Book of Jackson as commander of the Valley District and as head of the Second Corps was lost at Waynesboro March 2, 1865, along with other headquarters records but fortunately Jed. Hotchkiss had made a full abstract, which is preserved in the *Hotchkiss Papers*.

LT. GEN. T. J. JACKSON—His officiai Letter Book had the same history as his Order Book. The abstract is in the *Hotchkiss Papers*.

GEN. JOS. E. JOHNSTON—Extant papers of General Johnston and much correspondence by his biographer, R. M. Hughes, are in the Library of the College of William and Mary, Williamsburg, Virginia.

GEN. R. E. LEE—The nature and distribution of General Lee's papers is described in 4 *R. E. Lee*, 548 ff. Since the preparation of that bibliographical note, the Trustees of his military papers have deposited them in the Confederate Memorial Institute.

MAJ. H. B. McCLELLAN—"Jeb" Stuart's Assistant Adjutant General preserved some interesting papers of his chief and a few of other officers. These are in the Confederate Memorial Institute, to which they were presented by Mrs. Anne McClellan Holloway and Miss Margaret McClellan, of Lexington, Kentucky.

MAJ. GEN. J. B. MAGRUDER—A miscellaneous collection of his official papers is in the Confederate Museum.

DR. HUNTER McGUIRE—The large and interesting file of papers of the Medical Director of the Second Corps is in the Confederate Museum. Most of them are post bellum.

MAJ. R. J. MOSES—The charming memoirs of the splendid commissary of the First Corps contain much material on Longstreet.

BRIG. GEN. T. T. MUNFORD—The vast correspondence of General Munford, most of it post-bellum, now belongs to Duke University. Much of the correspondence relates to General Munford's controversy with General Rosser over the battle at Tom's Brook. Five Forks is the theme of many letters. A still larger collection was inherited by the General's grandson, William T. Munford, of Richmond.

MAJ. GEN. W. DORSEY PENDER—The admirably preserved and complete series of war letters written to his wife by General Pender, and many miscellaneous items relating to him, are in the custody of W. C. Pender, of Norfolk.

CAPT. JAMES PLEASANTS—Numerous interesting letters of this officer are in the D. H. Gordon Papers, cited *supra*.

BRIG. GEN. W. N. PENDLETON—His Order Book and his Letter Book, both of them used by the editors of *O.R.*, are in the Confederate Museum.

MAJ. CHANNING PRICE—The charming letters and the diary of Major Price, who was one of Maj. McClellan's predecessors as A.A.G. of the Cavalry corps, are owned by Miss Louise Price of Richmond.

MAJ. GEN. S. DODSON RAMSEUR—Many of his papers, his West Point text books, and his wartime letters, are owned by members of the family. The largest collections are in the keeping of V. D. Ramseur of New York and Paul W. Schenck of Greensboro, N. C.

MAJ. GEN. ROBERT RANSOM—Various papers, chiefly of the post-bellum era, remain in the hands of his widow, for whom Eugene M. Ransom of Atlanta has acted.

MAJ. GEN. THOMAS L. ROSSER—General Rosser's numerous extant papers belong to his granddaughter, Miss Barbara W. Rosser of Charlottesville, Va.

MAJ. GEN. W. B. TALIAFERRO—His military papers in considerable bulk are in the Confederate Museum, Richmond.

LT. COL. WALTER H. TAYLOR—The invaluable letters and papers of Gen. R. E. Lee's A.A.G. are described in 4 *R. E. Lee*, 552.

CADMUS M. WILCOX—An unfinished memoir is in the Library of Congress. Sundry other papers belong to his niece, Mrs. Moncure Burke of Washington, D. C.

SHORT-TITLE INDEX

Alexander. E. P. ALEXANDER. Military Memoirs of a Confederate.
Allan's Army. WILLIAM ALLAN. The Army of Northern Virginia in 1862.
Allan, William. WILLIAM ALLAN. History of the Campaign of Gen. T. J. (Stonewall) Jackson in the Shenandoah Valley of Virginia.
Avirett. J. B. AVIRETT. The Memoirs of General Turner Ashby and his Compeers.
Beale. R. L. T. BEALE. History of the Ninth Virginia Cavalry.
Beale, G. W. G. W. BEALE. A Lieutenant of Cavalry in Lee's Army.
Beauregard. P. G. T. BEAUREGARD. Commentary on the Campaign and Battle of Manassas.
B. & L. Battles and Leaders of the Civil War.
Brent. J. L. BRENT. Memoirs of the War Between the States.
Brock, Miss. "A Richmond Lady" [Sally Brock]. Richmond During the War.
Casler. JOHN O. CASLER. Four Years in the Stonewall Brigade.
Chamberlaine, W. W. W. W. CHAMBERLAINE. Memoirs of the Civil War.
Chamberlayne, Ham. C. C. CHAMBERLAYNE, *ed.* Ham Chamberlayne— Virginian.
Chesnut, Mrs. MARY BOYKIN CHESNUT. A Diary from Dixie.
C. M. H. CLEMENT A. EVANS, *ed.* Confederate Military History.
Companions in Arms. "A Distinguished Southern Journalist" [E. A. POLLARD]. The Early Life, Campaigns, and Public Services of Robert E. Lee, with a Record of the Campaigns and Heroic Deeds of his Companions in Arms.
Conner. Letters of General James Conner.
Cullum. G. W. CULLUM. Biographical Register of Officers and Graduates of the U. S. Military Academy.
C. V. Confederate Veteran.
D. A. B. Dictionary of American Biography.
Dabney. R. L. DABNEY. Life and Campaigns of Lieut.-Gen. Thomas J. Jackson.
Davis. JEFFERSON DAVIS. The Rise and Fall of the Confederate Government.
De Leon. T. C. DE LEON. Four Years in Rebel Capitals.
De Leon B. B. B. T. C. DE LEON. Belles, Beaux and Brains of the 60's.
Douglas. HENRY KYD DOUGLAS. I Rode With Stonewall.
Early. JUBAL A. EARLY. Autobiographical Sketch and Narrative of the War Between the States.
English Combatant, An. "An English Combatant" [ANON]. Battlefield-fields of the South.
Hamlin's Ewell. P. G. HAMLIN, *ed.* The Making of a Soldier; Letters of General R. S. Ewell.
Henderson. G. F. R. HENDERSON. Stonewall Jackson and the American Civil War.

Hood. J. B. Hood. Advance and Retreat.
Howard, McHenry. McHenry Howard. Recollections of a Maryland Confederate Soldier.
Jackson, Mrs. Mary Anna Jackson. Memoirs of Stonewall Jackson.
Johnston, R. M. R. M. Johnston. Bull Run, Its Strategy and Tactics.
Johnston's Narrative. J. E. Johnston. Narrative of Military Operations.
Journal C. S. Congress. Journal of the Congress of the Confederate States of America, 1861–1865 (Washington ed., 1904–05).
Laurel Brigade. W. N. McDonald. A History of the Laurel Brigade.
Lee, R. E. D. S. Freeman. R. E. Lee.
Lee's Dispatches. D. S. Freeman, *ed.* Lee's Dispatches.
Long. A. L. Long. Memoirs of Robert E. Lee.
Longstreet. James Longstreet. From Manassas to Appomattox.
McCabe. J. D. McCabe, Jr. Life and Campaigns of General Robert E. Lee.
Marshall. Frederick Maurice, *ed.* An Aide-de-Camp of Lee . . . The Papers of Col. Charles Marshall.
McClellan, H. B. H. B. McClellan. The Life and Campaigns of . . . J. E. B. Stuart.
McDonald, Mrs. Hunter McDonald, *ed.* Mrs. Cornelia McDonald. A Diary with Reminiscences of the War and Refugee Life in the Shenandoah Valley.
Moore, E. A. E. A. Moore. The Story of a Cannoneer under Stonewall Jackson.
Moore's Rebellion Record. Frank Moore, *ed.* The Rebellion Record.
N. C. Regts. Walter Clark, *ed.* Histories of the Several Regiments and Battalions from North Carolina in the Great War, 1861–65.
N. O. R. Official Records of the Union and Confederate Navies in the War of the Rebellion.
Oates. W. C. Oates. The War Between the Union and the Confederacy.
O. R. Official Records of the Union and Confederate Armies.
Pendleton. Susan P. Lee. Memoirs of William Nelson Pendleton.
Polley. J. B. Polley. Hood's Texas Brigade.
Roman. Alfred Roman. The Military Operations of General Beauregard.
Rowland. Dunbar Rowland, *ed.* Jefferson Davis, Constitutionalist, His Letters, Papers and Speeches.
R. W. C. D. J. B. Jones. A Rebel War Clerk's Diary.
S. H. S. P. Southern Historical Society Papers.
Sorrel. G. Moxley Sorrel. Recollections of a Confederate Staff Officer.
Southern Generals. Anon [W. P. Snow]. Southern Generals.
Smith, G. W. G. W. Smith. Confederate War Papers.
Stiles. Robert Stiles. Four Years Under Marse Robert.
Taylor, R. Richard Taylor. Destruction and Reconstruction.
Thomason. J. W. Thomason. "Jeb" Stuart.
Toombs, etc., Letters. Ulrich B. Phillips, *ed.* The Correspondence of Robert Toombs, Alexander H. Stephens, and Howell Cobb
von Borcke. Heros von Borcke. Memoirs of the Confederate War for Independence.
Wearing of the Gray. J. E. Cooke. Wearing of the Gray.
Wells. Edward L. Wells. Hampton and His Cavalry in '64.

Wingfield. H. W. WINGFIELD. Diary of (Bul. Va. State Lib., July, 1927).
Withers. R. E. WITHERS. Autobiography of an Octogenarian.
Worsham. J. H. WORSHAM. One of Jackson's Foot Cavalry.
Wright. MARCUS J. WRIGHT. General Officers of the Confederate Army.

INDEX

Unless otherwise indicated or generally familiar, all place names in this index are for Virginia, which in 1861 included the present State of West Virginia. The rank credited to officers is the highest held in either Union or Confederate service at any time and not merely during the period April, 1861–July 15, 1862, covered by this volume. In the case of men who held commission in the United States Army before secession and subsequently served as officers in the Southern Army, the Confederate rank only is given.

Abert, Capt. James W., 389 n.
Abraham's Creek, 395–6, 398, 482
Adams, Fort, 15
Alabama Regiments:
 Third, 245
 Fourth, 64–5, 730
 Fifth, 96, 171, 247–8, 533, 536
 Sixth, 171, 241, 244, 248, 250, 589
 Ninth, 192
 Tenth, 536
 Twelfth, 245, 248
 Fifteenth, 526, 533
 Eighteenth, 444
 Twenty-sixth, 533
Albemarle Sound, 696
Aldie, 43
Alexander, Brig. Gen. E. Porter, C.S.A., 37, 56, 57 n., 58, 63, 77 and n., 78, 97, 98 n., 575 n., 618, 642 n., 643, 734
Alexander, Bvt. Brig. Gen. Edmund B., U.S.A., 710 n., 721 n.
Alexander, Lt. Col. Thomas L., 710 n., 721 n.
Alexandria Loudoun and Hampshire Railroad, 680
Alexandria, 6–7, 39–40, 53, 90, 680, 682, 721, 725
Alice Gray (Toombs' mare), 624 n.–625 n.
Allan, Col. William, C.S.A., 315, 407 n., 414 n., 437 n., 442 n., 657
Allegheny Mountains, 332–4, 336–7, 368, 383, 417, 477, 678, 681–2, 686, 689, 692, 699, 701
Allen, Israel, 424
Allen, Col. James W., C.S.A., 325, 396 n., 397, 453–4, 536, 606 n., 730
Allen, Rev. L. W., C.S.A., 576–7, 589
Ammen, Brig. Gen. Jacob, U.S.A., 721 n.
Anderson, Gen. George B., C.S.A., 240 n., 242, 244, 533, 605 n., 653
Anderson, Brig. Gen. G. T., C.S.A., 543, 545, 672
Anderson, Brig. Gen. Joseph R., C.S.A., 202, 204, 208, 213, 218–9, 523, 588, 605 n., 653, 666, 668 n., 672, 706, 717 n.

Anderson, McKenzie, 652 n.
Anderson, Lieut. Gen. Richard Heron, C.S.A.; at West Point, 20 n.; early career, 157; character, xix, 157–8; commands D. R. Jones's Brigade, 157, 161 n.; his Brigade under Longstreet, 168, 176; in retreat toward Williamsburg, 176–9; praised by Longstreet, 189; as commander, 192, 249; at Seven Pines, 239, 244, 248–9, 252; losses in the Seven Days, 605 n.; his outstanding competence, 652; made Maj. Gen. in the reorganized Army, 672–3
Anderson, Col. S. S., C.S.A., 704
Anderson, Dr. W. W., 652 n.
Andrews, Maj. Gen. George Leonard, U.S.A., 392 n.
Appomattox River, 678, 697
Aquia Creek, 138, 337, 581, 680, 682, 688, 692, 697
Archer, Brig. Gen. J. J., C.S.A., 267, 270–1, 523
Arkansas (ram), 675
Arlington Heights, 39–40
Armistead, Drury L., 262 n.
Armistead, Col. F. S., C.S.A., 705
Armistead, Brig. Gen. Lewis A., C.S.A., 201 n., 226 n., 239 n., 246, 256, 258, 558 n., 592, 594–9, 601, 609 n., 612–3, 645, 650, 654, 673
Army of Northern Virginia, xv, xvii–xviii, xxiii, xxv, 49 n., 145, 207, 266, 273, 468, 477, 532, 565, 610–1, 614, 631, 667
 First Battle, 517–37
 Reorganization after the Seven Days, 670–5
 Problems of leadership, xxv–xxvii
Army of the Northwest, 123
Army of the Peninsula, 153–168 *passim*, 259, 264
Army of the Potomac (Confederate), 49 n., 91, 100, 103
Army of the Potomac (Union), 202, 214, 262, 275, 408, 661
Army of the Shenandoah Valley, 49 n.,

52 n., 103, 123, 149, 167, 318, 328, 344, 347, 359, 402, 431, 465, 503–5, 605, 658, 662, 731
Army Register, 703, 709
Arsenal Academy, The, 710
Asbury Chapel, 377
Ashby, Capt. "Jack," 308
Ashby, Brig. Gen. Turner, C.S.A., xvi, 11; family and early career, 308; appearance, 309, 437 n., 438; contrasted with Jackson, 308–9; his action at Bolivar Heights, 309–10; with Jackson in the withdrawal from Winchester, 311–3, 316; his recruiting, 324; trouble with his cavalry in the Valley, 337–41; plans for him there, 345–6; under Ewell there, 350, 353, 355, 359–60, 370–2, 377, 380, 382; details of his action, 385–433 *passim,* 472–5, 478–9, 481, 736–9; his gallant death, 433–5, 449, 674; appraisal of his generalship, 475–8
Ashby, Richard, 309
Ashcake road, 508
Ashland, 220, 497, 500, 503, 505–6, 508, 658
Atkinson, Lieut. W. G., C.S.A., 728
Atlee's Farm, 566
Atlee's Station, 509–11
August, Col. T. P., C.S.A., 606 n.
Austrian Infantry Evolutions of the Line, trans. by Cadmus M. Wilcox, 160
Avery, Col. C. M., C.S.A., 270 n.
Avirett, Chaplain J. B., C.S.A., 477
Ayers, Maj. Gen. R. B., U.S.A., 572 n.

Bainbridge, Lieut. Col. E. C., U.S.A., 705, 717 n.
Ball Family, 66 n.
Ball's Bluff, 111, 157, 269
Baltimore and Ohio Railroad, 9, 23, 406, 680–2, 691, 699
Baltimore Cross-roads, 208
Baltimore, Md., 149, 348, 415, 691
Bangor Democrat, 5
Banks, Maj. Gen. Nathaniel P., U.S.A., 138 n., 141, 306, 311, 317, 328–46 *passim,* 347–56 *passim,* 359–61, 363–5, 368, 371–2, 374, 383–9, 396, 406–9, 411, 413–4, 417–8, 428, 438, 466–7, 472–5, 477, 481–5, 657, 735–8
Barhamsville, 193–4, 208
Bark River, 17
Barksdale, Brig. Gen. William, C.S.A., 96, 97 n., 588, 598, 601–2, 607
Barrets Point, Va., 694
Barry, Maj. Gen. William F., U.S.A., 68 n., 155
Barton, Brig. Gen. Seth M., C.S.A., 704
Bartonsville, 315, 392
Bartow, Col. Francis S., C.S.A., 55, 64, 66, 70, 81, 89, 95, 162 n., 261, 262 n., 674, 728, 730–1, 734
Bartow, Mrs. Francis S., 81
Battle of Manassas, by Gen. Beauregard, 726
Battle of Young's Branch, by Warder and Catlett, 728
Baxter, Capt. George, C.S.A., 381
Baylor, Col. T. G., U.S.A., 705, 717 n.
Beale, George W., 297
Beale, Lieut. Col. R. L., C.S.A., 297, 299
Beauregard, Gen. Pierre Gustave Toutant, C.S.A., personality, xx, 3, 4, 22, 624; appearance and manner, 6–7, 111; early career, 709; called to Richmond defense, 1–9, 109, 725; popularity, 19, 22–3; learns about Harpers Ferry, 12–3; army increases, 38; popular appraisals, 38; plan of attack and strategy, 39, 43–4, 52–3, 103; Davis replies to him, 39–40; his regiments and leaders, 41, 86; plans offensive, 41–3, 46–8, 50 n.; uncertainty, 45–6; orders and action at First Manassas (Bull Run), 45–72, 89, 95, 726–30; returns command to Johnston, 73 n.; conference with Davis at Manassas, 76–8 and n.; promoted to be General, 79, 97; his valor, 79–80; uncritical public acclaim, 81; satisfaction after victory, 83; controversy with Cocke at Manassas, 90 n.; his officers who survived the action, 96–8; his letters on lack of support at Manassas, 99–101, 104; reply to Johnston's comment on his combat order, 726; political enmity toward Davis, 101, 104; attitude toward his command, 101, 109, 117–8; report on his Manassas plans, 101–3, 108, 726–7; resulting controversy with Davis, 104–11; explanatory letter to *Richmond Whig,* 105–7; loses command in Northern Virginia, 109, 121, 125, 156, 674; goes to Kentucky, 109, 133, 261, 445; made full General, 113–4; favors Bounty Act, 131; at Shiloh, 156. *See also* xviii, xxi, 14, 85 n., 113, 155, 157, 162–4, 273, 674
Beaver Dam, 492, 498, 500
Beaver Dam Creek, 220, 501, 513–5, 517–8, 538, 649, 658
Beckham, Maj. R. F., C.S.A., 232–3, 235, 238, 705
Bee, Brig. Gen. Barnard E., C.S.A., 41, 55, 57–8, 63–5, 66–7, 70, 81–3, 89, 95, 97, 157, 261, 674, 728, 730–1, 733–4
Belmead estate, 90
Benham, Maj. Gen. Henry W., U.S.A., 85 n.

Benjamin, Judah P., 2, 106, 109, 116–21, 124–34, 139–41, 143–5, 157, 170, 208, 237 n., 303, 308, 310, 324, 476, 671
Bennett, J. M., 128
Berthier, Marshal Pierre A., 734
Berryville, 413
Beverly, 23–25, 27, 29, 31, 33
Bible, The, 306–7, 492
Big Bethel Church, 17–19, 21, 23, 145, 152, 215, 545
Big Spring, 430
Black Creek, 292, 633
Blackburn's Ford, 45, 49, 54, 73, 101–2, 164, 247
Blackstone, Sir William, 269 n.
Blackwater River, 695–8
Blair, Maj. W. B., C.S.A., 704
Blakely gun, 310, 536, 646
Blanchard, Brig. Gen. Albert G., C.S.A., 201 n., 226 n., 239 n., 258, 266, 724
Bliss, Fort, 158
Blücher, Marshal G. L. von, 79
Blue Ridge Mountains, 330–8, 341, 344–5, 352, 354, 358–61, 364–5, 373, 383–4, 409, 413, 429, 431, 435, 450, 462, 466, 469–70, 481, 662, 678–9, 688–92, 699
Boatswain's Swamp, 520–2, 528, 531, 538, 542, 555, 594, 621, 663
Bohannon, Corp. William M., C.S.A., 646
Bolivar Heights, 309–10, 412
Bond, O. J., 710 n.
Bondurant, Capt. J. W., C.S.A., 252
Bonham, Gen. Milledge L., C.S.A., 7, 41, 53, 56, 58, 62, 64, 67, 70–1, 73–5, 77–8, 90, 97, 156 and n., 157 and n., 161–2 n., 164, 165 n., 674
Bonnycastle, Capt. John C., 704, 717 n.
Borcke, see von Borcke
Bory," "Old, see Beauregard, Gen. P. G. T.
Boswell, Capt. J. K., C.S.A., 426, 429, 455 n., 561
Boteler, Col. A. R., C.S.A., 128–9, 413–8, 431, 467, 469, 661–2
Bottom's Bridge, 212, 225, 638
Boyd, Belle, 378 and n.
Brackett's Ford, 539, 577
Bradford, Gamaliel, xvii
Bragg, Gen. Braxton, C.S.A., 85 n., 675, 709
Branch, Brig. Gen. L. O'B., C.S.A., 201, 213, 218–20, 358–9, 366–7, 497, 499, 501, 505, 508–13, 514 n., 515, 522–3, 605 n., 651
Bratton, Brig. Gen. John, C.S.A., 179, 187
Breathed, Maj. James, C.S.A., 279, 281, 291
Brent, Brig. Gen. Jos. L., C.S.A., 466 n.,

550, 551 n., 568–9, 582–3, 586, 592, 598, 600 and n., 612
Brice, Bvt. Maj. Gen. Benj. W., 710 n., 721 n.
Brightwell Farm, 558, 560, 566–7
Bristol, 279, 681–2
Brodhead, Brig. Gen. T. F., U.S.A., 407 n.
Brooks, Maj. Gen. W. T. H., U.S.A., 555 n.
Brown, Scout, 434
Brown, Maj. Campbell, U.S.A., 60 n., 261
Brown, Mrs. Pelham D., 248 n.
Brown, Col. Thompson, C.S.A., 618
Brown, Capt. William F., C.S.A., 416
Brown's Gap, 352, 354, 428, 448, 450, 462
Bryan, Maj. Henry, C.S.A., 561
Buchanan, President James, 160
Buck, Lucy R., diary quoted, 378–9
Buckhannon Pass, 25–28, 32
Buckton, 380
Buell, Maj. Gen. Don Carlos, U.S.A., 134
Buena Vista, Battle of, 20, 713
Buffalo Gap, 336–7
Bull Run, 7, 42, 45–72, 78–9, 89, 135, 138, 141, 195, 292, 674, 688
Bull Run, Order of Battle of Confederate Infantry, 728–32
Bull Run Mountains, 690
Bunker Hill, 405
Burke, Capt. Redmond, C.S.A., xxviii, 280–1, 292, 298
Burkeville, 697
Burks, Col. Jesse S., C.S.A., 313, 327–8
Burlington, Corp. John, C.S.A., 645
Burnside, Maj. Gen. Ambrose E., U.S.A., 108, 134
Butler, Maj. Gen. Benjamin F., U.S.A., 19, 152, 251
Butler, Gen. M. C., C.S.A., 269 n.
Byrd mansion (Westover), 603, 640

Cabeen, Thomas, 19
Cabell, Brig. Gen. W. L., C.S.A., 704
Cameron, Simon, 714 n.
Campbell, Capt. James D., U.S.A., 546 n.
Campbell, Col. John A., C.S.A., 396, 398
Campbell, Col. R. P., C.S.A., 536, 588, 606 n.
Cape Fear River, 274
Carlisle Barracks, 714
Carlyle, Thomas, xix, 307
Carpenter, Lieut. Joseph, C.S.A., 316, 396, 498–401, 453, 455
Carr, Col. George W., C.S.A., 704
Carr, Capt. M. T., 705, 717 n.
Carrick's Ford, 34, 35 n., 38, 317, 327
Carrington, Capt. E. C., U.S.A., 717 n

Carrington, Maj. James McDowell, C.S.A., 440 n., 442–3

Carroll, Maj. Gen. S. S., U.S.A., 443 n., 444 n., 461

Carter Farm, 597, 612, 650

Carter, Henry, 499

Carter, Robert, 66 n.

Carter, Col. Thomas H., C.S.A., 241, 252

Casey, Maj. Gen. Silas, U.S.A., 222 n., 237 n., 244

Casey's Redout, 240, 246, 268

Cash, Col. E. B. C., C.S.A., 731–2

Caskie, Capt. William H., C.S.A., 404

Casler, John O., 307 n.

Catlett, see Warder and Catlett

Catlett's Station, 409

Cedar Mountain, xvi, xxvi

Cedar Point, 374

Cedarville, 381–4, 388–9, 471–5, 482, 574, 735, 737–9

Central Railroad, see Virginia Central Railroad

Centreville, 43, 46–48, 50–51, 54–57, 59, 66, 73–75, 77–78, 105, 111, 141

Chaffin's Bluff, 581

Chambliss, Brig. Gen. J. R., 706 n., 717 n.

Champion, Private Frank, C.S.A., 526, 535, 645

Chancellorsville, xxvii, 692

Chapel road, 385, 473, 736, 738

Chapin, Bvt. Col. Gurden, 721 n.

Chapultepec, 9, 158, 574, 706–7, 715, 719

Charles City Court House, 298, 300, 640

Charles City road, 222, 225–9, 233–5, 239–40, 255–8, 539, 541, 548, 551, 553, 557–8, 565–7, 574, 612, 637

Charleston, S. C., 1–3, 6, 108, 150, 157, 273, 631, 677, 690, 707, 710

Charleston Mercury, 430

Charlestown, 406, 413–5, 418

Charlottesville, 470, 489–90, 680–1, 692–3

Charlottesville Artillery, 443

Cheat Bridge, 33

Cheat Mountain Expedition, 161

Cheat River, 25, 34

Chesapeake Bay, 677–9

Chesnut, Mrs. Mary Boykin (Mrs. James), 264 n.

Chesnut, Brig. Gen. James, C.S.A., 42–3, 103–4, 106–8

Chester Gap, 383, 472, 736–8

Chew, Lieut. Col. Robert Preston, C.S.A., 311, 373, 387, 477

His Battery, 311–2, 316, 385, 388 n., 391 n., 433, 477

Chickahominy River, 154, 208, 212–4, 220–1, 223, 225–6, 231, 238, 253, 275–7, 286–8, 293–9, 301, 471, 494–5,

497, 499–501, 506–9, 511, 515–7, 520, 523, 529, 532, 537–44, 547–8, 555, 558, 560–3, 570–1, 606, 616, 626, 628, 633, 636–8, 640, 647, 655, 658, 663, 674, 695, 698

Chickahominy road, 193, 206

Chilton, Brig. Gen. R. H., C.S.A., 85 n., 265, 500 n., 547, 586, 637–8, 704, 716–7, 722–3

Chinn House, 84, 731–2

Chipley, Capt. J. J., C.S.A., 437, 443

Chowan River, N. C., 696

Christian, Eli, 645

Christian, Lieut. Jonas, C.S.A., 295–6

Christian, Robert, 645

Christian, Thomas, 300

Churchill, Brig. Gen. Sylvester, U.S.A., 702 n.

Churubusco, 706–7

Citadel Academy, The, 710

City Point, 681, 697

Clark, Col. J. C., U.S.A., 461

Clarke's Gap, 680

Clark's battery, 617 n.

Clarksville, 681

Cleveland Plain Dealer, 5

Cobb, Maj. Gen. Howell, C.S.A., 160, 161 n., 213, 549, 598, 601–2, 609 n., 613, 622, 624 n.–625 n., 672

Cobb, Brig. Gen. T. R. R., C.S.A., 166 n., 607, 628 n., 630

Cocke, Brig. Gen. Philip St. George, C.S.A., 7, 41, 49 n., 54–6, 58, 63–4, 66–7, 70–1, 89, 90–1, 96, 97 n., 156 and n., 158, 261, 674, 705–6, 717 n., 721–2, 726–7, 731–2

Cold Harbor, 497–501, 517–8, 524, 540, 646

Cole, Lieut. Col. R. G., C.S.A., 705

Collins, Maj. W. D., U.S.A., 472 n.

Collis, Capt. C. H. T., U.S.A., 389 n.

Colquitt, Brig. Gen. A. H., C.S.A., 653

Colston, Brig. Gen. R. E., C.S.A., 161 n., 168, 178, 189, 201 n., 205 n., 234 n., 239 and n., 242, 246, 256

Columbia, S. C., 92

Columbia Bridge, 352, 422, 424

Columbia Furnace, 337–8

Confederate Military History, xvii

Confederate Portraits, by Gamaliel Bradford, xvii

Congress (man-of-war), 141

Conner, Brig. Gen. James, C.S.A., 95, 98 n.

Conner, Col. Z. T., C.S.A., 416–7, 479

Conrad's Store, Va., 332, 335, 341, 345–6, 348, 366, 373, 426–7, 429–30, 435, 437–8, 462, 481, 435

Conscription, 171–2, 322

Consideration of the Sermon on The Mount, by Gen. D. H. Hill, 20

Cooke, Miss Flora (Mrs. J. E. B. Stuart), 716
Cooke, John Esten, 289–90, 295–6, 301, 442 n.
Cooke, Brig. Gen. John R., C.S.A., 77 n., 716
Cooke, Brig. Gen. Philip St. George, U.S.A., 261, 286, 300, 633, 704, 715–7
Cook's Creek, 429
Cooper, Gen. Samuel, C.S.A., 43, 106–8, 113–4, 119, 121, 125, 328, 465 n., 709
Coppens, Lieut. Col. Georges G. A., C.S.A., 668 n.
Cornelius Creek, 656
Corse, Brig. Gen. Montgomery D., C.S.A., 97 n., 708, 718
Covington, 681, 690
Craighill, Brig. Gen. W. P., U.S.A., 705, 717 n.
Crenshaw's, 513
Crew Farm and House, 594, 598, 601, 650
Crittenden, Brig. Gen. George B., C.S.A., 348
Cromwell, by Thomas Carlyle, 307
Cross Keys, 429, 437, 444–8, 454, 461, 465, 479–80, 525, 654
  Battle, 444–8
Crozet, Col. Claude, 708
Crump, Col. C. A., C.S.A., 161 n., 170–1, 207 n.
Crutchfield, Col. Stapleton, C.S.A., 372, 379, 387, 390–1, 395 and n., 412, 424, 439–41, 443, 453, 471, 571, 573, 595, 649 n
Cub Run, 78
Culpeper Court House, 7, 90, 103, 142, 343, 352, 491, 692
Cumberland (man-of-war), 141, 679
Cumberland Gap, 678
Cummings, Col. Arthur C., C.S.A., 68–9, 325, 707, 723, 730
Cunningham, Lieut. Col. A. S., C.S.A., 705
Cunningham, Lieut. Col. Richard H., C.S.A., 84n., 418, 531, 588 n.
Custis, The Widow (Martha Washington), 634, 678
Cutshaw's Battery, 399, 401
Cutts, Lieut. Col. A. S., C.S.A., 618

Dabb House, 275, 494
Dabney, Capt. C. W., C.S.A., 492, 499, 503
Dabney, Maj. (Rev. Dr.) Robert Lewis, C.S.A., 362 n., 364 n., 372–3, 389 n., 391 n., 398 n., 399 n., 404 n., 406, 429 n., 438, 439 n., 441 n., 443, 447, 469, 589–92. 498–9, 503, 504 n., 505 n., 506, 508, 511, 528, 537, 560–1, 562 n., 563 and n., 568, 572 n., 604 n., 620 n., 630, 657, 659, 735

Daniel, John M., 664–6
Daniel, Capt. R. T., C.S.A., 645
Darbytown road, 541, 555, 557–8, 563, 565–6, 568, 574, 581, 585–6, 592, 597, 650
Daum, Col. Philip, U.S.A., 459 n.
Davidson College, 20
Davidson, Capt. John W., 704, 717 n.
Davis, Jefferson, xxiv; calls Beauregard to Richmond, 1, 3–6, 7–8; receives and answers Beauregard's plan of attack, 39–43, 45; appoints Brigadiers, 40; confers with leaders after Bull Run, 76–8 and n.; reads Beauregard's report on Manassas, 102–4; resulting controversy, 104–9; relations with Johnston, 112–8; difficulties with Miss. Brigades, 118–20; interferes with Jackson at Winchester, 124–6, 128–30; confers with Johnston on retreat, 134–6, 138; permanent inauguration, 173; uninformed during Johnston's retreat 142–4; puts Randolph in as Secretary of War, 144–5; approves Lee's plans to defend Richmond, 146–7; conference on Peninsula defense, 148–51; sends Johnson to help Magruder, 151; his "political" Generals, 160–1; disagrees with Johnston on Richmond defenses, 201–8; fails to learn Johnston's plans, 210–3; their strained relations shown in Magruder-Smith clash, 214–7; appoints more Major Generals, 218–9; left ignorant of Seven Pine's plans, 222–3, 205; at Johnston's headquarters there, 238, 262 n; in accord with Lee, 265, 267, 270; appoints new generals for Lee, 267, 270 n.; congratulates Jackson in the Valley, 431; comment and action in Richmond defense plans, 465–6, 495, 501 n., 504 n., 515, 574; receives Magruder's report on his action in the Seven Days, 608-11; comment on Jackson in the Seven Days, 657; Jackson appeals to him, to be sent against Pope, 661–2; judged after the War, xxiii. See also 46 n., 79, 100–1, 112, 157, 163, 166, 172, 230, 237 n.. 252, 262 n., 264, 266–7, 269, 270–1, 273, 365, 368, 371 n., 581, 616–7, 623, 625, 628–9, 643, 672, 709, 712
Davis, Mrs. Jefferson, 81, 222 n.
Davis, Lieut. J. Lucius, 706 n., 717 n.
Davis Legion, 279, 283 n.
Deal, John, 199 n.
Dearing, Brig. Gen. James, C.S.A., 98 n., 252
Deas, Col. George A., C.S.A., 11, 720 n
de Gouges, Countess Olympe, 24
de Lagnel, Brig. Gen. Julius A., C.S.A., under Garnett in Western Virginia,

27–31; at Hart house, 29, 36; details of his escape and recapture, 36
Delaware College, 614
de Leon, Tucker, 144
Denny, Bishop Collins, 706 n.
Denson, C. B., 271 n.
Deshler, Col. James, C.S.A., 582, 584
Detroit, 677
DeWitt, Lieut. Gen. J. L., U.S.A., 310 n.
Diascund Bridge, 193
Dickinson, Capt. A. G., C.S.A., 599 n.
Dictionary of American Biography, xvii
Dimick, Col. Justin, 15
Dispatch Station, 495
Donelson, Fort, 134
Donnally, Col. Dudley, U.S.A., 385 n.
Doswell, Turner, 297
Doubleday, Gen. Abner, 20 n.
Douglas, Col. H. K., C.S.A., 444 n., 499, 506 n.
Douglas, Gen. H. T., C.S.A., 532 n.
Douty, Col. Calvin S., U.S.A., 387 n., 472 n.
Dranesville, 217, 275, 281
Drewry's Bluff, 202, 209–11, 213, 273–4, 557, 698
Dumfries, 136, 137–8, 140
Dunkards, 322–3
Dyer, Bvt. Maj. Gen. Alexander B., U.S.A., 721 n.

Early, Lieut. Gen. Jubal Anderson, C.S.A., Early career, 85, 96, 706, 717, 723; appearance and manner, xix, 86; personality, 85-6; his orders at Bull Run, 62, 66 n., 726–7; his Brigade saves the day there, 72, 85, 89; his position there, 731–2; praised for his action there, 86; commands Brigade as Colonel, 86; his officers, 96; made Lieutenant General, 97; in Williamsburg retreat, 180–2; plans to attack the enemy, 181–2, 191; the futile attack, 182–8; wounded, 185, 190, 217, 262; his losses, 188–9; Longstreet reports on his action, 190; he disclaims responsibility, 190–1; assigned to Elzey's command, 588, 672, 674; character as commander, 192; battles in 1864, xvi. *See also* 41, 54–5, 58, 76 n., 87, 161 n., 170, 240 n., 248, 517
Echols, Brig. Gen. John, C.S.A., 98 n., 730
Edisto Island, 249
Edmonds, Col. E. C., C.S.A., 645
Edwards, Col. O. E., C.S.A., 718 n.
Elizabeth River, 679
Elk Run Valley, 332
Elsnitz, 734
Eltham, xix, 193–200, 204, 226
Elzey, Maj. Gen. Arnold, C.S.A., 71, 79, 83–86, 96, 97 n., 348–9, 351, 369

and n., 389, 413 n., 444–5, 447, 456 n., 487, 524, 525 n., 534, 536, 588, 605, 672, 674, 732, 735–6, 739
Enfield rifles, 532
English, Lieut. R. M., C.S.A., 455 n.
Enon Church, 284–5
Enroughty, Nathan, 591
Eufaula, Ala., 625
Evans, Brig. Gen. Nathan George ("Shanks"), C.S.A., 54–5, 58–9, 63–4, 66, 69, 72, 86–7, 88–9, 91, 96, 97 n., 111, 157, 262, 674, 728, 730
Evansport Battery, 135
Evelington Heights, 640–3, 647
Ewell, Lieut. Gen. Richard Stoddert, C.S.A., Personality, xix; training, early career, and appearance, 348–9; with Beauregard at Bull Run, 53–60, 62, 726–7; position after the rout, 75; his officers, 96; made Lieutenant General, 97; made Major General, 156; on the Blue Ridge, 201; in the Valley, 262, 334, 337, 342, 345; moves against Banks there, 330, 335, 341, 345–6, 350; heads Valley defense while Jackson aids Johnson, 347–61; his officers there, 348–50; "Jackson is crazy," 350–2; disgust in Valley situation and changing orders, 353–61; decides to consult Jackson, 361; retained by him to attack Banks at Front Royal, 362–82, 482; on the road to Winchester, 385, 388 n., 389–90, 392, 395 and n., 400–1, 403, 405, 416, 472, 735–9; in the retreat from Winchester, 420–1, 424, 429 n., 430, 432–3, 481; at Cross Keys and Port Republic, 437–64 *passim*, 471; praises troops in the Valley, 487; praises Jackson, 488; his part in the return to defend Richmond, 489, 491, 502, 505, 509–13; at Gaines' Mill, 517, 524–32, 534–5; in action at McClellan's retreat, 541, 560 n.; at Malvern Hill, 592, 602; losses in the Seven Days, 605; excellence as commander, 655, 667; sent again to the Valley, 662; his command, 671–2, 674. *See also* xvi, xviii, 7, 40–1, 50, 60 n., 171, 204, 213, 475, 478–9, 735

Fair Oaks Station, 225, 238, 244, 262, 548
Fairfax Courthouse, 111
Fairfax, Col. J. W., C.S.A., 578, 579 n.
Fairfax Station, 50
Fairfield Race Course, 231–2, 234
Faison, Lieut. Col. Franklin J., C.S.A., 534–5
Falkner, Col. W. C., C.S.A., 731
Farley, Samuel, 280 n.
Farley, Capt. William Downes, C.S.A., xxviii, 280–1, 293

Faulkner, Col. Charles J., C.S.A., 387 n., 448 n., 480 n.
Fauntleroy, Dr. A. M., 264 n.
Fauntleroy, Brig. Gen. Thomas T., C.S.A., 261, 703, 716–7, 722
Featherston, Brig. Gen. W. S., C.S.A., 97 n., 161 n., 171, 240, 268–70, 588, 605 and n.
Ferry, Maj. Gen. O. S., U.S.A., 641 n.
Field, Maj. Gen. Charles W., C.S.A., 202 n., 523, 649–50, 653
Finley, Rev. A. W., 256 n.
First Manassas, xvi, 45–72, 78–9, 89. *See also* Manassas
Fisher, Col. C. F., C.S.A., 52 n., 69, 70–1, 731–2
Fisher's Bridge, 539
Fisher's Ford, 539, 567, 577
Fisher's Gap, 330, 333–5, 358, 367, 481
Fletcher, Capt. John, C.S.A., 474 n.
Florida Regiment, Second, 179–81
Flournoy, Lieut. Col. Thomas S., C.S.A., 369, 377, 380–1, 385 n., 404–5, 406 n., 423, 574
Floyd, Maj. Gen. John B., C.S.A., 5, 37 n., 115 n.
Forge Bridge, Chickahominy, 288, 295, 297–8, 300, 636, 638
Forney, Maj. Gen. John H., C.S.A., 195 n.
Forrest, Lieut. Gen. Nathan B., C.S.A., 483
Fontaine, Private, C.S.A., 382
Franklin, W. Va., 408
Franklin, Gen. William B., U.S.A., 213, 539, 555, 626 n., 641 n., 657
Frayser, R. E., 289–91
Frayser's Farm, 583, 587–9, 591, 606, 611, 645, 650–3, 663–5, 670, 673
Fredericksburg, xxi, 42, 142, 145, 168, 205–6, 208, 213, 221, 337, 342, 344, 352, 358–9, 363, 408–10, 415, 491, 677, 682, 688, 692, 694, 697
Frederickshall, 491–2, 496, 502
Freeman, Lieut. Col. W. G, 706
Frémont, Maj. Gen. John C., U.S.A., 336, 342, 352 n., 358–9, 363–4, 368, 383, 389, 408–9, 414, 417–20, 422, 423 n., 425–8, 430, 435–7, 444–9, 451, 454, 461–2 and n., 466, 468, 477, 82–3, 485, 657
French Revolution, by Carlyle, xix
French, Col. S. B., 236
French, Maj. Gen. William H., U.S.A., 85 n.
Front Royal, 331–4, 343, 357–8, 363–82 *passim,* 383–6, 389–90, 395, 406, 412–3, 416, 419, 421, 435, 438, 471–3, 477–8, 480–2, 484, 502, 574, 674, 690, 736–7
Fulkerson, Col. Samuel V., C.S.A., 313–4, 327, 393, 442 n., 531, 536–7, 606 n., 643
Funsten, Col. O. R., C.S.A., 324, 338, 387–8, 391, 739 n.
Furlough and Bounty Act, 130–4, 171–3

Gaines, Dr., 652
Gaines' Mill, 517, 519, 524, 538, 539–40, 555, 560, 588, 597, 616, 620–1, 629, 633, 642, 645–6, 650, 652–5, 657, 663–4, 670–1; the Battle, 532–7
Gaines, Sam M., 35 and n.
Garibaldi, 88, 432
Garland, Brig. Gen. John, 261, 631 n., 703, 716
Garland, Brig. Gen. Samuel, C.S.A., ancestry and early career, 248; under Beauregard, 7; under Longstreet at Manassas, 96; as Colonel of Brigade, 97, 195 n.; assigned Ewell's troops, 217; his character as commander, 217–8, 248–9; at Seven Pines, 240, 242, 248, 252; losses there, 244; at Gaines' Mill, 533, 535, 601; losses in the Seven Days, 605 n.; praised by A. P. Hill, 653
Garlick's Landing, 290, 293–4
Garnett, Camp, 27–31
Garnett, Brig. Gen. Richard B., C.S.A., 123, 313–4, 316–9, 324–6, 328, 354, 479, 704
Garnett, Brig. Gen. Robert Selden, C.S.A., 399 n.; ancestry and early career, 25–5, 704, 716–7, 722; character, 25; operations in Western Virginia, 25–5, 32, 42–3; his officers, 27–8, 36 n.; at Laurel Hill, 32–3, 321; retreat from the Hill, 33; at Kaler's and Carrick's Ford, 34–5; rebuke to Gaines while under fire, 35; wounded, 35; his death, 36, 261, 317, 327, 674; Porter Alexander's estimate of him, 37
Garnett's Farm, 537
Gartrell, Col. Lucius J., C.S.A., 731
Gaston, N. C., 680
Geary, Maj. Gen. John W., U.S.A. 138 n., 409
Georgia Regiments:
First, 38
Seventh, 66, 730–1
Eighth, 730
Twelfth, 28, 416, **736**
Fourteenth, 195
Fifteenth, 537
Sixteenth, 608
Nineteenth, 195
Twentieth, 180
Twenty-first, 401, **526**
Thirty-fifth, 672
Forty-fourth, 515, 537, **605**
Gettysburg, xix, xxvi–xxvii
Gibbons, Col. S. B., C.S.A., **732**

Gibson, Maj. Gen. George, U.S.A., 702 n.
Gilbert, Corp. Cornelius, C.S.A., 645
Gildea, Lieut. James, 442 n.
Giles, Col. John R. R., C.S.A., 245
Gilham, Col. William, C.S.A., 127, 479, 713–4
Gillies Creek, 230, 234–5, 238, 253–5, 257–8
Gilman, Capt., 72 n.
Gist, Brig. Gen. S. R., C.S.A., 65 n., 98 n.
Glendale, 565, 591
Gloucester, 707
Gloucester Point, 148, 695, 724
Golding's Farm, 544–5, 626
Goode, Col. J. Thomas, 705
Gordon, Lieut. Col. George A., 705, 717 n.
Gordon, Maj. Gen. George H., U.S.A., 388 n., 391 n., 392 n., 474 n., 739 n.
Gordon, Maj. Gen. John B., C.S.A., appearance, xix; family, 251; action at Seven Pines, 241, 244, 250–2; at Gaines' Mill, 533; leads Rodes's Brigade at Malvern Hill, 589, 602, 629, 651; excellence as General, xxvi, 250–2
Gordon, Mrs. John B., 251, 252 n.
Gordon, Maj. William H., 704, 717 n.
Gordonsville, 6, 213, 219, 332, 351, 356, 358–9, 363, 366, 489–2, 501–2, 660, 662, 668; 671, 680–2, 692–3
Gorgas, Brig. Gen. Josiah, C.S.A., 170
Gooney Manor road, 376–7
Gosport Navy Yard, 202, 679
Grafton, 9, 23, 25, 37, 680–1
Graham, Maj. Campbell, 704, 716–7 and n.
Graham, Rev. Dr. and Mrs. James R., 128, 304
Graham, Brig. Gen. Lawrence P., U.S.A., 261, 704, 716
Grant, Gen. Ulysses S., U.S.A., 273
Grapevine Bridge, 541, 548, 551, 560, 563, 568, 637–8, 656, 658
Gregg, James, 518 n.
Gregg, Brig. Gen. Maxcy, C.S.A., described, 518 and n.; at Gaines' Mill, 519–22, 528–9, 532, 535, 653; losses in the Seven Days' Battles, 605 n. See also 202 n.; 280, 513 n., 665, 667 (his Regiment and Brigade)
Gregory, Corp. C. C., C.S.A., 645
Griffin, Maj. Gen. Charles, U.S.A., 68 n.
Griffith, Brig. Gen. Richard, C.S.A., 119, 161, 162 n., 549, 553, 588, 605, 674
Grigsby, Col. Andrew J., C.S.A., 363, 396 n., 398
Grimes, Capt. Carey F., C.S.A., 596, 616 n., 650

Gwynn, Brig. Gen. Walter (Va.), 229, 705–6, 717 n., 722, 724

Hagood, Brig. Gen. Johnson, C.S.A., 98 n.
Half Sink, 497, 499, 508
Halleck, Maj. Gen. H. W., U.S.A., 675
Halltown, 417
Hamilton, Dr. J. G. de R., xxvii
Hamlin, Dr. P. G., 726–7
Hampden, Artillery, 404
Hampden-Sydney College, 372, 708
Hampton, Anthony, 91
Hampton Legion, 70, 80–1, 83–4, 165 n., 195, 468, 529, 648, 730
Hampton Road, 174–8
Hampton Roads, 8, 679, 695
Hampton, 17, 169, 725
Hampton, Wade (the first), 91–2
Hampton, Wade (the second), 92 and n., 93 and n.
Hampton, Lieut. Gen. Wade (the third), C.S.A., xviii, 271; his ancestry and family, 91–3; his character, 94; his ability, 95, 195–6; his Legion, 70, 80–1, 93–4, 165 n., 195, 468, 529, 648, 730; at First Manassas, 57–9, 64, 66–7, 89, 91, 94–5; made Lieutenant General, 97; in Peninsula retreat, 161, 195–6; success at Eltham, 195–6, 199; becomes Brigadier General, 218; wounded at Seven Pines, 245, 262, 270; praised for his action there, 246; at McClellan's retreat, 571, 572 n., 575 n., 578–9; at Malvern Hill, 588; made Stuart's Senior Brigadier, 643, 673–4
Hampton's Battery, U.S.A., 389 n.
Hancock, Maj. Gen. W. S., U.S.A., 183 n., 188, 189 n., 555 n., 626 n.
Hancock, 138
Hanover Court House, 219, 284, 288–9, 367, 409, 496–7, 499, 501–2
Hanover Junction, 6, 522, 681, 692–4, 697
Happy Creek, 379
Hardee, Lieut. Gen. W. J., xxii, 709
Harman, Maj. John A., C.S.A., 304, 340, 345, 362 and n., 393, 411, 463–4, 476, 482, 489–92, 494 n., 498, 527–8
Harney, Maj. Gen. W. S., 24, 709
Harper, Maj. Gen. Kenton (Va. Mil.), 721, 730
Harpers Ferry, 9–13, 16, 21, 39, 44, 83, 112–3, 138, 308–10, 312, 321, 374, 404, 406, 409, 412, 414, 420, 486, 678, 680–3, 688, 691, 699, 721
Harris, Brig. Gen. D. B., C.S.A., 706 n., 717 n.
Harris, John T., 128
Harris, Mr. and Mrs. Nathaniel, 492

Harrisonburg, 330, 335-6, 341, 345, 348, 352, 360, 364, 408, 420, 425, 427, 429, 432, 435, 437, 462, 467, 690

Harrisonburg road, 346

Harrison's Landing, 603, 675

Hart house, 29, 36

Harvard University, 349

Harvie, Col. Edwin J., C.S.A., 705

Haskell, Col. J. C., C.S.A., 172, 535, 620 n., 623, 652 n., 734

Hatch, Brig. Gen. John P., U.S.A., 407 n.

Hatcher, Harry, 339

Hatton, Brig. Gen. Robert, C.S.A., 161, 218, 244 and n., 246, 262, 266, 270, 271 n.

Hatton, Mrs. Robert, 244 n.

Hawkinsville, Va., 424

Hawks, Maj. Wells J., C.S.A., 415

Haw's Shop, 285

Haxall's Landing, 639

Hays, Maj. Gen. Harry T., C.S.A., 96, 97 n., 454-5, 668, 672, 674

Hays, Bvt. Maj. Gen. William, 710 n., 721 n.

Heck, Lieut. Col. J. M., C.S.A., 27, 32

Heintzelman, Maj. Gen. S. P., U.S.A., 68 n., 223 n., 539, 555, 559, 568 n.

Henderson, Col. G. F. R., British Army, xvi, 490 n., 503 n., 512 n., 604 n., 733, 735

Henry, Fort, 134

Henry Hill, 64, 66 n., 70, 89, 648, 728

Henry House, 64, 66 n., 68, 84, 89, 728, 731

Henry, Judith, 64

Henry, Patrick, 284

Herring Creek, 641

Heth, Maj. Gen. Henry, C.S.A., 704

Hewes, M. Warner, 444 n.

Hickory Hill, 282

Hicksford, 680

High Meadows (Dabb House), 275, 494

Hill, Lieut. Gen. Ambrose Powell, C.S.A., education and early career, 159, 704; character, xix, 159, 192; as Brigadier General in Longstreet's Division, 159-60, 168, 170-1; in the retreat toward Williamsburg, 178, 189, 192; made Major General, 218-9; assumes command before Seven Pines, 219-20, 222, 231; action there, 248, 266; new Brigades given him, 271-2; in defense of Richmond, after Valley Campaign, 494, 497, 499-500, 505, 508-15; at Gaines' Mill, 517-8, 520, 522-32, 534; in action at McClellan's retreat, 541, 548, 557, 563, 566, 568; at Frayser's Farm, 581, 583, 585, 587, 611, 670; at Malvern Hill, 589-90, 592; his losses, 605-6; his praise of Pegram, 650-1; accomplishments of

his Division, 653, 667; Jackson's letter to Lee about him, 659 n.; Lee comments on his actions, 663; quarrels with Longstreet, 664-8; goes to reinforce Jackson, 668, 670-2. See also xxvii, 161 n., 195 n., 214 n., 217, 538, 649, 658

Hill, Lieut. Gen. Daniel Harvey, C.S.A., forebears, 19-20; education and early career, 17, 20; appearance and manner, 20-1; writings, 20; religious faith, 21; success at Big Bethel, 17-8; praised by Magruder, 21; goes to Yorktown, 21; becomes Brigadier General, 22; public acclaim, 22, 23; arrives late at Manassas, 96; becomes Lieutenant General, 97; receives Magruder's dispatches, 153; commands Division in Peninsula retreat, 169-70, 174; organizes Fort Macon defenses, 169; congratulates Randolph on his elevation as Secretary of War, 170; becomes Major General, 170; his Brigades, 170-1, 180, 189; plans to attack, during retreat to Williamsburg, 181-2, 191; the futile attack, 182-7; praised by Longstreet, 189-90; disclaims responsibility, 190-1; as commander, 192, 268; at Eltham, 194, 196 n.; orders and positions preliminary to Seven Pines, 222-3, 228-9, 233-6; action at Seven Pines, 238-41, 245, 248, 258, 259 n.; his heroic conduct, 246-7, 252-5; praises his officers, 246, 249-50; troubles in his Division, 265, 268-70; in defense of Richmond after Valley campaign, 494-7, 500, 508, 512-5; at Gaines' Mill, 517, 523-4, 526-35, 629, 650, 653; in action as McClellan retreats, 541, 570, 575-8, 585 n.; at Malvern Hill, 589, 592-5, 597-8, 600 n., 601-3, 609, 627, 670; losses in the Seven Days, 605 n.; possible critic of Magruder, 607 n., 608 n.; criticizes Holmes, 614; criticizes Whiting, 621; criticizes Toombs, 627; resulting quarrel, 627-8; praise of his generalship, 629-31; critical attitude caused by dyspepsia, 630-1, 667; sent to Charleston, S. C., 631, 674; praises his Division, 631-2; criticizes Jackson, 657; changes in his Division, 672-3. See also xviii, xxiv, 165, 214, 273

Hill, Maj. Henry, 704, 716-7, 723

Hill, James, 734

Hill, Col. R. C., C.S.A., 77 and n., 78 and n.

Hindman, Maj. Gen. T. C., C.S.A., 675

Hoke, Maj. Gen. Robert F., C.S.A., 651

Holkum Branch, 731

Holmes, Lieut. Gen. Theophilus H.

C.S.A., 45, 48, 51, 54–7, 60, 62, 75, 96–7, 140, 143, 145, 158, 165 n., 273–4, 541, 557, 565, 581–6, 589, 597, 608, 610, 614, 631, 643, 648, 726

Hood, Lieut. Gen. John Bell, C.S.A., early military career, 161 n., 196; promotions, 196, 198; his military discipline, 197–8; appearance and manner, 198; leads Texas Brigade, 198; gallantry at Eltham, 198–9; his Brigade at Seven Pines, 238, 246–7, 267; brilliant action at Gaines' Mill, 532, 534–5, 653; losses in the Seven Days' Battles, 605 n., 606; as commander, 270, 621; Lee's letter to him, May 21, 1863, xvii. See also 194 n., 468, 492, 511, 528–9

Hood, Pvt. William, C.S.A.; xxi

Hooe, Richardetta, 718–9

Hooker, Maj. Gen. Joseph, U.S.A., 85 n.

Hopewell Church, 290

Hopkins, Commodore Esek, 518 n.

Hotchkiss, Maj. Jedediah, C.S.A., xxvii, 23 n., 27–8, 28 n., 30, 32–3, 321–2, 329 n., 337, 339 n., 341 n., 342, 345, 387 n., 397, 415–6, 418, 423, 425 n., 427, 429 n., 430, 435, 438, 442 n., 447 n., 448 n., 455 and n., 469–70, 472 n., 473, 575 n., 481–2, 494 n., 498–9, 500 n., 503 n., 505 n., 514 n., 659, 735–7

Howard, Maj. McHenry, C.S.A., 310 n., 339 n., 399 n., 421 n., 439 n., 447 n., 486, 563 n.

Hoyt, Capt. James, C.S.A., 652 n.

Huger, Maj. Gen. Benjamin, C.S.A., 146, 154, 168, 201, 204, 206 n., 207, 213, 214 n., 219, 221, 223, 226, 228–31, 234–5, 237–9 and n., 246, 253–60, 262, 266–8 and n., 494, 508, 538, 541–4, 546–8, 550–3, 557–60, 563, 566–8, 574, 576–8, 583, 587; at Malvern Hill, 589–91, 597–9, 601–2, 605, 608, 610, 630; criticism of his action in the Seven Days' Battles, 611–4, 654, 658, 667, 675; losses, 605 n.; relieved and sent West, 613, 618, 674; illness as cause of his failure, 620

Huger, Lieut. Col. Frank, 705

Hughes, R. M., 237 n., 734

Hunt, Maj. Gen. Henry J., U.S.A., 584 n., 618 n.

Hunton, Brig. Gen. Eppa, C.S.A., 67, 72, 89, 96, 97 n., 588, 652, 730

Huntington, Capt. James F., U.S.A., 461

Hundley's Corner, 512, 514

Hupp's, 419

Huttonsville, 23, 25, 33

Imboden, Brig. Gen. John D., C.S.A., 97, 98 n., 449–50, 505

Indian Warfare, 24–5, 87, 91, 96, 123, 159, 268–9, 326, 707, 715

Indiana Thirteenth Regiment, 353

Iverson, Col. Alfred, C.S.A., 534–5

Jackson, Col. William L., C.S.A., 470

Jackson, Col. Andrew, Jr., C.S.A., 704

Jackson, President Andrew, 92, 328

Jackson, Maj. George, C.S.A., 705

Jackson, Lieut. Gen. Thomas Jonathan (Stonewall), C.S.A., in Mexican War, 9, 706 and n.; Colonel of Volunteers, 723; teaches at V. M. I., 11, 308, 706, 717; his personality, xix–xxi, 11, 417–8; his religious spirit, xxviii, 11, 305–6, 319–20, 328, 405–6, 422, 431, 439, 447, 461, 463, 492, 505, 570–1, 657, 717; precise military standard, 13; gives up Harpers Ferry command to Johnston, 12–3; appointed Brigadier General, 41; at First Manassas, 46, 56–9, 64–7, 69, 73, 89, 96–7, 305–6, 730–1; how he got his nickname, 81–3, 733–4; letters to wife, praising God for victory, 82–83; his action praised, 86; made Lieutenant General, 97; threatens to resign over Loring clash, 1861, 122–30, 133, 303–4; letter to Gov. Letcher, 126–7; on Longstreet's desire to reinforce him in the Valley, 167–8; his forces there, 201, 221, 236, 262; reinforced, 271, 274; victory in the Valley, 282; public appraisal of him, 303; his discipline at Winchester, 304; appearance and manner, 305, 307–8, 318, 348, 366; strategy of his withdrawal from Winchester, 306; personality and conduct, 307–8; contrasted with Ashby, 308–10; details of the retreat, 311–20; attitude toward Sunday fighting, 312–3, 319–21; as a hero, 313; reorganizes the Army of the Valley, 321–8; orders maps made, 321–2; treatment of conscientious objectors and AWOL's, 322–3; arms, 323–4; Sunday observance, 324; new officers, 324–8; his strategy in the Massanuttons, opposing Banks, 329–35; checkmated by Banks, 335–6; trouble with Ashby's cavalry, 337–41; alternatives of his next action, 342–4; decision to reinforce Johnson, 344–6; assigns Ewell to head Valley defense in his absence, 347; orders to Ewell there, 350, 352–3, 358–9; his action against Milroy, 354–61; wants to take offensive against Banks, 362–5; retains Ewell for that purpose, 365–8; decides to attack, 368; army discipline and command, 368–9, 630; the march north, 371–4; strategy and tactics of the attack, 374–8; the attack at Front

Royal, 378–82; pursuit of Banks and night march to Winchester, 383–94, 735–9; the attack and victory at Winchester, 395–405; gratitude for victory, 405–6; casualties of the engagement, 407; Jackson feared, as threat to Washington, 408–10; Union stores captured, 411–2; desires to press beyond the Potomac, 412; details of the retreat from Winchester, 413–34; strategic points involved, 428; Tom Strother incident. 429–30; Jackson's understanding of Negroes, 429–30; shock at Ashby's death, 432–3; success at Cross Keys and Port Republic, 435–69; personal incidents after the battles, 463–5; receives Lee's plans for Richmond defenses, 465–9; letter to Lee, 467; returns to Richmond, 470–1, 486; appraisal of his generalship in the Valley Campaign, 470–88—five questions: (1) inadequate batteries at Front Royal, 471, 481; (2) slow decision on May 24, 471–5, 481; (3) inadequate organization of cavalry, 475–9, 481; (4) difficulties with his subordinates 479–81; (5) routine infantry tactics 480–1; three superior qualities of generalship: (1) judgment of position, 481–2, 485; (2) balance of strategy, 482–3, 485; (3) by strategy, imposes his will on his adversary, 484–5; his popularity and public acclaim, 486–8; secrecy of his return toward Richmond, 490–3; conference at High Meadows with Lee and Generals, 494–8; his troops moved Southeast, 498–501, 636; a deserter tells Federals his strength, 492, 501–2; delays and disappointments in marches and action north of Richmond, 503–16; his delay and action before Gaines' Mill, 517–8, 523–4, 526–30, 670; meets Lee to organize the line, 530–1; the battle, 532–7; reconstructs Grapevine Bridge, 541, 548, 551, 554, 557, 560–3 and n., 656, 658; given post of danger, 555–6; delay at White Oak Swamp, 565–81 passim, 583, 587, 617 n., 629, 637–40, 655; at Malvern Hill and after, 588–92, 595–9, 603, 610, 628, 641–3, 655–6; losses in the Seven Days' Battles, 605; Whiting's jealousy of him, 620–1; praise of D. H. Hill, 629; his heroic officers, 647, 652–4; criticism of his comparative inaction in the Seven Days, 655–9 and n., 667, 673, 675; desires and is sent to attack Pope, 661–2, 668, 675; association with A. P. Hill, 663, 671; his enlarged command, 671–2, 674;

his position in this volume, xviii, xxi; his historical place, xv, xxx; his letters, after his death, xxvii; his conversational style, xxix; later estimates of his career, xxv. See also 4, 28 n., 149, 204
Jackson, Mrs. Thomas Jonathan, 82, 128, 304, 319, 321, 405–6, 422, 463, 500 n., 505 n., 570–1
Jackson's River, 681
James River, 9, 14, 16, 90, 146, 151, 168, 175, 201–11 passim, 270, 274, 495, 538–41, 548, 557, 560, 565, 570, 581, 583, 590, 593, 603, 632, 635–7, 639–40, 643, 675, 678, 681, 689, 694–5, 697–9
Jamestown, 695
Jeffers, Lieut. William N., 211 n.
Jefferson, Thomas, 18, 145
Jenkins, Brig. Gen. Micah, C.S.A., with D. R. Jones at Manassas, 96, 97 n.; at Williamsburg, 179; commands at Fort Magruder, 192, 242; praised for his action at Seven Pines, 249–50, 252; at Frayser's Farm, 651; promoted to Brigadier, 672, 674
Johnson, Maj. Gen. Edward, C.S.A., 28 and n., 85, 336–7, 342, 344–6, 352, 354, 362, 389 n., 416, 437, 481, 674
Johnson, Lieut. Col. B. J., C.S.A., 81, 95
Johnston, Gen. Albert Sidney, C.S.A., 83 n., 109, 113–4 and n., 115 n., 134, 162, 485, 709
Johnston, J. Ambler, 206 n., 678 n.
Johnston, Gen. Joseph Eggleston, C.S.A., appearance, manner, and character, 111–2, 120, 192; at opening of the War, 703, 714–7, 722–3; actions in early battles, xvi; commands at Harpers Ferry, 12–3, 16, 38, 113; his action planned by Beauregard, 39–44 and n., 46–8, 51–2, 726; his officers, 40; his rank, 97; at Manassas Junction, 46, 49 n., 50; details of his action at Bull Run, 51–3, 55–6, 58, 60–2, 65–7, 77–1, 726–30, 734; at Lewis House, 65–6, 72–5, 89; his command returned by Beauregard, 73 n.; tells Davis of victory, 76; confers with Davis and leaders, 76–8 and n.; suggests Beauregard's promotion, 79; praised after victory, 80–81; satisfaction over victory, 83; this officers, 83–4, 96–8; later account of his Manassas action, 83–5, 89; involved in Beauregard report controversy, 101, 103–11; in command near Centreville, 111; disapproves of Lee, 112; friendship with Davis, 112–3; made full General, 113–4; breaks with Davis over order of his nomination, 113–5; clashes with Benjamin, 116–25, 130, 131–3, 139,

476; clashes with Davis, 118–25, 129–30, 139; incident of Jackson's resignation at Winchester, 121–6, 129–30; letter to Jackson about this, 125; difficulties over Furlough and Bounty Act, 130–4, 172–3; discovers Cabinet's plan to withdraw from Manassas, 134–6; withdraws from Manassas, 137–42, 305–6; his weakened army, 137–8; supplies lost in retreat, 140; criticisms of his action, 141; his belief in Lee, 144–5; given most responsible command, 147; urges withdrawal from Peninsula, 148–51, 232; sent to help Magruder there, 151–4; details of the Peninsula retreat, 154–5, 175–80, 182, 191; officers and men in the retreat, 156–71, 189; on responsibility for Williamsburg attack, 191–2; his action at Eltham: officers and troops involved, 193–200; disagreement with Davis on Richmond defenses, 201–4, 264; desires concentration and unity of command, 201–7; exchange with Lee on control of troops near Fredericksburg, 204–8; orders new positions near Richmond, 208–12, 214; reticence in disclosing plans to Davis, 210–3, 265; their strained relations shown in Magruder-Smith clash, 214–7; plans offensive, 214; obtains more Major Generals, 218–9; his plans and orders before battle of Seven Pines, 219–29, 231–3, 236, 252, 430, 228–9; action in the battle, 236–8, 418; wounded, 262 and n., 264, 485, 674; his officers and troops involved, 245–52, 270–1, 325–6, 671; blamed for mismanagement, 252–4, 257, 259–60, 262; he blames Huger, 260; lays down command, 263–4, 431, 674; desires offensive in the Valley, 359–61; instructs Ewell there, 363–6, 368; dispatch to Jackson after Winchester, 415; disliked by Toombs, 623. See also xv, xvi, xviii, xix, xxi, xxv, xxvi, 157, 165 n., 166, 267, 270, 275–6, 281, 317, 327–30, 332, 349, 362 n., 363, 371 n., 408, 465, 615, 731
Johnston, R. M., 728, 733
Johnston, Col. Robert, C.S.A., 705
Jones, Maj. Gen. David R., C.S.A., 40–1, 54–60, 62, 75 n., 96–7, 157, 161 n., 162 n., 165 n., 174, 262, 272, 536, 544–6, 548, 550, 553, 562–3, 592, 598–600, 602, 605 n., 607, 672, 726
Jones, Lieut. Col. H. P., C.S.A., 572 n., 617 n.
Jones, Brig. Gen. John M., C.S.A., 704
Jones, Brig. Gen. John R., C.S.A., 588, 605 n., 671
Jones, J. William, 351 n.

Jones, Col. R. T., C.S.A., 245, 700 n., 717 n.
Jones, Maj. Gen. Samuel, C.S.A., 97 and n., 704
Jones, Brig. Gen. Thomas M., C.S.A., 705
Jones, Brig. Gen. William E., C.S.A., 279, 706 n., 717 n.
Jordan, Brig. Gen. Thomas, C.S.A., 51, 52 n., 56, 77, 78 and n., 97 n., 704
Jordan's Ford, 539, 558, 560, 567
Junction, N. C., 681

Kaler's Ford, 34
Kanawha River, 677, 678, 681, 699
Kanawha road, 690
Kearny, Maj. Gen. Philip, U.S.A., 559–60
Kearny's Bridge, 567
Keezletown road, 367
Kemper, Doctor, 439–40
Kemper house, 438–40, 44 ?–3
Kemper, Maj. Gen. James L., C.S.A., 70, 97 and n., 239, 241, 242 n., 249, 266–7, 651, 707, 718, 732
Kenly, 502
Kerfoot, Henry D., 439 n.
Kernstown, xvi, 312, 315–7, 324, 327–9, 377, 392, 406, 409, 475, 479–81, 483–4
Kershaw, Maj. Gen. J. B., C.S.A., 71, 84, 96, 97 n., 157, 161 n., 162 n., 176, 548–51, 553–4, 562, 603, 626 n., 672, 731–2
Keyes, Maj. Gen. Erasmus D., U.S.A., 223, 261, 539
Knight, Capt. O. M., C.S.A., 294
Kilby's Station, 282
Kimball, Gen. Nathan, U.S.A., 641 n.
King William Artillery, 241
King's School House, 611
Kirby, Brig. Gen. Edmund, U.S.A., 68 n.
Kirkland, Brig. Gen. W. W., C.S.A., 53 n., 97 n., 355, 356 n., 488, 736
Kirkland, Sergt. Richard, xxi
Knipe, Brig. Gen. J. F., U.S.A., 385 n.
Knoxville, Tenn., 682, 699

Laidley, Col. T. T. S., Jr., U.S.A., 704, 717 n.
Landers, Col. H. L., 525 n., 650 n.
Lane, Brig. Gen. James H., C.S.A., 17, 220 n., 270 n.
Latané, Capt. William, C.S.A., 286, 299
Latrobe, Lieut. Col. Osman, C.S.A., 545
Laurel Hill, 25–26, 28–33
Law, Col. E. M, C.S.A., 468, 534–5, 621, 673 n.
Lawson, Brig. Gen. Thomas, U.S.A., 702 n.
Lawton, Brig. Gen. A. R., C.S.A., 274,

465, 491–2, 502 n., 527, 529–34, 653, 671

Lay, Lieut. Col. George W., C.S.A., 704, 717, 722

Lay, Col. John F., C.S.A., 76 n.

Leavenworth, Fort, 15

Lebanon Church, 219

Lee, Col. C. C., C.S.A., 17, 606 and n.

Lee, Maj. Gen. G. W. Custis, C.S.A., 211–2, 705

Lee, Maj. Gen. Fitzhugh, C.S.A., early career, 705; serves under Ewell at First Manassas, 59, 96, 97 n.; chosen for Stuart's reconnaissance expedition, 278–81; action in this "ride around McClellan," 284–6, 289, 299–300; action in the Seven Days' Battles, 636; praised by Stuart and made Brigadier, 643–4, 673–4

Lee, Maj. John F., U.S.A., 261, 704, 716

Lee, Gen. Robert Edward, C.S.A., early career and reputation, 5, 703, 713–5, 717, 724; his character, xxiv–xxv, xxviii; his tact, 90–1, 145, 204, 212, 215; at West Point, 11, 615; his officers in this volume, xx–xxii–xxviii; on Magruder's plan to take Washington, 16; hears Beauregard's plans, 4–6, 43, 166–8; disapproved of by Johnston, 112; promotions, 722–3, 113–4 and n.; directs operations in Richmond defense, 144–7, 230, 423 n.; confers on Peninsula defenses, 148–51, 154–5; exchange with Johnston, on control of troops near Fredericksburg, 204–8; asks him for his plans of Richmond defense, 210–4; offers services to Johnston before Seven Pines, 223; at Johnston's headquarters there, 236–7; becomes Commanding General, xv–xvi, xxi, 263; as army administrator, xv, 264–6; problems of his command, xvii, 266–70; officers transferred and promoted, 267–74; on Brigades organized by States, 270; forms strategic plan for offensive north of Chickahominy, 275; sends Stuart to scout on McClellan, 275–8, 288, 297, 300–1; hears from Jackson in the Valley, 337, 340–1, 345; asked to reinforce him, 342, 344; orders to him, 352; messages to Ewell in the Valley, 353, 356, 359–60, 364, 366; messages to and from Jackson in the Valley, 363, 365–8, 371, 374, 406; plans Richmond defenses with Jackson, 465–9, 494; as strategist in the Valley, 485; view of the defenses, 495, 498, 500 and n., 501 n.; messages, and action north of Richmond, 504, 505 n., 506, 508–15; at Gaines' Mill, 517–9, 522, 524, 526, 529; organizes battle line there, 530–1; orders the advance, 532; details in the repulse of McClellan, 540, 542–8, 550–2, 554, 557, 560–1, 562 n., 563 n., 581; at White Oak Swamp, 565, 566 n., 568–9, 574; at Frayser's Farm, 553, 585–7, 628, 630, 665; at Malvern Hill, 588–604, 628; details of the Seven Days' Battles, with comment on action and officers involved, 607, 609–19, 636, 640, 642–3, 648, 658, 670; his dealing with disgruntled officers, 620-1, 629; questions Stuart on Seven Days' strategy, 635; promotes Stuart, 643; attitude toward Jackson, 658–63; toward A. P. Hill, 663–4, 666; adjusts Hill-Longstreet quarrel, 667–8; reorganizes Army after the Seven Days, 671–5; later public opinion of him, xxiv; his place in history, xv, xxx. See also xviii, xx–xxi, 7, 11–2, 24–5, 37, 83, 112, 123, 167 n., 200, 303, 496 n., 630, 649, 658, 685, 692 n.

Lee, "Rooney," see Lee, William H. F.

Lee, Capt. W. F., C.S.A., 576

Lee, Maj. Gen. William H. F. ("Rooney"), C.S.A., 278, 281–2, 284, 295 n., 296, 634, 643, 705

Lee, Mrs. William H. F., 282

Lee's Mill, 169

Leesburg, 170, 691, 715

Letcher, Gov. John, 4, 12, 15, 112, 126–9, 209 n., 300–1, 323, 712 n., 713–4, 721–2, 723 n.

Lewis, Lieut. Fisher A., 706, 717 n.

Lewis, General, 438, 450

Lewis House (Portici), 65–5, 70, 72–3, 76, 89

Lewisburg, 690

Lewiston (Lewis house), 438, 450–1, 453, 459, 482

Lewis's Ford, 649

Lexington, 11, 126, 321, 430, 614, 685, 705, 707–8

Lincoln, Mrs. Abe (of Lacy's), 328, 329 n.

Lincoln, President Abraham, 3, 8, 317 n., 329 n., 358 n., 408–9, 462 n., 485, 724

Lomax, Col. Tennent, C.S.A., 245

Long, Brig. Gen. A. L., C.S.A., 704

Long Bridge, 208, 636–7

Long Bridge Road, 540, 581, 586, 591, 612

Longstreet, Lieut. Gen. James, C.S.A., early career, 709; described, 166 n.; at Blackburn's Ford, 45; orders and action at Bull Run, 52, 54–6, 58–60, 62, 73–5, 726; his officers, 96, 158–9; made Lieutenant General, 97; favors Bounty Act, 131; retained by Johnston after Manassas, 144; at Peninsula defense conference, 148–51; on the Peninsula, 152; officers of his division in the retreat, 158–60, 169, 171; wishes to reinforce Jackson in the Valley, 167–8, 330; made Major General, 164–5; family tragedy, 166; Davis suggests he command near Fredericksburg, 168, 206–7, 219; given six Brigades in the retreat, 168–70; character as commander, 168–9, 189; in Peninsula retreat, 174–7; reinforces Anderson, 177–8; commands at Battle of Williamsburg, 180, 189; his attack, 182, 190–1; resulting losses, 188; his report, 189–91; at Eltham, 194; moved to Long Bridge, 208; hears Johnston's defensive plans, 210; his plans before Seven Pines, 221–3, 226, 228–9, 255; confuses the advance at Gillies Creek, 231–6; his part in the Battle of Seven Pines, 236–9, 242, 245–6, 253–60, 266; comments on his officers, 246, 249, 253–4; blames Huger for Seven Pines difficulties, 260; on Army conditions when Lee took over, 265–6; relationship to Whiting, 271–2; in defense of Richmond after Valley Campaign, 494–5, 497, 500, 506, 512, 514–5; at Gaines' Mill, 519, 523, 526, 529, 531–2, 534, 536; in action at McClellan's retreat, 541, 543, 547–8, 557, 563, 566, 568, 574, 578, 605, 641, 642 n., 658; at Frayser's Farm, 581, 583, 585–7, 651–3, 670; at Malvern Hill, 589–92, 596–9, 612, 628, 640, 648; losses in the Seven Days' Battles, 605; opinion of Jackson, 656–7; fine record in the Seven Days, 663–4, 667, 674; incensed at Daniel's praise of A. P. Hill, 664–8; arrests Hill, 666; his enlarged command, 671–2, 674–5; recommends R. H. Anderson's promotion, 673. See also xv, xvii, xviii, 20 n., 195 n., 214 n., 262, 276, 333, 607

Lookout Hill, 59
Loop Creek Shoals, 677
Lopez, Narciso, 88, 162 n.
Loring, Maj. Gen. W. W., C.S.A., 122–4, 126–7, 129, 133, 204, 303, 327, 476, 479, 709
Lossing, B. J., 634 n.
Loudoun, 339
Loudoun Heights, 412, 411
Louisa, 282–3, 681
Louisiana Regiments:
  Fifth, 668
  Sixth, 378–9, 423, 517
  Seventh, 353, 390, 423, 454–6, 458, 460, 464, 668
  Ninth, 349, 366, 370, 374, 378, 668

Louisiana Regiments (Cont'd):
  Fourteenth, 668
  Tigers, 87–8, 349, 378–9, 386–7, 401, 432, 517, 525, 537, 588, 739
Louisiana Zouaves, 87–8
Love, Maj. Gen. John, U.S.A., 721 n.
Lovell, Maj. Gen. Mansfield, C.S.A., 20 n., 162, 165 n.
Lownes family, 280 n.
Lumpkin House, 514
Luray, 332–6, 343–4, 350, 358, 359, 366, 422, 427, 448, 462, 466–7
Luray Valley, 331–5, 341–3, 358, 373–4, 393, 420–1, 435, 690
Lynchburg, 85, 247–8, 680–2, 724
Lyons, Judge James, 15, 115 n.

Macon, Fort, 169
Macrae, Col. N. C., U.S.A., 704, 716
Madison Court House, 330, 332, 334
Madison, Pres. James, 248
Madison's Run, 450
Magruder, Fort, 175–84, 187–8, 192, 242
  The Battle, 182–92
Magruder, Maj. Gen. John Bankhead, C.S.A., early career, 15, 703 n., 704, 716–7 and n., 722; personal appearance and manner, 19, 664; as host, 15; character, 15–6, 152, 214, 659; at York River, 14; Colonel of Virginia Volunteers, 16; commands on the Peninsula, 16, 146; demands more men, 16–17; first victory, 17–9; popularity, 19, 22, 23; praises Hill, 21; promoted, 40; his position threatened, 148–51; joined by Johnston's Army, 151; fourth in command, 152–3; his officers and men at the retreat, 156–73, 196; praised by Cobb, 160; his distinction, 161–2; his Division in retreat toward Williamsburg, 174–6, 189; troops diverted at Eltham, 193–4; clash with G. W. Smith, 214–7; position before Seven Pines, 226, 229; not used there, 252–3, 259; ordered to Texas, 262; attitude toward neighboring commands, 277; not selected in Richmond defense, 499; his front quiet, 508; delay in attacking the retreating McClellan, at Savage Station, 538–57, 560–2, 563–4, 636; shifted to lesser post, 556 n.; at White Oak Swamp, 566, 568–9; useless marches during Frayser's Farm action, 582–3, 585–7, 626; action at Malvern Hill, 589–92, 598–603, 612–3, 616, 630; losses in the Seven Days, 605 and n.; criticism of his action, 606–11, 614; writes self-justifying report, 608–11; sent to Trans-Mississippi Department, 607, 611, 614, 618, 667, 674; reasons

for his confused action, 620; praise of
Toombs, 624, 626; his mishandled
command, 654; his command disbanded, 672; his place in this volume,
xviii
Magruder, Lieut. William B., U.S.A.,
706
Mahone, Maj. Gen. William, C.S.A.,
xxvi, 201 n., 226, 246, 250, 369 n.,
557-8, 567-8, 597-600, 602, 609 n.,
612-3, 654, 673
Maine, Seventh Volunteers, 576
Mallory, Col. Francis, C.S.A., 705
Malvern Hill, 577, 582-4, 588-604,
606-11, 617-9, 620-1, 626, 628-30,
639, 643, 645, 648, 650-5, 670, 674
Manassas, x, 5-9, 13, 38-46, 48, 52,
71-87 passim; 97-105 passim, 107,
109, 113, 118, 135-46, 155-7, 159,
163-4, 166, 168, 171, 175, 180, 191,
198, 245, 248, 259-65 passim, 275,
278, 305, 325-6, 329, 348-9, 363,
373, 392, 472, 491, 494, 615, 623-4,
628, 648-9, 649, 661, 674, 690, 726
Manassas, First, xvi, 45-72, 78-9, 89.
See also Manassas
Manassas Gap Railroad, 9, 43, 52, 333,
376-7, 680, 682-3, 691
Manassas Junction, 44, 46, 49, 53, 59,
66, 75-6, 94, 680, 731, 734
Manassas, Second, xix, xxvi, xxx
Manning, Col. John L., C.S.A., aide to
Beauregard, 2
Maps and plans:
Strategical areas south of Harpers
Ferry, 10
Region of Garnett's operations in
Western Virginia, 26
Rich Mountain, 30
Confederate forces at Bull Run, 47
Fort Magruder and adjacent terrain,
178
Early's advance, Battle of Williams-
burg, 184
Lines of advance, Richmond to Seven
Pines, 227
Route of Stuart's "Ride around Mc-
Clellan," 287
Parallelogram of the Massanuttons,
331
Central Shenandoah Valley, 334
Jackson's alternative lines of advance,
April, 1862, 343
Environs of Front Royal, 375
Battle of Winchester, 397
Southern end of Massanuttons, 428
Port Republic and environs, 436
Battle of Port Republic, 452
Jackson's advance to Richmond Front,
493
Route of Jackson, Ewell and Branch,
June 26, 1862, 507

Maps and plans (Cont'd):
Battlefield of Gaines' Mill, 521
The environs of Savage Station, 549
White Oak Swamp, Huger's advance,
559
Vicinity of White Oak Swamp Bridge,
573
Malvern Hill terrain, 593
Northeastern frontier district of Vir-
ginia, 687
Shenandoah defensive area, 689
Rappahannock-North Anna area, 693
The Peninsula, the Norfolk zone, and
the Richmond-Petersburg area, 696
Order of battle, Confederate infantry,
First Manassas, 729
Marblehead (gunboat), 634, 642, 647
Marengo, 734
Marshall, Col. John, C.S.A., 536, 606 n.
Marshall, Lieut. Col. Louis H., U.S.A.,
704, 717 n.
Martin, Maj. Gen. Will T., C.S.A.,
278-9, 281, 283, 290, 638 n.
Martinsburg, 406, 682, 684
Maryland expedition, xxvi
Maryland Heights, 412
Maryland Regiment: First, 377-9, 381,
386, 433, 502, 732
Maryland Union Regiment: First, 381
Mason, Capt. C. R., C.S.A., 561-2
Mason's Hill, 164
Massanutton Gap, 373
Massanutton Mountains, 331-4, 341-5,
357, 359, 366, 371, 373-4, 420 422,
424, 426-7, 430, 475, 690-1
Mat River, 694
Mathias Point, 694
Mattapony River, 698
Maury, Maj. Gen. Dabney H., C.S.A.,
188 n., 264 n., 704
Maury, Capt. Matthew Fontaine, C.S.N.,
685 n., 699 n., 700, 703
Maxcy, Cornelia Manning, 518 n.
Maxcy, Mr. and Mrs Jonathan, 519 n.
Maynadier, Maj. Gen. Henry E., 704,
717 n.
McAllister, Capt. Thompson, C.S.A.,
316 n.
McClellan, Maj. Gen. George B., U.S.A.,
xx, 37, 42, 44, 133-4, 138, 146, 148-
51, 153-5, 167, 189 n., 202, 210,
211 n., 212-4, 220-1, 226, 229, 245,
261, 266, 275, 277, 283, 288, 290,
293, 300-1, 303, 317, 329 n., 356,
367, 408 n., 415, 418, 466 and n., 468,
485, 489, 494-7, 502, 510, 520, 522-3,
527, 538-42, 548, 555, 557, 560-3,
565-6, 568, 581, 583, 587, 589-90,
603-4, 618, 625, 628, 631 n., 633,
635-8, 640-3, 648, 655-6, 661, 674-5
McClellan, Maj. H. B., C.S.A., 285 n.
McCreery, Capt. W. W., C.S.A., 705

McCue, James, 470
McDonald, Mrs. Angus, *quoted,* 402
McDonald, Col. Angus W., C.S.A., 308–9
McDowell, Maj. Gen. Irvin, U.S.A., 41–44, 48, 58, 68 n., 85 n., 103, 133, 202, 212–4, 220–1, 275, 353, 356–7, 359, 371, 408–10, 412–5, 418, 423 n., 466 n., 485, 494 n., 659, 661
McDowell, 354, 362, 377, 450, 480, 674
McGaheysville, 437
McGowan, Brig. Gen. Samuel, C.S.A., 98 n., 529, 651
McGregor, Lieut. William, C.S.A., 291
McGuire, Dr. Hunter, 315, 439 n., 464 n., 562 n., 563 n., 656 n.
McIntosh, Col. W. M., C.S.A., 537
McIntosh's Battery, 512
McLaws, Maj. Gen. Lafayette, C.S.A., at West Point, 20 n.; in Yorktown retreat, 160 n., 161 n.; at Fort Magruder, 176, 189, 259 n.; excellence as commander, 192; assigned Magruder's troops, 216; made Major General, 218; plans for him, before Seven Pines, 226, 236, 288; in Magruder's command, 272, 548–9, 552–3, 598, 602, 608 n.; in reorganization after Malvern Hill, 607, 668 n.; losses in the Seven Days, 605 n.; his command in reorganized Army, 672
McLean's Ford, 49–50, 54
McPherson, Maj. Gen. James B., U.S.A., 196 n.
McRae, Col. D. K., C.S.A., 177 n., 185–8
McRae, Col. N. C., U.S.A., 261
Meade, Maj. Gen. George G., U.S.A., 85 n.
Meade, Maj. R. K., C.S.A., 582, 705
Meadow Bridges, 497, 500, 505–6, 512–3, 515, 522
Meares, Col. Gaston, C.S.A., 606 and n.
Mechanicsville, 213, 220, 497, 500–1, 508, 511–5, 518–9, 529, 537–8, 543, 596, 605, 616, 649, 653, 663–4, 670
Mechanicsville Turnpike, 506, 509
Mechum River Station, 354, 431, 470, 489
"Meem's Bottom," 425
Meems estate, 321
Meherrin River, 696
Mellert, Dr. J. H., 594 n.
Melton, Maj. Samuel W., C.S.A., 263 n.
Mennonites, 322
Mercer, Brig. Gen. H. W., C.S.A., 706 n., 717 n.
Merrimac (frigate), 679
Merrimac, Virginia- (C.S. warship), 141, 202, 209–10

Merry Oaks, 508
Mexican War, xvi, xxi', 2, 5, 9, 14, 19, 23, 24, 41, 68, 71, 85, 87–8, 112, 119, 157–9, 162, 164, 229, 273, 347, 350, 588, 705–7, 709, 711, 715–6, 718–9, 721, 724
Michler, Brig. Gen. Nathaniel, U.S.A., 572 n.
Middle River, 463
Middletown, 384–6, 388–90, 406, 408, 471–4, 480, 482, 735, 737–9
Mill Creek, 444
Millwood mansion, 92–3
Milroy, Maj. Gen. R. H., U.S.A., 342, 352 and n., 354–7, 364, 437 n.
Mississippi Regiments:
  Second, 730
  Eleventh, 730
  Twelfth, 248
  Thirteenth, 588
  Seventeenth, 269
  Nineteenth, 179
Mitchell, Capt. Samuel P., C.S.A., 728
Mitchell's Ford, 48–9, 53–6, 73
Molino del Rey, 709
Monitor (warship), 142
Monroe, Fortress, 8, 14 and n., 146, 151, 675, 695, 698, 725
Monterey, 36, 690, 713
Montgomery, Ala., 647
Moore, E. A., 391, 401 n.
Moore, Private, C.S.A., 382
Moore, Capt. Samuel J. C., C.S.A., 437, 439 n., 443
Mordecai's Station, 282
Morris, Maj. Robert, U.S.A., 300
Morrison, Robert Hall, 21 n.
Mosby, John S., 279–81
Moses, Maj. Raphael J., C.S.A., 622, 624 n.
Moss Neck, xx
Mossy Creek Academy, 27
Mott, Col. Gershom, U.S.A., 572 n.
Mott, Col. Chris. H., C.S.A., 179, 195 n.
Mount Airy, Meems estate, 321
Mount Crawford, 426
Mount Jackson, 306, 311, 322, 333, 353, 366, 425, 466–7, 680, 682
Mount Meridian, 435, 437, 440, 463
Mount Solon, 362–3
Mountain Top House, 469
Mullan, Lieut. John, 704, 717 n.
Munford, Brig. Gen. Thomas T., C.S.A., 98 n., 315, 355–7, 364, 369 n., 406 n., 423, 437 n., 469 n., 487–8, 571, 574–5, 577, 579, 639
Munson's Hill, 164
Murfee, Maj., 706 n.
Murfreesboro, 134
Myers, Capt. G. W., C.S.A., 438, 443, 477

Nansemond River, 696
Napoleon, 42, 110, 122, 531, 543, 708 n.
Napoleon gun, 536, 646
Neff, Col. John F., C.S.A., 325, 399
Negroes, xxiii, 429–30, 561–2
New Bridge, 540, 544
New Bridge Road, 232, 236
New Castle Ferry, 286
New Cold Harbor, 520, 528–30
New Jersey Regiments: First, 432
New Kent, 290
New Kent Court House, 200, 208
New Kent Road, 193, 206
New Market, 330, 332–7, 341–4, 350, 353, 357–60, 366–8, 419–20, 422, 424–5, 427, 562, 586
New Market Heights, 581–2
New Market Road, 581
New Orleans, La., 87–8, 92
New River, 699
New Road, 559–60, 577
New York, N. Y., 121, 149, 677
New York Herald, 163
New York Regiment: Eleventh, 731
New York Times, 38
Newbern, N. C., 144
Newman, Lieut. L. H., U.S.N., 211 n.
Newport, R. I., 15
Newport News, 17
Newton, Maj. Gen. John, U.S.A., 20 n., 704, 717 n.
Newtown, 315, 385, 390, 392, 472, 474, 477, 737, 739
Nicaragua, 88
Nine Mile road, 225–7, 231–4, 236, 238, 256, 272, 275, 494, 547
Ninevah, 472, 474, 735, 737–8
Norfolk, 134, 146–7, 149–51, 154, 201–2, 204, 229–30, 259, 264, 613, 677, 679, 695–9, 708, 721, 724, 734
Norfolk and Petersburg Railroad, 680
Norfolk Navy Yard, 7, 699
North Anna River, 692–4, 697–8
North Carolina Military Institute, 17, 20
North Carolina Regiments:
First, 515, 537
First Volunteers, 17–8, 21
Third, 606
Fifth, 180, 182–3, 185–8
Sixth, 67–70, 136, 187, 199, 731
Seventh, 509, 536
Sixteenth, 195
Twentieth, 534–5
Twenty-first, 401, 736
Twenty-third, 180, 182–3, 186–8
Thirty-seventh, 606
Fiftieth, 583
North Mountain Depot, 406
North River, 426–7, 430, 435–7, 439, 448, 454, 461–2, 485
Northern Neck of Virginia, 694, 716

Northrup, Col. L. P., C.S.A., 306 n.
Northwestern Virginia Railroad, 680–1
Norwood, Col. J. T., C.S.A., 606 n.
Nottoway River, 695
Ny River, 694

Oakwood Cemetery, 225–6, 234
Occoquan Creek and River, 7, 48, 135, 138, 143, 195, 688
Ohio River, 677–8, 681, 699
Old Capitol Prison, 281
Old Church, 282, 284–5, 289–91, 294, 300
Old Church Road, 514
Old Cold Harbor, 524, 527, 529–30
Orange, 6, 692
Orange and Alexandria Railroad, 139, 142, 367, 675, 680, 682–3, 688, 691–3
Orange Court House, 329–30

Page, Robert, 504 n.
Page, Rosewell, Jr., 504 n.
Palmetto Sharpshooters, 192, 242, 249
Pamunkey River, 205, 206 n., 275, 289, 495, 633, 642, 647, 678, 694, 698
Parker, Private Churchwell, C.S.A., 645
Parkersburg, 23, 25, 29, 122, 680–1, 690
Parkersburg Turnpike, 354
Parrott guns, 382, 385, 390, 398–9, 410, 441–2, 453–4
Parsons Farm, 532
Patterson, Gen. Robert, U.S.A., 41, 42, 44, 46–6, 58–9, 66, 71
Patton, I. W., 718 n.
Patton, Col. J. M., C.S.A., 398 n., 424, 448–9, 461
Pawnee (gunboat), 679
Paxton, Maj. E. Franklin, C.S.A., 325
Payne, Col. Matthew M., 261, 703–4, 716
Peabody, Lieut. F. W., U.S.A., 398 n.
Peaked Mountain, 340, 427
Peake's Turnout, 219
Peck, Maj. Gen. John J., U.S.A., 638 n.
Pegram, Maj. Gen. John, C.S.A., 27–34, 37, 649, 705
Pegram, Lieut. Col. William Jones, C.S.A., brilliant career in the Seven Days' Battles, 596, 649–51; his character and manner, 649
Pegues, Col. C. C., C.S.A., 536, 606 n.
Pelham, Maj. John, C.S.A., spectacular action under Stuart in the Valley, 192, 279, 536, 638 n., 640–1; brilliant career in the Seven Days' Battles, 646–7, 649; Stuart's praise of him, 647
Pelham's Horse Artillery, 279
Pemberton, Lieut. Gen. J. C., C.S.A., 85 n., 273, 719, 723
Pender, Gen. W. Dorsey, C.S.A., xvii,

xxvi, 136, 199, 267, 271, 514, 523, 605 n., 653
Pender, Mrs. W. Dorsey, xix
Pendleton, Lieut. "Sandie," C.S.A., 321, 404-5, 433-4, 447 n.
Pendleton, Brig. Gen. (Rev.), William Nelson, C.S.A., education, 614; early career, 705, 717 n.; captains Rockridge Artillery, 614; appearance, 615; distinguishes himself under Beauregard, 97 and n.; his prayers before shooting, 615; not found at Malvern Hill, 596; chief of Artillery, 614-6; report on Seven Days' Battles, 616-8; criticized, 614-8, 620
Pendleton, Mrs. William Nelson, 616
Peninsula, The, 14, 16, 21, 146-55, 156-73 passim, 205, 260, 363, 540, 548, 624-5, 635-6, 694-5, 698; details of the retreat, 174-7
Penn, Maj. David B., C.S.A., 388 n.
Pennsylvania Regiments: First, 281
Pensacola, Fla., 157
Petersburg, 201, 213, 230, 273-4, 678, 680-1, 692, 695, 697-8, 708, 711
Petersburg and Norfolk Railroad, 557, 698
Petersburg and Roanoke Railroad, 680, 682, 697
Pettigrew, Brig. Gen. Johnston J., C.S.A., 161 n., 244-6, 262, 266-7, 270, 271 n.
Peyton's Battery, 617 n.
Philadelphia, Pa., 149
Philippi, 23
Piatt, Donn, 713 n.
Pickens, Gov. F. W., 4, 157, 273
Pickett, Maj. Gen. George E., C.S.A., 158-60, 161 n., 168, 178, 189, 192, 239, 242-3, 250, 252, 526, 529, 535-7, 588, 605 and n., 652, 718
Piedmont, 678-9, 690
Piedmont Station, 46
Pike Bridge, 376, 379-80
Pikesville, Md., 719
Pikesville Arsenal, 268
Pilate, Pontius, 712
Pillow, Brig. Gen. Gideon, C.S.A., 273
Piping Tree Ferry, 285, 290
Plantation and Farm Instruction, by General Cocke, 90
Po River, 694
Poague, Col. W. T., C.S.A., 387, 388 n., 390-1, 398-9, 401, 441-2, 453-7
Poindexter farm, 591, 595, 597
Point Pleasant, 677
Pole Green Church, 509, 512
Polk, Maj. Gen. Leonidas, C.S.A., 162
Pope, Maj. Gen. John, U.S.A., 20 n., 659-62, 668, 675
Port Republic, xvi, 345-6, 354, 427-31, 435-8, 443-4, 446-9; the Battle, 451-65, 478, 480-3, 486-7, 489, 641

Porter, Maj. Gen. Fitz-John, U.S.A., 220 n., 409, 538, 585 n., 714 and n.
Porter, Capt. Josiah, C.S.A., 194 n.
Porterfield, Col. George A., C.S.A., 23
Portici, The Lewis House, 65-6, 70, 72-3, 76, 89
Portsmouth, 681
Potomac River, 9, 42, 45, 90, 107, 111, 138, 141, 143, 150, 155, 170, 305, 309, 363-5, 368, 383-4, 402-4, 406, 411-5, 486. 675-8, 680, 686, 688, 691, 694, 698, 738
Powhite Creek, 519-21, 531
Preston, Col. J. F., C.S.A., 7, 71, 730, 734
Preston, Col. J. L. T., C.S.A., 482
Preston, Brig. Gen. J. S., C.S.A., 89, 96, 97 n.
Preston, Col. R. T., C.S.A., 731
Price, Maj. Gen. Sterling, C.S.A., 216 n., 610
Providence Forge, 298
Provisional Army of the Confederacy, 122
Pryor, Brig. Gen. Roger A., C.S.A., 108, 161, 168, 176, 189, 239, 242, 256, 605 n., 653, 668
Purcell Battery, 649

Quaker road, 590-2, 608, 612
Queen's Creek, 177
Quince, Lieut. William, C.S.A., 172-3
Quitman, Maj. Gen. John A., U.S.A., 159

Radford, Col. R. C. W., 706, 717 n.
Rains, Gen. Gabriel J., C.S.A., 160 n., 161 n., 171, 182, 240-1, 246, 268-9; his land torpedoes, 268-9
Raleigh, 512
Ramsay, Bvt. Maj. Geo. D., 710 n., 721 n.
Ramseur, Maj. Gen. Stephen Dodson, C.S.A., xxvi, 651
Randolph, Brig. Gen. George W., C.S.A., 18, 21, 43, 145, 148, 150-3, 170, 216-7
Randolph, Lieut. Col. Thomas B., 705
Ransom, Maj. Gen. Robert, C.S.A., 273, 558 n., 597, 599-602, 606, 612-3
Rapidan River, 139, 142, 145-6, 166-7, 170, 195, 330, 367, 491, 660, 671, 688, 692-3
Rappahannock Bridge, 45, 143
Rappahannock River, 139-40, 142, 158, 195, 202, 207, 212, 343, 348, 677, 688, 692-4, 698
Rappahannock Station, 6
Reilly's Battery, 511
Religious spirit of the 1860's, xxviii
Reminiscences of Col. J. C. Haskell, 734
Reno, Maj. Gen. Jesse L., 721 n.

Responsibilities of the First Bull Run, by Gen. Johnston, 726
Reynolds, Capt. A. W., 704
Reynolds, Lieut. S. H., 705
Rhett, Maj. Burnett, C.S.A., 573, 617 n., 734
Rice, Doctor, 425
Rich Mountain, 25–31, 33, 37–8, 369, 649
Richardson, Col., 517 n., 575 n.
Richardson, Chaplain, 469
Richardson, Adj. Gen. W. H., 124 n.
Richmond and Danville Railroad, 680, 683, 697
Richmond and Petersburg Railroad, 680, 682, 698
Richmond and York River Railroad, 681, 698
Richmond Examiner, xix, 4, 102, 106, 664–5
Richmond, Fredericksburg and Potomac Railroad, 138, 140, 202, 205, 213, 282, 680, 682–3, 692, 694, 697
Richmond, xviii, 2, 3, 8, 11, 14, 16, 18, 23, 27, 39, 41–2, 46, 57, 76, 81, 87, 94, 102, 104, 107, 119–21, 124, 126, 128–9, 132–6, 138–55 *passim,* 162, 166–7, 200–16, 221, 225–7, 230–1, 251, 253, 262, 266, 268–9, 271, 273, 288, 293, 299–300, 318, 327–8, 330, 336, 338, 341–2, 351–2, 355–8, 365, 367, 370–1, 408, 413–4, 417, 526, 428, 430–1, 464–70, 481, 485–6, 488–93, 495, 497, 499, 506, 516, 537–42, 544–5, 555, 558, 581, 604–5, 608, 610, 615, 624–5, 649, 657, 660–2, 664, 668, 671–2, 678, 680–2, 691–2, 694–5, 697–8, 706, 713, 716, 718–9, 722, 724, 728, 733
Richmond Whig, 105, 107, 431, 666, 732
Ricketts, Capt. J. B., U.S.A., 68 n, 95, 730
Riddell's Shop, 565
Rifles and Rifle Practice, by Cadmus M. Wilcox, 159
Rio Grande River, 273
Ripley, Brig. Gen. Roswell S., C.S.A., 273, 514–5, 531, 602, 605 and n., 606, 653
River road, 581, 583, 589, 648, 663
Roanoke Island, N. C., 134, 169, 230, 259
Roanoke Valley Railroad, 681
Robertson, Brig. Gen. B. H., C.S.A., 704
Robertson, Judge John, 711–2
Robinett brothers, 220 n.
Robins, Lieut. W. T., C.S.A., 284, 292
Robinson, Capt. Lucius N., U.S.A., 461
Robinson House, 94, 730–1
Rockbridge Artillery, 385, 614
Rockfish Gap, 469–70

Rodes, Maj. Gen. Robert Emmett, C.S.A., education and early career, 247–8; appearance, 240; ability, 248; at Manassas, 96, 97 n.; in the Yorktown retreat, 161 n., 171; before Seven Pines, 226, 228–9, 235, 239 n.; action at Seven Pines, 240–2, 244, 247–8, 251–2, 255, 257, 268; wounded there, 245, 262, 653; action at Gaines' Mill, 533; his Brigade led by Gordon, 589, 602, 651; his death, xxvi
Rodgers, Commodore John, U.S.N., 211 n.
Romney, 122–3, 126–7, 130, 159, 161, 303, 317, 327, 476, 482
Ronald, Col. Charles A., C.S.A., 396 n.
Rose Hill, Ashby farm, 308
Rosecrans, Maj. Gen. W. S., U.S.A., 20 n., 37
Rosser, Maj. Gen. Thomas Lafayette, C.S.A., described, 647; his youth, 647; at Manassas, 97 and n.; at Lewinsville, 648; in the Seven Days' Battles, 648–9
Rouse, Lieut. Milton, C.S.A., 311
Rowland's Mill, 300
Roy, Maj. Jas. P., 721 n.
Rude's Hill, 329, 338
Ruffin, Edmund, 90
Ruggles, Maj. Daniel, 718–9, 721–3
Rust, Lieut. A. T. M., 706 n., 717 n.

Saint Peter's Church, 294
Salem, xix
San Francisco (vessel), 326
Santa Fe, N. Mex., 716
Saunders, Lieut. John S., 705
Saunders, Lieut. Thomas M., 705, 717 n.
Savage Station, 540, 549–55 *passim* (the battle); 560, 563–4, 566, 570, 611, 636, 658, 670
Savannah, Ga., 150
Saxon, Miss (Mrs. Samuel Farley), 280 n.
Saxton, Maj. Gen. Rufus, U.S.A., 409, 417
Schofield, Maj. Gen. John M., U.S.A., 196 n.
Schriver, Maj. Gen. Edmund, U.S.A., 708 n.
Scobey, Maj. W. P., U.S.A., 466 n.
Scott, Maj. John, C.S.A., 77 n.
Scott, Col. W. C., C.S.A., 369, 389 n., 424 n., 457 n., 459–60
Scott, Col. William G., C.S.A., 29 and n., 32–3
Scott, Lieut. Gen. Winfield, U.S.A., 5, 158, 229, 261, 703–4, 706, 711–3, 715, 717, 719
Seaboard and Roanoke Railroad, 681
Seawell, Col. Washington, U.S.A., 261, 704, 716–7
Second Manassas, xix, xxvi, xxx

Sedgwick, Maj. Gen. John, U.S.A., 85 n., 138 n.
Selden, Mr. and Mrs. Armistead, 84 n.
Selden, Miss Cassie, later Mrs. E. Kirby Smith, 84 n.
Selden, Capt. Joseph, 704
Selwyn, 519
Seminole Indians, 707
Semmes, Brig. Gen. Paul, C.S.A., 175, 176 n., 549, 554, 586, 603, 668, 672
Seven Days' Battles, xv, xix, xxvi, xxx, 611, 626, 630–3, 641, 646–9, 651, 653, 655, 657, 667, 670–3; losses in the battles, 605
Seven Pines, xvi, 221–3, 225–8, 266, 268, 271, 273–4, 276, 279, 418, 430, 494, 533, 535, 539–40, 548, 552, 558, 596, 613, 651, 672; the battle, 236–43; the commanders, 244–63
Sewell's Point, 724
Seymour, Col. Isaac G., C.S.A., 517, 525, 536, 588, 606 n.
Shady Grove Church, 509, 511–3
Sharpsburg, xvii, xxi
Sheetz, Capt. George F., C.S.A., 474 n.
Shelton, Dr., 509–10
Shenandoah River, 9, 331, 336–7, 344, 373–80, 412, 422, 424–7, 430, 435–66 passim, 574, 659, 678, 684, 690–1, 738
Shenandoah Valley, xxvii, 9, 24, 36, 39–51 passim, 58, 96, 122–30 passim, 141, 150, 159, 167, 201, 221, 236, 262, 282, 304–10, 317, 321–2, 327, 329–46 passim, 352–6, 358–61, 363–5, 367, 372, 384, 408, 411, 413, 415, 417, 419, 435–66 passim, 471–86 passim, 489, 494, 498, 518, 532, 535–6, 554, 564, 596, 615, 641, 654, 660, 664, 668–9, 678–9, 682–3, 686, 688–93, 739
Shenandoah Valley Pike, 312–3, 332–3, 373, 384–6, 388–9, 395, 400, 417–9, 423, 425, 429, 437, 448, 472, 474, 477, 484, 497, 684, 735, 737–8
Sheridan, Gen. Philip H., 196 n.
Shields, Lieut. H. L., U.S.A., 706, 717 n.
Shields, Maj. Gen. James, U.S.A., 311, 315, 353 n., 356–7, 360–1, 364–5, 367–8, 409, 412–3, 416–21, 425–8, 430–1, 435–8, 443 n., 444 and n., 448, 454, 461–3, 466–8, 482–3, 485, 487, 641, 657
Shiloh, 156, 628
Shotwell, R. A., 496 n.
Simcoe, Fort, 24
Sipe, Capt. Emanuel, C.S.A., 438
Slaughter, Lieut. James E., 704
Slocum, Maj. Gen. H. W., U.S.A., 568 n., 626 n.
Smead, Col. Abner, C.S.A., 415
Smith, 731

Smith, Maj. Albert J., 704, 716–7, 723 n
Smith, Lieut. Caleb, 704
Smith, Brig. Gen. E. Kirby, C.S.A., 41, 52 n., 66 n., 71, 76 n., 83–6, 89, 96–7, 130, 133, 156, 261, 348, 369 n., 613, 622, 674–5, 709, 724
Smith, Mrs. E. Kirby, 84 n.
Smith, Maj. Gen. Francis H. (Va.Mil.), 703, 706, 708, 717 n.
Smith, Maj. Gen. Gustavus W., C.S.A., early career, 20 n., 121, 149, 162–3; at Yorktown, 198; at Centreville, 163; as Major General, 121, 130, 163–5, 206; ill health, 144, 166, 262 and n., 263 and n., 674; his character and manner, 163; replaces Holmes, 145; at Peninsula defense conference, 148–51, 155; his distinction at time of Peninsula retreat, 162–3; Davis suggests he command near Fredericksburg, 168, 206–7, 219; action at Eltham, 193–6, 199–200; moved to Baltimore Crossroads, 208; clash with Magruder, 214–7; orders, plans and positions before Seven Pines, 220–3, 226, 228–9, 231–2, 235; vacillating action in the Battle, 237 n., 238, 242, 244–5, 254, 258, 260, 262; size of his command, 671; praise of his officers, 246; his report on the action, 256–7; leaves the Army, 264; Lee makes changes in his Division, 270–2; his men in the Valley, 468; wins approval of Toombs, 622–3. See also xviii, 119, 218 n., 259, 503
Smith, Maj. Larkin, 704
Smith, Maj. Gen. Martin L., C.S.A., 20 n.
Smith, Col. Robert A., C.S.A., 537, 606 n.
Smith, Col. William P., U.S.A., 705
Smith, Maj. Gen. William, C.S.A., xxii, 66–7 and n., 97 n., 731
Smithfield, 204
Somerville Heights, 353
Sorrel, Brig. Gen. G. Moxley, C.S.A., 98 n., 665–7
South Anna River, 282, 288, 490
South Carolina College, 92, 93
South Carolina Military Academy, xxiii, 249, 710
South Carolina Regiments:
First, 41, 64, 70–1
Second, 732
Fifth, 96, 179, 245
Sixth, 179, 185, 187, 326
Eighth, 732
Fourteenth, 529
Boykin Rangers, 279
South Fork Bridge, 379
South River, 427, 435–6, 438–9, 441, 449, 463, 483, 485, 694
South Side Railroad, 681, 697
Spangler's Ford, 377

Spartanburg, 91

Spaulding, Brig. Gen. O. L., U.S.A., 710 n.

Sperryville, 332, 343–4

Spotswood Hotel, Richmond, Va., 3, 215, 624

Spotsylvania. Wilderness of, 694

Stafford, Col. L. A., C.S.A., 588, 668

Stannardsville, 334, 341, 366

Stanton, Edwin M., 408–9

Starke, Brig. Gen. W. E., C.S.A., 645, 668 n.

Staunton, 9, 23–25, 28, 29, 122, 330–1, 334, 336–7, 342–6, 352, 353–5, 358, 362, 411, 414, 418, 426, 428, 435–6, 678, 681–2, 684, 690–2

Stephens, Vice-President Alexander H., 623, 625–6, 628, 723

Stephenson's Depot, 404

Steptoe, Maj. E. J., U.S.A., 261, 704, 716–7 and n.

Steuart, Brig. Gen. George H., C.S.A., 98 n., 270 n., 369 and n., 377, 379, 385–6, 403–5, 423, 424 n., 432–3, 447, 472–5, 487 n., 674, 732, 736–7, 739; appraised, 477–9

Stevens, Brig. Gen. W. H., C.S.A., 98 n., 582

Stevenson, Maj. Gen. C. L., C.S.A., 704

Stiles, Maj. Robert, C.S.A., 570 n.

Stokes, Col. M. S., C.S.A., 537, 606 n.

Stone Bridge, 49, 53–55, 57–58, 60, 63–64, 66, 70, 73, 86, 89, 95, 730

"Stonewall," origin of Jackson's name, 81–3, 733–4

"Stonewall Brigade," 313, 317–8, 324–5, 339, 398 n., 439, 451, 453, 455, 457, 459, 484, 531–2, 536

Stony Creek, 329, 338

Strange, Col. John B., C.S.A., 89, 588, 732

Strasburg, 306, 311–2, 330–1, 333, 352, 367, 371, 374, 376–7, 380, 383–7 passim, 389, 406–7, 417, 419–20, 425, 430, 438, 473–4, 477–8, 484, 682, 736–9

Strategic Areas of Virginia, 687–700

Stringfellow, Private Franklin, C.S.A., xxviii, 646

Strother, Tom, 429–30

Stubbs House, 232

Stubbs, Robert, 232

Stuart Horse Artillery, 279, 646–7

Stuart, Maj. Gen. James E. Brown, C.S.A., in U. S. Army, 161 n., 704; appearance and accoutrements, xix, 283; his marriage, 716; at Harpers Ferry, 11; at Bull Run, 731; cavalry charge at Henry Hill, 68, 96, 275; pursuit of the enemy, 73–4; praised by Johnston, 275–6; qualities as commander. 111.

189–90, 192, 275–6; character and self-assurance, 275–6; his cavalry in Yorktown retreat, 174; action near Williamsburg, 181, 276; reports on McDowell's northward move, 220–1; sent by Lee to scout on McClellan, xxviii, 275–9; his officers for the expedition, 279–81; the "Ride around McClellan," xx, 282–302; his report, 288; report on McDowell at Fredericksburg, 408; with Jackson north of Richmond, 505, 509–10, 514, 536, 567; his second raid, 604, 633–44, 655; rout of the gunboat Marblehead, 634; stores gained, 634–5; consulted by Lee on Seven Days' strategy, 635; raid at Evelington Heights, 640–3; criticisms of the useless raid, 641–3; promoted to be Major General, 643, 674; his officers and men in the Seven Days, 643–9, 651; commands cavalry in reorganized army, 673–4; his place in this volume, xx; his place in history, xv. See also 97 n., 213, 309, 369 n., 504 n.

Stuart, Mrs. James E. B., 716

Sturgis's Corps, 660 n.

Sudley Ford, 73, 76

Sudley road, 731

Suffolk, 204, 695–6

Summerall, Gen. C. P., U.S.A., 710 n.

Summit Point, 416

Sumner, Maj. Gen. E. V., U.S.A., 539, 555, 562 n., 703 n.

Sumter, Fort, 1–3, 38, 41, 81, 109, 273

Susquehanna River, 414

Swift Run Gap, 330, 332, 334–5, 341, 346, 352, 355, 358, 361, 429, 481

Sycamore Springs, 295–6, 298

Sydnor, Lieut. T. W., C.S.A., 514–5

Sykes, Maj. Gen. George, U.S.A., 20 n., 585 n.

Taliaferro, Col. A. G., C.S.A., 394 n.

Taliaferro, Brig. Gen. William B., C.S.A., 34 n., 34–5, 36 n., 327, 441–2, 448, 460, 479, 588, 671, 707, 718, 721, 723

Taliaferro's Mill, 284

Talley, Mrs. Fannie Gaines, 232 n.

Talleysville, 294–6, 300

Tangent, Ewell's horse, 347

Tarpley, Sergt. L. P. H., C.S.A., 645

Taylor, Maj. Gen. Zachary, U.S.A., 24, 349

Taylor County, 9

Taylor, Lieut. Gen. Richard, C.S.A., early career, 349; commands Brigade under Ewell, 349; discipline, 349; with Jackson in the Valley, 366–7, 370–1, 373–4, 377–9, 381–93 passim, 476. 735–7, 739; in the Battle of Win-

chester, 398–403, 405, 472 n.; in the retreat, 419–23, 429–30; at Port Republic, 437, 441, 446, 451 n., 453, 455–60, 480, 482, 484, 487; peacemaker in Jackson-Winder incident, 464–5; his Brigade not sent against Pope, 662; he is sent home, 669. See also 263 n., 315, 517, 524–5, 588
Taylor, Col. Walter H., C.S.A., 205, 338 n., 500, 524, 642 n.
Taylorsville, 282
Tennessee River, 134
Terrett, Col. G. H., C.S.A., 7, 41
Terrill, Brig. Gen. W. R., U.S.A., 705, 717 n.
Terry, Brig. Gen. W. H., C.S.A., 98 n.
Texas Regiments:
First, 198
Third, 732
Fourth, 197–9, 532, 536
Fifth, 198, 267, 528
Thomas, Brig. Gen. E. L., C.S.A., 589 n., 651, 672
Thomas, Col. F. J., C.S.A., 70
Thomas, Maj. Gen. George H., U.S.A., 261, 704, 713–5, 717
Thomson, Lieut. James, C.S.A., 311
Thornton's Gap, 332, 342–3, 358
Thoroughfare, 682
Thoroughfare Gap, 137, 140, 690
Tidball, Bvt. Maj. Gen. John C., 721 n.
Tidball's Battery, 646
Tignor house, 290
Timberlake, Lieut., C.S.A., 443
Timberlake's Store, 585
Toombs, Brig. Gen. Robert, C.S.A., at Savage Station, 543–6; at Malvern Hill, 602; criticism of his action there, 607, 608 n., 627; history of his career: causes of his discontent, 621–9, 656; his dislike of Johnston, Davis, Hill, etc., 623, 625–8, 667; story of his mare under fire, 624 n.–625 n.; his Brigade under D. R. Jones, 672. See also 161, 163, 180 n.
Tompkins, Capt. Christopher Q., 706 n., 717 n.
Totopotomoy Creek, 275, 285, 288, 510–2
Totten, Bvt. Brig. Gen. James, 721 n.
Townsend, Maj. Gen. E. D., U.S.A., 712 n.
Tredegar Iron Works, 672, 706
Trent House, 562
Trenhen, Lieut. Col. John F., C.S.A., 525, 535
Trimble, Maj. Gen. Isaac Ridgeway, C.S.A., under Ewell in the Valley, 348–9, 355, 356 n., 385, 401, 736; in action at Cross Keys and Port Republic, 444–9, 454, 461, 487–8, 512; at Gaines' Mill, 524–5, 532; at Malvern

Hill, 592, 603, 653–4. See also xvi, 664
Tunstall's Station, 288–92, 294–5, 300, 633
Tupelo, Miss., 675
Turkey Creek, 639
Turner, Bvt. Maj. Henry S., 706
Tuscaloosa, Ala., 247
Twiggs, Maj. Gen. D. E., C.S.A., 709
Tygart Valley and River, 9
Tyler, Col. C. H., C.S.A., 704
Tyler, Maj. Gen. E. B., U.S.A., 461–2, 643
Tyler, Maj. Nat, C.S.A., 31

Union Church, 444
Union Mills Ford, 50, 53–4, 57, 59, 75, 77, 96, 97
Union Theological Seminary, 372
United States Infantry:
Sixth, 123
Ninth, 158
Dragoons, 261
Mounted Rifles, 123
United States Cavalry:
First, 369
Second, 121
Fifth, 285
United States Artillery, Fourth, 461
United States Military Academy, West Point, xvi, xxii–xxiii, 3, 7, 11, 14, 16, 20, 24, 27, 41, 85, 87, 90, 97, 119, 136, 158–60, 162, 172, 268, 273, 308, 317, 325, 347–8, 413, 478, 489, 606, 614, 620, 623, 625, 647, 703–9, 711, 714, 718–21, 724, 734
University of North Carolina, xxvii
University of Virginia, 248, 279, 280, 649
Upper Kanawha Salt Wells, 699

Valley River, 33
Valley of Virginia, see Shenandoah Valley
Valley Pike, 312–3, 332–3, 373, 384–6, 388–9, 395, 400, 417–9, 423, 425, 429, 437, 448, 472, 474, 477, 484, 497, 648, 735, 737–8
van Dorn, Maj. Gen. Earl, C.S.A., 20 n., 121–2, 125, 133, 156, 165 n., 195 n., 261, 709
Vaughn, Brig. Gen. J. C., C.S.A., 97 n., 732
Vicksburg, 675
Vienna, 518
Virginia Agricultural Society, 90
Virginia and Tennessee Railroad, 681–2, 699
Virginia Cavalry:
First, 278–9, 284, 286, 295, 636
Second, 423, 444 475–6, 571, 574, 639, 713

Virginia Cavalry (Cont'd):
Fourth, 278, 282, 646
Fifth, 648
Sixth, 423, 475–6
Ninth, 278, 284, 295–7, 640
Thirteenth, 522
Jeff Davis' Legion, 284
Virginia Central Railroad, 219, 332, 354, 428, 469, 486, 489–91, 501, 503, 508–9, 660, 668, 681–2, 690, 692–4, 697
Virginia-Merrimac, 141, 202, 209–10
Virginia, Military Geography, 677–700; area, 677; waterways, 677; mountains, 678–9; shipyards, 679–80; railroads, 680–4; roads, 684–6; natural characteristics, 686; man-made characteristics, 686–9; effects of these factors, 687–8; Northeastern Frontier District, 687–8; Shenandoah Defensive Area, 689–92; Rappahannock-North Anna Area, 692–4, 698; Mid-Tidewater District, 694, 697; Peninsula District, 694–5, 697–8; Norfolk Zone, 695–7; Richmond-Petersburg Area, 696-8; Southwest Virginia Area, 699; West Virginia from the Alleghenies to the Ohio, 699–700
Virginia Military Institute, xvi, xxii, xxiii, 7, 11, 17, 83, 124 and n., 126–7, 161, 247–8, 308, 310, 329, 350, 372, 479, 536, 558, 703, 705, 707–8, 710–1, 713, 718
Virginia Regiments:
First, 448, 728
Second, 325, 369, 396–7, 403, 412, 421, 437, 451, 453–4, 484, 532, 536, 730
Fourth, 451, 453–4, 730, 734
Fifth, 396, 413, 455, 532, 730
Sixth, 369, 377, 403, 437
Seventh, 437
Eighth, 67, 96, 730
Ninth, 634
Tenth, 401, 730
Eleventh, 217, 248
Thirteenth, 96, 350
Eighteenth, 70, 537, 730
Nineteenth, 89, 91, 588, 732
Twentieth, 27, 31, 33
Twenty-first, 127, 418
Twenty-third, 34, 36 n., 68–9, 401
Twenty-fourth, 85, 170, 180, 182–8, 730
Twenty-fifth, 32
Twenty-seventh, 325, 396–8, 406, 428, 447, 455
Twenty-eighth, 70–1·
Thirty-first, 456
Thirty-third, 325, 392, 399, 453, 730
Thirty-eighth, 180, 182–3, 186–7, 645
Forty-second, 448

Virginia Regiments (Cont'd):
Forty-fourth, 29, 369, 457, 460
Forty-ninth, 66–7, 731
Fifty-eighth, 457, 460
Fifty-ninth, 433
Sixtieth, 645
Virginia Volunteers, 9, 11–3, 16, 45, 701–2, 707
von Borcke, Heros, 279, 281, 293

Waddy, Lieut. Col. John R., C.S.A., 705
Walker, William, 88
Walker, Charles D., 248 n.
Walker, C. Irvine, 652 n.
Walker, Brig. Gen. H. H., C.S.A., 705
Walker, Brig. Gen. James A., C.S.A., 350–1
Walker, Maj. Gen. John G., C.S.A., 77 n., 273
Walker, L. Pope, 116
Walker, Brig. Gen. R. Lindsay, C.S.A., 98 n., 522, 649 n.
Walker, Maj. Gen. William H. T., C.S.A., 85 n., 88
Wall, H. C., 191 n.
Walnut Grove Church, 518, 523
Ward, Col. G. T., C.S.A., 170–1, 179
Wardensburg, 419
Warder and Catlett, Battle of Young's Branch, 728
Warm Springs, 352
Warren, Maj. Gen. G. K., U.S.A., 585 n.
Warrenton, 103, 341–2, 344, 356
Warrenton turnpike, 49, 53, 55, 95, 726, 730
Warthen, Col. T. J., C.S.A., 606 n.
Warwick River, 148–9, 152, 154
Washington Artillery, 97, 647
Washington College, 20
Washington, D. C., 15, 23, 38–43, 78, 99, 103, 111, 149–50, 348, 406, 408–9, 415, 470, 491, 502, 659, 677, 682, 688, 691–2, 703, 706, 711, 714–5, 738
Washington, Gen. George, 66 n., 634, 678
Washington, Lieut. J. B., C.S.A., 233
Washington, John A., 12–3
Washington, Martha, 634, 678
Washington, Maj. T. A., C.S.A., 705
Watkins, Corp. L. D., C.S.A., 645
Waynesboro, 461
Weed's Battery, 646
Weisiger, Brig. Gen. D. A., 707–8, 718
Weldon, N. C., 680–2
West house, 593–4
West Point, United States Military Academy, xvi, xxii–xxiii, 3, 7, 11, 14, 16, 20, 24, 27, 41, 85, 87, 90, 97, 119, 136, 158–60, 162, 172, 268, 273, 308, 317, 325, 347–8, 413, 478, 489, 606, 614, 620, 623, 625, 647, 703–9, 711, 714, 718–21, 724, 734

West Point, Va., 205, 210, 678, 681, 694–5
Western Run, 590, 592–3
Westover, 603, 640, 642, 648
Weyer's Cave, 463
Wheat, Leo, 88 n.
Wheat, Maj. Roberdeau Chatham, C.S.A., 87–8, 350–1, 378, 386, 387 n., 401–2, 432, 447, 525, 537, 668, 730
Wheeling, 677, 680–1
White, Miss B., 378
White Hall, 352, 354
White House Bridge, 373, 422, 424
White House on Pamunkey River, 275, 288, 293, 495, 538, 566, 633–4, 642, 647, 678
White Oak Swamp, 225–6, 495, 539–41, 548, 551, 555, 557-8, 563, 565–80 passim, 587, 590, 611, 617, 621, 629–30, 637–9, 642, 655–8, 674
White Oak Swamp Bridge, 565–6, 570, 578–9
White, W. Margrave, 728
Whiting, Maj. Jaspar, C.S.A., 236–7, 503
Whiting, Maj. Gen. William Henry Chase, C.S.A., education and personality, 119; engineer at Harpers Ferry, 12; at Bull Run, 50, 75, 97; made Brigadier, 97 and n., 157; rejects Mississippi troops, 119–20, 143, 218; negligence in loss of equipment, 143; success at Eltham, 194–6, 198–9, 226; commands Division, 218; orders and action at Seven Pines, 222–3, 226, 229, 231–3, 236, 238, 244–5, 246–7, 257; as acting Divisional Commander, 270–2; under Jackson on return from the Valley, 489, 491–2, 495, 502, 505, 508, 653; at Gaines' Mill, 524, 527–32, 534–5, 620, 652; in action at Mc-Clellan's retreat, 541, 575; at Malvern Hill, 592, 595, 599, 530; losses in the Seven Days' Battles, 605; as disgruntled officer, 620–1; criticism of his actions, 621, 659, 667, 674. See also 121, 125, 133, 136 n., 140, 161 n., 466–9, 674, 734
Whittle, Lieut. Col. Powhatan B., C.S.A., 186, 645
Wickham, Sen. Henry T., 219 n.
Wickham, Brig. Gen. Williams C., C.S.A., 98 n., 278, 282
Wigfall, Brig. Gen. Louis T., C.S.A., 165 n., 197 and n., 198
Wilcox, Maj. Gen. Cadmus M., C.S.A., 152 n., 159, 161 n., 168, 178, 189, 192, 239 and n., 242, 255, 258, 605 and n., 645, 652–3
Wilcox, Col. J. M., C.S.A., 300
Wilkinson, Maj. Gen. James, U.S.A., 92

Williamsburg road, 222, 225–8, 233–4, 236, 238–40, 242, 253, 255, 257–8, 260, 541, 551–2, 562, 608, 688
Williamsburg, xvi, 169, 174–6, 180, 182–94 passim, 198, 217–9, 242–3, 245, 247–50, 261, 276, 281–2, 517, 646, 673, 695
Wilmington, Del., 108
Wilmington and Weldon Railroad, 682
Willcox, Maj. Gen. O. B., U.S.A., 68 n.
William and Mary College, 180
Williams, Maj. Gen. A. S., U.S.A., 474 n.
Williams house, 578
Williams, Lieut. J. H., C.S.A., 477 n.
Williams, Brig. Gen. Robert, U.S.A., 705, 717 n.
Williams, Maj. Gen. Seth, U.S.A., 20 n.
Williams, Col. Thomas G., C.S.A., 705
Williamson's, 426
Williamsport, 404, 406, 407, 413, 691
Willis Church, 591, 610, 612
Willis Church (Quaker) road, 590, 592, 597, 602, 612, 621
Willis, Col. Edward, C.S.A., 439, 443
Winchester, 44, 46, 48, 55, 58, 122–30 passim, 138, 304–6, 311–2, 315–6, 328, 333, 343, 358, 363, 376, 379, 382–4, 386, 388, 390, 391, 393, 411–2, 414–9, 421, 423, 431–3, 467, 472–3, 476, 479–80, 482, 484, 486, 525, 535, 681–2, 691, 735–9
the battle, 395–408
Winchester and Potomac Railroad, 681, 683
Winder, Brig. Gen. Charles S., C.S.A., xvi, 195 n., 325–7, 339, 354–5, 362, 390, 392, 396, 398–9, 412, 419–23, 441, 450–7, 459–60, 464–5, 469, 476, 479, 483, 486–7, 499, 504, 527–35, 563 n., 653, 671
Winston Farm, 282, 300
Wise, Brig. Gen. Henry A., C.S.A., 37 n., 90, 134, 230, 581, 672
Withers, Col. R. E., C.S.A., 70, 89, 537, 606 n., 730
Wooding, Capt. Geo. W., C.S.A., 596
Woodstock, Va., 337, 423, 691
Woodward, Col. J. J., C.S.A., 536, 606 n.
Wool, Maj. Gen. John E., U.S.A., 24, 706
Worth, Lieut. H. A. F., 705, 717 n.
Wright, Maj. Gen. A. R., C.S.A., 201 n.; 226 n., 266–7, 558 n., 560, 577–9, 592, 594, 597–602, 605 n., 609 n., 612–3, 652, 654, 668 n., 673
Wyndham, Sir Percy, 432–3
Wynne's Shop, 290

Yale University, 116, 349
York River, 9, 14, 16, 146, 148, 151,

175, 193, 202, 635, 677–8, 694–5, 724

York River Railroad, 208, 225, 239, 247, 249, 272, 288, 500, 548, 633, 636, 695

Yorktown, 16–18, 21, 146, 148–9, 151–4, 174, 194, 198, 218, 259, 265, 268, 374, 607, 624–5, 695; officers and army that retreated, May 3, 1862, 156–73

Yorktown Road, 174–8

Young's Branch, 728

Zouaves, Louisiana, 87–8

Zulich, Brig. Gen. S. M., U.S.A., 472 n.